Banks on
Sentencing

D1333861

Banks on Sentencing

Robert Banks, Barrister

Butterworths
LexisNexis™

Members of the LexisNexis Group worldwide

United Kingdom	LexisNexis Butterworths Tolley, a Division of Reed Elsevier (UK) Ltd, Halsbury House, 35 Chancery Lane, LONDON, WC2A 1EL, and 4 Hill Street, EDINBURGH EH2 3JZ
Argentina	LexisNexis Argentina, BUENOS AIRES
Australia	LexisNexis Butterworths, CHATSWOOD, New South Wales
Austria	LexisNexis Verlag ARD Orac GmbH & Co KG, VIENNA
Canada	LexisNexis Butterworths, MARKHAM, Ontario
Chile	LexisNexis Chile Ltda, SANTIAGO DE CHILE
Czech Republic	Nakladatelství Orac sro, PRAGUE
France	Editions du Juris-Classeur SA, PARIS
Hong Kong	LexisNexis Butterworths, HONG KONG
Hungary	HVG-Orac, BUDAPEST
India	LexisNexis Butterworths, NEW DELHI
Ireland	Butterworths (Ireland) Ltd, DUBLIN
Italy	Giuffrè Editore, MILAN
Malaysia	Malayan Law Journal Sdn Bhd, KUALA LUMPUR
New Zealand	LexisNexis Butterworths, WELLINGTON
Poland	Wydawnictwo Prawnicze LexisNexis, WARSAW
Singapore	LexisNexis Butterworths, SINGAPORE
South Africa	LexisNexis Butterworths, DURBAN
Switzerland	Stämpfli Verlag AG, BERNE
USA	LexisNexis, DAYTON, Ohio

A CIP Catalogue record for this book is available from the British Library.

ISBN 0 406 95130 6

Typeset by Kerrypress Ltd, Luton, Beds

Printed and bound by Clays Ltd, St Ives Plc

Visit Butterworths LexisNexis *direct* at www.butterworths.com

PREFACE

Sentencing has a peculiar ability to go wrong. The exercise is a potential graveyard. Mr Justice Leonard was one of the most experienced criminal High Court Judges. In February 1987, he passed sentence in the Ealing Vicarage rape case after which his reputation never recovered. The ferocious outcry about his sentences left the public with the impression that judges were unconcerned about rape and treated burglary as more serious a crime. In January 1982, Judge Richards, after passing sentence in another rape case, had to be provided with a police guard for months. In August 1987, Judge Brooks in a GBH with intent case gave the two defendants community service. The next day the judge saw most of the front page of the Daily Mirror newspaper enquire with a bitter attack against his sentence, 'Where do they get these Judges?' In July 1994, Judge Whitley passed a merciful but lenient sentence on man accused of indecent assault. The papers responded with angry attacks on the judge. The Sun newspaper carried the story for a week and even conducted a readers' poll about whether the judge should be sacked. The readers voted overwhelmingly for his dismissal. In October 1998, Judge (Susan) Hamilton QC described a defendant as, 'a complete dickhead' before sentencing him. The remark is now reprinted every time newspapers carry a silly judge story and want to pad out the article.

However, it is not only judges that suffer when their sentencing exercise goes wrong. Magistrates can go unnoticed for their whole services and then make a mistake which enables the local paper to have a field day. One magistrate fined an unemployed prostitute for soliciting and enquired, 'How long will it take you to earn the money?' The papers had their field day.

Perhaps the reason for the traditional problem with the sentencing exercise going wrong is that unlike trials the sentencer takes the dominant role. Juries are truly anonymous. A slip or lenient sentence is far more reportable than any wise sentence. The sentencing exercise is itself fraught with difficulties. For the newspapers who may not have the full facts there is a double human interest. It provides an opportunity to peep through the curtain into the lives of both the defendant and the judge or magistrate. These problems are why the Lord Chancellor's major concern for new judges or magistrates is the fear that they will appear in the newspapers for making a slip. His department knows that the public reads and remembers only the slip, not the coverage of the courts working well.

I hope this book will help sentencers as well as advocates, policemen, social workers, defendants and crime writers. It is designed to be comprehensive as well as portable, enabling the reader to find the case or point in 20 seconds.

I am grateful to the editorial team at LexisNexis Butterworths Tolley for their enthusiastic help and wholehearted support for the book. Bearing in mind that this work was scheduled for an impossibly early deadline causing the book to be written in the evenings and weekends, my fear is there will be some mistakes. I trust there are not but if a reader finds one I hope he or she lets me know so I can correct future editions. Of course I know one slip is more memorable than 650 pages of correct summaries. Please let me know, as I do not want this to be my graveyard.

Robert Banks   November 2002
DX 94252 Marylebone
London

ABBREVIATIONS

ABH	Assault occasioning actual bodily harm
CCC	The Central Criminal Court (The Old Bailey)
CCTV	Closed circuit television
CSO	A Community Service Order
GBH	Grievous bodily harm
gram(s)	gramme(s)
ID	Identification
kg(s)	Kilogramme(s)
LCJ	Lord Chief Justice
mg	Milligrammes (in drink drive cases milligrammes in 100 millilitres of blood)
News	News report in a newspaper
PDH	Pleas and Direction hearing in the Crown Court
QBD	The Queen's Bench Division in the High Court
ug	Microgrammes (in drink/drive cases milligrammes in 100 millilitres of breath
TDA	Taking and driving away (conveyances)
TIC	Offences taken into consideration
YOI	Detention in a Young Offenders Institute

HOW TO PREDICT SENTENCES

The basics

The traditional route for determining a sentence is as follows.

The court assesses:

(1) The legal framework namely any guideline case, guideline remarks and reported cases. If the case is a serious example of the offence the court will consider the maximum sentence available.

(2) The aggravating and mitigating features of the offence.

(3) The sentences of defendants connected with the case who have already been dealt with, (if there are any).

Taking into account (1) to (3) the court will decide the appropriate starting point. The court will next consider:

(1) The plea. (See GUILTY PLEA, DISCOUNT FOR)

(2) The character of the defendant both good and bad.

(3) The defendant's personal mitigation.

(4) The pre-sentence report if there is one.

(5) Whether it is appropriate to pass a longer than commensurate sentence (see LONGER THAN COMMENSURATE SENTENCES) or to pass an extended sentence (see EXTENDED SENTENCES).

Taking into account (1) to (5) the court will decide the appropriate sentence. Next it will consider:

(1) Whether costs should be awarded against the defendant.

(2) Whether compensation is appropriate.

(3) Whether there is an ancillary order linked to the offence that should be added to the sentence like disqualification, forfeiture, destruction, a drug trafficking offences order or a football banning order.

Aggravating and mitigating features of the offence

Most sentences are determined primarily by the offence. Very, very occasionally where the defendant has some terrible illness or has taken valiant steps to overcome his/her drug addiction and changed his/her whole lifestyle, courts can exercise mercy and impose a constructive sentence[1].

1   *A-G's Reference (No 83 of 2001)* [2002] 1 Cr App Rep (S) 589.

Character – General

There are potentially three parts to a defendant's character. First, there is the defendant's criminal record (if there is one). If there is no previous offending the defendant will normally receive a discount for his good character. Where there is only minor offending many years previously, the defendant will also usually receive a discount. The second part is the remarks in the pre-sentence report if one has been ordered. The judge or magistrate does not have to accept the views in the report if he thinks they are wrong but he or she should consider them. Many pre-sentence reports contain a risk assessment analysis which is of increasing importance. The third part is general evidence of good character. It is usually found in witness statements collected by the defence but it can be found in the prosecution case. If the victim of a theft by an employee describes the defendant as hard working and trustworthy over many years up until the theft, that would normally be taken into account.

Good character – How to apply it

It is not possible to apply mathematical principles about the discount that is applicable. It will all depend on the circumstances. Where there is serious professional criminal behaviour, for example conspiracy to commit armed robbery, good character will be of little significance[1]. At the other end of the scale good character can tip the balance in deciding whether it is necessary to give the defendant a custodial sentence. Good character is more important the older the defendant is. However, it can be very significant for defendants aged under 21. Courts try to avoid sending young people of good character into custody because it can be counter-productive. If the defendant in in employment, custody will normally destroy this and harm his or her chances of finding another position. Further, custody will introduce him or her to a corrupting influence, which will be hard to undo. Courts will prefer a lenient sentence, which may stop them re-offending than a custodial sentence, which may confirm his or her criminal behaviour.

1   *R v Turner* [1975] 61 Cr App Rep 67. The defendants appealed their sentences for armed robbery. The court in a guideline case said, 'the fact that a man has not much of a criminal record is not a powerful factor in cases of this gravity'.

Bad character – How to apply it

It is important that the defendant is not punished twice for the same offence. Therefore the courts will be careful not to add too much to the sentence because of the criminal record. But a criminal record is an important way of considering how the defendant has responded to previous sentences. If non-custodial sentences have not been effective the options of the court will be more limited. Where the criteria for imposing longer than commensurate sentences are satisfied bad character will be of crucial importance.

Personal mitigation

The majority of personal mitigation has little or no impact on the sentence. If a man with children commits an offence which deserves imprisonment the fact he has children will not normally influence the sentence. Serious offences are in one way aggravated by the fact the defendant committed the offence knowing that if caught the sentence would cause the children to be separated from their father. In principle it would be wrong for those without children to be necessarily sentenced to longer sentences than those with children. Each case will be dealt with on its own facts. However, where a mother appears for sentence the court will consider the impact on the children of the sentence. If she is the sole carer, or particular children will suffer badly, the court will adjust the appropriate sentence not to assist her but to protect the children, (see **MOTHERS**). If the father is the sole carer, the court will normally consider the impact on the children and then consider an adjustment in the same way.

Guideline cases

As the name implies these are only a guide. They assist in assessing the starting point. However, the aggravating and mitigating features for the offence may adjust the figure. Guideline cases rarely, if ever, create a maximum for an offence.

Finding and interpreting comparable cases

Non-guideline reported cases are also only a guide. Some of them are influential, others less so. They only show the operation of the basic principles. More recent cases are more useful than older ones. Some offences like manslaughter are very hard to index because of the infinite variety of ways the offence can be committed. It is important to look at more than one section. However, even if there is a very similar case it does not mean that the same sentence will be passed as in the reported case. Magistrates' Courts normally pass lower sentences than Crown Courts. Many Crown

Court judges pass lower sentences than the Court of Appeal judges. Judges differ in their approaches and the judge has a discretion when weighing up all the different factors before he or she passes sentence. The fact the Court of Appeal considers a sentence is not manifestly excessive does not mean that this is the sentence they would have passed. Where the Court of Appeal is considering an appeal by the prosecution (which are cited as *A-G's Reference (No 43 of 2001)* etc) the sentence that is substituted will be less than the appropriate sentence to take into account the stress etc of the defendant being sentenced twice.

The summaries in the book

The book contains all the cases listed in 1998–2002 in the Cr App Rep (S) law reports other than cases which deal with sentencing orders or procedure. The case summaries are intended to include all the relevant factors. Even cases, which seem out of line or unrepresentative are listed to ensure there is a complete picture.

Contents

Contents

TABLE OF CASES

Paragraph numbers printed in *italic* type indicate where a Case is set out.

A

B

C

G

H

K

L

M

N

S

U

V

W

X

Y

Z

TABLE OF STATUTES

References in the right-hand column are to paragraph number. Paragraph references printed in **bold** type indicate where the Act is set out in part or in full.

TABLE OF STATUTORY INSTRUMENTS

1 ABDUCTION

(Of a woman)

1.1 Sexual Offences Act 1956, s 17

Indictable only. Maximum sentence 14 years.

See also FALSE IMPRISONMENT/KIDNAPPING and RAPE – *Abduction/false imprisonment etc, and*

2 ABDUCTION OF A CHILD

2.1 Child Abduction Act 1984, s 1 (by parent) and s 2 (by other person)

Triable either way. On indictment maximum 7 years. Summary maximum 6 months and/or £5,000.

See also FALSE IMPRISONMENT/KIDNAPPING

General

Longer than commensurate sentences (frequently wrongly called extended sentences) – Is it a violent offence?

2.2 Powers of Criminal Courts (Sentencing) Act 2000, s 80(2)(b). . . . the custodial sentence shall be. . .where the offence is a violent or sexual offence, for such longer term (not exceeding the maximum) as in the opinion of the court is necessary to protect the public from serious harm from the offender (previously the Criminal Justice Act 1991, s 2(2)(b).)

Powers of Criminal Courts (Sentencing) Act 2000, s 161(3). . . . a violent offence is an 'offence which leads, or is intended or likely to lead, to a person's death or physical injury to a person.'

R v Newsome [1997] 2 Cr App Rep (S) 69. Look at the facts of the case. Next ask whether the restraining made it a violent offence. The false imprisonment may amount to a violent offence. The court also had to consider whether it was likely to lead to physical injury. Here they were likely to lead to that so it was a violent offence.

R v Nelmes (2001) Times, 1 February. The defendant pleaded guilty to attempted abduction. The defendant who smelt strongly of drink pulled a 3-year-old boy away from his mother who was at a bus station. He said calmly, 'I have come to take your child away.' The mother and boy became very distressed and the mother screamed for help. The mother was able to snatch the child back. The defendant was arrested. The defendant said he was drunk and on medication and could not remember being there or being arrested. He had no relevant previous convictions. Held. The judge purported to extend the sentence. That was not appropriate. The case failed the *R v Newsome* [1997] 2 Cr App Rep (S) 397 test that there should be physical injury or conduct that was likely to lead to physical injury.

Old cases. *R v Wrench* [1996] 1 Cr App Rep (S) 145.

See also LONGER THAN COMMENSURATE SENTENCES

Parent or stepparent, by

Court order, in breach of – Guideline remarks

2.3 *R v JA* [2001] EWCA Crim 1974, [2002] 1 Cr App Rep (S) 473. It is the interests of the child which are paramount not the interests or aspirations of the parent. Save in

1

quite exceptional circumstances a person who commits a s 2 offence commits a serious offence, especially if it is done to thwart orders of the court. Orders must be respected by parents who have access to the courts and to legal advice. Real punishment is called for to punish and to deter others.

Court order, in breach of

2.4   *R v Dryden-Hall* [1997] 2 Cr App Rep (S) 235. The defendant the mother of the victim pleaded guilty to two counts of child abduction and a theft. Her husband pleaded guilty to aiding and abetting the abduction. She divorced the father of the children and remarried. In 1993 she applied to her County Court to take her two children to Canada where she had lived and where her family lived. The welfare officer reported to the court and she withdrew her application. The court made an order prohibiting her from taking the children out of the jurisdiction for more than a month without the father consenting. She developed TB and became depressed. She ran up a bill of £1,328 on a store card, (the theft charge). She arranged for Pickfords to quote for a move to Canada. She told a neighbour she was going to Canada. She then flew to Canada with no intention of returning. The father brought proceedings in Canada, which she contested. The children were there for 21 months. The court ordered their return but she stayed behind. When she returned she and her husband were arrested. The welfare officer said the move had had a detrimental effect on the children. She had no previous convictions. Held 9 months was not wrong. However, because of her change in attitude and the interests of the children the sentence was reduced to **4 months** to enable her release very shortly.

R v JA [2001] EWCA Crim 1974, [2002] 1 Cr App Rep (S) 473. The defendant J and D pleaded to aiding an abetting the detention of their daughter, N. T who was J's mother pleaded to conspiracy to abduct a child. The pleas were on rearraignment. J and D had two children C and N. C was diagnosed as suffering from Munchausen Syndrome by Proxy when he was 11 and was accommodated by the council with an interim care order. It was said this had led to unnecessary treatment of the child amounting to abuse. J, J's sister and T were also diagnosed with the same syndrome. C remained in care with the consent of J and D. From then J and D raised many complaints about their son's health. They said he was starved, neglected and abused. In contact sessions C had extensive bruising and this was explained by the council in a number of ways. J and D did not accept the explanations and contacted organisations for help including the Child Protection Police. The Council then informed the parents that they were instituting care proceedings for the other child, N although they had no intention of taking her into care. The prosecution said there was a plan hatched by J, T and M, someone styled as a 'child abuse advocate' to remove N from the jurisdiction. T took N to Ireland where they stayed under false names. J reported her daughter missing. M and another arranged for various demands to be made over the Internet and in telephone calls to newspapers and the police. Until they were met T and N would not return. An interim care order and a recovery order were obtained from the High Court. There was also an order that anyone who had knowledge of the whereabouts of N should inform the authorities immediately. J and D knowing the location ignored this and spent a week with their daughter who had been moved to Scotland. D deposited £140 with a charity and an associate of M later withdrew it in Scotland. Police found the house and J, D and N. It was accepted the abduction was prompted in part by others. All defendants were of good character. J was 36. D was 34 and an engineer in the Royal Navy with good naval references. He was not at home for the majority of the relevant time. He had lost his marriage, his children and possibly his career. T was 63. There was a 2 year delay. The judge said the Council was beyond criticism. Held. It is the interests of the child which are paramount not the interests or aspirations of the parent. They had shown a complete contempt for the law. Save in quite exceptional circumstances a person who commits a s 2 offence commits a serious offence, especially if it is done to thwart orders of the court Those who did what the defendants did must expect prison sentences because real punishment is called for and to deter others. The judge took into account the mitigation. Accepting they were under the influences of others the appeals for J and T's **9 months** and D's **6 months** are dismissed.

Relative, friend etc, by

2.5   *R v Mawdsley* [2001] 1 Cr App Rep (S) 353. The defendant aged 43 pleaded guilty to two counts of abducting a child. He went with his son to the school of one of his son's friends aged 13. The defendant asked for the friend and said he was taking him to the dentist. The boy went with him because he was too scared to say no. His son then asked him to get another boy from another school. He again said he was taking him to the dentist. The boy aged 12 appeared willing to go. He took the boys to his house where they talked and watched TV. The defendant drank cider and on one occasion he took a boy by the ears and spat cider in his face. They stayed for about 2½ hours and nothing untoward happened. The defendant had an appalling record for dishonesty but had no convictions for sexual offences. **18 months** was substituted for 2 years.

Police advice, acting against

2.6   *R v Hutchinson* (1 October 1998, unreported). The defendant pleaded guilty to two offences of child abduction. Because of his previous convictions the defendant was known to the police paedophile unit. He was warned by officers to stay away from a 14-year-old boy. The boy asked him to give him a lift home as he was stranded and had no money. He gave him a lift and the police stopped the car and took the boy away. On another occasion he picked him up, and they went to visit a friend. Then they both went to a public lavatory and came out. The boy then went back in. Fifteen minutes later the defendant went to look for him and he wasn't there. The boy was arrested. Held. These were technical offences involving no kind of sexual conduct. **12 months** not 18.

R v A (14 September 1999, unreported). The defendant was convicted of child abduction. He was friendly with a 15-year-old girl. He visited her home and the mother telephoned the police who advised him not to take the girl with him. He met her later and they lived rough together. There was no contact with the mother for 5 days and she was away from home for 9 days. Held. **2 years** was at the top of the bracket but not manifestly excessive.

Stranger, by

General

2.7   *R v Dean* [2000] 2 Cr App Rep (S) 253. The defendant was convicted of abducting a 4½-year-old boy. He ordered the boy to come to him and not to speak. He threatened to kill him and took hold of his hand. His mother who was watching him shouted to him and the boy broke free and escaped. The defendant drove away. He always denied it. The defendant was then aged 29. When 17 he was put on probation for sending obscene material through the post. It was gay indecent material sent to young boys saying what he would like to do to them. There were 61 TICs. He was sentenced on the basis that it was not a spur of the moment offence because he had travelled away from his home territory. There was no proven sexual motive. The previous offending did give rise for concern. **5 years** was severe but a sentence that the judge was entitled to make to protect the public.

R v Nelmes [2001] Times, 1 February. The defendant pleaded guilty to attempted abduction. The defendant who smelt strongly of drink pulled a 3-year-old boy away from his mother who was at a bus station. He said calmly, 'I have come to take your child away.' The mother and boy became very distressed and the mother screamed for help. The mother was able to snatch the child back. The defendant was arrested. The defendant said he was drunk and on medication and could not remember being there or being arrested. He had no relevant previous convictions. Held. The judge purported to extend the sentence and extend the licence. That was not appropriate. The case failed the *R v Newsome* [1997] 2 Cr App Rep (S) 397 test that there should be physical injury or conduct that was likely to lead to physical injury. The case was appalling and caused tremendous distress to the mother, but **3 years** not 2.

Sexual motive, for

2.8 *R v Newsome* [1997] 2 Cr App Rep (S) 69. The defendant pleaded guilty to attempted child abduction. He was 43 and approached a girl aged 9 years old as she was gathering conkers in a field. He walked towards her and she backed away. He ran after her and grabbed her by the wrist and an arm. She screamed and kicked him and he let go. The child had feared she could have been pushed into a nearby river. He admitted the offence. He said his was intention was to take her towards the riverbank and indecently assault her. In 1972 he had a conviction for robbery. In 1975 he had a conviction for indecent assault on a girl aged 9. In 1988 he had a conviction for indecently assaulting a girl aged 15 for which he received 4 years. In 1991 he had a conviction for attempted abduction of a 6 year old for which the Court of Appeal gave him probation. The pre-sentence report said that he was a serious risk to young girls. A psychiatrist report said he had long standing paedophile interests. Held This offence was a 'violent' offence so the judge was right to extend the sentence. However, **5 years** substituted for 6.

R v Adamson (19 October 2001, unreported). 8 year old abducted by a paedophile. 33 months entirely appropriate.

3   ABH – ASSAULT OCCASIONING ACTUAL BODILY HARM

3.1   Offences Against the Person Act 1861, s 47

Triable either way. On indictment maximum 5 years. Summary maximum 6 months and/or £5,000.

Where the offence was committed relevant to a football match and where there are reasonable grounds to believe that making a banning order would help to prevent violence or disorder at or in connection with any regulated football match; the court must make a Football Banning Order, under the Football Spectators Act 1989, s 14A and Sch 1, para 1.

It is a violent offence for the purses of passing a longer than commensurate sentence [Powers of Criminal Courts (Sentencing) Act 2000, s 80(2)] and an extended sentence (extending the licence) [Powers of Criminal Courts (Sentencing) Act 2000, s 85(2)(b).]

[The categories listed are only one factor in the determination of sentence. Usually, the most important matter is the degree of injury inflicted.]

Guideline remarks

3.2   *R v Howells Re Robson and Howard* [1999] 1 Cr App Rep (S) 335 at 342 – LCJ. Gratuitous violence, directed at members of the public who are going about their business and doing nothing whatsoever to provoke such violence must attract and be understood to attract severe punishment. (For further details see **Stranger in the street, attack on**)

Magistrates' Court Sentencing Guidelines September 2000

3.3 Entry point. Are Magistrates' sentencing powers appropriate? Consider the impact on the victim. Examples of aggravating factors for the offence are deliberate kicking or biting, extensive injuries (may be psychiatric), headbutting, group action, offender in position of authority, on hospital/medical premises, pre-meditated, victim particularly vulnerable, victim serving the public and weapon. Examples of mitigating factors for the offence are minor injury, provocation and single blow. Examples of mitigation are age, health (physical or mental), co-operation with the police, voluntary compensation and genuine remorse. Give reasons if not awarding compensation.

For details about the guidelines see MAGISTRATES' COURT SENTENCING GUIDELINES at page 331.

Aircraft, on

See AIRCRAFT OFFENCES – *ABH*

Argument, after

3.4 *R v Jones* [1999] 1 Cr App Rep (S) 427. The defendant pleaded guilty at the Magistrates' Court to ABH. In the street, the defendant after drinking accused the victim of making too much noise. The allegation had been made before. The victim walked on. The defendant grabbed him by the back of the head, 'You better stop making noise at night because I'm fucking sick of it.' The victim walked off again and was struck a heavy blow to the jaw. He fell to the floor. The jaw was broken in two places and required lengthy surgery and a metal plate. The defendant had one conviction, which was for ABH 10 years earlier. The psychiatrist said there might be an element of paranoia. The pre-sentence report said he felt harassed because of an earlier incident on his estate. Held. Because of the serious permanent injuries the sentence of **18 months** was not altered although it was at the top end of the range.

Children, against

See CRUELTY TO CHILDREN – *ABH*

Defendant aged 14–15

3.5 *R v Howells Re Marston* [1999] 1 Cr App Rep (S) 335 at 344 – LCJ. The defendant pleaded guilty to ABH. While serving his 9 months detention he pleaded to a Public Order Act 1986, s 4 count for an offence which was committed before the first one and received 3 months consecutive. Both pleas were at the Crown Court. (For details of the first incident see PUBLIC ORDER ACT OFFENCES – s 4). The second incident was about 4 weeks later after the s 4 offence. The victim was in a shop and noticed some youths knocking over a sweet stand. He left and three youths from the shop approached him. One asked him a question and another told him to go. He carried on walking and the first youth punched him in the eye causing him to fall to the ground and repeatedly kicked him. The victim succeeded in tripping him up and stood up. The youth then stood up and seized the victim's jumper. The victim then seized the youth jacket and the other two shouted, 'If you hit him, we hit you.' They then punched and kicked him. The victim again fell where he curled up against the blows. He was pushed on the chest and the three ran off when someone shouted. The victim received bruising, grazing to his eye, cuts and a swollen jaw. The co-defendant was the main aggressor and there was no evidence the defendant kicked the victim. When interviewed he admitted pushing the victim. He was on bail for the first offence. He had a relatively minor dishonesty conviction and two dishonesty cautions. He was said to be remorseful and ashamed. He had been taken away from his family by the local authority. Held. The s 4 offence was an utterly disgraceful and inexcusable episode but abusive language by a 15 year old did not merit custody. For the ABH a very short term of detention would be appropriate. **4 months** YOI for the ABH and no separate penalty for the other not 12 months in all.

Information, to extract

3.6 *R v Reddy and Haslam* [2001] 2 Cr App Rep (S) 216. The defendant R pleaded guilty to a joint count with H and another count of ABH. H was convicted of the joint count of ABH. The victim was the same in both counts. The victim and another man who was having a relationship with R's girlfriend lived in the same block of flats. The victim intervened in a dispute between R and his girlfriend at the block of flats. The following day R was abusive to the victim and others at the same place. At about 3am, the victim tried to make R leave. R punched him in the face a number of times causing him to fall and kneed him in the face. He then grabbed his hair and punched him on the back of the head and kicked him in the face again. R then chased after someone who he feared was going to call the police and returned. He then struck the victim a number of times with his foot. The victim was taken to hospital where a cut to his nose and bumps to his head were seen.

Later the same day at 5pm the two defendants arrived at the block. They pushed their way into the victim's flat. The victim was forced to the floor and R sat on him punching him to the head asking him where his girlfriend and her baby were. H cut the telephone wire. R grabbed the victim by the hair, put him onto a sofa and again demanded to know where the girlfriend was. The victim's head was repeatedly hit against the wall and punched in the face by R. H kicked him to the thighs and knees. When the victim again was unable to say where the girlfriend was R once again kicked him in the face. H shouted, 'Old Bill, Old Bill' and R repeatedly karate kicked the victim. R also attempted to gouge out his eyes and headbutted him. The incident lasted about 20 minutes. The judge described it as a premeditated joint attack on a smaller defenceless man and an orgy of violence. He said he gave modest credit for the pleas because of the overwhelming evidence. He said H had participated fully till he shouted Old Bill to stop the violence. Both men were 21 and treated as of good character. The pre-sentence report for R indicated a lack of remorse and lack of insight into his behaviour. Held. The court could not conclude that there was a risk of further offences by these men of good character so as to evoke the powers of longer than normal sentences. R sentence was reduced from 5 years to **3 years** with the earlier ABH sentence of 2 years concurrent remaining. H's sentence was reduced from 5 years to **2½ years**.

Longer than commensurate sentence (frequently wrongly called an extended sentence)

3.7 Powers of Criminal Courts (Sentencing) Act 2000, s 80(2)(b) . . .the custodial sentence shall be. . .where the offence is a violent or sexual offence, for such longer term (not exceeding the maximum) as in the opinion of the court is necessary to protect the public from serious harm from the offender. [Previously the Criminal Justice Act 1991, s 2(2)(b).]

R v Reddy and Haslam [2001] 2 Cr App Rep (S) 226. The defendant R pleaded guilty to a joint count with H and another count of ABH. H was convicted of the joint count of ABH. The victim was the same in both counts. The victim and another man who was having a relationship with R's girlfriend lived in the same block of flats. The victim intervened in a dispute between R and his girlfriend at the block of flats. The following day R was abusive to the victim and others at the same place. At about 3am, the victim tried to make R leave. R punched him in the face a number of times causing him to fall and kneed him in the face. He then grabbed his hair and punched him on the back of the head and kicked him in the face again. R then chased after someone who he feared was going to call the police and returned. He then struck the victim a number of times with his foot. The victim was taken to hospital where a cut to his nose and bumps to his head were seen.

Later the same day at 5pm the two defendants arrived at the block. They pushed their way into the victim's flat. The victim was forced to the floor and R sat on him punching him to the head asking him where his girlfriend and her baby were. H cut the telephone wire. R grabbed the victim by the hair, put him onto a sofa and again demanded to know where the girlfriend was. The victim's head was repeatedly hit against the wall and punched in the face by R. H kicked him to the thighs and knees. When the victim again was unable to say where the girlfriend was R once again kicked him in the face. H shouted, 'Old Bill, Old Bill' and R repeatedly karate kicked the victim. R also attempted to gouge out his eyes and headbutted him. The incident lasted about 20 minutes. The judge described it as a premeditated joint attack on a smaller defenceless man and an orgy of violence. He said he gave modest credit for the pleas because of the overwhelming evidence. He said H had participated fully till he shouted Old Bill to stop the violence. Both men were 21 and treated as of good character. The pre-sentence report for R indicated a lack of remorse and lack of insight into his behaviour. Held. The court could not conclude that there was a risk of further offences by these men of good character so as to evoke the powers of longer than normal sentences. R sentence was reduced from 5 years to **3 years** with the earlier ABH sentence of 2 years concurrent remaining. H's sentence was reduced from 5 years to **2½ years**.

R v Smith [2001] 2 Cr App Rep (S) 160. The defendant pleaded guilty at the Magistrates' Court to ABH. He jumped on a bus ignoring the queue. An 85-year-old woman said something to the effect, 'There's a queue.' After she sat down he got up, approached her and spat in her face. She got up to remonstrate with him and pushed him. Because of their differing sizes it had no effect. He punched her in the face and she fell to the floor. A witness said that you could really hear the crack. She was knocked out for a short time. She was in a lot of pain. There was no medical evidence but the photographs were not a pretty sight. When interviewed he said he wanted her to behave and a man can strike a woman once for being cheeky. He claimed justification. He showed no remorse. The risk of re-offending was assessed as high. A psychiatrist said over the past 20 years there had been a number of incidents of the accused threatening people with a knife, intimidating others and hitting patients or staff. The risk increases when he is intoxicated. Another psychiatrist said the frequency and variety of these incidents indicated they would occur in the future with the same frequency and variety. The judge said the sentence started at 18 months and he extended it to 4 years. Held. It was a quite disgraceful piece of loutish and yobbish behaviour. The base sentence was not too high. It could have been considerably higher. Previously the court had suggested an uplift of 50–100% was appropriate. The extension to 4 years was abundantly justified. [The police CRO is not referred to].

See also **LONGER THAN COMMENSURATE SENTENCES**

Miscellaneous offences

3.8 *R v Regis and Marius* [1999] 2 Cr App Rep (S) 245. The defendants were convicted of ABH. The defendants were employed as security guards at a 'rave' where some 12,000 people attended. They received no training. The victim became violent and began assaulting someone. Security guards were instructed to remove him. They tried to and he struggled violently. The defendants and two others carried him via a fire exit to where some ambulances were. He continued to struggle. Two paramedics saw the victim being dropped after which he tried to kick the guards. M then kicked him in the head showing anger in his face. He continued to kick him as R joined in kicking him. The paramedics then intervened and stood over him to protect him. The victim later died of drug poisoning unconnected with the defendants. The victim had two or three bruises to the head. R was of good character and M had a number of previous including affray and possession of an offensive weapon. He also had references. Held. Those who kick others especially in the head should expect to go to prison. It was wrong not to differentiate between them. **2 years** for M and **18 months** for R not 3½ years for both.

Nurses, doctors etc

3.9 *R v Eastwood* [2001] EWCA Crim 155, [2002] 2 Cr App Rep (S) 318. The defendant changed his plea on the day of his trial to guilty of ABH. The defendant was drunk, beaten up and found in a ditch. He was taken to hospital and an ECG was thought appropriate. A nurse asked him to turn on his back for it to be done. He said, 'Leave me fucking alone,' and grabbed her index finger and squeezed it tightly. She said it was hurting and asked him to let go. He swore at her and sharply pulled her finger back causing a great deal of pain. He let go, she left and he continued to be abusive and aggressive. The police were called. The finger was swollen and had torn ligaments. Two fingers were splintered together and she was on light duties for a week and then had to stop work. Several months later she still hadn't returned to work. Her treatment was continuing and she might require surgery. When interviewed he said he was an alcoholic and didn't remember anything. He did not think the nurse was lying. He had an appalling record including offences of minor violence. Two years before he was convicted of ABH and received 4 months. Held. The assault was unprovoked and caused very considerable suffering and distress. The injury was serious. The need for a severe sentence is obvious. Nurses are particularly vulnerable. The starting point was somewhere between 21 and 24 months. **15 months** substituted for 21 because the late plea may not have been his fault.

Police officer, on

3.10 *R v Fletcher* [1998] 1 Cr App Rep (S) 7. The defendant was convicted of ABH. The victim and other officers were in full uniform enforcing parking regulations with a police truck. They approached a car with a police removal sticker on it, intending to tow it away. The defendant said he would move it. The defendant then pushed the police officer victim and said, 'You're not taking my car.' He was told to calm down and threatened with arrest for obstruction. He pushed pasted the victim. He slid under the officer's arm into the vehicle. The victim caught him round the neck. The defendant confronted the victim and was told he was arrested. The defendant drew back his right arm and the officer turned to avoid the blow. He then seized the victim's arm and pulled him from the car. The officer received a blow and fell back into the middle of the road. He got to his feet and the defendant drove the car away with the engine racing. The victim and another tried to get out of the way but the victim was hit by the car's wing mirror. The car sped off. The victim had a dislocated coccyx, which was an excruciatingly painful injury. He was off work for 6 months. Held. The defendant was 30 and had previous convictions for dishonesty and violence but none for 7 years. Officers deserve protection. **9 months** was not excessive.

R v Casey [2000] 1 Cr App Rep (S) 221. The defendant pleaded guilty to ABH at the Magistrates' Court and common assault at the Crown Court. The defendant drove the wrong side of a 'keep left' sign was followed by a police car and was stopped. The police tried to breathalyse him and the defendant tried to move away. A police officer took hold of him and the defendant shouted, 'You fucking bastard,' and he punched the officer. The defendant then pulled him into the road and punched him five or six times to the head. The officer fell to the ground and the defendant sat astride him and punched him repeatedly in the face. A member of the public came to his assistance and pulled the defendant away and the defendant leaned back and twisted the member of the public's knee. This caused ligament damage, which was the common assault matter. The officer returned to work after 3½ months. He had suffered bruising and swelling along with short-term memory loss. The defendant said he had taken cocaine and he thought he was being attacked. He had previous convictions including one for ABH when he received 9 months suspended. Held. 3 years reduced to **2 years 3 months** with 9 months concurrent for the common assault unchallenged.

R v Elliott [2000] 1 Cr App Rep (S) 264. The defendant pleaded guilty at a late stage to ABH. Outside a nightclub there were a number of scuffles and fights. Police arrived and tried to arrest the defendant. The defendant struck the officer twice in the back of the head. The officer fell to the ground grabbing the defendant's clothes. As the defendant tried to get away he dragged the officer behind him. The defendant hit him more than once from above. The officer suffered bruising. The defendant was 22 with one previous conviction for an unrelated matter. He was sentenced on the basis that initially he did not know it was a police officer. **8 months** not 12.

R v Broyd [2001] EWCA Crim 1437, [2002] 1 Cr App Rep (S) 197. The defendant pleaded guilty to ABH. Shortly after midnight police attended outside a nightclub and found the defendant being restrained on the ground by 3 door staff. He was struggling but the door staff had the upper hand. The defendant was allowed to get to his feet and was clearly drunk. He refused to co-operate and threatened to hit an officer. After a short struggle he was arrested for threatening behaviour. He was taken to the police vehicle still struggling and he turned to the arresting officer and headbutted him and said, 'Take that.' The blow split the officer's lip and chipped one of his teeth. He was interviewed and admitted the offence. The defendant was 36 with 8 convictions. The last one was in 1991. They were 5 for criminal damage, 2 for threatening behaviour and 1 for obstructing an officer. He had never received a custodial sentence. Held. **9 months** reflected the gravity of the offence. It was wholly appropriate to be of some length to punish and to make clear that custodial sentences will follow assaults on police which cause injury.

Prison officer, against

3.11 *R v Mills* [1998] 2 Cr App Rep (S) 198. The defendant made an early plea of guilty to ABH. He had a quarrel with an officer and was placed on report. The next day he threw a jug of boiling water over that officer and swung a sock with batteries at the officer who managed to restrain him. The officer was scalded and in considerable pain but was released from hospital the following day. The defendant was 22 and had a number of previous including affray. He had had four prison sentences. Held. As there was a plea and as it was not the worst case of ABH where the maximum is 5 years, **3 years** substituted for 4.

See also *R v Fryer* [2002] 2 Cr App Rep (S) 554 and PRISONERS – *Total sentence when sentence consecutive to the sentence being served*

Prison officers assaulting prisoners

3.12 *R v Fryer* (19 March 2002, unreported). [The report does not make it clear what the offences were but it was probably ABH. Three Wormwood Scrubs officers punched and kicked a prisoner in the segregation unit for 1½ to 2 minutes. The convictions followed bogus charges and disciplinary proceedings against the prisoner. Because of the breach of trust **4, 4 and 3½ years** upheld.]

Racially motivated

See **ABH – ASSAULT OCCASIONING ACTUAL BODILY HARM – RACIALLY AGGRAVATED**

Road rage

See **ROAD RAGE –** *ABH*

School teachers, medical staff etc

3.13   *R v Byrne* [2000] 1 Cr App Rep (S) 282. The defendant pleaded guilty at the Magistrates' Court to ABH. The defendant punched a teacher in the face in a private area at a primary school. The defendant was very angry and was talking about his son. The deputy head had warned the defendant and had tried to stop the defendant reaching the victim. The victim required two stitches for a cut lip and took 2 to 3 weeks to recover. He was teased at school about it and he had difficulty sleeping. He needed stress counselling. The defendant believed a teacher had pinned his son against a wall, which turned out to be entirely false. The victim did not recall his son. The defendant was in work, married with five children and had 10 previous convictions mainly for theft and burglary. None were for assaults. His last offence was in 1990. In 1984 he was convicted of a public order offence when he became angry in a hospital and made a though nuisance of himself. He expressed remorse. Held. Schoolteachers are in a particularly vulnerable position but **9 months** substituted for 15 months.

R v McNally [2000] 1 Cr App Rep (S) 535. The defendant pleaded guilty to ABH. The defendant was waiting for his son to be seen by a doctor started shouting at a staff nurse adding, 'You're fucking trying to kill my son.' A doctor tried to intervene and he was very aggressive to him. The doctor began to back away and the defendant hit him in the face causing him to fall backwards. As he fell he hit his head against a table. He suffered a haematoma on the temporamandibular joint, bruising, a cut to his chin and bleeding in the middle chamber of his ear. Hearing loss and tinnitus were present 8 months later. On arrest he apologised. He made a full confession in interview. The defendant was 41 with a good character and at the time was being treated for depression. He was a reliable employee and also had references. Doctors, nurses and their staff are entitled to whatever protection the courts can give. Held. People who use violence against them should expect prison. **6 months** not 12.

See also **STALKING –** *ABH*

Stranger in the street, attack on

3.14   *R v Marples* [1998] 1 Cr App Rep (S) 335. The defendant pleaded guilty to ABH. Late at night the victim was in a queue for taxis at a station. Some in the queue had been waiting 45 minutes. The defendant and another went from a seat to the head of the queue. An altercation developed and the defendant struck the man at the head of the queue and tried to push him out of a taxi. The victim then approached and said, 'Now lad.' or something similar. He punched him on the nose fracturing his nose. The defendant said he had been drinking and was feeling sick and had been on the seat for some time. He had marks to his neck from the tussle with the first man. He expressed genuine regret. He was 21 and had 11 previous court appearances but none for violence. He was sentenced to 6 months imprisonment with a concurrent 3 months for a revoked Community Service Order. Held. Because there was a plea of guilty 6 months was reduced to **4 months**.

R v Howells Re Robson and Howard [1999] 1 Cr App Rep (S) 335 at 342 – LCJ. The defendants R and H pleaded guilty to ABH. The defendants were in a market square and they saw the victim carrying a case of lager. R aged 18, shouted at him for a beer and the victim smiled and walked on. R ran up to him and punched him saying, 'Don't you grin at me'. The victim fell to the ground and was repeatedly kicked and punched by R and H aged 17. A member of the public shouted out and the two ran off. The victim received a severe black eye but was not detained in hospital. The defendants were arrested several days later and R said he had little recollection of the event and H said he went to help R as the victim was bigger than R. Both defendants were of good character with exemplary work records. They were also genuinely ashamed. Held. Gratuitous violence, directed at members of the public who are going about their business and doing nothing whatsoever to provoke such violence must attract and be understood to attract severe punishment. Conduct of this kind, cannot be tolerated. The custody threshold was passed. Apart from this they appear decent young men. A very short term will suffice. **2 months** detention not 6.

R v Smith [2001] 2 Cr App Rep (S) 160. See *Longer than commensurate sentence*

Victim over 65

3.15   *R v Smith* [2001] 2 Cr App Rep (S) 160. See *Longer than commensurate sentence*

4 ABH – ASSAULT OCCASIONING ACTUAL BODILY HARM – RACIALLY AGGRAVATED

4.1   Crime and Disorder Act 1998, s 29

Triable either way. On indictment maximum 7 years. Summary maximum 6 months and/or £5,000.

Where the offence was committed relevant to a football match and where there are reasonable grounds to believe that making a banning order would help to prevent violence or disorder at or in connection with any regulated football match; the court must make a Football Banning Order under the Football Spectators Act 1989, s 14A and Sch 1, para 1.

Magistrates' Court Sentencing Guidelines September 2000

4.2   Entry point. Are Magistrates' sentencing powers appropriate? Consider the level of racial aggravation and the impact on the victim. Examples of aggravating factors for the offence are deliberate kicking or biting, extensive injuries (may be psychiatric), headbutting, group action, offender in position of authority, on hospital/medical premises, pre-meditated, victim particularly vulnerable, victim serving the public and weapon. Examples of mitigating factors for the offence are minor injury, provocation and single blow. Examples of mitigation are age, health (physical or mental), co-operation with the police, voluntary compensation and genuine remorse. Consider committal for sentence. Give reasons if not awarding compensation.

For details about the guidelines see **MAGISTRATES' COURT SENTENCING GUIDELINES** at page 331.

General

4.3   *R v Saunders* [2000] 2 Cr App Rep (S) 73. The defendant was convicted of racially aggravated ABH. He had pleaded guilty to having a bladed article in a public place. Mr Ali parked his car outside his home. The defendant, when fuelled with drink, said, 'I don't like Pakis, fucking Pakis.' and 'kick them out.' Mr Ali went indoors and called the police. Believing they had arrived he went outside. Several of Mr Ali's friends attended. The defendant started pushing Mr Ali and throwing punches at him, wildly, causing him to fall to the ground. He got up and was punched in the face with a powerful blow. As he fell again he was continually hit. On the ground he was kicked in the face and head. As the victim left he held a knife and threatened Mr Ali's friends and sister. The victim had a cut lip grazing and bruising. The defendant denied hitting Mr Ali and said he assaulted him. The defendant was 35 with many previous convictions over 20 years including GBH in 1986 and wounding and affray in 1992. The sentence of **6 months** concurrent for the knife was not challenged. Held. The **42 months** sentence was not susceptible to attack.

Defendants aged 17–20

4.4   *R v Kelly and Donnelly* [2001] EWCA Crim 170, [2001] 2 Cr App Rep (S) 341. The defendants were convicted of a joint count of racially aggravated ABH and D was convicted of a count of racially aggravated ABH on his own. Mr Kapoor the victim of the joint count was driving in his S registered Porsche convertible with Mr Puri the victim of the other count and another. The defendants made racist remarks at them repeatedly using the word, 'Paki'. A witness said the defendants had goaded them and there were many references to the car. Donnelly stabbed Mr Kapoor with a biro and Kelly hit him with a bottle or some heavy object. Mr Kapoor headbutted Kelly. Mr Kapoor had a superficial wound to his chest and bruising. Kelly had a swelling and a small cut to the lip and a tooth was pushed back which he later lost. Kelly was 19 then and had previous convictions but none for violence. He had never lost his liberty. Donnelly was younger than Kelly, had more convictions and had lost his liberty more than once. Held. The judge was correct to give them the same sentence. The ABH was worth 18 months following a trial and the racial element was worth a further 9 months making **27 months** not 3 years' YOI. In the case of Donnelly that was consecutive to a sentence for breach of his release licence.

Racially motivated ABH before s 29 in force

4.5   *R v Williams* [1997] 2 Cr App Rep (S) 97. The defendant pleaded guilty at the earliest opportunity to affray. Police attended in the early hours of the morning after youths had been celebrating after a FA cup final. They found a group of youths facing a corner shop and broken glass on the pavement. The police explained there had been complaints about the noise and bottles being thrown. The group then moved about 5–10 yards and increased in size to about 35. The defendant who was in the group shouted, 'It's only a bastard Paki family complaining. We'll soon have those fuckers out of here.' He was warned by a police officer and said, 'They aren't human. They are fucking Paki bastards.' He was arrested and struggled with his escort. He admitted throwing a bottle at a corner shop but said he had drunk about 12 pints and didn't remember the remark. He was treated as of good character and was in work. **12 months** substituted for 21 months.

R v Earley and Bailey [1998] 2 Cr App Rep (S) 158. The defendants E and B both 18, made an early plea of guilty to ABH. At night the two approached a Pakistani in the street and asked for money. They were larger than him and were frightening and threatening. The victim showed them his empty wallet and he was told, 'You're going to be beaten up anyway, Paki.' He was pulled towards a doorway and punched six or seven times. He fell to the ground and was kicked on the upper part of the body about six times. Police arrived and they kept referring to him as a Paki. The victim was dazed and concussed but suffered no fractures. He was released from hospital after about 40 minutes. E said he had been drinking and had run out of money. E had previous for criminal damage, being carried and breach of bail for which he received a C/D. He was also on bail for assaulting a constable, (result not known). B was in breach of a C/D for ABH. Bailey had a Newton hearing about whether it was a racially motivated and lost. The judge started at 2 years and doubled it because it was racially motivated. He gave B 4 years with 3 months consecutive for the C/D. He gave E ⅓ off for his plea making 2 years 8 months with 1 month consecutive for the C/D. Held The 2 year starting figure was too low and the doubling of the figure was also wrong. B should have had some discount. Looking at it afresh B's sentence should be **3 years 3 months** with 3 months consecutive. E's sentence was unaltered. The sentences remain severe because they were racially motivated.

R v Miller [1998] 2 Cr App Rep (S) 398. The defendant pleaded guilty to affray. The defendant abused a black man aged 46 by shouting, 'Black bastard', 'Fucking nigger,' as he followed the man with other youths who lagged behind. Then the defendant who appeared to be in a rage hit and kicked the victim's back and head while shouting, 'Black bastard.' The victim was knocked to the ground. The defendant continued to kick him. The victim said he was terrified. The defendant was 20 and had convictions for dishonesty and criminal damage, but none for violence. Held. This offence comes towards the top of incidents that are charged as affray. Because of the aggressiveness of the defendant and the racial motivation **21 months** detention not reduced.

For basic principles about racially-aggravated offences see **RACIALLY-AGGRAVATED OFFENCES**

5   ABSTRACTING ELECTRICITY

5.1   Theft Act 1968, s 13

Triable either way. On indictment maximum 5 years. Summary maximum 6 months and/or £5,000.

Crown Court statistics England and Wales[1] – Crown Court – Males 21+ – Abstracting electricity

5.2

| Year | Plea | Total Numbers sentenced | Type of sentence% | | | | | Average length of custody (months) |
			Discharge	Fine	Community sentence	Suspended sentence	Custody	
2000	Guilty	3	0	0	100	0	0	0
	Not guilty	5	0	0	60	0	40	4.6

The cases are listed under **THEFT ETC** – *Electricity or gas (including abstracting electricity)*

1   Excluding committals for sentence. Source: Crime and Criminal Justice Unit, Home Office Ref: IOS 416-02.

ACCOUNTING, FALSE

See **FALSE ACCOUNTING**

If they were any cases they would be listed under **THEFT ETC**

6 AFFRAY

6.1 Public Order Act 1986, s 3

Triable either way. On indictment maximum 3 years. Summary maximum 6 months and/or £5,000.

Where the offence was committed relevant to a football match and where there are reasonable grounds to believe that making a banning order would help to prevent violence or disorder at or in connection with any regulated football match; the court must make a Football Banning Order, under the Football Spectators Act 1989, s 14A and Sch 1, para 1.

Magistrates' Court Sentencing Guidelines September 2000

6.2 Entry point. Are magistrates' sentencing powers appropriate? Consider the impact on the victim. Examples of aggravating factors for the offence are busy public place, group action, injuries caused, people put in fear and vulnerable victim(s). Examples of mitigating factors for the offence are offender acting alone, provocation, defendant did not start the trouble and it stopped as soon as the police arrived. Examples of mitigation are age, health (physical or mental), co-operation with the police, voluntary compensation and genuine remorse. Consider compensation. Give reasons if not awarding compensation.

For details about the guidelines see **MAGISTRATES' COURT SENTENCING GUIDELINES** at page 331.

Guideline remarks – Serious affrays

6.3 *R v Keys* (1986) 84 Cr App Rep 204 – LCJ. In cases of very serious affray where it is plain that there was some measure of preparation, central organisation and direction, those who are organisers and ringleaders can expect heavy sentences in the range of **7 years and upwards**. At the other end of the scale, acts of individual participants on the edges of the affray cannot be taken in isolation. Even though a particular defendant never hit an opponent, never threw a missile, never physically threatened anyone, nevertheless, even if he participated simply by encouraging others and shouting insults and threats, he thereby helps to promote the totality of the affray. He must accordingly take some share of the blame for the overall picture. The more he is shown to have promoted the affray, the greater must be his punishment. Where there has been not only a concerted major affray, but also a prolonged and vicious attack on the police, any participant, however slight his involvement may have been, can expect a sentence of at least **18 months to 2 years**. The carrying of weapons, the throwing of missiles and so on ought properly to be reflected in an increase in that minimum.

Aircraft, on

See **AIRCRAFT OFFENCES** – *Affray*

Football etc related

6.4 *R v Pollinger and Pearson* [1999] 1 Cr App Rep (S) 128. The defendants pleaded guilty to affray. Pollinger also pleaded to common assault. After an equalising goal had been scored at a football match there were two pitch invasions. Rival fans fought. At the first invasion, Pollinger was at the forefront, pushing a player, (the common assault). He was escorted off the pitch by policemen. At the second invasion one team cut the other team's players off from their exit. Pollinger ran the length of the pitch. Pearson in the first invasion confronted opposition players aggressively and gesticulated at them. He brushed or pushed a steward away. He was one of the first to invade the pitch in the second invasion and also ran the length of the pitch. The players who gave evidence at the trial of those who pleaded not guilty said they were frightened. Pollinger, aged 27 had a good work record and some previous convictions but none for violence and only one for a public order offence some years previously. Held. Pollinger's sentence of **4** months and 4 months consecutive was not wrong. However, because of very exceptional personal circumstances the sentences were **suspended**. Pearson aged 32, had convictions for public order offences and other matters up until he was 22. He was in work and had a family. His **4 months** sentence was not altered.

Partner/ex-partner, against

6.5   *R v Howells Re Jarvis* [1999] 1 Cr App Rep (S) 335 at 342 – LCJ. The defendant pleaded guilty to affray. He and his co-defendant made a large number of telephone calls to his ex-wife. He was amicable but the co-defendant was aggressive. After about eight calls she unplugged the telephone and later her boyfriend arrived and they went to bed. At about 3.40am they heard loud banging and the boyfriend got up and saw the defendant and the co-defendant coming up the stairs. When the defendant reached the top of the stairs he shouted, 'I'm going to get you, you bastard.' The boyfriend tried to shut the door but the defendant pushed it open and grabbed the boyfriend's hair. The ex-wife telephoned the police and the intruders left. After the police had arrived there were two further telephone calls from the co-defendant. The police discovered that the lower door lock had been damaged and the door forced. The defendant was arrested and outlined the friction between him and his ex-wife culminating in her refusal that night to let him have his passport which was at her house. He also said he resented the boyfriend living in what was the matrimonial home and said he had not formed an intention about what to do with the boyfriend but did agree he said he was going to 'get' him. He was 30 with a 15-year-old conviction for assaulting the police, an ABH conviction on his wife in 1994 (probation) and an assault on police conviction also in 1994 (fined £500). The pre-sentence report said his conduct was attributed to drink. He expressed regret. Held. The offence called for a custodial sentence. As it was his first custodial, he had learnt his lesson and there was no continuing danger to his ex-wife or her boyfriend **3 months** not 6.

Police officers, involving

6.6   *R v Sabeddu* [2001] 1 Cr App Rep (S) 493. The defendant was committed for sentence for an affray which was throwing an empty drinks bottle at the police at a May Day demonstration. The defence said it was a 'one man affray.' He was also committed for possessing a medicinal product for sale. Police stopped him before he went into a warehouse rave party. He was found to have 26 wraps of Ketamine in a wallet concealed up his trousers. He was 18 and of good character. Held. 3 months detention not 8 for the Ketamine. The affray merited a consecutive sentence and was committed on bail for the other. He was part of a large crowd. His action could have precipitated further violence. **6 months** detention was at the top of the bracket but not manifestly excessive.

R v Fox [1999] 1 Cr App Rep (S) 332. The defendant, aged 21 pleaded guilty at the first opportunity to affray at the Magistrates' Court and was committed for sentence. Police were called to an incident at a public house where a crowd of 40 had gathered. A friend of the defendant was arrested and the defendant who had been drinking was abusive and threatening. He produced a bottle, which fell to the ground and smashed. He struggled violently and attempted to strike an officer. The police used CS gas to subdue him. Held. He was of good character and full of remorse. **4 months** substituted for 9 months.

Racially motivated

See **RACIALLY-AGGRAVATED OFFENCES**

Public houses and chip shops etc

6.7   *R v Holmes and Holmes* [1999] 2 Cr App Rep (S) 100. The defendants, GH and AH pleaded guilty to affray at the magistrates and were committed for sentence. The defendants were in a chip shop and tension developed between them and other customers. GH swore, and hit someone on the head. AH joined in and both punched the victim. GH then punched someone who tried to intervene and the victim fell to the ground. GH said he had drunk 8–10 pints and didn't remember much. He did remember punching and kicking the victims. AH said he had 7 pints. They were both of good character with references and in work. **9 months** substituted for 15 months for both.

R v Howells [1999] 1 Cr App Rep (S) 335 at 338 – LCJ. The defendant pleaded guilty to affray. The defendant with two others visited a pub in the evening and behaved in a rowdy manner. One of the other two damaged a barmaid's shoes and the landlord asked the group to pay for the damage. An argument developed and they were asked to leave. The defendant left but the others remained and a fight broke out in which the landlord was punched several times. The fight then continued outside and the defendant was hit on the back of the head. The defendant then hit the assailant a number of blows in retaliation. The victim lost consciousness for 4 minutes and suffered pain, swelling and bruises to his cheek and jaw. One eye was closed and he had a 1″ laceration to his lip. Another hit the landlord fracturing his jaw in two places. The defendant's plea was on the basis of excessive self defence. He was 26 and had several convictions including a violent disorder when he was 19 for which he was fined. He had not received a custodial sentence before. He had sole parental responsibility for a very young child. Held. This did pass the custody threshold but **4 months** not 9.

AGENTS PROVOCATEURS

See **ENTRAPMENT/AGENTS PROVOCATEURS**

AGGRAVATED BURGLARY

See **BURGLARY – AGGRAVATED**

7   AGGRAVATED VEHICLE-TAKING

7.1   Theft Act 1968, s 12A

Triable either way unless the vehicle was only damaged and the value of the damage is less than £5,000 when it is summary only.

On indictment maximum 2 years, and where death is caused 5 years. Summary maximum 6 months and/or £5,000. Mandatory disqualification of 1 year and endorsement (3 to 11 points).

Crown   Court   statistics   England   and   Wales[1] *– Crown   Court – Males   21+ –*
Aggravated vehicle taking

7.2

Year	Plea	Total Numbers sentenced	Type of sentence%					Average length of custody (months)
			Discharge	Fine	Community sentence	Suspended sentence	Custody	
2000	Guilty	255	1%	0%	19%	0%	79%	12.4
	Not guilty	20	0%	0%	5%	0%	90%	12.9

1   Excuding committals for sentence. Source: Crime and Criminal Justice Unit, Home Office Ref:
IOS416-02.

Magistrates' Court Sentencing Guidelines September 2000

7.3   Entry point. Is it so serious that only custody is appropriate? Consider the impact
on the victim. Examples of aggravating factors for the offence are competitive driving:
racing, showing off, disregard of warnings eg from passengers or others in the vicinity,
group action, police chase, pre-meditated, serious injury/damage, serious risk, trying to
avoid detection or arrest and vehicle destroyed. Examples of mitigating factors for the
offence are no competitiveness/racing, passenger only, single incident of bad driving,
speed not excessive and very minor injury/damage. Examples of mitigation are age,
health (physical or mental), co-operation with the police, voluntary compensation and
genuine remorse. Give reasons if not awarding compensation. [Note The ability to
award compensation is restricted by the Powers of Criminal Courts (Sentencing) Act
2000, s 130(6) which is deals with motor vehicle accidents.]

For details about the guidelines see MAGISTRATES' COURT SENTENCING GUIDELINES at
page 331.

General considerations

7.4   *R v Bird* (1993) 14 Cr App Rep (S) 343 at 346 – LCJ. The most important of the
statutory criteria for the offence of aggravated-vehicle taking in judging the gravity of
the case is paragraph (a) that the vehicle was driven dangerously on a road or other
public place, for that concerns the culpability of the driver, whereas the incidence and
severity of any injury or damage under paragraphs (b), (c) and (d) are to some extent
a matter of chance.

Disqualification, for how long?

7.5   *R v Nicholls* (15 November 2001, unreported). See *Police car, being pursued
by a*

Drug abstinence order

7.6   Powers of Criminal Courts (Sentencing) Act 2000, s 58A(1). Where a person is
18 or over the court may make an order requiring the offender to abstain from misusing
specified Class A drugs and provide, when instructed to do so a sample to ascertain
whether he has any specified Class A drugs in his body. (3) The court must be of the
opinion the offender is dependant or has a propensity to misuse specified Class A drugs
and the offence is a trigger offence or the misuse of any specified Class A drug caused
or contributed to the offence in question. (7) An order shall be for not less than
6 months and not more than 3 years. (9) No order shall be made unless the court has
been notified that arrangements for implementing the order are available. [Criminal
Justice and Court Services Act 2000, Sch 6 specifies aggravated vehicle-taking as a
trigger offence.]

Police car, being pursued by a

7.7 *R v Frostick* [1998] 1 Cr App Rep (S) 257. The defendant pleaded guilty to aggravated vehicle-taking and driving whilst disqualified. Ten minutes after the car was stolen the police saw it and switched on their lights and their stop sign. The car driven by the defendant cut across the central reservation and accelerated away. It entered a 30 mph zone and travelled at speeds of about 85 mph. It crossed several mini roundabouts at speed and went right at a keep left sign. It stopped in a cul-de-sac. In interview he said he was paid to take the car and didn't stop because he was disqualified. The defendant was 23 and between 1992 and 1995 he had 24 previous convictions. Nearly all concerned motor vehicles particularly TDA and driving offences. He had received 21 months for dangerous driving, driving whilst disqualified and driving a conveyance when he knew it had been taken without authority. Held. As the maximum is 2 years, 18 months was a commensurate sentence, and because of the plea **15 months** not 21 months.

R v Nicholls (15 November 2001, unreported). The defendant pleaded guilty to aggravated vehicle taking, drink/drive, driving whilst disqualified and no insurance. He drove in a stolen car and was seen by police who put their light on to indicate him to stop. He did so but as the officers were about to get out of their car he sped away half on half off the pavement for about 100 metres. He drove through residential streets at between 50 and 60 mph and straight through red traffic lights at 60 mph. After travelling at over 80 mph over a brow of a hill he hit two vehicles at red traffic lights. When tested he was 3 times over the drink/drive limit. When interviewed he admitted speeds of between 80 and 100 mph. He was 29 with two findings of guilt and four convictions mostly for road traffic offences. He had three convictions for drink/drive. He was currently disqualified and had been disqualified six times for periods up to 3 years. The judge indicated the discount for pleading guilty was reduced because of the overwhelming evidence, his drinking and because he was a repeat offender. The sentences were ordered to run concurrently. Held. Credit must be limited because he was caught red-handed. **22 months** for the aggravated vehicle taking was in no way wrong. Because of employment prospects and rehabilitation 5 years' disqualification not 10.

AIDS

For the fear that the victim might contract AIDS although there was no evidence s/he had see VICTIMS – *Victim fears she will contact AIDS from sex attack*

For where defendant has AIDS see DEFENDANT – *AIDS, defendant has*

8 AIRCRAFT OFFENCES

Various offences and penalties.

General principles

8.1 *R v Oliver* [1999] 1 Cr App Rep (S) 394. Travelling on an aircraft places a special duty on passengers to co-operate and behave. The safety of the aircraft and the passengers may be put in jeopardy. A relatively small incident may have catastrophic consequences, which may not always be foreseen. Even on a guilty plea to affray it is correct to pass imprisonment.

ABH

8.2 Offences against the Person Act 1861, s 47

Triable either way. On indictment maximum 5 years. Summary maximum 6 months and/or £5,000.

R v Beer [1998] 2 Cr App Rep (S) 248. The defendant pleaded guilty to being drunk on an aircraft, and common assault. She was convicted of ABH. Before boarding a transatlantic flight the defendant told the staff she had a drink problem. She was monitored. She was abusive to the staff. She threw her part full wine glass and her tray at staff and pulled a tie clip off a member of staff who tried to calm her down. She went to the lavatory and consumed the best part of a bottle of whisky. She then fell asleep. On arrival police boarded the plane. She started to swear and shout. She kicked out at a constable with both legs hitting him in the groin. This was very painful. She was abusive and struggled. While handcuffs were placed on her she bent the same officer's hand back causing a painful injury. She lashed out as she was led away and landed a painful blow to the same police officer's leg by kicking him as she was put in a van. That officer was not back on duty 8 months later. One of his testicles was persistently swollen and painful. The wrist injury was still requiring treatment 4 months later. It caused him at times to have shooting pains. Except for a drink/drive offence she was of good character. She had a 12-year-old son. She was sentenced to 6 months, 2 months concurrent and 18 months consecutive. Held. The **18 months** sentence and the overall sentence of 2 years were not excessive.

Affray

8.3 Public Order Act 1986, s 3

Triable either way. On indictment maximum 3 years. Summary maximum 6 months and/or £5,000.

R v Oliver [1999] 1 Cr App Rep (S) 394. The defendant pleaded guilty to affray. The defendant travelled from America with his wife, young daughter and baby. The air steward asked the defendant to move the baby from a cot to one of their laps. He lost his temper, became abusive and moved towards the steward with his hands raised. He calmed down and a little later apologised. He again lost his temper this time with his wife. The cabin staff separated them and moved her away from him. He appeared to try to get to the flight deck and the steward blocked his path. The passengers were frightened and the captain considered diverting the plane. Held. Travelling on an aircraft places a special duty on passengers to co-operate and behave. The safety of the aircraft and the passengers may be put in jeopardy. A relatively small incident may have catastrophic consequences, which may not always be foreseen. Even on a guilty plea it is correct to pass imprisonment. If this offence had been committed on the ground a non-custodial might have been appropriate. However, here **12 months** not 18 months' imprisonment.

R v Oliver [1999] 1 Cr App Rep (S) 394. The defendant pleaded guilty on rearraignment to affray. He, his cousin and his father travelled from Newcastle to Spain. The defendant and his cousin were noisy and rude from the time they reached their seats. All three shouted and swore at each other. The cousin asked for and was found a seat and as she was leaving she pulled his head back by the hair. She pulled his head from side to side and threw a drink in his face. He punched her and she slapped him back. The staff had to intervene and moved them to different parts of the aircraft. With 2 hours still to go he ranted incoherently and kicked the seat in front shouting threats at his cousin. He threatened to open the aircraft door and the captain considered diverting the plane. The staff had to watch him in shifts for the rest of the flight. Police took him off the plane. He was receiving psychiatric treatment for a tendency to panic. Alcohol, drug abuse and his unwillingness to co-operate with the treatment worsened the condition. Held. The incident was over a very considerable time and for some 2 hours after the drink was thrown. There was considerable anxiety to staff and passengers. Conduct of this sort must be met with a significant sentence. **12 months** can't be criticised.

See also **AFFRAY**

Dangerous goods, delivering for loading

8.4   Air Navigation Order 2000, arts 60 and 122 and various regulations

Triable either way. On indictment maximum 2 years. Summary maximum £5,000 fine only.

R v Tropical Express Ltd [2001] EWCA Crim 1182, [2002] 1 Cr App Rep (S) 115. The defendant company pleaded guilty to delivering for loading onto an aircraft dangerous goods which he knew or ought to have known were capable of posing significant risk to health and safety etc contrary to the Air Navigation (Dangerous Goods) Regulations 1994, reg 4(2) and consigning 13 packages for carriage by air contrary to Air Navigation (Dangerous Goods) Regulations 1994, reg 6E. The company was a small company with 12 employees and shipped goods by air. It acted as middleman between those sending freight and air-carriers and their agents. Some of its employees were involved in smuggling cigarettes, which involved a loss to the Revenue of $7.5m. The effective sole Director of the company informed Customs about his suspicions and did all he could to help Customs about it. As an act of revenge against the company the employee involved in the smuggling presented a package property described as 'dangerous goods' at Stansted Airport for shipment to Nigeria. Twice it was rejected by the sales agent because of lack of proper paperwork and the boxes were damaged etc. Later the company, which had rejected the package, telephoned the employee and enquired about the packages. The employee said they had been shipped by Swiss Air without difficulty. This was not withstanding Swiss Air do not ship cargo to Nigeria. Next the employee presented the same goods wrapped up without proper labelling about it being dangerous goods to the same sales agent. They were suspicious and discovered they contained barrels and toxic liquid etc and informed the Civil Aviation Authority. The defendant company had conducted its affairs blamelessly for over 10 years. The sole Director gave evidence for the Customs in the trial about the cigarette trial and the employee was sent to prison. The company had lost its principle customer as a result of the prosecution. The defendant company was fined £20,000 with £18,000 costs. That put the company in a perilous position. Held. Normally the fine would be substantial. This is a wholly exceptional case so **£5,000 fine** and the costs to be taxed and include the sentencing hearing and preparation for that only.

Drunk, being

8.5   *R v Abdulkarim* [2000] 2 Cr App Rep (S) 16. The defendant pleaded guilty to being drunk on an aircraft and smoking in a prohibited part of an aircraft at the Magistrates' Court. The defendant who came from the United Arab Emirates was on a flight from Dubai to London. He smoked repeatedly in a non-smoking section of the plane. Passengers complained and he complied with the requests to stop from the staff only to light another one shortly afterwards. He dropped a lighted cigarette down the side of his seat and was unwilling to assist the staff in retrieving it. He had drunk about eight cans of beer and the staff refused to serve him with anymore. He demanded more and when refused showed his discontent in a forceful way. A doctor who examined him 3½ hours after the plane landed said he was still drunk. He was of good character. Held. Strong deterrent sentences are needed but **6 months** substituted for 12.

R v Ayodeji [2001] 1 Cr App Rep (S) 370. The defendant pleaded guilty to being drunk on an aircraft. A count of endangering an aircraft was left on the file. The defendant travelled from Lagos to London. It was a no smoking flight. He persisted in smoking even when told not to. He extinguished a cigarette on a bulkhead and a fire extinguisher had to be used. He was abusive calling a stewardess a 'white bitch' several times. He was very drunk. He suffered from schizophrenia. He had served several long prison sentences including 5 years for attempted robbery. Held. We take a very serious view of the case. Notwithstanding the endangering count being left on the file. The judge was entitled to sentence on the basis the passengers were utterly terrified. He had boarded the plane without his medication and deliberately got drunk. **8 months** was appropriate.

Endangering an aircraft or any passenger

8.6   Air Navigation Order 1989 and Civil Aviation Act 1982, s 61

Triable either way. On indictment maximum 2 years. Summary maximum £5,000 fine only.

R v Mullaly [1997] 2 Cr App Rep (S) 343. The defendant pleaded guilty to two offences under the Air Navigation Order and the Civil Aviation Act 1982 The first offence was the passenger's might be endangered and the second offence was he was drunk. The defendant, a US citizen, who was on a transatlantic flight to Manchester was suffering from a cocktail of alcohol and medication. He was asked several times to return to his seat because of his behaviour but he ignored the requests. He banged on the toilet door so it buckled. He banged the luggage rack. He went to the front of the aircraft where he clenched and unclenched his fists. He was incoherent. He pushed a steward while he tried to use a restraining kit. He managed to escape from the handcuffs while passengers guarded him. He got up and swore. The captain considered making an emergency landing in Ireland. The aircrew were in fear. A passenger described it as her worst nightmare. He was treated as of good character. Held. To reflect the plea and his good character the 2 year maximum was wrong. **18 months** substituted.

R v Ryan [2001] EWCA Crim 824, [2001] 2 Cr App Rep (S) 550. The defendant pleaded guilty, although not at the first opportunity to endangering the safety of an aircraft or persons therein contrary to the Air Navigation (No 2) Order 1995. On a flight from India the smoke alarm went off in the lavatory. Members of the crew armed with fire extinguishers knocked on the door but there was no response. They gained access and found the defendant there with burnt paper in the lavatory bowl. There was a smell of burnt paper. He said he lit paper to light a cigarette. The other passengers were frightened. He returned to his seat and caused no more trouble. He told police he was burning a receipt to avoid Customs duty. The aircraft materials were fire resistant. The defendant was 35 and had 94 previous convictions including robbery for which he received a 4½ year sentence. Held. Those who are tempted to endanger the safety of an aircraft or the passengers should expect deterrent sentences. **15 months** was not excessive.

Pilots

8.7   There are various offences that could be charged.

R v Grzybowski [1998] 1 Cr App Rep (S) 4. The defendant pleaded guilty to making false entries in his personal flying log, contrary to what is now Air Navigation Order 2000, art 83(2) at the Magistrates' Court. He was a pilot instructor teaching people to fly microlight aircraft. One of his trainees agreed to pay him petrol money and examination fees to learn to fly. The trainee was dissatisfied with the amount of flying he was receiving. However on his second flight in a particular aircraft when he was flying solo it crashed and he was killed. That evening the defendant handed to the Air Accident Investigation inspectors his log book. It included two entries for trips of the trainee, which hadn't taken place. There were five other entries on days which the trainee couldn't have flown because he was elsewhere. The log also contained his comments. The defendant claimed that the five trips were made but on other days. He claimed the entries helped the trainee to obtain a licence and that he was pressed to do it by the trainee. The trainees' father did not accept that. He was 48 and had a conviction for failing to record that he had taken possession of an aircraft, which was not properly licensed. Held. The log was a record of critical importance. It showed whether young pilots have or had not been properly trained. We profoundly disagree that the custody threshold was not crossed. It called for the sentence of **6 months**, which he had received.

R v Evans [2001] 1 Cr App Rep (S) 442. The defendant pleaded guilty to recklessly acting in a manner likely to endanger a helicopter and anyone therein, contrary to the Air Navigation (No 2) Order 1995 and flying otherwise in accordance with the air operator's certificate. Six months after obtaining a helicopter licence he gave some friends rides without charging at a carnival. He was then approached by someone who wanted to raise money for a registered charity in the name of his autistic son. He then gave rides to members of the public and raised £270. Children were allowed to sit on an adult's laps without being strapped in. One boy moved the control column and an adult had his feet on the control pedals while the helicopter was in flight. The defendant says he told the adult to take them off. An expert said that children sitting unrestrained put the helicopter and passengers in danger. The defendant was unemployed with two previous convictions for unrelated offences. The defendant's actions could have been catastrophic. Held. **3 months** for the endangering, £1,000 for the certificate offence and £5,127.29 prosecution costs were not wrong.

9 AMPHETAMINE

General properties

9.1 *R v Wijs* [1999] 1 Cr App Rep (S) 181 – LCJ. Amphetamine is a synthetic stimulant which, in powder or tablet form is a Class B drug. There are two very obvious differences between cannabis and amphetamine: (1) while market prices tend to fluctuate depending on the interplay of supply and demand, and there has been a sharp decline in the street value of amphetamine in the last two years or so, amphetamine has always, weight for weight, been vastly more valuable than cannabis; (2) it has always been the practice to retail amphetamine to consumers in a highly adulterated form. Based on seizures in the last year or two, amphetamine now has a higher concentration of the drug than was once generally the case. While goods seized at the points of importation may contain a high percentage of amphetamine, at a retail level the purity may well be no more than (say) 10% to 12% or even less. It follows that a trafficker in possession of amphetamine stands to earn very much larger sums than a trafficker in possession of the same weight of cannabis; that a relatively small weight of amphetamine of maximum purity will, when adulterated, convert into a very large number of individual doses; and that the weight of amphetamine which a user may hold for his own personal consumption is likely, in many cases, to be much smaller than the weight of cannabis held for personal consumption. For reasons clearly given in *R v Aranguren* (1994) 99 Cr App Rep 347 that with amphetamine sentence should depend not on market value but, on the quantity of the amphetamine calculated on the basis of 100% pure amphetamine base (ie the maximum theoretical purity of 73% amphetamine base in amphetamine sulphate, the remaining 27% being the sulphate). As was held in relation to Class A drugs in we should not attempt to distinguish between different drugs in Class B on the basis that one such drug is more or less pernicious than another.

See also **DRUG USERS; IMPORTATION OF DRUGS; POSSESSION OF DRUGS; PRODUCTION OF DRUGS** and **SUPPLY OF DRUGS (CLASS A, B AND C)**

10 ANIMAL CRUELTY

10.1 Protection of Animals Act 1911, s 1 etc

Summary only maximum 6 month and/or £5,000.

There is power to destroy the animal, deprive ownership of the animal and power to disqualify persons from having custody of any animal.

Magistrates' Court Sentencing Guidelines September 2000

10.2 Entry point. Is it serious enough for a community penalty? Examples of aggravating factors for the offence are adult involving children, animal(s) kept for livelihood, committed over a period or involving several animals, depriving pleasure from torturing or frightening, disregarding warnings of others, group action, offender in position of special responsibility towards animal, premeditated/deliberate, prolonged neglect, serious injury or death and use of weapon. Examples of mitigating factors for the offence are ignorance of appropriate care, impulsive, minor injury, offender induced by others and single incident. Examples of mitigation are age, health (physical or mental), and genuine remorse. Always consider disqualifying the offender from having custody and depriving him or her of owning the animal concerned.

For details about the guidelines see **MAGISTRATES' COURT SENTENCING GUIDELINES** at page 331.

11 ANIMAL RIGHTS ACTIVISTS

Various offences and penalties.

Guideline remarks

11.1 *R v Martin* [1999] 1 Cr App Rep (S) 477 – LCJ. Generally the sentences imposed for acts of violence relating to animal rights activism is in almost every case lower than for terrorist offences fuelled by political extremism. There are obvious reasons why this should be so. The political threat presented by such offences is much less potent; and the general level of sophistication is a very great deal lower.

See also **ANIMAL CRUELTY**

12 ANIMALS

Endangered species, purchasing selling etc

12.1 Control of Trade in Endangered Species (Enforcement) Regulations 1997, reg 8

Triable either way. On indictment maximum 2 years. Summary maximum 3 months and/or Level 5 fine (£5,000).

R v Eley and Bull [1999] 1 Cr App Rep (S) 252. The defendants E and B pleaded guilty to conspiracy to sell restricted animal specimens. B owned 128 rhinoceros' horn weighing 239 kgs which was 40 years old or older. He had acquired all but one of them before the regulations prohibiting the sale etc came into force. They were from between 77 and 128 rhinos. At least seven came from a critically endangered species. Their value was estimated to be £2.4m. In 1986 B was convicted of murder and sentenced to life imprisonment the sentence for which he was still serving. He asked A to help sell them and she approached E. E approached Christies and Sotheby's. A contacted the Stock Exchange who contacted the RSPCA. B had offered E a commission of 10% and 25% on anything above £10,000 per kg. Two RSPCA inspectors posed as buyers and met E and B who was on home leave. Negotiations continued and because of the sellers' suspicions the RSPCA inspectors were replaced by police officers posing as potential purchasers. Sophisticated arrangements were made to receive the money. There was a meeting in a hotel where £30,000 cash was shown by the police and shortly afterwards the defendants were arrested. E said that he thought it was legal to deal with the articles and if the man from the Stock Exchange had said it was illegal he would not have tried to sell the horn. B also said he thought it was legal. He also said the one horn bought in 1994 on his behalf had an exemption certificate. The pleas were tendered on the basis of recklessness as to the knowledge of the illegality of the activity. E was 54 and treated as of good character. He had character references and a letter from a commander of the Metropolitan police saying that he had performed a valuable service with his technical skill and equipment to trace stolen cars. He suffered from depression, renal damage, hypertension and tinnitus. He also said he was entrapped because throughout the meetings with the RSPCA inspectors and the police they continually avoided giving a straight answer to questions about whether the sales were legal. B was 63 and was an antique dealer at the time. Held. The offence is obviously serious. The quantity was very large. For E whilst not saying the original sentence was wrong, justice can now be made by **6 months** not 9 months. **15 months** for B was entirely correct but the forfeiture order could not stand because the horn had been acquired legally and there were no reasons given for rejecting the submissions made about hardship.

See also ANIMAL CRUELTY and ENVIRONMENTAL OFFENCES – *Slaughterhouses and animal incinerators*

APPREHENSION

For impeding the apprehension or prosecution of an another person see ASSISTING OFFENDERS

13 ARMED FORCES, MEMBERS OF

(Present and potential members)

Sentence may bar entry to services

13.1 Ministry of Defence Statement [1980] JP 697. Don't take into account the possibility of the defendant joining the forces as the Ministry of Defence judges the offence by the sentence imposed [Since this was issued the policy for recruitment in the armed forces has changed radically. This is only of persuasive force but is a policy which would be natural sentencing for Crown Court judges.]

14 ARSON

14.1 The section is divided into four sections: (1) arson (sometimes known as simple arson). The intent can be reckless or an intention to destroy property; (2) arson being reckless whether life was endanged; (3) arson with intent to endanger life and (4) a life sentence was/was not appropriate.

It is a violent offence for the purses of passing a longer than commensurate sentence [Powers of Criminal Courts (Sentencing) Act, s 80(2)] and an extended sentence (extending the licence) [Powers of Criminal Courts (Sentencing) Act 2000, s 85(2)(b)][1].

1 Powers of the Criminal Courts (Sentencing) Act 2000, s 161(3).

Crown Court statistics England and Wales[1] *– Crown Court – Males 21+ – Arson*

14.2

Year	Plea	Total Numbers sentenced	Type of sentence%					Average length of custody[2] (months)
			Discharge	Fine	Community sentence	Suspended sentence	Custody	
2000	Guilty	316	1%	1%	26%	2%	62%	33.4
	Not guilty	58	0%	0%	7%	2%	88%	42.6

1 Excluding committals for sentence. Source Crime and Criminal Justice Unit, Home Office Ref: IOS416-02.
2 Excluding life sentences.

Longer than commensurate sentences, how much extra?

14.3 *R v Jones* [2001] EWCA Crim 1524, [2002] 1 Cr App Rep (S) 214. The defendant pleaded guilty to two charges of arson and one charge of vehicle interference at the Magistrates' Court. There were three TICs for arson. Each charge was committed late in the evening or in the small hours after the defendant had been drinking. He set fire to a garage which was used to store furniture and ran off. A few days later he broke into a vehicle ripped the seats and set fire to the foam. He ran off. The vehicle charge was when he got in a van and left when he was seen. The suspicion was he might set fire to the van. He made full and frank confessions and said he was involved in an arson offence every weekend since his release from prison. Fire appeared to excite him. He was in breach of his licence by 278 days. The judge started at 3 years each concurrently and gave an uplift of 6 years making 9 years on each. Held. There were no fires at occupied or domestic premises. The uplift should be 3 so **6 years** instead. [Details of his record and the reports are not given.]

See also LONGER THAN COMMENSURATE SENTENCES

Psychiatric report, need for

14.4 *R v Calladine* (1975) Times, 3 December. It is unwise to pass sentence without a psychiatric report.

Arson (simple arson)

14.5 Criminal Damage Act 1971, s 1(1), (3)

The offence is triable either way. On indictment maximum life. Summary maximum 6 months and/or £5,000.

Defendant under 17

14.6 *R v Bool and White* [1998] 1 Cr App Rep (S) 32. Both defendants pleaded guilty to arson of an industrial premises, based on reckless intent. At the time of the offence they were 12 and 13. They lit a fire, which quickly got out of control causing between £2.4 and £2.55m worth of damage. There was also about £2m worth of lost business. Both had behavioural problem and a background of domestic violence to their mothers. Bool had a fascination with fires. Held. 3 years' detention reduced to **18 months** because of their age.

R v Nicholls and Warden [1998] 1 Cr App Rep (S) 66. Both defendants and two others entered a late plea of guilty to arson of a partly built house next to their school's playing field causing £50,000 worth of damage. The two appellants were then aged 12 and playing truant after a school break. Each blamed the others. Nichols had no previous convictions but had one caution for dishonesty. Warden also had no previous convictions but had one caution for TDA and because of his disruptive behaviour had been put into local authority care. The two other defendants were given deferred sentences. Held. Notwithstanding their ages because this was such a serious offence immediate custodial sentences were right. However, **1 year** detention substituted for 2.

R v Taylor [2000] 1 Cr App Rep (S) 45. The defendant pleaded guilty to arson. With three others he entered a yard on an industrial estate. A stack of paper was set alight which set fire to other stacks. £250,000 worth of damage was done to the paper. Other businesses also lost £50,000. The defendant admitted lighting the paper saying he was egged on. He also said he tried to put it out and failed. He was of good character. He was then 13, now 14. He had shown increasingly oppositional behaviour at home and was lighting fires at home. He was refusing to attend school. However, he had made good progress at the secure unit. **2 years** not 3 detention substituted.

R v Letham [2000] 1 Cr App Rep (S) 185. The defendant pleaded guilty to arson being reckless whether property was to be destroyed. When he was 16 he sat the last of his GCSE exams. The next day he and another returned to the school and threw stones at the windows causing over £800 worth of damage. The next morning a fire was started in the art block, which caused £400,000 worth of damage. The student's course work for the year was destroyed. He admitted both incidents to the police. He suffered from a depressive illness. He had no previous convictions. He received **2 years** YOI. Held. Less than that could not be justified.

R v Smith [2001] EWCA Crim 467, [2001] 2 Cr App Rep (S) 376. The defendants were convicted of simple arson. Four boys then aged 15 or 16 bought some petrol and set fire to a comprehensive school. The fire took several hours to extinguish. The damage and cost of hiring Portacabins was £721,000. A large amount of exam course work was lost. An expert concluded petrol had been poured through a broken window. The trial did not take place till about 18 months after the offence. The boys were either of good character or treated as such. There was no suggestion of mental or psychological disorder. The trial judge referred to the boy's boasting about it and the need for deterrent sentences because of the prevalence of these fires. Held. Where a crime is prevalent in an area it was right to pass deterrent sentences. He was right not to distinguish between them. An adult might well be facing 8 years after a trial. **6 years** detention was not excessive.

R v Tingle [2001] EWCA Crim 368, [2001] 2 Cr App Rep (S) 379. The defendant pleaded guilty at the earliest opportunity to simple arson. Another boy was concerned that his fingerprints might be found at a Primary school that he had burgled. The defendant then 15 after sniffing gas and taking cannabis, which made him less, inhibited went with the other boy to the school. The defendant threw a petrol bomb, which he had made earlier, through a window. The main part of the school, which had 460 children, was destroyed. The damage and the cost of replacement classrooms was assessed at £1.1m. All the work of the 4 to 7 year olds was destroyed. A video tape was found showing him, while the school burnt giving a commentary saying he was a hero and being absolutely delighted. The children were adversely affected. He had a previous conviction for causing damage. The pre-sentence report concluded that there was a high risk of him re-offending and a high risk of significant harm to the public. There was no mental disorder but he appeared to satisfy the criteria for, 'socialised conduct disorder.' However, he was genuinely remorseful. Held. Because of the authorities, particularly *R v Storey* [1984] 6 Cr App Rep (S) 104, his plea and so he would not be crushed by the sentence **5 years** not 8 detention.

See also *R v Marklew and Lambert* [1999] 1 Cr App Rep (S) 6 (Life imposed but sentences of 10 years considered appropriate if a life sentence had not been imposed.)

Defendant aged 17–20

14.7 *A-G's Reference (Nos 40-43 of 1997)* [1998] 2 Cr App Rep (S) 151. Three defendants pleaded guilty to simple arson. Arson with intent to endanger life counts were left on the file. The three defendants were told they could not come to a house where some young people had gathered. The three went to a public house and then made four petrol bombs from milk bottles and rags etc. They returned to the house and a petrol bomb was thrown at the wall of the house causing damage to a window frame and cracking the window. Another bomb was thrown at a car in the driveway causing damage of about £700. A third unlit bomb was left on the pavement. The fourth was found in a garden nearby.

The defendants were 16, 17 and 18 at the time of the offence. One defendant was in breach of a supervision order for offences, which included criminal damage. Another was in breach of a conditional discharge for criminal damage, which involved throwing glass bottles at a building. Held. The appropriate sentence would have been **2½ to 3 years** YOI and not the combination orders imposed. The sentences were unduly lenient but not increased because of what had happened since including the fact that the community service orders had been largely completed and the defendants were in work.

Domestic premises

14.8 *R v Hales* [1999] 2 Cr App Rep (S) 113. The defendant pleaded guilty to simple arson and was committed for sentence. A householder saw a piece of paper on fire sticking through his letterbox. He opened the door and saw the defendant. He put out the flames while the defendant ran away. When the defendant was arrested he admitted the offence but said he did not know why he did it. An expert said because there was no accelerant the fire would not have taken hold. The defendant was a lonely man who had a drink problem but no previous convictions. He lacked self-esteem. He told the psychiatrist that he had committed other anti-social behaviour when drunk. His employer attended court. Held. **15 months** substituted for 2 years.

Insurance money, to obtain

14.9 *R v Ellis* [1999] 1 Cr App Rep (S) 374. The defendant was convicted of conspiracy to commit arson and 9 counts of conspiracy to defraud. There was a very serious fire at the defendant's warehouse involving cloth and garments stored there by traders including some of his co-defendants. There was no evidence of an accelerant. Police found a list of payments to the loss assessor, which had been made by the conspirators. Investigations revealed that the insurance claims were also inflated. The defendant and the loss assessor arranged the fire and were at the centre of the conspiracies involving the others with an arrangement that the proceeds would be shared. The insurers made full or reduced payments. The defendant obtained 35% of the claims. The total claim was about £2m and £1.5m and was paid. The judge determined the defendant had probably received more than £200,000. He was 60 and of good character with depression. He was described as a ruined man. **7 years** was proper.

Petrol bombs

14.10 *A-G's Reference (Nos 40–43 of 1997)* [1998] 2 Cr App Rep (S) 151. Three defendants pleaded guilty to simple arson. Arson with intent to endanger life counts were left on the file. The three defendants were told they could not come to a house where some young people had gathered. The three went to a public house and then made four petrol bombs from milk bottles and rags etc. They returned to the house and a petrol bomb was thrown at the wall of the house causing damage to a window frame and cracking the window. Another bomb was thrown at a car in the driveway causing damage of about £700. A third unlit bomb was left on the pavement. The fourth was found in a garden nearby.

The defendants were 16, 17 and 18 at the time of the offence. One defendant was in breach of a supervision order for offences, which included criminal damage. Another was in breach of a conditional discharge for criminal damage, which involved throwing glass bottles at a building. Held. The appropriate sentence would have been **2½ to 3 years** YOI and not the combination orders imposed. The sentences were unduly lenient but not increased because of what had happened since including the fact that the community service orders had been largely completed and the defendants were in work.

Revenge

14.11 *R v Akhter* [2001] 1 Cr App Rep (S) 7. The defendant pleaded guilty to simple arson. The defendant began a probationary period at work and was spoken to about his performance. Just over a year from when he started he learnt from his line manager that things were not going well and he might lose his job. He stole a key and on a Saturday with another poured petrol over his line manager's desk and a severe fire started. £450,000 worth of damage was caused. Thirty people from other parts of the building had to be evacuated. The written basis of plea included that the co-accused put the petrol near the desk and lit it while he acted as look out. He had not intended to go that far or cause the damage that was caused. He was of good character and had 16 references referring to his impeccable character. **3 years** was not manifestly excessive.

Arson – reckless whether life would be endangered

14.12   Criminal Damage Act 1971, s 1(2) and (3)

Indictable only. Maximum sentence life.

Guideline remark

14.13   *A-G's Reference (No 1 of 1997)* [1998] 1 Cr App Rep (S) 54. The defendant pleaded guilty to arson being reckless whether life would be endangered. If you commit this sort of offence, save in the most exceptional circumstances, an immediate prison sentence must be imposed.

Crime of passion

14.14   *A-G's Reference (No 61 of 1996)* [1997] 2 Cr App Rep (S) 316. The defendant pleaded guilty to arson being reckless whether life would be endangered. He was also committed for sentence for animal cruelty and criminal damage. The defendant when worse for drink and in a jealous rage set fire to some of his girlfriend's clothes and maimed their dog with a sledgehammer. He then locked the door and left the terrace house burning. The fire brigade found the dog in a pool of blood and there was £2,000+ damage caused. An elderly man lived on one side and a couple lived on the other side. When asked about those people he said he never gave them a thought. He had only one previous conviction, which was for damaging the car of another boyfriend of his girlfriend. Held. Taking into account all the personal mitigation and that it was a reference, **2 years** not probation.

Death is caused

14.15   *R v Whitbrook and Smith* [1998] 2 Cr App Rep (S) 322. The two defendants aged 17 and 18 pleaded guilty at a late stage to arson being reckless whether life was endangered. A count of manslaughter was left on the file. The Smith family lived opposite to Mrs Mitchell and her three sons 9, 10 and 16. Accepting the defendant Smith's idea, Whitbrook lit a firework and put it through Mrs Mitchell's letterbox. The two boys then ran away. The house was engulfed in flames. The 10-year-old boy was found by firemen alive but with 53% burns to his body. He died 3 days later of brain damage and multi-organ failure. The defendants expressed remorse. The Smith family had to leave the area. One defendant was of good character and the other had nothing similar on his record. **3 years** YOI was not altered.

Where there is a conviction for manslaughter, see **MANSLAUGHTER** – *Fire, by*

Defendant under 17

14.16   *R v Spong and Bromham* [1999] 1 Cr App Rep (S) 417. The defendants pleaded guilty to arson being reckless whether life was endangered. The two boys then 15 and 16 were at a special needs school. They went to a storeroom and each lit a cigarette. They heard someone who they feared was a teacher. They both dropped their cigarettes and ran from the room. £400,000 worth of damage was caused. They were sentenced on the basis that they had given no thought either to the possibility of a fire being caused or to the possibility of lives being endangered. Both defendants were unlikely to re-offend and had responded well over 12 months to the bail support scheme. 21 months and 2 years detention reduced to **15 and 12 months** YOI.

R v Shaun C [2001] EWCA Crim 2007, [2002] 1 Cr App Rep (S) 463. The defendant appears to have pleaded guilty to two counts of arson being reckless whether life was endangered. [The judgment does not say what his plea was.] He asked for an offence of arson to be taken into consideration. A 73-year-old woman was asleep in bed alone at about 10.30pm. Her dog woke her up and she looked into the road outside and saw two male figures run off. They returned and they went towards her front porch. She opened the window and remonstrated with them and they ran off again. She went back to bed. Shortly afterwards, she smelt burning and went downstairs and found flames coming through her letterbox. She was able to put the fire out. A rolled up newspaper was in the letterbox. Police discovered a newspaper had been set alight under her car. Twelve days later at 6.15pm the victim was watching television. She smelt burning and found smoke coming through her letterbox. She managed to extinguish the flames and noticed a number of small fires on the hall carpet and the door itself was alight. The house was full of smoke. Police discovered lit firelighters had been put through the letterbox. The front door was badly damaged and the telephone lines had been burnt. The carpet was burnt in places and the wall was damaged by smoke. The victim found the experience terrifying. The defendant then 14 was arrested after setting fire to some bushes. This was the TIC. He admitted the house fire was his idea, and he knew someone lived there. He said the victim sometimes 'moaned at us and some years earlier had refused to return his football when it went into her garden.' He had no previous findings of guilt. He was not unduly sorry for the effects of his actions and was not willing to offer an apology. A child psychiatrist said he was suffering from an attention deficit hyperactivity disorder and an oppositional deficiency disorder. He had been given medication but had stopped taking it. Since then his behaviour had deteriorated and he had been excluded from school. Held. These offences were serious. The elderly lady was sleeping and caused terror. The second arson was even graver. The gravity of the offences and the apparent indifference by the defendant to the consequences called for a substantial sentence. **3 years** detention was entirely right.

See also **Arson – Life sentence was/was not appropriate** – *Defendant under 17*

Defendant aged 17–20

14.17   *R v Whitbrook and Smith* [1998] 2 Cr App Rep (S) 322. The two defendants aged 17 and 18 pleaded guilty at a late stage to arson being reckless whether life was endangered. A count of manslaughter was left on the file. The Smith family lived opposite to Mrs Mitchell and her three sons 9, 10 and 16. Accepting the defendant Smith's idea, Whitbrook lit a firework and put it through Mrs Mitchell's letterbox. The two boys then ran away. The house was engulfed in flames. The 10-year-old boy was found by firemen alive but with 53% burns to his body. He died 3 days later of brain damage and multi-organ failure. The defendants expressed remorse. The Smith family had to leave the area. One defendant was of good character and the other had nothing similar on his record. **3 years** detention was not altered.

R v J (4 October 2001, unreported). [A gas fire was used in a failed suicide attempt by a 17 year old. **2½ years** YOI not 4.]

R v Holliman [2001] EWCA Crim 2983, [2002] 2 Cr App Rep (S) 142.

See next section.

Domestic premises etc with other occupants

14.18   *A-G's Reference (No 1 of 1997)* [1998] 1 Cr App Rep (S) 54. The defendant pleaded guilty to arson being reckless whether life was endangered. The defendant started a fire in his ground floor flat by setting fire to a cushion. He then went to the public house while the owner of the building slept in another flat. The owner suffered minor burns and smoke inhalation. Several thousand pounds worth of damage was done. The defendant didn't know why he had done it but he was angry. The defendant's criminal record contained many burglaries, several offences of violence, and a great many offences of damage to property. Held. If you commit this sort of offence save in the most exceptional circumstances a custodial sentence must be imposed. One such circumstance is where there is mental trouble or a recommendation of medical treatment. Where the offence is recklessly endangering life, the sentence must be severe. The right sentence here would have been 6 years. Because it was a reference and that the defendant had made efforts to curb his drinking **4½ years** not probation.

R v Walker [1999] 1 Cr App Rep (S) 121. The defendant pleaded guilty to attempted arson being reckless whether life was endangered and reckless as to the starting of the fire. The defendant after drinking 6 pints of lager returned to his flat and had a serious row with his partner. He told her to leave and she did. Feeling sorry for himself he lit the wrong end of a cigarette and dropped it. He thought he had extinguished it. He then went to another room and fell asleep. He woke up with that room full of smoke and broke a vertebra when he escaped out of a window. Occupants in other flats were put at great risk. There was severe damage to the building estimated at £150,000. The defendant had no previous. As a result he had lost his home and his family. **2 years** was not excessive.

R v Parkhurst [1999] 2 Cr App Rep (S) 208. The defendant pleaded guilty to arson being reckless whether life would be endangered. He lived with a woman for 2 or 3 months and she decided she wanted to leave. The two had a lot to drink and he told her he was going to set fire to the place. She fell asleep and she was awoken by the smoke alarm. She was able to escape with her children. The expert said the fire had started in the bedroom with cloth and wood being ignited. A psychiatrist said he had a long history of acting impulsively in response to rejection. He was of 'relatively good character'. **5 years** was stern but not excessive.

A-G's Reference (No 84 of 1998) [1999] 2 Cr App Rep (S) 379. The defendant pleaded guilty to arson being reckless whether life would be endangered after the judge had indicated the appropriate sentence. The defendant was unable to accept that his relationship with his partner was over. He pursued her unsuccessfully with calls, letters and presents. She contacted the police who warned him but the letters and presents continued. Early one morning he poured petrol into her kitchen through the cat flap and set it alight. She woke up smelled the smoke and escaped. She was very upset and suffering from smoke inhalation. £10,000 worth of damage was caused. He had a recent conviction for criminal damage when he had placed glass under the wheel of the ex-girlfriend's new boyfriend's car He also had a conviction for making threats to kill in a letter sent to the girlfriend's new address. Held. **3 years** was lenient but as it was a reference and the sentence had been served the sentence was not altered.

A-G's Reference (No 66 of 1997) [2000] 1 Cr App Rep (S) 149. The defendant was convicted of arson being reckless whether life would be endangered. He had pleaded guilty to simple arson. He entered his mother-in-laws bungalow in the early hours. He squirted petrol onto the hallway carpet. He lit it. He also set fire to the carpet just outside the bedrooms where his wife, his son, his mother-in-law and brother-in-law were sleeping. He had removed a battery from the smoke alarm a week before. The fire was discovered before very much damage could be caused. He stood to gain between £100,000 and £110,000 on his wife's death. He was of good character and was clinically depressed. He expressed regret. Held. The appropriate sentence after a trial was within the range 8 to 10 years. **7 years** substituted for 3 years taking into account it was a reference.

R v Harding [2000] 1 Cr App Rep (S) 327. The defendant pleaded guilty at the earliest opportunity to arson being reckless whether life was endangered. His relationship with his wife was difficult and stormy with periods of separation. There were three children two of which were his. Shortly after midnight after he had spent the afternoon and evening drinking he had a violent argument with his wife and started to smash up furniture. With the help of her brother everyone left except the defendant. He lit separate fires in the house and then climbed out of a window and was found outside a police station screaming incoherently. He was distressed and admitted guilt immediately. There was very extensive damage to the house. Most if not all of the rooms of the property, which was owned by the local authority, were burnt out or smoke damaged. The adjoining house where an elderly lady lived was also damaged. Over £20,000 worth of damage was done to the two properties. He was 27 with convictions but nothing comparable. Held. The court takes a very serious view of arson where life is endangered albeit not intentionally because of the propensity of fire to spread rapidly. The offence was aggravated by the closeness of the elderly neighbour. **4 years** was not manifestly excessive.

A-G's Reference (No 98 of 2001) [2002] 2 Cr App Rep (S) 85. The defendant was convicted of two counts of arson being reckless whether life would be endangered. He was acquitted by the judge of two counts of arson with intent after the jury failed to agree on those counts. He lived with his wife and his daughter aged 16 and his son aged 11. He had married in 1982 and the relationship had become increasingly unstable. There had been recent incidents of violence. On the day of the fire he refused food his wife offered him and was not on speaking terms with his daughter. At night he called his daughter into his room and asked her why she would not speak to him. When she answered he pushed her onto the bed and slapped her twice. The wife intervened and told the daughter to go to her room which she did. The wife ran out and held onto the door handle to prevent the defendant leaving. The handle pulled out and the wife retreated to her daughter's room. The two prevented the defendant getting into the room by leaning against it etc for 30 minutes. The defendant demanded to get in and said, 'Or I'll set myself alight.' Finally he said, 'You can open the door now I have set myself alight.' Flames and smoke were seen below the door. Attempts to extinguish the flames failed and the daughter broke a window and screamed for help. The daughter climbed onto the window sill. A neighbour broke in through a window and found the front door locked and found the defendant outside his bedroom and told him to leave. He refused. The daughter jumped out of the window into a curtain which was held by neighbours. She broke her arm and hurt her back. She suffered cuts to the foot and a radial fracture to the radial head. The wife jumped onto a mattress. As she jumped flames could be seen flickering behind her. She suffered a 1″ deep cut to her hand from the broken window. The neighbour went back into the house where the defendant remained saying he was going to die there. The neighbour saw that the defendant had made no effort to tackle the flames or unlock the front door dragged him downstairs into the front room. It was discovered he had deactivated the smoke alarm and that there were two seats to the fire in the defendant's bedroom. They were consistent with burning items being dragged to the daughter's bedroom door. There was another seat outside that door. Her bedroom door and frame had been totally burnt away. The house was a mid-terrace property. The defendant was interviewed and denied starting the fires deliberately. He was 46 and of good character with references. He suffering from ill health and had served nearly 7 months. Held. The victims were effectively imprisoned by the fire. The judge overestimated the significance of the medical position. **At least 6 years** should have been imposed. Because it was a reference etc. **4 years** not a community rehabilitation order.

R v Holliman [2001] EWCA Crim 2983, [2002] 2 Cr App Rep (S) 142. The defendant pleaded guilty to arson being reckless whether life was endangered. Some travellers had set up an illegal camp in a car park and on tennis courts. There were 13 caravans. The defendant who had spent the evening drinking went to a petrol station at 2am and bought lighter fuel. He went to the camp site and poured the lighter fuel over a propane gas cylinder besides a caravan containing two adults and three children. He was seen holding something alight and placed it next to the cylinder. A fire was lit between the cylinder and the A frame of the caravan. A passer-by very quickly summonsed the police. They extinguished the fire. Only slight damage was caused. Had the fire been allowed to burn it was likely the cylinder would have heated up and exploded causing a fireball so the occupants of the caravan would have been unlikely to survive. The defendant was arrested. He was 20 and was serving in the Royal Navy with no convictions. A large number of character witnesses described him as conscientious, totally reliable etc. He regretted his actions and his risk assessment for re-offending was low. The YOI report described him as very polite and well behaved mature man. Held. There could have been appalling and fatal consequences. **4 years** YOI was severe but not manifestly excessive.

Insurance money, to obtain

14.19   See also *R v Zedi* (13 October 2001, unreported).

Police officers targeted

14.20   *R v Trowbridge* [2001] EWCA Crim 2984, [2002] 2 Cr App Rep (S) 154. The defendant pleaded guilty to arson being reckless whether life was endangered. His downstairs neighbours noticed water was coming from his maisonette through their ceiling. The defendant refused to let their plumber in or come to the door. A carpenter tried to gain entry and was sworn at and told to go away. The water flow increased and the supply had to be turned off. The defendant was seen pulling frantically at something in the bathroom. Eventually the police were summonsed and they were refused entry in an abusive manner. An officer said he would force the door and broke a glass panel. The defendant shouted, 'Fuck off, I've got petrol.' He then threw petrol at the officer and his clothing was splashed. Then he said he was going to burn the whole place down and lit the petrol causing the curtains to catch fire. The officer moved out of the way quickly and so avoided the flames, which spread to the stairs of the maisonette. A fire extinguisher put the flames out. The defendant jumped out of a rear window and was arrested. When interviewed he said he didn't intent to hurt anyone and he wanted to kill himself and be with his deceased mother. He was 50 and of good character and had no history of starting fires. He told the first psychiatrist that he wasn't going to his dump and marched off. The doctor said he had developed a marked antipathy to the people of Devon, which was where he lived. He was released on bail to be assessed and to see whether a probation order with treatment was suitable. He told them he would rather go to prison than there. The doctor said he was a man of limited intelligence who tended to take up fixed stances and was unable to retreat easily. Another said he needed social services assistance and it was surprising he has been neglected so long. The probation proposal is not feasible. The pre-sentence report said he was very vulnerable and unhappy with considerable difficulties coping with day-to-day issues. His risk assessment for re-offending was assessed as high. In 1996 the judge said he posed a significant risk to people and imposed a life sentence. Since then he had been released, recalled (not for offences but because of difficulties with the probation service supervising his release) and released again. The appeal was heard in December 2001. Held. Throwing petrol at a police officer is extremely grave and could have led to a loss of life. However, the criteria for a life sentence were not present. Since his sentence nothing had happened to suggest he constituted a risk to the public. **4 years** substituted which he had served.

Prison/police property

14.21   *R v Wilson* [2000] 1 Cr App Rep (S) 323. The defendant pleaded guilty to arson being reckless whether life was endangered. A prisoner set fire to his cell and caused about £500 worth of damage. A fire extinguisher put the flames out. His actions had 'been essentially a "cry for help" and to get him out of the health care centre, where he was being harassed and threatened.' He was nearing the end of an 8 year sentence for very serious sexual offences and at the time of the offence was exhibiting bizarre behaviour, including smearing and consuming faeces. He said everyone was against him. A psychiatrist said he met the criteria for narcissistic and paranoid personality disorders. He was not currently showing signs of mental illness. The probation officer, relying on psychiatrists said he was a danger to himself and others including his ex-wife and children. Held. The first pre-condition in *R v Chapman* [2000] was not met so life varied to **10 years** consecutive to sentence for which he was serving. The appropriate sentence of 3 years applying *R v Hales* [1999] 2 Cr App Rep (S) 113 at 115. However, the sentence was extended by 7 years for the protection of the public under [what is now the Powers of Criminal Courts (Sentencing) Act 2000, s 80(2)(b)].

Revenge

14.22   *R v Reynolds* [1999] 2 Cr App Rep (S) 5. The defendant pleaded guilty to arson being reckless whether life was endangered. The defendant who was 21 had a grudge against his brother believing he had burgled his room in the past. The defendant went to his brother's bedsit, kicked the door down and started a fire on the ground floor and another on the first floor. The damage was extensive. There was no-one else in the bedsitting rooms in the house but the defendant had no checked that. There was however a risk to the adjoining terraced houses. After initial denials to the police he pleaded guilty. Held. He had several previous convictions for burglary. Three of them were committed because of a grudge. There was little remorse. **6 years** was severe but not excessive.

A-G's Reference (No 23 of 2001) [2001] EWCA Crim 1008, [2001] 2 Cr App Rep (S) 514. The defendant was convicted of arson being reckless whether life was endangered. He had pleaded guilty to criminal damage. After a 4 year on-off relationship with his girlfriend, he told her he would always find her and burn her house down. After they were living apart he entered her house and was drunk and argumentative. He went to a public house and returned. He rammed his car into the back of her car pushing it towards her house. (This was the criminal damage matter.) She was so scared she left. He rang her saying, 'Get home or I'll burn your house down.' Ten minutes later he called again saying the house was burning and it would teach her a lesson. The blaze was extensive. Part of the house collapsed. It was also discovered that the smoke alarm had been removed before the fire started. The occupier of the adjourning house was away but had someone been there, there would have been a significant risk to anyone inside. He denied it but did not give evidence. He had a previous conviction for effectively a duplicate offence to this one when he had thrown petrol bombs through a girlfriend's window for which he received a 42 month imprisonment sentence. It was described as 'arson endangering life.' He had another conviction for smashing car windows when he thought he had been belittled. Held. The sentence to be expected was **between 6 and 7 years**. Therefore **5 years** substituted for 3½ years because it was a reference.

Similar previous convictions

14.23   *R v Firth* [2001] EWCA Crim 1570, [2002] 1 Cr App Rep (S) 309. The defendant pleaded guilty to arson being reckless whether life was endangered. The defendant lived in a hostel and he set fire to a chair and settee in his flat. He said it was to take his own life and voices in his head were telling him to kill himself and to set fire to the flat. After the room filled with smoke he panicked and changed his mind. He reported the fire to the fire brigade and handed himself in to the police. The flat sustained heavy smoke damage. There were convictions going back to 1976 and in 1997 he was sentenced to 3 years' imprisonment for arson and criminal damage committed in virtually identical circumstances. Again it was claimed he intended to take his own life. The pre-sentence report said the risk of harm to the public and the likelihood of re-offending were extremely high. He does not believe he has any control over his behaviour. There was a high risk of self harm and he was totally preoccupied with killing himself. The psychiatric report said the overall impression was of a disorder of adult personality with evidence for dependency, impulsively and antisocial behaviour particularly in a stressful situation. There was emotional instability and solitary traits. A hospital order was not proposed. He was sentenced to 10 years. Held. He poses a considerable risk to the public and there was a powerful need to protect the public from him. 10 years was manifestly too long but this was pre-eminently a case for a longer than commensurate sentence. Sentence varied to **10 years** as a longer than commensurate sentence.

Arson – Intending life would be endangered

14.24   Criminal Damage Act 1971, s 1(2) and (3)

Indictable only. Maximum sentence life.

Guideline remarks

14.25   *A-G's Reference (No 47 of 2000)* [2001] 1 Cr App Rep (S) 471. The bracket for arson with intent is 8–10 years.

Defendant under 17

14.26   *R v Johnson* [2000] 2 Cr App Rep (S) 235. The defendant pleaded guilty to burglary, arson with intent to endanger life, unlawful wounding, escape from custody, affray, aggravated vehicle-taking, TDA and damaging property. He received 9 years' detention concurrent for the arson and the escape counts. For the other offences he received no penalty other than disqualification. He and others stole petrol from a garage and one of them lit it near a house. Just over 3 weeks later he and another escorted an alcoholic home and brutally attacked him. They sprayed graffiti and lit a number of fires about the house. Due to the bravery of members of the public he was dragged unconscious from the property. He spent 5 days in intensive care. The defendant was arrested and detained in a secure unit. While a pool competition was in progress he was asked to return to his room because of his disruptive behaviour. Two staff escorted him and his co-accused attacked one of the staff with a pool cue. He and a third youth armed themselves with pool cues and threatened the staff. He and his co-accused threw pool balls towards the staff one of which caused a deep wound. Furniture was smashed and keys taken enabling the three to escape after they had scaled the perimeter fence with a ladder. A car was stolen and abandoned. The co-accused drove the three off in another stolen car, which crashed. The third youth was killed. These events were the subject matter of the other charges. Held. He had been to courts on five separate occasions. A report referred to all attempts to reintegrate him had failed. Taking into account the defendant's age and his pleas of guilty a **9 years** global sentence was not wrong.

Domestic premises with occupants

14.27   *A-G's Reference (No 57 of 1998)* [2000] 1 Cr App Rep (S) 422. The defendant was convicted of arson, threatening to destroy property and arson with intent to endanger life and two associated counts. He was estranged from his wife but continued to be violent to her after they separated. When she rejected his advances he set fire to the duvet on her bed, (count one). Shortly after he poured petrol through the letterbox of her flat and threatened to burn her out, (count two). Seven days later in the early hours, while his wife was out and her two young children were in the house with a babysitter he poured petrol through the letterbox in the front door and set it alight, (count three). He then left the scene. The front door was the means of escape. Damage was caused but the occupants suffered comparatively minor injuries. He showed no remorse. Held. The appropriate sentence was **8 to 10 years** so as it was a reference **7 years** substituted for 5.

R v McGrath [2000] 1 Cr App Rep (S) 479. The defendant pleaded guilty to arson with intent to endanger life. The defendant returned home after drinking although he wasn't drunk. His partner made a remark about his lorry and he erupted in anger. He kicked the furniture and was violent to her. He locked the back door and poured an inflammable wood preserver over the hall and other rooms. He tried to light it but was unsuccessful. Both doors were now locked. His partner told her son to escape but the defendant pulled him back. He poured the same fluid over the cooker and turned on the gas. The liquid ignited. While his partner tried to put the flames out he tried to fuel the fire. She then tried to escape using her key but he pulled the key out of the lock. She realised he wanted to kill them all. Breathing was now difficult. The son again tried to escape through a window but was stopped. He then stopped her leaving. Eventually he allowed them to leave. £5,000–£8,000 damage was caused. He was of good character. The judge concluded he was a very real danger to the public. **6 years** was not excessive.

A-G's Reference (No 4 of 1999) [2000] 2 Cr App Rep (S) 5. The defendant was convicted of arson with intent to endanger life. She and her husband argued and her husband said he wanted a receipt to prove she had been paying the mortgage. At 10pm she left the home saying she was going to work. She didn't go and when she was satisfied he was in bed she returned. Beneath the bed was a can of petrol she had put there sometime before. While he slept she sprinkled inflammatory material over the floor and she lit it. She shut the door and ignored her husband's screams. Three children were on the premises. Held. She had no previous convictions. One would expect a sentence of at least 8 years. Because it was a reference **6 years** was not altered.

A-G's Reference (No 47 of 2000) [2001] 1 Cr App Rep (S) 471. The defendant was convicted of arson with intent to endanger life. The victim who had a boy and a girl was depressed and left her flat to move in with her sister. He approached her and said he wanted to use her flat for dealing in crack cocaine. He said he wanted to start that night and he would pay to have the electricity connected and £30 a night. She changed her mind about moving out but allowed him to deal from the flat. The defendant and his associate would be there at night and the victim spent her money mostly on drugs. He went on holiday and on his return was told she had agreed to leave the flat for £7,000 from the council. He didn't think it was worth starting up again. Her children returned to live with her and on the night of the fire her stepson was there too. Shortly after midnight he and his associate knocked on her door and when she answered it the two rushed in. They searched the flat and asked, 'Where's the letter?' Five minutes later there was another knock and she could see it was the same two and she wouldn't let them in. The defendant told the other to kick the door in which he did. They ran upstairs and the defendant poured petrol from a can between the two bedrooms and the kitchen, the kitchen and the hall. She asked what was going on and he poured petrol over her T-shirt. She dialled 999 and he smashed the telephone. He was about to douse the bed where the two boys were asleep and she asked why. He struck her three times with a truncheon and poured petrol over the bed. She tried to wake them and his associate said, 'Not the kids.' She continued waking the boys and saw flames coming from the living room. The boys left taking the little girl with them. The rest left also. It took 30 minutes to extinguish the flames. The fire spread to all parts of the flat and caused £7,000 worth of damage. At his trial he relied on an alibi. He was 36 and had a substantial list of convictions mostly for dishonesty. They was also an ABH and procuring an abortion. His risk assessment was considered high. Held. The bracket for arson with intent is **8–10 years**. This case is at the top of the bracket. Because it was a reference **9 years** not 7.

Domestic premises with occupants – Serious injuries

14.28   *R v Manual* [2001] EWCA Crim 2290, [2002] 1 Cr App Rep (S) 526. The defendant was convicted of arson with intent to endanger life, arson being reckless whether life was endangered as an alternative to an intent count and criminal damage.

She was acquitted of GBH with intent. After drinking she returned home and as she went through the car park of her block and tore off a mirror from a car, (the criminal damage). Next she went to the flat of a woman who worked in a store and who she believed was responsible for reporting her for shoplifting. She put a rag through the letterbox, doused it in an inflammable liquid and set it alight. The occupant was able to extinguish it but was greatly distressed and shocked. The victim felt unable to live there for 2 months and the door and carpet was damaged. This was the reckless count. The defendant then did the same to another flat in the block. The occupant did not awake immediately and he collapsed in the smoke. He was rescued by the fire brigade and had very serious burns. They were 7.5% burns to his body surface and required full thickness skin grafts. There was smoke damage to his lungs and 3 months later he was still unable to walk more than a short distance. The door and hall were badly damaged and there was extensive smoke damage to the flat and the victim lost a large number of possessions, some of sentimental value. This was the intent count. The defendant was arrested and denied being in dispute with anyone in the block. She was 48 and then of good character. Before she was sentenced she pleaded to the shoplifting. She was divorced with children and had been under psychiatric care for 21 years. She was being treated for a depressive disorder and in 2000 she had been exhibiting very bizarre behaviour. The events occurred 2 weeks after she was discharged. The judge considered the motive for the second attack was to disguise she had committed the first arson. Held. Taking into account her good character **10 years and 8 concurrent** not 12 and 10 concurrent.

Domestic premises without occupants

14.29 *R v Stacey* [1999] 2 Cr App Rep (S) 298. The defendant pleaded guilty to arson being reckless whether life was endangered and arson. One hour after the occupant left her home the defendant poured lighter fuel or something similar through the letterbox of the house. He then lit a match and caused a small fire on a nylon mat. He then telephoned the emergency services and alerted neighbours. The householder's daughter arrived, as the fire services were about to break down the door. The fire was extinguished. The replacement door cost £595. He left a note for the occupier and was given a £5 reward. People were suspicious and the police questioned him. He denied starting the fire. About 6 weeks later firemen saw the defendant foraging in a roadside dustbin. A few minutes later the defendant called the fire station about a fire at a beach hut near where he had been seen. He was there when they arrived and helped to direct traffic and place cones in the road. Fireman found rubbish had been placed between two huts and ignited. £2,450 worth of damage was caused. The defendant was arrested and admitted the offence and said he started it because he was low and wanted attention. He was 38 and had been rejected for the fire service when he was 19. His only relevant conviction was in 1994 for setting fire to a car. It was more of an insurance fraud than a straightforward case of arson. Reports said he had been involved in a considerable amount of crime and was of low intelligence and vulnerable. The offences of arson were committed when he was depressed and upset and were linked to his mother's death. Held. His re-offending risk was described as considerable. Held. **4 years** not 5½ and **2 years** not 3 for the offences. The sentences remained concurrent.

Petrol bombs

14.30 *A-G's Reference (Nos 78, 79 and 85 of 1998)* [2000] 1 Cr App Rep (S) 371. Two defendants R and O'S were convicted of arson with intent to endanger life relating to two different houses. R had pleaded guilty to arson being reckless whether life was endangered which was not accepted. The third defendant, M was acquitted of those counts but convicted of arson being reckless whether life was endangered relating to the same two houses. R's father had separated from R's mother and had nothing to do with him. One day he heard something, which brought to the surface a long-standing resentment against his father. The three defendants met and R bought some petrol. Two petrol bombs were made and R and O'S threw them at two houses near his father's house. They intended to hit the father's house but made a mistake. The occupants at one house escaped without injury and relatively little damage. At the other house the father jumped from an upstairs window and injured himself. His two children suffered horrific injuries. One had 20% burns with extensive burns to the face hands and legs. The other also had 20% burns with severe burns to face, scalp and other parts of the body. R was now 23, O'S was now 20 and M was now 20. R was the instigator with no similar convictions. O'S was of good character. M was R's girlfriend and under his influence. The judge said she had been used unmercifully. Held. The appropriate sentence for R was **8–10 years** so his **8 years** sentence was undisturbed. It was a very severe sentence for a young man. The judge was entitled to make the distinction between that sentence and the other two defendants. O'S sentence was 5 years and M's was a combination order (probation and 100 hours' CSO).

Revenge

14.31 *R v Flanagan* [1999]1 Cr App Rep (S) 100. The defendant pleaded guilty to attempted arson being reckless whether life was endangered. The defendant called a hospital where she had previously received psychiatric treatment and said she intended to set fire to Orpington police station. She had previously attacked the station by attacking cars, striking a window with a hammer and had attempted to firebomb the station. For that she was convicted of arson. On the same evening as the call she was found in the foyer of the police station attempting to set fire to a pool of paraffin with a burning piece of paper. An officer put it out.

She was 49 and had two previous convictions for arson and a previous conviction for child cruelty. In that case the child had died and it had caused her strong feelings against the police. There were several previous convictions for assaulting the police. She had a history of alcohol abuse, self harm, and anger. One psychiatrist said she had a borderline personality disorder and the other one said she had a severe personality disorder. There was a belief she would commit arson again. Held. **Life was appropriate** but with a 3 year and not 5 year specified term.

A-G's Reference (Nos 78, 79 and 85 of 1998) [2000] 1 Cr App Rep (S) 371. Two defendants R and O'S were convicted of arson with intent to endanger life relating to two different houses. R had pleaded guilty to arson being reckless whether life was endangered which was not accepted. The third defendant, M was acquitted of those counts but convicted of arson being reckless whether life was endangered relating to the same two houses. R's father had separated from R's mother and had nothing to do with him. One day he heard something, which brought to the surface a long-standing resentment against his father. The three defendants met and R bought some petrol. Two petrol bombs were made and R and O'S threw them at two houses near his father's house. They intended to hit the father's house but made a mistake. The occupants at one house escaped without injury and relatively little damage. At the other house the father jumped from an upstairs window and injured himself. His two children suffered horrific injuries. One had 20% burns with extensive burns to the face hands and legs. The other also had 20% burns with severe burns to face, scalp and other parts of the body. R was now 23, O'S was now 20 and M was now 20. R was the instigator with no similar convictions. O'S was of good character. M was R's girlfriend and under his influence. The judge said she had been used unmercifully. Held. The appropriate sentence for R was **8–10 years** so his **8 years** sentence was undisturbed. It was a very severe sentence for a young man. The judge was entitled to make the distinction between that sentence and the other two defendants. O'S sentence was 5 years and M's was a combination order (probation and 100 hours' CSO).

Violent attack, part of a

14.32   *R v Griffin* [1999] 1 Cr App Rep (S) 213. The defendant pleaded guilty to arson with intent to endanger life and causing GBH with intent. The defendant was distressed with the break up of his relationship with the victim. He wrote to his family telling them what he was about to do. The victim came to the premises to pick up some clothing and he pointed a knife at her. She was told she would not get out alive and he stabbed her in the chest. He followed her to the bedroom where he locked the door. There was a struggle over the knife in which the defendant received severe injuries to his hands. After this he recovered the knife and stabbed her several times. By now she was having trouble breathing. Further stab wounds were inflicted and she was told to open her legs. The children then knocked on the front door and he told them to go away. He returned to the bedroom and stabbed her once again in the cheek. The victim became unconscious and awoke up to find he a burning duvet on the bed. She got up to get away and the defendant pushed her to the floor and threw the burning duvet over her, which she managed to throw off. She lost consciousness but awoke and escaped. She had burns to shoulders, arms, hands and feet. Held. The defendant had a significant mental illness and some minor previous convictions. Because of plea and the authorities **9 years** not 11 concurrent for both offences.

See also OFFENCES AGAINST THE PERSON ACT **1861**, S 18 – *Fire, by*

Arson – Life sentence was/was not appropriate

General

14.33   *R v Irving* [1998] 2 Cr App Rep (S) 162. The defendant was convicted of seven counts of arson and one count of threats to kill. During the night he set fire to three cars, one of which was valued at £25,000. Also that night he threw a brick through a window while the occupants, a married couple were asleep. Later that day, he telephoned the house and was abusive and threatening. In another call to the house he said he wanted £400 and was going to, 'burn them alive.' Other calls were made. Later the wife discovered her net curtains had been damaged by fire. Three other cars were damaged by fire that same day. The defendant was 25 years old and had no serious previous convictions. He was not suffering from a mental illness but was of very low intelligence. He had a mental age of about 12. He presented a real risk to the public. Held. **Life was appropriate** but the specified period should be 6 not 8 years.

R v Flanagan [1999] 1 Cr App Rep (S) 100. The defendant pleaded guilty to attempted arson being reckless whether life was endangered. The defendant called a hospital where she had previously received psychiatric treatment and said she intended to set fire to Orpington police station. She had previously attacked the station by attacking cars, striking a window with a hammer and had attempted to firebomb the station. For that she was convicted of arson. On the same evening as the call she was found in the foyer of the police station attempting to set fire to a pool of paraffin with a burning piece of paper. An officer put it out.

She was 49 and had two previous convictions for arson and a previous conviction for child cruelty. In that case the child had died and it had caused her strong feelings against the police. There were several previous convictions for assaulting the police. She had a history of alcohol abuse, self harm, and anger. One psychiatrist said she had a borderline personality disorder and the other one said she had a severe personality disorder. There was a belief she would commit arson again. **Life was appropriate** but with a 3 year and not 5 year specified term.

R v Simmonds [2001] EWCA Crim 167, [2001] 2 Cr App Rep (S) 328. The defendant pleaded guilty to arson. His plea of not guilty to arson with intent to endanger life and reckless whether life was endangered was accepted. These had been based on the other houses in the terrace. In 1998 he married his wife who he had known since 1993. He had a long history of mood swings and she eventually obtained an injunction to prevent him going to the matrimonial home. When he received a letter saying she was starting divorce proceedings he bought some petrol from a garage and drove to the former matrimonial home. At 2.50pm he gained entry by smashing a pane of glass and poured petrol round the unoccupied house. The fire took hold quickly. The building was saved but the contents were entirely destroyed. The defendant telephoned the police saying he had made sure the wife was not in the house and he had a shotgun and he intended to use it against people who had hurt him in the past. Knowing the police were pursuing him he said he would blow them out of the sky. When confronted by armed officers he indicated he had a weapon, which turned out to be a wooden-handled axe. The judge considered this was an attempt to invite them to shoot him. He immediately said I did it. He was 37 and of good character. Both of his wives complained of violence. He had had 40 mental health interventions including being sectioned. He had a personality disorder associated with loss of temper and control. There were no psychiatric recommendations from one psychiatrist. Others were more positive. He was considered highly manipulative and had a long and repetitive history of violence to his female partners which was escalating. There was an encouraging prison report. Held. It was a serious case of arson. There were several worrying features in his behaviour. We are concerned about the risk to the public. However, that itself does not justify a life sentence. Something more has to be established. There were no 'most exceptional circumstances.' **6 years** not life.

R v Trowbridge [2001] EWCA Crim 2984, [2002] 2 Cr App Rep (S) 154. See **Arson – reckless whether life would be endangered – *Police officers targeted***

Defendant under 17

14.34 *R v Stanley* [1999] 2 Cr App Rep (S) 31. The defendant pleaded guilty to arson being reckless whether life was endangered on the second day of her trial. A not guilty verdict was entered for a count for intending to endanger life. The defendant, a girl then aged 16 believed that her social worker had said something to those who ran her daughter's nursery so the daughter lost her place. She went to see her social worker. She was told she wasn't available. She then went and got some petrol and returned. She used a pushchair to jam open some doors. Her child was not present. She sprayed petrol from a container onto a counter and some doors. She set fire to it and ran out. There were about 40 people in the building. The damage was limited to about £2,300 because the fire brigade attended extremely quickly. She was arrested and was violent and abusive. There was a long-standing friction between the defendant and the social services. A High Court judge in 1990 had said she had not been served well by the authorities. Held. She had a previous conviction for arson for which she was conditional discharged. She had a child at the time of the fire who was 2 and one born while she was in prison. She appeared to be undergoing an abnormal personality development. The sentencing judge held that she would remain a danger for an unpredictable time. While in prison she and others had attacked a social worker. For that she had been convicted and sentenced to 12 months for affray and wounding. Also she had 10 adjudications in prison. **Life** with a fixed period of 18 months was appropriate.

Grave enough, is the offence?

14.35 *R v Chapman* [2000] 1 Cr App Rep (S) 377 – LCJ. The first pre-condition for imposing a life sentence for the purposes of public protection was that the offender had committed an offence grave enough to merit an extremely long sentence. *R v Hodgson* (1967) 52 Cr App Rep 113 applied.

R v Wilson [2000] 1 Cr App Rep (S) 323. The defendant pleaded guilty to arson being reckless whether life was endangered or property damaged. A prisoner set fire to his cell and caused about £500 worth of damage. A fire extinguisher put the flames out. His actions had 'been essentially a "cry for help" and to get him out of the health care centre, where he was being harassed and threatened.' The first pre-condition in *R v Chapman* [2000] 1 Cr App Rep (S) 377 was not met so life varied to **10 years** consecutive to sentence for which he was serving. The appropriate sentence of 3 years was extended (ie the licence was extended) by 7 years for the protection of the public under [what is now the Powers of Criminal Courts (Sentencing) Act 2000, s 80(2)(b)].

15   ASSAULT ON A POLICE OFFICER

15.1   Police Act 1996, s 89(1)

Summary only. Maximum 6 month and/or £5,000.

Magistrates' Court Sentencing Guidelines September 2000

15.2   Entry point. Is it so serious that only custody is appropriate? Consider the impact on the victim. Examples of aggravating factors for the offence are any injuries caused, gross disregard for police authority, group action, and premeditated. Examples of mitigating factors for the offence are impulsive action and unaware that person was a police officer. Examples of mitigation are age, health (physical or mental), co-operation with the police, voluntary compensation and genuine remorse. Give reasons if not awarding compensation.

For details about the guidelines see **MAGISTRATES' COURT SENTENCING GUIDELINES** at page 331.

16   ASSISTING OFFENDERS

16.1   Criminal Law Act 1967, s 4

Indictable only. Maximum sentence depends on the maximum offence for the other person's offence. When that maximum is fixed by law, the maximum is 10 years; when 14 years or more, 7 years; when 10–13 years, 5 years and in other cases 3 years.

Driving someone away from a crime

16.2   *R v Taylor* [2002] EWCA Crim 243, [2002] 2 Cr App Rep (S) 385. The defendant made an early plea to doing an act with intent to impede the apprehension of another. He gave his friend a lift to a supermarket where they were going to buy heroin. The friend went and robbed a woman of her handbag and ran back to the car whereupon the defendant drove them away. Police stopped the car. The defendant said he drove off because he feared members of the public might attack them. He was sentenced on the basis he had no knowledge that the friend intended to commit a crime when he got out of the car and when he saw him running with the bag he assumed that there had been a theft. The defendant had a number of convictions principally for drugs and theft. He showed remorse. The co-defendant pleaded guilty to robbery and received 30 months. Held. The level of sentencing to some extent is governed by the seriousness of the offence of the principle offender. **9 months** not 18.

See also **PERVERTING THE COURSE OF JUSTICE/CONTEMPT OF COURT ETC**

ATTEMPTS

Attempts are listed with the full offence except for **MURDER, ATTEMPTED – MURDER, CONSPIRACY TO**

17 BAIL OFFENCES

17.1 Bail Act 1976, s 6

The offence is tried at the court where the offence took place. Maximum sentence at Crown Court (including a committal for sentence) 12 months. Summary maximum 3 months and/or £5,000.

Crown Court statistics England and Wales[1] – Crown Court – Males 21+ – Failing to surrender to bail

17.2

Year	Plea	Total Numbers sentenced	Type of sentence%					Average length of custody (months)
			Discharge	Fine	Community sentence	Suspended sentence	Custody	
2000	Guilty	28	0%	25%	0%	0%	61%	1.6
	Not guilty	3	0%	33%	0%	0%	33%	4

1 Excluding committals for sentence. Source: Crime and Criminal Justice Unit, Home Office Ref: IOS416-02.

Magistrates' Court Sentencing Guidelines September 2000

17.3 Entry point. Is a discharge or a fine appropriate? Examples of aggravating factors for the offence are leaves jurisdiction, wilful evasion and appears after arrest. Examples of mitigating factors for the offence are appears late on day of hearing, genuine misunderstanding and voluntary surrender. Examples of mitigation are age, health (physical or mental), co-operation with the police and genuine remorse. **Starting point fine B.** (£100 when defendant has £100 net weekly income. See page 334 for table showing fines for different incomes.)

For details about the guidelines see **MAGISTRATES' COURT SENTENCING GUIDELINES** at page 331.

Absconding

17.4 *R v Deeley* [2001] EWCA Crim 1793, [1998] 1 Cr App Rep (S) 112. The defendant was convicted of failing to surrender to his bail. The defendant was committed to the Crown Court on four charges of burglary in custody. He was released on bail because of the expiry of the custody time limits and appeared when first required to. He then failed to attend his pleas and directions hearing. Three weeks later he was arrested. He said he was trying to face up to his drug addiction, his relationship was strained and he overlooked the date. He was not of good character. Held. This breach was not unusually serious. **3 months** not 6.

R v Clarke [2000] 1 Cr App Rep (S) 224. The defendant admitted failing to answer to his bail. He was arrested on an alcohol duty evasion case and bailed. It was suggested he was an important participant in a £1.2m duty fraud. He didn't turn up for his trial in July 1998 and the trial against the others proceeded. He was arrested in January 1999 after the main trial had finished. He was then tried and acquitted. In April 1999 he was dealt with for the bail offence. The judge considered his absence might have helped him and his co-defendants in their trials. The defendant had said he had received threats. Held. The judge might have given too much attention to the possible advantages of his absence. His criminality is unaffected by the verdict in the trial he absconded from. The judge was entitled to be critical of the suggestion of threats. Because the maximum is 12 months the sentence was reduced to 7½ months from 9 months. The court then reconvened itself as the Divisional Court and ordered the relevant period to start from January 1999.

R v Keane [2002] 1 Cr App Rep (S) 383. The defendant pleaded guilty to endangering the safety of rail passengers and failing to surrender to his bail. He was bailed to the Crown Court, failed to answer to his bail and was arrested nearly 4 months later. The defendant was 58 and had no convictions but had a long-standing problem with drink. There was a letter saying he was a hard working and conscientious member of the local community. Held. 15 months for the railway offence cannot be faulted. On the day in question it appears he just could not bring himself to face the music and at the last minute decided not to attend. Taking a broad view of all the circumstances, recognising his good character, the alcohol problems 3 months consecutive for the bail offence was more than necessary to mark what must be accepted as the great in convenience and cost in time and money caused by his failure to attend. **1 month consecutive** is sufficient.

Sentence should be consecutive to the sentence imposed for the other offence

17.5   *R v Aroride* [1999] 2 Cr App Rep (S) 406. The defendant pleaded guilty to attempting to obtain property by a deception at the Magistrates' Court and absconded. Held. Failure to surrender to bail is a serious and discrete matter and in principle should attract a separate and consecutive sentence.

18   BAIL, OFFENCES COMMITTED WHEN DEFENDANT IS ON

18.1   Powers of the Criminal Courts (Sentencing) Act 2000, s 151(2). In considering the seriousness of any offence committed while the offender was on bail, the court shall treat the fact that it was committed in those circumstances as an aggravating factor.

Magistrates' Court Sentencing Guidelines September 2000

18.2   Throughout the Guidelines each guideline for the offences says, 'If the offender is on bail this offence is more serious.'

For details about the guidelines see **MAGISTRATES' COURT SENTENCING GUIDELINES** at page 331.

Consecutive sentence, the offence on bail should attract a

18.3   *R v Stevens* [1997] 2 Cr App Rep (S) 180. It may be proper to make a sentence consecutive to one passed on an earlier occasion, particularly where the second offence was committed on bail for the first offence.

BANKRUPT

See **INSOLVENCY OFFENCES**

19 BASIC PRINCIPLES

Departing from the sentencing guidance

19.1 *A-G's Reference (No 83 of 2001)* [2002] 1 Cr App Rep (S) 589. What the authorities do not show are the cases where the individual circumstances of the defendant and the mitigation available to him have led to a justified departure from the guidance provided by the reported decisions. It is fundamental to the responsibilities of sentencing judges that while they must always pay proper regard to the sentencing guidance given, they are required also to reflect on all the circumstances of the individual case. Where sentencing judges are satisfied that occasion requires it, they have to balance the demands of justice with what is sometimes described as the calls of mercy.

A-G's Reference (No 84 of 2001) [2002] 2 Cr App Rep (S) 226. The defendant pleaded guilty to attempted robbery and having a firearm with intent to resist arrest. He tried to rob a Securicor guard delivering cash to a cash dispenser. Held. Personal factors in relation to offences of this gravity can have only a very small effect in determining what the appropriate sentence is.

Prison overcrowding

19.2 *R v Kefford* [2002] EWCA Crim 519, [2002] 2 Cr App Rep (S) 495 – LCJ. The defendant pleaded guilty to 12 thefts and asked for nine offences of false accounting to be taken into consideration. Held. It would be highly undesirable if the prison population were to continue to rise. The ability of the Prison Service to tackle a prisoner's offending behaviour and so reduce re-offending is adversely affected if a prison is overcrowded. Courts must accept the realities of the situation. In the case of economic crimes, eg obtaining undue credit by fraud, prison is not necessarily the only appropriate form of punishment. Particularly in the case of those who have no record of previous offending, the very fact of having to appear before a court can be a significant punishment. Certainly, having to perform a form of community punishment can be a very salutary way of making it clear that crime does not pay, particularly if a community punishment order is combined with a curfew order. The sentence for a theft from employer involving £11, 120 reduced from 12 months to 4 months. The message must go out that imprison only when necessary and for no longer than necessary.

Sentencing is an art etc/Rehabilitation

19.3 *A-G's Reference (No 4 of 1998)* [1990] 11 Cr App Rep (S) 517 – LCJ. It must always be remembered that sentencing is an art rather than a science; that the trial judge is particularly well placed to assess the weight to be given to various competing considerations; that leniency is not in itself a vice. That mercy should season justice is a proposition as soundly based in law as it is in literature. There were occasions where it was right to take a constructive course and seek to achieve the rehabilitation of the offender. The judge was satisfied it provided the best possible long-term solution for the community and the defendant. It was right to take a constructive course. So far he has been proved right. The prospects of re-offending are now lower than if he had had a custodial sentence. The sentence was lenient on paper but sentencing is not and never can be an exercise on paper; each case, ultimately, is individual. It would be wrong to interfere.

See also **DEFENDANT** and **MERCY**

BENEFIT FRAUD

See **SOCIAL SECURITY FRAUD/HOUSING BENEFIT FRAUD**

20   BIGAMY/MARRIAGE OFFENCES

20.1   Offences Against the Person Act 1861, s 57

Triable either way. On indictment maximum 7 years. Summary maximum 6 months and/or £5,000.

Perjury Act 1911, s 3
False statements etc with reference to marriage.

Triable either way. On indictment maximum 7 years. Summary maximum 6 months and/or £5,000.

Crown Court statistics England and Wales[1] – Crown Court – Males 21+ – Bigamy
20.2

Year	Plea	Total Numbers sentenced	Type of sentence%					Average length of custody (months)
			Discharge	Fine	Community sentence	Suspended sentence	Custody	
2000	Guilty	3	0%	33%	0%	33%	33%	3
	Not guilty	1	0%	0%	0%	100%	0%	0

1   Excluding committals for sentence. Source: Crime and Criminal Justice Unit, Home Office Ref: IOS416-02.

Immigration controls, to evade

20.3   *R v Cairns* [1997] 1 Cr App Rep (S) 118. The defendant pleaded guilty to bigamy. In August he married a Zimbabwean. This was legitimate. Three weeks later he married a Nigerian. Neither woman was traced. Both marriages were contracted for money. He had a previous conviction for dishonesty but none for this kind of offence. Held. A deterrent custodial sentence was inevitable but **9 months** not 15.

R v Zafar [1998] 1 Cr App Rep (S) 416. The defendants Z and B pleaded guilty to making a false oath or declaration to obtain marriage documents (s 3). The defendant G was convicted of the same offence. The conspiracy was to organise marriages of conveniences for Pakistani immigrants who had entered Belgium illegally. The ceremonies took place in the UK because the arrangements for weddings were easier in the UK. The men were unable to travel to the UK because they were illegal immigrants so their passports were forwarded to the organisers in the UK and a stand in groom would attend the ceremony. Other members of the conspiracy would attend as witnesses and guests. Shortly after the bride would be taken to Belgium where she would be introduced to the passport holder. They would then go to the Town Hall and register the marriage and that would give the husband the right to remain in Belgium. The authorities would then visit the home address and confirm that the marriage was genuine. The bride would return to the UK and would be paid between £700 and

£1,000. B and Z were at the heart of the conspiracy in the UK and played a major part in the recruiting of the brides and arranging the ceremonies. They were not at the 'top of the tree.' G was the partner of B and was also involved with the organisation. She drove the girls to the weddings, bought flowers and rings etc. Z pleaded at the last minute B pleaded at the first opportunity, gave help to the Belgium authorities and showed remorse. Held. There were close parallels between this offence and facilitating illegal entry. Z: **4½ years** not 5 ½. B: **3 years** not 4½. G: **21 months** not 2½ years.

See also IMMIGRATION OFFENCES and PASSPORT OFFENCES

21 BLACKMAIL

21.1 Theft Act 1968, s 21

Indictable only. Maximum sentence 14 years.

Crown Court statistics England and Wales – Crown Court – Males 21+ – Blackmail
21.2

Year	Plea	Total Numbers sentenced	Type of sentence%					Average length of custody[1] (months)
			Discharge	Fine	Community sentence	Suspended sentence	Custody	
2000	Guilty	47	2%	2%	15%	2%	79%	37.1
	Not guilty	23	0%	0%	17%	0%	83%	37.3

1 Excluding life sentences. Source: Crime and Criminal Justice Unit, Home Office Ref: IOS416-02.

Guideline remarks

21.3 *R v Hadjou* (1989) 11 Cr App Rep (S) 29 – LCJ. Blackmail is one of the ugliest and most vicious crimes in the calendar of criminal offences and it is perhaps due to the fact that the courts always impose severe sentences that one seldom, if ever, finds a person convicted for a second time for blackmail.

Bills, to enforce unreasonable

21.4 *R v Killgallon and Gray* [1998] 1 Cr App Rep (S) 279. The defendants K and G were convicted of seven counts of blackmail. G would approach small businesses and offer to tarmac their yard or car park for £25 saying he had some tarmac which might otherwise set because of a problem with a wagon etc. If an agreement was made, workman would appear and normally tarmac a greater area than had been agreed. Then G would reappear and demand £25 a square yard. When the customer protested, threats of an extremely intimidating nature were made. Another man who was not apprehended would then attack G, which would intimidate the customer. The threats included threats to burn down their premises, follow people home, firebomb their homes, assault their wives and children and inflict personal violence. K would then appear playing the part of a peacemaker. He would ask for the money and endorsed the threats made. The prosecution relied on 39 transactions for which £220,000 had been demanded. £98,000 had been obtained. The figures for the counts in the indictment were £46,000 and £17,000 respectively. G was 36 and effectively of good character and K was 41 and of good character. G was involved later than K. Held. Because the judge had based the sentence on the 39 transactions and not on the counts in the indictment and perhaps the judge had taken an exaggerated view of the offences **6 years** was substituted for 10.

Debt collecting

21.5 *R v Hart and Bullen* [1999] 2 Cr App Rep (S) 233. Just before a trial for conspiracy to cause GBH the prosecution added a count of conspiracy to blackmail to which the defendants pleaded guilty. Other counts were left on the file. The two defendants went to find a man called Thompson who had links with criminals. The purpose was to recover £20,000, which had been lent to him. They drove to the area where he lived and Thompson's girlfriend received a call saying they were coming to kill him. More calls were made. She was followed by a car, which at one point screeched to a halt and she was told, 'Thompson was going to die.' Threatening messages were left on her answering machine. The defendants went to Thompson's sister's home twice and demanded to know where he was. Threats were made to her and her family. She was terrified. They visited her a third time, entered her premises and forced her boyfriend against a wall. An object was thrust against his stomach and he was threatened with a stabbing if he did not help find Thompson. Next they re-visited his girlfriend.

The defendants were arrested in a hotel and a stun gun, a truncheon, a CS gas canister, a sheaf knife, two telephone pagers and a length of fishing wire were found. The basis of plea was that there was no intention to harm anyone, the debt was owed for a business and not connected with drugs and the weapons were not brought there at the behest of either defendant. One defendant was of good character and the other had a list of mostly drug convictions. He was on licence for a 3½ year supply of Class A drug sentence. Held. The judge was able to say that the weapons were ways of enforcing the debt. **4 years** was deserved. The 9 month sentence for breach of the prison licence remained consecutive.

R v Kewell [2000] 2 Cr App Rep (S) 38. He pleaded guilty to blackmail. The defendant's relationship broke up and the girlfriend left without making any provision for the money owing in their joint account. The defendant was having difficulty covering his other debts and commitments. She ignored his letters and his threats of legal action. He then sent a letter demanding £300 within 7 days or personal photographs would be distributed to her place of 'work or home or family or worse.' Fearing he might use the Internet she contacted the police. They found the photographs in his computer. The defendant was 25 with a new partner and her young son and was working as a software consultant. He had no previous convictions and expressed remorse. **12 months** substituted for 18 months.

Defendant aged 10–16

21.6 *R v Simmons* [2001] 2 Cr App Rep (S) 170. The defendant pleaded guilty to blackmail. A Cezanne painting worth more than £3m went missing from the Ashmolean Museum which attracted extensive publicity. The defendant then 16 was highly skilled in the use of computers and had a sophisticated knowledge of procedures. He telephoned the curator stating it would be returned for £1m. Two further calls followed and a computer-generated letter was sent saying, 'Your family might get upset if you make the wrong decision.' The curator was told not to tell the police. He sent five e-mails from an Internet café, which were disguised using an encryption programme one of which said the curator should, 'watch (his) family and friends die around (him).' The answer was expected by Friday or, 'The culling would start.' There were further threats. Substantial police resources were used to investigate the threats and he was after some difficulty traced. He said he only did it for a joke. The curator's family was extremely upset and suffered major disruption. The effect was devastating and they stopped going out. The defendant had cautions for theft a few months before the offence started. One involved an attempt to use his mother's credit card to obtain £10,000 worth of goods over the Internet. His parents had split up and he was recently told his father was not his biological father. He started a vendetta against his mother and had an overdraft of £2,600 and his family had paid off a large debt of his. The psychiatrist said he had a psychiatric disorder of a conduct disorder unsocial type and an unsettled personality. He was intelligent but had difficulty with authority. Held. Although in many ways he was vulnerable he was also very dangerous. The offence was serious and sophisticated pursued with intelligence and vigour. He had a cynical disregard to what he had done to the curator. **12 months** detention and training was exactly right.

Embarrassing material/allegations

21.7 *R v Kewell* [2000] 2 Cr App Rep (S) 38. The defendant pleaded guilty to blackmail. The defendant's relationship broke up and his girlfriend left without making any provision for the money owing in their joint account. The defendant was having difficulty covering his other debts and commitments. She ignored his letters and his threats of legal action. He then sent a letter demanding £300 within 7 days or personal photographs would be distributed to her place of 'work or home or family or worse.' Fearing he might use the Internet she contacted the police. They found the photographs in his computer. The defendant was 25 with a new partner and her young son and working as software consultant. He had no previous convictions and expressed remorse. **12 months** substituted for 18 months.

R v St Q [2002] 1 Cr App Rep (S) 440. The defendant was convicted of blackmail of his ex-wife. He pleaded guilty to indecent assault on a female (not his ex-wife). The defendant and his wife who was 8 years younger than him became involved in group sex with another couple and the sessions were video taped. Professional pornographic photographs were taken and the pictures sold in America with her face shaded out. There was an acrimonious divorce and a wrangle about the sale of the house. At the end the difference was she wanted £16,000 and he was prepared to settle for £7,000. He threatened to show the video tapes to her parents unless she settled for his figure. Both she and her parents sold their stories to newspapers. He was 34 and of good character. The judge described it as, 'an ugly and odious offence.' He said the defendant tried, 'to wreak as much muck' as he could and embarrass her during the trial. He described the defendant as 'cocky and arrogant and something of a predator'. Held. The defendant believed in his claim. **15 months** not 2½ years with the indecent sentence reduced to 3 months consecutive.

R v Daniels [2002] 1 Cr App Rep (S) 443. The defendant pleaded to blackmail. He delivered three letters to the victim demanding at first £2,000 and later £3,000 suggesting he had visited public lavatories several times to have sex with other men and that the writer had had oral sex with him. The notes made it clear that if the money was not paid the writer would inform his employers and his wife about the sex. The note also said the writer had followed the victim and it revealed personal details about the victim. The victim's secretary opened the second letter. The police and his wife were informed and the defendant was arrested when he went to pick up a package. The victim was married and was put under considerable strain. The defendant knew the victim slightly and they were once professional colleagues. The defendant showed animosity to him and over 30 years had gained pleasure from visiting lavatories and picnic sites to watch people having sex together. His motive was purely vindictive and there was no truth in the suggestions made. He was 52 and effectively of good character with a depressive illness for about 13 years. Held. The motives were to some extent strange and irrational. The offence was designed deliberately to cause pain to the victim. Bearing in mind his medical condition **2 years** not 3.

Kidnapping individuals for ransom

21.8   *R v Walters* [1998] 2 Cr App Rep (S) 167. The defendant pleaded guilty at the
first opportunity to conspiracy to possess cannabis, kidnapping, conspiracy to falsely
imprison, conspiracy to blackmail and three firearm offences. There was a drugs deal
involving 13 kgs of cannabis worth £27,000. The suppliers tricked the purchasers at the
point of sale and made off with some of the £24,000 purchase price. The defendant was
one of the buyers and he shouted for the return of the money. He held a gun to the
go-between's head and hit her in the face with it. She was kidnapped and taken to a
trading estate. She was told she was going to be killed and was punched three or more
times in the face. She was held for the return of the money. She didn't know the
identity of the suppliers and the defendant ordered the victim to strip naked or else she
would be killed. She was very distressed and placed in a car still naked and the gun
was held to her head while he counted, threatening to kill her. Her finger was held back
with the defendant again counting down from ten. They then decided to blackmail her
mother for £10,000 saying that unless the money was paid the victim would be killed.
The mother contacted the police. More threats to kill were made to the mother. The
victim was moved to a house. Her clothes were returned to her. At that house she was
stripped again and put in a cupboard. When she was taken out she was tortured by
electrocution using the exposed wires from a boiling kettle. Threats were made to put
the wires on her nipples and private parts to sterilise her. This event could not be
attributed to any one of the three kidnappers. She was moved again to another house
and the defendant grabbed handfuls of her hair and cut it off. During the journey the
defendant put one of the guns to her head and fired blanks at her. At the next house she
was repeatedly threatened. There were threats to blind her with acid. The mother was
called and there were threats to mutilate the victim. At the third house she overheard
them talking about killing her and a fellow kidnapper hit her with a mallet or hammer
because 'she hadn't felt pain yet'. An exchange of £9,000 was made under police
supervision and the defendant was arrested. He had 4 handguns, 17 rounds of
ammunition and the ransom money. The victim was released barefoot, injured and
hysterical. She had bruises around the nose and eyes and multiple bruises on the legs
and shoulders. There were injuries consistent with electrical burns. He was 38 and the
ringleader. Held. On any view it was a truly terrible case. The starting point was
15–16 years. Taking into account the plea and it wasn't pre-planned **11 years** not 14.

R v Mereu [1998] 2 Cr App Rep (S) 351. The four defendants K, Z, Mo and Me were
convicted of kidnapping, false imprisonment and blackmail. Men wearing balaclavas
and gloves abducted a wealthy member of a Greek shipping family from a car park. He
was threatened with a gun and told he would be killed if he shouted. He was
handcuffed, put in a boot of a car and taken to and locked in a windowless room. He
was stripped to his boxer shorts and held for 9 days. He was handcuffed, his legs were
tied and, he had to wear a mask and plaster was put over his eyes. K who was the
mastermind demanded $5m reduced to a not negotiable $3m. The victim was told that
unless that was paid he would be killed by injection. Syringes were left in the room and
he was made to make telephone calls to his family. There was a very sophisticated
telephone coupling system but the police eventually traced the calls. The flat was
raided and the defendants arrested. The victim was found in an awful state. His eyes
were sunken and red, his complexion was pale, he was distressed and looked gaunt. He
was terrified by the ordeal. The distress to his family, which was a close family, was
'indescribable' and 'immeasurable'. K had planned the kidnap for over a year and
recruited the others. The gun was not capable of firing. Mo and Me were of good
character. Character evidence showed that Z was capable of kindness and being a good
worker. Me spoke no English so would find prison particularly difficult. He and Mo
also showed certain acts of kindness to the victim when he was held. The defence at

trial was the victim faked the events because he was in financial difficulties. Held. These exceptionally grave offences required exemplary and deterrent sentences. We take into account the factors urged on us, the good character, the comparative youth of Z and the problems of serving sentences in a foreign country. **20 years** not 25 for K and **10 years** not 13 for the others.

Kidnapping individuals for ransom – Children taken

21.9 *R v Chong Kiong Hong* [2001] EWCA Crim 785, [2001] 2 Cr App Rep (S) 509. Three defendants pleaded guilty to blackmail and false imprisonment. A schoolboy aged 14 was kidnapped from Cambridgeshire and taken to London by all three defendants. The parents were asked for £250,000, which was later reduced to £100,000. They were told that otherwise the boy would be killed. The boy was well treated and not threatened with any violence. The men fled after a telephone call doubtless from someone higher up in the plot. The boy was unharmed. The false imprisonment was the more serious crime. Two had their sentences reduced from 12 to **10 years**. The third who had been recruited for his brawn rather than his brains had **9 years** substituted for 11.

Supermarkets and retail stores

21.10 *R v Riolfo* [1997] 1 Cr App Rep (S) 57. The defendant pleaded guilty to blackmail. Between January and April 1995, he threatened Tescos supermarket that the food had been contaminated with the AIDS virus. He also threatened to inform the press. He demanded £250,000. The money was to be transferred by bank cash machines. He received £7,500 by using a card 73 times. He was caught by police surveillance. It was a sophisticated operation. Nothing was actually infected but an inert substance was injected into certain produce. The defendant was of good character who had lived an industrious life. He had also co-operated with the police. He had had a heart attack and was depressed at the time. **6 years** not 8.

R v Banot [1997] 2 Cr App Rep (S) 50. The defendant pleaded to three counts of blackmail. Harrods received a letter threatening to sabotage their merchandise or their building and demanding £5m. It also said a coded message was to be put in the Evening Standard. This was done. The police mounted a covert operation. Another demand was received. This one contained a threat that food would be poisoned and rodents would be put in the store. Telephone calls were made and the defendant said she could go down to £1m. A threat to set fire to the store was also made. Another man was recruited and there were more telephone calls. The two were arrested. The defendant was 42 and was effectively of good character. She had a significant personality disorder. Held. The judge was right to refer how vulnerable well-known organisations were and how many resources had been deployed to deal with it. **5 years** substituted for 8 partly because of her personal circumstances.

R v Pearce [2000] 2 Cr App Rep (S) 32. See Explosive Offences – *Blackmail, and R v Dyer* [2002] 2 Cr App Rep (S) 490. [He pleaded guilty to nine counts of blackmail on stores over 6 months. **12 years** not 16 in total.]

See also Bomb Hoax – Placing or Dispatching Articles or Sending False Messages – *Sending false messages – Demands made* and Food etc, Contamination of

22 Bladed Article, Possession of a

22.1 Criminal Justice Act 1988, s 139

Triable either way. On indictment maximum sentence 2 years. Summary maximum 6 months and/or £5,000.

Magistrates' Court Sentencing Guidelines September 2000

22.2 Entry point. Is it so serious that only custody is appropriate? Consider the impact on the victim. Examples of aggravating factors for the offence are group action or joint possession, location of offence, people put in fear/weapon brandished and planned use. Examples of mitigating factors for the offence are acting out of a genuine fear, no attempt to use the weapon and offence not premeditated. Examples of mitigation are age, health (physical or mental), co-operation with the police, voluntary compensation and genuine remorse.

For details about the guidelines see MAGISTRATES' COURT SENTENCING GUIDELINES at page 331.

Weapon not produced

22.3 *R v Datson* [1999] 1 Cr App Rep (S) 84. The defendant pleaded guilty to possessing a bladed article. The defendant was in a public house and moved a knife from his belongings to beneath his jacket. Someone saw and informed the police. The defendant initially refused to be searched but then showed the police the knife in a sheaf in his waistband. He told police he had come across the knife when moving items from his former matrimonial home at the request of his partner. Held. We see no reason to disbelieve his account. He had convictions for violence but none for 8 years. The appropriate sentence was community service not immediate custody. As he had served 3 weeks in custody a **conditional discharge** not 2 months.

R v Baldwin [2000] 1 Cr App Rep (S) 81. The defendant pleaded guilty to possessing a bladed article. The defendant was stopped in a supermarket with a trolley with £200 worth of goods in it and arrested for stealing them. Police were called and they found a 5″ knife in his sock. He said it was for his own protection. He was 33 and a drug addict with a terrible record for dishonesty. There were no convictions for carrying a weapon. No evidence was offered on the shoplifting count. **6 months** not 18.

See also OFFENSIVE WEAPON, POSSESSION OF A

23 BOMB HOAX – PLACING OR DISPATCHING ARTICLES OR SENDING FALSE MESSAGES

23.1 Criminal Law Act 1977, s 51(1) and (2)

The two offences are: (1) placing . . .or dispatching an article . . .with the intention of inducing some other person a belief. . .that it will explode or ignite. . .and (2) communicating any information which he knows or believes to be false to another person with the intention of inducing in him . . .a false belief that a bomb or other thing. . .liable to explode or ignite is present etc.

Triable either way. On indictment maximum 7 years. Summary maximum 6 months and/or £5,000 fine.

Hostage, taking hostage as well

23.2 *R v Mason* [2002] 1 Cr App Rep (S) 122. The defendant pleaded guilty to communicating false information with intent. The prosecution dropped a count of endangering an aircraft and common assault. The defendant was politically active in

Trinidad and believed his life was in danger. He went to Switzerland to alert the United Nations about his plight and to claim political asylum. His application was refused and he was put on a plane to Gatwick so he could travel back to Trinidad. He wanted to draw attention to his plight and problems. About 10 minutes before the plane was due to land he took hold of a female member of crew and grabbed her by the neck. A blade of a pair of scissors was held to her throat. She was terrified and he said, 'This is a fucking hijack.' Another crew member came to help and she was told there was a bomb on the plane and he threatened to kill his hostage unless his demands were met. He indicated that his Dictaphone was a bomb, which he could activate by pressing a button. The captain arrived and he was told there was a bomb on the plane and that he was to radio the defendant's demands for political asylum to the UK authorities. The captain eventually persuaded the defendant to release his hostage who had been held for a few minutes. The defendant was arrested when the plane landed. He admitted the offence and said he wanted the hostage to feel as frightened as he did about returning to his own country. The hostage was severely traumatised. Some of the passengers were upset and frightened. He was 62 and had no convictions in the UK where he lived for 3 years in the 1990s. He said he had committed a robbery in Barbados. The judge referred to the serious situation of co-pilot landing the aircraft on his own and the injuries to the neck despite the charges, which had been dropped by the prosecution. Held. It was an extremely serious offence. The judge was entitled to take into account the danger to the aircraft. Sentences needed to deter others who wanted to secure their political ends. There was nothing wrong about the **4 years** sentence.

Placing an article

23.3   *R v Bosworth* [1998] 1 Cr App Rep (S) 356. The defendant pleaded guilty to placing an article. The defendant forced a DHL driver to stop and gave him a jiffy bag. The defendant said, 'Make sure Melvyn Ball gets this. Melvyn Ball at DHL.' The driver looked inside and saw there was a hand grenade. The defendant walked away saying, 'Make sure he gets it or you'll never fucking walk again.' The grenade was found to be genuine but with no pin or explosive. The defendant was an ex-employee of DHL with a grudge against them. He had been reprimanded for failing to find a suspicious parcel in a test. He was 29 and had no convictions. Held. It was a very serious and planned offence. A man had been caused great fear. **12 months** was the least he could have hoped to receive.

R v Spencer (1 October 1998, unreported). The defendant pleaded guilty at the Magistrates' Court to (it appears) placing an article and communicating a false message. A package looking like a home made bomb was found by police. The area was evacuated and a controlled explosion took place. Two to three weeks later a call to the ambulance service was made saying there had been a traffic accident. Later a call was made to the police saying there had been no response to the first call. The defendant admitted being responsible for the bomb and the calls. The defendant was mentally retarded and required a great deal of care from his family and others. He was of good character. Held. The court passed a lenient sentence taking into account the defendant's difficulties. The bomb constructed by the defendant was realistic. We are influenced that when he is released from his sentence he will be supervised. **12 months** was not manifestly excessive.

Sending false messages – Demands made

23.4   *R v Barker* (5 May 1997, unreported). The defendant pleaded guilty. He was in dispute with a company over an invention of his. He attached a wire round the company premises, which appeared to go to a parked car. He informed the police there was petrol in a bottle at the end of the wire and it would explode but not hurt anyone.

It turned out to be harmless. The police negotiated with the defendant who was demanding money from the company. His solicitor had told him his actions were not illegal. Held. The advice was remarkable. The sentencing bracket was 1–2 years. **9 months** was upheld.

See also **BLACKMAIL**

Sending false messages – No financial demands made

23.5   *R v Harrison* [1997] 2 Cr App Rep (S) 174. The defendant pleaded guilty at the Magistrates' Court to four charges of communicating false information. He made four calls to the London Coliseum Theatre within between 5.35 and 6.45pm. The first said there was a bag in the vicinity of the theatre that looked suspicious. The second said he was a member of the IRA and he had planted a bomb in a bin and it was due to go off at 6.30pm that evening and asking why the theatre had not been evacuated. The third said he had seen two men and it was a bomb. The fourth said he was going to operate the bomb by remote control at 7pm and it contained 100lbs. of Semtex. It was a rambling conversation lasting 6 or 7 minutes and it was plain he was under the influence of drink. He was found in a telephone box making the last call. He admitted the offence. The defendant was 34 and had many previous court appearances. First in 1984 for arson; second in 1988 for arson (probation); third and fourth for dishonesty; fifth in 1991, two for this offence – sending a false message (he had called the fire brigade twice saying there was a fire) (probation); sixth, four bomb hoax offences and using a telephone to send false messages to cause annoyance (he had called the emergency services saying there was a bomb) (2 years and 3 months for breach of probation); seventh in 1994 for calling the fire brigade to attend a non existent fire (fined) and eighth minor dishonesty. He had a personality disorder and needed help for his alcohol problem. His likelihood of reoffending was high. Held. The appropriate sentence for the offence before looking at the defendant was probably near 2 years before a discount for the plea. We have to bear in mind the danger to the public. The only answer is longer periods of custody. **4 years** was severe but not manifestly too long.

24   BUGGERY/ASSAULT WITH INTENT TO COMMIT BUGGERY

24.1   Sexual Offences Act 1956, s 12 – Buggery.

Indictable only. Maximum sentence if with a person under 16 or with an animal life imprisonment. If the defendant is 21 or over and the other party is under 18 maximum 5 years (This would apply if the offence was between men and not in private). Otherwise 2 years.

Sexual Offences Act 1956, s 16 – Assault with intent to commit buggery.

Indictable only. Maximum sentence 10 years.

For both offences the defendant must notify the police within 14 days (or 14 days from his release from imprisonment) of his name and home address etc, any change and addresses where he resides for 14 days or more in any 12 month period[1]. This does not apply when he is under 20 or the other party was 18 or over. See **SEX OFFENDERS' REGISTER**

1   Sex Offenders Act 1997, ss 1 and 2 and Sch 1, para 1(2)(a) and (b).

Crown Court statistics England and Wales – Crown Court – Males 21+ – Buggery 24.2

Year	Plea	Total Numbers sentenced	Type of sentence%					Average length of custody[1] (months)
			Discharge	Fine	Community sentence	Suspended sentence	Custody	
2000	Guilty	55	4%	0%	13%	0%	80%	58.6
	Not guilty	43	0%	0%	0%	0%	100%	72.1

1 Excluding life sentences. Source: Crime and Criminal Justice Unit, Home Office Ref: IOS416-02.

Guideline case

24.3 *R v Willis* (1975) 60 Cr App Rep 146 – LCJ. Judicial experience must be weighed against other sources of information and the main one is the Wolfenden Report. The younger the participating party, the greater is the need for protection. The sentencing bracket for offences which have neither aggravating nor mitigating factors is from **3 to 5 years**; and the place in the bracket will depend on age, intelligence, and education. The main aggravating factors are in order of importance: (1) physical injury to the boy. Offenders who use violence should be discouraged from repetition by severe sentences; (2) emotional and psychological damage; (3) moral corruption; (4) abuse of authority and trust. Those who have boys in their charge must expect severe sentences. The main mitigating factors are: (1) mental imbalance; (2) personality disorders; (3) emotional stress. [This case is hard to apply as it does not refer to specific ages for the other party and deals with non consensual buggery which should now be charged as rape.]

A-G's Reference (No 17 of 1990) (1990) 92 Cr App Rep 288 – LCJ. There are five aspects which the sentencing Judge should take into account for offences against young children. First, the overall gravity of the offence. Secondly, the necessity for punishment. Thirdly, the necessity to protect the public. Fourthly, the public concern for sexual offences on young children. Fifthly, the deterrent effect.

R v Alden and Wright [2001] EWCA Crim 296, [2001] 2 Cr App Rep (S) 401; *R v Willis* (1975) 60 Cr App Rep 146 remains the starting point.

Boy/girl fully consents

24.4 *R v Bradley* [1998] 1 Cr App Rep (S) 432. The defendant was aged 24. He a boy aged 15 in a gay club and buggery took place in the defendant's flat. He pleaded guilty. The court relying on authorities between 1981 and 1990 reduced the sentence from 30 months to **18 months**. [Since this decision the age of consent has been reduced to 16 and the courts are no longer permitted to discriminate over a man's sexual orientation, This authority is likely to be only of historic interest.]

R v Wells [1999] 1 Cr App Rep (S) 320. The defendant made an early plea of guilty to buggery and indecent assault. The defendant aged 28 met the boy aged 14 at a place well known for gay people to meet for casual sex. He asked the boy how old he was and was told 18. He and his co-defendant had oral sex and masturbation with the boy behind a sand dune. The defendant then buggered the boy. He was sentenced on the basis he thought the boy was over 16. The defendant had no previous convictions. **3 years** substituted for 4 years. [This authority is likely to be only of historic interest.]

R v Ali [2000] 1 Cr App Rep (S) 36. The defendant aged 23 pleaded guilty to buggery and gross indecency (kissing each other in bed 5 days later). He met the boy aged 14 in his brother's flat. The boy claimed he was 16 and he did look older than 14. On some waste ground he penetrated the boy but stopped when the boy said it was painful. The boy then buggered the defendant. The defendant expressed remorse. Held The court relying on *R v Bradley* [1998] 1 Cr App Rep (S) 432 reduced the sentence from 3½ years to **21 months**. [This authority is likely to be only of historic interest.]

Buggery charged when anal rape suggested

24.5 *R v Davies* [1998] 1 Cr App Rep (S) 380. The defendant aged now 21 was convicted of buggery and under age sex [Sexual Offences Act 1956, s 6(1)] with his girlfriend then aged 15. The judge sentenced him on the basis there was no consent. If a man is convicted of buggery it is wrong to sentence him for rape. Where non-consensual sexual intercourse is alleged it must be charged as rape.

Delay, long (before arrest)

24.6 *R v Leckey* [1999] 1 Cr App Rep (S) 57. The defendant was convicted of large number of counts of buggery and indecent assaults on boys (touching penises, masturbation simulated intercourse etc). There was a group of offences from 1972 to the late 1970s involving six boys aged from 8 to 15 and buggery aged from 11 years. Boys were given gifts and taken on trips. The second group was in 1995 and related to a boy aged 16 and involved masturbation and oral sex. The defendant had no previous convictions. 12 years for the 1970 offences upheld but the consecutive sentence for the later offences reduced from 6 to 3 years making **15 years** not 18 years in all. [Since the appeal the age of consent has been reduced so the second set of offences would no longer be criminal.]

R v Bowers [1999] 2 Cr App Rep (S) 97. The defendant pleaded guilty to five counts of buggery on 2 boys. The offences were committed when the defendant was between 15 and 18. He was 42 when convicted and was a member of a Lads club as a teenager and abused younger members of the group. The two boys were attacked over a period of 3 years when they were between 8 and 11. He co-operated with the police. The judge noted that the defendant, as an older boy, was in a position of responsibility at the club, and by a combination of encouragement, moneys and treats he systematically abused the boys. One boy suffered deep rooted psychological problems as a result. The defendant had two unrelated previous convictions. He had excellent references. Because he had now married and had four children the risk of re-offending was assessed as low. Held. The sentence that would have been passed at the time of the offences was a starting point and powerful factor in determining the sentence. That would have been Borstal so **2 years** not 7.

R v DR [2000] 2 Cr App Rep 314. The defendant was convicted of attempted buggery of his stepson then aged 10 in 1982–3 and indecent assault (touching and ejaculation) on his daughter when aged 4–5 in 1982–3. There were no threats. He tried to bugger the stepson but he stopped when told it hurt and told the boy to do the same to him but the boy couldn't get an erection. The defendant was now 69 and in poor health. He had no previous convictions. **4 years** and 1 year consecutive was not manifestly excessive.

R v Alden and Wright [2001] EWCA Crim 296, [2001] 2 Cr App Rep (S) 401. The first defendant A was convicted of 10 counts of buggery, five counts of indecent assault and gross indecency. There were four victims of the buggery and six in all. The second defendant W was convicted of six counts of attempted buggery and four counts of indecent assaults. There were four victims. The victims of both defendants were pupils at an approved school aged between 13 and 16. Many of the boys were vulnerable having been neglected, abused or assaulted. A now 66 committed the offences over a 17 year period from 1966 when he was house master to when he was deputy headmaster. Two boys experienced, 'pain nothing like I'd experienced before,' and 'unbearable pain.' Favours were given and threats made. W now 56 was a housemaster and was then 23–26. His offences were from 1966–9. He used home leave to bribe the boys. Both were of good character. **15 years** for A was fully deserved. **8 years** accurately reflects the factors in W's case.

Life sentence – Automatic life for second serious offence

24.7   Powers of Criminal Courts (Sentencing) Act 2000, s 109

Is an old offence of non-consensual buggery, (which would now be rape), a serious offence for the purposes of the Act?

R v Wood [2001] 1 Cr App Rep 20. No

Life sentence, is it appropriate?

24.8   *R v Bellamy* [2001] 1 Cr App Rep 116. The defendant pleaded guilty to 23 sex abuse counts on five boys aged 12–14 including four counts of buggery and one attempted buggery. The abuse lasted 5 years and included inserting objects into the boys' anuses and video recording the activity with the defendant directing every movement. The defendant was aged 50 with two appearances for indecent assaults on boys. The boy in the first case was 14 and the boys in the second case were 13, 14 and 15. The psychiatrist said he had a continuing history of sustained paedophile interest over many years and he falls into a high-risk group in relation to re-offending. He was not in a position of trust to the boys. **Life** was appropriate.

Life sentence – Fixing specified term

24.9   Crime (Sentences) Act 1997, s 28. The relevant section.

R v Archer [1999] 2 Cr App Rep 92. The defendant, a life long paedophile was sentenced to life for five buggery counts and 10 years in all for 10 indecent assaults counts. He had been sentenced for a string of sex offences since 1955. Held. The appropriate determinate sentence would have been 12 years. Dividing that amount by two and reducing that figure for the time he had spent in custody meant the period should be 5 years 8 months not 9 years. The 10 year sentence was reduced to **8 years** to ensure that he did not remain in prison for the less serious offences after he might have been released for the more serious matters.

Longer than commensurate sentences

24.10   Powers of Criminal Courts (Sentencing) Act 2000, s 80(2)(b) . . .the custodial sentence shall be. . .where the offence is a violent or sexual offence, for such longer term (not exceeding the maximum) as in the opinion of the court is necessary to protect the public from serious harm from the offender. [previously the Criminal Justice Act 1991, s 2(2)(b).]

A-G's Reference (No 7 of 1997) [1998] 1 Cr App Rep (S) 268. The defendant was convicted of seven counts of buggery with boys between 12 and 14 years, four counts of indecent assaults and one offence of possessing indecent photographs. The offences all related to boys between 11 and 15 over a 6 or 7 year period. Because of his good character the judge was not wrong to fail to use the [now s 80(2)(b)] provisions. However, the court said they were not saying the judge would have been wrong if he had used them.

See also LONGER THAN COMMENSURATE SENTENCES

Paedophiles

24.11   *R v Bowers* [1999] Crim LR 234. 2 years substituted for 7 for five counts on 8 and 11 year olds between 1971 and 1973 partly because had he been dealt with at the time he'd have received Borstal training.

R v Bellamy [2001] 1 Cr App Rep 116. The defendant pleaded guilty to 23 sex abuse cases on five boys aged 12–14 including four counts of buggery and 1 attempted buggery. The abuse lasted 5 years and included inserting objects into the boys' anuses and video recording the activity with the defendant directing every movement. The defendant was aged 50. He was not in a position of trust to the boys. Held. **Life** was appropriate (taking into account the protection of the public and his previous convictions.) The appropriate determinate sentence would have been 16 years.

R v Barker [2001] 1 Cr App Rep 514. The defendant pleaded guilty to two counts of buggery, gross indecency with a child and three counts of indecent assault on a male. They related to two boys then aged 12 and 16. He was also committed for sentence for gross indecency with a child. There were three offences taken into consideration, which were masturbation, and oral sex on a boy aged 10–11. After the 16 year old had been drinking, he and another had consensual sex with him. Later consensual sex took place between the defendant and the boy about 20 times. He met the 12 year old by being friendly with children who lived next door to his mother. The boy went to the defendant's flat and another flat. They had masturbation and oral sex. The gross indecency was touching and kissing the 12 year old. The defendant was arrested and admitted the offences. He was 34 and had two convictions for gross indecency with a child and an indecent assault on a male for which he received 6 years in 1993. The pre-sentence report said he posed a serious threat to young boys. The psychiatric report said he had a damaged personality and was emotionally unstable. He assisted the police by giving evidence in the murder trial for the other man who killed a schoolboy. Held. We accept the law reducing the age of consent will be enacted. The 2 year concurrent sentences for the buggery and gross indecency (all against the 16 year old) were not manifestly excessive. However, **8 years** not 10 is the suitable total. The 2 year sentences reduced to 1 year. One indecent assaults on the younger victim reduced from 4 to **3 years**. The other 2 remaining at 4 years extended so total is 1+3+4=8, not 2+4+4=10. The 2 years concurrent for the committal for sentenced and the **5 years** extended licence remained.

A-G's Reference (No 60 of 2001) [2001] EWCA Crim 2026, [2002] 1 Cr App Rep (S) 396. The defendant pleaded guilty to 11 counts of buggery, one of aiding and abetting buggery and 15 indecent assaults on five boys between 11 and 15. Between 1976 and 1991 he was Chairman of a naturist club. Between 1976 and 1991 he conducted systematic and persistent abuse on five boys. He gained the trust of the parents of the victims and then the victims were groomed, given treats and photographed naked. With each he masturbated, then had mutual masturbation and then buggered four of them. The treats were sweets, drinks, smoking and trips to London. The offences took place when he was 34–45 and he was now 62. Some were abused by his friends. The judge said, 'it was a terrible trail of corruption with a lasting and dreadful effect. Some were depressed, unable to take part in sport, form normal relations, lacked a social life, tried to commit suicide and attend psychiatric centres. You pose a real danger to the public.' He reduced the 15 year sentence to 9 because of the delay. Held. The 15 year starting point was right. It is right to make a discount for the delay but it cannot be very great because these offences tend not to come to light very quickly. Taking into account the delay and that it was a reference **12 years** substituted.

See the other sections because many of the offenders for buggery are paedophiles.

Paedophiles – With violence

24.12 *A-G's Reference (No 89 of 1998)* [2000] 1 Cr App Rep (S) 49. The defendant was convicted for attempted buggery, six counts of child abduction, six counts of indecent assault, and six counts of indecency with a child. Over a period of 4 years the defendant carried out five sexual attacks on six boys, aged between 11 and 14, as they were walking to or from school on the same common. The last attack was on two boys at the same time. The defendant travelled from Forest Hill to a common in Surrey to carry out these attacks. He seized the boys and forcibly took off their clothing. There was a variety of threats and force used. One was threatened he'd be killed. He inserted a glove in one of the boy's anus to extract faeces. In another he inserted a finger or a stick into the boy's anus. In three of the attacks he forced them to put their penises in his mouth and told them to urinate while he sucked the penis. One boy he tried to bugger but the boy was able to prevent it by tensing his buttocks. One attack was disturbed early on by a police helicopter. One boy was in such a state he was physically sick. The defendant assisted his escape by threats or by taking the boys footwear away or keeping their trousers down. Two were told to swallow his semen. All the victims suffered emotional and psychological harm. The defendant, who was 45, had no previous convictions. The maximum for attempted buggery was increased from 10 years to life after the offence. Held. As this was a campaign of premeditated abduction and grave sexual abuse the appropriate sentence was **18 years without passing a longer than commensurate sentence**. Consecutive sentences were appropriate. Taking into account it was a reference **15 years** in total not 10 years.

Stepfathers

24.13   *R v D* [2000] 1 Cr App Rep 120. The defendant was convicted of attempted buggery and two counts of indecent assaults on his stepdaughter when aged 14–15. All the counts were specimen counts. The attempted offence took place in a garden shed. The indecent assaults related to regular consensual sexual intercourse. He was treated as of good character. Sentenced by the Court of Appeal on the basis she might have consented to the attempt. **3 years** and not 7 years with 18 months concurrent for the assaults.

R v DR [2000] 2 Cr App Rep 314. The defendant was convicted of attempted buggery of his stepson then aged 10 in 1982–3 and indecent assault (touching and ejaculation) on his daughter when aged 4–5 in 1982–3. There were no threats. He tried to bugger the stepson but he stopped when told it hurt and told the boy to do the same to him but the boy couldn't get an erection. The defendant was now 69 and in poor health. He had no previous convictions. **4 years** and 1 year consecutive was not manifestly excessive.

Taking advantage when victim drunk etc

24.14   *R v Dalton* [2000] 2 Cr App Rep 87. The defendant aged 19 pleaded guilty to buggery of drunk woman aged 16. She approached him first and after having sex he entered her anally possibly by accident. She appeared to be consenting. Further vaginal intercourse took place. The defendant gave evidence during a Newton enquiry that he didn't know she was drunk. He was disbelieved. The defendant had an impressive reference from his employer. Because the defendant had been in custody after his arrest and after the sentence before being admitted to bail **3 months** not 6 months detention. [The public may question the necessity to use up valuable detention space for an offence most police forces would not consider processing]

Trust, gross breach of (teacher, foster parent etc)

24.15   *R v Paget* [1998] 1 Cr App Rep (S) 80. The defendant was convicted of eight counts of buggery and eight counts of indecent assaults on boys (masturbation and oral sex). It was persistently over 4½ years on five boys when aged 11–16. He was a foster parent to one and one was allowed to live with him. There were incidents of violence and intimidation. Rewards were given. The defendant had no previous convictions. Held. Buggery sentences of 4 and 5 years with indecent assault counts of 3 years and the five groups of counts being made consecutive totalling **20 years** was not manifestly excessive.

A-G's Reference (No 7 of 1997) [1997] 1 Cr App Rep (S) 268. The defendant was convicted of seven counts of buggery with boys between 12 and 14 years, four counts of indecent assaults and one offence of possessing indecent photographs. He entered a late plea to showing indecent photographs. The offences all related to boys between 11 and 15 over a 6 or 7 year period. The defendant now aged 29 showed the boys pornographic films and gave them alcohol and cannabis. Threats were made if the boys told anyone. He made a film about inserting a bottle into a boy's anus. The victims were vulnerable because of their home circumstances. One boy was given permission by the local authority to live with him. At least one had permanent psychological damage as a result of the offences. The defendant had no previous convictions. Held. The judge was not wrong to fail to use the longer than normal sentencing provisions. The appropriate sentence would have been at least 10 years. Taking into account it was a reference **9 years** not 7.

R v Alden and Wright [2001] EWCA Crim 296, [2001] 2 Cr App Rep (S) 401. The first defendant A was convicted of ten counts of buggery, five counts of indecent assault and gross indecency. There were four victims of the buggery and six in all. The second defendant W was convicted of six counts of attempted buggery and four indecent assaults. There were four victims. The victims were pupils at an approved school aged between 13 and 16. Many of the boys were vulnerable having been neglected, abused or assaulted. A, now 66 committed the offences over a 17 year period from 1966 when he was house master to when he was deputy headmaster. Two boys experienced, 'pain nothing like I'd experienced before,' and 'unbearable pain.' Favours were given and threats made. W now 56 was a housemaster and was then 23–26. His offences were from 1966-9. He used home leave to bribe them. Both were of good character. **15 years** for A was fully deserved. **8 years** accurately reflects the factors in W's case.

Victim aged 10–12

24.16 *R v Sullivan* [1999] 1 Cr App Rep (S) 89. The defendant pleaded guilty to three counts of buggery which took place between 1969 and 1972. He and his wife lived near the victim's family and invited the boy then aged 10 to help with some gardening. He took him to a box room ostensibly to show him some guns and records. After messing him around he pushed the victim face down on the floor, removed his jeans and underpants, forced his legs apart and buggered him. It was very painful. Over the next 2 to 3 years he buggered him on many weekends. He stayed over and was buggered on Friday night and Saturday afternoon. The boy stopped going when he was 12 and had heard it was wrong. The victim suffered trauma and hated the company of men. He found relationships with women difficult. He got married and had three children who he could not pick up. He told his wife about the offences and they split up. The victim reported the offences to the police when he saw the defendant with children. Earlier he had threatened the defendant that he would report him. The defendant was arrested and admitted the offences. He was 73 and of good character and spent his time caring for his wife who he had been married to for 48 years. After his arrest he attempted suicide and had been impotent for 14 years. The minister of the local Church said the defendant had confessed to him and the defendant was a well respected member of the church who helped the disadvantaged. His behaviour in prison was very much to his credit. Held. The sentence was not manifestly excessive. However, it was possible to show mercy particularly because of the defendant's age so **4 years** not 6.

R v Iverson [2000] 2 Cr App Rep 167. The defendant aged 36 pleaded guilty to buggery of a 12 year old girl, two specimen counts of under-aged sex, from when she was 13, and two specimen counts of indecent assault. The offences involved the same girl when she was 12–14. He was in a relationship with her. The buggery caused her pain and thereafter she always refused his requests to repeat it. Gross abnormalities were caused to her vagina and her anus because of her age. She had been seriously disturbed by what had happened. He admitted she expressed love for him but he used her for sex. He had no previous convictions and was married. **5 years** was severe but not manifestly excessive.

R v Clark [2001] 1 Cr App Rep 197. The defendant aged 36 pleaded guilty to three counts of attempted buggery of a boy when 11–13, and 4 counts of indecent assault on the same boy. There was also a TIC for an unspecified offence on a boy when he acted as a scoutmaster. The defendant was a friend of the family of the boy, took him on trips and gave him gifts. Each time the defendant tried to bugger the boy the boy flinched or otherwise indicated he wasn't enjoying it and he desisted. The activity was over a 2 year period. He made full admissions and showed deep remorse. **5½ years** not 7 with an extended supervision order.

Victim aged 13–15

24.17 *A-G's Reference (No 9 of 1996)* [1997] 1 Cr App Rep (S) 113. The defendant pleaded guilty at a late stage to buggery of a 14-year-old boy, G and three counts of indecent assault one on a boy of 10 (masturbation), one on a girl aged 12 (hand on her vagina) and one on a boy aged 9 (oral sex). In 1993, the defendant was released from prison after serving 4 years for attempted buggery and indecent assault on an 11-year-old boy. The defendant made friends with G and brought him presents. Sexually explicit material was sent to the boy's address and he threatened him on a number of occasions. The boy's mother sent him a solicitor's letter warning him. When questioned by the police the boy revealed buggery on one occasion. When the defendant's flat was searched sexually explicit material was found including scenes of buggery. Correspondence was found indicating he was seeking strangulation videos from Amsterdam. Held. The offences were carefully planned and two of the victims were threatened with violence. 8 years for the buggery and 4 years concurrent for the indecent assaults was not unduly lenient by reference to the tariff alone. However, taking into account the previous conviction for very similar offences and the fact that he was still on licence when he committed the first offence it was unduly lenient. The lower court should have exercised its powers to pass longer than normal sentences. Taking into account it was a reference **11 years** substituted for 8 on the buggery count with 4 years concurrent for the indecent assaults.

A-G's Reference (No 4 of 1997) [1998] 1 Cr App Rep (S) 96. The defendant was convicted of two counts of buggery with one boy when 15 and another boy whose age is unclear, three counts of indecent assaults and indecency with a child (all on boys between about 13 to 15, with masturbation and oral sex). The defendant, aged 54 set up two organisations and asked schoolboys if they would like to join. The intention was to obtain boys. Victims were tied up and blindfolded. One boy was confused about his sexuality and took an overdose of pills, which was not fatal. The defendant had no previous convictions. Held. It was in breach of trust. The correct sentence would have been 5 years and 5 consecutive for the buggery counts. Because it was a reference **4 years** and 4 consecutive with the rest concurrent not 5 years in all.

R v Brierley [2000] 2 Cr App Rep 278. The defendant aged 36–7 at the time of the offences was convicted of buggery of a 14-year-old girl and four counts of indecent assault. The offences involved the same girl over a 5 month period. He was in a relationship with her mother he turned her attentions to the daughter while the mother was out. The buggery was one incident. He had no previous convictions. Held. He had gravely abused the trust that was placed in him, but **3 years** not 4 for the buggery with the other sentences remaining consecutive.

R v Matthews [2001] 2 Cr App Rep (S) 112. The defendant made a plea not at the first opportunity to buggery. Allegations of rape and indecent assault were left on the file. The defendant aged 31 met the girl aged 15 at a public house. After both had been drinking sexual activity took place and he buggered her. It caused her some pain. The defendant had no previous convictions and an excellent work record. **18 months** substituted for 2½ years.

See also **RAPE** – *Anal*

25   BURGLARY

25.1   Theft Act 1968, s 9

Triable either way unless (a) the defendant could be sentenced to a minimum of 3 years[1] or (b) where the burglary comprises the commission of, or an intention to commit, an offence which is triable only on indictment or (GBH, rape etc)[2] or (c) where the burglary is a dwelling and a person was subjected to violence or the threat of violence[3]. In those cases the offence is triable only on indictment.

On indictment maximum 14 years when the building is a dwelling, 10 years otherwise. Summary maximum 6 months and/or £5,000.

Specified offence for a 3 year minimum sentence when the offence is a third domestic burglary.

1   Powers of Criminal Courts (Sentencing) Act 2000, s 111(2)
2   Magistrates' Courts Act 1980 , s 17(1) and Sch 1, para 28b.
3   Magistrates' Courts Act 1980 , s 17(1) and Sch 1 para 28c.

Crown Court statistics England and Wales[1] – Crown Court – Males 21+ – Burglary
25.2

Year	Plea	Total Numbers sentenced	Type of sentence%					Average length of custody (months)
			Discharge	Fine	Community sentence	Suspended sentence	Custody	
In a dwelling								
2000	Guilty	3,520	1%	0%	15%	1%	82%	24
	Not guilty	437	1%	0%	10%	0%	87%	26.4
Other than a dwelling								
2000	Guilty	638	2%	1%	26%	1%	69%	18.8
	Not guilty	108	1%	0%	25%	3%	70%	19.7

1   Excluding committals for sentence. Source: Crime and Criminal Justice Unit, Home Office Ref: IOS416-02.

Death is caused

See **MANSLAUGHTER** – *Burglars/robbers/thieves, by*

Drug abstinence order

25.3   Powers of Criminal Courts (Sentencing) Act 2000, s 58A(1) . . . Where a person is 18 or over the court may make an order requiring the offender to abstain from misusing specified Class A drugs and provide, when instructed to do so a sample to ascertain whether he has any specified Class A drugs in his body. (3) The court must be of the opinion the offender is dependant or has a propensity to misuse specified Class A drugs and the offence is a trigger offence or the misuse of any specified Class A drug caused or contributed to the offence in question. (7) An order shall be for not less than 6 months and not more than 3 years. (9) No order shall be made unless the court has been notified that arrangements for implementing the order are available. (Criminal Justice and Court Services Act 2000, Sch 6 specifies burglary as a trigger offence.)

Vehicle used to commit the offence

25.4 *R v Stratton* (1988) Times, 15 January. The defendant burgled an occupied house and an item from the house was found in his car. The defendant had no assets and his car was worth £1,500–£2,000. The court forfeited the car. Held. The forfeiture was extremely appropriate. Perhaps the power should be used more frequently.

Burglary – Domestic

Guideline case

25.5 *R v Brewster* [1998] 1 Cr App Rep 220, 1 Cr App Rep (S) 181 – LCJ. Domestic burglary is, and always has been, regarded as a very serious offence. It may involve considerable loss to the victim. Even when it does not, the victim may lose possessions of particular value to him or her. The record of the offender is of more significance in the case of domestic burglary than in the case of some other crimes. Generally speaking, domestic burglaries are the more serious if they are of occupied houses at night; if they are the result of professional planning, organisation or execution; if they are targeted at the elderly, the disabled and the sick; if there are repeated visits to the same premises; if they are committed by persistent offenders; if they are accompanied by vandalism or any wanton injury to the victim; if they are shown to have a seriously traumatic effect on the victim; if the offender operates as one of a group; if goods of high value (whether actual or sentimental) are targeted or taken; if force is used or threatened; if there is a pattern of repeat offending. It mitigates the seriousness of an offence if the offender pleads guilty, particularly if the plea is indicated at an early stage and there is hard evidence of genuine regret and remorse. The cases show:

(1)   that burglary of a dwelling-house, occupied or unoccupied, is not necessarily and in all cases an offence of such seriousness that a non-custodial sentence cannot be justified;

(2)   that the decision whether a custodial sentence is required, and if so the length of such sentence, is heavily dependent on the aggravating and mitigating features mentioned above and, usually to a lesser extent, the personal circumstances of the offender;

(3)   that the courts, particularly the higher courts, have generally reflected in their sentences the abhorrence with which the public regard those who burgle the houses of others.

Guideline remarks

25.6 *A-G's Reference (Nos 19, 20 and 21 of 2001)* [2001] EWCA Crim 1432, [2002] 1 Cr App Rep (S) 136. There can be little doubt that the two forms of criminal conduct which causes the public most concern are domestic burglary and street robberies. The effect of such offences goes way beyond the dreadful trauma suffered by the immediate victim and causes large sections of the public to alter their lifestyle to seek to avoid the danger. People are afraid to go out of their homes.

Magistrates' Court Sentencing Guidelines September 2000

25.7   Entry point. Are Magistrates' sentencing powers appropriate? Consider the impact on the victim. Examples of aggravating factors for the offence are at night, forcible entry, group offence, people in house, occupants frightened, professional operation, repeat victimisation, soiling, ransacking and damage. Examples of mitigating factors for the offence are low value, nobody frightened, no damage or disturbance, no forcible entry and opportunist. Examples of mitigation are age, health (physical or mental), co-operation with the police, voluntary compensation and genuine remorse. Give reasons if not awarding compensation.

For details about the guidelines see **MAGISTRATES' COURT SENTENCING GUIDELINES** at page 331.

Sentencing Advisory Panel Report 2002

25.8   For a low level burglary committed by a first-time burglar (and for some second-time domestic burglars), where there is no damage to property and no property (or only property of a very low value) is stolen, the starting point should be a community penalty. For a standard burglary (theft of electrical goods and/or personal items, damage caused by the break-in, some turmoil in the house and some trauma to the victims), the starting point for a first-time burglar should be 9 months. A case would on a guilty plea, be suitable for disposal in the Magistrates' Court. For a second-time burglar the starting point should be 18 months. Where the standard domestic burglary displays any 'medium relevance' factors (vulnerable victim, although not targeted as such, the victim was at home, goods of high value are taken (economic or sentimental) or the burglars worked in a group) the starting point should be 12 months. For a second time domestic burglar the starting point should be 2 years. For those with two or more previous convictions for domestic burglary the starting point is 3½ years. Where the standard domestic burglary has any 'high relevance' factors the starting point for a first-time burglar is 18 months, a second-time burglar 3 years and for a burglar with 2 or more previous convictions 4½ years. The presence of more than one 'high relevance' factor could bring the sentence level significantly above the suggested starting points. The high relevance factors are, force used or threatened against the victim; victim injured (as a result of force used or threatened); especially traumatic effect on the victim, professional planning, organisation or execution; vandalism of the premises, offence racially aggravated and vulnerable victim deliberately targeted (including cases of 'deception' or 'distraction' burglaries of the elderly). www.sentencing-advisory-panel.gov.uk [Note the first two factors should make the offence robbery. The Court of Appeal has not as yet adopted the suggestions.]

Custodial not necessary

25.9   *R v Brewster* [1998] 1 Cr App Rep 220, 1 Cr App Rep (S) 181 at 187 – LCJ Guideline case. The cases show: (1) that burglary of a dwelling-house, occupied or unoccupied, is not necessarily and in all cases an offence of such seriousness that a non-custodial sentence cannot be justified; (2) that the decision whether a custodial sentence is required, and if so the length of such sentence, is heavily dependent on the aggravating and mitigating feature

R v Finney [1998] 2 Cr App Rep (S) 239. The defendant pleaded guilty to burglary. He lost his job as a chef and with it his accommodation where others lived. The next year at night, he entered an occupied bebsitting room in the building and stole a number of cassettes and a jacket. He tried another room and the occupant recognised him and he left. He admitted the offence in interview. He said he was drunk at the time and he went there because the victim had some of his property, which he hadn't returned. Despite representations the victim had 'fobbed him off.' The defendant was of good character and genuinely remorseful. Held. Immediate imprisonment was not inevitable. Probation substituted for 9 months.

Sentencing Advisory Panel Report 2002: For a low level burglary committed by a first-time burglar (and for some second-time domestic burglars), where there is no damage to property and no property (or only property of a very low value) is stolen, the starting point should be a community penalty www.sentencing-advisory-panel.gov.uk. [The Court of Appeal has not as yet adopted the suggestions.]

Defendant aged 12–15

25.10   *R v Brewster Re RH* [1998] 1 Cr App Rep 220, 1 Cr App Rep (S) 181 at 187 – LCJ. The defendant, when 15 pleaded guilty to four burglaries committed in the space of little more than a week. The first involved an unoccupied dwelling where he stole nothing. The next three involved the dwellings of vulnerable people, starting within hours of his release. One involved an epileptic man and his disabled girlfriend, both of whom slept as property worth £225 was stolen. Next he burgled the house of an infirm pensioner in the early hours of the morning. She experienced 'terrible shock'. The next night he broke into the home of a 93-year-old lady and £150 was taken. The defendant had never known his father who was in prison for murder. He had lived with his mother to whom he was close. She suffered from domestic violence. At school he was persistently bullied. The mother disappeared in suspicious circumstances. Until then the defendant was a reasonably stable boy. Unable to come to terms with the situation, he began to use crack cocaine. The offences were committed to fund his addiction. His extended family saw his character change. He became unrecognisable and completely untrustworthy. He was in breach of a supervision order for a residential burglary. He did not receive any treatment at all for his addiction nor adequate counselling. Since his arrest he had absconded twice from local authority care. A psychiatric report said, 'He was clinically depressed and was a very vulnerable, fragile and somewhat immature youth. It was doubted whether he would have resources to survive in a prison environment and he is in urgent need of therapeutic help to address his bereavement, depression and drug addiction. His drug addiction is in fact very much secondary to his bereavement and depression.' He recommended a two-year supervision order including a direction to participate in specified activities for up to 90 days as an alternative to custody and 2 years' aftercare and monitoring. He had served 4 months. Held. The judge accurately described the offences as 'cruel and hateful burglaries' which resulted from 'deliberately targeting the weak and vulnerable'. There was quite exceptional mitigation. If he had been a little older or if the mitigation had not been so exceptional we would not have altered the 4 years' detention. **Supervision** substituted.

R v Winson and Poole [1998] 1 Cr App Rep (S) 239. The defendants W aged 15 and P aged 13 at the time pleaded to burglary. They entered a house while the owner was out. The door was unlocked. A purse, a treasured ring and £180 was stolen. The owner was very upset. W had a conviction for burglary committed about 1 month before this offence and 2 for theft. P had no previous convictions. Re-offending risks were considered to be 'posed a risk and quite high' respectively. Because of their ages **9 months** detention not 12.

R v Carr [1998] 2 Cr App Rep (S) 20. The defendant faced nine counts of burglary. He pleaded guilty to five and to four he pleaded guilty to theft as an alternative. When he was between 14½ and 15¾ he repeatedly stole from an extremely vulnerable 88-year-old lady who was frail and easily confused. Once he asked to use the lavatory and was allowed to enter. On another occasion he posed as a gasman and once he said he needed to read a meter. Frequently she was locked in the kitchen. He took on the nine occasions nothing twice, her purse three times, £70 twice, £300 and £60. She had been terrified. The defendant had previous convictions for public order offence, criminal damage and dishonesty. The judge said for an adult he would have received 7, which because of his age he reduced to 5. Held. The 7 and **5 years** figures were right.

R v Mills [1998] 2 Cr App Rep (S) 128 at 134 – LCJ The defendant pleaded to three burglaries committed in the space a little less than 4 months. He asked for another burglary to be taken into consideration. When 13 he burgled four houses when the occupants were out. On three occasions he broke a window and on two of them he was with other boys. He was arrested for the third burglary and released on bail. He then committed the fourth a month later. A variety of items were stolen. He had findings of guilt for non-domestic burglary and other offences. He was in care and had six placements in 9 months. He had served the equivalent of 11 months after sentence. Held. 18 months was at the top of the range but was not excessive. Taking into account the time serve and his need for assistance **supervision** instead.

R v O'Grady [2000] 1 Cr App Rep (S) 112. The defendant pleaded guilty to three distraction burglaries. Two pleas were entered late. The victims were all elderly ladies living alone. The first one involved three boys one of whom asked if she wanted any jobs done and when she said no they waited and entered. 60p was taken. In the second burglary boys entered the home and one asked her if she wanted any shopping done. Another boy went upstairs and stole her purse. The third burglary was very similar with the same two boys. It was clear elderly people had been targeted. The defendant had been sentenced to an attendance centre for common assault. Since his sentence his education had been taken in hand. Held. There had to be a balance between welfare and deterrent and punitive elements. The judge was able to use the then s 53(2) procedure. **6 months** detention was not excessive.

R v D [2001] 1 Cr App Rep (S) 202. The defendant pleaded guilty to burglary and was found guilty of handling stolen goods from another burglary. While the owners were away on holiday, he and the nephew of the victim entered a house by removing a pane of glass and stole a Play Station, games and power tools worth £684. A tap was left running which caused about £60 worth of damage to carpets and one of them urinated over a child's mattress. The nephew was 11. On the same day another house was burgled by a 14 year old and £157 worth of audio equipment and computer accessories were stolen. The defendant tried to sell some of the property on. He said he wanted money to buy his mother a present. He was 14 and had received three formal cautions for criminal damage, theft and common assault. He was sentenced to 12 hours at an attendance centre for theft of a cycle. He also failed to attend and was given no penalty. Held. The judge was entitled to consider the cautions when determining whether he was a persistent offender and to consider he was a persistent offender. Because of his age **8 months** detention not 12.

R v Elliott [2001] EWCA Crim 582, [2001] 2 Cr App Rep (S) 420. The defendant, aged 14 pleaded to burglary. He and the 13-year-old co-defendant forced the front door and ransacked the home of a friend of the co-defendant. A duvet was spayed and the co-defendant set it on fire. The defendant put it out. Property worth £1,500 was stolen and £1,000 damage was caused. The victim was very distressed. The defendant had two fairly recent non-domestic burglary convictions and a conviction for handling. The co-defendant's record was worse. The defendant had a disturbed family background and the risk of re-offending was described as high. The judge said it was worth 3 to 4 years for an adult and gave the co-defendant 12 months. Held. There was no reason to distinguish between them so **12 months** not 18.

Defendant aged 16–17

25.11   *R v Mills Re Lamb* [1998] 2 Cr App Rep (S) 128 at 137 – LCJ. The defendant pleaded guilty to burglary and aggravated vehicle-taking. He had changed his plea. He had when 16 taken a car without consent. He then picked two others and drove to a house where he burgled it while the others kept watch. It was unoccupied and he stole a substantial amount of electrical equipment, cameras, watches and a knife. Officers later saw the car and they were suspicious and one officer stood in the road signalling the car to stop. The defendant accelerated at him causing him to jump out of the way. He had nine court appearances and eight of them included a burglary. He had served two short YOI sentences. His most recent sentence was 5 months for offences including burglary, aggravated vehicle-taking and assaulting an officer with intent to resist arrest. The judge said he regarded him as a very dangerous man who needs to be kept away from the public because of his danger. He sentenced him to 2 years and 18 months consecutive for the vehicle offence. As this was unlawful he changed it to 3½ years as a global sentence on the burglary. Held. **2 years** was not wrong for the burglary nor was 3½ years globally wrong.

R v Mills Re Marsh [1998] 2 Cr App Rep (S) 128 at 140 – LCJ. The defendant pleaded guilty to a conspiracy to burgle, a conspiracy to steel, and two burglaries. He was committed for sentence for seven burglaries, six thefts, threatening behaviour and failing to surrender. The conspiracy to steal concerned elderly womens' purses. There was spate of such thefts in Portsmouth. He arrested for one and bailed. While his accomplice S distracted a lady in a supermarket he stole another purse. Later that day he and S with another burgled an Oxfam shop. The third person caused a distraction while the other two went upstairs, broke into staff lockers and stole purses. Four days later he and S stole another purse in a supermarket. Twelve days later the defendant entered a flat and stole cash and cigarettes. The next day he stole another purse in a supermarket. He was arrested and released on bail and police decided to follow him. He and S were talking to an old lady and S said they'd have to wait till she was on her own. The same day he and S entered a staff room at a health centre and stole £1,700 worth of camera equipment. They were arrested. Six months later they burgled the home of an elderly couple and stole a video and compact discs. They were arrested and much of the property was recovered. Twelve days later he burgled an elderly widower's home leaving it in disarray and his wife's jewellery and all his Christmas presents. Between July 1994 and December 1996 he had been arrested 49 times. Held. The totality was very serious. He targeted those who could ill afford to lose their purses. **5 years** was not manifestly excessive.

R v Sleeth [1999] 2 Cr App Rep (S) 211. The defendant a girl, now 17 pleaded guilty to three burglaries. She would get herself invited to the homes of elderly people and then wander round and steal. The victim's ages were 75, 86 and 84. At one she said she was looking for someone, at another she gave the impression she knew the lady and at the last she said she had some rings to sell. She started offending at 11 and her convictions included two burglaries, theft, and GBH with intent. Held. **3 years** detention substituted for 4 because of her age and because she had not served a custodial sentence before.

R v Chapple [2000] 1 Cr App Rep (S) 115. The defendant, when 17 pleaded guilty to a distraction burglary. At about 11.30pm the defendant broke a window and entered using a crowbar. A neighbour called police and they found him inside the flat holding a hammer. He said, 'Serves the bitch right, I'll do it again.' He had taken two penknives from the flat. The occupier was at work at the time. He admitted it in interview and when 15 he was convicted of three burglary offences. Each one was a business premise of the householder in the current case. He also had a conviction for theft. Six weeks before the burglary he said to the householder, 'I only got fined £150 at court don't worry I'll break in again at some point, I'll get you back.' **2½ years** detention not 4.

R v Fieldhouse and Watts [2001] 1 Cr App Rep (S) 361. The defendant W pleaded guilty to two counts of burglary, one count of theft and asked for four theft matters to be taken into consideration. F pleaded guilty to one of the burglaries. In the joint burglary the two entered a dwelling house and stole about £2,000 worth of property. F said he knew the occupants and that they would not be in. W's other burglary was at 11.20pm on a house with another while the householder's son was in bed. W's theft matter concerned £2,500 worth of property. W was found at 6am with another and the property that had been stolen from a house nearby. W's foru TICs were thefts from sheds and vehicles. Some of his offences were committed when he was on bail. They were both now 17. W had three convictions in 1999 for criminal damage, a public order offence and assaulting a police constable. His report said there was a risk of re-offending. F had minor convictions and cautions. F's prison report described him as quiet and well behaved. Held. The judge's approach was impeccable. The gravity of W's offending was such a long-term detention order under (what is now the Powers of the Criminal Courts (Sentencing) Act 2000, s 91) could well have been made. His 24 months could not be challenged. **8 months** detention for F not 12.

Defendant aged 18–20

25.12 *R v Hanrahan* [1999] 1 Cr App Rep (S) 308. The defendant, now 18 pleaded to a distraction burglary at the home of a 90 year old. He told the lady there was a water explosion and produced something to show he was from the council. He persuaded her to let him in and asked her where the mains tap was. He then persuaded her to go to the cellar while an accomplice stole a watch of great sentimental value worth £100. He had three previous court appearances but none for burglary and had no custodial sentences. He showed remorse and was said to be under the influence of others. Held. A deterrent sentence was called for and 4 years was suitable for someone older or someone who had been in custody before. However, because of the circumstances **3 years** detention not 4.

Where age is not a determining factor, eg where the defendant has already served a custodial sentence the case is listed in another category.

Distraction burglaries (entering by a trick and stealing)

25.13 *R v Henry* [1998] 1 Cr App Rep (S) 289. The defendant pleaded guilty very late to burglary. The defendant distracted a lady of 91 pretending to be a minicab driver wanting something written down. His brother then entered and stole items from her jewellery box. The victim now felt uneasy and anxious in her home. The defendant had several previous convictions for stealing from old people including one for which he had received 4½ years. When 16, he received 7 years for a rape which had started as a burglary. Held. The judge was right to start around 6 years so **5 years** after the discount was upheld.

R v Carr [1998] 2 Cr App Rep (S) 20. The defendant faced nine counts of burglary. He pleaded guilty to five and to four he pleaded guilty to theft as an alternative. When he was between 14½ and 15¾ he repeatedly stole from an extremely vulnerable 88 year old lady who was frail and easily confused. He was allowed to enter asking to use the lavatory once posing as a gasman and once to read a meter. Frequently she was locked in the kitchen. He took on the nine occasions nothing twice, her purse three times, £70 twice, £300 and £60. She had been terrified. The defendant had previous convictions for public order, criminal damage and dishonesty. The judge said for an adult he would have received 7, which because of his age he reduced to 5. Held. The 7 and **5 years** figures were right.

R v McCamon [1998] 2 Cr App Rep (S) 81. The defendant pleaded guilty to ABH and five counts of burglary. The defendant and others kicked a man outside a nightclub fracturing his right orbit round his eye. He was released on bail. Next he committed the first burglary when an 80-year-old man was tricked and his pension book and £40 was stolen. He was released on bail. There were then four similar burglaries. One involved a 95-year old lady in sheltered accommodation. He pretended to have lost his cat. Two purses containing some £600 were taken. The defendant had a number of previous convictions for dishonesty and a very recent one for obtaining money by deception from people in their homes while he pretended to be a charity collector. He had an unfortunate history of family rejection. Held. 4 not 5 years with the ABH 1 year consecutive so **5 years** not 6 years.

R v Wright [1999] 2 Cr App Rep (S) 327. The defendant pleaded guilty to burglary at the Magistrates' Court. The defendant approached the victim and asked to fill a bottle with water for his car. She invited him in. While she went to get a bucket to help him he stole her handbag. He was arrested and identified the bin he had put the bag in and it was recovered The contents less £35 and her bus pass were found. In 1984 he was convicted of theft when he entered an elderly person's home by asking for a glass of water. He stole two pension books and £94. In 1984 there were two convictions for burglary. In 1992 he was given at least 3 years for obtaining and attempting to obtain property by deception and breach of two suspended sentences. One of them related to a trying to cash someone's pension book. He showed genuine remorse. **3 years** not 4 years.

R v Woodliffe [2000] 1 Cr App Rep (S) 330. The defendant pleaded guilty to two burglaries. He went to an old age pensioner's home saying that he had come about the front light. He then said he needed to check the windows. He asked her to go to her bedroom and listen for banging while he stole her purse containing keys, her bus pass and £14. The same day he visited a 77-year-old man in an old people's complex and said the police and the council sent him. He also said it was cold and asked to be admitted. Once inside he said he was fitting alarms. The victim said he would not pay for any and followed him as he measured up. The defendant was told to leave. He ran out taking £30. The defendant was caught on video and admitted it in interview. He was on licence from a 5 year sentence for five burglaries and an attempted burglary. Those were similar offences to the two new ones. The new sentences were concurrent but consecutive to the order for breaching his licence. Held. *R v Henry* [1998] (above) did not lay down a sentence cannot ever be more than 6 years. **7 years** was severe but not excessive.

Sentencing Advisory Panel Report 2002: For a standard burglary (theft of electrical goods and/or personal items, damage caused by the break-in, some turmoil in the house and some trauma to the victim), the starting point where vulnerable victim are deliberately targeted (including cases of 'deception' or 'distraction' burglaries of the elderly) is for a first-time burglar 18 months, a second-time burglar 3 years and for a burglar with two or more previous convictions 4½ years. [www.sentencing-advisory-panel.gov.uk. The Court of Appeal has not as yet adopted the suggestions.]

See also *R v O'Brien* [2002] 2 Cr App Rep (S) 560.

Domestic, occupied – One offence

25.14   *R v Brewster Re Woodhouse* [1998] 1 Cr App Rep 220, 1 Cr App Rep (S) 181 at 187 – LCJ. The defendant, aged 49, pleaded guilty to one night time burglary. At about 4.30am the female occupant of a ground floor flat, who had not locked her front door, woke up to find the defendant in her bedroom. He told her the front door had been open and he had walked in. He then turned and left. Nothing was taken and he was arrested almost immediately. The defendant had 8 previous convictions of a relatively minor nature, and none for burglary. He had never served a custodial sentence before. He was an alcoholic and full of remorse. He acknowledged the traumatic effect on the victim. Held. For a burglar to enter the bedroom of someone who is asleep is a seriously aggravating feature. No doubt the appellant is a pathetic figure, but it must have been an utterly terrifying experience for the victim. **2 years** was right.

Sentencing Advisory Panel Report 2002: See extract at the beginning of the BURGLARY – DOMESTIC section.

Domestic, occupied – More than one offence

25.15 *R v Middlemiss* [1999] 1 Cr App Rep (S) 62. The defendant pleaded to one burglary. He asked for three offences to be taken into consideration. At night he entered a house occupied by a married couple and their two children. At 4.30am the couple were awakened by sounds. While they were investigating them the burglar ran off. Money jewellery, cards, and other property were stolen. The defendant was arrested and he helped locate some but not all of the property. He said he was in the getaway car. The family was distressed particularly the daughter who was referred to a doctor and counsellor. The TICs were two attempted burglaries on the same night and one burglary earlier. He said he was driver and lookout. He was 30 and treated as being of good character. He was genuinely remorseful and the risk of reoffending was assessed as being low. **3 years** was entirely justified.

Sentencing Advisory Panel Report 2002: See extract at the beginning of the domestic burglary section.

Domestic, unoccupied – One offence

25.16 Sentencing Advisory Panel Report 2002: In the case of a standard burglary (theft of electrical goods and/or personal items, damage caused by the break-in, some turmoil in the house and some trauma to the victim), the starting point for a first-time burglar should be 9 months. A case would on a guilty plea, be suitable for disposal in the Magistrates' Court. For a second-time burglar the starting point should be 18 months. [www.sentencing-advisory-panel.gov.uk. The Court of Appeal has not as yet adopted the suggestions.]

See also *R v Dawson* (26 July 2002, unreported). 3 years not 4.

Domestic, unoccupied – More than one offence

25.17 *R v Middlemiss* [1999] 1 Cr App Rep (S) 62. The defendant pleaded to one burglary. He asked for three offences to be taken into consideration. At night he entered a house occupied by a married couple and their two children. At 4.30am the couple were awakened by sounds. While they were investigating them the burglar ran off. Money jewellery, bank cards, and other property were stolen. The defendant was arrested and he helped locate some but not all of the property. He said he was in the getaway car. The family was distressed particularly the daughter who was referred to a doctor and counsellor. The TICs were two attempted burglaries on the same night and one burglary earlier. He said he was driver and lookout. He was 30 and treated as being of good character. He was genuinely remorseful and the risk of re-offending was assessed as being low. **3 years** was entirely justified.

Sentencing Advisory Panel Report 2002: In the case of a standard burglary (theft of electrical goods and/or personal items, damage caused by the break-in, some turmoil in the house and some trauma to the victim), the starting point for a second-time burglar should be 18 months. [www.sentencing-advisory-panel.gov.uk. The Court of Appeal has not as yet adopted the suggestions.]

Drug addicts – Guideline case

25.18   *R v Brewster* [1998] 1 Cr App Rep 220, 1 Cr App Rep (S) 181 – LCJ. It is common knowledge that many domestic burglars are drug addicts who burgle to satisfy their craving for drugs. This is often an expensive craving, and it is not uncommon to learn that addicts commit a burglary, or even several burglaries, each day, often preying on houses in less affluent areas of the country. Self-induced addiction cannot be relied on as mitigation. The courts will not be easily persuaded that an addicted offender is genuinely determined and able to conquer his addiction.

Drug addicts – Cases

25.19   *R v Brewster Re RH* [1998] 1 Cr App Rep 220, 1 Cr App Rep (S) 181 at 187 – LCJ The defendant, when 15 pleaded guilty to four burglaries committed in the space of little more than a week. The offences were committed to finance his addiction to crack cocaine. Because of wholly exceptional personal circumstances the court substituted a **supervision order** for an otherwise perfectly appropriate 4 years' detention. The court said, 'No one should interpret this judgement as detracting in any way from the general rule that there is no mitigation in drug addiction.'

Expensive properties with antiques etc

25.20   *R v Gibbs* [2000] 1 Cr App Rep (S) 261. The defendant pleaded guilty to seven counts of burglary and on three burglary counts pleaded to handling as an alternative. The seven properties were comparatively isolated country houses. Only high value items were taken. £46,000 worth of furniture was taken and £7,000 worth was recovered. Two of the victims were aged 88 and 75. The handling charges related to antique English furniture found in his property in Portugal. The furniture was worth £20,000 and had been burgled from English country houses. His houses were worth £110,000 and £115,000. He was 51 and since 12 had made 18 appearances at court mostly for dishonesty and half of them burglaries. He was sentenced to 10 years for the burglaries, 8 years concurrent for the handling offences, and ordered to pay over £70,000 confiscation, £45,000 compensation and £7,000 prosecution costs. **10 years** was justified.

GBH, with intent to inflict

25.21   *A-G's Reference (No 94 of 2001)* (21 January 2002, unreported). [Court would expect 5 years in this attack on the home of the defendant's ex-partner and her parents, with harassment before.]

Hotel rooms

25.22   *R v Massey* [2001] EWCA Crim 531, [2001] 2 Cr App Rep (S) 371. The defendant, aged 34 pleaded guilty to two burglaries at the Magistrates' Court. He broke into a guest's room at a hotel through a window. From the room and the guest's car he stole property worth £1,500. He also stole the car. The second burglary was also a guest's room at another hotel with access also gained through a window. The property stolen was worth £3,078. He admitted the offences in interview. He had many previous convictions including 36 for burglary and three for attempted burglary. The risk of re-offending was assessed as high. Held. The burglary of a guest's bedroom was much more akin to burglary of domestic premises rather than of a small business. It is close to the burglary of a bedroom. Two and 2 years consecutive not 2 and 3 years so **4 years** not 5 in all.

Persistent burglar – Minimum 3 years' custody

25.23 Powers of Criminal Courts (Sentencing) Act 2000, s 111. Where a person is convicted of a domestic burglary committed after 30 November 1999 and was 18 or over and he has been convicted of two other domestic burglaries one of which was committed after he had been convicted of the other and both of them were committed after 30 November 1999, the court shall impose a sentence of imprisonment of at least 3 years unless it is of the opinion that there are particular circumstances which relate to any of the offences or to the offender which would make it unjust. [This section is summarised and is slightly amended by the Criminal Justice and Court Services Act 2000.]

Persistent burglar – Minimum 3 years' custody – Plea of guilty

25.24 Powers of the Criminal Courts (Sentencing) Act 2000, s 152(3). Where a sentence is to be imposed under the Powers of the Criminal Courts (Sentencing) Act 2000, s 111 nothing in that section shall prevent the court from imposing a sentence of 80% or more of the minimum period. (Section summarised. The section means if he pleads guilty the court can impose a sentence, which is 80% or more of the minimum term.)

Persistent burglar with many previous convictions – One offence

25.25 *R v Brewster Re Thorpe* [1998] 1 Cr App Rep 220, 1 Cr App Rep (S) 181 at 188 – LCJ. The defendant, now aged 33, pleaded guilty just before a trial to one domestic burglary committed at night with another. The 14-year-old daughter of the house came home and heard voices inside. She looked through a blind and saw the defendant carrying her TV. Since the burglary she had received counselling for trauma and distress. The property actually removed was valued at £561, although property collected for removal downstairs was valued at approximately £2,000, and included the family's Christmas presents. The door forced to gain entry cost £300 to repair. The defendant had a significant criminal record, including 16 previous convictions for domestic burglary. Held. The judge rightly gave no great credit for the guilty plea and was also entitled to infer that the defendant was the leader. The judge was able to draw no distinction between this case, and one where the dwelling is occupied and the occupants are disturbed, because of the distress caused to the 14-year-old girl. The real point is to identify the distress caused to the victims. Held. There was nothing wrong with the **4 years** sentence.

R v Brewster Re Ishmael [1998] 1 Cr App Rep 220, 1 Cr App Rep (S) 181 at 188 – LCJ. The defendant, aged 32, pleaded guilty to one daytime burglary. Property worth some £7,000 was stolen. Significant damage was done on entry. The burglary was committed to feed a drug habit. The appellant has a large number of previous convictions, including 23 for burglary, with 23 other burglary offences taken into consideration. He told the probation officer (who assessed the risk of his re-offending as high) 'I am a burglar, it is what I do.' There is no merit in this appeal against the **4 years** sentence.

R v Brewster Re Blanchard [1998] 1 Cr App Rep 220, 1 Cr App Rep (S) 181 at 189 – LCJ. The defendant, aged 25, pleaded guilty not at the first opportunity to one night time burglary. The house was occupied by three children aged 15, 10 and 8. Fortunately they did not wake up. The defendant and another entered by breaking a window, and the third person drove the car. A neighbour raised the alarm. Minimal property was stolen. The defendant had an appalling criminal record, including 15 burglaries, although only two of dwellings. Held. The judge was entitled to infer that the appellant was the leader in the enterprise. The sentence of **2½ years** was entirely proportionate to the appellant's criminality. Had the sentence been longer he would still have had no cause for complaint.

R v Woods [1998] 2 Cr App Rep (S) 237. The defendant pleaded guilty to burgling a vicarage while the family were out. The Rector found the defendant, a vagrant half-asleep on the floor. A number of stolen items were in his bag ready to be taken away. The defendant said he had called at the vicarage to borrow a blanket and then had kicked the door in. He was 42 with 121 previous convictions including burglary. He had been released from prison 21 days earlier. The sentencing judge said in essence that there was no hope of rehabilitation and homes had to be protected from persistent burglars. Held. Without the previous convictions 2½ years was appropriate. Therefore **4 years** not 6 years.

R v Hollis [1998] 2 Cr App Rep (S) 359. The defendant pleaded guilty belatedly to burglary. He broke into a cottage while the owner was out. A window was forced and jewellery and a watch worth about £1,500 were stolen. The defendant was 29 and had 29 previous for burglary many of them of dwellings. His first burglary was when he was 13. **4 years** was not excessive.

R v Banks [1999] 2 Cr App Rep (S) 231. The defendant pleaded guilty at the Magistrates' Court to burglary. The victims returned to their flat at about 4am and heard a burglar. They went into the street, saw the defendant and gave chase. The defendant was caught nearby. Jewellery and ornaments from the flat worth £20,000 were recovered from a bag he dropped and his person. A report said it appeared he suffered from a personality disorder. In 1989 he was sentenced to 4 years for 29 burglaries and thefts. In 1993 he was sentenced to 3 years for burglary. It was said there was a serious danger he would re-offend. Therefore **4 years** not 5.

R v Jenkins [2001] EWCA Crim 1181, [2002] 1 Cr App Rep (S) 22. The defendant was convicted of burglary. During the day, the defendant broke into an unoccupied dwelling by forcing some French windows. Jewellery worth over £50,000 and a clock worth over £20,000 were stolen. His fingerprints were found near the scene and the clock was found in his garden shed. The jewellery was not found but he had £5,401 in cash was found. He relied on an alibi. He was 56 and on licence from a 2½ year sentence for burglary. There were twenty burglaries, seven handling offences, three attempted burglaries and four for either house-breaking or attempted house-breaking on his record. He had been a persistent offender for 38 years. The longest sentence was 5 years. His partner suffered from cancer. Held. He is a persistent, professional burglar. This case is similar to *R v Brewster* [1998] 1 Cr App Rep (S) 181 at 187. **8 years** was very severe but not manifestly excessive.

R v Humphreys (12 October 2001, unreported). 6 years not 9 for man with an appauling record for burglary convicted of a single offence

R v Comer [2001] EWCA Crim 1281, [2002] 1 Cr App Rep (S) 147. The defendant was convicted of burglary. The victim saw the defendant walk up the drive and walk into her hall. He said he hadn't done anything wrong and was with the postman delivering a parcel. He left and nothing was taken. He was identified sitting on a park bench nearby. When interviewed he said that he went to the house to look for milk and the door popped open. In November 1999 he received a combination order for a commercial burglary. In total he had four convictions for burglary and had convictions for possession of drugs and theft. He had served three prison sentences. Held. He was a somewhat low level professional burglar. **3 years** not 4

Persistent burglar with many previous convictions – More than one offence

25.26   *R v Brewster* [1998] 1 Cr App Rep 220, 1 Cr App Rep (S) 181 at 187 – LCJ. The defendant, aged 51, a professional burglar pleaded guilty to three offences of burglary. They were all daytime burglaries of unoccupied flats. A wristwatch valued at £10,000 was stolen. There was no ransacking of the premises. The offences were committed within 3 months, the first one taking place just six months after his release from prison. He made admissions in interview. He had a formidable criminal record, including no fewer than 33 previous convictions for domestic burglary. His criminal career began at the age of 8. Included in it was *R v Brewster* [1980] 2 Cr App Rep (S) 191, when a 10 years sentence was upheld on pleas of guilty to two burglaries in which some £70,000 worth of jewellery was stolen. Lawton LJ said: 'There is no hope of rehabilitating this man. There is no hope that he will be deterred by prison sentences. All that the courts can do with him and his like is to ensure that they do not carry out raids on other people's houses for very substantial periods.' Held. The judge was fully entitled to take into account his appalling record as aggravating the seriousness of the offences. **9 years** was a very severe sentence and was justified. It matters not whether it is structured as 9 years' concurrent or 3 years for each offence consecutive.

R v X [1999] 2 Cr App Rep (S) 294. The defendant pleaded guilty to 'a number of offences of burglary.' He was 30 years of age and had a 'substantial record'. He was a drug addict and his many offences were substantially committed to gain money to fund his habit. In September 1997, he was sentenced for three burglaries of homes, from which he had stolen electrical equipment. There were other less significant offences as well. He was put on probation for two years, with a condition that he reside for 12 months at an identified drug rehabilitation unit. Four days later, he left the unit without permission. A counsellor arranged for another rehabilitation centre and he went there and remained for about a month but left that centre unilaterally as well. Shortly afterwards, he committed a separate offence of a motoring kind, and served a short sentence for that. In March, he appeared before the justices and admitted the breach of probation. He was committed to the Crown Court for sentence, on bail. Accordingly, he was thereafter on bail as well as still on probation. In April, he broke into a house, divided into bed sitting rooms, during the day time, and stole from several of the rooms electrical equipment. Considerable damage was done to the property. Untidy searches were made and the possessions of the occupants were strewn about. Property worth just over £3,000 was stolen. He pleaded guilty and was sentenced to 4 years concurrently upon each offence. Held. Consecutive sentences would have been fully justified for the original offences and the recent ones. 4 years was appropriate. Because of information provided the offence was reduced to **3½ years**.

R v Burns [2000] 2 Cr App Rep (S) 198. The defendant, aged 19 pleaded guilty to three burglaries at the Magistrates' Court. He asked for five burglaries to be taken into consideration. The first victim was 66 years old who found the defendant in her kitchen. He asked for some directions and fled with £170, which was taken from the bedroom. Four rooms had been ransacked. Four days later the next victim also found the defendant in her kitchen. An hour later a couple aged 84 and 94 heard banging coming from a bedroom. They found jewellery of sentimental value worth £17,000 had been taken. He had an appalling record, which included 37 offences for burglary. The offences were to finance his heroin addiction. **5 years** was well merited.

Victim over 65

25.27 *R v Whittaker* [1998] 1 Cr App Rep (S) 172. The defendant was convicted of four burglaries. The first victim was aged 83 and lost £200 and personal property. He was wearing a balaclava. She was unable to stop him. The second he wore a mask. The victim was very frightened as he stole £100 and personal property. He was arrested and granted bail. The third victims were a 77-year-old woman and her disabled husband aged 81. He was wearing a hood and the woman tried to stop him but was unable to. He stole her handbag. The fourth involved another old woman who found him in her house. She screamed hysterically. He had a balaclava on. Her husband was knocked over as he took hold of him. He was later taken to hospital. She ran into the street and spoke to the police. The defendant was feeding a drug habit and in 1988 was sentenced to 5 years for burglary. Held. Burglaries against elderly people are regarded as extremely serious. 5 concurrent for each pair consecutive making **10 years** upheld.

R v Guigno [1998] 2 Cr App Rep (S) 217. The defendant was convicted of burgling a bungalow occupied by a married couple aged 87 and 91. At 2.15am he entered her bedroom and when she woke up he carried on searching. She put her hand out and she felt his head. He was challenged twice. Her panic alarm enabled the police to be called and the police outside found him. The contents of her bedroom cabinet had been spread on the floor. At the trial he accepted he was the burglar but said he was too drunk to form the necessary intent. The victims were not called to give evidence. The defendant had no previous convictions for burglary. **3 years** was right.

See also *R v O'Brien* [2002] 2 Cr App Rep (S) 560 and *Distraction burglaries* (where the victim is invariably elderly)

Burglary – Non domestic

Magistrates' Court Sentencing Guidelines September 2000

25.28 Entry point. Is it serious enough for a community penalty? Consider the impact on the victim. Examples of aggravating factors for the offence are forcible entry, group offence, harm to business, night time, occupants frightened, professional operation, repeat victimisation, school premises, soiling, ransacking and damage. Examples of mitigating factors for the offence are low value, nobody frightened, no damage or disturbance and no forcible entry. Examples of mitigation are age, health (physical or mental), co-operation with the police, voluntary compensation and genuine remorse. Give reasons if not awarding compensation.

For details about the guidelines see MAGISTRATES' COURT SENTENCING GUIDELINES at page 331.

Banks, places for money etc

25.29 *R v Richardson and Brown* [1998] 2 Cr App Rep (S) 87. The defendants pleaded guilty to burglary. An eight-man team used a JCB digger, lorry and car to ram raid a suburban branch of a bank. All the vehicles were stolen. Telephone wires were cut. The police arrived and the group scattered. The lorry was driven at and partly over a police car. The two defendants escaped in the car, which collided with numerous parked cars. The cash machine contained £75,000. R had more previous convictions than B. The judge thought not less than 7 years was appropriate and reduced it to 5 because of the plea. Held. The 2 year only discount was justified and **5 years** was no way too long.

Shops etc

25.30 *R v Anson* [1999] 1 Cr App Rep (S) 331. The defendant pleaded guilty very late to burglary. At night he burgled Woolworths of property worth £11,913 and caused £2,500 worth of damage. Half the property was recovered from his friends and relatives. He was 28 with a significant criminal record going back many years including burglary both domestic and commercial. **2½ years** was not wrong.

26   BURGLARY – AGGRAVATED

26.1   Theft Act 1968, s 10

Indictable only. Maximum sentence life.

Crown Court statistics England and Wales – Crown Court – Males 21+ – Aggravated burglary

26.2

Year	Plea	Total Numbers sentenced	Type of sentence%					Average length of custody[1] (months)
			Discharge	Fine	Community sentence	Suspended sentence	Custody	
In a dwelling								
2000	Guilty	92	0%	0%	1%	1%	96%	48.5
	Not guilty	37	0%	0%	0%	5%	92%	60.6
Not in a dwelling								
2000	Guilty	6	0%	0%	0%	0%	100%	57
	Not guilty	5	0%	0%	0%	0%	100%	64.8

1   Excluding life sentences. Source: Crime and Criminal Justice Unit, Home Office Ref: IOS416-02.

Guideline case

26.3   For some guidance see BURGLARY – DOMESTIC – *Guideline case R v Brewster* [1998] 1 Cr App Rep 220, 1 Cr App Rep (S) 181 – LCJ Guidelines. However, these guidelines do not deal with the very important element of aggravation.

Defendant aged 14–16

26.4   *R v Simpson* [1998] 1 Cr App Rep (S) 145. The defendant aged 16 made an early plea to aggravated burglary and ABH. The victim aged 83 found the defendant in her home in the early hours of the morning. She asked him what he was doing and didn't believe his answer. He tried to go upstairs and the victim called out to her neighbours. He left. A neighbour tried to take hold of him in the garden and the defendant pulled out two knives. A struggle ensued and the defendant bit the neighbour. The wound bled. The defendant also threatened the neighbour with a knife. The defendant had numerous previous convictions mainly for theft etc. He also had 18 burglary convictions many of them of dwelling houses. He had a sad and troubled background. Held. Even taking into account his age, the plea and the circumstances the 3½ year sentence was not manifestly excessive

A-G's Reference (No 24 of 1997) [1998] 1 Cr App Rep (S) 319. The defendant pleaded guilty to aggravated burglary. In the early hours of the morning he entered the home of a 78-year-old woman who lived alone. She woke up and checked downstairs and returned to bed. She then saw him standing next to her bed with a knife in his hand. His face was covered and he was carrying some tape. She screamed and he fled empty handed. She tried to call the police but the telephone was unplugged. She had seen him twice before when he asked to use her lavatory so he knew her age. He told his foster mother about it and he went with her to the police. He had many previous convictions including numerous for burglary. He had committed burglary the day before the offence. The right sentence would have been 4 years. Taking into account it was a reference **3½ years** detention not 2.

R v Vardy [1999] 1 Cr App Rep (S) 220. The defendant pleaded guilty to aggravated burglary. He asked for two burglaries and two attempted burglaries to be taken into consideration. Shortly after midnight when aged 16 he broke into the home of a 74 year old by smashing a window with a table leg he had brought with him. The householder came down the stairs and the defendant pushed pasted him and ran out of the house. After the householder had gone upstairs the defendant re-entered the house. The householder again came down the stairs and the defendant rushed at him and struck him over the head with the table leg and the householder fell to the ground. The defendant then struck him on the head at least six times and ran off. The victim had swelling over his head and some cuts. However, he suffered from severe trauma and the attack had severely effected him. The defendant was arrested and denied the offence. However, the police then found his name under some tape on the table leg he had left behind. Of the offences taken into consideration three of them involved dwelling houses. In one he stole £150 worth of Christmas presents and caused £1,700 worth of damage. When he was 14 he was given a conditional discharge for attempted theft. When 15 he was sentenced to 24 hours at an attendance centre for ABH. He had knocked a school friend to the ground and repeatedly kicked him. At the same time he was sentenced for two shopliftings. Later he received 3 months' detention for two ABH offences. He had repeatedly kicked and punched the victim. There was a Newton hearing and the judge found he had lied. The judge said he was a danger to the community. Held. There was gratuitous and severe violence. It was very serious. Had he been older 12 years could not be criticised. However as he is now only 17, **10 years** instead.

R v Bruce [2000] 2 Cr App Rep (S) 376. The defendant pleaded guilty to two burglaries and one aggravated burglary. When 16 he entered the flat of a woman in a housing complex for the elderly. He did not disturb her but took her purse. From then on she was afraid to stay in her flat alone and within a few weeks she died. On the same night in the same complex he entered another flat and stole a purse without waking the occupant. Less than 4 months later a resident aged 72 in the same complex found the defendant in her bedroom. He pulled her out of bed and as she lay on the floor he repeatedly stabbed her with a knife. He left taking no property. She was taken to hospital and found to have four wounds. They were each about 2½" long and 2 cm wide. All had been directed at a life threatening area of the body. The victim was in a lot of pain. He was under the effects of drink and sleeping pills, which would have had a disinhibiting effect. He had a number of previous convictions including five for burglary one of which was residential. **10 years** and 2 years concurrent was entirely right.

Drug abstinence order

26.5 Powers of Criminal Courts (Sentencing) Act 2000, s 58A(1). . .Where a person is 18 or over the court may make an order requiring the offender to abstain from misusing specified Class A drugs and provide, when instructed to do so a sample to ascertain whether he has any specified Class A drugs in his body. (3) The court must be of the opinion the offender is dependant on or has a propensity to misuse specified Class A drugs and the offence is a trigger offence or the misuse of any specified Class A drug caused or contributed to the offence in question. (7) An order shall be for not less than 6 months and not more than 3 years. (9) No order shall be made unless the court has been notified that arrangements for implementing the order are available. (Criminal Justice and Court Services Act 2000, Sch 6 specifies aggravated burglary as a trigger offence.)

More than one attack

26.6 *R v Daniel* [2000] 2 Cr App Rep (S) 184. The defendant was convicted of aggravated burglary and attempted aggravated burglary. Both the intents were to inflict GBH. The defendant lived in one of six flats in a house. On his way home early in the morning, the defendant was attacked by an unknown man in the street. The defendant arrived home and kicked the door to the flats open. He was bleeding and brandishing a rather blunt kitchen knife. He pushed past the occupant of the ground floor flat shouting, 'Where are they?' The occupier told him to call the police and he said, 'Well, you're dead then.' He left and started knocking loudly on another door. He threatened to kill the occupants. Things went quiet. Then he started hitting the door with a hammer saying he would kill them. The door was extensively damaged. The occupants of both flats were terrified. The police arrived. He was arrested in his flat and the hammer and knife were found. He was 27 with numerous previous convictions mostly for dishonesty and violence. There were numerous convictions for burglary. He had been to prison three times. **2½ years** substituted for 4.

Occupiers suffering injuries

26.7 *A-G's Reference (No 54 of 1996)* [1997] 1 Cr App Rep (S) 245. The defendant was convicted of aggravated burglary, based on an intent to inflict GBH. The victim held a party at his home. The defendant, then 20 and two others sought to gatecrash the party. They were told to leave. The victim was headbutted and punched but they were ejected. The following evening the defendant and about 15 others arrived at the victim's house and started breaking windows. The victim went out and saw people with baseball bats and metal piping. He was chased back and cornered in the kitchen. The defendant and three others attacked him with baseball bats, shouting, 'Don't fuck with us.' He was repeatedly struck about the head and upper body. The attack 'seemed to last for ages'. A great deal of damage was done to the property. The victim had lacerations on the scalp requiring 15 stitches and other injuries. The attack caused a recurrence of a psychiatric problem. The defendant was the organiser. He had previous convictions for which on four separate occasions he was conditionally discharged. Two were for non-residential burglary. He was in work and had good references. Held. There were very good features in this man but the appropriate sentence after a trial was 6 or 7 years. Taking into account that it was a reference **5 years** not 3.

A-G's Reference (No 36 of 1997) [1998] 1 Cr App Rep (S) 365. The defendant pleaded guilty to aggravated burglary. At 11.30pm he entered the home of his neighbour who he knew with a knife in his hand and demanded to know where his money was. The knife was pointed at his throat and drawn across his cheeks drawing blood. It was then pointed at his right eye and the defendant said he was going to gouge out his eyes. The victim was terrified and believed he was about to be killed. He was cut again and a large chunk of hair was torn from his scalp. After about a minute the defendant left threatening him he would kill him if he called the police. The police found the defendant next door. The victim had eight cuts including a deep and painful one between his thumb and finger. His throat was extremely sore having been seized by the defendant. When charged he said, 'This is a load of bollocks, I should have killed him.' The defendant was 31 and addicted to drink and drugs. He had one previous for violence for which only compensation was ordered and two convictions for burglary. He was in breach of orders made for theft and criminal damage. For those he was sentenced to 6 months each consecutive to each other and for the burglary. Held. The case would have merited 6 years. As it was a reference 4 years substituted for 18 months making **5 years** not 2½ years in all.

A-G's Reference (Nos 37 and 38 of 1997) [1998] 2 Cr App Rep (S) 48. The defendants A and D were convicted of two counts of aggravated burglary (the intent being inflicting GBH). The defendants and three others went to a flat of the victim and demanded ecstasy. They threatened violence and were given two pills. About 1 hour later a man from the flat was in the street and a vehicle driven by the D drove up and a man got out carrying a metal bar. D chased the man but he escaped. Later A with a razor-type blade and another with a metal bar forced their way into the flat. The man with the bar attacked an occupant with it on the head arms and legs, asking, 'Where is the stash?' The victim escaped. The victim thought he was going to die. D was outside as lookout. The victim required seven stitches to the scalp. The man attacked a second victim with the iron bar. He was hit on the side of the head, fell to the ground and was hit a number of times about the head and body. He had a 5 cm cut on his scalp and fractures to his shinbone, fibula and finger. D had convictions for threatening words, criminal damage and offences of dishonesty. He had a good work record. A had convictions for threatening words and two offences of GBH for which he got 15 months. After this offence he received 12 months for the supply of ecstasy. Held. **5 years** would have been appropriate for D and **7 years** for A. As it was a reference **4 years** on each concurrent not 2 for D and **6 years** on each concurrent not 4 for A.

A-G's Reference (No 47 of 1997) [1998] 2 Cr App Rep (S) 68. The defendant was convicted of aggravated burglary and ABH. In the early hours of the morning he forced his way into the flat of his former girlfriend armed with a baseball bat. He wrongly believed she had stolen the handbag of his current girlfriend. The victim who was 53 was beaten about the face. He damaged property and took a small quantity of her possessions of very modest value. Two telephones were pulled from the wall. He later apologised and said he would pay for the damage. He was there about 45 minutes. The bat was not used to injury or damage. The victim had bleeding, a swollen nose and bruising. The defendant was 37 and had convictions for assaulting the police, ABH to his partner, criminal damage and threatening behaviour for which he was on bail at the time of the offence. He had a good work record and there was strong evidence he had rehabilitated himself in the 2 years since the offence. Held. Taking into account it was a reference, **2½ years** not 9 months for the burglary and 12 months concurrent not 9 months concurrent for the ABH.

A-G's Reference (No 1 of 2000) [2000] 2 Cr App Rep (S) 340. The defendant pleaded to aggravated burglary. He entered a room at a home for nurses and awoke a nurse with a kiss. She moved away and he said, 'What is your problem?' She pulled the bedclothes over her head and the defendant tried to pull them off. He started stabbing her with a pair of scissors, which he had found in the room. He ran off. The victim had relatively minor injuries to her arms, neck and chest. He was of good character. Held. 5 years would be expected, but as it was a reference **4 years** not 18 months.

R v Barczi and Williams [2001] EWCA Crim 528, [2001] 2 Cr App Rep (S) 410. The defendants B and W pleaded guilty to aggravated burglary. The victim and his girlfriend broke up acrimoniously. The girlfriend then gave birth. She was the longstanding girlfriend of the brother of W. B lived with W and his family. The defendants travelled from Plymouth to Nottingham and went to the home of the victim wearing balaclavas and surgical gloves. One of them had a piece of wood. They knocked on the door and the victim opened it. Neighbours saw this and called the police. The victim was struck, pushed back in his house and hit repeatedly. He was wrestled to the floor and hit again. His feet and hands were bound with tape. A policeman arrived quickly and arrested the defendants. They didn't resist. The victim suffered from two fractured ribs, bruising, blood in his nose and a cut. Both defendants were of 'exemplary character.' B had served 6 years with the army and his conduct was described as 'exemplary'. W had been in the Royal Navy. Their current work records were good. They said the victim was over pursuing his rights with the children so unsettling the mother. It was feared he would abduct the children or harm the mother. Held. After a trial **7 or 8 years** would not have been out of place. **5 years** was not manifestly excessive.

See also *A-G's Reference (No 101 of 2001)* (14 January 2002, unreported) and *A-G's Reference (Nos 144–6 of 2001)* [2002] EWCA Crim 708, [2002] 2 Cr App Rep (S) 503.

Partner, spouse, ex-partner, ex-spouse, against

26.8 *R v Gordon* [2001] EWCA Crim 2194, [2002] 1 Cr App Rep (S) 523. The defendant pleaded guilty to aggravated burglary at an early stage. The defendant who had had two failed marriages and for nearly 2 months lived with the victim a single mother with her children. He didn't tell the truth about his background and he became aggressive and argumentative. When he moved out in August 2000 they remained in contact but she made it clear that she wanted the relationship to be mere friendship. At 3am in the beginning of October he rang her number and she by dialling 1471 discovered he was the caller. About an hour later he gained entry to her home by throwing a gas bottle through a glazed door. He was in combat clothing and was carrying five knives and a piece of rope. He told her to call the police saying he would be 'going down for what I'm going to do.' She did that. She was in the bedroom with 10-year-old daughter and he said he wanted revenge against two of her friends who he blamed for the break up of the relationship. He looked to see if there were signs of another man having been in her bed and threw a knife between her and her daughter. She pushed the daughter down and it missed the daughter by inches. The 3-year-old son came in and the defendant calmed down. The police arrived and found the victim and her daughter cowering against a wall. The defendant had two knives in one hand and three in the other and there was a stand off between him and the officers. He refused to do as he was told and only put the knives down when he was threatened with CS gas. In interview he said he had not intended to harm anyone and had had a moderate amount of alcohol. He was 36 and had convictions for drink/drive and driving whilst disqualified. His job, which had long hours, gave him a high degree of stress. The psychiatrist said it was totally out of character and he was remorseful. Held. This was a very serious offence causing very real terror. Because of the mitigation **5 years** not 7. [Whether the burglary had an intent to steal or cause GBH is not clear.]

Revenge attack on a burglar

26.9 *A-G's Reference (No 10 of 1996)* [1997] 1 Cr App Rep (S) 76. The defendant pleaded guilty to aggravated burglary. The defendant had spent much time and effort in building up his business. He was the victim of a burglary in which he lost £25,000 and his guard dog was attacked and seriously injured. He went to the home of the victim, the man he believed was responsible. He pretended he wanted to purchase the tools but was able to look at the inside of the house. Inside the house were the victim's wife, her two children and a neighbour. A few minutes later two cars pulled up and three men got out armed with pieces of wood and ran to the house. The defendant ran to the back door smashed the glass with a baseball bat and broke in. He then broke the lounge door with the bat and met the victim who was armed with a poker. The defendant struck him with the bat repeatedly leaving him lying in a pool of blood. The others in the house had fled upstairs. One of them had to free the victim's tongue, which had caught in his throat. The victim had a depressed occipital fracture of the skull. He was an in patient at hospital three times in the next 7½ weeks. The defendant was of good character and co-operated fully with the police. Held. Taking into account it was a reference **4 years** not 15 months.

See also **FALSE IMPRISONMENT/KIDNAPPING** – *Taking the Law into Your Own Hands*

Victim over 65 – Guideline

26.10 *A-G's Reference (Nos 32 and 33 of 1995)* [1996] 2 Cr App Rep (S) 346 – LCJ. Both defendants pleaded guilty to aggravated burglary. One also pleaded guilty to attempted robbery. The general effect of the (reported) cases is that where an elderly victim, living alone, is attacked by intruders and is injured the likely sentence will be in double figures. We wish to stress that attacks on elderly people in their homes are particularly despicable and will be regarded by the court as deserving severe punishment. Elderly victims living alone are vulnerable, not only because of their lack of assistance but also because of their own weakness and isolation. Any attack on such a person is cowardly and can only be expected to be visited with a very severe punishment indeed.

Victim over 65 – Cases

26.11   *R v Eastap, Curt and Thompson* [1997] 2 Cr App Rep (S) 55. The defendant E was convicted of aggravated burglary. The other two pleaded guilty to it. The victim was an 82-year-old lady living on her own. T knew the house was occupied by an elderly person and that the house contained antiques. At night T stood outside. The other two entered the house. The victim woke up, torches were shone in her face and she was struck twice. She was threatened with violence to her and her dog if she didn't reveal where the money was. She said she had no money. The place was ransacked. They returned and bound her to a bedpost. Something was put in her mouth. She had difficulty in breathing so they tied a towel round her mouth instead. They made threats to cover downstairs with petrol and set fire to the house. Her rings were taken off, one of which had her family's coat of arms on it. One man said they would cut her finger off. She was left tied up and discovered next day. E was 26 with previous convictions including burglary, C was 21 with no convictions and T was 39 with numerous convictions including burglary. E had pleaded guilty to a number of other offences and asked for 12 offences to be taken into account. T asked for six offences to be taken into account including five burglaries. E received **15 years**, C **7 years** and T **12 years**. Held. The sentences were justified.

R v Brady [2000] 1 Cr App Rep (S) 410. The defendant was convicted of aggravated burglary. The victim was 70 and lived alone. Late in the evening she saw the defendant running up her stairs holding a chisel pointing towards her. He told her to go back to her bedroom and threatened to kill her. He repeatedly asked where the money was. When told there was none he became more aggressive. Eventually she told him it was under the bed. He took it, and a radio and £50. He pulled the telephone from the wall. The defendant had three convictions for robbery and had a sociopathic personality disorder. **7 years** was not manifestly excessive.

A-G's Reference (No 19 of 2000) [2001] 1 Cr App Rep (S) 35. The defendant pleaded guilty to aggravated burglary, two counts of false imprisonment and obtaining by deception. He gained entry to the premises of a married couple by pretending to be a police officer. He said he was enquiring about a car and when the husband, aged 82 was in the garage he punched him in the face, gagged him and put material in his mouth and tape over his it. The punch broke a tooth and his top denture. He fell unconscious and his hands were bound. When unconscious the husband had been dragged along the garage floor. He was left in the garage. The defendant went into the house and attacked the victim's wife aged 76 by striking her in the face and knocking her down. Pressure was applied to her neck. He taped her mouth for a short time. He bound her hands with tape. She suffered from arthritis and this caused her considerable pain. He said he wanted money but she said she hadn't any. He stole camera equipment and a car. The couple remained bound for 7 hours. They were taken to hospital and suffered psychological problems. The defendant was 22 and had no convictions till about 21. They were for offences of dishonesty including theft from a dwelling. Held. We would have expected following a trial a sentence of **at least 10 years**. On a plea we would have expected 8 years (because of the strong evidence). As it was a reference **7 years** not 5.

A-G's Reference (No 35 of 2001) [2001] EWCA Crim 1271, [2002] 1 Cr App Rep (S) 187. The defendant pleaded to aggravated burglary. The victim aged 72 was in bed at 6am and woke up to find the defendant shining a torch in his face and pointing a carving knife at him. The victim was very frightened. The victim was told to sit on the bed and that it was a 'hold up.' The defendant demanded money and the victim said he had no money. The defendant began to search the bedroom and the victim offered £10 from his wallet downstairs. The victim was taken downstairs at knife point and the £10 was handed over. The defendant then ransacked the place. The victim asked him why he didn't get a job and the defendant told him to shut up or he'd use the knife. After 20 minutes the defendant left in the victim's VW Polo car. Property worth £2,000 was stolen including his pension book alcohol, share certificates and personal documents. The victim was so distressed he could no longer live in his own home. The defendant was 21 or 22 at the time with a conviction for burglary and addicted to heroin. He was in breach of a probation order. When arrested he denied it. Held. It was a terrifying offence. The proper sentence with substantial credit for a plea was **6 years**. As it was a reference **4½ years** not 3½.

R v Harrison [2002] 1 Cr App Rep (S) 470. The defendant pleaded guilty at the first opportunity to aggravated burglary. He asked for 2 shoplifting offences to be taken into consideration. The 61-year-old victim lived with and cared for his 91-year-old bedridden mother. The defendant rang the victim's doorbell at 9.45pm. When the door was opened the defendant said something about being a Catholic and held a crucifix in his hand. He barged in and threatened the victim with a knife and demanded money. The defendant forced him into a corner of the hallway and the victim agreed to give him money if his mother came to no harm, but the victim pushed him back causing a window to smash. The defendant continued to demand money and was given £140 in cash. Suddenly the defendant's behaviour changed and he began to apologise. A neighbour came to help and the defendant was detained. The mother was unaware of the intruder till he was detained. When interviewed the defendant said the knife was for opening sash windows and he thought the address was empty. He showed remorse. Held. This was a grave case with a knife, a vulnerable victim, late in the evening but because of the early plea **5 years** not 7.

See also **ROBBERY**

27   BURGLARY – RACIALLY AGGRAVATED

27.1   Theft Act 1968, s 9 and the Powers of the Criminal Courts (Sentencing) Act 2000, s 153

Triable either way unless (a) the defendant could be sentenced to a minimum of 3 years[1] or (b) where the burglary comprises the commission of, or an intention to commit, an offence which is triable only on indictment or (GBH, rape etc)[2] or (c) where the burglary is a dwelling and a person was subjected to violence or the threat of violence[3]. In those cases the offence is triable only on indictment.

On indictment maximum 14 years when the building is a dwelling, 10 years otherwise. Summary maximum 6 months and/or £5,000.

Specified offence for a 3 year minimum sentence when the offence is a third domestic burglary.

1   Powers of Criminal Courts (Sentencing) Act 2000, s 111(2).
2   Magistrates' Courts Act 1980, s 17(1) and Sch 1, para 28b.
3   Magistrates' Courts Act 1980, s17(1) and Sch 1, para 28c.

Cases

27.2 *R v Morrison* [2001] 1 Cr App Rep (S) 12. The defendant was convicted of burglary, which was racially aggravated and racially-aggravated criminal damage. He pleaded to affray. The defendant with friends was waiting for their food in a kebab shop. Also waiting was Mr Bashir. The defendant was heard to use the word, 'Paki'. He also said, 'I can't believe I've got to wait behind a Paki.' One of his friends apologised but the abuse continued. Mr Bashir said, 'Tell your mate he is a fucking prick.' At this the defendant lunged forward but was restrained. Mr Bashir was followed and there was a scuffle outside. Mr Bashir reached his home and closed the door behind him. The defendant broke a pane of glass in the door and opened the door. The defendant ran up the stairs brandishing a knife. Mr Bashir believed the defendant intended to kill him and ran into a bedroom and closed the door. As Mr Bashir leant on the door the defendant thrust the knife into the door several times, shouting, 'Fucking Paki, I'm going to get you' etc. This was the basis for the criminal damage count. The defendant then left before the police arrived. Mr Bashir and his friends moved from the area because of their fear. The defendant was 22 with no previous convictions. The judge said the defendant had caused terror to the victim and others in the flat and that normally a 4½ years sentence would be imposed the burglary and added 2 years for the racial element. Held. *R v Saunders* [2000] 1 Cr App Rep (S) 71 does not mean that the maximum that can be added is 2 years. The extra 2 years was not excessive. **6½ years** for this serious and horrifying case was justified.

Burial, Preventing

See **Obstructing the Coroner/Burial, Preventing**

28 Cannabis

Government plans

28.1 On 10 July 2002, the Home Secretary announced that: (a) he intended to downgrade cannabis from a Class B drug to a Class C drug; (b) the Lambeth experiment (where the police focus their energies on hard drugs) would be extended across London in a modified form; (c) the practice of police giving people a warning to those caught with cannabis and seizing it could apply across the county by the autumn; (d) he intended to keep the possession of cannabis an arrestable offence where public order was threatened or where children were at risk; (e) the penalty for dealing will be increased to 14 years, (the current penalty for Class B drugs including cannabis). (The Times 11 July 2002.)

How to assess the different types

28.2 *R v Ronchetti* [1998] 2 Cr App Rep (S) 100. Lord Lane's distinction in *R v Aramah* between cannabis, cannabis resin and cannabis oil should be read as cannabis and cannabis resin being equivalent and cannabis oil being ten times that, as 10 kgs of cannabis or cannabis resin are required to produce 1 kg of cannabis oil.

Cannabis, cultivation of/production of

28.3 Cultivation Misuse of Drugs Act 1971, s 6

Production Misuse of Drugs Act 1971, s 4(2)(a) and (b)

Triable either way. On indictment maximum 14 years. Summary maximum 6 months and/or £5,000.

Magistrates' Court Sentencing Guidelines September 2000 – Cultivation

28.4   Entry point. Is a discharge or a fine appropriate? Consider the impact on the victim. Examples of aggravating factors for the offence are commercial cultivation and large quantity. Examples of mitigating factors for the offence are for personal use, not commercial, not responsible for planting and small scale cultivation. Examples of mitigation are age, health (physical or mental), co-operation with the police, and genuine remorse. **Starting point fine B.** (£100 when defendant has £100 net weekly income. See page 334 for table showing fines for different incomes.)

For details about the guidelines see **MAGISTRATES' COURT SENTENCING GUIDELINES** at page 331.

Guideline remarks

28.5   *R v Dibden* [2000] 1 Cr App Rep (S) 64. There are four different categories. First, those who grow it for their own use. Secondly, those who grow it for their own use and also for friends who are supplied free of charge. Thirdly, those who supply friends for money, a commercial operation. Fourthly, those who grow no doubt massive quantities and supply all and sundry.

Book – producing a book giving advice on producing cannabis

28.6   *R v Marlow* [1998] 1 Cr App Rep (S) 272. The defendant was convicted of incitement to cultivate cannabis. He pleaded guilty to producing and possessing cannabis. He wrote a book about the cultivating and production of cannabis. It was advertised for sale in Private Eye, Viz and Hemp Nation. Some 500 copies were sold. Police visited his house and found evidence of cannabis production. The defendant was unemployed because of a heart condition, a blood problem and because he suffered from depression. His wife was diabetic and needed his care. He had convictions for possession of drugs, attempted arson, stealing and abstraction of electricity, but they were all before 1977. He was sentenced on the basis the book was not written to earn money and he received 12 months on each count concurrent. Held. The book was an active and widespread encouragement to produce cannabis. A custodial sentence was essential. **12 months** upheld for the book count with 6 months for the other counts substituted.

Own use

28.7   *R v Peters* [1999] 2 Cr App Rep (S) 334. The defendant pleaded guilty to cultivating cannabis and possession of cannabis at the Magistrates' Court. He was committed for sentence. Police searched the bedroom of his flat and found it had been converted for the hydroponic irrigation of cannabis plants. A wooden frame was covered with heavy-duty polythene. The walls were covered with silver reflective material. Water troughs contained 37 mature cannabis plants and 28 cannabis seedlings. 13.7 grams. of cannabis was found in other rooms. If the seedlings were allowed to grow to the height of the others the total yield would be 520 grams with a street value of £1,760. The basis of plea was that it was for his own use to alleviate a medical condition. He suffered from depression, migraine and a skin complaint. He was 34 and had convictions for possession of cannabis and production of cannabis for which he received a probation order. Held. Because of the medical condition **6 months** not 9.

R v Evans [2000] 1 Cr App Rep (S) 107. The defendant pleaded guilty to cultivating cannabis. Police searched his flat and discovered a bedroom had been converted into a hydroponics garden for the growing of cannabis. 21 plants were found in various stages of growth. There were heat lamps and an electric irrigation system. Walls were lined with insulation and plant food and gauges were found. Harvested leaves and flower buds were recovered from other parts of the house. He made full admissions to the police. The plea was based on 70.6 grams of flowering head material had been produced and the cannabis was for his own consumption. It was worth between £930 and £1,150 on the street. He was 47 and had numerous convictions including several for unlawful possession of drugs and one for supply for which he received 15 months. He had made a complaint about drug dealers and had had a petrol bomb through his letter box. His knee was injured and he received further threats. He said this caused depression and anxiety which was helped by cannabis. **9 months** not 12.

Old cases. *R v Marsland* (1994) 15 Cr App Rep (S) 665.

Own use and social supply free of charge

28.8 *R v Bennett* [1998] 1 Cr App Rep (S) 429. The defendant pleaded guilty to producing cannabis, possession of cannabis with intent to supply and possessing cannabis. The second count was entered 5 weeks after the other two. Police searched his house, garden and garden shed and found 87 cannabis plants, two of which had been cut down and some dried and drying cannabis leaf weighing 2.4 kgs. The cannabis' worth was said to be £7,000. There were no sophisticated systems like hydroponic growth or high intensity lighting. There was no evidence of commercial supply. He accepted his involvement in interview and said it was for his own use. The basis of plea was that the potential yield was between 2½–3 kgs which would last him 2 years if he had 1–2 oz a week. Some of the cannabis would be supplied to friends without payment. He was 55 and had one conviction for cannabis and that was 20 years old. He was a decent honest man who had always worked till prevented from doing so by an accident. He did charity work and had references. Held. **6 months** not 12.

R v Rafferty [1998] 2 Cr App Rep (S) 449 – LCJ. The defendant pleaded guilty before venue to producing cannabis and possessing cannabis. Police executed a search warrant at his home and in his loft they found ten cannabis plants most of which were 2″ high and covered in sticky buds. Two were a foot high. The loft was well equipped for the hydroponic cultivation of cannabis, which was described as a moderately sophisticated means of continuous plant production. There was a motorised heating and lighting unit and an oscillating fan etc. The yield was estimated to be two crops a year producing 428 grams of cannabis. The THC level for the tops of the plants was estimated to be 11% (the level of THC for imported cannabis was between 3 and 5%). The street value was between £2,500 and £3,750 with £900 for the remaining foliage. He was going to give the person who gave him the plants some of the cannabis. The rest he used and shared with friends. None was to be sold. He was 26 with three children and no assets. He had convictions for burglary, ABH and driving offences. He then received 4½ years for robbery and carrying a firearm with intent. Since his release in 1995 he had turned his life around and obtained a job as a telephone engineer. He had settled down with a partner and was buying a house on mortgage. He was granted bail after sentence. Held. **4 months** was not excessive.

R v Blackham [1997] 2 Cr App Rep (S) 275. Not clear whether the cannabis was to be sold or not.

Social supply for money

28.9 *R v Dibden* [2000] 1 Cr App Rep (S) 64. The defendant indicated a plea of guilty at the Magistrates' Court to possession of cannabis with intent to supply and producing cannabis. Police searched his premises and found cannabis growing in a bedroom and in a large garage. There were some skunk plants. Considerable effort had been devoted to ensure that the plants had optimum growing conditions. The plants were not ready for harvesting but were 'well on their way.' It was calculated there would be enough for 400 grams making 2,000 cannabis cigarettes. The defendant admitted the offence in interview and said he had fallen into debt. He was 39 with some old irrelevant convictions. Reverences said he was hard-working and honest. Held. This offence comes into the category of commercial supply to friends. **21 months** was not manifestly excessive.

Cannabis intended for commercial supply to the open market

28.10   *R v Green and Withers* [1998] 1 Cr App Rep (S) 437. The defendants pleaded guilty at the first opportunity to cultivating cannabis and possessing cannabis with intent to supply. Police searched an empty flat and found 48 cannabis plants and some cuttings. There were a motorised lamp heater, an irrigation system, and fertiliser. Also found in another place were eight further plants. The defendants both had bad previous convictions which had very little bearing on the present offences. They related to dishonesty not drug dealing. **3 years** not 4.

R v Knight and Dooley [1998] 2 Cr App Rep (S) 23. The defendants K and D pleaded guilty to producing cannabis and possessing cannabis with intent to supply. D also pleaded to two counts of possessing a prohibited weapon and possessing cannabis. Police watched D buying gardening equipment for hydroponic propagation. Documents showed £2,400 was spent on PH metres, lights, pumps, hydoponics and growing tanks. Police searched K's home and garage and found the windows and doors sealed with sheeting and tapes. Plants were growing in pumped water. Lamps, fans, seed trays, propagators, plant foods and instruction manuals were found. Eleven large plants from which cuttings had been taken were found. 47 plants were in grow-beds. The likely yield was about 555 grams worth between £10,500 and £15,000. In a bedroom plants were being dried. Police found in D's home two locked metal gun cabinets containing an electric stun gun which did not work because it did not have a battery and a pepper spray. £1,800 was found under a floorboard. He claimed the gun and pepper spray were for his own protection. He said he didn't know they were illegal. He bought them in South Africa where they were common defences. Held. The cannabis operation was clearly at the beginning of a sophisticated operation intended to be a serious financial enterprise. **3 years** for the production and supply counts concurrent upheld. The firearm sentences reduced from 18 months to 9 months. They remained concurrent to each other and consecutive to the cannabis offences.

R v Jubb [2002] 2 Cr App Rep (S) 24. The defendant pleaded guilty to producing cannabis and possessing cannabis with intent to supply. He rented an industrial unit and 3 months later the police searched it. There were five rooms in it. One was a nursery for plants and the other four contained cannabis plants with climate control, air conditioning etc. There was a large drying area and freezer facilities. There were 705 cannabis plants and 3.78 kgs of prepared flowering tops worth about £37,850. It was estimated there would be four or five harvests a year making £151,000 income for four and £190,000 for five harvests. When interviewed he admitted he was the sole lessee, constructed the entire hydroponic system and cultivated the plants. The written basis of plea said his involvement was to be for a year, he was not the principle and he received no direct share of the sale income. Others financed the project. He was 37 and had been self employed but was not making any 'meaningful money.' Held. He was a very important player in charge of the premises and crop production. The operation was on a very large scale and of the most sophisticated kind. His role was central. Deterrent sentences are needed. **5 years** was not in any way manifestly excessive.

Old case. *R v Booth* [1997] 1 Cr App Rep (S) 67.

Cannabis, being concerned in the management of premises

28.11   Being concerned in the management of premises and knowingly permitting the production of cannabis: Misuse of Drugs Act 1971, s 8(a).

Triable either way. On indictment maximum 14 years. Summary maximum 6 months and/or £5,000.

Cannabis intended for commercial supply to the open market

28.12   *R v Chamberlain* [1998] 1 Cr App Rep (S) 49. The defendant pleaded guilty to being concerned in the management of the premises used for the production of cannabis and possession of an offensive weapon. A count of being concerned in the production of cannabis was left on the file. The defendant was the freeholder of some industrial premises. He received a very good offer for the part he used and the part he let out. He gave his tenant notice. A year later the police watched him drive to the premises. He was arrested inside with the keys to the external and internal doors. They found 542 cannabis plants in various stages of growth. It was a highly sophisticated cannabis growing operation. There was a forced atmosphere of water and artificial light. On the basis of four crops a year the income would be between £200,000 and £240,000. There was some cannabis leaf and a CS gas canister in his car. The principles were not arrested. He was 36 and had a conviction for conspiracy to defraud for which he received 2 years. The conviction has made him bankrupt. The basis of plea was that he did not play any direct part in the production or supply, he obtained £1,200 and then £900 in rent, he did not receive any other benefit from the offence and he was not privy to the details of the operation. Held. We think there is an analogy with importing. He played a very important and crucial role. This activity is increasing and deterrent sentences are required to stop it. 6 years was not too high as a starting point before plea. **4½ years** upheld.

See also **Drug Users; Importation of Drugs; Possession of Drugs; Production of Drugs** and **Supply of Drugs (Class A, B and C)**

Car Ringing

See **Theft** – *Vehicles – Car ringing cases*

29   Careless Driving/Driving without Due Care and Attention

29.1   Road Traffic Act 1988, s 3

Summary only. Maximum fine Level 4 (£2,500).
3–9 points. Obligatory endorsement and discretionary disqualification

Magistrates' Court Sentencing Guidelines September 2000

29.2   Entry point. Is a discharge or a fine appropriate? Examples of aggravating factors for the offence are death, serious injury, damage done, excessive speed, high degree of carelessness, serious risk and using a hand-held mobile telephone. Examples of mitigating factors for the offence are sudden change in weather conditions, minor risk, momentary lapse and negligible/parking damage. Examples of mitigation are co-operation with the police, voluntary compensation and genuine remorse. Consider disqualification until test is passed (eg defendant's age, infirmity or medical condition).

Starting point fine B. (£100 when defendant has £100 net weekly income. See page 334 for table showing fines for different incomes.)

For details about the guidelines see **MAGISTRATES' COURT SENTENCING GUIDELINES** at page 331.

Guideline remarks

29.3 *R v Krawec* [1984] 6 Cr App Rep (S) 367 – LCJ. The primary considerations are the quality of the driving, the extent the defendant fell below the standard of the reasonably competent driver; in other words the degree of carelessness and culpability. The unforeseen consequences may sometimes be relevant to those considerations. Here the fact the defendant failed to see the pedestrian until it was too late and therefore collided with him was plainly a relevant factor.

Death results –General principles

29.4 *R v Krawec* [1984] 6 Cr App Rep (S) 367 – LCJ. The defendant was convicted of careless driving and acquitted of causing death by reckless driving. We do not think the fact the unfortunate man died was relevant to the charge of careless driving.

R v Morling [1998] 1 Cr App Rep (S) 420. The defendant was acquitted of causing death by dangerous driving and convicted of driving without due care and attention. Held. The principles in *R v Krawec* [1984] 6 Cr App Rep (S) 367 have been applied since then. The court must take care not to let the fact that a death occurred become an aggravating feature. But when examining the degree of culpability, the court is allowed to have regard to the consequences of such carelessness. Thus in this case, even if no death had occurred, it would be perfectly open to the court to say it was a serious act not to have lights because of the consequences which might follow.

R v Simmonds [1999] 2 Cr App Rep (S) 18. The defendant was indicted with causing death by dangerous driving. His plea to careless driving was accepted and no evidence was offered for the causing death count. Held. Considering the statutory changes that have taken place since *R v Krawec* [1984] 6 Cr App Rep (S) 367 we find the concept of a road traffic offence in which the sentencing court is obliged to disregard the fact that a death has been caused as wholly anomalous. The current approach is reflected in *A-G's Reference No 66 of 1996* [1998] 1 Cr App Rep (S) 16 (a case of causing death by careless driving having consumed alcohol) 'It is nonetheless the duty of the judge, to judge cases dispassionately and to do its best to reach the appropriate penalty, taking account of all the relevant circumstances.' Whether sentencing courts should take into account criminality alone or both the criminality and the consequences of an offence – and in the latter event in what proportions, is ultimately a question of choice and policy. *Krawec* was clearly valid in its context and at its time, but we do not see it as of assistance to sentencing courts in the different context of today. The judge was entitled to bear in mind the death.

R v King [2001] EWCA Crim 709, [2001] 2 Cr App Rep (S) 503. The decision in *R v Simmonds* [1999] 2 Cr App Rep (S) 218 has marked something of a reconsideration of the approach in this difficult area. The sentencer must still make it his primary task to assess culpability, but should not close his eyes to the fact that death has resulted, especially multiple death where as here, that was all too readily foreseeable.

Death results – Cases

29.5 *R v Simmonds* [1999] 2 Cr App Rep (S) 218. The defendant was indicted with causing death by dangerous driving. His plea to careless driving was accepted and no evidence was offered for the causing death count. Driving on a road that was unfamiliar to him the defendant missed his turning. Road conditions were good, but it was dark. He pulled into a wide entrance on his left and without pausing embarked on a sweeping right-hand turn to drive back. The victim, a motorcyclist travelling at 40 mph and in the same direction as the defendant had been travelling swerved and hit the defendant's Range Rover. The victim was catapulted through the air and died. The car behind was unable to stop and also hit the Range Rover. The defendant used his mobile phone to call for an ambulance and the police. At the scene he told police, 'I looked, it was all clear then suddenly this bike came from nowhere.' When interviewed he said, 'I cannot give an explanation as to why I didn't actually see him and I can only assume that he was invisible against the general illumination of other vehicles.' He was in his 60s of good character with an excellent driving record. The judge said it was a tragic error as a result of failing to keep a proper look out. Held. Neither the **£1,000 fine** nor the 12 months disqualification were excessive.

R v King [2001] EWCA Crim 709, [2001] 2 Cr App Rep (S) 503. The defendant was acquitted of three counts of causing death by dangerous driving and convicted of three charges of driving without due care and attention. [It would appear that two of them were entered in error, as they were all the same offence.] He had accepted the due care matters from the outset. There was a contraflow system in one lane of a dual carriageway with temporary traffic lights in place. The road was straight and visibility was good and warning signs were in place. The defendant drove his HGV vehicle into the back of a queue of traffic and killed three priests in the last car. The sole occupant in the next care was very badly injured. The vehicle before was a lorry. The impact speed was 43 mph in a 40 mph limit. 1¼ miles into the contraflow system and 350 metres before impact he was travelling at 50 mph. His defence was he looked down at his tachograph shortly before to calculate when he had to stop driving. He had a good driving record and his only trade was as a HGV driver. The judge described it as 'a quite appalling piece of careless driving.' Held. **£1,500 fine** not £2,250. 2 years not 3 disqualification.

See also **DEATH BY CARELESS DRIVING, CAUSING**

Disqualification, for how long?

29.6   *R v Morling* [1998] 1 Cr App Rep (S) 421. The defendant was acquitted of causing death by dangerous driving and convicted of driving without due care and attention. He drove his tractor on a dual carriageway at 14½ mph without amber flashing lights, rear lights or reflectors as required. The tractor had lights but they could have misled drivers about the position of the trailer. A car hit the trailer and the trailer was lifted into the air and it fell into the offside lane. Another car hit the trailer and the driver sustained head and arm injuries. His wife was killed and one of his children received serious head injuries and the other two received facial and stomach injuries. The defendant was of exemplary character with no convictions. He appealed the disqualification order only. Held. The fact the defendant is an HGV driver is two-edged. The disqualification will hit him hard, but being an HGV driver heightens the culpability of taking the risks he did. It was well within the judge's discretion to impose **12 months' disqualification**.

R v Johnson [1998] 2 Cr App Rep (S) 453. The defendant was acquitted of two counts of causing death by dangerous driving and convicted of two counts of careless driving. He tried to negotiate a bend when driving at 40–45 mph. He went on the wrong side of the road and hit a taxi head on and killed the driver and one of the passengers. The road was wet. The defendant was injured. One of his tyres was under inflated. He said the headlights of the taxi dazzled him. The judge said it was a momentary lack of concentration. The defendant was 23 and a student working hard and doing well. He had a lot of travelling to courses to do and was having difficulty with the trains and buses. He was sentenced to a **£500 fine** and appealed a 12 month disqualification order. Held. Applying *R v Krawec* (1984) 6 Cr App Rep (S) 367 the disqualification was too long so **5 months** not 12.

R v Simmonds [1999] 2 Cr App Rep (S) 218. See *Death results – Cases*

R v King [2001] EWCA Crim 709, [2001] 2 Cr App Rep (S) 503. See *Death results – Cases*

HGV drivers

29.7 *R v Morling* [1998] 1 Cr App Rep (S) 421. The fact the defendant is an HGV driver is two-edged. The disqualification will hit the defendant hard, but being an HGV driver heightens the culpability of taking the risks he did.

CHANGE IN TARIFF YEARS AFTER SENTENCE

See TARIFF, CHANGE IN TARIFF YEARS LATER

CHEATING THE PUBLIC REVENUE

See TAX FRAUD

CHILDREN

See CRUELTY TO CHILDREN and YOUNG OFFENDERS

30   CO-DEFENDANT'S PERSONAL MITIGATION

30.1 *A-G's Reference (No 73 of 1999)* [2000] 2 Cr App Rep (S) 209 – LCJ. The defendant's sentence was reduced because of the reduction made for the co-defendant because of his personal mitigation. The judge said it was to prevent him having a burning sense of injustice. Held. It is not a reason to reduce the sentence. **18 months** substituted for CSO.

31   COMMON ASSAULT

31.1   Criminal Justice Act 1988, s 39

Summary only. Maximum 6 months and/or £5,000.

However, through the Criminal Justice Act 1988, s 40 the offence is triable on indictment. According to the Divisional Court[1] it is then contrary to s 39 although certain academics and another set of judges at the Divisional Court[2] consider the offence is then contrary to common law. Maximum sentence 6 months (although this could be open to argument).

1   *DPP v Little* [1992] 95 Cr App Rep (S) 28.
2   *Haystead v DPP* [2000] Times 2 June 164 JP 396.

Magistrates' Court Sentencing Guidelines September 2000

31.2   Entry point. Is it serious enough for a community penalty? Consider the impact on the victim. Examples of aggravating factors for the offence are group action, injury, offender in position of authority, on hospital/medical premises, premeditated, victim particularly vulnerable, victim serving the public and weapon. Examples of mitigating factors for the offence are impulsive, minor injury, provocation and single blow. Examples of mitigation are age, health (physical or mental), co-operation with police, voluntary compensation and genuine remorse. Give reasons for not awarding compensation.

For details about the guidelines see **MAGISTRATES' COURT SENTENCING GUIDELINES** at page 331.

32   COMMON ASSAULT – RACIALLY AGGRAVATED

32.1   Crime and Disorder Act 1998, s 29

Triable either way. On indictment maximum 2 years. Summary maximum 6 months and/or £5,000.

Magistrates' Court Sentencing Guidelines September 2000

32.2   Entry point. Is it so serious that only custody is appropriate? Consider the level of racial aggravation and the impact on the victim. Examples of aggravating factors for the offence, group action, injury, offender in position of authority, on hospital/medical premises, premeditated, victim particularly vulnerable, victim serving the public and a weapon involved. Examples of mitigating factors for the offence, impulsive, minor injury, provocation and single blow. Examples of mitigation, age, health (physical or mental), co-operation with the police, voluntary compensation and genuine remorse. Consider compensation. Give reasons if not awarding compensation.

For details about the guidelines see **MAGISTRATES' COURT SENTENCING GUIDELINES** at page 331.

Cases

32.3   *R v Webb* [2001] 1 Cr App Rep (S) 112. The defendant was convicted of racially-aggravated common assault and racially-aggravated criminal damage. The defendant and another woman hired a minicab, which was driven by Mr Miah, the victim. There was a dispute over the fare and the two women passengers, who were drunk, screamed racial insults including, 'Paki bastard,' and 'Black Bastard.' The defendant who was sitting behind the victim grabbed his hair and pulled his head backwards. They were told to leave and the victim picked up his mobile phone to call the police. The other passenger threw it to the floor and the defendant left the car and kicked the car causing damage to the side panels, the doors, and the front and rear of the car. She also tore off the wing mirror and continued making racial insults. The other woman left the car. The defendant seized the victim by the shirt and punched and slapped him about the face. The other woman joined in the attack. The defendant was arrested and continued to be racially abusive to the victim and to Asians at the police station. The victim suffered multiple bruising, grazing and tenderness. There was £1,600 worth of damage to the car and it was a write-off. The defendant had no relevant previous convictions and had references. Held. 9 months for the assault and 6 months for the damage were not excessive. Nor was the total excessive when they were made consecutive. However, as she was the sole carer for her just widowed grandfather the **sentences were suspended**.

R v Bell [2001] 1 Cr App Rep (S) 376. The defendant was convicted of racially-aggravated common assault. The defendant after drinking blocked the path of a 65 year old and said, 'You black bastards. Why do you fuckers come to this country? You should be in a concentration camp and shot.' The victim ignored him. The defendant then hit him on the back of the head and he fell to the ground where the defendant hit and kicked him, saying, 'You black fuckers should be in a fucking camp and shot.' The victim had a cut and graze to his face and head and a cut to his knee. He was in pain and felt dizzy. The defendant had two previous convictions. One was for criminal damage in 1987 and the other one was in 1998 for assaulting a constable. Held. If 6 months was suitable for the common assault the 12 months extra was too great, so **12 months** not 18.

R v Foster [2001] 1 Cr App Rep (S) 383. The defendant was convicted of racially aggravated common assault. The defendant in a library approached a mother and child because the child was crying. The mother alleged the defendant touched the child inappropriately and she pushed or punched the defendant's hand away and shouted to the librarian. She also shouted at him, 'Fuck off' and he shouted back, 'Go away you fucking bitch. Fuck off.' More than once he referred to her as a, 'fucking black bitch.' He hit her either on the jaw or on the shoulder. The defendant was treated as of good character. Held. There was nothing wrong with **2 months** imprisonment.

R v Joyce [2002] 1 Cr App Rep (S) 582. The defendant was convicted of racially aggravated common assault, racially-aggravated harassment under s 4 and common assault. Because of her behaviour security guards spoke to her. She was abusive to a black one and emptied her bag on the floor. When she was told to pick the items up she said, 'Fuck off you black bastard,' and 'Fucking nigger, the BNP is going to get you.' As she was walked by the victim she struck him a backwards punch with a clenched fist. He punched her in the face. She struck out again and had to be restrained. She continued to swear, strike out and utter racist abuse at the victim. Police arrested her and she abused them and struggled, saying as an example, 'All black people are bastards, and they should not be in the country.' They told her they weren't interested in her views. She replied, 'You police are scared of niggers, you should try living in South London.' She kicked out at one of the officers and threatened to kill him and his family. She was given warnings and continued the abuse. She spat at another when being taken to the police van. She was now 39 and had 14 court appearances for theft, shoplifting, ABH, criminal damage, assault on police, threatening words, common assault, being drunk and disorderly and possession of a Class A drug. She hadn't received a custodial sentence. The pre-sentence report said there was a high risk of further offences and violence against the public, which would be reduced if she addressed her substance abuse and engaged in strategies to address issues of anger management. She had a glowing prison report and wanted to give birth to her child outside prison. Held. The assault without the racial element was worth 4 months. The racial element was worth 3 months extra so **7 months** not 15.

For basic principles about racially-aggravated offences see RACIALLY-AGGRAVATED OFFENCES

COMPANIES

The principles to follow are listed in the HEALTH AND SAFETY OFFENCES section.

For fraud see COMPANY FRAUDS AND FINANCIAL SERVICES OFFENCES

See also MANAGING ETC A COMPANY WHEN BANKRUPT

33   COMPANY FRAUDS AND FINANCIAL SERVICES OFFENCES

33.1   Various statutes and penalties including Companies Act 1985 and the Financial Services and Markets Act 2000.

Fraudulent trading Companies Act 1985, s 458

Triable either way. On indictment maximum 7 years. Summary maximum 6 months and/or £5,000.

A court may make a disqualification order against a defendant who is convicted of an indictable offence in connection with the management etc. of a company[1].

1   Company Directors Disqualification Act 1986, s 2.

Crown Court statistics England and Wales[1] – Crown Court – Males 21+ – Fraud by a company director

33.2

Year	Plea	Total Numbers sentenced	Type of sentence%					Average length of custody (months)
			Discharge	Fine	Community sentence	Suspended sentence	Custody	
2000	Guilty	29	0%	7%	24%	10%	59%	24.2
	Not guilty	12	0%	0%	8%	17%	75%	30.4

1   Excluding committals for sentence. Source: Crime and Criminal Justice Unit, Home Office Ref: IOS416-02.

Guideline remarks for fraud

33.3   *R v Feld* [1999] 1 Cr App Rep (S) 1 – LCJ. As well as the guidelines in *R v Barrick* [1985] 7 Cr App Rep (S) 142 the following are relevant considerations:

1   The amount involved and the manner in which the fraud is carried out.
2   The period over which the fraud is carried out and the degree of persistence with which it is carried out.
3   The position of the accused within the company and the measure of control over it.
4   Any abuse of trust which is revealed.
5   The consequences of the fraud.
6   The effect on public confidence in the City and the integrity of commercial life.
7   The loss to the small investors, which will aggravate the fraud.
8   The personal benefit derived by the defendant.
9   The plea.
10   The age and character of the defendant.

It is vitally important if confidence in the City is to be maintained documents sent out in support of rights issues should be honest and complete.

Copyright

See COPYRIGHT/TRADE MARK OFFENCES/TRADE DESCRIPTION OFFENCES

Fraudulent trading – Companies Act 1985, s 458 – Guideline remarks

33.4   *R v Smith and Palk* [1997] 2 Cr App Rep (S) 167. In broad terms, a charge of fraudulent trading resulting in a deficiency of a given amount was less serious than a specific charge of theft or fraud to an equivalent amount.

Fraudulent trading – Trading with intent to defraud creditors/Long firm fraud

33.5   *R v Thobani* [1998] 1 Cr App Rep (S) 227. The defendant made an early plea to trading in an attempt to defraud creditors. From 1981 the defendant ran what was effectively a one man company with a number of employees carrying out menial tasks dealing in frozen foods. Between July 1992 and March 1993, when the company ceased trading he ran up credit debts with suppliers and when he couldn't pay he bought from other suppliers. Till then the company had traded perfectly honestly. He sold nearly all the goods he obtained on credit to two other companies in both of which he was a director. By March he owed £165,000 with £86,000 owed to Lloyds Bank. Lloyds recovered their money from the sale of the defendant's home and from his parents on their personal guarantees. The total loss to creditors was £79,000. The defendant made full and frank statements to the Official Receiver. The Department of Trade and Industry wrote to him in October 1995 and the summons was issued in May 1996. He was of good character and unlikely to offend again. Held. 9 months was well within the range for this offence. The dishonesty affects the livelihood of other traders. Prison is to deter other businessmen. **3 years** was a proper period of disqualification. There was no evidence he could pay the £5,000 prosecution costs so they were quashed.

R v Elcock and Manton [1998] 2 Cr App Rep (S) 126. The defendants, E and M pleaded guilty to fraudulent trading. Between October 1995 and April 1996 the defendants operated a long firm fraud with companies pretending to deal in import/export, office supplies and other trades. They obtained rented accommodation and defrauded their suppliers. False references were provided and the supplies were sold at under cost price. There was no attempt to keep records. In December 1995 they were arrested and questioned about their activities but continued to operate the fraud. £56,000 was obtained. E was 35 with five court appearances for dishonesty. M was 54 and of good character. In 1993 he was made bankrupt and was thereby disqualified from managing companies. Held. Their position in running the businesses was the same. The continued trading after their arrest was an aggravating factor. **21 months** was correct.

A-G's Reference (Nos 80–1 of 1999) (13 December 1999, unreported). The Crown accepted the motive was to keep company trading rather than benefit personally. The defendants should have received 12 months.

R v Ward [2001] 2 Cr App Rep (S) 146. The defendant was convicted of two counts of fraudulent trading. He was in sole control of two companies. He failed to pay creditors properly or at all, continued trading and buying goods on credit knowing the companies were insolvent and misappropriated company assets. One company was a sham, which bought furniture on credit and sold it to the other company. The first company had shops and he borrowed £½m from a bank using his house as security, which was owned by his estranged wife. He was paying a separation agreement with his wife, which would eventually, result in the house being transferred to him. His spending on the house contributed to the collapse of the first company. He set up a third company and sold the assets to that company at about ½ their value. The company debts to creditors for the two companies were £684,000. He was 57 with convictions (not stated). He showed no remorse and lied continually. **3 years** not 4.

R v McHugh [2001] EWCA Crim 1857, [2002] 1 Cr App Rep (S) 330. The defendant pleaded guilty to three counts of fraudulent trading, two counts of acting as an insolvency practitioner without qualification and breach of bail. He and his then future wife were directors of an accountancy company. The company was wound up owing £374,000. The company described itself as chartered accountants which was untrue. The company also claimed that the debts it recovered would be paid into an 'insured and indemnity professional client account.' This was also untrue. There were a very large number of wrongful and fraudulent activities committed by the defendant. He told one prospective client that his wife was a Detective Sergeant and had access to a variety of information. This was also untrue as she was a traffic warden. The man asked him to collect a debt of £62,000 and advised him to settle for £34,000 with VAT. There was a long wait for the cheque and when it eventually came the cheque was signed by the defendant and his wife and it bounced. When the Trading Standards Deptartment and the DTI intervened he started running the same business under a different name. He held himself out to be a liquidator twice and gave people a false certificate saying he was. He was arrested and bailed to attend the Crown Court. He failed to attend and was found in the Orkneys. The basis of plea was that the company was not fraudulent at its inception. He was 44 and in 1977 he was convicted of making a false statement to obtain social security. In 1979 he was charged (presumably had convictions for) with false accounting, obtaining by deception and theft. **3 years** was well deserved. The 6 months for breach of bail remained consecutive.

Old cases. *R v Cook* (1995) 16 Cr App Rep (S) 917.

Investors, cheating etc

33.6 *R v Gibson* [1999] 2 Cr App Rep (S) 52. The defendant pleaded guilty to three counts of fraudulent trading. His pleas of not guilty to conspiracy to steal, falsifying documents 13 counts of procuring valuable securities by deception and six counts of theft were accepted. The defendant was an independent financial adviser dealing with investments and pensions. One of the defendant's companies became insolvent and he accepted in a 19 month period over £1m in investments from mainly the elderly or redundant employees. He undertook to invest the money in safe funds but in fact only placed a minute proportion in them and paid out the investors with the new money coming in. Some of the money he spent on himself and his friends. FIMBRA investigators discovered the irregularities and a restraining order was made. There was a £780,000 loss. Nearly all the investors were compensated through the Investors Scheme but they had suffered a great deal of distress. He was 62 and had no convictions. There was a delay of 6½ years between the offence and the sentence. Held. The public must be protected and others tempted warned that a custodial sentence is inevitable. We accept the denials to theft. There was a real impression that the judge in relying on *R v Clark* [1998] 2 Cr App Rep (S) 995 was treating the case as theft or fraud. That was in error. Because of the judge's lack of credit for the mitigation **3½ years** not 5. The 10 years disqualification was fully justified.

R v Chauhan and Holroyd [2000] 2 Cr App Rep (S) 230. The defendants C and H pleaded to two counts of engaging in a course of conduct which created a false impression as to the market in investments etc contrary to the Financial Services Act 1986, s 47(2), [now a slightly different Financial Services and Markets Act 2000, s 397(3)]. C also pleaded to making a false entry affecting the property or affairs of the company contrary to the Companies Act 1985, s 450(1). H pleaded just over 6 months after C. H was the principle shareholder and Managing Director of a food manufacturing company, which was floated on the Stock Market in 1992. C was a chartered accountant and finance director appointed in 1990 primarily to assist in the floatation. The two created false company accounts and a false value to the shares in the company by backdating sales contracts, substituting forged documents, inflating the stock values, removing parts of machines to disguise their age and make them appear more valuable and intercepting circulars. In 1990 the auditors were misled about £170,000 worth of debts. In 1992 the auditors were misled about £0.54m of debts. In 1992 for the floatation audit £0.97 m worth of false debt were confirmed. In 1992 a sales director discovered what was going on and reported his findings to the auditors. The defendants and H's father tried to discredit the sales director by false versions and printing duplicate invoices. After the floatation they tried to fool the auditor by claiming false amounts of money owing to the company and intercepting circulars sent out to their debtors. False debts to the company of £1.1m were created by forgeries. In 1993 Barclays Bank increased their overdraft to £2.2m. In 1994 receivers were appointed and the total deficit was £4.32m. The members' deficiency who were institutional investors was £1.78m and H and his father's deficiency was £0.45 m. H was 43 and of good character and clinically depressed. His gain was salaries and dividends which was £0.9m of which £0.38m had been paid back. He was made bankrupt and his marriage broke down as a result of the collapse of his company. He was a model prisoner and truly remorseful. C said he was manipulated by H and tried to restrain Directors from the plan and was worried he would be dismissed. Except for his salary of £35,000 a year he received no benefit. From 1997 he gave detailed assistance to the SFO. The judge described this assistance as 'massive'. Held. Having regard to *R v Buffrey* (1993) 14 Cr App Rep (S) 511 at 515 there was insufficient discount for the H's plea. **4 years** not 5 for him. C did not resign and gave respectability to the protracted and serious fraud. There were no exceptional circumstances to suspend his sentence. **18 months** was not manifestly excessive.

Raising money by deception

33.7 *R v Feld* [1999] 1 Cr App Rep (S) 1 – LCJ. The defendant was convicted of nine counts of using a false instrument and three counts of making misleading statements contrary to Financial Services Act 1986, s 47, [now a slightly different Financial Services and Markets Act 2000, s 397(3)]. The defendant was Managing Director of a company which owned and managed hotels. The company sought to raise money and a Rights Issue Circular was published which contained serious misinformation. The profit forecast was overstated by £1.6m, the liabilities were understated by £9.5m and the cash balance was stated to be £4.14m when it was only £127,000. The issue was supported by forged documents. The company was under pressure from its banks and was arguably insolvent. The rights issue raised £20.6m and the profits were announced to be £6.1m which was false. Forged documents were sent to the accountants to support that figure. The documents contained fictional income and bogus contracts. The following year the company went into liquidation. The individual shareholders received a voucher from the new owners for £250 and nothing else. The defence said that his family were the greatest losers when the company went into liquidation and the money had been applied to the company. However, it had allowed him to borrow £1.375m from banks, draw his salary for the extra time and continue to maintain his expensive lifestyle. He was of good character with references. Held. The defendant was the dominant figure in the company. His whole lifestyle depended on the continuation of the company. The sentences for the false statements should have been consecutive to the false instruments sentences so **6 years** not 8.

See also *Investors, cheating etc*

Take over bids, seeking to influence

33.8 *A-G's Reference (Nos 14–6 of 1995)* (21 March 1999, unreported). The three defendants were sentenced for (probably) conspiracy to defraud. They tied to create a false market in shares during a City takeover. No false market was created but that was not for want of trying. The exercise was carefully planned with painstaking organisation and with substantial dishonesty. The defendants were sentenced to CSO. Held. Influencing the fate of a take over is a very serious matter. Not only may it lead to a fraud on shareholders, but it causes considerable damage to the reputation of the

City of London, which is very important to the whole country; and damage to the confidence of the public in its institutions. Rigging a market is quite easy to do with expertise without it being realised. For the instigator and leader the right sentence was 3 years. As it was a reference 2 years. For the active and powerful second in command the right sentence was 30 months. As it was a reference 20 months. For someone who was not a main organiser and who pleaded guilty the right sentence would 15 months. As it was a reference and his failing health **12 months suspended**.

See also EMPLOYMENT, OTHERS WILL LOSE THEIR; INSOLVENCY OFFENCES; PENSION OFFENCES and THEFT ETC

34   COMPUTERS

34.1   Computer Misuse Act 1990, ss 1–3

Unauthorised access to computer material, unauthorised access with intent to commit or facilitate the commission of further offences and unauthorised modification of computer material respectively.

Section 1 is summary only. Maximum 6 months or a Level 5 fine (£5,000). Sections 2–3 are triable either way. On indictment maximum 5 years. Summary maximum 6 months and/or Level 5 fine (£5,000).

Interference with company data for revenge

34.2   *R v Lindesay* [2001] EWCA Crim 1720, [2002] 1 Cr App Rep (S) 370. The defendant pleaded guilty at the Magistrates' Court to three charges of causing unauthorised modifications to the contents of a computer contrary to s 3(1) and (7) of the 1990 Act. The defendant was a freelance computer consultant of very considerable experience and repute. He was working on a short-term contract with a computer firm which provided services for a number of clients including maintaining their websites. The company was not satisfied with his work and dismissed him. There was a dispute about the money owed which left him with a sense of grievance. A month later after he had been drinking and acting on impulse he gained unauthorised access to the websites of three companies who were clients of his former employer. They were a supermarket, a communications company and a tour operator. He made use of passports he had been given. He deleted some of the contents to cause inconvenience to his former employer. On two of the sites he moved images around. On the other site, the supermarket one he sent a number of emails informing their customers that prices would go up and they could go elsewhere if they did not like that fact. He changed some of the information on the site about recipes. The computer firm had to do considerable work to restore the sites. The supermarket had to send out E-mails apologising to their customers. Extra security had to be put in place. The site was closed for about 10 weeks. The other companies restored their sites in 3 and 3½ hours. The costs to date were approximately £9,000. There was no damage to the software and no direct revenue loss. When arrested the defendant deeply regretted his actions and wanted to apologise to the three client companies. The defendant was 47 and of good character. He was held in high esteem at Reading University where he was a part time teacher. The police said he was extremely candid. The judge said it was an act of pure unmitigated revenge after a slight. A community penalty was available. Held. The defendant had used the skill and knowledge acquired when working for the company to cause a great deal of work, inconvenience and worry to entirely innocent organisations. It was a breach of trust. **9 months** was not excessive let alone manifestly excessive.

Where the offence is to enable others to watch television without paying, see COPYRIGHT/TRADE MARK OFFENCES/TRADE DESCRIPTION OFFENCES – *Television, Enabling access to cable or satellite television for free*

35 CONSPIRACY

35.1 There are two different types of conspiracy. There are statutory conspiracies under Criminal Law Act 1977, s 1 which form the bulk of conspiracies charged. There are also common law conspiracies of which there are only two namely conspiracy to defraud and conspiracy to corrupt public morals or outrage public decency. For those see FRAUD and PUBLIC DECENCY, OUTRAGING

The Criminal Law Act 1977, s 3 provides for the following maximum penalties for statutory conspiracies:

(a)   life where the offence in question is murder, or is an offence which carries a maximum of life and where the offence has no maximum sentence provided,

(b)   the same maximum term of imprisonment to be available as for the offence in question carries and

(c)   in all other cases a maximum of a fine.

Conspiracy cases are listed under the offence which was agreed to.

Conspiracy not carried out

35.2   *R v Davies* (1990) Times, 3 October, unreported. The defendant was convicted of conspiracy to rob. Held. The fact that conspirators had desisted from the planned crime before carrying it out must be reflected in the sentence. If the conspirators desisted because they were overcome with better feelings then great credit must be given. If they desisted because they lost their nerve, none the less they should be not be sentenced as if they had gone ahead with their design.

Penalty for the offence alters during the conspiracy

35.3   *R v Hobbs* [2002] Crim LR 415. Where the maximum is raised during the conspiracy the maximum is the lesser sentence.

CONTAMINATING FOOD

See BLACKMAIL – *Supermarkets and retail stores* and FOOD ETC, CONTAMINATING OF

CONTEMPT OF COURT

See PERVERTING THE COURSE OF JUSTICE/CONTEMPT OF COURT ETC

36 COPYRIGHT/TRADE MARK OFFENCES/TRADE DESCRIPTION OFFENCES

36.1   Copyright, Designs and Patents Act 1988, s 107

Triable either way. On indictment maximum 2 years. Summary maximum 6 months and/or £5,000.

Trade Marks Act 1994, s 92

Unauthorised use of a trade mark etc.
Triable either way. On indictment maximum 10 years. Summary maximum 6 months and/or £5,000.

Trade Descriptions Act 1968, ss 1, 12, 13 and 14

Unauthorised use of a trade mark etc.
Triable either way. On indictment maximum 2 years. Summary maximum £5,000.

Crown Court statistics England and Wales[1] – Crown Court – Males 21+ – Trades Descriptions Act and similar offences

36.2

Year	Plea	Total Numbers sentenced	Type of sentence%					Average length of custody (months)
			Discharge	Fine	Community sentence	Suspended sentence	Custody	
2000	Guilty	76	11%	21%	30%	3%	34%	8.6
	Not guilty	23	9%	17%	13%	13%	48%	6.6

1 Excluding committals for sentence. Source: Crime and Criminal Justice Unit, Home Office Ref: IOS416-02.

Guideline remarks

36.3 *R v Kemp* (1995) 16 Cr App Rep (S) 941. Offences of counterfeiting normally attract at least a short sentence of imprisonment. They are difficult, time consuming and expensive to detect. The owners of copyright are entitled to be protected.

R v Ansari [2000] 1 Cr App Rep (S) 94. Trade Mark offences undermine reputable companies. The sentencer should consider how professional the enterprise was and the likely or actual profits made.

Car dealers

36.4 *R v Fellows* [2001] 1 Cr App Rep (S) 398. The defendant pleaded guilty to offences under the Trade Descriptions Act 1968, Fair Trading Act 1973, Consumer Transactions (Restrictions on Statements) Order 1976 and the Business Advertisements (Disclosure) Order 1977. There was an offence of supplying goods with a false description and obtaining property arising out of a false odometer reading. The defendant operated a second-hand car business from his home address for just over 18 months. He had dealt with 43 cars. He advertised in local papers giving the impression he was a private seller of a single car. He commonly said it was his daughter's car. The prosecution case was that he was targeting vulnerable people choosing low value cars typically aimed at first time buyers. He sold cars as seen. He accepted he misled buyers but he claimed he was under financial pressure and was ignorant of the law. Held. This was a particularly mean offence causing great anxiety and inconvenience to people whose cars developed faults. **18 months** was severe but not manifestly excessive.

Distributing articles in breach of copyright or with false trade marks or descriptions

36.5 *R v Ansari* [2000] 1 Cr App Rep (S) 94. The defendants M, H, L and S pleaded guilty to various unstated offences under the Trade Marks Act 1994, s 92(1)(c). Police raided H's house on an unconnected matter and found garments with well known fashion house labels on them. They started a surveillance operation. This revealed a large scale and sophisticated business in goods with false fashion labels like Versace and Calvin Klein. £74,000 worth of garments were found at one address. M sewed the false labels into every garment. H was in charge of storage of all the goods. He was a major player and the goods he pleaded guilty to were worth between £800,000 and £900,000. L was also a major player who had prior experience in the fashion trade and dealt with the buyers and sellers and the financing of the operation. S was a packer and machinist. £47,900 worth of goods was found in his premises. M was 46, married with three children and with no convictions. He had a legitimate job as a machinist and had lost a baby. H was 41 and effectively without any convictions. He was a trainee pub manager. L was 34 and was in breach of the suspended sentence. He worked in transport. S was 40, married with three children and had no convictions. He was a fork-lift driver. Held. Reputable companies were clearly undermined by this professional enterprise where the likely profits were high. There were no exceptional reasons to suspend M's sentence. **2 years** for M and S and **3 years** for H and L were correct.

Old cases. *R v Yanko* [1996] 1 Cr App Rep (S) 217.

Estate agents

36.6   *R v Docklands Estates Ltd* [year?] 1 Cr App Rep (S) 270 – LCJ. The defendant company was convicted of 3 offences of giving a false indication that services had been provided contrary to Trade Descriptions Act 1968, s 13. The company was a family firm of estate agents and had been established for about 6 years. They erected 'Sold' signs on properties in Docklands where they had received no instructions and no permission to erect the signs. Their defence was someone else had done it. The company had unencumbered assets of £77,000 and profits in the last 2 years of £16,000 and £33,000. The family salaries had been deducted. The company had no convictions. The court was shown material which showed fines of £100 being imposed at the Magistrates' Court for these offences. They were ordered to pay £5,203 costs. Held. The improper erection of signs is a nuisance of significant dimensions. It creates a false impression giving the public confidence in the company, which is not justified. Other honest companies are put at a disadvantage. The levels of fines we have been told about are not realistic. We hope the message will go out to Magistrates' Courts that the fines they are imposing are too low. **£2,000 for each** not £7,500 on each.

Making copies in breach of copyright or with false trade marks or descriptions

36.7   *R v Lloyd* [1997] 2 Cr App Rep (S) 151. The defendant was convicted of making an infringing article. Sixty one compact discs bearing counterfeit computer programs were seized from his home. Also found was a computer program, which facilitated the manufacture of compact discs, and a writer, which enabled programs to be recorded. Five hundred blank discs were found at the home of another man. The defendant had no previous convictions. Held. As the maximum was 2 years 12 months was wrong. **6 months** substituted.

R v Dukett [1998] 2 Cr App Rep (S) 59. The defendant pleaded guilty to four copyright offences. Three charged him with distributing the pirated compact discs and one with making them. He was the ringleader of seven defendants. In 1995 police confiscated all his equipment. However he continued to supply a small number of compact discs to others. Each disc contained material, which if purchased legitimately would probably cost several thousand pounds. The total value was very considerably in excess of £40,000. The defendant was 44 and had no similar convictions. He had made only modest profits. He received **9 months** (it appears for the last distribution) and **18 months consecutive** for the other counts. Held. Infringement of copyright is widespread and is able to cause serious damage to commercial interests. The sentence could not be faulted.

R v Bhad [1999] 2 Cr App Rep (S) 139 – LCJ. The defendant was convicted of two counts of applying a trade mark without consent (four polo shirts and a sweatshirt), possessing an article used to produce goods with a trade mark without consent (a multi-head embroidery machine) and four counts of unauthorised use of trade marks (19 polo shirt and a sweatshirt) in total. He ran an embroidery business whose premises were searched by Trading Standards Officers. They three large industrial embroidery machines one of which was connected to computer. On the computer screen was a 'Reebok' logo. There were the 'Reebok' polo shirts and a sweatshirt which were not genuine. He had no convictions of a similar kind. He was sentenced for just that day's occurrence only with a **£1,250 fine** for the three trade mark offences and 4 months on the four trade descriptions offences and £6,000 costs. The grounds of appeal argued that it was a single set of facts which gave rise to the seven counts. The trade mark offences were alternative counts it was wrong to impose custody on the less serious counts. Held. We recognise the damage done to the legitimate trade by fake products. However, we see force in the defence submissions. The defendant had built up an honest business. It was highly questionable whether the custody threshold was passed. It was anomalous to impose a custodial sentence on the less serious trade description offences and a financial penalty on the more serious trade mark offences. We quash the prison sentence and impose no penalty on those counts.

R v Gleeson [2001] EWCA Crim 2023, [2002] 1 Cr App Rep (S) 485. The defendant changed his plea at the latest possible stage to guilty of 19 counts of possessing goods bearing a trade mark contrary to s 92(1) of the Trade Marks Act 1994 and possessing goods for the labelling and packaging goods contrary to s 92(2)(c). He manufactured copies of music CDs from his home and acquired large quantities of labels, blank CDs and sophisticated printing and shrink wrap equipment. The CDs were indistinguishable from the genuine article. 14 trade marks were infringed. He had produced 4,000 CDs and hoped to produce 2,000 a week. The potential loss to the music industry was about £1.5m. The CDs were sold to a distributor for between £1.50 and £2 and he made 50p per CD. That gave him £20,000 and a loss to the owners of £20,000. He was 43 with a conviction for perverting the course of justice in 1988 and conspiracy to supply Class B drugs in 1997. He received 12 months for both. He lived with his elderly mother who was in poor health and had a legitimate job. Held. It is necessary to deter others. We do not tinker with sentences. **30 months** was not manifestly excessive.

Old cases. *R v Gross* [1996] 2 Cr App Rep (S) 189.

Market traders

36.8   *R v Adam* [1998] 2 Cr App Rep (S) 403. The defendant pleaded guilty to four offences of using an unauthorised trade mark, applying a false description and obstructing an authorised officer under the Trade Descriptions Act. In another indictment he pleaded guilty to three offences of using an unauthorised trade mark, and obtaining property by deception. Trading Standards Officers saw the defendant in a market selling illegitimate goods with names on them like, 'Calvin Klein, Ralph Lauren and Levi Strauss'. He lied to the officers about his name and address. A week later he was seen selling the same counterfeit goods. Seven months later in another market he was seen doing the same again. On the day of the trial of the first group of offences he pleaded guilty. He then changed his plea to the second group at a different court. It was his case that he was working for another and received £25 a day and the profits went to the stall holder. He was treated as having no convictions. He was 35 and married with four children. He was unemployed, in receipt of benefits and with no savings. Held. The judge was entitled to express scepticism that he was working for someone else. The offence calls for a deterrent sentence. 3 months and 4 months for each group was appropriate. The judge was fully entitled to make them consecutive. **7 months** was severe but he was entitled to pass a severe sentence.

Shops

36.9 *R v Burns* [2001] 1 Cr App Rep (S) 220. The defendant pleaded guilty at the Magistrates' Court to 22 offences of having counterfeit articles for sale in a shop and 31 offences for having counterfeit goods in another shop and storage unit. They were specimen offences. Trading Standard Officers attended his shop and found the clothing featuring counterfeit brand names like Adidas, Ralph Lauren Calvin Klein and Timberland. Five hundred items were seized. They took other clothing from another shop, a van and a storage unit. The value of all the goods was £15,000 and the value of the goods in the charges was £1,300. He was 34 with two recent convictions for trade mark infringement for which he was fined. He had financial difficulties. Held. The offences are prevalent. He had ignored the warning he received when last prosecuted. **12 months** was inevitable.

Television, enabling access to cable or satellite television for free

36.10 *R v Carey* [1999] 1 Cr App Rep (S) 322. The defendant pleaded guilty to conspiracy to defraud. Up until March 1994, he ran a company which made electronic devices. In July 1993, BSkyB a satellite television company had obtained a perpetual injunction against the company prohibiting it from making or trading the devices. In May 1995 the defendant set up another company in Ireland and successfully 'hacked' BskyB's smartcards so enabling viewers to watch programmes without paying BSkyB. BSkyB produced another smartcard and the company successfully hacked that card too. There were about 850,000 sales of the cards. The cost of introducing another smartcard by BSkyB was £30m, although such a figure could not be attributed to the defendant as others were also 'hacking' the cards. The defendant's profit was £20,000. He was 48 and of good character with family responsibilities. Held. The commercial damage was great. The judge was right to concentrate on the company's loss as well as the defendant's gain. **4 years** was not manifestly excessive.

R v Maxwell-King [2001] 2 Cr App Rep (S) 136. The defendant pleaded guilty to three counts of inciting computer misuse by supplying to third parties a device causing unauthorised modifications to a computer. He and his wife were also directors and sole shareholders in a company which pleaded to the same counts, which was not fined but ordered to pay £10,000 prosecution costs. He and his company manufactured and supplied a device, which allowed the upgrading of analogue cable TV so the viewer could access all channels regardless of how many s/he had paid for. Twenty were sold at £30 plus VAT. A number of customers returned the chips because the TV company had been able to disable them electronically. As a result he gave up the scheme. His advertisement had been withdrawn before he was arrested. The chips were advertised on his extensive website. When his premises were raided the FACT officers were able to virtually close him down as they seized all his technical equipment. The loss to the TV company was £14 a device per month. He was 36 and of exemplary character with excellent references. His risk for re-offending was assessed as very low. Held. It was effectively a form of theft. The custody threshold had not been crossed. The appropriate sentence would be a substantial fine or a community sentence. **150 hours' CSO** not 4 months.

See also **COMPANY FRAUDS AND FINANCIAL SERVICES OFFENCES**

CORONER, OBSTRUCTING THE

See OBSTRUCTING THE CORONER/BURIAL, PREVENTING

37   CORRUPTION

37.1   Public Bodies Corrupt Practices Act 1889, s 1

Prevention of Corruption Act 1906, s 1

Triable either way. On indictment maximum 7 years. Summary maximum 6 months and/or £5,000.

Local government

37.2   *R v Dearnley and Threapleton* [2002] 2 Cr App Rep (S) 201. The defend-ants were convicted after a retrial of corruption. The defendant D aged 56 was a principle valuer for a Metropolitan Council. He was responsible for its property management including a business centre. Tenders for the centre's security services were invited. A company called ESC was not approached. The defendant T aged 52, was a director of that company's parent company. ESC approached the defendant D and their quote was accepted although it was not the lowest. No formal documentation was presented just invoices. The council also gave the company other work. Two companies connected with T were paid £1m for services provided. Another company connected with T paid off a loan of £5,445 D had obtained to buy a car. The judge described T as greedy. Both had no convictions. The offence was 7 years old. T had spent £75,000 on his legal expenses and was ruined. Held. Custody is inevitable. There was no suggestion of lack of value for money. **12 months** not 18 for both.

Police officers as defendants

37.3   *R v Donald* [1997] 2 Cr App Rep (S) 272. The defendant pleaded guilty to four counts of corruption after 12½ weeks trial. The first matter was accepting £500 for police information, the second was agreeing to accept £10,000 for police information the third was agreeing to accept £40,000 for destroying a surveillance log; the fourth was accepting £18,000 for the removal of the log in the third matter. The defendant was a detective constable serving in No 9 Regional Crime Squad. He was at the heart of a sensitive and vitally important police operation. The money in each matter was negotiated by a criminal, who had gone to the BBC who then filmed and recorded the conversations between the two. The 1st matter was unsolicited and involved Michael Lawson. The second involved Michael Lawson and Kenneth Noye who were both two international criminals being investigated for major drug trafficking. The fourth was a down payment for the third. The defendant had 'glowing recommendations from his superiors.' He received 5 years for the first, 6 years for the second matter consecutive and 5 years concurrent for the other 2 (**11 years** in all). Held. The sentence was severe but not manifestly excessive.

R v Smith [2002] 1 Cr App Rep (S) 386. See *Police officers, trying to corrupt*

See also POLICE OFFICERS

Police officers, trying to corrupt

37.4   *R v Brown, Mahoney and King* [2000] 2 Cr App Rep (S) 284. The defendant K pleaded guilty to various conspiracies to pervert the course of justice, conspiracies to corrupt a police officer and corruption. The defendant B were convicted of one conspiracy involving K. The defendant M was convicted of two conspiracies involving K, forming one part of the case. The case fell into three parts. In the first part B was arrested for car fraud. four cars and £17,500 was seized. B's father approached K, a former policeman who approached another former police officer H who approached a Det Chief Inspector. The Inspector was suspicious and arranged for all further conversations to be recorded. H introduced K to the Inspector and H gave the Inspector £1,000. The Inspector then met B. The cars and the money were returned and K gave the Inspector £5,000. The officer then gave K a letter saying the enquiries into the fraud were at an end.

The second part of the case was when M was charged with two offences of GBH with intent. M's father knew K and he approached the same Det Chief Inspector. They both agreed that if the papers went missing the case would be tainted. K asked the officer if in exchange for payment he could make some enquiries. Later the Inspector told K he would need to tear up the officer's pocket books and the Identification book at the ID parade for that case. The Inspector asked what sort of money his client was prepared to pay and was told between £5,000 and £10,000. Eventually it was agreed two payments of £2,500 could be made. The first instalment was paid and the papers were produced and destroyed. A further meeting was arranged and K and M were arrested. They were in possession of £2,550.

The third part of the case involved a Henry Moore statue worth about £100,000, which had been stolen from a gallery. K asked the same Det Chief Inspector whether the £10,000 reward money could be obtained without anyone being arrested. It was agreed K could be registered as an informant in a false name. Later K handed the statue over and was paid the £10,000 reward from the insurance company and £3,000 out of the Informant's fund. He gave £2,000 to the Inspector.

K was 51 with no convictions. His business had gone wrong and he was in financial difficulties. M was 32 and was a builder. He had eight convictions including burglary, handling, theft and possession of cannabis. B was 25 and largely unemployed. He dealt with second-hand cars. He had no convictions. He was described as unsophisticated and somewhat gullible. K was said to have, 'called the shots.' K was given less than the normal credit for his plea because of the strength of the evidence in the tape recordings. Held. An important part of the sentencing process is deterrent. The starting point for K should have been 9 years. Taking into account the mitigation the appropriate sentence was 6 years for the first part of the case and the other sentences concurrent not the 9 he received. B sentence was reduced from 3 years to **21 months**. M's sentence was reduced from 5 to **3½ years**.

R v Smith [2001] EWCA Crim 1812, [2002] 1 Cr App Rep (S) 386. The defendants D and H pleaded guilty shortly after a jury was empanelled to a police corruption conspiracy which was over a 4 year period. D was a sergeant in CID and H was a drug dealer who was sentenced to 8 years for drug trafficking offences. £130,000 was found at H's home. H supplied D with money and information about other drug criminals and D provided H with information about police and customs operations against other drug dealers. H made tape recordings of the conversations which were found by the police. The corruption started at the beginning of the police officer's career. H suggested planting drugs on other criminals. D adopted H as an informant but did not tell his superior officers. D also dealt with his father's hotel business and it was in 1995 in a poor financial state. H put £10,000 into the hotel business. H then took over the running of the hotel and used it for the storing and distribution of drugs. D then lied about his involvement with H. Five offenders were able to escape when information about the raids on their addresses were leaked to H. The police started investigating and D ignored police instructions. He was told to stop seeing H and he met him the next day and again later. H and D were both arrested and D lied when interviewed. The prosecution could not be precise about the damage caused to the police and the profits made. However the integrity of the police force and its anti-drugs activities were very seriously compromised. H and his associates were major players in the drugs world. D received 7 years, the maximum and H received 5 years consecutive to the 8 years he had received in his drug case. The judge refused to give D a discount for the plea because the appropriate sentence was 10 years before a small discount for the plea which should have made it 8½ years. He said the situation was similar to a specimen charge where one count does not reflect the whole course of conduct. Held. Some discount for the plea should have been made so 6 years for D substituted. H's sentence reduced from 5 to **4½ years**.

See also MISCONDUCT IN PUBLIC OFFICE

38   COUNTERFEITING CURRENCY

38.1   Forgery and Counterfeiting Act 1981, ss 14(1), 15(1), 16(1) and 17(1)

Making, passing etc, having custody or control of counterfeit notes or coin intending the notes or coins to be passed; and making etc counterfeiting materials etc intending the notes or coins to be passed respectively.

Triable either way. On indictment maximum 10 years. Summary maximum 6 months and/or £5,000.

Forgery and Counterfeiting Act 1981, ss 14(2), 15(2), 16(2) and 17(2)

Making, delivering, having custody and control of counterfeit notes or coin without lawful excuse; and making etc counterfeiting materials etc without lawful excuse respectively.

Triable either way. On indictment maximum 2 years. Summary maximum 6 months and/or £5,000.

Guideline remarks

38.2   *R v Crick* [1998] 3 Cr App Rep (S) 275. The defendant pleaded guilty to possessing a press and he made about 150 fake 50p pieces. The coins could not have been put into general circulation and were to be used in vending machines. Held. Coining is a serious offence and calls for immediate imprisonment. However it must be recognised that not all such offences are of the same gravity. At one extreme is the professional forger, with carefully prepared plates, and elaborate machinery, who manufactures large quantities of bank notes and puts them into circulation. A long sentence of imprisonment is appropriate in such a case. At the other end is this case.

Large scale production

38.3   *R v Dossetter* [1999] 2 Cr App Rep (S) 248. The defendants D and J pleaded guilty to two counts of conspiracy to produce counterfeit currency. The defendants C, and M pleaded guilty to one of those counts. D's plea was very late and M's plea was extremely late. J was employed by D in the printing business. After J had left D who was the prime mover approached J to counterfeit US dollars. They needed help and J approached someone who had their own photographic business and who was able to make the necessary transparencies. D and J were able to produce some $200,000 worth of relatively unsophisticated notes. Some went to America where the authorities intervened. About 6 months later they started to produce with a different press and with improved technology $6m worth of notes. They were stored at C's premises and C was paid just over £3,000 for his help. D tried to sell the notes and M used his contacts and an undercover officer agreed to buy $2m. As the deal was about to be finalised officers arrested the courier and the minder at a hotel. J was arrested elsewhere in the hotel. J was interviewed and made admissions. He also showed the police where the other $3.5m worth of notes were and told the officers who else was involved. M was the organiser of the dissemination of the notes. No notes were ever circulated. J and C pleaded at the first opportunity and were prepared to give evidence for the prosecution. D was 46 and of good character. M was 52 with no convictions since 1986. C was 51 and of good character. Held. D's sentence of **7 years** was not manifestly excessive. M's sentence was reduced from 4 to **3 years**. C and J's sentences were reduced from 5 to **3 years** to reflect C's lesser role and J's assistance.

39   CRIMINAL DAMAGE

39.1   Criminal Damage Act 1971, s 1(1)

The offence is triable either way, where the value of damage is £5,000 or more. Otherwise summary only. On indictment maximum 10 years[1]. Summary maximum, when value is £5,000 or more 6 months and/or £5,000 fine; and 3 months and/or £2,500 otherwise.

1   This is irrespective of what the value is. So if a count is added to the indictment and the value is less than £5,000 the maximum is 10 years, *R v Alden* [2002] EWCA Crim 421, [2002] 2 Cr App Rep (S) 326.

Crown Court statistics England and Wales[1] – Crown Court – Males 21+

39.2

Year	Plea	Total Numbers sentenced	Type of sentence%					Average length of custody[2] (months)
			Discharge	Fine	Community sentence	Suspended sentence	Custody	
CriminalDamage endangering life								
2000	Guilty	36	0%	0%	19%	3%	75%	31.2
	Not guilty	5	0%	0%	20%	0%	80%	21.5
Other Criminal Damage								
2000	Guilty	340	20%	9%	49%	1%	18%	6.2
	Not guilty	40	8%	23%	33%	0%	20%	13.9
Threats etc. to commit Criminal Damage								
2000	Guilty	49	2%	2%	43%	8%	43%	17.2
	Not guilty	4	0%	0%	0%	0%	100%	21.8

1   Excluding committals for sentence. Source: Crime and Criminal Justice Unit, Home Office Ref: IOS416-02.
2   Excluding life sentences.

Magistrates' Court Sentencing Guidelines September 2000

39.3   Entry point. Is a discharge or a fine appropriate? Consider the impact on the victim. Examples of aggravating factors for the offence are deliberate, group action, and serious damage. Examples of mitigating factors for the offence are impulsive action minor damage, and provocation. Examples of mitigation are age, health (physical or mental), co-operation with the police, voluntary compensation and genuine remorse. Give reasons if not awarding compensation. **Starting point fine C.**

(£150 when defendant has £100 net weekly income. See page 334 for table showing fines for different incomes.)

For details about the guidelines see **MAGISTRATES' COURT SENTENCING GUIDELINES** at page 331.

Criminal damage – Threatening to destroy or damage property

39.4   Criminal Damage Act 1971, s 2

Triable either way. On indictment maximum 10 years. Summary maximum 6 months and/or £5,000.

Commercial premises

39.5   *R v McCann* [2000] 1 Cr App Rep (S) 495. The defendant pleaded guilty to threatening to destroy property. The defendant ordered a burger from a kebab shop over the telephone. After it arrived he complained over the telephone that there was sauce in the burger which he had not requested. He was offered a replacement which he declined. He then went to the shop and asked for a refund which was refused. He was abusive to the owner and falsely claimed he had served a long sentence for murder. He said he would return and burn down the shop with the proprietor inside. At 1.30am next morning he returned to the shop which was still open with customers and splashed diesel fuel on the floor and some on the customers. The proprietor's three young children were asleep upstairs. He had a cigarette in his mouth and a lighter in his hand and shouted he was going to burn the place down. The customers ran out in panic while the proprietor leapt on the defendant, took the petrol can and lighter off him and pushed him out of the shop. He restrained him till the police arrived. In interview he said he did not intent to set ignite the diesel but wanted to scare them with the fear of being killed. He had four convictions for criminal damage, one for a s 47 assault, one for threatening behaviour and one for possession of explosives. He was 35 and had received no adult custodial sentences. He was sentenced on the basis he had not intended to set the diesel alight. Held. The threat was an ugly and no doubt very frightening episode. In the diesel incident there was great fear but there was importantly no racial or terrorist element. Diesel is not as dangerous as petrol. **3 years** not 6.

Domestic

39.6   *R v Kavanagh* [1998] 1 Cr App Rep (S) 241. The defendant pleaded guilty to threatening to destroy or damage property in a way likely to endanger life. In March/April 1996 the defendant was a victim of an assault for which he required 48 stitches in his head. In August he quarrelled with his partner who told him to leave the house. The defendant responded with violence and the partner left the house. Police arrived and found him locked in the flat with the windows closed and a strong smell of gas. The defendant was armed with a large knife and a lighter. He threatened to blow the place up and to stab anyone who came near him. A police officer broke all the windows he could and switched off the gas at the meter. Police tried to calm him down but he brandished seven knives. He was eventually persuaded to leave the flat. A fire officer said the gas from the fire and the oven could easily have ignited and if someone in a neighbouring flat had even turned on a television there might have been an explosion. The defendant said he was on temazepan and painkillers and had drunk 4 pints and 2 large Bacardi rums. He said he did not know why he did it. He was 30 with many previous convictions mainly for dishonesty. A psychiatrist said he was not mentally ill but had symptoms which could be associated with post-traumatic stress disorder. The defendant told him he was very angry and wanted revenge. Held. People in the block were all put in danger. Action of this sort will be met with serious and heavy punishment. With mercy **3 years** not 4.

R v Bonehill [1998] 2 Cr App Rep (S) 90. The defendant made a late plea of guilty to two counts of damage property in a way likely to endanger life. The victim had had to give evidence at the committal proceedings. The defendant had a relationship with the defendant in which they lived together. After it broke up the house where she lived with her children aged 10 and 12 caught fire in the middle of the night. All three had to jump out of a window to escape. She suspected the defendant was responsible. He then began a campaign of intimidation and she had to move. A brick was thrown through her window and she had to move again. She then discovered that he knew her latest address. When at home with a friend and the children in bed she heard the door banging. She pressed her panic button and found on the floor by the front door a cassette tape in an envelope. A note said that she should play the B side which she did. That side had his voice on it saying how much he loved her. On the A side was him saying, 'I'm going to cut you up like a blood cock pussy whore, (sic) I'm going to torch the house when you're all in it.' The next day a friend told the victim that he was at the door again. Once again a cassette tape was delivered. On it he said he was going to cut her up and she should not go out of the house because he was watching her all the time. It concluded with him saying he would do what he did last time, 'when you were all in bed at our last house.' Three days later the victim's brother saw him and held him till the police arrived. After sentence a psychiatric report was written which gave the defendant no assistance. An adverse prison report was also written. Held. **4 years** was severe but it matched the offences which were very serious. Threats of arson are inevitably serious. They would have had an appalling effect on the victim's mind.

Fire, involving

39.7   *R v Bonehill* [1998] 2 Cr App Rep (S) 90. See **Criminal damage – Threatening to destroy or damage property – *Domestic***

Criminal damage – Reckless whether life would be endangered

39.8   Criminal Damage Act 1971, s 1(2)

Indictable only. Maximum sentence life imprisonment.

Court staff, offence directed at

39.9   *R v Dodd* [1997] 1 Cr App Rep (S) 127. The defendant pleaded guilty to criminal damage being reckless whether life was endangered. The defendant appeared at the Magistrates' Court and pleaded guilty. His case was adjourned. The court imposed interim disqualification, which upset the defendant. As he left court he made various threats and warned them to get out of the way. He got into his car, drove it up a ramp, through the glass front doors, through the inner doors and ended up at the rear wall of the court. On his way he demolished the reception desk. On impact the car was travelling at 35 to 40 mph and £34,000 damage was caused. He was 31 with ten court appearances latterly for repeated driving whilst disqualified. The psychiatrist said he had problems with his interaction with authority. **4 years** was entirely justified.

Motor vehicles, damage to

39.10   *R v Messenger* [2001] 2 Cr App Rep (S) 117. The defendant pleaded to guilty to criminal damage being reckless whether life was endangered. The defendant admitted cutting the brake hoses on a car. The driver discovered it, as he was about to take his son to school. The victim was the stepfather of the defendant's ex-girlfriend and there was bad feeling between them. It involved access to his child. The defendant was suffering from severe mental problems connected with the child and an abortion on an unborn child. His only convictions were drug related. **3 years** was not manifestly excessive.

Suicide attempt, connected with

39.11 *R v Mynors* [1998] 2 Cr App Rep (S) 279. The defendant pleaded guilty to criminal damage being reckless whether life was endangered. The defendant had arguments with his girlfriend and according to her hit her. She left the house. The police were called and found the girlfriend injured and distressed outside. They smelt gas and broke in. The defendant was found unconscious in a cupboard. A gas pipe had been severed. He told police it was an attempt to commit suicide. He was 43 and had five convictions for violence including rape and wounding and a conviction for arson. He was on probation. A report said he needed psychiatric assistance. **2 years** was not manifestly excessive.

For basic principles about racially-aggravated offences, see **RACIALLY-AGGRAVATED OFFENCES**

See also **ARSON – Arson – Reckless whether life would be endangered**

40 CRIMINAL DAMAGE – RACIALLY AGGRAVATED

40.1 Crime and Disorder Act 1998, s 30

Triable either way. On indictment maximum sentence 14 years. Summary maximum 6 months and/or £5,000.

Magistrates' Court Sentencing Guidelines September 2000

40.2 Entry point. Is it serious enough for a community penalty? Consider the level of racial aggravation and the impact on the victim. Examples of aggravating factors for the offence are deliberate, group action, and serious damage. Examples of mitigating factors for the offence are impulsive action minor damage, and provocation. Examples of mitigation are age, health (physical or mental), co-operation with the police, voluntary compensation and genuine remorse. Give reasons if not awarding compensation.

For details about the guidelines see **MAGISTRATES' COURT SENTENCING GUIDELINES** at page 331.

For basic principles about racially-aggravated offences, see **RACIALLY-AGGRAVATED OFFENCES**

CRUELTY TO ANIMALS

See **ANIMAL CRUELTY**

41 CRUELTY TO CHILDREN

41.1 Children and Young Persons Act 1933, s 1

Triable either way. On indictment maximum 10 years. Summary maximum 6 months and/or £5,000.

Dividing this section into the different categories etc is somewhat artificial as the important matters for sentence appear to be the defendant's intent, the injuries if any, the length of time over which the offences took place and most crucially of all the trauma of the victim(s). The courts stress their duty to protect the vulnerable and those who cannot protect them selves.

Crown Court statistics England and Wales[1] – Crown Court – Males 21+ – Cruelty to or neglect of children

41.2

Year	Plea	Total Numbers sentenced	Type of sentence%					Average length of custody (months)
			Discharge	Fine	Community sentence	Suspended sentence	Custody	
2000	Guilty	88	3%	0%	36%	9%	51%	18.7
	Not guilty	28	0%	0%	29%	11%	61%	23.5

1　Excluding committals for sentence. Source: Crime and Criminal Justice Unit, Home Office Ref: IOS416-02.

Danger, exposing child to

41.3 *R v Laut* [2002] 2 Cr App Rep (S) 21. The defendant pleaded guilty to cruelty. She lived with her husband and her four children, three of which were from a previous relationship. The husband was violent towards her and several times she made contact with the domestic violence unit. The lock on the washing machine was broken and the defendant asked her son aged 7 to hold it shut. He slipped on some water and his arm went into the exposed drum of the machine while it was on spin. It became entangled in a duvet and he suffered multiple fractures to his arm, which required internal and external fixation. He made a slow but successful recovery. Both his parents had been in the living room and his father knew what he was doing. About 6 weeks earlier a health visitor had seen the boy holding the door shut and had told her it was not appropriate. She said the boy liked doing it. There were insufficient funds to repair the machine. They were both arrested and she admitted the facts and the conversation with the health visitor. She showed remorse. The basis of the plea was it was wilful neglect likely to cause unnecessary suffering or injury to the boy. She was 30 and had no convictions. At the time she was pregnant and since then a baby was born. All her children including the baby were taken into care. She had started divorce proceedings. Her risk of re-offending was assessed as exceptionally low. The parents were treated the same and received 4 months. Held. Without the warning immediate custody would not necessarily be appropriate. The warning made the offence serious wilful neglect requiring imprisonment but because of her character and remorse **12 weeks** instead.

Medical help, delay in seeking

41.4 *R v S* [1999] 1 Cr App Rep (S) 67. The defendant pleaded guilty to cruelty. His girlfriend had his baby and although they were not living together he saw them 2–3 times a week. When his girlfriend returned home he drew her attention to the baby's breathing and telephoned for medical help. He took the baby to hospital and it was found to have bilateral subdural bleeding of two densities and massive retinal bleeding. The defendant confessed to shaking the baby after he was unable to stop him crying. The defence expert said that the injuries were very serious and had the potential to cause permanent blindness. The baby was taken into care and he was denied access. He had expressed shame and guilt. The basis for plea was he had shaken the baby without criminal intent or recklessness. He then realised the baby's health might suffer unless examined by a doctor and fearing what he might have done he delayed for an hour or so seeking medical assistance. He was 24 with no convictions. Held. Because of the basis of the plea, he fell to be sentenced for the delay and not the shaking. **3 months** not 6.

R v Edwards [1999] 1 Cr App Rep (S) 301. The defendant pleaded guilty to cruelty. It was based on a failure to seek medical help. His pleas of not guilty to assault and ill treatment were accepted. An 11-day-old baby suffered cruel injuries, which caused her terrible pain, but the prosecution could not prove which of the two parents had caused them. At 1pm a health visitor called and saw marks and red spots on the baby. The parents were advised to take the baby to a doctor. The doctor saw three marks probably caused by a burning cigarette. Other marks were seen on the soles of her feet, which could have been caused by a pin. The plea was based on a realisation during the evening before the injuries were seen that medical attention should have been sought. The mother had mental problems and was given probation. The defendant was 33 and had one conviction for a wholly dissimilar offence for which he was given a short prison sentence. **12 months** was entirely appropriate.

R v Taggart [1999] 2 Cr App Rep (S) 68. The defendant pleaded guilty to cruelty. It was based on a failure to seek medical help. His pleas of not guilty to assault and ill treatment were accepted. The defendant lived together with his co-defendant, the mother of the victim. He ran the bath taps with the baby in the bath and the plug out. He left the room and heard screams. He returned to find the victim had received severe scalding. Neither defendant sought medical help. The next day the health visitor was refused entry. Not until 5pm that day was a doctor contacted. He arrived and immediately called an ambulance. The bath water was estimated to be approaching 70°C. The hot water system was examined and found to produce hot water far hotter than normal. The baby recovered and was fostered. However, she still experienced flashbacks. The pictures of the baby were horrific. Held. **2½ years** not 4 ½

R v Bereton [2001] EWCA Crim 1463, [2002] 1 Cr App Rep (S) 270. The defendant pleaded guilty to cruelty on the first day of his trial. His partner was acquitted of the charge. They lived together and sometime between midnight and 4am their 12-day-old baby received serious injuries. The three were in the same bedroom. There was no call to the emergency services and he and his partner took the baby to the GP's surgery at about 11.15am. The baby was taken to hospital and found to have no external injuries but a drooping eyelid and possibly a bulging eye. A scan found serious injuries to the brain with internal bleeding and swelling. There was an emergency brain operation but the baby died from head injuries. They were caused by impact or shaking. The likelihood was she suffered a severe impact injury to the head, which may have been associated with some shaking. When interviewed he denied causing the injuries and said sometime around 3 or 4am he noticed the baby's eye was swollen. The child was upset, not taking food and vomiting. At 6am his partner had gone to a telephone box to try to obtain advice without success. The prosecution were unable to say which person caused the injuries. An expert said the baby from the moment of injury would not have been remotely normal. She would not have cried and any noises would have been from abnormal breathing. It would have been obvious that she was extremely ill and urgent medical attention was required. He was sentenced on the basis he knew something terrible had happened and he did not obtain medical help, which the baby plainly required. He was 28 and had a conviction for common assault in 1992. There was a delay of 17 months between the incident and the sentence and he showed remorse. Held. We bear in mind the need to protect children from unnecessary suffering and death. **3 years** not 4.

Neglect

41.5 *R v Weaver and Burton* [1998] 2 Cr App Rep (S) 56. W, aged 24 and B, aged 30 pleaded guilty to cruelty. They lived together and indulged in drugs in a squalid flat.

They had a son and 1 year later the health visitor was concerned at his weight loss. Three months later he was seen in hospital at the request of social services and had striking wasting due to depravation or illness. He was allowed home and 16 days later he died. The post-mortem found he was poorly nourished and had ingested cocaine. W, the mother and stronger personality pleaded on the basis of inadequate nourishment, failure to get medical help and a common assault when the baby was slapped and shook. B's plea was based on a failure to notice his declining condition and failure to stand up to the mother on behalf of his son. Held. The judge saw the death as crucial notwithstanding that the pathologist had failed to establish causation. **3 years** not 6 for W. **2 years** not 3 for B.

R v Jackson [2001] EWCA Crim 60, [2001] 2 Cr App Rep (S) 259. The defendant on the day his trial was to start, pleaded guilty to three counts of cruelty against his partner's three children. The mother pleaded to the same counts and another neglect count to another child. Each count was dated from the victim's birth to when the child was taken into care in 1997. The periods were nearly 4 years, 2 years 8 months and 14 months. In 1991 the couple started living together with his wife and their five children in total. She then gave birth to the three victims. He was domineering and she went to work delivering coal while he stayed at home doing very little. Support from health workers failed. They lived at various addresses and in each the conditions deteriorated. Clothes were unwashed, the children were dirty, nappies were not changed, medical advice not sought, dogs caused unsanitary conditions and there were concerns about the food. There were contrasts between the victims and his children by his wife. The victims aged 4 years, 2 years 8 months and 14 months were not toilet trained, were dressed in urine soaked clothes and the eldest was taking food from the dog's bowl. The house was squalid. The defendant was 50 and had no similar previous convictions. The mother received 1 year in total. Held. **3 years** was not manifestly excessive and the difference in the sentences was understandable.

Prevent ill treatment, neglect, etc failure to

41.6   *R v Adams and Sherrington* [1999] 1 Cr App Rep (S) 240. The defendants A and S pleaded guilty after their trial had begun to three counts of cruelty to A's baby girl. S was a new partner to A and S admitted squeezing the victim between his legs when she was 15–18 months old, (count two). A admitted biting the baby when she was 18 months old, (count five). They both admitted failing to prevent her ill-treatment, (count six) and failing to seek treatment for her injuries, (count seven). A was infatuated with S. The victim was subjected to a course of cruel and violent treatment leading up to her death. The prosecution was unable to say which had caused the particular acts save for the admitted counts. The incident when she was squeezed in a lock was recorded on a dictaphone. The child screamed in extreme pain. In the 4 weeks before her death bruises were seen by two doctors and a health visitor. Three days before her death S showed the baby to a neighbour, a nurse who saw her limp with bruises all over her face. They were both told to take her straight to hospital. They didn't. In the afternoon of the next day A called an ambulance. The various accounts for the injuries were in conflict. At hospital the baby was found to have several fractures to the skull and irreversible brain damage. There were also bruises of different ages and bite marks. Two days later the ventilator was turned off. A was 32 and treated as of good character and was of limited intelligence. She suffered from post-natal depression. S was 33 and of good character and was the dominant partner. Held. For A 2 years concurrent not 5 for counts six and seven. 2 years not 3 for count five but consecutive rather than concurrent so making **4 years** not 5 in all. S's total sentence of **7 years** was appropriate.

A-G's Reference (No 24 of 2001) [2001] 2 Cr App Rep (S) 535. The defendant pleaded guilty to 14 counts of cruelty to children on the third day of her trial and ABH. Her co-habitee subjected her three children to physical and sexual assaults. Eleven of the counts related to not protecting her children then aged 10, 8 and 6 years old. The children were kicked and punched, their heads were put down the toilet, an attempt to choke one was made, on three occasions paper was put up their anuses and there was digital penetration on another. When seen one was covered in injuries showing the assaults were very persistent and severe. The children gave details of assaults by the defendant and one seemed more afraid of the defendant than her partner. That one's hair was full of lice and she was very badly affected. The partner received 7 years and was described as having a sadistic personality. The defendant had no convictions. She had suffered from violence from her partner who dominated her. She had spent 8 months 1 week in custody before sentence. Held. **2½ years** would have been appropriate. However, now it would be wrong to interfere with the probation order.

R v Creed [2000] 1 Cr App Rep (S) 304. The defendant pleaded guilty not at the first opportunity to two counts of cruelty to her child (whose age is not in the judgment). Her co-accused and partner was convicted of the murder of the child. The first count was that her partner assaulted the child from time to time between March and October 1997 and the defendant knew this and she had allowed the child to remain at risk. During this time a number of people had noticed bruises, swelling and marks on her. Medical staff also saw a bite mark. At about 8am on 21 October 1997 neighbours of hers heard banging noises. The child had not been to school for 2½ weeks. Shortly after 9am the defendant received a telephone call at work. She was distraught and was allowed to go home. She arrived no later than 9.30am. After about an hour she made a 999 call saying the baby had fallen down the stairs. The ambulance took the child to hospital and there were no signs of life during the journey. The child was pronounced dead at 12.20pm. 167 bruises were found almost all less than a day old. Some were consistent with her being forcibly poked. Other larger ones were consistent with being hit with a fist or being kicked. She also had a haemorrhage to the intestines and a rib was fractured. Her liver had split which would have caused death within 15 to 20 minutes. The other count was based on causing unnecessary suffering by delaying making the 999 call. She was a senior aircraft woman in the RAF. She was given **3 years** (probably for the first count) and 2 years consecutive for the other count. Held. The sentences were entirely appropriate.

Punishments etc to the children, unlawful

41.7   *R v M* [1998] 2 Cr App Rep (S) 208. The defendant pleaded guilty to three counts of cruelty. The counts were based on bizarre punishments and humiliations. When one girl was about 13 she jokingly told her friend that her father had put her jewellery in the dustbin. The friend asked the father if it was true and his girl was hit in the face and stomach. She was then made to throw the jewellery in the bin and to hit her friend. He sent someone to check that it had been done. Once he required the girls to go to school in their oldest clothes and made the boys lead them with ropes shouting, 'dogs for sale.' His children were made to cut the lawn with nail scissors and to go to bed without food at 4pm. There were other bizarre punishments. The punishments on two children lasted from when they were 5 to 16, and on another between 5 and 14. The defendant aged 41 was of good character. He was frank with the police and he said he was exercising control and sometimes overreacted. He had a personality disorder. The risk of re-offending was minimal. **3 years** in total not 4.

Unsupervised, leaving a child or children

41.8   *R v Cameron and Senior* [2000] 2 Cr App Rep (S) 329. The defendants C and S pleaded guilty to three counts of cruelty and no evidence was offered on a count of manslaughter. S the mother of three children also pleaded to ABH. The children were 7, 9 and 13 years old and were left unsupervised while S and her partner C went to a couple of public houses. They were out from a little before 3.30pm and to 9.30pm. Witnesses saw the 13 year old behaving strangely as if drunk. He had tablets with him. The defendants returned home and at 5am an ambulance was called as the boy was having breathing difficulties. He died soon afterwards of methadone poisoning. Other drugs were also detected in his blood. C a drug addict had been proscribed methadone and hid it in the house. S had discovered it and it was kept in their wardrobe where the children were not allowed access. S's ABH was on a social worker, who arrived with police unexpectedly to take two of the children into police protection. She was struck in the face causing a bloody nose. C was 30 and had convictions for dishonesty, criminal damage and possession of cannabis. S was 32 and had one spent conviction. The judge referred to S's history of fecklessness in relation to the care of the children. Held. That remark was in error as she was to be sentenced for leaving the children unsupervised. **12 months** for that was not manifestly excessive nor was the 3 months consecutive for the ABH.

Violence to babies and toddlers (up to 2 years old)

41.9   *R v Isaac* [1998] 1 Cr App Rep (S) 266. The defendant pleaded guilty when first arraigned to cruelty to a child. The defendant had a difficult and unplanned pregnancy. The birth was extremely difficult and prolonged. A forceps delivery failed, as did a Ventouse extraction and she suffered a traumatic birth. An emergency Caesarean section had eventually to be performed. Her son was large, restless, hungry and colicky. He had to be treated for a urinary infection in hospital. When he was discharged the defendant found it very difficult to cope. Her family were supportive but were unable to help her to any great extent. The defendant's mother noticed that the baby had a swollen thigh and was bruised from the groin to the knee. The baby was taken to hospital and was found to have a displaced spiral fracture of the femur probably less than 10 days old and two fractures on both tibias and a fracture on the other femur 2–3 weeks old. The defendant who had learning difficulties denied causing any injury to the baby but could offer no explanation. Later she admitted to a probation officer that she had twisted the baby's legs on two occasions. She said he was crying continually and she felt isolated and physically exhausted. Later she was found to be suffering from depression with feelings of helplessness and an inability to cope. A Professor said her post-natal depression predated the injuries. The child was first fostered and then taken into care. Support for the Social Services was now available. Held. 3 years was quite inappropriate. It was totally different from the situation where a baby is injured by a father or other relative. Where injuries are inflicted by a mother suffering from post-natal depression with a difficult pregnancy and an even more difficult birth more than a short custodial is wholly inappropriate. A short custodial was appropriate but as she needs help and encouragement and she has served the equivalent of 8½ months **12 months' probation** instead.

R v Scammell and Mills [1998] 1 Cr App Rep (S) 321 – LCJ. The defendant M pleaded guilty to unlawful wounding (s 20) and two counts of cruelty to a child. S was convicted of two counts of cruelty to a child. S was the father of the victim and he had lived with M. They parted and S paid M to look after the child while he was at work. The child aged 21 months died of natural causes. However, the post-mortem revealed a skull fracture of 'some little age'; fractures to the fibulae consistent with twisting and pulling of the legs; skin loss to the back of the head underneath of which there was deep bruising; a burn on the back of the hand which extended to the lateral aspect of the elbow; and multiple abrasions and bruises to the head, neck, penis, buttocks and other parts of the body. At the flat the baby's blood was splattered against a wall. M admitted causing the burn. It was not suggested that S was responsible for the blood on the wall and M could not explain it. M gave evidence against S. S was of good character and had a record as a caring mother to her own children. Held. The burn was perhaps the most disturbing injury. The starting point for M was 9 years. The reduction to **6 years** was proper. As S had not committed the most serious assaults the starting point for him was **7 years** and not the 10 year maximum. There was nothing to mitigate that sentence.

R v Kelly [1998] 2 Cr App Rep (S) 368. The defendant pleaded guilty to ill-treating a 5-month-old child of his girlfriend. He and the mother abused drugs. Residents heard the baby screaming and several slaps. A doctor found severe facial bruising which was not part of the basis of his plea. His plea was based on him being responsible for bruising on the head and legs caused by slapping. The doctor concluded considerable force must have been used for those slaps. The defendant was now 23 and had extensive convictions for motor vehicles and one for ABH. The risk of re-offending was said to be high. The mother was given probation. Held. Because it was a plea **2 years** not 3.

R v Adams and Sherrington [1999] 1 Cr App Rep (S) 240. The defendants A and S pleaded guilty after their trial had begun to three counts of cruelty to A's baby girl. The defendant S who was a new partner to A and admitted squeezing the girl between his legs when she was 15–18 months old, (count two). A admitted biting the baby when she was 18 months old, (count five). They both admitted failing to prevent her ill-treatment, (count six) and failing to seek treatment for her injuries, (count seven). A was infatuated with S. The girl was subjected to a course of cruel and violent treatment leading up to her death. The prosecution was unable to say which had caused the particular acts save for the admitted counts. The incident when she was squeezed in a lock was recorded on a dictaphone. The child screamed in extreme pain. In the 4 weeks before her death bruises were seen by two doctors and a health visitor. Three days before her death S showed the baby to a neighbour, a nurse who saw her limp with bruises all over her face. They were both told to take her straight to hospital. They didn't. In the afternoon of the next day A called an ambulance. The various accounts for the injuries were in conflict. At hospital the baby was found to have several fractures to the skull and irreversible brain damage. There were also bruises of different ages and bite marks. Two days later the ventilator was turned off. A was 32 and was treated as of good character and was of limited intelligence. She suffered from post-natal depression. S was 33 and of good character and was the dominant partner. Held. For A 2 years concurrent not 5 for counts six and seven. 2 years not 3 for count five but consecutive rather than concurrent so making **4 years** not 5 in all. S's total sentence of **7 years** was appropriate.

Violence to children aged 5–10

41.10 *R v O'Gorman* [1999] 2 Cr App Rep (S) 280. The defendant pleaded guilty to cruelty and ABH at the Magistrates' Court. The victim on each count was the same. He was also sentenced for common assault on his co-habitee. The defendant returned home in a foul mood and drank a substantial amount of alcohol. He found his co-habitee's 8-year-old child's room untidy and on and off for 2 hours assaulted the two and broke furniture. The child was grabbed by the neck, thrown around the room, punched on the chin, struck on the eye, and had his head put down the lavatory and the chain pulled. The doctor found multiple areas of bruising and swelling on the boy. His lips were very swollen and there were multiple black bruises indicating where his teeth had knocked the lips. He said the injuries were consistent with repeated forceful blows. The defendant admitted the offences and he had one previous conviction for ABH on a woman in 1987 for which he was fined. He had been a postman for 14 years. Held.

Anyone who inflicts violence on a child like this will lose their liberty. Where it was prolonged like here substantial imprisonment will follow. Insufficient credit was given for the early plea so **21 months** concurrent for the attack on the boy not 2½ years with 6 months for the common assault concurrent.

See also MANSLAUGHTER – *Domestic (Children)*

Cruelty to children – ABH

41.11   Triable either way. On indictment maximum sentence 5 years. Summary maximum 6 months or £5,000

R v Burrows [1998] 2 Cr App Rep (S) 407. The defendant was convicted of ABH and cruelty to a child. The victim aged 10, said that while his father was away the defendant, his stepmother made him stay in his bedroom doing lines, (this was the cruelty count). When he was asleep she woke him and accused him of getting out of bed. She struck him with a slipper on both ears a number of times. She also beat him on the buttocks and thighs. The next day his teacher saw significant bruising. A doctor found extensive bruising. The defendant denied striking him and said he had made the allegations up. She was 47 with no previous convictions and described as inadequate. **12 months** and 3 months concurrent not 18 months on each concurrent.

R v Smith [1999] 2 Cr App Rep (S) 126. The defendant who had two children pleaded guilty to ABH on a 4-year-old child of his partner with whom he lived. He and his partner went out leaving the children, three of her sister's children and another child with a babysitter. The children were staying the night. After arriving home from a party and talking to her sister, the babysitter they decided to wake up the boy who was asleep to tell him he had been naughty while they were out. He started crying. The other children woke up and the partner and the babysitter left leaving him to look after a 'crisis'. The victim was told by the defendant who was intoxicated to come downstairs and he struck him in the face more than once causing extensive bruising and a cut lip. The defendant was of good character. **4 months** not 6.

R v Rayson [2000] 2 Cr App Rep (S) 317. The defendant made a late guilty plea to ABH. He lived with his girlfriend and her 18-month-old son. She went to visit a friend leaving the son in his care. He rang her to say he had accidentally dropped the son. She came home and saw the son's eye was swollen and bruised. The son was taken to hospital and the defendant repeatedly apologised for dropping him. The hospital found extensive bruising to the left side of the face from the ear to below the jawbone. On the right side there was bruising to the cheek and jawbone. On his forearm there were a collection of tiny petechial (red spots) on the forearm. The injuries to the left side indicated the son had been struck at least twice with considerable force by an adult with an open hand. A similar blow was struck to the right side. The forearm bruising could have arisen from handling or gripping during the assault. The defendant was 34 and of good character and said it was a single loss of temper. Held. Because of the authorities **6 months** not 18.

R v O'Gorman [1999] 2 Cr App Rep (S) 280. The defendant pleaded guilty at the Magistrates' Court to ABH and cruelty to a child. After drinking, the defendant committed a prolonged and fierce attack on his co-habitee's 8-year-old son lasting on and off for about 2 hours only stopping when his co-habitee returned home. He punched him, threw him across the room and put his head inside the toilet basin and flushed the toilet. The doctor found multiple areas of swelling, recent bruises on the head, face, jaw, lips, chin, and upper limbs. They were consistent with repeated forceful blows. The defendant admitted the offences in interview and expressed regret. He had one conviction in 1987 for ABH on a woman for which he was fined. Held. Anyone who uses violence of this nature over a prolonged period must expect a substantial period of imprisonment. Because of the very early pleas **21 months** not 2½ years concurrent on each, concurrent to 6 months for common assault on his co-habitee.

R v Dodgson [2001] 1 Cr App Rep (S) 291. The defendant pleaded guilty to ABH on the son of his co-habitee. When the mother returned she found extensive bruising to the boy's face measuring 10 cms by 7 cms and bruising to an ear. A doctor said the bruising was caused by several blows using a considerable degree of force. The defendant pleaded guilty on the basis of striking the boy twice. He said he was angry the boy had wet himself. Earlier he had said the injuries were an accident. He had been drinking and was remorseful. He was of good character with an employer's reference. The boy recovered quite quickly. The judge said there was substantial force used and it was an extremely dangerous thing to do. Held. It was an isolated incident. **3 months** not 6.

See also **ABH**

Cruelty to children – Offences Against the Person Act 1861, s 18

41.12   Indictable only. Maximum sentence life imprisonment.

A-G's Reference (No 34 of 2000) [2001] 1 Cr App Rep (S) 359. The defendant was convicted of GBH with intent. He pleaded guilty to s 20 GBH which was not accepted. The defendant was left in charge of his 5-month-old child while the mother went to do evening work. She returned home about 1½ hours later and noticed the baby's condition was not normal. A doctor was called and the baby was taken to hospital. She was found to have bruising to the head with subdural haemorrhage, extensive retinal haemorrhages to both eyes, cerebral contusion and soft tissue injury of the cervical spine. There was also severe brain injury (which was irreparable) and whiplash injury to the neck. The defendant had no convictions. He was not frank about how the injuries were caused. However, it was said to be an isolated incident by a decent and hard working man. Held. The sentencing bracket for an isolated incident by a man of good character following a trial was **4 to 5 years**. Taking it was a reference **3½ years** not 2½.

R v Murray [2001] EWCA Crim 1250, [2002] 1 Cr App Rep (S) 168. The defendant was convicted of GBH with intent. He had lived with the victim aged 2 years and 3 months and her mother for about 3½ months. One evening the mother went to buy a takeaway meal leaving the child asleep in her bedroom. Neighbours heard cries from the child for much if not most of the 15 to 20 minutes the mother was away suggesting the attack was sustained over most of the period. When the mother returned he put on a convincing performance that he had heard a scream and found the baby had fallen out of her cot. She had several discrete bruises to her face indicating a number of blows. The inside of her mouth and her frenulum was cut. Two different objects had also struck her. One might have been a belt and the other a shoe. When the mother returned the defendant was wearing only one shoe. There were injuries to her head, which indicated she had been struck by a hard surface, which was textured like the wallpaper in the bedroom. There was a long fracture to her occipital bone at the back of the head. For that an extremely severe blow would be required. There was retinal haemorrhage in one eye. The injuries could have led to the most serious consequences but she made a complete recovery although she remained withdrawn and timid which she wasn't before. He and the mother were arrested and he maintained his story. He was 25 and had been discharged from the army for a number of disciplinary incidents. There was a conviction for ABH and the psychiatrist said he was egocentric. Held. He had trouble controlling his temper. **8 years** not 10.

See also **OFFENCES AGAINST THE PERSON ACT 1861, S 18**

Cruelty to children – Offences Against the Person Act 1861, s 20

41.13 Triable either way. On indictment maximum sentence 5 years. Summary maximum 6 months or £5,000

Guideline remarks

41.14 *R v Durkin* (1989) 11 Cr App Rep (S) 313 – LCJ. The defendant pleaded guilty to a s 20 offence on a boy aged 19½ months. Held. These cases are among the most difficult a judge has to deal with. First, it is necessary to punish. Secondly, it is necessary to provide some form of expiation[1] of the offence for the defendant. Thirdly, it is necessary to satisfy the public conscience. Fourthly, it is necessary to deter others by making it clear this behaviour will result in condign punishment.

1 This means atonement.

Cases

41.15 *R v JH* [2000] 1 Cr App Rep (S) 551. The defendant pleaded guilty at the Magistrates' Court to s 20. The defendant and his wife took their nearly 3-month-old baby to hospital because he was vomiting. The defendant said he had tripped and knocked the baby's head against a door frame and that had occurred before some weeks earlier. Two days later the baby was re-admitted with an unusually large head. A 1 cm bruise was found above the eyebrow with a 5 mms bruise nearby. There was a fracture of the crown bones of the skull resulting in a subdural bleed. A brain scan showed a degree of brain atrophy (wasting of part of it). This might result in learning difficulties in the long term. The mother asked the police and social services to be informed as the defendant had admitted to her he had shaken the baby. When arrested he said he was sorry for what he had done and said his wife had no part in it. In interview he said the baby cried for prolonged periods and he was in pain after an in-growing toenail had been removed. He was agitated and distressed and had shaken the baby and lost his grip. The child had fallen and hit his head on the floor. The child screamed and vomited. His earlier account was false because he was scared. He was 24. His pre-sentence report noted remorse but poor co-operation with the professionals. Another report said he needed therapeutic intervention to address his depressive tendencies. The psychiatric report said he was of low intellectual ability with poor anger control. All the factors and poor verbal skills compromised his parenting ability. He was a risk to his son unless supervised. Treatment and probation was suggested. **2 years** not 4.

R v Busby [2001] 1 Cr App Rep (S) 454. The defendant pleaded guilty to s 20. A s 18 charge was left on the file. In November, his wife had his very premature triplets. They remained in hospital for some time. In February he was in charge of one of them while his wife was asleep. She rang the emergency services to say the child had stopped breathing. When asked he said he had fallen asleep and she was not breathing. The child was taken to hospital and found to have a large scull fracture and sheering to the brain at the site of the fracture and deep in the brain. The child suffered severe and irreversible brain damage. When interviewed the defendant said the child had lurched backwards and fell hitting her head on the coffee table. He then settled her and he fell asleep. The plea was on the basis of reckless or grossly negligent conduct. He had one previous conviction for assaulting a child which involved hitting the son of a former partner with a slipper. He had separated from his wife and expressed extreme remorse. **2½ years** not 4 because of the plea and the basis of plea.

R v Brown [2001] 2 Cr App Rep (S) 83. The defendant was convicted of s 20 GBH and cruelty to a child and acquitted of s 18. The defendant and his wife had two children. One was then aged 16 months and the other, the victim was 6 weeks old. The defendant was left alone with them and when the wife called him at about 1pm he said the baby was unwell and he was about to call an ambulance. It was agreed he would take the baby to her and then they both took the baby to hospital. The hospital discovered subdural blood over both cerebral hemispheres and a fracture of the femur. The fracture was the result of tractional forces such as pulling or twisting when the torso was violently shaken. The brain injury was consistent with this. The prosecution case for the cruelty count was that the baby was distressed and he did not assist him. When sentence was passed there was still general retardation of development of the baby. The defendant was 28 and of good character with letters in support. Held. **3 years** was at the upper end of the bracket for se 20 and reflected the mitigation. (The cruelty count was 1 year concurrent.)

See also OFFENCES AGAINST THE PERSON ACT 1861, S 20

CULTIVATION OF CANNABIS

See CANNABIS – **Cannabis, cultivation of/production of**

CURRENCY

See COUNTERFEITING CURRENCY

42   CUSTODY, DISCOUNT FOR TIME SPENT IN

42.1   Criminal Justice Act 1967, s 67 due to be replaced by the Powers of the Criminal Courts (Sentencing) Act 2000, ss 87 and 88.

Bail hostels
42.2   *R v Watson* [2000] 2 Cr App Rep (S) 301. The defendant was released on bail with a condition he reside at a bail hostel. He was not permitted to go into the garden or leave except when supervised. He only left to collect his benefit. He was there 11 months before sentence. For 5 months he had been tagged. Held. A Bail Hostel was not to be equated with imprisonment. However, the loss of liberty should be taken into account. More credit for that should have been given.

Defendant on remand but serving a sentence for an offence which is later quashed
42.3   *R v Roberts* [2000] 1 Cr App Rep (S) 569. The defendant was remanded in custody for drugs offences. Eighteen days later he was sentenced at the Magistrates' Court to 5 months' imprisonment. After he had served his sentence the Crown Court sentenced him to 42 months for the drugs offences. Later a different Crown Court quashed the sentence of 5 months and substituted a conditional discharge. Held. The **42 months** was a perfectly proper sentence. Considering *R v Governor of Wandsworth Prison, ex p Sorhaindo* [1999] 4 LS Gaz R 38 it would be appropriate to reduce the sentence by 5 months.

Detention and training orders
42.4   Powers of Criminal Courts (Sentencing) Act 2000, s 101(8).   In determining the term of a detention order for an offence, the court shall take into account any period for which the offender has been remanded in custody in connection with the offence, or any other offence the charge for which was founded on the same facts or evidence.

R v Ganley [2001] 1 Cr App Rep (S) 60. Time spent in custody on remand will not be deducted from a period to be served under a detention and training order. It has to be taken into account.

R v Inner London Crown Court, ex p I [2000] All ER (D) 612. The defendant had spent less than 24 hours in custody. Held. The duty under [what is now s 101(8)] is to take account of the time spent. It is not to reflect inevitable time spent and in some specific way in the sentence passed.

R v B [2001] 1 Cr App Rep (S) 303. The defendant had spent 3½ months in custody. The defence asked for twice the time spent in custody to be deducted from the sentence. The judge refused to do so. He passed a sentence which took into account of all the factors. Held. Taking into account the period in custody or secure accommodation for the purposes of [what is now s 101(8)] does not involve a 1 to 1, day for day or month for month, reduction in sentence let alone a 2 to 1 reduction. The reason for that is that the periods to which the court is entitled to sentence a young defendant to detention and training orders are specified in blocks and deducting precise amounts of time is in consistent with that provision. Doubling up is not available.

R v Inner London Crown Court, ex p N and S [2001] 1 Cr App Rep (S) 323. The defendants had spent 3 days in custody. Held. I would not regard it as appropriate or desirable that any precise reflection should be sought to be given, in making a detention and training order, of a day or two. It is impossible to fine tune by reference to a day or two the sentence which is appropriate.

R v Fieldhouse and Watts [2001] 1 Cr App Rep (S) 361. No rule of general application can be devised to cover the infinitely various situations which may arise. However, the proper approach can perhaps best be illustrated by taking by way of example, a defendant who has spent 4 weeks on remand, which is the equivalent of a 2 month term. The court is likely to take such a period into account in different ways according to the length of the detention and training order which initially seems appropriate. If that period is 4 months, the court may conclude a non-custodial sentence is appropriate. If that period is 6, 8, 10 or 12 months, the court is likely to impose 4, 6, 8 or 10 months respectively. If that period is 18 or 24 months, the court may well conclude that no reduction can properly be made, although the court will of course bear in mind for juveniles the continuing importance of limiting the period in custody to the minimum necessary. The observations to this effect in *R v Mills* [1998] 2 Cr App Rep (S) 128 at 131 still hold good. For those offenders for whom long-term detention under [what is now the Powers of the Criminal Courts (Sentencing) Act 2000, s 91] might otherwise be appropriate, a detention and training order of 24 months may be a proper sentence even on a plea of guilty and even when a significant period has been spent in custody. The weekend spent in custody in this case could not sensibly be reflected in the sentence.

R v Elsmore [2001] EWCA Crim 943, [2001] 2 Cr App Rep (S) 461. The sentence further reduced. (Little or no new matters of principle stated.)

R v Pitt [2001] EWCA Crim 1295, [2002] 1 Cr App Rep (S) 195. The defendant then aged 17 pleaded guilty to unlawful wounding and received 18 months. He had spent 4 months awaiting trial. The maximum was 24 months. Held. Taking the plea and the 4 months into account 15 months was appropriate. That wasn't available, as it was either 18 or 12 months. This Act puts the courts in a straitjacket. Therefore **12 months** substituted.

See also *R v March* [2002] EWCA Crim 551, [2002] 2 Cr App Rep (S) 448

Article about see Archbold News 17 March 2000.

Drug treatment centre

42.5   See *R v Armstrong* [2002] EWCA Crim 441, [2002] 2 Cr App Rep (S) 396.

Extradition, time in custody awaiting

42.6   Criminal Justice Act 1991, s 47(2). If, in the case of an extradited prisoner, the court by which he was sentenced so ordered, s 67 of the 1967 Act (computations of sentences of imprisonment) shall have effect in relation to him as if a period specified in the order were a relevant period for the purposes of that section. (Repealed and awaiting commencement order.)

R v De Simone [2000] 2 Cr App Rep (S) 332. The defendant absconded during his trial. He was convicted and sentenced in his absence to 6 years. He was arrested in Switzerland and spent 10 months in custody awaiting extradition. Held. The Act presupposes the extradition took place before sentence. Here it did not. Sentence reduced accordingly.

Criminal Justice Act 1991, s 47(2). New sub-section inserted by the Crime and Disorder Act 1998, s 119 and Sch 8, para 90 itself amended by the Powers of the Criminal Courts Act (Sentencing) Act 2000, s 165(1) and Sch 9, para 202(3) to make all days served automatically count. (Awaiting commencement order.)

R v Andre and Burton [2002] 1 Cr App Rep (S) 98. The defendants were extradited from New Zealand. The judge did not order all days to be deducted. Held. (Old law) He was entitled to do that on the facts of the case.

Local authority accommodation

42.7   Criminal Justice Act 1967, s 67(1A)(c). The relevant period means any period. . . he was remanded or committed to local authority accommodation . . . under section 23 of the Children and Young Persons Act 1969 or section 37 of the Magistrates' Court Act 1980 and in accommodation provided for the purposes of restricting liberty.

R v Secretary of State for the Home Office, ex p A [2000] 2 Cr App Rep (S) 263 – House of Lords. Held. *R v Collins* (1994) 16 Cr App Rep (S) 156 was wrongly decided. The time is not deducted automatically. A's position was closer to a person on bail than in custody. If an allowance was to be made it should be made by the sentencing court and not by an administrative officer of an institution.

Powers of the Criminal Courts (Sentencing) Act 2000, s 88(1)(c).Remanded in custody means, remanded or committed to local authority accommodation under section 23 of the Children and Young Persons Act 1969 and placed in secure accommodation [or detained in a secure training centre pursuant to arrangements under subsection (7A) of that section]. The words in brackets are added by the Criminal Justice and Police Act 2001. Section 88 is not yet in force and adds 'kept in secure accommodation' so affirming the decision in *ex pe A* in the House of Lords.

See also GUILTY PLEA, DISCOUNT FOR

43   DANGEROUS DRIVING

43.1   Road Traffic Act 1988, s 2

Triable either way. On indictment maximum sentence 2 years. Summary maximum 6 months or £5,000. Minimum disqualification 1 year. 3–11 penalty points. The defendant must be disqualified till he/she passes an extended driving test.

Sentencing trends. Parliament is likely to increase the maximum to 5 years to enable longer sentences to be passed in cases of very bad driving which cause very serious injures by people with bad similar previous convictions.

Crown Court statistics England and Wales[1] – Crown Court – Males 21+ – Dangerous driving

43.2

Year	Plea	Total Numbers sentenced	Type of sentence%					Average length of custody (months)
			Discharge	Fine	Community sentence	Suspended sentence	Custody	
2000	Guilty	726	1%	3%	28%	2%	65%	9.8
	Not guilty	143	1%	22%	26%	1%	49%	10.1

1 Excluding committals for sentence. Source: Crime and Criminal Justice Unit, Home Office Ref: IOS416-02.

Guideline cases

43.3 Some assistance can be found in DEATH BY DANGEROUS DRIVING, CAUSING – *Guidelines*

Magistrates' Court Sentencing Guidelines September 2000

43.4 Entry point. Are Magistrates' sentencing powers appropriate? Consider the impact on the victim. Examples of aggravating factors for the offence are avoiding detection or apprehension, competitive driving, racing or showing off, disregard of warnings eg from passengers or others in the vicinity, evidence of alcohol or drugs, excessive speed, prolonged, persistent, deliberate bad driving, serious risk and using a hand-held mobile telephone. Examples of mitigating factors for the offence are emergency, single incident and speed not excessive. Examples of mitigation are co-operation with the police, voluntary compensation and genuine remorse. Give reasons if not awarding compensation.

For details about the guidelines see MAGISTRATES' COURT SENTENCING GUIDELINES at page 331.

Alcohol, driving under the influence – 71 to 100ug in breath or equivalent

43.5 *R v Friend* [1998] 1 Cr App Rep (S) 163. The defendant pleaded guilty to dangerous driving and no insurance at the Magistrates' Court. The defendant ate and drank with friends and drove home in his van. His insurance had lapsed in the previous month. He was considerably affected by drink and drugs and was 2½ times over the limit and had taken diazepam. He failed to negotiate a left hand bend, crossed the central road markings and collided with an oncoming car. Both cars were very extensively damaged. The other driver received a 5″ cut to his forehead, whiplash injuries and bruising. The defendant told the police he was not the driver. He was 49 and from 1990 onwards had convictions for speeding, failing to provide a specimen, failing to report and failing to stop. He was on bail for and later fined and disqualified for 4 years for excess alcohol. Held. He is a menace to other road users. The photographs are chilling. Balancing the factors **15 months** was entirely appropriate. The £400 fine for the no insurance will be quashed because he has no money.

R v Nichols [1998] 2 Cr App Rep (S) 296. The defendant was convicted of dangerous driving. The defendant drifted from lane to lane on a three lane dual carriageway causing one driver to break heavily. Eventually he drifted into a barrier on the near side of the road of a two lane stretch and stopped. With smoke coming from the tyre and a tyre burst, he reversed at speed into the nearside lane and partly into the offside lane.

He drove down the road and into a layby where he got out and looked at his vehicle. Then he suddenly drove off again causing other drivers to avoid him. He drove with sparks coming from his nearside wheels at about 50 mph. Eventually he stopped. Police found that the car had extensive damage to the front. The wheel of the tyre that burst had been moved backwards. The steering and suspension was also damaged. Another tyre was deflated. His breath alcohol reading was 78ug. The expert couldn't dispute that the tyre might have burst before the impact. The defendant was now aged 40 and treated as of good character. He was hard working and his two youngest children were in poor health. The youngest was about to have an operation. There was a risk that his company which employed 26 people could collapse. Solicitors acting for Customs confirmed the company was in serious financial difficulties. He received 9 months and since then seven engineers and two apprentices had lost their jobs. Held. He had showed a singular lack of control which arose from excessive consumption of alcohol. With a great deal of hesitation the company mitigation means the sentence should be **6 months** not 9.

Alcohol or drugs charge, sentences should be concurrent with dangerous driving

43.6   *R v King* [2000] 1 Cr App Rep (S) 105. As the dangerous driving arose out of the fact drugs were taken the sentences should be concurrent. See *HGV drivers*

Asleep or being drowsy, driver is

43.7   *R v King* [2000] 1 Cr App Rep (S) 105. See *HGV drivers*

Death results

43.8   As the court is able to consider the victim's injuries it would be odd if the court could not take into account the ultimate injury, death. However, if there is no conviction for causing death by dangerous driving the defendant should not be sentenced for a more serious offence for which he has not been convicted.

R v Simmonds [1999] 2 Cr App Rep (S) 218. The defendant was indicted with causing death by dangerous driving. His plea to *careless driving* was accepted and no evidence was offered for the causing death count. The defence argued it was wrong to take into account the death caused. Held. Considering the statutory changes that have taken place since *R v Krawec* (1984) 6 Cr App Rep (S) 367 we find the concept of a road traffic offence in which the sentencing court is obliged to disregard the fact that a death has been caused as wholly anomalous. The current approach is reflected in *A-G's Reference (No 66 of 1996)* [1998] 1 Cr App Rep (S) 16 (a case of causing death by careless driving having consumed alcohol) 'It is nonetheless the duty of the judge, to judge cases dispassionately and to do its best to reach the appropriate penalty, taking account of all the relevant circumstances.' Whether sentencing courts should take into account criminality alone or both the criminality and the consequences of an offence – and in the latter event in what proportions, is ultimately a question of choice and policy. *Krawec* was clearly valid in its context and at its time, but we do not see it as of assistance to sentencing courts in the different context of today. The judge was entitled to bear in mind the death.

See also CARELESS DRIVING – *Death results*

Disqualification, for how long?

43.9   *R v Barker* [1999] 1 Cr App Rep (S) 71. The defendant pleaded guilty to dangerous driving. He drove a van on a country road in the dark. He knew the road well and was in an aggressive hurry. He drove too close to the car in front and the driver of the car gave two warnings by braking which he ignored. When the car and a lorry which was in front stopped to let an oncoming lorry pass at a narrow bridge he pulled out to overtake. He had to brake and his brakes screeched. He then had to reverse his van. He later overtook the car and the lorry and was behind a Range Rover and another lorry. He tried to overtake them both without being able see over a rise in the road. He said he was relying on not being able to see any vehicle headlights in front. However, a driver behind him did see oncoming vehicle lights. The van hit an oncoming motorcycle. The car driver described the defendant's driving as, 'outrageous and dangerous'. The motorcyclist who was driving at a moderate speed was very seriously injured. He was permanently disabled and is now paraplegic. The defendant was 30 with a drink/drive conviction 12 years before, a speeding conviction in 1993, which caused totting up disqualification and a no insurance conviction in 1995. Held. It was a sustained piece of bad driving and it caused very serious injury. He had ignored the brake light warnings and the warning of the incident at the bridge. The bridge incident and the accident were very similar. The maximum is 2 years and the judge must have started at about 20 months before the deduction for the plea. **16 months** was severe but not manifestly excessive. 4 years' not 6 years' disqualification.

R v Hicks [1999] 1 Cr App Rep (S) 228. The defendant pleaded guilty at the first opportunity to dangerous driving. When 19, he drove with friends at considerable speed in a 30 mph area and where there were traffic calming measures. He said he was trying to keep up with the car he was following. At a bend, which was marked with a slow sign, he did not slow down and lost control of the car. The car skidded across the carriageway, uprooted a tree and struck two teenage girls who were walking on the pavement. After the car had crashed through a wooden fence he did not try to leave the scene. It was estimated that the car was travelling at 71 mph. One girl was thrown into the air but fortunately only received cuts and bruises and a broken thumb. The other girl was trapped under the car, which went over her. She had a fractured femur and severe bruising. She was on crutches for 8 months. Her work and social life had been adversely affected. A witness thought he was going to overtake the car he was following. The defendant worked in the information technology industry and had started a BSc course in computer science. He was due to take his exams shortly. His employers spoke highly of him. He had had his licence for just over a year and had a conviction for doing 50 mph in a 30 mph area. He expressed remorse. The judge said the lowest sentence was 12 months which he reduced to **8 months** detention for the plea. Held. The judge was right to describe it as a dreadful piece of driving. The sentence was entirely appropriate. Because of his age and his employment needs 3 years' not 5 years' disqualification.

R v King [2000] 1 Cr App Rep (S) 105. 5 years appropriate here. See *HGV drivers*

R v Burman [2000] 2 Cr App Rep (S) 3. The defendant pleaded guilty at the first opportunity to dangerous driving. The victim was driving his car on a road with a 30 mph limit with his wife the other victim. He saw two cars driving at speed. The defendant's speed was estimated at 59 mph. The defendant clipped the kerb and lost control of his car, which collided with the victim's car. The victims had to be cut from their car and both had fractured sternums and bruising to the chest. The wife also had a broken clavicle. Both suffered from shock. The defendant had three fractured ribs. The court did not sentence him on the basis he was racing. He was 27 and his driving record was, 'not bad.' He had lost his business and his job as a result. His marriage was now over. He expressed remorse at the time and the likelihood of re-offending was assessed as low. He was sentenced to 18 months. Held. It was a bad case. Taking into account the 2 year maximum sentence the starting point was 18 months which we reduce to **12 months** for the plea. We reduce the disqualification from 4 to 3 years because a young man needs a licence to obtain suitable employment.

Drugs, when under the influence of

43.10   *R v King* [2000] 1 Cr App Rep (S) 105. See *HGV drivers*

HGV drivers

43.11   *R v King* [2000] 1 Cr App Rep (S) 105. The defendant pleaded guilty to dangerous driving and driving whilst unfit through drink or drugs at the Magistrates' Court. At 6.30am, the defendant was seen to drive his 7.5 tonne lorry in an erratic manner for some time. He drove into a layby and hit a parked car. The driver had just gone back into his car and was thrown into the air. The defendant stopped and went to the car. The defendant was certified unfit at the police station. He was unsteady on his feet and drowsy. He had traces of diazepam and barbiturates in his blood. Both could cause drowsiness. A combination would increase that effect. The defendant said he had taken five or six doses of diazepam in the previous 24 hours and he had been out the previous night and had not slept since 10am the previous day. The victim suffered extensive injuries to his shoulder and upper arm. He had a fracture at the base of his spine. He also suffered head injuries, which caused memory loss and other disabilities. He made a good recovery from his physical injuries but it was uncertain whether he had recovered from the head injuries. The defendant's last conviction was for disqualified driving and he was sent to prison for 3 months. The judge passed the maximum sentence of 2 years because he said the defendant had 'been caught red-handed' and the 6 month maximum for drink/drive and made the sentences consecutive. He was disqualified for 5 years. Held. This was a very serious case of dangerous driving made more serious by the drug taking. The drugs could have had a very grave impact on other road users. However, the consecutive sentences were wrong in principle because the dangerous driving arose out of the fact that drugs had been taken. **18 months** and 4 months concurrent substituted. The 5 years' disqualification was correct.

Overtaking

43.12   *R v Barker* [1999] 1 Cr App Rep (S) 71. The defendant pleaded guilty to dangerous driving. He drove a van on a country road in the dark. He knew the road well and was in an aggressive hurry. He drove too close to the car in front and the driver of the car gave two warnings by braking which he ignored. When the car and a lorry which was in front stopped to let an oncoming lorry pass at a narrow bridge he pulled out to overtake. He had to brake and his brakes screeched. He then had to reverse his van. He later overtook the car and the lorry and was behind a Range Rover and another lorry. He tried to overtake them both without being able see over a rise in the road. He said he was relying on not being able see to any vehicle headlights in front. However, a driver behind him did see oncoming vehicle lights. The van hit an oncoming motorcycle. The car driver described the defendant's driving as, 'outrageous and dangerous'. The motorcyclist who was driving at a moderate speed was very seriously injured. He was permanently disabled and is now paraplegic. The defendant was 30 with a drink/drive conviction 12 years before, a speeding conviction in 1993, which caused totting up disqualification and a no insurance conviction in 1995. Held. It was a sustained piece of bad driving and it caused very serious injury. He had ignored the brake light warnings and the warning of the incident at the bridge. The bridge incident and the accident were very similar. The maximum is 2 years and the judge must have started at about 20 months before the deduction for the plea. **16 months** was severe but not manifestly excessive. 4 years' not 6 years' disqualification.

R v Smith [2002] 2 Cr App Rep (S) 71. The defendant was convicted of dangerous driving. He drove his lorry laden with scrap iron and cars on a wet road in a 60 mph area. He approached a JCB digger at about 30 mph and overtook it on a blind bend without slowing down. The digger was travelling at about 15 mph. He collided head on with the victim who was driving her car at 40-45 mph in the opposite direction. With her was her 3yearold daughter strapped in the back. She tried to break and steer left but skidded on the damp road. Her face was covered in blood and the child was screaming. The front of her car was extensively damaged. The defendant kept approaching her and saying sorry. She had a broken leg, ankle, wrist, and lacerations to her face, scalp and leg. She suffered a whiplash injury and extensive bruising and swelling to her shoulder chest and stomach. She was in plaster for 10 weeks and the child suffered grazes and bruises. The sole cause of the accident was that he overtook on a blind bend. The defendant claimed the digger was indicating left at the time. He was 40 and of good character. The defendant suffered nightmares and had not driven for 6 months. Held. It was over a significant period he was on the wrong side of the road and he could have braked and returned to his side of the road. It was a bad case resulting in the most serious injuries. **4 months** was not manifestly excessive.

Police chases

43.13 *R v Scarley* [2001] 1 Cr App Rep (S) 86. The defendant pleaded guilty to dangerous driving and driving whilst disqualified. The defendant was on bail and disqualified from driving. Police were trying to arrest him for an assault. Police saw him in a car with his brothers. They followed him and lost him and then saw him driving towards them at speed. They had to take evasive action to avoid being hit. Two police cars blocked his path and he braked sharply but hit one of the cars. An officer suffered a whiplash injury, soreness and a headache. The defendant mounted the grass verge narrowly missing another officer. He drove on and abandoned the car and was arrested on foot. He was 36 with an appalling record. He had 157 offences on 40 occasions including violence and road traffic offences. The pre-sentence report said there was a high risk of re-offending. He was given the maximum sentence with no penalty for the other offence and the defence appealed because there was no discount for the plea of guilty. Held. There are exceptions to the rule that a guilty sentence results in a lesser sentence. First, being caught red-handed and having no practical defence to the charge *R v Rogers* (1991) 13 Cr App Rep (S) 80, *R v Landy* (1995) 16 Cr App Rep (S) 908, *R v Reay* [1993] RTR 189. Secondly, where there is a last minute tactical plea where there is a need to protect the public or where the charge was representative of a large number of offences, *R v Costen* (1989) 11 Cr App Rep (S) 182. The first example applies here. [The problem in these cases was the maximum sentence was clearly inadequate. It would be much better to have proper maximum sentences and a right to a discount, as having no defence does not always stop the defendant pleading not guilty. Alternatively there could have been a slightly lesser sentence and a consecutive sentence for the other offences.]

See also *R v Jones (Iain Mac)* [2002] EWCA Crim 414, [2002] 2 Cr App Rep (S) 412.

Police officers, traffic wardens, driving at

43.14 *R v Joseph* [2001] EWCA Crim 1195, [2002] 1 Cr App Rep (S) 74. The defendant was convicted of dangerous driving. He parked his jeep outside a bingo hall. When a parking attendant went across to issue a ticket he crossed the road and began a heated argument with him. Next he got in the vehicle turned the wheel towards the attendant and drove it at him. The attendant slid onto the bonnet and was carried for 150 yards. When the attendant got off the defendant drove away. The attendant received a cut finger and some pain to the back and ribs. He didn't require hospital treatment. The defendant surrendered but denied the offence. He was a man of good character who had built up a business. The judge said that those attendants, however unpopular motorists might find them to be, are carrying out an important public duty. They deserve the protection of the courts. Those that drive at them will receive substantial periods of custody as a deterrent to others. Held. We endorse the judge's comments. As the maximum is 2 years and that as a result of this his business had gone into bankruptcy **10 months** not 15. The 2 years' disqualification to remain.

Old case. *R v Charlton* (1994) 16 Cr App Rep (S) 703.

Racing, competitive driving etc

43.15   *R v Arthur* [2001] EWCA Crim 174, [2001] 2 Cr App Rep (S) 316. The defendant was tried for causing death by dangerous driving. At the close of the prosecution case the judge said there was no case to answer. The defendant then pleaded guilty to dangerous driving. The defendant and the victim raced their cars and the victim died when her car left the road at a bend. The count of causing death failed because the judge ruled that the prosecution could only rely on the final piece of driving. The defendant had driven at dangerous speeds on minor roads and raced through a town at 50–60 mph in a 30 mph area. The two cars were on the wrong side of the road and almost bumper to bumper. The defendant was 25 with convictions for dangerous driving, threatening behaviour, theft and criminal damage. The judge said it was very dangerous driving. He identified racing, excessive speed, prolonged course of driving, a very real danger to others and the death as aggravating factors. Held. The judge was entitled to make the findings he did. **20 months** was a severe sentence but not manifestly excessive.

Speeding

43.16   *R v Hicks* [1999] 1 Cr App Rep (S) 228. The defendant pleaded guilty at the first opportunity to dangerous driving. When 19, he drove with friends at considerable speed in a 30 mph area and where there were traffic calming measures. He said he was trying to keep up with the car he was following. At a bend, which was marked with a slow sign, he did not slow down and lost control of the car. The car skidded across the carriageway, uprooted a tree and struck two teenage girls who were walking on the pavement. After the car had crashed through a wooden fence he did not try to leave the scene. It was estimated that the car was travelling at 71 mph. One girl was thrown into the air but fortunately only received cuts and bruises and a broken thumb. The other girl was trapped under the car, which went over her. She had a fractured femur and severe bruising. She was on crutches for 8 months. Her work and social life had been adversely affected. A witness thought he was going to overtake the car he was following. The defendant worked in the information technology industry and had started a BSc course in computer science. He was due to take his exams shortly. His employers spoke highly of him. He had had his licence for just over a year and had a conviction for doing 50 mph in a 30 mph area. He expressed remorse. The judge said the lowest sentence was 12 months which he reduced to **8 months** detention for the plea. Held. The judge was right to describe it as a dreadful piece of driving. The sentence was entirely appropriate. Because of his age and his employment needs 3 years' not 5 years' disqualification.

R v Howells Re Ashby [1999] 1 Cr App Rep (S) 335 at 339 – LCJ. The defendant pleaded guilty to dangerous driving and driving with no insurance. The defendant produced some documents to the police about a car. He said he had just bought it. He said he had not driven it because he had had far too much to drink. The officers remained in the vicinity and saw him drive off in it. They followed the car and to start with it was driven slowly. When the police put on their blue light it accelerated to speeds of 60 mph. It drove across two 'Give way' signs and was chased for about a mile when the police lost it. The car was found abandoned nearby. The defendant was arrested and was not breath tested. However, he denied driving the car but admitted drinking a bottle of wine. He was 30 with a substantial record including motoring offences. He had been sent to prison before but had no dangerous driving convictions. Held. The judge was right to recognise the danger he had presented to other road users and that the offence was aggravated by drink. **4 months** was entirely appropriate.

R v Burman [2000] 2 Cr App Rep (S) 3. The defendant pleaded guilty at the first opportunity to dangerous driving. The victim was driving his car on a road with a 30 mph limit with his wife the other victim. He saw two cars driving at speed. The defendant's speed was estimated at 59 mph. The defendant clipped the kerb and lost control of his car, which collided with the victim's car. The victims had to be cut from their car and both had fractured sternums and bruising to the chest. The wife also had a broken clavicle. Both suffered from shock. The defendant had three fractured ribs. The court did not sentence him on the basis he was racing. He was 27 and his driving record was, 'not bad.' He had lost his business and his job as a result. His marriage was now over. He expressed remorse at the time and the likelihood of re-offending was assessed as low. He was sentenced to 18 months. Held. It was a bad case. Taking into account the 2 year maximum sentence the starting point was 18 months which we reduce to **12 months** for the plea. We reduce the disqualification from 4 to 3 years.

Victim(s) seriously injured

43.17   *R v Stokes* [1998] 1 Cr App Rep (S) 282. The defendant was convicted of dangerous driving. The defendant was late for work and was driving at about 30 mph in a 30 mph area. He drove across a pelican crossing when the lights were red and hit two 9-year-old twins who had just stepped out and were half-way across the lane. They were thrown in the air and suffered multiple injuries. The defendant stopped and was clearly shocked. One of the twins was in hospital for nearly a month and still suffered from anxiety. The other suffered from a fractured pelvis and was still suffering from dizziness and bladder problems. Their whole family was traumatised. The defendant was unable to drive afterwards and was on tranquilisers. He was 25 and of good character with references. The judge described him as a model citizen. He accepted it was careless driving but denied it was dangerous. Held. The criminality of the driving itself was very much at the bottom of the scale. The case was grave because of the injuries. **8 months** not 12 and 2 years' disqualification not 3.

R v Barker [1999] 1 Cr App Rep (S) 71. The defendant pleaded guilty to dangerous driving. He drove a van on a country road in the dark. He knew the road well and was in an aggressive hurry. He drove too close to the car in front and the driver of the car gave two warnings by braking which he ignored. When the car and a lorry which was in front stopped to let an oncoming lorry pass at a narrow bridge he pulled out to overtake. He had to brake and his brakes screeched. He then had to reverse his van. He later overtook the car and the lorry and was behind a Range Rover and another lorry. He tried to overtake them both without being able see over a rise in the road. He said he was relying on not being able see to any vehicle headlights in front. However, a driver behind him did see oncoming vehicle lights. The van hit an oncoming motorcycle. The car driver described the defendant's driving as, 'outrageous and dangerous'. The motorcyclist who was driving at a moderate speed was very seriously injured. He was permanently disabled and is now paraplegic. The defendant was 30 with a drink/drive conviction 12 years before, a speeding conviction in 1993, which caused totting up disqualification and a no insurance conviction in 1995. Held. It was a sustained piece of bad driving and it caused very serious injury. He had ignored the brake light warnings and the warning of the incident at the bridge. The bridge incident and the accident were very similar. The maximum is 2 years and the judge must have started at about 20 months before the deduction for the plea. **16 months** was severe but not manifestly excessive. 4 years' not 6 years' disqualification.

R v Hicks [1999] 1 Cr App Rep (S) 228. The defendant pleaded guilty at the first opportunity to dangerous driving. When 19, drove with friends at considerable speed in a 30 mph area and where there were traffic calming measures. He said he was trying to keep up with the car he was following. At a bend, which was marked with a slow sign, he did not slow down and lost control of the car. The car skidded across the carriageway, uprooted a tree and struck two teenage girls who were walking on the pavement. After the car had crashed through a wooden fence he did not try to leave the scene. It was estimated that the car was travelling at 71 mph. One girl was thrown into the air but fortunately only received cuts and bruises and a broken thumb. The other girl was trapped under the car, which went over her. She had a fractured femur and severe bruising. She was on crutches for 8 months. Her work and social life had been adversely affected. A witness thought he was going to overtake the car he was following. The defendant worked in the information technology industry and had started a BSc course in computer science. He was due to take his exams shortly. His employers spoke highly of him. He had had his licence for just over a year and had a conviction for doing 50 mph in a 30 mph area. He expressed remorse. The judge said the lowest sentence was 12 months which he reduced to **8 months** detention for the plea. Held. The judge was right to describe it as a dreadful piece of driving. The sentence was entirely appropriate. Because of his age and his employment needs 3 years' not 5 years' disqualification.

R v King [2000] 1 Cr App Rep (S) 105. See ***HGV drivers***

44 DEATH BY CARELESS DRIVING, CAUSING (WHEN UNDER THE INFLUENCE OF DRINK OR DRUGS OR AFTER FAILING TO PROVIDE A SPECIMEN)

44.1 Road Traffic Act 1988, s 3A

Indictable only. Maximum sentence 10 years. Minimum disqualification 2 years.

3–11 penalty points when the court finds special reasons. The defendant must be disqualified till he/she passes an extended driving test. Specified offence enabling defendant aged 14–17 to be detained[1].

Where a defendant has a conviction for driving while unfit, causing death under the influence of drink, driving with excess alcohol and failing to provide a specimen in previous 10 years' minimum disqualification is 3 years[2]. There is power to order reduced disqualification for attendance on courses[3].

1 Powers of the Criminal Courts (Sentencing) Act 2000, s 91(2)(a).
2 Road Traffic Offenders Act 1988, s 34(3).
3 Road Traffic Offenders Act 1988, s 34A.

Crown Court statistics England and Wales[1] – Crown Court – Males 21+ – Causing death by careless driving

44.2

Year	Plea	Total Numbers sentenced	Type of sentence%					Average length of custody (months)
			Discharge	Fine	Community sentence	Suspended sentence	Custody	
2000	Guilty	38	0%	0%	0%	11%	89%	38
	Not guilty	3	0%	0%	0%	0%	100%	53

1   Source: Crime and Criminal Justice Unit, Home Office Ref: IOS416-02.

Guideline cases and remarks

44.3   *A-G's Reference (Nos 24 and 45 of 1994)* (1995) 16 Cr App Rep (S) 583 at 586 – LCJ. This court is concerned primarily with the criminality of the person who has caused the death. The fact that the death is, of itself, a factor in contributing to the length of sentence which should be passed. But essentially we have to look at the cases in the light of the offender's criminality. The length of sentence will very much depend upon the aggravating and mitigating circumstances in the particular case, the extent of the carelessness or dangerousness, and the amount that the offender is over the limit in a case involving excess alcohol. Where an offender is not just over the limit, not even substantially over the limit, but 2½ to 3 times over the limit, the sentence which the court must pass is clearly a substantial one. It is insufficient excuse for failing to impose a sufficiently long sentence to look predominantly at the mitigating features and the remorse of the offender.

R v Cororan [1996] 1 Cr App Rep (S) 416 at 419 – LCJ. The defendant was convicted of causing death by careless driving after having consumed alcohol. Anyone who is driving with 2½ times the permitted alcohol limit must expect a substantial sentence.

R v Chippendale [1998] 1 Cr App Rep (S) 192. There is understandably grave concern about young men who have too much to drink and drive in the face of warnings and then kill. The court will have regard to the extent of the carelessness and the amount the defendant was over the limit. Personal elements of mitigation such as acute guilt feelings are not matters that should sound greatly in determining the proper sentence.

Alcohol – Guideline remarks

44.4   *A-G's Reference (Nos 14 and 24 of 1993)* (1994) 15 Cr App Rep (S) 640 – LCJ. Where a driver is over the limit and kills someone as a result of his careless driving a prison sentence will ordinarily be appropriate. In an exceptional case where the alcohol level is just over the border line and the carelessness is momentary, and there is strong mitigation, a non-custodial may be possible. But in other cases a prison sentence is required to punish the offender, to deter others from drinking and driving, and to reflect the public's abhorrence of deaths being caused by drivers with excess alcohol.

Alcohol level unknown but driver unfit

44.5   *A-G's Reference No 10 of 1997* [1998] 1 Cr App Rep (S) 147 – LCJ. The defendant pleaded guilty to causing death by careless driving when unfit through drink and aggravated vehicle-taking. A mother left her car on her driveway with a 'crook lock' attached and two boxes of beer in the boot. She went to Scotland with her husband and youngest son leaving her other son and a cousin at the house. Next day there were numerous visitors to the house and there was talk of taking the car. The defendant then 17 expressed reluctance to be involved. The radio and the beer were taken and the defendant and two others went to nearby woods and drank the beer. They came back and appeared drunk. The defendant drove the car with the other two at speed judged to be between 60 and 70 mph. The defendant lost control at a moderate left hand bend and the car left the road with no noise of skidding or brakes screeching. The car hit a tree and one passenger was killed. The car's speed near the accident was estimated to be between 70 and 90 mph. The speed limit was 60 mph but the greatest speed the bend could be negotiated was 50 mph. The road was dry. The defendant was unconscious for six days. The injury to his frontal lobe of the brain effected his personality. The defendant had a 'dis-social personality disorder.' One doctor said it was exacerbated by the accident and another said it was caused by it. He needed 12 weeks' observation and treatment in a specialist hospital. The judge sentenced him to probation and he was admitted to the hospital. It was not a success. The defendant was of good character. Held. The judge was correct to say 3 years was appropriate. We think 3–4 years if contested and 2–3 years if not. The 2 years since the offence, the injury, his plea and character are significant factors. **12 months** YOI substituted.

R v Roche [1999] 2 Cr App Rep (S) 105 – LCJ. The defendant pleaded guilty to causing death by careless driving when under the influence of drink. After 11pm he was driving his cousin after both had been in pubs. The weather was dry and the speed limit was 30 mph. He was driving in the region of 60 to 70 mph. He hit the kerb shortly after negotiating a bend and the car struck a telegraph pole and then a cast-iron post box. The car travelled through the air and partially demolished a bus shelter. His cousin died. The defendant was treated for a minor head injury and was arrested at the hospital. He declined to provide samples of blood or breath. He was subject to very severe stress at the time. The car was found to be defective but that had not contributed to the accident. He said he had had 7 or 8 pints of lager. The victim was not wearing a seat belt although he was. He was 27 and of good character. His re-offending risk was assessed as low and the accident had had a very severe effect on him. He was suffering from profound remorse. The defendant's parents were brother and sister of the victim's parents. The victim's mother treated the defendant almost as a son and had played a large part in bringing him up. The sentence of 4 years was delaying her grieving. Held. There is no room for the degree of indulgence which was shown in the past. Four years can be regarded as merciful. The injured party cannot dictate the sentence for vengeance or compassion. However, this is different and the court can be an instrument of compassion. **3 years** not 4.

Alcohol 36 to 70ug in breath or equivalent

44.6 *R v Ocego* [1998] 1 Cr App Rep (S) 408. The defendant pleaded guilty to careless driving after having consumed alcohol and perverting the course of justice. The defendant went to a party in public house. He left and gave a friend a lift in his pick-up truck. The victim and her husband were walking in single file on the edge of a country road facing the oncoming traffic. The defendant who was on the wrong side of the road hit the victim from behind. She died soon afterwards from severe head and neck injuries. He did not stop and dropped off the friend. He then took the truck to a field, doused it in petrol and set it alight. Six hours after he was arrested his blood/alcohol reading was 55mg. By backtracking the reading was estimated to be at the time of the accident between 113 and 200mg with a likely concentration of about 142mg (the equivalent of 62ug in the breath). He denied involvement in the accident. He was 25 and unemployed. He had convictions for violence, TDA and no insurance. He had served four prison sentences. Held. 6 years was entirely proper. The perverting sentence of 12 months should be concurrent not consecutive.

R v Stewart [1999] 2 Cr App Rep (S) 213. The defendant made a late plea to careless driving after having consumed alcohol. The defendant and a colleague who both worked at Heathrow airport took an unauthorised break and drove to a nearby football club. For 2½ hours they drank beer and then the defendant set off at about 6.30pm to drive the two of them back to work. He drove at speeds between 60–80 mph where there were limits of 40 or 50 mph. He also overtook and undertook other cars. When almost at the airport he was driving at nearly 50 in a 40 mph area on a slip road. A group of young people were crossing the road and he lost control of the car and hit a 13-year-old girl and her friend. He didn't stop and he abandoned the car when it broke down due to damage to it which was very substantial. The girl died and her friend suffered injuries of the utmost gravity. He suffered from multiple fractures and psychological trauma. He was in hospital for about 6 weeks and will suffer permanent and significant disability. The defendant was 1½ times over the limit when tested at 8pm. He accepted he required glasses to drive and was not wearing them. He was 35 and of good character. At work he was a team leader preparing aircraft. He had suffered threats and had had to sell his house and move his family. Held. The judge took into account the plea and the threats are not matters which can affect the sentence. The aggravating features were very serious and **5 years** was correct.

R v Thompson [2000] 1 Cr App Rep (S) 85. The defendant was convicted of causing death by careless driving after having consumed alcohol. The victim had spent the evening drinking with friends. They were looking for a minicab. One friend was on one side of the road negotiating with the driver of a cab, which had stopped at a red light. The lights changed and the victim who was wearing dark clothing and the other friend started to cross the road to join the one talking to cab driver. The victim was struck by the defendant's car and thrown into the air. He had major head injuries and died. The friend was also hit. The car on analysis seemed to have been travelling at 23 mph. The defendant remained at the scene and his blood alcohol level was 52mg. The limit is 35. An expert said the victim would have had about 3 seconds to react to the pedestrian and with dark clothing 1.4 seconds. The defendant said in interview he had overtaken a stationary bus and slowed down for the lights. As he approached them they changed and he saw two or three people in front. A witness who was a very experience car driver said the two leapt across very quickly. He said the pedestrians were the cause and the driver could not have done much about it. Others had differing accounts. An expert said alcohol and tiredness played a part for the main parties. The defendant was 44 and of good character and showed remorse. Since starting to drive at 16 he had one speeding conviction. He had references and a very impressive work record. Held. There was only one aggravating feature, he was 1½ times over the limit. **2 years** not 3.

R v McNiff [2001] EWCA Crim 79, [2001] 2 Cr App Rep (S) 275. The defendant then 18 pleaded guilty to causing death by careless driving when over the limit. The defendant spent the day drinking with friends. In the early morning he and a friend drove about 2 miles to a garage to buy cigarettes. On his way back he missed his turning and took the next one. He lost control of the car on a bend. The car hit a tree and the friend was killed. He did his best to help him. His blood reading was 51mg. When interviewed he admitted full responsibility and said he was driving too fast. He was of exemplary character with numerous testimonials. He was deputy head of his school and head boy at his college. The risk of re-offending was described as negligible. He showed deep regret. Held. If a person of older years had pleaded guilty 5 years would have been appropriate. Taking into account his age **3 years 9 months** was not manifestly excessive.

Alcohol 71 to 100ug in breath or equivalent

44.7 *A-G's Reference (No 11 of 1998)* [1999] 1 Cr App Rep (S) 145.   The defendant pleaded guilty to two counts of causing death by careless driving when over the limit at the first opportunity. The defendant then 21 attended a 21st birthday party where alcohol was freely available. He left in the early hours of the morning and drove in his mother's car on an unfamiliar unlit road. Five other young people were in the car which was designed to carry five people. He drove over a slight brow of a hill and after about 100 metres into a bend for which there was no warning. The car left the road and hit a tree. The defendant was probably the only person wearing a seat belt. Two passengers were thrown from the car and died instantly. One was the defendant's best friend. Another passenger was in hospital for 7 months with a fractured pelvis and severe head injuries. Two other passengers suffered fractured arms. He unsuccessfully tried to help one of those who had died. Two hours after the accident his alcohol reading was 93ug. He speed as he entered the bend was estimated to be between 40 and 50 mph. He told police he had intended to stay the night at the party. He was a university student of good character. He had many very impressive references. He showed deep, long-lasting remorse. The fathers of one of those killed and one of those injured said the tragedy would only be exacerbated if imprisonment were imposed. Held. We'd expect **4 years**. Taking into account it was a reference, his chance of resuming university in the autumn of next year and he had been at liberty **30 months** not 18 months suspended. 5 years' disqualification not 2.

R v Chippendale [1998] 1 Cr App Rep (S) 192. The defendant changed his plea to guilty to causing death by driving without due care when unfit through drink. The defendant went to a party intending to leave his car at a friend's house overnight. He then visited a pub, drank more alcohol and went back to the party. Just before 2am he offered to drive two men home. A third declined and advised the other two to get out of the car, as the defendant was not fit to drive. The car hit a brick wall and a passenger died and the defendant and the other man were slightly injured. The defendant said he swerved to avoid an animal but the other survivor didn't see anything. The speed limit was 30 mph and an expert estimated that the car was travelling at least 50 mph and the brakes had been applied very severely causing the wheels to lock. The blood alcohol reading was 68ug in breath. Backtracking made the reading at the time of the accident 80ug. The defendant was then 18 and of good character. He showed remorse, admitted the offence to the police and suffered grave emotional trauma from loosing a personal friend. Held. There is understandably grave concern about young men who have too much to drink and drive in the face of warnings and then kill. Personal elements of mitigation such as acute guilt feelings are not matters that should sound greatly in determining the proper sentence. The offence was aggravated by the extent he was over the limit, the excessive speed and failure to heed the warning given. **4 years** detention was not excessive.

A-G's Reference (No 91 of 2001) [2001] EWCA Crim 2135, [2002] 1 Cr App Rep (S) 466. The defendant pleaded guilty to causing death by careless driving when over the limit at the earliest opportunity. He drove in a built up area with his close friend as his passenger. He was revving very hard and travelling very fast. He was seen to cross the centre markings and to be too close to the kerb. He may have hit the kerb but in any event he lost control of the car and collided with a stationary taxi. He and the passenger were rendered unconscious but he was later able to leave the car. She died of a traumatic rupture of the thoracic aorta and he received minor facial injuries. An expert estimated he was driving at between 30 and 50 mph. When seen by police he said he did not know who was driving. His blood reading was 108mg (the equivalent of 98ug in the breath). The test revealed cocaine in the blood. He was 24 and of good character. He called evidence of his good character, the efforts both on him and his family and his remorse. He was sentenced to 18 months and had served it. Held. Driving with excess alcohol in any form is conduct which is to be deplored. When the levels reach the level in this case it is of the utmost seriousness. The particular nature of the driving was a straightforward manifestation of a drunken driver quite incapable of controlling his car. This was a bad case. He should have expected **4 or 5 years' imprisonment**. As it was a reference **3 years** instead.

Alcohol 101 to 130ug in breath or equivalent

44.8 *A-G's Reference (No 66 of 1996)* [1998] 1 Cr App Rep (S) 16 – LCJ. The defendant pleaded guilty to two counts of causing death by careless driving when over the limit at the first opportunity. The defendant drove his car out of a public house with the two victims. At a bend with an adverse camber on a wet road the car mounted the footway, went through a ranch style fence and dwarf conifers and continued till it hit a stone wall. The defendant said he was going at about 50 mph in a 40 mph area. He got out with difficulty but the passengers died. They were two of his closest friends. Police attended very quickly and volunteered that he was driving. His breath reading was 108mg. This was a little over three times the limit. He said he had drunk a lot in at least three pubs. He had lost control of the car because of the wet road. He had passed his test 8 months before. He had no relevant convictions. He had originally not intended to drive but due to problems with the car alarm he ended up with the keys when drunk. He expressed remorse. He had expressed a wish that he had died and not the victims. The probation officer found him devastated and reduced to tears. He had been plagued with nightmares and was on tranquillisers. He avoids his friends because he feels unable to accept their support. Held. Causing the death of both his passengers must be at the forefront of the courts' mind. The accident was a momentary and tragic loss of control. It wasn't dangerous driving. Applying *A-G's Reference (Nos 24 and 45 of 1994)* (1994) 16 Cr App Rep (S) 583, **3 years** was lenient and merciful but not unduly lenient such that it should be increased.

R v Ridley [1999] 2 Cr App Rep (S) 170. The defendant pleaded guilty to three counts of causing death by driving without due care after having consumed alcohol. The defendant and friends visited various public houses and each drank about 12 pints of beer. At about midnight they left a pub in Wigtown and he and four others got into a Fiesta to drive to Carlisle. The owner of the car who survived said 'Someone else had agreed to drive but that didn't happen. The defendant was the last to leave the pub and he got into the driver's seat as it was the only seat left. We all decided to get in the car. No one was dragged in against their will.' It was raining very heavily. The defendant accelerated over the crest of a hill and the car clipped a verge, skidded, turned over and span. The car was extremely badly damaged. Three were killed, the owner of the car spent 2 weeks in hospital and 6 months off work. He spent a lot of time in pain. The defendant's breath reading was 108mg. He suffered from shock and minor cuts and bruises. He came from a good and stable background and was unlikely to re-offend. He received 4 years detention and that had a very severe effect on him and his family. A psychologist said he was finding it extremely difficult to cope with it. Held. Three deaths are much worse than one. He is a vulnerable young man. **2½ years** substituted.

R v Ndlovu [2001] 1 Cr App Rep (S) 163. The defendant pleaded guilty to causing death by driving without due care after having consumed alcohol. The defendant and two others spent the evening drinking in three pubs with the victim who was due to be married the next day. They travelled back to where the car was parked in another town in a taxi. The defendant offered to drive the others home. There was no criticism of his driving until at a bend he braked heavily and sought to correct the steering. He was driving at about 50 mph in a 30 mph area. A cat came into the road and he lost control. The car hit a garage and the victim who was in the back and not wearing a seatbelt sustained head injuries from which he died. The other passengers sustained injuries of varying degrees. He remained at the scene and sought help. His breath reading was 84ug and by backtracking was estimated to be between 106 and 136ug at the time of the accident. He was 26 and of impeccable character. He was completely devastated. **3½ years** not 5 and 6 years' disqualification not 10.

R v Porter [2001] EWCA Crim 222, [2001] 2 Cr App Rep (S) 366. The defendant pleaded guilty to causing death by careless driving when over the limit. The defendant's son was born with breathing difficulties and was rushed to hospital in a critical condition. His wife went to hospital and he stayed at home with their three other young children. He drank 20 bottles of 5% proof lager during the early morning. That evening his wife rang him in a distress state and asked him to come to the hospital. Although he had family who could have driven him to hospital he drove himself in his van. He claimed he hadn't drunk during the day. He drove in a 40 mph area where there was a line of traffic doing 30–40 mph. He overtook a car causing the driver overtaken to break heavily to prevent him hitting an oncoming car. He then overtook the next car making an oncoming car to brake heavily which caused smoke to come from his wheels. The oncoming car had to go into the kerb. A witness said there the van, which was being driven erratically, could not overtake any cars safely, there were no gaps for the van and there was no reason the driver could not have seen the oncoming cars. Other witnesses described the driving as 'stupid', 'erratic' and 'suicidal'. His blood reading 3 hours after the accident was 270mg (the equivalent of 117ug in the breath). The van hit another car and the driver died 9 days later. The victim was a family man with young children. The defendant also suffered injuries and suffered a severe emotional reaction to the death. He was referred to the community health team. He was 28 and of good character. He was described as a good father and expressed remorse. Held. He was befuddled with alcohol. There are no grounds for interfering with the **4½ years** sentence.

Asleep, falling

44.9   *A-G's Reference (No 21 of 2000)* [2001] 1 Cr App Rep (S) 173.   The defendant pleaded guilty to causing death by careless driving and failing to provide a specimen. Shortly before 1am the defendant drove into the back of a heavy goods vehicle. His passenger died. The defendant was unable to provide a specimen when he was in the ambulance. At the hospital he initially consented to giving a blood test and then later refused. He told the doctor he had drunk 2½ pints. The HGV's speed was estimated at 43 mph and the defendant's speed was estimated at not less than 73 mph. When interviewed he said he had drunk three glasses of wine. He said he had fallen asleep. The speed limit was 70 mph. The victim was a very close friend of the defendant. They were almost inseparable. The defendant suffered very serious injuries in the accident. He was 40 and had an excess alcohol conviction in 1990. In 1997 he had a conviction for due care for which he was fined £60. He expressed remorse and became extremely morose. He was sentenced to 12 months and had already been approved for the tagging regime. Held. The proper inference to be drawn is that the accident and the death resulted in a substantial part from the alcohol consumed. Taking into account the mitigation, the plea and it was a reference **30 months** substituted.

Defendant aged 16–17

44.10   *A-G's Reference (No 10 of 1997)* [1998] 1 Cr App Rep (S) 147 – LCJ. See *Defendant seriously injured*

R v Brown [2001] 1 Cr App Rep (S) 195. The defendant pleaded guilty to causing death by driving without due care after having consumed alcohol. The defendant who was then 17 drove his mother's car ten days after he had passed his test. He went to a party and drank 2½ pints of lager. Under some pressure he agreed to drive three of his friends home. He lost control of the car at a bend and it hit a tree. One passenger died. He ran to a house for help and called the emergency services. His breath reading was

88ug. He said he had never received any skid training. He was in his sixth form and doing extremely well. He was expecting to go to university. He was of positive good character and had excellent references. The death had a devastating effect on him. The risk of reoffending was assessed as small. Held. The accident was the result of inexperience rather than alcohol. The judge had a difficult task. **1 year** YOI not 2.

Defendant aged 18–20

44.11   *R v Chippendale* [1998] 1 Cr App Rep (S) 192. The defendant changed his plea to guilty to causing death by driving without due care when unfit through drink. The defendant went to a party intending to leave his car at a friend's house overnight. He then visited a pub, drank more alcohol and went back to the party. Just before 2am he offered to drive two men home. A third declined and advised the other two to get out of the car, as the defendant was not fit to drive. The car hit a brick wall and a passenger died and the defendant and the other man were slightly injured. The defendant said he swerved to avoid an animal but the other survivor didn't see anything. The speed limit was 30 mph and an expert estimated that the car was travelling at least 50 mph and the brakes had been applied very severely causing the wheels to lock. The blood alcohol reading was 68ug in breath. Backtracking made the reading at the time of the accident 80ug. The defendant was then 18 and of good character. He showed remorse, admitted the offence to the police and suffered grave emotional trauma from losing a personal friend. Held. There is understandably grave concern about young men who have too much to drink and drive in the face of warnings and then kill. Personal elements of mitigation such as acute guilt feelings are not matters that should sound greatly in determining the proper sentence. The offence was aggravated by the extent he was over the limit, the excessive speed and failure to heed the warning given. **4 years** YOI was not excessive.

R v McNiff [2001] EWCA Crim 79, [2001] 2 Cr App Rep (S) 275. The defendant then 18 pleaded guilty to causing death by careless driving when over the limit. The defendant spent the day drinking with friends. In the early morning he and a friend drove about 2 miles to a garage to buy cigarettes. On his way back he missed his turning and took the next one. He lost control of the car on a bend. The car hit a tree and the friend was killed. He did his best to help him. His blood reading was 51. When interviewed he admitted full responsibility and said he was driving too fast. He was of exemplary character with numerous testimonials. He was deputy head of his school and head boy at his college. The risk of re-offending was described as negligible. He showed deep regret. Held. If a person of older years had pleaded guilty 5 years would have been appropriate. Taking into account his age **3 years 9 months** was not manifestly excessive.

Defendant distraught etc/What purpose does a prison sentence serve?

44.12   *A-G's Reference (No 36 of 1994)* (1994) 16 Cr App Rep (S) 723 at 726 – LCJ. The sentencing judge said that human life could not be brought back and he did not think any useful purpose would be served by sending the defendant to prison. Held. We cannot agree with that. There are many cases, unhappily, where offences of this kind are committed by persons of otherwise good character, who will be distraught by what has happened and who will have the fact that they have killed someone with them for the rest of their lives. But to say that no useful purpose is served by sending offenders to prison is to ignore the deterrent factor and the need to establish, to the knowledge of the public (and the driving public in particular) that where one drives with a substantial amount of drink, and one drives in such a way as to kill someone, then a sentence of imprisonment will almost always be required.

Defendant seriously injured

44.13 A-G's Reference (No 10 of 1997) [1998] 1 Cr App Rep (S) 147 – LCJ. The defendant pleaded guilty to causing death by careless driving when unfit through drink and aggravated vehicle-taking. A mother left her car on her driveway with a 'crook lock' attached and two boxes of beer in the boot. She went to Scotland with her husband and youngest son leaving her other son and a cousin at the house. Next day there were numerous visitors to the house and there was talk of taking the car. The defendant then 17 expressed reluctance to be involved. The radio and the beer were taken and the defendant and two others went to nearby woods and drank the beer. They came back and appeared drunk. The defendant drove the car with the other two at speed judged to be between 60 and 70 mph. The defendant lost control at a moderate left hand bend and the car left the road with no noise of skidding or brakes screeching. The car hit a tree and one passenger was killed. The car's speed near the accident was estimated to be between 70 and 90 mph. The speed limit was 60 mph but the greatest speed the bend could be negotiated was 50 mph. The road was dry. The defendant was unconscious for six days. The injury to his frontal lobe of the brain effected his personality. The defendant had a 'dis-social personality disorder.' One doctor said it was exacerbated by the accident and another said it was caused by it. He needed 12 weeks' observation and treatment in a specialist hospital. The judge sentenced him to probation and he was admitted to the hospital. It was not a success. The defendant was of good character. Held. The judge was correct to say 3 years was appropriate. We think **3–4 years** if contested and **2–3 years** if not. The 2 years since the offence, the injury, his plea and character are significant factors. **12 months** YOI substituted.

Disqualification, for how long?

44.14 A-G's Reference (No 11 of 1998) [1999] 1 Cr App Rep (S) 145. The defendant pleaded guilty to two counts of causing death by careless driving when over the limit at the first opportunity. The defendant then 21 attended a 21st birthday party where alcohol was freely available. He left in the early hours of the morning and drove in his mother's car on an unfamiliar unlit road. Five other young people were in the car, which was designed to carry five people. He drove over a slight brow of a hill and after about 100 metres into a bend for which there was no warning. The car left the road and hit a tree. The defendant was probably the only person wearing a seat belt. Two passengers were thrown from the car and died instantly. One was the defendant's best friend. Another passenger was in hospital for 7 months with a fractured pelvis and severe head injuries. Two other passengers suffered fractured arms. He unsuccessfully tried to help one of those who had died. Two hours after the accident his alcohol reading was 93ug. He speed as he entered the bend was estimated to be between 40 and 50 mph. He told police he had intended to stay the night at the party. He was a university student of good character. He had many very impressive references. He showed deep, long-lasting remorse. The fathers of one of those killed and one of those injured said the tragedy would only be exacerbated if imprisonment were imposed. Held. We'd expect 4 years. Taking into account it was a reference, his chance of resuming university in the autumn of next year and he had been at liberty **30 months** not 18 months **suspended**. 5 years' disqualification not 2.

Failing to provide a specimen, after – General principles

44.15 A-G's Reference (No 21 of 2000) [2001] 1 Cr App Rep (S) 173. The defendant pleaded guilty to causing death by careless driving and failing to provide a specimen. Held. Where the defendant has refused to provide a specimen the gravity lies in part in the fact the defendant has avoided the appropriate sentence for driving with excess alcohol. If the defendant asks to be sentenced on the basis he has drunk only limited alcohol the court should treat that with caution and circumspection. The onus of establishing that lies on the defendant. The court is likely to require him to give evidence. In the absence of evidence a court is able to draw adverse inferences about the amount of alcohol consumed. The ordinary inference will be he has refused because he knows he has consumed alcohol well in excess of the limit. Normally a substantial custodial sentence will be required.

R v Pinchess [2001] EWCA Crim 323, [2001] 2 Cr App Rep (S) 391. Held. Courts should not examine whether the defendant was below the limit or unaffected by the driving. They should approach the case as if there had been proven excess alcohol. (The court does not appear to have been referred *to A-G's Reference (No 21 of 2000)* [2001] 1 Cr App Rep (S) 173.)

Failing to provide a specimen, after – Cases

44.16 *A-G's Reference (No 21 of 2000)* [2001] 1 Cr App Rep (S) 173. The defendant pleaded guilty to causing death by careless driving and failing to provide a specimen. Shortly before 1am the defendant drove into the back of a heavy goods vehicle. His passenger died. The defendant was unable to provide a specimen when he was in the ambulance. At the hospital he initially consented to giving a blood test and then later refused. He told the doctor he had drunk 2½ pints. The HGV's speed was estimated at 43 mph and the defendant's speed was estimated at not less than 73 mph. When interviewed he said he had drunk three glasses of wine. He said he had fallen asleep. The speed limit was 70 mph. The victim was a very close friend of the defendant. They were almost inseparable. The defendant suffered very serious injuries in the accident. He was 40 and had an excess alcohol conviction in 1990. In 1997 he had a conviction for due care for which he was fined £60. He expressed remorse and became extremely morose. He was sentenced to 12 months and had already been approved for the tagging regime. Held. The proper inference to be drawn is that the accident and the death resulted in a substantial part from the alcohol consumed. Taking into account the mitigation, the plea and it was a reference **30 months** substituted.

R v Pinchess [2001] EWCA Crim 323, [2001] 2 Cr App Rep (S) 391. The defendant was convicted of causing death by careless driving and refusing to provide a specimen. The defendant drove his girlfriend on an unlit road when there was patchy fog. She was 16 and 7 months pregnant with his child. Because of his speed he failed to negotiate a 90° bend with no chevron markings. The car left the road and hit a grass bank. He helped his girlfriend and they walked over a mile to a telephone box to call an ambulance. Both went to hospital by ambulance and the girlfriend started to suffer epileptic fits. On arrival she had a Caesarean operation and her son was born suffering from severe injuries from oxygen starvation brought about by her fits. She had a fracture to her face, fractured ribs, internal bleeding, a blood clot in her arm and ten stitches in her knee. The defendant gave a false name and said they had been abducted by two men who had crashed the car. He said he was not driving the car. He refused to give a blood test and offered urine, which was not accepted by police. He said he had bought four cans of beer and had drunk only one. However, there were no empty cans in the car. He was abusive and unco-operative with the police. Eleven days later the boy died. When interviewed he said he was driving at 50 mph and shortly before the accident the girlfriend had kissed him. He turned to look and when he looked at the road again he was in a fog bank. Next he saw the bend. He admitted the car had failed its MOT. There were defective tyres and brakes but they were not the cause of the accident. He had convictions for assault, dishonesty and driving offences including drink/drive and driving whilst disqualified. He showed distress for the loss of his child and the mother's injuries. He suffered from Reiters syndrome which was very akin to arthritis. In a few years time he would be in a wheel chair. The accident caused the break up with the girlfriend. He had since married another girl and they have now a 2-year-old daughter. Held. We approach this case on the basis alcohol played a part. The aggravating factors were his behaviour at hospital, his denial of being the driver, the girlfriend's injuries and trauma, his record and the condition of the car. His disability was an important factor with the unlikelihood of his being able to drive on his release. There was also the case delay and his change of attitude. Seven years was not outside the appropriate bracket after a trial. However, **5 years** was appropriate taking into account the particular features.

Victim dies after defendant dealt with for careless driving

See DEATH BY DANGEROUS DRIVING, CAUSING – *Victim dies after defendant dealt with for dangerous driving*

Victims, the views of the relatives of the

See DEATH BY DANGEROUS DRIVING, CAUSING – *Victims, the views of the relatives of the*

45 DEATH BY DANGEROUS DRIVING, CAUSING

45.1 Road Traffic Act 1988, s 1

Indictable only. Maximum sentence 10 years. Minimum disqualification 2 years.

3–11 penalty points. The defendant must be disqualified till he/she passes an extended driving test[1]. Specified offence enabling defendant aged 14–17 to be detained[2].

1 Road Traffic Offenders Act 1988, s 36(2)(b).
2 Powers of the Criminal Courts (Sentencing) Act 2000, s 91(2)(a).

Crown Court statistics England and Wales[1] – Crown Court – Males 21+ – Causing death by dangerous driving

45.2

Year	Plea	Total Numbers sentenced	Type of sentence%					Average length of custody (months)
			Discharge	Fine	Community sentence	Suspended sentence	Custody	
2000	Guilty	90	0%	1%	3%	6%	89%	43.5
	Not guilty	47	0%	4%	6%	4%	83%	31.3

1 Source: Crime and Criminal Justice Unit, Home Office Ref: IOS416-02.

Guideline case

45.3 *R v Boswell* (1984) 79 Cr App Rep 277 – LCJ. Any driver who fails to realise that what he is doing at the wheel is creating a risk when to any ordinary person such a risk would be obvious, or even worse, sees the risk and nevertheless takes a chance and so kills, is prima facie deserving of severe punishment. Such punishment should in many cases involve immediate loss of liberty.

The following are aggravating factors:

a) Consumption of alcohol or drugs;
b) Racing, grossly excessive speed, showing off;
c) Disregarding warnings from passengers;
d) Prolonged persistent and deliberate course of very bad driving, someone who over a lengthy stretch of road ignores traffic signals, jumps red lights, passes

other vehicles on the wrong side, drives with excessive speed, drives on the pavement etc;

e) Committing other offences at the same time eg no licence, disqualified driving and driving whilst a learner without a supervisor;

f) Previous convictions for motoring offences particularly bad driving and excess alcohol;

g) Several people are killed;

h) Failure to stop after the accident or trying to throw off the victim from the bonnet by swerving to assist an escape and

i) Driving so to avoid detention or apprehension.

The mitigating factors are:

a) A one-off piece of dangerous driving, a momentary reckless error of judgment, eg briefly dozing off, failing to notice a pedestrian on a crossing;

b) Good character and a good driving record;

c) A plea of guilty;

d) The effect on the defendant if he is genuinely remorseful or if he is genuinely shocked and

e) The victim was either a close relative or a close friend and the consequential shock was likely to be great.

Where there are no aggravating factors a non-custodial sentence may well be appropriate.

A-G's Reference (Nos 14 and 24 of 1993) (1994) 15 Cr App Rep (S) 640 – LCJ. From 1993 Parliament has increased the sentence from 5 years to 10. *R v Boswell* [1984] 79 Cr App Rep 277 needs to be reconsidered. Clearly the statements of principle and the examples of aggravating and mitigating circumstances still stand.

A-G's Reference (Nos 24 and 45 of 1994) [1995] 16 Cr App Rep (S) 583 at 586 – LCJ. This court is concerned primarily with the criminality of the person who has caused the death. The fact that the death is, of itself, a factor in contributing to the length of sentence which should be passed. But essentially we have to look at the cases in the light of the offender's criminality. The length of sentence will very much depend upon the aggravating and mitigating circumstances in the particular case, the extent of the carelessness or dangerousness, and the amount that the offender is over the limit in a case involving excess alcohol. Where an offender is not just over the limit, not even substantially over the limit, but 2½ to 3 times over the limit, the sentence which the court must pass is clearly a substantial one. It is an insufficient excuse for failing to impose a sufficiently long sentence to look predominantly at the mitigating features and the remorse of the offender.

Alcohol, driving under the influence – Guideline case

45.4 *R v Boswell* (1984) 79 Cr App Rep 277 as adapted by *A-G's Reference (Nos 14 and 24 of 1993)* [1994] 15 Cr App Rep (S) 640 – LCJ. Drivers who drive with reckless disregard for the safety of others after taking alcohol should understand that in bad cases they will lose their liberty for upwards of 5 years. In the very worst cases, if contested sentences will be in the higher range of sentences permitted by Parliament. That type of driver should be removed from the road by a long period of disqualification.

Alcohol, driving under the influence – 36 to 70ug in breath or equivalent

45.5 *A-G's Reference (No 16 of 1998)* [1999] 1 Cr App Rep (S) 149. The defendant was convicted of two counts of causing death by dangerous driving. When 22 he went to a pub with two close friends and he drove away with them. None of them were wearing a seat belt. He overtook vehicles on a dual carriageway well in excess of 70 mph. He overtook another vehicle when the road narrowed to a single carriageway, which was potentially dangerous. He entered a roundabout at very close to 70 mph and lost control of the car, which hit a kerb and a crash barrier. Both his passengers were thrown from the car and died shortly after they had arrived in hospital. He left the scene in a state of shock. He gave a false name in hospital where he was treated for a broken shoulder, arm injuries and a head injury. The defendant pretended to the police that he was a passenger. At first he refused to supply a blood specimen but eventually did. By backtracking his reading was between 90 and 120mg at the time of the accident (equivalent to 39–52ug). In interview he accepted he was driving at about 70 mph and said the brakes had failed. He had two convictions of no relevance and a clean licence. He had an overwhelming sense of grief and was having difficulty in coming to terms with his responsibility. He had become a virtual recluse and had sought counselling. One of the mothers of the victims had written a moving letter saying she had forgiven him. The other mother had taken a very different position. He was sentenced to 240 hours' community service. The local press had described him as a murderer who had gone free. The offence was 18 months before and he had completed ¼ of his community service. Held. We would have expected 4½ years. Taking into account it was a reference and the CSO he had completed **3½ years** instead.

R v James [2001] 2 Cr App Rep (S) 153. The defendant was convicted of causing death by dangerous driving and driving whilst disqualified. After drinking in a pub with his two nephews he drove them away from the pub in his van. One of the nephews, the victim sat on the lap of the other in the front passenger seat. None of the three was wearing a seat belt and the defendant was disqualified from driving. The van was seen by police being driven at speed and they gave chase. The van went through a red light and the police put their lights on. Shortly after the van still driving at speed veered across the road and hit an oncoming coach. The victim was thrown from the van and killed instantly. The other nephew was severely injured with head injuries. He was in intensive care for several days. The defendant was also injured. He had 123mg reading of alcohol in his blood, (equivalent to 54ug in his breath). He showed shock and remorse. He was 28 and had an appalling driving record. He had 10 convictions for disqualified driving and two for dangerous driving. One of them was on a motorway when he was trying to escape the police. He also had a conviction for reckless driving and drink/drive. Held. The **8 years** sentence was entirely proper. However, as the judge had considered the fact he was disqualified in considering the aggravating factors it was wrong to make the disqualified driving sentence consecutive. The sentences were made concurrent.

R v Wood [1998] 2 Cr App Rep (S) 234. The defendant pleaded guilty to causing death by dangerous driving. The defendant drank with friends and then drove home with two of them. None of them wore seat belts. At the beginning of the journey he spun the wheels and was advised by one of them to calm down. He continued to speed and was cautioned again. A witness thought he was going 60 mph in a 30 mph area. He lost control of the car at a bend and slid sideways into an oncoming minicab. He and one of his passengers were thrown through the windscreen. The passenger suffered a fractured skull and died. The defendant's blood reading of alcohol was 93mg, (the breath equivalent was 40½ug). An expert said the accident was caused by a combination of a speed of at least 60 mph and drink. Shortly after this offence he drove with excess alcohol and was involved in a slight damage only collision. He didn't stop but was traced and given probation. He was 31 and had four possession of drug convictions. He had never been given a custodial sentence. He suffered from anxiety and a moderate degree of depression. He was drinking to alleviate the symptoms. He was 31. Held. Looking at the authorities and considering the factors including the plea and that he was only over the limit by a small margin **4 years** not 5.

A-G's Reference (No 3 of 2001) [2002] 2 Cr App Rep (S) 528 – LCJ. The defendant pleaded guilty to two counts of causing death by dangerous driving. The defendant collected her son and then went to a pub and drank on her account three bottles of Special Brew. At 3.30pm when conditions were fine and the road was dry the defendant overtook a two lorries just before the road went from a dual carriageway to a single one. Although there was a gap between the two lorries she overtook both. She cut in quickly after the second to avoid an oncoming lorry. She was travelling at about 80 mph when the limit was 60 mph and hit the grass verge and the car went out of control. She hit two cyclists who were thrown into the air and died. Her car went down an embankment. Both families of the victims were devastated. Her blood reading was 109mg (equivalent to 47ug of breath) She lacked remorse but depression might have masked that. After her sentence she did show remorse after receiving counselling. She had two speeding convictions. One of them was committed 5 weeks before the accident. Otherwise she was of good character with references. She was a single parent of her son now aged 8. Held. The appropriate sentence was **4–5 years**. Courts are very conscious of the impact of these offences on the relatives and friends of the victims. Courts should consider how bad the driving was and the quantity of alcohol consumed. The allowance made for a reference is about a year. Because of the son and the remorse 3 years not increased.

Alcohol, driving under the influence – 71 to 100ug in breath or equivalent

45.6   *R v Noble* (24 June 2002, unreported) The defendant was convicted of causing the death of 6 people with most of the aggravating features in *R v Boswell* (1984) 79 Cr App Rep 277 present and he was 2½ times over the limit. **10 years** not 10 and 5 consecutive making 15. For case details see *Multiple deaths*

Alcohol, driving under the influence – Defendant avoids test

45.7   *A-G's Reference (No 58 of 2000)* [2001] 2 Cr App Rep (S) 102.   The defendant pleaded guilty to causing death by dangerous driving after having pleaded not guilty. The defendant left a pub and drove to his girlfriend's house where they had an argument. He left and was seen by two pedestrians to be driving at about 50 mph in a 30 mph area. The car moved from the kerb to the centre of the road so that oncoming vehicles had to move towards their kerb. The engine was heard revving and after going over a bridge it collided head on with a motorcyclist. The accident was only a short distance from the house. The rider died. The defendant left the scene but surrendered to the police 18 hours later. Held. The defendant had prevented the police from determining his alcohol level. Applying *A-G's Reference (No 21 of 2000)* [2001] 1 Cr App Rep (S) 173 the court is able to draw an adverse inference about the amount of alcohol consumed. [For additional details see *Speeding*]

Asleep, falling

45.8   *A-G's Reference (No 26 of 1999)* [2000] 1 Cr App Rep (S) 394. The defendant pleaded guilty to causing death by dangerous driving. The victim's car broke down on the motorway. The victim lay underneath it and tried to repair it. It was on the hard shoulder. The police conned off the car. The defendant was in a van and was seen to weave about six times from the fast lane to the slow lane in such a way motorists were wary to overtake him. His van suddenly entered the hard shoulder and hit the victim's car. Witnesses did not see his brake lights illuminated. The van rolled over the victim and he was killed instantly. One of his passengers who was waiting outside the car was thrown into the road and suffered major fractures. The other two passengers who were also waiting outside the car also received fractures. One will not regain full use of their arm. The defendant climbed out of his overturned vehicle and scaled a high steel fence to escape. He received major injuries to his hand either in the accident or when climbing the fence. He went to a pub and asked his brother to collect him. When he went to hospital he was arrested and in interview he said he had had 4 hours sleep the previous night. Police found a broken whisky bottle in his van and he said he might have had a small amount. The minimum speed for the van was 45 mph and there was no evidence of braking. The basis of plea was that he must have fallen asleep and the dangerous driving was for no more than a mile. Further when he left the scene he was unaware there were serious injuries caused. The defendant was a professional driver with a very good driving record. He was sentenced to 100 hours' CSO and probation. He had completed the CSO. Held. It was not a momentary falling asleep. There would have been a period of drowsiness etc. 30 months would have been appropriate after a trial. Taking into account the late plea, his personal circumstances and his remorse **21 months** would have been appropriate. As it was a reference and the fact he had completed the CSO **9 months** instead.

R v Price [2001] 2 Cr App Rep (S) 114. The defendant pleaded guilty to two counts of causing death by dangerous driving. The defendant an HGV driver was told by his GP not to drive and see a consultant urgently. He saw the consultant next day who said he had sleep apnoea syndrome. He discovered the defendant had fallen asleep at the wheel of his lorry a month previously and the lorry went into a field. He was again told not to drive. Four days later his lorry was seen on the M1 weaving from the inside lane to the hard shoulder without any indications being given. Forty miles further on and just before a service station he ran into stationary traffic in the slow lane. Two cars were crushed between his lorry and another lorry. The cars and his lorry caught fire and both the car drivers died. The defendant stayed at the scene. He said he planned to pull into the service station. He was of good character and full of remorse. The judge held a Newton hearing about whether he had ignored medical advice and said he could no longer give a full discount for the plea. Held. **4 years** not 5.

R v Brown [2001] EWCA Crim 2108, [2002] 1 Cr App Rep (S) 504. The defendant pleaded guilty to causing death by dangerous driving. The defendant installed satellite dishes throughout Wales and the West Country. One Sunday after working 2 weeks without a break he spent the day installing dishes. He had a short break for lunch. At 4.30pm he drove normally with his employer who fell asleep. He then fell asleep and as the road turned to the left his van went head on into an oncoming car. The passenger of the car was killed. The defendant had 3 broken ribs and other injuries. He was married with two young children and of good character. He was visibly distressed and had character witnesses. The judge said, 'he was a sensible man and a sensible competent driver. He had dozed off monetarily.' Held. This was not a case where sleep was fought off over a protracted period. There were no *R v Boswell* aggravating features. **9 months** not 18.

R v Hart (2002) Times and Daily Telegraph, 12 January – High Court Judge at Crown Court. The defendant was convicted of 10 counts of causing death by dangerous driving. The defendant chatted on the telephone to a person he had contacted through the Internet for 6 (or 5 in the other report) hours until 3am. He set off on a 147 (or 154 in the other report) mile journey and fell asleep. His Land Rover, which was towing a 2 tonne load drifted off the M62. It ran along side it until it fell into a railway cutting containing the East Coast Main line. An express train ran into it and drove on for another 400 yards before crashing into an oncoming coal freight train. Ten men were killed and 76 injured. The defendant was 37. Judge's remarks. Every driver and I think I should include myself, has been in or very nearly in that position. Most acknowledge it by taking a break, taking a sleep or handing over to someone else if they can. A driver who presses on takes a grave risk. You chose not to have any sleep in the previous 24 hours. Choosing to drive after plenty of warnings was an aggravating feature. An accident was almost inevitable. There is very little to choose between you and a drink driver. Because of your arrogance in setting off on a long journey without sleep, you caused the worst driving-related accident in the UK in recent history. I accept you are a hard working and decent family man. **5 years** and 5 years' disqualification. [Treat news reports with care].

R v France (10 May 2002, unreported). Held. The authorities show in a case where a driver of good character falls asleep due to conventional tiredness and causes one death a sentence of around **21 months to 2 years** is likely on a plea. After a trial that sentence is likely to be in the bracket of **2½ to 3 years**. Where more than one death is caused, that fact must be reflected and sentences in such cases inevitably increase to a bracket of **2–4 years** on a plea. This period may go higher in cases where the conduct of the driver is particularly bad or the circumstances particularly horrific. Where more than one death is caused and other features are present, such as relevant previous convictions, a known medical condition, deliberate risk taking, or related tachograph offences a sentence of **4–5 years** is likely on a plea.

Consecutive or concurrent, should the other sentences be?

45.9 *R v James* [2001] 2 Cr App Rep (S) 153. The defendant was convicted of causing death by dangerous driving and driving whilst disqualified. The defendant was disqualified from driving. Held. As the judge had considered the fact he was disqualified in considering the aggravating factors it was wrong to make the disqualified driving sentence consecutive. The sentences were made concurrent. (For further details see *Alcohol, driving under the influence – 36 to 70mg in breath or equivalent*)

R v Noble (24 June 2002, unreported). It would be wrong in principle to impose consecutive sentences in respect of each death arising from a single piece of dangerous driving. For case details see *Multiple deaths*

See also *Multiple deaths*

Defendant aged 15–16

45.10 *R v Carroll* [1998] 2 Cr App Rep (S) 349. The defendant pleaded guilty to causing death by dangerous driving. The defendant then aged 15½ drove a young girl to a cash machine and on his way back he crashed the car into a substantial concrete lamp-post which fell onto the car and crushed and killed the girl immediately. He sought to claim he was not the driver but did assist others at the scene. His speed was assessed at 60–70 mph and 49 mph at the point of impact in a 30 mph area. When interviewed he admitted he was the driver. Held. Taking into account the feelings of the deceased's family and the other factors **2 years** YOI not 4 years.

R v Jenkins [2001] EWCA Crim 242, [2001] 2 Cr App Rep (S) 265. The defendant pleaded guilty to causing death by dangerous driving. The defendant then aged 16 drove his motorbike on a mountain road in Wales with his best friend on the back. He had been given the bike a month earlier and it was in very bad condition. He was wearing a helmet but the passenger was not. The throttle jammed open and was unable to take a bend. The bike hit a wall and the friend was thrown forward and hit his head on the wall. He died. The defendant said the throttle stuck and he was unable to brake. The collision was described as 'low impact'. The bike was found to be totally unroadworthy. The throttle cable was not rooted properly, and the brakes and wheels were also defective. The defendant was of good character. He had mild learning difficulties and showed the deepest remorse. He had become traumatised, very withdrawn, isolated and vulnerable. Held. The judge was faced with a very difficult sentencing problem. A custodial sentence was justified. His mental condition prevented him from fully appreciating the bike's dangerous condition. Taking into account the factors including the long delay before sentence, the fact he needs help and that he had served nearly 3 months, **2 years' supervision** not 12 months' detention. 3 years' disqualification not 4.

Defendant aged 17–18

45.11   *R v Hajicosti* [1998] 2 Cr App Rep (S) 396. The defendant was convicted of causing death by dangerous driving. She had pleaded to careless driving. The defendant applied for a provisional licence on her 17th birthday and her parents bought her a car. She passed her test on the third attempt. Two weeks later about 6pm when she when still 17 she followed in her car an acquaintance in his car. The road was damp. Her passenger on two or three occasions told her to slow down. The acquaintance stopped at a roundabout next to a motorcyclist. She hit the motorcyclist at between 32 and 43 mph. He was thrown across her bonnet and into the air and landed on a traffic island. Her car crashed into another car and the motorcyclist died. She suffered from back injuries, depression and post-traumatic stress disorder. She was of good character. She was remorseful. Detention was having a particular severe impact on her. Held. This is a very serious offence. We strongly suspect her inexperience was in part responsible for the accident. **2 years** YOI not 3.

R v Nijjer [1999] 2 Cr App Rep (S) 385. The defendant was convicted of two counts of causing death by dangerous driving. When 18 he left school in his Porsche at lunchtime with two friends. The car had been an 18th birthday present. It was drizzling, the road was damp and it was overcast. In a 30 mph area he overtook a car at 60 mph. He lost control of the car and it mounted the pavement and killed two elderly pedestrians. The defendant and his friends were uninjured and they remained at the scene. He was of good character and he and his family were devastated. The defendant said he never wanted to drive again. He was racked by guilt and self blame and suffered from depression. Held. This was a bad case. Bearing in mind his age, character and remorse **3 years** YOI not 4.

R v Adams [2001] EWCA Crim 1777, [2002] 1 Cr App Rep (S) 373. The defendant pleaded guilty to causing death by dangerous driving. When 17 and holding a provisional licence he took his mother's Ford Escort XR3i without permission. He was not insured. He picked up three friends of similar ages and started driving at a normal speed. The road was dry and the visibility good. He had had about 15 hours' driving experience. In a 40 mph area he accelerated to about 63 mph. A car in front was breaking to turn left into a petrol station. The defendant failed to pay sufficient attention and then swerved to the right to avoid the car, lost control of his car, went across the lane for on-coming traffic and crashed into a concrete bus shelter. The bus shelter collapsed on top of the car and killed the defendant's best friend who died of severe head injuries. Another friend suffered multiple injuries. His femur, left arm and pelvis were each broken in three places. One of his vertebrae was also fractured. His treatment will last 5 years. The car was in good mechanical order. At the time he had no convictions but since the offence he was made the subject of a combination order for assault and racially aggravated assault. He had completed the community service element faultlessly. The risk of re-offending was assessed as low. The judge said he was showing off and sentenced him to 4 years detention. Held. As it was a guilty plea the judge must have started too high. **3 years** YOI substituted.

Defendant not the driver of the car that killed the victim

45.12   *R v Padley* [2000] 2 Cr App Rep (S) 201. The defendant was convicted of causing death by dangerous driving. The defendant then aged 20 drove into a petrol station and challenged another driver to take part in a race. The man ignored him. Later that evening he challenged another man Cragg the co-defendant to race. Cragg agreed. They raced on a single carriageway road, which was a 30ft wide with houses on each side. The road was damp. Cragg whilst being pursued by the defendant lost control of his car and it veered across the carriageway and demolished a brick wall. The car somersaulted back across the road and came to rest on its roof. A girl aged 19 or 20 who was sitting in the back seat of the car was thrown from the vehicle and killed. Another passenger suffered very severe head injuries. The defendant stopped his car and ran back to help. The defendant had three driving convictions. One was for speeding at 40 mph in a 30 mph area when he was on bail for the present offence. It was on the same road as where the accident occurred. The judge said that the defendant was responsible for initiating the whole tragic sequence of events. Held. Cragg received an appropriate sentence of 4 years taking into account his guilty plea. The starting point for the defendant must be 6 years. Despite the fact that the defendant was not the driver of the car which killed the victim, **5½ years** YOI was appropriate.

Disqualification, for how long? – Guideline case

45.13   *R v Boswell* (1984) 79 Cr App Rep 277 – LCJ. There is a distinction to be drawn for disqualification between driving whilst disqualified and such offences where there is no question of bad driving and where the essence of the crime is the actual manner of driving. In the latter case where the defendant has shown himself to be a menace to others using the highway, he should be debarred from driving for a substantial length of time. In bad cases, **7–10 years** will not be too long.

R v France (10 May 2002, unreported). Periods of disqualification vary substantially. The bracket appears to that of 3-6 years, but likely to be near the top of that bracket where more than one death has been caused but a bad previous driving record is absent.

Disqualification, for how long? – Less than 5 years

45.14   *R v Garrod* [1999] 1 Cr App Rep (S) 172. 2 years. See *Ice, vision obscured by*

R v Everett [2001] EWCA Crim 2268, [2002] 1 Cr App Rep (S) 550. 4 years. See *Overtaking or starting to overtake, driver*

Disqualification, for how long? – 5 to 6 years

45.15   *R v Blackman* [2001] EWCA Crim 150, [2001] 2 Cr App Rep (S) 268. 5 years. See *Racing, competitive driving etc*

R v Corkhill [2001] EWCA Crim 2683, [2002] 2 Cr App Rep (S) 60. 5 years. See *Speeding*

A-G's Reference (No 32 of 2001) [2001] EWCA Crim 2120, [2002] 1 Cr App Rep (S) 517. 5 years. See *Speed, approaching a hazard at excessive*

R v France (10 May 2002, unreported). The defendant made an early guilty plea to six counts of causing death by dangerous driving. He was sentenced on the basis he was reading and had no effective control of his lorry on the A1(M). The lorry which was travelling at 55 mph drifted onto the hard shoulder and killed six people who were on the hard shoulder because they had been involved in an accident about 2 minutes earlier. The defendant was 55 and of good character with only one speeding offence which was 15 months before. **6 years** not 8.

Disqualification, for how long? – 7 or more years

45.16   *R v Lucas* [1998] 1 Cr App Rep (S) 195. See *Speeding – More than 2 years' imprisonment*

R v McGowan [1998] 2 Cr App Rep (S) 219. See *Overtaking or starting to overtake, driver*

R v Gilmartin [2001] 2 Cr App Rep (S) 212. 8 years. See *Drugs, driving under the influence of*

A-G's Reference (No 68 of 2001) [2001] EWCA Crim 1803, [2002] 1 Cr App Rep (S) 406. 7 years. See *Mobile phone, defendant using*

R v Noble (24 June 2002, unreported). The defendant was convicted of causing the death of six people with most of the aggravating features in *R v Boswell* (1984) 79 Cr App Rep 277 present and 2½ times over the limit. Held. In general very lengthy periods of disqualification should be avoided, but that is subject to the need to protect the public against someone who is a danger on the road. The defendant had already on three occasions either driven with excess alcohol or failed to provide a specimen of breath. He was drunk, but refused to recognise how that impaired his driving ability, with the result that six people died. The lack of recognition on his part is an extremely disturbing The judge found that this man would be a danger to other road users indefinitely. In those circumstances, this is one of those rare cases where there was nothing wrong with imposing disqualification for life. For case details see *Multiple deaths*

Disqualification, for how long? – Defendant under 18

45.17   *R v Jenkins* [2001] 2 Cr App Rep (S) 265. See *Defendant aged 15–16*

Disqualification, for how long? –HGV/tractor drivers

45.18   *R v Kallaway* [1998] 2 Cr App Rep (S) 228. The defendant pleaded guilty to three counts of causing death by dangerous driving. He disconnected the tachograph on his lorry and worked for 2 days well in excess of the permitted hours. He said it was to earn sufficient money. At 10.20pm the time of the accident he had been driving over the previous period some 39½ hours with less than 9 hours' rest. He had his last break 16 hours beforehand. The road went from two lanes to one and there were warning signs about this. There were also cones with amber light closing off a lane and a set of traffic lights. His lorry ploughed into a line a stationary traffic at about 50 mph. A driver in the last car heard no sign of braking and managed to escape. One car burst into flames. Three people died. Two drivers were significantly injured. Police found the defendant wandering round in a confused state. He was arrested and admitted his involvement. He denied he was asleep. He was 52 and had been a professional driver all his life. He had an unblemished record both as a driver and in work. He showed remorse. Held. The judge had perhaps been overly affected by the fact there were three deaths. That was clearly relevant but the number of deaths is sometimes a matter of chance and does not necessarily reflect the seriousness of the driving which caused the deaths. 3½ **years** not 6 and 5 years' disqualification not 10.

R v Lunt [1998] 2 Cr App Rep (S) 348. The defendant was convicted of causing death by dangerous driving. The defendant then 23, owned and maintained a tractor and trailer. He was an engineer at Rolls Royce whose work involved test driving vehicles. As a spare time occupation he collected straw bales from farmers' fields. When he started to drive the 21 miles home with a load of straw the trailer lights were working properly. Halfway through the journey they became completely inoperative. On an ill-lit single carriageway in the dark a car drove into the back and the driver was killed. The defendant showed deep remorse and was wholly respectable with references. He was a member of the Institute of Advanced Drivers. The judge said he must have realised the lights were not working and he took a gamble. Held. **8 months** upheld but 2 years not 5years' disqualification.

R v Wilsdon [1998] 2 Cr App Rep (S) 361. The defendant was convicted of causing death by dangerous driving. At dusk the defendant a farmer drove an unlit slow moving farm vehicle with trailer on an unlit single carriageway country road. It was equipped for crop spraying. A car travelling at about 50 mph drove up behind took avoiding action and swerved to avoid the tractor. It hit an oncoming car head on. The defendant located someone with a mobile to call an ambulance but the first car's passenger was already dead. The headlights of the tractor were obscured by a plastic tank and the rear mudguard, which carried the lights, and the reflectors had been removed to allow larger wheels to be fitted. The hazard lights were not visible as they were very dirty. The tractor would only have been visible at about 20 metres. The defendant said he had intended to drive the ½ mile home in his pick up truck taking the chemicals with him but the pick up got stuck in mud. Although he could have walked and collected another vehicle he took the tractor and took a chance. Held. The gravamen lies in causing the vehicle to go out at dusk with no visible lights. **12 months** was in no way excessive. 5 years' disqualification was not excessive either.

R v Neaven [2000] 1 Cr App Rep (S) 391. The defendant was convicted of causing death by dangerous driving. When it was dark he was driving a low loader which was carrying a dumper truck. He decided to do a U turn through a gap in the central reservation on a dual carriageway. While waiting for a gap in the traffic on the other carriageway the rear part of his lorry was protruding into the fast line of the road. The lights on his vehicle were not visible to those travelling in that lane. A car ran into the lorry and another car ran into that car. The driver of the first car was killed. He was a father of young children. The defendant remained at the scene and rang the police. The defendant was of impeccable character and had an impeccable driving history. He'd had an HGV licence for 25 years. Held. All motorists must realise that if they drive dangerously and thereby kill someone there must be a danger of imprisonment. It was a very dangerous piece of driving. **12 months** was not manifestly excessive. However, as he had always been a good driver so 2 years' disqualification not 4.

Drugs, driving under the influence of

45.19   *R v McGowan* [1998] 2 Cr App Rep (S) 219. The defendant pleaded guilty at the first opportunity to causing death by dangerous driving and driving whilst disqualified. The defendant left a public house where he had had a pint and a half or two in his girlfriend's car. When travelling at about 60 mph he overtook on a bend 'taking a chance.' He was only able to overtake slowly because his acceleration was poor. A car came into sight and he continued to try to overtake then braked. It caused a skid and he hit the other car head on. The defendant got out and tried to help his passenger who had suffered a ruptured bowel. The defendant left the scene without leaving details and telephoned his girlfriend and told her to report the car as stolen. She reluctantly did so but shortly after told the truth. The driver of the other car was trapped and died 2 weeks later in hospital. The defendant was arrested and denied being the driver. Later he admitted being the driver and expressed remorse. He had been disqualified from driving twice for drink/drive. The judge said he gave the minimum amount for the plea. Held. This case was not near the top of the scale although it was rank bad driving with a bad record. **5 years** not 7 and 8 years' disqualification not 15.

R v Gilmartin [2001] 2 Cr App Rep (S) 212. The defendant pleaded guilty to causing death by dangerous driving. The defendant and two friends spent several hours drinking. He took some ecstasy and later drove off with the two friends. He drove well above the 30 and 40 mph speed limits on residential roads. He lost control of the car, hit a tree and the two friends were thrown from the car. Just before the accident one of the friends shouted a warning. Initially he rang for a taxi to leave the scene but subsequently he stayed at the scene and gave considerable assistance to the police. One passenger died and the other was injured. His blood/alcohol reading was 74mg and by backtracking was 97mg, (the equivalent of 42ug in the breath). He also had 1,060ug of ecstasy in his blood which was so high it was mostly seen in fatal overdoses. The defendant had convictions in 1989 and 1990 for reckless driving and drink/drive. He was full of regret and remorse. There was a Newton hearing about whether the ecstasy was taken before or after the accident and the judge found it was taken before the accident although he said the defendant was not deliberately lying. The judge found the manner of driving was due to the effects of ecstasy making him drive faster and faster. Held. The defendant should have the full discount because of the judge's finding he wasn't lying and some of his evidence was accepted. The overarching consideration was the high level of ecstasy. Because of the plea and the other mitigation **6 years** not 7 and 8 years' not 10 years' disqualification.

Failing to see other vehicles, obstacles etc within time

45.20   *R v Lightfoot* [1999] 2 Cr App Rep (S) 55. The defendant pleaded guilty to two counts of causing death by dangerous driving. In daylight on a dry road where there was good visibility the defendant drove his tractor unit at excessive speeds. Shortly before the accident he was travelling at 67 mph. Ahead was a stationary car waiting to turn right into a layby. The speed limit was 60 mph and his permitted limit was 40 mph. Just before the accident his speed was 54 mph. He should have seen the white car 350 yards before but his concentration was such he only saw it when he braked. The brakes were defective and they locked. The tractor unit veered to the right and hit an oncoming a car head on. The driver and his 18-year-old daughter were killed and his wife and younger daughter were injured. The defendant was 33 and of good character with testimonials. He had been a lorry driver since he was 21 and had only one speeding ticket. He expressed genuine shock and remorse. There was a Newton hearing when the judge found the defendant was not aware of the defective brakes. **2 years** not 3.

R v Caucheteux [2001] EWCA Crim 2960, [2002] 2 Cr App Rep (S) 169. The defendant pleaded guilty to three counts of causing death by dangerous driving. In daylight on a dry road where there was good visibility the defendant drove his large lorry and a long trailer on the M6 at a consistent speed of 53 mph. As he approached a queue of traffic he didn't brake or slow down. The last car in the queue took evasive action but was still shunted into the hard shoulder barrier. The next car was propelled into the trailer of the van in front and all three young RAF technicians were killed. Their car was partly under the lorry, which veered into the barrier. The car was pushed under the barrier. Four other cars were pushed forward. Ten other people were injured some seriously. The defendant's lorry had no defects and the alcohol test was negative. There were no skid marks for the lorry. It was estimated he had 32 seconds to slow down for the queue. He could give no explanation for the accident. He was 29 and a French national who drove regularly in the UK. He had no convictions and was deeply effected by the accident and had very positive references. Genuine remorse was shown. In court he asked to speak and made an emotional apology to the relatives and asked for forgiveness. The judge said it was not a momentary loss of concentration, he could not have been looking properly. Held. We take into account the number of fatalities but **2 years** not 3.

See also *Speed, approaching a hazard at excessive*

Health problems, accident caused by

45.21 *R v Davies* [2001] EWCA Crim 2319, [2002] 1 Cr App Rep (S) 579. The defendant was convicted of causing death by dangerous driving. The defendant had been a lorry driver for over 40 years and a history of diabetes. In good conditions on a straight road his lorry veered over to the opposite carriageway and hit a Land Rover a glancing blow. It then hit a Skoda with four occupants and front part of the car virtually ceased to exist. The driver, his girlfriend and their 5-month-old daughter were killed. The other occupant the driver's mother suffered severe lacerations to her forehead and scalp which required about 90 stitches. She had multiple fractures to her cheekbone and eye socket and a fractured collarbone, two fractures to her arm and extensive lacerations to her chest and her underarm area. There were also lacerations to her elbow and arms and a complete loss of movement and feeling in that arm. The defendant was not injured but was in severe shock. He lost control of the lorry after a hypoglycaemic attack and the judge found, 'he didn't have his rations with him. When he felt the attack coming on he didn't stop but carried on.' In 1995 his lorry had also veered across a busy road after a similar attack. No one was hurt but he had received advice and he was authorised to continue driving on the basis he took proper precautions. He was about 65 and of exemplary character with references. He was deeply remorseful and had the strongest feelings of compassion. This judge disqualified him for life. Held. Three lives had been lost. A most serious aspect was the previous attack. Some judges might have imposed a lesser sentence because of the strong mitigation but **3 years** was not manifestly excessive. Disqualification for life remained.

HGV drivers – Guideline remarks

45.22 *R v Caucheteux* [2001] EWCA Crim 2960, [2002] 2 Cr App Rep (S) 169. Those who drove HGV vehicles owed a particular responsibility because of the nature of the vehicles they drove and because the results of the errors, could be as in this case catastrophic.

HGV drivers

45.23 *R v Neaven* [2000] 1 Cr App Rep (S) 391. See *Projecting into the road, vehicle*

R v Buckingham [2001] 1 Cr App Rep (S) 218. The defendant changed his plea to guilty to causing death by dangerous driving. The defendant was driving an articulated lorry on the motorway. He ran into stationary traffic which was queuing to leave the motorway. Eight cars were damaged and a fire started. One woman was unable to leave her car and died. The defendant was 62 and had one conviction for driving without due care in 1996. He was very remorseful and had suffered from post-traumatic stress disorder. Held. It is important to bear in mind the nature of the vehicle he was driving and the anger and grief of the family and friends of the deceased. In light of his age, trauma, character and remorse **18 months** not 3 years.

R v Price [2001] 2 Cr App Rep (S) 114. The defendant pleaded guilty to two counts of causing death by dangerous driving. The defendant an HGV driver was told by his GP not to drive and see a consultant urgently. He saw the consultant next day who said he had sleep apnoea syndrome. He discovered the defendant had fallen asleep at the wheel of his lorry a month previously and the lorry went into a field. He was again told not to drive. Four days later his lorry was seen on the M1 weaving from the inside lane to the hard shoulder without any indications being given. 40 miles further on and just before a service station he ran into stationary traffic in the slow lane. Two cars were crushed between his lorry and another lorry. The cars and his lorry caught fire and both the car drivers died. The defendant stayed at the scene. He said he planned to pull into the service station. He was of good character and full of remorse. The judge held a Newton hearing about whether he had ignored medical advice and said he could no longer give a full discount for the plea. Held. **4 years** not 5.

R v Taylor [2001] EWCA Crim 1106, [2002] 1 Cr App Rep (S) 76. See *Projecting into the road, vehicle*

Old cases. *R v Toombs* [1997] 2 Cr App Rep (S) 217.

HGV drivers – Exceeding permitted hours/fatigue

45.24   *R v Kallaway* [1998] 2 Cr App Rep (S) 228. The defendant pleaded guilty to three counts of causing death by dangerous driving. He disconnected the tachograph on his lorry and worked for 2 days well in excess of the permitted hours. He said it was to earn sufficient money. At 10.20pm the time of the accident he had been driving over the previous period some 39½ hours with less than 9 hours' rest. He had his last break 16 hours beforehand. The road went from two lanes to one and there were warning signs about this. There were also cones with amber light closing off a lane and a set of traffic lights. His lorry ploughed into a line a stationary traffic at about 50 mph. A driver in the last car heard no sign of braking and managed to escape. One car burst into flames. Three people died. Two drivers were significantly injured. Police found the defendant wandering round in a confused state. He was arrested and admitted his involvement. He denied he was asleep. He was 52 and had been a professional driver all his life. He had an unblemished record both as a driver and in work. He showed remorse. Held. The judge had perhaps been overly affected by the fact there were three deaths. That was clearly relevant but the number of deaths is sometimes a matter of chance and does not necessarily reflect the seriousness of the driving which caused the deaths. **3½ years** not 6 and 5 years' disqualification not 10.

R v Porter [2002] EWCA Crim 1121, [2002] 2 Cr App Rep (S) 222. The defendant pleaded guilty to three counts of causing death by dangerous driving. A count relating to a false entry on driver's hour's sheet was left on the file. At 6.55pm in February, the defendant was driving his articulated goods vehicle from Italy to Cheshire on a motorway and he drove into the back of a mobile crane. His vehicle crashed through the barrier, fell 30' and overturned. The driver of the crane lost control of his vehicle and went through the central reservation and overturned and collided with a car and another articulated vehicle. The drivers of all three vehicles died. There was no evidence of pre-impact breaking by the defendant. The estimated speed of the crane was the designated speed of 30 mph and the defendant at something less than 60 mph. One rear indicator light and one taillight on the crane were not lit. The written basis of plea was that he was under pressure to meet delivery deadlines that he pushed the limits of his driving hours and rest periods. He did not accept he had tampered with the tachograph. He failed to appreciate the speed of the crane and he must have lost his concentration for a few seconds when approaching the crane. He denied falling asleep. He had a conviction for perverting the course of justice involving a tachograph and driving convictions including speeding and showed remorse. There was a letter from one of the widows describing the devastation on her and her three children. Held. Any motor vehicle is potentially a lethal weapon and if it is driven by someone suffering from fatigue the chances of an accident are greatly increased **4 years** not 5. (The case was reheard after his earlier appeal had been dismissed when he wasn't there for the submissions, see *R v Porter* [2001] EWCA Crim 2653, [2002] 2 Cr App Rep (S) 67.)

HGV drivers/tractor drivers – Vehicle lit inadequately

45.25   *R v Lunt* [1998] 2 Cr App Rep (S) 348. The defendant was convicted of causing death by dangerous driving. The defendant then 23, owned and maintained a tractor and trailer. He was an engineer at Rolls Royce whose work involved test driving vehicles. As a spare time occupation he collected straw bales from farmers' fields. When he started to drive the 21 miles home with a load of straw the trailer lights were working properly. Halfway through the journey they became completely inoperative. On an ill-lit single carriageway in the dark a car drove into the back and the driver was killed. The defendant showed deep remorse and was wholly respectable with references. He was a member of the Institute of Advanced Drivers. The judge said he must have realised the lights were not working and he took a gamble. Held. **8 months** upheld but 2 years' not 5 years' disqualification.

R v Wilsdon [1998] 2 Cr App Rep (S) 361. The defendant was convicted of causing death by dangerous driving. At dusk the defendant a farmer drove an unlit slow moving farm vehicle with trailer on an unlit single carriageway country road. It was equipped for crop spraying. A car travelling at about 50 mph drove up behind took avoiding action and swerved to avoid the tractor. It hit an oncoming car head on. The defendant located someone with a mobile to call an ambulance but the first car's passenger was already dead. The headlights of the tractor were obscured by a plastic tank and the rear mudguard, which carried the lights, and the reflectors had been removed to allow larger wheels to be fitted. The hazard lights were not visible as they were very dirty. The tractor would only have been visible at about 20 metres. The defendant said he had intended to drive the ½ mile home in his pick up truck taking the chemicals with him but the pick up got stuck in mud. Although he could have walked and collected another vehicle he took the tractor and took a chance. Held. The gravamen lies in causing the vehicle to go out at dusk with no visible lights. **12 months** was in no way excessive. 5 years' disqualification was not excessive either.

R v Neaven [2000] 1 Cr App Rep (S) 391. The defendant was convicted of causing death by dangerous driving. When it was dark he was driving a low loader which was carrying a dumper truck. He decided to do a U turn through a gap in the central reservation on a dual carriageway. While waiting for a gap in the traffic on the other carriageway the rear part of his lorry was protruding into the fast line of the road. The lights on his vehicle were not visible to those travelling in that lane. A car ran into the lorry and another car ran into that car. The driver of the first car was killed. He was a father of young children. The defendant remained at the scene and rang the police. The defendant was of impeccable character and had an impeccable driving history. He'd had an HGV licence for 25 years. Held. All motorists must realise that if they drive dangerously and thereby kill someone there must be a danger of imprisonment. It was a very dangerous piece of driving. **12 months** was not manifestly excessive. However, as he had always been a good driver 2 years' disqualification not 4.

Ice, vision obscured by

45.26 *R v Garrod* [1999] 1 Cr App Rep (S) 172. The defendant was convicted of causing death by dangerous driving. The defendant drove in freezing conditions on a well lit road one evening. The car mounted a pavement hitting a pedestrian who was thrown into the air and landed on the car's bonnet. The defendant left the vehicle and told witnesses he hadn't seen the man. The man died. The car was examined and there was no evidence that the side window had been de-iced. Ice had formed on the inside and outside of the windscreen. It appeared an attempt had been made to clear a circular part of the windscreen in front of the driving position but ice had reformed. There were a few scratch marks on the nearside of the windscreen. There was no de-icer or scraper in the vehicle. He told police he left his home a few hundred yards away and had cleaned part of the windscreen. He hadn't cleaned the side windows and he had skidded on the corner. He was of good character. The prosecution put the case as comparable to driving a defective vehicle. Held. That would put it at the lower end of the criminality. **18 months** not 3 years' detention. As his employers would continue his employment if he had a licence 2 years' not 3 years' disqualification.

Mobile phone, defendant using

Guideline remarks

45.27   *R v Browning* [2001] EWCA Crim 1831, [2002] 1 Cr App Rep (S) 377. The use of a mobile phone to read and to compose text messages while driving is a highly perilous activity. Even the use of a handheld mobile phone by a driver whilst moving, a much more common feature of driving today, is self-evidently risky. But the risks of reading and composing text messages appear to us of a wholly different order and to be of the most blatant nature. An element of deterrence was appropriate for composing a message.

R v Browning [2001] EWCA Crim 1831, [2002] 1 Cr App Rep (S) 377. The defendant pleaded guilty to causing death by dangerous driving. The defendant was driving a lorry on a dual carriageway with a dangerous load, helium. 60 metres before a lay-by the lorry began to veer to the left. At the lay-by it scrapped the whole side of a BMW and hit the car in front. A man standing in the lay-by was killed instantly. The defendant stopped and later started crying. The weather was fine. He later claimed he was distracted by papers in his cab. After a Newton hearing the judge found he was composing a text message on his hand held mobile which was transmitted immediately after the accident. The judge concluded that the message had been composed over a distance of about 400 metres, which took the 27 seconds to travel. At the start of that distance he was travelling at 57 mph which he reduced to 49 mph. Also he had received an incoming text message while driving his lorry an hour earlier. Twenty minutes later while still on the move he composed and sent a reply. He had no convictions and a good work record. The judge said he was a decent family man and showed remorse. Since the accident he worked in a yard and he says he never intends to drive a lorry again. Held. The use of a mobile phone to read and to compose text messages while driving is a highly perilous activity. Even the use of a handheld mobile phone by a driver whilst moving, a much more common feature of driving today, is self-evidently risky. But the risks of reading and composing text messages appear to us of a wholly different order and to be of the most blatant nature. It was legitimate for the judge not to give full credit for the plea. An element of deterrence was appropriate for composing a message. **5 years** was not inappropriate.

A-G's Reference (No 68 of 2001) [2001] EWCA Crim 1803, [2002] 1 Cr App Rep (S) 406. The defendant was convicted of causing death by dangerous driving. The defendant was driving in a 60 mph area without a seat belt talking to his girlfriend on his mobile for 8 minutes. During which time he overtook three vehicles which was described as 'erratic'. He then overtook another car at the top of a hill which was considered by another motorist as dangerous. He was then behind a Mazda doing 55–60 with a Mitsubishi behind him. The Mazda was overtaken near a blind corner on the brow of a hill at a speed 20–30 faster than the Mazda. He lost control of his car and hit an oncoming Renault with three adults and a 5-year-old child. One adult was killed and the other two received serious injuries. The child was kept overnight in hospital. The defendant received a broken neck fortunately without spinal damage. When interviewed he said someone was tailgating him and he overtook to get away. He was 26 and was of good character. He had one speeding conviction in 1992 and was held in high regard by his family and friends. He expressed remorse and was sentenced to a community penalty with 180 hours community service. He had performed 66 hours. Held. We would have expected at least 3 years. Because it was a reference, the hours performed and it was his first custodial **18 months** substituted. The disqualification was increased from 3 to 7 years.

Multiple deaths

45.28 *R v Kallaway* [1998] 2 Cr App Rep (S) 228. The defendant pleaded guilty to three counts of causing death by dangerous driving. Three people died. Held. The judge had perhaps been overly affected by the fact there were three deaths. That was clearly relevant but the number of deaths is sometimes a matter of chance and does not necessarily reflect the seriousness of the driving which caused the deaths. (For further details see *HGV drivers – Exceeding permitted hours*)

R v Hart (2002) Times and Daily Telegraph 12 January – High Court Judge at the Crown Court. The defendant was convicted of ten counts of causing death by dangerous driving. The defendant chatted on the telephone to a person he had contacted through the Internet for 6 (or 5 in the other report) hours until 3am. He set off on a 147 (or 154 in the other report) mile journey and fell asleep. His Land Rover, which was towing a 2 tonne load drifted off the M62. It ran along side it until it fell into a railway cutting containing the East Coast Main line. An express train ran into it and drove on for another 400 yards before crashing into an oncoming coal freight train. Ten men were killed and 76 injured. The defendant was 37. Judge's remarks. Every driver and I think I should include myself, has been in or very nearly in that position. Most acknowledge it by taking a break, taking a sleep or handing over to someone else if they can. A driver who presses on takes a grave risk. You chose not to have any sleep in the previous 24 hours. Choosing to drive after plenty of warnings was an aggravating feature. An accident was almost inevitable. There is very little to choose between you and a drink driver. Because of your arrogance in setting off on a long journey without sleep, you caused the worst driving-related accident in the UK in recent history. I accept you are a hard working and decent family man. **5 years** and 5 years' disqualification. [Treat news reports with care.]

R v France (10 May 2002, unreported). The defendant made an early guilty plea to six counts of causing death by dangerous driving. He was sentenced on the basis he was reading and had no effective control of his lorry on A1(M). The lorry which was travelling at 55 mph drifted onto the hard shoulder and killed six people who were on the hard shoulder because they had been involved in an accident about 2 minutes earlier. He was 55 and of good character with only one speeding offence which was 15 months before. Held. Cases of causing death by dangerous driving pose a peculiar problem, particularly in multiple deaths cases because in the case of a serious accident, resulting from one particular piece of bad driving, it is very often a matter of chance how many people are killed. For example, if one car is knocked off the road and/or badly damaged, it is quite fortuitous whether there is a lone driver within it or an entire family. Equally, if a person drives recklessly fast round a corner it will be a matter of chance whether an ongoing vehicle is a motor cycle or a charabanc full of passengers. In either case, however many lives are lost, the level of dangerousness, lack of care, or recklessness of the driver will be exactly the same. For these reasons, the classic guideline case of *R v Boswell* (1984) 79 Cr App Rep 277, principally concentrated on features going to the degree and level of blameworthiness involved in the actions of the driver as dictating the proper level of sentence, rather than the number of people killed. Nonetheless, that feature was included as an element which the court must take into account. **5 years** not 6.

R v Noble (24 June 2002, unreported). The defendant was convicted of six counts of causing death by dangerous driving. He pleaded to driving whilst disqualified. He and friends spent the day drinking on a 'motorised pub crawl.' He said he had drunk about

12 pints of lager, 1 pint of mixed lager and cider and two Bacardi Breezers. He then drove with others on a wet busy A road at excessive speed. After the dual carriageway narrowed to a single carriageway there was a double bend. Because of his speed he lost control of his car and hit a wall and then two other cars. Three died from each other vehicle and others were injured. The defendant received relatively minor injuries and ran off. On his arrest he said someone else was driving. On his estimate of his drinking his blood/alcohol reading would have been 150 mg in his blood. (The court said he was 2½ times over the limit which gives a different figure.) He was 41 with the following convictions. 1990 failure to provide a specimen. 1991 drink/drive and driving whilst disqualified when he was disqualified for 3 years. In 1997 drink/drive when he received 100 hours' CSO and 4 years' disqualification. He was a family man with a good work record. The judge said he showed breathtaking arrogance in the witness box. Held. This was an horrendous case involving tragedy for many families. There were obvious aggravating features. The motorised pub crawl, the very bad driving record, being disqualified, running off, driving dangerously for a little while before the accident and blaming someone else. The element of chance in the number of people killed by a single piece of dangerous driving underlines the appropriateness of the general principle which applies throughout sentencing for criminal offences, namely that consecutive sentences should not normally be imposed for offences arising out of the same single incident. That is not an absolute principle. It may admit of exceptions in exceptional circumstances. But where such exceptional cases occur, they tend to be ones where different offences are committed. It seems to this court to be wrong in principle to impose consecutive sentences in respect of each death arising from a single piece of dangerous driving. We emphasise in saying that that it is right that the total sentence imposed in such cases should take account of the number of deaths involved. We have read the letters from relatives of several of those who died in the present case. They bring home to any reader the depth of the tragedy which has resulted from the behaviour of this appellant. At the same time, one has to recognise that no prison sentence of whatever length on the offender can make up for the anguish caused or bring back to life those who have been killed. While, therefore, the total sentence should take account of the number of deaths, it cannot be determined by it, if only because of the chance nature of the number of the deaths. The fact that multiple deaths have been caused is not of itself a reason for imposing consecutive sentences. The main focus of the sentencing judge in such cases has to be on the dangerousness of the driving, taking into account all the circumstances of that driving, including the results. It is difficult to imagine a worse case so **10 years** but the sentences should be concurrent so 10 years not 15.

See also *Consecutive or concurrent, should the other sentences be?*

Overtaking or starting to overtake, driver

45.29 *R v McGowan* [1998] 2 Cr App Rep (S) 219. The defendant pleaded guilty at the first opportunity to causing death by dangerous driving and driving whilst disqualified. The defendant left a public house where he had had a pint and a half or two in his girlfriend's car. When travelling at about 60 mph he overtook on a bend 'taking a chance.' He was only able to overtake slowly because his acceleration was poor. A car came into sight and he continued to try to overtake then braked. It caused a skid and he hit the other car head on. The defendant got out and tried to help his passenger who had suffered a ruptured bowel. The defendant left the scene without leaving details and telephoned his girlfriend and told her to report the car as stolen. She reluctantly did so but shortly after told the truth. The driver of the other car was trapped and died 2 weeks later in hospital. The defendant was arrested and denied being the driver. Later he admitted being the driver and expressed remorse. He had been disqualified from driving twice for drink/drive. The judge said he gave the minimum amount for the plea. Held. This case was not near the top of the scale although it was bad driving with a bad record. **5 years** not 7 and 8 years' disqualification not 15.

R v Richards [1998] 2 Cr App Rep (S) 346. The defendant pleaded guilty to causing death by dangerous driving. The defendant then 22, with his girlfriend overtook some friends who were in another car at speed well in excess of the limit. He then followed a car driven by an off duty police sergeant which was driving at the speed limit. He drove close to it, revved his engine and tried to overtake it. In effect he was showing his impatience. When the speed limit increased to 40 mph he overtook the car and the car in front of it at a speed in excess of 60 mph. He managed to move back into his side of the road but lost control as he tried to negotiate a bend. He had narrowly avoided hitting oncoming traffic and hit a telegraph pole. He suffered concussion. His girlfriend was killed. He was of good character with seven references and a clean driving record. He was greatly affected by the death and had not driven since. He had no intention of driving in the future. The girl's father said no member of his family wanted the defendant to go to prison and he could not have wished for a better future son in law. Held. Two years was on the high side but not necessarily manifestly excessive. However he has the burden of killing his own girlfriend and apparently his future wife. This was a grave sentence on its own. We also cannot ignore that he has retained the confidence and affection of the family who wanted him to marry the victim. Taking those matters into account **12 months** instead.

R v Nijjer [1999] 2 Cr App Rep (S) 385. See ***Defendant aged 17–18***

R v Kosola [2000] 1 Cr App Rep (S) 205. The defendant pleaded guilty to causing death by dangerous driving. He was driving with his wife and two children on a single carriageway and overtook some vehicles. He was driving at about 55 mph and collided head on with another car, which was also travelling at about 55 mph. The other car contained three people. One died. One was very badly injured and requires eight pain killing tablets a day. He will never work again. The third suffered fractures, bruising and dislocation. He was unable to work for 14 weeks and needed counselling. The defendant suffered two fractures to his leg, multiple fractures to his ankle and foot. He was in hospital for 9 weeks. He still requires further surgery and uses a crutch to walk. His wife and child suffered minor injuries. He immediately admitted responsibility. He said he still believed he was on a dual carriageway and that he had driven 10,000 miles on English roads in the previous year. He was 32 and was a Captain in the Finnish army who was studying at a military college in England. He had an impeccable character and showed remorse. He army career was very likely to be over and he suffered post-traumatic stress disorder. He claimed he had been confused by the road markings. There was a Newton hearing. He was disbelieved. The judge found he had overtaken a slow moving tanker dangerously. Held. Everybody's injuries and employment changes explain why this case is very serious. His sentence of **12 months** would normally be regarded at the bottom of the sentencing bracket. Exercising mercy because of his character, his probable loss of career, his serious injuries, that the sentence would be served in a foreign country and the effect on his family **8 months** instead.

R v Cusick [2000] 1 Cr App Rep (S) 444. The defendant was convicted of causing death by dangerous driving. He was driving on an A road in the dark between 55 and 60 mph. He didn't overtake the car in front although he could have done. Instead he tailgated it. As he approached a wide left hand bend he overtook the vehicle and within seconds hit an oncoming car. The driver was killed. The driver of the car that was overtaken did not see the accident but it was clear that the defendant's car was for unexplained reasons substantially over the centre line. The defendant's speed at the impact was estimated to be 65–70 mph in a 60 mph limit. He was 49 with an excess alcohol conviction in 1982. Otherwise his licence was for all practical purposes clear. Held. This was a bad case. There was excessive speed and aggression. **2 years** was severe but not excessive.

R v O'Brien [2001] 1 Cr App Rep (S) 79. The defendant pleaded guilty to causing death by dangerous driving on the day his case was listed for trial. In daylight the defendant was in a transit van. At a junction he overtook a car which was travelling at 30 mph. He hit a cyclist who had just emerged from the junction. A week later the cyclist died. The defendant showed remorse from the very beginning. He was 50 and was effectively of good character. The relatives said no useful purpose could be served by a custodial sentence. The judge said it was an impatient and aggressive piece of overtaking at an excessive speed. Held. It was more than a momentary lapse of attention. The judge was right to consider a stern sentence was unavoidable. **12 months** reflected all the factors.

A-G's Reference (No 68 of 2001) [2001] EWCA Crim 1803, [2002] 1 Cr App Rep (S) 406. See **Mobile phone, defendant using**

R v Everett [2001] EWCA Crim 2268, [2002] 1 Cr App Rep (S) 550. The defendant pleaded guilty to causing death by dangerous driving on the day his case was listed for trial. At 8.15pm the defendant overtook a car which was behind a bus on a narrow winding road with a 60 mph speed limit. He drove right behind the bus. Then on a blind left hand bend he overtook the bus and collided head on with an on coming car. The victim aged 18 with a bright future was burnt to death. His parents were shattered and overwhelmed. The defendant was 35. Held. This was a bad case of an impatient driver who overtook on a blind bend without making any attempt to ascertain whether it was safe to do so. It was a course of the utmost danger. **2 years** and 4 years' disqualification were not excessive.

See also *A-G's Reference (No 70 of 2001)* (31 October 2001, unreported) and *R v Penjwnini* (15 October 2001, unreported). 3 years not 4 for overtaking on a bend and *R v Braid* [2002] EWCA Crim 737, [2002] 2 Cr App Rep (S) 509.

Projecting into the road, vehicle

45.30   *R v Neaven* [2000] 1 Cr App Rep (S) 391. The defendant was convicted of causing death by dangerous driving. When it was dark he was driving a low loader which was carrying a dumper truck. He decided to do a U turn through a gap in the central reservation on a dual carriageway. While waiting for a gap in the traffic on the other carriageway the rear part of his lorry was protruding into the fast line of the road. The lights on his vehicle were not visible to those travelling in that lane. A car ran into the lorry and another car ran into that car. The driver of the first car was killed. He was a father of young children. The defendant remained at the scene and rang the police. The defendant was of impeccable character and had an impeccable driving history. He'd had an HGV licence for 25 years. Held. All motorists must realise that if they drive dangerously and thereby kill someone there must be a danger of imprisonment. It was a very dangerous piece of driving. **12 months** was not manifestly excessive. However, as he had always been a good driver so 2 years' disqualification not 4.

R v Taylor [2001] EWCA Crim 1106, [2002] 1 Cr App Rep (S) 76. The defendant was convicted of causing death by dangerous driving. He was driving his lorry and trailer which was 15.5 metres long and approached a junction with a dual carriageway from a side road. Wanting to turn right he crossed one carriageway and stopped in the central reservation with the front of the lorry protruding in the one carriageway and the trailer protruding in the other. It would have been possible to remain in the central reservation without protruding if the angle was right. The trailer had obstructed half of the outside lane of one of the dual carriageways. The deceased was driving her car at about 70 mph in the fast lane and hit the trailer. She didn't see the trailer in time. The dual carriageway was a busy truck road carrying fast moving traffic. It was dark and the speed limit was 70 mph. The road was wet but it wasn't raining. The rear lights of the trailer were not visible because of the angle of the vehicle and because of the colour of the vehicle it merged into the background. The judge said it was an error of judgment. The defendant was a businessman of good character with a good driving record. He had testimonials which spoke extremely highly of him. Held. Following *R v Ollerenshaw* [1999] 1 Cr App Rep (S) 65 [Courts should ask themselves for those who had not previously served custody whether an even shorter period might be equally effective] **4 months** not 8.

Racing, competitive driving etc

45.31 *R v Boswell* (1984) 79 Cr App Rep 277 as adapted by *A-G's Reference (Nos 14 and 24 of 1993)* [1994] 15 Cr App Rep (S) 640 – LCJ. Drivers who race should understand that in bad cases they will lose their liberty for upwards of 5 years. In the very worst cases, if contested sentences will be in the higher range of sentences permitted by Parliament. That type of driver should be removed from the road by a long period of disqualification.

R v Howell [1999] 1 Cr App Rep (S) 449. The defendant pleaded guilty to two counts of causing death by dangerous driving. The defendant with two friends went to Southend where young men raced high performance cars. On his way home at 1.30am he was driving his mother's Ford RS Turbo which had certain modifications made to it on a dual carriageway The speed limit was 70 mph and he saw a Fiesta car with a similar performance to his mother's car. The driver of the Fiesta had also been racing that day and had taken drink and drugs. He had two passengers. The two drivers decided to race each other. Side by side they travelled for over a mile at speeds of about 100 mph. The defendant was in the nearside lane and the Fiesta in the outer lane. A driver ahead also in the outer lane noticed the two cars driving at speed and stayed where he was. The Fiesta was forced to move into the nearside lane and it clipped the defendant's car causing the cars to crash. The driver and the passenger of the Fiesta were killed. The other passenger was injured. The defendant was quite seriously injured and one of his passengers was very seriously injured. The defendant was 24 and of good character and was a 'thoroughly decent' man with a good work record. **3½ years** not 4 which would reduce the sentence below the 4 year sentence.

R v Padley [2000] 2 Cr App Rep (S) 201. The defendant was convicted of causing death by dangerous driving. The defendant then aged 20 drove into a petrol station and challenged another driver to take part in a race. The man ignored him. Later that evening he challenged another man Cragg the co-defendant to race. Cragg agreed. They raced on a single carriageway road, which was a 30ft wide with houses on each side. The road was damp. Cragg whilst being pursued by the defendant lost control of his car and it veered across the carriageway and demolished a brick wall. The car somersaulted back across the road and came to rest on its roof. A girl aged 19 or 20 who was sitting in the back seat of the car was thrown from the vehicle and killed. Another passenger suffered very severe head injuries. The defendant stopped his car and ran back to help. The defendant had three driving convictions. One was for speeding at 40 mph in a 30 mph area when he was on bail for the present offence. It was on the same road as where the accident occurred. The judge said that the defendant was responsible for initiating the whole tragic sequence of events. Held. Cragg received an appropriate sentence of 4 years taking into account his guilty plea. The starting point for the defendant must be 6 years. Despite the fact that the defendant was not the driver of the car which killed the victim, **5½ years** was appropriate.

R v Blackman [2001] EWCA Crim 150, [2001] 2 Cr App Rep (S) 268. The defendant pleaded guilty to causing death by dangerous driving. The defendant stopped his TVR Sports car at traffic lights on a bypass. A motorbike pulled up beside him. When the lights changed the bike accelerated away and the defendant did the same. He kept close to the bike and crossed a humped railway bridge. Just the other side and 475 metres from the lights a pedestrian was crossing the road. The defendant then travelling at 63 mph braked. The wheels locked and he skidded into the pedestrian. The defendant stopped. He denied he was racing. He said he was squinting because of the sun. The impact on the widow was devastating. He was of good character with references and had a clean licence. He was in full time employment and terrified of going to prison. There was a Newton hearing and the judge found he was driving competitively. He had a good prison report. Held. There was very strong evidence to support the judge's finding. The balancing exercise is very difficult. **3 years** not 4½ and 5 years' disqualification not 7.

See also *R v Watson* (10 August 2001, unreported).

A-G's Reference (No 68 of 2001) [2001] EWCA Crim 1803, [2002] 1 Cr App Rep (S) 406. See **Mobile phone, defendant using**

Speed, approaching a hazard at excessive

45.32   *R v Wagstaff* [2000] 2 Cr App Rep (S) 205. The defendant changed his plea to guilty to three counts of causing death by dangerous driving. An accident had caused a build up of traffic on a dual carriageway. A 'slow' sign had been placed well in advance of the hold up. It had a warning strobe light. It was placed to provide maximum impact. In the early afternoon, the defendant drove a horsebox passed the sign and his passenger referred to it but the defendant did not take much notice of the remark. She shouted look there is a police car and he slowed down a bit. The horsebox hit the stationary traffic and a VW Polo car was almost completely crushed. A husband, wife and child all died. Earlier the passenger had observed the defendant was driving too fast and he was agitated. She had suggested he took a rest and he ignored the advice. The tachograph showed he was driving at 51 mph at the moment of impact. The horsebox speed limit was 50 mph. It also showed he had driven for 4½ hours with one break of 19 minutes. That 4½ hours was the maximum amount that was allowed. The defendant claimed he had no memory of the accident. He tried to substitute an earlier tachograph. He was of good character with references. A doctor provided a medical explanation for a loss of concentration. He had not been warned of this. He showed great remorse. Held. The doctor's opinion had to be considered with the warnings from the passenger. The judge had carried out the difficult balancing exercise and had taken into account all the factors. **3 years** was not manifestly excessive.

Speeding – 2 years' imprisonment or less

45.33   *R v Chahal* [1998] 2 Cr App Rep (S) 93 – LCJ. The defendant pleaded guilty to causing death by dangerous driving. The defendant was driving his taxi and was warned by police about driving 47 mph in a 30 mph area. Two hours later with a fare he hit a pedestrian when travelling 54 mph in a 30 mph area. The pedestrian had come from his offside on a three lane carriageway. He died. The defendant stayed at the scene, called an ambulance and admitted his guilt. He was of good character and showed remorse. The defendant at the time was 18 or 19 years old with a wife and 6-week-old son. It was a mixed marriage and they had both been disowned by their families. The wife had particular problems after the birth of the son. Held. The court takes a stern view of this offence. If he hadn't been warned a relatively short custodial might be appropriate. Taking into account the mitigation **18 months** not 30.

R v Hird [1998] 2 Cr App Rep (S) 241. The defendant was convicted of causing death by dangerous driving. The defendant then aged 18 drove his father's car at about 60 mph in a 30 mph area on a dual carriageway. He probably slowed down to some degree as the road became a single carriageway. There were pedestrians about and he failed to see one in time. He braked hard but it was too late and the victim was killed. The defendant was of positive good character undergoing an apprenticeship. The judge deferred sentence so he could complete his apprenticeship saying what sentence he would receive at the end. The victim's family said the final sentence of 30 months' detention was correct. Held. Courts should act with a degree of consistency. We must look at the feelings on both sides and above all loyally apply the guidance in the cases. **21 months** YOI not 30.

R v Richards [1998] 2 Cr App Rep (S) 346. The defendant pleaded guilty to causing death by dangerous driving. The defendant then 22, with his girlfriend overtook some friends who were in another car at speed well in excess of the limit. He then followed a car driven by an off duty police sergeant which was driving at the speed limit. He drove close to it, revved his engine and tried to overtake it. In effect he was showing his impatience. When the speed limit increased to 40 mph he overtook the car and the car in front of it at a speed in excess of 60 mph. He managed to move back into his side of the road but lost control as he tried to negotiate a bend. He had narrowly avoided hitting oncoming traffic and hit a telegraph pole. He suffered concussion. His girlfriend was killed. He was of good character with seven references and a clean driving record. He was greatly affected by the death and had not driven since. He had no intention of driving in the future. The girl's father said no member of his family wanted the defendant to go to prison and he could not have wished for a better future son in law. Held. 2 years was on the high side but not necessarily manifestly excessive. However he has the burden of killing his own girlfriend and apparently his future wife. This was a grave sentence on its own. We also cannot ignore that he has retained the confidence and affection of the family who wanted him to marry the victim. Taking those matters into account **12 months** instead.

R v Lightfoot [1999] 2 Cr App Rep (S) 55. See *Failing to see other vehicles, obstacles etc within time*

R v Ward [2001] EWCA Crim 1565, [2002] 1 Cr App Rep (S) 221. The defendant pleaded guilty to causing death by dangerous driving based on speed, being too close to the vehicle in front and inattention. The defendant drove four friends behind another a car driven by another friend. In a residential road with a 30 mph speed limit and a slight downhill gradient he was talking and didn't pay sufficient attention to the road. He was too close to the car in front. The car in front braked and he pulled out to avoid hitting it. He panicked, accelerated, overtook the friend's car and drove into a corner at over 50 mph. He hit it, skidded and lost control of the vehicle. It crossed the centre of the road, hit a lamppost and crashed into some parked cars. There was no oncoming traffic. During the manoeuvre his passengers shouted for him to stop but he did not. A passenger died and he and others were injured. He was then 20 of good character with character references. He showed remorse and the risk of re-offending was assessed as low. There was considerable delay, which was not the defendant's fault. Since the accident he had married and had a daughter. Held. This was not just a momentary lapse. **2 years** not 3.

A-G's Reference (No 50 of 2001) [2001] EWCA Crim 1475, [2002] 1 Cr App Rep (S) 245. The defendant was convicted of causing death by dangerous driving. After working at a public house she agreed to drive others in someone else's car to first a pub and then a party. The others were either too drunk or unable to drive. In a 30 mph area there was a lot of laughing in the car and she was driving at 45–50 mph. She approached a sudden blind corner and lost control of the car and went over to the wrong side of the road. One car just managed to get out of the way but she hit a scooter driven by a student. He was thrown onto her windscreen and onto the roof of a parked car and died. Her car hit three parked cars and hit a wall. It was severely damaged and found to have over-inflated tyres and an under-inflated tyre, which could well have affected the stability of the car. All the occupants of her car left the scene and she hid first of all in a garden. All had mobile phones and no one called for assistance. She then went to two pubs. When first interviewed she declined to answer questions and then said that others were joking and bouncing around in the back. One of them tugged her shoulder and she turned round to tell her to leave her alone and the crash happened. She was uninsured at the time. She was 20 with no convictions. Held. The most serious aspect was her simply leaving the scene. 18 months might just have been defensible on a plea of guilty. If contested the appropriate sentence was **3 years**. Because of her youth, her remorse and that it was a reference **2 years** not 18 months YOI.

See also *R v Hunter* (1 November 2001, unreported).

Speeding – More than 2 years' imprisonment

45.34   *R v Lucas* [1998] 1 Cr App Rep (S) 195. The defendant pleaded guilty at the earliest opportunity to causing death by dangerous driving and perverting the course of justice. The defendant drove so he could sell his car at a scrap yard to feed his heroin habit. He entered a bend at about 65 mph and lost control of his car. The car hit a kerb, mounted a pavement and hit a 77-year-old pedestrian. She was thrown into the air. The defendant drove on. His driving was effected by his withdrawal from heroin. An expert said the maximum speed the bend could be taken was 58 mph. The car's brakes were poorly maintained which contributed to the accident. A friend of his provided the scrap yard with false documents the day after which were in a false name. The registered keeper initially told police he had sold the car before the accident. He and the defendant later accepted this was not true. The victim had her leg amputated and 11 days later died. The defendant who was now 24 had motoring convictions but none for bad driving of any sort. His report said the shock of it had caused him to give up heroin. Held. There were serious aggravating features. **5½ years** not 7. 8 years' not 10 years' disqualification because of his age and because it is hoped he will find employment on his release.

A-G's Reference (No 58 of 2000) [2001] 2 Cr App Rep (S) 102. The defendant pleaded guilty at the earliest opportunity to causing death by dangerous driving. The defendant had a provisional licence, left a pub and drove to his girlfriend's house where they had an argument. He left and was seen by two pedestrians to be driving at about 50 mph in a 30 mph area. The car moved from the kerb to the centre of the road so that oncoming vehicles had to move towards their kerb. The engine was heard revving and after going over a bridge it collided head on with a motorcyclist. The accident was only a short distance from the house. The rider died and the passenger aged 7 suffered leg injuries. The defendant left the scene but surrendered to the police 18 hours later. An expert concluded the car was on the wrong side of the road and was travelling at about 52 mph. The defendant was 32 and showed every sign of genuine remorse. A basis of plea was accepted which said the speed of the car was about 40 mph and alcohol did not play any part in his manner of driving. Held. The defendant had prevented the police from determining his alcohol level. Applying *A-G's Reference (No 21 of 2000)* [2001] 1 Cr App Rep (S) 173 the court is able to draw an adverse inference about the amount of alcohol consumed. The judge should not have accepted the basis of plea, but the court was bound by it. Taking into account it was a reference and there were aggravating features **3½ years** not 30 months.

R v Corkhill [2001] EWCA Crim 2683, [2002] 2 Cr App Rep (S) 60. The defendant pleaded at the earliest opportunity to causing death by dangerous driving and driving whilst disqualified. The defendant was an unqualified driver who had been disqualified from driving for 6 months for speeding and driving without insurance or a licence. This was the second time he had been convicted for those offences. Two months later when 18 in the early hours he offered five people a lift in his friend's car. He drove through the centre of Liverpool at high speed. His passengers were terrified and repeatedly shouted for him to slow down but he took no notice. Three girls in the back started crying and asked him to let them out. He drove in excess of 50 mph despite the roads being busy with people and went through a number of red lights. Shortly before the accident he drove at about 50 mph and apparently aimed at a group of people standing in the roadway. Shortly after the victim was crossing the road and had almost reached the other side when the defendant came round a corner extremely fast on the wrong side of the road with the engine revving. The victim stood no chance and was run over. The defendant made no effort to brake or avoid the victim. He drove off at speed and continued to drive dangerously until he abandoned the car at Bootle. He surrendered to the police and accepted he was the driver although he disputed the speeds put to him. The victim's family was devastated by the loss. The defendant showed remorse. He had had a troubled background and had been severely injured by a car when he was 10. He had a clear learning disability, poor social skills and low self-esteem. In 1999 he was treated for depression and was in receipt of incapacity benefit. Held. This was a bad case but could not be described as among 'the very worst cases.' Because of his plea **5 years** not 7. The disqualification period reduced from 7 to 5 years too.

R v Noble (24 June 2002, unreported). The defendant was convicted of six counts of causing death by dangerous driving. He pleaded to driving whilst disqualified. He and friends spent the day drinking on motorised 'pub crawl.' He said he had drunk about 12 pints of lager, 1 pint of mixed lager and cider and two Bacardi Breezers. He then drove with others on a busy A road at excessive speed although the road was wet. After the dual carriageway narrowed to a single carriageway there was a double bend. Because of his speed he lost control of his car and hit a wall and then two other cars. Three died from each other vehicle and others were injured. The defendant received relatively minor injuries and ran off. On his arrest he said someone else was driving. On his estimate of his drinking his blood/alcohol reading would have been 150 mg in his blood. (The court said he was 2½ times over the limit which gives a different figure.) He was 41 with the following convictions. 1990 failure to provide a specimen. 1991 drink/drive and driving whilst disqualified when he was disqualified for 3 years. In 1997 drink/drive when he received 100 hours' CSO and 4 years' disqualification. He was a family man with a good work record. The judge said he showed breathtaking arrogance in the witness box. Held. This was an horrendous case involving tragedy for many families. There were obvious aggravating features. The motorised pub crawl, the very bad driving record, being disqualified, running off, driving dangerously for a little while before the accident and blaming someone else. While, therefore, the total sentence should take account of the number of deaths, it cannot be determined by it, if only because of the chance nature of the number of the deaths. The fact that multiple deaths have been caused is not of itself a reason for imposing consecutive sentences. The main focus of the sentencing judge in such cases has to be on the dangerousness of the driving, taking into account all the circumstances of that driving, including the results. It is difficult to imagine a worse case so 10 years but the sentences should be concurrent so **10 years** not 15.

Speeding with excess alcohol or drug taking

45.35 *R v Wood* [1998] 2 Cr App Rep (S) 234. The defendant pleaded guilty to causing death by dangerous driving. The defendant drank with friends and then drove home with two of them. None of them wore seat belts. At the beginning of the journey he spun the wheels and was advised by one of them to calm down. He continued to speed and was cautioned again. A witness thought he was going 60 mph in a 30 mph area. He lost control of the car at a bend and slid sideways into an oncoming minicab. He and one of his passengers were thrown through the windscreen. The passenger suffered a fractured skull and died. The defendant's blood reading of alcohol was 93mg, (the breath equivalent was 40½ug). An expert said the accident was caused by a combination of a speed of at least 60 mph and drink. Shortly after this offence he drove with excess alcohol and was involved in a slight damage only collision. He didn't stop but was traced and given probation. He also had four possession of drug convictions. He had never been given a custodial sentence. He suffered from anxiety and a moderate degree of depression. He was drinking to alleviate the symptoms. He was 31. Held. Looking at the authorities and considering the factors including the plea and that he was only over the limit by a small margin **4 years** not 5.

A-G's Reference (No 16 of 1998) [1999] 1 Cr App Rep (S) 149. The defendant was convicted of two counts of causing death by dangerous driving. When 22 he went to a pub with two close friends and he drove away with them. None of them were wearing a seat belt. He overtook vehicles on a dual carriageway well in excess of 70 mph. He overtook another vehicle when the road narrowed to a single carriageway which was potentially dangerous. He entered a roundabout at very close to 70 mph and lost control of the car which hit a kerb and a crash barrier. Both his passengers were thrown from the car and died shortly after they had arrived in hospital. He left the scene in a state of shock. He gave a false name in hospital where he was treated for a broken shoulder, arm injuries and a head injury. The defendant pretended to the police he was a passenger. At first he refused to supply a blood specimen but eventually did. By backtracking his reading was between 90 and 120mg at the time of the accident (equivalent to 39 and 52ug). In interview he accepted he was driving at about 70 mph and said the brakes had failed. He had two convictions of no relevance and a clean licence. He had an overwhelming sense of grief and was having difficulty in coming to terms with his responsibility. He had become a virtual recluse and had sought counselling. One of the mothers of the victims had written a moving letter saying she had forgiven him. The other mother had taken a very different position. He was sentenced to 240 hours' community service. The local press had described him as a murderer who had gone free. The offence was 18 months before and he had completed ¼ of his community service. Held. We would have expected **4½ years**. Taking into account it was a reference and the CSO he had completed **3½ years** instead.

R v James [2001] 2 Cr App Rep (S) 153. The defendant was convicted of causing death by dangerous driving and driving whilst disqualified. After drinking in a pub with his two nephews he drove them away from the pub in his van. One of the nephews, the victim sat on the lap of the other in the front passenger seat. None of the three was wearing a seat belt and the defendant was disqualified from driving. The van was seen by police being driven at speed and they gave chase. The van went through a red light and the police put their lights on. Shortly after the van still driving at speed veered across the road and hit an oncoming coach. The victim was thrown from the van and killed instantly. The other nephew was severely injured with head injuries. He was in intensive care for several days. The defendant was also injured. He had 123mg reading of alcohol in his blood, (equivalent to 54ug in his breath). He showed shock and remorse. He was 28 and had an appalling driving record. He had 10 convictions for disqualified driving and two for dangerous driving. One of them was on a motorway when he was trying to escape the police. He also had a conviction for reckless driving and drink/drive. Held. The **8 years** sentence was entirely proper. However, as the judge had considered the fact he was disqualified in considering the aggravating factors it was wrong to make the disqualified driving sentence consecutive. The sentences were made concurrent.

A-G's Reference (No 32 of 2001) [2001] EWCA Crim 2120, [2002] 1 Cr App Rep (S) 517. The defendant pleaded guilty to causing death by dangerous driving. He was committed for sentence for failing to stop, failing to report, driving without a licence and driving without insurance. He was also sentenced for perverting the course of justice, possession of heroin and two counts of possession of cannabis. He was released from YOI in January 2000 and obtained a provisional licence. He had some 4 hours of driving tuition. On 7 May 2000 he drove a stolen car at speed and mounted a pavement. He was arrested and cannabis and heroin were thrown from the car. He was released on bail. His girlfriend's mother left her powerful Ford Galaxy car outside her house and instructed one was to drive it. On 26 May 2000 the defendant used it for a number of journeys and on 27 May 2000 he drank rum in a pub and a club and then drove it at about 40 mph in a 30 mph area with his girlfriend who only had a provisional licence. He failed to see a Give Way sign in time and hit a taxi. His speed then was 20–25 mph. The taxi swung through 180 and the passenger of the taxi died. He got out, looked at the taxi and left the scene. The prosecution said this was to avoid a breath sample being taken. Two days later surrendered to the police. The defendant was either 18 or 19 (now 20) years old and in 1997 received 15 months YOI. In 1998 for burglary and robbery he received 3 years' detention. There were 439 days unexpired on his licence. He as sentenced to 2½ years for the driving and concurrent sentences on the other offences. No order was made for the breach of the licence. Held. We would expect **5 years** detention for the driving in addition to the breach sentence. As it was a reference **4 years** detention with 12 months for the breach of licence consecutive and 5 years' not 2 years' disqualification.

See also *Failing to see other vehicles, obstacles etc within time*

Unqualified driver

45.36   *A-G's Reference (No 32 of 2001)* [2001] EWCA Crim 2120, [2002] 1 Cr App Rep (S) 517. See *Speed, approaching a hazard at excessive*

Victim dies after defendant dealt with for dangerous driving

45.37   *R v Munro* [2001] 1 Cr App Rep (S) 205. The defendant pleaded guilty to dangerous driving and was sentenced to 15 months imprisonment. A week later the case was relisted and the judge suspended the sentence because of the defendant's family circumstances. At that stage which was 7 months after the accident the victim was still in hospital and was a quadriplegic. Thirteen months after the accident the victim left hospital but still required 24 hour care. A month later she died. The defendant was then charged with causing death by dangerous driving. She pleaded guilty and nearly 2 years after her first sentence was given 12 months imprisonment. The defendant had driven in a highly dangerous way to and from her children's school. She drove at high speed on a road with bends. She lost control of the car both before and after collecting her children. She finally mounted the pavement and knocked over an elderly lady. Since her first sentence she had been stricken with guilt and had difficulty living with what she had done. The sentence of imprisonment had had a very considerable effect on her children which was likely to increase. A recent report showed she had suffered from post-traumatic stress disorder and had attempted to take her life. Held. The judge was faced with a most difficult sentencing problem. The intrinsic culpability of the defendant's conduct had not significantly changed. The victim's quality of life had been destroyed when she had been knocked down. If the defendant had been dealt with for causing death by dangerous driving to start with the judge would have been obliged to pass a sentence of at least 3 years which he could not have suspended. Sentences should reflect the gravity of the offences. The judge had balanced all the competing interests and it was hard to criticise his decision. Notwithstanding the new information the appeal was dismissed.

Victims

See VICTIMS

Victims, the views of the relatives of the

45.38 *A-G's Reference (Nos 14 and 25 of 1993)* [1994] 15 Cr App Rep (S) 640 – LCJ. Human life could not be restored, or its loss measured, by the length of the prison sentence. No term could reconcile the family of the deceased to their loss, or cure their anguish.

A-G's Reference (Nos 24 and 45 of 1994) [1995] 16 Cr App Rep (S) 583 at 586 – LCJ. No court can bring back to life those who have been killed. We understand the feelings of those relatives and friends of the deceased who believe that there ought to be a correlation between the loss of life and the length of sentence. We also understand that no length of sentence will ever satisfy those who lose loved ones that a proper correlation has been made. We must emphasise that this court cannot be persuaded by campaigns or by clamour to pass extremely long sentences where the criminality of the offender does not justify it. This court is concerned primarily with the criminality of the person who has caused the death. The fact that the death is, of itself, a factor in contributing to the length of sentence which should be passed. But essentially we have to look at the cases in the light of the offender's criminality.

R v Nunn [1996] 2 Cr App Rep (S) 136. The opinions of the victim, or the surviving members of the family about the sentence do not provide any sound basis for reassessing a sentence. If the victim feels utterly remorseful towards the criminal, and some do, the crime has still been committed and must be punished as it deserves. If the victim is obsessed with vengeance, which can in reality only be assuaged by a very long prison sentence, as also happens, the punishment cannot be made longer by the court than would otherwise be appropriate. Otherwise cases with identical features would be dealt with in widely different ways leading to improper and unfair disparity.

A-G's Reference (No 66 of 1996) [1998] 1 Cr App Rep (S) 16 – LCJ. The families of the victims feel bitter and vindictive towards the defendant whom they see as the author of their irreparable loss. This case contains such a feature. The family of one of the victims has succeeded in reconciling themselves towards the consequences of this tragedy. The family of the other victim has not. Their feelings are understandable. No one who has not suffered such a loss is in a position to understand how they feel and it would be entirely inappropriate to disparage or belittle the emotions of those who suffer in this way. It is nonetheless the duty of the trial judge, and of this court to judge cases dispassionately. The court must of course take account of the understandable outrage felt against any defendant who has caused consequences such as these. That is a sense of outrage shared by the wider public, which feels acute anxiety about the cruel, avoidable loss of life which is a feature of cases such as this. On the other hand, the court must take account of the interests of the defendant who has often, as here, not intended these consequences and is often, as here, devastated by them. The court cannot overlook the fact that no punishment it can impose will begin to match the deep sense of responsibility which defendants often feel. It is important that courts should do their best to approach their task objectively and dispassionately. They should not be overborne or intimidated into imposing sentences, which they consider are unjust.

R v Richards [1998] 2 Cr App Rep (S) 346. The defendant pleaded guilty to causing death by dangerous driving. The defendant then 22, killed his girlfriend by overtaking at excessive speed. He had earlier overtaken another car at speed. He was of good character with seven references and a clean driving record. He was greatly affected by the death and had not driven since. He had no intention of driving in the future. The girl's father said no member of his family wanted the defendant to go to prison and he could not have wished for a better future son in law. Held. Two years was on the high side but not necessarily manifestly excessive. However, he has the burden of killing his own girlfriend and apparently his future wife. This was a grave sentence on its own. The court has a public duty to perform and must be careful not to be swayed by clamour or favour. However, the court cannot ignore that he has retained the confidence and affection of the family who wanted him to marry the victim. Taking those matters into account **12 months** instead. [For further details see *Overtaking*]

R v Roche [1999] 2 Cr App Rep (S) 105 – LCJ. The defendant pleaded guilty to causing death by careless driving when under the influence of drink. He killed his cousin when drunk and speeding. The defendant's parents were brother and sister of the victim's parents. The victim's mother treated the defendant almost as a son and had played a large part in bringing him up. It was very closely-knit family and the victim's mother had written a moving letter. The sentence imposed was delaying the time at which she can grieve. Other members of the family make the same point. A letter from the defendant's mother pointed out the very serious effect which the sentence was having on her and his father. Held. It is not for the injured party to dictate the sentence based on vengeance or compassion. Nonetheless the court can in appropriate circumstances become an instrument of compassion. That is an appropriate response to this case. Although there is no criticism of the 4 year sentence in light of the new material **3 years**.

R v O'Brien [2001] 1 Cr App Rep (S) 79. The defendant pleaded guilty to causing death by dangerous driving. The defendant showed remorse from the very beginning. The relatives said no useful purpose could be served by a custodial sentence. Held. The views of the family are to be greatly respected. Applying *R v Nunn* [1996] 2 Cr App Rep (S) 136 and *R v Roche* [1999] 2 Cr App Rep (S) 105 the views of the victims are not a relevant consideration whether they seek leniency or severity save in exceptional circumstances.

R v Porter [2002] EWCA Crim 1121, [2002] 2 Cr App Rep (S) 222. All judges are careful not to be overinfluenced by the devastation that is caused.

Practice Direction (Victim Personal Statements) [2002] 1 Cr App Rep (S) 482. The opinions of the victim or the victim's close relatives as to what the sentence should be are not relevant. Victims should be advised of this.

See also MANSLAUGHTER – *Vehicle, by*

DECENCY, OUTRAGING PUBLIC

See PUBLIC DECENCY, OUTRAGING

46 DECEPTION, OBTAINING PROPERTY ETC BY

46.1 Theft Act 1968, ss 15, 15A and 16. Theft Act 1978, ss 1 and 2

Triable either way. Maximum on indictment, 10 years for ss 15 and 15A, 5 years for ss 16, 1 and 2. Summary maximum 6 months and/or £5,000.

There is power to make a restitution order under the Powers of Criminal Courts (Sentencing) Act 2000, s 148.

Magistrates' Court Sentencing Guidelines September 2000

46.2 Entry point. Is it serious enough for a community penalty? Consider the impact on the victim. Examples of aggravating factors for the offence are committed over a lengthy period, large sums or valuable goods, two or more involved and victim particularly vulnerable. Examples of mitigating factors for the offence are for impulsive action, short period and small sum. Examples of mitigation are age, health (physical or mental), co-operation with police, voluntary compensation and genuine remorse. Give reasons for not awarding compensation.

For details about the guidelines see **MAGISTRATES' COURT SENTENCING GUIDELINES** at page 331.

Where the offence is in essence theft it is listed under **THEFT ETC**

Driving tests, trying to obtain a pass

46.3 *R v Adebayo* [1998] 1 Cr App Rep (S) 15. The defendant was convicted of conspiracy to obtain property by a deception. He arranged for an impostor to take his driving test. He was 36 and was treated as of good character. He had claimed political asylum and was working as a cleaner. The impostor pleaded guilty and received 3 months varied on appeal to community service. The judge said the difference was the defendant was the beneficiary and hadn't pleaded guilty. He had a good prison report. Held. This offence cannot be tolerated. **6 months** was right.

47 DEFENDANT

AIDS, defendant has

47.1 *R v Stark* [1992] Crim LR 384. The defendant was sentenced to 4 years for drug trafficking. Because of AIDS his life expectancy was estimated by one doctor as not more than a year and another 12–18 months. The offences had originally been allowed to lie on the file because of his condition but 5 weeks later he was arrested for a similar offence. Held. It was not for the Court of Appeal to manipulate a sentence to achieve a social end. That matter was for the Royal Prerogative of mercy. Adjustments could be made as an act of mercy but it would not be right to radically change a perfectly proper sentence. His arrest showed there was a grave risk he would continue to traffic in drugs as long as he was able to do so. The medical reports should be forwarded to the prison authorities.

Disabled, the defendant is

47.2 *A-G's Reference (No 2 of 2001)* [2001] EWCA Crim 1015, [2001] 2 Cr App Rep (S) 524. The defendant pleaded guilty to seven counts of indecent assault against his stepdaughter when she was between the ages of 8 and 15. The defendant, who was 100% disabled and wheelchair bound forced the victim to masturbate him and take his penis in her mouth. The defendant was 49 years of age. Held. The appropriate sentence was **5 years**. Having regard that this was a reference and the serious disability faced by the defendant which would render imprisonment more difficult to bear **2 years** was appropriate not a probation order.

Elderly

47.3   *R v Suckley* [2001] EWCA Crim 125, [2001] 2 Cr App Rep (S) 313. The defendant now aged 75 was convicted of attempted murder. Held. It is plain from *R v C* (1992) 14 Cr App Rep (S) 562; *R v S* [1998] 1 Cr App Rep (S) 261 and *R v Anderson* [1999] 1 Cr App Rep (S) 273 regard must be had to age and that a discount is appropriate. Any attempt at an actuarial basis for a discount is inappropriate. It may well be that there is greater scope for exercising mercy in cases where elderly men have committed sexual offences many years earlier. The present sentence has been significantly discounted from almost certainly 15 years which would have been appropriate for a younger man to **11 years**. Such a discount was proper and fair. Appeal dismissed.

Inadequate

47.4   *R v Turner* [2001] EWCA Crim 1331, [2002] 1 Cr App Rep (S) 207. The defendant pleaded guilty to manslaughter on the basis of lack of intent and he acted in panic when flustered and under stress. Also diminished responsibility would have been open to him because of his intellectual limitations. He lived with a girl who he had met at a special school. On 12 December 1999 they had a baby. They were both 17 and neither could look after themselves let alone a baby. The relationship was stormy and the arrival of the baby put the relationship under additional and severe strain. Occasionally he would look after the baby with her mother but he seemed not to understand the importance of careful handling. On 15 January 2000 he was left in charge of the baby for the first time. He called his aunt to say the baby was not breathing properly and had gone floppy. When the ambulance came he refused to let them take her because he was worried about his partner. Later the baby was taken to hospital and doctors found haemorrhaging behind both eyes. There was widespread bleeding in the brain. The next day the life support system was switched off. The injuries were consistent with shaken baby syndrome but experts could not say for how long or with what vigour the shaking had been. In interview the defendant admitted shaking his daughter. He said it was a particular difficult day with problems with the local authority etc. The baby started crying and he could not stop it. He shook her twice and supported her head. That he said usually quietened her. When she cried again he shook her without holding her head and he noticed she went floppy. He was of good character. The reports agreed he was a man with very real handicaps with profound social incapacity. He had a borderline learning disability with significant impairment of intellectual and social functioning amounting to an abnormality of the mind. He was vulnerable and dependent on others. If he remained in custody his partner would not be able to cope and would be taken into care. The overwhelming view of the doctors was that custody was entirely inappropriate for him. He had spent 5 months in custody, which he had been unable to cope with. He had to remain in the protection unit. Held. Parents could not escape all the responsibilities for their actions by relying on their own problems. That does not mean in every tragic case where a child is killed custody is inevitable. Exceptional cases merit exceptional sentences. He lacked the mental capacity to appreciate the consequences of his actions and intended no harm to the baby. He was vulnerable and needed protection. He was totally ill equipped to deal with the situation and should never have been put in that position. The sooner he receives support, guidance and medical treatment the better. A **3 year community rehabilitation order** with a condition of treatment and duty to live where approved not 2½ years YOI.

Mentally ill

47.5   *A-G's Reference (No 83 of 2001)* [2001] EWCA Crim 65, [2002] 1 Cr App Rep (S) 289. The defendant pleaded guilty at the first opportunity to robbery. He robbed a small off licence wearing a balaclava mask holding a 12" chrome object in his hand. He took money, cigarettes and a bottle of brandy. A few days later he went to hospital and admitted himself as a voluntary patient. He told the staff he heard voices and told them about the robbery and permitted them to tell the police. He admitted the offence to the police and said he had a metal bar. Without his help there would have been no evidence. He had minor convictions and was a crack addict. The report said he suffered from a serious mental illness namely schizophrenia. He needed long and consistent management, which would last for a number of years. He came to be sentenced from hospital where he had co-operated with the staff and his condition was stable. It was thought he would be ill equipped to deal with prison and that he would possible commit suicide if he was sent there. He was sentenced to a community rehabilitation order for 2 years with a requirement that he should reside as directed including hospital and he should take such medication as prescribed. The judge said he considered the normal tariff but considered the circumstances particularly the medical evidence. After sentence a report indicated he had taken advantage of his opportunity and was drug free. Held. What the authorities do not show are the cases where the individual circumstances of the defendant and the mitigation available to him have led to a justified departure from the guidance provided by the reported decisions. It is fundamental to the responsibilities of sentencing judges that while they must always pay proper regard to the sentencing guidance given, they are required also to reflect on all the circumstances of the individual case. Where sentencing judges are satisfied that occasion requires it, they have to balance the demands of justice with what is sometimes described as the calls of mercy. There were occasions where it was right to take a constructive course and seek to achieve the rehabilitation of the offender. The judge was satisfied it provided the best possible long-term solution for the community and the defendant. It was right to take a constructive course. So far he has been proved right. The prospects of re-offending are now lower than if he had had a custodial sentence. The sentence was lenient on paper but sentencing is not and never can be an exercise on paper; each case, ultimately, is individual. It would be wrong to interfere.

For two cases about whether life or hospital order should be imposed see *R v Moses* [1996] Crim LR 604 and *R v Mitchell* [1996] Crim LR 604.

Articles. Sentencing psychopaths: Is the 'Hospital and Limitation Direction' an ill-considered hybrid? 1998 Crim LR 93. Diversion of Mentally Disordered Offenders: Victim and Offender perspectives 1999 Crim LR 805.

Personal mitigation

47.6 *A-G's Reference (No 84 of 2001)* [2001] EWCA Crim 7, [2002] 2 Cr App Rep (S) 226. The defendant pleaded guilty to attempted robbery and having a firearm with intent to resist arrest. He tried to rob a Securicor guard delivering cash to a cash dispenser. Held. Personal factors in relation to offences of this gravity can have only a very small effect in determining what the appropriate sentence is.

Rich

47.7 Powers of Criminal Courts (Sentencing) Act 2000, s 128(3). In fixing the amount of any fine to be imposed... a court shall take into account. . .the financial circumstances of the defendant so far as they are known, or appear, to the court.

Powers of Criminal Courts (Sentencing) Act 2000, s 128(3). Sub-section (3) applies whether taking into account the financial circumstances has the effect of increasing or reducing the fine.

R v Jerome [2001] 1 Cr App Rep (S) 316. The defendant was convicted of handling. Computer and other equipment worth in all about £2,739 were stolen in a burglary. The computer was traced to the defendant when a message was sent from the computer to the Internet. His flat was searched and the equipment was found. He was an antiques dealer and his turnover was about £100,000. The judge said he was minded to imprisonment of the defendant but was concerned his business might be permanently wrecked. He was fined £10,000. Held. It is permissible to increase a fine for a wealthy or relatively wealthy offender. However, there must be some proportionality between the scale of the offence and the fine imposed. In handling the value of the goods must be taken into consideration. **£6,000 fine** not £10,000. [Many will consider the sentencing judge's proportionality of just under four times the value is more realistic than the Court of Appeal's proportionality of just over twice the value.]

See also ARMED FORCES, MEMBERS OF; BASIC PRINCIPLES; CUSTODY, DISCOUNT FOR TIME IN; CO-DEFENDANT'S PERSONAL MITIGATION; DISABILITIES, DEFENDANT'S; DRUG USERS; FATHERS; GUILTY PLEA, DISCOUNT FOR; MERCY; MOTHERS; SOLICITORS, and YOUNG OFFENDERS

DEFRAUD

See FRAUD

48   DELAY

Sexual offences

48.1 *A-G's Reference (No 60 of 2001)* [2001] EWCA Crim 2026, [2002] 1 Cr App Rep (S) 396. The defendant pleaded guilty to 11 counts of buggery, one of aiding and abetting buggery and 15 indecent assaults on five boys between 11 and 15. Between 1976 and 1991 he was Chairman of a naturist club. Between 1976 and 1991 he conducted systematic and persistent abuse on five boys. He gained the trust of the parents of the victims and then the victims were groomed, given treats and photographed naked. With each he masturbated, then had mutual masturbation and then buggered four of them. The treats were sweets, drinks, smoking and trips to London. The offences took place when he was 34–45 and he was now 62. Some were abused by his friends. The judge said, 'it was a terrible trail of corruption with a lasting and dreadful effect. Some were depressed, unable to take part in sport, form normal relations, lacked a social life, tried to commit suicide and attend psychiatric centres. You pose a real danger to the public.' He reduced the 15 year sentence to 9 because of the delay. Held. The 15 year starting point was right. It is right to make a discount for the delay but it cannot be very great because these offences tend not to come to light very quickly. Taking into account the delay and that it was a reference **12 years** substituted. (Crown Court judges give a greater discount than this which is less than a 1/5.)

See also INDECENT ASSAULT ON A MAN – *Delay, long delay before conviction*; INDECENT ASSAULT ON A WOMAN – *Delay, long delay before conviction* and RAPE – *Delay, long delay before conviction*

DEPENDANTS

See CRUELTY TO CHILDREN, FATHERS and MOTHERS

49   DISABILITIES, DEFENDANT'S

Circumstances change after sentence

49.1   *R v Nall-Cain* [1998] 2 Cr App Rep (S) 145. Obiter. Where, for example, there is a deterioration in the defendant's health, or it is impossible, by reason of a prisoner's physical disabilities for the prison to cope with him, the Court of Appeal may exercise mercy.

Disabled, the defendant is

49.2   *A-G's Reference No 2 of 2001* [2001] 2 Cr App Rep (S) 524. The defendant pleaded guilty to seven counts of indecent assault against his stepdaughter when she was between the ages of 8 and 15. The defendant, who was 100% disabled and wheelchair bound forced the victim to masturbate him and take his penis in her mouth. The defendant was 49 years of age. Held. The appropriate sentence was **5 years**. Having regard that this was a reference and the serious disability faced by the defendant which would render imprisonment more difficult to bear **2 years** was appropriate not a probation order.

DISCOUNT

For discount for a guilty plea see **GUILTY PLEA, DISCOUNT FOR**

For discount for time in custody see **CUSTODY, DISCOUNT FOR TIME SPENT IN**

For the principle that there is no discount for time served for a conviction which is later quashed see **SENTENCES SERVED FOR WHICH THE CONVICTION WAS LATER QUASHED**

50   DISQUALIFIED DRIVING

50.1   Road Traffic Act 1988, s 103

Summary only. Under the Criminal Justice Act 1988, s 40(3)(c) it may be included in an indictment.

Maximum sentence 6 months or £5,000. 6 penalty points. Discretionary disqualification.

Magistrates' Court Sentencing Guidelines September 2000

50.2   Entry point. Is it so serious that only custody is appropriate? Examples of aggravating factors for the offence are efforts to avoid detection, long distance driving, planned long term evasion and recent disqualification. Examples of mitigating factors for the offence are emergency established, full period expired but test not re-taken and short distance travelled. Examples of mitigation are co-operation with the police, and genuine remorse.

For details about the guidelines see **MAGISTRATES' COURT SENTENCING GUIDELINES** at page 331.

Is the defendant entitled to a discount for pleading guilty?

50.3   *R v Williams* (13 July 2001, unreported). The defendant pleaded guilty to dangerous driving and driving whilst disqualified. The judge considered 5 years was the appropriate penalty. He passed 2 years (the maximum) for the driving and 6 months consecutive (the maximum) for the disqualified driving. The defence appealed the disqualified driving sentence on the basis he was given the maximum because the judge thought the driving penalty was inadequate. Further the defendant had pleaded and the disqualified offence was not of the most serious. Held. We agree with the judge's description that one cannot conceive a more serious case of driving than this. The defendant was entitled to a reduction so **3 months** not 6.

51   DRINK DRIVING

51.1   Including driving under the influence of drugs

The Road Traffic Act 1988, ss 4 and 5 are relevant offences under the Football Spectators Act 1989, s 14A and Sch 1, para 1. Where (a) the offence was committed during a journey and the court makes a declaration that the offence related to football matches and (c) there are reasonable grounds to believe that making a banning order would help to prevent violence or disorder at or in connection with any regulated football match; the court must make a Football Banning Order, (except where the defendant is given an absolute discharge).

Drink driving – Excess alcohol

51.2   Road Traffic Act 1988, s 5(1)(a)

Summary only. Maximum 6 months or a Level 5 fine (£5,000). Minimum disqualification 1 year. 3–11 penalty points if special reasons not to disqualify are found. Where a defendant has a conviction for driving while unfit, causing death under the influence of drink, driving with excess alcohol and failing to provide a specimen in previous 10 years, minimum disqualification is 3 years[1]. There is power to order reduced disqualification for attendance on courses[2].

1   Road Traffic Offenders Act 1988, s 34(3).
2   Road Traffic Offenders Act 1988, s 34A.

Magistrates' Court Sentencing Guidelines September 2000

51.3   Entry point. Depends on reading. Examples of aggravating factors for the offence are ability to drive seriously impaired, causing injury/fear/damage, police chase, evidence of nature of the driving, type of vehicle, eg carrying passengers for reward/large goods vehicle and high reading (and in combination with above). Examples of mitigating factors for the offence are emergency, moving a vehicle a very short distance and spiked drinks. An example of mitigation is co-operation with the police. Offer a rehabilitation course.

Breath	Blood	Urine	Disqualify not less than	Guideline
36–55	80–125	107–170	12 months	B[1] fine
56–70	126–160	171–214	18 months	C fine
71–85	161–195	215–260	24 months	
86–100	196–229	261–308	24 months	Consider community penalty
101–115	230–264	309–354	30 months	
116–130	265–300	355–400	30 months	Consider custody
131+	301+	401+	36 months	

R v St Albans Crown Court, ex p O'Donovan [2000] 1 Cr App Rep (S) 344. The defendant was convicted of driving with excess alcohol. The guidelines only apply where there are no special reasons. For more details see **Disqualification, for how long?**

For details about the guidelines see MAGISTRATES' COURT SENTENCING GUIDELINES at page 331.

1   (B =£100, C=£150 when defendant has £100 net weekly income. See page 334 for table showing fines for different incomes.)

Disqualification, for how long?

51.4   *R v St Albans Crown Court, ex p O'Donovan* [2000] 1 Cr App Rep (S) 344. The defendant was convicted of driving with excess alcohol. The defendant was moving his car in a pub car park. He bumped another car and had 103mg of alcohol in his blood. The prosecution accepted that he lived 5 minutes' walk away and he was not going to drive out of the car park, but was simply moving his car to attempt to clear the access to the rear of the pub. The car was partially blocking a service gate. He was 39 with no relevant convictions. He was a forklift driver on building sites and his loss of job would effect his ex-wife and two daughters who he supported. He was sentenced to **£750 fine** and 20 months' disqualification with a 5 month reduction for going on a course. He appealed to the Crown Court who dismissed his appeal. Each court found special reasons to exist. The Crown Court relied on the Magistrates' Guidelines. Held. It would be hard to justify disqualification of more than 12 months. The guidelines only apply where there are no special reasons. The disqualification was reduced to 12 months with 3 month reduction for going on a course.

Drugs, under the influence of

51.5   *R v O'Prey* [1999] 2 Cr App Rep (S) 83. The defendant pleaded guilty to perverting the course of Justice, driving whilst disqualified and possession of cannabis. He was committed for sentence for driving whist unfit through drugs. Police stopped his car because it was being driven 'terribly' on the M3. He gave a false name (presumably the perverting matter). He admitted he had smoked cannabis and spat some out. He was then 24 with dishonesty convictions and had received custody for robbery. He was disqualified for 2 years for drink/drive. Held. The judge was in a difficult position because he had not been charged with dangerous driving. He could not be sentenced for it by using the cannabis count. The proper sentence for the driving whilst disqualified was 3 months, for the perverting count 3 months, for the unfit charge 6 months and 1 month (not 3 years) concurrent for the cannabis. The rest were consecutive making 12 months not 3½ years.

In charge

51.6   (Whilst unfit through drink or drugs, when refusing to provide a specimen and when over the alcohol limit.)

Road Traffic Act 1988, ss 4(2), 5(1)(b) and 7(6)

Summary only. Maximum 3 months or Level 4 (£2,500). Discretionary disqualification. Mandatory endorsement (subject to special reasons). 10 penalty points. There is power to order reduced disqualification for attendance on courses[1].

1   Road Traffic Offenders Act 1988, s 34A.

Magistrates' Court Sentencing Guidelines September 2000

51.7   Consider disqualification if evidence of driving or other aggravating factor. [This appears to offend the principle that courts are restricted to punishing for the offence charged and cannot punish for a different and more serious offence. More suitable would be to consider the intention to drive.] Offer a rehabilitation course if disqualifying for 12 months or more. **Starting point fine B.** (£100 when defendant has £100 net weekly income. See page 334 for table showing fines for different incomes.)

For details about the guidelines see MAGISTRATES' COURT SENTENCING GUIDELINES at page 331.

Failure to provide roadside breath test

51.8 Road Traffic Act 1988, s 6(4)

Summary only. Maximum fine Level 3 (£1,000). Discretionary disqualification. 4 penalty points. Mandatory endorsement (subject to special reasons).

Magistrates' Court Sentencing Guidelines September 2000

51.9 Starting point fine A. (£50 when defendant has £100 net weekly income. See page 334 for table showing fines for different incomes.)

For details about the guidelines see MAGISTRATES' COURT SENTENCING GUIDELINES at page 331.

DRIVERS' HOURS

See TACHOGRAPH AND OTHER DRIVERS' HOURS OFFENCES

DRIVING TEST

See DECEPTION, OBTAINING PROPERTY ETC BY – *Driving tests, trying to obtain a pass*

52 DRUG USERS

Guideline case

52.1 *R v Brewster* [1998] 1 Cr App Rep 220, [1998] 1 Cr App Rep (S) 181 – LCJ. It is common knowledge that many domestic burglars are drug addicts who burgle to satisfy their craving for drugs. This is often an expensive craving, and it is not uncommon to learn that addicts commit a burglary, or even several burglaries, each day, often preying on houses in less affluent areas of the country. Self-induced addiction cannot be relied on as mitigation. The courts will not be easily persuaded that an addicted offender is genuinely determined and able to conquer his addiction.

Determined efforts to break addiction

52.2 *A-G's Reference (No 34 of 1999)* [2000] 1 Cr App Rep (S) 322 – LJC. The defendant pleaded guilty to robbery 4 months after the PDH hearing. The defendant who had partly covered his face with a shirt came up to the victim in a park and grabbed him by his jacket. He also grabbed hold of a valuable gold chain, which was round his neck. The defendant produced a hypodermic syringe, which appeared to contain a brown liquid and accused the boy of selling drugs to his brother. He held the syringe about a foot away from his neck and threatened to give him AIDS if he didn't get the chain off. The boy was terrified and the syringe was moved close to the boy's legs in a stabbing motion. Eventually the chain was undone. The defendant ran off with it. The next day he went to the shop where the boy worked and asked if he was accusing him of being the robber. He warned the boy not to make trouble for himself. He was arrested and gave an alibi. He was 25 and had convictions for burglary, common assault, drink/drive and failing to provide a specimen. They were all drug related. He didn't co-operate with a probation order and was given CSO, which he breached and he then served a short period of custody. There were reports from drug rehabilitation units, which said he was committed to overcoming his addiction and was doing his utmost to sort out his life. He arranged his own interviews and all tests were negative. To interfere with the programme would jeopardise the recovery. He was now in a residential unit. The progress was very good. The stay would be for up to 9 months funded by the council. The risk to the public was now described as being very low. He was given 18 months suspended and suspended sentence supervision order. Held. What distinguishes this from the normal case of a defendant saying they will cure themselves is that here he has taken vigorous, persistent, constructive and determined action. That made it exceptional so the sentence could be suspended. The sentence did not fall outside the options open to the judge.

A-G's Reference (No 48 of 1999) [2000] 1 Cr App Rep (S) 472 – LCJ. The defendant pleaded guilty to conspiracy to steal. During a 9 month period he stole tools from vans during the night. Each loss was between £100 to £3,000 and he was arrested and bailed twice. He co-operated with the police and admitted involvement in 25 thefts. In all the property stolen was worth £25,000. He was 28 and had a long list of conviction including burglary and some which were similar to this offence. He looked after his disabled father who was 'highly dependant' on him. The defendant had been addicted to amphetamines but had voluntarily sought help at a clinic. The judge recognised he had made a determined effort to conquer his drug problem and the public interest was best served by a course of treatment. He was placed on **probation** for 2 years with a condition of attendance at a centre for 30 days. Although there had been one lapse back into drug taking the latest reports were positive. One said he had attended the regularly at the centre and the writer considered a custodial sentence would be counterproductive. Held. If he had been convicted the ordinary sentence would have been 18 months to 2 years. With a plea and his mitigation a sentence in the order of **12 months** would have been in no way excessive. Sentencing courts must retain an element of discretion. The sentence was merciful and one open for the judge to pass so not unduly lenient.

Drug abstinence order

52.3 Powers of Criminal Courts (Sentencing) Act 2000, s 58A(1). Where a person is 18 or over the court may make an order requiring the offender to abstain from misusing specified Class A drugs and provide, when instructed to do so a sample to ascertain whether he has any specified Class A drugs in his body. (3) The court must be of the opinion the offender is dependant or has a propensity to misuse specified Class A drugs and the offence is a trigger offence or the misuse of any specified Class A drug caused or contributed to the offence in question. (7) An order shall be for not less than 6 months and not more than 3 years. (9) No order shall be made unless the court has been notified that arrangements for implementing the order are available. [Criminal Justice and Court Services Act 2000, Sch 6 specifies theft, robbery, burglary, aggravated burglary, TDA, aggravated vehicle-taking, obtaining property by deception, going equipped and supplying, producing and possessing Class A drugs as trigger offences.]

Exceptional cases

52.4 *R v Brewster Re RH* [1998] 1 Cr App Rep 220, [1998] 1 Cr App Rep (S) 181 at 187 – LCJ. The defendant, when 15 pleaded guilty to four burglaries committed in the space of little more than a week. The offences were committed to finance his addiction to crack cocaine. Because of wholly exceptional personal circumstances the court substituted a **supervision order** for an otherwise perfectly appropriate 4 years' detention. The court said, 'No one should interpret this judgment as detracting in any way from the general rule that there is no mitigation in drug addiction.'

DRUGS

See **DRUG USERS; EXPORTATION OF DRUGS, IMPORTATION OF DRUGS; POSSESSION OF DRUGS; PRODUCTION OF DRUGS** and **SUPPLY OF DRUGS (CLASS A, B AND C)** and **AMPHETAMINE; CANNABIS; ECSTASY; LSD,** and **OPIUM**

For driving under the influence of drugs see **DRINK DRIVING**

DRUGS MONEY

For acquiring, possessing or using the proceeds of drug trafficking see **MONEY LAUNDERING ETC**

53   DRUNK

Aircraft, on

See **AIRCRAFT OFFENCES** – *Drunk, being*

Drunk and disorderly

53.1   Criminal Justice Act 1967, s 91

Summary only. Maximum fine[1] Level 3 (£1,000).

1   *R v Broughtwood* (26 June 2002, unreported). A sentence of one day's imprisonment is unlawful.

Magistrates' Court Sentencing Guidelines September 2000

53.2   Entry point. Is a discharge or a fine appropriate? Examples of aggravating factors for the offence are offensive language or behaviour, on hospital/medical premises and with a group. Examples of mitigating factors for the offence are induced by others, no significant disturbance and not threatening. Examples of mitigation are health (physical or mental), co-operation with the police, and genuine remorse. **Starting point fine A.** (£50 when defendant has £100 net weekly income. See page 334 for table showing fines for different incomes.)

For details about the guidelines see **MAGISTRATES' COURT SENTENCING GUIDELINES** at page 331.

DUE CARE

See **CARELESS DRIVING**

DUTY EVASION

See **TAX FRAUD**

EARNINGS, MEN LIVING ON IMMORAL

See **PROSTITUTION, MEN LIVING ON EARNINGS OF**

54 ECSTASY

Constituency

54.1 *R v Warren and Beeley* [1996] 1 Cr App Rep (S) 233 at 236 – LCJ. Most ecstasy tablets contain 100 mgs. of active constituents. Accordingly 5,000 tablets could contain 500 grams. That should equate with 500 grams of heroin or cocaine.

Dangers of

54.2 *R v Broom* [1993] 14 Cr App Rep (S) 677. Ecstasy in the odd unusual case can kill and does kill.

R v Wright [1998] 2 Cr App Rep (S) 333 at 335. Ecstasy is a drug whose dangerousness is not to be underestimated and which is unfortunately often retailed in premises where young people may be found gathered together who simply do not understand or appreciate the possible dangers.

See also DRUG USERS; IMPORTATION OF DRUGS; POSSESSION OF DRUGS; PRODUCTION OF DRUGS and SUPPLY OF DRUGS (CLASS A, B AND C)

EDUCATION

See SCHOOL, FAILURE TO SECURE REGULAR ATTENDANCE

ELDERLY DEFENDANT

See DEFENDANT – *Elderly*

55 ELECTION OFFENCES

55.1 Representation of the People Act 1983, ss 60–66A, 99–102 and 106–115

Impersonation, tampering, corrupt practices and many other offences.

Triable either way. On indictment maximum 1 year, (except s 60, 2 years). Summary maximum 6 months and/or £5,000.

Sections 63, 66, 97, 99–101, 107 and 110–113 summary only with varying penalties.

Forging proxy vote details

55.2 *R v Lewis* [1998] 1 Cr App Rep (S) 13. The defendant pleaded guilty to eight counts of making a false instrument and eight counts of using those instruments. The defendant was a candidate in local elections. When voters said they would be unable to attend the polling booth she persuaded them to sign proxy voting forms. She pleaded guilty on the basis that she forged the details but she had the specific authority of the voter. She denied any of the information was false and denied she had forged any of the signatures. She said all had expressed a willingness to vote for her and she was simply taking a short cut. Held. Prison was not wrong in principle. She was interfering with the electoral process and undermining confidence in it. **1 month** not 2 giving her immediate release.

ELECTRICITY

See ABSTRACTING ELECTRICITY

The cases are listed under THEFT ETC – *Electricity or gas (including abstracting electricity*

56 EMPLOYMENT, OTHERS WILL LOSE THEIR

56.1 *R v Nicholls* [1998] 2 Cr App Rep (S) 296. The defendant was convicted of dangerous driving. The defendant drifted from lane to lane on a three lane dual carriageway causing one driver to brake heavily. Eventually he drifted into a barrier on the near side of the road of a two lane stretch and stopped. With smoke coming from the tyre and a tyre burst and he reversed at speed into the nearside lane and partly into the offside lane. He drove down the road and into a layby where he got out and looked at his vehicle. Then he suddenly drove off again causing other drivers to avoid him. He drove with sparks coming from his nearside wheels at about 50 mph. Eventually he stopped. Police found that the car had extensive damage to the front. The wheel of the tyre that burst had been moved backwards. The steering and suspension was also damaged. Another tyre was deflated. His breath alcohol reading was 78ug. The expert couldn't dispute that the tyre might have burst before the impact. The defendant was now aged 40 and treated as of good character. He was hard working and his two youngest children were in poor health. The youngest was about to have an operation. There was a risk that his company which employed 26 people could collapse. Solicitors acting for Customs confirmed the company was in serious financial difficulties. He received 9 months and since then seven engineers and two apprentices had lost their jobs. Held. He had showed a singular lack of control which arose from excessive consumption of alcohol. With a great deal of hesitation the company mitigation means the sentence should be **6 months** not 9.

See also COMPANIES

ENDANGERED SPECIES

See ANIMALS – *Endangered species*

57 ENTRAPMENT/AGENTS PROVOCATEURS

Police etc collect evidence of continuing activity, eg drug dealing

57.1 *R v Springer* [1999] 1 Cr App Rep (S) 217. The defendant pleaded guilty at the Magistrates' Court to three charges of supplying heroin and was committed to the Crown Court. The defendant was a suspected drug dealer. The police tested their suspicions by making three telephone calls. He was asked, 'Have you got anything.' He replied, 'Yeah,' and arrangements were made to meet him. In response to each call a meeting was arranged and about 1.5 grams of heroin was supplied. The calls were recorded and the meetings were videoed. The defence argued that he was entitled to a discount because of entrapment. Held. There was a need for the police to adopt this method of detection. There was need for there to be more than one supply to provide evidence he was a dealer. This was not a case of entrapping a suspect into supplying drugs who would otherwise never have engaged in that activity. *R v Underhill* (1979) 1 Cr App Rep (S) 270 at 272 applied. Here there was legitimate police activity and not activity that could provide mitigation or a reduction at all.

R v Mayeri [1999] 1 Cr App Rep (S) 304. The defendant pleaded guilty at the earliest opportunity to 4 counts of supplying ecstasy. One tablet was involved in each case. Four undercover police officers approached him in a nightclub and he agreed to sell them a tablet for £10. He claimed there was an element of entrapment. The defendant relied on *R v Tonnessen* [1998] 2 Cr App Rep (S) 328 Held. The entrapment argument is not a good one. Where undercover officers discover a man is prepared to sell drugs by approaching him it is not a matter the courts need normally take into account as amounting to entrapment. It might be said 'Seller beware.' These premises are frequently used to sell drugs.

Journalists, by

57.2   *R v Tonnessen* [1998] 2 Cr App Rep (S) 328. The defendant pleaded guilty to supplying heroin. The defendant was approached by a man who claimed to know her. He was accompanied by two others who turned out to be from the *News of the World*. They said they worked for a Sheikh and they were instructed to buy drugs. She was a heroin addict and a cannabis user and said they were widely available. They said they wanted to buy heroin and asked her whether she was prepared to get it for them. They gave her £50 and she bought four wraps of heroin. She and a friend spent the rest of the evening with them. Immediately after her name and photograph appeared in the paper. The police felt obliged to arrest her and she admitted the offence. After the publicity she was assaulted and received a threat to her life. She was 31 and had already served a prison sentence for an unrelated offence. She had no supply convictions. She suffered from a serious pre-cancerous condition. The judge did not refer to the involvement of agents provocateurs and appeared not to have taken it into account. The defence said there can be considerable mitigation where it can be shown that the offence would not otherwise have been committed. It is legitimate for policemen to entrap criminals. When the entrapment is by journalist even more consideration and more weight should be given. Held. We consider there is substance in those submissions. However, it merited immediate custody. We cannot ignore she was set up. If these men had been police officers that would provide mitigation. Different considerations must apply to investigatory journalists. Their purpose was perfectly honourable. But we feel the public would be left with a sense of unease by the identification in the paper. The consequences were most unfortunate. It is appropriate to reflect the entrapment in the sentence. It should have been expressly mentioned in the remarks. In the exceptional circumstances we reduce the sentence from 12 months to **6 months**.

Refer to it in the sentencing remarks, must

57.3   *R v Tonnessen* [1998] 2 Cr App Rep (S) 328. The judge did not refer to the involvement of agents provocateurs and appeared not to have taken it into account. Held. Applying *R v Mackey* (1992) 14 Cr App Rep (S) 53, it should have been expressly mentioned in the remarks.

58   ENVIRONMENTAL OFFENCES

58.1   Various offences and penalties.

The principles to follow about dealing with companies as defendants are listed in the
HEALTH AND SAFETY OFFENCES section.

Crown Court statistics England and Wales[1] – Crown Court – Males 21+ – Public Health

58.2

Year	Plea	Total Numbers sentenced	Type of sentence%					Average length of custody (months)
			Discharge	Fine	Community sentence	Suspended sentence	Custody	
2000	Guilty	12	17%	58%	8%	0%	17%	13
	Not guilty	4	25%	75%	0%	0%	0%	0

1 Excluding committals for sentence. Source: Crime and Criminal Justice Unit, Home Office Ref: IOS416-02.

Magistrates' Court Sentencing Guidelines, amendment June 2001

58.3 Defendants in such cases are frequently companies with huge annual turnovers. Our aim should be for any fine to have an equal impact on rich and poor. Financial penalties must relate to the companies' means and we should accustom ourselves, in appropriate cases, to imposing far greater financial penalties than have been generally imposed in the past. In 1998, the Lord Chancellor spoke to the Magistrates' Association about the disquiet being expressed about the level of sentences for these offences. He particularly suggested the maximum penalties were there to be used in appropriate cases. He said, 'You should not flinch from using them if you believe that they are deserved.'

For details about the guidelines see MAGISTRATES' COURT SENTENCING GUIDELINES at page 331.

Slaughterhouses and animal incinerators

58.4 *R v Clutton Agricultural Ltd* (27 November 2001, unreported). The defendant company and two of its directors were convicted in total of 36 counts. The company was a family company operating incinerators and two directors who were brothers ran it. Local authorities attach conditions for incinerators to combat BSE and records had to be kept. For each count against the company there was one for a director. One pair was carrying out the operation in breach of conditions laid down. This was contrary to Environmental Protection Act 1990, s 23(1)(a). The company used three incinerators at a time although they were permitted to use only two in the conditions. The company had in fact applied to use three but their application was refused. Three years later on appeal permission was granted. The offences were committed when the appeal was pending. Two pairs of counts were for carrying out the operation otherwise than in accordance with the conditions. This was incinerating far in excess of the permitted 250 kilos of carcasses an hour. Twelve pairs of counts were either providing false figures or failing to provide accurate figures to the local authority. Accurate records were sent to the Intervention Board but false and lower figures were sent to the local authority to hide the amount of incineration and therefore the breach of conditions. Three pairs of counts were for failure to burn or deliver carcasses. The company had to incinerate carcasses within 6 days. When this couldn't be done in time the company was obliged to return them. Instead the carcasses were frozen till they could be burnt. One director was a solicitor and none of the defendants had any convictions. The company and the directors had access to considerable funds. The judge held neither environmental damage took place nor was there any danger to human health from the offences. He said the offences were committed for profit and it was wholly dishonest.

He fined the company **£25,000** and the directors **£15,500** and **£9,000**. A costs order of £80,000 out of £100,000 was made to take into account the defendants were not convicted on all the charges. Held. Courts need to show by the fines that this game is not worth the candle. There was no error in this sentence.

Waste, unauthorised keeping, treating or depositing

58.5   Environmental Protection Act 1990, s 33

Triable either way. On indictment maximum 5 years for special waste and 2 years otherwise. Summary maximum 6 months and/or £20,000.

R v Moynihan [1999] 1 Cr App Rep (S) 294. The defendant pleaded guilty to two counts of unauthorised keeping and depositing of controlled waste without a licence, obtaining services by a deception, two counts of forgery and an attempted obtaining by a deception. The defendant's family had a number of businesses including a company, which manufactured industrial incinerators and one which incinerated clinical waste. In the early 1990s the companies ran into financial difficulties and the defendant systematically cheated the Inland Revenue over VAT. In 1995 he started to accept large volumes of clinical waste before he had obtained the necessary licences. He tried to have the waste disposed of by another operator but that proved to be inadequate and he hired a number of containers to store the waste. An environmental protection officer ordered him to remove it and instead of deposing it lawfully he moved it to a disused factory. The Waste authority intervened and disposed of it at a cost to the Authority of £200,000. The nature of the waste created a potential risk to the public. It included incontinence pads, human tissue and syringes. The deception counts concerned the forging of an authorisation that he was able to use the incinerator, obtaining financial services by claiming he was able to use the incinerator, forging a performance bond to obtain a contract and stating a fictitious income in connection with a mortgage. He was 33 with a young family. In 1997 he had been convicted of cheating the Inland Revenue over the VAT. He received a 3 year sentence. He had no other convictions and was now a 'ruined man.' He received **18 months** in all for the environmental offences, consecutive to 9 months in all for the dishonesty offences consecutive to the VAT sentence he was still serving making 5¼ years in all. Held. There was nothing wrong with the sentences and we would expect the sentences for the dishonesty to be consecutive to the environmental offences. However the total was too long. The sentence was rearranged to make the total **4½ years**.

R v Ferguson [2001] 1 Cr App Rep (S) 311. The defendant pleaded guilty at the 11th hour to causing the disposal without a licence of controlled special waste in or on land. CSS an English company accepted for payment over 2,000 45 gallon drums labelled Nitrochlorobenzene (NCB) from an Italian company. Plans to recycle them were abandoned, as it wasn't economic. 1,120 drums were lawfully disposed of at £110 a drum. The defendant who worked for Blue Circle had an interest in blending chemicals. He set up a company with someone connected with a Belgium cement producer and the company was paid over £40,000 to take 738 drums of NCB. The contents were not suitable for the Belgium company and the venture was abandoned and he split from his partner. When the defendant was ordered to remove 184 drums from transport yard and he took them to a warehouse in Greenwich and contacted the London Waste Regulation Authority. They found the drums and disposed of them. The defendant disclaimed responsibility for them. The basis of plea included that he was told by CSS that it was a product and not waste and the drummed material was properly stored, did not suffer from significant leakage or deterioration and was not highly toxic. He was 56 and treated as of good character. The defendant was to receive a salary of £60,000 from the new company and was to receive payment of

£200,000 (defendant said £100,000) over a 5 month period. He had considerable other assets. Compensation was being claimed through the civil courts. He was **fined £30,000** (£25,000 within 2 months and then £2,000 a month) and **£50,000 prosecution costs**. Held. The defendant had avoided the cost of storage on specially licensed land for profit. Sometime before they were stored at the transport yard he knew it was waste. There was nothing wrong with the judge's approach.

R v O'Brien and Enkel [2000] 2 Cr App Rep (S) 358. The defendants O and E changed their plea to guilty to two counts of causing controlled waste to be deposited without a licence [s 33 (1)(a], no written description of controlled waste [s 33(1)(b)(ii)] and no signed transfer note [s 33(5)]. E was offered £4 a tyre to dispose of 2,000 tyres. He agreed. O and E were running a company and they said they could store the tyres or dispose them as mats in playgrounds or to farmers. O and E hired a van and rented a compound for £80 for 3 weeks. The tyres were dumped there and a neighbour complained. The total gain was £8,304 for 2 days' work. O was arrested and admitted he did not have a licence. The tyres were not removed. The cost of removal was £12,000–£12,500. O was 36 with no convictions for waste offences. E was 34 with a conviction in 1995 for counterfeiting but no waste convictions. Held. The lack of danger can be seen in the fact that no licence is needed to store the tyres. The case does not pass the custody threshold. A **fine or CSO** is appropriate. As they had served their 8 month sentence no order made.

Old cases. *R v Garrett* [1997] 1 Cr App Rep (S) 109.

Water Resources Act 1991, s 85

58.6 Polluting controlled waters.

Triable either way. On indictment maximum 2 years and unlimited fine. Summary maximum 3 months or a fine of £20,000.

R v Milford Haven Port Authority [2000] 2 Cr App Rep (S) 423. The company pleaded guilty to causing oil to enter controlled waters under s 85. A pilot of the company was guiding a tanker carrying about 130,000 tonnes of crude oil into Milford Haven dock. He committed a serious navigational error and the tanker grounded on rocks. Initially the tanker lost 2,500 tonnes of oil. Within 6 days the tanker losta further 69,300 tonnes of crude oil and some bunker oil. There was widespread pollution to the coastal waters which were beautiful and environmentally sensitive. There were many sites of special scientific interest and conservation. Various forms of marine life were killed and birds suffered as a result. Those who were dependent on visitors also suffered. The spill was among the largest ever recorded. The clean up costs were estimated to be £60m. The basis of plea was that the offence was one of strict liability and the authority was not at fault nor guilty of any breach of duty, whether negligent, reckless or deliberate or of any misconduct. There was no record of offending or history of non-compliance or warnings unheeded. The judge gave modest credit for the plea because there was no defence and the plea was late. The company was ordered to pay £825,000 prosecution costs. Held. Had it not been an offence of strict liability the culpability would have been much greater. However, Parliament creates an offence of strict liability when it considers the doing or not doing of a particular thing is so. Here the danger of oil pollution is so potentially devastating, so far reaching and so costly to rectify Parliament attaches a criminal penalty where no lack of care or due diligence need be shown. The company cannot escape a very substantial penalty. Public bodies are not immune from appropriate penalties because they have no shareholders and the directors are not in receipt of handsome annual bonuses. However, it is proper for the judge to take the factor into account. If a substantial financial penalty will inhibit the proper performance by a statutory body of the public function it has been set up to perform that factor should not be disregarded. It was understandable that the company delayed the plea until agreement had been reached about the basis even though a plea was inevitable. There is material to show the fine imposed could not be recouped from the customers. The judge did not have information we have which shows the authorities ability to borrow etc and pay the fine imposed without cutting back on expenditure or loosing business. **£750,000 fine** not £4m.

See also **COMPANIES** and **WATER**

59   ESCAPE FROM CUSTODY

59.1   Escape and breach of prison are common law offences. Indictable only. No maximum provided so the maximum is life.

Prison Act 1952, s 39

Aiding prisoner to escape etc.
Indictable only. Maximum 10 years.

Crown Court statistics England and Wales[1] – Crown Court – Males 21+ – Absconding from lawful custody

59.2

| Year | Plea | Total Numbers sentenced | Type of sentence% | | | | | Average length of custody (months) |
			Discharge	Fine	Community sentence	Suspended sentence	Custody	
2000	Guilty	129	5%	3%	16%	0%	75%	5.8
	Not guilty	4	0%	0%	25%	0%	75%	6.3

1   Excluding committals for sentence. Source: Crime and Criminal Justice Unit, Home Office Ref: IOS416-02.

Guideline remarks

59.3   *R v Sutcliffe* (1992) 13 Cr App Rep (S) 538. It is quite essential for the courts to mark out the seriousness of escapes from custody, whether in the Magistrates' Court or the Crown Court, by immediate sentences of imprisonment. It is not only intended as a punishment but also as a clear deterrent to others.

Carefully planned

59.4   Old cases. *R v Wilson* (1992) 14 Cr App Rep (S) 314.

Running from the dock – Opportunist

59.5   *R v Wilson* [1998] 2 Cr App Rep (S) 267 – LCJ. The defendant pleaded guilty to escape. The defendant was arrested for driving matters and appeared at the Magistrates' Court where his bail application was refused. As the dock officer moved towards him the defendant ran to the side of the dock, with the officer after him. The defendant vaulted over the door and ran into the court foyer. As the officer pushed the door open it swung sharply against an usher and injured her arm causing two cuts. The officer fell over the usher and they both fell to the ground. The defendant escaped. He visited his daughter in hospital and went home where he was arrested 2 days later. He said sorry in interview and when taken back to court he apologised personally to the officer. The driving offences were discontinued. He was 23 with 150 offences on 30 occasions. He had 18 custodial sentences including one for robbery for which he received 12 months. They included violence and drugs. He had an unfortunate family background and had a history of drug abuse. **9 months** not 18.

R v Roberts [1998] 2 Cr App Rep (S) 455. The defendant pleaded guilty to escape. The defendant appeared at a Magistrates' Court and without warning jumped over the dock. He was followed by officers but got away and he was at large for 6 weeks. He was 29. His sentence was consecutive to 18 months for other offences for which no appeal was made. Held. Escape is always a serious offence. An important factor is whether the escape was opportunist or carefully planned. **9 months** not 18.

See also *R v Jarvis* [2002] EWCA Crim 885, [2002] 2 Cr App Rep (S) 558 [6 not 12 months].

EVIDENCE

For giving evidence in a Newton hearing, see GUILTY PLEA, DISCOUNT FOR – *Newton hearing, defendant takes part in*

For giving evidence for the co-defendant, see GUILTY PLEA, DISCOUNT FOR – *Co-defendant, giving evidence for*

EVIDENCE – GIVING EVIDENCE FOR THE PROSECUTION

See INFORMANTS/GIVING EVIDENCE FOR THE PROSECUTION

EXCESS ALCOHOL

See DRINKDRIVING – **Excess alcohol**

EXCISE DUTY

See TAX FRAUD and DUTY EVASION

60   EXCISE LICENCE, FRAUDULENT USE ETC

60.1   Vehicle Excise and Registration Act 1994, s 44

Triable either way. On indictment maximum 2 years. Summary maximum £5,000.

Magistrates' Court Sentencing Guidelines September 2000

60.2   Entry point. Is a discharge or a fine appropriate? Examples of aggravating factors for the offence are deliberately planned, disc forged or altered, long term defrauding and LGV, HGV, PCV, PSV, taxi or private hire vehicle. Examples of mitigation are co-operation with the police and genuine remorse. **Starting point fine B.** (£100 when defendant has £100 net weekly income. See page 334 for table showing fines for different incomes.)

For details about the guidelines see MAGISTRATES' COURT SENTENCING GUIDELINES at page 331.

61 EXPLOSIVE OFFENCES

61.1 Explosive Substances Act 1883, ss 2, 3 and 4

Indictable only. Maximum Life for ss 2 and 3 is life and for s 4, 14 years.

With intent to endanger life

61.2 Explosive Substances Act 1883, s 2

Blackmail, and

61.3 *R v Pearce* [2000] 2 Cr App Rep (S) 32. The defendant pleaded to nine counts of blackmail, three ABHs, causing an explosion likely to endanger life, doing an act with intent to cause an explosion likely to endanger life, unlawful wounding, two counts of possessing firearms with intent to commit an indictable offence, possessing explosives and possessing a prohibited weapon. He was the 'Mardi Gras bomber' who over 3½ years waged a campaign against Barclays Bank and Sainsbury's. In the Barclays Bank campaign he deployed 25 devices of six different types intending to produce explosions. Some were boxes designed to fire shotgun cartridges, others were modified gas cylinders filled with diesel fuel and a detonating charge and some were designed to fire pellets from a two barrel shotgun. One victim received minor injuries, one narrowly avoided injury to the eye, and a passing car was engulfed with flames with the driver managing to escape. The devices could cause serious injury and death. In the campaign against Sainsbury's he used similar extremely ingenious mechanism involving shotgun cartridges. A man was injured another went off in someone's car and one struck a man causing multiple puncture wounds. That victim had to end his athletic career. Others exploded in the street without causing injuries. He wanted very substantial sums of money from the bank and £½m from Sainsbury's. For each there was an ingenious method of payment to avoid the risk of being caught. He was 62 and needed psychiatric treatment. His life expectancy was 4–5 years. Held. A hospital order was not appropriate. **21 years** in all was entirely appropriate.

See also **BLACKMAIL**

Kill the victim, intending to

61.4 *R v McDonald* [2001] EWCA Crim 2842, [2002] 2 Cr App Rep (S) 113. The defendant pleaded guilty to causing an explosion likely to endanger life. The defendant, the intended victim, W and the victim's wife worked for a firm of electrical engineers. The defendant was a technological systems manager. W's wife left him and went to live with the defendant. When she returned to W the defendant was openly talking about killing W and making it look like an animal rights act as the company was working on a large contract for a company which used animals for research. He wrote letters threatening to hurt employees of various companies if the company giving the contract continued animal testing. A sophisticated bomb was prepared packed with screws, which could be set off by remote control. He put the bomb beneath the driver's seat of W's van which was parked outside his home and waited. W went to the van and the defendant changed his mind. W saw the bag and went back home. The defendant detonated the bomb in part to cover his tracks. The screws were scattered over 200' and embedded themselves in window frames of houses. A gas meter nearby narrowly avoided being seriously damaged. The defendant left and wrote a letter to the companies saying, 'It could be you next.' When arrested he made a full confession. No report suggested there was anything aggressive about him. He was of good character and had been in the army but it was not suggested he had gained any bomb making skills there. His commanding officer wrote a testimonial for him. Held. It was jealous anger. **10 years** was severe but appropriate.

See also **MURDER, ATTEMPTED – MURDER, CONSPIRACY TO**

Making or possessing explosives

61.5 Explosive Substances Act 1883, ss 2

Defendant aged 14–15

61.6 *R v Milsom* [1998] 1 Cr App Rep (S) 306. The defendant pleaded guilty to making an explosive substance, having an explosive substance and possession of a prohibited weapon. He asked for offences of making an explosive device and stealing chemicals to be taken into consideration. In 1995 the defendant started experimenting with explosives. By the summer of 1996 he had an obsession with making explosives from common and domestic chemicals. In July 1996 he received a conditional discharge for setting off an explosion. Four days later he set off another explosion using icing sugar and weed killer in a biscuit tin with a fuse. It caused a ball of flame and a woman in a house nearby was terrified. He attended the police station and admitted making four explosions. In October 1996, the day before he was due to be interviewed about an offence of criminal damage for which he was later conditionally discharged, he was stopped by police who found on him another explosive device, two homemade pipe guns containing 10 grams of screwpin heads, tacks and ball-bearings. He said he was going to sell the device. A search of his room revealed further ingredients for explosive devices. The defendant admitted the equipment was for flares for Bonfire Night and said the pipegun was for self defence. He said he would never do any damage with his bombs. The pre-sentence report described him as arrogant, anti-authoritarian and reckless. The time on remand had shifted his views but he remained naïve and emotionally frozen. The risk of re-offending was estimated to be medium to high. A psychiatrist said he seemed to have an emotional disorder called 'conduct disorder' involving manic depressive mood swings. He recommended 18 months in a secure unit. Since his sentence he had made progress. Held. The defendant was presenting great risks to the public although he didn't intend the risks to be created. It was unfortunate he had been cautioned three times leading up to these offences. Custody was right but it ought to be kept to the minimum. **3 years** detention in total not 4.

R v O (17 July 2001, unreported). 6 months detention upheld for a 15 year old.

Home-made devices as a hobby

61.7 *R v Lloyd* [2001] EWCA Crim 600, [2001] 2 Cr App Rep (S) 493. The defendant pleaded guilty to making explosives. More serious charges were left on the file. He made four devices each about 8 cm long in the form of empty gas canisters containing a mixture of weedkiller and sugar. He handed them to a co-defendant who later told a prison officer about them after reading about a bomb in a newspaper. Police searched the defendant's home and found a closed copper pipe, a printed circuit board, 2″ silver CO_2 canisters and three full pots of weedkiller. He was sentenced on the basis the devices were to make a loud bang and enable him to show off. There was no intent to injure. He had a long standing hobby of making fireworks and explosives and had 14 convictions including firearm, and offensive weapon offences. There were none for explosives. He had a chronic personality disorder with depression. He made a witness statement against a co-defendant and was prepared to give evidence against him. Held. Explosive devices in the wrong hands are capable of causing untold injury and misery to innocent people. **3½ years** could not be criticised.

See also **TERRORISM**

62 EXPORTING DRUGS

For statute and penalties see IMPORTATION OF DRUGS

Basic principles

62.1 *R v Powell* (2000) Times, 5 October – LCJ. There was no difference in criminality between the importation and exportation of controlled drugs.

63 EXTENDED SENTENCES

63.1 An extended sentence is a sentence which has an extended licence period, Powers of Criminal Courts (Sentencing) Act 2000, s 85(2)(b).

The court can also pass a sentence which is longer than commensurate, Powers of Criminal Courts (Sentencing) Act 2000, s 80(2). This is frequently (wrongly) called an extended sentence but that is not what the section calls it. See LONGER THAN COMMENSURATE SENTENCES. It would have been much simpler if Parliament had called one an extended sentence and the other an extended licence.

Guideline case

63.2 *R v Nelson* [2001] EWCA Crim 2264, [2002] 1 Cr App Rep (S) 565. The first stage is to decide on the sentence which would be commensurate. The second stage is to consider whether a longer period in custody is needed to protect the public from serious harm from the offender. If so, a longer than commensurate custodial sentence will be called for. The third stage, in relation to a sexual offence or a violent offence for which the appropriate custodial sentence is 4 years or longer, is to consider whether that sentence, whether commensurate or longer than commensurate, is adequate to prevent the commission by the offender of further offences and secure his rehabilitation. If not, an extended sentence is called for. Also, there may be cases in which, because of the power to impose an extended licence period, a longer than commensurate sentence may not be necessary. Judges should always take care to use the correct terminology when passing sentence. In particular, a longer than commensurate sentence should be so described: it is not an extended sentence.

Commensurate term, and a

63.3 *R v Nelson* [2001] EWCA Crim 2264, [2002] 1 Cr App Rep (S) 565. One purpose of an extended sentence is to reduce the likelihood of re-offending, and it is therefore particularly suitable where a commensurate custodial term is too short for this to be done in prison and where the normal licence period, if any, will not be long enough to permit attendance at a treatment programme in the community. This will arise particularly in relation to less serious sexual offences, where the likelihood of re-offending appears high, but where a longer than commensurate sentence cannot be justified because the offender does not present a risk of serious harm to the public.

R v Creasey (1994) 15 Cr App Rep (S) 671 provides an example, although the option of an extended sentence was not, at that time, available to the court. The appellant there had a record of convictions for relatively minor indecent assaults, and he pleaded guilty to other comparatively minor offences. The trial judge imposed a longer than commensurate sentence of 5 years. The Court of Appeal substituted a sentence of 21 months as being commensurate because, although the offences were unpleasant and distressing, they did not require protection of the public from serious harm. The trial judge had fallen into the trap of assessing the seriousness of the risk of re-offending rather than the seriousness of the anticipated harm. Such a case might now be regarded as one where an extended sentence could and should be imposed with a commensurate custodial term. Similarly, in *R v JT* [2001] 1 Cr App Rep (S) 205, a 78-year-old offender pleaded guilty to comparatively minor acts of indecency. He had 10 previous convictions for sexual offences. He was sentenced to an extended sentence of 10 years, with a custodial term of 4 years expressed as a longer than commensurate sentence, together with an extension period of 6 years. Held. There was a clear risk of further offending but we are not satisfied that a longer than commensurate sentence was necessary to protect the public from serious harm. So that sentence is quashed and a commensurate sentence of 3 years is substituted. The extension period of 6 years, however, is upheld. These are the sort of cases where an extended sentence incorporating a commensurate sentence is appropriate. We add that the use of an extended sentence, with a relatively short custodial term, less than 12 months, was endorsed in *R v Ajaib* [2001] 1 Cr App Rep (S) 105.

Consecutive to other sentences

63.4   *R v Cridge* [2000] 2 Cr App Rep (S) 477. It should not be consecutive to other sentences.

R v Nelson [2001] EWCA Crim 2264, [2002] 1 Cr App Rep (S) 565. There have been conflicting views expressed in this Court as to whether the legislation permits the imposition of consecutive extended sentences. Whatever the position as a matter of statutory interpretation, we are in no doubt that sensible practice requires that extended sentences should not, generally, be imposed consecutively.

Counsel, should warn

63.5   *R v Nelson* [2001] EWCA Crim 2264, [2002] 1 Cr App Rep (S) 565. Where a sentencer is considering imposing an extended sentence, counsel should be warned of this.

Extended, the sentence should be

63.6   *A-G's Reference (No 89 of 2000)* [2001] 2 Cr App Rep (S) 309. 4 years imprisonment was substituted. The court was invited to consider an extended sentence. Held. It was plainly a violent offence. The court had to consider whether the licence period would be adequate for the purposes of preventing the commission of further offences and securing his rehabilitation. With 4 years the licence period would be between 4 and 12 months. That would not be adequate so the extension period will be 3 years That means 7 years in all he will be subject to an extended sentence. [For more details of the case see OFFENCES AGAINST THE PERSON ACT 1861, s 18 – *Domestic Men attacking wives and partners, or ex-wives and ex-partners 5 – 9 years appropriate*]

R v Green (31 July 2002, unreported). The defendant pleaded guilty to rape and was assessed as high risk. Held. There was nothing wrong with 6 years custody and 4 years extended licence.

How long should the sentence be? – Guideline case

63.7   *R v Nelson* [2001] EWCA Crim 2264, [2002] 1 Cr App Rep (S) 565. The court must decide what period will be adequate to secure the offender's rehabilitation and to prevent re-offending. This will often be difficult. But, in some cases, involving less serious sexual offences where the custodial term is relatively short, the court may be able to take advice on the availability and length of treatment programmes and tailor the extension period accordingly. In all cases the court should consider whether a particular extension period can be justified on the evidence available. A long extension period should usually be based on a clear implication from the offender's criminal record or on what is said in a pre-sentence report or a psychiatric report. The objective, where possible, should be to fix the length of the extension period by reference to what can realistically be achieved within it. When the defendant is clearly dangerous the custodial term will usually be longer than commensurate and a long period of extended licence will often be called for. The length of an extension period is subject to a statutory maximum of 5 years in relation to a violent offence and 10 years in relation to a sexual offence and the combined total of the custodial term and the extension period is limited to the maximum for the offence. It is clear from *R v Gould* [2000] 2 Cr App Rep (S) 173 that a court imposing an extended sentence should bear in mind that the offender may ultimately serve the whole or part of the extension period in custody. But, as the legislature's intention in introducing extended sentences is clearly to place an offender at risk of recall for some considerable time, it would be illogical to require strict proportionality between the duration of the extension period and the seriousness of the offence. Proportionality with the seriousness of the offence is, of course, of central importance to a custodial term. But it should not be a primary factor in determining the length of an extension period. It does, however have some relevance and the implications of the overall sentence should be borne in mind.

How long should the sentence be? – Cases

63.8 *R v Gould* [2000] Crim LR 311. The defendant was sentenced to a 5 year custodial term. Here 2 years extension not 5 appropriate. *R v Nelson* [2001] EWCA Crim 2264, [2002] 1 Cr App Rep (S) 565. The defendant was sentenced for indecent assault. The 15-year-old school girl victim was walking home and she noticed a man, in a parked car, apparently watching her. She arrived home and was alone. The defendant rang the doorbell. The girl saw him and, after a time, went downstairs, where she was confronted by the defendant, standing in the kitchen, by the back door. He asked if a man called Tony lived there and, when told he did not, he asked a further series of questions, including whether she would give her father his telephone number. When she bent over a table to write it down, the appellant seized her arm and put his other hand over her mouth. He threatened to kill her unless she was quiet. She was terrified. She found difficulty in breathing and started crying. The appellant dragged her upstairs, keeping her mouth covered, and saying 'shut up or I'll kill you'. He dragged her into the bedroom and threw her on the bed. He lay on top of her, starting to kiss her and simulating intercourse. He seemed angry. He squeezed her right breast, painfully. She begged him to get off. He asked her if he could feel her 'pussy'. She was very frightened and shaking and said no. The defendant said: 'It's all right I'm not going to rape you.' He reached inside her tracksuit bottoms and touched her vagina, without digital penetration. She was crying even more violently and feared she would be raped. The appellant stopped and got off the bed. He threatened he would return and kill her if she told anybody and left. The attack lasted about 5 minutes. When her father returned home the victim was distressed and hysterical and later had to take time off school. She had difficulty sleeping. The defendant was now 32 years and had convictions for blackmail and impersonating a police officer 1991. He received 2 years suspended. The pre-sentence report said there was a significant risk of the appellant re-offending. The psychiatrist's report said he had a 20% risk of re-offending. The judge passed a 5 year sentence with a 5 year extension. Held. This was a very serious offence committed by a stranger, in the victim's home. The judge was entitled to pass an extended period of licence. 2 not 5 years for the extension.

Longer than commensurate sentence, and a

63.9 *R v Thornton* [2000] Crim LR 312. Five years longer than commensurate changed to a 2 years custodial term with a 3 years extension period.

R v Nelson [2001] EWCA Crim 2264, [2002] 1 Cr App Rep (S) 565. The two sentences will be appropriate, where a violent or sexual offence is committed by a seriously dangerous offender, in relation to whom a life sentence, if available, might well be passed, thereby permitting the offender to be released only when the executive believes that the risk posed by him has been greatly reduced. In such a case, the offender would of course be subject to recall for the rest of his life. It is appropriate to combine an extended period of licence with a longer than commensurate custodial term for an offender who presents a serious danger to the public but where a life sentence is not available because the maximum penalty is, for example, a lesser determinate sentence. There may also be cases in which a discretionary life sentence is available for the offence but the criteria which have to be established before such a sentence can be passed may not all be present (eg *R v Chapman* [2000] 1 Cr App Rep (S) 377). Where a longer than commensurate sentence is called for, it should usually be accompanied by an extension period because a seriously dangerous offender, attracting a longer than commensurate sentence, may well commit further offences.

Magistrates' Courts

63.10 *R v Nelson* [2001] EWCA Crim 2264, [2002] 1 Cr App Rep (S) 565. Where magistrates think the normal period of licence is inadequate they should commit to the Crown Court for sentence. A Youth Court may have the power to pass an extended sentence but the legislation is obscure and the point may merit scrutiny on some future occasion.

Reduce the custodial term because the sentence is extended, don't

63.11 *R v Nelson* [2001] EWCA Crim 2264, [2002] 1 Cr App Rep (S) 565. It is not appropriate to reduce the custodial term because an extended licence period is being imposed [see *A-G's Reference (No 40 of 2001)* (9 May 2001, unreported).

Short sentences, and

63.12 *R v Ajaib* [2001] 1 Cr App Rep (S) 105. There is power to order an extended sentence when the sentence is 9 months imprisonment. However, the extension period should be reduced from 2 years to 15 months.

Treatment programmes

63.13 *R v Nelson* [2001] EWCA Crim 2264, [2002] 1 Cr App Rep (S) 565. One purpose of an extended sentence is to reduce the likelihood of re-offending, and it is therefore particularly suitable where a commensurate custodial term is too short for this to be done in prison and where the normal licence period, if any, will not be long enough to permit attendance at a treatment programme in the community. This will arise particularly in relation to less serious sexual offences, where the likelihood of re-offending appears high, but where a longer than commensurate sentence cannot be justified because the offender does not present a risk of serious harm to the public.

For definition of sexual and violent offence see LONGER THAN COMMENSURATE SENTENCES – *Sexual offence, what is?* and *Violent offence, is it?*

See also OFFENCES AGAINST THE PERSON ACT **1981**, S 18 – *Extended sentences*

EXTRADITION, TIME SPENT IN CUSTODY AWAITING

See CUSTODY, DISCOUNT FOR TIME SPENT IN – *Extradition, time in custody awaiting*

64 FAILING TO PROVIDE A SPECIMEN

64.1 Road Traffic Act 1988, s 7(6)

Summary only. Maximum 6 months or £5,000. Minimum disqualification 1 year, unless defendant in charge. 3–11 penalty points if special reasons not to disqualify are found. Where a defendant has a conviction for driving while unfit, causing death under the influence of drink, driving with excess alcohol and failing to provide a specimen in previous 10 years, minimum disqualification is 3 years[1]. There is power to order reduced disqualification for attendance on courses[2].

1 Road Traffic Offenders Act 1988, s 34(3).
2 Road Traffic Offenders Act 1988, s 34A.

Magistrates' Court Sentencing Guidelines September 2000

64.2 Entry point. Is discharge or a fine appropriate? Examples of aggravating factors for the offence are police chase, causing injury/fear/damage, type of vehicle, eg carrying passengers for reward/ large goods vehicle, evidence of nature of the driving, and ability to drive seriously impaired. Examples of mitigation are voluntary completion of alcohol impaired driver course (if available) and genuine remorse. Offer a rehabilitation course. Minimum 18 months disqualification. **Starting point fine C.** (£150 when defendant has £100 net weekly income. See page 334 for table showing fines for different incomes.)

For details about the guidelines see **MAGISTRATES' COURT SENTENCING GUIDELINES** at page 331.

65 FAILING TO STOP/FAILING TO REPORT

65.1 Road Traffic Act 1988, s 170

Summary only. Maximum 6 month and/or Level 5 £5,000. 5 to 10 points.

Magistrates' Court Sentencing Guidelines September 2000

65.2 Entry point. Is a discharge or a fine appropriate? Examples of aggravating factors for the offence are evidence of drinking or drugs, serious injury and serious damage. Examples of mitigating factors for the offence are believed identity to be known, failed to stop but reported, genuine fear of retaliation, negligible damage, no-one at scene but failed report and stayed at scene but failed to give/left before giving full particulars. Examples of mitigation are co-operation with the police and genuine remorse. **Starting point fine B.** (£100 when defendant has £100 net weekly income. See page 334 for table showing fines for different incomes.)

For details about the guidelines see **MAGISTRATES' COURT SENTENCING GUIDELINES** at page 331.

66 FALSE ACCOUNTING

66.1 Theft Act 1968, s 17

Triable either way. On indictment maximum 7 years. Summary maximum 6 months and/or £5,000.

Crown Court statistics England and Wales+[1] – Crown Court – Males 21+ – False accounting

66.2

Year	Plea	Total Numbers sentenced	Type of sentence%					Average length of custody (months)
			Discharge	Fine	Community sentence	Suspended sentence	Custody	
2000	Guilty	189	3	4	34	14	44	15.4
	Not guilty	41	7	7	27	15	44%	13.1

There are no cases, but similar cases are listed under THEFT ETC

1 Excluding committals for sentence. Source: Crime and Criminal Justice Unit, Home Office Ref: IOS 416-02.

67 FALSE IMPRISONMENT/KIDNAPPING

67.1 Both are common law offences.

Both are indictable only with a maximum sentence of life[1].

1 The penalty for false imprisonment is life *R v Szczerba* [2002] 2 Cr App Rep (S) 385 at 392.

Crown Court statistics England and Wales – Crown Court – Males 21+ – Kidnapping

67.2

Year	Plea	Total Numbers sentenced	Type of sentence%					Average length of custody[1] (months)
			Discharge	Fine	Community sentence	Suspended sentence	Custody	
2000	Guilty	153	1%	1%	19%	3%	76%	40.6
	Not guilty	67	0%	0%	9%	7%	81%	54

1 Excluding life sentences. Source: Crime and Criminal Justice Unit, Home Office Ref: IOS416-02.

Guideline case

67.3 *R v Spence and Thomas* (1983) 5 Cr App Rep (S) 413 – LCJ. The defendant pleaded to kidnapping. Held. There is a wide possible variation between one instance of the crime and another. At the top end of the scale comes the carefully planned abductions where the victim is used as a hostage or where ransom money is demanded. Such offences will seldom be met with less than 8 years or thereabouts. Where violence or firearms are used or there are other exacerbating features such as detention of the victim over a period of time, then the proper sentence will be very much longer than that. At the other end of the scale are those offences which can perhaps scarcely be classed as kidnapping at all. They very often arise as a sequel to family tiffs or lover's disputes, and they seldom require anything more than 18 months and sometimes a great deal less.

General

67.4 *R v Richardson* [2000] 2 Cr App Rep (S) 373. The defendant pleaded guilty to theft and false imprisonment. The defendant at night visited the victim, a lady of 89 who he knew. He asked to use the lavatory. She followed him. She said he should leave. He refused and appeared to be on drugs. He was aggressive and threatened to hurt her. He pushed her into her sitting room and forced her into an armchair. He tied a jumper over her face. He asked for £20. On a number of occasions she attempted to get out of the chair but he pushed her back. She was repeatedly threatened that she would be hurt if she told anyone about him. She allowed him to make a call for a taxi. When the taxi arrived he snatched her bag and stole £20. He tore the telephone wire from the wall. Because the telephone did not work and she could not manage the steps in the dark she had to stay in all night unable to contact anyone. Before the police started to look for him he went to a police station and confessed to a robbery. His account was very similar to the victim, although he claimed to have told her he wasn't going to hurt her. The defendant was very anxious she should not have to go to court and therefore did not contest her account. He had a bad record with 12 appearances in the last 10 years 7 of which were for robbery. He had three convictions for burglary, three convictions for theft in a dwelling house and three convictions for theft from a person. He expressed remorse. The reason for his offending was crack cocaine. Held. It was so serious a DTT order was inappropriate. In light of the mitigation **4 years** substituted for 5.

Arranged marriages, to force an

67.5   *R v Khan and Bashir* [1999] 1 Cr App Rep (S) 329. The defendants pleaded guilty to kidnapping and administering a noxious thing. The defendants were a husband and wife with three children. The eldest child was a girl aged 20. The parents tried to persuade her to go to Pakistan for an arranged marriage. She did not want to go and she left home and started a course at a local university. On 21 December 1997 she returned home when she discovered that her grandfather had died and agreed to stay there over the New Year period. On 27 December she was asked to wear some Asian clothes and she refused. Next day she was given some drinks which had sleeping pills in it. She was taken to Manchester airport and told she was in hospital. There were three plane tickets bought. One was for her, one for her mother and the other for her brother. She was very weak and drowsy. Her strange behaviour in not wanting to board the flight was spotted by security staff and the police were informed. She received medical treatment and recovered. The wife received 6 months 'out of mercy for her children' and the husband 2 years. Held. The wife's sentence even taking into account the children was an extremely merciful one. Her appeal has no merit. There was nothing which could justify suspending her sentence. The husband's sentence was reduced to **12 months** because of disparity.

Blackmail, and

See **BLACKMAIL**

Defendant aged 15–17

67.6   *A-G's Reference (Nos 36 and 37 of 1998)* [1999] 2 Cr App Rep (S) 7. The defendants L and J pleaded guilty to false imprisonment and L pleaded to wounding (the October incident). J also pleaded to wounding with intent and unlawful wounding and L also pleaded to affray (the September incident). In September at about 9.25pm the defendant J then 17 picked a fight with one of a group of students and punched one of them in the mouth and face several times. He then took a bottle of beer off the victim and smashed it over his head. The students made off. L then 15 and J pursued them throwing rubbish from a skip at them. A passer-by was walking her dog and J attacked her with a broken bottle. She had a 3″ wound to her cheek and 1″ wounds to her nose and chin. For a number of weeks she could not talk properly or eat solid foods and she was off work for 9 weeks. The defendants were released on bail and about 4 weeks later at about 9pm J and L approached a group of teenagers. J jumped on one of them aged 16, and started to struggle with him. L threatened the group, and was restrained by a member of his group. J then said to L 'Come on, let's go and get the filthy Paki'. J and L then followed three of them to a path running along a lake. J and L forced the three to climb over the gate into the park and threatened to 'batter' or kill them. Once in the park the three were forced to sit upon a bench. J punched one of them in the face and pushed a lighted cigarette into his face causing burn marks. L forced him against a tree, and J said he was going to kill him. The three were terrified and ran away, with L in pursuit. One climbed over some spiked railings, and suffered a 5 cm and 2 cm cut to his thigh. Both were deep. This was L's wounding charge. One of the three managed to run away and the third was forced by J and L to walk across the park until he too escaped. The three teenagers were so terrified that they were unable to estimate the period of time during which they had been detained. Both J and L were arrested and when interviewed disputed the victims' account of events. L was of good character. J had an ABH conviction involving an attack with two others on a man in the early hours. The man was knocked to the ground, kicked and punched. J had also been cautioned for affray and assaulting a police officer. A report indicated that L's use of drugs was the most significant factor in his aggressive behaviour. J also had a serious history of drug and alcohol abuse. The judge gave L a deferred sentence J received 3½ years for the wounding with intent and 6 months for the false imprisonment. Held. The intimidation of the teenagers was deliberate and sustained and the offence had a very unpleasant racist overtone which demanded an immediate custody. The deferred sentence was unduly lenient. Had L contested his guilt **15 months** detention would have been appropriate for the false imprisonment. With his plea **10–12 months** detention would have been merited. As it was a reference **8 months** detention with no separate penalty for affray. Had J pleaded not guilty a total of **7 years** detention would have been appropriate for the section 18 and false imprisonment offences. On a plea of guilty **5 years** would have been merited. Taking into account it was a reference and the false imprisonment **4 years** for the s 18 offence.

Domestic

67.7 *R v Lucas* [2000] 1 Cr App Rep (S) 5. The defendant was convicted of false imprisonment. He had had a relationship with a woman for 18 years. They had three children but they had separated. 6 months later he went to her home. He struck her on the head, which knocked her unconscious. He took her and his one-year-old daughter to his car. She was made to drive him and the baby to a park where he claimed to have dug a grave for her. The woman managed to escape. He followed and prized her from the hold of someone she had approached and took her back to his car. He drove off. When he heard his car being circulated as wanted by the police he drove her home. She was too frightened to make a complaint for 10 months. She had injuries of a cut above the right eye, a bite mark and bruising in various different places. He had no previous for violence. Held. Whether it is a domestic dispute or by a stranger is neither here nor there. It was a quite terrifying experience. **2 years** could not be faulted.

A-G's Reference (No 42 of 2000) [2001] 1 Cr App Rep (S) 393. The defendant pleaded guilty during his trial to four counts of false imprisonment, making threats to kill, ABH and inflicting GBH. The defendant had a troubled relationship with a 23 year old who from time to time returned to her mother. In June 1997, he slapped her and pulled her by the hair into the cellar. He pushed her into the coal cellar and shut her inside. He released her after two hours. He became angry again and told her to go back in. She did so because she feared an assault. This continued over 4 days although from time to time she was let out. This activity was the first count. In July 1997, she gave birth. A week later he punched her and pushed her down the cellar steps and locked her in the coalhouse. He let her out to feed the baby and picked up a crossbow and loaded it with a bolt. He told her he could kill her and get away with it. She believed she was going to be killed. This lasted for about a minute. He punched and kicked her and put a belt round her neck, which he pulled tight. This activity was the second false imprisonment count and the threats to kill. In November 1997 they moved to a flat. In December he punched kicked her. He grabbed her between the legs and twisted them. He tore her right labia majora, causing her bleeding and immense pain. She said she wanted to end her life and he said, 'go on then' and gave her some Tamazepam tablets, which she took. The offender became extremely violent and pushed her head through a plasterboard wall. He forced her to swallow shampoo to bring up the tablets, which she did. At 9–10pm he tied her to a stool with flex and put a sock in her mouth. He slapped and punched her till the early hours. This activity was the third false imprisonment. He was then sentenced to 30 months imprisonment for wounding etc which involved fighting men unrelated to the victim. The last false imprisonment was when he punched her, made her undress and tied her to the bedposts. He whipped her back and legs. She had black eyes, cut lips, a swollen face, bruising to her body and wheal marks. The ABH related to when he punched her and pushed a burning cigarette against her chest. This was followed by more punching. The GBH involved an incident when they out with friends and he slapped her. She refused to go home. He said he would break her jaw. He grabbed her hair and dragged her to the front door. The friends told him to stop. He kicked and punched her in the face. She was taken to the kitchen where it was repeated. She was pregnant again. He banged her head on the floor. She had to be taken to hospital. He was taking crack or heroin during all the false imprisonments and the occasion of the ABH. He was arrested and she gave evidence at the trial. Just before she was to be cross-examined he pleaded guilty. The defendant had helped police in an unrelated matter. He had two ABH findings of guilt as a juvenile as well as the 30 month sentence. **Held. 6 or 7 years** was appropriate. Because it was a reference **5 years** not 30 months, consecutive to 11 remaining of a 30 month sentence.

R v Hibbert [2001] EWCA Crim 2847, [2002] 2 Cr App Rep (S) 106. The defendant pleaded guilty to false imprisonment and was acquitted of two rapes. He had known the victim since they were teenagers at school. They had a short relationship then and remained friends. In 2000 they met in a pub and they started going out together. Four months later they moved into a flat together. Two months later she discovered he had run up a bill of £500 for sexual chat lines. She spoke to him about it but as he was so drunk she decided to go out. At 11.30pm she returned with a take away meal for them both but as he was drunk and arguing she went to bed and locked her door. He kicked open the door, pushed her backwards and placed his hand over her mouth to prevent her screaming. The argument continued in the bathroom where he grabbed her. They returned to the bedroom where he found her diary and read entries about her former boyfriend. He became very angry and tore up the diary. There a short struggle and he said he was going to commit suicide by jumping off the Humber Bridge. He told her to go to sleep and he lay in front of the door preventing her leaving. When she awoke he was asleep and she pushed a note though the bedroom window asking for help. When he awoke he left the room and locked the door behind him. She went back to sleep and 3 hours later they both woke up and started talking in a more reasonable manner. They had sex and then he fetched a Stanley knife and he was going to tie her up and jump off the bridge. He slashed his wrists with the knife and told her she could leave when he was dead. Then he rang his former partner and told her he had slashed his wrists. She rang back and persuaded him to let her go. The victim left about 13 hours after it all started. She was at times during the incident very frightened and made repeated requests to leave. The police arrived and arrested him, he said he was sorry. Five years before he had been convicted of wounding his previous partner when drunk. He stabbed her with a pair of scissors and received probation. **3½ years** was not manifestly excessive.

See also *A-G's References (No 73 and 74 of 2001)* [2001] EWCA Crim 1923, [2002] 1 Cr App Rep (S) 451 and *R v Ashbridge* [2002] EWCA Crim 384, [2002] 2 Cr App Rep (S) 408.

Drug offences, linked to

See SUPPLY OF DRUGS – *Drug gang using violence*

Firearms, with (real or imitation

67.8   *A-G's Reference (No 17 of 1999)* [2000] 1 Cr App Rep (S) 215. The defendant pleaded to false imprisonment, having a firearm in a public place and taking a vehicle without consent. The defendant arranged for a hire car to be delivered to his home. When it arrived the defendant threatened the driver with what the driver believed to be a shotgun. The defendant said he would, 'take your head clean off.' The victim heard two clicks. The defendant also said he had served 15 years already for shooting someone. He handcuffed the victim's hands behind him and ordered him upstairs at gunpoint. His legs and mouth were taped and he was asked for money. The defendant left the house taking the car keys with him. The victim escaped and called the police. Police found him at his sister's address. He had a loaded revolver in his waistband (the subject matter of the firearm count) and a large knife in his back pocket. He admitted the offences in interview. The defendant had been released from prison 11 months before for two robberies and firearm offences. He had received 12 years. He was sentenced on the basis the driver had believed he had been threatened by a gun but it was a hollow tube. Held. We would expect a total sentence of **at least 10 years**. Because it was a reference **4 years** for the false imprisonment, and for the firearm matter consecutive making **8 years** in all consecutive with the taking a vehicle 4 months concurrent not 5½ in all.

R v Wheeler [2002] EWCA Crim 65, [2002] 2 Cr App Rep (S) 263. The defendant pleaded guilty to possessing a firearm with the intent to cause a belief that violence would be used, having a firearm with intent to commit an indictable offence, possession of a prohibited weapon and false imprisonment. He had a relationship and moved in with the victim. He said he had it in the French Foreign Legion and was highly experienced in explosives, firearms and weapons. About a year later after arguments she told him to leave. He did so and found it hard to accept and made repeated efforts to see her. She felt pestered. Five months later he waited outside the garden centre where she worked and ¾ hour later he entered the centre and told her to go into an office. He had a pistol loaded with wo live rounds and told her and her colleague, A to telephone the police. He pointed the gun at her and said he wasn't messing about, he was serious. He talked about his relationship with her and she became extremely frightened. The gun appeared cocked and it appeared to remain so. He talked about Hungerford and Dunblane and said her son was going to be an orphan. She was detained for 12 hours and he wouldn't let her go to the lavatory. The defendant threatened to kill himself. A chose to remain although the defendant said he could go. Eventually the defendant surrendered to the police. A said he was not seriously worried about his or her safety. When interviewed the defendant said,' He waited till the school emptied. The victim had persuaded him not to let the police shoot him. He was at his lowest ebb ever and the gun was to stop her leaving.' The defendant was 44 and had no previous record for this kind of offence. He had had periods of depression. Held. The incident was terrifying. It was planned and the pistol was loaded with 2 bullets. These were very grave offences of the utmost seriousness. **7 years** was not manifestly excessive.

Hostage, more than one

67.9   *R v Cockeram* [1999] 2 Cr App Rep (S) 120. The defendant pleaded guilty to five counts of false imprisonment. At about 10pm, under the influence of alcohol the defendant entered a newsagent and purchased a packet of cigarettes. There were three members of staff present. As he received his change he produced a 12″ carving knife and shouted, 'Shut the fucking doors.' The knife was put to an assistant's throat. The doors were shut but not locked and a customer entered the shop. One assistant was ordered to bring the customer over to the counter. When another customer entered the first managed to escape and contacted the police. When another customer entered there were five hostages who were made to sit on the floor. The defendant pointed the knife at them and said he had nothing to lose. Armed police arrived and surrounded the shop. He became irrational. He smashed a display of Easter Eggs and threatened to cut the throat of an assistant. He also apologised and offered them cushions, cigarettes and drink. After time the hostages felt more comfortable with him and when he was arrested they shouted at the police not to hurt him because he hadn't hurt them. He released the hostages at 2.15am. One had in fact suffered a small bruise. All suffered some psychological harm. The defendant said he had not intended to rob the shop and expressed regret and remorse. He had a number of previous convictions and an impressive recent employment history. Held. This was not a case of solitary hostage taking which can be even more frightening. There was no material violence or pre-planning. These features put it at the lower end of the scale, so **5 years** not 6.

Longer than commensurate sentences (frequently wrongly called extended sentences) – Is it a violent offence?

67.10   Powers of Criminal Courts (Sentencing) Act 2000, s 80(2)(b). . . .the custodial sentence shall be. . .where the offence is a violent or sexual offence, for such longer term (not exceeding the maximum) as in the opinion of the court is necessary to protect the public from serious harm from the offender. (Previously the Criminal Justice Act 1991, s 2(2)(b).)

Powers of Criminal Courts (Sentencing) Act 2000, s 161(3). . . .a violent offence is an 'offence which leads, or is intended or likely to lead, to a person's death or physical injury to a person.'

R v Cochrane (1993) 15 Cr App Rep (S) 407. The defendant pleaded guilty to robbery. Held. The definition of a violent offence does not require that the physical injury be serious. It does not include psychological harm. Here no injury was actually done. Sometimes shock may amount to ABH. This was not that case. The defendant denied he intended to cause physical injury. The judge accepted that. It was not necessary to show that injury was a necessary or probable consequence. The only issue was whether the acts were likely to lead to physical injury. Here it could have done if the shopkeeper had resisted or the defendant had lost control. 6 years was arguably too high if the sentence was commensurate with the facts of the offence. However, it was a perfectly proper sentence for a man foreseeably likely to cause serious harm to the public.

A-G's Reference (No 113 of 2001) [2002] EWCA Crim 143, [2002] 2 Cr App Rep (S) 269. The defendant pleaded guilty to five counts of robbery. The victims were all elderly and attacked in their own homes after dark. He was masked and they were terrified. He demanded money and he put his hand over two of their mouths. He brushed passed one and caused her to fall. Another victim was tied up. The judge was not satisfied the offences were violent. Held. Bearing in mind the ages of the victims and what was done to each of them, the real possibility of fractures, asphyxia and cardiac arrest each was a violent offence. The defendant was lucky not to have caused physical injury and this demonstrates its likelihood.

R v Szczerba [2002] EWCA Crim 440, [2002] 2 Cr App Rep (S) 387. The defendant pleaded guilty to false imprisonment. He broke into the home of a 71-year-old widow who lived alone. The window was smashed and the telephone wires cut. The widow was terrified and he demanded money. He picked up her walking stick and threatened to kill her and threatened to punch and stab her. He sprayed her face with hair spray.

That caused discomfort for some weeks. He put his hands round her throat for some 2 minutes and applied pressure. She thought she was going to die. He was there for 1¾ hours. The judge found her physical and mental health had suffered. Held. The offence led to physical injury and the defendant's conduct was 'likely to lead to physical injury.' Although mere risk is insufficient to give rise to a violent offence, it does not have to be shown that injury was 'a necessary or probable consequence.' Conduct which could very well lead to injury is properly characterised as likely so to lead. It was a violent offence.

See also LONGER THAN COMMENSURATE SENTENCES

Public servants (Doctors etc)

67.11 *A-G's Reference (No 45 of 2000)* [2001] 1 Cr App Rep (S) 413. The defendant pleaded guilty to false imprisonment and robbery. A doctor visited a female patient who was a heroin addict. She was also the defendant's girlfriend. He explained to both of them that he was not going to prescribe any medication. They explained their displeasure and then the doctor tried to leave. The defendant's activity caused the doctor to ask, 'Are you barring my exit.' The defendant replied, 'I've done 7 years and I'll do it again.' He then armed himself with a large knife and held the knife at the doctor's chest. He demanded the doctor's bag. The doctor who was frightened gave the defendant two tablets. The defendant demanded a sleeping pill, which he was given. The doctor was allowed to leave but was in a highly distressed condition. Fortunately the doctor had a driver who became suspicious and called the police who arrived.

The defendant appeared to be under the influence of drink or drugs or both and the police found him incoherent. The defendant had an appalling record including offences of violence and dishonesty. He was on licence at the time. Held. A sentence of **4 or 5 years** would be appropriate. However, as it was a reference the **30 months** sentence was not altered.

Revenge

67.12 *A-G's References (Nos 73 and 74 of 2001)* [2002] 1 Cr App Rep (S) 451. The defendants W and S pleaded guilty to false imprisonment. W also pleaded to unlawful wounding. The pleas were entered on the day fixed for their trial. Over 6 months the victim and W had a casual sexual relationship. W called the victim and said she was coming to collect a TV set. W went to the victim's home and watched television with him for about an hour. About midnight she took a small fruit knife and accused him of raping her while she was asleep some days before because she had a love bite on her back and her knickers were wet. He denied it. She was very angry and waved the knife and stabbed him in the leg and smashed a mug over his head. She then took a pill probably ecstasy. She rang S to take her away from his flat. When S got there she repeated the rape allegation, shouted and stabbed the victim in his other leg. She said his life was in her hands. S spat at the victim's face and the victim became progressively more frightened. W said they would take the victim out of the flat and told S to tie him up. S tied him with electrical wire and slapped him across the face. The victim was put in a car next to S with W driving. W instructed S to cover the victim's eyes and S did so with sellotape. The victim's head was covered with a cloth. When the victim moved his head S punched him about the eye. The victim was also stabbed in the arm and a cigarette lighter was applied to his forehead. He heard W on her mobile saying the victim was dying and she was going to kill him. When the car came to a halt S told the victim to be quiet or he would be killed. The victim was headbutted and thereafter blacked out. He was released after an 8–10 hours ordeal and was terrified and distressed with three stab wounds requiring two, two, and three stitches, two small burns and bruising. Items of the victim's jewellery were found on

W. The defendants accepted violence took place but denied they did it. W was 42 and had previous convictions for violence. S was 21 and had no convictions for violence. S was sentenced **to 9 months** and had been released on a tag. The sentence was due to end in just over 2 weeks. Held. Those that perceive themselves to be victims of crime should not take matters into their own hands. The victim's detention was long and frightening with him not being able to see. There was considerable violence used. We would have expected **4 years** for W and **2 years** for S. As it was a reference **3 years** not 18 months for W. S's sentence not altered because of the progress he had made since it was passed.

Robbery, and
See **ROBBERY**

Sexual

67.13   *R v Williams* [1999] 1 Cr App Rep (S) 105. The defendant pleaded guilty to kidnapping, ABH, indecent assault and driving whilst disqualified.

R v Ellis [1999] 1 Cr App Rep (S) 245. The defendant pleaded guilty to kidnapping and indecent assault against a 23-year-old woman. The defendant followed the victim after she had been shopping and caused her to go into a graveyard where he indecently attacked her for a period of 45 minutes. The doctor found 10 areas of recent bruising around her neck, her ear, her arm, wrists, finger, both knees and damage to her private parts. The defendant was 37 and had a previous conviction of abduction and indecent assault against an 18-year-old girl. After that offence he did not accept offers of treatment. His risk of re-offending was assessed by a psychiatrist as serious. This was based on the similarity of the offences, his denial of important aspects of the offence, his unstable personality and his social isolation. The judge was of the opinion that the defendant was likely to commit similar offences in the future. Held. **Life** sentence for the kidnap was appropriate. 6 years concurrent for the indecent assault not 9 years.

A-G's Reference (No 77 of 1998) [1999] 2 Cr App Rep (S) 336. (The title in the law report is wrong.) 7 years was lenient but not varied.

R v Willoughby [1999] 2 Cr App Rep (S) 18. The defendant was convicted of false imprisonment, indecent assault and ABH. In the early hours, the defendant entered a student's accommodation block. He found an 18-year-old student in the bathroom. As she left a cubicle he came up behind her and put his hand over her mouth. She was pushed into a cubicle so she faced the wall. He slapped her three or four times and locked the door. He put what he claimed to be a knife against her neck and forced her to perform oral sex on him. After he had ejaculated he forced her to swallow, said he was sorry and left. At the time of the offence he was 43. He had 6 previous court appearances for assault and dishonesty, gross indecency with a child, kidnapping, indecent assault, attempted kidnapping, and false imprisonment. The psychiatric evidence indicated that he was 'a high risk' because of his repetitive sexual offending. Held. It was appropriate to look at the purpose of the imprisonment. **Life** was appropriate here.

A-G's Reference (No 22 of 1999) [2000] 1 Cr App Rep (S) 253. The defendant was convicted of false imprisonment, indecent assault and putting a person in fear of violence under the Protection from Harassment Act 1997. The victim after a long and violent relationship with another moved to next door to where the defendant lived. They began a sexual relationship and he moved in with her. That relationship deteriorated and he was asked to move out and he went back next door. She found another man. The defendant saw them together and resented it. She gave up her job and stayed with a girlfriend so the defendant could not find her. Because she had two dogs to look after she returned home. That same evening, at about midnight as she went to let the dogs out, the defendant jumped over a shared gate. He pushed her back in the house. He demanded to know who she had been talking to on the telephone. He dragged her into the living room. He took her car keys and threatened to set her car on fire. He pulled out the stereo plug and the telephone plug. At about 3am he said he wasn't leaving until they had sex. He put his arms around her and pressed his erection against her. She protested. He tried to kiss her. There was a struggle and he knelt astride her and unbuttoned his trousers. He then masturbated himself ejaculating over her breasts. At about 4.30am he left making her promise she would not get him into trouble. At 9am he returned and asked for the same assurance. The victim was so distraught she was admitted into a psychiatric hospital for 4 weeks where she had been treated before. On her release he harassed her persistently saying she was dead and he would get together with her old partner. She had to be re-admitted to hospital for 6 weeks. At the trial she had to give evidence. The defendant had previous for rape, receiving 4 years. He also had convictions for burglary and theft. Held. The appropriate sentence would have been **6 years** but as it was a reference **4½ years** not 3.

Old cases. *R v Ragusa* (1992) 14 Cr App Rep (S) 118.

Taking the law into your own hands

67.14 *A-G's Reference (No 15 of 1999)* [2000] 1 Cr App Rep (S) 128. The defendant was convicted of kidnapping, false imprisonment and having a firearm with intent to kidnap. The defendant was burgled and lost some jewellery. When seen by police he was very volatile, aggressive and threatened to kill whoever was responsible. Later he suspected the victim was responsible and one evening he with three others all wearing balaclavas kidnapped him using a handgun. He was pushed into a car and taken to an isolated lane. The handgun was put to his ear and he was told to retrieve the stolen property. The gun which was capable of firing blanks was discharged. The attackers made off and the victim was found 'absolutely terrified' with blood on his face and crying. His hearing was affected for 1½ days. He had been detained for ¼ hour. The defendant showed no remorse. He was 28 with some dissimilar convictions, which were not as serious. He was in good employment and had testimonials for charitable work. In 1992 he was given an award for saving a drowning man. The victim had a bad record. Police had to install a panic button in the defendant's home to protect him and his girlfriend from attacks. Held. There were serious aggravating features here. Three or 4 years was called for. As it was a reference **2½ years** not 18 months.

R v AS [2000] 1 Cr App Rep (S) 491. The defendant pleaded guilty to false imprisonment. The defendant's daughter complained of indecent assault. A man was interviewed by the police and denied it. The CPS decided there was insufficient evidence. The suspect was assaulted and the defendant was arrested and charged. He was obsessive in his views as to what should happen. He was kept in custody for 6 months and acquitted. He remained obsessed, which caused his marriage to break up and his business to collapse. He suffered from a form of depression and took to drink and drugs. Inflamed by a cocktail of cocaine, vodka, rage, and obsession he went to the suspect's house. The suspect was in bed and the defendant smashed a Calor gas bottle through the lounge window. He went in with a 5 litre oil can. He entered the bedroom and told the defendant to lie down. He showed him the oil can and threatened to set him alight. In fact the can contained water not oil. The police arrived. He said he had sufficient petrol to burn the suspect alive. Over 150 police became involved over 7 hours. He forced the man to write a confession, which he did. He considered it was not sufficient so he forced him to write another. He let the man go when the police promised to arrest him. He then barricaded himself in a room for a further 1½ hours. In interview he said he never had any intention of harming the man. At the Appeal

Court he said he now accepted the CPS decision. He had previous convictions for drugs and violence but nothing of this kind. Held. 4 years not improper, but as an act of mercy to a broken man **3 years**.

R v Meek and Meek [2001] 2 Cr App Rep (S) 12. The two defendants father and son pleaded guilty to six counts of false imprisonment. The father ran a company, which had factory area and a yard, which had skips and was also used as a car park. His son worked there. Intruders entered their premises and smashed windows, damaged vehicles and the like. The police were unable to track down the culprits. Later six boys aged 12 or 13 entered the yard. Men with airguns, sticks and bars and a hockey stick came on the scene. The boys tried to run away. Someone said 'Don't run or we'll shoot you.' Three boys were shot with an airgun. The younger defendant struck one with the hockey stick. The boys were herded into the factory. The older defendant was waiting for them in there. The boys were made to stand in six inches of dye and questioned about the damage. They denied it, which was not accepted. They then had to sit in the dye. One was punched and they were all threatened. The older defendant was sentenced on the basis he did not have a weapon. The younger defendant was sentenced on the basis that he had struck only two boys and only once and that he left the area after the boys were herded in. The father was 52 and the son 20. Both were treated as of good character and were hard working men. Nothing but good had been said about them. They were sentenced on the basis that they believed the boys had been involved in the earlier incidents. Their home was also attacked. **1 year** substituted for 2 years imprisonment and YOI.

R v McHale [2001] EWCA Crim 529, [2001] 2 Cr App Rep (S) 417. The defendant was convicted of kidnapping and two ABHs. He was the area manager of a construction company and with another interviewed a supervisor who they believed was responsible for stealing some company machinery. The supervisor denied it and the defendant lost his temper, became abusive and punched him. While the victim tried to defend himself he butted him in the face and pushed his head so it broke one of the windows. The attack continued and he was finally hit with a paving brick. The victim suffered pain, bruises to his head and back and a cut. Two days later he and two others went to see the next victim, another company employee and told the two to put the victim in the back of the van. The victim failed to escape and was questioned about the missing items in the back of the van. The defendant drove the van off and the victim was threatened which included using a knuckleduster which one of them had. When the van stopped the defendant went to the back of the van and asked where the stolen items were. He got in and said, 'Right lads, get him and break his legs.' The victim was punched repeatedly to the head and body and grabbed around the throat. The victim was exceedingly frightened. Eventually he was released and he had seven cuts to his head, numerous cuts to his hands and tenderness to his chest. The defence was he acted in self defence in the first matter and had nothing to do with the second matter. He was of good character with testimonials. The pre-sentence report said his risk of re-offending was low. He was sentenced on the basis he had acted out of character. Held. These were serious assaults. People cannot be permitted to take the law into their own hands. Severe prison sentences are virtually inevitable for this sort of conduct by people of good character. **3 years** not 3½.

See also *R v Chapman* (1993) 15 Cr App Rep (S) 196.

FALSE INSTRUMENT, USING A

Where the false instument is used to steal see **THEFT ETC**

See also **COUNTERFEITING CURRENCY, ELECTION OFFENCES** and **PASSPORT OFFENCES**

FAMILY

See CRUELTY TO CHILDREN and MOTHERS

FATHERS

See CRUELTY TO CHILDREN, and MOTHERS

68   FIREARMS

68.1   Various different penalties under the Firearms Act 1968 and the Firearms (Amendment) Act 1997, ss 2 to 8 and other legislation.

Crown Court statistics England and Wales[1] – Crown Court – Males 21+ – Firearms Act offences

68.2

Year	Plea	Total Numbers sentenced	Type of sentence%					Average length of custody[2] (months)
			Discharge	Fine	Community sentence	Suspended sentence	Custody	
2000	Guilty	219	5%	8%	16%	9%	61%	23.5
	Not guilty	18	6%	0%	6%	0%	72%	21.4

1   Excluding committals for sentence. Source: Crime and Criminal Justice Unit, Home Office Ref: IOS416-02.
2   Excluding life sentences.

Guideline case

68.3   *R v Avis* [1998] 1 Cr App Rep 420 – LCJ. The numbers convicted of some firearms offences has very sharply increased. The unlawful possession and use of firearms is generally recognised as a grave source of danger to society. The reasons are obvious. Firearms may be used to take life or cause serious injury. They are used to further the commission of other serious crimes. Often the victims will be those charged with the enforcement of the law or the protection of persons or property. In the conflicts, which occur between competing criminal gangs, often related to the supply of drugs, the use and possession of firearms provoke an escalating spiral of violence. The appropriate level of sentence for a firearms offence, as for any other offence, will depend on all the facts and circumstances relevant to the offence and the offender, and it would be wrong for this court to seek to prescribe unduly restrictive sentencing guidelines. It will, however, usually be appropriate for the sentencing court to ask itself a series of questions:

(1)   What sort of weapon is involved? Genuine firearms are more dangerous than imitation firearms. Loaded firearms are more dangerous than unloaded firearms. Unloaded firearms for which ammunition is available are more dangerous than firearms for which no ammunition is available. Possession of a firearm which has no lawful use (such as a sawn-off shotgun) will be viewed even more seriously than possession of a firearm which is capable of lawful use.

(2)   What (if any) use has been made of the firearm? It is necessary for the court, as with any other offence, to take account of all circumstances surrounding any use

made of the firearm: the more prolonged and premeditated and violent the use, the more serious the offence is likely to be.

(3)   With what intention (if any) did the defendant possess or use the firearm? Generally speaking, the most serious offences under the Act are those which require proof of a specific criminal intent (to endanger life, to cause fear of violence, to resist arrest, to commit an indictable offence). The more serious the act intended, the more serious the offence.

(4)   What is the defendant's record? The seriousness of any firearm offence is inevitably increased if the offender has an established record of committing firearms offences or crimes of violence.

Where there are breaches of ss 4, 5, 16, 16A, 17(1) and (2), 18(1), 19 or 21 of the Firearms Act, 1968 the custodial term is likely to be of considerable length, and where the four questions suggested above yield answers adverse to the offender, terms at or approaching the maximum may in a contested case be appropriate. An indeterminate sentence should however be imposed only where the established criteria for imposing such a sentence are met.

Some of the sentences imposed for these offences in the past, sometimes by this court, have failed to reflect the seriousness of such offences and the justifiable public concern which they arouse. Save for minor infringements which may be and are properly dealt with summarily, offences against these provisions will almost invariably merit terms of custody, even on a plea of guilty and in the case of an offender with no previous record.

[No cases heard before *R v Avis* [1998] are listed as that case indicates that past sentences were on occasions too low.]

Death results

See MANSLAUGHTER – *Firearms, with*

Debt collecting

68.4   *R v Lavin* [2000] 1 Cr App Rep (S) 227. The defendants KL, TL and SW pleaded guilty to possessing a firearm with intent to commit an indictable offence. TL also pleaded guilty to possessing prohibited ammunition. The pleas were entered late after a plea basis was agreed and the prosecution agreed to drop a more serious count. Police on surveillance duties saw a car containing the three defendants acting suspiciously near some shops and post offices. They stopped the car. SW was wearing a hood and gloves. A lump hammer, a holdall, two hats, a small handgun an earpiece and four further pairs of gloves were found. The safety catch on the firearm was down and the gun was cocked with live ammunition in the magazine and a live round in the chamber. A large amount of ammunition was found at TL's home. The basis of plea was that indictable offence was a debt owed to TL, which was not enforceable through the courts. The gun was only to be showed to the debtor and not to be used. The firearm had come into their possession because someone wanted it looked after rather than sought for the task. KL was 40 and had a number of convictions mostly for dishonesty but there was one firearm conviction. TL was 48 and had numerous convictions for motoring offences and dishonesty but none for firearm. SW was 40 with dishonesty convictions and no firearm offences. The judge said there was a local problem with the use of guns in Merseyside and SW was the least involved. He also said that gave a substantial discount for the pleas entered. Held. The judge was in the best position to judge local problems. KL, **6 years** not 7½. TL, **6 and 1 years consecutive** not 7 ½ and 1½ consecutive. SW, **5 years** not 6.

Defendant aged under 18 years

68.5 *R v Thomas* [2000] 2 Cr App Rep (S) 155. The defendant pleaded guilty to possessing a firearm when committing a Sch 1 offence and theft. The defendant went to a 'peep' show and asked for change. He left and returned and seized a cash bag containing £122 from the cashier. He was chased through the streets. A police officer caught him and an imitation handgun was found on him. It wasn't used but was of convincing appearance. He said he just liked carrying it. The defendant was 17 and had findings of guilt for failure to surrender to bail, criminal damage and possession of a bladed article. Held. The law on imitation firearms exists to prevent anyone minded to commit a criminal offence from carrying firearms or imitation firearm. If someone carries an imitation firearm when committing an offence but does not produce it and has some entirely credible or innocent reason for its possession the court might be persuaded to unusual leniency. Otherwise it calls for a substantial custodial sentence. Taking into account the defendant's youth and his plea 15 months cannot be described as excessive. **15 months and 3 months consecutive** YOI was not wrong.

R v Burnip (12 August 2002, unreported). The defendant pleaded guilty to having an imitation firearm with intent to resist arrest, threats to kill, having an offensive weapon and affray. He attacked police then they had been called by his mother because of his behaviour. We would have expected at least 18 months but because of his progress with his drug problem the community rehabilitation order was undisturbed.

False imprisonment, and

See **FALSE IMPRISONMENT** – *Firearms, with (real or imitation)*

Firearms Act 1968, s 1

68.6 Possession of a firearm

Triable either way. Maximum sentence 5 years. Summary maximum 6 months or £5,000

R v Baer [1999] 1 Cr App Rep (S) 441. The defendant pleaded guilty to possessing a firearm, possessing ammunition and handling stolen goods at the Magistrates' Court. He was committed for sentence. The police searched the defendant's home in connection with a motoring matter. The defendant told them he had a small handgun in the attic. It was duly found with 50 rounds of ammunition. The defendant said he had lawfully bought them in the US at the suggestion of his friend who he was living with. On his return to this country he had brought them back and they had remained in the house unused and untouched. The defendant was 38 with one minor conviction. Held. The gravity of the offence is the risk of them falling into the wrong hands. These facts are very unusual. **12 months** not 18 with the other sentences remaining concurrent.

R v Wharton [2000] 2 Cr App Rep (S) 339. The defendant made an early plea to possession of a firearm. The police executed a search warrant at the defendant's home and found a revolver hanging on the living room wall. It was of modern Italian reproduction with a cylinder with blocked chambers. However, in a cupboard was a cylinder which when fitted made a working firearm. The defendant said it was an ornament which he had had a number of years and had cost him £25. He was 44 with dissimilar convictions between 1974 and 1985, none of which were for violence. He was divorced who looked after his children 3 days a week. **2 months** not 6 months.

R v Lamb (24 September, unreported). The defendant pleaded guilty on the first day of his trial to possessing a firearm without a certificate and possession of ammunition. For many years he had had a turbulent relationship with his former wife. Police were called to her home and found on the kitchen table parts of a firearm which when assembled was a .2 self loading pistol. There was also ammunition which fitted the pistol. He was sentenced on the basis he owed money to another and when he defaulted that person asked him to take possession of it for a day or two. It was received in a disassembled state and the defendant never contemplated using it. He was 46 with many convictions, the last was in 1997 for a wholly different offence. The judge said he passed a deterrent sentence. Held. We are sceptical of the basis of plea, but we accept it. We support the judge in his views that severe sentences are appropriate, but because of the plea and the basis of plea **3 years** not 4.

Firearms Act 1968, ss 1 and 4(4)

68.7   Possession of a shortened shotgun or firearm which has been converted.

Triable either way. Maximum sentence 7 years. Summary maximum 6 months or £5,000

R v Gourley [1999] 2 Cr App Rep (S) 148. The defendant pleaded guilty to possessing a firearm. The police searched the defendant's home and found a single barrelled sawn-off shotgun and 17 shotgun cartridges in two plastic bags under a child's bed in one of the bedrooms. The gun was capable of being fired and the cartridges could be used in the gun. He said he had bought the gun off some gypsies for his own protection. The defendant had a conviction for violence and had a good wok record. The judge said that on a not guilty plea 6 years would be the sentence. Held 6 years was too close to the statutory maximum. **3 years** substituted for 4.

R v Holmes [1999] 2 Cr App Rep (S) 383. The defendant pleaded guilty to possession of a firearm whilst a prohibited person, possession of a shortened shotgun, and possession of a loaded shotgun in a public place. A householder went to look at a car and saw a sawn off shotgun in the passenger footwell through a partially open window. The police were called and found the shotgun, which was loaded with two cartridges. The police traced the defendant, aged 42 as the hirer of the vehicle and arrested him. He admitted the gun belonged to him and said he had bought it with the intention of committing suicide. He said he took some pills and ended up in hospital. In 1990 he was sentenced to 4 years for the possession of drugs with intent to supply. He had heart and artery problems, which he tended to exaggerate. The psychiatrist said the possession of the shotgun for a possible suicide fitted in with his presentation and his behaviour at the time. The prison report says he always uses his medical and psychological problems to get what he wants. Held. Leaving the firearm there was extreme irresponsibility and recklessness. We are quite unmoved by the submission that his intention to commit suicide means he is less culpable. There was nothing wrong with 2½ years on each concurrent.

R v Campbell [2000] 1 Cr App Rep (S) 291. The defendant appears to have pleaded guilty to possession of a shortened shotgun, and a prohibited firearm. Police officers searched his flat after a disturbance in which he threatened someone and kicked a car. For the disturbance he received 6 months in all for possession of an offensive weapon and criminal damage. In a cupboard they found a sawn off shotgun in pieces in a black bin liner. In another cupboard they found an automatic machine pistol, which was a prohibited weapon and over 900 rounds of ammunition in a suitcase. Neither was loaded but both were in working order. He was sentenced on the basis he thought the items were stolen goods and he didn't look at them. (This was no defence because of *R v Steele* [1993] Crim LR 298) He had had them for 10 days and was to receive no payment. [The judgment does not refer to his character.] Held. 3½ years would have been appropriate if he had known but as he didn't **2 years** substituted.

R v Herbert [2001] 1 Cr App Rep (S) 77. The defendant pleaded guilty to possession of a shortened shotgun and possession of a firearm when prohibited. Police officers executed a search warrant at the defendant's home address and found a sawn-off shotgun with two live cartridges concealed in a bed. The firearm was in working order and the cartridges fitted the shotgun. At a Newton hearing he claimed he was looking after it for a short while for £50 for a man he was terrified of. This was not accepted and he was sentenced on the basis it was for his own purposes. The defendant was 29 with eleven previous convictions including three for ABH one of which he was sentenced to 12 months. There were no convictions for firearms. Held. The weapon had no lawful use and was a criminal's weapon for use in violent and serious crime. Although there was no evidence of any contemplated offence the court was entitled to assume that it was for unlawful use should the occasion arise. His prohibition aggravated the offence. **4 years** on each concurrent was not manifestly excessive.

Firearms Act 1968, s 2

68.8   Possession of a shotgun

Triable either way. Maximum sentence 5 years. Summary maximum 6 months and/or £5,000.

Firearms Act 1968, ss 3(1)(a) and 5(1)

68.9   Manufacturing a firearm

Triable either way. On indictment maximum sentences 5 and 7 years respectively.

Summary maximum 6 months and/or £5,000.

R v Luty [1999] 2 Cr App Rep (S) 81. The defendant pleaded guilty to manufacturing a prohibited weapon and possession of ammunition. He asked for two offences of possession of a firearm to be taken into consideration. The defendant visited a photograph and said he had designed a weapon and he wanted the 80 parts photographed for a service and assembly manual. The photographer told the police who searched the defendant's home. They found a workshop with a very large number of assorted pieces of metal, weapon parts, gun magazines and diagrams. They also found a home-made sub-machine gun and six Luger cartridges. Residue showed the gun had been fired. It could only fire single shots but with adjustment it could probably fire bursts of ammunition. In interview he said he had been engaged in the project for 2 years for a book to be published in the US. The book was now published and it explained how to construct a sub-machine gun. Other prototypes were the subject matter for the TICs. The defendant had a conviction for possession of a loaded firearm in a public place for which he was fined. He was considered a loner with anger towards society. It was accepted the gun was not to be used for crime or to injure anyone. Held. The offence was aggravated by the deliberate breaking of the law, which he disapproved, and his previous conviction. A heavy sentence was inevitable. **4 years** was severe but the sentence properly reflects society's revulsion for guns and was not manifestly excessive.

Firearms Act 1968, s 4

68.10   Converting weapons and shortening the barrel of a shotgun.

Triable either way. Maximum sentence 10 years. Summary maximum 6 months and/or £5,000.

R v Avis [1998] 2 Cr App Rep (S) 178 – LCJ. Where there are breaches of s 4 of the Firearms Act 1968 the custodial term is likely to be of considerable length, and where the four questions suggested above (see *Guidelines*) yield answers adverse to the offender, terms at or approaching the maximum may in a contested case be appropriate.

Firearms Act 1968, s 5

68.11   Possession of a prohibited weapon or ammunition.

Triable either way. Maximum sentence 10 years. Summary maximum 6 months and/or £5,000.

R v Avis [1998] 2 Cr App Rep (S) 178 – LCJ. Where there are breaches of s 5 of the Firearms Act 1968 the custodial term is likely to be of considerable length, and where the four questions suggested above (see Guidelines) yield answers adverse to the offender, terms at or approaching the maximum may in a contested case be appropriate.

R v Wright [2000] 1 Cr App Rep (S) 109. The defendant pleaded guilty to possession of a prohibited weapon, possession of ammunition and possessing a firearm when prohibited. Police officers searched his flat and he managed to remove a revolver from his sofa without the officers noticing. He passed it to his partner but she was searched. It was a Smith and Wesson and fully loaded with six bullets. Because of its length it was prohibited. It was functioning normally. He said it was for his own protection and he was concerned because he had helped the police about the death of a close friend. The defendant had a conviction for conspiracy to rob where no robbery took place and no weapon was involved for which he received 4 years. Held. There was no actual use made of it, it was possessed for a short time and it was for self-defence. After considering the questions in *R v Avis* [1998], **2 years** not 4.

R v Campbell [2000] 1 Cr App Rep (S) 291. The defendant appears to have pleaded guilty to possession of a shortened shotgun, and a prohibited firearm. Police officers searched his flat after a disturbance in which he threatened someone and kicked a car. For the disturbance he received 6 months in all for possession of an offensive weapon and criminal damage. In a cupboard they found a sawn off shotgun in pieces in a black bin liner. In another cupboard they found an automatic machine pistol, which was a prohibited weapon and over 900 rounds of ammunition in a suitcase. Neither was loaded but both were in working order. He was sentenced on the basis he thought the items were stolen goods and he didn't look at them. (This was no defence because of *R v Steele* [1993] Crim LR 298) He had had them for 10 days and was to receive no payment. [The judgment does not refer to his character.] Held. 3½ years would have been appropriate if he had known but as he didn't **2 years** substituted.

R v Aplin [2000] 2 Cr App Rep (S) 89. The defendant pleaded guilty at the Magistrates' Court to possession of ten prohibited weapons and five charges of possessing prohibited ammunition. The defendant, aged 58 was a registered firearm dealer held in high regard by members of a Rifle and Pistol Club, which he ran and by members of the police force who used the club. A fire broke out in a bedroom above the garage of the house where the defendant was staying. The firemen discovered 46 prohibited firearms and ammunition in the garage and called the police. In the house the police discovered cabinets containing firearms. The firearms only became prohibited by the 1997 legislation. The firearms were stored without the knowledge of the family that lived there and before the change in the law were worth about £30,000. The defendant said that the firearms belonged in part to the club and the rest belonged to his business. When the charges to the law were taking place he stored the firearms in Germany at a gun club and club members used them there. However, because there were so many firearms he was asked to end the arrangement. He failed to sell them in Germany and then could not benefit from the UK surrender and compensated policy. He brought them back to the UK illegally. He claimed he held them in the hope of obtaining compensation. The family whose home the firearms were stored had problems with their insurance claim because of the illegal storage of firearms and the defendant had to compensate them £16,000 from his pension fund. Held. The prevailing purpose of the legislation was safety. Keeping lethal weapons in insecure conditions was serious. He treated himself above the law. The sentence had to have a deterrent element. He exposed his friends and others to a very significant level of risk. Applying *R v Avis* [1998] 2 Cr App Rep (S) 178, **18 months** not 3 years because of his age, character and the financial loss.

Firearms Act 1968, s 16

68.12 Possession with intent to endanger life

Indictable only. Maximum sentence life.

Section 16 is a specified offence for automatic life.

R v Avis [1998] 2 Cr App Rep (S) 178 – LCJ. Where there are breaches of s 16 of the Firearms Act 1968 the custodial term is likely to be of considerable length, and where the four questions suggested above (see **Guidelines**) yield answers adverse to the offender, terms at or approaching the maximum may in a contested case be appropriate

R v Avis [1998] *Re Thomas* 2 Cr App Rep (S) 178 at 189 – LCJ. Thomas pleaded guilty to two counts of possessing a firearm with intent to endanger life, six counts of selling or transferring firearms unlawfully; and two counts of selling or transferring ammunition unlawfully. The pleas were entered at the beginning of his trial after the judge had made a ruling on the evidence. Thomas was a firearms dealer who sold three revolvers and ammunition for them to an undercover police officer for £1,160 in a car park. Thomas told the officer that he could supply firearms regularly and easily. At a further meeting at a railway station Thomas sold the officer two pump action shotguns which had been shortened. He also sold three pistols and ammunition for all five weapons. The total price was £1,220. Thomas was arrested. He was 66 and had no convictions. He had a very large number of testimonials. He had for many years been involved with charity work and was held in high esteem. He was sentenced to 9 years on each endanger count; 4 years for the selling firearms counts and 2 years for ammunition counts. They were all concurrent making a total of **9 years**. Held. The judge's starting point would have been 12 years. The use of firearms by armed robbers and drug dealers is prevalent and on the increase. A person who provides firearms in the certain knowledge that they are going to be used by criminals commits a grave offence. The judge took the mitigation fully into account and he could not sensibly have reduced the sentence further.

A-G's Reference (No 49 of 1998) [1999] 1 Cr App Rep (S) 396. The defendant pleaded guilty 2 days before his trial to possession of a firearm with intent to endanger life, and other lesser and connected firearm offences. The defendant's flat was searched. The defendant struggled and kicked out at the officers. In the airing cupboard they found a plastic bin bag containing a self-loading pistol and a clip for the pistol containing six rounds of ammunition and 31 other rounds. The firearm was a prohibited weapon and in working order. In interview he said there had been a lot of gang related trouble and it was for his own protection. He accepted he was a member of one of the gangs. He was 23 and had convictions for drugs and wounding. Held. If the matter had been contested **8 years** would have been appropriate. For a late plea **7 years** was appropriate. As it was a reference **6 years** not 30 months.

A-G's Reference (No 2 of 2000) [2001] 1 Cr App Rep (S) 27. The defendant was convicted of possession a firearm with intent to endanger life and possessing ammunition. Police made an arrest and went to the man's home address. Inside was the defendant and the police saw him through a window throw an object into a cupboard. It was found to be a sock with a Smith and Wesson self-loading pistol with one round in the breech and 13 in the magazine. The safety catch was off. It was in good condition and was a prohibited weapon. The defendant was 33 and had no convictions.

Held. We would have expected a sentence of at least **7 years**. Because it was a reference **6 years** not 4.

R v Marney [2001] EWCA Crim 2111, [2002] 1 Cr App Rep (S) 506. See *Self defence, firearms for*

Firearms Act 1968, s 16A

68.13 To have in his possession any firearm or imitation firearm with intent (a) by means thereof to cause, or (b) to enable another person by means thereof to cause, any person to believe that unlawful violence will be used against him or another person.

Indictable only. Maximum sentence 10 years.

R v Avis [1998] 2 Cr App Rep (S) 178 – LCJ. Where there are breaches of s 16A of the Firearms Act 1968 the custodial term is likely to be of considerable length, and where the four questions suggested above (see *Guidelines*) yield answers adverse to the offender, terms at or approaching the maximum may in a contested case be appropriate.

Firearms Act 1968, s16A – Airguns, air rifles, air pistols

68.14 *R v Avis Re Thorrington* [1998] 2 Cr App Rep (S) 178 at 189 – LCJ. The defendant pleaded guilty to possessing a firearm with intent to cause fear of unlawful violence. In the early hours, the defendant's stepson, Roberts walked home from a local public house was confronted by about seven men. Abuse was exchanged and one of the men kicked him. The defendant, who had been drinking, was told about it and he fetched two air rifles, handing one to Roberts. Each was loaded and primed. The two men went to the scene of the earlier incident and Roberts identified a man called Sanjit Singh as the person who had kicked him. The defendant kicked Mr Singh and he pointed the gun at his face. Mr Singh pushed the gun away, but this caused the weapon to be accidentally discharged. The defendant then primed the weapon and reloaded. Mr Singh ran off in fear. The police then arrived. The defendant told the police where he had hid the guns. The defendant was of good character. He had been off work since January 1996 through ill health. He was also suffering from depression. Held. This case had the aggravating feature that loaded weapons were taken to a public place, where one was discharged, albeit accidentally. The **18 months** he received was the correct sentence.

R v Thompson [1999] 2 Cr App Rep (S) 292. The defendant pleaded guilty to possession of a firearm with intent to cause another to believe unlawful violence would used. The defendant aged 58, went to a public house with an air pistol. He had no ammunition with him. He was very drunk and he took exception to a remark about his age and produced the pistol, and said, 'No-one fucks with me.' The man who made the remark pulled up his shirt and pointed at his heart although he did not regarded it as a joke. The incident subsided. Later he was arrested. He had suffered from depression although the psychiatrist said the incident should be treated as an isolated offence and he was not psychiatrically disturbed. Between 1990 and 1993 he was convicted of ABH four times and affray. There were no convictions since. **4 months** not 2 years.

R v Carey [2000] 1 Cr App Rep (S) 179. The defendant was convicted of possession of a firearm with intent to cause fear or violence. Following reports of a male firing an airgun into the street, police went to the defendant's home. They saw him at an open window pointing a firearm in their general direction, shouting, 'Fuck off you lot. I'll let you have it if you come at me with a shotgun.' He was told not to be silly but he put the butt of the rifle to his shoulder and his eye to the sight pointing the gun at the police. He said, 'I'll do it. I'll fucking have you.' A crack was heard followed by a bang. A police cordon was mounted, and pupils were kept in at school. He was arrested and two air rifles and air pellets were found. He was 43 with a number of convictions but none between 1989 and 1997. The judge believed all the time in custody would count towards his sentence, but it didn't because of another conviction and sentence. Held. **2 years** cannot possibly be said to be manifestly excessive.

R v Doyle [2001] 2 Cr App Rep (S) 8. The defendant pleaded guilty to possession of a firearm with intent to cause a person to fear unlawful violence would be used. After 1am the defendant and two others went to a take away restaurant and she tried to buy a bottle of whisky. When the member of staff refused to sell the drink at she became angry and shouted at him that she would kill him. She produced a handgun and said, 'Give me the drink or I'll blow your fucking head off.' The member of staff who was used to firearms from his previous career did not think the gun was real and was not frightened. The customers of the restaurant gasped in disbelief. One of her friends pulled her away and they left. Just after that or before she entered the restaurant she discharged the gun through a window of an off-licence. The ball hit a bottle behind where the proprietor was standing. She was filmed on CCTV outside brandishing a gun and on one occasion waving in the direction of another man. She was arrested at her home and the gun was found in some undergrowth. It was an air pistol, which resembled a Browning 9mm handgun. On the night she had drunk a large amount of alcohol and had consumed anti-depressant drugs. She was 26 and had no convictions. She had suffered abuse as a child and had a history of alcohol abuse and suicide attempts. Held. **3 years** was not excessive.

Firearms Act 1968, s 16A – Handguns

68.15 *R v Avis* [1998] 1 Cr App Rep 420 – LCJ. The defendant was convicted of possessing a firearm with intent to cause fear of violence. Avis was involved in a serious dispute with his sister. A neighbour saw her face had blood on it and she was heading for her car, parked nearby and noticed Avis pursuing her shouting, 'you fucking want it'. Avis was holding a handgun, which he appeared to be trying to load with a magazine. He pointed the gun at her and made the gun click three times. He put the handgun to her head. She and her children reached the car and whilst she was trying to put the children in the car Avis was still trying to make the gun work. He approached her again and put the handgun to the back of her head. This time when he clicked the gun there was a loud bang and a wall was struck by a bullet and crumbled. A witness said she didn't know whether the sister moved her head or Avis purposely missed. The sister drove off in the car shouting to Avis 'I'll get you for this.' Shortly after this she drove back and it appeared she was going to confront Avis who appeared on the scene. Almost immediately the police arrived and Avis left. The gun was found nearby. It was a Colt .45 semi-automatic pistol with one live round in the magazine and in poor condition. Avis was arrested and was 35. He had convictions for violence. In 1995 he was placed on probation for affray. The sister, unlike many victims, did not appear to have suffered psychological distress. Held. The sentence of 8 years was above the prevailing level of sentence being imposed at the time. We reduce it to **6 years**. However, in future offences such as this could well attract sentences of the length first imposed.

R v Roker [1998] 2 Cr App Rep (S) 254. The defendant pleaded guilty to possessing a firearm with the intent to cause a belief that violence would be used, burglary and other dishonesty offences. The defendant with another burgled a house and stole property including an imitation 9mm Browning handgun. Three days later he saw a commotion outside a public house between two women one of which he knew. He produced the gun and held it at his side. The commotion ended and the defendant ran away. He was arrested and released on bail and committed further offences by obtaining £192 worth of goods. He was 20 and had a number of convictions but he had had no custodial sentences. Held. **2 years** detention for the firearm matter was not manifestly excessive. The total sentence of 3 years was too long so 3 months consecutive not 12 months for the other offences partly because of disparity with the co-defendant on the burglary offence. (The judgment does not refer to *R v Avis* [1998].)

R v Thynne (23 July 2001, unreported). 2½ years upheld on a plea. Attack on lover with violence.

A-G's Reference (No 7 of 2001) (29 November 2001, unreported. 1 year substituted for CSO.

R v Wheeler [2002] EWCA Crim 65, [2002] 2 Cr App Rep (S) 263. The defendant pleaded guilty to possessing a firearm with the intent to cause a belief that violence would be used, having a firearm with intent to commit an indictable offence, possession of a prohibited weapon and false imprisonment. He had a relationship and moved in with the victim. He said he had in the French Foreign Legion and was highly experienced in explosives, firearms and weapons. About a year later after arguments she told him to leave. He did so and found it hard to accept and made repeated efforts to see her. She felt pestered. 5 months later he waited outside the garden centre where she worked and ¾ hour later he entered the centre and told her to go into an office. He had a pistol loaded with two live rounds and told her and her colleague, A to phone the police. He pointed the gun at her and said he wasn't messing about, he was serious. He talked about his relationship with her and she became extremely frightened. The gun appeared cocked and it appeared to remain so. He talked about Hungerford and Dunblane and said her son was going to be an orphan. She was detained for 12 hours and he wouldn't let her go to the lavatory. The defendant threatened to kill himself. A chose to remain although the defendant said he could go. Eventually the defendant surrendered to the police. A said he was not seriously worried about his or her safety. When interviewed the defendant said,' He waited till the school emptied. The victim had persuaded him not to let the police shoot him. He was at his lowest ebb ever and the gun was to 'stop her leaving.' The defendant was 44 and had no previous record for this kind of offence. He had had periods of depression. Held. The incident was terrifying. It was planned and the pistol was loaded with two bullets. These were very grave offences of the utmost seriousness. **7 years** was not manifestly excessive.

Firearms Act 1968, s 16A – Imitation weapons, starting pistols etc

68.16   *R v Avis Re Barton* [1998] 2 Cr App Rep (S) 178 at 187. The defendant pleaded guilty to two dwelling house burglaries, possessing an imitation firearm contrary to s 16A of the Firearms Act 1968 and a count of commercial burglary. The last two were committed on bail. He also asked for three offences of domestic burglary and four of commercial burglary to be taken into account. In the early hours of a morning Barton, who had been drinking, approached a car containing three young men, produced a replica handgun and pointed it at them. He demanded a lift. He held the gun within inches of the face of one of them and immediately pulled the trigger and the gun clicked. It made a noise like an imitation pistol. The man was not sure whether it was imitation and was in shock. He aimed a blow at Barton who was leaning into the car and got out of the car and punched at Barton who fell but then got up again. The man chased him and he turned and fired the gun again. Although he did not think anything was fired from it, the man was still fearful. Barton was arrested and was 20. Between 1994 and 1996 he had been convicted on numerous occasions, including 21 offences of theft and taking vehicles and two public order offences, including his most recent conviction for affray for which he received 8 months' detention. The judge regarded the occupants of the car as absolutely terrified thinking their lives were in danger. He was sentenced to a total of **5 years** detention (3 years in all for the other offences and two years for the firearm offence consecutive). Held. The judge rightly said this was a terrifying offence. The total was not excessive.

R v Steele [1999] 1 Cr App Rep (S) 369. The defendant pleaded guilty to possessing an imitation firearm with intent to cause another to believe violence would be used. The defendant's relationship with his girlfriend F, aged 17 broke up and each accused the other of harassment. He said associates of her had used violence against him. He went to the police about it four days before the offence and was carrying a metal pole about 3' in length. He said it was for his self defence and it was taken off him. The police advised him against carrying weapons. He left blaming the police for taking her side. He then borrowed a starting pistol from a friend, which was capable of firing blanks. He had no cartridges for it. He went to the F's flat and was told F was not at home. F and two young women were abusive to one another and the defendant managed to get into the hall. He pointed the pistol at F and the two others and told the two to go away. F believed it was a real gun and was very fearful. All the women ran away and F went to the police station. The defendant admitted the offence. He was 22 and had been in minor trouble as a juvenile and had been cautioned for criminal damage. He had no convictions for violence. He was sentenced on the basis there had been provocation and he had ignored the advice given earlier. **9 months** not 18.

A-G's Reference (No 49 of 1999) [2000] 1 Cr App Rep (S) 436. The defendant pleaded guilty to possession of a firearm with intent to cause fear of violence. The defendant after drinking hired a taxi at about 1.30am to take him home. He was asked for £5 and he said his money was in the house. The defendant went in and after he didn't return the taxi driver knocked on his front door and then returned to his taxi. The defendant approached the taxi and demonstrated that he appeared to be holding a gun and magazine clip. He made a movement to suggest he was cocking a gun. He asked what the fare was and was told it was now £5.80. The defendant told the taxi driver to think again. There was a conversation during which he continued to make it appear he was prepared to use the gun. He said he was on crack cocaine and eventually the taxi driver left and contacted the police. Armed police attended and after ½ hour he was arrested. In the attic the police found a replica Beretta handgun and four rounds of replica ammunition. It was made of metal and plastic. He was 33 and his criminal record contained nothing of significant gravity. He was sentenced to 100 hours' community service, costs and compensation. Held. Anything less than **2 years** was inappropriate. **12 months** substituted because it was a reference and because he had performed 68 hours of the community service and had paid the £250 costs.

R v Crawford [2001] 1 Cr App Rep (S) 119. The defendant pleaded guilty to four counts of possession of a firearm to cause a person to fear unlawful violence, possession of a bladed weapon and common assault. The defendant was refused a drink at a public house because he was drunk. He swore and abused another customer. The relief manager of the public house told him to leave and the defendant headbutted him. He was ejected and the defendant was abusive and said he was going to shoot him. He pulled an imitation handgun from his pocket and the manager trapped the firearm in the doors of the public house. A customer said it was a toy and the defendant said, 'I'm having you,' and ran off. About 2½ hours later he went into a club and was refused a drink. He started to leave and was followed out. The defendant pulled out an imitation handgun and pointed it at the member of staff. He was told to behave himself. The defendant went home and got a kitchen knife and returned. The same member of staff saw him outside and saw him throw a glass into a builder's yard. He called the defendant a twat. The defendant took out the knife and there was a struggle. The defendant was headbutted and forced to drop the knife. A handgun fell to the ground and the defendant staggered off. He was arrested and released on bail. He failed to surrender to it.

About 6 months later he was drinking at a public house with two women and a man and telephoned his wife when he was emotional. Afterwards he became angry and pulled out a pistol and said he was going to kill someone and himself. The man said, 'Don't be stupid, you couldn't hurt a fly with that.' The defendant fired the gun at the wall and the woman he was with was terrified. He said he was going to shoot himself and put the barrel into his mouth. It was then realised the gun was for firing blanks. The defendant then fell asleep. The two men went to another public house and were so drunk that they practically fell over. The defendant asked a customer to change a £1 coin and he refused. The defendant removed an imitation gun and made a cocking motion. The customer was in fear of his life. They were ejected from the public house. The defendant was 43 with 16 mainly motoring convictions. **3 years** in total not 5.

R v Mernin [2001] 2 Cr App Rep (S) 24. The defendant made an early plea to possession of a firearm with intent to cause fear of violence. Shortly after midnight the defendant entered a shop of a petrol station with camouflage netting over his head. He asked to go to the kitchen area for water and this request was refused. He appeared unsteady on his feet and his speech was slurred. He was given a drink of water. He then asked the assistant what he would do if he pointed a gun at him and asked for the money in the till. The assistant was shocked but told the defendant he would not get any money and he would call the police. The defendant asked another customer for a cigarette and the panic button was pressed. The defendant made to leave and asked the assistant about another member of staff and told him to mention Mr Mernin, which was the defendant's name. He also said he had been released from prison that day. About 30–40 feet away he took a gun from his waistband and pointed it at the assistant and put his finger on the trigger. Three or 4 seconds later he put it back in his waistband, laughed and left the shop. The assistant was terrified and believed the firearm to be real and that the defendant was about to shoot him. Police arrested him nearby and he said, 'I've got HIV and Hepatitis C. I hope you lot get it.' and police found a blank cartridge firing imitation firearm resembling a Colt Magnum which was very realistic. The defendant was 29 and was a heroin addict. He had convictions but none that had attracted custody. He expressed remorse and had Hepatitis C and had been thought to be HIV positive. Held. **3 years** was a severe sentence for a man in the defendant's condition but it was not excessive.

R v Poggiani [2001] EWCA Crim 78, [2001] 2 Cr App Rep (S) 305. The defendant was convicted of possession of a firearm with intent to cause fear of violence. He had pleaded guilty to possession of ammunition at the Magistrates' Court. About 10 months before the offence the victim, a neighbour of the defendant had run out of his own house carrying a cap gun and had shouted at children who were playing with a ball near his car. He fired the gun twice. As a result the defendant's nephew had nightmares. This caused a dispute between the two. Six days before the neighbour was due to be sentenced, the defendant shouted abuse at him to provoke him into violence and it was not successful. The defendant left and returned with a toy pistol, which he pointed at the neighbour. He twice pretended to fire it and the neighbour's wife heard it click twice. He put the gun against the head of the neighbour's 6-year-old son and said, 'Bang, bang, you're dead.' The child ran into his house crying. The defendant surrendered to the police and they found three large bullets, 21 smaller bullets and 10 bullet heads in a hole in his kitchen wall. They had been both charged with similar offences and the neighbour was ordered to perform 150 hours' community service. The defendant was 30 and had convictions including two for threatening behaviour etc with intent to cause fear. **6 months** not 12.

A-G's Reference (No 71 of 2001) [2001] EWCA Crim 1489, [2002] 2 Cr App Rep (S) 79. The defendant pleaded guilty at the first opportunity to possession of an imitation firearm with intent to cause fear of violence. The defendant was driven to a job interview by a friend and produced a starting pistol. He fired two shots out of the window saying he was having fun and reloaded it. The friend protested but the defendant shouted at someone in the street and fired the pistol at him. The friend dropped him off and contacted the police. After the interview the defendant called his partner on his mobile and his behaviour was sufficiently odd for a man in a group of three to say something to the defendant. The defendant said he had nothing to do with the three and they should get on with their work. One said it was just funny to watch him. The defendant said, 'Just wait a minute, I'll fucking show you' and he produced, loaded and cocked the pistol. One tried to take cover and another was too frightened to move. The defendant discharged the pistol towards the ground. One of the three thought the pistol was aimed at one of his friends. The defendant went to a café apparently unconcerned and was arrested. The pistol was found to loaded with three blanks. He said the pistol just happened to be in his pocket and he used it to scare pigeons. Once he had an established relationship and a steady job. He started drinking which led to a drink/drive conviction and that led to the loss of his job and then the break up of his relationship. He was 36 with no convictions of 'particular relevance'. He had a serious altercation with his partner and when the police attended he threatened them with a pickaxe handle. He received 4 months. He was sentenced to 100 hours' CSO and had performed the 'greater part of it'. He refused to see a psychiatrist. Held. The gravity for this offence can vary enormously and in certain extreme circumstances a non-custodial might be appropriate. Less than **2 years** here was not appropriate. More than 2 would not necessarily be inappropriate. Taking into account it was a reference and the hours performed **1 year** instead.

A-G's Reference (No 36 of 2001) [2001] EWCA Crim 1928, [2002] 1 Cr App Rep (S) 241. The defendant pleaded guilty to possessing an imitation firearm with intent to cause fear of violence. He was a licensee and he and his friend were drinking heavily at another pub. An argument broke out with another group that had also been drinking heavily. The quarrel spilled out into the car park and his friend was knocked out. They defendant ran back to his pub which was in the same road and retrieved an 8mm replica self-loading pistol capable of firing blanks. He ran back with it and chased two from the other group waving his gun. One tried to get in a taxi and the defendant got in still brandishing the gun and demanded to know who had hit his friend. The name was revealed and the defendant threw the man out of the cab and he ended up sleeping on the ground. Four weeks later he was still off work on antidepressants. The defendant was arrested and the pistol was found under his bed. He claimed it was for his own protection. He was 40 and had three irrelevant dishonesty conviction when young. He had disposed of his share of the pub in which he had sunk his savings because of this case and had started a small grocers with his wife. They had both since become depressed. The pre-sentence report said he was industrious and law abiding. Held. An appropriate sentence would be **2 years**. Because of the sale of the pub and his character etc **18 months** would be justified. As it was a reference **9 months** not a £500 fine.

A-G's Reference No 75 of 2001 [2002] 2 Cr App Rep (S) 455. The defendant pleaded guilty to possession of an imitation firearm with intent to cause fear of violence at the first opportunity. The defendant a French lorry driver drove his lorry and trailer on the M25 at about 60 mph in the centre lane very close to a car. The two drivers both pulled into the fast lane and the defendant had to swerve back into the centre lane. The driver of the car made an offensive gesture with his finger at the defendant. The defendant responded by putting his arm out of the cab pointing a large pistol at the driver of the car for a few seconds. Other motorists were terrified and the police were contacted. An armed response was called and the defendant was questioned. A Desert Eagle pistol with an empty magazine was found, but no ammunition. It was designed to fire ball bearing but classified as an imitation firearm. In interview the defendant claimed the other driver had flashed his lights to allow him to go on. He said he carried the pistol to cause fear but in his own defence. He was 23 and only had a driving conviction. Held. The wielding of a firearm, by a driver of an HGV vehicle, travelling at considerable speed on a motorway and deliberately threatening a driver is a serious example of the use of a firearm albeit an imitation for the purposes of causing fear. The consequences of such activity are not difficult to imagine in terms of evasive driving by others immediately or indirectly threatened. For a foreign national for whom prison would be more difficult to bear we would expect **12–15 months**. Taking into account it was a reference and he had paid the fine of £250, **8 months** instead.

Firearms Act 1968, s 16A – Shotguns

68.17 *R v Hewitt* [1999] 1 Cr App Rep (S) 256. The defendant was convicted of possessing a firearm with the intent to cause fear, possession of a firearm when prohibited and possession of ammunition when prohibited. He visited his estranged wife's house and produced a sawn off shotgun which had been strapped to his leg and two cartridges. His wife asked him what the gun was for and he replied, 'Where's Sean?' No threats were uttered. She asked again and he ran away. The police searched his home and found six cartridges but no firearm. He was sentenced on the basis he did not intend his wife any harm but that he wanted her to believe that serious harm was intended to Sean his cousin. He was then 34 and had convictions but none since 1990. Held. The total should have been **3 years** not 4.

R v Corry [2000] 1 Cr App Rep (S) 47. The defendant pleaded guilty on the day his case was listed for trial to possession of a firearm with intent to cause fear of violence. The victim who knew the defendant heard someone outside his home and opened his front door. He saw the defendant about 2 feet from the door and being fearful he started to close the door. The victim was able to see the defendant produce a shotgun, which appeared shortened from behind his back. It was pointed at his head. He shut the door and heard someone say to the defendant, 'Why don't you do something about it?' The victim ran upstairs and the shotgun was discharged at the door. The pellets made a hole in the bottom of the door and hit the hall floor where the victim had been standing. The victim called the police. The defendant was arrested and denied the offence. He was then 23 and had five court appearances including two separate non dwelling house burglaries. There were no offences of violence. His basis of plea was that he had not fired the weapon and his intention was limited to threatening the victim with it. Held. This was gangsterism. The starting point is 6 years and he was entitled to only half of the usual discount. Therefore **5 years** not 7.

R v Wright [2000] 1 Cr App Rep (S) 109. The defendant pleaded guilty to shortening the barrels of a shotgun, possessing a shortened shotgun with intent to cause a person to fear violence and possession of 138 grams of amphetamine. Police executed a search warrant at the defendant's farm and found a van which contained six shotgun cartridges, the amphetamine worth at street value nearly £2,000, scales and a 12 bore shortened shotgun loaded with two live 12 bore cartridges. The stock of the gun had been broken off and the trigger guard was missing. The fore-end was held on by tape. The defendant claimed that his daughter had been attacked and he and his family had been threatened. He said intruders had put a gun to his throat and two weeks before he had been assaulted by a group of people who had broken his leg. He was treated at hospital where he gave a false name. He said he had stolen the firearm from a house and shortened it. He had used it in self-defence when he had discharged the gun over the heads of people who had arrived with lumps of wood and a hockey stick. He had not reported the attacks to the police. He was sentenced to 30 months for each of the firearm matters and 6 months for the drugs all concurrent. Held. It was important to remember the triggers were not protected, the condition of the gun was very poor, it was a classic weapon for serious crime, because of its aim and accuracy no one would use it for self-defence and it was loaded. The court needs to turn to only one authority, *R v Avis* [1998] 2 Cr App Rep (S) 178. People cannot take the law into their own hands. It cannot possibly be said that **30 months** was manifestly excessive.

R v Porter [2001] 1 Cr App Rep (S) 241. The defendant pleaded guilty to possessing a shotgun with intent to cause a person to fear violence and making threats to kill. A 21-month old girl was woken up in the evening by a car alarm on a housing estate. The car belonged to the defendant and the girl's father shouted out of his window for the alarm to be turned off. The woman next to the car said it wasn't her car and the father spoke to her again and she became abusive. About 10 minutes later the defendant knocked on the father's door and said he heard he wanted a word with him. The father who was carrying his daughter opened the door and explained it was about the car alarm. The defendant said he was talking to the wrong person and he was out of his league. He then pointed a sawn off shotgun at him and told him he wanted a word and he should leave the flat. He placed both his hands on the gun and the father heard two clicks. The gun was still aimed at the father and he was told he would be shot. There was a further verbal altercation and the father managed to close his door. The defendant was arrested and his father was later pursued by police in his car and the shotgun was thrown out of the car window. It hit the road and went off. A cartridge was in one barrel and there were 17 cartridges, which fitted the shotgun in a plastic bag. The defendant had a bad record, which included violence. The defendant said in a note for the judge that at the time the shotgun was unloaded. There was no Newton hearing and he was sentenced on the basis the gun was loaded. Held. **4 years** not 5 because of earlier decisions of the court and the defendant might have had a legitimate grievance about the sentencing comments.

Firearms Act 1968, s 17(1)

68.18 Making use of a firearm with intent to resist arrest.

Indictable only. Maximum sentence life imprisonment.

R v Avis [1998] 2 Cr App Rep (S) 178 – LCJ. Where there are breaches of s 17(1) of the Firearms Act 1968 the custodial term is likely to be of considerable length, and where the four questions suggested above (see ***Guidelines***) yield answers adverse to the offender, terms at or approaching the maximum may in a contested case be appropriate.

A-G's Reference (No 120 of 2001) (23 January 2002, unreported). [If there had been a trial 8 years' detention would have been appropriate. With the plea and other mitigation 5 years would be appropriate. As it was a reference 4 years.]

Firearms Act 1968, s 17(2)

68.19 Being arrested for a Sch 1 offence and being in possession of a firearm.

Indictable only. Maximum sentence life.

Firearms Act 1968, s 17(2) – Automatic life

68.20 *R v Buckland* [2000] 2 Cr App Rep (S) 217 – LCJ. Firearms Act 1968, s 17(1) and 17(2) are both 'serious offences' for the purposes of what is now the Powers of Criminal Courts (Sentencing) Act 2000, s 109, (automatic life).

Firearms Act 1968, s 17(2) – Cases

68.21 *R v Avis* [1998] 2 Cr App Rep (S) 178 – LCJ. Where there are breaches of s 17(2) of the Firearms Act 1968 the custodial term is likely to be of considerable length, and where the four questions suggested above (see Guidelines) yield answers adverse to the offender, terms at or approaching the maximum may in a contested case be appropriate

R v Tudor [1999] 1 Cr App Rep (S) 197. Tudor pleaded guilty to wounding and possession of a firearm whilst committing a Sch 1 offence. Three poachers armed with air rifles entered his land to shoot rabbits. Because of the problems he had had in the past with poachers and threats the defendant and his son were carrying guns. They saw the men and told them to give up their guns. The men appeared to comply with the request and then ran off. The defendant shouted at them to stop but they continued to run so he fired his gun aiming about 10 feet away from them when 30–40 feet away from them. One of the men was hit in the arm, nose and head. He fired again without incident. The plea was on the basis of recklessness. The defendant was 51 and of good character. The neighbourhood held him in high regard. Held. The wound to the nose was very close to the eyes. It must be made clear that anyone, even those who have a licence who in anger use a shotgun recklessly is almost invariably going to receive a custodial sentence. 18 months was too long so **3 months** substituted. (The court did not refer to *R v Avis* [1998].)

R v Thomas [2000] 2 Cr App Rep (S) 155. The defendant pleaded guilty to possessing a firearm when committing a Sch 1 offence and theft. The defendant went to a 'peep' show and asked for change. He left and returned and seized a cash bag containing £122 from the cashier. He was chased through the streets. A police officer caught him and an imitation handgun was found on him. It wasn't used but was of convincing appearance. He said he just liked carrying it. The defendant was 17 and had findings of guilt for failure to surrender to bail, criminal damage and possession of a bladed article. Held. The law on imitation firearms exists to prevent anyone minded to commit a criminal offence from carrying firearms or imitation firearm. If someone carries an imitation firearm when committing an offence does not produce it and has some entirely credible or innocent reason for its possession the court might be persuaded to unusual leniency. Otherwise it calls for a substantial custodial sentence. Taking into account the defendant's youth and his plea 15 months cannot be described as excessive. **15 months and 3 months consecutive** YOI was not wrong.

Firearms Act 1968, s 18(1)

68.22 Having a firearm or imitation firearm with intent to commit an indictable offence.

Indictable only. Maximum sentence life. Specified offence for automatic life.

R v Avis [1998] 2 Cr App Rep (S) 178 – LCJ. Where there are breaches of s 18(1) of the Firearms Act 1968 the custodial term is likely to be of considerable length, and where the four questions suggested above (see *Guidelines*) yield answers adverse to the offender, terms at or approaching the maximum may in a contested case be appropriate

R v Avis Re Marquez [1998] 2 Cr App Rep (S) 178 at 190 – LCJ. The defendant was convicted of having a firearm with intent to commit an affray, having an imitation firearm with intent to commit an affray and possession of a firearm. Police tried and failed to stop a car in which he was travelling with two other youths. There was a car chase. The defendant was seen to tumble from the passenger side and a police officer saw him throw an object from his jacket before running off. He was arrested and was returned to the point where he had emerged from the car. A self-loading automatic Colt pistol was recovered. A police car had followed the car until it collided with a wall. A search of the car revealed a black woollen hat with eye holes cut in it and an imitation gun. The Colt pistol was in full working order although no ammunition was found. The imitation firearm was a good copy of a Baretta self-loading pistol. The Crown were unable to say for what purpose the gun and the imitation gun were being carried but contended that they must have been intended an unlawful display of force that would inevitably cause considerable fear. The defendant was 19 and of good character. His girlfriend had given birth to a child and following her admission to hospital after a nervous breakdown; the defendant had had to shoulder a major part of the responsibility for care of the child. He was sentenced to **42 months** for having the firearm with intent and other concurrent sentences. Held. The aggravating features present in this case were that a real firearm was involved and that all the circumstances, including the adapted hat with the eye holes cut in it, suggest that whatever the precise objective was, it was something that involved a degree of preparation. Even allowing for the good character and age the sentence passed was not in any way manifestly excessive.

A-G's Reference (No 26 of 2001) [2001] EWCA Crim 919, [2002] 1 Cr App Rep (S) 3 – LCJ. The defendant was convicted of possession a firearm with intent to commit an indictable offence, two counts of threats to kill and an ABH. He pleaded guilty to possessing a firearm without a certificate, possessing a prohibited weapon and selling a prohibited weapon. The defendant married and early on the marriage deteriorated. After 'unhappy incidents' his wife obtained a non-molestation order. He went abroad but kept in touch. He returned without warning and at 3am he broke into the former family home where his wife, her sister and her mother were sleeping. He went into the sister's room and she woke up and began screaming. He grabbed hold of her and put a stun gun to her neck. Initially she thought it was an ordinary gun. Then he dragged her into his wife's bedroom. He had a leather holster, cable ties and handcuffs and said, 'I have come back to end it all and I'm taking you and your mother with me. I'm going to kill you and your mother.' He said he had no reason to live and asked to hold his baby and he treated her affectionately. The sister began to hyperventilate and a doctor was called. The ambulance arrived and he took the gun from the holster saying it was real. He removed and replaced the magazine so everyone knew it was loaded. At some stage he tried to handcuff the sister and the mother but he was easily dissuaded. The police arrived and he allowed the older three to go hospital leaving the baby with the defendant. An 18 hour siege followed and there was no harm to the baby. A large number of officers were involved. He threatened to kill himself. Eventually the defendant was distracted and he was seized. A self-loading pistol and stun gun designed to discharge electricity were recovered. The sister had bruising to the neck. The effect on the 3 victims was very substantial. He was 57, had no convictions and was depressed about the marriage. Held. The breach of the court order was very important indeed. The attack was premeditated and carefully planned. Women are very vulnerable to men who decide to behave in this way. 5 years would have been the very lowest sentence appropriate. As it was a reference **4 years** not 2½.

Firearms Act 1968, s 19

68.23   Having in a public place a loaded shotgun, a loaded air weapon or a firearm whether loaded or not.

Triable either way unless an airweapon when it is a summary only offence.

On indictment maximum 7 years. Summary maximum 6 months and/or £5,000.

R v Avis [1998] 2 Cr App Rep (S) 178 – LCJ. Where there are breaches of s 19 of the Firearms Act 1968 the custodial term is likely to be of considerable length, and where the four questions suggested above (see **Guidelines**) yield answers adverse to the offender, terms at or approaching the maximum may in a contested case be appropriate

R v Fatinikun [1999] 1 Cr App Rep (S) 411. The defendant pleaded to two counts of having a loaded firearm in a public place, possessing ammunition and possessing a firearm when prohibited at the Magistrates' Court. He was committed for sentence. The defendant tried to get into a nightclub and the doorman felt what he thought was a gun and refused him access unless he could be more fully searched. The police were called about an unconnected incident and approached the defendant who ran off. They chased and caught him. He was searched and the police found cannabis and two bullets. His car was searched and a derringer pistol with a sworn-off barrel loaded with two bullets of the same type as on the defendant was found. Also found was a revolver type pistol loaded with two bullets. The defendant was then almost 18 and had convictions for carrying a firearm with intent to commit an indictable offence and burglary. The risk of re-offending was assessed as high. The sentencing judge sentenced him on the basis the doorman had felt his telephone. The defendant was in breach of his licence for the burglary conviction and was ordered to serve an extra 4 months. Held. Because the maximum was 7 years the discount for the plea was inadequate. **4 years** substituted for 6 years with the 4 months remaining consecutive.

R v Morris [1999] 2 Cr App Rep (S) 146. The defendant pleaded guilty to possession of a firearm and ammunition in a public place, possession of a converted firearm and handling stolen goods. The defendant and the co-accused went to a wood to bury a shotgun and ammunition. The police intervened and the items were found. At the defendant's home was found a de-activated assault rifle, an AK Rifle under the floorboards. Both weapons had been stolen from a friend of his in a burglary a month before. After that the shotgun had been shortened and was for the co-defendant's use who said he had a buyer for it. He was of good character and had known the co-accused who received 10 years since school. Held. He was weak who was manoeuvred by a professional criminal to get himself out of his dilemma. Without those features 3½ years could not be criticised. With them **18 months** instead.

R v Holmes [1999] 2 Cr App Rep (S) 383. The defendant pleaded guilty to possession of a firearm whilst a prohibited person, possession of a shortened shotgun, and possession of a loaded shotgun in a public place. A householder went to look at a car and saw a sawn off shotgun in the passenger footwell through a partially open window. The police were called and found the shotgun, which was loaded with two cartridges. The police traced the defendant, aged 42 as the hirer of the vehicle and arrested him. He admitted the gun belonged to him and said he had bought it with the intention of committing suicide. He said he took some pills and ended up in hospital. In 1990 he was sentenced to 4 years for the possession of drugs with intent to supply. He had heart and artery problems, which he tended to exaggerate. The psychiatrist said the possession of the shotgun for a possible suicide fitted in with his presentation and his behaviour at the time. The prison report says he always uses his medical and psychological problems to get what he wants. Held. Leaving the firearm there was extreme irresponsibility and recklessness. We are quite unmoved by the submission that his intention to commit suicide means he is less culpable. There was nothing wrong with **2½ years** on each concurrent.

Firearms Act 1968, s 21(4)

68.24　Possession of a firearm when prohibited (when convicted of an offence and sentenced to certain terms of imprisonment)

Triable either way. Maximum sentence 5 years. Summary maximum 6 months and/or £5,000.

R v Avis [1998] 2 Cr App Rep (S) 178 – LCJ Where there are breaches of s 21 of the Firearms Act 1968 the custodial term is likely to be of considerable length, and where the four questions suggested above (see *Guidelines*) yield answers adverse to the offender, terms at or approaching the maximum may in a contested case be appropriate

R v Hill [1999] 2 Cr App Rep (S) 388. The defendant was convicted of possessing a firearm when prohibited, possession of a firearm, possession of a shotgun and possession of ammunition. Police officers conducted a search of the defendant's home and found a double-barrelled 12 bore shotgun, a .22 rifle without a bolt, 44 .22 cartridges and 32 .22 rifle cartridges. The defendant said the shotgun and rifle had been left at his home for safe keeping by a third party when he was in prison. The defendant had a long list of convictions all of them for dishonesty, except one in 1975 which was causing injury with an air pistol. Held. Although the maximum is the same for s 21(4) and possession of a firearm, *R v Avis* [1998] 2 Cr App Rep (S) 178 makes it clear it is more serious. There was nothing to suggest that he intended to use either of the firearms. **18 months** not 2½ years for the prohibited count with the other sentences remaining concurrent.

R v Holmes [1999] 2 Cr App Rep (S) 383. The defendant pleaded guilty to possession of a firearm whilst a prohibited person, possession of a shortened shotgun, and possession of a loaded shotgun in a public place. A householder went to look at a car and saw a sawn off shotgun in the passenger footwell through a partially open window. The police were called and found the shotgun, which was loaded with two cartridges. The police traced the defendant, aged 42 as the hirer of the vehicle and arrested him. He admitted the gun belonged to him and said he had bought it with the intention of committing suicide. He said he took some pills and ended up in hospital. In 1990 he was sentenced to 4 years for the possession of drugs with intent to supply. He had heart and artery problems, which he tended to exaggerate. The psychiatrist said the possession of the shotgun for a possible suicide fitted in with his presentation and his behaviour at the time. The prison report says he always uses his medical and psychological problems to get what he wants. Held. Leaving the firearm there was extreme irresponsibility and recklessness. We are quite unmoved by the submission that his intention to commit suicide means he is less culpable. There was nothing wrong with **2½ years** on each concurrent.

R v Brizzi [2000] 1 Cr App Rep (S) 126. The defendant was convicted of possessing a firearm when prohibited. Police officers observed the defendant riding a mountain bike next to another man who was walking beside him. As the officers approached he accelerated away and rode up a curb. He dropped the bike went up a small alleyway and put his hand in a privet hedge. He then walked towards the police who found a .25 Beretta semi automatic pistol at the spot in the hedge where he had put his hand. The gun was found to misfire repeatedly. After cleaning it was found to function normally. It was a prohibited weapon but was not linked to any recorded offending. The defendant was 30 and had a conviction for supplying drugs for which he received 5½ years. He had 22 court appearances but no firearm convictions. Held. As maximum sentence is 5 years, the gun could not be fired properly, there was no evidence it had been used, it was not loaded, the magazine had been removed and there was no ammunition **2½ years** 4.

R v Hair [2000] 1 Cr App Rep (S) 118. The defendant pleaded guilty to two counts of possession of a firearm and possession of ammunition. The defendant's house was searched and police found a Smith and Wesson revolver with a shortened barrel and 104 rounds of live ammunition. She said her stepson asked her to store them for him, when they lived in Sunderland and she took them with her when she moved to Blackburn. There was no lawful purpose for the revolver. The ammunition fitted the weapon. The defendant was 38 with no convictions. Held. The weapon was intended for using in crime. Just like drug offences persons of good character who do not appear to be criminally minded are used by others to lodge weapons. This offence is extremely serious. **2 years** was not manifestly excessive.

R v Corrish [2001] 1 Cr App Rep (S) 436. The defendant pleaded guilty to possessing a firearm when a prohibited person. A woman saw the defendant and another out of her window approach her door. One of them was carrying what appeared to be a shotgun. It was in fact a .22 air rifle. The barrel was wrapped in a bin bag. They knocked on her door and she asked what they wanted. They asked her to open the door and she was terrified. She didn't open the door and they shouted and swore at her. They then hammered on the door. She and her aunt who was with her ran and hid in a coal shed. The defendant was arrested. He was 30 and had a large number of convictions including several for violence and public order offences. In the last four years he had received custodial sentences for threats to kill, affray, possession of an offensive weapon, criminal damage, GBH, and robbery. There were no convictions for firearms. He was also sentenced to 254 days consecutive to the firearm sentence because he was in breach of his licence after his release from a robbery sentence. Held. Because the maximum is 5 years **18 months** was substituted for 2½ years. There was no reason to alter the consecutive sentence for the breach.

R v Allen [2001] EWCA Crim 302, [2001] 2 Cr App Rep (S) 359. The defendant made a plea not at the first opportunity to possession of a prohibited firearm. He had earlier pleaded guilty to possession of ammunition. Police visited the defendant's home to arrest him for an unrelated matter. They said they were going to search his home address and he told them he had a small .25 automatic pistol. He showed them where it was. It was a 6.35mm. Titan self-loading pistol with a missing pin. A cartridge, which fitted the pistol was also found. He said he had acquired it in America and had not fired it since 1974. At that time he was a serving member of the USAF in Germany. It was his property but he was then permitted to possess it. He brought the gun to England in 1979 and intended to move to Jamaica. When his partner died he changed his mind. He kept it as a souvenir He told the immigration service about it who told him to register it or remove the pin. He was 51 and had no relevant convictions. He had references and it was estimated there was a very low risk of him re-offending. Held. **6 months** not 12 months with the 3 months for the ammunition remaining concurrent.

R v M (11 October 2001, unreported). 2½ years not 3½.

Imitation firearms –Guideline remarks

68.25 *R v Avis* [1998] 1 Cr App Rep 420 – LCJ. Where imitation firearms are involved, the risk to life and limb is absent, but such weapons can be and often are used to frighten and intimidate victims in order to reinforce unlawful demands. Such imitation weapons are often very hard to distinguish from the real thing – for practical purposes, impossible in the circumstances in which they are used – and the victim is usually as much frightened and intimidated as if a genuine firearm had been used. Such victims are often isolated and vulnerable.

Imitation firearms –Automatic life

68.26 *R v Buckland* [2000] 2 Cr App Rep (S) 217 – LCJ. Possession of an imitation firearm under Firearms Act 1968, ss 16, 17 and 18 is a 'serious offence' for the purposes of the Crime (Sentences) Act 1997, s 2 (now the Powers of Criminal Courts (Sentencing) Act 2000, s 109) (automatic life).

Imitation firearms – Cases

68.27   *R v Thomas* [2000] 2 Cr App Rep (S) 155. The defendant pleaded guilty to possessing a firearm when committing a Sch 1 offence and theft. The defendant went to a 'peep' show and asked for change. He left and returned and seized a cash bag containing £122 from the cashier. He was chased through the streets. A police officer caught him and an imitation handgun was found on him. It wasn't used but was of convincing appearance. He said he just liked carrying it. The defendant was 17 and had findings of guilt for failure to surrender to bail, criminal damage and possession of a bladed article. Held. The law on imitation firearms exists to prevent anyone minded to commit a criminal offence from carrying firearms or imitation firearm. If someone carries an imitation firearm when committing an offence does not produce it and has some entirely credible or innocent reason for its possession the court might be persuaded to unusual leniency. Otherwise it calls for a substantial custodial sentence. Taking into account the defendant's youth and his plea 15 months cannot be described as excessive. **15 months and 3 months consecutive** YOI was not wrong.

Importation of firearms

68.28   Customs and Excise Management Act 1979, s 170(1) and (2)

Triable either way. On indictment maximum sentence 7 years. Summary maximum 6 months and/or £5,000 or three times the value of the goods which ever is greater.

R v Gal [2001] 1 Cr App Rep (S) 221. The defendant pleaded guilty to importing two handguns and ammunition. The defendant's car was searched at Dover docks. Customs found inside his luggage in the boot two semi-automatic pistols and 225 rounds of ammunition. About 200 of the rounds fitted one or other of the handguns. He was a foreign national and had no convictions. He was sentenced on the basis he was not a tourist but was here to deliver the guns and ammunition to someone involved in a criminal enterprise. His account was rejected. Held. The judge was right to say importing firearms was *every* bit as serious as importing drugs. It increases the arsenal of weapons in the country. **5 years** was severe but not manifestly excessive.

Knowledge that he possessed firearms, no

68.29   *R v Campbell* [2000] 1 Cr App Rep (S) 291. The defendant appears to have pleaded guilty to possession of a shortened shotgun, and a prohibited firearm. Police officers searched his flat after a disturbance in which he threatened someone and kicked a car. For the disturbance he received 6 months in all for possession of an offensive weapon and criminal damage. In a cupboard they found a sawn off shotgun in pieces in a black bin liner. In another cupboard they found an automatic machine pistol, which was a prohibited weapon and over 900 rounds of ammunition in a suitcase. Neither was loaded but both were in working order. He was sentenced on the basis he thought the items were stolen goods and he didn't look at them. (This was no defence because of *R v Steele* [1993] Crim L R 298) He had had them for 10 days and was to receive no payment. [The judgment does not refer to his character.] Held. 3½ years would have been appropriate if he had known but as he didn't **2 years** substituted.

Protecting your property

68.30   *R v Tudor* [1999] 1 Cr App Rep (S) 197. Tudor pleaded to wounding and possession of a firearm whilst committing a Sch 1 offence (s 17(2)). Three poachers armed with air rifles entered his land to shoot rabbits. Because of the problems he had had in the past with poachers and threats the defendant and his son were carrying guns. They saw the men and told them to give up their guns. The men appeared to comply with the request and then ran off. The defendant shouted at them to stop but they continued to run so he fired his gun aiming about 10 feet away from them when

30–40 feet away from them. One of the men was hit in the arm, nose and head. He fired again without incident. The plea was on the basis of recklessness. The defendant was 51 and of good character. The neighbourhood held him in high regard. Held. The wound to the nose was very close to the eyes. It must be made clear that anyone, even those who have a licence who in anger use a shotgun recklessly is almost invariably going to receive a custodial sentence. 18 months was too long so **3 months** substituted. (The court did not refer to *R v Avis* [1998].)

Robbery and

See **ROBBERY** *– Armed with firearm* and *Defendant aged 16–17 – Armed with firearm*

Self defence, firearms for

68.31   *R v Marney* [2001] EWCA Crim 2111, [2002] 1 Cr App Rep (S) 506. The defendant pleaded guilty to two offences of possessing a firearm with intent to endanger life, four counts of possessing ammunition, possessing a prohibited weapon and possessing a firearm. Police officers mounted a surveillance operation and watched him store items in three of his vehicles. He was arrested in one of his Landcruisers and they found a loaded Beretta pistol with a round in the breach. In his Skoda they found 45 rounds of ammunition which fitted the Beretta and a loaded .22 Ruger rifle with a round in the breach and nine rounds of ammunition in the magazine. There were 336 rounds of ammunition for the rifle and a silencer for it. In his other Landcruiser they found a silencer suitable for the Beretta. The defendant was 34 and a traveller. He had an extensive record for dishonesty and violence. In 1996 he sustained gunshot wounds to the elbow and buttocks. In 1997 he sustained gunshot wounds to the face, chest and buttocks. He nearly died. The reason for holding these guns was the attempt to murder him. Those incidents arose out of a feud, which had very serious criminal overtones. He broke from the normal code of those from his background and co-operated with the police and one of those he named was sent to prison. Others were arrested but proceedings against them were discontinued. The police advised him to leave the area but he refused. He installed video cameras, bullet proof windows, wore body armour and acquired the firearms. The basis of plea was that the firearms were intended to protect him and were not to be used against the public. Held. Firearm offences are always very serious more so when committed with men with substantial criminal records. The courts recognise the need for deterrent sentences and the acute public concern at the ever rising tide of possession of deadly weapons. The firearms were immediately available to use with deadly effect. This was a wholly exceptional case and the judge failed to reflect those exceptional circumstances. Nothing justified him in arming himself but **8 years** not 10.

Supplying firearms to criminals

68.32   *R v Avis Re Thomas* [1998] 2 Cr App Rep (S) 178 at 189 – LCJ. Thomas pleaded guilty to two counts of possessing a firearm with intent to endanger life, six counts of selling or transferring firearms unlawfully; and two counts of selling or transferring ammunition unlawfully. The pleas were entered at the beginning of his trial after the judge had made a ruling on the evidence. Thomas was a firearms dealer who sold three revolvers and ammunition for them to an undercover police officer for £1,160 in a car park. Thomas told the officer that he could supply firearms regularly and easily. At a further meeting at a railway station Thomas sold the officer two pump action shotguns which had been shortened. He also sold three pistols and ammunition for all five weapons. The total price was £1,220. Thomas was arrested. He was 66 and had no convictions. He had a very large number of testimonials. He had for many years been involved with charity work and was held in high esteem. He was sentenced to 9 years on each endanger count; 4 years for the selling firearms counts and 2 years for ammunition counts. They were all concurrent making a total of **9 years**. Held. The judge's starting point would have been 12 years. The use of firearms by armed robbers and drug dealers is prevalent and on the increase. A person who provides firearms in the certain knowledge that they are going to be used by criminals commits a grave offence. The judge took the mitigation fully into account and he could not sensibly have reduced the sentence further.

69   FISHING OFFENCES

69.1   Overfishing etc

Fisheries Act 1981, ss 5, 12, 17 and 30(2)

Many different orders made under the Act including some triable either way. Various penalties.

Overfishing

69.2   *R v Anglo-Spanish Fisheries Ltd* [2001] 1 Cr App Rep (S) 252. The defendant company pleaded guilty at the Magistrates' Court to an offence under the Fisheries Act 1981, s 30(2) and the relevant EEC regulations. There were three charges of failing to record accurately the quantity of fish, one of landing a quantity of undersized fish and one of failing to keep a drawing of a fish storage room. The Spanish company owned a British registered boat, which was boarded by officers from the Sea Fisheries Inspectorate. They weighed the fish on board and compared it to the entries in the logbook. There was significant under-recording of three fish. There was no recording of Megrim a fish much sought after in Spain in the book. 1,154 kgs of the fish was found on board. To conceal the Megrim an elaborate scheme of deception had been devised. The top layer of the boxes of fish was covered by Witch, a fish for which there was no quota and the boxes was labelled Witch. The Witch fish was over-recorded. Of the other two fish in the charges of failing to record, the fish was hidden under nets and empty boxes. The total value of the under declared fish was £12,400. In 1998 the company had four convictions before the same court as these charges for over-quota fishing. The company was fined £80,000 with £6,371 prosecution costs. The company was fined in total **£115,000** and ordered to **pay £3,869 prosecution costs**. It appealed the fine in this case for failing to record the amount of Megrim fish for which it was fined £80,000. Held. Policing and enforcement of the quota system is exceptionally difficult for ships nominally registered in the UK but who operate out of ports of other countries. There was a paramount need to protect the fishing stocks. The offences were extremely serious and were motivated by greed. Penalties must strip the offenders of the profits and act as a very real deterrent. The penalties imposed were no more than adequate. The judge would have been justified in imposing substantially larger fines on the other charges. We are surprised the judge did not suspend the fishing licence.

70   FOOD ETC, CONTAMINATING OF

70.1   Various offences including, Public Order Act 1986, s 38(1)

Contaminating goods with intent to cause the alarm, anxiety, injury or economic loss.

Triable either way. On indictment maximum 10 years. Summary maximum 6 months and/or £5,000.

Putting items in food in supermarket

70.2   *R v McNiff* [2001] EWCA Crim 79, [2001] 2 Cr App Rep (S) 275. The defendant pleaded guilty to two offences under s 38. He asked for seven offences to be taken into consideration. Customers of Tesco found pins, needles, and nails in food and the police were told. He pleaded in count one to a needle in some Turkish Delight and in a chicken and pins in other items. Police watched him push something into a packet of scones. A pin was found and this was count two. He was arrested and had a piece of paper with three pins attached. Videos of the store showed him handle items, which later were found to be contaminated. Some of the pins were not discovered till the customers were eating. Injuries were limited to a pierced tongue, pricks and soreness. The conduct was over a period of months. On three occasions the entire stock of pick and mix sweets were destroyed. The investigation involved considerable amount of police and store staff work. He was 56 with no convictions and references. Between 1995 and 1999 he became profoundly deaf. His motive was not clear but it wasn't financial. The cause might have been his difficulty in expressing his distress and difficulties. He cared for his mother in her 90s and expressed remorse. Held. The seriousness of the offence is shown by the 10 year maximum sentence. The potential for serious injury is obvious. Notwithstanding the personal mitigation the seriousness must be marked. **3 years** was not excessive.

See also BLACKMAIL – *Supermarkets and retail stores*

71   FOOD SAFETY

71.1   Food Safety Act 1990, ss 7, 8, 14, and 15

Rendering food injurious to health, selling food not complying with food safety requirements, selling food not of a nature or quality demanded, and falsely describing or presenting food etc.

Triable either way. On indictment maximum 2 years. Summary maximum 6 months and/or £20,000, (£5,000 for s 15).

If the defendant is licensed under Slaughterhouses Act 1974, ss 1 or 6 there is power to cancel the licence.

Crown Court statistics England and Wales[1] – Crown Court – Males 21+ – Adulteration of food

71.2

Year	Plea	Total Numbers sentenced	Type of sentence%					Average length of custody (months)
			Discharge	Fine	Community sentence	Suspended sentence	Custody	
2000	Guilty	1	0%	100%	0%	0%	0%	0
	Not guilty	1	0%	100%	0%	0%	0%	0

1   Excluding committals for sentence. Source: Crime and Criminal Justice Unit, Home Office Ref: IOS416-02.

Preparing food without a licence

71.3   *R v Altaf* [1999] 1 Cr App Rep (S) 429. The defendant elected trial for using premises for cutting of chickens without a licence, an offence under regulations made under the Food Safety Act 1990, ss 16 and 17. He then pleaded guilty at the Crown Court. He had been involved in the distribution and selling of chickens for some time.

He cut them up after they had been slaughtered elsewhere. His application for a licence was turned down. He was in the process of moving his business to premises where he had successfully obtained a licence. He continued using the other premises. Ministry inspectors visited the premises and found multiple breaches of the regulations. Flies were found in the work area, there was inadequate rodent protection, meat was stored in filthy cardboard boxes, meat contacted the cardboard and had spilt onto the floor, the reception, handling and dispatch of the exposed meat was unhygienic, chilling facilities were inadequate and there was dirty knives and other equipment. He had co-operated with the Ministry and was of good character. The offence was only punished by a fine at the Magistrates' Court. Held. It was quite impossible to say custody was wrong in principle for serious and multiple breaches of the regulations. Injury to health could have occurred. Because of the plea and other mitigation **3 months** not 6.

FOOTBALL OFFENCES

See also **AFFRAY** – *Football etc related*, and **OFFENCES AGAINST THE PERSON ACT 1861, s 20** – *Sporting*

FORGERY

Where the forgery is used to steal see **THEFT ETC**

See also **COUNTERFEITING CURRENCY, ELECTION OFFENCES** and **PASSPORT OFFENCES**

72   FRAUD

Various offences with differing penalties.

Crown Court statistics England and Wales[1] *– Crown Court – Males 21+ – Frauds other than by company director*

72.1

Year	Plea	Total Numbers sentenced	Type of sentence%					Average length of custody (months)
			Discharge	Fine	Community sentence	Suspended sentence	Custody	
2000	Guilty	1,137	5%	4%	29%	9%	53%	15.7
	Not guilty	278	2%	5%	22%	4%	68%	27.4

1   Excluding committals for sentence. Source: Crime and Criminal Justice Unit, Home Office Ref: IOS416-02.

Charity fraud

72.2   See *R v Day and O'Leary* [2002] EWCA Crim 503, [2002] 2 Cr App Rep (S) 421 and also **THEFT ETC** – *Charity offences*

Elderly victims

72.3   *R v Duggan* [1999] 2 Cr App Rep (S) 65. The defendant was convicted of six counts of procuring the execution of a valuable security. Theft and other counts were left on the file. He was an unqualified accountant who ran a perfectly legitimate business until he got heavily in debt over a speculative land development. He took £400,000 from the funds of a widow aged 85 by persuading her to invest in a particular account. By deception and forgery he kept his creditors at bay. He misled her to sign documents. When she asked for an explanation he lied. It carried on for about 3 years by which time £688,000 had been obtained. Held. The vulnerable victim was carefully targeted. It was a grave case of prolonged financial defalcation. There was no repayment. 4 years consecutive to 5 making **9 years** was entirely right.

See also *Wills*

Employers, frauds against the defendant's

72.4 *R v Oprey and Pinchbeck* [2001] EWCA Crim 1630, [2002] 1 Cr App Rep (S) 317. The defendants O and P pleaded to conspiracy to defraud and other dishonesty etc counts. A large hotel group employed them at one of their hotels in Harrogate. P was general manager between 1989 and 1997. O started working there before P arrived and was financial controller. P and O were paid at the end £47,000 and £21,000 in salaries. Between 1992 and 1997 P organised events at a nearby conference centre on his own behalf and for his own profit and used the hotel's facilities. Over the years the hotel paid for £140,000 of the costs. The company paid for the band at his wedding reception and £3,000 worth of hotel campaign was taken there and most was drunk. Other wine was taken for his own use. O was sentenced on the basis she failed to prevent the payment of the invoices by the hotel. She was also obstructive to the suppliers when their invoices were not paid. She didn't put the details on the computer so Head Office couldn't see them. There were unpaid invoices worth £130,000 found at her home. P was 52 and O was 61 with no convictions and had made no personal gain. She suffered from poor health. Both were made bankrupt. The defence said P was an extremely successful manager with a very respected reputation. O agreed to give evidence against P and then P made a late plea. The judge said the fraud was ingenious, sustained and profitable and P was dishonest, greedy and devious. Held. P had committed quite separate acts of dishonesty, which could have been made the subject of consecutive sentences. It was in P's favour the judge did not do that. P's plea although late was a very strong piece of mitigation so **3 years** not 4. Without O, P could not have continued the fraud and she had obstructed the investigation. Because of her health and mercy **9 months** not 12. It would be wrong to suspend her sentence.

Guilty plea, late

72.5 *R v Buffrey* (1992) 14 Cr App Rep (S) 511 – LCJ. The defendant made a late plea to conspiracy to trade fraudulently and other connected counts. The Court of Appeal considered to what extent – when someone pleads guilty at a late stage and so saves the holding of a very lengthy trial – ought the sentence which would otherwise have been imposed be discounted? Held. It must not be thought by those who are minded to commit fraud that after indulging in devious deception – which necessitates a long trial to unravel it – they can by pleading guilty at a late stage, earn such praise from the court for their public-spirited acceptance of what they have done that they can have a great reduction of their sentence. But some reduction must be made and because frauds of this kind are complex and do take a long time to unravel, they have become a burden on the criminal justice system. They are very costly, both in time and money. They cause stress to jurors, judges, those who conduct them and not least the witnesses and the defendants. These matters justify the jourt in applying a considerable discount where someone late in the day pleads guilty. There is no absolute rule as to what the discount should be. There will be considerable variance between one case and another. As a general guidance something of the order of one third would very often be appropriate.

R v Oprey and Pinchbeck [2001] EWCA Crim 1630, [2002] 1 Cr App Rep (S) 317. The defendants O and P pleaded guilty to conspiracy to defraud and other dishonesty etc counts. O agreed to give evidence against P and then P made a late plea. Held. P's plea although late was a very strong piece of mitigation.

Insurance frauds

72.6 *R v Nall-Cain* [1998] 2 Cr App Rep (S) 145. The defendant, Lord Brocket pleaded guilty to conspiracy to defraud. The defendant tried to develop Brocket Hall as a conference centre and heavily over-borrowed with a bank. The defendant overvalued for insurance four classic cars and some engines at £4.5m by using an inexperience valuer. They were worth about £3m. He induced two of his employers to join the scheme by threatening them with unemployment and loss of their housing if he went bankrupt. In May 1991 he arranged their removal to look like burglary. The three of them cut up the cars and engines and dumped or stored the pieces. He claimed on the insurance and the insurance company declined to pay. He sued them and in July or August 1994 discontinued the action, which in its concluding stages was being pursued by the bank. The insurer's irrecoverable costs were £200,000. The police interviewed his two employers and they admitted the offence. At his old style committal one of them gave evidence for the prosecution. The defendant was of good character and had done charitable work. The defendant said he was trying to protect his childrens' inheritance. The judge said it had been carefully planned and the suborning of his employees was one of the most serious aggravating factors. Later he pleaded guilty to obtaining by a deception and received 2 years. No complaint was made about that sentence. Held. **5 years** was not out of line.

R v Mehboob [2000] 2 Cr App Rep (S) 343. The defendant was convicted of four offences of conspiracy to defraud. Earlier he had pleaded guilty to three similar counts. There were 23 co-defendants. He was at the centre of seven separate conspiracies to defraud insurance companies by fabricating road traffic claims between September 1992 and April 1994. He was the central figure and the instigator of the fraud where the accidents were either fictitious or the accidents had not happened in the way the claimants stated. The fraud required a great deal of ingenuity and planning. He thought up the fictitious accidents, communicated with the insurance companies, filled in the documentation etc and corrupted others. The total claimed was £34,162. The total loss to the insurance companies was £13,358 and the total gain to the defendant was £6,147. He was of good character. Held. The mischief of this offence is that it is easy to commit and difficult to detect. **4 years** not 5.

Old cases. *R v Guppy* (1994) 16 Cr App Rep (S) 25.

Investments, bogus investment schemes

72.7 *R v Andre and Burton* [2001] EWCA Crim 1206, [2002] 1 Cr App Rep (S) 98. The defendant B pleaded guilty to conspiracy to defraud eight people of £185,659.54. The defendant A pleaded guilty to dishonestly retaining a wrongful credit of £93,770 and two counts of issuing a cheque (one for £500 and the other for £325) knowing or being reckless whether they would be honoured. The two defendants had lived together as a lesbian couple for many years. They went from Australia to America where they set up a company, which was later used in the frauds and came to the UK. They stayed in expensive hotels, employed a chauffeur and butler. They hired a Bentley and later a Rolls Royce and left the hotel bills unpaid. They created the impression they had access to enormous sums of money. B agreed to sponsor the Royal Windsor Horse Show for $250,000. Through that B promised someone involved that an investment of £75,000 could give a return of £6.8 m. He paid the money and the money went to America where the FBI retrieved it. A US businessman and a retired accountant were told that B was a very successful international bond dealer. They paid $300,000, which was spent within a month on staff, a horse and a car etc. B claimed to three other people she had just bought a German bank and profits were there for the taking. They were told an investment of $150,000 would offer a return of $13.5m in 10 months. They paid the money with a promised return of $1.5 m after 35 days. That money was spent within a month. B agreed to buy a farm from a Norfolk farmer. At the same time she persuaded the farmer to invest $300,000 which would raise $1.5m in 35 days. The cheque was payable to A. A kept half of it which was the wrongful credit offence she pleaded to. Two Swiss men were told a similar story and lost $300,000. £50,000 of that went into A's account. They left the country and went to New Zealand from where they were extradited. The total losses on B's defraud count were £557,000. A's 2 cheque offences related to her sponsoring the Arab Horse Show and the cheques were to the winners. She appreciated the cheques were unlikely to clear. A was 51 and had two unrelated convictions in Australia. B was 58 and had a substantial record for dishonesty in Australia and New Zealand between 1961 and 1999. While in New Zealand awaiting extradition she served 6 months for false pretences. Held. The judge was entitled to reduce the credit for the guilty plea because the pleas were late. A had benefited from all the high living in the defraud count and lent herself to the enterprise. Because A's was effectively of good character and had a lesser role the 8 months consecutive for the two cheque offences would run concurrently so 3 years in all. B's fraud was serious, sophisticated and large scale. It was on individual investors. **5 years** was entirely appropriate.

When by arson see ARSON – *Insurance money, to obtain* and ARSON – Arson – **Reckless whether life would be endangered** – *Insurance money, to obtain*

Wills

72.8 *R v Spillman and Spillman* [2001] 1 Cr App Rep (S) 496. The defendant A made a late guilty plea to conspiracy to defraud, two thefts of cheques from the testator and forgery of a will. The defendant D was convicted of the same conspiracy. They were husband and wife involved in a sophisticated scheme to swindle an elderly lady's beneficiaries out of £1.8m by creating and forging a will, which made them beneficiaries. A fake letter was sent to the elderly lady's long standing solicitor withdrawing her instructions from the firm. A's mother posed as the testator and made a will with a firm of solicitors the testator had never used. A and D witnessed it. After the testator died A and D continued to represent the fake will was valid. A's mother gave evidence for the prosecution and explained how D had recruited her and drove her to the victim's house where all the photographs of the testator had been removed. She then posed as the testator. Shortly after the testator died a vigilant solicitor intervened. The plot was very nearly successful. A had a conviction (not specified.) A's report detailed the abuse she had suffered from her mother, her stepfather and her husband. She suffered from battered woman syndrome. She was said to passively accept events. The judge said he rejected that and the views of the pre-sentence report after listening to the trial. Held. This was an extremely serious fraud involving an enormous sum and the grossest breach of trust. The judge's approach was entirely proper. **5 years 3 months** for A was severe and justified. D's sentence of **7 years** was not manifestly excessive.

For fraudulent trading and generally see COMPANY FRAUDS AND FINANCIAL SERVICES OFFENCES and THEFT ETC

FRAUDULENT TRADING

See COMPANY FRAUDS AND FINANCIAL OFFENCES – *Fraudulent trading*

GAY OFFENCES

See **BUGGERY**; **GROSS INDECENCY**; **HOMOSEXUAL OFFENCES** and **RAPE** (although at present there are no recent reported cases for anal rape on men.)

GBH – GRIEVOUS BODILY HARM

See **OFFENCES AGAINST THE PERSON ACT 1861, s 18** and **OFFENCES AGAINST THE PERSON ACT 1861, s 20**

73 GOING EQUIPPED TO STEAL

73.1   Theft Act 1968, s 25

Triable either way.

On indictment maximum 3 years. Summary maximum 6 months and/or £5,000.

If the offence concerns the theft or attempted theft of a motor vehicle the offence carries discretionary disqualification.

Crown Court statistics England and Wales[1] – Crown Court – Males 21+ – Going equipped for stealing

73.2

| Year | Plea | Total Numbers sentenced | Type of sentence% | | | | | Average length of custody (months) |
			Discharge	Fine	Community sentence	Suspended sentence	Custody	
2000	Guilty	85	6%	2%	40%	0%	52%	8.4
	Not guilty	38	0%	8%	24%	3%	66%	8.6

1   Excluding committals for sentence. Source: Crime and Criminal Justice Unit, Home Office Ref: IOS416-02.

Magistrates' Court Sentencing Guidelines September 2000

73.3   Entry point. Is it serious enough for a community penalty? Examples of aggravating factors for the offence are premeditated, group action, sophisticated, specialised equipment, number of items and people put in fear. Examples of mitigation are age, health (physical or mental), co-operation with police, and genuine remorse. Give reasons for not awarding compensation.

For details about the guidelines see **MAGISTRATES' COURT SENTENCING GUIDELINES** at page 331.

Drug abstinence order

73.4   Powers of Criminal Courts (Sentencing) Act 2000, s 58A(1). Where a person is 18 or over the court may make an order requiring the offender to abstain from misusing specified Class A drugs and provide, when instructed to do so a sample to ascertain whether he has any specified Class A drugs in his body. (3) The court must be of the opinion the offender is dependant or has a propensity to misuse specified Class A drugs and the offence is a trigger offence or the misuse of any specified Class A drug caused or contributed to the offence in question. (7) An order shall be for not less than 6 months and not more than 3 years. (9) No order shall be made unless the court has been notified that arrangements for implementing the order are available. [Criminal Justice and Court Services Act 2000, Sch 6 specifies going equipped to steal as a trigger offence.]

See also THEFT ETC – *Telephone boxes*

GRIEVOUS BODILY HARM

See OFFENCES AGAINST THE PERSON ACT **1861, s 18** and OFFENCES AGAINST THE PERSON ACT **1861, s 20**

74 GROSS INDECENCY

74.1 Sexual Offences Act 1956, s 13

Committing, being a party to the commission or procuring the commission of gross indecency.

Triable either way. Maximum sentence by man 21+ and boy under 16, 5 years. Otherwise 2 years. Summary maximum 6 months and/or £5,000.

Crown Court statistics England and Wales[1] *– Crown Court – Males 21+ – Indecency between Males*

74.2

Year	Plea	Total Numbers sentenced	Type of sentence%					Average length of custody (months)
			Discharge	Fine	Community sentence	Suspended sentence	Custody	
2000	Guilty	4	0%	0%	0%	0%	100%	21
	Not guilty	2	50%	0%	0%	0%	50%	24

1 Excluding committals for sentence. Source: Crime and Criminal Justice Unit, Home Office Ref: IOS416-02.

Boy aged 13–15 years

74.3 *R v Holland* [1998] 2 Cr App Rep (S) 265. The defendant pleaded guilty at the Magistrates' Court to attempting to procure an act of gross indecency with a boy. The defendant approached a 15-year-old boy as he waited for an Underground train. He asked him some indecent questions all of which were answered in the negative. He then asked, 'If I gave you 15 or 16 bob would you get an erection?' and 'If I gave you a video would you get an erection for me?' The boy got angry and jumped on a train leaving the defendant on the platform. When interviewed he said he got urges when he ran out of tablets. He was born in 1940 and between 1956 and 1994 he had 14 court appearances, all but one for indecency including four attempts to procure acts of gross indecency. The pre-sentence report said he claimed to be powerless to control his paedophilic behaviour and he lacked insight into the seriousness of his offending. Another report said he was on medication and had he taken some it would be very unlikely he would be in his current predicament. Held. As the sentencer had not passed a longer than commensurate sentence it had to be commensurate so **12 months** not 3 years.

75 GUILTY PLEA, DISCOUNT FOR

75.1 Powers of the Criminal Courts (Sentencing) Act 2000, s 152(1). In determining what sentence to pass on an offender who has pleaded guilty, a court shall take into account (a) the stage the offender indicated his plea and (b) the circumstances in which the indication was given. [Section summarised.]

Experience shows the full discount is a third so 3 years starting point becomes 2 years on a plea. As the sentence lengthens most judges reduce the fraction, so for 15 years starting point the defendant would receive 11–12[1] and not 10 years. There remains a significant discretion with some judges generous and others not so generous. The same principles apply to fines, community service hours etc. However, a guilty plea doesn't prevent a life sentence being passed.

1 For that calculation see *A-G's Reference (Nos 19, 20 and 21 of 2001)* [2001] EWCA Crim 1432, [2002] 1 Cr App Rep (S) 136.

Co-defendant, giving evidence for

75.2 *R v Lawless* [1998] 2 Cr App Rep (S) 176. The defendant pleaded guilty to affray and his co-defendant was convicted of the same offence. The defendant gave evidence for him. The judge sentenced them both to 21 months saying the defendant had thrown his credit away because the jury must have found his evidence to be lies and it was wholly discredited. Held. It is important that a co-defendant should not be inhibited from giving evidence. He was entitled to a discount so **15 months** instead.

R v Hickman [2000] 2 Cr App Rep (S) 171. The defendant made a late plea of guilty to robbery and his co-defendant pleaded not guilty and was convicted of the same offence. The defendant gave evidence for him. The Judge took the lying into account and sentenced them both to the same sentence. Held. The principle in *R v Lawless* [1998] 2 Cr App Rep (S) 176 has to be applied. **3½ years** not 4.

Conspiracy conviction which relates to many different offences

75.3 *R v Smith* [2001] EWCA Crim 1812, [2002] 1 Cr App Rep (S) 386. The defendants D and H pleaded guilty shortly after a jury was empanelled to conspiracy which was over a 4 year period and involved police corruption. C and S pleaded guilty to kidnapping. D was a sergeant in the CID and H was a drug dealer who was sentenced to 7 years for drug trafficking offences. £130,000 was found at his home. H supplied D with money and information about other drug criminals and D provided H with police and customs operations against other drug dealers. H made tape recordings of the conversations which were found by the police. The corruption started at the beginning of the police officer's career. H suggested planting drugs on other criminals. D adopted H as an informant but did not tell any superior. D also dealt with his father's hotel business and it was in 1995 in a poor state. H put £10,000 into the business. H then took over the running of the hotel and used it for the storing and distribution of drugs. D then lied about his involvement with H. Five offenders were able to escape when information about the raids on their addresses were leaked to H. The police started investigating and D ignored instructions. He was told to stop seeing H and he met him the next day. They were both arrested and lied when interviewed. The prosecution could not be precise about the damage caused to the police and the profits made. However, the integrity of the police force and its anti-drugs activities were very seriously compromised. H and his associates were major players in the drugs world. D received 7 years, the maximum and H received 5 years consecutive to the 8 years he had received in his drug case. The judge refused to give D a discount for the plea because the appropriate sentence was 10 years before a small discount for the plea to 8½ years. He said the situation was similar to a specimen charge where one count does not reflect the whole course of conduct. Held. Some discount for the plea should have been made so **6 years** substituted. H's sentence reduced from 5 to **4½ years**.

Detention and training orders where the adult maximum is less than 14 years

75.4   *R v Kelly* [2001] EWCA Crim 1751, [2002] 1 Cr App Rep (S) 40. The defendant pleaded guilty to causing GBH. He was aged 15. Held. As the maximum for the offence was 2 years' detention and training it was wrong to give him the maximum. **18 months** substituted.

R v Marley [2001] EWCA Crim 2779, [2002] 2 Cr App Rep (S) 73. The defendant pleaded guilty to violent disorder. He was aged 16 when the offence was committed. As the maximum for the offence was less than 14 years 2 years was the absolute maximum in this case. Held. Had not 2 years been the maximum this appeal would not have succeeded. As he pleaded guilty he was entitled to a discount so **18 months** not 2 years.

R v March (15 February 2002, unreported). The defendant had to be given a discount when he had pleaded and had spent 8 months on remand. Six months reduction given.

Early plea

75.5   *R v McDonald* [2001] EWCA Crim 2496, [2002] 1 Cr App Rep (S) 585. The defendant pleaded guilty to robbery at the first opportunity. His co-defendant pleaded 6 weeks later. They each received 4 years. Held. There was no ground for distinguishing between their culpability or criminality. It is important those who plead at the earliest opportunity should know that they will receive, and be seen to receive, the greatest possible credit for the early stage at which the plea is tendered. Although the offending might well have deserved a term of 4 years the sentence will be reduced to **3½ years** to mark positively the earliest stage at which the he gave his plea.

Early plea – Magistrates' Court, plea before venue

75.6   *R v Rafferty* [1998] 2 Cr App Rep (S) 449 – LCJ. The defendant pleaded guilty before venue. Held. It is no longer appropriate for counsel to say the defendant pleaded at the first opportunity if the plea was not entered before venue. If the plea is first entered at the Crown Court and there is no satisfactory explanation was it was not tendered earlier will receive less discount than if they pleaded at the Magistrates' Court and less discount than they received hitherto. (The part about receiving less discount than hitherto is not being followed by most Crown Courts judges because they are aware of the terrible pressures on their lists. Therefore they wish to encourage as many defendants as possible to plead guilty by giving those that plead when the indictment is first put the full discount.) In the usual case where a defendant who enters a plea before venue should be entitled to a greater discount than a person who delays making that plea until the Crown Court.

R v Barber [2001] EWCA Crim 2267, [2002] 1 Cr App Rep (S) 548. In many cases, the appropriate discount for a prompt plea of guilty, at the Crown Court to an offence triable only on indictment is of the order of one third. In relation to either way offences, where such a plea is entered before venue, a greater than 1/3 will often be appropriate.

Fraud

75.7   *R v Buffrey* (1994) 14 Cr App Rep (S) 511 – LCJ. The defendant made a late guilty plea to conspiracy to trade fraudulently and other connected counts. The Court of Appeal considered to what extent – when someone pleads guilty at a late stage and so saves the holding of a very lengthy trial – ought the sentence which would otherwise have been imposed be discounted. Held. It must not be thought by those who are minded to commit fraud that after indulging in devious deception – which necessitates a long trial to unravel it – they can by pleading guilty at a late stage, earn such praise from the court for their public-spirited acceptance of what they have done that they can have a great reduction of their sentence. But some reduction must be made and because frauds of this kind are complex and do take a long time to unravel, they have become a burden on the criminal justice system. They are very costly, both in time and money. They cause stress to jurors, judges, those who conduct them and not least the witnesses and the defendants. These matters justify the court in applying a considerable discount where someone late in the day pleads guilty. There is no absolute rule as to what the discount should be. There will be considerable variance between one case and another. As a general guidance something of the order of one third would very often be appropriate.

R v Oprey and Pinchbeck [2001] EWCA Crim 1630, [2002] 1 Cr App Rep (S) 317. In complex frauds where defendants plead guilty even late in the day and a long trial is avoided it is a very strong piece of mitigation.

Is a discount appropriate?

75.8 *R v Scarley* [2001] 1 Cr App Rep (S) 86. The defendant pleaded guilty to dangerous driving. He drove at police cars and an officer was injured. He received 2 years (the maximum) consecutive to the sentence he was serving. At the time he was on bail and a disqualified driver. He was 36 with 157 previous convictions. The judge said it was the worst record he had ever seen and he was giving no credit for the plea, as the defendant had no option but to plead guilty. There was no penalty for the other offence Held. There are exceptions to the rule that a guilty sentence results in a lesser sentence. First, being caught red-handed and having no practical defence to the charge *R v Rogers* (1991) 13 Cr App Rep (S) 80; *R v Landy* (1995) 16 Cr App Rep (S) 908; *R v Reay* [1993] RTR 189. Secondly where there is a last minute tactical plea where there is a need to protect the public or where the charge was representative of a large number of offences, *R v Costen* (1989) 11 Cr App Rep S 182. The first example applies here. (The problem in these cases was the maximum sentence was clearly inadequate. It would be much better to have proper maximum sentences and a right to discount as having no defence or the case being overwhelming does not always stop the defendant pleading not guilty.)

R v Williams (13 July 2001, unreported). The defendant pleaded to dangerous driving and driving whilst disqualified. The judge considered 5 years was the appropriate penalty. He passed 2 years (the maximum) for the driving and 6 months consecutive (the maximum) for the disqualified driving. The defence appealed the disqualified driving sentence on the basis he was given the maximum because the Judge thought the driving penalty was inadequate. Further the defendant had pleaded and the disqualified offence was not of the most serious. Held. We agree with the Judge's description that one cannot conceive a more serious case of driving than this. The defendant was entitled to a reduction so **3 months** not 6.

R v Hussain [2002] EWCA Crim 65, [2002] 2 Cr App Rep (S) 255. The defendant pleaded guilty to robbery at the very last possible moment before the trial. The defence declined a Newton hearing. The Judge said he gave no discount for the plea because the plea was late and the case was overwhelming. The defence argued that the Powers of the Criminal Courts (Sentencing) Act 2000, s 152 made credit for the plea mandatory. Held. That submission involves a misreading of the section. The court was obliged to take the stage he indicated his plea into account and not obliged to reduce the sentence. It remains in the discretion of the court whether to reduce it and if so by how much. In the present case the plea saved court time and particularly spared the victim from the ordeal of giving highly charged and distressing evidence. The judge was not justified in describing the case as so overwhelming as to make what would otherwise be an appropriate discount entirely inapplicable. It seems somewhat hard on the defendant for him to forego a Newton hearing and then receive no discount whatsoever. So **5 years** not 6.

Late plea

75.9   *R v Delaney* [1998] 1 Cr App Rep (S) 325. The defendant made a late plea to robbery and making use of a firearm with intent. The judge gave him **11½ years** saying there was a 2½ years' discount for the late plea. Held. The discount for the late plea was within the judge's discretion.

R v Okee and West [1998] 2 Cr App Rep (S) 199. The defendants pleaded guilty at the last minute. The judge passed a **4½ years** sentence saying with no plea it would have been 5 years. The defence said there was insufficient credit given. Held. Those who run their not guilty pleas to the wire should know that the discount will be substantially and visibly reduced. The 10% discount here was ample.

Magistrates' Court

75.10   Article. Sentence discounts in Magistrates' Courts [2000] Crim LR 436.

Minimum sentences for third Class A drug trafficking offence or third domestic burglary

75.11   Powers of the Criminal Courts (Sentencing) Act 2000, ss 110 and 111.

Powers of the Criminal Courts (Sentencing) Act 2000, s 152(3). Where a sentence is to be imposed under the Powers of the Criminal Courts (Sentencing) Act 2000, ss 110 and 111 nothing in that section shall prevent the court from imposing a sentence of 80% or more of the minimum period. [Section summarised. The section means if the defendant pleads guilty the court can impose a sentence, which is 80% or more of the minimum term.]

Newton hearing, defendant takes part in

75.12   *R v Hassall* [2000] 1 Cr App Rep (S) 67. The judge was entitled to reduce the discount that would otherwise be given where there was a Newton hearing and his account was disbelieved. The judge was wrong to give the defendant no credit for his plea. The sentence was reduced.

Plea indicated shortly after PDH

75.13   *R v Djahit* [1999] 2 Cr App Rep (S) 142. The defendant pleaded not guilty at his PDH hearing. His counsel then asked for an adjournment so a conference could take place. A few days later the conference took place and a letter was sent to the court saying he would plead guilty. At the sentencing hearing the judge said he would only give partial credit for the guilty plea, as it hadn't been entered at the earliest opportunity. Held. The fact he did not plead earlier appears to have been the responsibility of the solicitors who had failed to organise a conference before the PDH. The defendant was entitled to a full discount.

State that the sentence has been discounted, judge must

75.14   Powers of the Criminal Courts (Sentencing) Act 2000, s 152(2). If the court imposes a lesser sentence because of the guilty plea it shall state in open court it has done so. [Section summarised.]

See also *R v Bishop* [2000] 1 Cr App Rep (S) 432.

76   HANDLING

76.1   Theft Act 1968, s 22

Triable either way.

On indictment maximum 14 years. Summary maximum 6 months and/or £5,000.

Crown Court statistics England and Wales[1] – Crown Court – Males 21+ – Handling stolen goods

76.2

Year	Plea	Total Numbers sentenced	Type of sentence%					Average length of custody (months)
			Discharge	Fine	Community sentence	Suspended sentence	Custody	
2000	Guilty	1,331	6%	5%	37%	3%	50%	12.5
	Not guilty	272	2%	8%	35%	3%	52%	15.8

1   Excluding committals for sentence. Source: Crime and Criminal Justice Unit, Home Office Ref: IOS416-02.

Guideline case

76.3   *R v Webbe* [2001] EWCA Crim 1217, [2002] 1 Cr App Rep (S) 82 – LCJ. The difficulty of issuing guidelines in relation to handling arises from the enormous variety of possible sentences (which may be suitable) according to the circumstances. The offence can attract a penalty from a conditional discharge or modest fine at one end, up to 14 years (imprisonment) at the other. The relative seriousness of a case depends upon the interplay of different factors. One important issue is whether the handler has had advance knowledge of the original offence; or has directly or indirectly made known his willingness to receive the proceeds of the original offence, as compared with a handler who has had no connection with the original offence but who has dishonestly accepted the stolen goods at an undervalued (price). Where the handler has had knowledge of the original offence, the seriousness of the handling is inevitably linked to the seriousness of that original offence. The link to the original offence explains the need for the high maximum penalty of 14 years' imprisonment, which might otherwise look anomalous. Sentences approaching the maximum should clearly be reserved for the most serious and unusual cases where the handler had previous knowledge of a very serious offence such as an armed robbery, which itself carries life imprisonment as its maximum.

The replacement value of the goods involved is often a helpful indication of the seriousness of the offence. Monetary value in itself should not be regarded as the determining factor. There is an obvious difference, for example, between the gravity of receiving in a public house £100 worth of stolen television sets, and the gravity of receiving £100 in cash from the proceeds of a robbery which has taken place in the receiver's presence. Furthermore, accurate values in relation to the property received may very often be extremely difficult to ascertain. Other factors significantly affecting the relative seriousness of the handling offence, are the level of sophistication of the handler, the ultimate designation of the goods, the criminal origin of the goods, the impact on the victim, the level of profit made or expected by the handler, and, especially in cases of actual or intended disposal of goods, the precise role played by the handler. Handling cases at or towards the lower end of the scale are characterised by the handler having no connection with the original offence, an absence of sophistication on the part of the handler, the less serious nature of the original offence, the relatively low value of the goods and the absence of any significant profit.

The following nine factors aggravate the offence: (1) The closeness of the handler to the primary offence. [We add that closeness may be geographical, arising from presence at or near the primary offence when it was committed, or temporal, where the handler instigated or encouraged the primary offence beforehand, or, soon after, provided a safe haven or route for disposal]; (2) Particular seriousness in the primary offence; (3) High value of the goods to the loser, including sentimental value; (4) The fact that the goods were the proceeds of a domestic burglary; (5) Sophistication in relation to the handling; (6) A high level of profit made or expected by the handler; (7) The provision by the handler of a regular outlet for stolen goods; (8) Threats of violence or abuse of power by the handler over others, for example, an adult commissioning criminal activity by children, or a drug dealer pressurising addicts to steal in order to pay for their habit; (9) As is statutorily provided by s 151(2) of the Powers of Criminal Courts (Sentencing) Act 2000, the commission of an offence while on bail.

The mitigating factors are low monetary value of the goods, the offence was a one-off offence, committed by an otherwise honest defendant, there is little or no benefit to the defendant, and voluntary restitution to the victim.

Magistrates' Court Sentencing Guidelines September 2000

76.4   Entry point. Is it serious enough for a community penalty? Consider the impact on the victim. Examples of aggravating factors for the offence are adults involving children, high value and organiser or distributor. Examples of mitigating factors for the offence are for personal use, impulsive action, low value, no financial gain, not part of a sophisticated operation and single item. Examples of mitigation are age, health (physical or mental), co-operation with police, voluntary compensation and genuine remorse. Give reasons for not awarding compensation.

For details about the guidelines see **MAGISTRATES' COURT SENTENCING GUIDELINES** at page 331.

Antiques, valuable jewellery etc

76.5   *R v Dixon* [2001] EWCA Crim 2507, [2002] 2 Cr App Rep (S) 18. The defendant pleaded guilty to assisting in the retention etc. of stolen goods. While the victims were away attending a funeral, their house was burgled and antiques worth £255,000 were stolen including two clocks by Thomas Tompion worth together £230,000. Police searched the defendant's home and he showed them the stolen antiques. He said he was looking after them for someone else who he declined to name. He was 40 and was treated as of good character. His wife had a depressive illness and his daughter special needs. He was sentenced on the basis he was not a professional handler and had been prevailed upon against his better judgment to store the items. Nor could he be expected to know the clocks were so valuable. **18 months** not 3 years.

R v Chalcraft and Campbell [2001] EWCA Crim 2931, [2002] 2 Cr App Rep (S) 172. The defendant J pleaded guilty to four counts of attempting to handle stolen property. The defendant N pleaded to three such counts. They both had changed their plea. J had two jewellery shops. Following information jewellery was being received there an undercover officer started to sell them jewellery. J bought small items from him and then introduced him to N and he bought some items from him in pubs. As the contact developed the officer made it clear he was a burglar and the items were stolen. In fact the items were goods recovered which the owners had not claimed. N said the officer should take a gold watch and he would pay £1,000 for a 1930s Rolex. Next day he sold jewellery to J for £90. Six days later he told J a box saying he had stolen it from a house in Brighton. J said he would make enquires. Later he sold jewellery to J for £380. J warned him to be careful. There were further sales and J paid £40 and £50 and

N paid £30. They were told where items were stolen from. Again J told him to be careful. The officer then used four antique candlesticks, which had been provided by another dealer. They were worth £10,500 retail. On J's direction N was shown a single candlestick and he showed it to J. They agreed to pay £320 for them. Both were arrested and denied they knew the goods were stolen. J returned some items, which he had on display. J was 40 and of good character and spoken of highly. N was 39 and had a number of offences including in 1997 convictions for burglary, theft and 3 deceptions for which he received a deferred sentence followed by CSO. N's role was less than J. Held. Monetary value should not be the determining factor. The case was aggravated by the closeness to the primary offence, the items were thought to be from domestic burglary, the high level of profit and they were both a regular outlet. The fact they had been targeted by police and there were no victims was mitigation. **10 months** for J not 15. **8 months** for N not 12.

R v Gwyer [2002] EWCA Crim 102, [2002] 2 Cr App Rep (S) 246 – LCJ. The defendant was convicted of nine counts of handling stolen property. For almost 4 months he received property stolen from residential burglaries. It was mostly antiques - porcelain, silver, clocks, furniture and the like. He and his associate sold the items through auctioneers where £16,160 was obtained. The Judge considered the replacement value was substantially more. The property was handled shortly after the burglaries. The judge considered they were professional fences for antiques. He was 43 and a roofer. There were convictions for dishonesty, poaching, firearm offences but none for handling. He hadn't served a custodial sentence. There was a delay of 2½ years and he was under considerable stress. Held. Because of the delay and the stress **4 years** not 5.

Art, works of

76.6 *R v Davies* [1998] 2 Cr App Rep (S) 193. The defendant was convicted of three counts of handling. 'The Cook Report' investigated stolen art. A reporter met B the co-accused who introduced him to G and third accused. G showed the reporter some miniature pictures and other objects. Later at G's home B showed the reporter two more stolen pictures and sold them for £2,750. G said the defendant was in possession of the miniature painting mentioned earlier. The price was £9,000 each. It was agreed they would be seen in a hotel. A meeting was arranged. At the hotel the defendant produced the two miniatures from his pocket. G was there. Roger Cook and the police arrive. Investigations revealed that the miniatures were stolen in 1978 and the two pictures stolen in 1991. The defendant was aged 63 with no convictions. He was deaf and had a number of health problems. B pleaded to one count of handling a William and Mary inlaid chest and received **2 years**. The other was acquitted of two counts. Because of his age, character and health **3 years** not 4. [Unfortunately the report does not refer to the roles played or the value of the pictures.]

R v Love [1999] 1 Cr App Rep (S) 75. The defendants L and S were convicted of two counts of handling. Defendant T changed his plea at the beginning of the trial. They were all involved in the disposal of art. T was the principle, acting as broker to the thieves. He recruited L and S to assist. S made his flat available. L was responsible for transport. In 1995 a painting worth £10,000 was stolen from a country house. Also in 1995 a 42-item pottery collection was stolen from a museum valued at £100,000. It was regarded as part of the National Heritage. The following month T met an undercover police officer posing as an agent for a purchaser. T asked for £60,000 for the pottery. Next T and S met the officer and £52,000 was agreed for 37 items of pottery. T was followed to S's flat. £10,000 was handed over for the first tranche of property. S took the money to L who was in a car outside. The car dove off to collect the pottery and returned with the first tranche and the painting. S and L were arrested at the scene and T surrendered later. L was 50 with dishonesty convictions up to 1982. In 1981 he received 2½ years for handling stolen antiques. S was 44 and had 10 convictions including 6 for burglary. T was 34 and was effectively of good character. He was the sole carer for his ill wife. Held. **3 years 9 months** not 7 years for S and L. Because of his character, plea and mitigation **3 years 3 months** for T not 6.

Businessman defendant

76.7 *A-G's Reference (No 70 of 1999)* [2000] 2 Cr App Rep (S) 28. The defendant was convicted of conspiracy to steal computer equipment and conspiracy to handle stolen computer equipment. He pleaded guilty to conspiracy to handling stolen goods and taking part in a company when an undischarged bankrupt. The defendant ran a computer supply and repair business. He suffered 3 burglaries and he wasn't insured. The losses were substantial. He then started to sell substantial quantities of stolen computer equipment. He involved members of staff to act as drivers and payers of cash. He had discussions about stealing a lorry load of computers worth £250,000. He agreed to pay £50,000 for the computers. This was the conspiracy to steal count. The judge treated the defendant as a man of good character and the offences as rather stale. Held. The offences were worth at least 4 years following a trial. Because it was a reference and because the defendant had already been released from prison **30 months** not 12 months in all. [Unfortunately there is no reference to the estimated value of goods involved in the handling counts.]

Car ringing

See *Theft – Vehicles – Car ringing*

Compensation, confiscation and restitution

76.8 *R v Webbe* [2001] EWCA Crim 1217, [2002] 1 Cr App Rep (S) 82 – LCJ. A court should always have in mind the power to make restitution orders under ss 148 and 149 of the Powers of Criminal Courts (Sentencing) Act 2000, to make compensation orders under s 130 of the Powers of Criminal Court (Sentencing) Act 2000, and to make confiscation orders in relation to profits, under the Criminal Justice Act 1988 and the Proceeds of Crime Act 1995. A Magistrates' Court cannot, of course, make a confiscation order in a case of handling. But it is open to magistrates, in such a case, to commit to the Crown Court for sentence.

Custody threshold

76.9 *R v Webbe* [2001] EWCA Crim 1217, [2002] 1 Cr App Rep (S) 82 – LCJ. So far as the custody threshold is concerned, the defendant either with a record of offences of dishonesty, or who engages in sophisticated law breaking, will attract a custodial sentence. It is in relation to the length of that sentence that the aggravating and mitigating features will come into play, as will the personal mitigation of the offender, who may appropriately, in accordance with *R v Ollerenshaw* [1999] 1 Cr App Rep (S) 65, be dealt with by a somewhat shorter sentence than might, at first blush, otherwise have seemed appropriate. Note *R v Ollerenshaw* [1999] laid down, 'that where a court was considering imposing a comparatively short period of custody, of about 12 months or less, it should ask itself whether an even shorter period might be equally effective in protecting the interests of the public and punishing and deterring the criminal. There might be cases where 6 months might be just as effective as 9, or 2 months as effective as 4.'

Defendant aged 10–13

76.10 *R v T and F* [2001] 1 Cr App Rep (S) 294. The defendant F pleaded to robbery. The defendant T pleaded guilty to handling. The victim was walking home when F grabbed her from behind and pressed a closed penknife into her neck. F demanded her handbag and dragged and pushed her over a small fence. The victim fell and F grabbed her bag off her shoulder and ran off. The defendants both then 13 were arrested and T pointed out a bin where the bag was found. £15 and cash was missing. T admitted being given £5. A month later the victim still had a fear of being out alone. Without her admissions there was no evidence against T. T had been dealt with for 11 offences in less than a year. She had six robberies, two thefts and a common assault against her. Her mother had severe mental problems. She had tried to commit suicide and involve T in it. As a result she was taken into care. Her placement with foster parents broke down and she went to a community home. She made substantial progress but was volatile. She was said to be extremely emotionally and psychologically damaged. It was said there was no risk of re-offending. Held. Taking into account her age and that it was only £5 **12 months** not 18 months' detention and training.

Defendant aged 14–17

76.11 *R v Webbe Re Mitchell and Davis* [2002] 1 Cr App Rep (S) 82 – LCJ. The defend ants M and D pleaded guilty to handling. M's brother seized a lady's handbag as she was out walking. There was a short struggle and she screamed. She was punched once in the face. The defendants and others were standing nearby. The brother ran off with the handbag, which contained credit and bankcards, keys and £6. The others ran off with him. The woman was bruised and grazed. D received £5 and M nothing. The two Mitchell brothers contacted the police and were arrested. M admitted holding some of the items as the young men went through the victim's handbag. But he said he handed them back. He left the scene with the others. He told the police the names of the robbers. D was arrested and said they had searched the bag and shared the contents. He had had £5 from the robbery. He accepted that there had been a conversation beforehand about committing a robbery. M was then 17 He had a conviction for a serious sexual offence, for which he was sentenced to 3 years' detention but no convictions for dishonesty. D was then 16. He had a number of convictions for stealing. 1 month before the offence a supervision order was imposed on him. **12 months** detention not 18 for both.

Fines and compensation more appropriate than custody

76.12 *R v Webbe* [2002] EWCA Crim 1217, [2002] 1 Cr App Rep (S) 82 – LCJ. *R v Khemlani* (1981) 3 Cr App Rep (S) 208, shows the sentence that was appropriate for a man of good character, who pleaded guilty to handling 350 stolen watches (wholesale value £7,350). He was sentenced to 3 months' imprisonment. But the Court of Appeal took the view that the matter could be far better met by imposing a fine and making a compensation order in favour of the owners of the goods.

Monetary value – Value less than £1,000 – Guideline

76.13 *R v Webbe* [2001] EWCA Crim 1217, 1 Cr App Rep (S) 82 – LCJ. Where the property handled is of low monetary value and was acquired for the receiver's own use, the starting point should generally be a moderate fine or, in some cases (particularly, of course, if a fine cannot be paid by a particular defendant) a discharge. Such an outcome would, in our judgment be appropriate in relation to someone of previous good character handling low value domestic goods for his own use. By low value we mean less than four figures. A community sentence may be appropriate where property worth less than four figures is acquired for resale, or where more valuable goods are acquired for the handler's own use. Such a sentence may well be appropriate in relation to a young offender with little criminal experience, playing a peripheral role. But adult defendants with a record of dishonesty are likely to attract a custodial sentence.

Monetary value – Value less than £1,000 – Cases

76.14   *R v Osinowo* (23 October 2001, unreported). The defendant pleaded guilty on re-arraignment to handling. He also pleaded guilty to a bail offence for which he was fined. He allowed another, Q to use his bank account to pay in cheques. The victim discovered her chequebook had been taken and a cheque for £4,700 was paid into his bank account. He was charged and a verdict of not guilty was entered for that. Police searched his home and discovered a blank cheque. He said Q gave it to him. No attempt had been made to use the cheque. The defendant was a 23-year-old student of good character when the offence was committed. Since then he had been given a community service order and had not performed any work. His pre-sentence report said that another order would not be appropriate. Held. The offence of handling is always serious and that certainly applies to cheques. A short custodial sentence was right and the judge was justified in suspending it. However, **4 months suspended** not 12.

Monetary value – £1,000 – £100,000 – Guideline

76.15   *R v Webbe* [2001] EWCA Crim 1217, [2002] 1 Cr App Rep (S) 82 – LCJ. In the more serious cases there will be some for which the range of 12 months to 4 years are likely to be appropriate if the value of the goods involved is up to around £100,000. [Note this guideline only relates to offences in the 4th and most serious level of seriousness. The 3rd category is offences, which cross the custody threshold and the fourth is 'more serious offences'.]

Monetary value – £1,000 – £100,000 – Cases

76.16   *R v Jerome* [2001] 1 Cr App Rep (S) 316. The defendant was convicted of handling. Computer and other equipment worth in all about £2,739 were stolen in a burglary. The computer was traced to the defendant when a message was sent from the computer to the Internet. His flat was searched and the equipment was found. He was an antiques dealer and his turnover was about £100,000. The judge said he was minded to imprisonment the defendant but was concerned his business might be permanently wrecked. He was fined £10,000. Held. It is permissible to increase a fine for a wealthy or relatively wealthy offender. However, there must be some proportionality between the scale of the offence and the fine imposed. In handling, the value of the goods must be taken into consideration. £6,000 fine not £10,000. [Many will consider the sentencing judges' proportionality of just under four times the value is more realistic than the Court of Appeal's proportionality of just over twice the value].

R v Webbe [2001] EWCA Crim 1217, [2002] 1 Cr App Rep (S) 82 – LCJ. Webbe pleaded guilty to attempting to handle and handling stolen watches. Police officers found three watches and £250 in cash in the boot of his car. One was an 18-carat gold watch with a retail value of £7,700. That was the handling offence. The attempt count related to two other linked chronographs, each with a retail value of £1,150. In interview the appellant made no comment. But later, he said that he had paid £200 for the watches, to a man he had met in the street. He was of good character. A pre-sentence report indicated the defendant's regret and that he was not a man who had criminal attitudes or a general disrespect for the law. The risk of re-offending was minimal. The total retail value of the goods was slightly over £10,000. Held. The defendant was not forthcoming in interview and could have provided the police with more help about the source and circumstances of his acquisitions. Taking into account the good character, the goods were apparently for his own use, the plea and the observations made in *R v Ollerenshaw* [1999] 1 Cr App Rep (S) 65 (at custody threshold) **4 months** not 15 months.

Monetary value – Over £100,000 – Guideline case

76.17   *R v Webbe* [2001] EWCA Crim 1217, [2002] 1 Cr App Rep (S) 82 – LCJ. In the more serious cases where the value of the goods is in excess of £100,000, or where the offence is highly organised and bears the hallmarks of a professional commercial operation, a sentence of 4 years and upwards is likely to be appropriate, and it will be the higher where the source of the handled property is known by the handler to be a serious violent offence such as armed robbery. [Note. This guideline relates to offences in the fourth and most serious level of seriousness, although most offences of this value would fall into that category. The third category is offences, which cross the custody threshold and the fourth is 'more serious offences.']

Monetary value – Over £100,000 – Cases

76.18   *R v Webbe Re White* [2002] 1 Cr App Rep (S) 82 – LCJ. White pleaded guilty late to three counts of handling and a late count. The value involved was some £210,000. He leased a warehouse, which was searched by the police. There were found cigarettes, and alcohol, which had been stolen from two parked trailers two days before. The goods worth £72,000 were recovered. Also found were two trailers which, with their loads, had been stolen that day. Other stolen goods and trailers were found. At the time, he had been on bail for a remarkably similar offence. The judge concluded that the applicant had run a dishonest business yard, making it available to others for the disposal of dishonest goods. He was 36 and had convictions predominantly involving motor vehicles. He was sentenced to **2½ years** consecutive to 3 years he was currently serving. Held This was large scale professional receiving by a man with a criminal record. Goods reached him remarkably quickly after they had been stolen. The offences were committed while he was on bail for other serious offences. The sentence was a modest sentence.

Persistent offenders – Guideline

76.19   *R v Webbe* [2001] EWCA Crim 1217, [2002] 1 Cr App Rep (S) 82 – LCJ. *R v Battams* (1979) 1 Cr App Rep (S) 15, shows the sentence of imprisonment which was appropriate for a receiver of stolen goods, obviously known in the locality as a person willing to assist in the disposal of such goods, however modest the sums of money involved. In that case, a sentence of 18 months was reduced to **12 months**, to take account of the appellant's physical disability. In *R v Bloomfield* (1995) 16 Cr App Rep (S) 221, the Court of Appeal noted that the appropriate sentencing bracket for a receiver, who dealt regularly with thieves and burglars providing a regular outlet, was between 2 and 4 years' imprisonment, although, in that particular case, which was a one-off offence, a significantly lower sentence was imposed, namely 15 months for receiving three stolen caravans, for which he, a caravan dealer, had paid £9,000. As we have earlier indicated, sentences significantly higher than 4 years also may be appropriate where a professional handler, over a substantial period of time, demonstrated by his record or otherwise, has promoted and encouraged, albeit indirectly, criminal activity by others.'

Persistent offenders – Cases

76.20   *R v Webbe Re Moore* [2002] 1 Cr App Rep (S) 82 – LCJ. Moore pleaded guilty to two offences of handling. He asked for 47 other offences, including 17 burglaries and 27 thefts, to be taken into consideration. The total value of the goods in the indictment was somewhat less than £2,000. The value of the TIC property was some £20,000. Two houses were burgled on the same day. A day or two later the defendant converted some of the property into cash at a pawnbrokers. He tried to sell the stolen property again and was arrested by police. His home was searched and stolen items were seized. He was 26 and had 60 convictions including burglary, theft and handling. Held. It is not generally desirable that a very large number of offences should be taken into consideration when there are comparatively few offences in the indictment and when the offences taken into consideration are of a different kind from those in the indictment. It is far preferable for the indictment to reflect the general level of criminality of a particular defendant. **4 years** was not manifestly excessive.

Professional handlers

76.21 *R v Webbe* [2001] EWCA Crim 1217, [2002] 1 Cr App Rep (S) 82 – LCJ. In the more serious cases where the value of the goods is in excess of £100,000, or where the offence is highly organised and bears the hallmarks of a professional commercial operation, a sentence of 4 years and upwards is likely to be appropriate, and it will be the higher where the source of the handled property is known by the handler to be a serious violent offence such as armed robbery.

R v Gwyer [2002] EWCA Crim 102, [2002] 2 Cr App Rep (S) 246. See **Antiques, valuable jewellery etc**

Robbery, proceeds of

76.22 *R v Webbe* [2001] EWCA Crim 1217, [2002] 1 Cr App Rep (S) 82 – LCJ. The sentence will be higher where the source of the handled property is known by the handler to be a serious violent offence such as armed robbery.

R v Triumph and Ramadan (2 February 1999, unreported). T pleaded guilty to handling and R was convicted of it. Both were acquitted of robbery. There was a robbery of a Securicor van and CS gas was spayed in the driver's face. The stolen property was found in the possession of the defendants 8 hours later. Both had convictions for dishonesty. Held. **4 years and 6 years** was severe but due to the short time after the offence and that it was a violent offence the sentence was not manifestly excessive.

Vehicles, stolen

76.23 *R v Okoro* (7 October 1997, unreported). The defendant was convicted of 6 counts of handling stolen cars valued at £200,000. They were stolen in London and destined for Ghana. The defendant was a shipping agent who helped make arrangements for the containers and falsified details of payments. Held. It was a prevalent crime. **4 years** was not manifestly excessive.

77 HARASSMENT, S 2

77.1 Pursuing course of harassment.

Protection from Harassment Act 1997, s 2

Summary only. Maximum sentence 6 months and/or Level 5 fine (£5,000). There is power to make a restraining order to protect the victim etc from further conduct[1].

1 Protection from Harassment Act 1997, s 5.

Guideline case

77.2 *R v Liddle and Hayes* [2000] 1 Cr App Rep (S) 131. The court should consider: (1) Is the offence a s 2 or a s 4 offence? (2) Is there a history of disobedience to court orders in the past? (3) The seriousness of the defendant's conduct, which can of course range from actual violence through to threats, down to letters, which of course may even express affection rather than any wish to harm the victim. (4) Is there persistent misconduct by the defendant or a solitary instance of misbehaviour? (5) The effect upon the victim, whether physical or psychological. Does the victim require protection? What is the level of risk posed by the defendant? (6) The mental health of the offender. Is the defendant willing to undergo treatment or have the necessary help from the probation service, which is readily available under special schemes? (7) What is the defendant's reaction to the court proceedings? Is there a plea of guilty? Is there remorse? Is there recognition of the need for help? For a first offence a short sharp sentence may be appropriate, though much will depend on the factors of repetition and breach of court orders and the nature of the misconduct. Obviously, the facts of each case vary and the facts of any particular case may require a longer sentence. For a second offence longer sentences of about **15 months** on a plea of guilty wouldbe an appropriate starting point, and from then on it is possible to see from the maximum of 5 years where each case fits into the statutory frameworkworking from the figure of 15 months, which may be appropriate. [Unfortunately the court does not say whether the sentences are for ss 2 or 4 or both.]

Magistrates' Court Sentencing Guidelines September 2000

77.3   Entry point. Is it serious enough for a community penalty? Consider the impact on the victim. Examples of aggravating factors for the offence are disregard of warning, excessive persistence, interference with employment/business, invasion of victim's home, involvement of others, use of violence or grossly offensive material and where photographs or images of a personal nature are involved. Examples of mitigating factors for the offence are initial provocation and short duration. Examples of mitigation are age, health (physical or mental), co-operation with the police, and genuine remorse. Consider making a restraining order. Give reasons if not awarding compensation.

For details about the guidelines see **MAGISTRATES' COURT SENTENCING GUIDELINES** at page 331.

Ex-partners

77.4   *R v Liddle and Hayes* [2000] 1 Cr App Rep (S) 131. The defendant L pleaded guilty to two breaches of a restraining order. A Crown Court injunction was made restraining him from harassing his ex-wife. In breach of that he was convicted at the Magistrates' Court of harassment, (s 2), and of harassment, causing fear of violence (s 4). He was sentenced to a combination order including community service. A new restraining order was made for his ex-wife, his child and her parents. Four months later he was again convicted at the same court of three breaches of the new restraining order. He was conditionally discharged. Five months later he pleaded guilty at the Crown Court to two breaches of the order and was sentenced to 9 months imprisonment. He was released on 12th October 1998 and on 25 February 1999 he pleaded guilty to two more offences. They were sending two letters to his ex-wife, an exchange of words with her and sending three letters to her from prison. One of the offences was 2–3 weeks after his release from prison. His ex-wife was distressed and clearly annoyed. He was 32 and his pre-sentence report said he did not present a risk of serious harm to the public, but could pose such a risk to his wife and daughter should he persevere with his obsessional views about returning to his wife. A psychiatric report said he was not mentally ill and had no history of violent behaviour. Held. In the main he had only written letters. It is little mitigation that the letters were not threatening or objectionable. There was only one incident in the street. The effect on the victim and the need for protection are well in our minds. **8 months** and 4 months consecutive consecutive to the 3 months recall not 21 months.

Stranger

77.5 *R v Liddle and Hayes* [2000] 1 Cr App Rep (S) 131. The defendant H was convicted of two offences of harassment. He began to harass a young woman who he saw by chance. She rebuffed his advance but he persisted in harassing her. He was charged with harassment and sentenced to two months consecutive on each. The court madea lifetime restraining order. Eight months after the conviction he rang her door bell. He then ran away but was caught by a friend of the victim's. Six weeks later she received a letter written by him revealing his knowledge of her daily life and inferentially suggesting that he had been observing her in order to make those revelations. He was 39. A pre-sentence report said he was obsessional about this young lady. He has lived with his mother for a long period and has never been in full-time employment. Held. It was mainly letters. There was one incident at her home, which was at the bottomof the range. The effect on the victim was distress and annoyance rather than any more. **8 months** and 3 months consecutive not 2 years.

Telephone calls

77.6 *R v Sutton* [2001] EWCA Crim 291, [2001] 2 Cr App Rep (S)414. The defendant pleaded guilty to harassment. The defendant and an elderly man were good friends and the defendant helped him out for 15 years. When items went missing the elderly man asked a relation to tell the defendant not to visit again and to give him £500 as a thank you. The elderly man died. The relative, one of the victims gave the defendant the money and told him he didn't think the defendant was responsible for taking items.The defendant strongly denied the thefts and what the relative said. The defendant then made five threatening telephone calls and sent him a funeral brochure and two brochures of memorial headstones. Two further calls were made which were taken by the relative's wife demanding £10,000 or the relative would be killed. He eventually admitted making the calls and said he wanted to get his own back and he was very hurt by what the victims had said. He was 31 with no convictions. The pre-sentence report said it was very unlikely he would re-offend. He had depressive symptoms which had improved. They were linked to the death of the elderly man. The victims asked that the sentence should not be too harsh. Two prison reports commented favourably on his work and raised questions about his safety. **1 year** not 3 with a 5 year restraining order remaining.

See also **PUBLIC ORDER ACT OFFENCES** and **STALKING**

78 HARASSMENT, S 2 – RACIALLY AGGRAVATED

78.1 Pursuing course of harassment, which is racially aggravated.

Protection from Harassment Act 1997, s 2 and the Crime and Disorder Act 1998, s 32(1)(a)

Triable either way. On indictment maximum sentence 2 years. Summary maximum 6 months and/or £5,000. Power to make a restraining order to protect the victim etc from further conduct[1].

1 Protection from Harassment Act 1997, s 5 and the Crime and Disorder Act 1998, s 32(7).

Magistrates' Court Sentencing Guidelines September 2000

78.2 Entry point. Is it so serious that only custody is appropriate? Consider the level of racial aggravation and the impact on the victim. Examples of aggravating factors for the offence are disregard of warning, excessive persistence, interference with employment/business, invasion of victim's home, involvement of others, use of violence or grossly offensive material and where photographs or images of a personal nature are involved. Examples of mitigating factors for the offence initial provocation and short duration. Examples of mitigation are age, health (physical or mental), co-operation with the police, and genuine remorse. Consider making a restraining order. Give reasons if not awarding compensation.

For details about the guidelines see MAGISTRATES' COURT SENTENCING GUIDELINES at page 331.

Neighbours

78.3 *R v Shand* [2001] EWCA Crim 1582, [2002] 1 Cr App Rep (S) 291. The defendant pleaded guilty to racially aggravated harassment. The defendant and the victim were neighbours. They were both white. The victim's partner was Afro-Caribbean and her three children were of mixed race. One afternoon he started shouting, 'England, fucking blacks, nigger lovers,' outside his gate. He was looking towards the victim's flat and appeared drunk. She found it intimidating and called the police who spoke to him about it. A week later, the defendant saw the victim's partner and shouted, 'Nigger lover,' and continued shouting, 'England. If you're happy and white clap you're hands. Fucking black bastards.' He called the victim a 'whore,' 'drug dealer' and 'prostitute.' The police arrived about an hour later and talked to the defendant. He went back inside. At 11.30pm that night when she and the children were in bed he started shouting saying he was going to kill her and her days were numbered. The abuse continued till the police arrived and took him away. The next day at 8.30am he was back shouting loudly, 'Nigger lover, jungle bunnies, cock sucker, England.' 'Combat 18 was going to bomb you niggers out.' Eight days later there was further similar abuse and the next day he threatened to kill the victim and her children and set fire to her house. A month later there was more abuse. The victim was absolutely distraught. The defendant was 39 and had convictions for threatening behaviour, affray and in 1997 for racially threatening behaviour on the same victim for which he received 28 days imprisonment. He problem was drink. He showed remorse and had lost his home of 16 years. Held. This was the most disgraceful conduct. There was nothing wrong with **15 months**.

Police officers etc, directed at

78.4 *R v Jacobs* [2001] 2 Cr App Rep (S) 174. The defendant was sentenced for harassment (presumably s 2) which was racially aggravated and common assault. (The plea is not given in the report.) The defendant then 20 was arrested and taken to a police station. A police officer asked the defendant to remove two rings she was wearing. She said, 'I don't want you Paki filthy hands on me. I don't want that Paki touching me.' She also told the custody officer she didn't want a foreigner touching her. She was restrained and the rings were removed. She struggled and continued shouting racial abuse. In the cell she shouted abuse. Later she abused the same officer again. She admitted the offence in interview. She had a public order conviction in 1997 for which she received an attendance centre order. Her psychiatric report said she would respond to probation perhaps with psychiatric treatment. Held. Police officers are entitled to be protected from racial abuse but **3 months** not 9.

For basic principles about racially-aggravated offences see RACIALLY-AGGRAVATED OFFENCES

See also PUBLIC ORDER ACT OFFENCES and STALKING

79   HARASSMENT, S 4 (OR PUBLIC NUISANCE)

79.1   Putting people in fear of violence.

Protection from Harassment Act 1997, s 4

Triable either way. On indictment maximum sentence 5 years. Summary maximum 6 months and/or £5,000. Power to make a restraining order to protect the victim etc from further conduct[1].

Public Nuisance

Common law so indictable only. No maximum provided so the maximum is life.

1   Protection from Harassment Act 1997, s 5.

Guideline case

79.2   *R v Liddle and Hayes* [2000] 1 Cr App Rep (S) 131. The court should consider: (1) Is the offence a s 2 or a s 4 offence? (2) Is there a history of disobedience to court orders in the past? (3) The seriousness of the defendant's conduct, which can of course range from actual violence through to threats, down to letters, which of course may even express affection rather than any wish to harm the victim. (4) Is there persistent misconduct by the defendant or a solitary instance of misbehaviour? (5) The effect upon the victim, whether physical or psychological. Does the victim require protection? What is the level of risk posed by the defendant? (6) The mental health of the offender. Is the defendant willing to undergo treatment or have the necessary help from the probation service, which is readily available under special schemes? (7) What is the defendant's reaction to the court proceedings? Is there a plea of guilty? Is there remorse? Is there recognition of the need for help? For a first offence a short sharp sentence may be appropriate, though much will depend on the factors of repetition and breach of court orders and the nature of the misconduct. Obviously, the facts of each case vary and the facts of any particular case may require a longer sentence. For a second offence longer sentences of about **15 months** on a plea of guilty would be an appropriate starting point, and from then on it is possible to see from the maximum of 5 years where each case fits into the statutory framework working from the figure of 15 months, which may be appropriate. [Unfortunately the court does not say whether the sentences are for ss 2 or 4 or both.]

Magistrates' Court Sentencing Guidelines September 2000

79.3   Entry point. Is it so serious that only custody is appropriate? Consider the impact on the victim. Examples of aggravating factors for the offence are disregard of warning, excessive persistence, interference with employment/business, invasion of victim's home, involvement of others, threat to use weapon or substance (including realistic imitations), use of violence or grossly offensive material and where photographs or images of a personal nature are involved. Examples of mitigating factors for the offence are initial provocation and short duration. Examples of mitigation are age, health (physical or mental), co-operation with the police, and genuine remorse. Consider making a restraining order. Give reasons if not awarding compensation.

For details about the guidelines see **MAGISTRATES' COURT SENTENCING GUIDELINES** at page 331.

Obsessional behaviour to opposite sex

79.4   *R v Miah* [2000] 2 Cr App Rep (S) 439. The defendant was convicted of harassment and intimidating a witness. The defendant then 22 years old wanted to start a relationship with the victim who was a 15 or 16-year-old schoolgirl. He used to wait for her outside school and hug her and hold her hands. She didn't want a relationship with him at all. He threatened to cut her hands off with a knife. A man saw them and came and rescued her. Two weeks later she ran away from him and he caught up and shouted abuse at her and punched her in the face and kicked her on the ground. Onlookers called the police. She suffered bruises. Over 6 weeks later he came in to a fast food restaurant where she worked and she ran into the back office. He called out, 'Fucking bitch,' and said he had a gun and was going to get her. He was arrested and released on bail. 3½ months later the victim was walking home from work with a friend and he ran up to them with his fists clenched and said, 'Fucking bitch.' Her friend told him to leave her alone and there was a short argument. He then threw some papers down and said, 'Fucking bitch, read that. That is what you wrote,' referring to her witness statement. He took hold of her wrists and frog marched her to the station (police presumably) swearing at her. He dragged her to some gardens and his mood changed with him asking her not to leave him. His mood changed back and he said, 'Leave me, fucking bitch. You are going to pay in the end.' She walked away and he shouted after her. He was arrested and was remanded in custody. He was of good character. Those that wrote reports found he lied and continued to deny the offences. One report said he was irrational and might be obsessed with the victim. No treatment was suggested. There was no contrition and the risk of re-offending was described as high. Held. Here the persistent and impact on the victim must be regarded. The judge should assess the form of sentence and length of sentence most likely to lead to the defendant behaving and not breaching the restraint order. **18 months** not 2½ years with the intimidation sentence of 6 months concurrent and a retraining order remaining.

R v Onabanjo [2001] 2 Cr App Rep (S) 27. The defendant pleaded guilty at the Magistrates' Court to putting another in fear contrary to s 4 and common assault. He had a 2½ year relationship with the victim and they had an 18 month old son. She told him the relationship was over and she moved back to her old flat. He went to her flat argued with her and pulled her across the floor by her feet causing friction burns which were not serious. He was charge and released on bail. The there were a number of other incidents of which three were over 6 days and were; threatening to kill her twice on the telephone and once in the street after he had blocked her way. Within the 6 days he entered her flat through a window at 12.45 am. She awoke to find him at the foot of her bed repeatedly asking for them to get back together. He stayed for ½ hour and she said she wasn't frightened then. He also sent letters of affection. He said the conduct was connected with his concern for his son. He was then 21 and had 4 years before been bound over for threatening words and behaviour. Three years later he received 2 years detention for 3 robberies and 1 attempt. He had a problem with alcohol and expressed genuine remorse. Held. The repeated threats by a man who is capable of unpredictable behaviour made the offence particularly serious. The **12 months** and 3 months for the assault were not excessive. Neither was it wrong to make the sentences consecutive. Nor was the 15 months excessive.

Telephone calls

79.5 *R v Hill* [2000] 1 Cr App Rep (S) 8. The defendant made an early plea to harassment by putting someone in fear contrary to s 4. A 13-year-old girl left her bus pass on a bus. It had her personal details including her telephone number on it. She was unknown to the defendant but he repeatedly telephoned her at her home in Rotterdam. Generally the calls were made at night between 7.15pm and 9am. Sometimes he would hang up, sometimes he started heavy breathing and sometimes he asked her questions about what she was doing. There were also questions about what she was wearing and threats to see her at school. He also claimed to know personal details about her. The girl became very frightened and was frightened to leave her home. On one day he told her he wanted to shag her and talked about coming to her house and ripping her clothes off. Eventually the telephone number was changed and this caused considerable inconvenience to her father over his business calls. The defendant was 24 when he appeared at court he had no convictions. Later he pleaded guilty to a similar offence for which he received 2 months concurrent. He had a history of depressive symptoms and an inadequate and immature personality. Held. The victim was at a vulnerable stage. However, **12 months** not 18.

R v Eskdale [2001] EWCA Crim 1159, [2002] 1 Cr App Rep (S) 118. The defendant pleaded guilty to causing a nuisance to the public by making threatening, obscene and malicious telephone calls. Over 2 weeks he made about 1,000 telephone calls. There were 15 complainants. Four were telephoned in the middle of the night, three very late in the evening and the rest very late in the morning. In some he said he had followed them or was outside their homes. They were made for his sexual gratification. As an example he telephoned a pregnant 28-year-old wife whose telephone was ex-directory and spoke to her by name and asked if her husband was in. He then said he was outside and said, 'I'm going to come inside and fuck you. Don't put the telephone down or you'll regret it.' She did put the telephone down and tried to ring her husband but the defendant was blocking the line. Eventually she went to a neighbour who assisted her. In another he threatened to stab the female victim if she put the telephone down. The worst case was when he rang a young woman whose flat overlooked a darkened car park. At 1am it woke her up and he said she had better do as he said or he would come and rape her. She was alone and very frightened. He made her stand in front of the window and take her clothes off and threatened to enter the flat if she refused. It was clear he was watching her. He told her to touch her breasts and vagina and told her to put her bottom against the window and part her cheeks. He also told her to stop crying or he'd come and fuck her. She was also made to simulate sex with a banana and her mouth. She was told not to tell anyone or he'd come and get her. She felt disgusted and violated. She had to leave her flat and live with her father. The defendant was arrested. He had in 1990 a conviction for using the telephone system to send offensive matter and several burglaries and threats to kill. The burglaries were to steal underwear. Later in 1990 a conviction for using the telephone system to send indecent matter. In 1993 he received 5½ years for indecent assault. In 1996 a conviction for using the telephone system to send offensive matter and to cause annoyance for which he received imprisonment. When serving the 5½ year sentence he received treatment but after his release he committed further offences and was recalled to prison. The probation officer considered his offending was escalating in a dangerous way. There was considered a serious risk of harm to the public. The psychiatrist described his abnormally high sex drive with anger, social isolation and little self-control and the likelihood he gains gratification from humiliating women. Adding despite extensive treatment he was a danger to women. Held. The judge was confronted with an exceptionally difficult sentencing exercise. **9 years** was a very severe sentence but it was justified.

R v Preston [2002] 1 Cr App Rep (S) 419. The defendant pleaded guilty to harassment causing fear at the Magistrates' Court. Within 6 of her release from prison she made 46 menacing calls to a 63-year-old lady who was a complete stranger. The victim lived with her sister and suffered from high blood pressure. The calls were abusive and threatening. One day there were 19 calls containing threats to stab her, burn her house down and kill her. Sometimes the calls would be silent. She was arrested and told the police, 'I am going not guilty because I want to know what the bitch looks like.' She was 27 with a substantial history of offending. She had convictions for repeated offences of theft, assault, Public Order offences, intimidating a witness, harassment and racially aggravating threatening behaviour. In 2000 she received 19 months for threats to kill, threatening behaviour, affray and common assault. The psychiatrist's report said she suffered from an emotionally unstable personality disorder. The judge sentenced her to the 10 months for the breach of her licence and **2½ years consecutive**. Held. There was a history of disobedience to the court orders in the past. The sentence was inevitable.

See also **PUBLIC ORDER ACT OFFENCES** and **STALKING**

80   HARASSMENT, S 4 – RACIALLY AGGRAVATED

80.1   Putting people in fear of violence, which is racially aggravated.

Protection from Harassment Act 1997, s 4 and the Crime and Disorder Act 1998, s 32(1)(b)

Triable either way. On indictment maximum sentence[1] 7 years. Summary maximum 6 months and/or £5,000. Power to make a restraining order to protect the victim etc from further conduct[2].

1   Where they convict of s 4 as an alternative to the racially-aggravated offence the maximum sentence at the Crown Court is the Magistrates' Courts maximum, Public Order Act 1986, s 7(4). Where the jury convict the defendant of s 4A as an alternative the maximum sentence is the Magistrates' Courts maximum, *R v Alden* [2002] 2 Cr App Rep (S) 326.
2   Protection from Harassment Act 1997, s 5 and the Crime and Disorder Act 1998, s 32(7).

Magistrates' Court Sentencing Guidelines September 2000

80.2   Entry point. Are magistrates' sentencing powers appropriate? Consider the level of racial aggravation and the impact on the victim. Examples of aggravating factors for the offence are disregard of warning, excessive persistence, interference with employment/business, invasion of victim's home, involvement of others, threat to use weapon or substance (including realistic imitations), use of violence or grossly offensive material and where photographs or images of a personal nature are involved. Examples of mitigating factors for the offence initial provocation and short duration. Examples of mitigation are age, health (physical or mental), co-operation with the police, and genuine remorse. Consider a committal for sentence. Consider making a restraining order. Give reasons if not awarding compensation.

For details about the guidelines see **MAGISTRATES' COURT SENTENCING GUIDELINES** at page 331.

Cases

80.3   *R v Joyce* [2001] EWCA Crim 2433, [2002] 1 Cr App Rep (S) 582. The defendant was convicted of racially-aggravated common assault, racially aggravated harassment under s 4 and common assault. Because of her behaviour security guards spoke to her. She was abusive to a black one and emptied her bag on the floor. When she was told to pick the items up she said, 'Fuck off you black bastard', and 'Fucking nigger, the BNP is going to get you.' As she was walked by the victim she struck him a backwards punch with a clenched fist. He punched her in the face. She struck out again and had to be restrained. She continued to swear, strike out and utter racist abuse at the victim. Police arrested her and she abused them and struggled, saying as an example, 'All black people are bastards, and they should not be in the country.' They told her they weren't interested in her views. She replied, 'You police are scarred of niggers, you should try living in South London.' She kicked out at one of the officers and threatened to kill him and his family. She was given warnings and continued the abuse. She spat at another when being taken to the police van. She was now 39 and had 14 court appearances for theft, shoplifting, ABH, criminal damage, assault on police, threatening words, common assault, being drunk and disorderly and possession of a Class A drug. She hadn't received a custodial sentence. The pre-sentence report said there was a high risk of further offences and violence against the public, which would be reduced if she addressed her substance abuse and engaged in strategies to address issues of anger management. She had a glowing prison report and wanted to give birth to her child outside prison. Held. The assault without the racial element was worth 4 months. The racial element was worth 3 months extra so **7 months** not 15.

See also **PUBLIC ORDER ACT OFFENCES** and **STALKING**

For basic principles about racially-aggravated offences see **RACIALLY-AGGRAVATED OFFENCES**

81   HARASSMENT, S 5

81.1   Breach of a restraining order.

Protection from Harassment Act 1997, s 5

Triable either way. On indictment maximum sentence 5 years. Summary maximum 6 months and/or £5,000.

Breach after some compliance

81.2   *R v Kasoar* [2001] EWCA Crim 12, [2002] 2 Cr App Rep (S) 260. The defendant pleaded guilty to breaching a restraining order. He had a relationship with the victim for about a year and a half from 1995. After the break up he used to park his car outside her place of work. She ignored that. After she got married in 1996 he constantly followed her from her work to her home. That disrupted her relationship and she separated from her husband. In January 2000 there was harassment and assault and he was convicted and sentenced to CSO. The day after the sentence he started telephoning her. It lasted for 'months.' In July 2000 he was arrested for it and sent to prison. A restraining order was made. After nearly a year he went to her home where she was with her boyfriend and shouted, 'You fucking bitch.' She went inside and he continued to shout. She was upset and angry about his interference in her life again. All his convictions were for pestering the victim. The pre-sentence referred to the defendant being unable to recognise that his behaviour constitutes harassment and that he does not wish to address this continuing domestic violence. His risk assessment for re-offending was high. **12 months** was severe but wholly justified.

Early breach

81.3   *R v Burke* (26 July 2001, unreported). The defendant pleaded guilty to breach of a restraining order and criminal damage and later he made a belated plea to threats to kill. He had a 6 year stormy relationship with the one of the victims. He harassed her and in 1994 stabbed her. For that he was convicted of wounding with intent and received 4 years. On his release he resumed the relationship and it remained extremely stormy. Many incidents were reported to the police and she feared for her life. In May 2000 the relationship ended and in August 2000 he was sentenced to 3 months for harassment and a restraining order was made. Because of time served on remand he was released immediately. The victim was so scared she stayed overnight with friends and visited her disabled elderly mother during the day. 5 days after the order was made he entered the mother's flat from the garden. He pushed the arthritic lady to the ground, used foul and abusive language and threatened to shoot both victims. The flat was ransacked and he damaged a window, a table, china ornaments, a clock, a gas fire, a kettle and electrical equipment. The mother went outside to get help and he told her he was going to shoot her daughter and her current boyfriend. He also said, I've got a gun. Do you want to see it.' He then sat on a wall until the police arrived. When he was charged he threatened to repeat his behaviour. He was 37 with 23 convictions and had had 10 periods of custody. As well as the offences already mentioned he had convictions for GBH with intent, assault on police, two affrays and two threatening words or behaviours. Held. The offences were in breach of the court order. It was permissible to make the 2 years for the breach of the order consecutive to the threats to kill, because the threats to kill were outside the flat after the breach offence was committed. The total of **5 years** was appropriate but the criminal damage sentence should be made concurrent not consecutive.

Persistent breaches

81.4 *R v Lumley* [2001] 2 Cr App Rep (S) 110. The defendant pleaded guilty to breaching a restraining order. The offence took place 3 weeks after his release from prison for a similar offence. In August 1998, he was sentenced to 8 months for two counts of harassment and a threats to kill. A restraining order was made. It contained a prohibition from contacting either directly or indirectly his former partner, the victim. There were persistent breaches of the order, although the victim did write to him when he was in prison. In April 1999 he was put on probation for common assault, threatening behaviour and harassment. In October 1999, he was sentenced to 6 months for breaching the restraint order and the probation. The probation order continued. Two weeks later, at 9.15pm he and another went to the victim's home and rang the bell twice. The police were called but when they arrived he had gone. The victim and her new partner were distressed, angry and extremely afraid. The defendant was arrested and gave a false alibi. In March 2000, he was sentenced for breaching the probation order on a date after the current offence. He received 6 months and the probation order was revoked. He was 28 with a long history of offending. His pre-sentence report said his heroin use had depleted what self control he had left. Held. The harassment (not revealed) was at the lower end of the scale. The persistent nature of the breaches did call for a more substantial sentence. The fact he had served a 6 month sentence since the offence was important. **18 months** not 2½ years. [Factually the judgment is far from clear.]

See also **PUBLIC ORDER ACT OFFENCES** and **STALKING**

82 HARASSMENT AND UNLAWFUL EVICTION OF TENANTS

82.1 Protection from Eviction Act 1977, s 1

Triable either way. On indictment maximum 2 years. Summary maximum 6 months and/or £5,000.

Crown Court statistics England and Wales[1] – Crown Court – Males 21+ – Protection from Eviction Act 1977
82.2

Year	Plea	Total Numbers sentenced	Type of sentence%					Average length of custody (months)
			Discharge	Fine	Community sentence	Suspended sentence	Custody	
2000	Guilty	2	0%	0%	0%	0%	0%	0
	Not guilty	3	0%	0%	33%	0%	67%	10.5

1 Excluding committals for sentence. Source: Crime and Criminal Justice Unit, Home Office Ref: IOS416-02.

Threats and aggression

82.3 *R v Khan* [2001] EWCA Crim 912, [2001] 2 Cr App Rep (S) 553. The defendant was convicted of interfering with the peace or comfort of an occupier, unlawful eviction, theft and doing an act intending to pervert the course of justice. The victim a single mother aged 33, her boyfriend and her three children including her baby rented a flat owned by the defendant. There was some delay in the rent being paid because of benefit problems and that situation was explained to the defendant. She was told her 6 month agreement would not be renewed His agent started legal proceedings but said this was just a formality because he was expecting the rent money. However the defendant started calling round and saying he needed the flat for his wife. While the victim was out he and four associates went to the flat and kicked in the door breaking the frame. They disturbed and broke much of its contents. The stereo and speakers were smashed, the TV was broken, the beds were turned upside down, and one of them was broken in two. The baby's cot and toys were also broken. After discovering this the family went to the victim's mother. A number of items were taken from the flat including an electric fan. After a couple of hours, the boyfriend went to the flat to pick up some of the baby's clothes. He was met by the defendant and four others and he said they had no right to be there. One of them replied it was 'fuck all to do with him' and the defendant wanted his house back. That man was aggressive and threatening and the boyfriend found him intimidating. The boyfriend was told to leave immediately and if the victim returned to the flat her face would be rearranged. The lock on the flat door was changed. Police attended and found the defendant and four other men inside and the defendant said he was repossessing the flat for non-payment of rent. The defendant was released on bail with a condition not to contact directly or indirectly any prosecution witness. Two months later, a car in which the defendant was a passenger approached the boyfriend. The man who had intimidated him got out of the car and asked to see the victim. They both went to where the victim was living and the man asked her how much she wanted to drop the case. When she told him to deal with the solicitors the man became aggressive and told her if the defendant went to prison she would get nothing. He also said the most she would get would be £1,500, with half paid now and the rest when the case was dropped. The defendant was 26 and of good character. His wife was ill and spoke no English. Held. There was no basis for interfering with the **16 months** for the three flat offences. Perverting offences are treated seriously because they undermine justice. 8 months for it was not excessive. Neither was **2 years** in total in any way excessive.

Old case. *R v Madarbakus* (1992) 13 Cr App Rep (S) 542.

83 HEALTH AND SAFETY OFFENCES

83.1 (and principles when the defendant is a company)

Various statutes, regulations and penalties. The main one is the Health and Safety at Work etc Act 1974, ss 2(1) and 33(1) and (1A) (failing to discharge the duty to ensure the health, safety and welfare of the employees.)

Triable either way. On indictment maximum an unlimited fine. Summary maximum £20,000. For offences against ss 33(1)(g) or (o) the maximum on indictment includes 2 years and the summary maximum includes 6 months' imprisonment.

Sentencing trends. The prosecution tends to under indict perhaps because of lack of confidence or because they want to avoid trials where they may not obtain their costs. Defence counsel's current tactic is to provide a list of very selective cases at the Crown Court and the Court of Appeal to try to minimise the fine. Those lists often ignore the fact that the low fines are because of lack of means rather than lack of culpability. The Lord Chancellor and the Court of Appeal have made it clear that the current level of fines are too low. Poor health and safety standard continue to maim and kill at work particularly in the construction industry. Judges are likely to reflect these factors in higher fines particularly where the company is a large one. Unless the fines are large it will not cause shareholders or directors to notice the orders of the court. Where there is doubt that the company will carry through adequate changes to their Health and Safety procedures deferring sentences will become routine. This power is not restricted to occasions where the court is considering a custodial sentence.

Crown Court statistics England and Wales[1] – Crown Court – Males 21+ – Health and Safety at Work etc Act 1974

83.2

Year	Plea	Total Numbers sentenced	Type of sentence%					Average length of custody (months)
			Discharge	Fine	Community sentence	Suspended sentence	Custody	
2000	Guilty	14	14%	71%	0%	0%	0%	0
	Not guilty	2	0%	100%	0%	0%	0%	0

1 Excluding committals for sentence. Source: Crime and Criminal Justice Unit, Home Office Ref: IOS416-02.

Guideline remarks

83.3 *R v F Howe & Son (Engineers) Ltd* [1999] 2 Cr App Rep (S) 37. There had been increasing recognition in recent years of the seriousness of health and safety offences. In assessing the gravity of the breach look at how far short of the appropriate standard the defendant fell. It is often a matter of chance whether death or serious injury results from even a serious breach. Generally where death is the consequence of a criminal act it is regarded as an aggravating feature of the offence. The penalty should reflect public disquiet at the unnecessary loss of life. Financial profit can often be made at the expense of proper action to protect employees and the public. Cost cutting is a crucial tool in achieving a competitive edge. A deliberate breach of the health and safety legislation with a view to profit seriously aggravates the offence. There is some evidence that proportionately more accidents occur in companies with less than 50 employees than those with a large staff. The standard of care imposed by the legislation is the same regardless of the size of the company. Other matters that may be relevant to sentence are the degree of risk and extent of the danger created by the offence; the extent of the breach or breaches, for example whether it was an isolated incident or continued over a period and, importantly, the defendant's resources and the effect of the fine on its business. Particular aggravating features will include (1) a failure to heed warnings and (2) where the defendant has deliberately profited financially from a failure to take necessary health and safety steps or specifically run a risk to save money. Particular mitigating features will include (1) prompt admission of responsibility and a timely plea of guilty, (2) steps to remedy deficiencies after they are drawn to the defendants attention and (3) a good safety record.

The objective of prosecutions is to achieve a safe environment for those who work there and for others who may be affected. A fine needs to be large enough to bring that message home where the defendant is a company not only to those who manage it but also to its shareholders. The level of fines imposed generally for offences of this nature are too low.

R v Colthrop Board Mills Ltd [2002] EWCA Crim 520, [2002] 2 Cr App Rep (S) 359. The company pleaded guilty to an offence under the Health and Safety at Work etc Act 1974, s 2(1) and the Provision and Use of Work Equipment Regulations 1974, reg 11. An experienced charge-hand either slipped or became entangled in a machine. His arm was passed or pulled through a join and he received a serious crush injury to his hand and arm. He was in hospital for 4 weeks. The company discontinued trading and realised assets of about £17m. Held. Companies like this can expect to receive penalties up to at least £½ m for serious defaults and proportionately lesser sums if the limitation upon means or some lesser blame justifies it. The £½m figure should not be seen a maximum. As time goes on and awareness of the importance of safety increases, the courts will uphold sums of that amount and even in excess of them in serious cases, whether or not they involve what could be described as major public disasters.

Magistrates' Court Sentencing Guidelines September 2000

83.4   It is important to seek guidance from the clerk in all these serious cases. Matters to consider when assessing seriousness include: (1) offence deliberate breach of the law rather than carelessness; (2) financial motive – profit or cost-saving or neglecting to put in place preventative measures or avoiding payment for relevant licence; (3) considerable potential for harm to workers or public; (4) regular or continuing breach, not isolated lapse; (5) failure to respond to advice, cautions or warning from regulatory authority; (6) death or serious injury or ill-health has been a consequence of the offence; (7) ignoring concerns raised by employees or others; (8) having knowledge of risks, but ignoring them; (9) previous offences; (10) extent of damage and cost of rectifying it; (11) attitude to the enforcing authorities and (12) offending pattern. When computing penalties for a company look at net turnover. 'Costs: follow event'. Consider the fine first and then the costs.

Magistrates' Court Sentencing Guidelines amendment June 2001

83.5   Defendants in such cases are frequently companies with huge annual turnovers. Our aim should be for any fine to have an equal impact on rich and poor. Financial penalties must relate to the companies' means and we should accustom ourselves, in appropriate cases, to imposing far greater financial penalties than have been generally imposed in the past. In 1998, the Lord Chancellor spoke to the Magistrates' Association about the disquiet being expressed about the level of sentences for these offences. He particularly suggested the maximum penalties were there to be used in appropriate cases. He said, 'You should not flinch from using them if you believe that they are deserved.'

Basis for sentence, there must be a proper

83.6   *R v Friskies Petcare (UK) Ltd* [2000] 2 Cr App Rep (S) 401. Problems can arise when there is a dispute about whether the court sentenced the defendant on the basis on which the case was presented. This case illustrates the problem. The Health and Safety Executive should list in writing not merely the facts of the case but the aggravating features as set out in *R v F Howe & Son (Engineers) Ltd* [1999] 2 Cr App

Rep (S) 37. It should be served and the defence should set out in writing the mitigating features. If there is an agreed basis it should be in writing.

Costs

83.7   *R v F Howe & Son (Engineers) Ltd* [1999] 2 Cr App Rep (S) 37. The power to award costs is contained in s 18(1) of the Prosecution of Offences Act 1985 and permits an order that the defendant pay to the prosecutor such costs as are just and reasonable. This includes the cost of the prosecuting authority carrying out investigations with a view to prosecution, see *R v Associated Octel Ltd* [1997] 1 Cr App Rep (S) 435. Sometimes costs awarded have been scaled down so as not to exceed the fine. Neither the fines nor the costs are deductible against tax and therefore the full burden falls upon the company.

Magistrates' Guidelines amendment June 2001: The enforcing authorities' costs should be fully recouped from the offender. The order for costs should not be disproportionate to the level of the fine imposed. The court should fix the level of the fine first, then consider awarding compensation, and then determine the costs. If the total exceeds the defendants' means, the order for costs should be reduced rather than the fine. Compensation should always take priority over both the fine and costs.

Death is caused

83.8   *R v Hall and Co Ltd* [1999] 1 Cr App Rep (S) 306. The company pleaded guilty to an offence under the Health and Safety at Work etc Act 1974, 2(2) at the Magistrates' Court. At the company's builder's' yard an employee was helping to load a lorry. The lorry reversed, ran over him and killed him. The injuries were very serious. The following failures were identified: (1) the vehicle could not be reversed without danger to pedestrians; (2) there were no fixed mirrors to assist drivers to see round blind corners; (3) the vehicle had no reversing alarm; (4) the procedure for lookouts was regularly flouted. On the day there were none; (5) there was no proper risk assessment as required by reg 3 of the Management of Health and Safety at Work Regulations 1992. Six months before the incident the company was fined £750 for another s 2 breach but the circumstances were far removed from this case. The company was part of the Ready Mix Group of companies. The defendant's turnover was £180m and the parent company's turnover was £4 billion. The judge said the failures created an obvious risk to the safety of employees. Held. That risk necessarily encompassed the risk of a fatal accident. A severe penalty was required. £150,000 was a proper fine.

R v F Howe & Son (Engineers) Ltd [1999] 2 Cr App Rep (S) 37. It is often a matter of chance whether death or serious injury results from even a serious breach. Generally where death is the consequence of a criminal act it is regarded as an aggravating feature of the offence. The penalty should reflect public disquiet at the unnecessary loss of life.

R v Rimac Ltd [2000] 1 Cr App Rep (S) 468. The company pleaded guilty to an offence under the Health and Safety at Work etc Act 1974, s 2 at the Magistrates' Court. The victim a 19-year-old trainee who was asked to move some plastic piping in an area which was used for storage. He fell through a suspended ceiling onto the floor 9 feet below. He died 2 days later of head injuries. The area was not load bearing. The only safe way to cross the ceiling was to use crawling boards. No verbal instructions of any kind were given on how he should do the task. There was no real recognition of this being a hazardous area despite access to it being easy. No warnings were displayed. The use of the area as a storage area may well have misled someone into believing that it was in fact load bearing. There was no supervision of the deceased. The company was **fined £60,000** (payable in four quarterly instalments) and ordered to pay

£9,723 costs. Held. The risk was obvious, foreseeable and continuing. The penalty should reflect the public disquiet at the unnecessary loss of life. The mitigating factors were: (1) prompt admission of responsibility; (2) the good safety record of the company: and (3) steps had been promptly taken to remedy the deficiency. The accounts show the company can well afford both the fine and the costs. A fine needs to be large enough to bring the message home not only to those that manage it but also to its shareholders. The fine and costs were right.

R v Friskies Petcare (UK) Ltd [2000] 2 Cr App Rep (S) 401. The company pleaded guilty to an offence under the Health and Safety at Work etc Act 1974, s 2(1) at the Magistrates' Court. The company was a large manufacturing concern producing cat food. A company welder and process technician went into a silo in which the meat was mixed by metal stirrers to repair a stirrer. The welder was wearing steel toe capped boots and was connected to an electric arc welding unit. The welder remained still and the technician realised he was undergoing an electric shock. The technician had to go 30 metres up a ladder, along a gantry and through a locked gate to turn the power off. The welder died of electrocution in a damp environment. The inspector concluded that the victim came into contact with the exposed and live parts of the welding electrode holder and/or the welding electrode itself while in contact with the metal silo creating a complete electrical circuit. The clothing did not provide sufficient resistance. The power point was too far away. The breaches had been going on for some time and no-one's attention was drawn to the Health and Safety pamphlets about welding. There was no system in place, which alerted the technicians to the risks. No steps were taken to avoid the risks. The inspector said it was well known in the trade that those circumstances were potentially dangerous. The company disputed this. There was a prompt admission of responsibility, steps were taken to remedy the deficiencies and the company had a good safety record. The company's pre-tax profits were some £40m. The judge said the company had put profit before safety. The defence said in mitigation that this wasn't the case and no one questioned that assertion at the time. After the sentence the prosecution wrote saying that was not their case. Held. Reported cases show that fines in excess of £½m tend to be reserved for cases where a major public disaster occurs eg the collapse of the Heathrow railway tunnel – that is to say where the breaches put large numbers of people at risk of serious injury or more. A fine of £425,000 was imposed on a major retail company when the trial judge said that the working practices dated back to the dark ages and safety was sacrificed for profit. This case was in neither of those categories. We agree with the judge's description that the defendants fell a long way short of doing what was reasonable and practical. Applying *R v F Howe & Son (Engineers) Ltd* [1999] 2 Cr App Rep (S) 37, **£250,000 fine** not £600,000.

R v Keltbray Ltd [2001] 1 Cr App Rep (S) 132. The company pleaded guilty to Health and Safety at Work etc Act 1974, s 2(1). It was based on breaches of Construction (Health, Safety and Welfare) Regulations 1996. The company was demolishing a building. Two workmen were cutting a well hole and a floor slab on the eighth floor collapsed. They fell and died. Before the work started there had been written risk assessments. A dangerous method was used to do the cut on the eighth floor. The workman chose a quicker method than the one planned. They were being paid on the basis of a full day's work even if they managed to finish early. This was approved by the ganger even though the company did not approve it. There was no harness or other protection provided. No foreman was supervising contrary to the risk assessment. After the accident procedures were altered. The company had an excellent work record for demolition. They had no convictions and were not the subject of any complaints from the Health and Safety Executive. It had won awards. The company made profits of £191,000 in 1997 and £211,000 in 1998. The company was ordered to pay

£8,037.87 costs. Held. This potentially dangerous operation requires firm supervision. A highly dangerous operation was permitted. Harnesses which were the fall back means of safety were not present. The **£200,000 fine** was appropriate.

R v Aceblade Ltd [2001] 1 Cr App Rep (S) 366. The company pleaded guilty to failing to ensure the health and safety of an employee. The victim was lifting a piece of stone on his crane and the crane fell over. The driver's cab was crushed and he was killed. A warning device had been bypassed a few weeks before the accident. The directors did not know this. The tyres were under-inflated which contributed to the instability. The crane had been inspected a month before when it was working properly. There was no proactive system for the inspection of the crane. There was a prompt admission of responsibility and a timely plea. Steps were made to remedy the deficiencies and the company had a good safety record. In 1999 the company profit was £113,608 and in 2000 there was a £7,901 loss. Legal expenses in this case, health and safety spending and investment had contributed to the fall. The directors' remuneration remained the same. The accountants said the cost of the accident was about £134,000 including loss of production. They were **fined £20,000** with £6,648.98 legal costs and £15,000 health and safety costs. The fine was payable over 42 months. Held. The payment period was not too long. The penalties were entirely justified.

Death is caused – not directly attributable to the breach

83.9   *R v Cardiff City Transport Services* [2001] 1 Cr App Rep (S) 141. The company pleaded guilty to an offence under the Health and Safety at Work Act etc 1974, s 2 at the Magistrates' Court. On a Sunday, at the company's bus depot an employee moved a bus into an allocated space. He ran off the bus and was knocked to the ground by another bus, which was travelling at the regulation 10 mph. The other driver had no opportunity to avoid him. The victim struck his head on the ground and died shortly after. The Health and Safety inspectors concluded that there was no risk assessment for pedestrians and vehicle movements. There were three specific failings: (1) the bus was travelling the wrong way in the one way system. The one way system was not enforced at all times, as Sunday was seen as an exception; (2) high visibility clothing was needed for those engaged in moving vehicles round the depot; (3) the speed limit should not have been increased from 5 to 10 mph. The prosecution accepted that there was no causal link between the death and the breaches. The death did however highlight the unsafe system and increase the risk of the type of collision, which in fact occurred. The basis of plea was that the company had failed make the risk assessment about pedestrians and vehicles, failed to identify the need for high visibility clothing and failed to enforce the one way system. The company had a good safety record and had no convictions. It had always co-operated with the Health and Safety Inspectorate. The company profits were between £300,000 and £½m in the previous 3 years. The failings were not connected with increasing profit. Held. It is essential that employers are made acutely aware of the need to ensure the highest possible standards. However, the company had behaved very responsibly since the accident. No one had suggested high visibility clothing before the accident. The change of speed limit was after they had consulted an expert. Had the death been caused by the breaches a fine of considerably more than £75,000 would have been appropriate. **£40,000 fine** not £75,000.

Directors etc

83.10   Health and Safety at Work etc Act 1974, s 37. Power to convict director etc who consent, connive etc to an offence committed by a body corporate.

R v Davies [1999] 2 Cr App Rep (S) 356. he defendant was a director and pleaded guilty to neglecting his duty under the Health and Safety at Work etc Act

1974, s 2(1). His company and two other companies also pleaded guilty to breaching their duties. His company made plastic cases. The process created heat, which was dispelled in a cooling tower. That created the risk of legionnaires' disease. In an earlier incident at another plant the production manager caught the disease and died. As a result that company went into liquidation. It was not suggested that was the fault of the defendant. The defendant then became the director of the new company. Neither he nor the person responsible for the cleaning of the towers had any knowledge of the regulations or the guidelines for cleaning the towers. The system was shut down over Christmas for 11 days when it remained stagnant. One of the defendants, a cleaning company wrote in a survey 8 years before of the problem of bacteria which was present and chlorination but pointing out the cost of having the towers shut down for a full clean. They were regular inspections and chlorination but no actual cleaning. The defendant said he was relying on the cleaning company, as neither he nor anyone from his company were experts. The basis of the plea was that the defendant believed he had taken all the necessary steps and the system was being properly supervised by the cleaning company. The only neglect was his failure to ensure that their company's employer who was responsible for the cleaning went on a course. His ability to pay was not in question. The defendant was bought into the proceedings at a late stage and argued that he should not be responsible for the costs before he was a defendant. The cleaning company was fined £15,000 and he and his company was fined £25,000. Held. The primary responsibility must remain with the employers. It is not adequate to simply transfer it to an expert third party. At all stages the employer must supervise the independent contractor rather than the independent contractor supervise the employer. They must carry the greater responsibility. Because of the basis of plea **£15,000 fine** not £25,000. At whatever stage the defendant was brought in costs would have been incurred and the defendant must pick up his share of the responsibility for those costs. £10,000 costs order for him upheld.

Directors and small companies both prosecuted. Avoid double punishment

83.11   *R v Rollco Screw and Rivet Co Ltd* [1999] 2 Cr App Rep (S) 436 – LCJ. The defendant company and two of its directors who were father and son pleaded guilty to failing to ensure the health and safety of employees and persons other than their employees. The defendants were prosecuted for stripping out asbestos in breach of the regulations and exposing employees and others to risks. The father was in charge of the contractual arrangements. The son was considered the father's lieutenant and did not fully appreciate the risks. The total fines and costs for the company was £40,000 fine and £30,000 costs. The father was fined £6,000 and £2,000 costs. The son was fined £4,000 and £2,000 costs. Held. In a small company the directors are likely to be the shareholders and therefore the main losers if a severe sanction is imposed on the company. One must avoid a risk of overlap and must not impose double punishment. On the other hand it is important that fines should be imposed which make it clear that there is a personal responsibility on directors and they cannot simply palm off their responsibilities to the corporation of which they are directors. The proper approach is to answer two questions. First, what financial penalty does the offence merit? Secondly, what financial penalty can a defendant, whether corporate or personal reasonably be ordered to meet? Addressing the first question the total fine for the company and the directors was £50,000. In considering that question we have to bear in mind the glaring public need for effective sanctions where the health and safety of the public are so obviously at risk. The situation is the more important when, as here, the ill-effects of exposure to brown asbestos may take many years to appear. In the interim of course no individual can know whether he will ultimately suffer or not. The division of £40,000 and £10,000 was an appropriate split. The total sum divided between the two was an appropriate recognition of the gravity of this offending. The directors' appeal was dismissed. The fine on the company was reduced on other grounds.

Employees etc partly/fully to blame

83.12   *R v Patchett Engineering Ltd* [2001] 1 Cr App Rep (S) 138. The company pleaded guilty to Health and Safety at Work etc Act 1974, s 2(1). The company supplied an egg collecting machine to a farm. A young worker who was collecting eggs caught his jacket in the machine and was found suspended from a drive shaft. The clothing had tightened round his neck and he was strangled. The worker must have climbed up the frame of the cage to reach the position where his clothing was caught. The likely explanation was that he noticed the top tier tray was not in place and he climbed up to let it down without turning the machine off. The defence argued that there was no need for the worker to act in the unorthodox way he did and it was not foreseeable. The judge rejected this. Held. The judge was right. Workers will take short cuts and not follow proper practices. The need to guard the shaft should have been apparent. When it was designed someone should have considered operatives do on occasions take short cuts. The statutory duty has as one of its objects, the protection of workers who may be neglectful of their own safety in a way, which should be anticipated.

Health and Safety at Work etc Act 1974, ss 2(1), 33(1) and (1A)

83.13   Failing to discharge the duty to ensure the health, safety and welfare of the employees

Triable either way. On indictment maximum sentence unlimited fine. Summary maximum £20,000. For offences against ss 33(1)(g) or (o) the maximum on indictment includes 2 years and the summary maximum includes 6 months imprisonment.

(The cases are broken up into financial groups to assist but many state principles, which apply to all the groups)

Less than £50,000 fine

83.14   *R v F Howe & Son (Engineers) Ltd* [1999] 2 Cr App Rep (S) 37. The company pleaded guilty to (1) an offence under the Health and Safety at Work etc Act 1974, s 2(1), (2) failing to maintain an electric cable to a machine under reg 4(2) of the Electricity at Work Regulations 1989, (3) failing to make a suitable and sufficient assessment of the risks of the electric cable to the machine, contrary to reg 3 of the Management of Health and Safety at Work Regulations 1992, and (4) failing under reg 11 of the Electricity at Work Regulations 1989 to ensure that means were provided to protect the electrical system supplying the machine from excess current. A 20-year-old employee of the company was electrocuted when he was cleaning the factory when it was shut down for that purpose. A cable to a machine called Freddy was damaged and the machine became 'live' and the boy was unable to let go. The damage to the cable was consistent with the cable having been crushed by a heavy load. The socket into which the 15 amp cable had been plugged was fitted with 32 amp fuses, which had been subsequently bridged by fuse wire. There was a circuit breaker called an RCD that had been deliberately interfered with so it was inoperable. A Health and Safety Inspector found in a number of instances that someone had tried to install contactors but the piece of equipment was not working and he had to rectify it. A fitter had advised the company both orally and in writing that they were overloading the electrical supply. The fitter was never asked to look at Freddy. The judge sentenced on the basis that the company's employees did not themselves interfere with the RCD. There was 13 months between the installation of the RCD and the accident. During this time the company made no effort to check the RCD or indeed even to check whether the test button was operating. The test button could have been pressed at any time and would have revealed that the device was not working. Good practice dictated that it should have been checked every 3 months. The company was a small precision engineering company then with 12 employees. It is now 10. The company accounts reveal that for 1996–7 the annual turnover was £355,000 and the net profit after tax was £26,969 and the net book value of the company was £129,288 but this included £68,227 in respect of assets held under finance leases and hire purchase contracts. The company did not pay any dividends and retained its annual profit in order to finance improvements and acquire further machinery. Neither of the working directors received an income in excess of £20,000 per annum. There was no pension scheme and no company car. Following the accident the company spent £15,000 on a complete overhaul of its electrical system. The company had no previous convictions nor has it received warnings from the Health and Safety Executive. Held. The company had no system at all for checking its electrical equipment. The fatality was an accident waiting to happen. This was a bad case and the electrical state of the equipment was appalling. There appears to have been a flagrant disregard for the safety of the company's employees. Corners were cut and no real attention was paid to electrical safety. The judge gave inadequate weight to the financial position of the company maybe because such financial information as he had was not supplied until the very last moment. This is a small company with limited resources. The appropriate fine was one totalling **£15,000** on count one of the indictment with no separate penalty in respect of the other offences not £48,000 in all. There was no reason to scale down the £7,500 costs when the prosecutor's total costs exceeded £12,000.

R v Cappagh Public Works Ltd [1999] 2 Cr App Rep (S) 301. he company pleaded guilty to failing to discharge its duty under Health and Safety at Work etc Act 1974, s 2(1). An employee was cleaning a concrete crushing machine. Safety guards to prevent access to the crushing part had not been fitted and were lying derelict some 50 yards away. The supervisor told him to turn the machine on. The employee was drawn into the machine some way and was crushed to death. The judge took into account the good safety record of the company but said the facts were extremely disturbing. The company's profits for 1996–7 were £150,000. Held. The 'judge's approach was proper and there was no basis to say the **£40,000** fine was excessive.

R v Rollco Screw and Rivet Co Ltd [1999] 2 Cr App Rep (S) 436 – LCJ. The defendant company and two of its directors who were father and son pleaded guilty to failing to ensure the health and safety of employees and persons other than their employees, [Section 2(1) and 3(1)]. The company employed 12 or more employees in the manufacture of screws and rivets. Both directors were keen that the roof, which was in poor condition, should be repaired and knew it contained asbestos. The company contracted two co-defendants from another company to remove the brown asbestos from the roof. Brown asbestos is the most dangerous of all kinds of asbestos and requires the greatest care in handling. An asbestos worker, Mr Evans contracted with the two co-defendants to remove the asbestos. None of them possessed an asbestos licence. A vehicle hired by Mr Evans was seen unloading bags of asbestos at a number of unauthorised sites. An investigation took place. That discovered that the asbestos was removed with inadequate equipment, with an absence of air locks, effective masks and protective clothing. Asbestos was disseminated over the factory premises. 200–300 bags had been fly-tipped. Children had taken an interest in some of them. During the work father and son visited the premises regularly. When the work was finished employees were directed to clear up the mess. The son organised this. The father was in charge of the contractual arrangements. The son was considered the father's lieutenant and did not fully appreciate the risks. The company's profits were £51,000 in 1994–5, £24,000 in 1995–6 and £33,000 in 1996–7. There was a loss of

£122,000 in 1997–8 which attributable in part to roof costs, fines, court costs and legal fees. A modest profit was expected in 1998–9. The total fines and costs for the company was **£40,000 fine** and £30,000 costs. The father was fined **£6,000** and £2,000 costs. The son was fined **£4,000** and £2,000 costs. Held. We give the guidelines in *R v F Howe & Son (Engineers) Ltd* [1999] 2 Cr App Rep (S) 37 our unqualified support. The proper approach is to answer two questions. First, what financial penalty does the offence merit? Secondly, what financial penalty can a defendant, whether corporate or personal reasonably be ordered to meet? Addressing the first question the total fine for the company and the directors was £50,000. In considering that question we have to bear in mind the glaring public need for effective sanctions where the health and safety of the public are so obviously at risk. The situation is the more important when, as here, the ill-effects of exposure to brown asbestos may take many years to appear. In the interim of course no individual can know whether he will ultimately suffer or not. The division of £40,000 and £10,000 was an appropriate split. The total sum divided between the two was an appropriate recognition of the gravity of this offending. We are not persuaded there was disparity between the father and son and the contractors on the other hand because the judge made it plain that the business of the contractors had plummeted and that the fines on the two contractors would have been very much greater had that not been so. We are not satisfied that the fine for the son who is relatively young with commitments and a young child is one he can't pay. The directors' appeal was dismissed. The company's costs were reduced to £20,000 because the period of payment over 6 years 5 months was too long a period.

R v Cardiff City Transport Services [2001] 1 Cr App Rep (S) 141. The company pleaded guilty to an offence under the Health and Safety at Work etc Act 1974, s 2 at the Magistrates' Court. On a Sunday, at the company's bus depot an employee moved a bus into an allocated space. He ran off the bus and was knocked to the ground by another bus, which was travelling at the regulation 10 mph. The other driver had no opportunity to avoid him. The victim struck his head on the ground and died shortly after. The Health and Safety inspectors concluded that there was no risk assessment for pedestrians and vehicle movements. There were three specific failings: (1) the bus was travelling the wrong way in the one-way system. The one-way system was not enforced at all times, as Sunday was seen as an exception; (2) high visibility clothing was needed for those engaged in moving vehicles round the depot; (3) the speed limit should not have been increased from 5 to 10 mph. The prosecution accepted that there was no causal link between the death and the breaches. The death did, however, highlight the unsafe system and increase the risk of the type of collision, which in fact occurred. The basis of the plea was that the company had failed make the risk assessment about pedestrians and vehicles, failed to identify the need for high visibility clothing and failed to enforce the one way system. The company had a good safety record and had no convictions. It had always co-operated with the Health and Safety Inspectorate. The company profits were between £300,000 and £½m in the previous 3 years. The failings were not connected with increasing profit. Held. It is essential that employers are made acutely aware of the need to ensure the highest possible standards. However, the company had behaved very responsibly since the accident. No one had suggested high visibility clothing before the accident. The change of speed limit was after they had consulted an expert. Had the death been caused by the breaches a fine of considerably more than £75,000 would have been appropriate. **£40,000 fine** not £75,000.

£50,000 to £100,000 fine

83.15 *R v Firth Vickers Centrispinning Ltd* [1998] 1 Cr App Rep (S) 293. The defendant company pleaded guilty to failing to ensure the health and safety of employees from 1 to 3 November 1995. Failure to maintain plant and provide safe systems of work were particularised. The firm had a foundry employing about 300 people. On 2 November 1995 the foundry was making a ring which was heavier than anything cast before. Two tons of molten metal at 1,500°C was poured into a mould and some escaped. It sprayed out in a jet and four men were caught. Three received substantial injuries. One received 40% burns and was in hospital for 10 weeks. He will probably not return to work. Another was in hospital for 6 nights. The machine was designed to hold 5 tons. The Health and Safety report said parts had become worn and the accident was caused by the top plate, which was inadequately retained by enough and strong enough pins. The top plate and the side wall were found to be distorted. There was no effective seal. The company overhauled their whole safety procedures with a new officer audits and training etc. That cost £60,000. A new managing director was appointed. An employee had been burnt in a fault on a different machine in 1993. For that the company was fined £10,000. It also involved the spray of molten metal. There was another incident in April 1994 when no one was injured. Two employees were splashed in September 1994. That incident was not reported to the Health and Safety Executive. In 1994–5 employees expressed their concerns about the ejection of molten metal. Throughout 1995 the employee that was most seriously injured who was also splashed in 1994 complained about the unrepaired top plate. On the day of the offence that employee had made requests about the steel plate. Those requests were ignored. The company was fined £100,000 and ordered to pay £6,600 costs. It was suggested the judge gave undue weight to the earlier incidents and requests. Held. The previous incidents are very relevant for they showed that no proper re-assessment of the risks was made in due time. Potentially this machinery could cause very serious injuries and yet its guarding was known to be defective. The relatively modest cost of the guard eventually fitted underlined the company's failure to take any proper care in this hazardous employment. The judge had properly considered the history to see if it was an isolated oversight or indicative of something greater. The history was relevant in considering their inactivity. It was a serious case. The criminality was not wrongly inflated. The fine was upheld.

More than £100,000 to £½m fine

83.16   *R v Hall & Co Ltd* [1999] 1 Cr App Rep (S) 306. The company pleaded guilty to an offence under the Health and Safety at Work etc Act 1974, s 2(2) at the Magistrates' Court. At the company's builder's yard an employee was helping to load a lorry. The lorry reversed, ran over him and killed him. The injuries were very serious. The following failures were identified: (1) the vehicle could not be reversed without danger to pedestrians; (2) there were no fixed mirrors to assist drivers to see round blind corners; (3) the vehicle had no reversing alarm; (4) the procedure for lookouts was regularly flouted. On the day there were none; (5) there was no proper risk assessment as required by reg 3 of the Management of Health and Safety at Work Regulations 1992. Six months before the incident the company was fined £750 to another s 2 breach but the circumstances were far removed from this case. The company was part of the Ready Mix Group of companies. The defendant's turnover was £180m and the parent company's turnover was £4 billion. The judge said the failures created an obvious risk to the safety of employees. Held. That risk necessarily encompassed the risk of a fatal accident. A severe penalty was required. £150,000 was a proper fine.

R v Friskies Petcare (UK) Ltd [2000] 2 Cr App Rep (S) 401. The company pleaded guilty to an offence under the Health and Safety at Work etc Act 1974, s 2(1) at the Magistrates' Court. The company was a large manufacturing concern producing cat food. A company welder and process technician went into a silo in which the meat was mixed by metal stirrers to repair a stirrer. The welder was wearing steel-toe capped boots and was connected to an electric arc welding unit. The welder remained still and the technician realised he was undergoing an electric shock. The technician had to go 30 metres up a ladder, along a gantry and through a locked gate to turn the power off. The welder died of electrocution in a damp environment. The inspector concluded that the victim came into contact with the exposed and live parts of the welding electrode holder and/or the welding electrode itself while in contact with the metal silo creating a complete electrical circuit. The clothing did not provide sufficient resistance. The power point was too far away. The breaches had been going on for some time and no-one's attention was drawn to the Health and Safety pamphlets about welding. There was no system in place, which alerted the technicians to the risks. No steps were taken to avoid the risks. The inspector said it was well known in the trade that those circumstances were potentially dangerous. The company disputed this. There was a prompt admission of responsibility, steps were taken to remedy the deficiencies and the company had a good safety record. The company's pre-tax profits were some £40m. The judge said the company had put profit before safety. The defence said in mitigation that this wasn't the case and no one questioned that assertion at the time. After the sentence the prosecution wrote saying that was not their case. Held. Reported cases show that fines in excess of £½m tend to be reserved for cases where a major public disaster occurs eg the collapse of the Heathrow railway tunnel – that is to say where the breaches put large numbers of people at risk of serious injury or more. A fine of £425,000 was imposed on a major retail company when the trial judge said that the working practices dated back to the dark ages and safety was sacrificed for profit. This case was in neither of those categories. We agree with the judge's description that the defendants fell a long way short of doing what was reasonable and practical. Applying *R v F Howe & Son (Engineers) Ltd* [1999] 2 Cr App Rep (S) 37 **£250,000 fine** not £600,000.

R v Colthrop Board Mills Ltd [2002] EWCA Crim 520, [2002] 2 Cr App Rep (S) 359. The company pleaded guilty to an offence under the Health and Safety at Work etc Act 1974 , s 2(1) and the Provision and Use of Work Equipment Regulations 1974, reg 11. The company produced carton board on a very large machine. In 1999 a Health and Safety inspector visited the factory and issued an improvement notice requiring the company to carry out a risk assessment. The inspector identified employees accessing dangerous areas of machinery to carry out cleaning and maintenance work as particular problems and asked for action without delay. The company's risk assessment which took place after a delay and a successful application for an extension of time found the joins between the rollers in the machine as carrying a substantial risk of death or serious injury to an employee in the event of an accident. The gravity of the injury was assessed as 'at its highest' and the likelihood of an accident as 'moderate'. No remedial steps were taken. An experienced charge-hand leant through the handrails of the machine and he either slipped or became entangled in the machine. His arm was passed or pulled through a join and he received a serious crush injury to his hand and arm. Several bones were broken in the hand, there were friction bones to the shoulder and back and a deep cut to his palm. He was in hospital for 4 weeks. After the accident the danger was removed promptly, simply and inexpensively. The company discontinued trading and realised assets of about £17m. In about 40 years the joins in the machine must have been cleaned about 126,000 times without accident. In 1994 the company had a s 2(1) conviction when a hand had been drawn into another join on another machine. It was fined £6,500. In 1995 there was a conviction under the Factories Act 1961, s 14(1) for an accident when another employee was drawn into another join on another machine. The fine was £3,000 with £1,000 costs. Held. Companies like this can expect to receive penalties up to at least £½m for serious defaults and proportionately lesser sums if the limitation upon means or some lesser blame justifies it. The £½m figure should not be seen a maximum. **£200,000** not £350,000 fine in total with £5,000 costs unaltered.

R v Keltbray Ltd [2001] 1 Cr App Rep (S) 132. The company pleaded guilty to an offence under the Health and Safety at Work etc Act 1974, s 2(1). It was based on breaches of Construction (Health, Safety and Welfare) Regulations 1996. The company was demolishing a building. Two workmen were cutting a well hole and a floor slab on the eighth floor collapsed. They fell and died. Before the work started there had been written risk assessments. A dangerous method was used to do the cut on the eighth floor. The workman chose a quicker method than the one planned. They were being paid on the basis of a full day's work even if they managed to finish early. This was approved by the ganger even though the company did not approve it. There was no harness or other protection provided. No foreman was supervising contrary to the risk assessment. After the accident procedures were altered. The company had an excellent work record for demolition. They had no convictions and were not the subject of any complaints from the Health and Safety Executive. It had won awards. The company made profits of £191,000 in 1997 and £211,000 in 1998. The company was ordered to pay £8,037.87 costs. Held. This potentially dangerous operation requires firm supervision. A highly dangerous operation was permitted. Harnesses which were the fall back means of safety were not present. The **£200,000 fine** was appropriate.

83.17

Health and Safety at Work etc Act 1974, ss 3(1) and 33(1)(a) and (1A)

Failing to discharge the duty to ensure the health, safety and welfare of persons other than employees.

Triable either way. On indictment maximum sentence unlimited fine. Summary maximum £20,000. For offences against ss 33(1)(g) or (o) the maximum on indictment includes 2 years and the summary maximum includes 6 months.

R v Rollco Screw and Rivet Co Ltd [1999] 2 Cr App Rep (S) 436 – LCJ. The defendant company and two of its directors who were father and son pleaded guilty to failing to ensure the health and safety of employees and persons other than their employees, [s 2(1) and 3(1)]. The company employed 12 or more employees in the manufacture of screws and rivets. Both directors were keen that the roof, which was in poor condition, should be repaired and knew it contained asbestos. The company contracted two co-defendants from another company to remove the brown asbestos from the roof. Brown asbestos is the most dangerous of all kinds of asbestos and requires the greatest care in handling. An asbestos worker, Mr Evans contracted with the two co-defendants to remove the asbestos. None of them possessed an asbestos licence. A vehicle hired by Mr Evans was seen unloading bags of asbestos at a number of unauthorised sites. An investigation took place. That discovered that the asbestos was removed with inadequate equipment, with an absence of air locks, effective masks and protective clothing. Asbestos was disseminated over the factory premises. 200–300 bags had been fly-tipped. Children had taken an interest in some of them. During the work father and son visited the premises regularly. When the work was finished employees were directed to clear up the mess. The son organised this. The father was in charge of the contractual arrangements. The son was considered the father's lieutenant and did not fully appreciate the risks. The company's profits were £51,000 in 1994–5, £24,000 in 1995–6 and £33,000 in 1996–7. There was a loss of £122,000 in 1997–8 which attributable in part to roof costs, fines, court costs and legal fees. A modest profit was expected in 1998–9. The total fines and costs for the company was **£40,000 fine** and £30,000 costs. The father was fined **£6,000** and £2,000 costs. The son was fined

£4,000 and £2,000 costs. Held. We give the guidelines in *R v F Howe & Son (Engineers) Ltd* [1999] 2 Cr App Rep (S) 37 our unqualified support. The proper approach is to answer two questions. First, what financial penalty does the offence merit? Secondly, what financial penalty can a defendant, whether corporate or personal reasonably be ordered to meet? Addressing the first question the total fine for the company and the directors was £50,000. In considering that question we have to bear in mind the glaring public need for effective sanctions where the health and safety of the public are so obviously at risk. The situation is the more important when, as here, the ill-effects of exposure to brown asbestos may take many years to appear. In the interim of course no individual can know whether he will ultimately suffer or not. The division of £40,000 and £10,000 was an appropriate split. The total sum divided between the two was an appropriate recognition of the gravity of this offending. We are not persuaded there was disparity between the father and son and the contractors on the other hand because the judge made it plain that the business of the contractors had plummeted and that the fines on the two contractors would have been very much greater had that not been so. We are not satisfied that the fine for the son who is relatively young with commitments and a young child is one he can't pay. The directors' appeal was dismissed. The company's costs were reduced to £20,000 because the period of payment over 6 years 5 months was too long a period.

Instalments, paying fines etc by

83.18 *R v Olliver and Olliver* (1989) 11 Cr App Rep (S) 10 – LCJ. There is nothing wrong in principle for the period of payment (for a fine) being longer than a year providing it is not an undue burden and so too severe a punishment having regard to the offence and the nature of the offender. A 2 year period will seldom be too long and in an appropriate case 3 years will be unassailable. Every effort is required to find alternatives to custodial sentences.

R v Rollco Screw and Rivet Co Ltd [1999] 2 Cr App Rep (S) 436 – LCJ. The defendant company and two of its directors who were father and son pleaded guilty to failing to ensure the health and safety of employees and persons other than their employees, [s 2(1) and 3(1)]. The defendants were prosecuted for stripping out asbestos in breach of the regulations and exposing employees and others to risks. The father was in charge of the contractual arrangements. The son was considered the father's lieutenant and did not fully appreciate the risks. The total fines and costs for the company was £40,000 fine and £30,000 costs, (£5,000 within a year and the rest at £1,000 a month). The father was fined £6,000 and £2,000 costs, (£1,000 a month). The son was fined £4,000 and £2,000 costs. Held. Reminding ourselves of *R v Olliver and Olliver* (1989) 11 Cr App Rep (S) 10 the court was at pains to avoid stipulating any period which should not be exceeded. With a personal defendant there are arguments for keeping the period within bounds. Those arguments are much weaker, if indeed they apply at all when one is considering a corporate defendant. There is not the same anxiety as is liable to afflict an individual and it is acceptable for a fine to be payable by a company over a substantially longer period than might be appropriate for an individual. It is not necessarily a more severe course to order a larger sum over a longer period than a smaller sum over a shorter period, since the former course may give the company a greater opportunity to control its cash flow and survive difficult trading conditions. If it wants the company can pay the sums sooner than it need. This period of payment over 6 years 5 months was excessive. Because of that the fine is reduced to £20,000 so the payment period is **5 years and 7 months** which is an appropriate payment period.

R v Aceblade Ltd [2001] 1 Cr App Rep (S) 366. The company pleaded guilty to failing to ensure the health and safety of an employee. They were fined £20,000 with £15,000 costs. The fine was payable over **42 months**. Held. The payment period was not too long

Magistrates' accepting jurisdiction

83.19 *R v F Howe & Son (Engineers) Ltd* [1999] 2 Cr App Rep (S) 37. Magistrates should always think carefully before accepting jurisdiction in health and safety at work cases, where it is arguable that the fine may exceed the limit of their jurisdiction or where death or serious injury has resulted from the offence. [This guidance is repeated in the Magistrates' Guidelines.]

Means, the defendant/company

83.20 Magistrates' Court Sentencing Guidelines amendment June 2001

Defendants in such cases are frequently companies with huge annual turnovers. Our aim should be for any fine to have an equal impact on rich and poor. Financial penalties must relate to the companies' means and we should accustom ourselves, in appropriate cases, to imposing far greater financial penalties than have been generally imposed in the past. In 1998, the Lord Chancellor spoke to the Magistrates' Association about the disquiet being expressed about the level of sentences for these offences. He particularly suggested the maximum penalties were there to be used in appropriate cases. He said, 'You should not flinch from using them if you believe that they are deserved.' In all cases with corporate offenders the company's financial circumstances must be carefully considered. No single measure of ability to pay can apply in all cases. Turnover, profitability and liquidity should all be considered. It is not unusual for an expert accountant to be available. If a company does not produce its accounts the court can assume that the company can pay whatever fine the court imposes. In most cases it is hard to imagine a company failing to provide such information, although with large (well) known companies of national or international standing this may not be a necessary requirement. Where necessary the payment of fine can be spread over a longer period that the usual 12 months, if payment in full would be unduly burdensome on say, a smaller company. The fine should be substantial enough to have real economic impact. Care should be taken to ensure that fines imposed on smaller companies are not beyond their capacity to pay. The court might not wish the payment of the fine to result in the company not being able to pay for improved procedures or cause the company to go into liquidation or make its employees redundant.

R v F Howe & Son (Engineers) Ltd [1999] 2 Cr App Rep (S) 37. Any fine should reflect not only the gravity of the offence but also the means of the offender, and this applies just as much to corporate defendants as to any other. See s 18 (3) of the Criminal Justice Act 1991. Difficulty is sometimes found in obtaining timely and accurate information about a corporate defendant's means. The starting point is its annual accounts. If a defendant company wishes to make any submission to the court about its ability to pay a fine it should supply copies of its accounts and any other financial information on which it intends to rely in good time before the hearing both to the court and to the prosecution. This will give the prosecution the opportunity to assist the court should the court wish it. Usually accounts need to be considered with some care to avoid reaching a superficial and perhaps erroneous conclusion. Where accounts or other financial information are deliberately not supplied the court will be entitled to conclude that the company is in a position to pay any financial penalty it is minded to impose. Where the relevant information is provided late it may be desirable for sentence to be adjourned, if necessary at the defendant's expense, so as to avoid the risk of the court taking what it is told at face value and imposing an inadequate penalty. Where a defendant is in a position to pay the whole of the prosecution costs in addition to the fine there is no reason in principle for the court not to make an order accordingly. The court must look at the whole sum (fine and costs) and consider the impact upon him.

R v Patchett Engineering Ltd [2001] 1 Cr App Rep (S) 138. The company pleaded guilty to an offence under the Health and Safety at Work etc Act 1974, s 2(1). A worker died. The company was fined £75,000 and ordered to pay £5,000 costs. Held. *R v F Howe & Son (Engineers) Ltd* [1999] 2 Cr App Rep (S) 37 and *R v Hall and Co Ltd* [1999] 1 Cr App Rep (S) 306 suggest subject to the defendant's ability to pay the fine could have been higher. The judge did take the means into account. We have more information than he did. Six of its 11 staff have been laid off. The £80,000 fine and costs would be likely to mean that the company could not keep its head above water. **£20,000 fine** substituted.

R v Supremeplan Ltd [2001] 1 Cr App Rep (S) 71. The company pleaded to an offence under the Health and Safety at Work etc Act 1974, s 2. It ran a mobile delivery hot food business. A safety device on a warmer was bypassed and there was a build up of gas in a compartment. When an employee lit the burner in a van there was a flash flame and she received burns to her face and hands. The company was owned by two directors who had taken out in the previous year less than £10,000 on a turnover of £140,000. The year's profit was £11,500. The judge described the van as a death trap. He made a compensation order for £3,000. Held. The company fell far short of the appropriate standard of care. Taking into account the means of the company **£7,500 fine** not £25,000.

Previous incidents/convictions

83.21   *R v Firth Vickers Ltd* [1998] 1 Cr App Rep (S) 293. The defendant company pleaded guilty to failing to ensure the health and safety of employees from 1 to 3 November 1995. Failure to maintain plant and provide safe systems of work were particularised. The firm had a foundry employing about 300 people. On 2 November 1995 the foundry was making a ring which was heavier than anything cast before. Two tons of molten metal at 1,500°C was poured into a mould and some escaped. It sprayed out in a jet and four men were caught. Three received substantial injuries. One received 40% burns and was in hospital for 10 weeks. He will probably not return to work. Another was in hospital for 6 nights. The machine was designed to hold 5 tons. The Health and Safety report said parts had become worn and the accident was caused by the top plate, which was inadequately retained by enough and strong enough pins. The top plate and the side wall were found to be distorted. There was no effective seal. The company overhauled their whole safety procedures with a new officer audits and training etc. That cost £60,000. A new managing director was appointed. An employee had been burnt in a fault on a different machine in 1993. For that the company was fined £10,000. It also involved the spray of molten metal. There was another incident in April 1994 when no one was injured. Two employees were splashed in September 1994. That incident was not reported to the Health and Safety Executive. In 1994–5 employees expressed their concerns about the ejection of molten metal. Throughout 1995 the employee that was most seriously injured who was also splashed in 1994 complained about the unrepaired top plate. On the day of the offence that employee had made requests about the steel plate. Those requests were ignored. The company was fined **£100,000** and ordered to pay £6,600 costs. It was suggested the judge gave undue weight to the earlier incidents and requests. Held. The previous incidents are very relevant for they showed that no proper re-assessment of the risks was made in due time. Potentially this machinery could cause very serious injuries and yet its guarding was known to be defective. The relatively modest cost of the guard eventually fitted underlined the company's failure to take any proper care in this hazardous employment. The judge had properly considered the history to see if it was an isolated oversight or indicative of something greater. The history was relevant in considering their inactivity. It was a serious case. The criminality was not wrongly inflated. The fine was upheld.

Public Bodies

83.22 *R v British Railways Board* (1991) unreported extract at [2000] 2 Cr App Rep (S) at 430 – High Court Judge at CCC. The company was sentenced for Health and Safety offences following the Clapham rail crash. Held. In the case of a public authority that is funded by the taxpayer or, as here, by a combination of the taxpayer and the fare-paying public, the question of penalty raises an acute problem. A swingeing fine of the magnitude that some might consider appropriate could only be met by the board either by increasing the burden on the fare-paying passengers – which is hardly logical, having regard to the fact that it is for the benefit of the fare-paying passengers that this legislation exists – or by reducing the funds available for improvements in the railway system in general. That can hardly be regarded as a desirable state of affairs. On the other hand, I must bear in mind the necessity of marking the disapproval of society at the failures demonstrated by those charged with British Rail management leading up to and causing this accident. An insignificant fine would rightly bring down on myself and upon the whole system of justice universal condemnation. I therefore have to steer a narrow course between those two alternative hazards. **£250,000 fine** imposed.

R v Milford Haven Port Authority [2000] 2 Cr App Rep (S) 423. The company pleaded guilty to causing oil to enter controlled waters. A pilot committed a serious navigational error and a tanker grounded on rocks causing a crude oil spill which was among the largest ever recorded. The authority was a public trust port. Held. Public bodies are not immune from appropriate penalties because they have no shareholders and the directors are not in receipt of handsome annual bonuses. However, it is proper for the judge to take the factor into account. If a substantial financial penalty will inhibit the proper performance by a statutory body of the public function it has been set up to perform that factor should not be disregarded.

Railway accidents

83.23 *R v Great Western Trains Co Ltd* (1999) unreported extract of judgment see [2000] 2 Cr App Rep (S) at 431 – High Court Judge at CCC. The company pleaded guilty to Health and Safety failures, which led to the Southall train crash which caused seven deaths and 150 casualties. The company had a good safety record. Prompt action was taken to prevent further breaches of Health and Safety requirements. Held. The company fell short of the standard required and it was a serious failure. The court needs to bring home to those who run substantial transport undertakings that eternal vigilance is required to ensure accidents do not occur. The company operated a system where there was no alternative in place when the AWS system was isolated. It was a serious fault of senior management. **£1.5m fine.**

For an extract of the judgment in the Clapham rail crash prosecution see *R v British Railways Board* (1991) unreported extract at [2000] 2 Cr App Rep (S) at 430.

84   HEALTH, DEFENDANT'S POOR STATE OF

Circumstances change after sentence

84.1   *R v Nall-Cain* [1998] 2 Cr App Rep (S) 145. Obiter. Where for example there is a deterioration in the defendant's health, or it is impossible, by reason of a prisoner's physical disabilities for the prison to cope with him the Court of Appeal may exercise mercy.

HEROIN

See IMPORTATION OF DRUGS; OPIUM; POSSESSION OF DRUGS; PRODUCTION OF DRUGS and SUPPLY OF DRUGS (CLASS A, B AND C)

85   HOMOSEXUAL OFFENCES

85.1   The main offences are buggery, rape and the Sexual Offences Act 1956, ss 13 and 32

Gross indecency and soliciting.

Both triable either way with the same penalty. On indictment maximum 2 years. Summary maximum 6 months and/or £5,000.

Sentencing trends. The pace of the ending of discrimination against homosexuals will speed up and the 2002 Queen's speech contained a commitment to 'modernise the laws on sexual offences'. Journalists were told the Government would 'sweep away offences targeting only homosexuals'. (Evening Standard, 13 November 2002).

R v T [1999] 2 Cr App Rep (S) 304. The seven defendants pleaded guilty or were convicted of buggery, gross indecency, incitement to commit buggery and attempted buggery. Police executed a search warrant and found two videos of gay sex. All the participants were over 18 except one who was 17½. All said they consented to the activity and it was agreed the video was not for commercial exploitation. The case was based on the fact that it was not in private because there were more than two people present and one of the parties was under 18, the then age for homosexual consent. They were sentenced to probation, CSO of 100 or 150 hours with probation and 9 months' imprison suspended. Held. The judge was entitled to consider the offences were serious enough to warrant **community sentences**. They may be more serious than a single act in a public lavatory out of view of the public. Some of the sentences were reduced. [It is hard to make any sense of this bizarre prosecution and judgment.]

See also BUGGERY, and RAPE [although at present there are no recent reported cases for anal rape on men, there are cases involving boys].

HOSPITALS

See PATIENTS, ILL TREATING ETC

ILL TREATING

See ANIMAL CRUELTY; CRUELTY TO CHILDREN and PATIENTS, ILL TREATING ETC

86   IMMIGRATION OFFENCES

86.1   Immigration Act 1971, s 25

Assisting illegal entry and harbouring

Triable either way. On indictment maximum 10 years. Summary maximum 6 months and/or £5,000. The penalty was increased from 7 to 10 years from 14 February 2000.

Immigration Act 1971, s 24A

Obtaining leave etc by deception

Triable either way. On indictment maximum 2 years. Summary maximum 6 months and/or £5,000.

Crown Court statistics England and Wales[1] – Crown Court – Males 21+ – Assisting entry of illegal immigrants

86.2

Year	Plea	Total Numbers sentenced	Type of sentence%					Average length of custody (months)
			Discharge	Fine	Community sentence	Suspended sentence	Custody	
2000	Guilty	65	0%	0%	2%	9%	89%	20.1
	Not guilty	37	0%	0%	0%	5%	95%	36.8

1   Excluding committals for sentence. Source: Crime and Criminal Justice Unit, Home Office Ref: IOS416-02.

Guideline case

86.3   *R v Le and Stark* [1999] 1 Cr App Rep (S) 422 – LCJ. The problem of illegal entry is on the increase. The offence calls very often for deterrent sentences. The following are aggravating features: (1) where the offence has been repeated; (2) where there is financial gain; (3) where it involves a stranger rather than a spouse or a close member of the family; (4) in a conspiracy where it has been committed over a period; (5) high degree of planning, organisation and sophistication; (6) there are a large number of illegal immigrants as opposed to one or a very small number. Plainly the more prominent the role of the defendant the greater the aggravation of the offence.

Guideline remarks

86.4   *R v Ali Nasir* [2001] EWCA Crim 2814, [2002] 2 Cr App Rep (S) 115. The defendant pleaded guilty to an offence under s 24A. Held. Previous good character and personal circumstances are of very limited value. Cases will be sentenced on a deterrent basis.

Disqualification from driving

86.5   *R v Woop* [2002] EWCA Crim 58, [2002] 2 Cr.App Rep (S) 281. The defendant pleaded guilty on rearraignment to facilitating the illegal entry of 35 people. He drove his lorry to the freight depot on the French side of the channel tunnel. A Customs officer asked him what he was towing and he said, 'Quartz sand.' A custom officer found movement and 35 people were found. The defendant denied knowledge of them. He was a 38-year-old German man of good character with two young children. The trip was to fund treatment for his wife's chronic asthma. That treatment was not covered by their health insurance. Held. The gravity and prevalence of this offence requires no special emphasis. Sentences are heavy and intended to deter. Six years was too long so **5 years** substituted. The offence had nothing to do with his driving. He earns his living from driving. The disqualification was reduced from 5 to 3 years.

Driving illegal immigrants through ports etc – Commercial motive

86.6   *R v Winn* [1999] 1 Cr App Rep (S) 154. The defendant pleaded guilty to facilitating an illegal entrant. He drove his lorry off a ferry and was stopped by Customs. He said he was on his own but 16 illegal immigrants were found in the back of the vehicle. The sentencing judge reluctantly accepted that he only knew there were four of them. He was 40 and of good character with financial difficulties. He received 4 years. Held. Sentences will contain a deterrent element. Suppose the judge had in mind a sentence of 6 years following a trial that would be 1 year less than the maximum of 7 [now 10]. That could not be right for a first offence. **3 years** substituted.

R v Le and Stark [1999] 1 Cr App Rep (S) 422 – LCJ. The defendant S, pleaded guilty to facilitating illegal entry at the Magistrates' Court. The defendant and another were questioned when they arrived in England from France in a camper van. They both said they were only two people travelling in the van. They said the large number of bags in the van were being taken to friends. The van was searched and two men were found in the luggage locker and a woman and six children were found under bedding. Two of them said they had paid a large sum of Deutschmarks to be conveyed from Kosovo to England. The defendant said he had only been paid 4,400 DM as expenses and one of his employees had asked him to bring members of his family to the UK. He was of good character with references. **3½ years** not 5.

R v Liddle [2000] 2 Cr App Rep (S) 282. The defendants L and B were convicted of assisting illegal entry. V pleaded guilty to the same count. Police came across a lorry driven by L with V as the co-driver. Also found was a transit van driven by B with 20 illegal immigrants in the back. L and V had gone abroad to collect goods and the immigrants were picked up and brought over. The van was to collect the immigrants. The motive for all three was money. L was to receive £200 and the other amounts were not known. V's basis of plea was he had not gone abroad to pick the immigrants up. He admitted telephoning numbers on both sides of the Channel. L was 47 and treated as of good character. He had been a hard worker as a driver. B was 43 with no convictions. He was the sole carer of three children. V was 30 with no convictions. He had a good military record but was in financial difficulties He had two children aged 15 and 12 and showed remorse. The judge said he started at 6 years and he would give a discount for the delay and would have given a substantial discount to V for his plea but had to take into account the part he had played. Held. Each had played a vital part in the operation. The smuggling in of strangers was an aggravating factor. The judge was entitled to sentence them to the same sentence. With a maximum of 7 years to start at 6 was wrong. **3 years** not 4 for all.

R v Woop [2002] EWCA Crim 58, [2002] 2 Cr App Rep (S) 281. The defendant pleaded guilty on rearraignment to facilitating the illegal entry of 35 people. He drove his lorry to the freight depot on the French side of the channel tunnel. A Customs officer asked him what he was towing and he said, 'Quartz sand.' A custom officer found movement and 35 people were found. The defendant denied knowledge of them. He was a 38-year-old German man of good character with two young children. The trip was to fund treatment for his wife's chronic asthma. That treatment was not covered by their health insurance. The Judge sentenced him to 5 years and when told the maximum was increased to 10 years he increased it to 6 years. Held. The gravity and prevalence of this offence requires no special emphasis. Sentences are heavy and intended to deter. It was permissible for the judge to increase the sentence but 6 years was too long so 5 years substituted. The disqualification was reduced from 5 to 3 years.

R v Wacker [2002] Crim LR 839. The defendant was convicted of conspiracy to facilitate illegal entry and 58 counts of manslaughter. 60 illegal immigrants travelled from China to Holland where they were loaded into an adapted container on the defendant's lorry. The only ventilation was a small vent at the front. 4½ kilometres from Zeebrugge the lorry stopped and the vent was closed. The deaths were caused by lack of air. The basis for the manslaughter was gross negligence. The defendant was a Dutch national. It was not suggested that he intended to harm the victims in anyway. He received 8 years for the conspiracy and 6 consecutive for the manslaughter counts. The defence argued the total was too much and the Attorney General argued the 6 years for the manslaughter counts was too lenient although the total sentence was not challenged. Held. Professional smuggling of large numbers of illegal immigrants is in itself a serious matter. The causing of so many deaths to avoid detection puts this case in a category of its own. 14 years was not manifestly excessive. Concurrent sentences were the correct approach so 14 years for the manslaughter, which would not have the appearance of devaluing the loss of life.

See also *R v Nikalakos* [2002] EWCA Crim 673, [2002] 2 Cr App Rep (S) 526.

Old cases. *R v Goforth* [1997] 1 Cr App Rep (S) 234; *R v Aziz and Niaz* [1996] 2 Cr App Rep (S) 44; *R v Ungruth* [1996] 2 Cr App Rep (S) 205; *R v Brown* [1997] 1 Cr App Rep (S) 112; *R v Matloob Hussain* [1997] 1 Cr App Rep (S) 298; *R v Farah* [1997] 2 Cr App Rep (S) 333.

Driving illegal immigrants through ports etc – Compassionate motive

86.7 *R v Angel* [1998] 1 Cr App Rep (S) 347. The defendant pleaded guilty to facilitating an illegal entry. The defendant was from Sri Lanka and was detained and ill-treated by the police. On his release he went to France where he was granted refugee status and became a French national. He worked for a hire car company for 10 years. His family became friendly with B who was 26, who had entered France illegally. It was agreed B should be taken to the UK using the defendant's son's passport. The son was 19. The defendant took his wife, B and two of his children to Dover by car and was questioned by immigration. He was asked who B was and he said he was his son. He was arrested and fully admitted the offence. He said he feared B would be discovered and deported back to Sri Lanka where he feared he would be arrested, tortured and possibly die. The defendant was 46 and of good character. He was sentenced to **15 months** and as a result lost his employment. The house which he had bought on mortgage was likely to be repossessed Held. The deterrent element was entirely justified. We agree with the judge's remark that it has to be marked out to all others tempted how very seriously it is viewed. Even though there was a humanitarian motive rather than a commercial motive and there was only one entrant involved there is no reason to disturb this sentence.

R v Le and Stark [1999] 1 Cr App Rep (S) 422 – LCJ. The defendant L, a Vietnamese refugee was convicted of facilitating illegal entry. He arrived from Ostend with a fellow Vietnamese and showed a Customs officer two Home Office travel documents one in his name and one in another. Looking at his companion the officer considered the age in the document didn't match the companion. When interviewed the defendant said he had met his passenger in Belgium and he had agreed to give him a lift to England. The judge did not decide it was for commercial gain and left the issue open. The defendant was 35 with a conviction for an entirely different matte. He was separated from his wife and had responsibility for his 6-year-old son. Held. While he might have received payment there was no evidence of financial gain nor participation in a commercial operation. **2½ years** not 3½.

R v Ahmetaj [2000] 1 Cr App Rep (S) 66. The defendant a Dutch national pleaded guilty at the Magistrates' Court to assisting illegal entry. He was committed for sentence. The defendant's car was searched and 2 Yugoslav nationals were found hiding in the boot. He was a former Yugoslav national from Kosovo who said an acquaintance had asked him to give the two men a lift from Holland to France and the two men had persuaded him to take them to England for a small sum to contribute to the petrol money. He was 31 and of good character. Held. It is inevitable he would be sympathetic to their plight when Kosovo had suffered ethnic cleansing. It was an isolated offence with no financial gain or commercial organisation. **18 months** not 2 years.

Old cases. *R v Ozdemir* [1996] 2 Cr App Rep (S) 64.

Obtaining leave etc by deception

86.8   *R v Nasir Ali* [2001] EWCA Crim 2814, [2002] 2 Cr App Rep (S) 115. The defendant pleaded guilty to seeking to obtain leave to enter by a deception at the Magistrates' Court (s 24A). Immigration officials were investigating Pakistanis who were claiming asylum pretending to be Afghans. They spoke to the defendant who gave a false name and falsely said he was born in Afghanistan. Checks revealed he was a Pakistani who had entered the country on a different date than he claimed. He was arrested and admitted the deception. He was 24 and had no convictions. He worked in a bakery and had never claimed any benefits. He regularly sent money to his ill parents in Pakistan. He said he wanted to return to Pakistan. He had a good prison report. Held. Offences will be treated very seriously. The offence was prevalent. Previous good character and personal circumstances are of very limited value. Cases will be sentenced on a deterrent basis. As the maximum is 2 years, **12 months** not 18.

See also BIGAMY – *Immigration controls, to evade* and PASSPORT OFFENCES

IMMORAL EARNINGS, MEN LIVING ON

See PROSTITUTION, MEN LIVING ON EARNINGS OF

IMPEDING

For impeding the apprehension or prosecution of an another person see ASSISTING OFFENDERS

87   IMPORTATION OF DRUGS (CLASS A, B AND C)

87.1   Customs and Excise Management Act 1979, s 170(1)(b) and (2)(b)

Triable either way unless the defendant could receive the minimum sentence of 7 years for a third drug trafficking offence when the offence is triable only on indictment.

On indictment maximum Class A – life, Class B – 14 years, and Class C – 5 years. On summary conviction 6 months (3 months for Class C drugs) and/or £5,000 or three times the value of the goods which ever is greater.

Specified offence for minimum 7 years for third Class A drug trafficking offence.

For drugs on the high seas destined for other countries the offences are prosecuted under Criminal Justice (International Co-operation) Act 1990, s 19 which has the same penalties (save the three times the value of the goods is omitted) and has the same 'triable either way' provisions.

Crown Court statistics England and Wales[1] – Crown Court – Males 21+ – Unlawful Importation

87.2

Year	Plea	Total Numbers sentenced	Type of sentence%					Average length of custody[2] (months)
			Discharge	Fine	Community sentence	Suspended sentence	Custody	
Unlawful importation Class A								
2000	Guilty	268	0%	0%	1%	0%	99%	77.3
	Not guilty	156	0%	0%	0%	0%	99%	133.6
Unlawful importation Class B								
2000	Guilty	125	0%	1%	1%	3%	94%	26.1
	Not guilty	74	0%	0%	0%	0%	100%	59.5
Unlawful importation Class C								
2000	Guilty	2	0%	0%	0%	50%	50%	36
	Not guilty	2	0%	0%	0%	0%	100%	30

1 Excluding committals for sentence. Source: Crime and Criminal Justice Unit, Home Office Ref: IOS416-02.
2 Excluding life sentences.

General Principles

Guideline cases – Class A

87.3 *R v Aramah* (1982) 76 Cr App Rep 190 – LCJ. Large scale importations, that is where the weight of Class A drugs at 100% purity is of the order of 500 grams. or more, sentences of **10 years** and upwards are appropriate. Where the weight at 100% purity is of the order of 5 kgs or more, sentences of **14 years** and upwards are appropriate. It will seldom be that an importer of any appreciable amount will deserve less than **4 years** [as adapted by *R v Bilinski* [1987] 86 Cr App Rep 146 – LCJ and *R v Aranguren* [1994] 99 Cr App Rep 347 – LCJ.]

R v Van der Leest (16 June 1997, unreported). Where a massive quantity of Class A drugs has been imported, a sentence significantly in excess of 20 years, after a trial, should be reserved for exceptional cases eg where the amount of drugs is truly enormous, or the defendant is to be sentenced for more than one such importation, or he has a previous record for serious drug dealing or he is at the pinnacle of responsibility for the particular importation. Here 170 kgs of ecstasy worth £10m merited 20 not 25 years after a trial and 15 not 18 after a plea for those very close to the centre of the operation.

Assisting the Crown

87.4 *R v Aramah* (1982) 76 Cr App Rep 190 – LCJ. It is particularly important that offenders should be encouraged to give information to the police, and a confession of guilt coupled with considerable assistance to the police can properly be marked by a substantial reduction.

Believing goods to be a different drug

87.5 *R v Bilinski* (1987) 9 Cr App Rep (S) 360. The drugs were heroin although the defendant believed they were cannabis. Held. It was a relevant sentencing consideration.

Cannabis – Guideline cases

87.6 *R v Aramah* (1982) 76 Cr App Rep 190 – LCJ. Importation of very small amounts for personal use can be dealt with as if it were simple possession. (See **POSSESSION OF DRUGS**). Otherwise importation of amounts up to about 20 kgs of herbal cannabis, or the equivalent in cannabis resin or cannabis oil, will, save in the most exceptional cases, attract sentences of between **18 months and 3 years**, with the lowest ranges reserved for pleas of guilty in cases where there has been small profit to the offender. There are few, if any, occasions when anything other than immediate custodial sentence is proper in this type of importation. Medium quantities over 20 kgs will attract sentences of **3 to 6 years** imprisonment, depending on the amount involved, and all the other circumstances of the case. As adapted by later cases.]

R v Ronchetti [1998] 2 Cr App Rep 100. Following a trail, the importation of 100 kgs of cannabis by persons playing more than a subordinate role, should attract a sentence of **7 to 8 years**. Following a trial, for importations of 500 kgs or more, by such persons **10 years** is the appropriate starting point. Larger importations will attract a higher starting point. That starting point should rise according to the role played, the weight involved, and all the other circumstances of the case up to the maximum of 14 years. The fact that, in a particular case of massive importation, an even greater quantity of the drug might one day have to be dealt with by the courts, is not in itself, a reason for not imposing the maximum sentence for those at the top of the organisation.

Couriers

87.7 *R v Rimmer* [1999] 1 Cr App Rep (S) 234. The defendant pleaded to importing amphetamine. Held. A courier can be involved in a wide variety of ways. The critical fact is the degree and extent of his involvement and the nature of the enterprise.

Defendant under 18 – Class A

87.8 *R v J* [2001] 1 Cr App Rep (S) 280. The defendant pleaded guilty to importing 1.66 kgs of pure cocaine. When aged 15, she went to Jamaica with another aged 22 to buy drugs for resale in UK. They each had a bag with a hidden compartment in which the drugs were hidden. The drugs were found at Gatwick. They expected to be paid between £4,000 and £5,000. She had no previous convictions. She had started working and had become addicted to drugs. She lost her job and was unable to purchase drugs. The pre-sentence report said she had a pattern of frequently wilful behaviour since she was 13 and was vulnerable. Held. Because of her age **5½ years** not 6 ½ detention.

Defendant aged 18–20 – Class A

87.9 *R v Bristol* [1998] 1 Cr App Rep (S) 47. The defendant was convicted of importing cocaine. She arrived from Jamaica with almost 1.5 kgs of cocaine concealed in the soles of three sandals. The drugs were 85% pure with a street value of £96,000. She was 18 with no convictions. She had been in care since the age of 9. She was said to be vulnerable and easily influenced by a man much older than herself. Held. The sentence was perfectly proper save for the age and vulnerability of the defendant. Those who intend to bring drugs into the country will select the vulnerable, the young and those of good character. Those factors which will justify a substantial discount carry less weight in importation cases. However, in all the circumstances **8 years** YOI not 10.

Drugs not destined for UK

87.10 *R v Mouzulukwe* [1996] 2 Cr App Rep (S) 48. The defendant claimed the drugs were destined for the US. Held. That made no difference whatsoever to the sentence.

R v Maguire [1997] 1 Cr App Rep (S) 130. The defendant was convicted of being concerned with cannabis in transit on the high seas, contrary to the Criminal Justice (International Co-operation) Act 1990, s 19(2)(b). The boat carrying the drugs was on the high seas in international waters and not in UK waters. The boat was going to Holland where the maximum would have been 4 years. The likely sentence would have been 18 months. Held. That was irrelevant. Courts should use English cases.

See also *Foreign penalties are irrelevant, future*

Drugs worth less than defendant thought
87.11   Old cases. *R v Afzal* (1991) 13 Cr App Rep (S) 145.

Exporting drugs
87.12   *R v Powell* (2000) Times, 5 October judgment 10 July 2000 – LCJ. There was no difference in criminality between the importation and exportation of controlled drugs.

Foreign penalties are irrelevant, future
87.13   *R v Nwoko* (1995) 16 Cr App Rep (S) 612. A Nigerian defendant faced a further term imprisonment on his return. Held. It was not a relevant consideration.

Old cases. *R v Ogburu* (1992) Times, 14 October. (Ignore the foreign penalty in the future.)

See also *Drugs not destined for UK*

Good character
87.14   *R v Aramah* (1982) 76 Cr App Rep 190 – LCJ. Good character of a courier of drugs was less important than good character in other cases. The large scale operator looks for couriers of good character and for the people of a sort which is likely to exercise the sympathy of the court if they are arrested. Consequently one will frequently find students and sick and elderly people are used as couriers for two reasons: first of all they are vulnerable to the offer of quick profit, and secondly, it is felt that the courts will be moved to misplaced sympathy in their case.

Own use
87.15   *R v Aramah* (1982) 76 Cr App Rep 190 – LCJ. Importation of very small amounts of cannabis for personal use can be dealt with as if it were simple possession. (See **POSSESSION OF DRUGS**)

R v De Brito [2000] 2 Cr App Rep (S) 255. The defendant is entitled to a discount if the importation is solely for the consumption of the offender, but the larger the amount the smaller the discount. This is because whatever the intention of the offender may be, the larger the amount the greater the danger that the drugs may pass into the hands of others.

Old cases. *R v McLean* [1994] 15 Cr App Rep (S) 706.

Persistent Class A offender – Minimum 7 years
87.16   Powers of Criminal Courts (Sentencing) Act 2000, s 110. Where a person is convicted of a class A drug trafficking offence committed after 30 November 1999 and was 18 or over and he has been convicted of two other class A drug trafficking offences one of which was committed after he had been convicted of the other, the court shall impose a sentence of imprisonment of at least 7 years except where the court is of the opinion that there are particular circumstances which relate to any of the offences or to the offender which would make it unjust. [This section is summarised and is slightly amended by Criminal Justice and Court Services Act 2000.]

Persistent Class A offender – Minimum 7 years – Plea of guilty

87.17 Powers of the Criminal Courts (Sentencing) Act 2000, s 152(3) Where a sentence is to be imposed under the Powers of the Criminal Courts (Sentencing) Act 2000, s 110 nothing in that section shall prevent the court from imposing a sentence of 80% or more of the minimum period. [Section summarised. The section means if he pleads the court can impose a sentence, which is 80% or more of the minimum term.]

Purity – What is required?

87.18 *R v Morris* [2001] 2 Cr App Rep (S) 297. We have considered a large number of authorities. The relevant principles are the amount of Class A or B drug with which a defendant is involved is a very important but not solely the determinative factor in sentencing. Evidence as to the scale of dealing can come from many sources other than the amount with which a defendant is directly connected. Amounts should generally be based on the weight of drug involved at 100% purity, not its street value; see *R v Aramah* (1982) 4 Cr App Rep (S) 407 at 409 and *R v Ronchetti* [1998] 2 Cr App Rep (S) 100 at 104 as to cannabis; *R v Aranguren* (1994) 99 Cr App Rep 347 at 351 as to cocaine; *R v Warren and Beeley* [1996] 1 Cr App Rep 120 at 123A as to ecstasy and *R v Wijs* [1999] 1 Cr App Rep (S) 181 at 183 as to amphetamine. But, in some circumstances, reference to the street value of the same weight of different drugs may be pertinent, simply by way of cross check, eg 1 kg of LSD is worth very much more than 1 kg of heroin, and 1 kg of amphetamine is worth very much more than 1 kg of cannabis. Weight depends on purity. The purity of drugs such as cocaine and heroin, and amphetamine powder, can be appropriately determined only by analysis. The weight of drugs such as ecstasy, in tablet, or LSD, in dosage, form, can generally be assessed by reference to the number of tablets or doses and, currently, an assumed average purity of 100 mgs of ecstasy (*R v Warren and Beeley* [1996] 1 Cr App Rep (S) 233 at 236) and 50 micrograms of LSD (*R v Hurley* [1998] 1 Cr App Rep (S) 299 at 304) unless prosecution or defence, by expert evidence, show the contrary (*R v Warren and Beeley* [1996] 1 Cr App Rep (S) 233 at 236, and *R v McPhail* [1997] 1 Cr App Rep (S) 321 at 322) Purity analysis is essential for sentencing purposes for cases of importation, or in other circumstances, where 500 grams or more of cocaine, heroin or amphetamine are seized. It may be desirable in cases where quantities less than 500 grams of those substances are seized. But, bearing in mind the cost of purity analysis and that analysis may cause delay, purity analysis will not generally be required where a defendant is in possession of only a small amount consistent with either personal use or only limited supply to others. In such a case the court can be expected to sentence only on the basis of a low level of retail dealing, but taking into account all the other circumstances of the particular case. But, as purity can indicate proximity to the primary source of supply, if there is reason for the prosecution to believe that a defendant in possession of a small quantity of drugs is close to the source of supply and is wholesaling rather than retailing, it will be necessary for purity analysis to be undertaken before a court can be invited to sentence on this more serious basis. In the absence of purity analysis or expert evidence, it is not open to a court to find or assume levels of purity, except in the case of ecstasy and LSD in the circumstances to which we have referred.

Amphetamine – Class B

Amphetamine – Class B – Guideline case

87.19 *R v Wijs* [1998] 2 Cr App Rep 436. On conviction of importing amphetamine a custodial sentence will almost invariably be called for save in exceptional circumstances or where the quantity of the drug is so small as to be compatible only with personal consumption. The ordinary sentence following a contested trial (subject to all other considerations, and on quantities calculated on the basis of 100% purity) should be (1) Up to 500 grams: **up to 2 years**. (2) More than 500 grams but less than 2½ kgs: **2–4 years**. (3) More than 2½ kgs but less than 10 kgs: **4–7 years**. (4) More than 10 but less than 15 kgs: **7-10 years**. (5) More than 15 kgs: **upwards of 10 years**, subject to the statutory maximum of 14 years. We have considered a number of cases. Some of these fall comfortably within the guidelines set out above: eg *R v Fitzgerald* (1993) 15 Cr App Rep (S) 236, *R v Brougham* [1996] 2 Cr App Rep (S) 88. Others do not such as *R v Coughlan* (1995) 16 Cr App Rep (S) 519.

Amphetamine – Class B – Less than 5 kgs

87.20   *R v Rouse* (22 October 1996, unreported). The defendant pleaded guilty to importation of 2.25 kgs at 45%. He was a mere courier. **4 years** not 5 years.

R v West [1998] 2 Cr App Rep (S) 310. The defendant was convicted of importing 3.1 kgs of amphetamine at a minimum purity of 95%. A DHL parcel was intercepted in Belgium. It was addressed to UK. The drugs were removed and the Customs made a controlled delivery. There was no answer so they left a card. The defendant's co-accused picked up the parcel from the depot and took it to a van outside. The defendant who was in the van drove him away at speed. The van was lost and but some time later was found and the two were arrested. The defendant was now 27 and had a degree of mental handicap. He had convictions for theft and burglary but nothing for drugs. Held. The defendant was if not at the heart of the enterprise very near it. **6 years** not 8.

Old cases. *R v Purcell* [1996] 1 Cr App Rep (S) 190.

Amphetamine – Class B – 5 kgs and more

87.21   *R v Wijs Re Donaldson* [1999] 1 Cr App Rep (S) 181 at 184. The defendant was convicted of importing 33 kgs of amphetamine (equivalent to 30 kgs at 100% pure amphetamine base) with a street value of about £4.7m. Two other defendants were convicted of importing cannabis, which were bought in at the same time. The drugs were brought into this country by another by car, in bags. The car was stopped at Harwich and the drugs were removed. The bags were re-filled. The car went to a meeting place at a hotel where Donaldson was seen in a gold Mercedes. The judge described him as a substantial organiser in a vastly profitable enterprise. Held. The judge having heard the evidence was entitled to sentence on that basis. **12 years** was not excessive.

R v Rimmer [1999] 1 Cr App Rep (S) 234. The defendant made a very late plea to importing amphetamine. Four boxes of 74.5 kgs of amphetamine (32 kgs at 100%) arrived at Heathrow Airport from Belgium. Their street value was between £3.75m and £4m. Sugar was substituted for the drugs. The man who collected them took them to his home. The defendant arrived there and put the boxes in his car and took them to Liverpool. As he approached Liverpool he conducted some very odd manoeuvres on the road. In interview he claimed it was contraband tobacco. He was a 29-year-old happily married family man with a good character and references. He was unemployed and in financial difficulties. The judge said he was in sole charge of a very valuable cargo over quite a significant time. Held. A courier can be involved in a wide variety of ways. The critical fact is the extent of his involvement and the nature of the enterprise. **6 years** was severe but because of the late plea, the extent of his involvement and that it was a very substantial enterprise it was not manifestly excessive.

Old cases. *R v Fitzgerald* (1993) 15 Cr App Rep (S) 236,

See also **AMPHETAMINE**

Cannabis – Class B

Cannabis – Class B – Guideline cases

87.22 *R v Aramah* (1982) 76 Cr App Rep 190 – LCJ. Importation of very small amounts for personal use can be dealt with as if it were simple possession (see **POSSESSION OF DRUGS**). Otherwise importation of amounts up to about 20 kgs of herbal cannabis, or the equivalent in cannabis resin or cannabis oil, will, save in the most exceptional cases, attract sentences of between **18 months and 3 years**, with the lowest ranges reserved for pleas of guilty in cases where there has been small profit to the offender. There are few, if any, occasions when anything other than immediate custodial sentence is proper in this type of importation. Medium quantities over 20 kgs will attract sentences of **3 to 6 years** imprisonment, depending on the amount involved, and all the other circumstances of the case. (As adapted by later cases.)

R v Ronchetti [1998] 2 Cr App Rep (S) 100. Following a trial, the importation of 100 kg of cannabis by persons playing more than a subordinate role, should attract a sentence of **7 to 8 years**. Following a trial, for importations of 500 kgs or more, by such persons **10 years** is the appropriate starting point. Larger importations will attract a higher starting point. That starting point should rise according to the role played, the weight involved, and all the other circumstances of the case up to the maximum of 14 years. The fact that, in a particular case of massive importation, an even greater quantity of the drug might one day have to be dealt with by the courts, is not in itself, a reason for not imposing the maximum sentence for those at the top of the organisation.

Cannabis – Class B – Under 1 kg

87.23 *R v Aramah* (1982) 76 Cr App Rep 190. For very small amounts for personal use deal with as simple possession which is often met with a fine.

R v Browne (31 March 1999, unreported). The defendant made a late guilty plea to importing through the post three packages of herbal cannabis from South Africa. The combined weight of cannabis was about 500 grams worth about £1,750 on the street. He was 33 and of good character. Held. It wasn't a single instance and the benefit of the plea was diluted by the lateness of it but **2 months** not 3.

Old cases. *R v Elder and Pyle* (1993) 15 Cr App Rep (S) 514.

Cannabis – Class B – 1–19 kgs

87.24 *R v Astbury* [1997] 2 Cr App Rep (S) 93. The defendant pleaded guilty at the Magistrates' Court to importing 1,100 grams of herbal cannabis and a little over 20 grams of cannabis resin. They drugs were found in his car at Dover. The prosecution accepted it was for own use. He was committed for sentence. Held. **3 months** not 9.

Old cases. *R v Blyth* [1996] 1 Cr App Rep (S) 388, *R v Klitzke* (1995) 16 Cr App Rep (S) 445.

Cannabis – Class B – 20–99 kgs

87.25 *R v Damen* (12 December 1997, unreported). The defendant was convicted of importing cannabis resin. While on bail for a drugs supply case he arrived by ferry from France. His car was searched and 29 kgs of cannabis resin worth about £96,000 was found. He denied any knowledge of it. He was 45 and had been sentenced for the drugs matter to 3 months a few weeks after his arrest for this matter. The judge described him as a knowing courier. **4½ years** not 6.

R v Frazer [1998] 1 Cr App Rep (S) 287. The defendant pleaded guilty to importing 36 kgs of herbal cannabis. He took the drugs through the green channel and he was stopped. He was 50 and it was his third time conviction for importing cannabis into the country. He had received 6 months and 2 years. Held. **6 years** was a high sentence at the top end of the bracket but because it was a commercial importation by someone convicted three times before it was not manifestly excessive.

R v Wijs Re Church and Haller [1999] 1 Cr App Rep (S) 181 at 186. The defendants H and C were convicted of importing 39 kgs of cannabis resin with a street value of £132,900. The drugs were brought into this country by car by another. The car was stopped at Harwich and the drugs were removed by Customs. They were re-filled. The car went a hotel where H and C arrived. H was given two bags, which had contained cannabis. H and C were arrested. H had met the driver once in Holland and once at the hotel to arrange the delivery. H was sentenced on the basis that he was substantially involved and C was involved on a lesser basis. For H, **5 years** not 7. For C, **4 years** not 5.

Cannabis – Class B – 100 kgs to 1 tonne

87.26   *R v Ronchetti* [1998] 2 Cr App Rep (S) 100. Following a trial, the importation of 100 kgs of cannabis by persons playing more than a subordinate role, should attract sentences of **7 to 8 years**. **10 years** is the appropriate starting point for importations of 500 kgs by such persons. That starting point should rise according to the role played, the weight involved and all the other circumstances to the 14 year maximum. Here with this well planned and sophisticated conspiracy with three separate importations in the false roof of a van, the probable total was around 600 kgs. Sentences on two who were convicted and played much more than a subordinate role reduced from 12 to **10 years**. Other three defendants who played a more than subordinate role reduced from 9 to **6 years** to reflect lesser role and plea.

R v Vickers [1999] 2 Cr App Rep (S) 216. The defendant was convicted of importing 402 kg of cannabis and 301 kgs of cannabis resin. The cannabis was found in his lorry when it searched at Dover ferry port. Held. As it was his lorry he could not be described as in a subordinate role. He was not an ordinary courier, he was master of his own lorry. Therefore **10 years** was not excessive.

R v Golder [2000] 1 Cr App Rep (S) 59 – LCJ. The defendant, a lorry driver pleaded guilty to importing cannabis resin. In May 1998 he was seen transferring boxes from his lorry to a van. Sixteen days later he entered the country at Dover and drove his lorry to Warwickshire. He transferred boxes containing 141 kgs of cannabis to his car and then drove the car to a meeting place where he transferred the boxes to another car. He and the driver of the other car were arrested. The cannabis was worth about £½m. He agreed he had smuggled six similar boxes in May. He said he was paid £8,200 for the first trip and £200 a box for the second trip. He was now 35 and effectively of good character and had co-operated with the Customs officers. He was sentenced on the basis he knew the second consignment was drugs but not the first. Held. Applying *R v Ronchetti* [1998] 2 Cr App Rep (S) 100, **5½ years** not 7.

A-G's References (Nos 36–89 of 1999) [2000] 2 Cr App Rep (S) 303. The defendants D, B and H were convicted of a conspiracy to import and supply cannabis. The defendant N pleaded guilty on a limited basis. D was the prime mover and the others were his lieutenants. Police conducted a surveillance operation. D was seen to pay £10,000 into a bank. The cashier said, 'Paying in again.' He said, 'Yes.' D made three visits to Spain one year. N, B and H also visited Spain. 400 kgs of cannabis resin with a street value of about £800,000 was packed in containers in two cars. N drove it and he was stopped. D was the prime mover and appeared to be reasonably affluent. The others were said to be lieutenants. B had no signs of wealth. He worked as a minicab driver. H worked as a valet for cars. N was an unemployed warehouseman. D was

35 and the rest varied from 29–39. They had no convictions. N had served his sentence. Held. D should have received 9 years. As he has absconded it didn't matter it was a reference so 9 not 7. B and H should have received **6 years**. However, it was not now appropriate to increase their 4 year sentences. N should have received **3½ years** not 2½ but as he has been released the sentence will not be increased.

Old cases. *R v Sturt* (1992) 14 Cr App Rep (S) 440 and *R v Rescorl* (1992) 14 Cr App Rep (S) 522.

Cannabis – Class B – Over 1 tonne

87.27 *R v Maguire* [1997] 1 Cr App Rep (S) 130. The defendant was convicted of being concerned with cannabis in transit on the high seas, contrary to Criminal Justice (International Co-operation) Act 1990, s 19(2)(b). The boat carrying 1,850 kgs of cannabis resin was on the high seas in international waters and not in UK waters. The boat was going to Holland where the maximum sentence would have been 4 years. Customs boarded the boat. The defendant had purchased the boat in 193. Held. The dutch sentence was irrelevant. Courts should use English cases. **9 years** was not manifestly excessive.

R v Bisset and Wray [2000] 2 Cr App Rep (S) 397. The defendants B and W pleaded guilty to importing 1,151 kgs of cannabis in a very sophisticated false compartment of a lorry. B was acting on behalf of the Spanish principle who had arranged the exportation. B also supervised the unloading of the lorry in London and the transfer of the drugs to the next in the chain. Customs videoed the unloading of the drugs and then arrested both defendants. W was not the principle in the UK but very close to him. The judge said he was an able lieutenant. W had recruited the man who had the premises where the drugs were stored in this country. B was 40 and of good character. W was 36 and had an old conviction for theft. Held. The **11 years** sentences were severe but not excessive because of the amount of drugs, the roles played, and the limit for the credit for the plea of guilty because they were caught red-handed.

Old cases. *R v Fishleigh* [1996] 2 Cr App Rep (S) 283.

See also **CANNABIS**

Cocaine – Class A

Cocaine – Class A – Under 1 kg (at 100% purity)

87.28 *R v Aranguren* (1994) 99 Cr App Rep 347. Where the Class A drugs are 500 grams or more (at 100% purity) the sentences will be **10 years** and upwards.

R v White [1999] 1 Cr App Rep (S) 325. The defendant pleaded guilty to importing 477 grams of cocaine, (386 grams at 100% purity). A man was approached to import drugs and he informed the police who put him in touch with customs. He agreed to take part in the plan and inform customs. He was told two women would visit him. The defendant and another woman visited him and she assessed his suitability and was the go-between. She attended further meetings where instructions were given and spending money handed over. The informer was told that as this was his first trip he would be returning with a Class C drug. He was instructed to go to Jamaica and there was given a pair of training shoes to wear. He returned to the UK and the shoes were found to contain the drug, the street value of which was £59,390. She was sentenced on the basis that she believed the cannabis was to be imported. She was a 38-year-old mother with three children and two foster children and some spent convictions. There was some evidence of her attempting to assist the authorities. Held. **5½ years** not 6½.

R v De Brito [2000] 2 Cr App Rep (S) 255. The defendant pleaded guilty to two counts of importing cocaine. He had received two envelopes and together they contained

21.5 grams of cocaine. One was 5.59 grammes and the other 4.94 grammes at 100% purity. He was sentenced on the basis it was for his own use. The defendant was 37 and of good character. Held. **2 years** could not be criticised.

Old cases. *R v Ashley* (1993) 14 Cr App Rep (S) 581; *R v McLean* (1994) 15 Cr App Rep (S) 706; *R v Bell* (1994) 16 Cr App Rep (S) 93; *R v Nwoko* (1995) 16 Cr App Rep (S) 612.

Cocaine – Class A – 1–9 kgs (at 100% purity)

87.29   *R v Aranguren* (1994) 99 Cr App Rep 347 – LCJ. Where the Class A drugs are 500 grams or more (at 100% purity) the sentences will be 10 years and upwards. Five kgs or more (at 100% purity) is worth **14 years** and upwards.

R v Guy [1999] 2 Cr App Rep (S) 24. The defendant pleaded guilty to importing cocaine. Customs Officers at Gatwick airport stopped the defendant, his then girlfriend and her child after they had travelled from Jamaica. They were on route to Manchester. A search of their luggage revealed packages of 3.95 kgs of cocaine, which at 100% purity was 2.29 kgs. The packages were replaced with dummies. Guy and his girlfriend were arrested and he was frank with the customs officers and he co-operated with them. Later that day different Customs Officers met the defendant in Manchester. The co-accused was expected to meet the defendant at there and he too was arrested. His co-accused was tried, convicted and received 12 years. The defendant gave evidence against him. He also gave also gave significant information to Customs. The defendant received 8 years. The co-accused's conviction was quashed on appeal and he was acquitted at the retrial. The defendant did not give evidence in that trial. He was 26 and was a person of positive good character. Held. The sentence on the co-accused was entirely appropriate. The defendant was significantly less involved than him. The starting point in the case of Guy ought to have been **10 years**. He was entitled to 50% discount so **5 years** instead.

Old cases. *R v Brougham* [1996] 2 Cr App Rep (S) 88; *R v Bristol* (28 April 1997, unreported); *R v McLeary* (10 April 1997, unreported) and *R v Watson* (10 March 1997, unreported).

Cocaine – Class A – 10–24 kgs (at 100% purity)

87.30   Old cases. *R v Scamaronie* (1992) 13 Cr App Rep 702; *R v Serdeiro* [1996] 1 Cr App Rep (S) 251; *R v De Four* [1996] 2 Cr App Rep (S) 106.

Cocaine – Class A – Over 25 kgs (at 100% purity)

87.31   Old case. *R v Richardson* (1994) 15 Cr App Rep (S) 876.

Ecstasy – Class A

Ecstasy – Class A – Guideline case

87.32   *R v Warren and Beeley* [1996] 1 Cr App Rep (S) 233 at 237 – LCJ. For the importation of 5,000 tablets or more of ecstasy tablets (assuming that each tablet contained an active constituent close to the average of 100 mgs) the appropriate sentence would be of the order of **10 years** and upwards. For 50,000 tablets or more **14 years** or more.

Ecstasy – Class A – Less than 5,000 tablets or equivalent

87.33   *R v Warren and Beeley* [1996] 1 Cr App Rep (S) 233 – LCJ. Both defendants W and B in unconnected cases pleaded guilty to importing ecstasy tablets. W was searched by customs officers at Ramsgate and they found 1011 tablets taped to his chest. He was 43 with three unrelated convictions. Held. **5 years** not 6. Customs

Officers at Sheerness searched B after he arrived from the continent. They found 1,585 tablets of ecstasy in his sock. He was expecting £500 and a debt of £800 he owed the person organising it to be written off. He claimed the dealer had made threats. He had no relevant convictions. Held. **6 years** not 7.

R v Wijs [1999] 1 Cr App Rep (S) 181 at 184. The defendant pleaded guilty to importing ecstasy, amphetamine and cannabis, obstructing a customs officer and impeding the detention of drugs. A customs officer searched the defendant, who with his 17-year-old girlfriend after he had disembarked from a ferry from Holland. The defendant was searched and he produced 1.34 grams of cannabis from his shoe. His girlfriend was also searched and she produced 15 ecstasy tablet from inside her sock. There was 35.9 grams of cannabis concealed in her vagina. The appellant was taken to hospital and he dropped 58 amphetamine tablets, and five tablets of ecstasy which had been concealed in his rectum. While at the hospital he tried to grab the packages and abscond, which gave rise to the last two counts. The street value of the 20 ecstasy tablets (containing somewhat over 1 gram of pure ecstasy) was £240, the value of the 58 amphetamine tablets (containing 2.03 grams of pure amphetamine) was £205 and the value of the 37.24 grams of cannabis was £151.56. The judge regarded it as a commercial importation by the defendant who had used his girlfriend as an assistant. The judge gave only a nominal discount for his plea since the evidence was quite overwhelming. He received 7 years for the ecstasy, 15 months' concurrent for the amphetamine and 6 months consecutive for the obstructing and impeding counts making 7½ years in all. The girlfriend, who pleaded guilty to all the counts except the last two, received a total of 6 months detention. Held. The judge was entitled to say he had involved his young girlfriend. Although the defendant certainly merited a longer sentence than she did the difference was too great. The guideline decisions are not to be applied with mathematical precision. This court in *R v Warren and Beeley* [1996] 1 Cr App Rep (S) 233 at 237, indicate that for the importation of 5,000 tablets or more of ecstasy tablets (assuming that each tablet contained an average of 0.1 grams) the sentence would be of the order of 10 years and upwards. The appellant pleaded guilty and the importation was of 20 tablets only, which contained less of the active ingredient than was assumed in *R v Warren and Beeley* to be the norm, so **2 years** not 5. In view of the very small quantity of amphetamine 15 months for that was excessive. 9 months substituted making 2½ in all.

Ecstasy – Class A – 100,000 tablets or more

87.34 *R v Van der Leest* (16 June 1997, unreported). The defendant V pleaded guilty to importing 170 kgs of ecstasy worth £10m. G was convicted of the same offence. 630,000 tablets of ecstasy was sent by lorry from Holland to Manchester. In a surveillance operation V was seen flying from Holland to Manchester shortly before the importation and he was met by G. V was arrested as the lorry was unloaded. G left the scene in a car at the same time as V's arrest and seven boxes of ecstasy were recovered from that car. G had made many telephone calls to Holland and visited Holland in the months before. The judge said V was equally involved as G. Held. The judge was right to say that G was 'very close to the centre of the operation.' However, **20 years** not 25 years for G and **15 years** not 18 for V.

R v Main and Johnson [1997] 2 Cr App Rep (S) 63. The defendants M and J were convicted of attempting to import 1.2 million tablets of ecstasy worth £23.5m in a van, and conspiracy to supply ecstasy. Officers searched premises and found 25 kgs and 111,275 tablets of ecstasy and the two defendants. The house received deliveries of imported ecstasy. Both were considered 'main persons' in the organisation in this country. J was 54 and had heart disease. Held. **24 years** concurrent on each defendant upheld.

R v Ellis and Avis [2000] 1 Cr App Rep (S) 38. Both defendants E and A were convicted of a conspiracy to import 115,000 ecstasy tablets from Belgium. Another person was arrested in Belgium with the tablets before they could be imported. The defendants were under surveillance and seen making preparation for the importation and flying around in a small aircraft. The drugs were about 75% purity representing 88,000 at 100%. Their street value was about £1m. The trial judge sentenced A as the principle. The prosecution said they were equally involved. Held. The appropriate bracket for this amount is more than 14 years and less than 20. Because the conspiracy was not successful **16 years** for both not 18 and 22 years.

Old cases. *R v Tattenhove* [1996] 2 Cr App Rep (S) 91.

See also Ecstasy

Heroin – Class A

Heroin – Class A – Guideline case

87.35   *R v Aramah* (1982) 76 Cr App Rep 190 – LCJ. Large-scale importations of Class A drugs, that is where the weight of the drugs at 100% purity is of the order of 500 grams or more, sentences of **10 years** and upwards are appropriate. Where the weight at 100% purity is of the order of 5 kgs or more, sentences of **14 years** and upwards are appropriate. It will seldom be that an importer of any appreciable amount will deserve less than **4 years**, [as adapted by *R v Bilinski* (1987) 86 Cr App Rep 146 – LCJ and *R v Aranguren* (1994) 99 Cr App Rep 347 – LCJ.]

Heroin – Class A – Under 1 kg (at 100% purity)

87.36   *R v Aranguran* (1994) 99 Cr App Rep 347. Where the Class A drugs are 500 grams or more (at 100% purity) the sentences will be 10 years and upwards.

R v Siebers [2001] EWCA Crim 2757, [2002] 2 Cr App Rep (S) 28. The defendant pleaded guilty to the importation of 0.496 kgs of heroin (at 100%). She was stopped at Waterloo Station after travelling from Brussels on the Eurostar. Her ticket showed she was due to return in about an hour. She said she had come to see her boyfriend. Underneath her clothing were found four packages held by elasticised back support. They contained 1.986 kgs of heroin at 25%. The street value was £70,000. She was a foreign national, 18 and of good character. She had an unhappy background and had been pressurised to do it by an older man who offered marriage and money. Held. Couriers very often have a sad background, immaturity, youth and vulnerability. The judge made proper allowance for these factors. The appeal over **5 years** detention is dismissed.

Old cases. *R v Daniel* (1995) 16 Cr App Rep (S) 892; *R v Mouzulukwe* [1996] 2 Cr App Rep (S) 48.

Heroin – Class A – 10–50 kgs (at 100% purity)

87.37   *R v Aranguren* (1994) 99 Cr App Rep 347 – LCJ. Five kgs or more (at 100% purity) is worth **14 years or more**.

R v Kayar [1998] 2 Cr App Rep (S) 355. The defendant was convicted of importing 10.3 kgs (purity unknown). The heroin was concealed in the sides of 20 boxes of clothing which arrived at Stansted airport from Turkey. The defendant was in charge of the UK end of this operation. He planned and tested the system and arranged with others the actual importation. He was considered to be 'a ruthless character' but he had no previous convictions. He was 35 and Turkish and had been in the UK for 18 years. He spoke little English and had a disabled son of 17. Held. **16 years** not 20. The deportation order was confirmed.

See also *R v Billson* [2002] EWCA Crim 665, [2002] 2 Cr App Rep (S) 521 [49 kgs, 14 years].

Old cases. *R v Latif and Shahzad* (1994) 15 Cr App Rep (S) 864; *R v Patel* (1995) 16 Cr App Rep (S) 267; *R v Serdeiro* [1996] 1 Cr App Rep (S) 251.

Heroin – Class A – Over 50 kgs (at 100% purity)

87.38   *R v Kaynak* [1998] 2 Cr App Rep (S) 283. The defendant A pleaded guilty and K, H and S were convicted of conspiracy to import 200 kgs of heroin (100 kgs at 100% purity). None of the defendants were at the top of the chain. H was a Czech coach driver who was seen to hand packages from his coach to S and A. K and A were stopped in a car and 66 kgs of heroin were found. S was found to have large sums of cash and a bag identical to one in which heroin had been packed. A's car was parked in the car park of S's apartment block and 73 kgs of heroin was found in the car. Nine kgs was found in K's flat. H's coach was again seen at the place where packages were seen being transferred but no-one turned up. He drove back to Ramsgate Dock to leave the country and 50 kgs of heroin was found in the coach. K was a courier-cum-errand boy who was not a middle ranker more a cog. At the trial he claimed duress. H was a high ranking courier. He also claimed duress. S was a mid ranker who claimed not to be involved. A was also a mid ranker but slightly below S. He provided some assistance to the authorities. Held. K **18 years** not 24. H was assigned too high a role by the judge so **18 years** not 26 years. S, **24 years** not 30. A, **15 years** not 20.

R v Dimitrov and Nedelkov (14 June 1999, unreported). The defendants D and N were convicted of importing 65.1 kgs of heroin worth in excess of £10m. N drove the lorry with the drugs from Bulgaria to Hull. Customs discovered it and took N to hospital. They then created the fiction he was still in hospital when he was taken into police custody. D came over from Bulgaria and collected the lorry believing the drugs were still on board. For 5 days he drove round England till he was arrested. N was 52 and D 43. They were of good character. The judge described it as a very sophisticated and professional operation based on a legitimate consignment of furniture. He did not regard N as one of the top men but someone who took the load through seven countries. He thought D had been sent over to retrieve the situation. N knew no English. Held. N **18 years** not 24 and D **12 years** not 16.

R v Kulunk (14 April 2002, unreported). The defendant pleaded guilty on the eighth day of his trial to conspiracy to supply heroin. Well in excess of 44 kgs of heroin was found. The deliveries were 80 kgs of heroin a week. The amount involved was well in excess of £100m. The judge considered the defendant to be the prime mover and started at **30 years**. He took into account his plea and his good character and sentenced him to **26 years** which was upheld.

R v Izzigil (25 April 2002, unreported). The defendants were co-conspirators with Kulunk (above) and they were convicted of importation. Held. The scale of the importation required exceptional and severe sentences. **18 years** and **20 years** upheld.

Old cases. *R v Richardson* (1994) 15 Cr App Rep (S) 876; *R v Middelkoop and Telli* [1997] 1 Cr App Rep (S) 423; *R v Kaya* (12 June 1996, unreported); *R v Mulkerrins* (20 June 1997, unreported).

See also OPIUM

LSD – Class A

87.39   Old cases. *A-G's Reference (Nos 3, 4, and 5 of 1992)* (1992) 14 Cr App Rep (S) 191.

See also **LSD**

Opium – Class A

Opium – Class A – Guidelines

87.40   *R v Mashaollahi* [2001] 1 Cr App Rep (S) 330. The court should proceed on the assumption that any given consignment of opium is unadulterated and of 100% purity. Should the defence wish to persuade a judge that the active ingredient was of a lesser percentage it is open to them to call the evidence. Heroin is eight times more valuable than opium, so 40 kgs of opium at 100% would be equivalent to 5 kgs of heroin at 100%. There is at least the remote possibility that opium might be imported to convert it into morphine or heroin. Then base the sentence on the amount of heroin or morphine that could be produced from the opium seized. The ratio to apply would be 10:1 ie 10 kgs of opium would be needed to produce 1 kg of morphine or heroin assuming average levels of purity. The guideline for the importation of opium should be based on weight, crosschecked with street value to ensure that at least an approximate equivalence with heroin and cocaine is maintained. For importation of opium, the appropriate guidelines would be, **14 years** and upwards for 40 kgs or more of opium, **10 years** and upwards for 4 kgs or more of opium. To this rule of thumb we would make one exception and that is in cases where it is established that the importation of opium was carried out for the purpose of conversion into morphine or heroin we consider that the appropriate sentence should be based on the equivalent value of those drugs.

See also **OPIUM**

Steroids – Class C

87.41   *R v Abdul* [2001] 1 Cr App Rep (S) 8. The defendant was convicted of conspiracy to import steroids, conspiracy to supply steroids, and theft of cash and drugs from his employers. The defendant was a qualified pharmacist who used his position at work as a locum pharmacist to import 'massive quantities' of steroids and supply them. He was a bankrupt who was in severe financial difficulties. Held. The steroid offences were very serious indeed. **3 years** concurrent for the steroids, 1 year for the thefts consecutive upheld.

See also **DRUG USERS**

IMPORTATION, OTHER

See also **TAX FRAUD** and **DUTY EVASION**

88   IMPORTATION OF PORNOGRAPHY

88.1   Customs and Excise Management Act 1979, s 170(2)

Triable either way. On indictment maximum 7 years. On summary conviction 6 months and/or £5,000 or three times the value of the goods which ever is greater.

The defendant who is involved with indecent photographs of persons under 16 must notify the police within 14 days (or 14 days from his release from imprisonment) his name and home address etc, any change and addresses where he resides for 14 days or more in any 12 month period[1].

R v Dunn (28 October 1999, unreported). The defendant pleaded guilty to importing two obscene video-tapes and had seven computer disks containing 6428 indecent images of children. He and was sentenced to 8 months' imprisonment. It was accepted that that material was for his own use, and he was in a poor state of health. For that reason in particular, his sentence was halved to **4 months**.

R v Hirst [2001] 1 Cr App Rep (S) 152. The defendant pleaded guilty to conspiracy to import indecent or obscene material. He was involved in a sophisticated and cleverly set up operation to import hard core pornography. The main man absconded and the defendant was described as his right-hand man. The defendant's prime role was the use of his home to receive pornographic video spools and to copy them onto blank video cassettes. He also arranged forward transmission of the videos to customers and addressed jiffy bags with addresses in England knowing they would be sent to Belgium for the pornographic material to be dispatched. He was involved for about 5 weeks and was paid £500 a week. 236 videos were found at his home some of which were blank. Also found were materials for copying videos, mailing lists, customer orders and a large quantity of jiffy bags. The material was revolting and sickeningly vile. It included coprophilia, defecation, scatophagy, urolagnia, enema, domination, bestiality, sado-masochism and simulated rape. He was 51, of good character and under extreme financial pressure. He showed remorse and the risk of re-offending was assessed as very low. Held. He played an important role. **12 months** might be regarded as severe but it was not manifestly excessive.

1   Sex Offenders Act 1997, ss 1, 2 and Sch 1, para 1(1)(e) and 1(2)(c).

INADEQUATE DEFENDANT

See **DEFENDANT** – *Inadequate*

89   INCEST

89.1

Sexual Offences Act 1956, s 10

Indictable only. Maximum sentence if girl under 13 Life imprisonment. Otherwise 7 years. Maximum for an attempt if girl under 13, 7 years otherwise 2 years.

The defendant, unless the other party was 18 or over, must notify the police within 14 days (or 14 days from his release from imprisonment) his name and home address etc, any change and addresses where he resides for 14 days or more in any 12 month period[1].

Sexual Offences Act 1956, s 11

Indictable only. Maximum sentence 7 years. For attempted offences 2 years.

1   Sex Offenders Act 1997, ss 1, 2 and Sch 1, para 1(2)(b).

Crown Court statistics England and Wales – Crown Court – Males 21+ – Incest
89.2

Year	Plea	Total Numbers sentenced	Type of sentence%					Average length of custody[1] (months)
			Discharge	Fine	Community sentence	Suspended sentence	Custody	
2000	Guilty	24	8%	0%	4%	4%	75%	47.4
	Not guilty	7	0%	0%	14%	0%	86%	57

1   Excluding life sentences. Source: Crime and Criminal Justice Unit, Home Office Ref: IOS416-02.

Guideline case

89.3   *A-G's Reference (No 1 of 1989)* (1989) 90 Cr App Rep 141, 11 Cr App Rep (S) 489 – LCJ. The view taken by the legislature of the gravity of this offence has to be judged by the maximum penalties which can be imposed. Incest by a man with a girl under 13 has a maximum penalty of life. Incest by a man with a female over 13 carries a maximum sentence of 7 years. The gravity of the offence of incest varies greatly according, primarily, to the age of the victim and the related matter, namely the degree of coercion or corruption. Aggravating factors, whatever the age of the girl may be, are:

(1)   If there is evidence that the girl has suffered physically or psychologically from the incest;

(2)   If the incest has continued at frequent intervals over a long period of time;

(3)   If the girl has been threatened or treated violently by or was terrified of the father;

(4)   If the incest has been accompanied by perversions abhorrent to the girl, eg buggery or fellatio;

(5)   If the girl has become pregnant by reason of the father failing to take contraceptive measures;

(6)   If the defendant has committed similar offences against more than one girl.

Possible mitigating features are:

(1)   A plea of guilty. It should be met by an appropriate discount, depending on the usual considerations, that is to say how promptly the defendant confessed and his degree of contrition and so on;

(2)   If it seems that there was a genuine affection on the part of the defendant rather than the intention to use the girl simply as an outlet for his sexual inclinations;

(3)   Where the girl has had previous sexual experience;

(4)   Where the girl has made deliberate attempts at seduction;

(5)   Where, as very occasionally is the case, a shorter term of imprisonment for the father may be of benefit to the victim and the family.

(The rest of the guidelines are split up into the various sections for the different ages for the victim.)

Girl under 13 years – Guideline case

89.4   *A-G's Reference (No 1 of 1989)* (1989) 90 Cr App Rep 141, 11 Cr App Rep (S) 489 – LCJ. The most difficult area is that involving girls under the age of 13. As in the case of those between 13 and 16, sexual intercourse is an offence, quite apart from the parental relationship. For victims under 13, however, a further factor comes into play. Although the girl may 'consent' to the act of intercourse in such a way as to render a charge of rape inappropriate, the girl is from the very relationship in a particularly vulnerable position, which the father is in a position to exploit due to her dependence and inexperience and, possibly, fear of disrupting relations between mother and father if she lets it be known what is happening, or fear of her father if she refuses to comply with his demands. In those circumstances the crime, although falling far short of rape, has some of the unpleasant aspects of that particular crime.

A broad guide to the level of sentence where the girl is under 13 and where there has been no plea of guilty is as follows. It is here that the widest range of sentence is likely to be found. If one can properly describe any case of incest as the 'ordinary' type of case, it will be one where the sexual relationship between husband and wife has broken down the father has probably resorted to excessive drinking and the eldest daughter is gradually, by way of familiarities, indecent acts and suggestions, made the object of the father's frustrated sexual inclinations. If the girl is not far short of her 13th birthday and there are no particularly adverse or favourable features on a not guilty plea, a term of about **6 years** on the authorities would seem to be appropriate. The younger the girl when the sexual approach is started, the more likely it will be that the girl's will was overborne and accordingly the more serious would be the crime. [Note. The imprisonment figures in this guideline case were issued before the charges to the release dates brought about by the Criminal Justice Act 1991, ss 32 to 40. The figures should be considered in line with the Practice Statement (Crime Sentencing) (1992) 95 Cr App Rep 948. However, since then the actual release dates are not greatly different and in recent years the courts have been slow to make reductions because of the 1991 changes.]

Girl under 13 years – Brother, by – Aged 13–15

89.5   *R v C and C* [2001] EWCA Crim 916, [2002] 1 Cr App Rep (S) 14. The defendants pleaded guilty to acts of incest with their sisters when they were younger. The offences were committed 14 years before conviction when the defendants were between 14 and 16 and the sisters between 9 and 13. Held. **8 months** not 3 years.

Girl aged 13–15 years – Guideline case

89.6   *A-G's Reference (No 1 of 1989)* (1989) 90 Cr App Rep 141, 11 Cr App Rep (S) 489 – LCJ. Where the girl has achieved the age of 13 will in most cases mean she has achieved puberty. This of course is the demarcation line chosen in the 1956 Act. Sentences in this area seem to vary between about **2 years to 4 or 5 years** on a plea of guilty, depending on the mitigating or aggravating factors. A broad guide to the level of sentence where the girl is 13 to 16 and where there has been no plea of guilty is: Here a sentence between about **5 years and 3 years** seems on the authorities to be appropriate. Much the same principles will apply as in the case of a girl over 16, though the likelihood of corruption increases in inverse proportion to the age of the girl. [Note. The imprisonment figures in this guideline case were issued before the charges to the release dates brought about by the Criminal Justice Act 1991, ss 32 to 40. The figures should be considered in line with the Practice Statement (Crime Sentencing) [1992] 95 Cr App Rep 948. However since then the actual release dates are not greatly different and in recent years the courts have been slow to make reductions because of the 1991 changes.]

Girl 13–15 years – Fathers

89.7   *R v MH* [2001] EWCA Crim 761, [2001] 2 Cr App Rep (S) 454. The defendant pleaded guilty to seven counts of incest with his daughter over a period of 6 years when the girl was 15 to 21. When the girl started a sexual relationship with a boyfriend he resented it and after an incident between him and the boyfriend that relationship broke up. He decided he was going to teach her about sex. He engaged in sexual activity with her when she was aged 14 without active protest on her part. She simply suffered what was going on. On her 15th birthday he first had sexual intercourse her. He would sleep in her bedroom and have intercourse with her 2–3 times a week often with his with his wife's (the girl's mother) knowledge. He moved out of the family home with his daughter and the two effectively lived as husband and wife. She permitted that to keep the peace and because she was financially dependant on him. He was 47 and had no relevant convictions. The sentencing judge said that the defendant had destroyed the young womanhood of his natural daughter and destroyed the trust that should exist between a father and daughter. Held. The sentencing judge was correct in his remarks, therefore **4½ years** was high but we will not disturb it.

Victim aged 16 or more – Guideline case

89.8 *A-G's Reference (No 1 of 1989)* (1989) 90 Cr App Rep 141, 11 Cr App Rep (S) 489 – LCJ. At one end of the scale is incest committed by a father with a daughter in her late teens or older who is a willing participant and indeed may be the instigator of the offences. In such a case the court usually need do little more than mark the fact that there has been a breach of the law and little, if anything, is required in the way of punishment. A broad guide to the level of sentence where there has been no plea of guilty is: where the girl is over 16, generally speaking a range from **3 years down to a nominal penalty** will be appropriate depending, in particular, on whether force was used, on the degree of harm, if any, to the girl, and the desirability, where it exists, of keeping family disruption to a minimum. The older the girl the greater the possibility that she may have been willing or even the instigating party to the liaison, a factor which will be reflected in the sentence. In other words, the lower the degree of corruption, the lower the penalty.

Girl 16–20 years – Fathers

89.9 *R v B* [1999] 1 Cr App Rep (S) 174. The defendant pleaded guilty to incest with his daughter and supplying cannabis to her. The defendant, who was 42 years of age, had spent the evening with his daughter, who was aged 20. Both of them had been drinking heavily and shared a cannabis cigarette. The defendant and his daughter were sleeping in the same room, though in separate beds. During the night the defendant asked his daughter to join him in his bed and engaged in sexual intercourse with her. The woman did not move nor communicate with her father during the act. She pretended to be asleep. When he pleaded guilty she said she wanted to withdraw the complaint and that she loved him. The defendant had no relevant convictions. The sentencing judge noted that the defendant had abused his position of trust and had taken advantage of his daughter's vulnerability as she was under the influence of alcohol and cannabis. Held. The hitherto good relationship between the father and daughter should not be disrupted longer than was necessary therefore **6 months** not 18 months.

See also *R v GM* [2001] EWCA Crim 1107, [2002] 1 Cr App Rep (S) 112. 3½ years imposed on a father who committed incest with his daughter when she was 17 and she became pregnant.

See also **RAPE**

INDECENCY WITH CHILDREN

For gross indecency with a girl under 14 (Indecency with Children Act 1960, s 1(1)) see **INDECENT ASSAULT ON A WOMAN**

INDECENCY, GROSS

See **GROSS INDECENCY**

90 INDECENT ASSAULT ON A MAN

90.1 Sexual Offences Act 1956, s 15

Triable either way. On indictment maximum 10 years. Summary maximum 6 months and/or £5,000.

The defendant must notify the police within 14 days (or 14 days from his release from imprisonment) his name and home address etc, any change of addresses and where he resides for 14 days or more in any 12 month period[1]. This does not apply where the other party was 18 or over unless the defendant was sentenced to 30 months or more or admitted to a hospital with a restriction order[2].

1   Sex Offenders Act 1997, ss 1, 2 and Sch 1, para. 1(1)(a)(viii).
2   Sex Offenders Act 1997, Sch 1, para 1(2)(a) and 1(3).

Crown Court statistics England and Wales[1] – Crown Court – Males 21+ – Indecent assault on a male

90.2

Year	Plea	Total Numbers sentenced	Type of sentence%					Average length of custody (months)
			Discharge	Fine	Community sentence	Suspended sentence	Custody	
2000	Guilty	163	2%	1%	22%	7%	67%	29.8
	Not guilty	86	0%	1%	14%	5%	79%	29.9

1   Excluding committals for sentence. Source: Crime and Criminal Justice Unit, Home Office Ref: IOS416-02.

Magistrates' Court Sentencing Guidelines September 2000

90.3   Entry point. **Is it so serious that only custody is appropriate?** Consider committal for sentence. Consider the impact on the victim. Examples of aggravating factors for the offence are age differential, breach of trust, injury (may be psychiatric), prolonged assault, very young victim, victim deliberately targeted, victim serving the public and vulnerable victim. An example of mitigating factors for the offence is slight contact. Examples of mitigation are age, health (physical or mental), co-operation with the police, voluntary compensation and genuine remorse.

For details about the guidelines see MAGISTRATES' COURT SENTENCING GUIDELINES at page 331.

Guideline remarks – Child victims

90.4   *R v Lennon* [1999] 1 Cr App Rep (S) 19. The defendant, was convicted of indecent assault on the 9-year-old daughter of his co-habitee. The court reviewed 43 authorities on indecent assault on a child. Held. It is never easy to sentence in these cases. The circumstances of each case will vary greatly. The judge must tailor the sentence to the particular facts. In most cases the personal circumstances of the defendant will have to take second place behind the plain duty of the court to protect victims and to reflect the clear intention of Parliament that offences of this kind are to be met with greater severity than in former years when the position of the victim may not have been so clearly focused in the public eye.

Breach of trust – Educational

90.5   *R v Bromiley* [2001] 1 Cr App Rep (S) 255. The defendant pleaded guilty to 10 counts of indecent assault on five boys aged 12 and 14 in her residential school for those with learning difficulties. She was a care assistant at a residential for boys with learning difficulties. She was later promoted to senior care assistant. The offences took place in 1984, 1986/7 and between 1995 and 1999. On two she approached one boy in a dormitory and had sexual intercourse with him. On another occasion she invited another victim to her flat, initiated sexual activity and engaged in sexual intercourse with him. She had sexual intercourse with another boy who sent her a love letter. She said she loved him. She had sexual intercourse with two further boys both at her flat and on the school premises. The boys were all willing parties. She was 37 and of previous good character. She had a history of failed relationships with men. Her risk of re-offending was assessed as high. The judge noted the frequency and severity of the abuse on vulnerable boys. He also noted she had a 9-year-old son who would suffer should his mother face a custodial sentence. He said that her punishment would be nothing like as severe as it would have been had she been a man. Held. Sexual abuse of the young in residential homes is currently a matter of serious and acute public concern. Those of either sex, who are in positions of trust in such homes, must expect to go to prison for a substantial time if they prey sexually on those in their care. The offences were a grave breach of trust and had a man had sexual intercourse with girls of such an age he would have faced a very long sentence. Therefore **5 years** was not manifestly excessive.

Breach of trust – Friend of the victim's family

90.6 *R v Nicholson* [1998] 1 Cr App R (S) 370. The defendant was convicted of nine counts of indecent assault on two brothers who were aged 12 and 10. The defendant, who was 56 years, befriended the victims and persuaded their mother that he was suitable person to take them out for the day. The abuse included touching the victims private parts both over and underneath their trousers. The defendant had two previous convictions of indecent assault and one conviction of indecency with children. The judge noted that the defendant did not accept that he had a problem and believed what he was doing was for the benefit of the young boys. Held. The assaults were serious and the conduct may affect the future of the victims. **4½ years** not 6 years was appropriate.

Breach of trust – Youth clubs etc

90.7 *R v Staples* [2001] EWCA Crim 1017, [2001] 2 Cr App Rep (S) 517. The defendant was convicted of 17 counts of indecent assault on boys who were between the ages of 8 and 11. The defendant was a leader of a Cub group and over a period of 3 years abused the boys in his care. The offences happened after the defendant had managed to separate the victims from the rest of the boys. The abuse included touching the victims' penises both over and underneath their clothing and removing both his and one of the victims' trousers and lying on top of him. There was no evidence any of the boys had been harmed by the experience. The defendant was 33 and of good character. Held. On all the offences except one there was minimal touching usually over rather than under their clothing. The offences were pre-meditated and involved a gross breach of trust, therefore **4 years** was not a manifestly excessive sentence.

Delay, long delay before arrest

90.8 *A-G's Reference (No 5 of 2001)* [2001] EWCA Crim 771, [2001] 2 Cr App Rep (S) 473 – LCJ. The defendant was convicted of three offences of indecent assault against an 8-year-old boy. In 1986, two older friends of the victim who were 13 or 14 took the boy to the defendant's flat and the defendant then 31 asked him to perform oral sex on him. The abuse was secured in the first instance by preventing the victim from escaping and pushing on his chest. The acts had a marked effect on the boy who in his middle teens became reclusive anxious and confused. The defendant was now 45. In 1987, he was convicted of indecent assault against the other two boys. He was put on probation and since then he had behaved responsibly. Held. To corrupt a child of the victim's age was a serious matter. If the offences had been committed recently the appropriate sentence would be **4 years**. Having regard to the age of the offences, the successful probation order and that it was a reference **2 years** was appropriate not 6 months.

See also **DELAY**

Female defendant

90.9 *R v Bromiley* [2001] 1 Cr App Rep (S) 255. See *Breach of trust – Educational*

R v TF [2000] 2 Cr App Rep (S) 292. See *Victim aged 13–15*

Longer than commensurate sentences

90.10 *R v Nicholson* [1998] 1 Cr App Rep (S) 370. The defendant was convicted of nine counts of indecent assault on two brothers who were aged 12 and 10. The defendant, who was 56 years, befriended the victims and persuaded their mother that he was a suitable person to take them out for the day. The abuse included touching the victims' private parts both over and underneath their trousers. The defendant had two previous convictions of indecent assault and one conviction of indecency with children. Held. Although the assaults were serious they could not be said to be the kind of assaults which would expose the public to serious harm.

See also **LONGER THAN COMMENSURATE SENTENCES** and *Persistent offender*

Victim under 10

90.11 *A-G's Reference (No 5 of 2001)* [2001] EWCA Crim 771, [2001] 2 Cr App Rep (S) 473. See *Delay, long delay before arrest*

R v Staples [2001] EWCA Crim 1017, [2001] 2 Cr App Rep (S) 517. See *Breach of trust – Youth clubs etc*

Victim aged 10–12

90.12 *R v Nicholson* [1998] 1 Cr App Rep (S) 370. See *Breach of trust – Friend of the victim's family*

R v Bromiley [2001] 1 Cr App Rep (S) 255. See *Breach of trust – Educational*

Victim aged 13–15

90.13 *R v TF* [2000] 2 Cr App Rep (S) 292. The defendant, a woman pleaded guilty to five counts of indecent assault on two 15-year-old boys and two counts of permitting premises to be used for the smoking of cannabis. She had three children and children used to visit her. On three occasions one of the victims visited the defendant where consensual sexual intercourse and oral sex took place. On two other occasions the second victim participated in consensual sexual foreplay with the defendant. The victims drank freely and used cannabis with her and her children. Her 5-year-old boy was curious about cannabis and sniffed some from a bucket and was sick. The defendant had not interfered. The pre-sentence report said she was a vulnerable and dependant personality with a degree of leaning difficulty. She 'presented as extremely immature.' Held. The defendant was neither a predatory sex offender nor a risk to the public therefore **6 months** not 12.

R v Lee [1998] 2 Cr App Rep (S) 272. The defendant, who was aged 45, pleaded guilty to indecent assault on a consenting 14-year-old boy. The counts were specimen counts. The defendant met the victim near public lavatories where they engaged in mutual masturbation. For a period of 5 months thereafter the victim visited the defendant in his flat and consented to mutual masturbation and fellatio. The victim asked for money and was given it on every visit. He showed the boy some pornographic films. The defendant had previous convictions for gross indecency in 1987 with a consenting male and was fined £150. In 1991 he had a conviction for indecent assault on a

15-year-old girl. He received 28 days suspended. In 1993 he was convicted of two indecent assault offences on a physically and mentally disabled man. The offences were committed in the lavatory of a public house. He was given probation for that. The pre-sentence report recommended a 3 year probation order involving a Sex Offender Treatment programme. The judge said that the defendant presented a potential risk to young boys or children, certainly to vulnerable members of the public. Held. Young boys must be protected against themselves. **2½ years** not 3½ years.

A-G's Reference (No 41 of 2000) [2001] 1 Cr App Rep (S) 372. The defendant pleaded guilty to two counts of indecent assault on a 13-year-old boy and three counts of taking indecent photographs of a child. The victim attended a school for children with special needs and on his way to school bumped into the defendant, whom he did not know. The victim began to talk to the boy and took him for something to eat at McDonalds. The defendant took the boy swimming and then drove him home. The defendant arranged to meet the victim later the same evening and took him to his flat. They watched an '18' film and the victim was given a mobile phone. They met again and the defendant asked the boy to pose for him for £20. The photographs included one with the victim naked with his legs apart and the defendant on top of him simulating intercourse. Another photograph showed the roles reversed. These were the basis for the indecent assault. There were other photographs of the boy masturbating and others that showed him with an erection. In addition photographs of other children were found. The defendant was 39 and had two convictions for gross indecency. They involved masturbation of a mentally defective teenage boy. For this offence he was sentenced to probation with a Sex Offender Treatment programme. He had left his accommodation without notifying anyone and had ignored the treatment programme. Held. The gravity of the appropriate sentence lay in the grooming of the handicapped victim and the giving of money and gifts. **2½ years** substituted.

91 INDECENT ASSAULT ON A WOMAN

91.1 Sexual Offences Act 1956, s 14

Indecency with Children Act 1960, s 1(1)[1] (gross indecency with a child under 14).

Both offences are triable either way. On indictment maximum 10 years. Summary maximum 6 months and/or £5,000.

The defendant must be placed on the Sex Offenders Register, which requires him/her to notify the police within 14 days (or 14 days from his release from imprisonment) his name and home address etc, any change of addresses and where he resides for 14 days or more in any 12 month period[1]. This does not apply where the other party was 18 or over unless the defendant was sentenced to 30 months or more or admitted to a hospital with a restriction order[2].

1 The maximum sentence was increased from 2 to 10 years from 1 October 1997, Crime (Sentences) Act 1997, s 52.
2 Sex Offenders Act 1997, ss 1, 2 and Sch 1, para 1(1)(a)(viii).
3 Sex Offenders Act 1997, Sch 1, para 1(2)(a) and 1(3).

Crown Court statistics England and Wales[1] – Crown Court – Males 21+ – Indecent assault on a female

91.2

Year	Plea	Total Numbers sentenced	Type of sentence%					Average length of custody (months)
			Discharge	Fine	Community sentence	Suspended sentence	Custody	
2000	Guilty	719	2%	1%	22%	5%	68%	27.2
	Not guilty	518	1%	2%	12%	2%	83%	26.9

1   Excluding committals for sentence. Source: Crime and Criminal Justice Unit, Home Office Ref: IOS416-02.

Magistrates' Court Sentencing Guidelines September 2000

91.3   Entry point. Is it so serious that only custody is appropriate? Consider committal for sentence. Consider the impact on the victim. Examples of aggravating factors for the offence are age differential, breach of trust, injury (may be psychiatric), prolonged assault, very young victim, victim deliberately targeted, victim serving the public and vulnerable victim. An example of mitigating factors for the offence is slight contact. Examples of mitigation are age, health (physical or mental), co-operation with the police, voluntary compensation and genuine remorse.

For details about the guidelines see MAGISTRATES' COURT SENTENCING GUIDELINES at page 331.

See also RAPE

Guideline remarks – Child victims

91.4   *R v Lennon* [1999] 1 Cr App Rep (S) 19. The court reviewed 43 authorities on indecent assault on a child. Held. It is never easy to sentence in these cases. The circumstances of each case will vary greatly. The judge must tailor the sentence to the particular facts. In most cases the personal circumstances of the defendant will have to take second place behind the plain duty of the court to protect victims and to reflect the clear intention of Parliament that offences of this kind are to be met with greater severity than in former years when the position of the victim may not have been so clearly focused in the public eye.

R v Stapley [2001] 1 Cr App Rep (S) 302 – LCJ. The defendant, aged 67 and of good character, fondled the breasts of a 13 year old. He showed her indecent photographs. Held. The courts have to have regard to the public perception of the way offences of this sort are treated and have to make it plain, in order to discourage and to deter others that custodial sentences will invariably be passed.

Guideline remarks – The victim

91.5   *A-G's Reference (No 31 of 2000)* [2001] 1 Cr App Rep (S) 386. The effect on the victim is a very important consideration. Women are entitled to walk home without fear of being attacked by men.

Breach of trust – Doctor

91.6   *R v Ghosh* [1999] 1 Cr App Rep (S) 225. The defendant was convicted of two counts of indecent assault on a patient aged 20. The victim had been receiving treatment for breast pain when the defendant handled her breasts in an examination, which did not conform to the usual clinical guidelines. The victim also complained of back pain and the defendant suggested that a massage would reduce the discomfort. The following day whilst performing the massage the defendant squeezed the victim's bottom and breasts and inserted a finger several times into her anus and vagina. As a consequence the victim found it difficult to go to the doctor. The defendant who was aged 57 had one unrelated conviction. As a consequence of the conviction the defendant has lost his income, his wife and his profession. He suffered from ill health. Held. As these offences were committed in breach of trust, 3 years cannot be criticised. As an act of mercy **2 years** not 3 was appropriate.

A-G's Reference (No 6 of 1999) [2000] 2 Cr App Rep (S) 67. The defendant, an osteopath was convicted of four counts of indecent assault on patients. We would expect at least **30 months**.

Breach of trust – Friend of victim's family – Less than 4 years appropriate

91.7 *A-G's Reference (No 54 of 1997)* [1998] 2 Cr App Rep (S) 324. The defendant pleaded guilty to three counts of indecent assault on three girls, one count of indecent assault on a boy and four counts of indecency with children. The four victims, who were aged between 9 and 13 and were children of friends of the defendant, were allowed to stay overnight on the defendant's boat. The defendant touched and digitally penetrated the girls' vaginas, touched the boy's penis, drew over the victims naked bodies with washable pens and procured them to draw over his penis whilst he was naked. The offences were over 'a long time'. The defendant, who was 53, was of previous good character. The sentencing judge rejected the defendant's denials of sexual motivation and that the children were lying. Held. Having regard to position of trust the defendant was in, the age of the victims and the degree of indecent assault a total sentence in the region of **3 years** would have been appropriate. As it was a reference, **27 months**, not 12 months.

R v W [1999] 2 Cr App Rep (S) 150. The defendant, who was 34 years of age, pleaded guilty to two counts of indecent assault on his niece, who was aged 6 years. The victim had to stay with the defendant and his wife because her mother was in hospital. The defendant entered the victim's bedroom, removed her underwear and touched her vagina; on one occasion he digitally penetrated her. The conduct caused the victim pain and as a result she became tearful and clingy and often reluctant to go upstairs or sleep on her own. The defendant was of previous good character. Held. It was inappropriate for the sentencing judge to note that these offences were 'not much short of rape'. The risk of the defendant molesting children in the future was medium to low and he accepted the impact that his conduct had had on the victim. **2½ years** not 5 years was appropriate.

A-G's Reference (No 46 of 1999) [2000] 1 Cr App Rep (S) 310. The defendant pleaded guilty to nine counts of indecent assault and eight counts of indecency with a child. Some were sample counts. The defendant assaulted three children aged between 7 and 8, one child aged between 5 and 6 and one girl of 15 years of age. The defendant was a friend of the victims' families and would occasionally visit their houses. The younger victims suffered digital penetration and were forced to touch the defendant's penis and take it in their mouths. In addition the defendant touched the 15-year-old victim's breasts over her clothing. The defendant, who was 55 years of age, had no relevant similar convictions. The risk of re-offending was assessed as significant. He was sentenced to 3 years probation with the condition of attendance at sex offenders' programmes. In breach of the conditions he had gone abroad. After sentence although prohibited from seeing his grandchildren by his daughter he said, 'She'll come round in time.' His attitude to the offences had not changed. Held. The appropriate sentence if he had contested the case was **6 years** and **4 years** as he pleaded. As it was a reference **3 years** substituted. His licence should be extended so it was 3 years from his release.

A-G's Reference (No 77 of 1999) [2000] 2 Cr App Rep (S) 250. The defendant was convicted of three counts of indecent assault. The defendant indecently assaulted his niece for about a year when she was between the ages of 10 and 11, when she was staying at his house. The defendant put his hand inside the girl's knickers and touched the victim's vagina and would occasionally expose his penis to her. The defendant, who was 46 years of age, had no relevant previous convictions and after conviction he admitted the offences and expressed deep remorse. The defendant was given probation with conditions. Since his sentence a report told of his high level motivation and that his relationship with his partner was in tact and that his own children were not at risk. His risk of re-offending was described as being relatively low. Held. Having regard to the progress the defendant has made a **3 years** probation order was not unduly lenient, it was within the residual discretion of the judge to take an exceptional course.

A-G's Reference (No 1 of 2001) [2001] EWCA Crim 766, [2001] 2 Cr App Rep (S) 469 – LCJ. The defendant was convicted of indecent assault on a 10-year-old girl. The defendant was a good friend of the victim's stepfather and would visit their home with his wife once a fortnight. The defendant sat the victim on his lap and digitally penetrated her. The defendant, who was 55 years of age, had one previous conviction for indecent assault against his daughter when she was 6 years old. When bathing the child the defendant inserted a finger into her vagina. The defendant was in ill health. The sentencing judge noted that the defendant had breached the trust not only of the victim but also of her parents and that his plea of not guilty had meant that the victim had had to give evidence. Held. The appropriate sentence was 3 years. As it was a reference **21 months** was appropriate not a probation order.

See also *A-G's Reference (No 27 of 2001)* [2001] EWCA Crim 1283, [2002] 1 Cr App Rep (S) 175. **27 months** on a man who indecently assaulted friends of his daughter.

Breach of trust – friend of victim's family – 4 to 6 years appropriate

91.8   *R v D* [2001] EWCA Crim 248, [2001] 2 Cr App Rep (S) 281. The defendant pleaded guilty to two counts of indecent assault on a girl who was aged 5. The defendant was married to the victim's grandmother and had offered to look after the victim and her brother. The defendant began to tickle the victim's stomach and then removed her trousers and digitally penetrated her. The defendant then took the girl upstairs and made her lie on top of him so that her vagina touched his penis; he then digitally penetrated her again. The defendant, who was 29, had four convictions for indecent assault against his stepdaughter aged 11, who was the victim's aunt. That abuse involved digital penetration. The sentencing judge said that this was a very revealing previous conviction. Where children are concerned 'once is too often, twice is completely and utterly unacceptable. You are an ongoing danger to children'. Held. **4 years** longer than commensurate and an extension period of 3 years was not a manifestly excessive.

Breach of trust – Friend of victim's family – 7 years or more appropriate

91.9   *R v Sweeney* [1998] 2 Cr App Rep (S) 43. The defendant, who now was 65, pleaded guilty to 17 counts of indecent assault on seven girls aged between, 6 and 14 between 1962 and 1993. The six victims were either related to the defendant or he was a friend of their families. The abuse for the most part consisted of frequent digital penetration of their vaginas but also included attempts to make the victims masturbate him. The abuse had caused one of the girls to bleed and another was in such pain that she would lie awake all night crying. One of the victims took an overdose as a result of the abuse. The defendant had no previous convictions and was a pillar of the community. The pre-sentence report said he was a continuing risk to children. The sentencing judge noted that the offending did not involve violence. Held. Because of the relatively moderate nature of the sexual activity **7 years** not 9.

R v Burton-Barri [1999] 2 Cr App Rep (S) 252. The defendant, who was 63 when convicted, pleaded guilty to 44 counts of indecent assault, taking indecent photographs of a child and gross indecency with a child. 23 counts were for indecent assault, 16 on females and 7 on males. The ages were from 8 upwards. The abuse took place over a period of 25 years with children of friends of the defendant and his own stepchildren. He inveigled his way into the confidence of the parents by acts of kindness and generosity. The offences took place when the defendant offered to babysit the victims and included videoing the defendant performing oral sex on the victims and having the act reciprocated. Vaginal and anal penetration took place and he inserted objects into one of the victims' anus. Presents were given. The defendant was 63 with convictions in 1992 for gross indecency with a child and taking indecent photographs. Held. The sentence had to reflect the fact that although the abuse was appalling it was not as appalling as it could have been. It had to be borne in mind that the defendant should not have been sentenced as he might have been for committing rape or buggery. **10 years** not 14½ years was appropriate.

Breach of trust - Police officer

91.10 *R v Cairns* [1998] 1 Cr App Rep (S) 434. The defendant pleaded guilty to three counts of indecent assault on girls who were between the ages of 13 and 14. They were specimen counts. The defendant, who was 23 at the time of the first assault, was a serving police officer who assisted in the running of a youth club. The defendant persuaded the first victim, who was aged 14 to enter into a sexual relationship with him. The indecency progressed from the defendant kissing the victim and fondling her breasts over her clothing to engaging in mutual oral sex and digital penetration of her vagina. This conduct took place both in the defendant's flat and in the countryside. The second victim was abused just before she was 13. The defendant touched the victim's breasts and vagina over her clothing when they were in a stockroom together and on occasions forced her to masturbate him and perform oral sex upon him. The second victim also engaged in sexual activity when the first victim was also present. The defendant kissed the third victim, who was 13, when he was driving her home. Intimacy progressed as with the other two victims. The defendant was 36 and of previous good character. Held. The defendant was not only in a position of trust but as a serving police officer a position of authority. The offences were not the worst kind of indecent assault, therefore **5 years** not 7 years was appropriate.

Breach of trust – Taxi driver

91.11 *R v Saboor* [2000] 1 Cr App Rep (S) 40. The defendant was convicted of indecent assault against a passenger in his minicab. The victim and her male friend travelled in the defendant's minicab after an evening out. The companion was dropped off whilst the victim was asleep. The defendant moved into the backseat and digitally penetrated the woman. The defendant, who was 28, had no previous convictions. The sentencing judge noted that this assault was made worse as it was committed by a person in a position of trust. Held. This was a very serious assault. Society rightly looks to the courts to offer what protection it can to those who use taxicabs and expose themselves to the possibility of attack by the drivers. **3 years** was an appropriate sentence. Having regard to the personal circumstances of the defendant including his wife was unable to speak English and the death of three of their children from an inherited lung disorder and as an act of mercy **2 years**.

R v Sailani (13 July 2001, unreported). The defendant was convicted of indecent assault. He was a taxi driver who kissed one of his passengers at night on the cheek and tried to kiss her on the lips. She refused to allow him and he brushed his hand across her breasts. Held. The trust between the taxi driver and the passenger must be maintained. People who travel at night need protection. The breach of trust was serious but **9 months** not 2 years. The deportation order quashed.

Breach of trust – Teachers etc

91.12 *A-G's Reference (No 44 of 2000)* [2001] 1 Cr App Rep (S) 460. The defendant pleaded guilty to eight counts of indecent assault on a girl, five of which related to girls under 13 and one count of indecent assault on a male. They spanned from 1969–1977. The victims were pupils aged 11–13 at a private preparatory school where he was deputy headmaster and then headmaster. He would administer punishment for poor spelling etc. He required them to lie across his lap and sometimes he would remove their knickers to expose their buttocks. He would then perform circular hand movement on the girls. The offences came to light in 1977 and nobody told the police or thought it appropriate to inform the police. He was 67. He pleaded guilty after the judge had indicated that he would not go to prison. The judge gave him **18 months suspended**. Held. We doubt there were exceptional circumstances to suspend the sentence, but no order made because the prosecution had been involved in the plea bargain.

See also SEXUAL INTERCOURSE, BREACH OF TRUST – *Teachers*

Breach of trust – Workplace

91.13 *A-G's Reference (No 25 of 1997)* [1998] 1 Cr App Rep (S) 310. The defendant was convicted of two counts of indecent assault on a girl aged 15 years. The defendant, who was 64 years of age owned a pet shop and the victim was placed him on work placement. Over the course of the first week he made lewd comments towards her, cuddled her, squeezed her bottom on several occasions, ran his hand over her bare back, kissed and bit her neck, stroked her upper thigh, felt her right breast underneath her clothing and squeezed her vagina over the top of her jeans. The acts were done despite the protestations of the victim. He gave her £5 and told her not to tell anyone. She was worried about being given a bad report. The victim was very distressed and became withdrawn. There was no remorse. The defendant had a previous conviction for indecent assault 11 years earlier. Held. He was in a position of trust. The conduct was a campaign of sexual harassment towards a girl, though it was not the worst indecent assaults. The only mitigation was his age. **12 months** was the appropriate sentence. As it was a reference **8 months** not a £500 fine.

See also *Workplace*

Deception, by – Pretending to be a Doctor

91.14 *A-G's Reference (No 62 of 1998)* [2000] 2 Cr App Rep (S) 286. The defendant, who was now 59 years of age, was convicted of four offences of indecent assault on women, six of obtaining property by deception, three of unlawful wounding, two of supplying prescription-only medicines, and nine of perverting the course of justice. For 8 years the defendant passed himself off as a doctor, establishing a laboratory and styling himself as Dr, BSc, MSc, PhD, and DSc. The defendant was not medically qualified and an expert said that he had very little knowledge and experience. He carried out vaginal examinations on female patients. A 15-year-old girl had something inserted between her legs, and she screamed. The defendant inserted his finger into the vagina of a 25-year-old woman and on the next day he pretended to take a sample from her by inserting a stick into her vagina. He then inserted his finger and touched her clitoris. The victim was very upset. The defendant told her that she was suffering from a sexually transmitted disease. Other women were told that they had sexually transmitted diseases and one had a wooden spatula inserted into her vagina and the other was examined with a speculum. The 3 older victims' relationships with their partners broke up. The defendant had convictions for ABH for which he received 3 months and obtaining property by deception for which he received 6 months. Held. The appropriate sentence for the indecent assault and related offences was **5–6 years** with 2 years consecutive on the second indictment for perverting the course of justice. The sentence of 5 years was unduly lenient. Having regard to the age of the defendant, his state of health and that this was a reference it was not necessary to increase the **5 years** sentence.

Defendant aged 10–13

91.15   *R v W* [1999] 1 Cr App Rep (S) 488. The defendant was convicted of indecent assault on a 12–year-old girl. He was acquitted of attempted rape. The victim was walking home in the early evening when the defendant caught up with her and started to kiss her. The defendant, who was aged 13, then put his hand down the victim's clothes and touched her vaginal area. The victim pulled his hand away and attempted to escape whereupon the defendant tripped her over, pulled her jogging bottoms down and simulated sexual intercourse on her. The defendant had no previous convictions. Held. These cases are extremely difficult to deal with. It is extremely important that if any woman, whatever age, and in particularly if a child, is sexually assaulted then that is an extremely serious matter and must be dealt with by appropriate punishment. On the other hand when the attacker is no more than a child, the overriding consideration is to do the best to see what can be done to assist him, but at the same time to mark the seriousness of the offence. Here the two principles clash. It was a gratuitous assault but a **supervision order** rather than 8 months was appropriate.

Defendant aged 14–15

91.16   *R v D* [1998] 2 Cr App Rep (S) 292. The defendant, then aged 15, pleaded guilty to three counts of indecent assault on a 4–year-old girl. The defendant was the son of a friend of the victim's mother and was a babysitter for the victim and her brothers. On two occasions he placed his finger in the victim's anus and vagina and on one occasion placed his penis into her mouth. He also masturbated himself. The abuse became apparent when the victim claimed that the defendant had 'shagged' her. He tried to bribe her into silence. The defendant had no convictions but had two cautions for offences of buggery against his sister and brother. He had buggered his sister once when she was aged five and he was 12 years old, and buggered his brother who was aged ten on a number of occasions. He had then failed to respond to the help that was available. The pre-sentence report said unless he received help the risk of re-offending was high. A supervision order was recommended. The sentencing judge held that the defendant constituted a significant risk to children and that a custodial sentence was essential. Held The defendant is plainly a dangerous man in relation to sex offences and children. The offences were extremely serious. There was no doubt he needed therapy and deserved punishment. There were no Sexual Offenders programmes in YOI. Until he had the therapy he constituted a significant risk to young children. A substantial custodial sentence was required to punish him and protect young children. If it was [the then s 53] detention he would receive therapy in a secure environment. **4 years' detention** was severe but not manifestly excessive.

R v B [2000] 1 Cr App Rep (S) 177. The defendant, pleaded guilty to three counts of indecent assault on a female child, one count of indecent assault on a boy aged 3 years, and one count of committing gross indecency with a child. One of the counts was a specimen count. The defendant when aged 14 and 15 baby-sat the victims, two of whom were his half-sisters, who were aged 4 and 6. The male victim was the son of a friend of the defendant's stepmother. The defendant touched and sucked the boy's penis, touched the female victims vaginal area, encouraged one of the victims to perform oral sex on him and simulated sexual intercourse upon her. The defendant was of previous good character. He showed signs of being unable to control his behaviour without therapeutic help. The pre-sentence report said a high level of therapeutic input was required. Held. This type of offence will always pose problems for a court. Balanced against the interests of the offender in seeking a way to prevent further offending are, of course, the damage to his victims and the public abhorrence for this type of crime. We are not saying custody was wrong in principle, but now he has served a short period of custody it is possible to take a different course. **Supervision order** not 2 years' detention.

A-G's Reference (No 61 of 1999) [2000] 1 Cr App Rep (S) 516 – LCJ. The defendant pleaded guilty to indecent assault on a girl aged 12. His not guilty plea to attempted rape was accepted. The victim was walking home from school when the defendant, who was 14, approached her. She agreed to go into some bushes with him where he asked her to have sexual intercourse with him. When she refused he pushed her to the ground and forced his penis into her mouth. On withdrawing his penis he ejaculated over her leg. Held. Such behaviour was not less unacceptable because it was committed by one of such youthful age. A supervision order was an unduly lenient sentence; the appropriate sentence was 12 months detention. As this was a reference the court could not impose more than 6 months and it would not be in the public interest that he should serve such a short period of detention; therefore a **supervision order** was undisturbed.

R v TW [2001] 1 Cr App Rep (S) 128. The defendant pleaded guilty to three counts of indecent assault on a girl of 5 or 6 years of age. A not guilty verdict was entered on two rape counts. The defendant knew the victim through her brother, as they were school friends. Over the period of a year, the defendant, put his penis into the victim's mouth, lay on top of her with his penis between her thighs and touched the outside of her vagina. The defendant, who was 14 years of age, had no previous convictions. The risk of the defendant re-offending was low, particularly if the defendant became involved in a relationship with a child of his own age, but that only a custodial sentence would do. After sentence the education he received was undemanding and obstructed by others. Held. Looking at it from the defendant's point of view it would be better if he was seeing a psychiatrist and being educated outside. The sentencing judge was imposed the correct sentence of **15 months**. Sentence reduced to **12 months** so as not to interfere with the next academic year.

Defendant aged 16–17

91.17   *R v Oldfield* [2000] 1 Cr App Rep (S) 73. The defendant pleaded guilty to indecent assault on a 20 year old woman as she walking home in the early hours of the morning. The defendant, who was 16 years of age, grabbed the victim from behind and pushed her to the ground and pinned her down. He put one hand over her mouth and the other seized her wrists. He forced his hand down her trousers and inside her underwear where he touched her vagina. The force broke the top button and the zipper. A man who was nearby frightened the defendant and the defendant escaped, stealing the victim's purse. The victim was hysterical and had scratches to her neck and breastbone. The defendant had two previous convictions for ABH, which had no sexual element. The risk of offending and the risk to the public was assessed as high. There was no sign of any mental illness. The sentencing judge noted that the defendant was lucky that the man intervened as he may have been facing a charge of attempted rape. An indefinate supervision order was made. Held. Having regard for the age of the defendant **3 years** not 4 years.

See also *R v Gallagher* [2002] EWCA Crim 653, [2002] 2 Cr App Rep (S) 523.

Delay, long delay before conviction

91.18   *R v Sweeney* [1998] 2 Cr App Rep (S) 43. The defendant, who now was 65, pleaded guilty to 17 counts of indecent assault on seven girls aged between, 6 and 14 between 1962 and 1993. The six victims were either related to the defendant or he was a friend of their families. The abuse for the most part consisted of frequent digital penetration of their vaginas but also included attempts to make the victims masturbate him. The abuse had caused one of the girls to bleed and another was in such pain that she would lie awake all night crying. One of the victims took an overdose as a result of the abuse. The defendant had no previous convictions and was a pillar of the community. The pre-sentence report said he was a continuing risk to children. The sentencing judge noted that the offending did not involve violence. Held. Because of the relatively moderate nature of the sexual activity **7 years** not 9.

R v Burton-Barri [1999] 2 Cr App Rep (S) 252. The defendant, who was 63 when convicted, pleaded guilty to 44 counts of indecent assault, taking indecent photographs of a child and gross indecency with a child. 23 counts were for indecent assault, 16 on females and 7 on males. The ages were from 8 upwards. The abuse took place over a period of 25 years with children of friends of the defendant and his own stepchildren. He inveigled his way into the confidence of the parents by acts of kindness and generosity. The offences took place when the defendant offered to babysit the victims and included videoing the defendant performing oral sex on the victims and having the act reciprocated. Vaginal and anal penetration took place and he inserted objects into one of the victims' anus. Presents were given. The defendant was 63 with convictions in 1992 for gross indecency with a child and taking indecent photographs. Held. The sentence had to reflect the fact that although the abuse was appalling it was not as appalling as it could have been. It had to be borne in mind that the defendant should not have been sentenced as he might have been for committing rape or buggery. **10 years** not 14½ years was appropriate.

R v JW [2000] 1 Cr App Rep (S) 234. The defendant, who was now aged 80 years, pleaded guilty to 14 counts of indecent assault on his daughter over a period of 4 years when the girl was aged between 11 and 15. The counts were specimen counts. The offences were committed 40 years earlier. The assaults included digital penetration of her vagina, forcing the victim to touch his erect penis and to masturbate him and simulating sexual intercourse with her. The victim was threatened with violence if she did not comply. The pre-sentence report referred to his lack of insight into his responsibility. The sentencing judge noted that these offences occurred when the maximum sentence was 2 years, save where the victim was under 13, where the maximum was 5 years. Held. The offences had grave consequences. According to modern sentencing standards the appropriate sentence would perhaps go into **double figures**. For the sentencing standards at the time 8 years would have been likely on a guilty plea. Delay is a factor to be taken into account but the weight to be attached is limited. Great caution is required lest discount is accorded for what is in truth an aspect of the crime itself. Age is another factor but there is no particular ailment or hardship here. The present and future interest of the victim is of high priority. Taking into account the time that has passed and the age of the defendant **3½ years** was appropriate and will send the right message to him.

R v R [2000] 1 Cr App Rep (S) 244. The defendant pleaded guilty at a late stage in the trial to four counts of indecent assault against his niece and nephew over a period of 4 years. Counts of rape and attempted buggery were not persued. When the assaults began in 1971 the victims were aged 10 and 8 respectively and the defendant was

14 years of age. The defendant digitally penetrated the female victim and performed oral sex on her. The male victim was forced to masturbate the defendant and perform oral sex on him. The defendant was arrested in 1997. He was now 41 with a number of convictions for dishonesty and violence but no sex convictions. There was no sexual misconduct for 25 years. Held. The correct approach is to sentence him for the penalty which would then have then been appropriate. These offences included a significant degree of breach of trust, however consideration must be given to the fact that the defendant was little more than a child when he committed these offences. **2 years** not 4 years was appropriate.

R v North [2001] 1 Cr App Rep (S) 109. The defendant pleaded guilty to four counts of indecent assault on a girl who was between the ages of 10 and 13. The offences took place between 1979 and 1982. The defendant befriended the victim's mother and became a frequent visitor to her home. The defendant touched the girl on her vagina and masturbated in front of her. On one occasion the defendant took the victim to his home and showed her a pornographic film and held a vibrator against her, outside her clothing. There was no penetration nor digital penetration. From 1988 the defendant sent the victim money, first, through her mother and subsequently directly. In 1998 the victim made the allegations. The defendant, who was now 73 years and was treated as of good character. He showed remorse and was in failing health. The sentencing judge noted that there was not a high risk of the defendant re-offending but there was some risk to the public. Held. The defendant had groomed and trained a young girl for his own sexual gratification, and there was a grave breach of trust. If recent the sentence would in no way be excessive. The court must take into account the maximum sentence available at the time that the offences were committed, which was 5 years. On this basis alone **2 years** not 3.

A-G's Reference (No 15 of 2000) [2001] 1 Cr App Rep (S) 82. The defendant was convicted of nine counts of indecent assault on a girl, four counts of indecency on a boy and two counts of indecency with children. The defendant sexually abused his three children over a period of 11 years from 1966 to 1977. The defendant abused his eldest daughter when she was between the ages of 9 and 15 by touching her vaginal area with his hand and his penis, digitally penetrating her and masturbating in her presence. The defendant abused his adopted son when he was between the ages of 5 and 12 by forcing the boy to masturbate him and reciprocating the act and forcing his penis into the boy's anus. The defendant's adopted daughter was abused over an 18 month period between the ages of 12 and 13. The defendant masturbated in her presence, digitally penetrated the victim, forced his penis into her mouth and achieved slight vaginal penetration with his penis. The defendant who was 71 when convicted was arrested over 20 years after the offences occurred. He had no previous convictions. Due to the date that the offences took place the maximum sentences were 5 years for the counts on a girl under 13, 2 years for the offences with a female over the age of 13 and 10 years for the indecent assault on a male. Held. The appropriate sentence in this instance would have been at least **6 or 7 years**. Taking into account the defendant's age and the fact that he had poor health and his reliance on a wheelchair for movement 6 was appropriate. As it was a reference **4 years** not 2 years **suspended**.

A-G's Reference (No 28 of 2000) [2001] 1 Cr App Rep (S) 307 – LCJ. The defendant pleaded guilty to two counts of indecent assault on a girl under the age of 10 and two counts of indecency with a child. The offences began in 1973 when the victim was 4 and continued until 1980. The abuse took place on an almost daily basis, where the defendant would fondle the victim, and coerce her to masturbate him. When the girl asked him to stop he did so. The defendant, who was 51 years of age, also indecently assaulted the son of a woman with whom he lived after the failure of his marriage to the first victim's mother. His new partner found the defendant in the kitchen with the defendant's penis in the boy's mouth. He said to the boy, 'Come on swallow it.' The relationship also ended. He showed remorse and took very seriously the gravity of his offending. The reports indicated that he was not predatory and offences would only occur in the family context. He was sentenced to probation and the order was progressing well and the defendant had obtained employment. Held. The appropriate sentence would have been **3 years** on a plea. As it was a reference 2 years would have to be imposed of which the defendant would only serve 1 year. The probation order imposed by the sentencing judge was for 3 years, therefore the public would be better protected by the continuation of this order. **3 years probation order** was appropriate in these exceptional circumstances.

[Note. The maximum penalty for indecent assault was increased from 2 years to 10 years for victims 13 and over from 16 September 1985.]

Se also **DELAY**

Extended sentences (ie licence extended)

91.19 Powers of Criminal Courts (Sentencing) Act 2000, s 85 (previously the Crime and Disorder Act 1998, s 58).

R v Barros [2000] 2 Cr App Rep (S) 327. The defendant pleaded guilty to indecent assault of a female. The defendant left a pub and about 1am he met the victim outside a supermarket. She was under 16 and they began kising. The defendant touched the victim over her clothes and pulled her skirt up and digitally penetrated her vagina. The girl said that she wanted to go. The defendant took the victim's hand and put it on his penis over his trousers. After pulling the victim to the ground and holding her, she struggled free and ran away. At that stage the defendant said he was not trying to have sex with the victim. When interviewed the defendant admitted the offence. The defendant, now aged 36, had no previous convictions. He was sentenced on the basis that he thought the victim to be 17 years old the sentence was 4 years with an extended period of licence of 3 years under what is now s 85. Held. 4 years cannot be justified after a guilty plea and this was not an appropriate case for an extended licence.

R v Thornton [2000] 2 Cr App Rep (S) 47. 5 years extended sentence for man who put his hand up the victim's skirt and pulled down her tights.

R v Pullen [2001] EWCA Crim 1071, [2002] 1 Cr App Rep (S) 60. 3½ years with an extension period of 2 years for a man who dragged a woman off her bicycle and squeezed her breast.

See also *R v Horrobin* [2002] EWCA Crim 566, [2002] 2 Cr App Rep (S) 566 and **EXTENDED SENTENCE**

Factual basis for sentence after an acquitted of rape

91.20 *R v Gillespie* [1998] 2 Cr App Rep (S) 61. The defendant was acquitted of attempted rape, but pleaded guilty to indecent assault on a 14–year-old girl. The defendant was a door-to-door salesman and gained access to the victim's house when she was alone by asking to use the lavatory. The victim alleged that the defendant forcibly undressed her and attempted to rape her though only succeeded in touching the outside of her vagina with his penis. The jury rejected this account. Held. The judge when sentencing the defendant on the count of indecent assault either based his judgment on the evidence of the victim, which is wrong as this was rejected by the jury, or failed to make clear which part of the victim's evidence he was accepting. The court did not know on what factual basis the judge sentenced and was left with a feeling that it was inconsistent with the jury's acquittal of attempted rape. The indecency was not of the worst kind, therefore **6 months**, not 4 years.

R v Iles [1998] 2 Cr App Rep (S) 63. The defendant was acquitted of rape but convicted of indecent assault on a 15-year-old girl, arising out of the same facts. The defendant had admitted the act of intercourse to the police. The victim was very drunk and had been raped earlier by a third party; the defendant was aware of this. The defendant then had consensual sexual intercourse with the victim, which amounted to indecent assault as the victim was under 16 and in law could not consent. The defendant has previous convictions but not for sexual offences. Held. The maximum sentence for unlawful sexual intercourse is 2 years, *R v Hinton* 1995 16 Cr App Rep (S) 271. The defendant should be treated as though he pleaded guilty therefore **15 months** not 2 years.

See also: *R v Gore* [1998] 1 Cr App Rep (S) 413. The sentencing basis of the judge could not stand. It will have to be based on a consenting victim here.

Father/stepfather, by – Victim under 10 – Less than 3 years appropriate

91.21   *R v Lennon* [1999] 1 Cr App Rep (S) 19. The defendant, who was 52, was convicted of indecent assault on the 9–year-old daughter of his co-habitee. The defendant had masturbated and subsequently jumped onto the victim, pulled off her trousers and underwear and attempted to penetrate her with his penis. It was treated as a single act. Held. Each sentence must be tailored to the particular facts. **2 years** was not manifestly excessive. [Facts are in short supply in this case.]

A-G's Reference (No 35 of 1998) [1999] 1 Cr App Rep (S) 400. The defendant, who was 61, pleaded guilty to four counts of indecent assault on two girls aged between 7 and 11. The victims were the daughters of the defendant's girlfriend with whom he was staying. The defendant invited the victim's into his bed when he was naked and subsequently placed his penis between their legs. The defendant was arrested but without any evidence except for the girls there was no prosecution for a year. This conduct occurred on a second occasion after the defendant had shown the victims a pornographic video. The defendant was treated as being of good character. The judge noted the defendant remained a high risk unless his behaviour was fully addressed. Held. The appropriate sentence was **12–18 months** considering his age and the plea. As it was a reference **9 months** was appropriate not a probation order.

A-G's Reference (No 20 of 1998) [1999] 1 Cr App Rep (S) 280. The defendant pleaded guilty to four counts of gross indecency and three counts of indecent assault on the daughter of his co-habitee, who was between 8 and 11. The counts were specimen counts. The defendant had touched the victim's vagina with his penis, his finger and a vibrator and masturbated in front of her, and ejaculated onto her naked leg. It was accepted that he had not digitally penetrated her. The defendant, who was 37, had a record but no previous convictions of this kind. The Jjudge gave him a 3½ years probation order. The girl was dismayed the defendant might lose his liberty. Held. This was very grave conduct, considering the defendant was in a position of responsibility and that the offences were repeated on several occasions over a number of years. We would have expected **4 years**. As it was a reference and going to prison for him will be particularly harsh **2 years**.

A-G's Reference (No 72 of 1999) [2000] 2 Cr App Rep (S) 79. 2½ years imposed on a man who touched his stepdaughter's vagina whilst she was between the ages of 4 and 8.

Girl under 10 – Stepdaughter

91.22   *A-G's Reference (No 15 of 2001)* [2001] EWCA Crim 850, [2001] 2 Cr App Rep (S) 532 – LCJ. The defendant was convicted of gross indecency on his 4-year-old stepdaughter and perverting the course of justice. The defendant had consumed a considerable amount of alcohol when his wife found him astride the girl.

The defendant had pulled down the child's underwear and was masturbating over her. His wife came in and found him astride the girl and there was semen on the crotch of her knickers and her T-shirt. The defendant tried to destroy the evidence by putting the sheet in the washing machine while she attempted to prevent it. She also tried to call the police and he ripped the phone out of the socket. When she tried to use her mobile to call the police he snatched it. He was arrested and denied the incident. The defendant, who was 23 years of age, had no relevant convictions. He was in the Navy with promotion prospects. He was dismissed from the services, lost £8,000 in pension rights and lost Navy quarters. He also lost being with his two daughters and his stepdaughter. He received 6 months for the indecency and 2 months consecutive for the pervert. Held. The 2 months was adequate and rightly consecutive. A sentence must be imposed as a deterrent. The appropriate sentence was **2½ years**. As it was a reference **18 months** not 6 months.

Father/stepfather, by – Victim under 10 – 3 to 4 years appropriate

91.23 *A-G's Reference (No 32 of 1998)* [1999] 1 Cr App Rep (S) 316. The defendant pleaded guilty to five offences of indecent assault and one of indecency, with the daughter of his co-habitee, who was between the ages of 6 and 8. The defendant, who was aged 44, admitted to behaving indecently with the child on between 15 and 20 occasions, which included simulating sexual intercourse, digital penetration of the victim's vagina and anus, and mutual oral sex. The child was extremely traumatised and had to receive treatment for her mental condition. The defendant had no previous convictions and had demonstrated genuine remorse. The psychiatrist's report stated that the defendant had distorted the boundaries between affection and sexuality with his stepdaughter. The judge noted that the defendant was not a 'true paedophile' and presented a low risk of re-offending. Held. **3 years** was lenient but not an unduly lenient.

A-G's Reference (No 61 of 1998) [1999] 2 Cr App Rep (S) 226 – LCJ. The defendant pleaded guilty to eight counts indecent assault on the handicapped daughter of the woman with whom he cohabited. The victim suffered from quadriplegia, cerebral palsy and dystonia, which affected her limb movements and voice. The defendant was the father figure of the house. Over a 2 year period when the victim was between the ages of 9 and 11 the defendant forced the victim to masturbate him, digitally penetrated her, performed oral sex on her and forced her to reciprocate. The acts were not reported and it wasn't till 3 years later her school nurse was told about it. The defendant, who was 40, had no previous convictions for similar behaviour. The judge noted that the child's trust had been abused and the child's innocence betrayed. Held. The appropriate sentence on a trial was 4 years or more. On a plea it should have been **3 years**. As it was a reference **2 years** not a probation.

Father/stepfather, by – Victim under 10 – More than 4 years appropriate

91.24 *R v Densley S* [1998] 2 Cr App Rep (S) 17. The defendant pleaded guilty to 12 counts of indecent assault on his daughter over a period of 5 years and his step-daughter over a period of 8 years. The abuse began when both victims were aged 8. The first abuse started in 1988 and the abuse on the second child started in 1991. The defendant required the victims to masturbate him, perform oral sex on him and he digitally penetrated their vaginas. He showed one child pornographic videos. Once he pinned one down and put his tongue in her vagina. He offered £50 and £100 for sex and then refused her to use the telephone unless she had sex with him. One of the victims caught a vaginal infection as a result of the abuse. The judge noted that the defendant had breached his position of trust. Held. It was appalling sexual abuse. A starting point of **9 years** without a plea is appropriate. As the guilty plea had prevented the victims giving evidence and the defendant had expressed remorse at an early stage **6 years** was proper.

A-G's Reference (No 66 of 1999) [2000] 1 Cr App Rep (S) 558. The defendant was convicted of seven counts of indecent assault on his three daughters, who were aged between 7 and 13 over a period of 4 or 5 years. The defendant's wife had died and he had been left to look after the victims and a fourth child, a boy aged 10. The conduct included digital penetration touching the victim's breasts, simulating sexual intercourse and forcing the victims to masturbate him. Two of the victims left home at the age of 13 because of the defendant's conduct. The defendant, who was 51, had previous convictions though none had a sexual element and these were not taken into account by the sentencing judge, though the serious breach of trust was noted. Held. Taking into account the case of *R v Lennon* [1999] 1 Cr App Rep (S) 19 and *R v L* [1999] 1 Cr App Rep (S) 347 the appropriate sentence for these offences was **4½–5 years**. As this was a reference, **3½ years** not 2½ years.

A-G's Reference (No 77 of 2000) [2001] 2 Cr App Rep (S) 94. The defendant was convicted of six counts of indecent assault against his two daughters who were between the ages of 9 and 14. The defendant was a strong disciplinarian and as such his daughters feared him. The defendant began to abuse his eldest daughter when she was 10. The defendant touched the girl's breasts and vagina, digitally penetrated her and simulated sexual intercourse with her. When the defendant's younger daughter was between the ages of 9 and 13 he subjected her to abuse such as digital penetration, sucking her breasts and simulating sexual intercourse with her. The abuse was over a 4 year period. The defendant, who was 52 years of age at the time of conviction, had no previous convictions. Held. The appropriate sentence was **4 years**. As it was a reference **3 years** was appropriate not 12 months.

A-G's Reference (No 2 of 2001) [2001] EWCA Crim 1015, [2001] 2 Cr App Rep (S) 524. The defendant pleaded guilty to seven counts of indecent assault against his stepdaughter when she was between the ages of 8 and 15. The defendant, who was 100% disabled and wheelchair-bound forced the victim to masturbate him and take his penis in her mouth. The defendant was 49 years of age. Held. The appropriate sentence was **5 years**. Having regard that this was a reference and the serious disability faced by the defendant which would render imprisonment more difficult to bear **2 years** was appropriate not a probation order.

Father/stepfather, by – Victim aged 10–13

91.25   *R v L* [1999] 1 Cr App Rep (S) 347. The defendant pleaded guilty to six counts of indecent assault on his daughter aged 12. The offences took place over a period of 3 months when the victim was in the sole care of her father and consisted of, touching the victim's breasts and vagina, placing her hand on his erect penis when it was exposed and through his clothing and pinning her down whilst kissing her. The defendant, who was 46 years of age, had no previous convictions. The pre-sentence report said unless he addressed his offending there was a high risk of re-offending. The trial judge had regard that there was no force, no threats and no penetration but that children were entitled to protection from the courts. Held. These offences were a gross breach of trust and as the defendant was unwilling to accept the seriousness of what had happened **2 years** was not manifestly excessive.

A-G's Reference (No 43 of 1999) [2000] 1 Cr App Rep (S) 398 – LCJ. The defendant was convicted of two counts of indecent assault on his daughter, who was aged between 10 and 11, and one count of gross indecency. The offences took place when the victim's mother was either asleep or out of the house. The defendant rubbed his penis on the victim's vaginal area, stroked her breasts and forced the victim to hold his penis. The defendant, who was 45, had no previous convictions. The probation officer said he was unlikely to offend again. The judge noted that these were not the worst assaults imaginable as there had been no violence or threat of violence and no penetration. The defendant was sentenced to 6 months. Held. The sentence was unduly lenient. The appropriate sentence for these offences was **15–18 months**; having regard that this was a reference **9 months**. As the defendant had already served his 6 months it would be destructive and advanced no relevant public interest for him to be returned to prison.

Kidnapping, and

See FALSE IMPRISONMENT/KIDNAPPING – *Sexual*

Kissing – (not breach of trust)

91.26   *R v Tabit* [2000] 2 Cr App Rep (S) 298. The defendant, who was aged 42, was convicted of indecent assault. Both the victim, who was 18 years of age, and the defendant worked in a shop. The defendant had attempted to kiss the victim but she had said 'no'. She was frightened. The next day the victim was in the stock room and she saw him outside and locked the door. For 25 minutes the defendant kept calling the victim's name and trying to open the door. As she left the stockroom when she thought he had gone he grabbed her in a bear hug and pushed her onto some crates. He tried to kiss her twice but she pushed him away, she felt very scared. The defendant was much bigger than the victim. The victim was tearful and shaken. After the incident the victim had to leave her job. The defendant had no previous convictions. At trial the judge commented that the serious aspect was that the defendant was more than twice as old as the victim and that his actions had frightened her. The defendant's risk assessment was described as high because he continued to deny the offence. Held. This was not the most serious offence of indecent assault, therefore **4 months** not 9 months.

Longer than commensurate sentences

91.27   *R v Langton* [1998] 1 Cr App Rep (S) 217. The defendant pleaded guilty to indecent assault on a 10-year-old girl. The defendant was a friend of the family of the victim and had offered to baby-sit her and her two brothers. When the victim was preparing for bed the defendant went into her bedroom and watched her undress. Later in the evening the victim got up and went downstairs wearing only her nightdress and underwear. The defendant cuddled her, invited her to sit on his knee and touched her over her clothing near her vagina. She got off and ran upstairs. In interview the defendant added that he touched the girl on her chest. The defendant had two convictions for buggery of an 8–year-old boy when he was 14; a conviction for indecently assaulting a young boy when he was 15 and a conviction for indecently assaulting a 6–year-old girl when he was 17. The pre-sentence report said he constituted a danger particularly to young children. The sentencing judge noted that the defendant constituted a danger to young children, and there remained a risk that he would re-offend. He passed a longer than commensurate sentence. Held. No strictly mathematical approach should be adopted in longer than commensurate cases, and it may well be that a much longer sentence than a commensurate sentence is perfectly proper, particularly in an extreme or particularly difficult case. Having regard to the risk the defendant posed **4 years** was proper.

See also *R v Osman* [2000] 2 Cr App Rep (S) 112. The defendant touched a woman's bottom on a tube train. He had seven convictions for indecent assault on a woman. The judge gave him 30 months as a longer than commensurate sentence. Held. That power could not be invoked. The public did not require protection from serious harm. **12 months** substituted.

R v D [2001] EWCA Crim 248, [2001] 2 Cr App Rep (S) 281. The defendant pleaded guilty to two counts of indecent assault on a girl who was aged 5. The defendant was married to the victim's grandmother and had offered to look after the victim and her brother. The defendant began to tickle the victim's stomach and then removed her trousers and digitally penetrated her. The defendant then took the girl upstairs and made her lie on top of him so that her vagina touched his penis; he then digitally penetrated her again. The defendant, who was 29, had one previous court appearance for four offences of indecent assault against his stepdaughter aged 11, who was the victim's aunt. That abuse involved digital penetration. The sentencing judge said that this was a very revealing previous conviction. Where children are concerned 'once is too often, twice is completely and utterly unacceptable. You are an ongoing danger to children'. Held. **4 years** longer than commensurate and an extension period of 3 years was not a manifestly excessive sentence.

R v Parsons [1999] Crim LR 918 judgment 31 August 1999 (the date in the report is wrong). The defendant was convicted of gross indecency with a child. In an alleyway he came towards three girls aged 13, 14 and 14 with a young boy. His penis was exposed and he was masturbating. The girls were very frightened and embarrassed. They reported it to the police who arrested the defendant who denied the offence. He was 38 and had 28 sexual convictions. Since he was 13 there was a pattern of indecent assaults or indecent exposures with women and in one case a young boy. All the other victims were teenage girls or women who were strangers to him. The last one was an attempted abduction of a girl under 16 for which he received 4 years and 3 months for indecent exposure. He was in breach of his licence for that with 11 months outstanding. The psychiatric report made plain that, 'he was a recidivist sex offender. There was little evidence to indicate that any of the treatment he had received had any beneficial effect. There was a high risk of re-offending.' The defendant claimed his victims enjoyed his behaviour and that it had no impact on them. He didn't want treatment because he considered those giving it were unreasonable. The Judge considered he was a grave risk and untreatable. Held. The sentence for the offence had been increased and that reflects Parliament's view that the offence is potentially very serious and damaging and should be dealt with more severely than in the past. Because of his past offending **6 years** as a longer than commensurate sentence was not manifestly excessive. The breach of licence should be consecutive not concurrent.

See also **LONGER THAN COMMENSURATE SENTENCES** and *Persistent offender*

Partner/pick up, on

91.28 *R v Coles* [1999] 1 Cr App Rep (S) 372. The defendant was convicted of indecent assault on a woman who consented to go to his hotel room with him. He was acquitted of attempted rape. The victim had spent the evening drinking at a hen night in a hotel. The defendant met the victim in a hotel bar and they began to drink together. In the early hours of the morning the victim went with the defendant to his hotel room. As the victim tried to leave the defendant pushed her onto the bed and removed her lower clothing and all of his own clothes. When the victim escaped the defendant followed her to the lift doors and prevented her from escaping. He told her, 'You're drunk. No one will believe you.' He returned to his room but the door had closed. The victim tried to wake her room-mate and others for help. Eventually the room-mate opened the door and she ran in distressed and crying. He tried to follow her in. The incident had lasted 5–10 minutes. The defendant, who was 31 years of age, had a number of previous convictions though none involved a sexual element. Held. This was serious offence and outrageous behaviour. **2½ years** not 4 years was appropriate.

R v C [2000] 1 Cr App Rep (S) 533. The defendant pleaded guilty to indecent assault on his partner, with whom he had lived for 10 years. The victim and the defendant who had been drinking had gone to bed, at which point the defendant removed her nightdress and attempted to perform oral sex upon her without her consent. He demanded that she perform oral sex on him and pulled her head to his penis. When she refused to perform oral sex he digitally penetrated her anus and vagina. This caused her pain. He threatened to bugger her unless she performed oral sex on him, which she subsequently did. She was crying and very upset. He then inserted his fingers into her vagina and anus which was painful. She attempted to escape by going to the lavatory but he accompanied her and ordered her back upstairs. She was so frightened she complied. She thought he was a different person and was treating her like an animal. He again forced her to perform oral sex while fingering her anus and vagina. When she said she had had enough he slapped her and pushed her back on the bed. Eventually he released and she ran to her mother's house which was across the road. The incident had lasted about an hour. When interviewed he said he had been drinking heavily and admitted his behaviour to the victim had changed over recent weeks. The defendant, who was 35 years old, had previous convictions for violence but none for sexual offences. Before the offence there had been no violence in the relationship. The relationship ended but she visited him in prison. The incident happened on Friday and he pleaded guilty at the Magistates' Court on the following Monday. Held. Conduct such as this, when it takes place in a well-established relationship, was just as unacceptable and unlawful as when the parties knew nothing of each other. **2½ years** not 3½ years was appropriate.

R v Sully [2000] 1 Cr App Rep (S) 62. The defendant pleaded guilty to two counts of indecent assault on his girlfriend. The victim and the defendant had engaged in a sexual relationship for 6 years, during which time the defendant had used such objects as a vibrator and a carrot on the victim. The victim did not enjoy this form of sexual activity. On the evening of the offence the defendant drove the victim to a car park and he started to masturbate himself. She demanded to be taken home but he drove them to a remote area after stopping off to buy a cucumber. He had already equipped himself with a roll of tape and a knife. She again demanded to be taken home. The defendant told her that he wanted to have sexual intercourse with her, to which she refused. He then threatened her with a knife and said he would tape up her mouth if she refused. She begged him to let her go. He pulled down her trousers and underwear, rubbed Vaseline onto her vagina and inserted a cucumber into her whilst digitally penetrating her anus. She screamed. He forced his fingers into her anus saying he was going to bugger her. He was unable to because of her struggling. He took the cucumber out of her vagina. The victim refused to take the defendant's erect penis in her mouth and he ejaculated over her face. He released her and apologised. Throughout the incident he remained on top of her. When he arrived home he apologised and said he was going to commit suicide. The victim had scratch marks on her breast thigh and arm. The defendant, who was 34, had eight previous convictions, two of which were for violence, but were for sexual offences. For a number of years he had fantasised about violent sex particularly anal rape. The judge noted that this attack was planned and that the defendant was totally merciless in treating the victim as a sex object. Held. This was a dreadful case. The combination of sexual perversions was worse than rape. **7 years** was severe but not manifestly excessive.

Persistent offender

91.29 *A-G's Reference (No 47 of 1998)* [1999] 1 Cr App Rep (S) 464. The defendant pleaded guilty to five counts of indecent assault on five different women as they were using a multi-storey car park. They were on 5 different days. The defendant targeted the victims when they were alone and seized their bottoms, twice he exposed himself and on one occasion he placed his hand up the victim's skirt and touched the top of the inside of her leg. The victims were all effected by the incidents and some were psychologically damaged. The defendant was 25 and had 8 convictions for indecent assault including a conviction in 1994 for burglary with intent to commit rape, indecent assault and ABH for which he received 5 years. On his release he started to attend a Sex Offenders programme. His first group therapy meeting was on the same day as the first offence. The psychiatrist said progress was slow and he had no victim empathy. He concluded the defendant was a grave danger to the public. His later report said, 'he was extremely dangerous partly because the defendant considers treatment a waste of time. He is an untreatable psychopath whose offending behaviour was likely to escalate.' Held. The defendant constituted a serious risk to the public and there was a serious risk that he would re-offend. **6 years** not 2 years was appropriate as a longer than normal sentence being passed under the then Criminal Justice Act 1991, s 2 (2)(b).

See also *R v Osman* [2000] 2 Cr App Rep (S) 112. The defendant touched a woman's bottom on a tube train. He had seven convictions for indecent assault on a woman. The judge gave him 30 months as a longer than commensurate sentence. Held. That power could not be invoked. The public did not require protection from serious harm. **12 months** substituted.

A-G's Reference (No 46 of 2000) [2001] 1 Cr App Rep (S) 407 – LCJ. The defendant pleaded guilty to indecent assault on a 35–year-old woman in her car. The victim was visiting shops in the course of her business as a sales consultant. Having returned to her car she wrote up her report. The defendant got into the car and asked the victim for a lift. The victim found the man cheeky but not, at this point, threatening. The defendant tried to steer the car into an alley though it came to rest in a lay-by. She demanded he get out of her car. The defendant then grabbed the her thigh and said, 'Come on love.' She tried to hit him and he pushed something into her ribs, saying, 'I've got a knife'. The defendant then put his hands over her breasts. He got out of her car and sped away. The whole incident lasted 10 minutes. The defendant, who was 46 years of age, had previous convictions for offences against the person, four convictions for sexual offences in 1981–8, of which three were for rape (one included an act of buggery), 21 convictions for theft and others for offences involving weapons. The 1981 three rapes were on lone women on footpaths at night. He received 7 years. In 1988 he received 6 years for robbery. The sentencing judge noted that whilst he was able to pass an extended sentence this would still not be long enough for the defendant to benefit from a sexual offender treatment programme whilst in prison. Therefore a treatment programme to last for the duration of his probation order was more appropriate. Held. The judge weighed up the competing considerations in a fair and appropriate manner. **3 years probation order** with a requirement to attend a sexual offenders treatment programme for the duration was not unduly lenient.

See also *R v De Silva* [2000] 2 Cr App Rep (S) 408. Children aged 6 and 8. Touching their vaginal areas in the bath. Previous for rape, buggery, indecent assault etc. **3 years** not 5 years longer than commensurate.

See also **Longer than commensurate sentences**

Prostitute, on a

91.30   *A-G's Reference (No 65 of 1999)* [2000] 1 Cr App Rep (S) 554. The defendant, who was aged 43, pleaded guilty to indecent assault on a prostitute on the day his case was listed for trial. The victim was engaged by an escort agency to provide sexual services for the defendant. She visited the defendant at his flat and during sexual activity the defendant put live maggots into her vagina. She was unable to see this. As he inserted them with his finger he held her head in a tight grip. When she could see she saw a plastic bag on the bed with live maggots in it. She tried to get out but the defendant prevented her from leaving by sitting on her. She panicked and he became aggressive. He then held a knife to her face and thrust it at her four times as she tried to escape. She ran out of the house naked. The victim said the offence had had a devastating effect on her. Her college work and her family life had suffered she said beyond recognition. She didn't want to be cuddled by her husband or her children. The defendant had three previous convictions for sexual offences. The pre-sentence report said he was not motivated to reduce the risk of re-offending. Held. This was an exceptionally unpleasant and serious sexual assault and the victim was threatened with a knife, therefore **3 years** not 12 months was appropriate. [The sentence was not extended as a longer than commensurate sentence.]

Public place, in a – Stranger

91.31   *R v Amin* [1998] 1 Cr App Rep (S) 63. The defendant pleaded guilty to two counts of indecent assault and one count of common assault against three women in public during the early hours of the morning. The defendant approached two of the victims as they walked together and assaulted one and indecently assaulted the other by grabbing her left breast with so much force as to cause her pain. Twenty minutes later the defendant offered the third victim a lift home. When the victim declined the defendant grabbed her right breast. The defendant, who was 25, had no convictions. There was a very low risk of the defendant re-offending and his conduct was considered to be out of character. Held. These offences lay at the lower end of the scale of gravity. **6 months** not 18 months was appropriate.

A-G's Reference (No 29 of 1999) [2000] 1 Cr App Rep (S) 209. The defendant, who was 37 years of age, was convicted of indecent assault on a 28-year-old female. He was acquitted of rape. The defendant offered to buy the victim a drink in a public house, which she refused. When the victim delayed leaving the pub to avoid him. However, when she left she found the defendant at a bridge waiting for her. He put his hand round her shoulders and attempted to kiss her. When she resisted he placed her hands down her shorts and tried to touch her vagina. He pushed her into the driveway of a bungalow and placed both hands over her bottom and pulled her towards her. He undid his belt and pushed her on her shoulders and caused her to fall to the ground. He took hold of her shorts and underwear and pulled them to her ankles. He tried to persuade her to masturbate him but she refused. He then masturbated himself and ejaculated over her. He then rubbed his semen around her vaginal area. When she got home she was crying and shaking. The defendant had no previous convictions and a good work record. At trial he contended she consented. The sentencing judge noted that the defendant had targeted the victim and then lay in wait for her. Held. Having regard for the seriousness of the offence the proper sentence should have been 3½–4 years. Taking into consideration that this was a reference **2 years 9 months**.

Train, on a – Stranger

91.32   *R v Tanyildiz* [1998] 1 Cr App Rep (S) 362. The defendant was convicted of indecent assault on a woman who was travelling on a tube train. Two plain clothes police officers noticed the defendant, who was 34, boarding different tube trains and standing close behind female passengers. He was described as being sexually aroused on at least one occasion. The victim described how the defendant had pushed his erect penis against her bottom on three separate occasions during her journey. The defendant was a political asylum seeker and was of good character. Held. Offences of this nature were easy to commit and difficult to detect and were highly unpleasant and could be frightening for the victim. Taking account of his inability to speak English and his problem in Turkey, **3 months** not 6 months was appropriate.

R v Yazbek [1998] 1 Cr App Rep (S) 406. The defendant was convicted of indecent assault on a woman who was travelling on an underground tube train. The defendant stood unnaturally close to the victim and was reluctant to move as other passengers wanted to board the train. The victim felt the defendant rubbing himself against her groin area and was observed rubbing his right upper arm across her right breast. The defendant, who was 62 years of age, had no previous convictions. The sentencing judge noted that the defendant had caused the victim shock, humiliation, and degradation and took advantage of her intentionally. Held. **3 months** was not an excessive sentence.

R v Diallo [2000] 1 Cr App Rep (S) 426. The defendant was convicted of indecent assault on a woman on an underground train. The victim was travelling to work, and had to stand, as there were no seats on the tube. The victim felt the defendant rubbing himself across her buttocks. The defendant, who was 30, was French and of previous good character. He was assessed as suitable for CSO but in need of supervision. The judge noted that this assault was pre-meditated and was serious because it lasted several minutes, rather than a matter of seconds. Held. **3 months** was not an excessive sentence.

See also *R v Osman* [2000] 2 Cr App Rep (S) 112. The defendant touched a woman's bottom on a tube train. He had seven convictions for indecent assault on a woman. The judge gave him 30 months as a longer than commensurate sentence. Held. That power could not be invoked. The public did not require protection from serious harm. **12 months** substituted.

Uninvited intruder – Stranger

91.33   *R v Woodcock* [1998] 1 Cr App Rep (S) 383. The defendant was convicted of indecent assault. At 1.55am the defendant, who was 35, was let into the victim's house by someone else and then barged his way into the victim's bed-sitting room. She was 21 and made it plain she did not want him there. He was drunk, and she was undressed ready for bed. He put his hand under her quilt and touched the victim's knee and made lewd comments about her body. The defendant requested that the victim masturbate him, although she refused he exposed his penis to her. She said she was crying with fright. The defendant fell asleep and she was able to escape. Wearing only a nightdress she went to a call box and called the police. Rear terror could be heard in her voice. The defendant had several previous convictions for violence, though none for sexual violence. Held. The barging in was a serious aggravating feature. **2 years** not 33 months was appropriate.

Victim under 10

91.34   *A-G's Reference (No 54 of 1997)* [1998] 2 Cr App Rep (S) 324. See ***Breach of trust – Friend of victim's family – Less than 4 years appropriate***

A-G's Reference (No 46 of 1999) [2000] 1 Cr App Rep (S) 310. See R v D 2001 2 Cr App Rep (S) 58 – See ***Breach of trust – Friend of victim's family – 4 to 6 years appropriate***

Victim aged 10–12

91.35   *A-G's Reference (No 77 of 1999)* [2000] 2 Cr App Rep (S) 250. See ***Breach of trust – Friend of victim's family – Less than 4 years appropriate***

A-G's Reference (No 1 of 2001) [2001] EWCA Crim 766, [2001] 2 Cr App Rep (S) 469. See ***Breach of trust – Friend of victim's family – Less than 4 years appropriate***

Victim aged 13–15 – Less than 2 years appropriate

91.36   *A-G's Reference (No 25 of 1997)* [1998] 1 Cr App Rep (S) 310. See **Breach of trust – Workplace**

R v Martley [2000] 1 Cr App Rep (S) 416. The defendant pleaded guilty to indecent assault on a 15-year-old girl. The victim was walking home at night having spent the evening drinking a considerable amount of alcohol. The defendant met the victim and began to help her home. The two kissed each other and the victim voluntarily pulled down her trousers and underwear. The defendant attempted, unsuccessfully, to have sexual intercourse with the victim and subsequently digitally penetrated her. This caused a small tear. She became nauseous and vomited. All sexual activity stopped. She tried to resume kissing but he wasn't interested. She was sick again and offered to take her home. She declined the offer and asked him to leave, as she would look after herself. An hour later a woman found her and the victim made no complaint. The defendant saw police tape at the scene and thought she had been murdered and went to the police station. The age gap between the two was 'limited.' The defendant was of previous good character and in work. The judge noted that the defendant, knowing the victim was drunk, had taken gross advantage of the situation. Held. As the activity was consensual the offence could have been charged as attempted unlawful sexual intercourse, for which the maximum is 2 years. The judge did take into account the defendant's guilty plea therefore he must have had a starting point which exceeded that for unlawful sexual intercourse therefore **9 months** not 2 years.

R v Stapley [2001] 1 Cr App Rep (S) 302 – LCJ. The defendant pleaded guilty to indecent assault on a 13–year-old girl at the Magistrates' Court. The defendant met the victim through her 15-year-old friend who delivered newspapers to the defendant's home. The two girls were walking past the defendant's home just after Christmas when he told them that he had a present for them and invited them into his house. The defendant showed the girls two photographs of himself, one showed him with an erect penis and the other with a naked woman. The defendant undid the blouse of the victim and placed his hands on her breasts and fondled them. The girls left and he gave them £10. They went to a shop and he followed them and remained outside for about 20 minutes. The girls left after he had gone. The defendant, who was 67 years of age, had no previous convictions. As a result of his conviction he had lost his home. Held. The defendant did not use violence towards the victim and the girls were not involuntarily detained. **1 year** was appropriate not 2.

Victim 13–15 – Cases – 2 years or more appropriate

91.37   *R v Blackman* [1998] 2 Cr App Rep (S) 280. The defendant was convicted of indecent assault on a 14-year-old girl. He was acquitted of attempted rape. The defendant went driving with the victim whom he knew. The victim accepted that she comforted the defendant whose grandfather had recently died and that she kissed him and lowered her own trousers and underwear. The defendant then attempted to have sexual intercourse with her and masturbated over her pubic area. The victim who was a virgin found it very, very distressing. The defendant, who was 20, had no previous convictions. He was sentenced that knew that the victim did not consent. **Held. 2½ years** was severe but not excessive.

R v Wellman [1999] 2 Cr App Rep (S) 162. The defendant was convicted of indecent assault on a 13-year-old girl. The victim was a friend of the defendant's 14-year-old daughter, with whom he lived. The defendant supplied the girls with a considerable amount of alcohol and eventually the victim became sick. The victim and her friend shared the defendant's double bed, whilst he slept on the sofa. The victim woke three times during the night and found the defendant in the bed. On the second occasion he had his hand down the girl's pyjama trousers and on the third occasion his hands were inside her underwear after which he digitally penetrated her vagina. The defendant, who was 58, had previous convictions though none of a sexual nature and none of any kind in recent years. Held. **2 years** was entirely appropriate.

R v Parsons [1999] Crim LR 918 judgment 31 August 1999 (the date in the report is wrong). See *Longer than commensurate sentences*

Violence, injuries caused

91.38 *A-G's Reference (No 39 of 1997)* [1998] 2 Cr App Rep (S) 336. The defendant was convicted of indecent assault. The victim aged 25, was walking home in the early hours of the morning when the defendant who was a stranger to her attacked her from behind and held her in a bear hug. He fondled her breasts, tore her T-shirt and attempted to tear off her bra. She thought he was attempting to drag the victim to his car. There was a struggle and he lost his balance and fell over. The victim had bruising and slight scratches to the chest and breasts. At the time of sentence the defendant had no previous convictions though subsequently he was convicted of another indecent assault. For that he was sentenced to 12 months consecutive. The defendant was 29. Held. The court must do what it can to keep the streets safe from incidents of this kind. 9 months was an unduly lenient sentence. The appropriate sentence in this case would be between **3 and 3½ years**. Having regard that this was a reference **2½ years**.

A-G's Reference (No 31 of 2000) [2001] 1 Cr App Rep (S) 386. The defendant pleaded guilty to indecently assaulting an 18-year-old female student and to common assault. After an evening out the victim waited to board a bus and became aware of the defendant and his companion. On the bus she was very worried about the defendant and his companion. He left the bus at the same time as her and ran up behind her without warning. He grabbed her vaginal area from behind. She pushed her hands back and he released his grip. He then attempted to grab her breasts from behind but her heavy jacket prevented him from doing it. She was able to pull free. The defendant then attempted to put his hand up the victim's skirt. He said words to the effect, 'you really want it'. She tried to walk away but he kept grabbing her. When a couple came near he walked away and when they were out of sight he ran after her. He then tried to put his hand up her skirt a third time. She screamed for her mother and he punched her in the face. Her screams were heard and he ran off. She sustained bruising. The incident effected the victim very adversely. She had nightmares and avoided the company of men. Her studies were affected. The defendant, was also 18 years, and of good character. Held. The effect of this on the victim is a very important consideration. Women are entitled to walk home without fear of being attacked by men. A probation order was an unduly lenient sentence. **18 months YOI** was an appropriate sentence. It was not necessary to extend the licence.

A-G's Reference (No 83 of 1999) [2001] EWCA Crim 1008, [2001] 2 Cr App Rep (S) 511. The defendant was convicted of indecent assault on a woman at a New Year's Eve party. The victim attended the party with her boyfriend. She proposed to him over the loudspeaker and he accepted. She later went outside to get some fresh air. The defendant aged 31, approached her and threatened her with a 9″ metal file. He then punched and dragged her away from the club where he inserted the metal file into her vagina several times. The defendant then inserted his fist inside her. The defendant punched the victim whilst the file was inside her. The blows rendered her unconscious. She was taken to hospital in an ambulance in considerable pain. She had bruises to her forehead, grazing on the nose, swollen lips and friction type graze marks in her private parts. She also had an unpleasant vaginal discharge. He had no convictions and was of exemplary character. Held. The appropriate sentence was **6 years**. As it was a reference **5 years** was appropriate not 3 years.

Workplace, at

91.39   *R v Wakefield and Lancashire* (2001)   Times, 12 January judgment 6 November 2000. The defendants W and L were convicted of indecent assault on a work colleague aged 50. They were 41 and 33. L in front of others pushed the victim against a filing cabinet and simulated intercourse with her and grabbed her between the legs. It was repeated and she had to leave work as she was severely depressed. Held. This was prolonged, humiliating and degrading. L was a cowardly bully and W was in a position of authority and did nothing about it. W then assaulted her. Women were entitled to be protected. **12 and 21 months** were unimpeachable.

See also *Breach of trust – Workplace*

Indecent Photographs of Children

See **Photographs of Children, Indecent** and **Obscene Publications**

92   Informants/Giving Evidence for the Prosecution

92.1   The going rate for a plea of guilty at the Crown Court is up to ⅓ off. If the plea is indicated at the Magistrates' Court more than ⅓ can be discounted. If the defendant gives evidence for the prosecution s/he can expect up to another ⅓ off. The Court of Appeal tends to work on a 50% discount for giving evidence and plea, which is not so generous. It is expected the Crown Court will continue with their approach as a person who risks his life and will endure a difficult time in prison should expect at least the same discount for giving evidence, (⅓), as the man who pleads guilty (⅓).

General principles

92.2   *R v King* (1985) 82 Cr App Rep 120 at 122 – LCJ. One then has to turn to the amount by which the starting figure should be reduced. The quality and quantity of the material disclosed by the informer is one of the things to be considered, as well as accuracy and the willingness or otherwise of the informer to confront other criminals and to give evidence against them in due course if required in court. Another aspect to consider is the degree to which he has put himself and his family at risk by reason of the information he has given; in other words the risk of reprisal. The reasoning behind this practice is expediency. It is to the advantage of law-abiding citizens that criminals should be encouraged to inform upon their criminal colleagues. They know that if they do so they are likely to be the subject of unwelcome attention, to say the least, for the rest of their lives. They know that their days of living by crime are probably at an end. Consequently, an expectation of substantial mitigation of what would otherwise be the proper sentence is required in order to produce the desired result, namely the information. The amount of that mitigation, it seems to us, will vary from about ½ to ⅓ reduction according to the circumstances.

R v A and B [1999] 1 Cr App Rep (S) 52 – LCJ. Where defendants co-operate with the prosecuting authorities, not only by pleading guilty but by testifying or expressing willingness to testify, or making a witness statement which incriminates a co-defendant, they will ordinarily earn an enhanced discount, particularly where such conduct leads to the conviction of a co-defendant or induces a co-defendant to plead guilty. It has been the long standing practice of the courts to recognise by a further discount of sentence the help given, and expected to be given, to the authorities in the investigation, detection, suppression and prosecution of serious crime: see for example

R v Sinfield (1981) 3 Cr App Rep (S) 258; *R v King* (1985) 7 Cr App Rep (S) 227 and *R v Sivan* (1988) 10 Cr App Rep (S) 282. The extent of the discount will ordinarily depend on the value of the help given and expected to be given. Value is a function of quality and quantity. If the information is accurate, particularised, useful in practice, and hitherto unknown to the authorities, enabling serious criminal activity to be stopped and serious criminals brought to book, the discount may be substantial.

Danger, the defendant exposes him/herself to

92.3   *R v A and B* [1999] 1 Cr App Rep (S) 52 – LCJ. Where by supplying valuable information to the authorities, a defendant exposes himself or his family to personal jeopardy, it will be ordinarily recognised in the sentence passed.

Document handed to the judge about an informant – Procedure

92.4   *R v X (No 2)* [1999] 2 Cr App Rep (S) 294. The defendant pleaded guilty to a number of burglaries. A confidential document prepared by a police officer at a high level was passed to the judge. Prosecution counsel began a Public Interest Immunity application before the judge over the document. The defence asked to see the document and the judge refused the request. Held. The proper principles to be followed are:

1   It is convenient to remember that a document of this kind is supplied at the request of the defendant.

2   Except to the extent that the defendant's contention that he has given assistance is supported by the police, it will not generally be likely that the sentencing judge will be able to make any adjustment in sentence. A defendant's unsupported assertion to that effect is not normally likely to be a reliable basis for mitigation.

3   The courts must rely very heavily upon the greatest possible care being taken, in compiling such a document for the information of the judge. The judge will have to rely upon it, without investigation, if police enquiries are not to be damaged or compromised and other suspects, guilty or innocent, are not to be affected. The document in the present case had not been prepared with sufficient care. Those who prepare such documents, and senior officers who verify them, must realise the importance of ensuring that they are complete and accurate.

4   Except in very unusual circumstances, it will not be necessary, nor will it be desirable for a document of this kind to contain the kind of details which would attract a public interest immunity application.

5   If very exceptionally such a document does contain information attracting a public interest immunity consideration, then the usual rules about the conduct of such an application will apply. In particular, the Crown Court (Criminal Procedure and Investigations Act 1996) (Disclosure) Rules 1997 will apply. The defence can and should be told of the public interest immunity application.

6   Absent any consideration of public interest immunity, which we take to be the general position, a document of this kind should be shown to counsel for the defence, who will no doubt discuss its contents with the defendant. That is not, we emphasise, because it will be necessary to debate its contents, but it is so that there should be no room for any unfounded suspicion that the judge has been told something potentially adverse to the defendant without his knowing about it. A defendant is entitled to see documents put before the trial judge on which he is to be sentenced. Expeditions to the judge's chambers should not be necessary in these cases. There should never normally be any question of evidence being given, nor of an issue being tried upon the question of the extent of the information provided.

7   If the defendant wishes to disagree with the contents of such a document, it is not appropriate for there to be cross-examination of the policeman, whether in court or in chambers. The policeman is not a Crown witness, he has simply supplied material for the judge, at the request of the defendant. It would no doubt be possible, in an appropriate case, for a defendant to ask for an adjournment to allow any opportunity for further consideration to be given to the preparation of the document. Otherwise, if the defendant does not accept what the document says, his remedy is not to rely upon it. Cross-examination on the usefulness of the information would almost inevitably be contrary to the public interest. It would be likely to damage enquiries still in train, trials yet to come, suspects guilty or innocent and quite possibly the defendant in the instant case.

8   No doubt, the learned judge should ordinarily disregard such a document, if asked by the defendant to do so. In such case, he will no doubt not then be minded to entertain any submission that the defendant has given valuable assistance to the police.

9   If the judge does take the document into consideration he will, no doubt, say no more than is in accordance with the present practice, namely that he has taken into consideration all the information about the defendant, with which he has been provided.

Giving evidence in the first trial but not in the re-trial

92.5   *R v Guy* [1999] 2 Cr App Rep (S) 24. The defendant gave evidence in the first trial and the co-defendant was convicted. The Court of Appeal quashed the conviction and the defendant did not give evidence at the retrial. The co-defendant was acquitted. Held. The appropriate discount here is 50%. His failure to give evidence in the 2nd trial should not be held against him. If he had given evidence, a further slight reduction might have been justified.

Family informing on the defendant's family

See SUPPLY OF DRUGS (CLASS A, B AND C) – *Informing on the defendant, family*

Future help

92.6   *R v A and B* [1999] 1 Cr App Rep (S) 52 – LCJ. Account will be taken of help given and reasonably expected to be given in the future.

See also *Sentence, information given after*

Giving evidence in major cases

92.7   *R v Sehitoglu and Ozakan* [1998] 1 Cr App Rep (S) 89. The defendants S and O made early guilty pleas to conspiracy to possessing heroin. S gave information and evidence in a linked murder case, which his part had been crucial. He had also given information and assistance in a significant drugs conspiracy. He was due to give evidence in that case and he was described as the lynch pin in both cases. He and his family were very seriously at risk. The police were satisfied his account was true and accurate. The judge started at 25 years for S and reduced it to 15 because of the assistance he had given. Held. The case falls into the highest category of drug trafficking. On a trial the sentence for O and S would be in the region of 24 years. The information, assistance, evidence, given and the risks to S and his family mark this as a case where the maximum possible reduction should be made. Applying *R v King* (1985) 7 Cr App Rep (S) 227 the reduction for S should be ⅔ off the starting figure before one considers the plea. The sentence should then be reduced to **8 years**.

R v Guy [1999] 2 Cr App Rep (S) 24. The defendant pleaded guilty to importing cocaine. The defendant, his then girlfriend and her child were stopped by customs officers at Gatwick airport after a flight from Jamaica when they were on route to Manchester. A search of their luggage revealed packages of 3.95 kgs of cocaine, which at 100% purity was 2.29 kgs. The packages were replaced with dummies. Guy and his girlfriend were arrested and he was frank with the customs officers and he co-operated with them. Later that day different customs officers met the defendant in Manchester. The co-accused was expected to meet the defendant there and he too was arrested. His co-accused was tried, convicted and received 12 years. The defendant gave evidence against him. He also gave also gave significant information to Customs. The defendant received 8 years. The co-accused's conviction was quashed on appeal and he was acquitted at the retrial. The defendant did not give evidence in that trial. He was 26 and was a person of positive good character. Held. The sentence on the co-accused was entirely appropriate. The defendant was significantly less involved than him. The starting point in the case of Guy ought to have been 10 years. He was entitled to 50%. discount so **5 years** instead.

Poor information

92.8 *R v A and B* [1999] 1 Cr App Rep (S) 52 – LCJ. If the information given is unreliable, vague, lacking in practical utility or already known to the authorities, no identifiable discount may be given or, if given, any discount will be minimal.

Sentence, information given after

92.9 *R v A and B* [1999] 1 Cr App Rep (S) 52 – LCJ. The defendants A and B pleaded guilty to importing ecstasy. The sentencing judge was told they were already assisting Customs. At the Court of Appeal the police said there was additional information given which related to a major mostly international crime. This information was found to be correct. Also there was further information which was described as high in the scale of valuable intelligence. Held. If a defendant is sentenced following a contested trial without supplying valuable information before sentence or expressing willingness to do so, the Court of Appeal will not ordinarily reduce a sentence to take account of information supplied by the defendant after sentence. So much is made clear by *R v Waddingham* (1983) 5 Cr App Rep (S) 66 at 68–9, with commentary at [1983] Crim LR 492; *R v Debbag and Izzet* (1991) 12 Cr App Rep (S) 733 at 736–7 and *R v X* (1994) 15 Cr App Rep (S) 750 with commentary at 1994 Crim LR 469. The reason for this general rule is that the Court of Appeal is a court of review; its function is to review sentences imposed at first instance, not to conduct a sentencing exercise of its own from the beginning. Thus it relies entirely, or almost entirely, on material before the sentencing court. A defendant who has denied guilt and withheld all co-operation before conviction and sentence cannot hope to negotiate a reduced sentence in the Court of Appeal by co-operating with the authorities after conviction. In such a situation a defendant must address appropriate representations to the Parole Board or the Home Office. To this general rule there is one apparent, but only partial exception. It sometimes happens that a defendant pleads guilty and gives help to the authorities, for which help credit is given, explicitly or not, when sentence is passed. In such a case the sentencing court will do its best to assess and give due credit for information already supplied and information which, is reasonably hoped, will thereafter be supplied. But it may be that the value of the help is not at that stage fully appreciated, or that the help greatly exceeds, in quantity or quality or both, what could reasonably be expected when sentence was passed, so that in either event the credit given did not reflect the true measure of the help in fact received by the authorities. In such cases this court should review the sentence passed, adjusting it, if necessary. Applying those principles A and B are entitled to some additional credit. Therefore A's sentence reduced from 13 to **11 years** and B's from 14 to **12 years**.

R v R (2002) Times, 18 February judgment 28 January 2002 – LCJ. The defendant provided significant information in relation to the offence he pleaded guilty to after he has been sentenced. Held. He was entitled to rely on it. However, it would not have the same weight, as it would have carried if it was given before sentence.

See also *Future help*

93 INSOLVENCY OFFENCES

93.1 Insolvency Act 1986, ss 206–211, 262A and 353–362 and 389 (and many other sections)

Fraud, misconduct and falsification etc when a company is to be or is wound up.

Non disclosure, concealment of property, falsification, making false statements and fraudulent disposal of property etc. by a bankrupt.

The offences are triable either way[1]. On indictment maximum 7 years (except for ss 207, 354(3), 357–358, 360–362 and 389 where it is 2 years). Summary maximum 6 months and/or £5,000.

Where the defendant is convicted in connection with the liquidation or receivership of a company etc there is power to disqualify from being a director, receiver etc[2].

1   Insolvency Act 1986, s 431 and Sch 10.
2   Powers of Criminal Courts (Sentencing) Act 2000, s 146.

Crown Court statistics England and Wales[1] – Crown Court – Males 21+ – Bankruptcy offences

93.2

Year	Plea	Total Numbers sentenced	Type of sentence%					Average length of custody (months)
			Discharge	Fine	Community sentence	Suspended sentence	Custody	
2000	Guilty	38	13%	13%	42%	8%	24%	10.1
	Not guilty	3	0%	0%	33%	67%	0%	0

1   Excluding committals for sentence. Source: Crime and Criminal Justice Unit, Home Office Ref: IOS416-02.

Guideline remarks

93.3 Some guidance can be found in *R v Theivendran* (1992) 13 Cr App Rep (S) 601. See below.

Failing to disclose property to a liquidator

93.4 *R v Bevis* [2001] EWCA Crim 9, [2001] 2 Cr App Rep (S) 257. The defendant changed his plea to guilty for failing to disclose company property and details of its disposal to the liquidator contrary to the Insolvency Act 1986, s 208(1)(a). He was a 'partner or present office holder' in a company which was wound up. (What the property was and how much it was worth is not revealed in the report.) He was 53 and of good character. The defence said there was no self-enrichment. Held. The section implies dishonesty so he has a defence if he wants to prove he had no dishonesty. He did not seek to do so. There is a distinction between this offence and fraudulent trading but it strikes at the root of winding up companies. **9 months** not 18. 2 not 4 years disqualification from being a director.

Managing a company when bankrupt

93.5 Company Directors Disqualification Act 1986, s 11

Triable either way. On indictment maximum 2 years. Summary maximum 6 months and/or £5,000.

Guideline remarks

93.6 *R v Theivendran* (1992) 13 Cr App Rep (S) 601 – LCJ. The underlying purpose of the Acts (Insolvency Act 1986 and Company Directors Disqualification Act 1986) is to rationalise the law of insolvency and in general to enable those who have suffered business failure to get back on their feet as rapidly as may be consistent with fairness to the creditors. If the contravention has been flagrant. . .a custodial sentence would in principle be appropriate. If, on the other hand, there are no aggravating features, such as previous offences of the same kind or personal profit gained in the fraud of creditors, that may be taken into account as justifying suspension of the sentence. [The need for exceptional circumstances to suspend sentences was in force shortly after the judgment.]

Cases

93.7 *R v Ashby* [1998] 2 Cr App Rep (S) 37. The defendant was convicted of four counts of taking part in the management of a company when an undischarged bankrupt. The offences were over a 2 year period. The companies were Tottenham Hotspur Football Club and its associated companies. The defendant effectively ran the company on behalf of Terry Venables. He signed cheques, chaired meetings and gave executive orders. He was 53 and of good character with references. The defence said he turned the company round from near bankruptcy to prosperity and there was no allegation of fraudulent personal enrichment. They also said the sentence had an utterly devastating effect on him. The sentencing judge described it as wholly flagrant and over a considerable time and said the more blatant and repeated the offences the greater the necessity for a clear deterrent warning to others. Held. Under the current legislation the judge did not have the option of suspending the sentence. Unhesitatingly we conclude **4 months** was not too long.

See also *R v Vanderwell* [1998] 1 Cr App Rep (S) 439.

See also COMPANY FRAUDS AND FINANCIAL SERVICES OFFENCES ETC and THEFT ETC

INSTRUMENT, USING A FALSE

Where the forgery is used to steal see THEFT ETC

See also COUNTERFEITING CURRENCY; ELECTION OFFENCES and PASSPORT OFFENCES

INSURANCE

See FRAUD – *Insurance frauds*

94 INSURANCE, NO

94.1 Road Traffic Act 1988, s 143

Summary only. Maximum Level 5 fine, £5,000. Discretionary disqualification. Obligatory endorsement. 6–8 points.

Magistrates' Court Sentencing Guidelines September 2000

94.2   Entry point. Is a discharge or a fine appropriate? Examples of aggravating factors for the offence are deliberately driving without insurance, gave false details, LGV, HGV, PCV, PSV, or minicabs and no reference to insurance ever having been held. Examples of mitigation for the offence are accidental oversight, genuine mistake, responsibility for providing insurance rested with another – parent/owner/lender/hirer and smaller vehicle eg moped. Examples of mitigation are difficult domestic circumstances and genuine remorse. **Starting point 2 months' disqualification and fine B.** (£100 when defendant has £100 net weekly income. See page 334 for table showing fines for different incomes.)

For details about the guidelines see **MAGISTRATES' COURT SENTENCING GUIDELINES** at page 331.

Magistrates' Association Guidance May 2001

94.3   Supplementary Guidance May 2001: The offence causes particular concern to magistrates who sometimes say that 'it is cheaper to pay a fine rather than insure one's car'. However, although it is possible to purchase a roadworthy car for £200 or £300, for a young male driver to insure that car third party only, will cost three or four times that and as we know only too well, the temptation is to drive the car without insurance. The chances of being caught are slim and if he is caught he will only face a very small fine since he is on low income. The implied alternative is that he should be fined at least the cost of the insurance, regardless of the fact that the fine will be way beyond his ability to pay and will probably end up being written off. Magistrates should have regard to the advice in the Guidelines which suggests that for driving with no insurance they should carefully consider the option of disqualification, a much greater penalty than any fine. Even if the driver is not disqualified he will have 6–8 points on his licence and face disqualification on a second offence under the totting up procedure. The outcome of this however is that it is unlikely that he will become legally insured in the future and the cycle often ends with a term of imprisonment for disqualified driving.

Certainly the solution to the problem is not in imposing fines which the defendants are unable to pay and which bear no relation to their income. A more efficient system of enforcement of the law, so that the chances of a driver getting away with it are greatly reduced may be a part of the solution.

The prevalence of the offence of driving without insurance must relate in part to the difference between the cost of the car and the cost of insurance. Magistrates must continue to administer the law by following the current edition of the Magistrates' Court Sentencing Guidelines.

JURY OFFENCES

For interfering with jurors etc see **PERVERTING THE COURSE OF JUSTICE/CONTEMPT OF COURT ETC** – *Jury interference*

JUSTICE, PERVERTING THE COURSE OF

See **PERVERTING THE COURSE OF JUSTICE/CONTEMPT OF COURT ETC**

KIDNAPPING

See FALSE IMPRISONMENT/KIDNAPPING. When for ransom see BLACKMAIL – *Kidnapping individuals for ransom*

KILL, THREATS TO

See THREATS TO KILL

LANDLORDS

See HARASSMENT AND UNLAWFUL EVICTION OF TENANTS

LAUNDERING, MONEY

See MONEY LAUNDERING

95   LICENCE, BEING IN BREACH

95.1   Powers of the Criminal Courts (Sentencing) Act 2000, s 116(1) and (2)

Courts have power to return to prison those who were sentenced after 30 September 1992 and during his licence period commits an offence punishable with imprisonment. The return may be for the whole or part of the remaining term of imprisonment. Magistrates' Courts have no power to return to prison for more than 6 months but may commit the defendant to the Crown Court for sentence on bail or in custody.

This section of the book does not deal with the details of the provisions but just how long should be imposed.

Basic principles

95.2   *R v Taylor* [1998] 1 Cr App Rep (S) 312 at 318 sub nom *R v Secretary of State for the Home Department, ex p Probyn* (a QBD and Court of Appeal case). First decide the appropriate sentence for the new offence. Then consider whether to order a return to prison. Consider the nature and the extent of any progress made by the defendant since his release and the nature and gravity of the new offence and whether it calls for a custodial sentence. Have regard to the totality both in determining whether to return to prison and whether the period of return should be concurrent or consecutive and how long the return term should be.

R v Blades [2000] 1 Cr App Rep (S) 463 – LCJ. The fact there is a discretionary power makes clear that no iron rules can be or should be laid down which would pervert the nature of the discretionary power. The commission of a further offence during the licence period shows that a defendant has not availed himself of the opportunity to live a law abiding existence and has not taken advantage of the probationary opportunity offered. There is a public interest in making quite clear to defendants and to the public in general that if a defendant commits serious further offences or offences while on licence there is a real and not simply a theoretical price to pay.

323

Examples – Reduced period appropriate

95.3 *R v Cox* [2000] 2 Cr App Rep (S) 57. The defendant was sentenced to 4 months consecutive for two charges of dangerous driving and was ordered to serve the whole of the 2 years and 73 days of his breached licence following an 8 year sentence for robberies and related offences. The pre-sentence report said he had made very determined efforts to rehabilitate himself. Held. The judge had not applied his mind to whether or the term should be reduced in accordance with *R v Taylor* [1998] 1 Cr App Rep (S) 312. The breach term should be reduced to **1 year 73 days**.

R v Griffiths [2000] 2 Cr App Rep (S) 224. On 27 May 1999 the defendant was sentenced to 15 months for burglary which was committed on 31 March 1998 and 20 months and 21 days for a breach of his licence for a sentence of 6 years for manslaughter. Since the burglary he had given up drugs and settled down with a girlfriend who confirmed he was not taking drugs. He had also found work and kept out of trouble. In prison he had a successful record of negative tests for drugs. Held. Applying *R v Taylor* [1998] 1 Cr App Rep (S) 312, the considerable progress during the relevant period is very much to his credit. A person must generally expect to go back to prison. However, his efforts must be reflected in the total sentence. Accordingly **6 months** substituted consecutive to the new sentence.

A-G's Reference (Nos 32 of 2001) [2001] EWCA Crim 2120, [2002] 1 Cr App Rep (S) 517. The judge should have ordered detention for the breach. 439 days left. 12 months consecutive to the sentence for the new matter added.

See also *R v Russell* [1998] 2 Cr App Rep (S) 375 and *R v Martin* [2002] EWCA Crim 775, [2002] 2 Cr App Rep (S) 516 [second offence minor].

Examples – Full amount ordered to be served

95.4 *R v Walker* [1998] 2 Cr App Rep (S) 245. The defendant pleaded guilty at his first appearance to three counts of supplying crack cocaine. In August 1994 he was sentenced to 3 years for supplying crack cocaine. Two months after his release he was seen by an officer in Brixton conducting an undercover drugs operation. The officer asked if he had any crack. The officer was asked to follow him and he did. A short distance away the defendant broke off a piece of crack from a large piece and sold it to the officer for £50. It weighed 321 mgs. A few days later there was another meeting and two wraps were sold for £40 each. Their total weight was 253 mgs. The next day he sold 197 mgs of crack for £20 to another undercover officer. That wrap was spat from his mouth. He was arrested 3 months later and lied in his interview. The risk of re-offending was described as considerable, although there were some indications that he was trying to lead a more settled life. The judge sentenced him to 3 years 11 months consecutive to 16 months for being in breach of his licence for the previous supply offence. The sentenced had been varied because the judge had misstated his parole position. Held. *R v Taylor* [1998] 1 Cr App Rep (S) 312 applied. The **3 years 11 months** sentence was entirely proper. He could not have complained if it had been longer. These offences were committed in flagrant breach of his licence. Some judges might have given a reduction for the 3 month after the offences when he was not offending but the judge could not be criticised for not doing so. The total was not excessive.

A-G's Reference (No 89 of 1999) [2000] 2 Cr App Rep (S) 382. The full period should have been made to run consecutively. For details see **ROBBERY** – *Domestic premises – Victim over 65 – Victim injured or attacked*

R v Bolt [1999] 2 Cr App Rep (S) 202. The defendant pleaded guilty to theft. His accomplice stole a handbag from the floor of a pub near a customer and the two drove off together. The police caught them. He was 28 and had an appalling record. There were 30 convictions since he was 11. He had been sentenced to 3 and 5 years. This offence was committed 3 months after his release from the 5 years. The judge ignored the defence version that it was an impulse theft. Held. The judge should have indicated his view to counsel. An impulse theft is worth **12 months** not 2 years. The earlier sentence had not deterred him. He had been released very shortly before. There was no reason he should not serve the remainder of the earlier sentence.

R v Taylor [2002] 1 Cr App Rep (S) 490. The defendant pleaded guilty to robbery in which knives were used. The offence was committed 3 months after his release from a 7 year sentence for an armed robbery on a post office. He had two other convictions for robbery. There were 684 days unexpired on his licence. The defendant who was equally to blame received 6 years. The co-defendant had an appalling record but no convictions for robbery. Held. The defendant's sentence was reduced from 12 years to 10. We do not ignore that he had difficulties in coming to terms with life in the community but it was wholly outweighed by the offence being committed 3 months from a precisely the same offence. There was no element of double punishment. All he had done was deprived himself of the benefit of his licence. The total was not too long. The 684 days were not reduced and were to remain consecutive. That was within the judge's discretion.

Judge does not say whether the days to be served are to be consecutive or not

95.5   *R v Cargill* [1999] 2 Cr App Rep (S) 72. The defendant pleaded guilty to offering to supply cocaine. He was in breach of his licence following his release from a 2½ year sentence for robbery. There were 224 days left to serve. Held. The sentence should be reduced to 12 months. Although the judge when he activated the 224 days left to serve didn't say whether they were consecutive or concurrent they should be served consecutively. The amount should be 6 months consecutive not 224 days.

R v Twisse [2001] 2 Cr App Rep (S) 37. The defendant was convicted of possessing heroin with intent to supply, possessing cocaine with intent to supply. He had pleaded guilty to simple possession of ecstasy. Police officers stopped the defendant as he was about to get into a car. They searched him, and his flat. They found 23 ecstasy tablets, 23.37 grams of cocaine, the street value was up to £2,200, 42.5 grams of heroin the street value was up to £3,400. The appellant was arrested and interviewed and claimed the drugs were for his own use. He was 35 years of age and had nine previous court appearances mostly for robbery, sometimes including firearms. In 1993, he was sentenced to 11 years for attempted robbery and carrying a firearm with intent to commit an indictable offence. He was released on licence in 1998. He was sentenced to 6 years and ordered to serve the whole 1,670 days of an unexpired term of the 11 year sentence. (That was illegal, as the maximum is the time from the breach to the end of the sentence). Held. The judge did not pay sufficient regard either to the appellant's history following his release on licence or to the principle of totality. **2½ years** consecutive substituted.

Longer than commensurate sentences, consecutive to

See LONGER THAN COMMENSURATE SENTENCES – *Consecutive to other sentences, the longer than commensurate sentence should not be*

LIVING OFF THE EARNINGS OF PROSTITUTION

See PROSTITUTION, MEN LIVING ON EARNINGS OF

96   LONGER THAN COMMENSURATE SENTENCES

96.1   Powers of Criminal Courts (Sentencing) Act 2000, s 80(2)(b). The custodial sentence shall be. . .where the offence is a violent or sexual offence, for such longer term (not exceeding the maximum) as in the opinion of the court is necessary to protect the public from serious harm from the offender, (previously Criminal Justice Act 1991, s 2(2)(b)).

An extended sentence is a sentence which has an extended licence period, Powers of Criminal Courts (Sentencing) Act, s 85(2)(b).

The court can also pass a sentence which is longer than commensurate, Powers of Criminal Courts (Sentencing) Act, s 80(2)(b). This is frequently (wrongly) called an extended sentence but that is not what the section calls it. It would have been much simpler if Parliament had called one an extended sentence and the other an extended licence. Where judges refer to a longer than commensurate sentence as an extended sentence, 'longer than commensurate' is substituted to distinguish the sentence from a real extended sentence.

This book only deals with the *tariff* for offences and not the sentencing orders. However, as passing a longer than commensurate sentence increases the tariff there is a section on this order.

Duty to pass

96.2   *R v Avis Re Goldsmith* [1998] 2 Cr App Rep (S) 178 at 192 – LCJ. The defendant pleaded guilty to attempted robbery and having a firearm with intent to commit an indictable offence. The defendant was 49 and was a persistent armed robber. The judge said that viewed in isolation 10 years' imprisonment was the correct sentence but when he considered the need to protect the public, a longer sentence of **15 years** was appropriate. Held. The long sentences the defendant had served had done nothing to deter him. Even without resorting to s 2(2)(b) of the 1991 Act 10 years was justified for this armed robbery. The judge was right that the s 2(2)(b) power should be exercised. It is clear the defendant is likely to commit further offences of this very serious kind. The sub-section requires that the court 'shall' pass such sentence 'as is in the opinion of the court necessary to protect the public from serious harm from the offender'. Since a previous 15 year sentence did not deter him from re-offending, it is difficult to see how the necessary period of protection required should be any shorter. The sentence was an entirely proper one.

Consecutive to other sentences, the longer than commensurate sentence should not be

96.3   *R v Johnson* [1998] 1 Cr App Rep (S) 126. The defendant pleaded guilty to three robberies and a s 20 wounding. The offences were committed 3 months after he was released from a 5 year sentence for robberies. The judge passed a longer than commensurate sentence of 10 years and ordered it to be consecutive to the unexpired portion of his previous sentence. Held. After considering *R v King* (1995) 16 Cr App Rep (S) 987 and the words of the s 2(2)(b) it was illogical to order that the period assessed for the protection of the public should commence on some date in the future. It was therefore in principle generally undesirable to order an extended sentence to run consecutive to any subsisting sentence. They should be ordered to run concurrent thus ensuring that the extended sentence runs from the date the sentence is passed.

R v Cuthbertson [2000] Crim LR 61. Same rule applied.

R v Sullivan [2000] 2 Cr App Rep (S) 318; *R v King* (1995) 16 Cr App Rep (S) 987 and *R v Johnson* [1998] 1 Cr App Rep (S) 126 applied. The sentences should not be ordered to run consecutively. Sentence of **4 years** made concurrent to the 167 days for breach of licence.

R v Sowden [2000] 2 Cr App Rep (S) 360. The defendant pleaded guilty to robbery and theft. He had a bad record. He received 1 year for the theft and 5 years extended for the robbery consecutive. Held. We are bound to follow *R v Walters* [1997] 2 Cr App Rep (S) 87 and hold the extended sentence should not be consecutive to the other sentence.

R v Ellis [2001] 1 Cr App Rep (S) 148. Rule applied.

R v Everleigh [2001] EWCA Crim 1276, [2002] 1 Cr App Rep (S) 130. Rule applied.

See also *R v Fletcher* [2002] EWCA Crim 834, [2002] 2 Cr App Rep (S) 568.

Extended sentence, and an

96.4 *R v Thornton* [2000] Crim LR 312. 5 years longer than commensurate changed to a 2 years custodial term with a 3 years extension period.

R v Nelson [2001] EWCA Crim 2264, [2002] 1 Cr App Rep (S) 565. The two sentences will be appropriate, where a violent or sexual offence is committed by a seriously dangerous offender, in relation to whom a life sentence, if available, might well be passed, thereby permitting the offender to be released only when the executive believes that the risk posed by him has been greatly reduced. In such a case, the offender would of course be subject to recall for the rest of his life. It is appropriate to combine an extended period of licence with a longer than commensurate custodial term for an offender who presents a serious danger to the public but where a life sentence is not available because the maximum penalty is, for example, a lesser determinate sentence. There may also be cases in which a discretionary life sentence is available for the offence but the criteria which have to be established before such a sentence can be passed may not all be present (eg *R v Chapman* [2000] 1 Cr App Rep (S) 377). Where a longer than commensurate sentence is called for, it should usually be accompanied by an extension period because a seriously dangerous offender, attracting a longer than commensurate sentence, may well commit further offences.

Sentence must not be out of proportion/out of scale

96.5 *R v Mansell* (1994) 15 Cr App Rep (S) 771 – LCJ. The judge has to balance the need to protect the public on the one hand with the need to look at the totality of the sentence and see that it is not out of all proportion to the nature of the offending.

R v Crow (1994) 16 Cr App Rep (S) 409 – LCJ. Where (the then) s 2(2)(b) is applied, the sentence should, whilst long enough to give necessary protection to the public, still bear a reasonable relationship to the offence for which it is being imposed.

R v Howatt (8 July 1997, unreported). The defendant was convicted of rape. He forced his way into flat, and threatened the victim with a knife. He then raped her. He had 4 previous convictions for indecent assault. Held. The use of the section must not result in a sentence out of all proportion to the sentence that would otherwise be imposed. 15 years not 18.

R v Gabbidon and Bramble [1997] 2 Cr App Rep (S) 19. One defendant was sentenced to 27 for very grave domestic robberies. The judge had considered 18 years suitable for the overall figure and added 50% under the then s 2(2)(b). Held. That was out of scale. Without extending the sentence 15 years would have been appropriate. To reflect the need to protect the public 5 additional years is right making **20 years** in all.

R v Langton [1998] 1 Cr App Rep (S) 217. The defendant pleaded guilty to indecent assault on a 10-year-old girl. The defendant had two convictions for buggery of an 8-year-old boy when he was 14; a conviction for indecently assaulting a young boy when he was 15 and a conviction for indecently assaulting a 6-year-old girl when he was 17. The pre-sentence report said he constituted a danger particularly to young children. The sentencing judge noted that the defendant constituted a danger to young children, and there remained a risk that he would re-offend. He passed a longer than commensurate sentence. Held. No strictly mathematical approach should be adopted in longer than commensurate cases, and it may well be that a much longer sentence than a commensurate sentence is perfectly proper, particularly in an extreme or particularly difficult case. Having regard to the risk the defendant posed 4 years was proper. For further details see INDECENT ASSAULT ON A WOMAN – *Longer than commensurate sentences,*

R v Winfield [1999] 2 Cr App Rep (S) 116. The defendant was convicted of robbery. He and two others were in a public house. One followed the victim who had drunk about 5 pints into the lavatory. The victim's gold chain was seized and there was a struggle. The victim received a bite on the finger. The defendant and the other man joined them and all three kicked and punched the victim. The door was closed to stop those who had heard the commotion from entering. The victim became unconscious and lost his gold chain, his bracelet, a gold watch, a ring and £30. Police found him covered in blood with a boot mark on his forehead. At hospital he was found to have a 2″ cut to his head and bruising to his temple, nose, cheek and near his eye. He stayed there for a few days. The defendant had a bad record (details not given). He was given a longer than commensurate sentence of 8 years. Held. Ordinarily the offence would warrant 5 years. The court had to balance the need to protect the public and ensure the sentence is not out of all proportion to the nature of the offending. It must also ensure there is no double counting. Double counting is when a sentence has a deterrent factor built in and is extended without taking into account that existing deterrent factor. That deterrent factor caters for the necessity to protect the public. **6 years** not 8.

R v Smith [2001] 2 Cr App Rep (S) 160. The defendant pleaded guilty to ABH. The judge said the sentence started at 18 months and he extended it to 4 years. Held. It was a quite disgraceful piece of loutish and yobbish behaviour. The base sentence was not too high. It could have been considerably higher. Previously the court had suggested an uplift of 50–100% was appropriate. The extension to **4 years** was abundantly justified.

See also ARSON – *Longer than commensurate sentences, how much extra?* and OFFENCES AGAINST THE PERSON ACT 1861, S 18 – *Longer than commensurate sentences, how much extra?*

Serious offences, should it be used for the most

96.6   *R v Chapman* (1994) 15 Cr App Rep (S) 844. The defendant was a persistent armed robber. Held. He is a dangerous man who is a menace to society. It is clearly necessary to protect the public. We apply (the then) s 2(2)(b) provisions.

R v Christie (1994) 16 Cr App Rep (S) 469. It is incumbent when considering whether to apply (the then) s 2(2)(b) to guard against the danger of effectively imposing an element of the sentence twice. That is because the commensurate sentence is likely to contain an element which is designed to achieve the protection of the public, it is wrong in principle to apply s 2(2)(b) in order to achieve a sentence of greater length.

R v Gabbidon and Bramble [1997] 2 Cr App Rep (S) 19. he defendants were sentenced **to 27 and 17 years** for very grave domestic robberies. Held. *R v Chapman* (1994) 15 Cr App Rep (S) 844 and *R v Christie* (1995) 16 Cr App Rep (S) 469 were clearly in conflict. There was a clear need to protect the public. We prefer the approach in *Chapman*. It is better the courts applies Lord Taylor (LCJ)'s balance, the need to protect the public and the need to look at the totality of the sentence.

Sexual offence, what is?

96.7   Powers of Criminal Courts (Sentencing) Act 2000, s 161(2)   In this Act, 'sexual offence' means any of the offences in the following acts:

Sexual Offences Act 1956 other than an offence under ss 30–31 or 33–36;

Mental Health Act 1959, s 128;

Indecency with Children Act 1960;

Theft Act 1968, s 9 when committed with intent to commit rape;

Criminal Law Act 1977, s 54;

Protection of Children Act 1978; and

Conspiring to, or attempting to or inciting another to commit those offences.

Use of powers wrong but sentence correct

96.8   *R v Rai and Robinson* [2000] 2 Cr App Rep (S) 120. The defendants received a longer than commensurate sentence of 15 years. The judge did not state that the reason for that was their propensity to violence. Held. It was unnecessary to extend the sentence, as 15 years was not inappropriate. Where the court passes an extended sentence but the sentence was correct this court will not reduce that sentence even if it considers the use of the statute was wrong. The sentence was upheld without relying on the statute.

R v Sowden [2000] 2 Cr App Rep (S) 360. The defendant pleaded guilty to robbery and theft. He had a bad record. He received 1 year for the theft and 5 years extended for the robbery consecutive and an extended licence. Held. We are bound to follow *R v Walters* [1997] 2 Cr App Rep (S) 87 and hold the extended sentence should not be consecutive to the other sentence. However, 5 years could be imposed without extending the sentence. 1 year consecutive was correct. Appeal dismissed.

Violent offence, is it?

96.9   Powers of Criminal Courts (Sentencing) Act 2000, s 161(3). A violent offence is an 'offence which leads, or is intended or likely to lead, to a person's death or physical injury to a person.'

R v Robinson [1993] 96 Cr App Rep 418. Attempted rape was a violent offence under the Act.

R v Cochrane (1994) 15 Cr App Rep (S) 708. The defendant pleaded guilty to robbery. Held. The definition of a violent offence does not require that the physical injury be serious. It does not include psychological harm. Here no injury was actually done. Sometimes shock may amount to ABH. This was not that case. The defendant denied he intended to cause physical injury. The judge accepted that. It was not necessary to show that injury was a necessary or probable consequence. The only issue was whether the acts were likely to lead to physical injury. Here it could have done if the shopkeeper had resisted or the defendant had lost control. **6 years** was arguably too high if the sentence was commensurate with the facts of the offence. However, it was a perfectly proper sentence for a man foreseeably likely to cause serious harm to the public.

R v Johnson [1998] 1 Cr App Rep (S) 126. The defendant pleaded guilty to three robberies and a s 20 wounding which were concerning four separate attacks on minicab drivers. He had 3 previous convictions for robbery. The defence contended that in the three robberies there was no evidence that he intended injury to the victims. Held. Applying *R v Cochrane* (1994) 15 Cr App Rep (S) 708 the judge was entitled to come to that view. In little more than a week four drivers were subjected to attacks with a knife. In three the defendant produced a knife to reinforce demands for money and/or jewellery. In one case a driver was stabbed in the chest. One driver was told he would be killed.

See also ABDUCTION OF A CHILD – *Longer than commensurate sentences*, ABH – *Longer than commensurate sentences*; BUGGERY – *Longer than commensurate sentences*; FALSE IMPRISONMENT/KIDNAPPING – *Longer than commensurate sentences*; INDECENT ASSAULT ON A MAN – *Longer than commensurate sentences*; INDECENT ASSAULT ON A WOMAN – *Longer than commensurate sentences*; OFFENCES AGAINST THE PERSON ACT 1861, S 18 – *Longer than commensurate sentences*; PUBLIC DECENCY, OUTRAGING – *Longer than commensurate/Extended, can the sentence be?*; ROBBERY – *Longer than commensurate sentences* and THREATS TO KILL – *Longer than commensurate sentences*

97   LSD

Don't treat the drug as less serious than other Class A drugs

97.1   *R v Hurley* [1998] 1 Cr App Rep (S) 299 at 302 – LCJ. Principle stated.

How should the amount be presented to court?

97.2   *R v Hurley* [1998] 1 Cr App Rep (S) 299 at 303 – LCJ. Don't use resale value. Although it may be appropriate for the street value to be given to give an idea of the scale of the operation. The number of impregnated squares usually of approximately ¼ inch in size, provides the best way. There is however evidence that it is now the fashion for dosage units to approximate to 50 microgrammes and since any effect is unlikely to be detectable very much below 25 microgrammes a dose of 50 microgrammes is accepted as being a realistic dose. The practical evidence suggests that in the market place this is the average level of dose as judged by the seizures which are made. Of course, one would not expect the squares to be impregnated with exactly 50 microgrammes. There must be a plus or minus. If, however, one takes the number of squares as the primary starting point, then allowance must be made appropriately upwards or downwards if there is convincing evidence that the squares are significantly more or less heavily impregnated. By 'significantly' we have in mind something in excess of 10 microgrammes one way or the other. It is therefore possible, where weaker dosage units are intentionally produced, to adjust the scale accordingly, while bearing in mind that in such a situation those who produce these squares may well have done so quite deliberately in order to maximise their profits. Since the object of the legislation is to deter the use of unlawful drugs and strip dealers of their profits, it seems to us appropriate that the penalties should be related to the number of dosage units put, or to be put, on the market, subject to such adjustment as may be appropriate in the light of a significant deviation from the standard dose. The sentence therefore should ordinarily be based on the number of squares to be marketed, assuming an LSD content of about 50 microgrammes of pure LSD per square, plus or minus about 10 microgrammes, but with discretion in the sentencer to vary the sentence upwards or downwards where there is any more significant variation.

Scientific evidence

97.3   *R v Hurley* [1998] 1 Cr App Rep (S) 299 at 302 – LCJ. Dr Jansen and Professor Nichols told us that in the 1960s and 1970s LSD was regularly used in much larger quantities than is usual today. They testified that it was at about a dose of 50 microgrammes that most people start to begin to experience hallucinatory effects.

See also **DRUG USERS**; **IMPORTATION OF DRUGS**; **POSSESSION OF DRUGS**; **PRODUCTION OF DRUGS** and **SUPPLY OF DRUGS** (**CLASS A, B AND C**)

98   MAGISTRATES' COURT SENTENCING GUIDELINES

98.1   Implementation date: 1 September 2000

Quotes

'They are of course only guidelines. They do not curtail your independent discretion to impose the sentences you think are right, case by case. But they exist to help you in that process. To give you a starting point. To give you more information in reaching your decisions. And, importantly, they help to assist the magistracy to maintain an overall consistency of approach.' Lord Irvine of Lairg (Lord Chancellor)

'I think it most important that, within discretionary limits, magistrates' courts up and down the country should endeavour to approach sentencing with a measure of consistency, and I have no doubt that these Guidelines will contribute powerfully to that end.' Lord Bingham of Cornhill (former Lord Chief Justice)

R v Krawec (1984) 6 Cr App Rep (S) 367 – LCJ. It cannot be emphasised too strongly the guidelines are not a tariff.

Section 1 – User Guide

98.2   These Sentencing Guidelines cover offences with which magistrates deal regularly and frequently in the adult criminal courts. They provide a sentencing structure, which sets out how to: establish the seriousness of each case and determine the most appropriate way of dealing with it. They provide a method for considering individual cases and a guideline from which discussion should properly flow; but they are not a tariff and should never be used as such.

Using the sentencing structure

98.3   The sentencing structure used for these Guidelines was established by the Criminal Justice Act 1991. This reaffirms the principle of 'just desserts' so that any penalty must reflect the seriousness of the offence for which it is imposed and the personal circumstances of the offender. Magistrates must always start the sentencing process by taking full account of all the circumstances of the offence and making a judicial assessment of the seriousness category into which it falls. In every case, the Criminal Justice Act 1991 requires sentencers to consider: Is discharge or a fine appropriate? Is the offence serious enough for a community penalty? Is it so serious that only custody is appropriate? If the last, in either way cases, justices will also need to consider if Magistrates' Courts' powers are appropriate.

The format of the Sentencing Guidelines

98.4   1. Consider the seriousness of the offence

Magistrates must always make an assessment of seriousness following the structure of the Criminal Justice Act 1991. However, the Sentencing Guidelines do give a starting point guideline for each offence. Where the starting point guideline is a community penalty, refer to the guidance under '*Community Penalties*', below. Where the starting point guideline is custody, think in terms of weeks or months and discount as appropriate for a timely guilty plea. For some either way offences the guideline is 'are magistrates' sentencing powers appropriate?' This indicates that magistrates should be considering whether the seriousness of the offence is such that 6 months (or 12 months in the case of two or more offences) is insufficient, so that the case must be committed to the Crown Court. If the case is retained in the Magistrates' Court a substantial custodial sentence is likely to be necessary. It should be noted that if magistrates consider (say) 9 months to be the appropriate sentence, to be reduced for a timely guilty plea to six months, then the case falls within their powers and must be retained. Subject to offender mitigation, six months would appear to be the appropriate sentence.

2. Consider aggravating and mitigating factors

Make sure that all aggravating and mitigating factors are considered. The lists in the Sentencing Guidelines are neither exhaustive nor a substitute for the personal judgment of magistrates. Factors which do not appear in the Guidelines may be important in individual cases. If the offence was racially aggravated, the court must treat that fact as an aggravating factor under statute (Crime and Disorder Act 1998, s 82). If the offence was committed while the offender was on bail, the court must treat that as an aggravating factor under statute (Criminal Justice Act 1991, s 29 as amended). [Note. Now the Powers of Criminal Courts (Sentencing) Act 2000, a 151(2)].Consider previous convictions, or any failure to respond to previous sentences, in assessing seriousness. Courts should identify any convictions relevant for this purpose and then consider to what extent they affect the seriousness of the present offence.

3. Take a preliminary view of seriousness, and then consider offender mitigation

When an initial assessment of the seriousness of the offence has been formed, consider the offender. The Guidelines set out some examples of offender mitigation but there are frequently others to be considered in individual cases. Any offender mitigation that the court accepts must lead to some downward revision of the provisional assessment of seriousness, although this revision may be minor. A previous criminal record may deprive the defendant of being able to say that he is a person of good character.

4. Consider your sentence

The law requires that the court to reduce the sentence for a timely guilty plea but this provision should be used with judicial flexibility. A timely guilty plea may attract a sentencing discount of up to one third but the precise amount of discount will depend on the facts of each case and a last minute plea of guilty may attract only a minimal reduction. Discount may be given in respect of the amount of a fine or periods of community service or custody. Periods of mandatory disqualification or mandatory penalty points cannot be reduced for a guilty plea.

5. Decide your sentence

Magistrates have a duty to consider the award of compensation in all appropriate cases, and to give reasons if compensation is not awarded. See *Compensation Orders*

Section 2 – The guidelines (these are listed under the various offences)

Section 3 – Establishing the seriousness of the offence

98.5 In establishing the seriousness of the case before them, courts should: (1) make sure that all factors, which aggravate or mitigate the offence are considered. The lists in the Guidelines are neither exhaustive nor a substitute for the personal judgment of magistrates. Factors which do not appear in the Guidelines may be important in individual cases; (2) consider the various seriousness indicators, remembering that some will carry more weight than others; (3) note that, by statute, racial aggravation increases the seriousness of any offence, Crime and Disorder Act 1998, s 82, but see the note on specific racially-aggravated offences created under ss 29–32 of the same Act; (4) always bear in mind that, by statute, the commission of an offence on bail aggravates its seriousness; (5) consider the effect of using previous convictions, or any failure to respond to previous sentences, in assessing seriousness. Courts should identify any convictions relevant for this purpose and then consider to what extent they affect the seriousness of the present offence; (6) note that, when there are several offences to be sentenced, the court must have regard to the totality principle.

When the court has formed an initial assessment of the seriousness of the offence(s), consider any offender mitigation.

The impact of the offence upon the victim should be taken into account as a seriousness factor.

In deciding what sentence to pass on a person who has pleaded guilty the court has to take into account the stage in the proceedings at which that plea was indicated and the circumstances in which the indication was given, (Criminal Justice and Public Order Act 1994, s 48). If the court imposes a less severe penalty than it would have given, it must state this in open court.

The principles of 'discount' apply as much to magistrates' courts as they do to Crown Courts. A timely guilty plea may attract a sentencing discount of up to a third but the precise amount of discount will depend on the facts of each case. A change of plea on the day set down for trial may attract only a minimal reduction in sentence; the court must still consider whether discount should be given.

Discounts apply to fines, periods of community sentences and custody. Mandatory periods of disqualification and mandatory penalty points cannot be reduced for a guilty plea. Reasons should be given for decisions.

The purpose of a Pre-Sentence Report (PSR) is to provide information to the sentencing court about the offender and the offences charged so that the court has sufficient relevant information to enable it to decide a suitable sentence.

The revised National Standards require a PSR to contain: an assessment of the offending behaviour, an assessment of the risk to the public, and a clear and realistic indication of the action, which can be taken by the court to reduce re-offending. When adjourning a case for receipt of a PSR the court should indicate to the officer preparing the report (preferably in writing): (1) the court's preliminary view of the level of seriousness, (2) the aim of the sentence and (3) any particular issues to be addressed in the report

The court must make it clear to all that the sentencing bench is not bound by the preliminary indication of seriousness.

A PSR must be provided within a maximum of 15 working days of the court's request or any shorter time agreed. Any delay must be explained in writing.

The Specific Sentence Report (SSR) has a similar purpose to the PSR but, while still in writing, is in an expedited form. The SSR is intended for the more straightforward cases where the required information is readily available from the probation officer in court. The SSR is designed to be available on the same day on which the court's request is made, unless there are exceptional circumstances or the probation officer preparing the report considers further investigation and a full PSR to be necessary.

Giving reasons

98.6 Magistrates should normally give reasons for their findings and decisions; this is obligatory under the Human Rights Act 1998: (1) the offender should be told the reasons for the decision; (2) the victim will want to know the reasons for the decision; (3) the public is entitled to know what is going on in the criminal justice system, and to have confidence in it. (4) If a sentence is unusual the case for reasons is doubly important; (5) ill-informed criticism in the media may be reduced if reasons have been given in public and recorded; (6) in preparing an SSR or a PSR, or in implementing a community sentence, the probation service must know what the magistrates had in mind; (7) if a case has to be adjourned, and a differently constituted bench sits next time, the later bench must know the reasons for the decisions of the earlier bench; (8) the reasons will be necessary if there is an appeal by way of case stated.

There are now many instances where the giving of reasons is required by law: (1) why bail is refused; (2) why the offence is so serious as to justify prison; (3) why a defaulter is being sent to prison; (4) if a compensation order is not awarded; (5) if a sentence discount is given; (6) if the court does not disqualify the driver or endorse his licence for 'special reasons'.

Fining

98.7 Fines are suitable as punishment for cases which are not serious enough to merit a community penalty, nor so serious that a custodial sentence must be considered. The aim should be for the fine to have equal impact on rich or poor and before fixing the amount of a fine, the court must inquire into the offender's financial circumstances, preferably using a standard means form. The fine must reflect the seriousness of the offence and must be proportionate both to the offence and the offender. Where compensation is awarded this must take priority over fines or costs (see *Compensation Orders*). The suggested fines in these Guidelines are given as either A, B or C.

This guidance should not be used as a tariff and every offender's means must be individually considered. Where a defendant is to be fined for several offences and his means are limited it may be better to fix the relevant fine level for the most serious offence and order 'no separate penalty' on the lesser matters.

It is useful if the defendant can be given a document, which sets out the total fines, rate of payment, date of first payment and place of payment before leaving the court.

Adjusting fine to take into account net income
98.8

Weekly income less Tax and Nat Insurance	£100	£130	£160	£190	£220	£250	£300	£350	£400
Fine A	£50	£65	£80	£95	£110	£125	£150	£175	£200
Fine B	£100	£130	£160	£190	£220	£250	£300	£350	£400
Fine C	£150	£195	£240	£285	£330	£375	£450	£525	£600

Increase the fine when the offence is aggravated and reduce it when it is mitigated and for a timely plea of guilty. If there is insufficient income to pay a fine and compensation consider ordering the compensation only.

Assessing means

98.9 Criminal Justice Act 1991, s 18 requires the court to inquire into the financial circumstances of the offender so far as they are known. The means form is the starting point, then any necessary further questioning about income and expenditure can be done by the clerk and/or the magistrates. The first figure needed is net income which is income net of tax and National Insurance contributions. An assessment should then be made of the disposable or spare income left to the offender after unavoidable ordinary living expenses, such as food, housing, clothing, council tax and essential services have been deducted. The court should discover whether the offender has savings or other disposable or realisable capital assets. The financial circumstances of third parties, eg other members of the family, are irrelevant, save insofar as the offender derives income or benefit from such persons. Before the actual fine has been announced, inquiry should be made to establish the extent of any outstanding fines and consideration as to the appropriate course of action, which may be to transfer the fine to be collected by the local court.

If for any reason the magistrates are not satisfied with the information they have received, and they feel they cannot sentence until they have such information, they may adjourn the case for further information to be supplied, and they may make a financial circumstances order requiring a statement of means to be provided, see the Criminal Justice Act 1991, s 20.

The fine is payable in full on the day and the defendant should always be asked for immediate payment. If periodic payments are allowed, the fine should normally be payable within a maximum of 12 months. It should be remembered, however, that for those on very low incomes it is often unrealistic to expect them to maintain weekly payments for as long as a year.

The fine should be a hardship, depriving the offender of the capacity to spend the money on 'luxuries', but care should be taken not to force him or her below a reasonable 'subsistence' level.

Fining in the defendant's absence

98.10 If, having been given a reasonable opportunity to inform the court of his means, the offender refuses or fails to do so, the magistrates may draw such inference as to means as they think just in the circumstances. It is inappropriate simply to fine the maximum level.

Costs

98.11 The following guidance was given by the Court of Appeal in *R v Northallerton Magistrates' Court, ex p Dove* [2000] 1 Cr App Rep (S) 136, 163 JP 657, [1999] Crim LR 760, DC: (1) an order for costs to the prosecutor should never exceed the sum which, having regard to the defendant's means and any other financial order imposed upon him, he is able to pay and which it is reasonable to order him to pay; (2) such an order should never exceed the sum, which the prosecutor had actually and reasonably incurred; (3) the purpose of the order is to compensate the prosecutor and not to punish the defendant; (4) the costs ordered to be paid should not in the ordinary way be grossly disproportionate to the fine imposed for the offence. If the total of the proposed fine and the costs sought by the prosecutor exceeds the sum which the defendant could reasonably be ordered to pay, it is preferable to achieve an acceptable total by reducing the sum of costs ordered than by reducing the fine; (5) it is for the defendant to provide the justices with such data relevant to his financial position as would enable them to assess what he could reasonably afford to pay, and if he fails to do so the justices are entitled to draw reasonable inferences as to his means from all the circumstances of the case; (6) it is incumbent on any court, which proposes to make any financial order against a defendant to give him a fair opportunity to adduce any relevant financial information and to make any appropriate submissions.

Community penalties

98.12 The purpose of a community penalty is to provide a rigorous and effective punishment for an offender whose offence requires more than a financial penalty but is not so serious as to necessitate imprisonment. A community penalty has three principal elements: restriction of liberty, reparation and prevention of re-offending. Community sentences include: (1) attendance centre orders, (2) probation orders with or without special requirements, (3) community service orders, (4) combination orders and (5) curfew orders.

The restrictions on liberty imposed by the sentence must be commensurate with the seriousness of the offence and the order must be the one most suitable for the offender.

It is generally good practice to require a Pre Sentence or Specific Sentence Report when considering whether to impose a community penalty. In ordering such a report the court should indicate its view of the level of seriousness and the aim of the sentence. In pronouncing sentence the court should stress the need of the offender to co-operate and the consequences of breach.

Penalties for breach of a community sentence are: (1) a fine of up to £1,000, the order to continue, (2) community service of up to 60 hours, the order to continue, (3) revocation and re-sentencing for the original offence (in which case the probable sentence will be custody) and (4) attendance centre order. (See the revised National Standards and the new inter-agency publication *Towards Good Practice – Community Sentences and the Courts.*)

The court may ask to be kept informed of the offender's progress under the order.

Electronic monitoring of curfew orders

98.13   Curfew orders enforced by electronic monitoring are available for offenders aged 16 and over. The curfew order is a community sentence requiring an offender to remain at a specified place from 2 to 12 hours a day on from 1 to 7 days a week, for a maximum period of 6 months. The court must obtain and consider information about the proposed curfew address including the attitude of others affected by the order. The order must take account of religious beliefs, employment, education and the requirements of other community orders. The offender's consent is not required. The aims of the order are: (1) to restrict liberty in a systematic controlled way; (2) to make it harder for the offender to commit further crimes; (3) to interrupt the pattern of offending by removing the offender from the circumstances of his/her offending and (4) provide clear evidence of curfew compliance

The order can be used as a stand alone order, in combination with any other community order, or can be added to a pre-existing community order.

When considering whether to impose an order the offence must be assessed by the court to be 'serious enough', and the level of punishment appropriate. When ordering a Pre-Sentence Report the court must specifically ask the probation service to carry out a curfew assessment even if an 'all options open' report is specified.

Breach of court orders

98.14   The breach of court orders should never be treated lightly. They should be rigorously enforced. In making any pronouncement on sentence the breach should be given special mention. A failure by the court to respond effectively to a breach can: (1) erode public confidence in the courts, (2) undermine the work of the agency supervising the order and (3) allow the offender to feel he has 'got away with it'.

The offender should be clearly told of the seriousness of the offence and, if the court decides to allow an order to continue, be told what is expected of him/her and the likely consequence of any further breach. In the case of community sentences there are National Standards revised in April 2000 which lay down strict enforcement requirements for the probation service. The seriousness of any offence should be matched not just by the severity of the sentence but also by the intensity of the enforcement.

Compensation orders

98.15 Having assessed the seriousness of the offence, including the impact on the victim, and any aggravating and mitigating factors affecting the offender, the court is under a duty to consider compensation in every case involving death, personal injury, loss or damage (Powers of Criminal Courts Act 1979, s 35), whether or not an application has been made.

If the sentence is to be financial, then the order of priorities is compensation, fine, costs.

Compensating the victim is more important than paying money to the state. If the sentence is to be a community penalty, the court should consider carefully the overall burdens placed on the offender if a compensation order is to be made too. If the sentence is to be custody, then a compensation order will be unlikely unless the offender has financial resources available with which to pay.

If, having considered making a compensation order, the court decides that it is not appropriate to make one, it has a statutory duty to give its reasons for not ordering compensation.

Limitations on powers: Magistrates have the power to award compensation for personal injury, loss or damage up to a total of £5,000 for each offence. An exception is where the injury, loss or damage arises from a road accident: a compensation order may not be made in such a case unless there is conviction of an offence under the Theft Act or if the offender is uninsured and the Motor Insurers' Bureau will not cover the loss. If in doubt, seek advice from the clerk. Compensation should only be awarded in fairly clear, uncomplicated cases: if there are disputes and complications, the matter should be left to the civil courts.

Any victim may bring a civil action for damages against the offender: if that action is successful, the civil court will deduct the amount paid by the offender under a compensation order. In this way, there should be no double compensation. The same applies where the victim receives a payment under the Criminal Injuries Compensation Scheme. The magistrates' court should therefore take no account of these other possibilities.

The Criminal Injuries Compensation Scheme provides state compensation for the victims of crimes of violence, particularly those who are seriously injured. The minimum award is currently £1,000. Courts are encouraged to make compensation orders, whether or not the case falls within the Criminal Injuries Compensation Scheme, in order to bring home to offenders themselves the consequences of their actions.

The purpose of making a compensation order is to compensate the victim for his or her losses. The compensation may relate to offences taken into consideration, subject to a maximum of £5,000 per charge. Compensation for personal injury may include compensation for terror, shock or distress caused by the offence. The court must have regard to the means of the offender when calculating the amount of the order. Up to 3 years can be allowed for the compensation to be paid in certain cases.

In calculating the gross amount of compensation, courts should consider compensating the victim for two types of loss. The first, sometimes called 'special damages', includes compensation for financial loss sustained as a result of the offence – eg the cost of repairing damage, or in cases of injury, any loss of earnings or dental expenses. If these costs are not agreed, the court should ask for evidence of them. The second type of loss, sometimes called 'general damages', covers compensation for the pain and suffering of the injury itself and for any loss of facility.

Calculating the compensation: The amount of compensation should be determined in the light of medical evidence, the victim's sex and age, and any other factors, which appear to the court to be relevant in the particular case. If the court does not have sufficient information, then the matter should be adjourned to obtain more facts.

The Table below gives some general guidance on appropriate starting points for general damages.

Once the court has made a preliminary calculation of the appropriate compensation, it is required to have regard to the means of the offender before making an order. Where the offender has little money, the order may have to be scaled down significantly. However, even a compensation order for a fairly small sum may be important to the victim.

Type of injury	Description	Starting point
Graze	Depending on size	Up to £75
Bruise	Depending on size	Up to £100
Black eye		£125
Cut: no permanent scar	Depending on size and whether stitched	£100–£500
Sprain	Depending on loss of mobility	£100–£1,000
Finger	Fractured little finger, recovery within month	£1,000
Loss of non-front tooth	Depending on cosmetic effect	£500–£1,000
Loss of front tooth	Depending on cosmetic effect	£1,500
Eye	Blurred or double vision	£1,000
Nose	Undisplaced fractured of nasal bone	£1,000
Nose	Displaced fracture of bone requiring manipulation	£1,500
Nose	Not causing fracture but displaced septum requiring sub-mucous resection	£2,000
Facial scar	However small, resulting in permanent disfigurement	£1,500
Wrist	Simple fracture, recovery within month	£3,000
Wrist	Displaced fracture, limb in plaster, recovery in 6 months	£3,500
Leg or arm	Simple fracture of tibia, fibula, ulna or radius, recovery within month	£3,500
Laparotomy	Stomach scar 6-8 inches (resulting from operation)	£3,500

Road traffic offences

98.16   *Disqualification.* Some offences carry mandatory disqualification. This mandatory disqualification period may be automatically lengthened by the existence of certain previous convictions and disqualifications. Sentencers should not disqualify in the absence of the defendant but should take steps to ensure the defendant attends the court.

Penalty points and disqualification. All penalty points offences carry also as an alternative discretionary power to disqualify for a selected period and also discretionary power to disqualify until a test is passed. The number of variable penalty points or the period of disqualification is targeted strictly at the seriousness of the offence and in either case must not be reduced below the statutory minimum, where applicable. Penalty points and (non-totting) disqualification cannot be awarded for the same offence, or even for offences being convictions on the same occasion.

Disqualifications for less than 56 days. A disqualification for less than 56 days is also more lenient in that it does not revoke the licence and cannot increase subsequent mandatory periods. The precise amount of discount for a timely guilty plea will depend on the facts of each case. It should be given in respect of the fine or periods of community penalty or custody, but does not apply to mandatory periods of disqualification.

The multiple offender. Where an offender is convicted of several offences committed on one occasion, it is suggested that the court should concentrate on the most serious offence, carrying the greatest number of penalty points or period of disqualification.

The application of the totality principle may then result in less than the total of the suggested amounts of fines for the remaining individual offences, or the court may decide to impose no separate penalty for the lesser offences.

Totting. Repeat offenders who reach 12 points or more within a period of three years become liable to a minimum disqualification for 6 months, and in some instances 12 months or 2 years – but must be given an opportunity to address the court and/or bring evidence to show why such disqualification should not be ordered or should be reduced. Totting disqualifications, unlike other disqualifications, erase all penalty points. Totting disqualifications can be reduced or avoided for exceptional hardship or other circumstances. No account is to be taken of non-exceptional hardship or circumstances alleged to make the offence(s) not serious. No such ground can be used again to mitigate totting, if previously taken into account in totting mitigation within the 3 years preceding the conviction.

Driver not supplying details. This offence is now prevalent and must be regarded more seriously.

New drivers. From June 1997, newly qualified drivers who tot up 6 points or more during a two year probationary period from the date of passing the driving test will automatically have their licence revoked and will have to apply for a provisional licence until they pass a repeat test. The totting must also include any points imposed prior to passing the test provided they are within 3 years.

Goods vehicles over 3.5 tonnes, buses and coaches. Owners and drivers of such vehicles are often in the average or high income scale. If, exceptionally, low income is applicable, seek documentary evidence and reduce the fine as appropriate.

Fixed penalties. If a fixed penalty was offered, consider any reasons for not taking up and, if valid, fine the amount of the appropriate fixed penalty and endorse if required, considering whether costs should be waived.

99 Making Off Without Payment

99.1 Theft Act 1978, s 3

Triable either way. On indictment maximum sentence 2 years. On summary maximum 6 months and/or £5,000.

There is power to make a restitution order under Powers of Criminal Courts (Sentencing) Act 2000, s 148.

For the tariff for general dishonesty offences see Theft etc

Magistrates' Court Sentencing Guidelines September 2000

99.2   Entry point. Is a discharge or a fine appropriate? Consider the impact on the victim. Examples of aggravating factors for the offence are deliberate plan, high value, two or more involved and victim particularly vulnerable. Examples of mitigating factors for the offence impulsive action and low value. Examples of mitigation are age, health (physical or mental), co-operation with the police, voluntary compensation and genuine remorse. Give reasons if not awarding compensation. **Starting point fine B**. (£100 when defendant has £100 net weekly income. See page 334 for table showing fines for different incomes.)

For details about the guidelines see MAGISTRATES' COURT SENTENCING GUIDELINES at page 331.

MANAGING A COMPANY WHEN BANKRUPT

See INSOLVENCY OFFENCES

100   MANSLAUGHTER

100.1   Offences Against the Person Act 1861, s 5, and the Homicide Act 1957, s 2(3)

Indictable only. Maximum sentence life imprisonment.

When committed by a driver of a motor vehicle, there is obligatory disqualification for 2 year unless there are special reasons and endorsement with 3-11 points. The court must order him to be disqualified till he has passed the appropriate driving test unless there are special reasons. There is power to deprive the defendant of the vehicle used[1].

There is a power to make a compensation order for the deceased's funeral expenses[2].

Manslaughter is a specified offence for automatic life.

The cases are in part divided into sections for the weapon that was used, as that part of the case is usually clear. Much more important factors are the intent and the surrounding circumstances. One of the most critical factors is whether there was an intent to kill or cause GBH, which would be present, when the offence is based on diminished responsibility or provocation. It is not possible to divide the cases by intent because many of the cases provide insufficient information.

1   Powers of the Criminal Courts (Sentencing) Act 2000, s 143.
2   Powers of Criminal Courts (Sentencing) Act 2000, s 130(1)(b) See *Funeral expenses of the deceased, power to order for compensation for the*

Crown Court statistics England and Wales – Crown Court – Males 21+
100.2

Year	Plea	Total Numbers sentenced	Type of sentence%					Average length of custody[1] (months)
			Discharge	Fine	Community sentence	Suspended sentence	Custody	
Manslaughter								
2000	Guilty	118	0%	0%	7%	1%	86%	59.2
	Not guilty	53	0%	0%	0%	2%	96%	69.3
Manslaughter due to diminished responsibility								
2000	Guilty	11	0%	0%	9%	0%	45[2]%	84
	Not guilty	2	0%	0%	0%	0%	100%	84

1 Excluding life sentences. Source: Crime and Criminal Justice Unit, Home Office Ref: IOS416-02.
2 The reason the figures do not add up to 100% may be because Hospital Orders are omitted.

Guideline remarks

100.3 *R v Boyer* (1981) 3 Cr App Rep (S) 35. The offence of manslaughter attracts the widest band of sentences for any offence known to this court. The sentence can vary from life imprisonment to a conditional discharge.

R v Butler [1999] 2 Cr App Rep (S) 339. Little use is gained in sentencing in manslaughter cases from an exhaustive view of the authorities since it is clear that this court has repeatedly said that sentencing in manslaughter cases is (a) very difficult, and (b) turns on the particular facts of the cases under consideration.

A-G's Reference (Nos 19, 20 and 21 of 2001) [2001] EWCA Crim 1432, [2002] 1 Cr App Rep (S) 136. First, the court will examine the context in which the death was caused. If it is particularly reprehensible conduct or conduct that calls for deterrence, the court is bound to impose a longer sentence than otherwise might be the case. Consider whether violence of any kind was contemplated or intended by the defendant. When actual violence is intended the sentence must inevitably reflect both the fact of that intention and the extent of the violence contemplated. The court must then consider the risk inherent in what was being done of really serious injury or death and the extent to which this must have been apparent to those involved. A further factor to consider is the behaviour of the defendant after inflicting the unintended serious injury.

Guideline remarks – Diminished responsibility

100.4 *R v Chambers* (1983) 5 Cr App Rep (S) 190 – LCJ. In diminished responsibility cases there are various courses open to a judge. His choice of the right course will depend on the state of the evidence and the material before him. If the psychiatric reports recommend and justify it, and there are no contrary indications, he will make a hospital order. Where a hospital order is not recommended, or is not appropriate, and the defendant constitutes a danger to the public for an unpredictable period of time, the right sentence will, in all probabilities, be one of life imprisonment. In cases where the evidence indicates that the accused's responsibility for his acts was so grossly impaired that his degree of responsibility for them was minimal, then a lenient course will be open to the judge. Provided there is no danger of repetition of violence, it will usually be possible to make such an order as will give the accused his freedom, possibly with some supervision. There will however be cases in which there is no proper basis for a hospital order; but in which the accused's degree of responsibility is not minimal. In such cases the judge should pass a determinate sentence of imprisonment, the length of which will depend on two factors: his assessment of the degree of the accused's responsibility and his view as to the period of time, if any, for which the accused will continue to be a danger to the public.

Babies

See *Domestic (Children)*

Body, dismembering and disposing of the

100.5   *R v Frisby* [2001] EWCA Crim 1482, [2002] 1 Cr App Rep (S) 289. The defendant was convicted of manslaughter on the basis of provocation. Held. The dismembering and disposal of the body was not a proper matter to take into account. It would have been a proper matter in relation to murder as showing some form of pre-planning but not for manslaughter. Sentence reduced from 8 years to **6 years**.

Burglars/Robbers/Thieves, by

100.6   *R v De Jesus Amarel* (11 June 1999, unreported). The defendant pleaded guilty to manslaughter and robbery. The victim, aged 72 had befriended the defendant aged 26. However the defendant and another agreed to steal from him. They gagged him, and the other punched him. They found £180 and tied him up and gagged him. They left him to die while they went to buy drugs. The defendant played the lesser role in the violence but took a full part in the manslaughter. He was due to give evidence against the other. Held. **10 years** and 8 concurrent was not excessive.

A-G's Reference (Nos 19, 20 and 21 of 2001) [2001] EWCA Crim 1432, [2002] 1 Cr App Rep (S) 136. The defendants B, F and C pleaded to attempted robbery. They denied murder. On the third day of their murder trial B and F pleaded to manslaughter and C pleaded to conspiracy to rob. A 59-year-old Norwegian man was walking in Blackpool town centre and the three defendants attacked him from behind. He was pushed to the ground and kicked to the head and body. They didn't find his wallet. People came to his help and the three fled. The victim was very badly beaten and suffered extensive bruising to the face. Ninety minutes later a 60-year-old man was walking home nearby. He was attacked from behind and robbed of £270 and a sovereign ring. He staggered home, collapsed and died. There were nine fractures to seven of his ribs. Four penetrated his chest cavity. The victim had pre-existing emphysema and respiratory problems caused by the fractured ribs which led to his rapid decline. The cause of death was 'blunt force chest and neck injuries'. The manslaughter basis of plea was that the chest injuries were caused by F falling on him and/or sitting on him in order to restrain him while his property was stolen. C's basis of plea to the conspiracy was he withdrew before the violence begun and he wasn't responsible for the death. B was 36 and of effective good character. He was married with two children. He had a good work record as a security guard and had been discharged from the army with exemplary character. He was separated from his wife and at a low ebb in a hostel. F was 26 and the Judge ignored his record. He broke the 'wall of silence' and assisted in the recovery of part of the property. C was 16 at the time and had spent a 'very considerable period' in custody and none of it would count to his sentence. B and F received 7 years for the manslaughter with 5 concurrent for the attempted robbery. C received **2 years detention and training** but the effective sentence would be a little short of **4 years**. Held. The offences were not opportunist. The first offence involved considerable gratuitous violence. Even without a death or unintended serious injury resulting, these two offences following pleas of guilty merited for an adult **at least 6 years**. The risk of serious harm was a high one. Deterrent sentencers were demanded. There was no good reason why the sentences for the 2 attacks were concurrent. They were quite distinct matters. We would have imposed a sentence of 12 years for the manslaughter and **3 years consecutive** for the attempted robbery making **15 years**. For a plea that would be **11 to 12 years**. Taking into account it was a reference 10 years for B and F, made up of **9 years** for the manslaughter and 1 year consecutive for the attempt. The 1 year is artificially low to take account it was a reference. C when 16 had faced a murder charge when he bore no responsibility for the death. As the appropriate sentence for an adult was 6 years C's sentence was not unduly lenient.

R v Simpson [2002] EWCA Crim 25, [2002] 2 Cr App Rep (S) 234 – LCJ. The defendant made an early guilty plea to manslaughter and two robberies. The first victim, an 89-year-old lady was returning to her flat after picking up her pension and doing some shopping. As she was walking up the stairs to the flat the defendant pulled her shopping bag firmly backwards. It contained her purse with £6 in it. She tried to resist and he gave it a heavier pull. She fell backwards and slid down the concrete stairs. He ran off with the bag. She was found to have a fracture to her neck and femur. A plate and screws were inserted. The operation appeared straightforward but she suffered two consequential chest infections and died about a month after the robbery. Almost immediately after the first robbery, the defendant 'thumped' a 76-year-old lady in the back and then pulled at her bag. It contained her pension book, documents and purse. The victim had just returned from collecting her pension. He pulled at it until she let go and drove away. The defendant was now 40 with convictions going back to the early 1970s. Over the years he had been in and out of prison for dishonesty and driving offences. In 1995 he received 4 years for two robberies and one of the victims was an 83 year old lady who was followed from picking up her pension and knocked to the ground. The second robbery was similar. After the manslaughter offence he was sentenced to 3 years for burglary and serious driving offences. He needed £200 a day for heroin. Held. These offences are mean beyond words, easy to commit, highly prevalent and dangerous both to life and limb of the elderly victims. When they are committed by dangerous acts and death occurs severe sentences are called for. There can be no fault with the sentence of 7 years for the robberies because of his record and the circumstances. The **10 years** for the manslaughter as an overall sentence could not be faulted. The sentences remained consecutive to the sentence he was serving.

R v Ginley [2002] EWCA Crim 209, [2002] 2 Cr App Rep (S) 277. The defendant was convicted of manslaughter and attempted robbery. The 57-year-old victim and his disabled wife were helping out at their frozen food warehouse. Because of ill health they were semi-retired and their sons had taken the business over. In 1987 the victim had had a triple bypass and his wife was paralysed down one side and in a wheelchair. In the late morning the defendant and another entered the warehouse. One pulled a balaclava down over his face and demanded to know where the safe was. He put a knife with a 10″ blade to the victim's throat and put him in a headlock. There was a scuffle in which the victim was prodded in the ribs a number of times with the knife. The wife pointed to the safe in the office and picked up a stick to go to her husband's aid. The second man who was masked grabbed her stick and pushed her in her wheelchair to the other side of the office away from the panic button. The victim shouted the police were on their way and the robbers left believing the panic button had been pressed. The victim then pressed the panic button and the police attended quickly. The victim gave the number of the car to an officer, collapsed and died of a heart attack. The pathologist said, 'death could have occurred at any time but trauma and excitement could precipitate a heart attack. More likely than not the victim would have been alive had it not been for the struggle.' The defendant was 21 when sentenced and had convictions but none for violence. Held. The judge quite rightly took the view that this was a robbery of an extreme kind. It was a prepared robbery. There was nothing wrong with 9 years for the robbery without considering the death. The 3 years extra for the death was wholly appropriate. **12 years** upheld. (The poor health of the victim is not listed as a factor in the judgement confirming the principle defendants do not receive a reduction when the defendant is of poor health.)

R v Clark and Lappin [2002] EWCA Crim 222, [2002] 2 Cr App Rep (S) 353. The defendant L pleaded guilty to manslaughter and robbery at the first opportunity. C pleaded guilty to robbery. At about midnight the 32-year-old alcoholic victim was walking in the street with two bottles of cider. He was beaten and robbed of the two bottles. L punched him and caused quite 'horrific injuries'. They were a closed and swollen eye, which required three stitches, a cut to the lip and a broken nose. The victim was discharged from hospital and asked to return in the morning. Unfortunately he suffered from a liver disease and his blood would not clot. When he returned the next morning his nose would not stop bleeding and he suffered a cardiac arrest. He died 16 days later of multiple organ failure as a result of bleeding caused by his facial injuries. The pathologist said the injuries were consistent with several punches and could be one rather forceful punch and a lesser punch. The basis of plea was, 'C asked the victim for a cigarette and the victim probably thought he was going to be robbed and swung a bottle at L. At that stage they didn't intend to rob him and L punched him and both men fell to the ground. When L was on top of the victim he told C to take the bottles which he did. As L walked away the victim grabbed his jumper and L punched him on the nose causing the fatal injury.' L was then 19 with 12 convictions including attempted robbery, theft, assault on police, criminal damage, threatening behaviour, burglary and possession of an offensive weapon. He had served 4 months YOI. Held. The aggravating feature was that the offence occurred during a robbery. **6 years** YOI was not obviously too long.

Old cases. *A-G's Reference (No 2 of 1993)* [1994] 15 Cr App Rep (S) 358; *R v McGee* (1994) 15 Cr App Rep (S) 463; *R v Sowrey* (1994) 15 Cr App Rep (S) 870; *R v Brophy* (1994) 16 Cr App Rep (S) 652; *A-G's Reference (No 68 of 1995)* [1996] 2 Cr App Rep (S) 358.

Concurrent, should the sentence be concurrent or consecutive to the sentence for the illegal activity

100.7 *R v Wacker* (31 July 2002, unreported). The defendant was convicted of conspiracy to facilitate illegal entry and 58 counts of manslaughter. Sixty illegal immigrants travelled from China to Holland where they were loaded into an adapted container on the defendant's lorry. The deaths were caused by lack of air. The basis for the manslaughter was gross negligence. He received 8 years for the conspiracy and six consecutive for the manslaughter counts. The defence argued the total was too much and the Attorney General argued the 6 years for the manslaughter counts was too lenient although the total sentence was not challenged. Held. The causing of so many deaths to avoid detection puts this case in a category of its own. Concurrent sentences were the correct approach so there is no danger of punishing the underlying criminality twice. Therefore 14 years for the manslaughter substituted, which would not have the appearance of devaluing the loss of life.

Crime of passion

100.8 *R v Henry* [1999] 2 Cr App Rep (S) 412. The defendant pleaded guilty to manslaughter. He had indicated his plea at the first opportunity. The defendant's wife went out for the evening leaving the defendant to look after the children aged 5 and 1. Leaving one child with his in-laws and taking the other with him, he drove to pick up his wife. However, she had left a public house with another man. He then saw them in the street with arms linked and saw them stop and kiss each other. The defendant shouted across but the wife refused to get into the car. The defendant ran across the road and punched the other man in the face who fell backwards, and struck his head on a manhole cover. He died of injuries to his skull and brain caused by the fall. The blow was of considerable force. It broke the victim's jaw and had lifted him off the ground. The defendant after initial denials expressed remorse. He was 31 with no previous convictions and had excellent character references. He told the probation officer he didn't drink and had never hit anyone before. He was a model prisoner. Held. **18 months** substituted for 4 years. Had the blow been less ferocious it would have been less.

R v Gratton [2001] 2 Cr App Rep (S) 167. The defendant pleaded guilty to manslaughter. The defendant and the victim were friends. The deceased believed the defendant fancied his girlfriend (wrongly they said). After drinking a lot during the day, they went home when the public house closed. The defendant and the victim were seen arguing. The defendant was put to bed on the sofa by his girlfriend and the victim. The defendant's girlfriend went into the garden and was joined by the victim. They sat opposite each other on chairs. The victim leaned forward put his hands on her knees and gave her a quick kiss on the lips as a thank you gesture. Unfortunately the defendant had come out and had seen it. He walked up to them quickly saying, 'You fucked up with your missus, now you are trying it on with mine.' He threw two or three punches to the victim's face causing the victim and his chair to tip back. His head hit some rocks in a rockery. He appeared to be dead when the ambulance attended. The defendant showed great remorse. He thought he saw a 'snog.' He was 31 and was treated as of good character. He had an excellent work record. There were many references. The defendant received **9 months**. Held. It would not be right to suspend it.

R v Rumbol [2001] EWCA Crim 238, [2001] 2 Cr App Rep (S) 299. The defendant was convicted of manslaughter. The defendant, a professional boxer formed a relationship with a 17-year-old girl, called Carlie. It faded and she resumed her relationship with the victim, her former boyfriend. The defendant who was possessive of her when they were together became consumed with jealousy. Shortly before his 21st birthday he lay in wait for the victim as he walked to the bus for work. The victim was struck by one blow, which caused him to fall to the ground. The defendant was heard to say, 'Stay away from Carlie, just stay away from her.' The defendant ran off. The victim died the next morning. The pathologist said the rupture of the vertebral artery was cause by a single hard blow. The defendant had never been in trouble before. Held. Because of his character and because he never intended to cause any serious harm to the victim **6 years** not 7.

Old cases. *R v Gussman* (1993) 15 Cr App Rep (S) 440; *R v Light* (1995) 16 Cr App Rep (S) 824.

See also **Domestic**

Defendant aged under 16

100.9 *A-G's Reference (Nos 68 and 69 of 1996)* [1997] 2 Cr App Rep (S) 280. Two girls L and H who were aged 13 and 12 at the time of the offence pleaded guilty to manslaughter. At a fairground there were a number of incidents involving girls fighting. Two who had been involved on earlier occasions sought to leave the site but were followed by the two defendants who were part of a much larger group. One girl was encouraged to fight H and she eventually agreed to do so. They fell to the ground and H managed to sit on her punching the girl in the chest and on the head. The victim of the manslaughter said the girl had had enough and intervened. L seized her by the hair and pulled her off balance and kicked her chest and head as she lay on the ground. H also kicked her between the eye and the ear. After a Newton hearing both were sentenced on the basis of one kick as victim lay defenceless on the ground. Both had no previous convictions. Held. It was worth **2 to 3½ years** detention, so the 2 year sentence remained undisturbed.

Old cases. *R v G* (1992) 14 Cr App Rep 349; *R v Coffey* (1994) 15 Cr App Rep (S) 754.

Defendant aged 16-17

100.10 *R v Swatson* [1997] 2 Cr App Rep (S) 140. The defendant pleaded guilty to possession of a firearm with intent to endanger life and manslaughter. The defendant who was then 17 was believed to have been involved in a robbery in which a handgun was used and £12,000 was stolen. The deceased and another visited the defendant and demanded money from him. He went with them to his mother's address claiming he would find some money. Later the deceased forced open the front door. Three shots were fired and the deceased left and then bled to death. The defendant at first claimed it was self-defence. He had had the gun in his possession for some weeks. Sentenced on the basis that it was a shooting in panic when under attack. Held. Although there was a need for deterrence the starting point was **12 years** discounted for plea to **9 years** not 12 years detention.

A-G's Reference (No 51 of 1997) [1998] 2 Cr App Rep (S) 313. The defendant pleaded guilty to manslaughter by reason of provocation. The victim attacked the defendant's girlfriend, by calling her a slag, pushing chips and gravy into her face and pushing or punching her so she fell onto a bonnet of a car. The defendant then aged 17, went home, got a chisel and found the victim. He then plunged the chisel into the victim's head to the full length of the blade. He surrendered to the police. He had no previous convictions and was full of remorse. Held. Taking into account it was a reference **3½ years** not 2½ detention.

R v Hamilton [1999] 1 Cr App Rep (S) 187. The defendant was convicted of manslaughter. The defendant aged 17 at the time visited his grandmother aged 83 to steal money from her to pay for drugs. She disturbed him and he strangled her. There was no sign of mental illness. Held. In view of the defendant's youth, his minor record and the fact the attack was not persisted or repeated **8 years** detention substituted for 10 years.

R v Jeans [1999] 2 Cr App Rep (S) 257. The defendant pleaded guilty to manslaughter. There were two different parties attended by young people. One was orderly and attended by the victim and the other was disorderly and drunken and attended by the defendant then aged 16½. Later in the street when people from the two parties met, three youths from the defendant's group heckled the other group. Either the defendant or someone else from his group struck someone from the other group on the head with a piece of wood. The defendant then struck the victim with his piece of wood on the upper lip. The victim's nasal septum was torn away at the base. The victim lost consciousness and fell backwards. Unusually the shock to the brain caused the heart and breathing to stop. The defendant had two previous convictions for ABH and common assault. He had suffered abuse as a child. Remorse was shown from the outset. Held. Because of his youth and the surprising consequences of what he did, **4 years** detention substituted for 6 years.

R v Murray [2001] 2 Cr App Rep (S) 17. The defendant was convicted of manslaughter of his stepfather after years of abuse. The defendant's mother married the victim when the defendant was 14. The relationship between the victim and his wife and his stepson deteriorated. The victim was seriously violent to his wife. He ripped down a curtain rail, smashed a telephone, threatened to break the TV set with a meat cleaver, tore off cupboard doors and threw knives at the defendant's bedroom door. The defendant, who was 17, told his mother that he did not want his stepfather at the flat. The stepfather was told about the remark and said he was not going to be dictated to by a 17 year old.

He left a public house and went home. He found the defendant in and seized him by the shirt. He produced an iron bar weighing about 2lbs. The defendant was told to return to his flat. He refused and the victim hit him and threatened to hit and harm him. He prodded the defendant in the stomach with the bar quite firmly. The bar was raised. The defendant punched him to the face and grabbed the bar. The victim fell to his knees and the defendant managed to take the bar. The victim started to rise and the hit him up to eight times with the bar. The victim's skull was hopelessly shattered. The defendant gave himself up to the police. He gave a full and frank account to the police. The defendant had no previous convictions and had many very positive reports. **18 months** detention and training order not 5 years detention.

A-G's Reference (No 63 of 2001) [2001] EWCA Crim 1652, [2002] 1 Cr App Rep (S) 326. The defendant was convicted of manslaughter by reason of provocation. He had earlier pleaded guilty to manslaughter on the basis of a lack of intent and the prosecution had not accepted the plea. After a trial he was acquitted of murder and convicted of manslaughter. When 17, he was a regular at the pub where the victim was the manager. He was warned about his behaviour on a number of occasions. Shortly before the incident he was barred. He went to a party and then with friends at about 9.30pm he went to the victim's pub. He hid behind the pillar and the victim saw him and went to speak to him. An argument developed and the defendant punched him once, hard on the jaw. The victim was propelled backwards onto a gaming machine and then fell. He never regained consciousness. The defendant was dragged from the pub by a friend kicking as he went to another pub where he boasted he had beaten up the victim. The cause of death was bleeding in the skull because of a rupture to an artery. The blow had rotated the head. The defendant was arrested having tried to run away. In interview he said he had drunk about 12 bottles of beer and the victim had started talking to him as though he was 'a thicky' and showing him up to his friends. He also lied. In 1994 he was cautioned for ABH. In 1998 he pleaded to common assault on a fellow schoolboy. In 2000 there was another common assault when he punched another boy. He received 3 months detention. In December 2000 there was another ABH in which he kicked the victim twice in the head. He received 5 months detention. He was on bail for this when he killed the victim. His parents were heroin addicts and he had been drinking alcohol since 15. Since leaving school he had always been in work. His father and uncle were 'hard men' and he had been taught that men deal with conflict through violence. His risk of re-offending was assessed as high. He showed genuine remorse. Held. The judge appreciated the importance of affording protection to landlords particularly from those they have excluded. There was no weapon. Some judges would have passes more than 3 years. It was lenient but not unduly lenient.

Defendant aged 16 – 17 – Knives

100.11 *R v Mills Re Holder* [1998] 2 Cr App Rep (S) 128 at 143 – LCJ. The defendant was acquitted of murder and convicted of manslaughter. There was a trivial dispute in a playground not involving the defendant in which a boy was chased. The police were called and it ended. The boy was chased again by a large number of boys and sticks and bottles were thrown at him. The defendant caught up with him and stabbed him with a 2–2½" knife which penetrated his heart. He had been to the Youth Court twice for TDA and for handling and assault with intent to resist arrest. There were testimonials. Held. Where a defendant deliberately goes out with a knife which is carried as a weapon, and uses it to cause death, even if there is provocation, he should expect a sentence in a contested case in the region of **10 to 12 years**. **9 years** detention was not too long.

R v Saif [2001] EWCA Crim 541, [2001] 2 Cr App Rep (S) 458. During a murder trial the defendant pleaded guilty to manslaughter on the basis of insufficient intent The defendant knew the victim but was not a friend of his. When aged 16, at the end of a party the host, the defendant, the victim and a girl remained. There was an exchange of insults and the defendant called the deceased, 'green teeth.' The deceased replied with words like, 'smelly Arab.' The defendant who had been drinking a great deal was challenged to go outside. He declined. There was some evidence that the defendant was egged on to fight and he was frightened of a fight. The deceased then went upstairs to the lavatory and the defendant followed him with a knife. The deceased emerged and the defendant lunged at him saying, 'If you want me to fight him, I will fight him.' They went to the ground. A punch was thrown. The victim was holding his chest and an ambulance was called. He was found to have five stab wounds with one to the heart. The defendant started crying and the victim died. The trial judge described it as close to murder. The defendant had one caution and no previous convictions. **7 years** detention not 9 was appropriate.

See also *R v Turner* [2001] EWCA Crim 1331, [2002] 1 Cr App Rep (S) 207 and **Domestic (Children)**

Old cases. *A-G's Reference No 24 of 1991* (1992) 13 Cr App Rep (S) 724; *A-G's Reference (No 8 of 1992)* (1993) 14 Cr App Rep (S) 130; *A-G's Reference (No 28 of 1994)* (1995) 16 Cr App Rep (S) 589.

Defendant aged 18–20

100.12 *R v McLean* [1998] 2 Cr App Rep (S) 250. The defendant was convicted of manslaughter and acquitted of murder. The victim went to the defendant's house and head-butted the defendant after a dispute over some money. The defendant's father intervened and the victim was evicted. The defendant then obtained a knife and returned to the victim and the father who was now in a poor state. The defendant stabbed the victim once in the shoulder and once in the aorta. The defendant was aged 19 with a number of previous including convictions for violence. Remorse was shown. **5 years** YOI was not excessive.

R v Anucha [1999] 2 Cr App Rep (S) 74. The defendant pleaded guilty to manslaughter, two counts of robbery and a count of battery. The defendant and another stole £60 by pulling a shop assistant away from the till. Six days later the defendant returned and was recognised and the assistant refused to open the till. The defendant tried to open it. The assistant went next door to call the police and returned. The defendant accused him of injuring him on the earlier occasion and punched him three times in the face. Thirteen days later the defendant who was then aged 19, used a minicab. The driver was the deceased and he drove it to a petrol station to fill up with petrol. The deceased became worried and tried to ring the police. The defendant left the cab became aggressive and shouted, 'You don't want to take me'. He then punched the victim twice in the face causing him to fall hitting his head hard on the ground. On the same day the defendant returned to the shop and opened the till while another held the assistant as £200 was stolen. Three weeks later the victim died. The defendant had seven previous convictions for robbery, one for attempted robbery, three for theft and two for assault. A report indicated crack cocaine lay behind the offending. The sentencing judge invoked the 'longer than normal sentence' statutory provisions. **6 years** YOI not 8 for the manslaughter consecutive to 3 years for the two robberies.

R v Bosanko [2000] 2 Cr App Rep (S) 108. The defendant pleaded guilty to manslaughter. On the defendant's 18th birthday, he, the victim and another sat outside a public house drinking strong lager. The defendant became aggressive to the victim and others. The three then visited the home of a women. The three continued drinking and the victim and defendant continued quarrelling. The defendant was unsettled and hyperactive. There was a scuffle between the two inside and a fight outside. The third person described them both as equally to blame and both stupid. The victim was next seen getting up and at the same time made an extremely insulting remark about the defendant's mother. The defendant struck the victim with a single blow, which knocked him over, and his head cracked against the ground. He died in hospital of fractures and swelling of the brain. The defendant had a conviction for unlawful wounding with a knife the previous year and one for ABH when he had knocked down a female who fractured her cheek bone and caused her head to hit the pavement. **4½ years** YOI substituted for 6.

R v Al-Hameed [2000] 2 Cr App Rep (S) 158 – LCJ. The defendant was convicted of manslaughter to which he had been prepared to plead guilty to when he faced a murder count. The age of defendant is not recorded but would be less than 21. The defendant and the victim had a bad relationship due to a problem between the defendant and the victim's half-sister. On account of this the victim had confronted and assaulted the defendant twice. The defendant was told the victim was looking for him and was going to beat him up. The defendant went from his house to where the victim lived with a knife. The victim arrived there at about 11pm. There was an exchange of words and the victim went to the garden and challenged him to a fight. The defendant did not respond. The victim returned and they met in the kitchen. The defendant produced his knife. He later said he did this because he feared the victim was going to attack him. The victim fell on the knife, which penetrated his chest. There was no evidence of a deliberate stab or a lashing out at the victim. The conviction was based on the defendant producing and holding the knife and that the victim may have fallen or stumbled on the knife. He had no previous convictions. **4 years** YOI upheld.

R v Thompson [2001] 1 Cr App Rep (S) 249. The defendant was convicted of manslaughter on an insufficient intent basis after a murder trial. When aged 18 the defendant was celebrating the New Year when a confrontation developed. He and another were pursued by the deceased and two others who were older and bigger than the defendant was. The defendant picked up a yard brush and a scuffle developed. After the defendant had been injured, he hit the deceased with the brush on the neck, which caused extensive internal bleeding. The defendant had no previous convictions and had impressive references. **3½ years** YOI substituted for 4½.

R v Refern [2002] 2 Cr App Rep (S) 155. Three defendants R, B and O pleaded guilty to manslaughter. All three after drinking heavily and taking drugs attacked a 40 year old in a car park. He was punched to the ground and kicked by all three in a deliberate and violent beating. He died of an extensive brain haemorrhage. R was 28 (all ages are taken from the time of the offence), and had been to the courts on 23 occasions for offences of dishonesty, criminal damage, arson and possession of an offensive weapon. One had resulted in custody. He had a good prison report and had an excellent work record in prison. B aged 19, had had 17 court appearances including offences of dishonesty, criminal damage, affray, and three convictions for ABH. Those three did not appear particularly serious. He had had several custodial sentences. He expressed remorse. O who was 21, had 18 court appearances mostly for dishonesty. He had had four custodial sentences. He expressed remorse. The prison report said he was quiet and polite. All were dealt with equally. Two were sentenced to 6½ years imprisonment, the other to 6½ years YOI. Held. All reduced to **5½ years**. An order under the Crime and Disorder Act 1986 extending the supervision to 8 years was undisturbed.

R v Murphy [2001] EWCA Crim 288, [2001] 2 Cr App Rep (S) 384. The defendant was convicted of manslaughter. The defendant aged 19, left his home to walk to Plaistow to meet his girlfriend. He met some teenagers who told him that, 'A madman was going nuts.' Further that he was sniffing glue and chasing little kids. One of the teenagers was in possession of a knife. The defendant took it, put it in his back pocket and went to confront the glue-sniffer, the victim. The defendant found him and challenged him. He also took the knife out of his pocket. The victim told the defendant he did not want a fight. The defendant said he was going to stab him. The two moved together and started to fight. They fell to the ground and the defendant stabbed the victim. The defendant ran away and fled to Ireland. The wound had penetrated the heart. Later he surrendered. He claimed self-defence. He had three convictions. One was for robbery. One was for being aggressive to two boys in a park, being arrested and becoming violent and assaulting two police officers. The third was a non-domestic burglary. He was using Class A drugs. There was no mental disorder. Held. The sentencing bracket was **8–10 years** detention so **9 years** with an extended period of supervision on licence was undisturbed.

R v Harty [2001] EWCA Crim 90, [2002] 2 Cr App Rep (S) 253. See *Fighting (no knife)*

R v H (22 October 2001, unreported). Because of his plea, remorse and he was 18, 2 not 4 years YOI.

Old cases. *A-G's Reference (No 8 of 1992)* [1992] Crim LR 678; *R v Brereton* [1993] 14 Cr App Rep (S) 719.

Diminished responsibility – Homicide Act 1957, s 2

100.13 The basis for a conviction for manslaughter is not as important as the individual circumstances. The diminished responsibility cases are listed under the general categories. However if there is a plea based on diminished responsibility it means the defendant accepts that he or she intended to kill or cause GBH to the victim.

Domestic (Children) – Neglect, starvation etc

100.14 *R v Watts* [2001] EWCA Crim 1427, [2002] 1 Cr App Rep (S) 228. The defendant changed her plea to guilty to manslaughter. She was a single mother and sole carer for her 20-month-old daughter and her 9-month-old son, the victim. During the pregnancy of the son she made it clear she did not want the baby. Afterwards she would deny his existence and told her GP that she hated him. Nannies were employed and found a catalogue of neglect. Some were not paid. While she was at work she provided childcare for the older child but saved money by not providing it for her son. She made a 999 call and emergency services found the boy dead. He was unchanged, unwashed, unfed and had been in a cold room for hours. He was caked with faeces and grossly underweight. He had a bedsore and had been starved over a long period. There was severe skin breakdown on both the buttocks and the penis. The cause of death was severe malnutrition and dehydration. She was of normal intelligence and led an active social and sex life. She had no friends and was estranged from her family. She had a severe untreatable personality disorder of an anti-social and histrionic variety and was an inveterate and skilful liar. One psychiatrist said, 'She will remain concerned with her own hedonistic satisfaction and short term gratification. She will continue to lie, fail to meet her financial obligations, steal and defraud. She will place blame and responsibility on others and take none herself.' Held. The photographs are horrific. The prolonged history of starvation, dehydration and cruel neglect are appalling. It is difficult to think of a more serious case of manslaughter by neglect. There was no sufficient evidence to suggest she posed a grave risk to the public so **10 years** not life.

Domestic (Children) – With violence

100.15 *R v Pigott* [1999] 1 Cr App Rep (S) 392. The defendant was convicted of manslaughter when the prosecution had rejected that plea before the trial for murder. The defendant aged then 23, lived with his son aged 9 months and the son's mother. When the mother was out he consumed four cans of lager and 2 litres of cider. The baby cried and he struck him with his hand or fist. The baby died due to head injuries including a fracture to the left parieto-occipital bones. There was no previous history of violence to the baby. **6 years** YOI substituted for 10

R v Yates [2001] 1 Cr App Rep (S) 428. The defendant pleaded guilty to manslaughter. The defendant was caring for his 3-month-old baby girl while the mother was in bed unwell. He was unable to stop the baby crying. He shook her violently causing the baby to be limp and silent. She was taken to hospital where her head was swollen because of bleeding in her brain. Surgery was not successful and her life support systems were turned off. A post-mortem revealed that significant trauma to the baby's brain had been sustained 1 to 2 weeks before her admission to hospital. The left-sided subdural haematoma, which had led to her death, was probably inflicted on the same day as her admission. There was also a fracture of the skull. He was sentenced on the basis, 'that he had lost his temper when he had been unable to calm her. He had shaken her on two occasions. There were no direct blows and he was not responsible for the fracture. As soon as he realised harm had been done he immediately told his wife.' He had six previous spent convictions for violence, but had served no period of custody. The other children of theirs were said to be well parented. Held. The cases reveal the bottom bracket for baby cases is 2 years but in a most exceptional case a non-custodial is appropriate. Here **5 years** not 7 was appropriate.

R v Webb [2001] 1 Cr App Rep (S) 524. The defendant pleaded guilty to manslaughter and cruelty to a child. The defendant lived with his wife and baby daughter. He became agitated with her. He scalded her accidentally but was reluctant to obtain medical advice. Later, his wife noticed that the baby screamed when her left arm was touched. Five days later when in hospital for an infection she was found to have a fractured rib. Eighteen days later the baby was rigid and her vision was unfocused. She was sent to hospital. Bruising on the neck, breastbone and rib cage developed. Three days later she died. At hospital the defendant said he had accidentally dropped her on her head. The baby was found to have a substantial skull fracture, the rib fracture seen earlier and three other fractures. The skull fracture could not have been accidental. Severe squeezing had caused the rib fracture. The injuries had been caused on no less than four separate occasions, and must have resulted in severe pain for something like 7 days. He later made admissions to a doctor saying he had deliberately hit her head on the cot and had pushed her head violently on to the bed dropping her twice. He had no previous convictions. It would be wrong to reduce the **5 years** sentence.

R v Turner [2001] EWCA Crim 1331, [2002] 1 Cr App Rep (S) 207. The defendant pleaded guilty to manslaughter on the basis of lack of intent and he acted in panic when flustered and under stress. Also diminished responsibility would have been open to him because of his intellectual limitations. He lived with a girl who he had met at a special school. On 12 December 1999 they had a baby. They were both 17 and neither could look after themselves let alone a baby. The relationship was stormy and the arrival of the baby put the relationship under additional and severe strain. Occasionally he would look after the baby with her mother but he seemed not to understand the importance of careful handling. On 15 January 2000 he was left in charge of the baby for the first time. He called his aunt to say the baby was not breathing properly and had gone floppy. When the ambulance came he refused to let them take her because he was worried about his partner. Later the baby was taken to hospital and doctors found haemorrhaging behind both eyes. There was widespread bleeding in the brain. The next day the life support system was switched off. The injuries were consistent with shaken baby syndrome but experts could not say for how long or with what vigour the shaking had been. In interview the defendant admitted shaking his daughter. He said it was a particular difficult day with problems with the local authority etc. The baby started crying and he could not stop it. He shook her twice and supported her head. That he said usually quietened her. When she cried again he shook her without holding her head and he noticed she went floppy. He was of good character. The reports agreed he was a man with very real handicaps with profound social incapacity. He had a borderline learning disability with significant impairment of intellectual and social functioning amounting to an abnormality of the mind. He was vulnerable and dependent on others. If he remained in custody his partner would not be able to cope and would be taken into care. The overwhelming view of the doctors was that custody was entirely inappropriate for him. He had spent 5 months in custody, which he had been unable to cope with. He had to remain in the protection unit. Held. Parents could not escape all the responsibilities for their actions by relying on their own problems. That does not mean in every tragic case where a child is killed custody is inevitable. Exceptional cases merit exceptional sentences. He lacked the mental capacity to appreciate the consequences of his actions and intended no harm to the baby. He was vulnerable and needed protection. He was totally ill equipped to deal with the situation and should never have been put in that position. The sooner he receives support, guidance and medical treatment the better. A **3 year community rehabilitation order** with a condition of treatment and duty to live where approved not 2½ years YOI.

Old cases. *R v White* (1994) 16 Cr App Rep (S) 705; *R v Brannan* (1994) 16 Cr App Rep (S) 766; *R v Staynor* [1996] 1 Cr App Rep (S) 376; *R v Leggett* [1996] 2 Cr App Rep (S) 77; *R v Cawthorne* [1996] 2 Cr App Rep (S) 445.

Domestic (Women killing husbands and partners)

100.16 *R v Cutlan* [1998] 1 Cr App Rep (S) 1. The defendant pleaded guilty to stabbing her last husband after years of physical abuse from her second husband and other partners. After spending the afternoon in a public house together the defendant and the victim walked home telling people how good it was to be married. He went to bed and was probably asleep while she armed herself with a kitchen knife and stabbed him twice. She was sentenced on the basis that the husband was affectionate and loving and was never violent towards her. The defendant was now over 60 and had no relevant previous convictions. There was evidence of brain damage by reason of alcohol abuse and physical violence. **4½ years** was not wrong.

R v Howell [1998] 1 Cr App Rep (S) 229. The defendant was convicted of manslaughter by reason of provocation and acquitted of the murder of her husband. She was abused by four men over many years. The victim and the defendant lived in an inn. A year after the relationship with the victim began the violence started. In one incident she required hospital treatment and the in another police were called. Two residents who lived in the same premises heard the continuing violence and saw the effect it had on the defendant. One night, after both had finished working at the inn and after the victim had drunk an exceptional amount of alcohol, she was battered about the head six or seven times. She went to the kitchen where he dragged out and punched her several times. Fearing that she was going to be attacked again she took a gun that belonged to someone else. She loaded it because when she had used it before unloaded it had been ineffectual. He came up towards her and she shouted, 'Keep away' and shot him. The defendant was treated as of good character. **3½ years** not 6.

R v Fell [2000] 2 Cr App Rep (S) 464. The defendant pleaded guilty to manslaughter. The defendant started having sex with the victim when she was 14 and he was 19. When she was 16 they started living together. He recruited her to take part in his criminal activities. Once he left her and she took an overdose. She briefly went into care and was expelled from school. She had a miscarriage and took a further overdose. She said he became violent to her two or three times a week. She was depended on him. As her depression deepened she began to take cannabis. He was sent to prison and on his release continued to beat her up. He frequently locked her up. She handled a cheque-book stolen by him and was given probation. She did not respond well to the order. She was seen by a psychiatrist and because of the injuries twice by the police. She would respond to the violence by attacking him. Those who lived nearby frequently heard shouting, screaming and crying. On the day she decided to leave there was an argument and the defendant punched him. He grabbed her and locked her in the bathroom. A visitor let her out and she picked up a knife and waved it at him. He picked up the knife, put it down and went to attack her. She picked it up, there was a struggle and as he grappled with her. The struggle continued and the knife went into his back. She was seen to be immediately distressed. She was arrested and found to have bruising to her upper arms, breasts, neck, back and legs. During the interviews she sobbed uncontrollably. A psychiatrist found a number of features of battered women's syndrome namely: (a) a chronic depressive illness; (b) a feeling of hopelessness and helplessness and despair; (c) inability to act effectively; (d) inability to see any escape from the situation or any future; (e) self blame for the violence inflicted upon her by her male partner; (f) a failure to see that what was happening was abnormal because she was isolated from reality; shame and a poor sense of worth and (g) submission as a form of self protection. The prosecution psychiatrist also found a number of features of battered women's syndrome. The probation officer listed the new improvement to her character and life and said a custodial sentence was likely to destroy the very positive steps, which had been achieved. There was a job, a new relationship and reconciliation with her family. She had been in custody about a year. **2 years' probation** not 4 years YOI.

See also *Crime of passion*

Old cases. *R v Harrison* (1991) 13 Cr App Rep (S) 40; *R v Gardner* (1992) 14 Cr App Rep (S) 364; *R v Stubbs* (1993) 15 Cr App Rep (S) 57; *R v Brennan* (1994) 15 Cr App Rep (S) 874; *R v Higgins* [1996] 1 Cr App Rep (S) 271.

Domestic (Men killing wives and partners)

100.17   *R v Tzambazles* [1997] 1 Cr App Rep (S) 87. The defendant was convicted of manslaughter of his wife when the marriage had broken down. A fight developed in which the defendant suffered superficial injuries and the wife suffered extensive bruising to head, face upper body, arms and hands. There were no fractures but there was a severe laceration to the head. After hearing screaming he refused to let the police in and he didn't call the emergency services for over 4 hours. The police arrived and found her dead under an upturned wardrobe. He was sentenced on the basis that it was a vicious attack and that he had shown a callous disregard for the victim's well-being. **6 years** was justified.

R v Caswell [1999] 1 Cr App Rep (S) 467. The defendant pleaded guilty to manslaughter on the grounds of diminished responsibility. A boy now aged 21 killed his older gay lover after the relationship was over following a row about money. He severely beat, kicked and stamped on the deceased causing grievous multiple injuries to the face head and body. The defendant was found to have a severe emotional and personality disorder. He was sentenced to life, which was not challenged. Held. If there had been a determinate sentence passed **8 years** would have been appropriate.

R v Butler [1999] 2 Cr App Rep (S) 339. The defendant pleaded guilty to manslaughter. The defendant, aged 22, was released from custody and spent his time drinking and taking amphetamine and cocaine. He also resumed living with his girlfriend. One week after being released he had an argument with her in the street. She punched him and he punched her. She then got a knife and threatened him. Both went to their house where a violent struggle took place in the hallway. She tried to use the knife again. He then strangled her. The force of that had caused her to have a vasovagal reflex. He pleaded on the basis that he had injured her in the course of disarming her but had gone beyond self-defence. He had a bad record including five appearances for violence including actual bodily harm involving a weapon. 6 years was entirely correct.

R v Sexton [2000] 2 Cr App Rep (S) 94. The defendant pleaded guilty to manslaughter on the grounds of diminished responsibility based on depression. The defendant's business got into difficulties so he mortgaged his house and eventually went bankrupt. He hid this from his wife to whom he was devoted. The bailiff's possessed the home but to prevent his wife discovering he re-entered the premises. She was very devoted to the house. Five days later they were leaving the house together and she remarked a plant needed to be replanted. At this he seized a spade from the garage and hit his wife hard across the head. He drove around in his car for 28 hours with her body in the boot. Then he surrendered himself to the police. He said he had been trying to tell the wife but never found a suitable opportunity. He showed deep remorse. He had a blameless character, to whom violence of any kind was alien. He was considered sane. Held. Partly because it was a crime based on love not hatred **3 years** not 5.

R v Hampson [2001] 1 Cr App Rep (S) 288. The defendant pleaded guilty to manslaughter on the grounds of diminished responsibility based on depression. The defendant's wife was reported missing. He said she had left home after their marriage had broken down. This he repeated later. When formally arrested for murder he admitted killing her because of years of friction and arguments. He said she went on and on and he had to shut her up. After continual verbal abuse he picked up a hammer and struck her three times. He buried her in the garden where the police found her. He felt he couldn't leave his wife because his daughter was extremely close to him. He was 44 with no previous convictions. He also had had mild to moderate personality problems over the years. He was suffering from moderate to severe depression. **4 years** substituted for 6.

R v Frisby [2001] EWCA Crim 1482, [2002] 1 Cr App Rep (S) 289. The defendant was convicted of manslaughter on the basis of provocation after a murder trial. After his marriage to the victim in 1994 she continued to see her boyfriend and drank. Over Christmas 1999 she disappeared. Fifteen months later a dog found her skull. The defendant wrote a note saying the victim had grabbed their eldest child and kicked her in the buttocks. They had argued and she threw a hammer at him. He picked it up and struck her on the head several times and he then dismembered and disposed of the body. The torso was cut up and put in the sea and river. The head was buried. He was 42 and of good character. Held. The dismembering and disposal of the body was not a proper matter to take into account. It would have been a proper matter in relation to murder as showing some form of pre-planning but not for manslaughter. Sentence reduced from 8 years to **6 years**.

See also *A-G's Reference (No 118 of 2001)* [2002] EWCA Crim 958, [2002] 2 Cr App Rep (S) 537 [Drunk, lump of wood – 5 years proper].

Old cases. *R v Murphy* (1992) 13 Cr App Rep (S) 717; *R v Taylor* (1993) 15 Cr App Rep (S) 120; *R v Sanderson* (1993) 15 Cr App Rep (S) 263; *R v Anderton* (1993) 15 Cr App Rep (S) 532; *R v Silver* (1994) 15 Cr App Rep (S) 837; *R v Irons* (1995) 16 Cr App Rep (S) 46; *A-G's Reference No 43 of 1995* [1996] 2 Cr App Rep (S) 74.

See also **Crime of passion**

Drug abuse

100.18   *R v Atherton* [2001] EWCA Crim 2109, [2002] 1 Cr App Rep (S) 498. The defendant pleaded guilty on re-arraignment to manslaughter. The defendant was a heroin addict and lived in a hostel for the homeless where he supplied other residents with heroin. The victim a 33-year-old alcoholic and heroin addict knocked on the defendant's door and was told to go away. Later the defendant said to others he planned to take the victim's medication in return for heroin. Later again the defendant injected himself and the victim with heroin. The victim fell unconscious and the defendant and another carried him to the bathroom where they left him. The defendant left the hostel and when he came back in the evening he pretended to find the body and shouted for help. The victim was found dead. Next day he told a friend that he had cleaned the syringe and placed it in the victim's hand. The cause of death was multiple drug toxicity. The defendant was arrested and denied he knew how the victim had died. He had been present once before when a resident had died of heroin injection. Another had died in similar circumstances. Held. The judge was entitled to take into account the prevalence of his offence in South Wales but **5 years** not 6.

See also *R v Edwards* (28 April 1998, unreported) and *R v Davison* (22 March 2001, unreported).

Old cases. *A-G's Reference (No 5 of 1995)* [1996] 1 Cr App Rep (S) 85; *A-G's Reference (No 39 of 1995)* [1996] 2 Cr App Rep (S) 125.

See also SUPPLY OF CLASS A, B AND C DRUGS – *Death is caused*

Farm accident

100.19   *R v Crow* [2001] EWCA Crim 2968, [2002] 2 Cr App Rep (S) 219. The defendant and his father were convicted of manslaughter on the grounds of gross negligence though their reckless disregard for safety over months. They were co-owners of a farm, which employed a 16-year-old placement from an agricultural college who was enthusiastic and popular. The boy drove a JCB telescopic farm loadall with a brush attachment to clear mud from an A road next to a field which had been recently harvested. He parked the vehicle off the road but the raised bucket protruded at the height of its boom 1½ metres into the road. A passing lorry hit the bucket and the JCB rolled onto the boy and crushed him. He died that night. The defendants had failed to heed warnings from the Health and Safety Executive that the boy should not be permitted to drive the JCB till he had undergone a course. Despite this he had used the vehicle regularly and on the day of the accident the father had instructed him to brush the farmyard and a road. The son was away on his honeymoon. They boy had used the JCB on the A road before. The son had a positive good character and there was an excellent safety record at the farm. The business (income?) was assessed as £300,000. The parents of the victim wrote a moving letter saying nothing would be achieved by sending them to prison. Their defence was to blame their employees. The Judge identified three aggravating features. There was a high degree of recklessness, forseeability of serious injury or death and failure to heed explicit warnings. He determined that the son was marginally more responsible because his role was 'chief executive.' He expressed a wish to ensure someone was looking after the farm when the son was in prison. The father received 12 months suspended based on health and life expectancy. Held. There was no error in the judge's approach. However since sentence the father's health had deteriorated and to fulfil the judge's wish the **15 months** sentence was **suspended**.

Fighting (no knife)

100.20   *R v Lloyd-Williams* [1997] 1 Cr App Rep (S) 41. The defendant was convicted of manslaughter after claiming self-defence in his trial. The defendant and another went to help the victim who they lived with. The victim was drunk and couldn't open the front door because of a chain lock. An altercation developed between the deceased and the other man, after which all three went upstairs. A fight developed on the landing and the defendant struck the victim, which fractured his jaw, projecting him through the air. The deceased fell onto the hall floor below. The defendant had no previous. **4 years** could not be faulted.

R v McMinn [1997] 2 Cr App Rep (S) 219. The defendant was convicted of manslaughter on the basis of provocation, which the prosecution had earlier rejected. The deceased 'flew' at the defendant in a nightclub. The deceased was ejected by the doorman and defendant was asked to leave a little later. Sentenced on the basis that outside the victim ran at the defendant and punched him. The defendant, a karate champion, pulled and twisted the victim who fell to the ground. The defendant then kicked the victim in the head causing a fractured scull and haemorrhage in the brain. The defendant had previous conviction for wounding and was described by the judge as a dangerous man. Held. The judge was entitled to pass a high sentence of **10 years**.

R v Elton [1999] 2 Cr App Rep (S) 58. The defendant was convicted of manslaughter and causing GBH with intent both charges involving the same victim. He had also pleaded guilty to common assault on Adrian Berry. In a public house the defendant struck Adrian Berry forcibly twice for no apparent reason. This was the common assault. The defendant was ejected. Adrian Berry and others returned to their hotel and the defendant arrived there. The defendant and the victim, one of Adrian Berry's group, got into a verbal altercation, which degenerated into a fight. The defendant chased the victim out of the hotel and the victim was next seen lying in the road. The defendant admitted punching the victim several times and kicking him once in the face. Forensic evidence revealed that the victim had been killed by being crushed by a heavy vehicle. It also revealed that the victim had injuries to his face and mouth, which were typical of those produced by a violent assault. The injuries were consistent with the victim receiving a severe kick to the face, but being alive when hit by the vehicle. The basis for the prosecution case was that the victim had been left in a situation where he would be 'subject to some harm'. The defendant when 16 and 18 had been convicted of common assault. Held. Four not 5 years for the GBH because it should be detached from the death. The manslaughter was completely unintended and it should be dealt with as a bad case of manslaughter by gross neglect. **6 years** substituted for 8. One year for the common assault unaffected with all sentences concurrent.

R v Harty [2002] EWCA Crim 90, [2002] 2 Cr App Rep (S) 253. The defendants pleaded to manslaughter at the first opportunity. He and the victim were brothers and part of a large family of travellers. After a christening party there was hard core drinking and the two were driven back to their caravan site and they shouted at each other, 'I can beat you.' This was not an uncommon exchange. When the van neared the site the defendant jumped out and the two men started fighting. The victim fell back in the van and his wife drove him to her cousin's caravan leaving the defendant behind. She wanted to stop the fighting. The defendant went to the caravan, stripped to the waist and challenged his brother again. They started fighting and the victim fell to the ground. The defendant kicked him in the mouth and deliberately jumped on his stomach with both feet. His wife took him to hospital and he died of massive internal bleeding. The fights were not uncommon. The defendant was then 19 and had a dissocial personality disorder. He had a great deal of suppressed anger which related to his dislocated and deprived childhood. The anger was brought to the fore when he drank. He showed genuine remorse. Held. There were serious features particularly the stamping and the excessive and unwarranted violence. But because of the plea, his age, it was his own brother and the remorse **4 years** YOI not 5.

See also *R v Powell* [2002] EWCA Crim 661, [2002] 2 Cr App Rep (S) 532.

Old cases. *R v Morbey* (1993) 15 Cr App Rep (S) 53; *R v Small* (1993) 15 Cr App Rep (S) 534; *R v Badhams* (1993) 15 Cr App Rep (S) 616; *R v Crimp* (1995) 16 Cr App Rep (S) 346; *R v Harrison* [1996] 2 Cr App Rep (S) 250.

Fighting with the death being caused by the fall not any blow – Guideline remarks

100.21 *R v Coleman* (1991) 13 Cr App Rep (S) 508 – LCJ. We are considering a person who receives a blow, probably one blow only, to the head or face, is knocked over by the blow and unfortunately cracks his head on the floor or the pavement, suffers a fractured skull and dies. It is to be distinguished sharply from the sort of case where a victim on the ground is kicked about the head. It is to be distinguished sharply from the sort of case where a weapon is used in order to inflict injury. It is to be further distinguished from where the actual blow itself causes the death. This is the case of a fall almost accidentally resulting in a fractured skull. The starting point for this type of offence is **12 months** on a plea of guilty. Then one looks at the mitigation and aggravating features. No premeditation, a single blow of moderate force, remorse and immediate admissions are all mitigation. Indications that the defendant is susceptible to outbreaks of violence, the assault was gratuitous and unprovoked, more than one blow all tend to aggravate the offence.

Fighting with the death being caused by the fall not any blow – Cases

100.22 *R v Henry* [1999] 2 Cr App Rep (S) 412. The defendant pleaded guilty to manslaughter which he had indicated at the first opportunity. The defendant's wife went out for the evening leaving the defendant to look after the children aged 5 and 1. Leaving one child with his in-laws and taking the other he drove to pick his wife up. However, she had left a public house with another man. He then saw them in the street arms linked. They stopped and kissed each other. The defendant shouted across but the wife refused to get into his car. The defendant ran across the road and punched the other man in the face. The victim fell backwards, and struck his head on a manhole cover. He died of injuries to his skull and brain caused by the fall. The blow was of considerable force. It broke the victim's jaw and had lifted him off the ground. The defendant after initial denials expressed remorse. He was 31 and had no previous convictions. There were excellent character references. He told the probation officer he didn't drink and had never hit anyone before. He was a model prisoner. Held. **18 months** substituted for 4 years. Had the blow been less ferocious it would have been less.

R v Cannon [2001] 1 Cr App Rep (S) 286. The defendant pleaded guilty to manslaughter, which he had been tendered at an early stage. The defendant's brother broke the glass door of a restaurant as he was leaving. The proprietor, Mr Lau left the restaurant to talk to him The defendant then left the restaurant The defendant mistakenly thought that Mr Lau was striking the brother whereas he was merely grabbing hold of him to detain him. There was an altercation in which Mr Lau struck the defendant causing pain and the defendant struck Mr Lau twice in the face with a clenched fist. Mr Lau fell backwards and struck his head on the pavement receiving his fatal injury or injuries. The defendant had been drinking heavily. He had previous convictions for violence including assaulting a constable. He showed remorse. Held. The court accepted the need to protect shopkeepers at night. **3½ years** substituted for 7.

R v Gratton [2001] 2 Cr App Rep (S) 167. The defendant pleaded guilty to manslaughter. The defendant and the victim were friends. The deceased believed the defendant fancied his girlfriend (wrongly they said). After drinking a lot during the day, they went home when the public house closed. The defendant and the victim were seen arguing. The defendant was put to bed on the sofa by his girlfriend and the victim. The defendant's girlfriend went into the garden and was joined by the victim. They sat opposite each other on chairs. The victim leaned forward put his hands on her knees and gave her a quick kiss on the lips as a thank you gesture. Unfortunately the defendant had come out and had seen it. He walked up to them quickly saying, 'You fucked up with your missus, now you are trying it on with mine.' He threw two or three punches to the victim's face causing the victim and his chair to tip back. His head hit some rocks in a rockery. He appeared to be dead when the ambulance attended. The defendant showed great remorse. He thought he saw a 'snog.' He was 31 and was treated as of good character. He had an excellent work record. There were many references. The defendant received **9 months**. Held. It would not be right to suspend it.

R v Edwards [2001] EWCA Crim 862, [2001] 2 Cr App Rep (S) 540. The defendant was convicted of manslaughter. At a country club the victim and the defendant who did not know each other had an argument. The defendant was aggressive and offered to see the other outside. One of the defendant's friends tried to pull him away. The victim left the club and was followed by the defendant. The victim suddenly turned and squared up to the defendant. The defendant punched the victim once with his fist to the mouth and chin. The victim fell back and struck the base of his head on the hard surface of the car park. The defendant was aggressive and offensive to someone who sought to explain that the victim had gone over to apologise. The victim died two days later. The fall and not the blow caused the death. The skull had fractured. The defendant, who had been a keen amateur boxer, was 40 with two previous convictions. One was for s 20 wounding in 1979. He had a large number of letters and testimonials. The judge spoke of his positive good character and described the blow as not a blow of great force. **18 months** not 30 months.

R v Matthews and Hewson [2001] EWCA Crim 1421, [2002] 1 Cr App Rep (S) 279. The defendants M and H now 20 and 19 pleaded to manslaughter. M also pleaded to burglary. While staff were busy at 11pm in a pub M went behind the bar and took £133. This was the burglary. Outside he saw G a 17-year-old quiet lad and asked to him to hide the money. The next day he asked G for it back and G said it had gone missing. He gave M £20 but M threatened him saying, 'If I don't get the rest soon I'm gonna smash your face in.' G promised to get the money and invented a story so he got £50 from his grandfather and gave it to M. M still wasn't satisfied. The next day, M boasted to H and a group of youths what he would do if he didn't get the money. He would smash him in the face and knock him out with one blow. H picked up a broom handle and said he would wrap this round his head while you punch him. H continued to encourage M to hit G and asked, 'Are you going to hit him? Bet you don't hit him. Could you one time him.' One timing means knocking someone out with one punch. They came across G with others in the street. M confronted him and G pleaded with him saying he would get the money somehow. H continued to incite M saying, 'You're a shit bag. I thought you were going to knock him out,' and 'Come on hurry, I've got somewhere to go.' This incitement continued. Eventually M punched G who fell backwards and hit is head on a paving slab. G went into a fit or spasm. It was clear he was badly hurt save perhaps to M and H. They appeared to revel in the violence and M said, 'Oh yes, sweet punch,' 'Check that punch out' and 'Knock out.' H said, 'That was a bad punch. Check it out he's having a fit. I'm buzzing off. It was a sweet punch.' While G lay unconscious M took his watch. Because of the fit he was unable to prise open the fingers so he forced his fingers apart with his teeth. M then told the witnesses to lie about the attack. Eventually G was taken to hospital and died of double basal fracture to the skull caused by the head hitting the stone. M changed his account in interview but in the second admitted hitting him. Later he said it was an accident. H denied inciting him but admitted laughing as G lay on the ground. M had convictions for five ABHs, intimidating witnesses, three of threatening behaviour, battery and offences of dishonesty. H had fewer including ABH, arson, threatening behaviour and dishonesty. Held. There is an important distinction between the one punch cases and

M's case. The fatal violence had been pre-meditated. It was to obtain the proceeds of the burglary. He announced his intention to do so. He made unwarranted demands above and beyond the return of the ill-gotten gains. H did everything possible to encourage M to attack G. At the scene there was no remorse. This was wholly unprovoked and pre-meditated violence which led to the death of this very young man. M's **4½ years** detention with 6 months consecutive for the burglary and H's **2 years** detention were sentences of some severity but entirely justified.

See also *A-G's Reference (No 124 of 2001)* (22 January 2002, unreported).

A-G's Reference (No 100 of 2001) [2002] EWCA Crim 294, [2002] 2 Cr App Rep (S) 365. The defendant pleaded guilty to manslaughter and two counts of ABH. After drinking heavily the defendant was in a pick up truck with another in a city centre. At around 2.00-2.20am he called three people over to him and punched them in the face. Each bent down to hear what he was saying. The first victim was struck a hard punch and the defendant drove off at speed. The first two victims suffered bruising. The third victim was knocked backwards and his head struck the pavement and he was rendered unconscious. The defendant told his colleague to, 'Quick, drive, drive.' The victim died within 36 hours and the pathologist found injuries to the nose and lips, which were consistent with a single blow of at least moderate force. Death was due to a blunt force injury to the back of the head as a result of the fall. The victim was 34 and about to finish his 4 year degree course and had bright prospects. When interviewed the defendant lied and said the victim had thrown at punch at him. The defendant was 22 and of good character with most favourable references. He showed remorse. Held. This was a premeditated, deliberate and wholly unprovoked blow to an innocent passer-by. The defendant drove off. This was a serious case. 5 years would be appropriate. As it was a reference **4 years** not 3.

Old cases. *R v Bryant* (1993) 14 Cr App Rep (S) 621; *R v Williams* [1996] 2 Cr App Rep (S) 72.

Fire, by

100.23 *R v Archer* [1998] 2 Cr App Rep (S) 76. Eaton, Archer, and Purnell all pleaded guilty to manslaughter and to committing arson when reckless whether life was endangered. The pleas were entered, as the trial was about to start. Following a grievance between Archer and another because Archer believed that the other had informed on him to the police, the three defendants went to what they believed was his house. In fact he no longer lived there but four others did. The defendants soaked a pair of shorts in petrol, lit it and pushed it through the letterbox. One resident escaped breaking a leg. One jumped through a window and broke a foot. One died from smoke inhalation. The last was rescued but only after 20–30% of her body had been burnt. Her lungs were damaged and her body was scarred for life. All defendants had long criminal records. Archer denied it at first but offered the pleas at the PDH. Eaton served an alibi notice. Purnell denied it. Held. **12 years** correct but Archer's sentence reduced to **11 years** because of his early offer to plead.

R v Hills [1999] 2 Cr App Rep (S) 157. The defendant was convicted of manslaughter. The defendant visited an estate to pick up a car he had just purchased. He had with him some car accessories including an empty petrol can. A group of youths approached him, as he appeared drunk. He went to a garage and filed the can with petrol. He met up with the youths again and after some banter chased two girls in a drunken manner. He said to them, 'Do you want to see something freaky?' As a boy reached him he poured petrol on to him and lit a cigarette lighter over the neck of the can. The boy was thrown to the ground and covered in flames. He had 47% burns to his body and died. The defendant said he had taken methadone that morning. Held. This offence was consistent with the sentences where a knife has been used but its use was entirely unpremeditated. **8 years** substituted for 10 years.

Old cases. *R v Herbert* (1993) 14 Cr App Rep (S) 792; *R v Snarski* (1993) 15 Cr App Rep (S) 19; *R v Kennedy* (1993) Cr App Rep (S) 141; *R v England* (1995) 16 Cr App Rep (S) 776.

See also ARSON - *Death is caused*

Firearms, with

100.24   *A-G's Reference (No 2 of 1997)* [1998] 1 Cr App Rep (S) 27. The defendant was acquitted of murder but convicted of manslaughter by reason of provocation. After many years of animosity between the victim and the defendant, they met and insults were traded. The defendant obtained a gun and went to outside the deceased's home. The defendant was ushered away. The deceased armed with a knife then left his house and went to confront the defendant and punched him or more likely he stabbed him with the knife. He was then shot in the chest and head. The wound to the chest caused no damage to any vital organs while the head injury was fatal. Held. The lowest sentence that could be imposed was **10 years** but because it was a reference **9 years** not 7.

R v Howell [1998] 1 Cr App Rep (S) 229. The defendant was convicted of manslaughter by reason of provocation and acquitted of the murder of her husband. She was abused by four men over many years. A year after the relationship started with the victim the violence started. One incident required hospital treatment and the another police were called. Two residents who lived in the same premises, an inn heard the continuing violence and saw the effect it had on the defendant. One night, after both had finished working at the inn and after the victim had drunk an exceptional amount of alcohol, she was battered about the head six or seven times. She went to the kitchen where he dragged out and punched her several times. Fearing that she was going to be attacked again she took a gun that belonged to another. She loaded it because when unloaded before it had been ineffectual. He came up towards her and she shouted, 'Keep away' and shot him. The defendant was treated as of good character. **3½ years** not 6.

R v Jackson [1999] 2 Cr App Rep (S) 77. The defendant leaded guilty to manslaughter and to doings acts tending to pervert the course of justice. The victim was living with one woman and also having an affair with the defendant's daughter. The daughter thought she was pregnant by him but in fact wasn't. The defendant received a telephone call saying the victim wanted the daughter to stop pestering him. The defendant's partner on hearing this got into a rage and demanded that the defendant speak to the victim. The defendant went to the victim's house. The victim went into the street with a bulletproof vest. They both got into the defendant's car. He was sentenced on the basis the victim cocked the gun and held it to the defendant's neck. The gun was knocked out of his grasp and picked up by the defendant. The defendant made threats and a struggle developed in which the gun was discharged twice. The defendant disposed of the gun and initially relied on an alibi. He also had the car cleaned and disposed of which was the background to the perverting charge. The defendant had one deception offence in the last 20 years. Held. **5 years** substituted for 8 with 2 years consecutive for the perverting remaining as before.

Old cases. *R v McGee* (1993) 15 Cr App Rep (S) 463; *R v Klair* (1994) 16 Cr App Rep (S) 660; *R v Pittendrigh* [1996] 1 Cr App Rep (S) 65.

Frightened to death,

100.25   *R v Scammell* [2001] EWCA Crim 1631, [2002] 1 Cr App Rep (S) 293. See *Victim's health precarious/eggshell skull*

Funeral expenses of the deceased, power to make an order for compensation for the

100.26   Powers of Criminal Courts (Sentencing) Act 2000, s 130(1). The court may on application or otherwise make an order requiring him to make payments for funeral expenses or bereavement in respect of a death resulting from an offence other than death due to an accident arising out of the presence of a motor vehicle on a road.

Powers of Criminal Courts (Sentencing) Act 2000, s 130(3). A court shall give reasons if it does not make a compensation order in a case where this section empowers it to do so.

R v Williams (10 March 1989, unreported). It is important sentencers bear in mind the words (which had just been added to the then statute giving the court power to order compensation for funeral expenses). If the court decides not to order compensation it must give its reasons.

Glassing

100.27   Old cases. *R v Brereton* (1993) 14 Cr App Rep (S) 719.

Harassed by neighbours, after being

100.28   Old cases. *R v Wright* (1995) 16 Cr App Rep (S) 877.

Health

See *Victim's health precarious/eggshell skull*

Knife, with – Guideline case

100.29   *A-G's Reference (No 33 of 1996)* [1997] 2 Cr App Rep (S) 10. Where a defendant deliberately goes out with a knife which is carried as a weapon, and uses it to cause death, even if there is provocation, he should expect a sentence in a contested case in the region of **10 to 12 years**.

R v Mills Re Holder [1998] 2 Cr App Rep (S) 128 at 143 – LCJ. The above case does provide a tariff for manslaughter.

Old cases. Ignore all cases before *A-G's Reference No 3 of 1996*, above.

Knife, with – General

100.30   *R v Pitt* [1998] 1 Cr App Rep (S) 58. The defendant was convicted of manslaughter by reason of provocation. Bad feeling existed between the victim's girlfriend and other women including the appellant's wife. While the defendant was at home with his daughters, there was an argument in a public house between the women where various drunken men demanded to know where the defendant's wife lived. They were told and the victim and two of his friends went to the house. They were abusive and demanded the defendant's wife should be brought out. Instead of telephoning the police the defendant armed himself with two knives and confronted them. Words were exchanged and the defendant cut one on the arm. The victim tried to intervene and he was stabbed in the chest. The defendant was of good character and with a good work record. **7 years** was substituted for 8.

A-G's Reference (No 3 of 1999) [1999] 2 Cr App Rep (S) 433. The defendant pleaded guilty to manslaughter. Two drunken men walked past the defendant's home and one of them appeared to damage the defendant's wife's car. She protested and they swore at her. The defendant became aware of this and he armed himself with a hunting knife, which he removed from its sheath. The knife had been in a cupboard. He and his wife followed the young men and they turned and confronted them. One picked up some timber and the other was carrying a bottle. A fight ensued initiated by the two young men. The defendant was hit by the timber and the bottle. The defendant then knifed one of them three times and he died. One stab was to the head, one was to upper chest and the third to his right chest. Genuine remorse was expressed. The defendant had an excellent record with character references showing his integrity, his generosity and his lack of aggression. Held. The case would merit a 4 year sentence. It might have merited 3 years because of the exceptional circumstances, but not less than that. Since the conviction his family has had to move and his wife's health had suffered. **2 years** immediate imprisonment substituted for 2 years suspended.

A-G's Reference (No 19 of 1999) [2000] 1 Cr App Rep (S) 287. The defendant was convicted of manslaughter on the grounds of provocation. He had agreed to plead to that before the trial but it was not accepted. Some neighbours became annoyed at the defendant's dog. The RSPCA was contacted but the found the dog to be in perfectly good condition. After the dog had barked all one evening, neighbours gathered to complain and the police were called. Eventually when the defendant came home, neighbours expressed their anger and the victim and others surrounded his car. Some witnesses described the deceased trying to pull the car door off and pull the defendant out. The children in the car were terrified. The car drove off and someone shouted that they would kill the dog. The defendant went to the home of a friend and armed himself with a knife. He returned with another and found damage to his windows and the fence of his home. The deceased was standing by a front door four doors away from the defendant's home and directed abuse at the defendant. The defendant walked towards him and a fight ensued. They fell to the ground and the defendant stabbed him in the neck. The stab wound would have required moderate force. He died within a few minutes. The defendant was 22 and was effectively of good character. Held. This case was significantly different from the *A-G's Reference (No 33 of 1996)* [1997] 2 Cr App Rep (S) 10 where a 10–12 year starting point was set. The sentence of **5 years** was lenient but within the permissible parameters for this offence. It was not unduly lenient.

R v Wade [2000] 2 Cr App Rep (S) 445. The defendant was convicted of manslaughter after a murder trial. There was a history of violence between the defendant and the victim who had known each other for about 10 years. For 9 months before the killing they had been involved in selling drugs. The victim accused the defendant of stealing from their joint supply of heroin. The victim demanded payment and later stole some of the defendant's property from his address. The defendant threatened the victim with a shotgun and most of the property was returned. However the victim maintained he was owed £2,000 for the heroin. The victim, armed with a knife, visited the defendant's address with another. The victim had given the other visitor £2,000 to look after. They were refused access. Later the victim visited the address alone and was stabbed to death. The defendant who had a cut on his hand was seen with a large wad of notes which it was suggested he had taken from the victim. The victim was found to have 11 stab wounds five of which were to the head, one to his shoulder, one to the neck and three to his chest. Any of the three could have been fatal. The room was in disarray and a knuckle-duster was found. The defendant surrendered himself to the police and said, 'I did it. I fucking killed him' In interview he said the defendant had beaten him in the past. He said the victim had threatened him and a struggle took place and the defendant took the knife from him. The fatal blows were then struck. The jury rejected self defence but concluded he had been provoked. **7 years** not 9.

R v Bowen [2001] 1 Cr App Rep (S) 282 – LCJ. The defendant was convicted of manslaughter after a murder trial. The defendant had drank beer and was carrying a knife, which was carried so he could cut cocaine. In a snooker hall the two victims approached him and he stabbed them both in the neck. Then he kicked one of them. The fatal wounds were severe. The defendant claimed self-defence, which was rejected. Held. The basis was manslaughter because of provocation. One witness had heard one of the victims saying, 'Paki bastard.' The two deaths were an important aggravating factor. The defendant had previous convictions for violence but none since 1986. **12 years** concurrent substituted for 14 concurrent.

R v Dillon [2001] EWCA Crim 1342, [2002] 1 Cr App Rep (S) 172. The defendant was convicted of manslaughter by reason of provocation after a murder trial. The victim believed the defendant had stolen his girlfriend's purse. The defendant was angry because he claimed the victim had threatened the defendant's ex-wife and their daughter in numerous telephone calls. He threatened to kill the victim and his girlfriend. The victim went in search of the defendant to confront him and during the day had a great deal to drink. He told a barmaid the defendant was going to 'get it.' When he found the defendant in a pub he abused him and both squared up to each other. A scuffle broke out with both exchanging punches. The fight was short and the defendant forced the victim to the floor face down. The defendant sat astride his legs and stabbed him twice with a knife in the lower back. The first blow did not penetrate very far but the second blow was with great force and the blade went up to the hilt penetrating 10 cm. The defendant left and the victim was taken to hospital. The victim had very severe internal bleeding and major damage to the arteries and veins. He died the following morning. When arrested the defendant said, 'The bastard got what he deserved. He threatened my daughter and missus.' The defendant had swelling on his temple caused by a blunt instrument. The victim was found to have had a knuckleduster. The defendant was sentenced on the basis it was not known who originally had the knife. The defendant was about 36 and had a conviction for robbery in 1985. Held. **7 years** not 9 and the judge was wrong to consider he was danger to the public so the extension to the licence quashed.

Old cases. Ignore all the cases before the guideline case, *R v Mills* [1998], which increased the tariff.

Life sentence is appropriate, a

100.31   Old cases. *R v Sanderson* (1993) 15 Cr App Rep (S) 263.

Life sentence/Automatic life sentence – Fixing specified term

100.32   *R v Secretary of State for Home Department, ex p Furber* [1998] 1 Cr App Rep (S) 208. The general rule for young offenders is to fix the period at half the determinate period.

R v Caswell [1999] 1 Cr App Rep (S) 467. Consider first what would be appropriate if a determinate sentence was passed. Divide that term by two although not every prisoner is entitled to have ½ deducted. Then deduct the time the defendant has been on remand. Here it was worth 8 years. Because the defendant had not done well in prison after division 4½ years. Deducting 6 months for the time he had spent in custody **4 years** substituted.

Old cases. *R v Iqbal* [1997] 2 Cr App Rep (S) 226.

Medical

100.33   Old cases. *R v Saha* [1994] 15 Cr App Rep (S) 342.

Neglect, gross

100.34   *R v Sogunro* [1997] 2 Cr App Rep (S) 89. The defendant was convicted of manslaughter and false imprisonment. The defendant shut his fiancé in a room without food or drink because he believed she was possessed by the devil. She died of starvation and neglect but was not found till 10 months after her death. Defendant had no previous convictions. **6 years** and 3 years concurrent upheld.

R v Elton [1999] 2 Cr App Rep (S) 58. The defendant was convicted of manslaughter and causing GBH with intent both involving the same victim. He had pleaded guilty to common assault on Adrian Berry. In a public house the defendant struck Adrian Berry forcibly twice for no apparent reason. This was the common assault. The defendant was ejected. Adrian Berry and others returned to their hotel and the defendant arrived there. The defendant and the victim, one of Adrian Berry's group, got into a verbal altercation, which degenerated into a fight. The defendant chased the victim out of the hotel and the victim was next seen lying in the road. The defendant admitted punching the victim several times and kicking him once in the face. Forensic evidence revealed that the victim had been killed by being crushed by a heavy vehicle. It also revealed that the victim had injuries to his face and mouth, which were typical of those produced by a violent assault. The injuries were consistent with the victim receiving a severe kick to the face, but he was alive when hit by the vehicle. The basis for the prosecution case was that the victim had been left in a situation where he would be 'subject to some harm'. The defendant when 16 and 18 been convicted of common assault. Held. Four not 5 years for the GBH because it should be detached from the death. The manslaughter was completely unintended and it should be dealt with as a bad case of manslaughter by gross neglect. **6 years** substituted for 8. One year for the common assault unaffected with all sentences concurrent.

See also *Domestic (Children) – Neglect, starvation etc*

Negligence, gross

100.35 *R v Devine* [1999] 2 Cr App Rep (S) 409. The defendant was convicted of manslaughter. The defendant had after drinking heavily jumped, ran or walked into the path of a motorcyclist. The bike skidded and the rider hit a lamp-post and died. The defendant received minor injuries. He said he had mixed alcohol with his medication for depression. The defendant had previous convictions for domestic burglary (receiving 30 months' youth custody), common assault, possession of an offensive weapon and threatening behaviour. He had been warned on earlier occasions about drinking when on medication. He had also on occasions staggered into the road, no doubt imperilling motorists. Held. Gross negligence manslaughter cases are notoriously difficult. He had pleaded not guilty but he could hardly be criticised for asking for a jury's verdict. The **3½ years** sentence, consecutive to 3 months for unrelated offences was reduced to 2½ years.

Old cases. *A-G's Reference (Nos 26 and 27 of 1994)* (1994) 16 Cr App Rep (S) 675; *R v Kite* [1996] 2 Cr App Rep (S) 295.

No reason/Minor provocation

100.36 Old cases. *R v Bourne* (1995) 16 Cr App Rep (S) 237; *R v Bamborough* (1995) 16 Cr App Rep (S) 602.

Provocation

100.37 *R v Byrne* [2002] Crim LR 754 judgment 27 June 2002. After some mild provocation the defendant had struck the victim with a pool cue. *A-G's Reference (No 33 of 1996)* [1997] 2 Cr App Rep (S) 10 had set an upper bracket for provocation at 10 years. As the degree of provocation was not extreme the sentence did not fall to be reduced by a great extent. 8 years was not manifestly excessive.

[For other cases of provocation see the individual sections for the type of death etc.]

Rapists, by

100.38   Old cases. *A-G's Reference (No 33 of 1992)* [1993] 14 Cr App Rep (S) 712.
See also *Sexual*

Reckless

100.39   This ground for manslaughter is listed under the different types of situation,
namely medical, sexual and negligent etc.

Religious beating/imprisonment

100.40   *R v Sogunro* [1997] 2 Cr App Rep (S) 89. The defendant was convicted of
manslaughter and false imprisonment. The defendant shut his fiancé in a room without
food or drink because he believed she was possessed by the devil. She died of
starvation and neglect but was not found till 10 months after her death. Defendant had
no previous. **6 years** and 3 years concurrent upheld.

Old cases. *R v Patel* (1995) 16 Cr App Rep (S) 827.

Revenge attack

100.41   *A-G's Reference (Nos 33 and 34 of 2001)* [2002] 1 Cr App Rep (S) 400. The
defendants were convicted of manslaughter. [The case is unclear about what the
prosecution case was so is not summarised.]

Road Traffic

See *Vehicle, by*

Robbers

See *Burglars/Robbers/Thieves, by*

Sexual

100.42   *R v Blakemore* [1997] 2 Cr App Rep (S) 255. The defendant was convicted of
manslaughter and doing an act to pervert the course of justice. The defendant sold
some land and workmen found a young man's body buried. The body was wrapped in
plastic and tied with a rope. Marks on the neck indicated that he had been strangled
with a rope or ligature. The boy had been dead for some 10 years. Sentenced on the
basis he had died posing for bondage photographs taken by the defendant. **5 and
3 years consecutive** not 7 and 5 years consecutive.

Old cases. *R v Barrell* [1992] 13 Cr App Rep (S) 646; *R v Williamson* (1993) 15 Cr App
Rep (S) 364; *R v Billia* [1996] 1 Cr App Rep (S) 39.

See also *Rapists, by*

Two or more killings

100.43   *R v Bowen* [2001] 1 Cr App Rep (S) 282. The defendant was convicted of
manslaughter after a murder trial. In a snooker hall the defendant drank beer. He was
carrying a knife, which he had so he could cut cocaine. The two victims approached
him and he stabbed them both in the neck. Then he kicked one of them. The fatal
wounds were severe. The defendant claimed self-defence, which was rejected. Held.
The basis of the conviction was manslaughter because of provocation. One witness had
heard one of the victims saying, 'Paki bastard.' The two deaths were an important
aggravating factor. He had previous convictions for violence but not since
1986. **12 years** concurrent substituted for 14 years concurrent.

R v Wacker (31 July 2002, unreported). The defendant was convicted of conspiracy to
facilitate illegal entry and 58 counts of manslaughter. Sixty illegal immigrants travelled
from China to Holland where they were loaded into an adapted container on the

defendant's lorry. The only ventilation was a small vent at the front. 4½ kms from Zeebrugge the lorry stopped and the vent was closed. This was to avoid discovery and the defendant's fingerprints were found on the outside covering of the vent. The ferry trip took longer than expected and nearly 6 hours later customs officers searched the container and found the victims. The two survivors told how 2 hours after the vent was closed those inside became distressed and found difficulty in breathing. There was also a lot of screaming and no one came to help. The deaths were caused by lack of air. The basis for the manslaughter was gross negligence. The defendant was a Dutch national. It was not suggested that he intended to harm the victims in anyway. He received 8 years for the conspiracy and six consecutive for the manslaughter counts. The defence argued the total was too much and the Attorney General argued the 6 years for the manslaughter counts was too lenient although the total sentence was not challenged. Held. Professional smuggling of large numbers of illegal immigrants is in itself a serious matter. The causing of so many deaths to avoid detection puts this case in a category of its own. **14 years** was not manifestly excessive. Concurrent sentences were the correct approach so 14 years for the manslaughter, which would not have the appearance of devaluing the loss of life.

Uncertainty over jury's verdict

100.44 *R v Cawthorne* [1996] 2 Cr App Rep (S) 445. There were three bases for this manslaughter conviction, insufficient intent, provocation or gross negligence. The foreman was asked if he wanted to indicate the basis and he declined. The judge sentenced the defendant on the basis of lack of sufficient intent. Held. It was quite proper for the foreman to decline. Having considered the authorities, we are quite clear that whether the judge asks is entirely a matter for the trial judge's discretion. In many cases the judge will not wish to do so, and doing so will throw an unnecessary addition burden on the jury. In a case like the present, and there are many other cases of this nature, there are grave dangers in asking juries. For example they may not all have reached it by the same route. The judge was entitled to decide the basis of the sentence.

R v Bowen [2001] 1 Cr App Rep (S) 282. The jury was not asked which it was. The judge did not indicate whether it was provocation or lack of sufficient intent. Held. It was for the Court of Appeal to decide.

R v Byrne [2002] Crim LR 754 judgment 27 June 2002. The defence case in the defendant's murder trial was there was a lack of intent. The judge left the issue of provocation to the jury. The jury convicted of manslaughter and the judge decided it was not appropriate to ask them for the basis of their verdict. Held. The judge was entitled not to ask and decided that the basis of the verdict was provocation. The judge has a duty to explain his decision and it would have been better if he had gone into greater detail. The sentence was upheld.

Unprovoked attach with fists and/or feet

100.45 *R v Harrison* [1996] 2 Cr App Rep (S) 250. An unlucky punch in the course of a spontaneous fight is very different from a wholly unprovoked blow to an innocent bystander.

R v Anucha [1999] 2 Cr App Rep (S) 74. The defendant pleaded guilty to manslaughter, two counts of robbery and a count of battery. The defendant and another stole £60 by pulling a shop assistant away from the till. Six days later the defendant returned and was recognised and the assistant refused to open the till. The defendant tried to open it. The assistant went next door to call the police and returned. The defendant accused him of injuring him on the earlier occasion and punched him three times in the face. Thirteen days later the defendant who was then aged 19, used a minicab. The driver was the deceased and he drove it to a petrol station to fill up with petrol. The deceased became worried and tried to ring the police. The defendant left the cab became aggressive and shouted, 'You don't want to take me'. He then punched the victim twice in the face causing him to fall hitting his head hard on the ground. On the same day the defendant returned to the shop and opened the till while another held the assistant as £200 was stolen. Three weeks later the victim died. The defendant had seven previous convictions for robbery, one for attempted robbery, three for theft and two for assault. A report indicated crack cocaine lay behind the offending. The sentencing judge invoked the 'longer than normal sentence' statutory provisions. Held. **6 years** not 8 years detention for the manslaughter consecutive to 3 years for the two robberies.

A-G's Reference (No 44 of 1998) [1999] 1 Cr App Rep (S) 458. The defendant was convicted of manslaughter. The defendant after drinking went to his former matrimonial home where he kicked in the door. When his wife and another man returned, the defendant started shouting. He then attacked the other man. He was punched and knocked to the ground and then kicked 7 or 8 times, including on the face. The deceased suffered a myocardial insufficiency by reason of hypertensive heart disease. The attack had significantly contributed to his death. The defendant had no previous convictions. Held. Taking into account it was a reference **3½ years** not 2½.

R v Keaney [2001] 1 Cr App Rep (S) 126. The defendant was convicted of manslaughter. After drinking about 14 pints the defendant came across a group of Asian taxi drivers. A dispute developed and a number of punches were thrown. The defendant was knocked to the ground. He got up punched an entirely innocent 62-year-old West Indian bystander. He fell over causing injury to the back of the head and severe brain damage from which he died. The defendant ran away and was arrested the next day. The pathologist said the blow was heavy and above moderate. He was sentenced on the basis it was not a racially-aggravated attack. There was some remorse and he was treated as of good character. Held. This the case is more serious that the cases cited. There was a substantial age gap (62 and 30), the victim was blame-free, the blow was described as severe, guilt was contested and the defendant had had far too much to drink. However, **3 years** substituted for 7.

R v Refern [2002] 2 Cr App Rep (S) 155. Three defendants R, B and O pleaded guilty to manslaughter. All three after drinking heavily and taking drugs attacked a 40 year old in a car park. He was punched to the ground and kicked by all three in a deliberate and violent beating. He died of an extensive brain haemorrhage. R was 28 (all ages are taken from the time of the offence), and had been to the courts on 23 occasions for offences of dishonesty, criminal damage, arson and possession of an offensive weapon. One had resulted in custody. The defendant had a good prison report citing an excellent work record in prison. B aged 19, had had 17 court appearances including dishonesty, criminal damage, affray, and three convictions for ABH. Those three did not appear particularly serious. He had had several custodial sentences. He expressed remorse. O who was 21, had 18 court appearances mostly for dishonesty. He had had four custodial sentences. He expressed remorse. The prison report said he was quiet and polite. All were dealt with equally. Two were sentenced to 6½ years imprisonment, the other to 6 ½ years detention. Held. All reduced to **5½ years**. An order under the Crime and Disorder Act extending the supervision to 8 years was undisturbed.

R v Hamar [2001] EWCA Crim 114, [2001] 2 Cr App Rep (S) 295. The defendant pleaded guilty to manslaughter. Having drunk about 12 pints, the defendant joined a taxi queue in which the victim was standing. There was a scuffle involving the victim in which the defendant was struck. They both left and a CCTV camera recorded what happened. The defendant gratuitously struck the victim a single bow to the side of his head causing him to fall to the ground banging his head. The defendant walked away.

The victim was taken to hospital and died. The post mortem disclosed the cause of death was fractures to the skull with associated bruising and swelling. Further the injuries were consistent with a fall onto the back of the head. Sentenced on the basis of striking the victim a, 'haymaking blow of tremendous force.' The defendant had been released from custody 3 months before. Held. The judge was right to take a serious view and **4½ years** was severe but not excessive.

A-G's Reference (No 100 of 2001) [2002] EWCA Crim 294, [2002] 2 Cr App Rep (S) 365. See **Fighting with the death being caused by the fall not any blow – Cases**

See also **Fighting**

Vehicle, by

100.46   Road Traffic Offenders Act 1988, Sch 2, Part II

Obligatory disqualification and endorsement when by the driver of a motor vehicle. 3–11 penalty points

R v Gault (1995) 16 Cr App Rep (S) 1013 – LCJ. The gap that exists in relationship to statutory vehicle offences does not exist for manslaughter. The maximum is life.

R v Ripley [1997] 1 Cr App Rep (S) 19. The defendant pleaded guilty to manslaughter on the basis that he drove when drunk (and possibly concussed) at the deceased to frighten him and with no intention of hitting him. The defendant, a friend of the deceased, had an altercation with him in and outside a pub. The defendant was punched by the deceased after which the deceased helped the defendant up and walked off with him. Later the defendant drove his transit at the deceased when he was on the pavement. The speed was estimated at 10–20 mph. He drove off but was arrested and found to be three times over the drink drive limit. He had previous convictions for drink drive but the offence was out of character. Held. Defendants can expect heavy sentences. **6 years** was stiff but not manifestly excessive.

A-G's Reference (No 16 of 1999) [2000] 1 Cr App Rep (S) 524 – LCJ. The defendant was convicted of manslaughter, theft and conspiracy to cause actual bodily harm. There was bad blood between the defendant's co-defendant, Marsh and Danny Marlow, the victim. It was about money and snooker. About a month before the incident, the co-defendant had approached a taxi which Danny Marlow was driving and hit the driver's window with a brick. Marsh became obsessed with him and approached someone requesting that he should put the 'frighteners on him'. He refused and Marsh approached the defendant to frighten him with telephone calls and assaulted him causing minor injuries. This was the basis of the conspiracy conviction. One evening Marlow left a public house and on his way home was assaulted and knocked to the ground. The defendant hit him with the stolen car he was driving and made no attempt to stop. He suffered a severe injury and died. The medical evidence indicated he had been run over by a car and dragged along the road. It also suggested that the victim was lying in the road when hit. The stolen car was set on fire. **5 years** was not unduly lenient.

A-G's Reference (No 14 of 2001) [2002] 1 Cr App Rep (S) 106. The defendant was convicted of manslaughter and pleaded to attempting to pervert the course of justice. The defendant had defective vision which requires spectacles for driving. Without spectacles his vision was blurred from 30 cm and from there on the blurring increased. Shortly after his release from custody he left his spectacles in Salisbury and decided to drive from Bournemouth to Salisbury in a car he had just bought. It had no insurance. He was warned by a colleague before he set off and he said he was prepared to take the risk and would leave early to avoid the dark. In fact he left as it was getting dark and after driving 20 miles at 40 mph he hit an 18-year-old girl who was crossing the road.

It was a 40 mph area but he was not speeding. She was in dark clothing and the road was poorly lit. It was accepted even if wearing glasses he probably would not have been unable to avoid her but it would have given him an opportunity to slow down and sound the horn. It was accepted he never really saw her at all. He carried on driving and another car passed over her legs. She died from being hit by the defendant's car. Next he set the vehicle alight and removed the registration plates. His defence to the manslaughter was that he was wearing glasses and in interview he said, 'I won't get in my car without my glasses on. I'm lethal. I wouldn't even make it down the road. I wouldn't be able to see about 3 ' in front of me.' The jury were directed that to convict they must be sure he wasn't wearing glasses. He was 22 and was genuinely remorseful from early on. *Held.* Had he been convicted of death by dangerous driving the proper sentence should not have been less than 5 years. For manslaughter the sentence should have been of the order of **5–6 years** with 9 months for the perverting count consecutive. As it was a reference **4 years 3 months** for the manslaughter not 3 years and 9 months consecutive for the perverting matter not concurrent.

A-G's Reference (No 64 of 2001) [2001] EWCA Crim 2028, [2002] 1 Cr App Rep (S) 409. The defendant offered to plead guilty to manslaughter and his offer was rejected. Later it was accepted and the murder charge was dropped. The defendant lived near the victim and was close to her sister and the sister's boyfriend who lived with her. The relationship between the victim and her sister soured, probably because of the victim's resumption of drug taking. The defendant was drawn into the dispute and he discovered that yellow paint had been poured over his van, a window had been smashed and its tyres were slashed. He blamed (no doubt in good faith) the victim and blamed her for causing the general disruption in his life. There was a discussion between the defendant and the sister and their partners and the defendant stormed out very angry stating he was going to get the deceased. He lost his temper and drove off at speed. He chatted to some people and said, 'Watch this.' He revved his engine and drove the van at the victim and another. The van mounted the pavement, went across a grass verge and hit the victim who was walking on the pavement. It had travelled 50 yards. She went onto the bonnet, struck her head, travelled some distance, fell to the ground and later died of head injuries in hospital. The defendant drove off at speed smiling. The sister's boyfriend persuaded him to contact the police and he did so. He claimed he tried to avoid her. The victim was 35 with four children but only one living with her. He was sentenced on the basis it was to frighten her and deliberate and the van was travelling at 15 mph. He was 24, extremely deaf and had no convictions. He was deeply remorseful and not a violent man by nature. *Held.* The sentence should have been **6 years** not 3½. Because it was a reference and of his difficulties **4½ years** substituted.

Old cases. *R v Mahmood* (1992) 14 Cr App Rep (S) 8; *R v Pimm* (1993) 14 Cr App Rep (S) 730; *R v Sherwood* (1995) 16 Cr App Rep (S) 513; *A-G's Reference (No 68 of 1995)* [1996] 2 Cr App Rep (S) 358.

Victim over 65

100.47 *A-G's Reference (Nos 57, 58 and 59 of 1997)* [1999] 1 Cr App Rep (S) 31. All three female defendants pleaded guilty to manslaughter, two by reason of no intent to cause serious harm and the third on account of diminished responsibility. All three went to the flat of a 74-year-old man who was being cared for by one of them, Beveridge. They wanted revenge because the old man had answered questions from the police about a social security claim made by Beveridge. The claim had involved the old man. He was attacked by being smothered by bedclothes and his belt was used to strangle him. He was also struck. His body was not discovered for 4 or 5 days during which time Beveridge used his pension book to obtain his pension. Beveridge who was the leader and who at the plea showed remorse was given **7½ years detention and 3½ concurrent** for the pension book robbery. The second girl showed early remorse but had stamped on the victim's face and was given 5 years and 3½ years concurrent. The last girl, who was of very limited intelligence and susceptible to pressure, and had relied on diminished responsibility received **3½ years** for the manslaughter. None of the sentences were held to be unduly lenient.

R v Kime [1999] 2 Cr App Rep (S) 3. The defendant was convicted of manslaughter having earlier offered to plead guilty to it. He was acquitted of murder. At about 10pm, the defendant who was then aged 21 was drunk. He was with his girlfriend and he heard the victim aged 80 and others laughing in the street. He went over to them and asked him, 'Are you fucking laughing?' Before there was an opportunity to reply he shouted again and punched the victim in the head with moderate force. There was some evidence of a second blow. He collapsed and during the following evening the victim suffered a cardiac arrest which had been hastened by the shock and the facial injuries. The injuries had caused heavy bleeding. The defendant had a number of previous convictions including common assault, criminal damage and had served a custodial sentence. A psychiatric report said he had a propensity to act very dangerously when under the influence of alcohol. Held. **6 years** was severe but not excessive.

Victim's health precarious/eggshell skull

100.48 *R v Harrison* [1996] 2 Cr App Rep (S) 250. A blow sufficient to fracture an eggshell skull is very much less culpable than one which fractures a normal skull. [This means that the sentencing factor is the force of the blow and not the victim's individual characteristics.]

R v Scammell [2001] EWCA Crim 1631 [2002] 1 Cr App Rep (S) 293. The defendant pleaded guilty to manslaughter. The defendant lived near the victim and heard the victim had blamed him for breaking his neighbour's window. The next day the defendant got drunk and called the victim 'queer' to his friends. He went to the victim's house and banged on the door. The victim closed it, which the defendant tried to prevent. The defendant then attacked the door and was bitten by the victim's Alsatian dog. He threw red paint on the door, kicked it and began to scream and shout. A friend caught up with him and found him in a temper about the bite. The friend tried to calm him down and another friend arrived and both tried to restrain him. But the defendant threw six or seven stones or rocks through the window and into the room the victim lived. He continued to shout threats including threats to kill him. Later the victim was found dead and the windows smashed. There was glass everywhere including on top of the victim. A wheelbrace and baseball bat was found on the bed which it was suggested the victim had to protect himself. The victim was 68 and suffered from severe coronary heart disease. Any stressful incident could have led to cardiac arrhythmia and death. It was not suggested the defendant knew about the bad heart. The defendant was 21 and in 1998 had a conviction for criminal damage. He had abused a bus driver and was ejected from the bus. He kicked out at the bus door and smashed the glass in the door. When the bus returned he threw a brick though the bus windscreen. The pre-sentence report said he needed to give up intoxicants, mature and get a job. The psychiatric report said he was being treated for depression and threatened self harm. The judge said the victim died of fright. Held. The intention was to damage property rather than commit physical harm. The plea to manslaughter indicates an acknowledgment there was a risk of harm to the deceased from his conduct but not that death was envisaged. It was aggravated by drunkenness and his decision to go there. The misconduct was over a period of time. Taking into account his age 4 years would have been appropriate after a trial so **2 years 9 months** not 3½ years.

R v Ginley [2002] EWCA Crim 209, [2002] 2 Cr App Rep (S) 277. See **Burglars/Robbers/Thieves, by**

R v Clark and Lappin [2002] EWCA Crim 222, [2002] 2 Cr App Rep (S) 353. See **Burglars/Robbers/Thieves, by**

Victims, the views of the relatives of the

100.49 The law is most clearly stated in the cases about causing death by dangerous and careless driving. See **DEATH BY DANGEROUS DRIVING, CAUSING** – *Victims, the views of the relatives of the*

MANUFACTURE OF DRUGS

See **PRODUCTION OF DRUGS**

MARRIAGE OFFENCES

See **BIGAMY/MARRIAGE OFFENCES**

101   MEDICINE OFFENCES

101.1   Medicines Act 1968, ss 7, 8, 31, 31 and 34

Sell, supply, export etc medicinal products, substances etc.

Triable either way. On indictment maximum 2 years. Summary maximum £5,000.

Selling – Defendant aged 18–21

101.2   *R v Sabeddu* [2001] 1 Cr App Rep (S) 493. The defendant pleaded guilty at the Magistrates' Court to possessing a medicinal product for selling. Police stopped him before he went into a warehouse rave party. He was found to have 26 wraps of Ketamine in a wallet concealed up his trousers. He was 18 and of good character. He also faced sentence for committal for an affray which was throwing an empty drinks bottle at the police at a May Day demonstration. Held. No guidelines exist for Ketamine. We are not fully informed of its dangers so this should not be seen as a precedent in a case where there is such evidence. **3 months** YOI not 8.

See also **DRUG USERS; IMPORTATION OF DRUGS; POSSESSION OF DRUGS; PRODUCTION OF DRUGS** and **SUPPLY OF DRUGS (CLASS A, B AND C)**

MENTALLY ILL DEFENDANTS

See **DEFENDANT** – *Mentally ill*

102 MERCY

Mercy should season justice

102.1 *A-G's Reference (No 4 of 1998)* [1990] 11 Cr App Rep (S) 517 – LCJ. It must always be remembered that sentencing is an art rather than a science; that the trial judge is particularly well placed to assess the weight to be given to various competing considerations; that leniency is not in itself a vice. That mercy should season justice is a proposition as soundly based in law as it is in literature.

A-G's Reference (No 83 of 2001) [2002] 1 Cr App Rep (S) 589. What the authorities do not show are the cases where the individual circumstances of the defendant and the mitigation available to him have led to a justified departure from the guidance provided by the reported decisions. It is fundamental to the responsibilities of sentencing judges that while they must always pay proper regard to the sentencing guidance given, they are required also to reflect on all the circumstances of the individual case. Where sentencing judges are satisfied that occasion requires it, they have to balance the demands of justice with what is sometimes described as the calls of mercy. There were occasions where it was right to take a constructive course and seek to achieve the rehabilitation of the offender. The judge was satisfied it provided the best possible long-term solution for the community and the defendant. It was right to take a constructive course. So far he has been proved right. The prospects of re-offending are now lower than if he had had a custodial sentence. The sentence was lenient on paper but sentencing is not and never can be an exercise on paper; each case, ultimately, is individual. It would be wrong to interfere.

See also **DEFENDANT**

103 MISCONDUCT IN PUBLIC OFFICE

103.1 Common law offence.

Indictable only. Maximum sentence is large so life.

Police officers selling information

103.2 *R v Keyte* [1998] 2 Cr App Rep (S) 165. The defendant was convicted of conspiracy to commit misconduct in a public office. He was a police officer who made 192 unauthorised enquiries on police national computer. They were mainly about the registered keepers of motor vehicles. He supplied the information to a private investigation company, which was connected with his co-accused who was a friend of the defendant and an ex-police officer. The sums gained were not large. The defendant was 42 and of good character. He was a father of four children and his partner was suffering from ill health. He had lost his job. Held. The integrity of the police national computer is of absolutely vital importance. Police officers are given considerable powers and privileges. If they dishonestly abuse their position and do so for profit, then not only must a prison sentence follow but it must of necessity be a severe one. We take into account the devastating effect of the prison sentence and the mitigation but **2 years** was not manifestly excessive.

See also **CORRUPTION** and **POLICE OFFICERS**

MOBILE PHONES

See DANGEROUS DRIVING – *Magistrates' Court Sentencing Guidelines September 2000* and DEATH BY DANGEROUS DRIVING, CAUSING – *Mobile phone, defendant using*

MONEY

See COUNTERFEITING CURRENCY

104 MONEY LAUNDERING ETC

104.1 Criminal Justice Act 1988, ss 93A, 93B and 93C. (Criminal conduct money)

Drug Trafficking Act 1994, ss 49, 50 and 51 (drug trafficking money)

Triable either way. On indictment maximum 14 years. Summary maximum 6 months and/or £5,000.

[When the Proceeds of Crime Act 2002 is in force, the above provisions will be repealed and replaced with:

Proceeds of Crime Act 2002, ss 327–9

Section 327: concealing etc criminal property.
Section 328: entering into an arrangement etc about criminal property.
Section 329: acquiring using and possessing criminal property.
Triable either way. On indictment maximum 14 years. Summary maximum 6 months and/or £5,000.]

The Court of Appeal has ruled that the prosecution can indict for the Criminal Justice Act 1988 Sections and the Drug Trafficking Act 1994 together[1] so the counts in the indictment do not always distinguish between drug trafficking and other money.

1   *R v El-Kurd* [2001] (26 July, unreported), Crim LR 234 .

Guideline remarks

104.2 *R v O'Meally and Morgan* (1994) 15 Cr App Rep (S) 831 – LCJ. It is impossible to lay down guidelines. Cases are infinitely variable.

R v Greenwood (1995) 16 Cr App Rep (S) 614. The defendant pleaded guilty to assisting another to retain the proceeds of drug trafficking. Launderers are nearly as bad but not quite as bad as those that do the actual dealing.

R v Basra [2002] EWCA Crim 541, [2002] 2 Cr App Rep (S) 469. Held. Money laundering is a stand alone offence where the constituent elements may be many and varied. There may be circumstances where the launderer has no knowledge of the source of the money laundered and indeed may choose not to know. He may know that it represents the proceeds of criminal activity, but beyond that he is careful not to ask any questions. Many such offenders say they are ignorant of the origin of the proceeds in question and that this should isolate them from the original crime. In this case the maximum sentence for money laundering is 10 years, (Note in fact it is 14 years) whereas the maximum sentence for the evasion of duty was 7 years. The former makes allowance for the many and varied antecedent offences to which it could relate. There is no necessary direct relationship between the sentence for the laundering offence and the original antecedent offence. The criminality in laundering arises from the encouragement and nourishment it gives to crime in general. Without it many crimes would be rendered much less fruitful and perhaps more difficult to perpetrate. Nonetheless the sentence for laundering cannot be wholly disproportionate to the sentence for the original antecedent offence, where the offence is that of being involved in an arrangement whereby the retention or control of the proceeds of criminal conduct.

Criminal conduct money – £1m and up to £20m

104.3   *R v Everson* [2001] EWCA Crim 2262, [2002] 1 Cr App Rep (S) 553. The defendants S and B pleaded guilty to conspiracy to convert and remove from the jurisdiction criminal conduct money. The judge gave them the full discount for the plea. The defendant E was convicted of the same count. The conspiracy was over nearly 2 years and masterminded by S's brother in Gibraltar. Stirling notes, all the proceeds of crime were exchanged for foreign currency of higher denomination, bank drafts and electronic transfers. Over £15m was laundered through a Bureau de Change in Victoria in London. There were at least 150 transactions. Some of the amounts were very large. S was the runner making most of the deposits. The money came from B and E. B was stopped as he was about to board a flight to Athens with his cleaner. They had nearly £169,000 worth of Swiss francs and Deutchmarks in their hand luggage. E was arrested and found to have a large amount of cash and a note in his jeep. The note referred to a shipment of training suits. When the consignment was intercepted it was found to contain £8.67m worth of cigarettes. He was deeply involved in the smuggling of cigarettes and the investment of the proceeds. His role was to cloak the operation with respectability. £1 m was transferred by shares. His laundering was close to £2m. None of the defendants were principles. The personal profits were said to be relatively modest. The judge found B was deeply involved in the regular laundering of the proceeds of cigarette smuggling. S was of good character. In 1984 B was convicted of evading duty and received 2 years. In 1991 he was sentenced to 10 years for drug smuggling. E was of good character and his partner had health problems. The defence relied on the fact the maximum for smuggling cigarettes was 7 years. The prosecution could not say what the duty evaded was. Held. As it was a conspiracy count it did not relate to just one evasion of duty so we are not impressed with counsel's argument. The Judge had looked at the totality of the sums. However, **3½ years** not 4 ½ for S, **5 years** not 6 for B and **6 years** not 7 for E.

R v Basra [2002] EWCA Crim 541, [2002] Cr App Rep (S) 469. The defendant pleaded guilty to assisting another to obtain the benefit of criminal conduct money. He exchanged £1.2m into foreign currency at a bureau at Victoria Station. He was sentenced on the basis it was the proceeds of jewellery smuggled from Uganda. His role was a middleman and the VAT evaded was £215,000. He carried on exchanging after his first arrest. **3½ years** not 5.

Criminal conduct money – £20m or more

104.4   *R v El-Kurd* [2001] Crim LR 234. The defendant was convicted of two conspiracies to remove criminal conduct money and two conspiracies to convert criminal conduct money. He was the proprietor of a Bureau de Change where over £70m was laundered over a 2 year period. Suitcases and holdalls of low value sterling notes were exchanged for high value foreign notes particularly Dutch guilders, Deutschmarks and Swiss Francs. The laundering activities did not appear in the exchange's books and the defendant had the defendant had 55 bank accounts in England, Wales and Jersey. Held. As he wasn't convicted of laundering drugs money and the maximum was 14 years. **12 years** not 14.

Old cases. *R v Hanna* (1993) 15 Cr App Rep (S) 44; *R v Greenwood* (1994) 16 Cr App Rep 614.

Drugs money – Up to £50,000

104.5 *R v Gray* [2001] 1 Cr App Rep (S) 99. The defendant pleaded guilty to the acquisition, possession or use of the proceeds of drug trafficking and possession of cannabis. Police searched his home and he produced a small piece of cannabis. Another piece was found in a speaker. They also found a letter from a man in prison asking for help with some 'dosh' and in another speaker they found £15,725 which contained traces of cocaine, cannabis, heroin and amphetamine. He told police it was his savings for a business buying and selling houses. His plea was entered on the basis that he had received a call from the man in prison the night before who informed him there was cash in the speakers which he had previously asked him to remove from the premises. He realised the cash was stored in the speakers was the proceeds of drugs. He had not responded to the letter and was relieved that his dilemma about what to do with the money ended with the arrival of the police. He was 41 with convictions and a low risk assessment for offending from the probation officer. Held. It was surprising the Crown accepted the basis of plea. As it was he had to be sentenced on that very limited role and that he stood to gain nothing. Therefore **15 months** not 2 years.

Old case. *R v Greenwood* (1995) 16 Cr App Rep (S) 614.

Drugs money – £200,000

104.6 *R v Simpson* [1998] 2 Cr App Rep (S) 111. The defendants S, F and L pleaded to conspiracy to possess the proceeds of drug trafficking. A and D pleaded to possessing the proceeds of drug trafficking. G pleaded to assisting another to retain the benefit of drug trafficking. They were part of a well-organised drug syndicate, which during 1995 was raising £½m every 2–3 weeks principally selling Class A drugs. The money was taken to Ireland to be laundered. S made regular trips to Ireland. F and L delivered £540,000 to S in London and S was arrested with the cash at Heathrow airport. From tape recordings F and L were thoroughly familiar with workings of the whole organisation. After S's arrest A visited him in prison on a number of occasions. It was agreed he would take over S's role in dealing with the Croydon end and receive the cash generated there. A was arrested with £½m of cash which he had been handed at Victoria Station by D. D had earlier been contacted at home by the dealers and asked to take the money there. He had the money for a maximum of 1½ hours and was paid £200. The judge said this was not the first time F and L were involved in disposing of the proceeds of drug trafficking. They were very much higher up than the bottom rung of the conspiracy. L was subordinate to F and became involved later than F did. A's criminal responsibility was considered the same as F. G's basis of plea was that he had twice in 1995 facilitated the export of money and on each occasion didn't know the amount involved and his role was back up. The judge said he knew S, F, L and A well and played quite a prominent role in the business. However, he didn't seem to have made much money out of his involvement. D was sentenced for the one occasion and he knew there was substantial amount of cash but didn't know how much money there was. F had convictions for a number of offences of dishonesty but none for drugs. L was of good character. A was 42 and had a number of convictions. There were no drug trafficking convictions and he had testimonials. D was 31 and for practical purposes of good character. G was 29 and of good character with testimonials. F and L's benefit was assessed at £20,000 and £10,000 and they were ordered to pay £10,000 and £8,800 respectively. A's benefit was £519,500 and the judge made a confiscation order in that amount. No order was made against G. Held. S's 11 years was severe but not manifestly excessive. F's **9 years** and L's **7 years** were not manifestly excessive. The judge was wrong to equate A with F so 7 years not 9 for A. Although D did not plead at the first opportunity, **4 years** not 5. The judge by saying

G had played a prominent role was implicitly rejecting the basis of plea so **5 years** not 6. (For details about S see the next paragraphs.)

Drugs money – £1m and up to £20m

104.7   *R v Simpson* [1998] 2 Cr App Rep (S) 111. The defendant S pleaded guilty at an early stage to conspiracy to possess the proceeds of drug trafficking. He was part of a well-organised drug syndicate, which during 1995 was raising £½ m every 2–3 weeks principally selling Class A drugs. The money was taken to Ireland to be laundered. S made regular trips to Ireland. F and L delivered £540,000 to S in London and S was arrested with the cash at Heathrow airport. He admitted his involvement in interview. S was sentenced on the basis he had made five earlier trips, the total sum transported by him being approximately £2.5m and he was paid £25,000 to £30,000 per trip. S received 11 years with a £948,700 confiscation order. It was contended that **11 years** on a plea equated with 14 years if contested which was the maximum. Held. S's role was crucial and pivotal. As he was caught red-handed we doubt whether a 3 year discount would have been appropriate. It was a severe sentence but not manifestly excessive. (For details about the co-defendants see *Drugs money – £200,000–£1m)*

Drugs money – £20m or more

104.8   *R v Sabharwal* [2001] 2 Cr App Rep (S) 373. The defendant was convicted of conspiracy to facilitate the proceeds of drug trafficking. He exchanged £52m into guilders and £1,288,000 into other currencies between April 1998 and May 1999 using two London exchange centres who kept no records of the transactions. The £½m notes were seized and analysed. They were contaminated throughout with heroin, cocaine and two forms of ecstasy. He was living on benefits. Held. **12 years** was entirely appropriate.

Solicitors

104.9   *R v Duff* (30 July 2002, unreported). The defendant pleaded guilty to two counts of failing to disclose knowledge or suspicion of money laundering contrary to the Drug Trafficking Act 1994, s 52(1). They involved £60,000 and £10,000. The defendant qualified as a solicitor in 1984. In 1991 he established his own practice, 90% of his work was conveyancing and the rest was personal injury work. In 1993 or 1994 he met G through their mutual interest in motor racing. He started to act for G and his business associate, H. They also became friendly. In April 1997 the defendant was given £60,000 in cash by G of which £10,000 was to pay for litigation. The rest was to be invested in an office run by the defendant and G. In May 1997 G paid the defendant £10,000 as an investment in a company to solicit personal injury work. The venture failed. In 1998 G and H were arrested for possession of cocaine worth £5m. To start with the defendant acted for G and H and then just G. Six months later a charge of conspiracy to import was added. The defendant accepted from then he had doubts about G's innocence. The defendant returned the £50,000 investment money. In October 1998 he obtained literature from the Law Society and concluded he was not under any duty to disclose. In 1999 G and H were tried and convicted and the trial focused on the defendant's dealing with G. After the trial the defendant took advice from another solicitor who advised he had no duty to report the dealings. The defendant was arrested and was not frank about the facts. There was a 15 month delay between his arrest and charge and 18 months before the case came to court. The defendant was of good character with a wife and three children. He suffered from adverse and sometimes inaccurate publicity and his firm collapsed. The judge said the clear message had to go out that offences of this type would not be overlooked. Held.

Money laundering is a very serious matter and we agree with the judge. **6 months** was not in any way excessive.

105   MOTHERS

Dishonesty, offences of when of good character

105.1   *R v Bowden* [1998] 2 Cr App Rep (S) 7. The defendant pleaded guilty to four counts of theft and asked for 12 similar matters to be taken into consideration. The defendant was elected Treasurer of a Parent Teacher Co-operative. She held the cheque books etc and persuaded her co-signatory to sign blank cheques. She didn't prepare the accounts when they were due. A member of the group attended her house to request the books at the next day's meeting. The next day the books were not available and she submitted a letter of resignation saying she couldn't juggle the roles of mother and treasurer and saying the paperwork had been lost. In fact she had taken £2,983 in 16 withdrawals. She made full admissions in interview. She was 35 and of good character. She said she intended to pay the money back but it had got out of hand. She was a single mother with four children aged 15, 14, 11 and 8. She had spent the money on necessities. She lived on benefit and disability benefit. The pre-sentence report said the behaviour stemmed from difficult home circumstances, stress, debts and poor health. Two of the children suffered from chronic asthmatic, one from depression, one from attention deficit, hyperactivity disorder and a language disorder and one from brain damage, epilepsy and severe learning difficulties. The pre-sentence report said separation would be very traumatic for the children. She was given 12 months and a special needs worker had moved in to her home. Held. 12 months was excessive. The compensation order of £2,983 was too heavy. Custody was not in principle incorrect. The appropriate sentence was **6 months** and 1 day. The exceptional circumstances justified a **suspended sentence** and a suspended supervision order. Both orders made with the compensation order upheld but varied to £100 a month.

R v Mills [2002] 2 Cr App Rep (S) 229 – LCJ. The defendant pleaded guilty to two offences of obtaining services by deception. She completed an application for credit at a store and claimed that the Merseyside Fire Service had employed her for 3 years. This was untrue. Credit facilities were granted. For 12 months she had made the minimum payments. She made no more payments. With interest and charges, the account was £5,682.66 in debt. She also purchased goods to the value of £714 from another store. A 10% deposit was paid. She applied for credit to finance the balance. In her application she claimed to have been employed by Allwood Joinery for 6 years. This was quite untrue. Some months after a finance company issued a credit card to the appellant, which she then used. She said she had not knowingly applied for, or expected to receive, the card. By the time that account was closed, it was approximately £5,438 in debit, and only £43.76 had been paid. She was arrested and when interviewed she admitted that she had made the false representations on each application. She had borrowed £4,000 from her mother to pay off part of the debt. She was 33 years of age and the sole carer of two children aged 11 and 4. She had no previous convictions or cautions and had references. They said that she did voluntary work at a local charity shop and gave her time to a voluntary agency assisting parents with young children. A pre-sentence report recommended a community sentence. The judge said, 'Those who commit offences of this kind, knowing perfectly well that there is really no chance of them ever being able to pay for the goods concerned, go to prison.' Held. The appellant was deeply sorry for the way she had behaved and the offences had been committed to provide for her children. The first factor that has to be take into account is that apart from 'the clang of the prison door' type of sentence, which gives a prisoner the opportunity of knowing what is involved in imprisonment, the ability of the prison service to achieve anything positive in a short prison sentence is very limited. Secondly, with a mother who is the sole supporter of two young children, you must consider them if the sole carer is sent to prison. Finally, take into account the current situation with the female prison population. Since 1993 there has been a remarkable increase. Short prison sentences are always difficult for the prison service to accommodate. The ability to imprison mothers close to their homes in the community is difficult. The difficulties in the prison population to which we have referred does not mean that if an offence is such that it is necessary to send an offender to prison, they should not be sent to prison. But in a borderline case, where the offence does not in particular involve violence but is one with financial consequences to a commercial concern, it is very important to take into account the facts to which we have referred. The courts should strive to avoid sending people like her to prison and instead use punishments in the community. It is true that obtaining credit is easy. Commercial concerns are entitled to the protection of the courts. It was wrong in principle to send her to prison. The minimum period should be passed for this category of offending. If it was necessary to send her to prison, all that would be required was the clang of the prison door. One month not 8 months should have been imposed. It would have been right to impose a **community punishment** order in this case then but now we will make a community rehabilitation order for 6 months.

Exceptional circumstances to enable sentence to be suspended

105.2 *R v Hier* [1998] 2 Cr App Rep (S) 306. The defendant pleaded guilty to GBH with intent. She lived with the victim and their two sons aged 2 and 3 and her three other children. The victim admitted he had been violent to her and had been arrested for it three times. Several times the defendant had moved with her children to a woman's refuge. She instigated a reconciliation and when the relationship broke down moved back to the refuge with the children. She, when slightly intoxicated and some women friends went to a bar where the victim was. He asked about the children and she said they were being looked after. She asked him to dance and they did. He went to another public house. The defendant went in and accused him of chatting up the girls. He calmed her down and then they argued. She suggested they go outside and he walked away to join his girlfriend. She started crying and he and the girlfriend might have goaded her. He went to buy a drink and stood besides her. She hit him with a bottle more than once causing a large laceration to his ear, four cuts to the back of the head, one to his temple and one to his other ear. She told a barman it had given her satisfaction. She was arrested and accepted responsibility and shock at the extent of the injuries. She was 39 and in breach of a C/D for ABH. She had struck a female on the head causing bruises. There were four convictions including the ABH and an assault on police in 1981. She expressed affection for the victim and expressed genuine regret. She was on anti-depressants. The refuge expressed concern for the children. Three were with their father all sharing a bedroom in his brother's three bedroom house with three other children. Two ran away to a mountain nearby. The youngest were with the victim who was also staying with his brother and sharing a room with the children. The victim also expressed concern about his children. Held. It was a very serious offence. The living conditions of each of the children is highly unsatisfactory. The circumstances are now so exceptional to enable the sentence to be suspended. **18 months suspended** for 12 months (reduced because of the time in custody) with a supervision order not 18 months immediate imprisonment.

R v Smith [2002] EWCA Crim 1476, [2002] 1 Cr App Rep (S) 258. The defendant pleaded guilty to evading duty on tobacco etc. 105 trips were made with £365,000 evaded. She made 35 return trips evading some £70,000. Her father, mother and sister were co-defendants. The father was the prime mover. All 4 had been stopped by Customs. She was 28, with three children aged 7 and 2½ years and 8 months. The middle one was epileptic. Her husband was the breadwinner and was experiencing extreme difficulty in arranging adequate care for the children. She was of good character. She received **12 months** and the defence asked for it to be suspended. Held. This was a sustained participation in a major fraud notwithstanding warnings when they were stopped. The circumstances are of course harrowing from the perspective of the children. No one can fail to be moved by the children's plight but sadly the picture painted is all too familiar in cases where a young mother becomes involved in serious criminal activity. This Court is always most reluctant to see a mother of young children sentenced to imprisonment. Unhappily sometimes it is inevitable. The sentence was merciful. A suspended would not have been justified.

See also CRUELTY TO CHILDREN

106   MURDER

Common law. Mandatory sentence of life. There is a power to make a compensation order for the deceased's funeral expenses.

Crown Court statistics England and Wales[1] – Crown Court – Males 21+ – Murder
106.1

Year	Plea	Total Numbers sentenced
2000	Guilty	35
	Not guilty	173

1   Source: Crime and Criminal Justice Unit, Home Office Ref: IOS416-02.

Defendant under 18 at the time of the offence
106.2   Powers of Criminal Courts (Sentencing) Act 2000, s 90. Where a person convicted of murder appears to the court to have been aged under 18 at the time the offence was committed, the court shall (notwithstanding anything in this or any other Act) sentence him to be detained during Her Majesty's pleasure.

Defendant under 21 on the day of conviction
106.3   Powers of Criminal Courts (Sentencing) Act 2000, s 93. Where a person aged under 21 is convicted of murder the court shall sentence him to custody for life unless he is liable to be detained under s 90 (of this Act).

Defendant 21 or over on the date of conviction
106.4   Murder (Abolition of the Death Penalty) Act 1965, s 1.   No person shall suffer death for murder and a person convicted of murder shall be sentenced to imprisonment for life.

Funeral expenses of the deceased, power to make an order for compensation for the
106.5   Powers of Criminal Courts (Sentencing) Act 2000, s 130(1). The court may on application or otherwise make an order requiring him to make payments for funeral

expenses or bereavement in respect of a death resulting from an offence other than death due to an accident arising out of the presence of a motor vehicle on a road.

Powers of Criminal Courts (Sentencing) Act 2000, s 130(3). A court shall give reasons if it does not make a compensation order in a case where this section empowers it to do so.

R v Williams (10 March 1989, unreported). It is important sentencers bear in mind the words (which had just been added to the then statute giving the court power to order compensation for funeral expenses). If the court decides not to order compensation it must give its reasons.

Recommendations to the Secretary of State

106.6 Murder (Abolition of the Death Penalty) Act 1965, s 1(2) On sentencing any person convicted of murder to imprisonment for life the Court may at the same time declare the period which it recommends to the Secretary of State as the minimum period which in its view should elapse before the Secretary of State orders the release of that person on licence.

Setting the minimum term

106.7 Practice Statement as to Life Sentences Unreported Issued 31/5/02: The word minimum term should replace the word 'tariff'. The normal starting point for an adult is 12 years and the higher starting point is 16 years. (As this book is about sentences passed not recommendations the text is not summarised.)

107 MURDER, ATTEMPTED – MURDER, CONSPIRACY TO

107.1 Attempted murder. Common law indictable only. Maximum is life[1].

Conspiracy to murder. Criminal Law Act 1977, s 1(1). Indictable only. Maximum is life[2].

Attempted murder, conspiracy to murder, incitement to murder and soliciting to murder are specified offences for automatic life.

1 Criminal Attempts Act 1981, s 4(1)(a).
2 Criminal Law Act 1977, s 3(1)(a) and (2)(a).

Crown Court statistics England and Wales – Crown Court – Males 21+ – Attempted murder

107.2

| Year | Plea | Total Numbers sentenced | Type of sentence% | | | | | Average length of custody[1] (months) |
			Discharge	Fine	Community sentence	Suspended sentence	Custody	
2000	Guilty	20	0%	0%	5%	0%	75%	98.6
	Not guilty	30	0%	0%	0%	0%	97%	133

1 Excluding life sentences. Source: Crime and Criminal Justice Unit, Home Office Ref: IOS416-02.

Guideline remarks – Attempted murder

107.3 *R v Powell* [1998] 1 Cr App Rep (S) 84. Attempted murder is often more serious than murder as it involves the intention to kill which is not necessary in murder cases.

R v Smith [2000] 2 Cr App Rep (S) 212. Factors to have particular regard to are: (1) an intent to kill will have been established; (2) the failure to implement the intent will not normally be a cause for indulgence or credit to be accorded to the defendant; (3) the motive and the premeditation; (4) the recognition of some proportional correlation between the sentence and the minimum recommendation the judge would have made had murder been committed; (5) the plea; (6) the defendant's age; (7) where there are other sentences, the totality.

Assisting others who want to kill

107.4   *R v Chapman* [1999] 2 Cr App Rep (S) 374   The defendant was convicted of conspiracy to murder. His co-accused was violent to his girlfriend and they separated. He became obsessed by her, obtained a gun and made a number of threatening calls to her. He was arrested and met the defendant in prison. While there he recruited others to make threatening calls to the girlfriend. He was returned to prison and expressed an intention to kill her. He persuaded the defendant to write a letter at his dictation which included threats to kill. The defendant was charged with that and was acquitted by a jury. The co-accused then persuaded the defendant to assist him kill the girlfriend. He told others in prison about the plan and an undercover police officer approached the co-accused posing as a contract killer. The co-accused's instructions were taped. The co-accused then exchanged letters with the defendant who was also still in prison about plans to kill her. Both their cells were searched and the correspondence was found. The defendant was arrested. At his trial the defendant said he had no real intention of carrying out the plan. He was 26 with an appalling record for dishonesty but no convictions for violence. The co-defendant had three convictions for ABH, two for kidnapping, one each for arson, false imprisonment and possession of a firearm. The psychological reports on the defendant differed in their conclusions. They were both sentenced to 8 years. *Held.* The defendant should have received less than the co-accused. One had convictions for violent acts of retribution against former girlfriends. The other had no convictions for violence. The co-accused was the prime mover and had issued earlier threats. **6 years** substituted.

Contract killings – Guideline remarks

107.5   *R v Smith* [2000] 2 Cr App Rep (S) 212. The range for (vengeance) cases is **14 to 20 years**. Contract killing or for enforcement of drugs (disputes) gives rise to sentences at the upper end.

Contract killings – Cases

107.6   *R v Mason and Sellars* (22 March 2002, unreported). The defendants M and S were convicted of conspiracy to murder. M was also convicted of possessing a firearm with intent to endanger life. There was a history of conflict between them and the victim. They all drank in the same pub. They plotted over months to kill him and paid a hit man £6,000 to kill the victim who died in the street. He was shot in the neck with a shotgun. The victim was a violent and unpleasant man. M had an extensive criminal record principally for dishonesty and a conviction for armed robbery and was sentenced to automatic life. *Held.* We must take into account the plan succeeded. The appropriate determinate sentence for M was **22 years**. As S did not represent a serious danger to the public **20 years** not life.

Criminal gangs, killings by

107.7   *R v Powell* [1998] 1 Cr App Rep (S) 84. The defendant was convicted of attempted murder and possessing a firearm with intent to endanger life. The defendant was acquitted of three other shooting incidents in Birmingham, Stoke Newington and Peckham in London. The victim was 17 and sold cannabis. Near midnight he was in the Ladbroke Grove area of London with two others involved in selling drugs. They were joined by two women. A car pulled up and the defendant and another two men got out. The defendant pulled out a gun and fired it at the victim who fell to the ground. He was taken to hospital and it was found a bullet had entered his chest and damaged his spine. The victim was left permanently paraplegic. Held. This was either a contract killing or a killing concerned with the enforcement of order amongst drug dealers. It was at the top end of the scale for this kind of offence. However, **20 years** not 25.

Defendant over 65

107.8   *R v Suckley* [2001] EWCA Crim 125, [2001] 2 Cr App Rep (S) 313. The defendant who was now 75 was convicted of attempted murder, GBH with intent and ABH. He was a neighbour of the victims, a husband and his wife and their son. He had built his house and their house. In 1990 they exchanged properties. In 1995 when his wife died his personality changed and the relationship with the neighbours deteriorated. By 1999 he had become obsessed with complaining about them. He said they moved his tools and scratched his windows. The complaints appeared to be trivial and ill founded. He left two telephone messages for the police but they were not followed up. The next day the husband aged 52, started early to cut his hedge. He wanted to avoid the heat of the day. At 9am his wife and son were sweeping up the cuttings. The defendant revved his engine and reversed his Transit van at them. He hit all three. The wife was knocked into the hedge unconscious and the husband was knocked away. The son was hit by the central part of the bonnet and hit the windscreen which broke, and he landed on the road. The defendant reversed over the son and knocked the husband who was trying to rescue him. He drove forward and reversed over the son three or four times. Then he parked his van and told a neighbour, 'These people have made my life hell for the past 3 years.' The son had a fractured nose and femur with multiple fractures to the rib, pelvis, spine and foot bones. He was in intensive care for 3 weeks and in hospital for 4 weeks. He was in a wheel chair and it was hoped he would be able to walk again. The wife had a fractured pelvis with a head injury. She was in intensive care for 5 days and in hospital for a month. She continued to suffer from memory and concentration problems. The husband suffered bruising and was in hospital for 2 days. The psychiatric report said the defendant had a paranoid psychotic illness of an unknown cause. Another said his persecution delusions were evidence of a mental disorder specifically paraphrenia. Held. It is plain from *R v C* (1992) 14 Cr App Rep (S) 562; *R v S* [1998] 1 Cr App Rep (S) 261 and *R v Anderson* [1999] 1 Cr App Rep (S) 273 that regard must be had to age and that a discount is appropriate. Any attempt at an actuarial basis for a discount is inappropriate. The present sentence has been significantly discounted from almost certainly 15 years, which would have been appropriate for a younger man to **11 years**. Such a discount was proper and fair. Appeal dismissed.

Domestic/emotional – Guideline remarks

107.9   *R v Davis* [2001] 1 Cr App Rep (S) 186. The defendant pleaded guilty to attempted murder. Held. Decisions of this court show offences involving savage attacks by a partner who either does not want himself removed or does not want the partner to go a sentence of **12 years** on conviction is certainly not unusual, and may well be appropriate and usual.

Domestic/emotional – Cases

107.10   *R v John D* [1998] 1 Cr App Rep (S) 110. The defendant pleaded guilty to two counts of attempted murder. After 18 years his marriage broke down and the separation was very bitter. His wife accused him of rape and threatening to kill her. He was remanded in custody and then released on bail for the offences. Under the bail conditions he was allowed contact with his children two boys aged 17 and 13 and a girl aged 9. He met all three and gave the eldest boy 200 cigarettes saying he could not afford to take him to Blackpool. He took the other two to Blackpool and on the way home he took a detour and drove to an isolated wood. In the car he told them 'We are all going to die tonight.' They became upset. He said their mother had hurt him so much that he was going to get his revenge by taking them away from her. He gave them the choice of tablets, strangulation or suffocation. He said they should go to sleep first and he would kill them. He said he would not hurt them but he would kill them in ½ hour whether they were asleep or not. They were told to swallow paracetamol with lager, which they did. They didn't go to sleep and he tried to suffocate the youngest. She and her brother fought back and he then tried to suffocate the boy. He then tried to strangle him by squeezing his neck and then suffocate him by placing a bag over his head. This failed because of the children's resistance. Next he took the boy out of the car and tried again to strangle him and to hang him by lifting him up with his arm under the chin. The boy fought back. The paracetamol was by now having an effect and they were drowsy, weak and physically sick. They pleaded with their father to let them go and they were told to walk to the nearest house. He said he would kill himself. The children walked 4 miles and arrived at a house at 6.30am. They were taken to hospital and the boy had a massive sub-conjunctival haemorrhage with petechical haemorrhage around both eyes, neck and chest. He needed emergency treatment for the paracetamol to prevent liver damage. The defendant was found and was suffering from a paracetamol overdose. He admitted trying to kill his children several times. He said he let them go because he couldn't go through with it. He was 42 and found to have a fragile personality and possibly a psychotic disorder. One doctor said his mental state would have been sufficient to support a diminished responsibility defence if he had been charged with murder. He was later acquitted of the rape. Held. The degree of his responsibility was the cardinal consideration. **10 years** was fully justified.

R v Wooton [1998] 1 Cr App Rep (S) 296. The defendant pleaded guilty to attempted murder. The plea was entered late. The defendant aged 42, was arrested for serious sexual offences against his wife's daughters, (later to lie on the file). He was released on bail on condition he did not have unsupervised access with his wife or her children. Her two older daughters lived with her parents and her 12-year-old son and her 3-year-old daughter lived with the mother. The defendant was the father of the 3 year old. Four months later his wife, after she had been drinking telephoned him and invited him to her home. The defendant said he wanted to take his daughter to France and the son was concerned and rang his grandfather. The grandfather aged 68 arrived and the defendant took hold of his daughter and refused to hand her over. An argument took place. The defendant seized the grandfather by the throat, pushed him onto a bed, knelt over him and threatened to kill him if his daughter went into care. The police were called but the defendant had left before they arrived. As he left he told the grandfather 'I'll will get you.' The grandfather stayed the night and was afraid the defendant would return so he armed himself with a frying pan. He had been in bed 15 minutes when he heard the gate being opened. He got up and went to the top of the stairs holding the frying pan. He saw the defendant climbing the stairs carrying a carving knife and wearing gloves. The mother and the boy saw two knives. The grandfather told him to be sensible but the defendant swore and repeatedly said he was going to kill him and 'You are not going to take my baby away.' As the defendant reached the top of the stairs the grandfather hit him on the head with the pan. The defendant continued to advance and threatened to kill him. He aimed blows at him with the knife and stabbed him in the lower stomach. The grandfather started to bleed profusely and the defendant stabbed him twice more in the stomach and slashed him in the chest. The wife and son appeared and shouted at him to stop. The defendant continued to advance striking out at the grandfather who sustained further injuries to his hands and chest. The grandfather barricaded himself in the bedroom but the defendant attacked the door with the knife and continued to make threats. The knife pierced the door and narrowly missed the grandfather's head. The defendant burst into the room and the son who was in there cried hysterically and pleaded with him to stop. The defendant was still shouting 'I'm going to kill you.' Eventually the defendant threw the knife on the bed and ran down stairs. As he left he cut the telephone wires and the grandfather's car tyres. The grandfather was taken to hospital and found to have a 10 cm wound which penetrated his liver. There was also a 6 cm chest wound. The defendant was arrested and the reports suggested his hypoglycaemia would affect his risk of further offending and was the possible or likely cause of the offence. After his sentence a report said the risk of re-offending had been reduced. Held. The starting point was **12 years**. Taking into account the plea and the hypoglycaemia **8 years** not 11.

R v Rahman [1998] 1 Cr App Rep (S) 391. The defendant pleaded guilty to attempted murder. From 1990 to 1992 the defendant had a sexual relationship with the victim. He then had an arranged marriage, which ended in divorce. In 1995 they briefly lived together until the victim was reconciled with her husband. In 1996 there was an emotional scene between the victim and the defendant and she resolved to finish the relationship. She asked him not to contact her. When she heard his pleas for her to see him and that he was suffering from depression and emphysema she again started to visit him. After one visit she got up to leave and he approached her from behind with a knife. He slashed her throat and she collapsed. He watched her in silence and then repeatedly cut her. She thought she was going to die but managed to escape and a neighbour who was outside helped her. The victim's epiglottis had been completely cut across the vocal chord opening the palette for ⅔ of its circumference. 2″ of the jugular vein was visible. There were many other lacerations. Some were extremely deep. The neck required 120 stitches. She required tendon repairs to her hand. She recovered but remains appallingly scarred. He was born in Bangladesh and was now 30. He had served a prison sentence for a wholly different offence. He had no history of serious medical problems but had suffered from stress from cultural value conflict. He did not want to take anti-depressants. No mental disorder was found. Held. There was evidence of potential continuing dangerousness which would have justified a life sentence after a trial for this almost fatal attack. Because of the plea **11 years** not 14.

R v Davis [2001] 1 Cr App Rep (S) 186. The defendant was convicted of attempted murder. His relationship with the victim broke down after a domestic argument and she asked him to leave. He chased her and stabbed her in the back and stomach. He dragged her down the road and slashed her face substantially with a kitchen knife. The victim was expected to have permanent and cosmetically disfiguring scars on her face and to have facial muscle weakness. Her life had been altered and she had problems eating and drinking. She could not sleep and felt the events would haunted her forever. He was 37 and she was 36. Held. The photographs show very frenzied injuries. There was no mitigation. **12 years** upheld.

R v Hough [2001] 1 Cr App Rep (S) 258. The defendant pleaded guilty to attempted murder. After a 20 year relationship the victim, aged 36 left the defendant, aged 66 and took their five children with her. She blamed the deterioration of the relationship on his violence. He blamed it on her affair with another man. He met her and two of the children in the street and tried to persuade her to return home. She refused. They went to a friend's house, as neutral territory and talked. He tried to persuade her to return and she continued to refuse to do so. He went home which was close by and returned shortly afterwards. He asked her to go upstairs so they could speak privately. She feared he would attack her but he assured her he would not. They went upstairs and he asked her to sit down. He asked to see her personal alarm as she had said she had one. In fact she didn't have one. He leant towards her, she thought to cuddle her but he produced a knife. Using both hands he tried to stab her in the stomach. Luckily as she was wearing a strong fabric the knife buckled. She kicked him and he pulled out a second knife and stabbed her in the top of the forehead and the knife passed between the skin and the skull. The knife exited 4″ further down her forehead just above the right eye. She screamed and he ran off leaving the knife in place. She went to hospital and he went to the police station and told them he had stabbed her because she was messing with another man and he wished her dead. In interview he said he tried to 'get rid of the bitch.' He said he went home to get the knives and he wanted to make sure he got rid of her. He said he intended to kill her because she deserved it. His last conviction was in 1976 for sex with a girl under 16. His last custodial sentence was in 1961. He was unemployed and had earlier told the third man he had nothing to live for. Held. On a fight the sentence would be **8–9 years**, so with the mitigation **6 years** not 8.

A-G's Reference (No 117 of 2001) [2002] EWCA Crim 144, [2002] 2 Cr App Rep (S) 274. The defendant was convicted of attempted murder. About 5 years before the offence he separated from his wife and started a relationship with the victim. The new partner believed it was a good, open and honest relationship. He was loving and affectionate and never violent. He hid from her his debts but his partner's death would not have helped with that. At 5.45am he approached her in bed, held her hands and said he loved her. He took up a pillow on which he had wrapped some cling film. He forced it over her face and she struggled. She was able to scream and he abandoned his attempt. She asked him what he had done and he said he didn't know what she was talking about. A pathologist found petechial haemorrhages in her eyes consistent with her nose and mouth being covered for at least a minute. The defendant denied the offence in interview. His former wife said he had never been violent or aggressive and there was no sign of a mental disorder. He was of good character and his manager said he was responsible and trustworthy. No explanation for the offence emerged. Held. The range of sentences for attempted murder is wide. **5 years** was lenient but not unduly lenient.

Old case. *R v Turner* (1990) 12 Cr App Rep (S) 110; *R v Gibson* [1997] 2 Cr App Rep (s) 292.

Obsessive attacks

107.11 *R v Suckley* [2001] EWCA Crim 125, [2001] 2 Cr App Rep (S) 313. See **Defendant over 65**

Police officers, on

107.12 *R v Morrison* [2001] EWCA Crim 2806, [2002] 2 Cr App Rep (S) 75. The defendant was convicted of three counts of attempted murder and a count of wounding with intent. He married in 1988 and had two children. In 1995 his wife discovered he was having an affair and in 1997 they were divorced. In June 1999 he accused his ex-wife of turning the children against him. He threatened to kill her and they rarely spoke although contact with his daughters continued. In August 1999, she borrowed his car and collected her daughter from a previous relationship. 45 minutes later she returned and he became angry because he did not accept where she had been. That evening he rang her and sounded drunk. He said he loved her, asked her why she had been away so long and called her a bitch because she wouldn't take him back. There were further calls during that evening and he said he was going to kill her. The calls were recorded and in the last one he said 'I'm coming up now. I've decided what to do with you. I'm going to kill you and get you out of the way.' 15 minutes later he arrived at her home with a Samurai sword. He used the sword to break down the door. She ran upstairs and shut the door and held onto the handle of the door of the bedroom to stop him coming in. He thrust the sword through the door three times but she wasn't hit. (This was the first attempted murder – 10 years.) Police arrived and an officer got out of a van. The defendant ran towards him with the sword raised. The officer retreated to the van and sat in the driver's seat. The defendant raised the sword and brought it down on the windscreen twice but it didn't break. He followed the van as it reversed and raised the sword again. That officer decided to wait for an armed response unit to arrive. A dog van attended and the defendant hid behind an electricity junction box. Suddenly he ran at the dog van which reversed. The defendant caught up with it and brought the sword down on the windscreen in a dagger like movement aiming at the driver. It went through the windscreen but missed the officer. The driver drove away. (This was the second attempted murder – 15 years.) Another officer arrived in a patrol car and saw the attack on the van. He decided to disarm the defendant by knocking him over. His bonnet hit the defendant's knees. The defendant fell down but got up, picked the sword up, walked towards the car and raised the sword which he brought down like an axe smashing the windscreen in front of the PC The PC panicked and his attempts to drive away failed. The defendant struck the roof of the car with the sword a number of times. He then drove the sword through the open window towards the officer's head. He slashed and stabbed at the PC's head and body. The roof was hit again. The PC managed to run away. The tendons to his wrists had been cut. (This was the third attempted murder – 16 years.) Another officer arrived, knocked the defendant over and he was arrested. The defendant was 40 with three convictions, two of which were for ABH. He expressed remorse. Held. It was a very serious incident. **16 years** in all was not excessive.

Sadistic offences

107.13 *R v Dalziel* [1999] 2 Cr App Rep (S) 272. The defendant made a late guilty plea to attempted murder. Just under a month after being released from a 2 year sentence for blackmail the defendant then 19 called at the front door of an 82-year-old widower who was blind and lived with his guide dog. The defendant claimed he was from Age Concern and was invited in. They talked and the defendant was given strawberries and cream. After taking the dirty dishes to the kitchen the two returned to the living room and the defendant drew the curtains. He then seized the victim from behind and held a knife to his throat. He was threatened that his throat would be cut if he did not do what he was told. The victim's hands were tied behind his back with flex and over ½ hour he removed his trousers and underwear and buggered him. He took him to the bathroom where he made the victim lie on the floor while he had a shower. Next he took him to his bedroom and ransacked it. Then he was taken to the living room where he was tied up with flex round the legs and throat and gagged. The defendant found and sprinkled a can of lighter fuel and whisky over the victim and the room. Finally he set light to a piece of paper and left the house to burn. The victim was terrified for himself and the dog which had been tethered. The flames spread quickly and travelled up between the victim's bare legs which began to burn. He managed to remove the gag and shout for help. Neighbours heard the screams, kicked the door down and dragged him free. The victim had reddening to the scrotum and penis and multiple partial thickness burns to the legs, stomach, hand and soles of the feet. They required skin grafts. The defendant had the blackmail conviction and dishonesty offences but none for violence. Psychiatric reports indicated he was very dangerous. He had fantasies of torturing and killing people and had tortured animals. His psychopathic disorder was untreatable. Held. Examination of comparable horrific cases of attempted murder and similar offences indicate a broad range of **14–18 years** for a contested case. It was not surprising the defendant was given life. **18 years** or close could have been the starting point. Taking into account the plea and his youth **14 years** would not be too high. His dangerousness should not increase the sentence, as that's why it was life. The specified period was therefore ½ the 14 years so **7 years** not 12 years.

Vengeance – Guideline remarks

107.14   *R v Smith* [2000] 2 Cr App Rep (S) 212. The range for (vengeance) cases is **14 to 20 years**. Contract killing or for enforcement of drugs (disputes) gives rise to sentences at the upper end.

Vengeance – Cases

107.15   *R v Smith* [2000] 2 Cr App Rep (S) 212. The defendant was convicted of murder and attempted murder. There was a history of bad feeling and violence between the victim and another, K. The defendant took a gun to a nightclub. He and K watched the two victims leave the club and the defendant gave the gun and ammunition to K saying 'Cap him, cap him'. K fired at one victim and missed. He fired again and the victim fell to the ground. The other victim ran to K and tried to kick him but slipped and fell. The defendant said to K 'Ain't you going to end him?' K then shot him on the floor. The bullet passed through his heart sac. The defendant and K left. The first victim through a miracle survived. The second victim died. The defendant was serving a sentence for rape and was sentenced to custody for life and 25 years. Held. A clear motive is absent. We conclude that there was a grievance, which ran so deep to cause these offences. That puts it at the upper end of the range of 14 to 20 years. Had it not been that he was serving the rape sentence and his age the sentence might be at the top namely 20. However, **18 years** substituted concurrent to custody for life. [The report does not state the defendant's age or any details of the rape or the sentence for the rape.]

See also EXPLOSIVE OFFENCES – *Kill the victim, intending to*

MUTINY

See PRISON MUTINY

NEWTON HEARING

See GUILTY PLEA, DISCOUNT FOR – *Newton hearing, defendant takes part in*

NOXIOUS THING

For administering etc a noxious thing see OFFENCES AGAINST THE PERSON ACT **1861, s 23** and OFFENCES AGAINST THE PERSON ACT **1861, s 24**

NUISANCE, PUBLIC

See PUBLIC NUISANCE

Where the offence is connected with obtaining money dishonestly see THEFT ETC

Where the offence is connected with harassment see **HARASSMENT (S 4 OR PUBLIC NUISANCE)**

See also **PUBLIC ORDER ACT OFFENCES** and **STALKING**

108   OBSCENE PUBLICATIONS

108.1   (Including videos, the Internet etc.)

Obscene Publications Act 1959, s 2

Publishing an obscene article or having an obscene article for publication for gain.

Triable either way. On indictment maximum 3 years. Summary maximum 6 months and/or £5,000.

Crown Court statistics England and Wales[1] – Crown Court – Males 21+ – Possession of obscene material

108.2

Year	Plea	Total Numbers sentenced	Type of sentence%					Average length of custody (months)
			Discharge	Fine	Community sentence	Suspended sentence	Custody	
2000	Guilty	94	3%	16%	21%	7%	51%	9.2
	Not guilty	23	9%	17%	17%	0%	57%	11

1   Excluding committals for sentence. Source: Crime and Criminal Justice Unit, Home Office Ref: IOS416-02.

Guideline remarks

108.3   *R v Holloway* (1982) 4 Cr App Rep (S) 128 at 131. Fining pornographers does not discourage them. The only way of stamping out this filthy trade is by imprisonment for first offenders and all connected with the commercial exploitation of pornography: otherwise front men will be put up and the real villains will hide behind them.

R v Pace [1998] 1 Cr App Rep (S) 121. The sale of pornographic books, films and tapes on a commercial sale justify sentences of imprisonment for first offenders. The sentences will be comparatively short when appropriate. Salesmen, projectionists, owners and suppliers behind the owners should be at risk of losing their liberty.

R v Tunnicliffe and Greenwood [1999] 2 Cr App Rep (S) 88. There may be cases where prison was not necessary.

Mail order

108.4   *R v Lamb* [1998] 1 Cr App Rep (S) 77. The defendant pleaded guilty to five counts of having obscene articles for gain. Each count concerned a different video. Four involved sadomasochism and one involved animals. Police raided his premises and they found five obscene videos, some video recorders and postage bags and stamps. The defendant said he made his living by running a mail order business. His address book and sales showed the sales were not trivial. He said he had obtained the animal video unintentionally. He was 38 with three similar previous convictions. They involved the sale of pornography on a larger scale than the present offence. He received consecutive offences totalling 5 years. Held. The judge may have been too greatly influenced by the previous convictions. The total exceeded the maximum and was too long. **30 months** on each concurrent substituted.

Sadomasochism and animals

108.5   *R v Lamb* [1998] 1 Cr App Rep (S) 77. The defendant pleaded guilty to five counts of having obscene articles for gain. Each count concerned a different video. Four involved sadomasochism and one involved animals. Police raided his premises and they found five obscene videos, some video recorders and postage bags and stamps. The defendant said he made his living by running a mail order business. His address book and sales showed the sales were not trivial. He said he had obtained the animal video unintentionally. He was 38 with three similar previous convictions. They involved the sale of pornography on a larger scale than the present offence. He received consecutive offences totalling 5 years. Held. The judge may have been too greatly influenced by the previous convictions. The total exceeded the maximum and was too long. **30 months** on each concurrent substituted.

Shop assistants

108.6   *R v Pace* [1998] 1 Cr App Rep (S) 121. The defendant was convicted of possessing an obscene article for gain. He worked for about 4 months in an unlicensed sex shop in Soho. Much of the stock was hard pornography. He was there on both days 3 months apart when police raided the shop. He was tried in respect of three videos and acquitted of two. The video he was convicted of showed digital penetration of female anuses and vaginas by the female or other females and scenes of urination, buggery and anal and vaginal 'fisting.' The sentencing judge said he was a 'front man' who was either unable or unwilling to identify the operators of the shop. The defendant was 50 with no relevant convictions. He suffered from a history of depressive illnesses. Held. The sale of pornographic books, films and tapes on a commercial sale justify sentences of imprisonment on first offenders. The sentences will be comparatively short when appropriate. Salesmen, projectionists, owners and suppliers behind the owners should be at risk of losing their liberty. **3 months** was not manifestly excessive.

R v Ibrahim [1998] 1 Cr App Rep (S) 157 – LCJ. The defendant pleaded guilty to 13 counts of possessing obscene articles for gain. They were videos and magazines depicting bondage, flagellation and cruelty to women. There was violence and torture to women which glorify their degradation. No children or animals were depicted. Six articles related to the first police visit. Two to the second police visit and five related to a third police visit. In October 1994 police found the defendant behind a counter in Soho talking to people and pointing to a screen where bound and gagged women were being whipped by a man. He said he was in charge of the premises but refused to answer questions how the business worked. In January 1995 there was another police visit and the defendant was again behind the counter. He said he had been employed for 3 months and his job was to sell the videos and magazines. Six days later he was seen arriving at the shop with another. Two laundry bags of videos were taken into the shop and the defendant said he was in charge of the shop. The defendant had convictions but of a different character. He was sentenced on the basis he was a salesman but not the owner. He received **18 months** on each while the other man received 150 hours' community service at the Magistrates' Court. Held. It is difficult to imagine material more degrading to women. The October matter was a low level offence. He was minding the shop and not taking the profits. **6 months** was appropriate. His later persistent conduct was a serious aggravating factor. The other two groups of offences were worth **12 months** concurrent but **consecutive** to the 6 months. So the original sentence was rearranged but the length was the same.

R v Tunnicliffe and Greenwood [1999] 2 Cr App Rep (S) 88. The defendants T and G pleaded guilty on the day of their trial to having an obscene article for gain. Police officers went to a partitioned-off area of a shop in Manchester which was not licensed and found T behind a till, magazines and videos. The police officer requested videos and T went to the rear of the shop and returned with five videos. The officer asked to look at them. He did so and left. They showed three people having sex and oral sex. Ten days later a search warrant was executed. T was again behind the counter and G arrived saying the shop had nothing to do with him. T admitted selling the videos and receiving 10% of the money paid. The videos were not of the worst kind. None showed children or animals. G's basis of plea was he was allowed to use the flat above in exchange for performing a supervisory role in the shop. He paid the bills and was paid £50 on occasions. T involvement was for 2 months and G's for 4 months. T was 27 and treated as of good character. G was 47 with some irrelevant convictions. Held. We are surprised the Crown asked the Magistrates to decline jurisdiction. There was no evidence that the problem in Manchester was the same as the problem in West End of London at the time of *R v Holloway* (1982) 4 Cr App Rep (S) 128. There may be cases where prison was not necessary. Applying *R v Ollerenshaw* [1999] 1 Cr App Rep (S) 65, **6 weeks** not 3 months for G and **1 month** not 2 for T.

Shop owners

108.7   *R v Singh* [1999] 2 Cr App Rep (S) 160. The defendant pleaded to nine counts of having obscene articles for sale and was committed for sentence. The police visited the defendant's shop and seized magazines. Most were returned and some were destroyed. The defendant continued to sell pornography. A police offer visited the shop and was shown some videos by an assistant (not the defendant). He then asked for 'more unusual stuff.' The assistant went to a back room and came back with two videos depicting acts of torture and 'anal fisting.' A week later a search warrant was executed and videos and magazines were seized. [The report does not indicate what seven of the counts related to.] He was 52 with no convictions and a wife and five children. Held. The police visit should have warned the defendant. **6 months** was fully merited.

See also **PUBLIC DECENCY, OUTRAGING** and **PHOTOGRAPHS OF CHILDREN, INDECENT**

109   OBSTRUCTING A POLICE OFFICER

109.1   Police Act 1996, s 89(2)

Summary only. Maximum 1 month and/or Level 3 (£1,000).

Magistrates' Court Sentencing Guidelines September 2000

109.2   Entry point. Is a discharge or a fine appropriate? Consider the impact on the victim. Examples of aggravating factors for the offence are group action, and premeditated. Examples of mitigating factors for the offence are genuine misjudgment, impulsive action and minor obstruction. Examples of mitigation are age, health (physical or mental), subsequent co-operation with the police, and genuine remorse. **Starting point fine B.** (£100 when defendant has £100 net weekly income. See page 334 for table showing fines for different incomes.)

For details about the guidelines see **MAGISTRATES' COURT SENTENCING GUIDELINES** at page 331.

110   OBSTRUCTING THE CORONER/BURIAL, PREVENTING

Both offences are against the common law. Indictable only. No maximum provided so the maximum is life.

Guideline remarks

110.1 *R v Godward* [1998] 1 Cr App Rep (S) 385 at 388 – LCJ. The defendant pleaded guilty to obstructing the Coroner. The most important factor is the intention of the accused. If it appears that the intention was to obstruct the course of justice by disposing of or concealing a body, and so making it difficult or impossible to bring home a charge against the defendant or another person, then the offence merits a sentence at the top endof the appropriate scale.

Obstructing the Coroner

110.2 *R v Godward* [1998] 1 Cr App Rep (S) 385 – LCJ. The defendant pleaded guilty to obstructing the Coroner. She complained to the police that her boyfriend who had recently been released from prison had broken into her flat. Officers visited the flat and noticed a strong smell and discovered a body in a cupboard. It had been there for over five months. Parts were severely decomposed and it was infested with maggots and flies. The hands of the deceased were tied behind his back with cords, which secured a bloodstained towel. He was wearing only a vest and socks and there were slash marks. In the cupboard was a pair of bloodstained trousers. Pathologists found no fractures or wounds to the body and there were no signs of a heart attack or stroke. It was impossible to certify a cause of death. The deceased was 51 and he had had a sexual relationship with the defendant. There was evidence that the defendant was violent and domineering towards him. The defendant said she left him in her house with a prostitute and another woman and returned to find the deceased slumped on the floor. She realised that he was dead and she and one of the women put him in a cupboard. She was in a state of blind shock and panic. Before the body was found police had twice called on her when they were trying to trace him after he was reported missing. The judge said he did not accept her explanation and that there had been some form of violence but she was not necessarily involved in it. Held. It was not possible to infer that her intention was to conceal from the authorities that violence had occurred. It is at least possible and perhaps more likely that the defendant's intention was shock and panic. There was persuasive evidence that the smell had preyed on her imagination and had been a form of torment. **3 years** not 4.

Preventing burial

110.3 *R v Peddler* [2000] 2 Cr App Rep (S) 36. The defendant, a heroin addict, pleaded guilty to preventing the burial of a corpse. Residents complained of a foul odour at his flat and the police attend and found a badly decomposing body. It was estimated death had taken place six weeks before. The defendant said the deceased had wanted heroin and may have used his syringe, which contained heroin of great strength. He said he was frightened because the circumstances were similar to those when his wife died. He was 37 and had a long list of previous convictions. Held. 18 months was appropriate. However, because he had now rehabilitated himself from drugs and his partner had MS, **12 months** not 18 months.

R v Whiteley [2001] 2 Cr App Rep (S) 119. The defendant, a heroin addict, pleaded guilty to conspiracy to prevent the burial of a corpse. He also failed to answer his bail for which he received 3 months consecutive. The deceased, D, a heroin addict, and recently released from prison arrived at a block of flats either drunk or under the influence of drugs. He was unsteady, muddled and drowsy. At 10.30pm a neighbour heard an occupant of the flat of his girlfriend say, 'Take him out of the flats.' Later she heard an occupant say he was unable to move D. She next saw D being dragged to a green at the rear of the flats. His body was next taken wrapped in a carpet, curtain and newspapers to a ditch in a country lane. He was found three days later and death had been caused by opiate poisoning. The flat was described as a drugs den. The defendant was arrested and said they panicked and he had bought a car to dispose of the body. He had also helped with the wrapping of the body. He was 35 and had two drug convictions and a conviction for possession of a bladed article. Held. It was a serious offence capable of interfering with the administration of justice and causing real grief to the bereaved. As the defendant was not present at the time of the death, so didn't make the initial decision and because he had fewer convictions and played a lesser role than his co-defendant who received 30 months, **18 months** not 30.

See PERVERTING THE COURSE OF JUSTICE/CONTEMPT OF COURT ETC – *Evidence, interfering with – Bodies*

OBSTRUCTIONS ON A RAILWAY LINE, PLACING

See RAILWAY OFFENCES

OBTAINING PROPERTY AND SERVICES BY DECEPTION

See DECEPTION, OBTAINING PROPERTY AND SERVICES BY; where the offence is in essence theft it is listed under THEFT ETC

111 OFFENCES AGAINST THE PERSON ACT 1861, S 18

111.1 Indictable only. Maximum sentence life.

It is a specified offence for automatic life.

The division of the cases into categories does not mean that each category has its own sentencing tariff. The number of categories only indicates how many cases have been reported recently.

Where the offence was committed relevant to a football match and where there are reasonable grounds to believe that making a banning order would help to prevent violence or disorder at or in connection with any regulated football match; the court must make a Football Banning Order, under the Football Spectators Act 1989, s 14A and Sch 1, para 1.

It is a violent offence for the purses of passing a longer than commensurate sentence [Powers of Criminal Courts (Sentencing) Act 2000, s 80(2)] and an extended sentence (extending the licence) [Powers of Criminal Courts (Sentencing) Act 20000, s 85(2)(b)].

Crown Court statistics England and Wales – Crown Court – Males 21+ – 'Wounding or other act endangering life'[1]

111.2

Year	Plea	Total Numbers sentenced	Type of sentence%					Average length of custody[2] (months)
			Discharge	Fine	Community sentence	Suspended sentence	Custody	
2000	Guilty	490	0%	0%	5%	2%	88%	45.3
	Not guilty	435	0%	0%	1%	1%	96%	52.9

1 It is assumed this means s 18. Source: Crime and Criminal Justice Unit, Home Office Ref: IOS416-02.
2 Excluding life sentences.

Guideline remarks

111.3   *A-G's Reference (No 44 of 1994)* [1995] 16 Cr App Rep (S) 865 – LCJ. The general level of sentencing for an offence under s 18 is of the order of 4 years and upwards. It is frequently a misconception that unless some object is held in the hand, no weapon has been used. An attacker who uses shod feet, or who bites someone is just as much using a weapon as someone who wields an object in his hand.

A-G's Reference (Nos 59, 60 and 63 of 1998) [1999] 2 Cr App Rep (S) 128 – LCJ. All offences under s 18 are serious because they involve the deliberate or intentional causing of serious injury. Some instances are more serious than others: the use of a firearm, a razor, a knife, a broken bottle, a club, a baseball bat, or a pick helve, or something of that sort, has usually been held to aggravate the offence. The courts have also, however, been obliged to recognise that injuries of almost equal seriousness can be caused by kicking with a shod foot or biting. It is also of course possible to inflict serious injury with the bare fist, although this is usually regarded as less serious, partly because in that instance the offender may lack the premeditation usually shown by a defendant who has armed himself with a dangerous weapon. Perhaps the least inexcusable example of an offence under s 18 is where a defendant entitled to defend himself responds with unreasonable and excessive force directed against an aggressor. Even then a custodial sentence, probably of some length, will usually be appropriate. In any other case a custodial sentence will almost invariably follow.

A-G's Reference (No 29 of 2001) [2001] EWCA Crim 1491, [2002] 1 Cr App Rep (S) 253. A sentence of only 18 months, without the benefit of a plea will only be merited in the most exceptional circumstances. The essence of the offence which marks it out for a substantial custodial sentence, is the specific intent to do serious bodily harm, which even in cases of provocation or stress simply cannot be excused. In s 18 cases the court is less flexible in its approach than in relation to lesser assaults and is much less inclined to leniency in the face of personal mitigation. Nonetheless in appropriate cases, the courts will be merciful and sentences towards the bottom end of a wide ranging band which is likely to range between 2½ years when the injury is relatively minor, and the circumstances of the offence and the defendant deserving of leniency, up to as much as 10 years in the case of horrific or sadistic injuries where mitigating circumstances are absent.

Acid etc attack

111.4   *R v Newton* [1999] 1 Cr App Rep (S) 438. The defendant was convicted of GBH with intent and robbery. The defendant was having extreme difficulty in coming to terms with the separation from his wife. He bought paint stripper and was warned it would burn. He discussed it with the safety officer at work. It contained phenol capable of causing serious burns to skin and eyes. He added hydrochloric acid to the mixture and put it in Flash bathroom cleaner bottle. It was potentially cancer inducing. He went to the shop his wife worked at on a motor cycle wearing a motor cycle helmet, balaclava and gloves. He paid for a packet of cigarettes and when the wife opened the till he squirted the mixture into her face. She ran to the storeroom and he followed her. He sprayed more of the mixture on her front, head and back. He ran back into shop and stole £65 and some cheques. The wife was in extreme pain. The burns covered about 10% of her body. She was in hospital for 5 days. Her burns healed remarkable well. After the police had released the defendant, an anonymous letter was received by the police saying he would be attacked. He staged a fake attack on himself. The judge described him as evil, vengeful and scheming. He had no previous convictions. **12 years** for the GBH not 15 and 8 not 10 concurrent for the robbery.

R v Jones [1999] 1 Cr App Rep (S) 473. The defendant was convicted of GBH with intent and false imprisonment. In a gangland feud the defendant was seeking revenge. The defendant, the victim and others were involved in a substantial credit card fraud. He maintained that the victim owed him several thousand pounds and made attempt to recover it. The victim stopped his car to make a telephone call. The defendant sprayed him with acid from a squeezy bottle shouting abuse. The victim tried to run away and the defendant followed squirting the acid over his face and arms. The victim was put in his car and questioned about the money while the car was being driven. His requests to be taken to hospital were ignored. The defendant jumped out at some traffic lights. The acid had ¾ hour to wreak havoc on his face. He had extensive full thickness burns and the loss possibly permanently of an eye. The defendant was 30 and had nine court appearances for criminal damage, burglary, theft, drugs, two ABH and other matters. The defendant was sentenced for conspiracy to defraud for the credit card offences and possession of a loaded firearm and received 4 years imprisonment. Held. **16 years** for the GBH was in the proper range for such a determined, remorseless and vicious attack. The fact the victim was a former confederate does not necessarily entitle him to a discount. However, the sentence should have been concurrent not consecutive to the 4 years.

R v Carrington [1999] 2 Cr App Rep (S) 206. The defendant was convicted of GBH with intent. The victim and the defendant lived together for almost 6 years. She asked him to leave her flat, which he did. He agreed to pay his contribution to the bills. The following day he visited her and she was unrelenting. She asked him to leave and he became rather upset. Some time later he approached her when she was on the way to work. He said he wanted to talk to her. She stepped back, saw a Lucozade bottle and liquid was thrown on her face. She ran into her work place and colleagues doused her face with water. She spent 1 week in hospital. Gradually her eyes improved and she no longer suffers from any disability. She was expected to have eye discomfort up to 8 to 11 months after the attack. For a period after that they would feel abnormal. The damage to her clothing was consistent with sulphuric acid. Had she not received prompt assistance there could have been very severe consequences for her sight. The defendant was 57 and showed no remorse. 9 years previously he had a conviction for ABH on his wife. Held. Despite his ill health **6 years** was appropriate.

R v Rai and Robinson [2000] 2 Cr App Rep (S) 120. The defendants K and E was convicted of conspiracy to commit GBH with intent. E was also convicted of GBH. K's girlfriend broke off the relationship when he went to prison because she did not want to mix with criminals. He would not accept it was over and pestered her and her family over the telephone. The calls also contained threats, like, 'If I can't have you, then no-one can'. On his release he was warned by the police to stay away from her. He continued to call her and was twice more warned. To stop him calling she said she was going to marry someone else but he followed her and drove past her when she was in the street. She walked to work and E who had been in prison with K threw concentrated nitric acid over her from a bottle. Perhaps anticipating the attack she moved her head and the acid hit the side of her head. The side of her head and her neck dissolved. She suffered the most acute agony. She was taken to hospital and she lost her right ear with significant scarring to her face, neck, scalp and chest. Her facial appearance was altered. Seven months later K called her again. The judge passed longer than commensurate sentence of 15 years. He did not state that the reason was their propensity to violence. Held. The injuries were horrific. It was unnecessary to extend the sentence, as **15 years** was not inappropriate. (The previous convictions were not listed.)

Old cases. *R v Ismail* (1991) 13 Cr App Rep (S) 395.

Baseball bat, plank of wood etc

111.5   *A-G's Reference (No 56 of 2000)* [2001] 1 Cr App Rep (S) 439. The defendant was convicted of wounding with intent. The victim after drinking went to stay in someone's house and among others there was the defendant aged 27 whose group had also been drinking. That group was watching an adults only channel on television which caused some embarrassment to the women in the victim's group. There was an atmosphere, which led to words being exchanged. The victim and one of the women went into the garden. After a while one of the woman complained that the defendant had tried to kiss her. The victim told the defendant that he should leave the house. There was a baseball bat by the front door. At some stage, the victim picked up the baseball bat and took it outside. An argument developed about some property being taken to the garden where some people were going to sleep. The baseball bat was passed to victim and then seized by the defendant. The defendant then struck the victim on the head with the bat three times, twice when he was on the ground. One of the women tried to get between the defendant and the victim, but the defendant side-stepped her and kicked the victim in the stomach. The victim had two wounds, one 10 cmlong and the other 6 cm long, which required stitching. He had bruising on his arm. The judge accepted that the offender had struck the first blow in the mistaken belief that the victim had been intending to hit him with the bat. The offender was of good character and had expressed remorse. He was sentenced to 200 hours' community service and £1,500 compensation. He had carried out just over 160 hours' community service. Held. We would have expected a sentence within the bracket of **2 to 3 years**. Taking into account it was a reference and one where he will now looe his liberty for the first time and he had performed a substantial amount of the community service **9 months** substituted with the outstanding amount of the compensation quashed.

Biting

See **Fighting – Biting**

Burglary, and

See **Robbery/Burglary, and**

Children against

See CRUELTY TO CHILDREN – **Cruelty to Children – Offences Against the Person Act 1861, s 18**

Defendants aged under 21 – Guidelines

111.6   *A-G's Reference (Nos 59, 60 and 63 of 1998)* [1999] 2 Cr App Rep (S) 128 – LCJ. In sentencing young offenders the court will of course have regard to the welfare principle expressed in s 44 of the Children and Young Persons Act 1933: the younger the offender the less the justification in any ordinary case for treating the offender exactly as if he or she were an adult. It must be recognised that an effective means of protecting the public in the future is to reform a criminal whether young or old. Sentencers must, however, always bear in mind that the welfare of the young offender is never the only consideration to be taken into account. When an offender, however young, deliberately inflicts serious injury on another there is a legitimate public expectation that such offender will be severely punished to bring home to him the gravity of the offence and to warn others of the risk of behaving in the same way. If such punishment does not follow, public confidence in the administration of the criminal law is weakened and the temptation arises to give offenders extra-judicially the punishment, which the formal processes of law have not given. When we speak of the public we do not forget the victim, the party who has actually suffered the injury, and those close to him. If punishment of the offender does little to heal the victim's wounds, there can be little doubt that inadequate punishment adds insult to injury.

Defendant aged under 14

111.7   *R v Haley* [1998] 2 Cr App Rep (S) 226. The defendant pleaded guilty to GBH with intent. Two girls persuaded the victim aged 13 to go to a flat. At the flat the defendant and another were there and the victim was accused of stealing a benefit book. The defendant aged 12 and one of the girls kicked and punched the victim. The victim was threatened with a ferret and was twice burnt with a cigarette. She was given the opportunity to confess and then the kicking would start again. It lasted for about 1½ hours until the occupier returned. The victim had severe bruising and abrasions to her head, face back and chest. She also had burns and remains severely disturbed by the experience. The defendant had no convictions. He had had a very disturbed childhood. He was in care and had many expulsions from school because of disruptive behaviour and fighting. Held. The offence could properly be described as torture. We have considered the extreme youth of the victim and the sustained nature of the detention and the attack. **3 years** detention was upheld.

A-G's Reference (Nos 60 and 61 of 1997) [1998] 2 Cr App Rep (S) 330. The defendants were convicted of wounding with intent. The defendant W aged 12 enquired of another girl whether she had been writing things about someone. She denied it. B also 12 handed W a razor blade and said 'Go on, slash her.' They approached another girl aged 14 and asked her the same question. She also denied it. W hit her across the face with the razor blade. She needed 26 stitches and is permanently scarred. B had convictions. Three days before the offence a supervision order had been made for theft, two assaults with intent to resist arrest, assault on police and obstruction. Less than 3 weeks before the wounding she committed ABH and robbery. Six weeks after the wounding she committed affray. In the same month and 3 months later she committed three criminal damage offences. W had no convictions. The judge imposed a supervision order on each. W had responded well to it. Held. If they had been adults a sentence of 5 years would have been imposed. Taking into account it was a reference, B sentence increased to **18 months** detention and W's to **12 months**.

Defendant aged 14–15

111.8   *R v Baldwin* [1997] 2 Cr App Rep (S) 260. The defendant pleaded guilty to wounding with intent. The defendant who was just 15 and friends were refused entry to a party because they were uninvited and drunk. ¾ of an hour later near the party the defendant threatened and attacked a 15-year-old girl who had left the flat to use a telephone. The police were called and the girl did not want to pursue the allegations. The police took the defendant home and left him there. The defendant however left home with a very sharp kitchen knife taped to his arm. He approached the victim who was carrying some drink in a bag on his way home from work. He asked for a can of drink and was refused. The defendant pulled the knife out and pointed it at the victim. A scuffle developed and the defendant's friends tried to pull him off. However, the defendant managed to stab the victim once. He walked away as his friends stopped a passing motorist who took the victim to hospital. He had a deep wound, which was sucking in air. His left lung had collapsed. A drainage tube saved his life. His behaviour when in foster care awaiting trial was impeccable. He showed a very high degree of remorse. Held. This was an appalling crime. To go out armed after you have been brought home after already being in trouble with a knife taped to your arm is conduct, which can only be treated with extreme gravity. His report was about as good as you could have. We agree the end of the sentence must not be out of sight. Taking into account the welfare provisions of Children and Young Persons Act 1933 and the mitigation **4 years** detention not 5.

R v Fokrul Islam [2001] EWCA Crim 2950, [2002] 2 Cr App Rep (S) 118. The defendant pleaded guilty to robbery and GBH with intent. He was acquitted of racially-aggravated GBH with intent. The victim, a 75-year-old man was walking home with a bag, which contained a flask and his cap. The defendant who was in a group of three approached him, grabbed the plastic bag and punched him. The victim struggled and he either fell or was pushed to the ground. He was then kicked in the head on a number of occasions. The victim became disorientated and confused. He was taken to hospital and he had facial swelling, a virtually closed eye, cuts over and under that eye, a broken nose, fractures to his cheekbone and both orbital rims. He had a number of operations with plates and splints inserted. He was there for 10 days and was unable to go home so went to a rest home. He needed new teeth, had problems with his balance and nose. Seven months later he had not recovered. The defendant boasted about it to friends. He was 14 with findings of guilt for ABH, battery and burglary. The pre-sentence report said he showed remorse. Held. The injuries are truly horrific. Age has to be looked at in the greatest detail. This joint attack with shoes or boots compares with those where weapons are held in their hands. **4 years** detention was in no way manifestly excessive.

See also *R v Tabu* [2002] EWCA Crim 626, [2002] 2 Cr App Rep (S) 500.

Defendant aged 16–17 – Baseball bat, plank of wood etc

111.9   *A-G's Reference (Nos 56 and 57 of 1996)* [1997] 2 Cr App Rep (S) 286. The defendants were convicted of wounding with intent and affray. M was also convicted of common assault. The defendants M then 16 and S then 21 were brothers spent New Year's Eve drinking and afterwards outside S's home an argument developed between S and his girlfriend. A group of loud boisterous people who had been drinking passed the house and approached the defendants. The defendants went inside to arm themselves with a golf club and mop handle. A fight developed. They kicked one of them after he had been knocked down and was lying curled up and defenceless. They also used their weapons on him. Someone from the group tried to intervene and was attacked with the weapons with such force the head came off the club and the mop handle broke. The first victim was taken to hospital with wounds to his head, the bridge of his nose and under his eye were stitched. He also had bruises to the head, neck and shoulders. The second victim did not go to hospital and had a swollen and cut head. M told the police the group had interfered with their argument. He said the group had tried to kick in the front door. There was no damage to the door. The judge said the truth lay somewhere between the two conflicting versions and there was an element of provocation and self defence. S was on bail for one offence at the time of the offence and M two offences. S had convictions for breach of the peace and causing harassment etc. That offence related to a fight. M had no convictions when the offence took place. Since then he had pleaded guilty to attacking a fish and chip shop owner after he had accused him of being gay. He had also been convicted of affray after he and others had entered a supermarket where a member of staff was beaten up and the defendant had produced an air pistol and threatened to kill a member of staff. He was given a community sentence order for both incidents. Both were sentenced to a Community Service Order and had completed their of 180 and 200 hours and M had paid the compensation of £400 ordered. Held. Making the most generous assumptions in favour of the defendants the appropriate sentence would have been between **12 and 15 months**. Because of their behaviour since and the circumstances the Community Service Orders would not be altered.

Defendant aged 16–17 – Bricks etc

111.10 *A-G's Reference (No 18 of 1998)* [1999] 1 Cr App Rep (S) 142.The defendant pleaded guilty on the day after his trial was due to start to wounding with intent. He was also committed for sentence for dangerous driving and disqualified driving. At 10.30pm outside a supermarket, the defendant then 16 approached the victim aged 18 apparently looking for a fight. A fist fight developed. The defendant picked up a brick and threw it in the victim's face causing heavy bleeding. As the victim staggered away the defendant threw the brick again into his face with full force. A friend intervened. The victim required 30 stitches. He suffered severe headaches. He was permanently scarred. He lost 2% of his vision in one eye. He feels nervous when he goes out alone. The defendant had 24 convictions for burglary, theft, criminal damage, ABH and offences in relation to motor cars. He had been sentenced to detention three times. One of the two ABH convictions was with a baseball bat on a woman. She was hit on the head and required seven stitches. He was sentenced to 1 year and 6 months consecutive for the driving offences. Held. The appropriate total was 4 years detention. As it was a reference **3 years** detention substituted.

Defendant aged 16–17 – Glassing

111.11 *A-G's Reference (Nos 36 and 37 of 1998)* [1999] 2 Cr App Rep (S) 7. The defendants L and J pleaded guilty to false imprisonment and L pleaded guilty to wounding (the October incident). J also pleaded to wounding with intent and unlawful wounding and L also pleaded guilty to affray (the September incident). In September at about 9.25pm the defendant J then 17 picked a fight with one of a group of students and punched one of them in the mouth and face several times. He then took a bottle of beer off the victim and smashed it over his head. The students made off. L then 15 and J pursued them throwing rubbish from a skip at them. A passer-by was walking her dog and J attacked her with a broken bottle. She had a 3" wound to her cheek and 1" wounds to her nose and chin. For a number a weeks she could not talk properly or eat solid foods and she was off work for 9 weeks. The defendants were released on bail and about 4 weeks later at about 9pm J and L approached a group of teenagers. J jumped on one of them aged 16, and started to struggle with him. L threatened the group, and was restrained by a member of his group. J then said to L 'Come on, let's go and get the filthy Paki'. J and L then followed three of them to a path running along a lake. J and L forced the three to climb over the gate into the park and threatened to 'batter' or kill them. Once in the park the three were forced to sit upon a bench. J punched one of them in the face and pushed a lighted cigarette into his face causing burn marks. L forced him against a tree, and J said he was going to kill him. The three were terrified and ran away, with L in pursuit. One climbed over some spiked railings, and suffered a 5 cm and 2 cm cut to his thigh. Both were deep. This was L's wounding charge. One of the tree managed to run away and the third was forced by J and L to walk across the park until he too escaped. The three teenagers were so terrified that they were unable to estimate the period of time during which they had been detained. Both J and L were arrested and when interviewed disputed the victims' account of events. J had an ABH conviction involving an attack with two others on a man in the early hours. The man was knocked to the ground, kicked and punched. J had also been cautioned for affray and assaulting a police officer. J had a serious history of drug and alcohol abuse. J received 3½ years for the wounding with intent and 6 months for the false imprisonment. Held. The intimidation of the teenagers was deliberate and sustained and the offence had a very unpleasant racist overtone, which demanded an immediate custody. Had J pleaded not guilty a total of **7 years** detention would have been appropriate for the s 18 and false imprisonment offences. On a plea of guilty

5 years would have been merited. Taking into account it was a reference and the false imprisonment **4 years** detention for the s 18 offence.

A-G's Reference (Nos 59, 60 and 63 of 1998) Re O'Brien [1999] 2 Cr App Rep (S) 128 – LCJ. The defendant, O was convicted of GBH with intent. The victim challenged O about some rumours O was said to have spread. O denied the matter and the victim became annoyed. The victim then punched O in the face and a fight began. After a few minutes the victim and O became tired and stopped. The victim had had the better of the fight. O, nursing a cut lip, entered a local shop was in a 'very excited mood' and asked to borrow a toy cricket bat so that he could hit someone with it. He left the shop empty-handed. O then approached the victim, holding an empty beer bottle, which he broke against a lamp-post and then ran at the victim, holding it. The victim ran but fell. O caught up with him and stabbed him more than once to the body using the broken bottle, causing immediate heavy bleeding. Someone pulled O back and O ran. Two builders ran to the victim's assistance he was taken to hospital in their van. He had a ½ cm cut to his arm, a 4 cm superficial laceration to his chest and a deep laceration to his left armpit. He had lost a substantial loss of blood. The main artery to the arm had two large wounds in it and the main vein to the arm was completely divided, as were several major nerves, which provided nerve supply to the left arm. His operation lasted some 5 hours. The armpit wound was life threatening. The prompt actions of the builders helped to prevent a fatal consequence. The victim remained in hospital for a week. On his discharge he was unable to use his left arm, which was devoid of any feeling. He continues to be disabled with regard to his arm. He has had to learn to write with his other hand and is permanently scarred. O admitted that he had been involved but contended that it was self-defence. O had one conviction when 14 for robbery. He had shown remorse and had a good employment record. O received a £1,000 compensation and combination order. Since the sentence favourable reports had been received. Held. Following a contested trial the appropriate sentence, even for someone of this age, would have **5 years** detention. It was right to make a very substantial reduction to reflect the efforts, which the offender has undoubtedly made. **3 years** detention substituted. The compensation order was quashed.

Defendant aged 16–17 – Kicking man on ground

111.12   *A-G's Reference (No 51 of 1996)* [1997] 2 Cr App Rep (S) 248. The defendant pleaded guilty to wounding with intent and robbery. In the early hours of the morning in a town centre the defendant who was worse for drink and two others approached the victim. The victim recognised one of them and conversation developed while the defendant went behind a wall and came back with half a brick. He threw the brick which hit the victim and the defendant and others chased him. He escaped and then was seen again. This time the defendant had a bottle with him. There was the sound of breaking glass and the defendant was found on the ground. The defendant made off saying, 'He's dead. I've murdered him. Leg it.' Police found him with a very deep gash and swelling to his left eye. At hospital the victim was found to have 2½ cm laceration which required stitching in two layers. He had another laceration to his eyelid and a piece of skin was missing. The defendant said he did it for no particular reason and admitted jumping on his head. The case was there was 6–7 stamps on the head. He had one conviction for assault with intent to rob committed 1½ months after this. He received 100 hours' community service. Held. The seriousness of the offence lay in the stamping on the head of a defenceless man. Taking into account the plea, his age, and that it was a reference **3 years** detention not 1 year. [What the robbery referred to is not revealed.]

R v Robinson and McManus [1998] 1 Cr App Rep (S) 72. The defendant M pleaded guilty to GBH with intent. The defendant R pleaded guilty to just GBH. The white defendants who were drunk came across the victim who was black walking home from work. M aged 16 ran after him and knocked him out the way. He was raving and shouting. R aged 18 started pushing him in the chest and grabbing his suit lapels. As he wouldn't let go the victim took a swing at him. R still would not go and a fight ensued. The victim was knocked out. A witness saw M punch him to the ground and kick him in the head. The witness moved in between them. Punches were thrown at him and the M continued to kick the victim. The witness ran and was chased by R. M then jumped on the victim's head. The victim required 22 stitches to his head and face. He had multiple lacerations round the eye. There was a danger his retina might become detached. His scarring to his right eye might be permanent. His headaches and vertigo would take several months to resolve. He was afraid to leave his home. R plea was based on a late participation in the joint enterprise and preventing the witness from assisting the victim. Held. It wasn't racially motivated but it was horrific. Taking into account the mitigation particularly the remorse **4 years** detention not 3 for M and **2 years** not 3 for R.

Defendant aged 16–17 – Knives

111.13   *A-G's Reference (Nos 30 and 31 of 1998)* [1999] 1 Cr App Rep (S) 200. The defendants pleaded to GBH with intent. At 10.30pm, the defendant K then 16 who was with 15–20 other youths in the street, ran towards the victim. K challenged him about an earlier incident and held him in a headlock. K punched him several times on the head and held his hands while others struck him. G also hit him with a crutch. The victim fell to the ground and G hit him across the back of the head with a crutch. K kicked him on the head. K jumped in the air and landed with both feet on the victim's head. Others asked him to stop and he carried on. It only stopped when someone said he had been killed. An ambulance arrived and his pulse was found to be weak. There were no fractures or brain damage. He was confused. He had bruising, lacerations and grazing. He was in hospital for 2 weeks. He had unreliable memory problems. He required psychiatric counselling. He made a remarkable complete physical recovery. G admitted punching him five or six times and kicking him in the face. G had a conviction for damaging property. K had convictions for common assault, handling, burglary, damaging property and possession of an offensive weapon. He had had a short sentence of detention. Held. Taking into account the ages of the defendants, the mitigation, the plea and it was a reference K **21 months** detention and G **12 months** detention not 8 and 4 months.

A-G's Reference (Nos 59, 60 and 63 of 1998) Re Hussein [1999] 2 Cr App Rep (S) 128 – LCJ. The defendant Hussein, H pleaded guilty to wounding with intent. H aged 16 and the victim aged 17 attended the same school. They were both queuing up for lunch and H pushed in front of the victim and others in the queue. The victim objected and a teacher intervened H was told to leave. Both H and the victim swore at each other. The H left threatening to hit the victim. A teacher spent 10 minutes trying to calm him down. After lunch H confronted the victim and challenged him to a fight. The victim was reassured by H and his friends that it would only be a fist fight involving the two of them. One of the H's friends assured the victim that H did not have a knife. H raised his open hands in the air to confirm that that was so. H and the victim then walked to a small car park followed by a large group of other pupils wanting to watch the fight. A fist fight started. The victim appeared to be getting the better of H, which involved punching and kicking. three of H's friends tried to join in by kicking out at the victim. They were, however, stopped by the others. The victim, fearing that the offender's friends would try and join in again, decided to stop the fight. He turned away from H to return to school. H produced a knife, which he had concealed in his clothing, and he stabbed the victim in the back with it. The victim immediately ran off, pursued initially by the offender and ran down onto a railway track in order to escape. He was found slumped at the side of the track in a semi-conscious state. The victim had a single stab wound to his back. The knife had penetrated the chest and cut the lung, causing severe internal bleeding. The victim was left with a permanent and disfiguring scar to his back. H's record contained some minor offences of theft. H had spent 5 months in a secure unit and had shown 'a good deal of remorse'. He had responded well to that. H was sentenced to a supervision order with attendance at a Youth Justice Centre. The Centre said H's attendance had been excellent, both for his time keeping and his level of participation. Held. The proper order on a plea of not guilty would have been of the order of **4½ years** detention. For a plea of guilty the appropriate sentence would have been **3½ years** detention. Because of H's progress **2½ years** substituted.

A-G's Reference (No 75 of 1999) [2000] 2 Cr App Rep (S) 146 – LCJ. The defendant was convicted of wounding with intent. The victim aged 40 left a shop with his young son and heard the defendant's friend swearing. He asked him to be quiet and the defendant aged 17 and his friend told him to 'Fuck off.' The victim asked again for them not to use such language in earshot of his son. The defendant ran up to the victim and a scuffle ensued. The victim tried to defend himself. The victim was held in a headlock and was punched three or four times to the head. They fell to the ground. They got up and the defendant crouched in front of the victim and began swaying as the friend shouted encouragement. The two youths then walked away. They were very drunk. The son was very upset. The victim was bleeding profusely. The defendant was then heard to boast he had laid into the man with a knife. The knife was thrown onto some waste ground. The victim had a 2 cm cut and there was haematoma. He was in hospital for 2 days and a month later he had to have an operation to remove a blood clot. The defendant had no previous convictions for violence and had not served a custodial sentence. The juvenile centre where he was detained spoke highly of him. Held. **4 years** would have been appropriate. Taking into account the mitigation and it was a reference **3 years** detention not 15 months.

R v Reed [2001] EWCA Crim 1371, [2002] 1 Cr App Rep (S) 219. The defendant pleaded guilty to wounding with intent. The victim with friends visited a number of pubs and in one saw the defendant aged 17 looking through a window at one of them. He had been to school with her and she tried to ignore him. The group left the pub and saw the defendant with his friends waiting outside. The defendant's group set about trying to provoke a fight. The victim's group made it clear they were not interested. With no provocation the victim was stabbed in the chest. He then sat on the ground and was kicked in the face. Fortunately there was an ambulance nearby and he was rushed to hospital. He had a stab wound to the lower chest and his chest wall was penetrated. He was in hospital for a week and then had to be re-admitted in a serious condition 4 days later in severe pain. He then remained in hospital for 3 weeks. The defendant was arrested and said he took the knife in case he met a group he disapproved of. He said he just swung and hit the victim. He did not suggest the victim was any threat to him. He was in breach of a conditional discharge for obstructing the police and threatening behaviour. The risk of re-offending was assessed as high. He had a favourable prison report although he had been involved in a fight. Held. We bear in mind his age. It was sheer good fortune the injury was not life threatening. He deliberately set out armed with a knife looking for a fight. Too many young men have knives all too ready to use them on innocent members of the public. Offences of this kind are far too prevalent. **4 years** was not excessive.

Defendant aged 16–17 – Punishing the victim, motive to

111.14 *A-G's Reference (No 25 of 1998)* [1999] 1 Cr App Rep (S) 351. The defendant was convicted of GBH with intent. The victim aged then 16 parked his caravanette in the street and it was damaged. The victim sought to discover the culprit and was told it was the defendant. He and two male friends approached the defendant and the situation escalated. The defendant went into his house and came back armed with a sword and struck the two friends. Neither was cut. The victim and the two friends left to play golf and returned with the victim's uncle and a golf club. Words were exchanged and the golf club was put on the ground. The victim asked the defendant to come round the corner to talk. The defendant then struck the victim in the face with the club. A large area of skin was gouged out and the jawbone was broken. He was in hospital for 3 days. Six metal plates were inserted in his face to repair the fractures. He will be permanently scarred and have shooting pains. The defendant maintained it was self-defence. He had two convictions for ABH, an assault on police and various offences of dishonesty. Before trial he was convicted of burglary and theft. He was sentenced on the basis he felt threatened. Held. Because of the defendant's age, the fact he felt threatened and other mitigation the sentence of **18 months** detention was not unduly lenient.

Defendant aged 16–17 – Robbery/Burglary, and

111.15   *R v Mills Re Holder* [1998] 2 Cr App Rep (S) 128 at 143 – LCJ. The defendant pleaded guilty at the earliest opportunity to wounding with intent. In the early hours he when 16 broke into the home of a couple in their mid 70s. He took a large knife from the kitchen went upstairs and confronted the man who had been disturbed. He demanded money and told the man not to look at him. The wife appeared and he pointed the knife at the man's temple. The man tried to persuade him there was no money. He ignored this and continued intimidating the couple. He started searching and became increasingly aggressive and threatening telling them he would kill them. It seems that he made as if to stab the woman and her husband pushed her backwards and tried to avoid the knife. The man managed to seize the defendant's wrist for a minute and shortly after the defendant left with money and jewellery. In fact the man had been stabbed and he collapsed. He had a punctured lung with injuries to his head and back. He was in hospital for 8 days. The defendant claimed to be very drunk at the time and he had a problem with alcohol. He showed little remorse. The defendant was unemployed with nine findings of guilt mostly for theft and criminal damage. Held. He had menaced this couple and the man was fortunate to survive. **9 years** was entirely appropriate.

A-G's Reference (Nos 33 of 2000) [2001] 1 Cr App Rep (S) 355. The defendant pleaded guilty at a late stage to wounding with intent. He was also committed for sentence for burglary and handling. The defendant entered the flat of a vulnerable man who was something of a recluse through an unlocked door at 1.00 am. The man had an artificial leg, was of low intellect and suffered from depression. He was too frightened to sleep in the bedroom because it had been broken into before. The defendant entered the living room where the victim was and started to shout abuse. The victim went into the bedroom and the defendant followed. The defendant hit the victim with his walking stick till the stick broke. The victim retreated into the kitchen and the defendant followed and repeatedly shouting, 'Motherfucker.' The victim was struck with a saucepan and a crutch. The victim escaped to the front garden and the defendant followed again and attacked him with fists and feet. The blows were aimed at his head and shoulders. The victim fell and the defendant aimed a kick at his head and a neighbour intervened. The neighbour went to call an ambulance and the defendant renewed the attack by running over his body and kicking him. He then left and told a friend a false story to explain his lack of shirt, which was not believed. He took the friend to the front garden and showed him the victim motionless body. He continued to call the victim 'Motherfucker.' The victim had extensive bruising to the head, face, trunk and arm with other bruising. He had a 2 cm laceration on his forehead, which required stitching. Four ribs were fractured. A psychiatrist said the offence had had a serious impact upon his social functioning. He had to be moved to hospital as a place of safety. The defendant was just 16 and on bail at the time. He had three convictions and since the offence he was given a conditional discharge for possession of a bladed weapon, criminal damage and failure to surrender. He showed some signs of remorse. Held. This was a very serious offence because the victim was vulnerable, he was attacked at home, a variety of weapons were used, the attack was sustained and in different areas, there were serious consequences for the victim's physical and mental health and he was on bail. We would have expected **5 years** detention. Taking into account it was a reference **4 years** not 3.

Defendant aged 16–17 – Transport company etc, victim working for

111.16   *A-G's Reference (No 69 of 1999)* [2000] 2 Cr App Rep (S) 53. The defendant pleaded guilty when the case was listed for trial to GBH with intent. The defendant then 16 and a friend boarded a bus. The defendant recognised the driver as someone who had ordered him off a bus before and he told his friend if he tried it again he was going to hit him. The defendant produced a Saver ticket, which the driver thought had an altered date. The defendant became aggressive. The driver took the ticket and asked the defendant to leave. The defendant became irate and produced a knife with a 4 to 6" blade. He then held the driver with his hand and thrust the knife towards the ribs. The driver raised his arm and was stabbed just below the elbow. The friend who had tried to stop it pulled the defendant off the bus. The friend took the knife and gave it to the police. The victim had a 9 cm wound and had an operation to repair the muscles, tendons and nerves. He suffers from weakness in the power of his grip and it was anticipated he would be able to return to work. The defendant admitted it in interview and showed remorse. The defendant had a caution for possession of an offensive weapon namely a knife but no convictions. He spent 6 months in custody awaiting trial. The psychological report described him as on the borderline of mental retardation and naïve and simplistic. He was given probation and had made excellent contact in the 16 weeks since then. It was said if the constructive work continued his risk for re-offending could be reduced from low to medium to very low. Held. Applying *A-G's Reference (Nos 59, 60 and 63 of 1998)* [1999] 2 Cr App Rep (S) 128 the sentence was unduly lenient. We would have expected **3½ years** detention. Taking into account his progress and that it was a reference **2½ years** detention not probation.

Domestic – Men attacking wives and partners, or ex-wives and ex-partners – Less than 5 years appropriate

111.17   *R v Mannion* [1999] 2 Cr App Rep (S) 240. The defendant pleaded guilty to GBH with intent ABH and common assault. After 17 years of married life the defendant's wife left the matrimonial home. About 2 weeks later they met to discuss the end of their marriage and the financial arrangements. The wife returned to where she was living. As she was sitting in her car outside the house the defendant appeared. He opened the car door, struck her in the face and pulled her hair, saying, 'You're not having half. I'll kill you first.' He was angry and walked off. The police arrested him and she suffered from two cuts and a graze. Nine days later his wife spent the evening with a male friend, the victim and they both went home to his house. The victim noticed a car was following their car home. They entered the house. There was a loud banging on the front door. Fearing that it might be the defendant because the victim had received abusive telephone calls from him he asked the defendant's wife to go upstairs. He did not answer the door and rang the police. The defendant smashed the front window and ran upstairs after the victim. The victim tried to barricade the defendant's wife and himself in the bedroom but the defendant burst in and hit him on the head with a small wrench. The wrench belonged to the victim. He beat the victim with the wrench until the victim seized it. He then struck the victim with a hammer. The wife tried to intervene and was repeatedly punched as she tried to intervene. The police arrived and arrested the defendant. The victim had multiple fractures to his arm and lacerations to his head and forehead. The wife had a cut to her eye and bruising to her legs. The defendant said he had employed a private detective to prove to his family that the victim was a confidence trickster. The basis for the plea was he went unarmed to the house to reason with his wife. The victim was armed with a hammer. He did not intend to assault or injure his wife. The defendant aged 56 was effectively of good character. He had many positive attributes. Held. Because the judge strayed from the agreed basis of plea and the mitigation **3 years** not 4. The other 1 month and 12 month concurrent sentences would remain.

A-G's Reference (No 92 of 1998) [2000] 1 Cr App Rep (S) 13. The defendant pleaded guilty at the first opportunity to wounding with intent and assault with intent to resist arrest. In January 1998 after 12 years of marriage the defendant aged 40 separated from his wife, the victim. The wife left taking the three children with her. At 2am on 31 May 1998 the defendant after drinking went to where his wife was living with a hatchet and a kitchen knife. He broke into the house by breaking panes of glass. He climbed the stairs with the knife in one hand and the hatchet in the other and told his wife (who had woken and moved to the landing) that she was a dead woman. He raised the hatchet and hit her on her face with the blunt side. He raised it again and she pulled it from him and tried to take refuge between the children's bunk beds. He began a sustained attack with fists booted feet and she became unconscious. Most of this took place in front of the children aged 13, 10 and 7 one of whom called the police. His 7-year-old son tried unsuccessfully to get the knife off his father. The defendant was present in the house for about 10 minutes. He then left. The victim was taken to hospital and stayed there for 9 days. She had extensive bruising on the back of her neck and shoulder, a huge haematoma on her head, swelling and bruising to both thighs and above the eye, and a huge swelling above the temple. She also had swellings to both ears, both cheeks, her lip, neck, chest and under her armpit. There were no fractures. When police arrested him he stripped to the waste and wielded a wooden walking stick at them and punched an officer a number of times. In interview he said he was devastated when his wife left him. The victim had continuing pain and has lost concentration and memory. The children had sustained distressing consequences also. The defendant at the time was profoundly disturbed following a mining accident, which caused a depressive illness resulting in a change of character. Since the offence he had improved. He had expressed deep and genuine remorse. He had been imprisoned for 3 months for assaulting a police officer during the miner's strike. There were no convictions for the best part of 20 years nor evidence of any prior violence to wife or children. The risk of re-offending was low. The prison report was 'glowing.' Held. Were it not for the exceptional circumstances a sentence very considerably in excess of 4 years would have been appropriate. 2 years was on the border between lenient and unduly lenient. The mitigation was very substantial. The **2 years** sentence was not altered.

A-G's Reference (No 61 of 2000) [2001] 2 Cr App Rep (S) 66. The defendant pleaded guilty to two counts of GBH with intent and unlawfully wounding. The defendant had a relationship with the victim. Both sides claimed the other was violent. The defendant did not accept it was over. On the day of the offence he was at her flat mending her stereo and gave her and her daughter lifts. He said he wanted to see her and he loved her. That evening she went with her father to a public house. He remained nearby parked in a van. They communicated by text messages and she indicated she did not want to see him. He twice offered her a lift. The victim left the public house and as she was walking to a nightclub with a friend he approached her and he was persuaded to leave her alone. He was on CCTV in the town centre from 12–2am. He then approached her in a club and grabbed her by the shoulder and stormed out. A taxi took her and a man to her flat and as they crossed some grass the defendant told the man to get away from her. He lunged at her in the neck, face and back. The man tried to assist her and he later discovered he had a number of cuts to his fingers. The defendant then called the police and said he had stabbed his girlfriend. When they arrived he said he did it and told the police who had arrested the other man that he didn't do anything. Two knives were found on the ground. Her neck wound was 2.5 cm long and was superficial to a major blood vessel. The other wounds were 1.5 and 2 cm long. The defendant was 31 and had no convictions. He told police that he saw them snogging and she taunted him. Held. The appropriate sentence was in the order of **4½ years**. As it was a reference **3½ years** not 3.

Domestic – Men attacking wives and partners, or ex-wives and ex-partners – 5–9 years appropriate

111.18   *A-G's Reference (No 42 of 2000)* [2001] 1 Cr App Rep (S) 393. The defendant pleaded guilty during the trial to four counts of false imprisonment, making a threats to kill, ABH and inflicting GBH. The defendant had a troubled relationship with a 23-year-old woman who from time to time returned to her mother. In June 1997, he slapped her and pulled her by the hair into the cellar. He pushed her into the coal cellar and shut her inside. He released her after two hours. He became angry again and told her to go back in. She did so because she feared an assault. This continued over 4 days although from time to time she was let out. This was the first count.

In July 1997, she gave birth. A week later he punched her and pushed her down the cellar steps and locked her in the coalhouse. He let her out to feed the baby and picked up a crossbow and loaded it with a bolt. He told her he could kill her and get away with it. She believed she was going to be killed. This lasted for about a minute. He punched and kicked her and put a belt round her neck, which he pulled tight. This activity was the second false imprisonment count and the threats to kill.

In November 1997 they moved to a flat. In December he punched kicked her. He grabbed her between the legs and twisted them. He tore her right labia majora, causing her bleeding and immense pain. She said she wanted to end her life and he said, 'go on then' and gave her some Tamazepam tablets, which she took. The offender became extremely violent and pushed her head through a plasterboard wall. He forced her to swallow shampoo to bring up the tablets, which she did. At 9–10pm he tied her to a stool with flex and put a sock in her mouth. He slapped and punched her till the early hours. This activity was the third false imprisonment.

He was then sentenced to 30 months imprisonment for wounding etc which involved fighting men unrelated to the victim. The last false imprisonment was when he punched her, made her undress and tied her to the bedposts. He whipped her back and legs. She had black eyes, cut lips, a swollen face, bruising to her body and wheal marks. The ABH related to when he punched her and pushed a burning cigarette against her chest. This was followed by more punching. The GBH involved an incident when they were out with friends and he slapped her. She refused to go home. He said he would break her jaw. He grabbed her hair and dragged her to the front door. The friends told him to stop. He kicked and punched her in the face. She was taken to the kitchen where it was repeated. She was pregnant again. He banged her head on the floor. She had to be taken to hospital.

He was taking crack or heroin during all the false imprisonments and the occasion of the ABH. He was arrested and she gave evidence at the trial. Just before she was to be cross-examined he pleaded guilty. The defendant had helped police in an unrelated matter. **6 or 7 years** was appropriate. Because it was a reference **5 years** not 30 months, consecutive to 11 months for breach of his licence.

R v Carrington [1999] 2 Cr App Rep (S) 206. The defendant was convicted of GBH with intent. The victim and the defendant lived together for almost 6 years. She asked him to leave her flat, which he did. He agreed to pay his contribution to the bills. The following day he visited her and she was unrelenting. She asked him to leave and he became rather upset. Some time later he approached her when she was on the way to work. He said he wanted to talk to her. She stepped back, saw a Lucozade bottle and liquid was thrown on her face. She ran into her work place and colleagues doused her face with water. She spent 1 week in hospital. Gradually her eyes improved and she no longer suffers from any disability. She was expected to have eye discomfort up to 8 to 11 months after the attack. For a period after that they would feel abnormal. The damage to her clothing was consistent with sulphuric acid. Had she not received prompt assistance there could have been very severe consequences for her sight. The defendant was 57 and showed no remorse. 9 years before he had a conviction for ABH on his wife. Held. Despite his ill health 6 years was appropriate.

A-G's Reference (No 3 of 2000) [2001] 1 Cr App Rep (S) 92. The defendant was convicted of GBH with intent. The defendant had an intermittent relationship with the victim for about 5 years. The defendant returned home about 2am under the influence of crack cocaine. He found the victim and two male friends there and demanded to know what had happened to his motor car. He believed the three had sold it to buy heroin. He was armed with a knife and his manner was threatening. He was also asking for £100 to buy crack. He left and returned carrying a full jug sized kettle of boiling water. He poured it over the victim's back and shoulders. He fetched a sheet soaked in cold water and she wrapped herself in it. She was terribly burnt and in agony. She suffered from 16% to 22% mixed depth burns. Some 80% of her back was scarred. She was in hospital for 3½ weeks. The defendant claimed it was an accident. He had 16 court appearances as an adult. He had convictions for robbery, dishonesty and two for ABH. Held. We would have expected a sentence of **at least 6 years**. Taking into account it was a reference **5 years** substituted for 3.

A-G's Reference (No 89 of 2000) [2001] EWCA Crim 137, [2001] 2 Cr App Rep (S) 309. The defendant pleaded guilty on the day his trial was listed to GBH with intent, ABH and criminal damage. The defendant was married for 18 years and there were a number of incidents of his violence to her. She moved out and he discovered where it she was living. He went there and she would not let him in so he forced his way in. He punched and kicked her. Their younger son went to find help. The older son pleaded with him to stop. The defendant pulled her into the kitchen and armed himself with a wine bottle. A neighbour persuaded him to put it down and he picked up a knife and stabbed her in the abdomen and shoulder. The police arrived and he was arrested. The victim had two wounds one through her liver. The victim of the ABH was someone who the defendant thought was associating with his wife. The victim was driving his car and the defendant parked his car so as to block the victim's route. The defendant opened his car door and struck him a number of times. He pulled his shirt off and kicked the car causing a large indentation, (the criminal damage). The victim had swelling and bruising. The defendant was 37 and had no convictions. Held. The appropriate sentence was **5 years**. As it was a reference **4 years** not 30 months. The time on licence should be extended to 7 years under the Powers of the Criminal Courts (Sentencing) Act 2000, s 85.

R v Symeon [2002] 1 Cr App Rep (S) 211. The defendant was convicted of GBH with intent. He pleaded guilty to an offence under s 20, which was not accepted and was acquitted of attempted murder. The victim moved in with him and she found him extremely possessive and jealous. He tried to control her. The relationship was extremely stormy and the police were called at least once. She broke it off twice but took him back at his request. After about 9 months she moved out and he made abusive and threatening telephone calls to her. He also sent her text messages. She made it plain the relationship was over and she wanted no contact with him. She consulted the police who advised her to obtain an injunction and they warned him to stay away from her. The threatening messages continued and he said the children would have a dead mother and threatened to tell them she was a prostitute. At around midday she arrived from work and received a text message saying he was going to get her for this. Then she received another threatening phone call and he said he had been following her and watched her with another man. At short time later he broke in to the house with a loud crash and ran towards her shouting, 'Prostitute. You're a dead mother. If I can't have you, no one can. I'd rather we both die.' He then punched her several times and started to throttle her. She struggled and fell to the floor and he kicked her repeatedly to the face, nose, chest and body. Suddenly he stopped and he sat on the floor crying saying she did not deserve to live. Seeing he had a knife she ran to a neighbour's house and banged on the door. The neighbours were too frightened to open the door. He followed her shouting, 'I'm going to kill you.' He trapped her in the porch grabbed her hair, dragged her backwards and punched her to the face and chest. She fell to the floor and he kicked her in the head, chest and arms until she lost consciousness. The neighbour called the emergency services and she was taken to hospital. She had four cuts to her scalp the largest of which was 17 cm and exposed the scull bone, It needed 30 stitches. There were cuts and bruising elsewhere to her head, two black eyes, other bruising to her face, neck, hands and legs. She had two broken teeth and suffered from severe headaches for some time. The defendant was arrested and found to have a 9″ knife on him and another knife in his car. He was of good character. Held. This was not a sudden unpre-meditated explosion of violence by a man at the end of his tether marked by immediate remorse. It was a campaign of intimidation of a particularly unpleasant nature despite a police warning. The attack could have proved fatal. **8 years** was not excessive.

Domestic – Men attacking wives and partners, or ex-wives and ex-partners – 10 or more years appropriate

111.19 *R v Newton* [1999] 1 Cr App Rep (S) 438. The defendant was convicted of GBH with intent and robbery. The defendant was having extreme difficulty in coming to terms with the separation from his wife. He bought paint stripper and was warned it would burn. He discussed it with the safety officer at work. It contained phenol capable of causing serious burns to skin and eyes. He added hydrochloric acid to the mixture and put it in Flash bathroom cleaner bottle. It was potentially cancer inducing. He went to the shop his wife worked at on a motor cycle wearing a motor cycle helmet, balaclava and gloves. He paid for a packet of cigarettes and when the wife opened the till he squirted the mixture into her face. She ran to the storeroom and he followed her. He sprayed more of the mixture on her front, head and back. He ran back into shop and stole £65 and some cheques. The wife was in extreme pain. The burns covered about 10% of her body. She was in hospital for 5 days. After the police had released the defendant, an anonymous letter was received by the police saying he would be attacked. He staged a fake attack on himself. The judge described him as evil, vengeful and scheming. He had no previous convictions. **12 years** for the GBH not 15 and 8 not 10 concurrent for the robbery.

R v Moseley [1999] 1 Cr App Rep (S) 452. The defendant pleaded guilty to GBH with intent and wounding with intent. The defendant and the woman (the second victim) intended to get married. However, she became increasingly concerned, disillusioned and depressed about it. She needed medication. She confided in the licensee of a public house (the first victim). She became attracted to him and spent a night with him. She told the defendant who was upset, very angry and for the first time was violent to her. He punched her and the engagement was broken off. He was asked to leave her house where they were living. Later there was much discussion and she said she wanted to be with the first victim. He appeared to accept it and moved out. One night the two victims spent the evening at a nightclub and went back to her house. At about 4 or 5am the defendant entered the house with a wheel brace. The first victim was struck several hard blows to his head and body. She was hit on the head as well. Her pleas to stop were ignored and the attack went on for a while. The defendant went straight to the police. He told them his mind had gone. The first victim had a large depressed fracture of the skull causing permanent disability. He had to be re-educated to read and write and to communicate. He suffered severe headaches. His skin was de-sensitised. His business came to an end. He was unable to go out alone. His stuttering and inability to pronounce many words was unlikely to improve. The second victim had lacerations to her head, which required 18 stitches. She had bruising to her arm and swelling to her hands. She found it extremely difficult to come to terms with what had happened and became something of a recluse. The defendant showed considerable remorse and had no convictions for violence. A psychiatrist did not consider he posed a risk to the public in general. Held. There was no provocation. We accept he was under emotional strain and the attack was out of his normal character. The sentence was severe and the crime merited it. **10 years** in total (6 +4) upheld.

Drug offences, linked to

See Supply of Drugs – *Drug gang using violence*

Extended sentences – (Powers of the Criminal Courts (Sentencing) Act 2000, s 85)

111.20   *A-G's Reference No 89 of 2000* [2001] 2 Cr App Rep (S) 309. Held. 4 years imprisonment was substituted. The court was invited to consider an extended licence. It was plainly a violent offence. The court had to consider whether the licence period would be adequate for the purposes of preventing the commission of further offences and securing his rehabilitation. With 4 years the licence period would be between 4 and 12 months. That would not be adequate so the extension period will be **3 years**. That means 7 years in all he will be subject to an extended sentence. (For more details of the case see *Domestic – Men attacking wives and partners, or ex-wives and ex-partners – 5–9 years appropriate*)

See also Extended Sentences

Fighting – Biting

111.21   *A-G's Reference (No 44 of 1994)* [1996] 11 Cr App Rep (S) 265 – LCJ. It is frequently a misconception that unless some object is held in the hand, no weapon has been used. An attacker who uses shod feet, or who bites someone is just as much using a weapon as someone who wields an object in his hand.

A-G's Reference (No 29 of 2001) [2001] EWCA Crim 1491, [2002] 1 Cr App Rep (S) 253. The defendant pleaded guilty to ABH. She was convicted of wounding with intent and common assault. She was in a pub with her sister and saw a group of workers from a bakery having a belated Christmas party. She used to work there. There had been a dispute between her husband and one of their husbands. Previously the wives had been friends for 15 years. There was an attempt to resolve the dispute and the sister ended up assaulting one of them and being ejected from the pub. The argument continued outside and the defendant struck the woman she had fallen out with. This was the

ABH. At some stage the defendant suffered a blow to the head possibly by hitting the pavement. The situation calmed down and one of the victim's colleagues tried to take her back inside. The defendant grabbed the colleague's hair and pulled her to the ground. This was the common assault. A woman from the bakery, G intervened and there was a struggle with the defendant. G held the defendant's face while the defendant had her hair. G pushed her finger into the defendant's mouth and the defendant bit it. She gripped it for some time. She let go and then bit her nose so some of the flesh was bitten off. The defendant was scratched to the face. G lost the lowest part of her nostril which the police preserved. The graft was unsuccessful. Her injury was disfiguring. She had a small wound to her finger. The first victim had a badly swollen eye and other bruises and swellings to her arms, legs and head. The second victim had hair loss and bruising. The defendant was 41 and of positive good character. She had a stable family, two teenage children and she was suffering stress at the time. The judge said the usual sentence is 3 years and the least he could impose was 18 months. Held. The judge was at liberty to take a lenient view of the case. There was strain at work, the offence was in anger and after a struggle and it was wholly out of character. But it was a vicious attack with permanent disfigurement. The lowest sentence was **2½ years** but because it was a reference the sentence will remain.

Fighting when the major injuries are caused by the fall, not any blow – Guideline remarks

111.22   *R v Coleman* (1992) 13 Cr App Rep (S) 508 – LCJ. The defendant was sentenced for manslaughter. We are considering a person who receives a blow, probably one blow only, to the head or face, is knocked over by the blow and unfortunately cracks his head on the floor or the pavement, suffers a fractured skull and dies. It is to be distinguished sharply from the sort of case where a victim on the ground is kicked about the head. It is to be distinguished sharply from the sort of case where a weapon is used in order to inflict injury. It is to be further distinguished from where the actual blow itself causes the death. This is the case of a fall almost accidentally resulting in a fractured skull. The starting point for manslaughter for this type of offence is 12 months on a plea of guilty. Then one looks at the mitigation and aggravating features. No pre-meditation, a single blow of moderate force, remorse and immediate admissions are all mitigation. Indications that the defendant is susceptible to outbreaks of violence, the assault was gratuitous and unprovoked, more than one blow all tend to aggravate the offence.

R v Hickman [2001] EWCA Crim 239, [2001] 2 Cr App Rep (S) 261. The defendant pleaded guilty to GBH (s 20). The principles in *R v Coleman* [1992] 13 Cr App Rep (S) 508 were applied. (So they would also apply to s 18, but to a lesser extent than manslaughter and s 20 because in a s 18 case there is an intent to cause GBH unlike the other two offences.)

Fire, by

111.23   *R v Griffin* [1999] 1 Cr App Rep (S) 213. The defendant pleaded guilty to arson with intent to endanger life and causing GBH with intent. The defendant was distressed with the break up of his relationship with the victim. He wrote to his family telling them what he was about to do. The victim came to the premises to pick up some clothing and he pointed a knife at her. She was told she would not get out alive and he stabbed her in the chest. He followed her to the bedroom where he locked the door. There was a struggle over the knife in which the defendant received severe injuries to his hands. After this he recovered the knife and stabbed her several times. By now she was having trouble breathing. Further stab wounds were inflicted and she was told to open her legs. The children then knocked on the front door and he told them to go away. He returned to the bedroom and stabbed her once again in the cheek. The victim became unconscious and awoke up to find a burning duvet on the bed. She got up to get away and the defendant pushed her to the floor and threw the burning duvet over her, which she managed to throw off. She lost consciousness but awoke and escaped. She had burns to her shoulders, arms, hands and feet. The defendant had a significant mental illness and some minor previous convictions. Held. Because of the plea and the authorities **9 years** not 11 concurrent for both offences.

R v Parker [2000] 2 Cr App Rep (S) 60. The defendant was convicted of GBH with intent. He had earlier pleaded guilty to arson being reckless whether life would be endangered. The defendant and the victim lived in the same block of flats. They spent an evening together and the defendant in the early hours returned to his flat and decided someone had entered it. He with others went to the victim's other address and would not accept his denials. They took him back to the defendant's flat by car and the victim noticed that the defendant had a petrol can on his lap. After they arrived at the defendant's flat the defendant continued to assert that the victim had entered his flat. He was kept there in all 1 hour. At 10.30pm he said he had till 11.00pm or I'll burn you. As 11.00 drew closer the defendant counted off the minutes. At 11.00pm he unscrewed the lid on the petrol can and the victim felt petrol splashing over his head and body. He then heard the click of a cigarette lighter and the petrol ignited. The victim ran from the flat in great pain. He heard the defendant shouting for him to get his coat off and felt water going over him. He had skin hanging off his chin and elbows and his hands looked as if his fingers had split open. The defendant who had burnt his own hands trying to help had followed him. A motorist took him to hospital. He had 19% burns to his entire head, chest and upper arms. 12% of the area was partial thickness and the remaining 7% was full thickness. He sustained burns to both hands. He had dreadful scarring. The defendant said the victim was his best friend and he would regret it for the rest of his life. He was 27 and had two convictions for possession of an offensive weapon, two public order offences drug possession and dishonesty. **10 years** was in no way manifestly excessive.

See also ARSON – **Arson – Intending life would be endangered** – *Violent attack, part of a*

Glassing – Guideline remarks

111.24   *A-G's Reference (No 20 of 1993)* (1994) 15 Cr App Rep (S) 797 – LCJ. We have been referred to a number of decisions indicating the level of sentence appropriate for 'glassing cases.' In *R v Harwood* (1979) 1 Cr App Rep (S) 354, Lord Widgery LCJ said that nothing less than **3 years** would be appropriate for deliberate glassing. We have been referred to *R v Ronaldson* (1990) 12 Cr App Rep (S) 91, where in circumstances similar to those in the present case a sentence of **5 years** was upheld. Other authorities tend to suggest that the appropriate sentence for offences of this kind is of that order.

A-G's Reference (No 14 of 2000) [2001] 1 Cr App Rep (S) 55. Glassing offences are extremely dangerous. Terrible and permanent injuries can be inflicted in a split second.

Glassing – Less than 3 years' imprisonment

111.25   *A-G's Reference (No 15 of 1998)* [1999] 1 Cr App Rep (S) 209. The defendant pleaded guilty to wounding with intent. The victim who knew the defendant from schooldays saw what he thought was the defendant and others pestering a woman outside a public house. The woman came over and spoke to the victim about it. The victim asked the defendant, 'Do you have a problem with that.' The defendant said, 'No.' About 1½ hours later the defendant, who appeared drunk, approached and threatened the victim. He said, 'I have now got a problem with you.' He was told to go away but he pushed the victim backwards. He was told to go away again but he continued putting his face very close to the victim. Eventually the victim thought he was about to throw a punch and he pushed him and he fell over. Shouts were exchanged. The defendant was told to desist by a friend of his but didn't. He attempted to get round the friend and reach the victim but didn't. He then went into the public house for 3–5 minutes and came out. There was the sound of breaking glass and the victim's face was cut open. He had multiple lacerations. There was a deep 2 cm cut and a deep 3 cm cut. The saliva duct was cut. He was in hospital for a couple of days and will have permanent scarring to the face. The defendant accepted he had a pint glass in his hand. The defendant was then 18. He pleaded not guilty to an offence under s 18 but guilty to s 20. It was set down for trial but there was no time to hear it. The trial was put back and he then failed to answer his bail and had to be arrested. Two months later he pleaded guilty to an offence under s 18. He had a conviction for common assault. He was sentenced on the basis the glass was not broken before the single blow. Held. *A-G's Reference (No 20 of 1993)* (1993) 15 Cr App Rep (S) 797 makes it clear that 6 months was unduly lenient. If the defendant had not been released 2½ years would be substituted. However, as the defendant had been at liberty for 4 months, was in work and now drinks in very small amounts **2 years** substituted.

A-G's Reference (No 79 of 1999) [2000] 2 Cr App Rep (S) 124. The defendant pleaded guilty to wounding with intent. He had earlier pleaded guilty to an alternative s 20 offence. The defendant then 18 had been drinking and was standing outside an Indian restaurant. He had a beer glass from the restaurant in his pocket and the victim, a 20-year-old student seems to have slightly bumped into him. There may have been a mumbling and the victim and his friend walked on. The defendant approached the victim from behind and there was a confrontation. After a very short fight he took the glass from his pocket and smashed it into the victim's face. Immediately the defendant said, 'Oh no, what can I have done?' The victim needed 16 stitches to cuts on his eyebrow, cheek, chin and lip. His scars will be permanent. He suffered from nightmares and from a complex about his face. The defendant had references and an excellent character. He showed real remorse. He received 8 months and had been released from the sentence with a tag. Held. The judge was in error to say in chambers that in the region of 12 months was merited, there no great distinction between ss 18 and 20 and to consider drink as a mitigating factor. Our approach must be tempered by the fact the judge said there was not much to distinguish ss 18 and 20 before the plea. Giving maximum value to the factors in mitigation the least sentence that could properly be imposed was **18 months**. Taking into account his release and that it was a reference we substitute **12 months** detention.

A-G's Reference (No 67 of 1999) [2000] 2 Cr App Rep (S) 380. The defendant pleaded guilty to GBH with intent. The defendant's partner of 3 years left her and started a relationship with the victim. She appeared to accept the situation. In the early hours of New Years Day 1999 she went into a club where the victim was drinking. Someone heard the defendant say while pointing at the victim, 'She's getting it tonight. She is definitely getting it tonight.' The defendant picked up a lager bottle and asked whether it was empty. She was asked what she wanted it for and was informed, 'You'll see in a minute.' She then walked over to the victim and struck the victim in the face with it. It broke quite easily and caused a dreadful wound, which required 17 stitches. The victim was disfigured for life. The defendant surrendered to the police. The defendant was 24 and had a daughter aged 8. Six weeks before the offence she had a miscarriage and she was expecting another child. She suffered from depression. She had convictions for possession of an offensive weapon and prostitution. Held. Taking into account it was a reference **2 years** not probation.

Glassing – 3 years and less than 4 years' imprisonment

111.26   *A-G's Reference (No 67 of 1997)* [1998] 2 Cr App Rep (S) 420 – LCJ. The defendant pleaded guilty to wounding with intent and criminal damage. The defendant's girlfriend had separated from him after a difficult relationship. There had been a number of separations before. The victim and the defendant's ex-girlfriend attended a company party and she invited the defendant back for coffee. When they arrived the defendant appeared and asked, 'What's going on here.' The victim turned round and was struck by a glass bottle. The victim fell to the ground. He was struck again with the bottle. The defendant saw the ex-girlfriend making a telephone call through the window and threw the bottle breaking the window. As it went through it appeared it was still unbroken. The victim required 29 stitches for five lacerations to the face and head. He had bruising and grazing and his glasses were smashed. The defendant admitted he was jealous. He had several convictions for dishonesty and two recent convictions for minor violence. Held. If he contested the allegation **4 years** would have been appropriate. The lowest sentence for plea at first instance was **3 years**. Because it was a reference and he was expecting to be released shortly **2 years** not 14 months.

A-G's Reference (No 24 of 1998) [1999] 1 Cr App Rep (S) 278. The defendant was convicted of wounding with intent. The victim was with his girlfriend at a public house. They went to the bar and the victim was next to the defendant who said something. The victim couldn't hear it and asked the defendant what he had said. The defendant smashed a beer glass into his face. The defendant aged 27 had convictions over 13 years principally for theft, motor vehicle and motoring offences. However, there were offences for two assaults on police, ABH and common assault. He had received for those 3 months detention, probation and a community service order. Held. We would have expected a sentence in the order of **5 years**. However, as it was a reference and the defendant had 7 weeks before his planned release **3 years 9 months** not 2 years.

A-G's Reference (Nos 59, 60 and 63 of 1998) [1999] 2 Cr App Rep (S) 128 – LCJ. The defendant G pleaded guilty to wounding with intent. G then aged 18, and the victim, aged 15, attended a birthday party at a nightclub. G was observed behaving in an intimidating way towards some other youths, who did not include the victim. G accosted a guest who sought to avoid any further confrontation and walked away. However, he told the victim what had happened. The victim then approached G to calm down the situation. He asked the offender what was the problem, but the offender did not respond. The victim then said to the offender, 'Just chill out, it's a party'. About 5–10 minutes later G beckoned the victim to come over to him. An argument developed and G suddenly turned and threw a pint glass into the victim's face. The glass broke, causing immediate wounds to his face and heavy bleeding. The victim was found to have a deep 4 cm laceration to the cheek, which extended down to the bone, a 2 cm laceration across his nose, which also extended down to the bone, a laceration to his lip, and other small superficial lacerations. A fragment of glass was removed from his eye. The victim has received permanent facial scarring as a result of the assault. The attack had a profound effect on his schooling. He was very reluctant to return to school at all because of his embarrassment at his facial appearance and his loss of confidence and interests had been marked. In interview he admitted being drunk. He denied that he had assaulted the victim. He expressed remorse. The offender has some offences of dishonesty on his record, but no violence and no custodial sentences. He was expelled from school. Held. Had the offender pleaded not guilty the appropriate sentence would then have been **4 years** detention. As he pleaded guilty the appropriate sentence would have been **3½ years**. As it was a reference **2½ years** not 18 months.

Glassing – 4 years or more imprisonment

111.27   *R v Dooley* [1999] 2 Cr App Rep (S) 364. The defendant pleaded guilty to wounding with intent. The victim and the defendant were in a public house. The defendant walked passed the victim, stopped walked back, picked up a pint glass, raised it and smashed it into the back of the victim's head. The glass broke and the defendant punched him on the back of the head. The defendant then picked up a chair and raised that. The landlord approached and the defendant left. The victim had four lacerations of 5, 5, 4 and 1½ cm long. He required 17 stitches. When arrested the defendant said the victim called his sister a slag. He was sentenced on the basis the attack had lasted 3 seconds and the victim had discharged himself from hospital on the same day. The defendant had been detained under s 38 of the Mental Heath Act 1959 from 10 months after the offence and it was continuing. It was for intermittent psychotic illness. He had an emotionally unstable personality disorder of the borderline type as well as features of a dyssocial personality disorder. He did not meet the treatment criteria for a mental health disposal. The defendant was 28 with numerous convictions for violence and dishonesty. The longest sentence he had received was 21 months for burglaries. **4 years** not 6.

R v Gould [2000] 2 Cr App Rep (S) 173 – LCJ. The defendant changed his plea to guilty of GBH with intent. He and his friend went drinking together and had an argument about computer games. The defendant stood up and punched his friend to the head and body. The friend tried to defend himself and the defendant picked up a glass and drove it into the area round his ear causing the glass to break. The defendant ran off. The victim had a large, flap laceration, which extended from the neck up over his chin as far as the ear and back. He needed 25 stitches. When interviewed the defendant could not explain his conduct. The defendant was now 21. In 1996 he was convicted of affray. When 19 he was convicted of a Public Order Act 1986 offence and a s 20 offence (6 months). The defendant after drinking and an argument threw a glass at another man causing severe facial injuries. As he ran off he threw a concrete boulder at him which hit the victim's chest. The pre-sentence report referred to a need to control his drinking and develop anger management techniques. The psychiatric report referred to a likelihood of further violent offending. There were references saying he was responsible when not in drink. Held. The **5 years** detention was not at the top of the bracket. It was entirely appropriate.

R v Bishop [2000] 2 Cr App Rep (S) 416. The defendant was convicted of GBH with intent. The victim and the defendant were in the ladies' lavatory in a nightclub together and there was a harmless exchange. An altercation developed involving hair pulling and both of them ended up on the ground. Things calmed down and the victim left the lavatory. Outside the defendant thrust a beer bottle into the victim's face. There was a 15 to 17cm cut to the victim's cheek. The defendant was then 20 with a debilitating disease called Lupus, asthma and eczema. She also had a young son. **4 years** not 6.

R v Reader [2000] 2 Cr App Rep (S) 442. The defendant was convicted of GBH with intent, ABH and criminal damage. Mr Bhangra, Mr Sheldrick and Mr Bhogal went to a public house, then went to buy some food and then Mr Bhangra went back to the public house. When he didn't return Mr Sheldrick went in. There was then an altercation between the three as to whether they should go home. The defendant with a half-full glass of beer approached Mr Bhangra and Mr Sheldrick who were at a van and asked, 'Did you smash my glasses? I hope it was an accident. I'm the only one who smashes glasses.' A girl who he was with told him to stop. He punched Mr

Bhangra in the face and he fell down unconscious. This was the ABH. Other men joined the defendant and he asked, 'What are you doing standing up for a Paki?' The defendant and three others started to kick the van. This was the criminal damage. Someone opened the rear doors of the van and Mr Sheldrick got out and as he stood up the defendant struck him with his glass of beer shattering the glass. The victim had a deep 3cm laceration to his forehead with two superficial lacerations to each side. He was left with scarring and developed depression. When he went out he feared he would be attacked. Mr Bhangra had bruising and soreness to his eye and cheek. The van had dents to its side panels, wings and bonnet. The back door had been pulled off its hinges. Held. As there was a racist motive **4½ years** with other concurrent sentences was appropriate.

A-G's Reference (No 14 of 2000) [2001] 1 Cr App Rep (S) 55. The defendant was convicted of wounding with intent. The defendant who had drunk 5 to 6 pints of lager and the victim aged 17 who had drunk ½ pint of lager were in the same wine bar. The defendant who was tipsy was acting in a partly aggressive manner on the dance floor. He was staring at the victim and his friends. The defendant thought they were laughing at him and he spoke to one of the victim's friends and said, 'Have you got a problem.' The friend said there wasn't and said they didn't want any trouble. He waved a wine glass in the man's face. He then asked, 'Have you got a problem now.' He was told three times they didn't want any trouble. He then picked up a pint glass and waved in the victim's direction. The victim stood up to attract the attention of a doorman and the defendant swung the glass into the victim's face and punched him. The victim bled heavily and became unconscious. He had a deep laceration to his face stretching from the bridge of his nose around the cheek to his lip. His wounds required 44 stitches. The scarring was likely to be permanent. He had problems with his right eye. The defendant said he feared he would be attacked. The defendant was 35 and had six court appearances. Five of which were for public order offences or ABH. He suffered from post-traumatic stress due to an attack on him in 1995. His nose was severed with a knife when he went to the assistance of a publican who was in trouble with some youths. He also had been good in preventing serious clashes between clients at a charity dealing with people with tempers. The risk of re-offending was assessed as high due to mental illness and alcohol. Held. Glassing offences are extremely dangerous. Terrible and permanent injuries can be inflicted in a split second. Taking into account he had been a victim, his charity work and it was a reference **3½ years** not 2.

A-G's Reference (No 43 of 2000) [2001] 1 Cr App Rep (S) 381. The defendant was convicted of wounding with intent. The defendant was separated from his wife and was living with another woman. The wife and the victim were in a relationship. She moved out of the matrimonial home and shortly before the offence she moved back in. In the evening the defendant was seen to be in a rage looking wild and very angry. He was angry because his wife would not leave the matrimonial home. He went to the public house where his wife and her friend were and picked up a wine glass and thrust it into the friend's face. The glass shattered. The victim had a large laceration in his left eye, and lacerations to his forehead and cheek. A piece of glass was protruding from his lower left eyelid. The surgeon said it was one of the most severe ocular injuries he had seen for some time. He had lost virtually all his sight in the left eye and the right eye was at risk of developing symptomatic inflammation. It was becoming very sensitive to light. He was unable to return to work. The defendant was 37 and had convictions for violence. In 1984 and 1996 he was convicted of criminal damage and in 1997 burglary. In 1997 he was convicted of ABH and threatening words with intent to cause fear or provocation of violence. These offences were committed against his wife. He had an excellent work record. Held. This was a very grave offence. Taking into account the mitigation and that it was a reference **5 years** not 3½.

Hammer, bars and shovels etc, with

111.28   *A-G's Reference (No 19 of 1998)* [1999] 1 Cr App Rep (S) 275. The defendant was convicted of two wounding with intent counts and affray. He was committed for sentence for ABH. The ABH matter related to an unprovoked attack on a white victim with a bottle. The victim had just left a restaurant with his girlfriend. The defendant was with three to five Asians. He left sniggering. The victim's nose was cut and his spectacles were broken. He was convicted. While on bail for that offence and 3 weeks after the offence he made an unprovoked attack on a young man who had just left a nightclub with his girlfriend. He used a lump hammer and the victim suffered a 3 and 2 cm cut. He also lost consciousness. The defendant was arrested nearby and lashed out at the police officer with a belt. He was released on bail. Less than a week later he committed the second GBH offence. A girl knocked on the victim's door saying there were two men she wanted to get rid of. The victim saw the defendant and another and walked the girl to a telephone box. The two men approached the victim and he was threatened. The other man tried to start a fight. The victim's friends managed to calm things down. The victim returned home and then decided to tell the father of the other man he was causing trouble. The victim and his friends left and the defendant and the other man appeared. They were shouting and trying to start a fight. Without any warning the defendant lunged forward and struck the victim on the top of the head with a claw hammer. The victim had a 7 and 10 cm long cut. Beneath was a skull fracture and the brain had been lacerated indicating a blow of extreme force. There was a risk of brain damage and epilepsy. There was a comparatively superficial 3 cm wound on the back of the head. The defendant was 19 and had no relevant previous convictions. Held. We would have expected a sentence of 6 years in total. Taking into account it was a reference and he was showing signs of maturity 6 months for the ABH, 3 years and 5 years for the GBH concurrent substituted for **3½ years** in total.

A-G's Reference (No 81 of 2000) [2001] 2 Cr App Rep (S) 90. The defendant pleaded guilty to GBH with intent on the day his trial was listed. The defendant lived near the victim and at 1am repeatedly hit his head and body with a shovel. He said, 'I'm going to fucking kill you.' The victim's daughter saw the attack from her bedroom and ran out. He ignored her pleas to him to stop. The victim had a large skull fracture, a fracture to his forearm, a 5 cm laceration to his temple, a deep 5 cm laceration to his elbow and a superficial laceration to his forearm. He was in hospital for 5 days and made a good recovery. The defendant was 36 and had no convictions. The judge sentenced him on the basis that the victim had been aggressive, thrown stones at his house and made a noise early in the morning. The victim ran at him swinging his fist. The defendant used excessive self-defence. The prosecution did not accept that account. Held. Accepting the defence version, which was in stark contrast to the victim's without evidence, was wrong. It is difficult to see how the judge found severe provocation. Taking into account it was a reference **15 months** immediate imprisonment not 18 months suspended.

A-G's Reference (No 68 of 2002) (12 August 2002, unreported). The use of a claw hammer was no less serious than when a glass was used. Here following a trial **5 years** was appropriate.

R v Laker [2001] EWCA Crim 1070, [2002] 1 Cr App Rep (S) 64. The defendant pleaded guilty to GBH with intent and affray. After drinking he was argumentative and aggressive to all and sundry and threatened the victim who he suggested had forced himself on his sister 16 years previously. This suggestion was quite untrue. Eventually he was arrested and the police took him home and de-arrested him because they thought he had calmed down. When they had left he took a hollow metal bar weighing 0.4 kgs to the victim's house and knocked on the door. When the victim's girlfriend answered it he pushed her out of the way and stormed into the lounge where he confronted the victim about his sister. The victim said he didn't know what he was talking about. With the victim defenceless in the chair he struck him about the head and face multiple blows. He also struck him on the inside of his forearm which was extremely painful. Next he ripped his watch off cutting his arm and smashed it. Also smashed was his mobile phone. Then he struck the victim's knees causing him to fall to the ground where he struck him with the bar 23 times. The victim was told, 'You're fucking dead. 'and was in agony. He was blinded by blood and spat his teeth out until he became unconscious. The victim was taken to hospital and three fractures to the jaw and eight lacerations were found. Seven teeth had been knocked out and 36 stitches were required. There were other injuries. The doctor said the injuries were significant but not life threatening. Police found him near a taxi office and he climbed onto the roof of some shops. When a police officer approached he said, 'I've got a 9mm. I'm going to blow you away.' He was eventually overpowered. This was the affray matter. The victim's life had permanently changed and he had to give up his job which he was proud of. He was permanent scarred. Parts of his teeth were embedded in his lips. The defendant was 29 and had an unattractive record but only one conviction for violence in very different circumstances. There was 141 days left of his licence to serve from an earlier sentence. Since his sentence he had performed well in prison and now displayed remorse. Held. This dreadful case called for a severe sentence. **8 years** was richly deserved.

Kicking – Guideline remarks

111.29   *A-G's Reference (No 44 of 1994)* [1995] 1 Cr App Rep (S) 256 – LCJ. It is frequently a misconception that unless some object is held in the hand, no weapon has been used. An attacker who uses shod feet, or who bites someone is just as much using a weapon as someone who wields an object in his hand.

R v Fokrul Islam [2001] EWCA Crim 2950, [2002] 2 Cr App Rep (S) 118. Attacks by kicking with shoes or boots compares with those where weapons are used.

Kicking victim on ground after drinking

111.30   *R v Reynolds* [1997] 2 Cr App Rep (S) 118. The defendant pleaded guilty to attempting to cause GBH with intent. The defendant heard the victim was making a nuisance of himself including making some modest sexual advances to the defendant's wife. The victim then saw the defendant in a public house and asked him to go outside to clear the air. The defendant who had had about 6 or 7 pints went outside with him and an argument developed. The victim then made provocative 'come on' gestures and punches were exchanged. The victim fell to the ground. The defendant was seen kicking the victim's head very hard and jumping on his head. The defendant walked away. The victim was bleeding heavily and was having difficulty breathing. The defendant's brother then kicked him twice in the head. The victim was in a deep coma yet was able to be discharged from hospital 2 days later. He made a complete recovery. The defendant was of good character with references saying that he was not aggressive. Held. The appropriate sentence for GBH on a guilty plea was 4 to 5 years. However, he was only charged with an attempt so he fell to be sentenced for an unsuccessful attempt. The appropriate sentence for that was 3 years. Because of the mitigation it could be reduced to **2½ years**.

R v Richards [1998] 1 Cr App Rep (S) 87. The defendant pleaded guilty to GBH with intent. The defendant who had been drinking threw a beer bottle across the road, which smashed against a wall near the victim. The victim crossed the road to remonstrate with the defendant and threw the first punch. A fight developed and the victim fell to the ground where he was kicked in the face, throat and head. The victim was so drunk he could not defend himself. The victim had fractures to his skull, eye socket, cheekbones, nose, and a cut above his eye. He was in hospital for 2 weeks. The defendant attended the police station and made full admissions. He was 23 with no significant convictions. He had a chronic drink problem. Held. This was a sustained and merciless attack on a man who could easily have died. **7 years** after a trial would not be excessive. **5 years** on a guilty plea was not manifestly excessive.

A-G's Reference (Nos 33 of 1997) [1998] 1 Cr App Rep (S) 352. The defendant pleaded guilty to GBH with intent and ABH. The two victims E and W were out celebrating the birthday of one of them and had a considerable amount to drink. At about 1.45am they walked along a road looking for a taxi. The defendant then 22 and H had also had a lot to drink and an argument developed between the two couples. As E walked passed he was hit on the back of his head and fell to the ground. The defendant struck E in the face knocking him backwards and his head hit the pavement and rendered him unconscious. As E lay on the ground the defendant repeatedly kicked him on the head and stamped on it with considerable force, causing bleeding. The defendant then joined H in assaulting W. Passers-by gave first aid to E and succeeded in preventing further attacks on W. The defendant then returned to E and as a police car arrived he jumped on his head, kicked it and stamped on it. The defendant and H walked off and were caught and than ran off again. They were eventually apprehended. E was bleeding profusely from the head and was unconscious. In hospital he showed no verbal or eye-opening responses. X-rays revealed no internal injury apart from soft tissue trauma to the neck. There was bruising to the eye, swelling to his cheek and grazes to the shoulder. He regained consciousness a day later. The defendant was of good character and showed remorse. Held. The appropriate sentence giving generous construction to the facts in favour of the defendant was **3 years**. The best for him on a guilty plea would have been **2 years**. As it was a reference **12–15 months** would have been appropriate. As he had completed the 240 hours' community service ordered, was now in full time employment and with hesitation it was not appropriate to order a short sentence.

A-G's Reference (No 18 of 2001) [2001] EWCA Crim 107, [2001] 2 Cr App Rep (S) 521. The defendant was convicted of GBH with intent. He had pleaded to GBH without the intent. The defendant then 19 and the victim had been drinking. At about 1.15am the victim who owed a bicycle shop and two young women were sitting on a bench and the defendant joined them. The defendant's larger brother and two others came up to them and the victim said to the brother, 'You're a fat bastard.' The defendant punched him in the face and others crowded round punching him in the head. The brother kicked him in the head. The victim was pulled to the ground and as he lay motionless the defendant kicked him four or five times with considerable force. Witnesses said it was sickening. The victim had a large bruise on the back of the head and blood from the mouth. He had a serious brain injury. His responses were tested and were the lowest possible. He was still effected. His co-ordination was poor, he was unsteady on his feet, he had reduced mental faculties and he was unable to ride a bicycle. Two years after the incident he was expected to have recovered most of his lost functions. The defendant had no convictions for violence. He showed remorse. Held. We would have expected a sentence of **5 to 6 years**. Taking into account it was a reference **4 years** not 3.

Kicking victim on ground after drinking – Group attack

111.31   *A-G's Reference (Nos 62 and 63 of 1997)* [1998] 2 Cr App Rep (S) 300. The defendant M made a late guilty plea to GBH with intent and two violent disorder counts. The defendant C was convicted of GBH with intent and violent disorder. In the late afternoon in a shopping centre two youths were scuffling on the ground. A group of six to eight youths approached including M and C who had been drinking. M launched himself on top of one of the youths and banged his head on the ground. As he was holding the victim C and other friends delivered a series of violent kicks to his head and body. A woman intervened and as she pushed one away others would steam in. At the end M sank his teeth into the cheek of the victim's cheek so deeply that when someone tried to pull him off the victim's head was lifted from the ground. The victim's ribs were fractured and one punctured his lung. His jaw was fractured in several places and in the centre it was completely severed. In the central area his teeth were displaced into his left cheek. He had extensive bruising to his face and body. His epilepsy was permanently worsened. The second violent disorder matter was an entirely separate matter in which M attacked another young man and punched him in the face. The victim had a wound over his eye, which required two stitches and he lost two teeth. M was 21 and C was 19 and had no convictions. Held. For this kind of barbaric brutality an exemplary sentence must be passed. Taking into account it was reference M's sentence was increased from 30 months twice and 3 months concurrent to **4½ years** for the GBH and 3 months consecutive for the separate violent disorder. [No mention is made of the sentence for the first violent disorder count.] C's sentence was increased from 17 and 12 months concurrent to 3 years on each concurrent.

A-G's Reference (No 76 of 1998) [1999] 2 Cr App Rep (S) 361. The defendant made an early guilty plea to GBH with intent. The victim and the defendant aged 28 had been drinking. The victim was chased into a car park by a group of youths. There was no escape and he was knocked to the ground and kicked. He got up. Someone punched him and they both fell to the ground and youths began kicking the victim. He was curled up in a defensive position. Someone called out that they had called the police and the youths moved away. There was nothing to say the defendant had played a part in any of this. The defendant then walked up and asked if he was alright. The victim believing the defendant was part of it said, 'I'll get you back one day.' The defendant replied, 'I didn't hurt you, but if you want me to. . .' He then stamped on his head six times. A witness said it was vicious. He was said to be very drunk but able to boast as to what he had done afterwards. The victim was described as slipping into a coma and had blood coming from his nose and mouth. He had bleeding in the back and side of his brain. It was a traumatic brain injury from which it is unlikely he will make a full recovery. Three months later he was allowed home from hospital for weekends but needed constant care. Eight months later he could only walk with difficulty and his sight and speech were still impaired. The basis of plea was that the complainant abused him and struck the defendant. The defendant had four violent convictions one of which was punished with imprisonment. The defendant expressed remorse. His partner and child were facing difficulties. Held. Taking into account that it was a reference and the mitigation **5 years** not 3.

R v Jama and Oliver [2000] 2 Cr App Rep (S) 98. The defendants J and O made a late plea to GBH with intent. A minor incident developed in a public house between O and the victim. Later O was evicted and waited outside. As the victim left J and O were together. O approached the victim and there was a scuffle. They were parted and the victim walked away. He next saw J, O and another coming towards him. O confronted the victim and J took an estate agent's board and hit the victim with its post. He made heavy determined blows to the head. A witness thought he was going to be killed and telephoned the police. A witness saw a second man punching out with both fists at the victim. He saw a third man watching. Another witness said he saw three men punching and kicking a man on the floor. That witness told them to leave him alone and two stopped and one carried on kicking and stamping on his face, head and body. The victim had fractured ribs and a ruptured spleen, which had to be removed. This has affected his immune system. He has permanent tinnitus in his ear and blurred vision.

The injuries were life threatening. He wanted to be a sound engineer, which is now not practical. The defendants expressed shame and remorse. J was 30 and had a long list of convictions including wounding, ABH, two for cruelty to animals and possession of an offensive weapon. O was 23 and had less violent convictions but had one for robbery. J's basis of plea was that he struck one blow with the estate agent's board and delivered two or three kicks. Held. This was a truly brutal, sustained attack with consequences that the victim will have to endure long after the defendants are released. If there was a trial **7½ to 8 years** could not be criticised. **6 years** was not manifestly excessive.

A-G's Reference (Nos 44 and 45 of 2001) [2001] EWCA Crim 1483, [2002] 1 Cr App Rep (S) 283. The defendant S was convicted of GBH with intent. G pleaded guilty to the same offence. No one saw the start of the attack near a kebab van. The victim who had spent the evening in pubs was slightly built and 5' 2" One witness saw S then 21 holding the victim against a wall punching him 8–12 times in the face and head. The victim fell to the ground and lay motionless on his back. A group then kicked him to the head and upper body. S delivered 10–15 hard kicks like a footballer kicking a ball. G then 19 kicked him 10 times and said, 'That's how you fucking do it.' A witness tried to stop it and lay across the prone body. He shouted for them to stop and he was kicked powerfully and frequently to the body, head and chest. A woman tried to use her mobile phone to call the police and another woman punched her. A witness who had been in the army and was trained in first aid saw the victim and found no pulse or signs of life. He found the victim had swallowed his tongue and cleared the victim's airway. He commenced resuscitation and the victim remained unconscious throughout. The victim was taken to hospital and on the Glasgow coma scale he was 3. He was in hospital for nearly 3 weeks. Six months afterwards he was still having nightmares and had only just returned to work. He was on anti-depressants and his concentration wasn't what it should have been. He was seeing a clinical psychologist. The man who lay prone on the body had bruising to his eye, jaw and ribs. When interviewed, S said he had been drinking and had taken an ecstasy pill. He made no comment about the attack. G said he had no memory of the attack. S had convictions mostly for dishonesty and motoring offences. There was a s 20 glassing. G's record was not as bad and included ABH. S showed no remorse. Held. This was a particularly bad case. The facts are too shocking to require any further elaboration. This was a sustained and vicious unprovoked assault, which could have resulted in the death of the victim. The appropriate sentence for S after his trial was **7 years** and for G on his plea **5 years**. As it was a reference **6 years** not 4 for S and ordinarily we would have imposed on G 4 years. However, because of the delay and 4 years would make him a long-term prisoner **3 years 9 months** not 3 years detention instead.

Knives, with

111.32   *R v Pollin* [1997] 2 Cr App Rep (S) 356. The defendant pleaded guilty to aggravated vehicle-taking and other driving offences. He also pleaded guilty to wounding with intent. The defendant lived in the victim's house. The victim spoke to the defendant about the financial arrangements for paying the rent. The victim then went to another property and the defendant was driven there in a car. He stabbed the victim on his arm and upper body repeatedly and without warning with a 12" kitchen knife. The victim tried to get away, fell and was stabbed again twice. The driver of the car pleaded with him to desist and he was ignored. The victim's artery was severed and some nerves were cut. The victim's jacket took the brunt of the attack so many of the wounds did not penetrate. There were 21 stab wounds and 11 wounds where the knife had penetrated the jacket. The victim was left with a disability to his hand. The defendant was 23 with a number of previous although none for violence. He received concurrent sentences for the driving offences. He received a 9 year sentence. Held. A higher level of sentence is now properly imposed for offences involving a knife. Where knives are used and serious injuries are caused the courts must impose severe sentences. Even after a guilty plea this merited a sentence of **9 years**.

R v McPhee [1998] 1 Cr App Rep (S) 201 – LCJ. See *Life was not appropriate*

A-G's Reference (No 4 of 1998) [1998] 2 Cr App Rep (S) 388 – LCJ The defendant made an early guilty plea to wounding with intent. The defendant was in a public house in a belligerent mood. The victim and friends of his entered and he accused them of stealing his drink and of someone putting their hand up his girlfriend's skirt. They denied it. He threatened to 'cut' someone. One of the group punched him twice causing him to fall over. They grappled on the floor and the victim parted them. The defendant left. ½ hour later he returned and without any warning stabbed the victim in the back. The defendant was restrained by some of the group and received some injuries. The condition of the victim was critical and without surgery would have been fatal. He had severe internal bleeding. The wound had penetrated the full thickness of his chest, severed a rib, passed through the diaphragm, cut the spleen in two and made a shallow cut on the kidney. He was on a ventilator for 3 days. He was in hospital for a month. He had now returned to work but was desk-bound. He suffered depression and flashbacks. Further surgery may be necessary. The defendant had a long record mostly for dishonesty. It included wounding with a hammer and assault on police. Held. If he had pleaded not guilty a sentence of **7–8 years** would have been appropriate. If he had pleaded guilty at trial the sentence would have been **5–6 years**. As it was a reference **4½ years** not 3.

A-G's Reference (No 86 of 1998) [2000] 1 Cr App Rep (S) 10. The defendant was convicted of wounding with intent, ABH and having an offensive weapon. In the early hours of New Year's Day the victim and his girlfriend paused to kiss outside a block of flats on their way home. Two girls told them to do that outside their own house. As they started to leave the defendant who had been drinking arrived. He said, 'I'm telling you to leave.' He ran after them stood in front of them and punched the victim several times. The victim punched back. A co-accused arrived tried to separate them. He was punched by the victim and then joined in the attack. The defendant then produced a knife and the victim raised his arm to defend himself. The knife cut through his jacket and the muscle and tissue of his arm and caused a chip fracture to his left elbow and an 8 x 7 cm wound in his forearm. The co-accused called an ambulance. The ambulance arrived and the crew were confronted by about seven people. The crew did not think it safe to render any assistance and called the police. In a further attack on the victim he was knocked to the ground, punched and kicked. He was assaulted again by the defendant who then went into the block of flats where he lived and came out carrying a baseball bat. The victim fled. The victim's fracture required a metal plate and 25 stitches. He was in hospital for 4 days. He fell behind with his Master's Degree. When the defendant was sentenced the victim still had restricted movement of his arm. The defendant had no convictions for violence. Held. We would have expected a sentence of **6 years**. Because it was a reference **4½ years** not 2.

A-G's Reference (No 27 of 1999) [2000] 1 Cr App Rep (S) 237. The defendant was convicted of wounding with intent. In July 1996, the victim who was black was with a group of mostly black friends. They visited a night club and group of white youths started making insulting remarks to his group. A slanging match developed which the defendant then 21, was not part of. A missile hit the victim then he and others left and a fracas developed outside. A Mr Selby spat in the victim's face and the victim threw him to the ground and stood over him. He also stabbed the victim in the right leg. While the victim was dealing with Mr Selby the defendant stabbed the victim in the buttocks. The victim ran off. A Swiss army knife was found close by with the victim's blood and the defendant's fingerprints on it. The victim had 11 lacerations in the buttocks and a 2 cm cut to his thigh. The defendant said he had been drinking and could not recall much. The defendant was not tried till March 1999 through no fault of his. The defendant had a lengthy criminal record although he had never had a custodial sentence before. He was on probation at the time. Held. Taking into account the mitigation the sentence should have been **2½ years**. As it was a reference **22 months** not 15.

A-G's Reference (No 26 of 2000) [2001] 1 Cr App Rep (S) 188. The defendant pleaded guilty to wounding with intent. It was not at the first opportunity. The victim who was 18 drunk about 7 or 8 pints of lager. The defendant aged 21 and the victim both ended up in a nightclub. The defendant was involved in two incidents with other young men there. The victim left the club and saw his friend being attacked by the defendant and another. Witnesses said it was unprovoked. The victim intervened and witnesses said the victim was getting the better of the defendant until they saw four or five jabs to the victim's face. The victim shouted he's got something in his hand. Blood was seen on the victim's face. The victim remembered the defendant squared up to him and the defendant's hand flashed in front of the victim three or four times really fast. The victim had four lacerations cause by a very sharp knife. Two were over the forehead penetrating down to the bone and required nerve and muscle repair. Another one caused cartilage damage. One was 14 cm and one 12 cm long. The scarring was extremely serious, as it was permanent and very disfiguring. The victim was changed from an ambitious outgoing man to a withdrawn one who finds profound difficulties with his work and social life. The defendant had convictions although he had never had custody before. He was of limited intelligence. Because of medical opinion he was sentenced on the basis he used a very sharp knife. Held. When a victim is seriously injured in an unprovoked attack the offender must be seriously punished. Were it not for the particular factors and that it was a reference the sentence would be substantially higher. **4½ years** not 3½ years.

A-G's Reference (No 52 of 2001) (30 July 2001, unreported). 7 years would be the least sentence for this attack with a Stanley knife on the partner of girl who the defendant fancied.

[The sentences have risen following the court's change in attitude to knives. A similar trend can be found in the cases listed at **MANSLAUGHTER**]

Old cases. Ignore them.

Life was appropriate

111.33 *A-G's Reference (No 88 of 1998)* [1999] 2 Cr App Rep (S) 346. The defendant, a serving prisoner was convicted of wounding with intent. Another prisoner was talking to a police officer in a therapy workshop. He approached from behind and plunged a screwdriver into the prisoner's back, saying, 'That's for you, you fucker, 'and later, 'The fucker deserved it.' The screwdriver was used with considerable force and was buried up to its 10 cm hilt. The defendant had asked for the screwdriver 10 minutes before. The victim was taken to hospital and the screwdriver was seen on X ray to be 1 cm from the heart. He was lucky to be alive and lucky not to have suffered catastrophic injuries. The defendant said the victim had made repeated unwanted advances to him and he just flipped. The defendant had 26 previous court appearances including robbery, and burglary. In the robbery he threatened a pharmacist with a knife demanding drugs. While serving his sentence for that offence he attacked a fellow prisoner with a Stanley knife. He slashed the back of his neck and stabbed him in the side of the body. He received 2 years for a an offence under s 20. Psychiatrists said he suffered from marked instability of mood and behaviour. He had a strong sense of being persecuted. Not particularly frequently he heard voices. He had a severe personality disorder. He presents a risk of further violent offences. Treatment was unlikely to be successful. The judge sentenced him to 7 years as a longer than commensurate sentence. Held. The instance offence was very serious. It required a very long sentence. He was unstable. He cannot be dealt with under the Mental Health Act. There is a substantial risk he will re-offend. He represents a grave danger to the public and will remain so for the indefinite future. The appropriate sentence was **life** with 5 years specified.

Life was not appropriate

111.34 *R v McPhee* [1998] 1 Cr App Rep (S) 201 – LCJ. The defendant pleaded guilty to wounding with intent. He was 27 and had been a serving soldier for 4 or 5 years. Two days before the incident the victim and the defendant were drinking and the defendant was taking ketamine, a drug with psychedelic properties. At one stage the victim was aggressive. The next day the victim again spent a substantial time drinking and went to bed before midnight. He was awoken by loud banging on his front door. The defendant was outside and when the door was opened the defendant punched the victim about the head and face. The victim said the defendant had a metal rod but the defendant denied this. The victim was knocked back into a chair and the defendant was shouting incoherently. He said, 'I'm going to do you in,' and he accused the victim of stitching up one of the defendant's friends and that he was going to kill him. Two others came in and assaulted the victim. One claimed the victim owed him money but the victim told him to 'piss off'. As the victim stood up to hand over some money the defendant stabbed him in the chest and lower back. The defendant told him not to go to the police but did assist in trying to stem the blood. He then said if he went to the police his brother would come down from Scotland and 'finish him off'. The defendant left and the victim went to a friend's room to recuperate. 45 minutes later the defendant returned under the influence of drugs with a machete. The threats were repeated and he left. The victim went to hospital and the wound was sutured. One wound was a 1″ laceration involving skin and fat. The other was 1″ and very shallow. The defendant was arrested and admitted the offence and said that he was under the influence of drugs and that he picked up the knife and was so worked up in his head. In 1988 he had convictions for breach of the peace, and two assault on police officers for which he was admonished. In 1994 he was fined for common assault. He had punched the manager of a restaurant during a fracas. In 1995 he was fined for vandalism. In 1996 he was given probation for ABH on his wife who was accused of infidelity. The psychiatric report said, 'he posed a high risk of further offending. His anger remains whether or not he is under the influence. He fails to see he has a choice or could have acted differently. The public need to be protected from his potential to commit violent offences.' Another report said, 'the defendant described feelings of intense anger and he thought about stabbing and beating up people. He has a personality disorder characterised by an incapacity to experience guilt and antisocial behaviour. There was also a pattern of escalating violence.' The judge described the attack as savage, mindless, and very dangerous. He also said the defendant posed a serious danger to the public for an indefinite time. Since then a report said he did not have a personality disorder but had severe difficulty with anger control. Held. It cannot be said that he is likely to represent a serious danger to the public for an indeterminate time. Accordingly life is inappropriate. The previous convictions are not of a type or number which by themselves would justify anything other than a commensurate sentence. A commensurate sentence is sufficient and it is not necessary to pass a longer than normal sentence. It was worth 9 years and because of the guilty plea **7 years** not life.

Life – Sentence/Automatic life sentence – Fixing specified term

111.35   *R v Lee* [2001] 1 Cr App Rep (S) 1. The defendant pleaded guilty to GBH with intent. The defendant had convictions for GBH with intent, and wounding. He was sentenced to automatic life and the judge considered 12 years was appropriate if a determinate sentence was passed. He thought 8 years should be specified. This was reduced to 6 years 9 months to take into account the period on remand. Held. 6 years would have been appropriate for a determinate sentence. He was entitled to ½ not a ⅓ discount so 3 years specified making it **1 year 9 months**.

See also *A-G's Reference (No 82 of 2000)* [2001] EWCA Crim 65, [2001] 2 Cr App Rep (S) 289

Longer than commensurate sentences (frequently wrongly called extended sentence)

111.36   Powers of Criminal Courts (Sentencing) Act 2000, s 80(2)(b). . . .the custodial sentence shall be. . .where the offence is a violent or sexual offence, for such longer term (not exceeding the maximum) as in the opinion of the court is necessary to protect the public from serious harm from the offender. (previously the Criminal Justice Act 1991, s 2(2)(b).)

R v McPhee [1998] 1 Cr App Rep (S) 201 – LCJ. Not appropriate here. See *Life was not appropriate*

See also LONGER THAN COMMENSURATE SENTENCES

Motorists

See VEHICLES

Police officers, against

111.37   *R v Hall* [1997] 1 Cr App Rep (S) 62. The defendant was convicted of driving whilst disqualified, aggravated vehicle taking and GBH with intent. He was in breach of a probation order for handling and burglary. After visiting public houses he drove another in a stolen car. Police officers followed them. He drove in stages of 60–65 mph, 90 mph and 75 mph in a 30 mph limit. The conditions were poor because of frost. The car skidded, hit a wall and mounted a gate. A WPC approached the car and the defendant reversed at speed into her causing her to be thrown against the police car and dragged backwards as she screamed. As she was partially underneath the car it was revving and not moving. He was told she was trapped. He applied heavy acceleration. The car suddenly sprang forward and she was turned on her chest and run over. A traffic examiner said it was only on the second movement that the movement was far accidental. The victim had fractures in three vertebrae in the back. 11 months later she was still in pain. There was nothing objectionable about a **12 years** sentence with other concurrent sentences.

A-G's Reference (No 78 of 2001) [2001] EWCA Crim 2114, [2002] 1 Cr App Rep (S) 500. The defendant was convicted of four counts of GBH with intent and two counts of ABH. All the victims were police officers on duty in police cars. Two police offers decided to stop the defendant's Nissan four-wheel drive after they did a vehicle check. They flashed the lights of their car and the Nissan stopped. As the officers got out the Nissan drove across a grassy area and the officers were unable to follow. They caught up with it when it returned to the road and the Nissan stopped and reversed twice into their car at considerable speed. There was a further chase and the Nissan reversed into their car again at speed. These were the ABH counts. One officer received acute neck strain and back strain. The other sustained neck strain. Shortly after the Nissan rammed another police car, a Vectra on the off-side front wing and then rammed it on the nearside pillar. The Nissan then drove at a third police car, a Fiesta, and the car was badly damaged. The Vectra then pursued the Nissan and the Nissan rammed the police car six times. The defendant was arrested shortly after he left the vehicle with another man. He denied being the driver. The two occupants of the Fiesta received whiplash injuries and received cuts to the face and arm, the two occupants of the Vectra also received whiplash injuries and one had misaligned teeth. All the officers returned to work. The defendant was 30 and had convictions for perverting the course of justice, assaulting a constable (3 months), reckless driving (9 months), reckless driving (12 months) and threatening behaviour for which he was fined. Held. The gravity of using a vehicle as a weapon increases when it is used repeatedly and at police officers. In many authorities the vehicle is used at a body. Here it was used at a car in which officers were in. Happily the officers were not as injured as they might have been. We would expect **6 to 7 years**. As it was a reference **5 years** not 4.

Prison officers, against

111.38 *A-G's Reference (No 88 of 1998)* [1999] 2 Cr App Rep (S) 346. The defendant, a serving prisoner was convicted of wounding with intent. Another prisoner was talking to a police officer in a therapy workshop. He approached from behind and plunged a screwdriver into the prisoner's back, saying, 'That's for you, you fucker, 'and later, 'The fucker deserved it.' The screwdriver was used with considerable force and was buried up to its 10 cm hilt. The defendant had asked for the screwdriver 10 minutes before. The victim was taken to hospital and the screwdriver was seen on X ray to be 1 cm from the heart. He was lucky to be alive and lucky not to have suffered catastrophic injuries. The defendant said the victim had made repeated unwanted advances to him and he just flipped. The defendant had 26 previous court appearances including robbery, and burglary. In the robbery he threatened a pharmacist with a knife demanding drugs. While serving his sentence for that offence he attacked a fellow prisoner with a Stanley knife. He slashed the back of his neck and stabbed him in the side of the body. He received 2 years for a s 20 offence. Psychiatrists said he suffered from marked instability of mood and behaviour. He had a strong sense of being persecuted. Not particularly frequently he heard voices. He had a severe personality disorder. He presents a risk of further violent offences. Treatment was unlikely to be successful. The judge sentenced him to 7 years as a longer than commensurate sentence under the longer than normal provisions. Held. The instance offence was very serious. It required a very long sentence. He was unstable. He cannot be dealt with under the Mental Health Act 1983. There is a substantial risk he will re-offend. He represents a grave danger to the public and will remain so for the indefinite future. The appropriate sentence was **life** with 5 years specified.

See also **PRISONERS** – *Total sentence when sentence consecutive to the sentence being served*

Punishing the victim, motive to

111.39 *A-G's Reference (No 49 of 1996)* [1997] 2 Cr App Rep (S) 144 – LCJ. The defendant pleaded guilty to wounding with intent. The victim was walking with four friends to a town centre. The defendant was with a group of young men and he approached the victim from behind and struck him with an unbroken beer bottle on the back of the head. The victim fell to the ground and the defendant continued to punch and kick him. The bottle did not break. A friend of the victim attempted to intervene and the defendant threatened him. The victim had a deep laceration in the back of the head, which needed five stitches. He also had a broken finger. The defendant said the attack was because the victim had punched his younger brother some days before. The defendant had convictions for (a) criminal damage, affray and ABH and (b) ABH and other offences. Both times he was given supervision. The defendant was in work with a stable relationship and had been out of trouble for 3 years till this offence. Held. Wanton, thuggish violence is all too prevalent. **9 months** substituted taking into account he had performed ⅓ of his Community Service Order and that it was a reference. That is the shortest sentence we can impose.

A-G's Reference (Nos 8 and 9 of 1997) [1998] 1 Cr App Rep (S) 98. The defendants made a late guilty plea to GBH with intent on the first victim, AP, and just GBH on the second victim MP. The defendants N and A were brothers. N cohabited with the victim's sister. AP was a regular visitor to his sister. N believed AP was making adverse comments about him to his sister. N was heard to speak about, 'going to have' AP. The two defendants and AP were drinking in a public house when suddenly N jumped to his feet, grabbed AP and threw him to the floor. Both defendants kicked him in the body and head. This continued for some time. N also hit him on the head with a bar stool. An ambulance was called and the defendants left. However, they soon returned and dragged the victim out of the public house. One held him while the other punched him. They took him to his home and continued to attack him. They only stopped because they feared their fish tank might be damaged. So they took him out to the garden and attacked him again. A neighbour thought he looked dead. He was kicked and N stamped on his head. The two then pulled the victim up banged his head against a metal post several times. Then they carried on kicking him and stamping on his groin. The victim's brother, MP then arrived at the scene and took a pickaxe from the van and tried to strike N with it. A took hold of him and took him across to a walled area where N laid into him with the pickaxe handle and A kicked him. He fell to the ground where the defendants carried on kicking him. He was unconscious.

The victims were taken to hospital. N had a severe head injury resulting in impairment of higher cerebral functions such as speech. He had a skull wound. It was too early to say what the long term effects would be. MP had scars and so many teeth knocked out he needed five false teeth in his upper jaw. He suffered from headaches and dizzy spells. Both defendants had convictions for violence but nothing as serious as this. Held. It was a severe, sustained and vicious attack. If there had been a trial the sentence should have been **9 years and 2 consecutive**. On a guilty plea the sentences should have been **7 years and 1½ consecutive**. Because it was a reference **6 years** and 1 consecutive not 3 and 1 consecutive.

R v McDonagh [1998] 2 Cr App Rep (S) 195. The defendant pleaded guilty to two counts of wounding with intent. The defendant learnt that his sister's common law husband had been saying he was cracking up again. The defendant joked about it. He returned home and seemed fine. Later he became furious and drove to his sister's home. His sister shouted and argued with him. Her common law husband held a cricket bat. The defendant then took a machete and swung it down a few times. One swing caught her sister's arm and almost amputated the hand. Another did the same to the common law husband. At hospital the hands were stitched back. Both would suffer residual disability. The defendant said the common law husband had swung the cricket bat at him. He was 29, unemployed with no relevant convictions. He had suffered from manic depression. There was some evidence of paranoid beliefs. The victims had forgiven him. Everyone said it was out of character and he had a good prison report. Held. Without some hesitation **5 years** not 6.

R v Lee [2001] 1 Cr App Rep (S) 1. The defendant pleaded guilty to GBH with intent. The victim who worked in a store sold and delivered a bed to the defendant's girlfriend. The victim was attracted to her and sent her a letter expressing his feelings.

The defendant and two other men went to the store. The defendant grabbed him, pushed him back and told him to leave his girlfriend alone. He then repeatedly punched him and the victim fell to the floor. He knelt on his neck and punched him in the face. He stood up and kicked the victim in the ribs. The two other men prevented a colleague of the victim from helping him. Later the defendant kicked the victim again on the back of the head two or three times and stamped on his head five times. The attack lasted about 2 minutes and the blows might well have killed him. The victim had a fractured skull but no brain damage. He had a small bruise above his eye, a swelling on the jaw and some scrapes over the temple. He was in hospital for 2 days twice. The defendant had convictions for GBH with intent, and wounding. He was sentenced to automatic life. Held. It was a very serious and vicious attack. It was premeditated. It was amazing no more serious damage was caused. **6 years** would have been appropriate for a determinate sentence.

R v Frost [2001] 2 Cr App Rep (S) 124. The defendant pleaded guilty to GBH with intent. The victim who knew the defendant visited a friend in a block where the defendant lived. As he was leaving he saw the defendant and the co-accused and he was seized and bundled into the defendant's flat. He was put on a bed, the door was blocked and an iron was turned on. The victim said he had done nothing wrong. Both punched him in the face and head and then pulled him to the floor where he was kicked in the side and back. The defendant held his arms and neck tightly while the other put the hot iron on his naked back. While he screamed the others laughed. He was dragged into the hallway where the other man hit him in the face with the iron. The defendant held his hands and kicked him. His face was hit against a cupboard. The victim managed to struggle free and escape. [No medical report is referred to.] He was told the defendant wanted to give him £2,000 to keep his mouth shut. The defendant had a significant number of convictions for violent, driving and dishonesty offences. In 1991 when 15, he was found guilty of an offence under s 18 and received a supervision order. He had stabbed a police officer in the face with a screwdriver after a car chase. He told the probation officer that the victim had burgled his flat. His risk of re-offending was assessed as high but he had a good prison report. He was sentenced to automatic life, which was quashed because there were exceptional circumstances. Held. This was a very nasty attack. It was persistent, calculated and vicious and involved two people. **5 years** substituted.

Racist attack

111.40 *A-G's Reference (Nos 29, 30 and 31 of 1994)* [1995] 16 Cr App Rep (S) 698 – LCJ. It cannot be too strongly emphasised that where there is a racial element in an offence of violence, that is a gravely aggravating feature.

R v Reader [2000] 2 Cr App Rep (S) 442. The defendant was convicted of GBH with intent, ABH and criminal damage. Mr Bhangra, Mr Sheldrick and Mr Bhogal went to a public house, then to a buy some food and then Mr Bhangra went back to the public house. When he didn't return Mr Sheldrick went in. There was then an altercation between the three as to whether they should go home. The defendant with a half-full glass of beer approached Mr Bhangra and Mr Sheldrick who were at a van and asked, 'Did you smash my glasses? I hope it was an accident. I'm the only one who smashes glasses.' A girl who he was with told him to stop. He punched Mr Bhangra in the face and he fell down unconscious. This was the ABH. Other men joined the defendant and he asked, 'What are you doing standing up for a Paki?' The defendant and three others started to kick the van. This was the criminal damage. Someone opened the rear doors of the van and Mr Sheldrick got out and as he stood up the defendant struck him with his glass of beer shattering the glass. The victim had a deep 3 cm laceration to his forehead with two superficial lacerations to each side. He was left with scarring and developed depression. When he went out he feared he would be attacked. Mr Bhangra had bruising and soreness to his eye and cheek. The van had dents to its side panels, wings and bonnet. The back door had been pulled off its hinges. As there was a racist motive **4½ years** with other concurrent sentences was appropriate.

See also RACIALLY-AGGRAVATED OFFENCES

Razor blades

111.41 *A-G's Reference (Nos 60 and 61 of 1997)* [1998] 2 Cr App Rep (S) 330. The defendants were convicted of wounding with intent. The defendant W aged 12 enquired of another girl whether she had been writing things about someone. She denied it. B also 12 handed W a razor blade and said 'Go on, slash her.' They approached another girl aged 14 and asked her the same question. She also denied it. W hit her across the face with the razor blade. She needed 26 stitches and is permanently scarred. B had convictions. Three days before the offence a supervision order had been made for theft, two assaults with intent to resist arrest, assault on police and obstruction. Less than 3 weeks before the wounding, she committed ABH and robbery. Six weeks after the wounding she committed affray. In the same month and 3 months later she committed three criminal damage offences. W had no convictions. The judge imposed a supervision order on each. W had responded well to it. Held. If they had been adults a sentence of **5 years** would have been imposed. **18 months** detention for B and **12 months** detention for W substituted.

Robbery/Burglary, and

111.42 *R v Rogers* [1998] 1 Cr App Rep (S) 402. The defendant pleaded guilty to causing GBH with intent and two burglaries. The victim was aged 87 and lived on her own in a large detached house. In January 1995 the defendant broke into her house and was sentenced to 9 months detention for it. After being released on 1 November 1996 he broke in again and stole milk and other items. On 25 November 1996 he broke in again after the victim had gone to bed. He entered her bedroom and repeatedly struck her in the face. He put his hands around her throat as if to throttle her. When she regained consciousness she had difficulty in breathing. He was under the influence of heroin. The victim went to hospital and numerous cuts and bruises were found. The doctor believed pressure would have to be applied for some time to leave the marks he found on her neck. The defendant's prints were found and he was arrested the next day. The defendant was 20 when sentenced. He had five drug-related cautions for burglary, theft, TDA etc. The judge described the photographs as, 'truly revolting.' He was sentenced to 2 years for the first burglary, 5 years' concurrent for the second burglary and 12 years' consecutive to the 2 years for the GBH. Held. If there had been a trial **12 years** would have been appropriate for the GBH. For a plea **9 years** was appropriate. The 5 years concurrent was right. The consecutive sentence of 2 years was right because he had preyed on the house. Therefore **9 years** and 2 consecutive not 12 and 2 years.

R v Dudeye [1998] 2 Cr App Rep (S) 430. The defendant pleaded guilty to wounding with intent and robbery. The defendant then 18 and the victim were on a train. As the train pulled out of a station the defendant sat next to the victim and produced a knife. He tried to grab her briefcase and she wouldn't give it to him. A struggle developed. He wanted her shoulder bag and said, 'Give me the fucking bag or I'll kill you to death.' He stopped her getting off at the next station and repeated the threat to kill her. She managed to alight at the station after that and he followed. He was holding the strap of the bag and he stabbed her four times. He cut the handle of the bag and ran off leaving her bleeding profusely. She had a punctured lung, internal chest bleeding and stab wound that required stitching. In interview he admitted it and said he was sorry.

He said he was drunk at the time. He had convictions for robbery, threatening behaviour, common assault and several previous for burglary and dishonesty. He had previously been sent to detention. The longest period was 6 months. The robbery was on a woman travelling on a tube train. He told her he would punch her in the face. The defendant left Somalia when he was 9. His mother and her children were refugees. He was taken into care. He used alcohol as an escape. **8 years** not 10 YOI.

Self defence, excessive

111.43   *A-G's Reference (No 81 of 2000)* [2001] 2 Cr App Rep (S) 90. The defendant pleaded guilty to GBH with intent on the day his trial was listed. The defendant lived near the victim and at 1am repeatedly hit his head and body with a shovel. He said, 'I'm going to fucking kill you.' The victim's daughter saw the attack from her bedroom and ran out. He ignored her pleas to him to stop. The victim had a large skull fracture, a fracture to his forearm, a 5 cm laceration to his temple, a deep 5 cm laceration to his elbow and a superficial laceration to his forearm. He was in hospital for 5 days and made a good recovery. The defendant was 36 and had no convictions. The judge sentenced him on the basis that the victim had been aggressive, thrown stones at his house and made a noise early in the morning. The victim ran at him swinging his fist. The defendant used excessive self-defence. The prosecution did not accept that account. Held. Accepting the defence version, which was in stark contrast to the victim's without evidence, was wrong. It is difficult to see how the judge found severe provocation. Taking into account it was a reference **15 months** immediate imprisonment not 18 months suspended.

Series of offences

111.44   *A-G's Reference No 19 of 1998* [1999] 1 Cr App Rep (S) 275. The defendant was convicted of two wounding with intent counts and affray. He was committed for sentence for ABH. The ABH matter related to an unprovoked attack on a white victim with a bottle. The victim had just left a restaurant with his girlfriend. The victim was with three to five Asians. He left sniggering. The victim's nose was cut and his spectacles were broken. He was convicted. While on bail for that offence and 3 weeks after the offence he made an unprovoked attack on a young man who had just left a nightclub with his girlfriend. He used a lump hammer and the victim suffered a 3 and 2 cm cut. He also lost consciousness. The defendant was arrested nearby and lashed out at the police officer with a belt. He was released on bail. Less than a week later he committed the second GBH offence. A girl knocked on the victim's door saying there were two men she wanted to get rid of. The victim saw the defendant and another and walked the girl to a telephone box. The two men approached the victim and he was threatened. The other man tried to start a fight. The victim's friends managed to calm things down. The victim returned home and then decided to tell the father of the other man he was causing trouble. The victim and his friends left and the defendant and the other man appeared. They were shouting and trying to start a fight. Without any warning the defendant lunged forward and struck the victim on the top of the head with a claw hammer. The victim had a 7 and 10 cm long cut. Beneath was a skull fracture and the brain had been lacerated indicating a blow of extreme force. There was a risk of brain damage and epilepsy. There was a 3 cm comparatively superficial wound on the back of the head. The defendant was 19 and had no relevant previous convictions. Held. We would have expected a sentence of **6 years** in total. Taking into account it was a reference and he was showing signs of maturity 6 months for the ABH, 3 years and **5 years** for the GBH concurrent substituted for 3½ in total.

R v Moseley [1999] 1 Cr App Rep (S) 452. The defendant pleaded guilty to GBH with intent and wounding with intent. The defendant and the woman (the second victim) intended to get married. However, she became increasingly concerned, disillusioned and depressed about it. She needed medication. She confided in the licensee of a public house (the first victim). She became attracted to him and spent a night with him. She told the defendant who was upset, very angry and for the first time was violent to her. He punched her and the engagement was broken off. He was asked to leave her house where they were living. Later there was much discussion and she said she wanted to be with the first victim. He appeared to accept it and moved out. One night the two victims spent the evening at a nightclub and went back to her house. At about 4 or 5am. the defendant entered the house with a wheel brace. The first victim was struck several hard blows to his head and body. She was hit on the head as well. Her pleas to stop were ignored and the attack went on for a while. The defendant went straight to the police. He told them his mind had gone. The first victim had a large depressed fracture of the skull causing permanent disability. He had to be re-educated to read and write and to communicate. He suffered severe headaches. His skin was de-sensitised. His business came to an end. He was unable to go out alone. His stuttering and inability to pronounce many words was unlikely to improve. The second victim had lacerations to her head, which required 18 stitches. She had bruising to her arm and swelling to her hands. She found it extremely difficult to come to terms with what had happened and became something of a recluse. The defendant showed considerable remorse and had no convictions for violence. A psychiatrist did not consider he posed a risk to the public in general. Held. There was no provocation. We accept he was under emotional strain and the attack was out of his normal character. The sentence was severe and the crime merited it. **10 years** in total (6 + 4) upheld.

R v Iyegbe (18 October 2001, unreported). The defendant was convicted of two woundings with intent and pleaded guilty to five robberies on minicab drivers. 10 years not 12 in all.

Unprovoked attack

111.45   *R v Thomas* [1997] 2 Cr App Rep (S) 148. The defendant then 20 and another were convicted of GBH with intent. They had both pleaded guilty to violent disorder and ABH on another man. The defendant then aged 20 with a co-defendant left a public house after drinking and went to a burger bar. Inside the public house there was talk of someone getting a good kicking. Immediately behind them in the queue were some strangers. One of them, one of the victims, was talking to the others with his back to the defendant. Without warning he was punched from behind on the back of the head. He turned round and saw five or six youths including the defendant facing him. He was then set upon and received blows to the head. He fell to the ground and was kicked by the two defendants (the ABH). The second victim went forward to try to split up the fight. It looked as if peace had been restored. The co-defendant then went over to the second victim and punched him hard in the face, which knocked him to the ground. The two defendants then started kicking and stamping on him about 20 times. That victim had widespread facial injuries and fractures to cheekbone and eye socket. He was in hospital for 4 days. He had memory, walking and speech difficulties caused by brain damage. He would never be able to work again and cannot look after himself. He had a major personality change and was disabled. His wife was overwhelmed by the changes and his need to be cared for 24 hours a day. **10 years** YOI was not excessive.

A-G's Reference (No 19 of 1998) [1999] 1 Cr App Rep (S) 275. The defendant was convicted of two wounding with intent counts and affray. He was committed for sentence for ABH. The ABH matter related to an unprovoked attack on a white victim with a bottle. The victim had just left a restaurant with his girlfriend. The victim was with three to five Asians. He left sniggering. The victim's nose was cut and his spectacles were broken. He was convicted. While on bail for that offence and 3 weeks after the offence he made an unprovoked attack on a young man who had just left a nightclub with his girlfriend. He used a lump hammer and the victim suffered a 3 and 2 cm cut. He also lost consciousness. The defendant was arrested nearby and lashed out at the police officer with a belt. He was released on bail. Less than a week later he committed the second GBH offence. A girl knocked on the victim's door saying there were two men she wanted to get rid of. The victim saw the defendant and another and walked the girl to a telephone box. The two men approached the victim and he was threatened. The other man tried to start a fight. The victim's friends managed to calm things down. The victim returned home and then decided to tell the father of the other man he was causing trouble. The victim and his friends left and the defendant and the other man appeared. They were shouting and trying to start a fight. Without any warning the defendant lunged forward and struck the victim on the top of the head with a claw hammer. The victim had a 7 and 10 cm long cut. Beneath was a skull fracture and the brain had been lacerated indicating a blow of extreme force. There was a risk of brain damage and epilepsy. There was a 3 cmcomparatively superficial wound on the back of the head. The defendant was 19 and had no relevant previous convictions. Held. We would have expected a sentence of **6 years** in total. Taking into account it was a reference and he was showing signs of maturity 6 months for the ABH, 3 years and 5 years for the GBH concurrent substituted for 3½ in total.

A-G's Reference (No 24 of 1998) [1999] 1 Cr App Rep (S) 278. The defendant was convicted of wounding with intent. The victim was with his girlfriend at a public house. They went to the bar and the victim was next to the defendant who said something. The victim couldn't hear it and asked the defendant what he had said. The defendant smashed a beer glass into his face. The defendant aged 27 had convictions over 13 years principally for theft, motor vehicle and motoring offences. However there were offences for two assaults on police, ABH and common assault. He had received for those 3 months detention, probation and a community service order. Held. We would have expected a sentence in the order of **5 years**. However, as it was a reference and the defendant had 7 weeks before his planned release **3 years 9 months** not 2 years.

R v Richards [2002] 1 Cr App Rep (S) 133. The defendant was convicted of wounding with intent. The defendant then 19 and a friend met a 44 to 45-year-old gay man, the victim through a gay chat line. The man paid for their train fares from London to Swansea and took them to his house where they had sex. He provided them with food, accommodation, drink and money for 3 days. On the fourth day the man was asked to pick them and another up from a club and he did so. On the way home they bought food and cannabis. When they got home they drank beer and whisky and smoked the cannabis. The friend left the room and the defendant without warning or cause cut the victim across the throat using a serrated kitchen knife. He also stabbed him and as the victim tried to get away the defendant continued to attack him causing multiple wounds to the victim's head and body. Eight were serious and the attack only stopped when the friend re-entered the room. The three men left leaving the victim who managed to telephone for an ambulance. The friend returned to London and told his mother who told the police. The knife was left at the scene and was 19 cm long with a serrated double edge. It had a forked tip which had one fork broken off and the blade was bent at right angles to the handle. In hospital the victim was found to have a 6–7 cm laceration on his neck and a 5 cm stab wound. There were multiple complications and he was on an artificial ventilator for nearly a month. The defendant was arrested and said the victim wanted sex, he was resisting and the victim tried to stab him. The defendant had a conviction in 1995 for two robberies with an imitation firearm and an aggravated burglary. He was then 14½ and received 2 years' detention. His risk of re-offending was described as high. The judge said the victim was only saved by the prompt and highly competent medical treatment. The judge did not pass an automatic life sentence because the defendant did not create an unacceptable danger to the public and the other offence was when he was 14½ and there was no actual violence on his record. Held. **12 years** was not manifestly excessive.

Vehicles, after using – (including road rage)

111.46   *A-G's Reference (No 60 of 1996)* [1997] 2 Cr App Rep (S) 198. The defendant was convicted of ABH and wounding with intent. The defendant after drinking heavily argued with his sister in the street. He threw a can of drink into the road and it struck a car. The driver got out to remonstrate with the defendant. The defendant threatened him and kicked him hard in the testicles, (the ABH). The sister and the driver tried to push the defendant away and the passenger, an off duty police officer got out of the car. He tried to restrain the defendant and told him to calm down. The defendant pushed him back and forced him against a wall. The defendant persistently bit his ear growling and roaring like a wild animal. The driver and the sister tried to pull the defendant away but failed. The driver went to the boot of the car to find a torch to hit him with. Unable to find one he returned with a wheelbrace and hit the defendant with it. The defendant then turned to face the driver, shouted abuse and moved towards him aggressively. The sister managed to push him away and he left. The driver followed him and he was threatened. Both the victims were detained overnight in hospital. The driver had swollen testicles. The passenger had 18 stitches for three bite marks in the ear of 2.5, 3.5, and 0.8 cm long. He was off work for 5 weeks and he and his family suffered great stress and upset. Four months later he was still in pain. The victim required five stitches to his head. The defendant had convictions for ABH and criminal damage. He had forced his way into his former girlfriend's flat and had punched and kicked her current boyfriend about the face and head. The probation officer thought he posed no significant risk. There was significant personal mitigation. Held. Giving weight to that the minimum sentence for the wounding was 3 years. Because of the delay and it was a reference **2 years** substituted for the wounding and 6 months concurrent for the ABH remaining.

Vehicles, using vehicle as a weapon

111.47   *A-G's Reference (No 13 of 2001)* [2001] EWCA Crim 137, [2001] 2 Cr App Rep (S) 497. The defendant pleaded guilty on the day fixed for his trial to GBH with intent and dangerous driving. A month earlier he pleaded guilty to driving whilst disqualified and perverting the course of Justice. The defendant tailgated a number of vehicles including a van. He shouted to his passenger about the van driver, 'Hurry up,' and flashed his lights and made gestures. The driver pulled over and the defendant pulled up behind the van. The van driver got out and walked towards the defendant who drove his car straight at him at speed. The van driver was thrown onto the bonnet of the car and hit his face on the windscreen. He fell off and the defendant drove away. The victim had a badly broken wrist and cuts and bruises to his face. The defendant went to the police station with a bogus receipt for his car and made a statement saying he had sold his car. The defendant was 25 and had convictions for dangerous driving (twice) and disqualified driving (7 times) with 36 similar offences taken into account. He had had three probation orders, a 6 month detention order and a combination order. He had references. He was sentenced to a combination order with 100 hours' community service and 3 years' probation. He had performed 60 out of the 100 hours' community service and was within 6 weeks of completing the course he was required to undertake. Held. We would have expected the order of **5 years** made up of 4 years for the GBH and 1 for the perverting count. Taking into account it was a reference, the partial completion of the community service, 2½ years for the GBH and 6 months consecutive for the perverting matter and 2 for ABH making **3 years**.

R v Bradley Evans [2001] EWCA Crim 2631, [2002] 2 Cr App Rep (S) 34. The defendant was convicted of GBH with intent, ABH and dangerous driving. He went to a pub and drank 'quite an amount of alcohol'. There was an incident with C but it all calmed down. When the pub closed he went outside and started some horseplay which developed into a fight. His ex-girlfriend intervened to try to calm the situation and he made a threatening gesture towards her as if to hit her. Two brothers who were both judo experts intervened and had no difficulty in inflicting one or two punches on him and putting him on the ground. The defendant in a rage about being humiliated, went home, got his pick up truck and went to the road where the brothers were walking home with C. He drove onto the pavement and deliberately straight at the three men. C was struck a glancing blow and was not seriously injured. One brother got out of the way. The other was hit and carried for about 20 metres before he fell to the ground. He sustained fractures to the spinal column and it was initially thought he would be totally paraplegic. He could have been killed, but made a remarkable recovery. He had recovered the use of his legs, although the use of his hands and arms had been gravely impaired and would not recover further. The defendant was 23 and effectively of good character with references, which said the offence, was out of character. Held. The aggravating factors were it was a relatively heavy truck used as a weapon of revenge. After the perceived insult there was ample time for the defendant to come to his senses. The injuries were severe and permanently disabling. **8 years** was on the high side but not manifestly excessive.

See also *A-G's Reference (No 78 of 2001)* [2001] EWCA Crim 2114, [2002] 1 Cr App Rep (S) 500. See **Police officers, against**

Victim caused permanent disability

111.48   *R v Meredith and Craven* [2000] 1 Cr App Rep (S) 508. The defendant C was convicted of GBH with intent. In October 1997 the victim and the defendant C's brother got in an argument in a public house. They then fought and the victim seemed to be getting the better of the brother. They were separated and the brother was bleeding. The victim got into a chair. Then C punched the victim and he fell to the floor and was motionless. A fracas developed between a bystander and C. M then punched the victim in the head three or four times and kicked him in the stomach. M also stamped and kicked his head and shoulders. C then picked up a chair and brought it down on the victim's head four or more times. The injuries were the worst the consultant had seen. An eye was knocked out of its socket and was on his cheek held by the optic nerve, which was damaged. He was blind in that in that eye and had reduced vision in the other. Every bone in his face was broken. His mid face area was mobile. He was on a ventilator for 4 days and they could not operate on him for 13 days because of his condition. There was no hint of remorse or regret. C was 40 and had a long record. Most were minor but in 1985 he received 2½ years for robbery and in 1996 he received 6 months for unlawful wounding and violent disorder. In December 1996 he was arrested for supplying cannabis in a public house. In 1998 he was sentenced to 27 months for it. M was given automatic life because he had a conviction for manslaughter. Held. It was sadistic and sustained cruelty. **12 years** was towards the top of the sentencing bracket but was not outside it. However, the total sentence of 12 years and 27 months consecutive for the drugs was too long so the sentences were made concurrent.

R v Cloud [2001] EWCA Crim 510, [2001] 2 Cr App Rep (S) 435. The defendant was convicted of GBH with intent. Around midnight there was an argument and then a fight outside a public house involving the defendant and his two younger brothers. The victim aged 35, told them to break it up and he was attacked. He went back into the pub and returned with a fire extinguisher which was wrested from him and he was thrown or knocked to the ground. The fire extinguisher was discharged and the defendant swung it in a golf swing at the victim's head as he lay on the ground. He suffered two skull fractures and nearly lost his life. There was serious and irreversible brain damage. He will need full time care for the rest of his life and could regain limited speech and possibly some degree of continence. **10 years** not 13. [The age and character of the defendant is not revealed.]

Water, boiling

111.49   *A-G's Reference (No 3 of 2000)* [2001] 1 Cr App Rep (S) 92. The defendant was convicted of GBH with intent. The defendant had an intermittent relationship with the victim for about 5 years. The defendant returned home at about 2am under the influence of crack cocaine. He found the victim and two male friends there and demanded to know what had happened to his motor car. He believed the three had sold it to buy heroin. He was armed with a knife and his manner was threatening. He was also asking for £100 to buy crack. He left and returned carrying a full jug sized kettle of boiling water. He poured it over the victim's back and shoulders. He fetched a sheet soaked in cold water and she wrapped herself in it. She was terribly burnt and in agony. She suffered from 16% to 22% mixed depth burns. Some 80% of her back was scarred. She was in hospital for 3½ weeks. The defendant claimed it was an accident. He had 16 court appearances as an adult and he had convictions for robbery, dishonesty and two for ABH. Held. We would have expected a sentence of at least 6 years. Taking into account it was a reference **5 years** substituted for 3.

112   OFFENCES AGAINST THE PERSON ACT 1861, S 20

112.1   Malicious GBH or wounding

Triable either way. On indictment maximum 5 years. Summary maximum 6 months and/or £5,000.

It is a violent offence for the purposes of passing a longer than commensurate sentence [Powers of Criminal Courts (Sentencing) Act 2000, s 80(2)] and an extended sentence (extending the licence) [Powers of Criminal Courts (Sentencing) Act 2000, s 85(2)(b)]

Where the offence was committed relevant to a football match and where there are reasonable grounds to believe that making a banning order would help to prevent violence or disorder at or in connection with any regulated football match; the court must make a Football Banning Order, Football Spectators Act 1989, s 14A and Sch 1, para 1.

Crown Court statistics England and Wales[1] – Crown Court – Males 21+ – 'Other wounding[2]'

112.2

Year	Plea	Total Numbers sentenced	Type of sentence%					Average length of custody (months)
			Discharge	Fine	Community sentence	Suspended sentence	Custody	
2000	Guilty	4,808	5%	3%	34%	5%	51%	14.2
	Not guilty	1,230	3%	4%	25%	3%	60%	15.4

1   Excluding committals for sentence. Source: Crime and Criminal Justice Unit, Home Office Ref: IOS416-02.
2   This is assumed to be primarily s 20 offences.

Magistrates' Court Sentencing Guidelines September 2000 – Wounding

112.3   Entry point. Are Magistrates' sentencing powers appropriate? Consider the impact on the victim. Examples of aggravating factors for the offence are deliberate kicking or biting, extensive injuries, group action, offender in position of authority, on hospital/medical premises, pre-meditated, victim particularly vulnerable, victim serving the public and weapon. Examples of mitigating factors for the offence are minor wound, provocation and single blow. Examples of mitigation are age, health (physical or mental), co-operation with the police, voluntary compensation and genuine remorse. Consider committal for sentence. Give reasons if not awarding compensation.

For details about the guidelines see MAGISTRATES' COURT SENTENCING GUIDELINES at page 331.

Aircraft, on a

See AIRCRAFT OFFENCES

Defendant 18–20

112.4   *R v Robinson and McManus* [1998] 1 Cr App Rep (S) 72. The defendant M pleaded guilty to GBH with intent. The defendant R pleaded to just GBH. The white defendants who were drunk came across the victim who was black walking home from work. M aged 16 ran after him and knocked him out the way. He was raving and shouting. R aged 18 started pushing him in the chest and grabbing his suit lapels. As he wouldn't let go the victim took a swing at him. R still would not go and a fight ensued. The victim was knocked out. A witness saw M punch him to the ground and kick him in the head. The witness moved in between them. Punches were thrown at him and the M continued to kick the victim. The witness ran and was chased by R. M then jumped on the victim's head. The victim required 22 stitches to his head and face. He had multiple lacerations round the eye. There was a danger his retina might become detached. His scarring to his right eye might be permanent. His headaches and vertigo would take several months to resolve. He was afraid to leave his home. R plea was based on a late participation in the joint enterprise and preventing the witness from assisting the victim. Held. It wasn't racially motivated but it was horrific. Taking into account the mitigation particularly the remorse 4 years not 3 for M and **2 years** YOI not 3 for R.

R v Clarke [1999] 2 Cr App Rep (S) 400. See *Serious but unexpected injuries*

Fighting with the injuries are caused by the fall not any blow – Guideline remarks

112.5   *R v Coleman* (1991) 13 Cr App Rep (S) 508 – LCJ. The defendant was sentenced for manslaughter. We are considering a person who receives a blow, probably one blow only, to the head or face, is knocked over by the blow and unfortunately cracks his head on the floor or the pavement, suffers a fractured skull and dies. It is to be distinguished sharply from the sort of case where a victim on the ground is kicked about the head. It is to be distinguished sharply from the sort of case where a weapon is used in order to inflict injury. It is to be further distinguished from where the actual blow itself causes the death. This is the case of a fall almost accidentally resulting in a fractured skull. The starting point for manslaughter for this type of offence is 12 months on a plea of guilty. Then one looks at the mitigation and aggravating features. No premeditation, a single blow of moderate force, remorse and immediate admissions are all mitigation. Indications that the defendant is susceptible to outbreaks of violence, the assault was gratuitous and unprovoked, more than one blow all tend to aggravate the offence.

Fighting with the injuries are caused by the fall not any blow – Cases

112.6   *R v Hickman* [2001] EWCA Crim 239, [2001] 2 Cr App Rep (S) 261.   The defendant pleaded guilty to a Section 20 GBH and ABH at the first opportunity. The defendant and his girlfriend went to a party and then a pub. When she said she was leaving he followed her down the street and shouted at her. Two people D and R told him to leave the girl alone. He punched R once to the back of the head and the D intervened to separate them. The defendant threw a punch at D which missed. The girlfriend and D tried to calm him down. Someone seized the defendant and D and the girlfriend again intervened to separate them. The defendant punched D to the face. D fell and his head hit a raised part of the pavement. The girlfriend walked him away and unsuccessfully attempted to phone an ambulance. D and R were taken to hospital. D's injuries were catastrophic. He was found to have a large blood clot over his brain with bruising and trauma to the brain. He suffered dense spastic weakness to an arm and leg, disordered eye movements, which produced double vision, and a significant loss of vision in both eyes. The defendant attended voluntarily at a police station after he had seen a newspaper report of the incident. He said he was in temper and struck D. D's recovery was slow. He had severe cognitive impairment, memory impairment, poor concentration and an impaired bladder and bowel function. He was unable to read and write had had depression and anxiety which at times were overwhelming. A year later he had not significantly improved. He remained unable to walk and was incontinent. R had tenderness around an eye and his jaw. The defendant was 19 in employment and an amateur boxer. He was of good character and showed genuine remorse. Held. It was a difficult sentencing exercise. It was a one-off loss of self-control. It was unprovoked and he didn't stop when people tried to make him. The principles in *R v Coleman* (1991) 13 Cr App Rep (S) 508 were applied. **2 years** YOI not 3.

R v Gilbert [2001] EWCA Crim 615, [2001] 2 Cr App Rep (S) 450. The defendant pleaded guilty to GBH on the first day of his trial for that and a section 18 count. There was an altercation between the defendant aged 21 and the victim aged 26 over something trivial. They were both affected by alcohol. Each felt increasingly provoked by the other. Anger escalated and each refused to heed the calls made to them to back off. The victim was as anxious to continue the confrontation and was as provocative. The defendant then punched the victim once very hard in the face. The victim fell back and struck his head on the ground causing bleeding in the brain. When the defendant heard that the police wanted to see him he surrendered himself saying he hadn't had any sleep and his conscious made him go to the police. The victim underwent two brain operations. Nine months later he was still suffering language difficulties both in comprehension and expression. It was doubted whether he would ever return to work. When 17, the defendant had a conviction for assault on the police and was given community service. When 18 he was conditionally discharged for damaging property. The CSO was ordered to continue. When 19 there was another conviction for damaging property. There were later convictions for threatening behaviour and drunk and disorderly. The basis of plea was that he acted initially in self-defence but his response was an over reaction. Held. Concentrating on the blow **21 months** was severe but not manifestly excessive. (The medical details are scant.)

Old cases *R v Ambrose* [1997] 1 Cr App Rep (S) 404.

See also *Serious but unexpected injuries*

Glassings

112.7 *R v Robertson* [1998] 1 Cr App Rep (S) 21. The defendant pleaded guilty to a s 20 wounding. The defendant was watching football in a public house with friends. The victim realised he was being spoken to by the defendant said, 'Pardon.' The defendant said do you want to be scarred. The victim said, 'No thanks.' The defendant grabbed him and showed him a glass and said, 'You would be if I pushed that in your face.' The victim did not take this as a threat as he thought he was drunk. The defendant then faced the victim and thrust a glass into his face, which broke. The defendant was arrested and said he did not recall the incident and was drunk at the time. He expressed remorse. The victim suffered a 2½″ cut above the eye and two cuts below. The defendant was suffering anxiety about work and had difficulty controlling his drinking. He had only a drink/drive conviction. His medical notes referred to unexplained acts of violence when he had been drinking. The defendant has now accepted his alcohol problem. Held. Considering *R v McLoughlin* (1985) 7 Cr App Rep (S) 67 and *R v Doak* (1992) 14 Cr App Rep (S) 128 the court should look with care at sentences over 2 years. It was a serious offence involving a glass. **2 years** not 30 months.

R v Singleton [1998] 1 Cr App Rep (S) 199. The defendant was convicted of unlawful wounding. He was acquitted of an offnec under s 18. The defendant was in a wine bar with his sister and his girlfriend. The victim spoke to his sister in an objectionable and sexual way. The victim went to order drinks and on his way back walked past the defendant who stood up on the foot rest of his stool and picked up a glass. He swung his arm and smashed the glass into the victim's face. The defendant was taken out of the bar and he told the owner the victim had started it. The victim had very serious injuries to his eye and face. At the trial over 6 months later he was still undergoing treatment. The left eye remains at significant risk of severe visual loss or blindness. It was a 'very severe injury.' There was a small life long risk of the healthy right eye being affected by sympathetic ophthalmia. The defendant was arrested and said it was an accident after the victim had punched him. He was of good character with references. Held. We have regard to the very serious injuries and the strong personal mitigation. **2 years** not 3.

Public houses/After drinking

112.8 *R v Byrne* [1998] 1 Cr App Rep (S) 105. The defendant pleaded guilty at the first opportunity to unlawful wounding and affray. The defendant with a group of friends went to his local pub and he drank about 7 or 8 pints of lager. He asked the manager to turn the jukebox up and the manager refused to do it. The defendant continued to be abusive and the manager still refused to turn it up. The defendant was calmed down by a member of his party. Ten minutes later his son who was barred from the pub came in and the staff refused to serve him. The defendant got involved in an argument about this. The manager tried to calm the situation but the defendant lost his temper and wanted in his words, 'to harm the pub.' He picked up a bar stool and threw it across the bar intending to damage the optics. Unfortunately it hit a female member of staff rendering her unconscious. A head wound required six stitches. The defendant showed remorse and paid £500 to the victim. His last violent conviction was in 1979 and he had character witnesses. His business which employed 20 staff was in jeopardy. He received 18 months for the wounding and 6 months for the affray. Held. **9 months** not 18.

R v McNellis [2000] 1 Cr App Rep (S) 481. The defendant pleaded guilty to unlawful wounding on an indictment for wounding with intent. After a lengthy drinking session there was an argument between him and his friend, the victim in a flat. The defendant waved a knife at the victim, which he had earlier used to open bottles. The victim obtained a meat cleaver from the kitchen and a fight developed in which the victim hit him with it on the shoulder causing a wound 4.5 cm long and 1.5 cm deep. The defendant then stabbed the victim four times in quick succession in the shoulder, upper arm and twice in the chest with the knife. In hospital the victim deteriorated rapidly due to the severity of the wounds. Holes were found in his left and right ventricles of his heart. He was 4 days in intensive care and was in hospital for 24 days. The defendant was 37 and had numerous convictions for a variety of offences with many for dishonesty. He had served prison sentences. The longest was 9 months. The judge accepted the he was not entirely to blame. On appeal it was argued there was insufficient discount for the plea. Held. The wounds were of the utmost severity and could have led to death. The plea should not have been accepted. **4½ years** was a severe sentence but it did not cross the threshold of being manifestly excessive.

Knives

112.9   *R v Farrar* [2002] 2 Cr App Rep (S) 63. The defendant changed his plea to guilty to unlawful wounding and ABH. A section 18 count was dropped. The defendant held a house warming party and at about 12.20am one of the guests made an unfortunate but well meaning joke. There was then an argument between him and his partner who was one of the people present. The maker of the joke approached and said to the defendant, 'Sorry, cheer up' and patted him with a friendly gesture. The defendant headbutted him which cut his forehead. That victim was taken to hospital and the cut required six stitches. There was bruising to the bridge of the nose and discolouration to an eye. The party continued and at about 5am the defendant became involved in an argument with his partner's brother about a long standing family issue about the different ethnicity between the defendant and his partner. It culminated in a struggle but no one was injured. The brother left the house and a short while afterwards the defendant followed with a large carving knife. Outside a neighbour was being dropped off by a friend. The neighbour saw the defendant's demeanour and was concerned about walking past him. The friend decided to reverse into a side street and take a different route. The defendant approached the car and asked, 'What are you doing hanging around here?' The friend said, 'Nothing.' The defendant kept on asking him what he was doing and then asked him for a lift home. He did this in a threatening manner. The friend said, 'Get lost.' The defendant then smashed the car window and lunged at him with a knife. The friend who was a doorman opened the car door, forced the defendant backwards and punched out at him. He managed to restrain the defendant who kept on struggling violently. Police arrived and arrested the defendant. The victim was taken to hospital and found to have a deep wound to his index and ring finger. The radial digital nerve was divided and he would have permanent loss of normal sensation. The defendant was interviewed and admitted hitting the window but claimed he was set upon by the victim. Afterwards he was an in patient for 5 days at an acute psychiatric unit. He was 29 and had a conviction for ABH in 1996 for which he received CSO. He had been teased at school because of his gypsy origins. He had become an apprentice welder, which led to him graduating from University in computer studies. He worked for Rolls Royce and was buying his house with his partner. A psychiatrist said he suffered from anxiety in crowds and with strangers. In 1999 he had been badly assaulted in a nightclub. The risk of the defendant causing further harm to the public was assessed as high. Held. This was an extremely bad case of wounding. It was very nasty but **2½ years** not 3½. There was nothing wrong with the 6 months consecutive for the ABH.

Serious but unexpected injuries

112.10   *R v Jane* [1998] 2 Cr App Rep (S) 363. The defendant pleaded guilty at the Magistrates' Court to GBH. The defendant bought some tins of lager from a shop and drank them. He returned and stole two more cans. A few minutes later he tried to steal some more but the shopkeeper locked the door. He tried to leave but the shopkeeper stood in his way and held his arm telling him to wait till the police arrived. A struggle developed and the shopkeeper fell to the floor. A friend of the defendant pushed the door open and the shopkeeper continued to try to stop him leaving. The defendant kicked him in the face and left. The shopkeeper's eye was serious injured. There was no likelihood of the vision returning to normal. There was a small risk of sympathetic ophthalmia occurring in the uninjured eye causing reduced vision in that eye. The defendant was arrested and made full admissions. He said he kicked out in frustration and had not intended to cause any injury. He was 23 and had been in the army and the experience had effected him mentally. He had a conviction for threatening behaviour. He showed remorse and had a number of impressive character references. He also had attended an alcohol rehabilitation course. Held. He lashed out in a panic. There was no suggestion that he intended to do serious harm. **2½ years** not 3½.

R v Clarke [1999] 2 Cr App Rep (S) 400. The defendant pleaded guilty at the first opportunity to GBH and threatening words and behaviour. After the defendant's Rugby team had won the League cup the defendant and players etc. went to celebrate and ended up in a nightclub. Shortly after 1am the doorman of the club said the defendant had bumped into him. The defendant said it was accidental but was asked to leave and did so. He began shouting at the doorman and kicked the door. This was the Public Order offence. At about the same time, the victim a complete stranger to the defendant left the club and walked down an alleyway. The defendant overtook him and punched him in the face with the back of fist. The defendant thought he was the doorman. The force of the blow knocked the victim to the ground and he hit his neck and head against a building. The defendant walked off not realising he had been seriously injured. Members of the public flagged down a passing ambulance and he was taken to hospital. His neck was fractured at the base of the skull and he was placed in a halo jacket, which he had to wear for 6 months. Five months later it was hoped that the fracture would unite and the outlook was 'good.' The injury was potentially fatal and there was the possibility of severe and irreparable neurological damage. The defendant surrendered voluntarily to the police. He showed genuine remorse and apologised unreservedly to the victim. He was 19 and of good character and with an admirable record and 15 testimonials about charity work etc. Held. For any unprovoked blow of this nature, which causes the serious, albeit fortunately not even long term injury which this blow caused, the assailant must expect to go straight to custody. There was a great deal of mitigation and the attack was limited and unpremeditated. **6 months** YOI not 18 and 1 month not 6 for the Public Order Act offence remaining concurrent.

Sporting

112.11   *R v Calton* [1999] 2 Cr App Rep (S) 64. The defendant pleaded guilty to GBH. His plea of not guilty to GBH with intent was accepted. He was aged 19 and played in a schools' rugby match. The victim was on the ground after a ruck and was getting up. The defendant who was on the opposing side kicked him to the side of the head. There was a loud crack. He was sent off and when interviewed said he kicked him because the victim had tried to grab his ankles. The victim had a fracture to his mandible. Six months later he was still having problems with his jaw and was still in pain. The defendant was a student with no convictions and five testimonials. He didn't want to play rugby again. The risk of re-offending was assessed as low. The judge sentenced him on the basis it was a fit of temper. There was a good prison report. Held. Custody was necessary but **3 months** detention not 12.

R v Moss [2000] 1 Cr App Rep (S) 307. The defendant was convicted of GBH. According to the victim he was at the bottom of a ruck in a rugby game and was getting up when the defendant who was on the opposing team punched him in the face knocking him to the ground. He was disorientated and his eye bled. A witness said they it was 10' from the ruck and both players were throwing punches. The defendant denied hitting the victim. The victim was found to have a blow out fractured eye socket with entrapment of both fat and muscle. This had to be reduced and a titanium mesh was inserted to reconstruct the orbital floor. He was in hospital for 5 weeks. 10 days after his release he was suffering from diplopia. There was 16 months delay before sentence. The defendant was 35 with a conviction for conspiracy to defraud. There were no convictions for violence. The risk for re-offending was assessed as extremely unlikely. He was married with children and his small business would suffer severe hardship or collapse if he remained in custody. There were eight character references. His prison conduct was commendable. Held. **8 months** was not too long.

R v Bowyer [2001] EWCA Crim 1853, [2002] 1 Cr App Rep (S) 448. The defendant was convicted of GBH. In the final of a Rugby Union competition there was a scrum and when it broke up the victim went to defend his team's line. The defendant struck him a very severe blow which knocked him off his feet. The blow broke his jaw in two places and split his gum. His lower incisors were pushed backwards. Two plates were inserted which would remain there permanently. The defendant faced three trials after the first jury could not agree and the second was struck by illness. The defendant was 36 and treated as of good character although he had old convictions for ABH and threatening behaviour. It was out of character and he was a hard working family man with children. Held. This kind of gratuitous violence on the field is not to be tolerated. Acts of physical violence off the ball in sporting events must receive custodial sentences. **8 months** was severe but not excessive let alone manifestly excessive.

R v Tasker [2001] EWCA Crim 2213, [2002] 1 Cr App Rep (S) 515. The defendant pleaded guilty to unlawful wounding at the Magistrates' Court. The defendant was playing in a local Sunday league football match. The score was 0-0 until the victim's team scored a disputed goal. His players protested but it was allowed. Thereafter things deteriorated rapidly. He was later cautioned by the referee after an incident with one of the opposing players and spoken to by the referee after that. Matters came to head following a foul and there was a flare up between the players during which the victim was pulled to the ground. Before he could get up the defendant came across the field and kicked him in the face. The victim could hardly see and the game was abandoned. An X-ray of the victim showed a fracture of the lower eye socket and possibly another one under the cheek bone. When interviewed the defendant said it was, 'just a rush of blood, silly moment'. He was 29 and of good character in full time employment. Held. There was no provocation. He had been cautioned and deliberately went over and kicked him. Very serious injuries were caused. Looking at the authorities **6 months** not 12.

See also *R v Ahmed* [2002] EWCA Crim 779, [2002] 2 Cr App Rep (S) 535.

Stalking

See STALKING – *Offences Against the Person Act 1861, s 20*

Strangers in street, attack on

112.12   *R v Byrne* [1998] 1 Cr App Rep (S) 105. The defendant pleaded guilty to unlawful wounding which had been offered and rejected by the prosecution months earlier. His plea of not guilty to a s 18 offence was accepted because of his drunkenness at the time. The defendant became very drunk and met a complete stranger in the street. He asked the stranger, 'Where is my misses?' and 'No one comes before my misses.' He then punched him and stabbed him with a chisel. He went home and told his mother he had killed someone. The victim was taken to hospital and stab wound in his arm with a 10 cm laceration dividing 75% of one of the muscles was found. His mother phoned the police because the defendant was trying to kill himself by throwing himself in front of traffic. He was 22 and unemployed. He had four previous convictions including robbery and theft (for which he received 30 months). He had a personality disorder and alcohol 'released the angry person within him.' Held. This was a grave offence. The plea was rightly accepted. Because of the plea **30 months** not 4 years.

R v Curry [1998] 2 Cr App Rep (S) 410 – LCJ. The defendant changed his plead when his trial was due to start to guilty of unlawful wounding and ABH. A s 18 count was left on the file. At about 11pm two brothers were getting into a taxi after an evening drinking and the defendant approached them and asked for a cigarette. One reached in his pocket to get one and the defendant said, 'No one fucking ignores me.' The defendant punched him in the back of the head and seized his hair. Then he banged his head on the roof of the taxi and was pulled onto the ground where he was further assaulted. The other brother pushed the defendant back into some metal shutters of a shop. A struggle ensued in which the defendant punched the second victim two or three times in the face. A female asked the defendant to stop and the attack ceased and the brothers ran off. The first victim had bruises to the face, shoulder and elsewhere. He needed a sling for his shoulder injury. The other had two fractures in the lower jaw. The jaw had to be wired. Both received counselling. When arrested the defendant said he had been drinking since 2pm and had drunk 13 pints of lager. He said he was pushed against the shutters but was not the man who asked for a cigarette. He had a number of convictions for violence and was on licence with 19 months to serve. Held. The offence called for a severe penalty. However, **3 years** not 4 for the Section 20 offence. The period for the breach of licence reduced from 19 months to 12 consecutive. The ABH sentence remained 18 months concurrent.

See also *R v Clare* [2002] EWCA Crim 619, [2002] 2 Cr App Rep (S) 445.

Vehicle used as a weapon

112.13   *R v Wildman* [1998] 1 Cr App Rep (S) 236. The defendant was convicted of unlawful wounding and dangerous driving. He was acquitted of s 18. The defendant had a somewhat stormy relationship with his girlfriend over 3 years and they had two children. In one of the many separations the girlfriend met the victim and she said they were never more than friends. The defendant became reconciled with his girlfriend but was jealous of the victim. On Boxing Day the victim had too much to drink and sat beside the girlfriend. The defendant stared at him and she stood up. As she did so the victim stroked her leg and the victim was ejected from the club. At 1 am on New Years Day the defendant after drinking told some acquaintances that he was looking for the victim. The defendant then drove away and saw the victim after he had left a pub worse for drink. He turned his car round and drove it at the victim. There was an issue whether the victim was on the pavement or in the road at the time. The defendant told the girlfriend the victim had walked into the middle of the road and he had put his foot down. The victim was very seriously injured. He had a fracture to his face with multiple lacerations and contusions. He stopped breathing in the ambulance. He was paralysed and unconscious initially. By the trial he had improved considerably but was left with a personality change which was likely to be permanent. The defendant was 25 and had no convictions for violence but had one for criminal damage arising out of an argument with his girlfriend. Held. The courts treat very seriously any offence committed by means of misuse of a motorcar. It is indeed a lethal weapon. If a car is driven at speed at someone it is always likely that serious injury may result. **4 years** was correct. (The report does not refer to the estimated speed of the car.)

See also CRUELTY TO CHILDREN – **Cruelty to Children – Offences Against the Person Act 1861, s 20**

113 OFFENCES AGAINST THE PERSON ACT 1861, S 20 – RACIALLY-AGGRAVATED

113.1 Crime and Disorder Act 1998, s 29

Triable either way. On indictment maximum 7 years. Summary maximum 6 months and/or £5,000.

Where the offence was committed relevant to a football match and where there are reasonable grounds to believe that making a banning order would help to prevent violence or disorder at or in connection with any regulated football match; the court must make a Football Banning Order under the Football Spectators Act 1989, s 14A and Sch 1, para 1.

Magistrates' Court Sentencing Guidelines September 2000 – Wounding

113.2 Entry point. Are Magistrates' sentencing powers appropriate? Consider the level of racial aggravation and the impact on the victim. Examples of aggravating factors for the offence are deliberate kicking or biting, extensive injuries, group action, offender in position of authority, on hospital/medical premises, pre-meditated, victim particularly vulnerable, victim serving the public and weapon. Examples of mitigating factors for the offence are minor wound, provocation and single blow. Examples of mitigation are age, health (physical or mental), co-operation with the police, voluntary compensation and genuine remorse. Consider committal for sentence. Give reasons if not awarding compensation.

For details about the guidelines see MAGISTRATES' COURT SENTENCING GUIDELINES at page 331.

For basic principles about racially-aggravated offences see RACIALLY-AGGRAVATED OFFENCES

114 OFFENCES AGAINST THE PERSON ACT 1861, S 23

Administering etc poison or noxious thing etc so as to endanger life or inflict GBH. Indictable only. Maximum sentence 10 years.

Drugs – Class A

114.1 *R v Dorosz* [2001] EWCA Crim 769, [2001] 2 Cr App Rep (S) 476. The defendant pleaded guilty at the first opportunity to two counts of supplying heroin and administering heroin so as to endanger life. The victim visited his flat. At the request of the victim he injected her with heroin. Later she injected herself. One evening she brought heroin and cocaine to his flat. They both injected themselves with heroin and cocaine probably four or five times. He probably gave her two of them and she gave herself the rest. He asked her several times whether she was alright and she always said she was. She seemed to be enjoying it. Apart from one occasion he always put the heroin in the syringe to ensure she was taking less than he was. He left her to sleep on the sofa. In the morning he rang his workplace to say he was unwell and went back to bed. He woke again at 1pm and could not wake her. He called for an ambulance and she could not be resuscitated. Police arrived and he gave them above account although in less detail. An expert said she possibly died from heroin and cocaine. He also said she had taken heroin up her nose, which the defendant said he had not seen. He was 28 and of good character. He gave a full account to the coroner although he was not obliged to. He was arrested 2 months later. He was a computer programmer, which rewarded well. He had developed a fascination with altered states of the mind and had abused drugs including heroin from time to time. He had impressive character witnesses. He was genuinely remorseful and the pre-sentence report said that the event had been devastating for him. Held. There were many factors in his favour. **2½ years** on each count concurrent not 3½.

Neighbours

114.2   *R v Cronin-Simpson* [2000] 1 Cr App Rep (S) 54. The defendant was convicted of three counts of causing a noxious thing to be administered so as to endanger life. The defendant's mother lived next door to the victims who detected a strong smell of fumes in their house. It appeared to be either petrol or ammonia. Liquid was seen to be pouring down the walls. The three occupants began to feel ill and suffer from nausea. One of them discovered a brick had been removed in the loft between the two houses. Police found a number of containers of petrol and other liquids in the mother's house. Local authority inspectors also found three pipes running in a cavity wall into the neighbours' house which were found to contain petrol. There were also holes in the plasterwork. The defendant was unfit to be interviewed and spent a short time in a psychiatric hospital. She gave no clue as to the reason for the offence. She gave detail of some disputes with the neighbours but said she had not had any problems with them. She was 62 with some minor convictions for criminal damage and abusive behaviour. She refused to co-operate with a psychiatric report. The judge said the ammonia and petrol mix was extremely dangerous. After sentence a report said she had a hysterical personality disorder and a paranoid personality. She was suspected of suffering paranoid delusions. There were no signs of a major mental illness. Her prison behaviour was above standard. Held. Because the neighbours did not suffer more than feeling ill and nausea and her medical condition **4 years** not 6.

115   OFFENCES AGAINST THE PERSON ACT 1861, S 24

Administering etc poison or noxious thing etc with intent to injure, aggrieve of annoy. Indictable only. Maximum sentence 5 years.

General principles

115.1   *R v Jones* (1990) 12 Cr App Rep (S) 233. The right approach is to equate the offence with either an Offences Against the Person Act 1861, s 20 offence or a serious ABH.

Neighbours etc, unexplained administering to

115.2   *R v Nasar* [2000] 1 Cr App Rep (S) 333. The defendant pleaded guilty to three counts of causing a noxious thing to be administered with intent. On three occasions she mixed a sleep inducing tablet with food or drink and gave it to friends or relations on the pretext it was beneficial for some supposed ailment. On the last occasion having drugged the woman she tied her up and bundled her unconscious into a suitcase and took her from her house into a car to move her to another house. She asked two friends who had come to visit her to give her a lift. As she was struggling with the suitcase the friends heard the victim calling from inside the suitcase. They opened the case and found the victim semi-conscious inside. On two of the occasions the victims were hospitalised and all three victims lost consciousness. The first drug was fluoxetine, which the defendant had been prescribed for her depression. The second drug was probably sleeping pills, which were also proscribed to her or her disabled daughter. The third drug was most probably Temazepan and an anti-depressant drug called Dothiepin. She was arrested and claimed the last victim asked for the tablets and she put her in the box because the victim was nearly unconscious and she could not find a pushchair. She couldn't speak English and showed a lot of concern for her mentally disabled daughter who required constant attention. The psychiatrist diagnosed a somatised anxiety state, which was a form of mental illness. She was sentenced on the basis the true explanation was unknown but she did not intend to cause any permanent harm. She received 1, 1 and 12 months concurrent. Held. Because of the defendant's age (not stated) and antecedents **12 months** was a severe sentence but it was fully merited for these deliberate acts which certainly in relation to the last matter could well have caused death. [The serious aspect seems to be the false imprisonment of the last victim, which was not a something she was charged with.]

Prank etc

115.3   *R v Callaghan* [2001] EWCA Crim 198 [2001] 2 Cr App Rep (S) 339. The defendant pleaded guilty to causing a noxious thing to be administered with intent to injure or annoy and common assault. He had known the young victim for some time and she had recently purchased a house from him. He agreed to do some carpentry work in the house for her before she moved in if she helped him. While she was out of the room he slipped a prescription only drug into her glass. Its effects were sedation, drowsiness and confusion. Combined with alcohol the effects could be more severe. She became unconscious. When she came round the next morning, on her skin just below the knicker line the defendant had written 'In here' and an arrow pointing to her private parts. She was horrified and she became frightened. The next day he asked her if she remembered falling over in the garden and said he had written over her to show how inebriated she was. Traces of the drug were found in her glass and a half-consumed packet of the same drug was found at the defendant's home. He denied the offence when interviewed. The basis of plea was that there was no indecent motive and it was a joke. Also he had not needed to remove any of her clothing. He was 52 and of good character with character witnesses. Held. The dominant consideration is the victim. The drug was calculated to render her unconscious and the drawing on her which was an invasion of her person aggravated the offence. **6 months** was just as it should have been.

Security staff, directed at

115.4   *R v Tre Sky* [2000] 2 Cr App Rep (S) 260. The defendant pleaded guilty to causing a noxious thing to be taken with intent, common assault, theft and breach of bail. A security guard at Marks and Spencer was informed the defendant had stolen a bottle of vodka. Outside the store he tried to apprehend him and the defendant sprayed a substance in his face. The guard was temporarily blinded and had difficulty in breathing. He also had a burning sensation to his face. The defendant escaped. The guard's eyes were bloodshot and he was treated with antibiotics and eye drops. When interviewed the defendant said he acted out of panic. He had been given the substance by another and did not known what it was. He was 28 with numerous convictions for dishonesty including 22 for theft. One was for failing to surrender. The majority were spent. Held. **21 months** for the spray offence was not manifestly excessive. The theft sentence, 1 month and breach of bail sentence, 2 months remained consecutive making **2 years** in all.

Victim under 10

115.5   *R v Liles* [2000] 1 Cr App Rep (S) 31. The defendant pleaded guilty to causing a noxious thing to be administered. Two brothers aged 5 and 6 years visited the defendant who was 52. They knew the defendant and they lived in the same road. The defendant used isobutyle nitrate which was similar to amyl nitrate. During their visit he allowed them to inhale some. The boys felt dizzy and unwell. Some was spilt on the face and clothing of the youngest. His mother noticed that his eyes were full of tears and his face bright red. He was taken to hospital and allowed home. The defendant had been in trouble in the past for a number of different matters. He was sentenced on the basis that there was no sexual content. Held. Because of the plea and frankness **2 years** not 3.

116   OFFENSIVE WEAPON, POSSESSION OF AN

116.1   Prevention of Crime Act 1953, s 1

Triable either way. On indictment maximum sentence 4 years. Summary maximum 6 months and/or £5,000.

It is a relevant offence under the Football Spectators Act 1989, s 14A and Sch 1, para 1. Where (a) the accused was at or attempting to enter or leave the premises or journeying to and from the football premises or the offence related to a match, the offence was committed during a journey and the court makes a declaration that the offence related to football matches and (b) there are reasonable grounds to believe that making a banning order would help to prevent violence or disorder at or in connection with any regulated football match, the court must make a Football Banning Order (except where the defendant is given an absolute discharge).

Magistrates' Court Sentencing Guidelines September 2000

116.2   Entry point. Is it so serious that only custody is appropriate? Consider the impact on the victim. Examples of aggravating factors for the offence are group action or joint possession, location of offence, people put in fear/weapon brandished, planned use and very dangerous weapon. Examples of mitigating factors for the offence are acting out of a genuine fear, no attempt to use the weapon and offence not premeditated. Examples of mitigation are age, health (physical or mental), co-operation with the police, voluntary compensation and genuine remorse.

For details about the guidelines see **MAGISTRATES' COURT SENTENCING GUIDELINES** at page 331.

Self protection, claim of

116.3   *R v Proctor* [2000] 1 Cr App Rep (S) 295. The defendant was convicted of possessing an offensive weapon. Police spoke to him and he was taken to a police station and was searched. They found a plastic bottle containing ammonia. He said it was for his own protection and had been carrying it for 2–3 days. He also feared a particular individual was going to stab him. The ammonia strength was similar to household solutions and if sprayed into the eyes could cause extreme discomfort. He was 23 with convictions for dishonesty. He had served 12 months for burglary and theft but had been out of trouble for some time. Held. Offences of this nature are serious. **9 months** was severe but not manifestly excessive.

See also **Bladed Article, Possession of a**

117 Official Secrets Acts

117.1 Official Secrets Act 1911, s 1

Indictable only. Maximum sentence 14 years.

Official Secrets Act 1920 and 1989

Various penalties. Some offences triable only on indictment, some either way and some summary only.

Selling defence secrets, unsuccessful

117.2 *R v Bravo* (2002) Times and Daily Telegraph 2 February and Internet sites – CCC The Recorder of London. The defendant pleaded guilty to five counts under the Official Secrets Act (presumably including 1911 Act, s 1) and five theft counts. He asked for two secrets counts to be taken into consideration. He was a security guard for a private firm at British Aerospace and obtained documents from unlocked security cabinets while on night patrols. He tried to sell the documents, which contained British, and Nato secrets. The documents related to defence systems for Harrier jump jets to stop radar locking onto them, electronic decoy systems for warships and electronic warfare. The documents had a colour system indicating that the documents could threaten life and cause serious damage to operational effectiveness etc. He telephoned the Russian Embassy but only reached an answerphone. He therefore posted the documents with his pager number. When the documents were found to be missing he was suspected. His fingerprints were found at the scene. He was followed. Shortly after the theft, an MI5 agent contacted him and arranged a meeting. Bravo said he had more documents. He was asked what he wanted and he said, 'Money, as much as I can get.' He was arrested and 200 pages of defence secrets were found in the carriers of his motorbike. There was no evidence that national or allied secrets were prejudiced. Had he succeeded those interests would have been substantially prejudiced. He considered he was in a dead-end job and wanted money to go to Spain. He was 30 and a British National of Spanish descent with financial problems. He was described as a loner and typical opportunist spy. He claimed that he had not appreciated the seriousness of what he had done. Sentencing remarks. Although I accept you were motivated by financial gain a lengthy jail term was necessary to deter others. Anyone who has put at risk his country's security must receive long sentences. **11 years**.

Old Defendant

See **Defendant** – *Elderly*

118 Opium

General characteristics

118.1 *R v Mashaollahi* [2001] 1 Cr App Rep (S) 330. Opium is most often imported from traditional opium growing countries in small quantities for personal use. It is not commonly traded on the street and there is no evidence that its use is widespread or that it is likely to increase significantly. The current classification of opium as a class A drug is on the premise that it is to be regarded as being every bit as harmful as other class A drugs. Weight for weight, where street value is concerned, heroin is considered to be approximately eight times more valuable than opium. On this basis, a consignment of 40 kgs of opium at 100% purity would be equivalent in value to five kgs of heroin at 100% purity, importation of which, under the current sentencing guidelines, attracts a sentence of 14 years and upwards on a contested case. We understand that the ratio to apply to convert opium to morphine or heroin would be 10:1 ie 10 kgs of opium would be needed to produce 1 kg of morphine or heroin assuming average levels of purity. In practice, it is virtually impossible to buy heroin or cocaine of 100% purity on the street. They are invariably cut or otherwise adulterated by the admixture of some harmless substance. The extent of criminality depends on the extent of the drug itself and not of the harmless substance. But with opium the position is different. It is a crude mixture of many different chemicals contained in the juice of the seed capsule of the opium poppy, papaver somniferum. Incisions are made in the capsule from which the latex oozes out and when collected and allowed to dry in the air forms a dark sticky mass known as raw opium. For non-medical purposes, such as either smoking or eating the substance, the raw opium is boiled in water, strained to remove insoluble materials and then evaporated to form a sticky paste known as prepared opium. The significant feature is that it is still the natural derivative of the plant, and, save exceptionally, it is not adulterated by the addition of any further substances. It was pointed out to us that the morphine constituent of opium tended to show a considerable variation. However, since we are dealing with the composite product of the plant, we think that any enquiry as to the percentage of one particular constituent, even though it is by itself a Class A drug, would introduce a needless complication to the sentencing process.

For details of the sentences imposed see **SUPPLY OF DRUGS (CLASS A, B AND C) – Opium**

See also **DRUG USERS; IMPORTATION OF DRUGS; POSSESSION OF DRUGS; PRODUCTION OF DRUGS** and **SUPPLY OF DRUGS (CLASS A, B AND C)**

OUTRAGING PUBLIC DECENCY

See **PUBLIC DECENCY, OUTRAGING**

119 PASSPORT OFFENCES

119.1 Various offences and penalties

Old cases. All cases before *R v Singh* [1999] should be ignored.

Guideline case

119.2 *R v Singh* [1999] 1 Cr App Rep (S) 490. There have been a number of inconsistent cases in offences involving false passports. The use of false passports appears to be on the increase. A passport is an important document, that confers rights upon the lawful holder. It is, in our judgment, necessary that the integrity of passports should be maintained. It follows that to use a false passport is a serious offence, whatever the precise nature of the offence. Good character and personal circumstances are of very limited value. Sentences should generally be on a deterrent basis, for the reasons given in *R v Osman* [1999] 1 Cr App Rep (S) 230. Extensive or sophisticated alteration of a passport will always be an aggravating feature. Cases involving the use of false passports will almost always merit a significant period of custody. Taking into account *R v Ollerenshaw* [1999] 1 Cr App Rep (S) 65, this will usually be within the range of **6 to 9 months**, even on a guilty plea by a person of good character.

Guideline remarks

119.3 *R v Takyi* [1998] 1 Cr App Rep (S) 372. The integrity of the passport system is of such public importance that other than in unusual circumstances custodial sentences will follow convictions for the improper use of a passport. The length of the sentence will vary infinitely with the facts of the case.

False passport, using or possessing

119.4 *R v Olorunnibe* [1998] 2 Cr App Rep (S) 260. The defendant pleaded guilty to using a false instrument namely a passport at the Magistrates' Court. He checked in at Gatwick for a flight to Canada. He presented a passport and checks revealed that it was a forgery. He admitted the offence in interview and said he was a political refugee from Nigeria and awaited a decision about his application for asylum. He was desperate to visit his wife and baby in Canada and had provided a photograph and paid £200 for the passport. He wanted to settle in Canada. He expressed remorse and had no convictions. Held. Custody is rightly considered for this offence. That should be the norm indeed the almost inevitable result in any case of using a false passport. Such offences are archetypally committed by persons under great pressure. A loud and clear message must go out that custodial sentences will be imposed. Here **6 months** not 9 months was sufficient.

R v Singh [1999] 1 Cr App Rep (S) 490. The defendant pleaded guilty to using a false instrument at the Magistrates' Court. He presented a false British passport with his photograph inserted for the original one at Gatwick airport, in an attempt to travel to Canada. He was arrested and admitted the offence in interview. He came from India and had no convictions. He was here illegally and expected to be deported. **8 months** was appropriate.

R v Siliavski [2000] 1 Cr App Rep (S) 23. The defendant pleaded guilty to possessing four forged passports at the Magistrates' Court. The defendant arrived at Heathrow on a flight from Bulgaria. He was legitimately entering the country. He was searched and was found to have four counterfeit Greek passports hidden in his trousers. In interview he said he had been asked to bring them here but didn't know what was in the envelope till he looked inside during the flight. He said he was going to be paid £150. **6 months** not 12. [This case was disapproved of in *R v Cheema* [2002] EWCA Crim 325, [2002] 2 Cr App Rep (S) 356.]

R v Balasubramaniam [2001] EWCA Crim 2680, [2002] 2 Cr App Rep (S) 57. The defendant pleaded guilty to using a false instrument. He had indicated that plea at the Magistrates' Court. The defendant tried to fly from Gatwick airport to Canada using a false Danish passport which had his name and photograph in it. He told police he was an asylum seeker and he had been told his mother who lived in Canada was very ill and he knew he would not be able to leave the country with his appeal against the refusal of his asylum application. He had tried unsuccessfully to gain permission to leave the country. He bought the passport for £1,000. Letters confirmed his mother was very seriously ill. He was 34 and of good character. Held. There were no aggravating features. Applying *R v Singh* [1999] 1 Cr App Rep (S) 490 this case is at the bottom of the 6–9 month bracket so 6 months not 12.

False passport, using or possessing – part of large organisation

119.5 *R v Cheema* [2002] EWCA Crim 325, [2002] 2 Cr App Rep (S) 356. The defendant was convicted of having custody or control of false instruments namely 12 false passports. The defendant arrived at Birmingham airport from Amsterdam with 12 counterfeit Greek and German passports with Asian names and £2,500. He had been in Amsterdam 1 day and the passports were not of the best quality and were unlikely to deceive an immigration official. He was treated as a courier. He was 65 with two convictions in 1974 for conspiracy to assist illegal entry for which he received 42 months. In 1996 he received 7 years for importing 17 kgs of heroin. Held. A courier in the drugs trade is not treated less seriously than a person carrying drugs for his own use. The same approach is required in the illegal trade in false passports. We disagree with any principle in *R v Siliavski* [2000] 1 Cr App Rep (S) 23 suggesting the contrary. Couriers are a necessary element in this unlawful trade. Sentences need to deter others. But **3 years** not 4.

Making false statements

119.6 *R v Walker* [1999] 1 Cr App Rep (S) 42. The defendant pleaded guilty to making a false statement to obtain a passport. The defendant came to Britain from Zimbabwe and remained after the permitted period had expired. He applied for a passport in a different name with a false date and false place of birth. He was 31 and of good character. He had given evidence for the prosecution in a serious criminal matter. Held. Passport application offences are to be treated seriously. They have the potential to undermine the immigration control system. As the maximum is **2 years 9 months** not 18 was appropriate to take into account the plea and to leave room for more serious offences.

Obtaining a passport using false documents

119.7 *R v Wardenier* [1999] 1 Cr App Rep (S) 244. The defendant pleaded guilty to obtaining property by a deception at the Magistrates' Court. The defendant met a Russian woman and offered her a holiday in the UK. She had difficulty in obtaining a visa and he persuaded a friend to apply for a passport. A local councillor endorsed her photograph. The defendant then took a photograph of the Russian woman and wrote an endorsement on it purporting to be from the councillor. A passport was received and the defendant altered the date of birth by 10 years. In November 1995, he flew to Warsaw and met the Russian woman and they both tried to leave for the UK. The passport was detected and she was sent home to Russia. He wasn't charged till January 1998. Held. It was an extremely serious offence. It was his plan. **6 months** could not be faulted. If it had been slightly longer he could not have complained.

Someone else's passport, using

119.8 *R v Takyi* [1998] 1 Cr App Rep (S) 372. The defendant pleaded guilty to attempting to obtain an air flight by a deception namely that he was the owner of another's passport. The defendant engaged in political activity in Ghana and was arrested. Complaints were made about the conditions of his detention and he was released. In May 1994 he came to the UK using a friend's passport which had a visa to enter the country. When he arrived he applied for political asylum and obtained his own passport in Ghana, which he surrendered to the authorities who kept it. After 6 months he was given permission to work and he worked constantly from then. When his application to remain was refused he decided to travel to Canada where he thought his chances of asylum would be greater. With his passport still kept by the authorities he went to a check in desk at Gatwick and handed over someone else's passport and a ticket to Canada in the same name. The official noticed the photograph did not match the defendant. It was said he would have revealed his true identity when he arrived in Canada. Held. The integrity of the passport system is of such public importance that other than in unusual circumstances custodial sentences will follow convictions for the improper use of a passport. The length of the sentence will vary infinitely with the facts of the case. Here where the passport was genuine, and the motivation was not devious entry into a country where there was reason to believe he would be unwelcome **3 months** not 9. [The court in *R v Osman* [1999] 1 Cr App Rep (S) 230 said this decision in effect was not to be followed.]

R v Osman [1999] 1 Cr App Rep (S) 230. The defendant pleaded guilty to using a false instrument at the Magistrates' Court. The defendant went to Gatwick Airport to board a flight to the US. He produced a passport in the name of Morgan and was arrested. When interviewed he said he wanted to start a new life in the US because he feared that his application for political asylum would fail in this country. He had left Sudan because he claimed he had been tortured. Held. *R v Takyi* [1998] 1 Cr App Rep (S) 372 should be confined to its own facts and should not be treated as an indication of what the appropriate sentence is. In future rely on *R v Hadzic* (17 June 1997, unreported) where on broadly similar facts 12 months was upheld. The only difference between the two is that in Hadzic the passport was altered. The fact a defendant is under personal pressure e.g. a refugee does not excuse the conduct. The courts must discourage those attempting to abuse the system. **9 months** was right.

See also **BIGAMY** – *Immigration controls, to evade* and **IMMIGRATION OFFENCES**

120   PATIENTS, ILL TREATING ETC

120.1   Ill treatment or neglect mental patients

Mental Health Act 1983, s 127

Triable either way. On indictment maximum 2 years. Summary maximum 6 months and/or £5,000.

Elderly patients

120.2   *R v Spedding* [2001] EWCA Crim 2190, [2002] 1 Cr App Rep (S) 509. The defendant was convicted of 11 counts of ill-treating patients. He was a registered mental nurse working in a home for elderly mental patients. The prosecution said he was a lazy, heavy-handed, cruel nurse whose ill treatment was systematic, prolonged and distressing. It ran from February 1997 to May 1999. None of the patients were fit to give evidence. The judge sentenced him to **12 months** on two counts and 9 months on the rest. The sentences were all concurrent and the defendant only appealed the 12 month sentences. One of the sentences was reduced because of the judge's approach and the other was confirmed. [The facts are not listed because the approach of the judge was criticised and the appeal did not centre on whether the sentences were manifestly excessive.]

121   PENSION OFFENCES

Various offences including many under the Pensions Act 1995.

Failing to pay money into employees' company fund

121.1 *R v Dixon* [2000] 2 Cr App Rep (S) 7. The defendant pleaded guilty at the Magistrates' Court to nine offences contrary to the Pensions Act 1995, ss 49(8) and 115(1). He was company secretary and finance director of a ceramic company and trustee of the occupational pension scheme involving payment of part of the 60 employees' pay to the managers of the scheme. Six of the charges related to payments of about £80,000 in total from the company to the scheme which were all made but were 10 to 53 days late. The last three charges related to payment of about £40,000 due but not made. This sum will be replaced from public funds with the possibility of lost interest to the fund as a result. A cheque was issued when there appeared sufficient overdrawing facilities but the bank did not honour it and soon after the company went into receivership at the instigation of the bank. During the period of the offences the bank was reducing the overdraft facilities month by month from £1.5m. The defendant was unaware the delay of payments was a criminal offence. A letter from the pension adviser said payments should be made to avoid late payment fees but said nothing about it being a criminal offence. When he discovered it was an offence he wrote to the regulatory authority and explained the position. When interviewed he candidly accepted his failure and explained the reasons for it. He delayed payment in an attempt to preserve the jobs when the company was beset with debts. He was of good character. A £2,500 penalty had already been paid. Held. The offences have only recently been introduced and were being replaced with one which requires fraudulent evasion of payment. The desire to keep the company going rather than a selfish motive and his frankness with the authority were significant mitigation. 3 and 6 months custody was wrong and it should have been a financial penalty. £250 fine for the first six charges and £500 for the others making **£3,000** fine in total.

See also COMPANY FRAUDS AND FINANCIAL OFFENCES

PERJURY

See PERVERTING THE COURSE OF JUSTICE/CONTEMPT OF COURT ETC

For Perjury Act 1911, s 3 see BIGAMY/MARRIAGE OFFENCES

PERMITTING

For permitting premises to be used for drug supply see the end of the SUPPLY OF DRUGS (CLASS A, B AND C)

For permitting premises to be used by a girl under 13 or under 16 for sexual intercourse see SEXUAL OFFENCES ACT 1956, SS 25 AND 26

122 PERVERTING THE COURSE OF JUSTICE/CONTEMPT OF COURT ETC

122.1

Perverting the course of justice. Common law offence.

Indictable only. No maximum provided so the maximum is life.

Contempt of Court Act 1981, s 12 (Mags), s 14 (and all other courts which have power to commit to prison for contempt)

Contemnors aged 18–20 may be sentenced to YOI[1]. There is no power to sentence a contemnor under 18 to custody[2].

Triable at the court the offence was committed. Maximum 2 years except for Magistrates' Court where 1 month and/or £2,500.

Perjury Act 1911, s 1

Perjury in judicial proceedings.
Indictable only. Maximum 7 years[3].

Criminal Justice and Public Order Act 1994, s 51

Intimidation of witnesses, jurors etc.
Triable either way. On indictment maximum 5 years. Summary maximum 6 months and/or £5,000.

1   Powers of the Criminal Courts (Sentencing) Act 2000, s 108.
2   *R v Byas* [1995] 16 Cr App Rep (S) 869.
3   See the Criminal Justice Act 1948, s 1(1) and (2).

Crown Court statistics England and Wales – Crown Court – Males 21+

122.2

Year	Plea	Total Numbers sentenced	Type of sentence%					Average length of custody[1] (months)
			Discharge	Fine	Community sentence	Suspended sentence	Custody	
Perverting the course of justice								
2000	Guilty	1,076	3%	2%	31%	5%	59%	6.4
	Not guilty	109	0%	4%	15%	2%	76%	18.3
Perjury								
2000	Guilty	46	0%	7%	13%	4%	76%	10
	Not guilty	10	0%	10%	10%	30%	50%	11.6

1   Excluding life sentences. Source: Crime and Criminal Justice Unit, Home Office Ref: IOS416-02.

Guideline remarks – Perjury

122.3   *R v Archer* (2001) Times, 2 August, unreported. There are many factors to be considered when determining the appropriate level of sentence for perjury and related offences. There is not any distinction to be drawn whether the proceedings contaminated were civil or criminal. Perjury may be comparatively trivial in relation to criminal proceedings or very serious in relation to civil proceedings. No doubt whether the proceedings were civil or criminal is one of the factors proper to be considered. There are many others. We do not purport to give an exhaustive list. They include the number of offences committed; the timescale over which they are committed; whether they are planned or spontaneous; whether they are persisted in; whether the lies which are told or the fabrications which are embarked upon have any actual impact on the proceedings in question; whether the activities of the defendant draw in others; what the relationship is between others who are drawn in and the defendant.

Guideline remarks – Perverting the course of justice etc

122.4   *R v Williams* (1995) 16 Cr App Rep (S) 191. The defendant was convicted of an attempt to intimidate a witness in civil proceedings. Held. People who are tempted to involve themselves in seeking to deter witnesses from giving evidence, or true evidence, must realise that a prison sentence is inevitable, whatever their own personal mitigation and good character might be.

R v Khan [2001] EWCA Crim 912, [2001] 2 Cr App Rep (S) 553. Such offences undermine the whole process of justice and they are to be treated seriously and will in most cases merit a custodial sentence to run consecutively to any other sentence.

Evidence, interfering with – Bodies

122.5   *R v Lang* [2001] EWCA Crim 2690, [2002] 2 Cr App Rep (S) 44. The defendant changed his plea to guilty of perverting the course of justice in concealing a body knowing he had been killed and two counts of supplying cocaine. The defendant's uncle shot and killed a fellow criminal at close range with a shotgun probably over a dispute over drugs. The defendant dug a grave in his uncle's garden and helped his uncle bury the body. The grave was covered by a patio. Later he spent time with his brother in a hotel at his uncle's expense. He was nearby when his uncle was arrested and firearms attributed to the uncle were found in a vehicle not far away. His fingerprints were found on wrappings associated with two overalls found by police in the uncle's garden. The uncle was convicted of the murder of the fellow criminal. The defendant told police that while he was digging the grave the uncle was mopping up blood inside the house. He said he was called unexpectedly to assist and couldn't say no because he was scared of the uncle who had been violent to him before and threatened him on the day. The uncle was drunk and had a shotgun in his hand. On two occasions he bought cocaine for another when he bought his own cocaine. He owed that person money. He was 33 and had a number of dishonesty convictions. In 1995 he received 4½ years for possession of firearms and a CS canister, possession of drugs with intent to supply and possession of counterfeit currency. He was released 11 months before the pervert offence. The judge said the facts which lie behind the offences bear all the hallmarks of professional organised crime. It was professional crime to conceal a professional execution by a professional criminal. Held. It was possible to infer that the judge was associating the defendant with the killing. **6 years** not 8 consecutive to the 1 year for the drugs' convictions.

Old case. *A-G's Reference (No 19 of 1993)* (1994) 15 Cr App Rep (S) 760.

See also OBSTRUCTING THE CORONER/BURIAL, PREVENTING

False name or information to the police, giving

122.6   *R v Johnson* [1998] 1 Cr App Rep (S) 169. The defendant pleaded guilty to perverting the course of justice. Following a complaint that someone was masturbating police visited a car park and found the defendant. He gave his brother's name who was sent a court summons. When the brother attended court the officer realised it was not the culprit. The defendant was arrested and admitted the offence. He had minor motoring and dishonesty convictions none of which 'bore on the matter.' He had recently served a prison sentence and had become a father again. Held. The fact of prison is all important. **2 months** not 6.

R v Saxon [1999] 1 Cr App Rep (S) 385. The defendant pleaded guilty to perverting the course of justice. Police stopped him when he was driving a car. He gave his brother's name because he was disqualified from driving. He was asked to produce documents at a police station. When they were not produced his brother was summonsed for failing to produce. The brother spoke to the defendant and the defendant went to the police and said he had lied. He was 22 with a conviction for drink/drive. The pre-sentence report recommended community service, said he had expressed remorse and said the chance of re-offending was low. Held. Custody was right but applying *R v Howells* [1999] 1 Cr App Rep 335 **2 months** not 4 months.

A-G's Reference (Nos 62-65 of 1996) [1998] 1 Cr App Rep (S) 9. The defendants S, J, M and B pleaded guilty to perverting the course of justice at the earliest opportunity.

S also pleaded guilty to dangerous driving, failing to stop and failing to report. S drove his car with M at between 38 and 47 and the car was swerving. There was a 30 mph speed limit and he hit a pedestrian who was thrown into the air. He didn't stop. He abandoned the car and the two went to the home of J and B. The four agreed to report that the car had been stolen. The car was set on fire and it was effectively destroyed. The victim was taken to hospital. She had a massive head injury and fractures to her cheek bone, eye socket, jawbone and knee. She had a large wound on her forehead and blood in her ear. She was in hospital for 16 days. The police were told it had been stolen. Next day the four confessed to the police and were arrested. The victim made a full recovery but has permanent scarring. The prosecution suggested the driving was borderline between careless and dangerous driving. S and J were 22, M 28 and B 27. S had a speeding conviction in 1990. The rest were of good character. M was a mother of four children one of whom was 11 and blind. B was a mother of two children and was expecting a third. She suffered from cerebral palsy and has since married J. The four showed remorse. There was almost a year's delay before sentence. The judge gave S 6 months suspended and conditionally discharged the rest. Held. Remorse and delay were not reasons to suspend the sentence. For S a total sentence of **12 months** would have been appropriate. As it was a reference 8 months would have been appropriate. As the prosecution said **6 months** was the appropriate sentence we substitute 3 months on each consecutive making 6 months. J's sentence is **2 months**. M's sentence is **1 month** and because of the child that would be **suspended**. B sentence is **1 month** and as an act of mercy with the sentence passed on M that would also be **suspended**.

R v Sookoo (20 March 2002, unreported). The defendant gave a false name on arrest. Held. In many cases the addition of a perverting count was unnecessary and only served to complicate the sentencing process. Where as in this case, the defendant had attempted to hide his identity and failed, a specific separate count should not be laid. Where there were serious aggravating features like a great deal of police time and resources were involved or innocent members of the public had been arrested as a consequence, a specific count could be justified. The attempt here was unsophisticated and it was inevitably going to fail. **3 months** not 9 concurrent to 6 months for the other matter.

Incriminating innocent people

122.7   *R v Sadiq* [1999] 2 Cr App Rep (S) 325. The defendant pleaded guilty to perverting the course of justice. In June 1996 the defendant started to live with his girlfriend, the victim. On 28 April 1997 the relationship ended and 3 days later he visited her and there was an argument and he was excluded from the flat. She borrowed his car and returned it on 12 May 1997. They met in the street near her home and he took her house keys and said he was going to her flat to collect his passport. She said she would call the police and he said if she did she would be in one hell of a lot of trouble. She did contact the police who took her home and it was clear he had been in the flat. He gave the keys to a neighbour. Later the same day he called the police claiming to be her previous boyfriend. He tried to disguise his voice and said the victim was about to receive a delivery of drugs. Police thought the call was a hoax in response to the keys. The next day he made another call pretending to be the ex-boyfriend and said he was aware they had been to the flat and told them they had missed the drugs. He suggested they look under the washing machine. Later he made another call giving his true name and said he understood they wanted to talk to him about the keys. The flat was searched and 11 grams of amphetamine and 20 grams of cannabis were found under the washing machine. The drugs were made up in several bags to make it look like she was dealing in drugs. The judge said it was a 'deliberate, calculated attempt' to get the young woman of good character into serious trouble with the police. The defendant had 'serious convictions.' **2 years** not 3.

A-G's Reference (No 85 of 2001) [2002] 2 Cr App Rep (S) 13. The defendant was convicted of doing acts tending to pervert the course of justice. In November and December 1998 the defendant had sex with the victim unbeknown to her boyfriend. She falsely told the victim that her relationship with her boyfriend was over. She arranged to go out with the victim and some of his friends on 24 December but never arrived. In the early hours of Christmas Day she was with her boyfriend at his home. The victim went to her home saw the gas fire on and assumed she was in. The defendant was worried as she was often drunk and had often had to climb in through her window as she was too inebriated to let him in. He climbed in through a window and telephoned the boyfriend using her telephone assuming she was there pretending to be a friend of the boyfriend. two calls were received and the telephone display showed they were being made from the defendant's home. She called the police. When the police went to her home they found the victim with a knife and a tape which he had used to break the window and saw where entry had been gained. He was arrested for burglary and kept in custody. The defendant that day made two witness statements saying the defendant had developed an obsession with her and had sent her flowers, love songs etc at work. He had arrived uninvited at her home although she had not told him where she lived. She said she was frightened of him and had had to improve her security. She had not given him permission to enter her home and as a result of the break in she was terrified. The victim was charged with burglary and harassment and was remanded into custody. Police found photographs of the defendant at the victim's home and she claimed in another witness statement she had not given them to him saying they must have been removed from her house without authority. She gave the police letters, a tape and a card which he had given her. The victim remained in custody till 12 January 1999 when the proceedings were discontinued. She continued with her account and said she wanted the proceedings against the victim to continue. The effect on the victim was severe and he needed psychiatric help. Because of the allegations he had problem in obtaining access to see his son and found difficulty in forming relationships because of his distrust of others. She wasn't interviewed until November 1999 when she maintained her story. Her second trial started 2 years and 4 months after the offence. She was 41 with no convictions except some for drink/drive. The relationship with the boyfriend ended and she had since married someone else. They had taken over a pub and had invested a lot of energy and money into it. She was sentenced to 180 hours CSO, £1,000 costs and £700 compensation to the victim. 69.5 hours were performed and the penalties had been paid. The court heard the appeal nearly 3 years after the offence. **Held.** False complaints of a serious offence sexual or otherwise leading to the arrest of an innocent man/woman call for sentences of immediate imprisonment even on a plea of guilty. It is even more serious when the alleged offence is very grave. Burglary and harassment are grave offences. If the conviction had been obtained in 1999 the sentence would have been counted in months if not years. In light of the delay, her marriage, the way she had established herself, the CSO performed and the payment of penalties the judge was entitled to ask whether custody was necessary. Although we do not say we would have reached the same decision the sentences were not disturbed.

A-G's Reference (Nos 6-8 of 2000) [2002] EWCA Crim 264, [2002] 2 Cr App Rep (S) 341 – LCJ. [The defendants J and R were convicted of conspiracy to commit acts tending to pervert the course of justice. The defendant a police officer pleaded guilty to the same offence. They were involved in planting Class A drugs in the car of the policeman's estranged wife. The starting point was **10–12 years.**]

Jury interference

122.8 *R v Mitchell-Crinkley* [1998] 1 Cr App Rep (S) 368. The contemnor was judged to be guilty of contempt after a trial. He was a friend of someone being retried for obtaining property by deception. He sat in the public gallery and recognised a juror as the son of an old drinking friend. A police officer heard him repeating the names of the jurors with another man. Early next day he obtained the telephone number of the juror from directory enquires and at 6.50am he telephoned the juror. He said without giving his name that the first jury was hung and some inconsequential matters like garden furniture. The juror reported the conversation to a court official and said he was very unnerved, indeed intimidated, and he had lost his appetite for some time. The whole jury was discharged. The contemnor was interviewed and said he only told the juror that he knew something of the man on trial and that he had suggested the juror gave up the case. Further when he was asked by the juror for his name he put the telephone down and he was trying to help the juror. The contemnor was 67. Held. This was a very serious matter indeed. Jurors must be free to come to a fair and informed decision untainted. There was no more important aspect of the judicial process. The effect on the juror was all too apparent. **12 months** was appropriate.

R v Boodhoo [2001] EWCA Crim 1027, [2002] 1 Cr App Rep (S) 33. The defendant pleaded guilty to perverting the course of justice. He acted as a juror and on the second day of the trial he asked his fellow jurors, 'What if they offered us a bribe?' There was then a series of calls and meetings between him and the defendants in the trial. He was paid £1,000 in cash and told them the views of the jurors and was told to do what he could. In fact the jury was not corrupted. Another juror pleaded guilty and gave evidence for the prosecution. Some of the defendants in the first trial were convicted and others acquitted in the pervert trial. The judge said he was the central figure. He was 37 and had co-operated with the police. Held. Any event which threatens the integrity of the jury system will inevitably attract a custodial sentence. **4 years** was entirely appropriate.

Newspaper reporting

122.9 *R v MGM* (2002) Daily Telegraph, 20 April – High Court. The defendant, a publishing company accepted they were in contempt of court. There was a trial of Leeds United footballers at Hull Crown Court about an attack on an Asian student. The judge had stressed to the jury that any issue of racism was not part of the prosecution's case. While the jury was considering their verdict the Sunday Mirror printed an interview with the victim's father. The report said the father said it was a racist attack. The father had agreed to the interview on condition it would not be published till after the verdicts. It caused the trial to be 'derailed' which would be 'lengthy, expensive and traumatic for the complainant, his family, witnesses and defendants alike.' The total cost for the aborted trial was £1.113m and the retrial was £1.25m. The company said it was the result of wrong legal advice and they apologised unreservedly. Two lawyers had been dismissed and the Editor had resigned on the basis that he was ultimately responsible. Held. In the absence of mitigating information we find it difficult to escape the conclusion that the assurances given to the father were simply overridden. The defendant's good record and their attitude since this matter came to light make it possible to reduce the fine to £75,000. The costs to be paid were £54,160. [News reports should be treated with care.]

Outbursts in court

122.10 *R v Lewis* (22 October 1999, unreported). The six defendants were judged to be in contempt of court. They went to court to see a friend being sentenced. The friend was given 6 months. The Assistant Recorder heard a disturbance and cries of 'terrible' and 'disgusting' with people pointing at the bench. The defendants said they were upset because the court had been misled by the victim's impact statement. The defendants were all of good character and apologised unreservedly. Each was in gainful employment or had home responsibilities. Held. In a situation like this it is often tactically wise for a judge merely to rise and leave the courtroom, and for those who wish to behave badly to do so in his absence. It was not suitable for the contempt to be dealt with by another court because that would have blown the whole thing out of proportion. The defendants should be dealt with quickly and they should know their fate as soon as possible. This contempt was at the low end of the scale. The custody threshold was not crossed. The situation could have been dealt with by a strong judicial reprimand coupled if necessary with a fine or discharge. 7 days was wholly wrong in principle and quashed. **No order** substituted.

Perjury – To assist your own case

122.11   *R v Dunlop* [2001] 2 Cr App Rep (S) 133. The defendant pleaded guilty to two counts of perjury. In 1991, the defendant was tried for murder and gave evidence that he had not gone to the victim's house shortly before her death. The jury failed to agree and he gave the same evidence again at the retrial. That jury couldn't agree and he was discharged. In fact shortly before her death he had been in a fight at a stag do and beaten a man and gouged his eyes such that he was in hospital for 4 days. Afterwards he went round to see the victim of the murder and on his account she made fun of him and his injuries and he lost his temper and strangled her. After the trials he formed a relationship with another woman and they had a child. The relationship didn't last and she found another boyfriend. He then stabbed her several times and smashed the facial bones of the boyfriend with a baseball bat. He received 7 years for those offences. In prison he confessed to the murder to a prison officer. He said he was sick of violence and wanted help. He also wrote a letter to an ex-girlfriend confessing to the murder. He was sincere in accepting the distress he had caused to the family of the deceased. He was about 37 when sentenced with convictions for a firearm offence, an offensive weapon offence, eight offences against the person and 18 offences for dishonesty. A psychiatric report said he suffered from a number of abnormal personality traits. Held. The offences were very serious. The case was aggravated by the perjury being at a very grave trial and it was repeated. No criticism could be made if the judge had given 3 years on each consecutive so there was no fault with **6 years** concurrent on each but consecutive to the 7 years.

R v Archer (2002) Times, 2 August. The defendant, Lord Archer was convicted of procuring a false alibi, two counts of perverting the course of public justice, swearing a false affidavit and perjury. In 1986 he was a successful writer, ambitious politician and deputy chairman of the Conservative Party. The News of the World published articles saying he had sex with a prostitute and that money was handed to her at Victoria Station to silence her. The Star newspaper effectively repeated the News of the World's allegation with added details. The co-accused who was a casual friend created a false alibi for the appellant. He received £12,000 in cash and was told the defendant would help him with his film script. At the libel trial against The Star newspaper the prostitute gave her account and the defendant gave false evidence. A diary with false entries written by his secretary was relied on. In 1999 the co-accused approached Max Clifford, a public relations man. Held. The secretary was an employee and therefore vulnerable to suggestions made by her employer. The co-accused was corrupted by money. Considering the length of time over which these offences were committed, the perceived involvement of others, and the persistence in dishonest conduct **4 years** was not manifestly excessive.

Prosecution/conviction, to avoid

122.12 *R v Saxena* [1999] 1 Cr App Rep (S) 170. The defendant a doctor, pleaded guilty to two counts of perverting the course of justice. They were not entered at the first opportunity. The defendant was in a minor traffic accident and was charged with failing to stop, failing to report and due care. He was interviewed and denied being the driver. He approached a colleague who worked as a doctor in prison and asked her if she would like to earn £200. He asked her to write a note saying he was on duty in the prison at the time of the accident. She contacted the police. After he was convicted of the offences he repeatedly contacted her and she told the police about it. The police arranged for her to meet him with a tape recorder on her. He again asked her to give evidence for him at his appeal despite the fact she repeatedly said she could not recall whether he was working that day. He encouraged her to make false entries in her diary and offered her money and a trip to India. The defendant was arrested and denied the offences. He had a conviction for obtaining property by a deception for which he received a suspended sentence. He was about 47 and would be struck off as a doctor. He had health difficulties and was the sole carer of his 6-year-old son. Held. The case was serious. The offence was repeated. **3 months and 6 months consecutive** was not manifestly excessive.

R v Wake [1999] 2 Cr App Rep (S) 403. The defendant pleaded guilty to perverting the course of justice. The defendant after celebrating in a pub drove his car into two elderly men who had just got off a bus. Both died very shortly afterwards. His car was very seriously damaged. He did not stop but drove the car to a wood where he abandoned it. He wrenched off the cowling around the ignition to make it look like it had been hot-wired. He went back to the pub and asked a friend to drive him home. On the way he threw some clothing out of the window because it was impregnated with glass. He told his wife if the police called he should say the car had been stolen. He went back to the pub and when he arrived home the police were there and he was told the two victims had died. He denied any knowledge of the accident and lied during several interviews but admitted it in a later interview. He had convictions but had not served a custodial sentence. He was only prosecuted for due care. The judge said the sentence had to be more than the charges he avoided namely two death by dangerous driving. Held. That approach was wrong. The offences were separate. Within 24 hours the defendant had given his account of what had happened and the prosecution could have charged whatever offence they liked. He had drawn his wife into the offence. **2 years** not 4½.

R v Dowd and Huskins [2000] 1 Cr App Rep (S) 349. The defendants D and H changed their plea to guilty of perverting the course of justice. H also pleaded to driving without due care and attention when originally charged with dangerous driving. H drove D in his father's car on a bendy unlit road with no pavement just less than an hour after lighting up time. The victims were walking in the same direction on the right hand side of the road. The car was on the wrong side of the road and hit the victims. One died instantly and the other was very seriously injured. H drove on and told a witness he thought he had knocked someone over. The car's front indicator surround was broken. H and D returned to the scene to retrieve the missing pieces. H met C who he knew and told him that he thought he had hit someone and was told, 'he looks all right he's sat' and was advised to leave. That person when he leant of the fatality told the police of the conversation. H was insistent that D and others agreed to dispose of the car. H and D drove to a field and set the car on fire. H then reported the car as stolen and with D and others agreed a false version of events. C then told H of the fatality and that he had told the police that H was the driver. H went to the police and told then he had been involved in an accident and that subsequently the car had been stolen. In interview he gave the agreed version but later admitted he had lied about the car being stolen and admitted burning the car. D was then arrested and told the truth. H was 27 and had convictions for a public order offence, theft and in 1996 perverting the course of justice. In that case he had an accident causing damage, fled and reported the car stolen. D was 25 and had convictions for theft and attempted theft for which he ultimately received probation. Held. **18 months** not 3 years for H and **9 months** not 18 for D.

R v Charlton and Mealing [2000] 2 Cr App Rep (S) 102. The defendants C and M pleaded guilty to conspiracy to pervert the course of justice. C also pleaded to perverting the course of justice. M was a director of a car repair company, which employed C. A customer was lent a car while his Nissan was being prepared. His wife was killed in it in an accident and the tyres were found to be faulty and that might have contributed to the accident. The car was also found to be uninsured. The defendants said the Nissan was received as payment and the other car was sold by M to C. This was to avoid blame for the lack of insurance. When C was interviewed he produced false receipts as proof of the transfer. Later they admitted the truth. Three days later C was stopped for speeding and he gave his brother's name and an incorrect address. He was found to be almost twice over the alcohol limit. C was 29 and M was 43 and neither had any relevant convictions. M's pre-sentence report referred to panic attacks and stress as a result of the offence and said it was an ill-judged attempt to protect his business. C's report referred to stress. Held. Because M was older and the employer he should receive more for the conspiracy. **18 months** not 3 years for him. C **15 months and 3 months consecutive** not 2 and 1 years consecutive.

Statement, making a false witness

122.13 *R v Evans* [1998] 2 Cr App Rep (S) 72. The defendant pleaded guilty at the first opportunity to perverting the course of justice. The defendant was in a pub with his friend Y. There was bad feeling between Y and M. M assaulted Y and they were both ejected from the pub. The defendant remained inside and when he went out he found Y outside injured. Y told him he had been assaulted by M and another. The defendant made a witness statement describing events he said he had seen outside implicating M and another. He attended an ID parade and picked out H as the other man. He confirmed that with another witness statement. A few days before the trial of M and H at the Crown Court he withdrew his statement. He was interviewed and admitted he hadn't seen anything outside and made the statement out of misguided loyalty. He was 25 with minor unrelated convictions and a good work record. The employer wrote a testimonial. Held. The offence struck at the heart of the administration of justice. It created the risk of an innocent man being convicted. The judge was entitled to be influenced by the prevalence the making of false statements in his area. As the maximum sentence for giving a false statement (under the Criminal Justice Act 1967, s 89) is 2 years the sentence was reduced from 2 to **1 year**.

Witness interference – Guideline remarks

122.14 *R v Khan* [2001] EWCA Crim 912, [2001] 2 Cr App Rep (S) 553. Cases where threats are used against potential witnesses are generally more serious than those where the offender merely tries to persuade (with or without a bribe) a witness to retract or change his or her evidence. Where threats are used the sentence may well be in the range of **12 months to 2 years** depending on the circumstances, including the seriousness of the threats.

R v Chinery [2002] EWCA Crim 32, [2002] 2 Cr App Rep (S) 244. The defendant was convicted of two counts of witness intimidation. Held. The offences are very serious.

Witnesses are indispensable. They must not be pressurised. Sentences invariably contain an element of deterrence.

Witness interference – Cases – Threats, no

122.15 *R v Khan* [2001] EWCA Crim 912, [2001] 2 Cr App Rep (S) 553. The defendant was convicted of interfering with the peace or comfort of an occupier, unlawful eviction, theft and doing an act intending to pervert the course of justice. The victim a single mother aged 33, her boyfriend and her three children including her baby rented a flat owned by the defendant. He harassed her and unlawfully evicted. He broke much of her property and stole some of her property. After a couple of hours after they discovered the damage, the boyfriend went to the flat to pick up some of her baby's clothes. He was met by the defendant and four others and he said they had no right to be there. One of them replied it was 'fuck all to do with him' and the defendant wanted his house back. That man was aggressive and threatening and the boyfriend found him intimidating. The boyfriend was told to leave immediately and if the victim returned to the flat her face would be rearranged. The lock on the flat door was changed. Police attended and found the defendant and four other men inside and the defendant said he was repossessing the flat for non-payment of rent. The defendant was released on bail with a condition not to contact directly or indirectly any prosecution witness. Two months later, a car in which the defendant was a passenger approached the boyfriend. The man who had intimidated him got out of the car and asked to see the victim. They both went to where the victim was living and the man asked her how much she wanted to drop the case. When she told him to deal with the solicitors the man became aggressive and told her if the defendant went to prison she would get nothing. He also said the most she would get would be £1,500, with half paid now and the rest when the case was dropped. The defendant was 26 and of good character. His wife was ill and spoke no English. Held. There was no basis for interfering with the 16 months for the three flat offences. Perverting offences are treated seriously because they undermine justice. **8 months** for it was not excessive. Neither was 2 years in total in any way excessive. (For more details see HARASSMENT AND UNLAWFUL EVICTION OF TENANTS)

Old cases. *R v Singh* (1992) 13 Cr App Rep (S) 123; *R v Postlethwaite* [1992] 13 Cr App Rep (S) 260.

Witness interference – Cases – Threats, with

122.16 *R v Bryan* [1998] 2 Cr App Rep (S) 109. The defendant was found to be in contempt of court. He was in the public gallery while his brother was on trial for murder. The court rose at the end of the day while an important witness Miss Pakey was giving evidence. That witness was in custody and was with a dock officer. The dock officer saw the defendant lean over and point at the witness and mouth, 'I'm going to have you.' Miss Pakey became upset and began to cry. The brother was convicted of murder. The defendant was 37 and treated as of good character. His imprisonment was causing rent arrears problems. Held. **6 months** was entirely appropriate.

R v Smith [2001] 1 Cr App Rep (S) 229. The defendant pleaded guilty to nine charges of intimidating a witness at the Magistrates' Court. A complaint was made that the defendant had indecently assaulted a young lady. In February 1999 the defendant drove his car at one of the witnesses and another young lady saw it. The defendant was arrested and released on bail on condition he did not contact that lady. In June 1999 he made a number of threatening and abusive telephone calls to her home. A recorder was installed on the telephone. The first was abusive and threatening. Three threatened death. Another asked to speak to her saying he was going to kill her. The rest were similar. She was terrified. The defendant was arrested and he denied making the calls. His plea was only forthcoming after an expert had identified his voice. He was convicted of the indecent assault and had served the 6 months detention. He was 20 and was of previous good character. Held. The judge said it was an ongoing campaign of harassment and intimidation with the aim of striking fear and to persuade her not to give evidence. He gave limited credit for the plea because it was extremely late. **2 years** YOI not 2½.

R v Rogers [2001] EWCA Crim 1528, [2002] 1 Cr App Rep (S) 272. The defendant pleaded guilty to witness intimidation. A 12-year-old boy gave a statement to the police, which concerned his grandmother and the defendant's two younger brothers. The victim was walking to a park and the defendant started to abuse and threaten him saying if he got his brothers into trouble he would kill him and his family and attack him with a bottle. Further he was not to tell anyone or he would be killed and if his mother contacted the police she would be killed as well. The defendant's speech was slurred and he smelt of alcohol. The boy was very frightened but the grandmother who had heard what was going on came out and told him to stop. The victim ran home and told his mother who told the police. The defendant was interviewed and denied the offence. The boy said the defendant headbutted him but he was sentenced on the basis their heads came close together. He was 18 and on probation for criminal damage. Held. The offence was not premeditated and was an isolated occasion. The defendant did not seek out the witness nor did he pursue a campaign of threats or violence against him. But there was actual and direct physical confrontation accompanied by intimidating threats of violence. We take into account his youth but he was on probation. A significant custodial sentence was justified but **18 months YOI** not 2 years.

R v Chinery [2001] EWCA Crim 32, [2002] 2 Cr App Rep (S) 244. The defendant was convicted of two counts of witness intimidation. He was a DJ in a nightclub where there was a fight in the ladies' lavatory between his former wife and a barmaid, his wife to be. There were three witnesses. The wife to be was charged with common assault and appeared at the Magistrates' Court. The next day the three witnesses were in the nightclub and the defendant pulled one of them that had made a statement to the police to one side and said, 'Why did you give a statement? Bad things happen to people who grass. You want to watch your back.' She said, 'Don't threaten me.' He replied, 'I am just warning you. Watch your back.' She was upset, shocked and in fear for her safety. The victim told her friends and one of them spoke to the defendant and said he should not threaten her friend. He said, 'You're all grasses and you best watch your backs.' She was infuriated and very intimidated. The next morning the first victim called the police and asked to withdraw her statement. Five days later the second victim gave a statement about both incidents. The defendant was arrested and denied the incidents. He was 43 and of good character with references. He supported his four children and his now wife's two children. Held. The offences are very serious. Witnesses are indispensable. They must not be pressurised. Sentences invariably contain an element of deterrence. It was not wrong to pass consecutive sentences. The judge was entitled to pass 3 and 3 months making **6 months** in all.

Witness interference – Cases – Violence to the witness or damage to his/her property, with

122.17   *R v Watmore* [1998] 2 Cr App Rep (S) 46. The defendant was convicted of an offence under the Criminal Justice and Public Order Act 1994, s 51. The defendant's girlfriend and the victim's girlfriend's quarrelled in a pub. The victim tried to defuse it but the defendant struck the victim on the head with a bottle. The victim became unconscious and suffered a gash. The defendant was charged with assault and tried at the Magistrates' Court. The victim gave evidence and the defendant was convicted and committed for sentence. Three weeks later the defendant and the victim and his girlfriend were again in the same pub. The victim kept away from the defendant. Half an hour later the defendant said to him, 'Ken, mate, I apologise for what I am going to do later,' in a threatening manner. When the victim went to the lavatory, the victim followed him in, pushed his head onto the tiles, punched him in the face and half throttled him. He said, 'No witnesses, all three of you are dead one way or another (sic).' He punched the victim again several times and finally headbutted him. There was no lasting injury but the victim had severe cuts and bruising to his face. The judge sentenced him to **4 years** and 6 months for the assault concurrent. Held. Intimidating witnesses either before or after they have given evidence is becoming endemic and is getting worse. Violent young thugs believe they can avoid justice by threatening witnesses. The sooner the defendant and others discover their mistake the better. There is no distinction between revenge afterwards and intimidation before giving evidence. Often the assault will be comparatively minor but it is an attack on justice itself. The appeal is dismissed.

R v Edmunds [1999] 1 Cr App Rep (S) 475. The defendant was convicted of an offence under the Criminal Justice and Public Order Act 1994, s 51. The defendant had a relationship with the victim who was 16. He assaulted her twice and the police were told. She did not support a prosecution. They were further assaults and she started a relationship with someone else. He stayed at her address, as she was afraid to make him leave. She realised he was stealing cars and property from cars. He assaulted her again and was given a lift by him in a car which she realised was stolen. She then informed the police about his stolen cars and made a statement about it. That evening she received a telephone call from him after he had been released on police bail saying he was, 'going to carve her up and stab her. It won't be worth her walking the streets because I've got so many people after her. If they don't get her I will' A quarter of an hour later he rang again saying he was going to smash her place up. When she returned home she found, 'Grass. Remember this.' in nail polish on a mirror with an arrow pointing to a decapitated teddy bear. A table lamp was smashed, her belongings were strewn across her room and all the photographs were taken from their frames. The judge said that his violence had led to her withdrawing three complaints. He was now 22 with a substantial record for dishonesty. He had lost his liberty more than once but had no convictions for violence or threatening violence. **3 years** not 4.

See also ASSISTING OFFENDERS

123 PHOTOGRAPHS OF CHILDREN, INDECENT

123.1 Protection of Children Act 1978, s 1

Taking, distributing, publishing etc indecent photographs etc.

Triable either way. On indictment maximum 10 years[1]. Summary maximum 6 months and/or £5,000.

Criminal Justice Act 1988, s 160

Possession of indecent photographs etc.

Triable either way. On indictment maximum 5[2] years. Summary maximum 6 months and/or level 5 fine (£5,000).

Under both sections the defendant must be placed on the Sex Offenders' Register, which requires him/her to notify the police within 14 days (or 14 days from his release from imprisonment) his name and home address etc, any change of addresses and where he resides for 14 days or more in any 12 month period[3]. This does not apply where the other party was 18 or over unless the defendant was sentenced to 30 months or more or admitted to a hospital with a restriction order[4].

As the maximum has been increased by Parliament significantly for both offences those cases before 2001 should not be considered a true guide to the likely sentence for offences committed after that date.

Sentencing trends. The sentences will be faithful to *R v Toomer* [2001] 2 Cr App Rep (S) 30. However, the practice of giving conditional discharges as a 'shot across the defendant's bow' will cease because it is not then possible to make an order for sexual registration, *R v Wild (No 2)* [2001] EWCA Crim 1433, [2002] 1 Cr App Rep (S) 162.

1   This was increased from 3 years to 10 years on 11 January 2001, Criminal Justice and Court Services Act 2000, s 41(1).
2   This offence was until 11 January 2001 a summary only offence, Criminal Justice and Court Services Act 2000, s 41(3).
3   Sex Offenders Act 1997, ss 1, 2 and Sch 1, para 1(1)(a)(viii).
4   Sex Offenders Act 1997, Sch 1, para 1(2)(a) and 1(3).

Guidelines case/remarks

123.2   *R v Toomer* [2001] 2 Cr App Rep (S) 30. The defendant pleaded guilty to taking and distributing photographs of children. Held. It is clear that the most severe sentences will be imposed on those who make and distribute such photographs on a substantial scale for commercial ends, especially if they have previous convictions for offences of this nature. But even the young inexperienced amateur who downloads one image for his or her personal gratification does a significant criminal act which adds to the scale of human misery because, if there was no market for these images children would not be degraded producing them. The authorities indicate the following principles: (1) sentences up to statutory maximum should be imposed where there is a contested case, and there is evidence of commercial or large-scale exploitation, and the amount of material is significant, especially if the offender has previous convictions; (2) non-custodial disposals should normally be reserved for isolated offences where the amount of material is very small, and it is for personal use, or use within a very restricted circle, as for example by passing it to one other recipient, when there is no commercial element and the defendant has pleaded guilty and is a first offender; (3) where between those two extremes a particular case falls, will depend on the circumstances, and in particular on, first of all, the quality and nature of the material and the quantity thereof. Secondly, whether there is any element of exploitation or commercial gain; (4) whether the offence is simply one of making; that is to say, in most cases downloading and saving or also involves distribution and, if so, to what extent there has been distribution, whether it has been by email to a single specified recipient, or whether the distribution has been significantly more widespread; (5) the character of the defendant is an important factor, and also the effect of the conviction upon the individual; (6) it is of great importance to consider whether there has been a plea of guilty coupled with co-operation from the outset in the investigation.

R v Wild [2001] EWCA Crim 1272, [2002] 1 Cr App Rep (S) 156. Distribution or further dissemination of obscene material is almost inevitably likely to be an aggravating factor. Whether it causes the custody threshold to be passed depends on the extent of the distribution. The degree of the obscenity will bear upon the gravity of the offence because it reflects the degree of corruption on the child. Those who receive the images have an indirect responsibility for the corruption of the child because unless they were people willing to possess the images they would not be created in the first place. The aspects of the image which give rise to aggravating features are, the age and number of the children involved, whether they were one or both sexes and the nature of the conduct depicted.

Internet, downloading from

123.3   *R v Bowden* [2000] 2 Cr App Rep (S) 26. The defendant pleaded guilty to 12 counts of taking indecent photographs and nine counts of possessing indecent photographs of children. The defendant had taken his computer hard drive for repair where the repairer found indecent material on it. Police in a different operation police seized his computer hard drive and floppy discs. That material contained indecent images of boys under the age of 16. The defendant had downloaded the images from the Internet and either printed them out or stored them on disk. All images were downloaded for the defendant's own use. The defendant who was a schoolteacher had no previous convictions. Held. The defendant was not a risk to the public therefore a **conditional discharge for 12 months** was appropriate, not 4 months' imprisonment.

R v MS [2000] 2 Cr App Rep (S) 388. The defendant pleaded guilty to one count of taking indecent photographs of children. His estranged wife found pornographic images of children on his computer. They were of a sexual nature. Police then searched his home and seized the equipment. In interview he admitted downloading the material from the Internet. It was accepted the material was for his own use. He was a 33-year-old architect and of positive good character. There were six references. He had undertaken private psychiatric counselling. The psychiatric report said, 'the defendant was not a paedophile and was unlikely to become one. He was responding to therapy and was unlikely to re-offend.' Held. Taking into account the sentence in *R v Bowden* [2000] 2 Cr App Rep (S) 26, 4 months was a manifestly excessive sentence. A **conditional discharge for 12 months** was appropriate.

R v Makeham [2001] 2 Cr App Rep (S) 41. The defendant pleaded guilty to three offences of taking an indecent photograph of a child. The defendant asked for 61 other such offences to be taken into consideration. The defendant's girlfriend became concerned about file names found on the defendant's computer and contacted the police. The police found images on a power box of young children engaging in mutual masturbation and oral sex and a video clip of a young girl being abused by an older man. The defendant, who was 41 years of age, had no previous convictions. The sentencing judge noted that the defendant did not have the pictures in his possession for profit or gain. Held. By downloading images of children from the Internet the defendant was perpetuating child abuse therefore a custodial sentence was necessary. **6 months** not 9 months was appropriate.

R v Malone [2001] 2 Cr App Rep (S) 203. The defendant pleaded guilty at the Magistrates' Court to taking indecent photographs of a child. The defendant's employer became aware that the defendant was using the Internet at work to visit pornographic websites and informed the police. The police seized his computer and found no indecent images. But they found indecent images of children on a back-up cartridge, mostly of girls between 13 and 14 naked or performing sex acts on adults. The defendant had no convictions and had lost his job. The pre-sentence report emphasised his insight into the seriousness of what he had done. The sentencing judge noted that the defendant had downloaded the images for personal use but could not conceive that anyone would download such photographs unless they had paedophile tendencies. Held. Taking into account *R v Toomer* [2001] 2 Cr App Rep (S) 30 custody was not required. As the defendant was not distributing the images and had lost his job and spent 4 weeks in custody a **conditional discharge** was appropriate not 6 months. [The court reduced the period of Registration to 5 years which appears illegal because there can be no registration when the defendant is conditionally discharged.]

R v Wild [2001] EWCA Crim 1272, [2002] 1 Cr App Rep (S) 156. The defendant pleaded guilty to 15 counts of taking indecent photographs. Police executed a search warrant at his home. He was asked about indecent images and he told them he had deleted the images from his computer. Experts were able to recover the images from the hard drive of the computer. The images involved children of both sexes from about 2 to 3 months to 13 years. Many showed children engaged in sexual activity including apparent intercourse and oral sex. He said he had been sent the pictures unsolicited. They had been stored. Held. This was grave conduct because of the ages and numbers of children. However it did not cross the custody threshold and could have been dealt with by a **substantial fine**. As he had served a custodial sentence **conditional discharge** substituted for 4 months. [His age and character are not revealed. The judgment was considered a nullity because there is no appeal for a committal for sentence case when less than 6 months is imposed, *R v Wild (No 2)* [2001] EWCA Crim 1272, [2002] 1 Cr App Rep (S) 162.]

R v Turpin [2001] EWCA Crim 1600, [2002] 1 Cr App Rep (S) 323 LCJ. The defendant pleaded guilty to 19 counts of taking indecent photographs. He asked for 21 other offences to be taken into consideration. Police executed a search warrant at his home and seized his computer which had indecent images on it. The images involved children from about 5 to 12 years who were in a variety of indecent situations. Some children were alone, some with other children and some indulging in explicit sexual acts with children and adults. The defendant said he had downloaded them from the Internet over a 4 month period. He was 29, married, in work and of good character. A psychiatrist said there was no evidence of psychosexual abnormality by way of deviant interest with sexual arousal. Although the defendant denied it, the pre-sentence report concluded he derived sexual pleasure from the images, but presented a low risk of re-offending. He had suffered high level of anxiety before sentence. Held. The degree of obscenity was high. However, there was no distinction between this case and *R v Wild* [2002] 1 Cr App Rep (S) 156, so the case did not cross the custody threshold. Therefore 1 year **community rehabilitation order** not 8 months.

R v Owens [2001] EWCA Crim 1370, [2002] 1 Cr App Rep (S) 216. The defendant pleaded guilty to five counts of taking indecent photographs. They were not specimen counts. Trading Standards Officers searched his home during a trade mark investigation and took some floppy disks. Four contained images of young girls displaying their vaginas and the fifth showed a naked boy touching a naked girl's vagina. He admitted that he had downloaded the material from the Internet. There was no suggestion he had links with others or that he had distributed the material. He was now 40 and of good character with very positive references. He was dishonourably discharged from the RAF after 21 years' service and had lost his family home. He received 6 months' imprisonment which he had almost served. Held. The pictures were very nearly at the bottom of the scale of indecency. However upsetting this material may be there is an element of the pathetic as well. He looked at five indecent pictures, briefly obtaining some lonely sexual gratification and now faced a very bleak future. The conviction had had a devastating effect on his unfortunate wife and their family. An immediate custodial sentence was not appropriate. We would have imposed a probation order with treatment so his interest could be addressed. Alternative a substantial fine would be sufficient punishment. As he had nearly served his sentence conditional discharge substituted. [The court reduced the period of Registration to 5 years which appears illegal because there can be no registration when the defendant is conditionally discharged.]

Internet, downloading from – Relevant previous convictions

123.4 *R v James* [2000] 2 Cr App Rep (S) 258. The defendant pleaded guilty to six counts of taking indecent photographs. Police search the address of his co-defendant where the defendant also lived. Items connected with the co-defendant were seized. They also searched the defendant's computer and discs and found 18,500 indecent photographs depicting the images of 'young' children and animals. The defendant said he had downloaded the images from the Internet and they were for his personal use. The defendant, who was 37, had a previous conviction for possessing indecent photographs of children (he received 4 months). He said he wanted help. The sentencing judge noted that to download such images perpetuated the abuse of children. Held. We agree with the judge. This is a disgusting trade. He had plenty of opportunity to obtain help after his last conviction. But **18 months** not 2 years.

R v Hopkinson [2001] EWCA Crim 84, [2001] 2 Cr App Rep (S) 270. The defendant pleaded guilty at the Magistrates' Court to six offences of taking indecent photographs of a child. They were sample counts. The police executed a search warrant at the defendant's home and seized his computer. About 550 images of males under the age of 16 were found. There were also duplicates. The images depicted children in nude poses or engaging in sexual activity with other children or adults. They had been down loaded from the Internet or sent by email. The defendant had co-operated with the police and claimed the material had been sent unsolicited. The judge rejected that. The defendant was 66 and had previous convictions for taking indecent photographs of children, two offences of buggery and one of gross indecency. He showed no remorse. The pre-sentence report said until he changed his attitudes the risk of re-offending could not be discounted. The judge gave credit for the images not being used to corrupt children or anyone else and that the defendant was not using the pictures for commercial gain. Held. The matters to be borne in mind are the number of images and the convictions for similar offences. The offence was not an isolated case and it appeared to some degree to be systematic. It was more serious because of his history and his involvement with a group who he had corresponded with called 'Gay Teen boys'. Therefore **12 months** was not a manifestly excessive sentence.

Internet, posting images on

123.5   *R v Bolingbroke* [2001] 1 Cr App Rep (S) 277 – LCJ. The defendant pleaded guilty at the Magistrates' Court to six offences of distributing indecent photographs of a child and ten offences of processing indecent photographs of a child for distribution. After an investigation the defendant was identified as the person responsible for posting indecent images of children on a bulletin board on the Internet. Over 3 months he had posted numerous articles all with indecent photographs of children. On the last day he posted 61 articles attaching 145 images. Police seized his computer equipment and found 6,000 similar images. The images were of children who were between the ages of 5 and 8 some of whom appeared to be distressed. He made immediate admissions and said he started using chatrooms and it had snowballed and he'd been involved for 18 months. There were records of chatroom conversations in which he had boasted of his part in obtaining the images. It was not suggested the offences were committed for gain. The defendant was of good character and was a cleaner. The judge made the sentences for distribution consecutive to those for possession. Held. These images are available to a very, very large audience. They can have a corrupting effect. Even if persons of good character were committing these offences without any desire for profit a very firm stance had to be taken. As the distribution could not have taken place without possession the offences should be concurrent so **3 years** not 4.

Internet, sending images to others

123.6   *R v Toomer* [2001] 2 Cr App Rep (S) 30. The defendant pleaded guilty to 30 offences of taking indecent photographs or pseudo photographs of children and to two offences of distributing the same photographs. He approached a friend and gave him a computer disc to do some printing work. The disk contained (in a part not for printing) pornographic pictures of children. Police were informed and his premises were searched. The pornographic images were of children between the ages of 3 and 13 engaging in sexual intercourse with other children and adults (both vaginal and anal) and oral sex were found. He explained that he had gained access to the material through chat rooms and logging on to the ICQ system. He said he had been doing it for 2 years and he was hooked. Not only had he downloaded the material he had traded in the images but not commercially. He was of good character. He showed remorse and recognised the seriousness of the offences. The sentencing judge noted that he was not involved in the abuse or incitement of children. Held. Having regard to the personal use of the images, the maximum was (then) 3 years the appropriate sentence for the distributing offences was **18 months** not 24 months.

R v Toomer Re Powell [2001] 2 Cr App Rep (S) 30 at 35. The defendant pleaded guilty to an offence of taking an indecent photograph of a child, two offences of possessing an indecent photograph of a child and one offence of distributing an indecent photograph of a child. He asked for 50 offences including distribution to be taken into consideration. Police executed a search warrant at his home address and he immediately admitted being in possession of obscene material on his computer and disks. When interviewed he admitted he had possessed pictures of children and distributed them to others on the Internet. He had downloaded 16000 images from the Internet and created 229 pseudo photographs. A large number were of children and many showed them in sexual positions. There was no obvious commercial element. This defendant was of positive good character and had been Mayor of his town. The images were not produced for commercial gain. Held. The sentences should have been concurrent. Having regard to the personal use of the images the appropriate sentence was **18 months** not 3 years.

R v Wild [2001] EWCA Crim 1272, [2002] 1 Cr App Rep (S) 156. Distribution or further dissemination of obscene material is almost inevitably likely to be an aggravating factor. Whether it causes the custody threshold to be passed depends on the extent of the distribution.

Internet, sending images to others – There must be a count in the indictment

123.7   *R v Wild* [2001] EWCA Crim 1272, [2002] 1 Cr App Rep (S) 156. The defendant pleaded guilty to 15 counts of taking indecent photographs. The judge took into account that the defendant had sent the images to others. This was admitted. Held. Before that can be taken into account it should be reflected in a specific count.

Magazines etc, producing etc

123.8   *R v Caley* [1999] 2 Cr App Rep (S) 154. The defendant was convicted of distributing indecent photographs of a child and possessing indecent photographs of children for distribution. He wanted to produce a magazine and approached a friend and asked for his help. He gave the friend a CD-ROM containing sexually explicit photographs of children. He told the friend he wanted to sell copies at £50 each. The friend looked at the file and found photographs of young children in various sexual poses and states of undress. The friend was so shocked he phoned the police. The police searched the defendant's home and found computer equipment and 26 floppy disks containing 670 images of children, aged between 3 and 16. The images were of children with each other and with adults. The defendant said he had obtained the pictures from the Internet and claimed he wanted to infiltrate a paedophile ring. He had no relevant convictions. The sentencing judge noted 'there must be an element of deterrence in this sentence'. Held. We agree. The material was foul. The (then) penalties may be thought to be somewhat inadequate. **30 months** was not manifestly excessive.

Taking etc photographs – Victims aged 13–15 – Guideline remarks

123.9 *R v Bayliss* [2000] 1 Cr App Rep (S) 412. Where there is a commercial aspect to the taking of indecent photographs of children the courts will take a strong line intending to discourage that kind of activity.

Taking etc photographs – Victims aged 13–15

123.10 *R v Bayliss* [2000] 1 Cr App Rep (S) 412. The defendant pleaded guilty to three counts of taking indecent photographs of a child and one count of unlawful sexual intercourse with a girl under 16. The defendant, who was 52 at the time of conviction, picked up a 15-year-old girl who was working as a prostitute. The defendant had sexual intercourse with the girl and then took a series of indecent photographs of her. This was the basis of two of the photograph counts. On that and other occasions he videoed his sexual intercourse with the girl. He met the second victim, through an escort agency when she was 13 years of age. Her mother organised her availability to men. 34 photographs were taken of the second victim. The photographs showed the girls with provocative expressions and standing in sexually suggestive positions. The police searched his home and found pictures of women of various ages in varying degrees of indecency. There was also video and computer equipment. He was sentenced on the basis he thought the girls were 16 or over but was reckless about their ages. The defendant had no convictions and was a retired school inspector. He had had a 'life time of honourable service to the community'. The judge noted that this was an extraordinarily difficult and unusual case as the girls had consented to the photographs as part of their sordid trade. He gave 6 months for the unlawful sex and concurrent sentences for the taking of photographs on that girl and 3 months consecutive for the photograph of the other girl. Held. The purpose behind the offences is the protection of children and that includes protection from themselves. Neither girl was corrupted by him. We might well have made up the sentences in a different way. However, **9 months** in total was not an excessive sentence.

R v Grigg [1999] 1 Cr App Rep (S) 443. The defendant pleaded guilty to two counts of taking indecent photographs of children. He was a friend of the father of the victims who were girls aged 14 and 10 at the time. He had friends who ran a model agency and he asked the girls if they would like to be models. Primitive contracts were drawn up. Legitimate videos were made of the children wearing sundresses ostensibly to help them obtain contracts for modelling children's clothes. Others were in in their underwear and he paid them small sums. As a school governor he became involved in converting an air-raid shelter into a museum. The victims came along to help. He then asked the girls to pose without their clothes on in the air-raid shelter. The girls reluctantly agreed and there were indications that he put pressure on the victims to consent. He withdrew while they undressed and wasn't present while they filmed each other naked. There was no sexual activity involved in the filming, nor were there any close-up shots. The girls told their parents who told the police. He was 52, in poor health and of good character. Held. Maybe the videos were not obscene but he had prevailed upon the girls one of whom was only 10 to pose naked for a camera. We accept that the film was not for his own sexual gratification. The breach of trust not only to the victims' parents but also as a school governor meant it had to be a custodial sentence. **9 months** was not manifestly excessive.

124 PLANNING OFFENCES

124.1 Town and Country Planning Act 1990, ss 179, 187, 189, 194 and 210 etc

Offences concerning enforcement notices, orders requiring discontinuance, making false statements in an application and tree order offences respectively.

All triable either way. On indictment maximum fine only (except for s 194 where the maximum is 2 years). Summary maximum £20,000 for ss 179, 187 and 210, and £5,000 for ss 189 and 194.

Crown Court statistics England and Wales[1] – Crown Court – Males 21+ – Town and Country Planning Act 1990

124.2

Year	Plea	Total Numbers sentenced	Type of sentence%					Average length of custody (months)
			Discharge	Fine	Community sentence	Suspended sentence	Custody	
2000	Guilty	3	0%	100%	0%	0%	0%	0
	Not guilty	1	100%	0%	0%	0%	0%	0

1 Excluding committals for sentence. Source: Crime and Criminal Justice Unit, Home Office Ref: IOS416-02.

Enforcement notices

124.3 Old case. *R v Ayling* [1996] 2 Cr App Rep (S) 266.

PLEA

See **GUILTY PLEA, DISCOUNT FOR**

POISON

For administering etc poison see **OFFENCES AGAINST THE PERSON ACT 1861, s 23** and **OFFENCES AGAINST THE PERSON ACT 1861, s 24**

125 POLICE OFFICERS

Defendants, as

125.1 *R v Keyte* [1998] 2 Cr App Rep (S) 165. Held. Police officers are given considerable powers and privileges. If they dishonestly abuse their position and do so for profit, then not only must a prison sentence follow but it must of necessity be a severe sentence.

See also **OBSTRUCTING A POLICE OFFICER**; **CORRUPTION** – *Police officers as defendants*; **MISCONDUCT IN PUBLIC OFFICE** and **THEFT ETC** – *Police officers as defendants*.

126 POSSESSION OF DRUGS

126.1 Misuse of Drugs Act 1971, s 5(2)

Triable either way. On indictment maximum 7 years for Class A drugs, 5 years for Class B drugs and 2 years for Class C drugs. Summary maximum 6 months and/or £5,000 for Class A drugs, 3 months and/or £2,500 for Class B drugs and 3 months and/or £1,000 for Class C drugs.

Crown Court statistics England and Wales[1] – Crown Court – Males 21+ – Unlawful possession of controlled drug

126.2

Year	Plea	Total Numbers sentenced	Type of sentence%					Average length of custody (months)
			Discharge	Fine	Community sentence	Suspended sentence	Custody	
Unlawful possession – ClassA								
2000	Guilty	506	8%	13%	40%	2%	37%	10
	Not guilty	55	0%	25%	33%	0%	42%	14.2
Unlawful possession – Class B								
2000	Guilty	435	16%	33%	31%	1%	17%	7.1
	Not guilty	29	21%	34%	14%	3%	28%	5.9
Unlawful possession – Class C								
2000	Guilty	4	25%	25%	25%	0%	25%	0.9

1 Excluding committals for sentence. Source: Crime and Criminal Justice Unit, Home Office Ref: IOS416-02.

Guideline case – Class A

126.3 *R v Aramah* (1982) 76 Cr App Rep 190 – LCJ. It is at this level that the circumstances of the individual offender become of much greater importance. Indeed the possible variety of considerations is so wide, including often those of a medical nature, that we feel it is impossible to lay down any practical guidelines. On the other hand the maximum penalty for simple possession of Class A drugs is 7 years and there will be very many cases where deprivation of liberty is both proper and expedient.

Guideline case – Cannabis

126.4 *R v Aramah* (1982) 76 Cr App Rep 190 – LCJ. When only small amounts are involved being for personal use, the offence can very often be met with a fine. If history shows, however, a persistent flouting of the law, imprisonment may become necessary.

Magistrates' Court Sentencing Guidelines September 2000 – Class A

126.5 Entry point. Is it serious enough for a community penalty? Example of aggravating factors for the offence are an amount other than a very small quantity. An example of a mitigating factor for the offence is very small amount. Examples of mitigation are age, health (physical or mental), co-operation with the police, and genuine remorse. Consider forfeiture and destruction.

For details about the guidelines see **MAGISTRATES' COURT SENTENCING GUIDELINES** at page 331.

Magistrates' Court Sentencing Guidelines September 2000 – Class B

126.6 Entry point. Is a discharge or a fine appropriate? An example of an aggravating factor for the offence is large amount. An example of a mitigating factor for the offence is small amount. Examples of mitigation are age, health (physical or mental), co-operation with the police, and genuine remorse. Consider forfeiture and destruction. **Starting point fine B.** (£100 when defendant has £100 net weekly income. See page 334 for table showing fines for different incomes.)

For details about the guidelines see **MAGISTRATES' COURT SENTENCING GUIDELINES** at page 331.

Drug abstinence order

126.7 Powers of Criminal Courts (Sentencing) Act 2000, s 58A(1). Where a person is 18 or over the court may make an order requiring the offender to abstain from misusing specified Class A drugs and provide, when instructed to do so a sample to ascertain whether he has any specified Class A drugs in his body. (3) The court must be of the opinion the offender is dependant or has a propensity to misuse specified Class A drugs and the offence is a trigger offence or the misuse of any specified Class A drug caused or contributed to the offence in question. (7) An order shall be for not less than 6 months and not more than 3 years. (9) No order shall be made unless the court has been notified that arrangements for implementing the order are available. (Criminal Justice and Court Services Act 2000, Sch 6 specifies possession of Class A drugs as a trigger offence.)

Causing dangerous driving, taking while

126.8 *R v O'Prey* [1999] 2 Cr App Rep (S) 83. The defendant pleaded guilty to perverting the course of justice, driving whilst disqualified and possession of cannabis. He was committed for sentence for driving whist unfit through drugs. Police stopped his car because it was being driven 'terribly' on the M3. He gave a false name (presumably the perverting matter). He admitted he had smoked cannabis and spat some out. He was then 24 with dishonesty convictions and had received custody for robbery. He was disqualified for 2 years for drink/drive. Held. The judge was in a difficult position because he had not been charged with dangerous driving. He could not be sentenced for it by using the cannabis count. The proper sentence for the driving whilst disqualified was 3 months, for the perverting count 3 months, for the unfit charge 6 months and 1 month (not 3 years) concurrent for the cannabis. The rest were consecutive making **12 months** not 3½ years.

Individual drugs

Cannabis – Class B

126.9 *R v Djahit* [1999] 2 Cr App Rep (S) 142. The defendant pleaded guilty to possession of heroin with intent to supply and possession of cannabis. The cannabis was found at his home. Held. The proper sentence for this low level retailing of heroin was 4 years. 12 months concurrent for the cannabis was manifestly excessive. **2 weeks** concurrent substituted.

R v Hughes [1999] 2 Cr App Rep (S) 329. The defendant was convicted of possession of 1.35 kgs cannabis. Police stopped a car and searched the defendant for drugs. The cannabis was found in his pocket. He was arrested and denied the drugs were found in his pocket. He was 22 and of good character and unemployed. The pre-sentence report said he was continuing to deny it and recommended CSO. Held. *R v Aramah*

(1982) 76 Cr App Rep 190 does not imply the only appropriate penalty is a financial one. The offence will usually cross the CSO threshold. However, **40 hours' CSO** not 80.

Cocaine – Class A

126.10   *R v Nawaz* [1999] 1 Cr App Rep (S) 377. The defendant pleaded guilty to possessing crack cocaine. A count of supplying was left on the file. Police watched the defendant and the co-defendant, H leave H's house. They separated and H picked up something on the ground near a fence. He rejoined the defendant and they both walked back to the H's house. They were arrested and the police found three wraps of crack cocaine on the defendant. He was a widower aged 31 with two children. He was in receipt of benefits. He had a number of previous convictions but none for drugs. He had been to prison before for perjury (12 months) and assault on police (3 months concurrent). H was convicted of supply. **8 months** not 12 months.

Old cases *R v Scarlett* (1994) 16 Cr App Rep (S) 745.

Heroin – Class A

126.11   *R v Campbell* [2001] EWCA Crim 262, [2001] 2 Cr App Rep (S) 369. The defendant was convicted of possession of heroin and crack cocaine. It was treated as a plea of guilty. He was acquitted of possessing the same amounts with intent to supply. Police saw him behaving suspiciously in an area known for the sale of drugs. He appeared to be buying drugs. They moved in and he ran off. He was caught and tried to swallow something. He eventually spat out four wraps. Three contained 383 mgs of heroin and the fourth contained 193 mgs of crack cocaine. The total value was £20. He was a drug addict and in 1996 he had been convicted of three offences of supplying cocaine and received 4 years. Afterwards he was deported. **10 months** not 18.

See also AMPHETAMINE; CANNABIS; DRUG USERS; ECSTASY; LSD; OPIUM and SUPPLY OF DRUGS (CLASS A, B AND C)

PREMISES

For permitting premises to be used for drug supply see the end of the SUPPLY OF DRUGS (CLASS A, B AND C)

For permitting premises to be used by a girl under 13 or under 16 for sexual intercourse see SEXUAL OFFENCES ACT 1956, SS 25 AND 26

PRISON

For need to consider prison overcrowding see BASIC PRINCIPLES – *Prison overcrowding*

See also ESCAPE FROM CUSTODY and PRISONERS

127   PRISON MUTINY

127.1   Prison Security Act 1992, s 1

Indictable only. Maximum sentence 10 years.

R v Mitchell and Pipes [1995] 16 Cr App Rep (S) 924 – LCJ. The defendants M and P were the ringleaders of a prison riot in which £117,000 worth of damage was caused and a prison van was 'hot wired' and used to ram the hospital gate. The van then drove round the perimetre wall and it was then used as a launch pad in an attempt to scale a wall. It was also driven at speed at prison and police officers. M attacked an officer while keys were snatched and stopped others going to his aid. P was armed and masked and tried to stop people surrendering. Held. The Prison Security Act 1992 was passed because Parliament was concerned about unrest and riots in prison. **5 years** and 5 years YOI concurrent to sentences being served were entirely appropriate.

128   PRISON OFFICERS AS DEFENDANTS

Breaching their trust to prisoners

128.1   *R v Fryer* (19 March 2002, unreported). [The report does not make it clear what the offences were but it was probably ABH.] Three Wormwood Scrubs officers punched and kicked a prisoner in the segregation unit for 1½ to 2 minutes. The assault was followed by bogus charges and disciplinary proceedings against the prisoner. Held. Breach of trust does not simply mean protection of the prisoner. A prisoner is entitled to receive protection that the law provides him with from prison officers. It is a breach of trust so far as the responsibilities of the prison officers are concerned, to society generally. The damage does not stop with the damage such as it may be to the prisoner. The damage is to the fabric of the prison system, to the proper administration of the prisons, to the need for those who are in prison, and for those who regard the prison system as playing a significant social role, to have confidence in it. Those who are in prison are not to be abused in a way which is likely to undermine yet more their alienation from society. Prisoners are entitled to the protection of the law, from assaults on them by prison officers. Society is entitled to the proper discharge of the onerous responsibilities which prison officers undertake. They are heavy responsibilities.

See also **ABH** – *Prison officers assaulting prisoners*

PRISON OVERCROWDING

For need to consider prison overcrowding see **BASIC PRINCIPLES** – *Prison overcrowding*

See also **ESCAPE FROM CUSTODY** and **PRISONERS**

129   PRISONERS

Defendant badly treated by other prisoners

129.1   *R v Nall-Cain* [1998] 2 Cr App Rep (S) 145. The defendant, Lord Brocket was sentenced to 5 years for a false £4.5m insurance claim. While in prison his diary was stolen by a gang of prisoners for sale to the press. Other prisoners blackmailed him and threats were made to him and his family. A prisoner went to his aid and was assaulted and wounded. The leader of the gang was arrested and charged with theft, GBH, and blackmail but none of the other prisoners who could give evidence were prepared to give evidence. He was moved from one prison to another on a number of occasions.

When prison officers were absent he was accused of being a grass. He was stabbed in the hand and repeatedly kicked and punched. His shoulder was dislocated and he received a black eye. Since he moved to an open prison 12 months ago there were no further incidents but he said he was fearful. Held. The different wording of the Criminal Appeal Act 1907, s 4(3) and the Criminal Appeal Act 1968, s 11(3) means there is now a wider power to alter sentences. The authorities do not speak with one voice. *R v Kirby* (1979) 1 Cr App Rep (S) 214; *R v Kay* (1980) 2 Cr App Rep (S) 284 and *R v Parker* [1996] 2 Cr App Rep (S) 275 show that a defendant's treatment by other inmates is not generally a factor the Court of Appeal can have regard to. A prisoner maltreated has a number of avenues of redress open to him. The difficulties of adjudicating upon the disputes preclude us from taking them into account. The appeal is dismissed.

Total sentence when sentence consecutive to the sentence being served

129.2   *R v Ali* [1998] 2 Cr App Rep (S) 123. The defendant was convicted of prison mutiny, and two counts of GBH with intent. A prisoner P hit two prison officers with a metal part of a bed causing serious injuries to their heads. The short- and long-term damage to them was great. Neither had been able to return to work. P said he had been threatened to do this by the defendant and it was the signal for a riot. P gave evidence for the prosecution. The defendant was 32 with 20 previous including manslaughter and wounding with intent. He was sentenced to 6 years for the mutiny and 12 years for each GBH. The sentences were concurrent to each other and consecutive to the 9 year sentence for the wounding which he was serving making **21 years** in all. The judge said, the regard the principle of totality should be minimal. The defence did not appeal the individual sentences but appealed the total sentence. Held. The total is very long indeed. The judge is to be commended for the stern attitude he took which the court supports. We hope the message will be conveyed to anyone contemplating acts of this sort. It is inevitable the sentences should be consecutive. The judge was right not to be persuaded by the arguments of totality.

R v Singh [1999] Crim LR 173. The defendant was convicted of possession of 4.9 grams of heroin with intent to supply. He was a serving prisoner with about 9 months to serve of a 12 year sentence. The judge thought he should serve his sentence and then 2 years extra and passed originally a 4 year sentence consecutive. When informed that this would make him a long-term prisoner he reduced the sentence to 3 years 10 months. Held. He was still a long-term prisoner because of the 12 year sentence and both sentences were treated as one term. So **3 years** substituted to achieve the judge's intention of 2 extra years.

R v Parker [2000] Crim LR 494. The judge considered that a sentence which kept him a short-term prisoner was too short. Held. The authorities established that the effect of converting a short-term prisoner to a long-term prisoner was a relevant consideration. If the effect of that was disproportionate then make an appropriate discount. However, here the sentence was appropriate.

See also **ABH** – *Prison officers, against*; OFFENCES AGAINST THE PERSON ACT **1861**, S **18** – *Prison officers, against* and PRISON MUTINY

PROCURING

For procuring the execution of a valuable security in which the defendant intended to steal see THEFT ETC

130 PRODUCTION OF DRUGS

130.1 Misuse of Drugs Act 1971, s 4(2)(a) and (b)

Triable either way, unless the defendant could receive the minimum sentence of 7 years for a third drug trafficking offence when the offence is triable only on indictment.

On indictment maximum life for Class A drugs, 14 years for Class B drugs and 5 years for Class C drugs. Summary maximum 6 months and/or £5,000 for Class A and B drugs and 3 months and/or £2,500 for Class C drugs.

Specified offence for minimum 7 years for third Class A drug trafficking offence.

Drug abstinence order

130.2 Powers of Criminal Courts (Sentencing) Act 2000, s 58A. (1) Where a person is 18 or over the court may make an order requiring the offender to abstain from misusing specified Class A drugs and provide, when instructed to do so a sample to ascertain whether he has any specified Class A drugs in his body. (3) The court must be of the opinion the offender is dependant or has a propensity to misuse specified Class A drugs and the offence is a trigger offence or the misuse of any specified Class A drug caused or contributed to the offence in question. (7) An order shall be for not less than 6 months and not more than 3 years. (9) No order shall be made unless the court has been notified that arrangements for implementing the order are available. [Criminal Justice and Court Services Act 2000, Sch 6 specifies production of Class A drugs as a trigger offence.]

Magistrates' Court Sentencing Guidelines September 2000 – Class A

130.3 Entry point. Are Magistrates' sentencing powers appropriate? Consider the impact on the victim. Example of aggravating factors for the offence are commercial production, large amount, deliberate adulteration, venue, eg prison or educational establishment, sophisticated operation and supply to children. An example of a mitigating factor for the offence is small amount. Examples of mitigation are age, health (physical or mental), co-operation with the police, and genuine remorse. Consider forfeiture and destruction.

For details about the guidelines see MAGISTRATES' COURT SENTENCING GUIDELINES at page 331.

Persistent Class A offender – Minimum 7 years

130.4 Powers of Criminal Courts (Sentencing) Act 2000, s 110 Where a person is convicted of a class A drug trafficking offence committed after 30 November 1999 and was 18 or over and he has been convicted of two other class A drug trafficking offences one of which was committed after he had been convicted of the other, the court shall impose a sentence of imprisonment of at least 7 years except where the court is of the opinion that there are particular circumstances which relate to any of the offences or to the offender which would make it unjust. [This section is summarised and is slightly amended by the Criminal Justice and Court Services Act 2000.]

Persistent Class A offender – Minimum 7 years – Plea of guilty

130.5 Powers of the Criminal Courts (Sentencing) Act 2000, s 152(3). Where a sentence is to be imposed under the Powers of the Criminal Courts (Sentencing) Act 2000, s 110 nothing in that section shall prevent the court from imposing a sentence of 80% or more of the minimum period. [Section summarised. The section means if the defendant pleads guilty the court can impose a sentence, which is 80% or more of the minimum term.]

For production of cannabis see **CANNABIS**

See also **IMPORTATION OF DRUGS**; **POSSESSION OF DRUGS** and **SUPPLY OF DRUGS** (**CLASS A, B AND C**)

PROSECUTION, GIVING EVIDENCE FOR THE

See **INFORMANTS/GIVING EVIDENCE FOR THE PROSECUTION**

131 PROSTITUTION, MEN LIVING ON EARNINGS FROM

131.1   Sexual Offences Act 1956, s 30

Triable either way. On indictment maximum 7 years. Summary maximum 6 months and/or £5,000.

Sentencing trends. The sentences are likely to remain stable or fall where there is no coercion but there will a much more concerted effort to strip the defendant of his profits.

Guideline case

131.2   *R v Farrugia* [1979] 69 Cr App Rep 108 at 113. In the absence of any evidence of coercion, whether physical or mental, or of corruption **2 years** is probably adequate. Anything exceeding 2 years should be reserved for a case where there is an element of coercion or there is some strong evidence of corruption.

Coercion, violence or threats, with

131.3   *R v Powell* [2001] 1 Cr App Rep (S) 261. The defendant was convicted of living on prostitution. He was acquitted of ABH. The defendant met the victim socially and moved into a flat he owned. He offered her work in a sauna and she agreed. When she went there and saw girls in skimpy underwear she realised what she was being asked to do and left. When she got back to the flat he demanded she work as a prostitute. She agreed because she was frightened of him. She started working as a prostitute between 10am and 4pm and he demanded all the money she earned. She said she was unable to leave because he threatened her. She took drugs to take her mind off what she was doing and her weight dropped from 10 to 8 stone. After 6 weeks she was allowed to go home. She estimated she had earned £7,000. A month later she suffered a breakdown and tried to harm herself. It was considered she had suffered personality damage as a result of her experiences. He was 38 and had convictions for theft, handling, offensive weapon and criminal damage. In 1997 he had received 18 months concurrent for two domestic burglaries. Held. **5 years** was severe having regard to the maximum but not too long.

Owner etc of premises used for prostitution

131.4   *R v Malik* [1998] 1 Cr App Rep (S) 115. The defendant was convicted of living on prostitution over a 21 month period. The defendant owned three flats in West London, which were ostensibly massage party houses, which were in fact used for prostitution. He also ran an escort agency with 20 women on the books, which served the same purpose. At one of the flats the prostitute would pay £120 a day rent and he advised on the charges. At another the woman would pay £20 per client of which the defendant received £15. This rose if there were more than six clients. The escort service women charged £150 of which £50 went to the defendant. Police posed as clients and as an applicant for a job as a maid. The applicant was told to say services started at £30 and if they wanted to discuss sex they should speak to the lady. The defendant was interviewed and denied the women were prostitutes. He said he forbid prostitution. Accounts disclosed £17,000 rent money from the three massage flats over a 3 month period. The gross receipts appeared to be some £89,000. There were no young women and no drugs. There was also no violence or coercion. The defendant contended he thought it was legitimate and that he kept records and account was made to the Inland Revenue. Held. In light of the authorities **2 years** was not excessive.

R v Elul [2001] EWCA Crim 177, [2001] 2 Cr App Rep (S) 321. The defendant pleaded guilty to four counts of living off prostitutes. The defendant came to this country in 1997 and from 1999 he and his wife were in the business of providing sexual services. He advertised for prostitutes in South Africa and 20 came over to the UK. The business started at one flat and then police kept observations on two other flats and typically there were two girls at each of the flats. There was no coercion or corruption and the business was run hygienically. The defendant took 50% of the earnings less a fee for the receptionist. His benefit was £105,600 and there was a confiscation order for £12,340 made. He was 30 and of good character. His wife was cautioned. Held. It was a carefully organised and professional criminal enterprise but **12 months** not 18.

132   Public Decency, Outraging

132.1   Common law

Indictable only. There is no maximum fine or term of imprisonment provided the sentence is not inordinate *R v Morris* (1951) 34 Cr App Rep 210.

Children, involving

132.2   *R v Gaynor* [2000] 2 Cr App Rep (S) 163. The defendant was convicted of outraging public decency. He had been sentenced to 4½ years for indecent assault on a male. Three weeks after his release on licence police who had mounted a surveillance operation on him and saw him looking at children in a playground 30 to 40 yards away. He took out his penis and masturbated. He was not calling out or gesticulating to any child. No child came near. When arrested he denied it. He was 63. He had an appalling record. In 1976, 1979, 1980, 1985, 1992, and in 1996 he was sentenced to 6 months, 2, 3, 5 years, 4 years 9 months and 4½ years respectively for various indecent assault offences on children under 14. The total convictions for indecent assault was 11. Held. He has to be kept out of the way of children for a long time. **3 years** not 5 years consecutive to the 1 year, 22 weeks and 4 days passed for breach of the licence.

Longer than commensurate/Extended, can the sentence be?

132.3   *R v Gaynor* [2000] 2 Cr App Rep (S) 163. As the offence is not listed in the definition under the Criminal Justice Act 1991, s 31 [now the Powers of Criminal Courts (Sentencing) Act 2000, s 161(2)] extended sentences cannot be passed.

See also **Obscene Publications**

Public Health

See **Environmental Offences**

PUBLIC NUISANCE

Common law so indictable only. No maximum provided so the maximum is life.

Where the offence is connected with obtaining money dishonestly see THEFT ETC

Where the offence is connected with harassment see HARASSMENT (S 4 OR PUBLIC NUISANCE)

See also PUBLIC ORDER ACT OFFENCES and STALKING

PUBLIC ORDER ACT OFFENCES, S 2

See VIOLENT DISORDER

133   PUBLIC ORDER ACT OFFENCES, S 4

133.1   Public Order Act 1986, s 4

Summary only. Maximum sentence 6 months[1] and/or Level 5 fine (£5,000).

1   Where the jury convict the defendant of an offence under s 4 as an alternative to a racially-aggravated offence the maximum sentence at the Crown Court is the Magistrates' Courts maximum, Public Order Act 1986, s 7(4).

Magistrates' Court Sentencing Guidelines September 2000

133.2   Entry point. Is it serious enough for a community penalty? Consider the impact on the victim. Examples of aggravating factors for the offence are group action, on hospital/medical premises; people put in fear, victim serving the public and vulnerable victim. Example of mitigating factors for the offence are minor matter and short duration. Examples of mitigation are age, health (physical or mental), co-operation with the police, voluntary compensation and genuine remorse. Give reasons if not awarding compensation.

For details about the guidelines see MAGISTRATES' COURT SENTENCING GUIDELINES at page 331.

Defendant aged 15–16

133.3   *R v Howells Re Marston* [1999] 1 Cr App Rep (S) 335 at 344 – LCJ. The defendant pleaded guilty to ABH. While serving the 9 months detention he pleaded guilty to the Public Order Act 1986, s 4 count for an offence which was committed before the first one and received 3 months consecutive. Both pleas were at the Crown Court. In the first offence (second plea) the victim was returning home in his car with his 14-year-old son and sounded his horn to encourage two youths who were fighting to move off the road. One of them shouted abuse and his car was hit. He stopped and he was sworn at so he left the car. A youth ran at him and fearing for his safety the victim struck him. A group of youths surrounded him shouting, 'You're going to die' and other threats. The victim got back in his car and his car door was struck by a baseball bat. The bat was swung at the victim who ducked and it missed him. He drove home, called the police and went outside where about 20 youths were approaching the house. Wooden fencing was ripped up and wood and bricks were thrown at him and his family. A brick struck his father on the leg and a piece of wood struck his girlfriend. The police arrived and the group dispersed and when they left the group returned. More abuse was shouted. None of the witnesses identified the defendant then 15 in taking part in any of the violence and the case against him was based on an admission that he had been shouting abuse. The second incident was about 4 weeks later, (for details see **ABH**). He had a relatively minor dishonesty conviction and two dishonesty cautions. He was said to be remorseful and ashamed. He had been taken away from his family by the local authority. Held. The first incident was an utterly disgraceful and inexcusable episode, but abusive language by a 15 year old, however deplorable, **did not merit custody**. 4 months detention for the ABH and no separate penalty for the s 4 offence not 12 months in all.

134   PUBLIC ORDER ACT OFFENCES, S 4A

134.1   Using threatening, abusive or insulting words or behaviour etc causing harassment etc with intent to cause harassment etc.

Public Order Act 1986, s 4A

Summary only[1]. Maximum sentence 6 months and/or Level 5 fine (£5,000).

1   Where the jury convict the defendant of an offence under s 4A as an alternative to a racially-aggravated offence the maximum sentence at the Crown Court is the Magistrates' Courts maximum, *R v Alden* [2002] 2 Cr App Rep (S) 326.

Magistrates' Court Sentencing Guidelines September 2000

134.2   Entry point. Is it so serious that only custody is appropriate? Consider the impact on the victim. Examples of aggravating factors for the offence are football hooliganism, group action, high degree of planning, night time offence, victim specifically targeted and weapon. An example of a mitigating factor for the offence is short duration. Examples of mitigation are age, health (physical or mental), co-operation with the police, voluntary compensation and genuine remorse. Give reasons if not awarding compensation.

For details about the guidelines see **MAGISTRATES' COURT SENTENCING GUIDELINES** at page 331.

135   PUBLIC ORDER ACT OFFENCES, SS 4 AND 4A – RACIALLY AGGRAVATED

135.1   Crime and Disorder Act 1998, s 31 and the Public Order Act 1986, ss 4 and 4A

Triable either way. On indictment maximum 2 years. Summary maximum 6 months and/or £5,000.

Magistrates' Court Sentencing Guidelines September 2000 – Section 4

135.2   Entry point. Is it so serious that only custody is appropriate? Consider the level of racial aggravation and the impact on the victim. Examples of aggravating factors for the offence are group action, on hospital/medical premises, people put in fear, victim serving the public and vulnerable victim. Example of mitigating factors for the offence are minor matter and short duration. Examples of mitigation are age, health (physical or mental), co-operation with the police, voluntary compensation and genuine remorse. Give reasons if not awarding compensation.

For details about the guidelines see **MAGISTRATES' COURT SENTENCING GUIDELINES** at page 331.

Magistrates' Court Sentencing Guidelines September 2000 – Section 4A

135.3   Entry point. Are magistrates' sentencing powers appropriate? Consider the level of racial aggravation and the impact on the victim. Examples of aggravating factors for the offence are football hooliganism, group action, high degree of planning, night time offence, victim specifically targeted and weapon. An example of a mitigating factor for the offence is short duration. Examples of mitigation are age, health (physical or mental), co-operation with the police, voluntary compensation and genuine remorse. Consider committal for sentence. Give reasons if not awarding compensation.

For details about the guidelines see MAGISTRATES' COURT SENTENCING GUIDELINES at page 331.

Police officers, against

135.4   *R v Jesson* [2000] 2 Cr App Rep (S) 200. The defendant pleaded guilty at the Magistrates' Court to racially aggravated threatening, abusive or insulting words or behaviour with intent to cause harassment etc. Police officers tried to arrest the defendant's cousin and the defendant intervened. He was abusive to an Asian police officer and brought his face close to the officer repeatedly. Each time the officer stepped back and told him to calm down. The defendant shouted, 'You Paki' and repeatedly shouted, 'Fuck off Paki.' He was arrested and in the interview said he was drunk. He had several previous convictions including a number for threatening behaviour and one for ABH for which he was sent to prison for 12 months. **6 months** substituted for 9 months.

R v Jacobs [2001] 2 Cr App Rep (S) 174. The defendant was sentenced for racially-aggravated harassment and common assault. [Her plea is not revealed.] She was arrested and taken to a police station. While she was being searched a police officers asked her to remove her rings. She replied, 'I don't want you Paki filthy hands on me, I don't want that Paki touching me.' She spoke to the custody sergeant and continued to shout racial abuse and began to struggle. Later she shouted racial abuse in the cell. She admitted the offence in interview. She was 20 and had one public order previous conviction in 1997. **3 months** substituted for 9 months.

Public officials, ticket collectors etc, against

135.5   *R v Miller* [1999] 2 Cr App Rep (S) 392. The defendant pleaded guilty at the Magistrates' Court to racially aggravated threatening words and behaviour and travelling on a railway without a ticket. He was committed for sentence. Mr Shafi, a railway conductor approached the defendant on a train and asked to see his ticket. He hadn't got one and pretended he had lost it. The conductor pressed him and the defendant became abusive calling him a Paki. He was ordered to leave the train. The defendant refused and said, 'What's your problem? You're all the same you Pakis, why don't you fucking go back to India.' He was left on the platform and he continued to swear at Mr Shafi. He said, 'I feel like head-butting you. You fucking Paki, why don't you fuck off?' and 'You cunts are all the same, you Pakis.' The victim thought he was going to be hit and he found the incident so upsetting he went off work sick. The defendant was arrested and was abusive to the police. He was 35 with an appalling record. It included three robberies, three public order offences, two possessions of an offensive weapon, an affray, an ABH and a wounding. Held. The facts were weighted so heavily against him the discount for the plea was marginal. **18 months** was severe but fully justified.

For basic principles about racially-aggravated offences. See RACIALLY-AGGRAVATED OFFENCES

136 PUBLIC ORDER ACT OFFENCES, s 5

136.1 Using threatening, abusive or insulting words or behaviour etc likely to cause harassment etc.

Public Order Act 1986, s 5

Summary only. Maximum sentence Level 3 fine (£1,000).

The offence is a relevant offence under the Football Spectators Act 1989, s 14A and Sch 1, para 1. Where (a) the offence was committed during a period relevant to a football match and (b) the accused was at or attempting to enter or leave the premises or journeying to and from the premises or the offence related to a match the court must make a Football Banning Order, where there are reasonable grounds to believe that making a banning order would help to prevent violence or disorder at or in connection with any regulated football match (except where the defendant is given an absolute discharge).

Magistrates' Court Sentencing Guidelines September 2000

136.2 Entry point. Is a discharge or a fine appropriate? Consider the impact on the victim. Examples of aggravating factors for the offence are group action and vulnerable victim. Examples of mitigating factors for the offence are stopped as soon as police arrived and trivial incident. Examples of mitigation are age, health (physical or mental), co-operation with the police, voluntary compensation and genuine remorse. Give reasons if not awarding compensation. **Starting point fine B**. (£100 when defendant has £100 net weekly income. See page 334 for table showing fines for different incomes.)

For details about the guidelines see **MAGISTRATES' COURT SENTENCING GUIDELINES** at page 331.

137 PUBLIC ORDER ACT OFFENCES, s 5 – RACIALLY AGGRAVATED

137.1 Crime and Disorder Act 1998, s 31 and the Public Order Act 1986, s 5

Summary only. Maximum fine Level 4, (£2,500).

The offence is a relevant offence under the Football Spectators Act 1989, s 14A and Sch 1, para 1. Where (a) the offence was committed during a period relevant to a football match and (b) the accused was at or attempting to enter or leave the premises or journeying to and from the premises or the offence related to a match the court must make a Football Banning Order, where there are reasonable grounds to believe that making a banning order would help to prevent violence or disorder at or in connection with any regulated football match (except where the defendant is given an absolute discharge).

Magistrates' Court Guidelines September 2000

137.2 Entry point. Is it serious enough for a community penalty? Consider the level of racial aggravation and the impact on the victim. Examples of aggravating factors for the offence are group action and vulnerable victim. Examples of mitigating factors for the offence are stopped as soon as police arrived and trivial incident. Examples of mitigation are age, health (physical or mental), co-operation with the police, voluntary compensation and genuine remorse. Give reasons if not awarding compensation.

For details about the guidelines see **MAGISTRATES' COURT SENTENCING GUIDELINES** at page 331.

For basic principles about racially-aggravated offences. See **RACIALLY-AGGRAVATED OFFENCES**

QUEEN'S EVIDENCE, GIVING

See **INFORMANTS/GIVING EVIDENCE FOR THE PROSECUTION**

138   RACIALLY-AGGRAVATED OFFENCES

138.1   Crime and Disorder Act 1998, ss 29–32

On indictment Offences Against the Person Act 1861, s 20, ABH, and Protection from Harassment Act 1997, s 4 – 7 years. Common assault, Public Order Act 1986, ss 4 and 4A and Protection from Harassment Act 1997, s 2 – 2 years. Summary maximum 6 months and/or £5,000.

Public Order Act 1986, s 5 Summary only Maximum Level 4 fine (£2,500).

Magistrates' Court Sentencing Guidelines September 2000

138.2   The present position on sentencing for racial harassment and racially aggravated offences has been substantially clarified by the Crime and Disorder Act 1998. As previously stated, the new offences have been created by ss 29–32 which carry increased maximum sentences when compared with the basic offences from which they are derived. The increase in maximum sentence must lead sentencers to reach a provisional sentence in excess of the appropriate one for the basic offence. Parliament has given a specific message to sentencers that it expects those who have been convicted of offences which are defined as having a racial element to receive higher tariff penalties. Conversely, as indicated, if there is a conviction for one of the non-aggravated offences, the sentence must be on the basis that the offence was not racially aggravated otherwise the decision would amount to sentencing for a more serious offence than the one for which the offender has been convicted.

General approach

138.3   *R v Saunders* [2000] 2 Cr App Rep (S) 71. Racism must not be allowed to flourish. The message must be received and understood in every corner of our society. Racism is evil. Those who indulge in racially aggravated violence must expect to be punished severely. Generally speaking following a trial a period of up to 2 years should be added to the term of imprisonment otherwise appropriate. Consider the sentence in two stages. Relevant factors will include the nature of the hostile demonstration, its length, whether isolated, repeated, or persistent; its location, whether public or private; and the number both of those demonstrating and those demonstrated against.

R v Morrison [2001] 1 Cr App Rep (S) 12; *R v Saunders* [2000] 1 Cr App Rep (S) 71 does not mean that the maximum that can be added is 2 years. The amount will depend on all the circumstances.

R v Kelly and Donnelly [2001] EWCA Crim 170, [2001] 2 Cr App Rep (S) 341. First determine what the appropriate sentence was for the offence without the racial element and then determine the appropriate sentence for the racial element. Each part should be publicly identified. The factors seriously aggravating the racial element in relation to the offender's intention, are planning, the offence being part of a pattern of racist offending, membership of a group promoting racist activity, and the deliberate setting up of the victim for the purposes of humiliating him or being offensive towards him. The factors seriously aggravating the racial element in relation to the impact on the victim are if the offence took place in the victim's home, or the victim was particularly vulnerable, or providing a service to the public, or if the timing or location of the offence was such to maximise the harm or distressed caused, or the expressions of racial hostility were repeated or prolonged, or if fear and distress throughout a particular community resulted from the offence or if particular distress was caused to the victim or the victim's family. These factors should be added to the factors in *R v Saunders* [2000] 2 Cr App Rep (S) 71

Offences other than under the Crime and Disorder Act 1998, ss 29–32

138.4   Powers of Criminal; Courts (Sentencing) Act 2000, s 153. If an offence other than one under sections 29–32, was racially aggravated, the court shall treat that fact as an aggravating factor (ie to increase the sentence) and shall state in open court that the offence was so aggravated. [Summarised.]

For index of racially-aggravated offences, see **RACIST OFFENCES**

139   RACIST OFFENCES

Guideline remarks

139.1   *A-G's Reference (Nos 29–31 of 1994)* (1994) 16 Cr App Rep (S) 698 – LCJ. It cannot be too strongly emphasised that where there is a racial element in an offence of violence, that is a gravely aggravating feature.

Possession of racially inflammatory material

139.2   Public Order Act 1986, s 23

Triable either way. On indictment maximum 2 years. Summary maximum 6 months and/or £5,000.

R v Gray [1999] 1 Cr App Rep (S) 50. The defendant pleaded guilty to possession of racially inflammatory material with a view to distribute it. Three months after serving a 3 year sentence for assaulting a police officer police raided his address where he was living as a lodger. The prime occupier was his landlord. The house was used for the production of a right-wing magazine designed to appeal to the British National Party and football fans. The magazines contained violent intolerance of groups because of their race, religion and political views. The landlord was also the prime mover in the magazine. 500 copies were found and 88 were in the defendant's bedroom. Held. Old cases are no longer an adequate guide to sentencing practice. **12 months** was not in any way excessive. As the offence was committed so soon after his release it was entirely appropriate for him so serve the outstanding period of the first sentence which the sentencing judge had made concurrent.

See also **ABH – RACIALLY AGGRAVATED; BURGLARY – RACIALLY AGGRAVATED; COMMON ASSAULT – RACIALLY AGGRAVATED; CRIMINAL DAMAGE – RACIALLY AGGRAVATED; HARASSMENT, S 2 – RACIALLY AGGRAVATED; HARASSMENT, S 4 – RACIALLY AGGRAVATED; OFFENCES AGAINST THE PERSON ACT 1861, S 20 – RACIALLY AGGRAVATED; PUBLIC ORDER ACT, SS 4 AND 4A – RACIALLY AGGRAVATED; PUBLIC ORDER ACT, S 5 – RACIALLY AGGRAVATED; RACIALLY-AGGRAVATED OFFENCES** and **THREATS TO KILL** – *Racist defendants*

140 RAILWAY OFFENCES

140.1 Various offences and penalties

Malicious Damage Act 1861, s 35

Placing wood etc on a railway etc with intent to obstruct or overthrow any engine etc.
Indictable only. Maximum Life.

Malicious Damage Act 1861, s 36

Obstructing engines or carriages on railways etc.
Triable either way. On indictment maximum 2 years. Summary maximum 6 months
and/or £5,000.

Offences Against the Person Act 1861, s 32

Placing wood etc on railway etc with intent to endanger passengers.
Triable either way. On indictment maximum 2 years. Summary maximum 6 months
and/or £5,000.

Offences Against the Person Act 1861, s 33

Casting stones etc on railway etc with intent to endanger passengers.
Indictable only. Maximum Life.

Offences Against the Person Act 1861, s 34

Doing or omitting anything so as to endanger passengers etc.
Triable either way. On indictment maximum 2 years. Summary maximum 6 months
and/or £5,000.

*Crown Court statistics England and Wales[1] – Crown Court – Males 21+ –
Endangering railway passengers*

140.2

Year	Plea	Total Numbers sentenced	Type of sentence%					Average length of custody (months)
			Discharge	Fine	Community sentence	Suspended sentence	Custody	
2000	Guilty	3	0%	0%	0%	0%	100%	14
	Not guilty	3	0%	0%	0%	0%	100%	14

1 Excluding committals for sentence. Source: Crime and Criminal Justice Unit, Home Office Ref:
IOS416-02.

Defendant under 16

140.3 *R v AH* [2000] 2 Cr App Rep (S) 280. The defendant pleaded guilty to three
counts of placing obstructions on a railway. (Because of the sentence imposed it is
assumed it was under s 35.) He, when 14 placed a concrete troughing lid on a railway
line which was struck by a train. He did the same again 4 days later and the lid was also
hit by a train. Three days later a train hit another obstruction. In no case was there any
injury or serious accident. The defendant and his co-defendant aged 22 were arrested
and made full admissions. However, they both blamed each other. They had envisaged
themselves as some sort of private army and gave themselves a quasi-military status.
They wore military style clothing. The defendant was given 5 years and since his
sentence had made excellent progress. A report said he had learnt a salutary lesson and
developed a heightened awareness of the reason he had offended. Held. The danger
was plain for all to see. Obstructions can cause the most horrendous accidents. The age
differential was so great the primary responsibility must be borne by the older
defendant. Because of his age, the reports and mercy **3 years** detention substituted.

Defendant aged 16–17

140.4   *R v Leech* (8 November 2001, unreported). (A 16 year old pleaded guilty to three counts of endangering passengers (s 34). He dropped a 32 lb boulder on to the track which was hit by a train. The other offences were a piece of wood and a stone on other days. He was of good character. **18 months** detention and training upheld.

Endangering passengers

140.5   *R v Keane* [2001] EWCA Crim 1793, [2002] 1 Cr App Rep (S) 383. The defendant pleaded guilty to endangering the safety of rail passengers (Offences Against the Person Act 1861, s 34) and failing to surrender to his bail. The defendant dragged a bench along the platform of South Croydon Station and threw it on the track. Moments later a train travelling at 55 mph struck the bench which caught under its front and it became entangled with the train's front axle. After the train had stopped the driver spoke to the defendant. The defendant said he had worked on the railways for 30 years. In fact he was sacked from his job on the railway in 1995 because of alcohol problems. After the conductor had left the train the defendant entered the conductor's van with a key he already had. He stole the conductor's jacket and £20 cash which was in a pocket. No-one was injured but an expert said if the bench had wrapped round one of the wheels the train would probably have derailed. Police stopped the defendant and he was heavily intoxicated. He said he had little recollection of what had happened but was angry about being sacked. He failed to answer to his bail and was arrested nearly 4 months later. The defendant was 58 and had no convictions but had a long-standing problem with drink. There was a letter saying he was a hard working and conscientious member of the local community. The judge said he must have caused the driver very considerable alarm and a great deal of inconvenience to passengers. Held. **15 months** cannot be faulted, but 1 month not 3 months consecutive for the bail offence.

See also **HEALTH AND SAFETY OFFENCES** – *Railway accidents*

141 RAPE

141.1   Sexual Offences Act 1956, s 1

Indictable only. Maximum sentence life. It is a specified offence for automatic life.

The defendant must notify the police within 14 days (or 14 days from his release from imprisonment) his name and home address etc, any change and addresses where he resides for 14 days or more in any 12 month period[1]. See **SEX OFFENDERS' REGISTER**

Sentencing trends. The sentences passed have been very loyal to *R v Billam* (1986) 82 Cr App Rep 347. There is a consistency and predictability absent in the sentencing of many other offences. This and the growing use of life sentences is likely to continue.

1   Sex Offenders Act 1997, ss 1 and 2.

Crown Court statistics England and Wales – Crown Court – Males 21+ – Rape
141.2

Year	Plea	Total Numbers sentenced	Type of sentence%					Average length of custody[1] (months)
			Discharge	Fine	Community sentence	Suspended sentence	Custody	
Rape of a female								
2000	Guilty	170	0%	0%	2%	2%	95%	80.6
	Not guilty	309	0%	0%	0%	0%	99%	90
Rape of a male								
2000	Guilty	6	0%	0%	0%	0%	100%	94
	Not guilty	21	0%	0%	0%	0%	100%	91.6

1   Excluding life sentences. Source: Crime and Criminal Justice Unit, Home Office Ref: IOS416-02.

Guideline case

141.3   *R v Billam* (1986) 82 Cr App Rep 347 – LCJ. For an adult in a contested case with no aggravating or mitigating features the starting point is **5 years**. Where a rape is committed by two or more men acting together, or by a man who has broken into or otherwise gained access to a place where the victim is living, or by a person who is in a position of responsibility to the victim, or by a person who abducts the victim and holds her captive, the starting point should be **8 years**.

At the top end of the scale comes the defendant who has carried out a campaign of rape, committing the crime upon a number of different women or girls. He represents more than ordinary danger and a sentence of **15 years or more** may be appropriate.

Where the defendant's behaviour has manifested perverted or psychopathic tendencies or gross personality disorder, and where he is likely, if at large, to remain a danger to women for an indefinite time, a life sentence will not be inappropriate.

The crime should be treated as aggravated by the following factors: (1) violence is used over and above the force necessary to commit the rape; (2) a weapon is used to frighten or wound the victim; (3) the rape is repeated; (4) the rape has been carefully planned; (5) the defendant has previous convictions for rape or other offences of a serious sexual or violent kind (Note this would now normally be dealt with under the automatic life provisions); (6) the victim is subjected to further sexual indignities or perversions; (7) the victim is either very old or very young; (8) the effect on the victim, whether physical or mental, is of a special seriousness. Where any one of these aggravating features are present, the sentence should be substantially higher than the figure suggested as the starting point.

Aiding and abetting etc

141.4   *R v Reid* [1998] 2 Cr App Rep (S) 10. The defendant was convicted of assisting the rape and the unlawful wounding of a 16-year-old girl. At about 2.30am, the victim aged 16 was walking down the street and she saw the defendant and O, a 23 year old. They exchanged greetings and she walked on. They followed her and the O grabbed her by the hair and pushed her over a wall and up a staircase. The defendant kicked her in face several times. O took her clothes off and she fought back. He watched while O raped her and he laughed. O gave the defendant a lighter and told him to burn her clothes. They left her naked. It wasn't till just before 4am she made her way to a bus station. Her face was bleeding heavily and she had injuries all over body. She was in a drowsy state for days. The defendant was 19 and immature. He had received sentences of youth custody. He was unable to read and write. He was also sentenced for a bail offence and two counts of burglary for which he received 6 months' consecutive. O who pleaded guilty received 9 years. After his sentence a psychiatrist said the defendant was immature but not mentally ill. Held. It was not appropriate to add a short consecutive sentence. To reflect the role **10 years** YOI not 12 years with the unrelated matters concurrent not consecutive.

A-G's Reference (No 12 of 2001) [2002] EWCA Crim 353, [2002] 2 Cr App Rep (S) 382. [The defendant aided and abetted the rape of a baby of some friends by her partner. 4 years was lenient but not disturbed.]

Abduction/false imprisonment etc, and

141.5   *R v Billam* (1986) 82 Cr App Rep 347 – LCJ. For an adult in a contested case, who abducts the victim and holds her captive the starting point should be **8 years**.

R v Masood [1997] 2 Cr App Rep (S) 137. See *Prostitutes, on*

A-G's Reference (No 27 of 1998) [1999] 1 Cr App Rep (S) 259. The defendant was convicted of false imprisonment, ABH, rape, attempted rape and indecent assault. In 1995 there was an arranged marriage in Pakistan between the defendant and the victim. She came to England and lived with the defendant and his brother, mother and sister. She was prevented from leaving and when they moved from Preston she was humiliated, abused and mocked. She was prevented from speaking to her family in Pakistan and having contact with the outside world. She did not share her husband's bedroom. She was not permitted to do anything without the permission of her mother in law. When she passed a note to a neighbour he told her not to speak to neighbours without his permission. He hit her, threw her against the floor and raped her. He tried to anally rape her. The police arrived and the victim was seen by a doctor. She had a healing laceration to her neck, two small lacerations and tenderness to her face and three anal fissures, which were sufficiently tender that an internal examination was not possible. She had lacerations and/or abrasions on her hand, back, legs and breast. The false imprisonment lasted 8–10 weeks. He was 28 and was of good character with testimonials. He was under the influence of his mother. The victim had discussed with him the possibility of reconciliation. His mother, brother and sister were also convicted of false imprisonment. Held. The sentences of **4½ years** for the rape and **1 year consecutive** for the false imprisonment **were lenient**. The judge was particularly well placed to impose appropriate sentences. Neither sentence nor the total were unduly lenient.

R v ABE [2000] 1 Cr App Rep (S) 78. The defendant pleaded guilty to two rapes and false imprisonment Five months after his release from prison he lay in wait in the evening for a 58-year-old widow who lived in the same block of flats as he did to return. When she did he forced her into his flat and brutally raped her. Threatening her with a knife he forced her upstairs to her flat and raped her again. The victim was then kept in her flat against her will till the next afternoon. The first rape was violently painful. In 1992 he had been convicted of two counts of rape on his stepdaughter when she was between the ages of 12 and 16. He repeatedly raped her over 4 years. He had received 10 years. After 8 years he was released on licence. The judge passed an automatic life sentence considering 18 years would have been appropriate otherwise. Held. The rapes were extremely bad. The appropriate determinate sentence would have been **15 years** not 18.

Old cases. *R v Farmer* (1993) 14 Cr App Rep (S) 664; *R v Dooley* (1994) 15 Cr App Rep (S) 703; *A-G's Reference (No 16 of 1993)* (1994) 15 Cr App Rep (S) 811.

AIDS

See **DEFENDANT** – *AIDS, Defendant has* and **VICTIMS** – *Victim fears she will contract AIDS from sex attack*

Anal rape

141.6   *R v Stepton* [1998] 2 Cr App Rep (S) 319. 9 years not 7 for buggery of this 9 year old by 44 year old who pleaded guilty.

R v Bowley [1999] 1 Cr App Rep (S) 232. The defendant was convicted of anal rape of a woman. The defendant had been drinking with the victim, who was a 34-year-old married woman and other patrons in a pub. The group drunk a lot and engaged in a game of strip poker. The defendant had made it clear to the victim that he wanted sex with her and during the evening had kissed her. In the early hours of the morning the victim drove herself home and was followed by the defendant. The victim's car suffered two burst tyres and she was persuaded by the defendant to accept his offer of a lift home. The defendant did not stop at the woman's house but drove to a nearby car park. The victim feared for her safety and jumped from the car, however as a consequence she lost consciousness. When the victim awoke she was on the backseat of the car and the defendant was having anal intercourse with her. She received bruises and abrasions. The defendant was 37 and had no convictions. The judge described it as dreadful, humiliating, degrading and painful. Held. The fact that this was anal rape was a powerful aggravating feature. The fact that the victim was unconscious or semi-conscious, D had taken advantage of her drunken state and he drove past her house to a car park were all also aggravating factors. **7 years** was not so severe we should quash it.

R v H [1999] 1 Cr App Rep (S) 470. The defendant pleaded guilty to two counts of rape on his estranged wife and one count of possessing a firearm with intent to cause fear. The defendant had been married for 13 years although the marriage had deteriorated. Following incidents of violence and sexual abuse the wife moved out of their home. The victim went to the defendant's house during her lunch break after a request by the defendant and was detained for 4–4½ hours. During this time she was sexually assaulted, anally raped twice and terrified by the defendant brandishing a handgun. She was also assaulted and threatened and in constant fear of being shot. She received bruises and abrasions and was in considerable pain. The defendant was a fireman who had been traumatised by the misery and violence he had seen. He had laspsed into drink, drugs and violence. Since his conviction the defendant realised the full extent of his actions He had sought and obtained help. His wife had considerably forgiven him his conduct. He received 10 years for the anal rape and lesser concurrent sentences for the other counts. Held. Due to the defendant's improvement of attitude **7 years** was more appropriate than 10 years.

R v Triggs [2000] 2 Cr App Rep (S) 179. The defendant was convicted of attempted rape and anal rape. The victim aged 13 had an argument with her mother, packed her bags and left home. She went to some grassland and was reading a book when the defendant approached her from behind. He dragged her into some bushes and held a knife to her throat. He undressed her and unsuccessfully tried to rape her. Then he anally raped her. The victim had three small tears in her anus. The defendant was 28 with 14 previous convictions including a firearm offence but no sex offences. He had a very rudimentary knowledge of sexuality and relationships. He had little education and a number of other problems from his childhood. The judge said there was a very real risk of further offending and causing serious harm. Later an expert said the risk was low. **12 years** not 14 years.

See also *R v Ishizawa* [1998] Unreported Judgment 10/12/98.

See also **BUGGERY**

Attempted rape – Is it a violent offence?

141.7 *R v Robinson* [1993] 96 Cr App Rep 418. Attempted rape was a violent offence for the purposes of the Powers of Criminal Courts (Sentencing) Act 2000, s 80(2)(b) previously the Criminal Justice Act 1991, s 2(2)(b). (The court is able to pass longer than normal sentences and extend the sentences.)

Attempted rape (including Theft Act 1968, s 9(1) (a)) – Guideline case

141.8 *R v Billam* (1986) 82 Cr App Rep 347 – LCJ. The starting point for attempted rape should normally be less than for the completed offence, especially if it is desisted at a comparatively early stage. But, attempted rape may be made by aggravating features into an offence even more serious than some examples of the full offence.

See also *A-G's Reference (No 6 of 1998)* [1998] 2 Cr App Rep (S) 423. 8 years' imprisonment for a series of attempted rapes on a social worker over the period of about one hour.

Old cases. *A-G's Reference (No 11 of 1993)* [1994] 15 Cr App Rep (S) 490; *R v Diggle* (1995) 16 Cr App Rep (S) 163.

Breach of trust/in a position of responsibility to victim

141.9 *R v Billam* (1986) 82ˑCr App Rep 347 – LCJ Guideline case. For an adult in a position of responsibility to the victim in a contested case the starting point is **8 years**.

R v Sellars [1998] 1 Cr App Rep (S) 117. The defendant pleaded guilty at the beginning of the trial to rape. The victim, a 16-year-old family friend who he treated as if she was his uncle went to visit him. They had known each other for 6 years. He gave her wine, which made her drunk. Later he had sexual intercourse with her while she was asleep. She woke up to find his mouth on vagina. He jumped back and pulled his trousers up. Her blouse was undone and her knickers and her tights had been pulled down. She had a small abrasion to the posterior fourchette and was very distressed. In interview he denied the offence. She later found she was pregnant and feared it was the defendant's baby. She was very troubled by this. It turned out not to be his. He was 29 and had a large number of previous convictions mainly for burglary but including one for underage sex with his then 15-year-old girlfriend for which he was given probation. **6 years** not 8.

R v Maishman [2000] 1 Cr App Rep (S) 419. See *Victim aged less than 10*

A-G's Reference (No 51 of 2001) [2001] EWCA Crim 1635, [2002] 1 Cr App Rep (S) 334. 8 years' imprisonment for a man who raped an 18 year old girl who was the daughter of his friend, and whom she called 'uncle'.

Old cases. *A-G's Reference (No 11 of 1993)* (1993) 15 Cr App Rep (S) 490; *R v Angol* (1994) 15 Cr App Rep (S) 727; *R v Mason* (1995) 16 Cr App Rep (S) 860.

See also *Fathers, by; Stepfathers/stepgrandfathers; Victim aged less than 10* and *Victim aged 13–15*

Brother, by

See also **INCEST**

Burglars/robbers, by

141.10 *R v Shafiq* [1998] 2 Cr App Rep (S) 12. The defendant pleaded guilty to rape, robbery and possession of an imitation firearm with intent. At about 10pm the victim was walking from her garage to her flat. She saw the defendant, then 19, and another walking towards her. The defendant had a firearm and she was terrified. When the two were less than a yard from her the defendant pointed the gun at her while the other took her handbag. She was told to open the garage doors which she did. She was then told to go inside and ushered to the back. The defendant fondled her breast and tried to kiss her. He put his tongue in her mouth. The victim tried to escape but was threatened with the gun. The other youth wanted to leave and he was told to shut the garage door when he left which he did. The defendant ordered the victim to get in the car while pointing the gun at her. She decided not to resist and took her clothes off and he pulled at her underclothes. She managed to get the gun but he seized it back off her. The defendant became angry and she again decided not to resist. He couldn't enter her fully and ejaculated over her lower stomach. After having difficulty with the garage door he managed to escape while telling her if she told anyone he'd kill her. The victim was not injured but needed counselling to overcome the trauma. She became a frightened reclusive lady. She couldn't organise her life and had to stay with friends. Her concentration was zero. Previously she had been very confident and outgoing. The defendant had no previous convictions but had been cautioned for robbery, theft and handling. He was a heroin addict and he said he was out of his head at the time. He had lost his mother and had been abused by his father. Held. There were a number of aggravating features which added to the starting figure of 8 years. For an adult it was worth **12–14 years** if contested. Because of his guilty plea and age **9 years** YOI not 11.

A-G's Reference (No 47 of 1999) [2000] 1 Cr App Rep (S) 446. The defendant was convicted of having a firearm with intent to commit robbery, indecent assault and rape. After midnight, a 15-year-old boy answered a knock at the front door and the defendant and another chased the boy in. There were with five or six children in the flat asleep. A loaded gun was held to a 15 year old's head. They ordered all four people in the room to get on the floor and not look at them. Money, jewellery and drugs were demanded. Personal items were seized from them. Two were hit with the gun for no obvious reason and one was tied up with a sheet. Oral sex was demanded at gunpoint. The other man attempted to rape a 19-year-old girl, then ordered her into kitchen and raped her. He hit her with the gun. Then the defendant made her perform oral sex at gunpoint and raped her. The house was searched and they left. The gun was thought to have been loaded. The victim was very seriously traumatised. The defendant was arrested and denied involvement. He was then 20 and had no convictions. He was an illegal overstayer from Jamaica in the process of being deported. There was no underlying psychiatric condition. Held. The sentence should have been **14 years**. But because it was a reference, his good character and youth **11½ years** not 9.

See also *R v Akram* (13 March 1997, unreported).

Old cases. *A-G's Reference (No 16 of 1993)* (1994) 15 Cr App Rep (S) 811; *R v Thomas* (1994) 16 Cr App Rep (S) 686.

Concurrent or consecutive sentences for two or more rapes
141.11 *R v Khan* [2001] EWCA Crim 104, [2001] 2 Cr App Rep (S) 285. Consecutive sentences for these two rapes was not wrong.

Date rape
141.12 *R v Devitt* [2001] EWCA Crim 563, [2001] 2 Cr App Rep (S) 354. The defendant was convicted of rape. Previously he had had sex with the victim about six times. She said they were dating rather than in a serious relationship. He said he was in love. He arrived at their house and asked for sex but she told him to leave, which he did. The next day she decided he was to be told that she did not want to see him again. Three days later he went to her house with a friend and was told she did not

want to see him again and to leave. He did but he tapped on the window and eventually she let him back in to talk. They talked for about 2½ hours with her children upstairs. He began to touch her thigh and she made it clear she wasn't interested in sex. He put his leg over hers and pulled down his tracksuit bottoms. He pulled her head towards his groin. She pushed him away and moved to another sofa. She made it clear she wanted him to go and he locked the front door and put the key in his pocket. He called her a bitch and threatened her. She was extremely frightened and he pushed her head aggressively. She was worried about the children and that he had the key. She went upstairs because she didn't think he would do anything with her daughter in the bedroom. He grabbed the daughter and lashed out at the victim. He apologised to the daughter and took her to her room. He returned, ordered the victim about and kicked her several times in the chest. He told her how he had battered a friend and she was going to be taught a lesson and that she made him sick. She was told how he was going to hurt her, and he forced oral sex on her and performed oral sex on her. He raped her after he had put his fingers in her vagina. After 5 minutes he ejaculated. The victim suffered bruising. When interviewed he said she consented. He was 27 years old, and had served 15 months in custody before but had no sex convictions. Held. **8 years** not altered, but it was wrong to extend the licence by 4 years.

Old case. *R v Diggle* [1995] 16 Cr App Rep (S) 163.

Defendant under 18 – Guidelines case

141.13   *R v Billam* [1986] 82 Cr App Rep 347 – LCJ. About one third of those convicted of rape are under 21 and thus fall within the scope of Criminal Justice Act 1982, s 1, (now the Powers of the Criminal Courts (Sentencing) Act 2000, s 79(2)). Although the criteria to which the Court is required to have regard by that Act must be interpreted in relation to the facts of the individual case rather than simply by reference to a legal category of the offence, most cases of rape are 'so serious that a non custodial sentence cannot be justified' Make some reduction to reflect the youth. In the case of a juvenile, the court will in most cases exercise the power to order detention under Children and Young Persons Act 1933, s 53(2), (now the Powers of the Criminal Courts (Sentencing) Act 2000, s 91). 'A man of 20 will not receive much less than a man of 22, but a youth of 17 or 18 will receive less.

Defendant aged 10–13

141.14   *A-G's Reference (No 18 of 1999)* [2000] 1 Cr App Rep (S) 246. The defendant was convicted of a number of counts of rape, incest, indecent assault, buggery and attempted buggery against his sisters and brother over a 7 year period beginning when the defendant was 12 or 13. The abuse started when the defendant was 10 or 11. The defendant raped his older sister when she was 14 or 15 and the defendant was 12 or 13. The defendant raped his younger sister, O when she was 11, and the defendant was 15. His abuse of her had started when she was 9. He would attack her in her bed and in the shower. It is estimated that she was abused over 50 times. The abuse continued until she was 15. She put up with the activity because her father had also raped her. The defendant began to abuse his brother when he was 13 and the defendant was 15 or 16. The defendant made his brother, S masturbate him and perform oral sex on him and eventually buggered him. Force and inducements were used. O now lives as a lesbian saying she cannot bear a penis near her after what the defendant and her father did to her. All the victims were gravely damaged. S eventually ran from home and went to live with his aunt never to return. The defendant, who was 31 at the time of conviction, had committed no sexual offences since his adolescence. The defendant did not pose a danger to the community now. Held. The sentencing task was immensely difficult. **3 years 8 months** was a lenient sentence, but not unduly lenient.

R v KB [2001] 1 Cr App Rep (S) 431. The defendant aged 12 pleaded guilty to four rapes on a boy aged 11. 2 years not 4 detention but the 11 months on remand remaining consecutive.

Defendant aged 14–15

141.15 *R v M* [2000] 1 Cr App Rep (S) 188. The defendant pleaded guilty to two attempted rapes of an 18-year-old woman. The defendant, who was 14 at the time of the offences, followed the woman and a girlfriend after they left a party. He led the woman into an estate on the pretext that she could find a telephone box pretending to help her. He began to touch her and she pushed him away. He persisted and pinned her against a car and grabbed her breasts and put his hand between her legs and squeezed her vagina. She screamed and he put his hand over her face and then bit her cheek. She screamed again. He touched her breasts and kissed them and then pulled down her trousers. Her pleas for him to stop were ignored and he turned her round and attempted to penetrate her anus. He then pushed her to the ground and then let her get up and dragged her to a dustbin area. She cried uncontrollably and she was pushed to the ground again. He attempted to penetrate her vagina but police who had been summonsed by neighbours arrived. She was crying hysterically. When interviewed he pretended she was consenting. The defendant had breached a conditional discharge for indecency. Held. It was a terrifying attack carried out with grim persistence. The defendant was of a young age. A good secure unit report contributed to a reduction from 5 to **3½ years** detention.

See also *R v Bennett* (1 March 1997, unreported); *R v Tack* (7 July 1997, unreported); *R v Stepton* [1998] 2 Cr App Rep (S) 319.

Old cases. *R v Robinson* [1993] 14 Cr App Rep (S) 448; *A-G's Reference (No 3 of 1993)* (1993) 98 Cr App Rep 84; *R v Connors* (1992) 13 Cr App Rep (S) 666; *R v McIntosh* (1994) 15 Cr App Rep (S) 163; *R v Suleman* (1993) 15 Cr App Rep (S) 569; *R v Powell* (1993) 15 Cr App Rep (S) 611; *R v Stone* (1995) 16 Cr App Rep (S) 407; *R v Brumwell* [1996] 1 Cr App Rep (S) 213.

Defendant aged 16–17

141.16 *R v HS* [2001] 2 Cr App Rep (S) 491. The defendant was convicted after a trial of rape. The defendant then aged 16, raped a 17-year-old virgin from the school he had attended. He called out to her while she was waiting for a friend and invited her to his house. She refused. He pulled her in. After she resisted, she was pushed onto a sofa and he inserted his fingers into her vagina. He then forced her onto the floor and put his fingers in again. She was struggling. He then raped her while she struggled. There were no injuries. He had been excluded from school with a bad school report. When on bail he also earned an unfavourable assessment from a NACRO programme, which he had to leave. At the trial he alleged consent. He was treated as of good character. Held. Because of his age **4 years** not 5 detention.

R v S (14 September 2001, unreported). The defendant pleaded guilty to rape. He was aged 16 at conviction. The victim was 15 years old. He thought she consented to start with and during the act she tried to push him off. He was sentenced on the basis he was reckless and had carried on regardless. Held. Because of *R v Greaves* [1999] 1 Cr App Rep (S) 319, the court had to pass a sentence that was less than *Greaves*. Therefore **12 months** detention and training not 30 months.

Defendant aged 18–20

141.17 *R v Matthews* [1998] 1 Cr App Rep (S) 220. The defendant was convicted of rape, and two counts of indecent assault. They related to the same incident. The defendant when 19 came up behind a 14-year-old girl who was walking in a wood and listening to her stereo. He put his hand over her mouth and pulled her off the footpath. She suffered superficial abrasions to her leg and was taken through the undergrowth to a small clearing. He told her not to scream and pushed her so she fell on her hands and knees. She said, 'Please leave me alone,' but he hit her three times on the head with an object like a stone or piece of wood. Her underwear was pulled down and he put his hand over her eyes. He undid her trousers and forced oral sex on her. She was then pushed forward onto her hands and knees. Fearing rape she told him she was 14 and a virgin. He nonetheless raped her causing her considerable pain. He then pushed his penis into her mouth and pushed it in and out. He withdrew, pushed her head to the ground and made off. She sustained injury to her back rib area and to her wrist because of his tight grip on it with his hand and his fingernails. Semen was found on her clothing. He volunteered to give a specimen and his DNA matched the specimen. He was arrested and he denied the rape. He had no previous convictions. At the trial the cross-examination was restricted to the identity of the rapist. A psychiatric report said he was simple. Held. There were aggravating features. 10 years would be merited for an adult but here **8½ years** YOI not 10.

R v Reid [1998] 2 Cr App Rep (S) 10. See *Aiding and abetting etc*

R v Shafiq [1998] 2 Cr App Rep (S) 12. The defendant pleaded guilty to rape, robbery and possession of an imitation firearm with intent. At about 10pm the victim was walking from her garage to her flat. She saw the defendant then 19 and another walking towards her. The defendant had a firearm and she was terrified. When the two were less than a yard from her the defendant pointed the gun at her while the other took her handbag. She was told to open the garage doors which she did. She was then told to go inside and ushered to the back. The defendant fondled her breast and tried to kiss her. He put his tongue in her mouth. The victim tried to escape but was threatened with the gun. The other youth wanted to leave and he was told to shut the garage door when he left which he did. The defendant ordered the victim to get in the car while pointing the gun at her. She decided not to resist and took her clothes off and he pulled at her underclothes. She managed to get the gun but he seized it back off her. The defendant became angry and she again decided not to resist. He couldn't enter her fully and ejaculated over her lower stomach. After having difficulty with the garage door he managed to escape while telling her if she told anyone he'd kill her. The victim was not injured but needed counselling to overcome the trauma. She became a frightened reclusive lady. She couldn't organise her life and had to stay with friends. Her concentration was zero. Previously she had been very confident and outgoing. The defendant had no previous convictions but had been cautioned for robbery, theft and handling. He was a heroin addict and he said he was out of his head at the time. He had lost his mother and had been abused by his father. Held. There were a number of aggravating features which added to the starting figure of 8 years. For an adult it was worth **12–14 years** if contested. Because of his guilty plea and age **9 years** YOI not 11.

R v Broadhead [2000] 1 Cr App Rep (S) 3. The defendant pleaded guilty to the rape of his stepbrother's wife. The defendant, who was 19, was a frequent visitor to the house. One day the defendant entered the house, where the victim and her two young children were. He was holding a knife and refused to put it down. He grabbed the woman and held the knife to her face. The defendant made threats towards the children and made the woman go into a bedroom and remove her clothing. He raped her, performed oral sex on her and made her reciprocate. The sentencing judge recognised that the defendant posed a significant risk within the community. The defendant had previous convictions, which were not relevant. A guilty plea did not hold as much credit as for others as the defendant was caught in the act. Held. Taking into account that a weapon was used to frighten the victim and her children and that the offence included sexual indignities over and above rape **9 years** YOI was not a manifestly excessive sentence.

A-G's Reference (No 54 of 1998) [2000] 1 Cr App Rep (S) 219. The defendant was convicted of two counts of rape, both per anum and vaginally, on a 17-year-old student. The defendant, who was 19 at the time of conviction was drinking in the pub where the victim worked. He offered to walk her home but she declined. At 4.30pm she left the pub and the defendant followed her. He called the victim offensive names and eventually picked her up in bear hug and dragged her along 100 yards to a thorny thicket. He threatened to kill her if she did not do what she wanted. The defendant tore off the victim's clothes and anally raped her briefly. He then placed his penis in her mouth and then penetrated her vagina. He pulled her hair, sucked her breasts and then took £15 from the victim. He then returned £10. During the incident he slapped her causing red marks. She suffered stress and trauma. The defendant was treated as of previous good character. Held. We would have expected **7 or 8 years** YOI. As it was a reference, the sentence of **6 years** was upheld.

See also *R v Barrie* (18 July 1997, unreported).

Old cases. *R v Dooley* (1994) 15 Cr App Rep (S) 703.

Defendant over 65

141.18   *R v Anderson* [1999] 1 Cr App Rep (S) 273. The defendant was convicted of three attempted rapes, seven indecent assaults, and three indecency with children counts. The offences occurred between 1972 and 1982 on three girls. The defendant was a lodger of the first victim's grandmother. The victim and her family stayed there for 7 months when the girl was 11. She recalled that she was assaulted on more than one occasion. The first time the defendant touched her vagina under her knickers. The second victim, A, was the granddaughter of the defendant's partner, and cousin of the first victim. When A was 7 or 8 the defendant would baby-sit for her. He would walk around the house naked and invite A to touch his penis. D would masturbate in front of A and digitally penetrate her vagina. On one occasion the defendant masturbated over her arm. When the victim was 10 the defendant attempted to have intercourse with her. Between the ages of 10–14, A was indecently assaulted about twice a week by the defendant. When A was 15 the defendant attempted to rape her again, however, A held a knife to his throat and he never touched her again. The third victim was a friend of A's. She was indecently assaulted many times over a 3 year period and when she was aged 10 the defendant attempted to rape her. The defendant who was about 56 when the offences began and 77 at the time of conviction had no previous convictions. The sentencing judge said that the victims and their families were entitled to trust the defendant but his conduct had caused them irreparable damage. Held. **8 years** accurately reflected the scale and criminality of the defendant's behaviour. However, due to the defendant's age and as an act of mercy, **6 years** not 8 years.

R v S [1998] 1 Cr App Rep (S) 261. Defendant aged 82. See *Grandfather, by*

Delay, long delay before conviction

141.19   *R v Anderson* [1999] 1 Cr App Rep (S) 273. See *Defendant over 65*

R v Matthews [1999] 1 Cr App Rep (S) 309. The defendant pleaded guilty to two counts of attempted rape and two counts of indecent assault on a girl of 10. The defendant who was then 18 was the brother of the victim's stepfather. The defendant admitted that on two occasions his penis had touched the outside of the victim's vagina, but that he had stopped when he realised what he was doing was wrong. The defendant also admitted that he had had oral sex with the child on more that one occasion. The victim, a mother of five, stated how the defendant's conduct has stifled her ability to communicate with others over the past 30 years and how she had received counselling. He admitted the matters when interviewed and expressed remorse. The defendant, who was 49 at the time of conviction, was of exemplary character. He had been in the same job for 29 years and was buying his house on mortgage. Held. Had he been dealt with at the time he would have received Borstal. Taking into account the delay of 30 years before the case came before the court and that the defendant was a man of limited intellect with learning difficulties 30 months was excessive. Therefore **12 months**.

R v King [1999] 2 Cr App Rep (S) 376. The defendant was convicted of one count of rape, two counts of buggery and 16 counts of indecent assault. The defendant targeted seven children who came from vulnerable and deprived backgrounds. He would buy them presents and show an interest in them while belittling their families. He introduced them to alcohol and cannabis. The offences took place over a period of 19 years and involved touching the genital areas of the children, forcing the children to masturbate him and then engaging in sexual intercourse. The first victim was 7 when the abuse began and it lasted 4 years. Her sister was abused from when she was 4 and when she was 11 or 12 he raped her. He continued raping her regularly after that and she took an overdose at 19 and had psychiatric treatment. The abuse on her then stopped. Her brother was abused from 11 and he was given cannabis as a reward. The boy was forced to masturbate him regularly. On one occasion he tried to bugger him. Another boy was abused from 10 leading to masturbation, oral sex and then buggery. The defendant had three-way sex with him and his 19-year-old girlfriend. The abuse ended when the boy was 13. Three other girls were abused through oral sex etc from when they were aged 15, 12 and sometime after she was 8. His control was mostly emotional. The abuse seriously affected the children. The defendant, who was 52 at the time of conviction, had no previous convictions. He was blind in one eye and had severe arthritis. One blow could cause him to lose the sight in his other eye. He was not considered a serious threat to children now. The judge said that the defendant had sexually corrupted young children chosen by him for their vulnerability. Held. For this prolonged insatiable depravity involving children of both sexes a long sentence was called for. It was to punish and deter. **18 years** was not manifestly excessive.

A-G's Reference (No 64 of 1998) [1999] 2 Cr App Rep (S) 395. See *Victim aged less than 10*

A-G's Reference (No 18 of 1999) [2000] 1 Cr App Rep (S) 246. See *Defendant aged 10–13*

A-G's Reference (No 13 of 2000) [2001] 1 Cr App Rep (S) 89. At least 8 years was expected for a father, now 70 and in bad health, who committed a series of rapes on his daughters 27 years earlier.

See also *R v S* (3 December 1998, unreported) and *R v Fowler* [2002] EWCA Crim 620, [2002] 2 Cr App Rep (S) 463. See also **DELAY**

Fathers, by

141.20 *A-G's Reference (No 23 of 1997)* [1998] 1 Cr App Rep (S) 378. The defendant was convicted of five counts of rape, one of indecent assault, and one of ABH on his daughters aged 5 and 13. The 5-year-old girl was raped and the defendant put his penis into her mouth and he also attempted to tie her down. The elder daughter was raped when she was between the ages of 13 and 15. The defendant also digitally penetrated her whilst wearing rings on his fingers. This caused her considerable pain. She was also hit over the head with a stick and punched in the eye on a separate occasion. This was the ABH and caused her difficulty in breathing. The offences occurred in two separate households. Held. If the offences for the elder daughter stood on their own 10 or 11 years would be appropriate. The offences on the younger girl merited 8 years. If together **13 years** would have been appropriate. As it was a reference **11 years**.

R v C [1998] 2 Cr App Rep (S) 303. [10 years for a father who was convicted of two counts of rape, one of buggery and one of indecent assault on his daughter when she was 15 upheld.]

A-G's Reference (No 29 of 1998) [1999] 1 Cr App Rep (S) 311. The defendant pleaded guilty to three rapes and five indecent assaults on his daughter over a period of 6 years when she was between the ages of 11 and 17. When the victim's mother was away from the house the defendant would return home to his daughter and abuse her. The abuse began by touching her genitals over and under her clothing. When the girl was 13 or 14 the abuse progressed to digital penetration of her vagina. He abused her weekly over 6 years. The rapes took place when the victim was 15. The defendant was 49 years of age and of good character. At the time of conviction, continued to have a close relationship with his daughter, the girl was extremely fond of her father. The sentencing judge had passed sentence as though this offence was one of incest. Held. Substantial allowance should be given for the fact that these offences of rape were akin to incest. The appropriate sentence was if not **5 years** very close to 5. As this was a reference **3½ years** not 2 years.

A-G's Reference (No 8 of 1999) [2000] 1 Cr App Rep (S) 56. The defendant was convicted of five counts of rape and one count of indecent assault. Four counts of rape were on his daughter and one on his daughter's friend. He and his wife were divorced and his daughter lived with her mother. He looked after her daughter, who was 8, when her mother was in hospital. First he indecently assaulted her and thereafter raped the child on a number of occasions. The defendant made the child smell amyl nitrate and would perform oral sex upon her. The defendant took his daughter and another child, who was 13, to a caravan site. During the stay he anally raped the second child and again raped his daughter. The rapes were over 3 years. He was 37 and a warrant officer in the army and of good character. He would be dismissed from the army and lose considerable pension rights. Held. The defendant was in a position of responsibility to both victims. The lowest sentence that could be imposed was **12 years**. Taking into account that this is a reference **10 years**.

A-G's Reference (No 75 of 1998) [2000] 1 Cr App Rep (S) 102. The defendant pleaded guilty to four rapes, three buggeries and six indecent assaults against his two daughters over a period 11 years in one case and 4 years in the other. Some were specimen counts. The pleas were very late. He placed his penis against the girls' genital areas and digitally penetrated their anuses and vaginas. The defendant also used sex aids on the children. The defendant raped and buggered the victims. He would place a pillow over the face of the older child to prevent her sounds being heard. The defendant administered entinox from a gas cylinder to the younger child. The older child was abused from the age of 6 to 17 and the younger child from 6 to 10. The defendant was 45 at the time of conviction and lacked remorse. Held. These were grave offences against victims of a tender age. Taking into account the late guilty plea and the lack of remorse the appropriate sentence was **12–14 years**. As it was a reference **10 years** not 7 years.

R v DR [2000] 2 Cr App Rep (S) 239. The defendant pleaded guilty to three rapes and other sex offences on his daughter over 9 years. The first offence was rape when she was 13. **14 years** not 16 years.

See also Incest by a Man

Fathers/mothers by – with torture

141.21   *R v W and W* [1999] 1 Cr App Rep (S) 268. The defendant F, the victim's father, pleaded guilty to 11 counts of rape, four counts of GBH with intent, four counts of indecent assault and five counts of cruelty to a child. The defendant M, the victim's mother pleaded guilty to four counts of GBH with intent, four counts of indecent assault and two counts of cruelty to a child. The defendants were a married couple who had five children who were aged between 17 and 3 when the case came before the court. They lived with their children in squalor with rubbish being collected inside the house and the only lavatory facilities being a bucket. He disconnected the water and there was an overpowering smell in the house. They denied access to health visitors. W had had sexual intercourse with his eldest child since her 12th birthday. The child was also forced to perform oral sex and masturbate her father; she was paid £1 a time. She was also paid £25 for her mother to beat her. M tied her daughter to a bed, used a vibrator on her vagina and urinated in her mouth whilst the male defendant videoed the act. Videos were found depicting the eldest child being beaten and tortured by her mother with the father watching. The girl was tied to a metal bar on the ceiling and vaginally penetrated by a vibrator vaginally and anally. The victim was also made to tie her baby brother to his playpen and suck his penis. The 15-year-old daughter also described how she had been repeatedly raped since her 12th birthday. She was tied up and hit by the father with a cane. She was found to have knife and cigarette burns on her. The children were withdrawn and one aped the sexual behaviour she had seen. The sentencing judge said that the defendants had descended deep into a pit of human degradation. Held. No parallel could be drawn between the facts of this case and any other case. The judge did not err. **Life imprisonment**, with 21 years as the notional determinate sentence and 14 years as the specified period for the male defendant not wrong. **15 years** for the female defendant not altered.

R v M and M [2000] 1 Cr App Rep (S) 296. The defendant, F, and his wife, M were convicted of repeatedly raping, buggering and indecent assaulting their seven children and grandchildren over a period of 34 years. F was sentenced for 11 rapes and four buggery on his children and nine rapes and buggery on his grandchildren. M was sentenced for three rapes and two buggeries. Their children suffered abuse for 13 years between 1961 and 1974 and their grandchildren were abused from 1982 to 1995. The defendant's engaged in vaginal and anal intercourse with the victims, and inserted such items as screwdrivers, part pickaxe handles, razor blades, pins and knitting needles into the victims. One had his foreskin pinned over his penis and another razor blades inserted into her vagina. One had both ends of a pitchfork inserted into their bodies. A daughter and granddaughter had knitting needles inserted into their vaginas in an attempt to procure abortions. The children were forced to abuse each other and the defendants invited family members, neighbours and friends to use the victims for sexual gratification. Some were taken away for the weekend by strangers in exchange for money. Degradation and humiliation was used as a tool to subjugate them. M held their heads and watched. She humiliated them and when they wet their beds she made them stand for hours in soiled sheets. The children were still disturbed and one continues to mutilate herself. F was now 68 with a heart condition. He was of good character and had been in the RAF. M was 67 and not in good health. The sentencing judge considered that it would not be appropriate to pass an indeterminate sentence because at the end of a substantial sentence it would be unlikely that the defendants would represent a serious danger to the public. He considered F was the prime mover. Held. It was beyond belief. They were abused and tortured for pleasure. The offences were of unique gravity and sentences of very substantial length had to passed. **25 years** for F and 14 years for M were neither excessive nor wrong in principle.

Firearm, with

141.22   *R v Shafiq* [1998] 2 Cr App Rep (S) 12. The defendant pleaded guilty to rape, robbery and possession of an imitation firearm with intent. At about 10pm the victim was walking from her garage to her flat. She saw the defendant then 19 and another walking towards her. The defendant had a firearm and she was terrified. When the two were less than a yard from her the defendant pointed the gun at her while the other took her handbag. She was told to open the garage doors which she did. She was then told to go inside and ushered to the back. The defendant fondled her breast and tried to kiss her. He put his tongue in her mouth. The victim tried to escape but was threatened with the gun. The other youth wanted to leave and he was told to shut the garage door when he left which he did. The defendant ordered the victim to get in the car while pointing the gun at her. She decided not to resist and took her clothes off and he pulled at her underclothes. She managed to get the gun but he seized it back off her. The defendant became angry and she again decided not to resist. He couldn't enter her fully and ejaculated over her lower stomach. After having difficulty with the garage door he managed to escape while telling her if she told anyone he'd kill her. The victim was not injured but needed counselling to overcome the trauma. She became a frightened reclusive lady. She couldn't organise her life and had to stay with friends. Her concentration was zero. Previously she had been very confident and outgoing. The defendant had no previous convictions but had been cautioned for robbery, theft and handling. He was a heroin addict and he said he was out of his head at the time. He had lost his mother and had been abused by his father. Held. There were a number of aggravating features which added to the starting figure of 8 years. For an adult it was worth **12–14 years** if contested. Because of his guilty plea and age **9 years** YOI not 11.

R v H [1999] 1 Cr App Rep (S) 470. See **Anal rape**

A-G's Reference (No 47 of 1999) [2000] 1 Cr App Rep (S) 446. See **Burglars/Robbers, by**

Old cases. *R v C* (1993) 14 Cr App Rep (S) 642; *R v Suleman* (1993) 15 Cr App Rep (S) 569.

General

141.23   *R v Billam* (1986) 82 Cr App Rep 347 – LCJ Guideline case. For an adult in a contested case with no aggravating or mitigating features the starting point is **5 years**.

A-G's Reference (No 23 of 2000) [2002] EWCA Crim 858, [2001] 1 Cr App Rep (S) 155. The defendant pleaded guilty to rape. The victim and the defendant had helped each other in past as they lived in adjacent flats. They had been friendly for about 2 years. She had occasionally cooked meals for him. She had not responded to his interest in her. At 11pm she knocked on his door and asked his help to move a box into her children's bedroom. He got out of bed, agreed to help and got dressed. After helping her they smoked and had tea. She told him about her debts and he said he would pay them off if she had sex with him. She declined. He asked her to masturbate him and she again declined. He pulled down his trousers and pants and started to masturbate in front of her. She avoided looking at him. After a few minutes, he pulled down her shorts and raped her. Eventually she pushed him off and he continued to masturbate and ejaculated over her carpet. He then left. The rape was very brief. During the night he left a number of telephone messages apologised for his behaviour. The next morning he put £10 note through the door. When arrested he made immediate admissions. The victim found it difficult to remain in her flat and often had nightmares about the rape. The defendant was 37 and a farm labourer. He had no previous offending of any gravity and was of very limited intelligence. He had very few close friends and his family was somewhat over protective of him. He showed remorse. Held. It is axiomatic that in a rape case a non-custodial sentence cannot be justified save in wholly exceptional circumstances. **3½ years** was appropriate. Because it was a reference, **2½ years** not probation with treatment.

A-G's Reference (No 44 of 1999) [2000] 1 Cr App Rep (S) 317 – LCJ. The defendant pleaded guilty to two counts of rape on women with whom he was previously acquainted. Both were committed when he was drunk. The defendant met the first victim at a fun fair and sometimes visited her house, staying the night. After a period of time the victim sought to avoid the defendant. The defendant came to her door one evening and was let in by the victim's young daughter. The defendant made advances towards the victim, which she rebuffed. The defendant then became angry and ordered that the child be put to bed. He said they were going to have some fun tonight and she indicated it was time he left. The child became distressed but the defendant made threats to the victim if she did not put the child to bed. When the woman returned from putting the child to bed she was frightened and in tears. He ordered her to remove her clothing and he removed his trousers and underwear. Fearful of what might happen she complied with the request. The victim realised that she was about to be raped and asked the defendant to wear a condom, which she provided; he refused to do this. He raped her then attempted to penetrate her anus and then raped her vaginally again. The victim felt physically sick. He stayed the night on her sofa and told her nothing was going to stop him doing the rape. They had sex in the morning because she wanted to get rid of him. The defendant knew the second victim and would often arrive at her house drunk. The defendant was found banging on her window and she let him in so that he did not wake her 18-week-old baby. The defendant produced a knife and claimed he had stabbed six people with it. She asked him to leave and he told her he was having her tonight. She began to cry and he waved the knife about. The defendant forced the woman to perform oral sex on him. He then pushed her onto the sofa and raped her. She managed to flee and ran to another house and by chance the first victim came to help her. The police were called and the defendant was arrested on the second victim's sofa. The defendant, who was 24, was of good character. Held. The fact that a knife was used in the second attack and that in both cases young children were present made this a very serious case. As the prosecution suggested he had initially been a welcome guest in both rapes the appropriate sentence was **5 years**. As it was a reference **4 years** not altered.

See also *A-G's Reference (No 43 of 2001)* [2001] EWCA Crim 1275, [2002] 1 Cr App Rep (S) 125 and *A-G's Reference No 69 of 2001* [2002] 2 Cr App Rep (S) 593 [Woman with mental disabilities].

Old cases. *R v Shields* (1994) 15 Cr App Rep (S) 775; *A-G's Reference (No 28 of 1993)* (1994) 16 Cr App Rep (S) 103; *R v Doe* [1995] 16 Cr App Rep (S) 718.

Grandfather, by

141.24 *R v S* [1998] 1 Cr App Rep (S) 261. The defendant was convicted of four rapes and three indecent assaults on his granddaughter over an 11 year period from 1983. Some were specimen counts. The abuse began when she was 3 and the first rape was when she was 13. He would digitally penetrate the victim and asked her to masturbate him. When the victim was older the defendant began to teach her to drive and asked to touch her genitalia as payment. The girl was pulled to the floor and cried during the first rape. On the second she was again pulled to the floor. She resisted and he held her wrists. The third and fourth occasions were similar. There was a lack of remorse. He was now 87 years of age and was 69 when the abuse began. He was in poor health. The pre-sentence report said there was no risk of re-offending. Held. **3 years** was appropriate.

See also INCEST BY A MAN

Guilty, plea of

141.25   *R v Billam* (1986) 82 Cr App Rep 347 – LCJ Guideline case. The extra distress which giving evidence can cause a victim means that a plea of guilty, perhaps more than in other cases, should normally result in some reduction from what would otherwise be the appropriate sentence. The amount of the reduction will of course depend on all the circumstances including the likelihood of a finding of not guilty had the matter been contested.

See also *R v B* (23 June 1999, unreported).

Husbands, by – Guideline remarks

141.26   *R v Berry* (1988) 10 Cr App Rep (S) 13. In some instances the violation of the person and defilement and inevitable features where a stranger rapes a woman are not always present to the same degree when the defendant and victim previously had a long-standing sexual relationship.

R v W (1992) 14 Cr App Rep (S) 256 at 260 – LCJ. It should not be thought that a different and lower scale of sentencing attaches automatically to rape by a husband as against that set out in Billam. All will depend on the circumstances of the individual case. Where the parties were cohabitant normally at the time and the husband insisted on intercourse against his wife's will, but without violence or threats, the considerations identified in *R v Berry* (1988) 10 Cr App Rep (S) 13 and approved in *R v Thornton* (1990) 12 Cr App Rep (S) 1 will no doubt be an important factor in reducing the level of sentencing. Where, however, the conduct is gross and does involve threats or violence, the facts of the marriage, of long cohabitation and that the defendant is no stranger will be of little significance. Between these two extremes there will be many intermediate degrees of gravity which judges will have to consider case by case.

Husbands/partners, ex-husbands/ex-partners, by – living together

141.27   *R v M* (1994) 16 Cr App Rep (S) 770 – LCJ. Principles considered. There must be a distinction between those who are estranged and return as an intruder and those who share the same house or bed. Here, where the victim consented to sharing the same bed, no violence was used, the defendant showed remorse and pleaded guilty, **18 months** not 3 years.

R v Dredge [1998] 1 Cr App Rep (S) 285. The defendant pleaded guilty to two rapes and two indecent assaults on his girlfriend. The defendant lived with his girlfriend and her 12-year-old son. He was jealous and suffered from depression and was moody especially when drunk. His wife served him with her divorce papers and his girlfriend noticed his behaviour was not right. At work the next day he told her on the telephone his thoughts were getting worse and he could not handle the situation. When he came home he started drinking. He raised with her the time she had slept with another man, J, which he often raised. He asked whether she had made a sex video and she denied it. He shook her and said he had to make the decision whether she lived or died. He left and said he would return. Fearing violence she asked her parents to collect her son which they did. She heard one of her cats cry out with pain and he entered the bedroom with a Stanley knife and two lengths of rope. He said he had killed the cat and he threw her on the bed and pulled off her clothing. He made her kneel and asked her questions about J. He inserted his finger into her anus as far as it would go. She cried out in pain and he told her to be quiet. He removed his clothing and buggered her entering as far as possible which was extremely painful. He then raped her and she could tell he was very angry. He held the rope against her neck and said he would slit her son's throat.

He then said he'd slit his throat while she watched and then slit hers. He marked the skin of her thigh and she thought she would be killed. He told her to suck his penis and when she tasted the faeces on it she was sick. She became hysterical and cried uncontrollably. He apologised and gave her the knife. However, he would not let her leave the bedroom. After pleading for 10 minutes he let her go to the kitchen and she was able to telephone the police. When interviewed he said he could not remember much of what had happened but the victim would tell the truth. She refused to give evidence and said it was out of character. The prosecution relied on his admissions. She wanted her relationship to continue and to marry him. He was 30. His risk of re-offending was considered high. Held. Each of the four offences was extremely serious. **6 years** was high but was appropriate.

R v W [1998] 1 Cr App Rep (S) 375. The defendant was convicted of two rapes on his wife while they were cohabiting. When he was drunk he used to become difficult and sometimes violent. In February 1996 he returned home drunk, woke his wife and told her she was going to be raped. He pinned her down and despite her protestations he raped her. The next day she went to a Women's Refuge taking the children with her. About 3 weeks later she attempted a reconciliation and during it consensual intercourse took place. The defendant believed things were developing satisfactorily but the relationship was not always peaceful. In August 1996 there was an argument and he threatened to kick her. He ripped her sweatshirt, knelt on her chest, tried to strangle her, and dragged her round the flat. She said she did not want sex but he persisted. As she was frightened of the consequences she didn't resist. She was sick and upset and left the flat the next day never to return. At the trial his defence was consent. Held. The aggravating features were the violence and that there were two rapes. 5 years is the *R v Billam* [1986] 82 Cr App Rep 347 starting figure. 3½ years consecutive (total 7) reduced to 3½ and **5½ years** concurrent.

R v Mountaine [1998] 2 Cr App Rep (S) 66. The defendant was convicted of three rapes, indecent assault and ABH. The defendant had a stormy relationship with the victim over 10 years. They had two children. There were separations and he drank and was violent to her. They went out and the defendant got drunk. Another man flirted with the victim and when they got home he said if anyone else could have her so could he. He punched holes in the living room door and the victim ran upstairs. He followed and threw her on the bed. He ripped off her shirt and bra and shouted abuse. He pushed her in the face causing her nose to bleed. He held his hand over her nose and mouth preventing her from breathing. He tried to remove her underwear and she started to choke on her blood. She thought she was going to die but managed to run to a neighbour's house. She called the police and they attended but she decided not to make a complaint. She returned home to look after the children. He dragged her upstairs and said he hadn't had sex the previous night and he wanted it now. She refused. He pulled off her underwear and she tried to punch and head-but him. He had sex with her for 10–15 minutes and ejaculated. He apologised and she told him to leave, which he did. He went to Italy and a month after the rape the two spent the day with the children. They went home and when he didn't leave she asked him to leave. He didn't but he went to the kitchen and came back with a knife and held it to her throat. He pulled at her clothes and had sex with her for about ½ hour. He withdrew his penis and cut her with the knife. He then had sex with her for another ½ hour and withdrew and forced his penis into her mouth and attempted to penetrate her anally. They both fell asleep and he woke her up saying he hadn't ejaculated the night before. She struggled and screamed and he raped her again. He was arrested and denied the offence. He had previous convictions but none for sex or violence. He received 5, 5, and 7 years for the rapes with the last one sentence made consecutive. Held. **12 years** in all was amply justified.

A-G's Reference (No 24 of 1999) [2000] 1 Cr App Rep (S) 275. The defendant pleaded guilty to raping his estranged wife. He and his wife were no longer in a relationship but they continued living in same house. The victim went to bed and the defendant jumped on her and pinned her down. He placed tape over her mouth and nose so she had difficulty breathing. She was dragged downstairs and struck three or four times across the face. He tied her legs to the bed with rope and told her he was going to kill himself. He added he had not decided whether she was also going to die. She was told she was not going to see the children again. He held the Stanley knife against her wrist and had oral sex with her while saying he had been planning it for days. She begged him not to have oral sex but he continued for about 10 minutes. She cried and he raped her. She believed she was going to be killed. He attempted to commit suicide with pills. The defendant, who was now 26 years of age, had no previous convictions and had a good work record. He suffered from acute depression. Held. The appropriate sentence was **6 years** but as the defendant was in state of acute depression **5 years** was appropriate. As this was a reference and he had not been given custody before, **3½ years** not probation with treatment.

R v KG [2000] 1 Cr App Rep (S) 70. The defendant was convicted of three counts of rape, one ABH and one common assault on his wife. He was 34 and she 44. The defendant had been married to his wife for 13 years when the offences took place. He became violent towards her and put pillows over her face until she almost passed out. On two occasions she did pass out. He forced his wife to have sex with him every night for 3 months until she left. He would put his wife in a headlock and then force her to have sex with him. She repeatedly told him she did not want sex. It hurt her every time they had sex and that was the basis of the ABHs and common assault. Once when she was scared after being raped he wrapped a tie around her neck and tightened it until she could not breathe. Her head was pulsating and she lost her voice for 4–5 days. Her lower lip was blue. One of the rapes was anal while she cried. When interviewed he made a complete denial of the offences. He was mentally retarded with some long spent convictions. The judge concluded he was dangerous and he enjoyed the violence on his wife. Held. This was a particularly distasteful and persistent episode of serious sexual misconduct and violence over a considerable time. **10 years** was severe not a manifestly excessive.

R v H [2001] 1 Cr App Rep (S) 181. The defendant was convicted of rape on his wife and two specimen counts of indecent assaults on his daughter (from 13 years onwards). They had lived together since 1983. His wife was pinned down on the bed and raped despite the fact she was unwilling. They had consensual sex after the rape and before sentence. The daughter said from when she was 13 she was regularly assaulted by her father who touched her breasts and vagina area despite her objections. It happened weekly for over a year. The investigation into the daughter's assault caused the rape to come to light and there was a considerable delay between the rape in September/ October 1998 and the sentence a year later. He was aged 36 with no previous convictions and a good work character. He was not thought a danger to young girls in the future. He had lost his family, his job and his home. **3 and 2 years consecutive** not 4 and 2 years consecutive.

Old cases. *R v W* (1992) 14 Cr App Rep (S) 256; *R v T* (1993) 15 Cr App Rep (S) 318; *R v Henshall* (1995) 16 Cr App Rep (S) 388; *R v Pearson* [1996] 1 Cr App Rep (S) 309; *R v Thorpe* [1996] 2 Cr App Rep (S) 246.

Husbands/partners, ex-husbands/ex-partners, by – Living apart

141.28 *R v Mills* [1998] 2 Cr App Rep (S) 252. The defendant pleaded guilty to attempted rape, having called the victim as a witness at the committal hearing. Two weeks after being told his relationship with the victim was over he waited for her to return to her house. He had been drinking. When she returned at about 2am he dragged her down the road and pushed her to a grassy area. He took out his penis but had no erection. He made threats to kill her and ripped away at her tights. She struggled and after a verbal exchange he desisted. He pulled her to her feet and punched her. He started to take her to a nearby garage but she managed to escape. He told police he had drunk 10 pints of beer. He had a conviction for manslaughter when after drinking he had fought with another man. Both he and the victim had weapons. The rape victim attended the Court of Appeal saying they 'were back together'. Held. The fact the offence was not completed was not without its importance. **3 years** not 6.

R v H [1999] 1 Cr App Rep (S) 470. The defendant pleaded guilty to two counts of rape on his estranged wife and one count of possessing a firearm with intent to cause fear. The defendant had been married for 13 years although the marriage had deteriorated. Following incidents of violence and sexual abuse the wife moved out of their home. The victim went to the defendant's house during her lunch break after a request by the defendant and was detained for 4–4½ hours. During this time she was sexually assaulted, anally raped twice and terrified by the defendant who was brandishing a handgun. She was also assaulted and threatened and in constant fear of being shot. She received bruises and abrasions and was in considerable pain. The defendant was a fireman who had been traumatised by the misery and violence he had seen. He had lapsed into drink, drugs and violence. Since his conviction the defendant realised the full extent of his actions. He had sought and obtained help. His wife had considerably forgiven him his conduct. He received 10 years for the anal rape and lesser concurrent sentences for the other counts. Held. Due to the defendant's improvement of attitude **7 years** was more appropriate than 10 years.

A-G's Reference (No 64 of 1999) [2000] 1 Cr App Rep (S) 529. [For this rape and kidnap at least 4 would be imposed.]

R v H [2001] 1 Cr App Rep 181. 4 years upheld.

See also *R v Kearney* [1996]

Old cases. *R v Hind* (1993) 15 Cr App Rep (S) 114; *R v Hutchinson* (1993) 15 Cr App Rep (S) 134, *R v Hopkins* [1994] 15 Cr App Rep (S) 373; *R v C* (1994) 15 Cr App Rep 757; *R v Cox* (1995) 16 Cr App Rep (S) 72; *R v Malcolm* (1995) 16 Cr App Rep 151; *R v D* [1996] 2 Cr App Rep (S) 342.

Intruders – Breaking into premises etc as a trespasser

141.29 *R v Billam* (1986) 82 Cr App Rep 347 – LCJ Guideline case. For an adult in a contested case who has broken into or otherwise gained access to a place where the victim is living the starting point should be 8 years.

A-G's Reference (No 51 of 1999) [2000] 1 Cr App Rep (S) 407. The defendant pleaded guilty to the rape of a woman while she was asleep. He broke into the house of the victim, who was an ex-neighbour. On previous occasions he had made inappropriate comments towards the victim. On the night of the offence the victim had consumed a great deal of alcohol and had gone to bed. She awoke in the night when she realised that someone was having sexual intercourse with her. At first she thought it was her boyfriend, when she realised it was not she shouted and the defendant left. The victim rang a friend and was sobbing violently and was very upset. When interviewed the defendant denied he had been at the house. When intimate samples were analysed he then said she had consented. The defendant, who was 46, had no relevant convictions. Held. The claim of consent was a very unattractive feature of the case. The appropriate sentence taking into account it was a reference, his character and other matters was **6 years** not 4 years.

Old cases. *R v Guniem* (1993) 15 Cr App Rep (S) 91; *R v Hutchinson* (1993) 15 Cr App Rep (S) 134; *A-G's Reference (No 10 of 1995)* [1996] 2 Cr App Rep (S) 122.

Life sentence is appropriate

141.30   *R v Billam* (1986) 82 Cr App Rep 347 – LCJ Leading case. A life sentence would not be inappropriate where the offender's behaviour has manifested perverted or psychopathic tendencies or gross personality disorder and where he is likely, if at large, to remain a danger to women for an indefinite time.

R v Low [1998] 1 Cr App Rep (S) 68. The defendant was convicted of attempted rape, robbery and indecent assault. The defendant when 19 came up behind a 19-year-old girl in the street at 10.55pm. She was 6 months pregnant. He mumbled something and pushed a knife close to her neck. She was told to get on her fucking front and she did so. He went through her pockets and shouted at her to lie on her back. She thought she was going to be killed. He asked her to undo her blouse and when she had done that he slid the knife underneath her bra until he had cut it down the middle. He fondled and licked her breasts and told her to take her clothes off. He took out his erect penis but resisted intercourse when told about her pregnancy. He fondled and performed oral sex on her and made her reciprocate. He made her perform oral sex on him. She was terrified of damage to her baby. He said he was taking her back to his place but she refused to go. He left stealing her necklace, some cash and her stereo. A baseball hat covered his face and he told her if she told the police he would kill her. He was unemployed. He had three previous convictions for indecent assault for which he had received 14 days, 3 and 9 months. The probation officer said he was completely out of control and the risk of further offending was very substantial. A medical report said he was illiterate, innumerate, and severely intellectually handicapped. He was not mentally ill. After being sentenced a psychologist said there was a high risk of re-offending. Held. **Life** was justified. Because a sentence in excess of 15 years could not be justified the specified period was reduced from 10 to 7 years.

R v Rodwell [1998] 2 Cr App Rep (S) 1. See **Series of rapes**

A-G's Reference (No 5 of 1998) [1998] 2 Cr App Rep (S) 442 – LCJ. The defendant pleaded guilty to one count of rape and one of inflicting GBH. The defendant, who was 21 years of age, knew the victim as he lived close to her boyfriend. On one occasion where the defendant was socialising with the victim and her boyfriend the defendant touched the woman's bottom over her jeans. The victim ignored the advance but when the defendant repeated the act he told her that he 'fancied' her and that she should leave her boyfriend. The victim replied that the defendant had no chance. The victim did kiss the defendant affectionately but later told him that she wanted to forget the whole incident. The defendant continued to make advances towards the woman who resisted them. On one occasion the defendant arrived at the victim's boyfriend's flat when the latter was away. The victim left but then returned to the defendant's flat to tell him she was going to her own home. The defendant tried to kiss her. As the victim pushed him away the defendant punched her in the face and kicked her as she lay on the floor. The defendant stripped the victim and dragged her to his bedroom. He made her masturbate him whilst he digitally penetrated her and then he raped her twice. The victim was again punched and had her throat squeezed when she tried to escape. The defendant's mood change and he accompanied the victim to the police station where the matter was reported. The defendant had three previous convictions for ABH and for attempted murder and arson and for threats to kill and again assault occasioning actual bodily harm. Held. The defendant was untreatable and had an unstable personality. He was a serious risk and danger to the public. Therefore **life** not 9 years. 5 years relevant period.

A-G's Reference (No 14 of 1998) [1999] 1 Cr App Rep (S) 205. The defendant pleaded guilty to rape and GBH (s 18). At about 2am he attacked the victim aged 42 from behind as she was walking home. He struck her on the head with a house brick, causing her to lose consciousness more than once and dragged her along a road. For over 2 hours he used repeated violence including kicks to the head and striking her with her belt which had a metal buckle. The victim managed to break free and ran to her home. He chased her and started attacking her again. There she managed again to break free but was recaptured again. He said she had done it now and told her to take her clothes off. She was raped while her throat was squeezed and her head hit. She had difficulty in breathing. Suddenly he stopped, apologised and tried to comfort her. She asked him to knock on her door to wake her son and he did so. He was arrested nearby and later expressed remorse. She was bleeding extensively and was in hospital for 3 days. She had extensive bruising to her face, her throat and upper body. There were multiple lacerations to her face which required stitching. There were multiple lacerations to her face. Her facial scars would be permanent. Six months later she was still suffering pain with permanent tinnitus. She had to move home with her children aged 16 and 13. It appeared he was only aroused when violence was used. He had been released from an 18 month sentence for indecent assault and ABH one month earlier. At 1am he had forced entry into the victim's house where she lived with her two young children. He woke her and pulled lumps of hair from her head. He tore her clothes and demanded money. He struck her with his fists knocking her to the floor. He was 29. Held. He did represent a serious danger to the public for an indeterminate time. Therefore **life** not 11 years. 7 years specified.

R v W and W [1999] 1 Cr App Rep (S) 268. See **Fathers, by**

See also *A-G's Reference (No 5 of 1998)* [1998] 2 Cr App Rep (S) 442; *R v Jabble* [1999] 1 Cr App Rep (S) 298; *R v Pullen* [2000] 2 Cr App Rep (S) 114.

Old cases. *A-G's Reference (No 6 of 1993)* (1993) 15 Cr App Rep (S) 375.

Life sentence/Automatic life sentence – Fixing specified term

141.31   Crime (Sentences) Act 1997, s 28.

R v ABE [2000] 1 Cr App Rep (S) 78. The defendant pleaded guilty to two rapes and one false imprisonment. He had many previous convictions including two rapes (10 years' concurrent). Held. If it hadn't been automatic life, 15 years would be appropriate, taking into account the guilty plea. The trial judge fixed the specified period too high at 12 years. The practice is to fix it at ½ the appropriate determinate sentence, unless there was good reason not to. As the defendant had spent 145 days in custody before sentence, **8 years** for the specified period substituted.

R v Stokes [2000] 2 Cr App Rep (S) 187. The defendant pleaded guilty to seven counts of indecent assault, one attempted rape and seven counts of rape. Previously convicted of attempted rape and sentenced to 4 years. The judge had indicated that without life provisions 9 years would be appropriate. The judge wrongly told to deduct a third. Should deduct a half and time on remand. So **4 years 2 months** not 5½ years specified.

See also *R v Rodwell* [1998] 2 Cr App Rep (S) 1; *R v Jabble* [1999] 1 Cr App Rep (S) 298; *R v Pullen* [2000] 2 Cr App Rep (S) 114

Old cases (before procedure slightly altered). *R v Hann* [1996] 1 Cr App Rep (S) 267; *R v Arnold* [1998] 1 Cr App Rep (S) 416.

See also MANSLAUGHTER – *Life Sentence/Automatic life sentence – Fixing specified term*

Longer than commensurate sentences

141.32 Powers of Criminal Courts (Sentencing) Act 2000, s 80(2)(b) . . .the custodial sentence shall be. . .where the offence is a violent or sexual offence, for such longer term (not exceeding the maximum) as in the opinion of the court is necessary to protect the public from serious harm from the offender. (Previously the Criminal Justice Act 1991, s 2(2)(b).)

R v Robinson [1993] 96 Cr App Rep 418. Attempted rape was a violent offence under the Act.

R v Howatt (8 July 1996, unreported). The defendant was convicted of rape. He forced his way into the victim's flat, threats with a knife then raped her. He had four previous convictions for indecent assault. The use of the section must not result in a sentence out of all proportion to the sentence that would otherwise be imposed. **15 years** not 18.

R v L [2000] 2 Cr App Rep (S) 177. The defendant pleaded guilty to two counts of rape and one of indecent assault on his 12-year-old stepson. He touched the boy and was told to stop. The defendant got him to the floor and the boy screamed and was buggered. His mother walked in and the defendant stopped. On a caravan holiday the defendant buggered him again. The defendant was 53 and had 21 convictions including attempted rape (receiving 18 months) and two indecent assaults (receiving C/D and CSO). The last offence was 15 years ago. The judge passed a longer than commensurate sentence of 9 years. Held. As his last offence was 15 years ago it was taking things too far to say there was current dangerousness. Therefore it was wrong to pass a longer than commensurate sentence so **9 years** substituted.

See also LONGER THAN COMMENSURATE SENTENCES and *Persistent offender*

Manslaughter, and

See MANSLAUGHTER – *Rapists, by*

Mothers

See *Fathers, by – With torture*

Murder, attempted, and

See MURDER, ATTEMPT – *Rapists, by*

Newspapers, and

141.33 See the article about rape sentences and newspaper reporting [1998] Crim LR 455.

Robbers

See *Burglars/Robbers, by*

Previous conviction for rape or attempted rape/serious offence

See *Life sentence/automatic life* and EXTENDED SENTENCES

Prostitutes, on

141.34 *R v Cole* (1993) 14 Cr App Rep (S) 764. The law will uphold the prostitute's right to say 'no'. But by the very nature of her trade she is prepared to have sex with any man who pays for it and the hurt she may suffer is to some extent different from another woman and that is a factor the court can take into account.

R v Masood [1997] 2 Cr App Rep (S) 137. The defendant, aged 20, pleaded guilty to rape and false imprisonment. He picked up a 16-year-old prostitute in his car punched her 3–4 times and she lost consciousness. The attack involving various sexual activity lasted over 4 hours. He had no convictions. Held. We do not disagree with *R v Cole*

(1993) 14 Cr App Rep (S) 764, but the remarks are not germane here. The very act of intercourse to someone who has never experienced it before, if she is unwilling and is taken by surprise, can be in itself an inexpressibly appalling event. Intercourse by itself with a prostitute might be to some extent less appalling, but the catalogue of other indecencies, of gratuitous violence, of false imprisonment, of gratuitous additional insults and threats is something which is as painful to a prostitute as it would be to anyone else. It was for the courts to give the protection to prostitutes they sadly too often need. We take no account of the fact she was a prostitute. **9 years** concurrent was severe but not manifestly excessive.

A-G's Reference (No 28 of 1996) [1997] 2 Cr App Rep (S) 206 – LCJ. The defendant was convicted of five rapes over 6 years. Each was on different prostitutes. He always refused to wear condom just before sex. Held. Prostitutes were entitled to the protection of the law as much as anyone else. They were in particular need of protection. **8 years** was the least sentence appropriate. Because it was a reference **6 years**.

R v Khan [2001] EWCA Crim 104, [2001] 2 Cr App Rep (S) 285. The defendants N, T, and K were convicted of two rapes, three false imprisonment and a robbery. The defendant J was convicted of one rape, two false imprisonments and a robbery. There were three attacks on prostitutes. J was only involved in two and the others in all three. The first and third victims were the same. The first victim was persuaded by N to get in a car. The car was driven off to a nearby car park. T and K got in and a hand was placed over her mouth. She was forced by the threat of a knife to have sex with the three in turn. She supplied them with a condom. The second victim was picked up by J, driven to a secluded spot and the other three defendants got in. She struggled, punched and kicked them. They took £25 from her and ejected her from the car. The first victim was attacked again shortly after. She went through the same ordeal as she had on the first occasion. The defendants were now aged 20, 19, 21 and 20 respectively. All had no previous convictions. N had received cautions. T, K, and J were assessed as a risk for re-offending. The judge gave N and J an extra ½ year because they had been the ones who had picked up the girls in question. Held. The attacks were planned. The robbery was very unpleasant. Consecutive sentences for the two rapes was not wrong. The picking up of the girls did not add to N and J's responsibility so **10 years** not 10½ years detention for N. **10 years** detention for T upheld. **8 years** detention for K upheld. **6½ years** detention not 7 for J.

Old cases. *R v Cole* (1993) 14 Cr App Rep (S) 764.

Series of rapes

141.35   *R v Billam* (1986) 82 Cr App Rep 347 – LCJ Guideline case. At the top end of the scale comes the defendant who has carried out a campaign of rape, committing the crime upon a number of different women or girls. He represents more than ordinary danger and a sentence of **15 years** or more may be appropriate.

A-G's Reference (No 28 of 1996) [1997] 2 Cr App Rep (S) 206. See **Prostitutes, on**, *R v Rodwell* [1998] 2 Cr App Rep (S) 1. The defendant was convicted of attempted rape, two counts of buggery, rape and two counts of indecent assault. The defendant attacked five women over a 2½ year period. The first victim was grabbed from behind and dragged into bushes. He threatened to kill her and using a knife attempted to rape her and then buggered her. The second victim, aged 63 was also grabbed from behind and buggered. The third victim was attacked on a towpath and dragged into the undergrowth and raped. The fourth victim was also dragged into the undergrowth and he used a knife to force her to allow his fingers to enter her vagina and his penis to enter her mouth. She was left tied up. The last victim was knocked to the ground and punched two or three times on the head. He forced her to masturbate him. At his trial he disputed the DNA evidence and the victims were not called. The judge did not have psychiatric evidence but considered the offences showed the danger he posed. He was sentenced to life and appealed the specified term. Held. **Life** was entirely appropriate. In none of the considered cases were two of the victims buggered, a most terrible indignity. Each one of the offences would be punishable with sentences in the region of **10 years**. A starting point of 22–23 years was not manifestly excessive.

R v Mountaine [1998] 2 Cr App Rep (S) 66. The defendant was convicted of three rapes, indecent assault and ABH. The defendant had a stormy relationship with the victim over 10 years. They had two children. There were separations and he drank and was violent to her. They went out and the defendant got drunk. Another man flirted with the victim and when they got home he said if anyone else could have her so could he. He punched holes in the living room door and the victim ran upstairs. He followed and threw her on the bed. He ripped off her shirt and bra and shouted abuse. He pushed her in the face causing her nose to bleed. He held his hand over her nose and mouth preventing her from breathing. He tried to remove her underwear and she started to choke on her blood. She thought she was going to die but managed to run to a neighbour's house. She called the police and they attended but she decided not to make a complaint. She returned home to look after the children. He dragged her upstairs and said he hadn't had sex the previous night and he wanted it now. She refused. He pulled off her underwear and she tried to punch and head-but him. He had sex with her for 10–15 minutes and ejaculated. He apologised and she told him to leave, which he did. He went to Italy and a month after the rape the two spent the day with the children. They went home and when he didn't leave she asked him to leave. He didn't but he went to the kitchen and came back with a knife and held it to her throat. He pulled at her clothes and had sex with her for about ½ hour. He withdrew his penis and cut her with the knife. He then had sex with her for another ½ hour and withdrew and forced his penis into her mouth and attempted to penetrate her anally. They both fell asleep and he woke her up saying he hadn't ejaculated the night before. She struggled and screamed and he raped her again. He was arrested and denied the offence. He had previous convictions but none for sex or violence. He received 5, 5, and 7 years for the rapes with the last one sentence made consecutive. Held. **12 years** in all was amply justified.

R v W and W [1999] 1 Cr App Rep (S) 268. See *Fathers, by*

A-G's Reference (No 45 of 1998) [1999] 1 Cr App Rep (S) 461. The defendant was convicted of two counts of rape on two separate women. The defendant, who was now 26 years of age, began a consensual sexual relationship with the first victim, but the relationship ended. The defendant continued to pester the girl, who was then 18 years old. One evening after he had been drinking the defendant called at the victim's flat and persuaded her to let him in. The defendant pushed her onto the sofa, tore her nightdress, called her a bitch and raped her. The victim repeatedly pleaded with the defendant to stop. After the victim was allowed to use the toilet she was raped again. The defendant was arrested but released on bail. During this time the defendant raped a second woman who was the fiancé of a relative of his. The defendant called at her flat and was admitted. The defendant made advances towards the woman and would not leave. He picked her up in a fireman's lift and carried her upstairs, then raped her. The defendant ejaculated over the right side of her face and hair. The defendant left saying that he would return the following night. The defendant had a history of violence predominately on men. However, two convictions were for offences of violence on his then partner. The court took into account that the defendant committed an offence whilst on bail and that he attacked the victims when he knew they would be alone. Held. Taking into account it was a reference **9 years** not 6 years.

A-G's Reference (No 8 of 1999) [2000] 1 Cr App Rep (S) 56. See *Fathers, by*

A-G's Reference (No 44 of 1999) [2000] 1 Cr App Rep (S) 317. See *General*

A-G's Reference (No 47 of 1999) [2000] 1 Cr App Rep (S) 446. See *Burglars/Robbers, by*

R v Khan [2001] EWCA Crim 104, [2001] 2 Cr App Rep (S) 285. See *Prostitutes, on*

See also *R v Ishizawa* (10 December 1998, unreported) and *Concurrent or consecutive sentences for two or more rapes*

Old cases. *R v McArthur* (1993) 14 Cr App Rep (S) 659; *R v Angol* (1994) 15 Cr App Rep (S) 727; *R v Henshall* (1995) 16 Cr App Rep (S) 388; *R v M* [1996] 2 Cr App Rep (S) 286.

Stepfathers/stepgrandfathers

141.36 *R v Billam* [1986] 82 Cr App Rep 347 – LCJ Guideline case. For an adult in a contested case the starting point is 8 years for a person in a position of responsibility to the victim.

A-G's Reference (No 12 of 1998) [1999] 1 Cr App Rep (S) 44. The defendant pleaded guilty to two rapes and three indecent assaults. The prosecution was told of the guilty pleas a day before his trial. The offences were on his stepdaughter aged then between 11 and 13 over an 18 month period. The mother left her children in his care while she worked long hours in the evening. The defendant due to his epilepsy was unable to work. The offences started when he was 23 with touching her breasts and vagina over her clothing. Later there was digital penetration, oral sex and then full sex. He gave her cigarettes. He was 23 when the offences started and of good character. Held. The discount for the plea should be reduced because the girl had been left in suspense for so long. The appropriate sentence was **at least 7 years**. Because it was a reference and the other circumstances **6 years** not 4.

A-G's Reference (No 23 of 1999) [2000] 1 Cr App Rep (S) 258. The defendant was convicted of two counts of indecent assault and one count of rape against his stepdaughter when she was between the ages of 11 and 13. The defendant was convicted 20 years after the offences took place. When the victim was 11 the defendant married her mother. The abuse began almost immediately. The defendant touched the girl's vagina over her underwear. She told him to stop. When the victim was 12 she had to go to hospital for an injection. She became drowsy and fell asleep. When she awoke in a car in a country lay-by. She found the defendant on top of her trying to force her legs open. She screamed and cried and he slapped her across her face and called her a frigid bitch. He drove her home and sent her to bed. Just before her 13th birthday the defendant came into her bedroom, put his hand over her mouth and raped her. Her vagina was bleeding. He bullied her and told her if she told anyone her mother would die. The victim suffered considerably as a result of the abuse. She had very low self-esteem and could not relate to her husband. She was forced to seek counselling. The defendant, who was 57 at the time of conviction, suffered ill health. He had a conviction for unlawful sexual intercourse with a girl under 13 and was released from prison only months before this abuse began. The victims of those offences were his stepdaughters from a previous relationship. Held. Taking into account the short period of time from the defendant's release from prison and when this new abuse started and the effect on the victim 4 years was unduly lenient. The appropriate sentence was **9 years**. As this was a reference **7 years**.

A-G's Reference (No 71 of 1999) [2000] 2 Cr App Rep (S) 83. The defendant was convicted of three rapes, one indecent assault and one gross indecency. The offences were over a 9 month period against his stepdaughter when she was 7 or 8 years old. While his wife was out he raped her and tried to make her suck his penis. It went close to her face. He also performed oral sex on her. The medical evidence referred to the injury to the girl as being slight. The defendant was 38 and had convictions (no details given). The pre-sentence report said he was holding the girl responsible for the offences. There was a significant risk of re-offending. Held. There was no mitigation. The sentence should have been **10 or 11 years**. Because it was a reference **9 years** substituted for 6. 2 years for the indecent assaults increased to 3 but remaining concurrent.

See also **BUGGERY** – *Stepfathers*

Old cases. *R v M* [1996] 2 Cr App Rep (S) 286; *A-G's Reference (No 5 of 1996)* [1996] 2 Cr App Rep (S) 434.

Street attack on victim

141.37   *R v Chowdury* [1999] 2 Cr App Rep (S) 269. The defendant was convicted of rape on a stranger. The victim, who was partially deaf in both ears, was walking home at about 2am. She had drunk about 13 bottles of beer. The defendant began to follow her and then caught up with her said, 'I want you to come home with me.' He tugged at her sleeve and she managed to pull free. He continued to walk behind her and then dragged her off the road to a secluded spot. He pushed her to the ground and raped her. The victim went back to the road and screamed hysterically. The victim said she felt humiliated, violated and ashamed. She found her dealings with the police extremely traumatic. The defendant, who was 30 years old, was of extremely limited intellect and was a continuing danger to women. Held. The serious impact the offence had on the victim was the strongest aggravating factor making the starting point 8 years. The other factors including the dragging her to a quiet spot and him being a continuing danger to women means **10 years** was entirely justified.

R v Maidment [2000] 1 Cr App Rep (S) 457. The defendant pleaded guilty, to rape. The plea was indicated 4 days before trial. At about 2.30am the 17-year-old victim was walking home. He attempted to engage her in conversation and she ignored him. As she continued walking he followed her and she became increasingly uneasy. As she quickened her pace he caught up with her and placed his hand on her buttocks. She removed his hand and he moved in front of her to block her path. He seized her and pinned her against a wall. Her struggling was in vain. He slapped or punched her on her head several times and ended up on the ground. He got on top of her and put his fingers in her vagina. He produced a bottle of amyl nitrate and told her to sniff it and she refused to do it. He then raped her. He told her to get up and she continued with her journey shaking with fear. When she reached her home he followed her in. She went to her brother's room and when she and her brother went to the hall he had left. She had bruising, a cut lip and scratches. When arrested he continued to deny the offence until confronted with the evidence of a DNA match. He was 32 with no relevant convictions. Held. His conduct was very serious indeed. Because of the gratuitous violence and her being waylaid at night after a trial it would have warranted a sentence of the dimension of **8 years**. Taking into account his late plea that would be discounted to **6 years**.

Two or more men acting together

141.38   *R v Billam* (1986) 82 Cr App Rep 347 – LCJ Guideline case. Where two or more adult men acting together in a contested case, the starting point is **8 years**.

R v Khan [2001] EWCA Crim 104, [2001] 2 Cr App Rep (S) 285. See *Prostitutes, on* Old cases. *R v Cole* (1993) 14 Cr App Rep (S) 764; *R v Suleman* (1993) 15 Cr App Rep (S) 569.

Victim, bad effect on

141.39 *R v Billam* (1986) 82 Cr App Rep 347 – LCJ Guideline case. For an adult in a contested case with no aggravating or mitigating features the starting point is 5 years. The crime should be treated as aggravated by the following factors: . . . the effect on the victim, whether physical or mental, is of a special seriousness. Where any one of these aggravating features are present, the sentence should be substantially higher than the figure suggested as the starting point.

R v Chowdury [1999] 2 Cr App Rep (S) 269. The defendant was convicted of rape on a stranger. The victim, who was partially deaf in both ears, was walking home at about 2am. She had drunk about 13 bottles of beer. The defendant began to follow her and then caught up with her said, 'I want you to come home with me.' He tugged at her sleeve and she managed to pull free. He continued to walk behind her and then dragged her off the road to a secluded spot. He pushed her to the ground and raped her. The victim went back to the road and screamed hysterically. The victim said she felt humiliated, violated and ashamed. She found her dealings with the police extremely traumatic. The defendant, who was 30 years old, was of extremely limited intellect and was a continuing danger to women. Held. The serious impact the offence had on the victim was the strongest aggravating factor making the starting point 8 years. The other factors including the dragging her to a quiet spot and him being a continuing danger to women means **10 years** was entirely justified.

Victim less than 10

141.40 *R v Anderson* [1999] 1 Cr App Rep (S) 273. See *Defendant over 65*

R v King [1999] 2 Cr App Rep (S) 376. See *Delay, long delay before conviction*

A-G's Reference (No 64 of 1998) [1999] 2 Cr App Rep (S) 395. The defendant pleaded guilty at an early stage to 11 charges of rapes and indecent assault against his two nieces. There were three rapes and an attempted rape. They took place over 9 years. The offences came to light 12 years after the offending against the two girls stopped. The victim's mother died when the nieces were 5 and 6 so they had to live with their grandmother. After her death the girls had to live with the defendant and his wife. The defendant had already begun to indecently assault the younger of the two girls before she lived with him. It started when she was 5. When she was 9 the abuse turned into rape. This became a regular event. The defendant then began to indecently assault the older girl. The assaults were of a particular unpleasant character. The offences came to light 10 to 12 years after they had been committed. The effect on the girls was very serious. From time to time they would run away from home and the elder girl tried to commit suicide. The defendant had a conviction for attempted rape of the third sister when she was 15 years old (he received an 18 month suspended sentence). There were no offences since then. He was 46. The girls, now women, asked that the defendant be allowed home. Held. **10 years** would have been appropriate. Taking into account the time that had elapsed since the offences and the fact that this was a reference, **7 years** not 3 years.

A-G's Reference (No 18 of 1999) [2000] 1 Cr App Rep (S) 246. See *Defendant aged 10–13*

A-G's Reference (No 28 of 1999) [2000] 1 Cr App Rep (S) 314 – LCJ. The defendant pleaded guilty to two counts of attempted rape, four counts of indecent assault and one count of indecency with a child at the first opportunity. The victim was the 6 year old daughter of the woman with whom he was living with. The defendant asked the victim to put his penis in her mouth and to masturbate him, which she refused to do. The defendant then masturbated in front of her. The defendant lay with his penis exposed and made the girl lie on top of him. The defendant also digitally penetrated the girl at least three times and placed his penis between her legs and pushed his penis between the cheeks of her bottom. On a later occasion he penetrated her anally. She said it hurt and he stopped. The victim told her mother and he left the house that evening. The child's anus was not damaged but her character had been effected by the events. Previously she was affectionate and cheerful but now she was quiet, withdrawn, tearful and afraid of men. Her sleep was disturbed. The defendant admitted the matters in interview. He was 24 and of good character. He was assessed as having a high risk of re-offending. He expressed regret and disgust towards himself. Held. After a trial the appropriate sentence would have been in the order of **6 years**. Taking into account the early plea, which saved the victim the trauma of the fear of giving evidence, and that he had spent time in a bail hostel **4 years** would be appropriate. However, as it was a reference **3 years** was suitable. **30 months** was unduly lenient, but it would not be appropriate to increase the sentence by 6 months.

R v Maishman [2000] 1 Cr App Rep (S) 419. The defendant pleaded guilty to two rapes and ABH of a 7-year-old girl. He rented a room in the girl's stepfather's public house where she lived. The defendant on Christmas evening had a few drinks with her family and played with the children. After the girl had had a happy day she went to bed. At night he entered her bedroom and carried her to his room. Once in his room she called for her mother and he punched her in the eye and told her to be quiet. He undressed her and then had vaginal and anal sex with her. He tried to make her perform oral sex on him. He also punched her on the nose causing it to bleed. At one stage he covered her face with a pillow. Next morning when the mother asked the girl about the injuries the defendant seemed overprotective towards her. The girl said she had fallen over. At hospital she was treated for a black eye and a bruised nose and forehead. Later the girl was able to say what had happened. The defendant was arrested and said he could recall little of what had happened on Christmas Day because he was drunk. Four days after the rapes a paediatrician found bruising to the inside of her mouth and a tear on the inside of her lip. There was a deep cut at the base of her hymen and an acute fissure in her anus. The child's personality changed. She now wakes up crying, wets her bed and has nightmares. She plays by herself and is clingy and frightened. He was now 45 and had no relevant convictions. The judge said the offence was cruel and vicious and would have long lasting effects on her. Held. The effect on her was devastating and disastrous. The attack was depraved. The aggravating features were the age of the child; the age gap between them; the two rapes; the violence before and after the rapes; the attempt to perform oral sex; the effects on the victim and the breach of trust. If there had been a trial **14–16 years** would be appropriate. Because the case was overwhelming **14 years** was at the top of the bracket but not manifestly excessive.

A-G's Reference (No 12 of 2001) [2002] 2 Cr App Rep (S) 382. [The defendant aided and abetted the rape of a baby of some friends by her partner. 4 years was lenient but not disturbed.]

See also *Stepfathers/stepgrandfathers*

Victim aged 13–15

141.41   *R v Matthews* [1998] 1 Cr App Rep (S) 220. See *Defendant aged 18–20*

R v Canavan Re Shaw [1998] 1 Cr App Rep (S) 243 at 251 – LCJ. The defendant was convicted of rape and eight counts of indecent assault. There were six victims. The victim of the rape was his niece and the count was a specimen account reflecting about seven rapes over a 2–3 year period from when she was 11. He started indecently assaulting her when she was 5. The indecent assaults were over a 36 year period. He was now 73. Because of the circumstances and his pitiful medical condition **8 years** not 12.

R v Geary [1998] 2 Cr App Rep (S) 434. **14 years** for the rape and indecent assaults on a girl over a 3 year period beginning when she was 12 and other sex offences.

R v Triggs [2000] 2 Cr App Rep (S) 179. The defendant was convicted of attempted rape and anal rape. The victim aged 13 had an argument with her mother packed her bags and left home. She went to some grassland and was reading a book when the defendant approached her from behind. He dragged her into some bushes and held a knife to her throat. He undressed her and unsuccessful tried to rape her. Then he anally raped her. The victim had three small tears in her anus. The defendant was 28 with 14 previous convictions including a firearm offence but no sex offences. He had a very rudimentary knowledge of sexuality and relationships. He had little education and a number of other problems from his childhood. The judge said there was a very real risk of further offending and causing serious harm. Later an expert said the risk was low. **12 years** not 14 years.

R v S (14 September 2001, unreported). The defendant pleaded guilty to rape. He was aged 16 at conviction. The victim was 15 years old. He thought she consented to start with and during the act she tried to push him off. He was sentenced on the basis he was reckless and had carried on regardless. Held. Because of *R v Greaves* [1999] 1 Cr App Rep (S) 319, the court had to pass a sentence that was less than *Greaves*. Therefore **12 months** detention and training not 30 months.

See also **Stepfathers/stepgrandfathers** and *R v Tack* (7 July 1997, unreported).

Old cases. *R v Powell* (1993) 15 Cr App Rep (S) 611; *R v Angol* (1994) 15 Cr App Rep (S) 727; *R v Stone* (1995) 16 Cr App Rep 407; *R v Brumwell* (1996) 1 Cr App Rep (S) 213; *A-G's Reference (No 36 of 1995)* [1996] 2 Cr App Rep (S) 50; *R v M* [1996] 2 Cr App Rep (S) 286.

Victim aged 16–17

141.42 *R v Maidment* [2000] 1 Cr App Rep 457. The defendant pleaded guilty, to rape. The plea was indicated 4 days before trial. At about 2.30am the 17-year-old victim was walking home. He attempted to engage her in conversation and she ignored him. As she continued walking he followed and she became increasingly uneasy. As she quickened her pace he caught up with her and placed his hand on her buttocks. She removed his hand and he moved in front of her to block her path. He seized her and pinned against a wall. Her struggling was in vain. He slapped or punched her on head several times and she ended up on the ground. He got on top of her and put his fingers in her vagina. He produced a bottle of amyl nitrate and told her to sniff it and she refused to do it. He then raped her. He told her to get up and she continued with her journey shaking with fear. When she reached her home he followed her in. She went to her brother's room and when she and her brother went to the hall he had left. She had bruising, a cut lip and scratches. When arrested he continued to deny the offence until confronted with the evidence of a DNA match. He was 32 with no relevant convictions. Held. His conduct was very serious indeed. Because of the gratuitous violence and her being waylaid at night after a trial it would have warranted a sentence of the dimension of **8 years**. Taking into account his late guilty plea that would be discounted to **6 years**.

Victim aged 18–21

141.43   *R v Ford* [1998] 2 Cr App Rep (S) 74. The defendant pleaded guilty on re-arraignment to the rape of a 17 year old. The victim had an argument with her parents and left her home in Blackpool and went to Manchester. She wandered the streets and started crying. The defendant approached her at about 6pm and asked if he could help. He offered her money to telephone home which she declined. They held hands and eventually they entered a car park where he tried to kiss her. He held her round the waist and put his hand inside her clothing and fondled her breasts. He later undid her jeans, stroked her buttocks and vagina and pulled down his trousers and her jeans. She began to cry and pleaded with him. He raped her and ejaculated. Then he walked off and she eventually sought help. She sustained some bruising on her arm and upper thigh. There was tenderness above the pubic bone and injuries to the genitalia consistent with recent penetration. When given the DNA match he admitted the intercourse but claimed it was with her consent. He was 29 with some minor convictions and expressed regret. He was then on bail for two other offences of rape, which were left on the file. **4 years** not 6.

R v Bamforth [1999] 1 Cr App Rep (S) 123. The defendant pleaded guilty to rape. He when 23, wandered round the streets looking for and fantasising about sexual intercourse. The victim aged 19, was walking at night with her boyfriend and the defendant took a fancy to her. He followed them for some while until the victim about two streets from her home persuaded the boyfriend he should leave her to make her way the last few yards. Once she was alone he stole up behind her and seized her from behind. He put his hands over her breasts and held her by the neck. He squeezed the neck tightly and when she screamed he pushed her fingers down her throat. He dragged her to a playing field and notwithstanding her desperate struggles and her screams pushed her to the ground. He stripped her and raped her and left her naked to make her way to the nearest house. Nearly a year later his DNA was matched and when told of the match he admitted the offence. The victim became withdrawn, depressed and left her university without completing the first year. She continued to experience nightmares. Held. Had he fought the case 8 years would have been appropriate. Because of his plea at the first opportunity, **6 years** not 8.

Victim aged over 65

141.44   Old cases. *R v Guniem* (1993) 15 Cr App Rep (S) 91; *R v McIntosh* (1993) 15 Cr App Rep (S) 163; *A-G's Reference (No 11 of 1993)* (1993) 15 Cr App Rep (S) 490; *R v Dooley* (1994) 15 Cr App Rep (S) 703; *R v Thomas* (1994) 16 Cr App Rep (S) 686; *R v Mason* (1995) 16 Cr App Rep (S) 860.

Victim initially consents

141.45   *R v Greaves* [1999] 1 Cr App Rep (S) 319. The defendant pleaded guilty to the rape of a 17-year-old woman after she initially consented but then withdrew her consent. The victim was friendly with the defendant and asked him to come to the flat where she was staying. Shortly after his arrival sexual intimacy took place and the couple began to have sexual intercourse. However the victim at this late stage said, 'No Steve. This isn't what I want. Stop'. The defendant did not stop until the act of sexual intercourse was completed. The defendant, who was 34 years of age had no previous convictions of a sexual nature. The trial judge attached a great deal of significance to the disparity in ages between the defendant and the victim; this was not appropriate, the girl was over the age of consent. Held. **18 months** not 3½ years.

R v S (14 September 2001, unreported). The defendant pleaded guilty to rape. He was aged 16 at conviction. The victim was 15 years old. He thought she consented to start with and during the act she tried to push him off. He was sentenced on basis he was reckless and had carried on regardless. Held. Because of *R v Greaves* [1999] 1 Cr App Rep (S) 319, the court had to pass a sentence that was less than *Greaves*. Therefore **12 months** detention and training not 30 months.

Victim, defendant initially believed victim consented

141.46   Old cases. *R v Brookes* [1993] 14 Cr App Rep (S) 496.

Victim does not want the defendant sent to prison/Victim has forgiven him

141.47   *R v Dredge* [1998] 1 Cr App Rep (S) 285. The victim suffered an extremely painful and degrading rape. However, she said wanted the relationship to continue and to marry him. The victim was not prepared to give evidence. Held. The views of the victim are always a factor to be taken into account. That also has to be balanced, however, against the public interest that a sentence which is appropriate is passed. For further details see *Husbands/partners, ex-husbands/ex-partners, by – living together*

R v Mills [1998] 2 Cr App Rep (S) 252. The defendant pleaded guilty to attempted rape, having called the victim as a witness at committal hearing. Two weeks after being told his relationship with the victim was over he waited for her to return to her house. He had been drinking. He dragged her down the road and pushed her to a grassy area. He took out his penis but had no erection. He made threats to kill her and ripped away at her tights. She struggled and after a verbal exchange he desisted. He pulled her to her feet and punched her. He started to take her to a nearby garage but she managed to escape. He told police he had had 10 pints of beer. He had previous for manslaughter when he fought with another man. Both had weapons. The victim attended the Court of Appeal saying they 'were back together'. Held. The victim of a crime cannot tell the court that because she has forgiven the defendant they should treat the crime as not having happened. But we can take it into account. **3 years** not 6.

R v S (3 December 1998, unreported). Insufficient account taken of the view of the victim so sentence reduced.

R v Perks [2000] Crim LR 606 judgment 19 April 2000. The opinions of the victim and the victim's close relatives on the appropriate level of sentence should not be taken into account except (a) where the sentence passed on the offender was aggravating the victim's distress and (b) where the victim's forgiveness or unwillingness to press charges provided evidence that his or her psychological or mental suffering must be very much less than would normally be the case. For further detail see VICTIMS – *Victim impact statements etc*

See also VICTIMS and DEATH BY DANGEROUS DRIVING, CAUSING – *Victims, the views of the relatives of the* and *R v N* (5 May 1999, unreported).

Old cases. *R v Henshall* [1995] 16 Cr App Rep (S) 388.

Victim exposing herself to danger

141.48   *R v Billam* (1986) 82 Cr App Rep 347 – LCJ. Victim exposing herself, eg accepting a lift, is not a mitigating factor.

Victim's previous sexual experience

141.49   *R v Billam* (1986) 82 Cr App Rep 347 – LCJ Guideline case. It is irrelevant

Violence, with (including offences of GBH etc)

141.50   *R v Billam* (1986) 82 Cr App Rep 347 – LCJ Guideline case. The crime should be treated as aggravated where violence is used over and above the force necessary to commit the rape. The sentence should be substantially higher than the figure suggested as the starting point.

R v Masood [1997] 2 Cr App Rep (S) 137. See *Prostitutes, on*

R v Matthews [1998] 1 Cr App Rep (S) 220. See *Defendant aged 18–20*

R v Reid [1998] 2 Cr App Rep (S) 10. See *Aiding and abetting etc*

A-G's Reference (No 14 of 1998) [1999] 1 Cr App Rep (S) 205. See *Life sentence is appropriate*

R v W and W [1999] 1 Cr App Rep (S) 268. See *Fathers, by*

R v Maishman [2000] 1 Cr App Rep (S) 419. See *Victim less than 10*

Old cases. *R v Hind* (1993) 15 Cr App Rep (S) 114; *R v Dooley* (1994) 15 Cr App Rep (S) 703; *R v Shields* (1994) 15 Cr App Rep (S) 775; *R v Thomas* (1994) 16 Cr App Rep (S) 686; *R v Thorpe* [1996] 2 Cr App Rep (S) 246.

REMAND

See CUSTODY, DISCOUNT FOR TIME SPENT IN

REPORT

See FAILING TO STOP/FAILING TO REPORT

REVENUE, CHEATING THE PUBLIC

See TAX FRAUD

RICH DEFENDANT

See DEFENDANT – *Rich*

142   RIOT

142.1   Public Order Act 1986, s 1

Indictable only. Maximum sentence 10 years.

Crown Court statistics England and Wales[1] *– Crown Court – Males 21+ – Riot*
142.2

Year	Plea	Total Numbers sentenced	Type of sentence%					Average length of custody (months)
			Discharge	Fine	Community sentence	Suspended sentence	Custody	
2000	Guilty	1	0%	0%	0%	100%	0%	0

1   Source: Crime and Criminal Justice Unit, Home Office Ref: IOS416-02.

Guideline remarks

142.3   *R v Tyler* (1992) 96 Cr App Rep 332. Two defendants were convicted of riot and two offences of violent disorder. After a poll tax demonstration buildings were damaged and police attacked. Held. It is not the individual act that is the essence of the offence here. It is the using of violence in circumstances where so many people are present as to cause or inspire fear in the general public. One must look at the individual act in the context of that fear. When it occurs in a busy street the dangers are obvious.

143   RISK ASSESSMENT

Can defence counsel cross-examine the probation officer?

143.1   *R v Green* (31 July 2002, unreported). Where there is a challenge it is an appropriate procedure.

144   ROAD RAGE

Guideline remarks

144.1   *R v Hassan and Schuller* [1989] RTR 129 – LCJ. The habit of drivers getting out of their cars, loosing their tempers and striking other road users seems to be increasing. If it occurred a prison sentence will follow.

ABH

144.2   Offences Against the Person Act 1861, s 47

Triable either way. On indictment maximum 5 years. Summary maximum 6 months and/or £5,000.

R v Maben [1997] 2 Cr App Rep (S) 341. The defendant was convicted of ABH. The victim thought the defendant was indicating he was turning off a main road. The defendant then turned right into the main road and the defendant tailgated him and flashed him. At a red light the defendant gesticulated to the victim to open his window. The defendant was shouting and swearing. The defendant left his car, ran round to the victim's door and punched the victim through the open car window. He told the victim to get out of his car, which he didn't. The victim's glasses were broken and his face was bleeding. The defendant turned to walk to his car. The victim reached for his mobile phone and the defendant turned back and struck the victim again on the head. The defendant ran self-defence. The defendant was of good character. 9 months reduced to **6 months**.

R v Doyle [1999] 1 Cr App Rep (S) 383. The defendant was convicted of ABH. The defendant, driving a lorry sounded his horn at a woman in a car. At the giveway lines at a roundabout he got out and went to the car. Another motorist, the victim fearing he was going to assault or abuse the women went over to the car. The defendant without saying a word punched him five or six times in the face causing him to fall to the ground. He then kicked him five times in the legs. The victim was in his 60s and had bruising to an eyebrow a 5mm cut to an eye and a bleeding nose. The defendant was 36 with a number of previous for dishonesty and two for violence (GBH and common assault). The court was entitled to take a more serious view that in earlier cases as the offence has become more prevalent. Use the more recent cases. **12 months** was not excessive.

R v Sharpe [2000] 1 Cr App Rep (S) 1. The defendant was convicted of ABH. The defendant started to reverse into a parking space the victim had found. The victim then left his car to stand in the space. The defendant's car continued to reverse. The victim went over to the defendant's car and opened the driver's door. The defendant then got out of the car and headbutted the victim causing a broken nose. The defendant was treated as being of good character. These attacks are on the increase and the courts must indicate that they will not be tolerated. Custody is almost inevitable. Where there is any significant injury the period will be months rather than weeks even if the defendant is of good character. A substantial sentence was justified, but **8 months** substituted for 12 months.

Old cases. Ignore them. The tariff has gone up.

145 ROAD TRAFFIC

The following offences are listed separately: CARELESS DRIVING; DANGEROUS DRIVING; DEATH BY CARELESS DRIVING; DEATH BY DANGEROUS DRIVING; DISQUALIFIED DRIVING; DRINK DRIVING; EXCISE LICENCE, FRAUDULENT USE; FAILING TO PROVIDE A SPECIMEN; FAILING TO STOP; INSURANCE, NO; ROAD RAGE; SPEEDING; TACHOGRAPH AND OTHER DRIVERS' HOURS OFFENCES; TAKING MOTOR VEHICLES and VEHICLE INTERFERENCE.

Magistrates' Court Sentencing Guidelines September 2000

145.1 In all cases, consider the safety factor, damage to the roads, commercial gain and if the driver is not the owner, with whom prime responsibility should lie.

Offence	Penalty points	Maximum penalty	Suggested penalty	Fixed Penalty[1]
Driver offences				
Not supplying details	3[2]	Level 3 E	B	–
Licence offences				
● No driving licence, where could be covered[3]	-	Level 3	A	£30
● Driving not in accordance with provisional licence[4]	3–6	Level 3 E	A	£60 and 3 points
● No excise licence	–	Level 3 or 5 times annual duty (whichever greater)	Actual duty lost and penalty of Guideline fine[5]	£30
Lights				
Driving without lights	–	Level 3	A	–
Ownership				
Not notifying DVLA of change etc	–	Level 3	A	–
Parking				
● In a dangerous position	3	Level 3 E	A	£60
● In a Pelican/Zebra crossing area	3	Level 3 E	A	£60
Test Certificate				
Not held	-	Level 3	A	-
Traffic Offences				
● Failing to comply with height restrictions	3	Level 3 E	A	£60
● Failure to comply with red traffic light	3	Level 3 E	A	£60
● Failure to comply with stop sign	3	Level 3 E	A	£60
● Failure to comply with double white lines	3	Level 3 E	A	£60
● Failure to give precedence at Pelican or Zebra crossing	3	Level 3 E	A	£60

Offence	Penalty points	Maximum penalty	Suggested penalty	Fixed Penalty[1]
Motorway Offences				
Driving				
• Driving in reverse on motorway	3	Level 4 E	B	£60
• Driving in reverse on slip road.	3	Level 4 E	A	£60
• Driving in wrong direction on motorway.	3	Level 4 E	B[6]	£60
• Driving off carriageway – central reservation	3	Level 4 E	A	£60
• Driving off carriageway – hard shoulder	3	Level 4 E	A	£60
• Driving on slip road against no entry sign	3	Level 4 E	A	£60
• Doing U turn	3	Level 4 E	A6	£60
Fast lane				
• Vehicle over 7.5 tonnes or drawing trailer in fast lane	3	Level 4 E	A	£60
Learners				
• Learner or excluded vehicle	3	Level 4 E	A	£60
Stopping				
• Stopping on hard shoulder of motorway	–	Level 4	A	£30
• Stopping on slip road of motorway	–	Level 4	A	£30
Walking				
• Walking on motorway or slip road	–	Level 4	A	£30
• Walking on hard shoulder or verge	–	Level 4	A	£30
Vehicle defects up to and including 3.5 tonnes gross vehicle weight				
Defects				
• Brakes	3	Level 4 E	A	£60
• Steering	3	Level 4 E	A	£60
• Tyres (per tyre)	3	Level 4 E	A	£60
• Loss of wheel	3	Level 4 E	A	£60
• Exhaust emission	–	Level 3	A	£30
• Other offences	–	Level 3	A	£30
Loads, danger of injury by				
• Condition of vehicle, access – ories and equipment	3	Level 4 E	A	£60
• Purpose of use/number of passengers/how carried	3	Level 4 E	A	£60
• Weight position or distribution of load	3	Level 4 E	A	£60
• Insecure load	3	Level 4 E	A	£60
• Overloading or exceeding maximum axle weight	–	Level 5	A[7]	£30
Buses and Goods vehicles over 3.5 tonnes gross vehicle weight				
Brakes	3	Level 5 E	C	B
Steering	3	Level 5 E	C	B
Tyres (per tyre)	3	Level 5 E	C	B
Loss of wheel	3	Level 5 E	C	B
Exhaust emission	–	Level 4	C	B
Other offences	–	Level 4	C	B
Loads				
Condition of vehicle, access – ories and equipment	3	Level 5 E	C	B
Purpose of use/number of pass – engers/how carried	3	Level 5 E	C	B

Offence	Penalty points	Maximum penalty	Suggested penalty	Fixed Penalty[1]
Weight position or distribution of load	3	Level 5 E	C	B
Insecure load	3	Level 5 E	C	B
Overloading or exceeding maximum axle weight	–	Level 5	C[9]	B8
Operator's licence				
Not held	–	Level 4	C	B
Speed limiters-When applicable				
Not being used or incorrectly calibrated	–	Level 4	C	B
Key				
A, B and C stand for suggested starting point fines. When defendant has £100 net weekly income A = £50, B = £100 and C = £150. See **page 334** for table showing fines for different incomes.)				
Level 3 fine = maximum fine is £1,000				
Level 4 fine = maximum fine is £2,500.				
E = Must endorse if no special reasons and may disqualify.				
● All these offences are eligible for a fixed penalty offer. If a fixed penalty was offered, consider any reasons for not taking it up and if valid fine amount of appropriate fixed penalty and endorse if required to. Consider whether costs should be waived and allow a maximum of 28 days to pay. Or if a fixed penalty was refused or not offered, consider whether known circumstances merit any discount for guilty plea (but never go below the fixed penalty) or if there are aggravating factors which merit increasing the fine.				

For details about the guidelines see MAGISTRATES' COURT SENTENCING GUIDELINES at page 331.

1   Fixed Penalty Order 2000. It only applies when the fixed penalty procedure is used.
2   If company owned, use higher fine when unable to apply endorsement as a minimum.
3   Eg If licence not renewed, but would have covered class of vehicle driven, or holder of full licence has lost or misplaced it.
4   Includes where no licence ever held.
5   Guideline fine is Starting point A (1–4 months unpaid duty), Ax2 (4–6 months), Ax3 (6–12 months) subject to a maximum of twice the duty.
6   Consider disqualification.
7   Plus increase in proportion to % overloading. Examine carefully evidence of responsibility for overload and if for commercial gain relating to the owner increase the fine.
8   For an owner/driver take net turnover into account as appropriate.
9   Plus increase in proportion to % overloading.

146   ROBBERY

146.1   Theft Act 1968, s 8

Indictable only. Maximum sentence life imprisonment.

There is power to make a restitution order under Powers of Criminal Courts (Sentencing) Act 2000, s 148.

Robbery is a specified offence for automatic life if the offender had in his possession a firearm or imitation firearm.

It can be a violent offence for the purses of passing a longer than commensurate sentence [Powers of Criminal Courts (Sentencing) Act 2000, s 80(2)] and an extended sentence (extending the licence) [Powers of Criminal Courts (Sentencing) Act 2000, s 85(2)(b)]

Sentencing trends. Hopefully a new and comprehensive guideline case will be issued. The sentences for street robbery are likely to continue to rise to take into account the dramatic increase in those offences and the terrible effect those offences have on the victims. Many victims become too frightened to leave their home.

Crown Court statistics England and Wales – Crown Court – Males 21+ – Robbery 146.2

Year	Plea	Total Numbers sentenced	Type of sentence%					Average length of custody[1] (months)
			Discharge	Fine	Community sentence	Suspended sentence	Custody	
2000	Guilty	1750	0%	0%	6%	1%	92%	44.3
	Not guilty	478	0%	0%	3%	1%	95%	59.6

1   Excluding life sentences. Source: Crime and Criminal Justice Unit, Home Office Ref: IOS416-02.

Guideline remarks

146.3   *A-G's Reference (Nos 20 and 21 of 1992)* (1993) 15 Cr App Rep (S) 152. Those who seek to prey upon the vulnerable carriers of money will be treated severely by the courts.

Armed with firearm – Guidelines

146.4   *R v Turner* (1975) 61 Cr App Rep 67 at 90. It is not in the public interest that even for grave crimes, sentences should be passed which do not correlate sensibly and fairly with the time in prison which is likely to be served by someone who has committed murder in circumstances in which there were no mitigating circumstances. The courts must have a range of penalties to deal with abnormal crime like bad cases of espionage, horrid violence like the *Richardson* torture case and bomb outrages. Bank robberies, which are common occurrences, should not be treated as abnormal crimes but as crimes of gravity. The normal sentence for anyone taking part in a bank robbery or the hold-up of a security or Post Office van should be **15 years** if firearms are carried and no serious injury done. The fact that a man has not much of a criminal record is not a powerful factor in cases of this gravity. The total sentence for those that commit two or more should not normally be more than **18 years**. This is about the maximum for the category of offences we describe as, 'wholly abnormal.' The judge was right to make a distinction between the look out and those who went into the bank and held up the staff with guns.

R v Adams and Harding [2000] 2 Cr App Rep (S) 274 at 277. The starting point must be *R v Turner* (1975) 61 Cr App Rep 67 which suggests that the maximum sentence for more than one armed robbery should be 18 years. However, *R v Turner* [1975] was decided when the sentencing climate was very different from today. For one thing remission was one third. Recent examples of sentencing is *R v Schultz* [1996] 1 Cr App Rep 451 in which sentences of 25 years were upheld for more than one offence of armed robbery. Here but for the fact that life sentences were imposed we would not consider 25 years as manifestly excessive.

Armed with firearm – Automatic life – Exceptional circumstances

146.5   *R v Buckland* [2000] 2 Cr App Rep (S) 217 – LCJ. The defendant was convicted of attempted robbery and possessing a firearm on arrest [Firearms Act 1968, s 17(2)]. The defendant entered a branch of Barclays Bank and joined a queue for Customer Service. When his turn came, he passed an envelope with a note which read 'This is a robbery, give us the money, I have a gun.' The note was signed by him in his correct name and on the back of the envelope was typed his name and address. He made no attempt to disguise himself and produced no gun. The clerk who took it seriously told him he needed to go to the counter. The defendant said 'You better go and get it. I want £100,000.' The clerk activated the alarm and the defendant sat and waited quietly. At one point he went to the cashier's window and said he hadn't got all day. He was told to sit down and obediently did so. He was arrested without a struggle and an imitation handgun costing £1.50 was found in his tracksuit pocket. He gave his occupation as 'Saving the planet.' The defendant was 31 and was a persistent but relatively minor offender with a conviction for having a firearm with intent to resist arrest. He had picked up a starting pistol, which fired caps and he was stopped by police for firing it and his boisterous and drunken behaviour. He ran off and fired the pistol once. He was sentenced to 4 years' imprisonment. He suffered from drug-induced psychosis. He had a glowing prison report. He was sentenced to automatic life after the judge found no exceptional circumstances. Held. The incompetence, lack of aggression, the fact no physical injury could have been caused and the imitation gun was not produced, no gain was made, and any distress caused to the staff was far from extreme were exceptional circumstances. He did not present a serious danger to the public. The judge's starting point of 7 years was too high. Sentence varied to **4½ years**.

Armed with firearm – Imitation – Banks, security guards etc

146.6 *R v Law* [1998] 2 Cr App Rep (S) 365. The defendant pleaded guilty to robbery. He and another wearing masks attacked a security guard as he was delivering cash to a bank. They threatened the guard with a machete and what turned out to be an imitation gun. £6,000 was stolen. They escaped in a waiting van, which was found abandoned nearby. There a passer-by was threatened and the three men left in a car that had been parked there the day before. The car was followed and all but £1,200 was recovered. The judge said it was carefully planned and executed. The defendant was now 22. Held. The authorities indicate sentences a little lower than the 10 year sentence had been passed for similar offences and age of the defendant. The LCJ has said age and personal mitigation can play but a limited part. Severe sentences must be passed. Sentences will vary according to how prevalent the offence is. **10 years** was entirely appropriate.

R v Buckland [2000] 2 Cr App Rep (S) 217. See *Armed with firearm – Automatic life – Exceptional circumstances*

Armed with firearm – Imitation – Domestic

146.7 *R v Delaney* [1998] 1 Cr App Rep (S) 325. The defendant D made a late plea to robbery and making use of a firearm with intent. The defendants M and H were convicted of the same counts. At about 4.20am four men wearing balaclava masks broke into the first floor of a pub where the publican and his family lived. One carried an imitation but realistic firearm. They entered the bedroom of the publican's 12-year-old daughter. The publican came in and the man with the gun seized him. The publican believed he would be killed if he did not co-operate. At gunpoint he handed over the keys to the safe and deactivated the alarm. They threatened to tape his mouth and he begged them not to, as he was asthmatic. He showed them the cash tills and deactivated a further alarm. £1,893 and some jewellery was taken. The police arrived as the gang was leaving and the gun was pointed at an officer. 'Firearm' was shouted out and police had to stand back and the gang escaped. D was 34 with a substantial number of previous convictions including robbery and manslaughter. M was 42 with 15 convictions including burglary, robbery and rape. H was 27 and had four convictions including GBH and burglary. The judge said the family was terrorised and he gave 2½ years' discount for D's late plea. D received **11½ years** and the other two received **14 years**. Held. This was a very grave offence. It is imperative courts impose exemplary sentences. Applying *R v Brewster* [1998] 1 Cr App Rep (S) 181, **14 years**

was tough but not manifestly excessive. The discount for the late plea was within the judge's discretion.

Armed with firearm – Imitation – Post Offices etc

146.8   *R v Lea* [1997] 2 Cr App Rep (S) 215. The defendant pleaded guilty to robbery. He put false plates on a hired car and bought an imitation air pistol. He went into a Post Office and produced the pistol that was taken to be real. There were three people in the Post Office and one was seized. He demanded money and was given £905. He fled. The car number was taken and he was arrested. He admitted the offence immediately. The postmistress was unable to serve in her Post Office for some time and a customer was became very nervous. The defendant had financial problems with loan sharks. He had a good work record and was of good character. **6 years** not 8.

A-G's Reference (Nos 52 to 55 of 1999) [2000] 1 Cr App Rep (S) 450. The defendants T, L, B and J pleaded guilty to robbery. L also pleaded to attempted robbery. After 1½ hours reconnaissance and careful planning the four defendants entered a sub-Post Office and newagency. They were dressed in camouflage clothing and wore masks. T had a hammer, which he used to smash the security video. Two imitation firearms were carried. There were four customers and four members of staff. The defendants shouted, 'Get to the floor.' A firearm was waved and those inside were terrified. Two of the staff were working in the Post Office part and they were told to 'Open the fucking door.' The guns were pointed at them and they opened the door. The staff left leaving the keys inside. The door closed and the robbers demanded the door be opened again. The staff tried to explain that couldn't be done as the keys were inside. The guns were discharged and one of the staff thought her colleague had been shot. The demands and the explanations continued till they left. A robber demanded the till be opened and £200 was taken. They ran to a hostel because there was no getaway transport. The defendants were arrested and the guns recovered. They were both blank firing pistols and one had a live round in it. They were granted bail. Eight months later L confronted a boy who went to the same school as him. L and his friends bullied him. L asked to use his mobile and tried to grab it. The boy tried to run from L but was followed. L produced a Stanley knife and held it to his stomach. The boy thinking he was to be stabbed broke free and escaped. T and B were 17, J 16 and L 15 years old. T had no previous convictions, B had been cautioned, J had a conviction and a caution. L had been dealt with for violence. L received an indication that on a guilty plea to the attempted robbery he would receive a concurrent sentence. Held. Had they been adults the sentence would be in the region of **10 years**. Bearing in mind their youth and the mitigation **7 years** would be appropriate. Because it was a reference **5 years** detention not 2.

A-G's Reference (No 74 of 1999) [2000] 2 Cr App Rep (S) 150 – LCJ. The defendant was convicted of theft, attempted robbery and having a firearm with intent. The defendant and another entered a village shop and post office wearing masks and gloves. One had what appeared to be a handgun and the other a knife. The gunman shouted, 'It's a hold up,' and 'Give us your money.' The gunman shouted at the two customers, one of whom was retired and the other 79 years old to lie on the floor. The door to the Post Office section was kicked open. The men attempted to open the safe but the assistant did not have a key. The alarm went off and the two men fled. The defendants were arrested driving away in a stolen car. The assistant had experience of another robbery and did not want to return to work. One customer feared for his life and the other couldn't stop crying. The weapon was found and it was low powered unloaded air pistol which was not in working order. The defendant was 22 and had a bad criminal record although he had not served a prison sentence. He was released on bail and committed further offences. Held. The vulnerability of Post Offices has not decreased. **6 years** would be the minimum. Because it was a reference **5 years** substituted.

For sentencing principles about Post Offices, see *Post Offices*

Armed with firearm – Imitation – Shops, public houses, petrol stations etc

146.9 *A-G's Reference (No 17 of 1998)* [2000] 1 Cr App Rep (S) 174. The defendant pleaded guilty to robbery, supplying cannabis, supplying amphetamine sulphate, being concerned in the supply of cannabis, two counts of handling stolen goods and affray. A month after his release from prison and when on licence he supplied a small quantity of cannabis to undercover police officers. Just over a month later he supplied the same officers in the same place amphetamine sulphate. He introduced the officers to someone who supplied cannabis. He was arrested. He handed seven stolen T-shirts to the manager of an amusement arcade and was connected with three others worth in total £190. He was again arrested. He next walked over some parked cars when drunk and seized a man who told him to get off. He pushed him against a wall and threatened him. The victim went home to telephone the police and the defendant banged on his front door loudly. He barged his way in and seized the victim by the throat. The victim was pinned against the wall and threatened with a beating if he reported the matter to the police.

Five days later when on bail for two sets of charges he entered a petrol station wearing a balaclava, and gloves. He was carrying a handgun. He told the attendant to hand him the money in the till. The attendant handed over £100. The defendant made off and discarded the gun, balaclava and outer clothing in a stream. They were recovered and the gun was a plastic pistol but resembled a firearm and was able to discharge a pellet. He was arrested. Next someone who worked in a hostel where the defendant was living found a cassette player and stereo system in a communal room. They had been stolen from a daytime burglary of an 84-year-old man. He was arrested again. He had recently served an 18 month sentence for burglary. He was a chronic alcoholic and had deeply sad personal circumstances. He pleaded guilty to robbery at the earliest opportunity. He was given 4 years for the robbery with the other sentences concurrent with no order for the breach of licence. Held. We would expect **at least 7 years** for the robbery even with a plea. We would also expect the 8 months unexpired period of his licence to be activated and consecutive sentences for the offences on bail. We would expect a total of **at least 8 years**. As it was a reference **6 years** substituted.

Armed with firearm – Imitation – Street robbery

146.10 *A-G's Reference (No 13 of 1998)* [1999] 1 Cr App Rep (S) 140. The defendant pleaded guilty at the first opportunity to robbery and having an imitation firearm with intent. The victim aged 69 was confronted by the defendant as he walked along road. The defendant aged 18 held up an air gun and said, 'Give me your money or I'll blow your head off.' The victim gave him his wallet with some small change in it. He assured him that all he had and the defendant walked away. The area was searched and the defendant was found with an airgun in his waistband with two pellets in the breech. The defendant said he had been drinking and expressed remorse. He was of good character. He was given a deferred sentence. Since them he had spent £3,000 to go on a course. The money was said not to be recoverable. Held. We would have expected a **4 years** sentence. Because it was a reference and the other features **2½ years** detention.

R v McDonald [2001] EWCA Crim 860, [2001] 2 Cr App Rep (S) 546. The defendant pleaded guilty to two counts of robbery and possessing a firearm at the same time as the robbery. Two students were walking home and they were followed. They were eventually surrounded and someone, not the defendant produced an imitation pistol. They were told to put their cash etc on the ground. A wallet, credit cards and cash was taken. The pistol was found at the defendant's address. The defendant was arrested and he said he received £5 from the robbery. He was sentenced on the basis the pistol was produced without his complicity or consent. In 1986 he was sentenced to 5 years for two robberies, a s 18 wounding and 'two other similar offences', an aggravated burglary and offences of criminal damage. He cared for his ill mother. His automatic life sentence was quashed and **4½ years** substituted.

Armed with firearm – Imitation – Taxi drivers, delivery staff etc

146.11   *R v Jackson* [1998] 1 Cr App Rep (S) 259. The defendant pleaded guilty to robbery. He directed a taxi driver to a car park and ordered him to stop. He put a metal object into the back of the driver's neck and said, 'Give us your fucking money. I've got a gun.' The threat was repeated and the driver handed over £40. The driver said he did not have any more. The defendant said, 'I'm IRA. If you go to the police I will kill you and your family. If I find any money on you I'll kill you.' £1.50 was handed over. The defendant was 24 and had convictions for dishonesty between 1989 and 1993. In 1994 he received 15 months for an affray. In 1995 he had received 3 years for robbery and was released on licence 4 months before the offence. The robbery was at a bus station when he forcibly removed a neck chain from a 17-year-old youth and threatened him with a knife. He forced him to take off his jacket and ran off with it. Held. **4½ years** consecutive to the 8 months of the unserved sentence not 6 consecutive.

R v Shaw [1998] 2 Cr App Rep (S) 233. The defendant pleaded guilty to robbery on the day his case was listed for trial. The defendant and another directed a taxi driver to a car park. A gun was pointed at the driver and he was struck by a spanner. He lost consciousness for a few seconds while his keys and about £65 was taken. The two drove off in his cab, which was later found. The gun was found to be an imitation. The driver's colleagues were able to identify the defendant and he was maltreated. The police were called. He put forward an alibi. The defence said the defendant had the spanner and the other the gun and it was a spur of the moment offence. **5½ years** was not manifestly excessive. [There is no reference to the defendant's character.]

R v Wright [2000] 2 Cr App Rep (S) 459. The defendants H and S pleaded guilty to two robberies. The defendant W pleaded to a robbery and aiding and assisting an offender. A taxi driver went to pick up a fare and H got in the cab and pointed a replica pistol at the driver's chest. The driver handed over the cab keys, about £10 in coins and £34 from the driver's wallet. H ripped the radio hand set out and ran to a waiting car throwing the keys in a nearby alleyway. W was the driver of the car and S was a passenger. They drove off. The pistol was capable of firing blanks. 27 hours later another taxi driver went to pick up a fare. H approached him, asked for the keys and produced a gun. H opened the cab door, demanded money and was given £316 and a cheque for £95. As H walked away he pointed the gun at the taxi and the gun went off. H again ran to a car where W drove them off with S as a passenger. Both taxi drivers were in fear of their lives. H was sentenced on the basis the gun went off accidentally and W on the basis on the second occasion he only knew afterwards there had been a robbery. S's role was as a lookout. H was 18 with eight convictions including burglary, assault and theft. He had not been sentenced to a custodial term before. H was treated as the dominant personality. S and W were treated as of good character. S was 20 and W 21. W bitterly regretted his involvement. H received **8 years**, S **7 years** and W **6 years**. Held. The use of the gun and the discharge of it even accidentally were major aggravating factors. Taxi drivers are vulnerable and attacks on them are increasing. Taxi drivers, milkmen and postmen go about the streets carrying money and are entitled to look to the courts for protection. If taxi drivers are not protected members of the public, including women will be forced to make their own way home. The offences were planned. The judge could have passed consecutive sentences. The sentences were rightly severe and not excessive let alone manifestly excessive.

R v Harvey [2002] 1 Cr App Rep (S) 127. The defendant pleaded guilty to robbery. A take-away meal was delivered to the defendant's address and as he paid for it he noticed a considerable sum in the employee's wallet. Two hours later he ordered another meal to another address and when the employee arrived he and another robbed him of £700 with a gun. There were no substantial physical injuries caused. Later the victim saw the defendant in a car and told the police. He was 37. Six weeks earlier he had been released from a 7 year sentence for robbery with 3 years concurrent for indecent assault. It was a Post Office robbery in which £15,000 had been stolen by a violent assault by him and others. He also had convictions for s 20 wounding, ABH, indecent assault and assault with intent to resist arrest. He had served the unexpired period of his licence. Held. It was deliberately planned. There were a number of aggravating features including the firearm, the trick to lure the victim, the vulnerability of those running the service and his record, but **8 years** not 12.

See also *Taxi drivers etc*

Armed with firearm – No firearm count

146.12   *R v Eubank* [2002] 1 Cr App Rep (S) 11 – LCJ. The defendant pleaded guiltyto a single count, robbery. There was an issue whether the defendant had a firearm. The judge held a Newton hearing and concluded that the defendant at least had an imitation weapon. Held. Before the defendant is convicted of such a grave offence he is entitled to have a verdict of the jury. The appropriate course was to include a count in the indictment to make their position clear. As there was no count it was wrong to sentence him on the basis he had a firearm.

Armed with firearm – Persistent offenders

146.13   *R v Woodruff and Hickson* [1998] 1 Cr App Rep (S) 424. See **Armed with firearm – Post Offices**

R v Avis Re Goldsmith [1998] 2 Cr App Rep (S) 178 at 192 – LCJ. Goldsmith pleaded guilty to attempted robbery and having a firearm with intent to commit an indictable offence. In June 1997, he entered a jeweller's shop and asked to see a ring. He left returning an hour later and again asked to see the ring. He produced a starting pistol threatening to shoot the jeweller if he did not open the till. The jeweller tried to 'bluff him'. The gun was fired into the ceiling and Goldsmith left the shop. He was arrested nearby. The gun was a .22 pistol capable of firing .22 pellets. The jeweller and his wife were terrified. The defendant later wrote to the jeweller expressed the hope that he had not been too upset. He suggested that if the jeweller had been on his own he might have shot him but that he wouldn't do that in front of a lady. He advised that the next time someone came to rob him with a gun, he should let them take what was there. The defendant was 49 and was a persistent armed robber. In 1968 he had two convictions for assault with intent to rob involving firearms. In 1971, he was sentenced to 2 years for offences that included using a firearm with intent to resist arrest. In 1979, he went to prison for 6 years for offences that included possession of a firearm and ammunition. In 1985 he was sentenced to 15 years for six armed robberies or attempted robberies and in 1994 he was sentenced to 8 years concurrent for armed robbery. He was released in August 1996. The judge said that viewed in isolation 10 years' imprisonment was the correct sentence but when he considered the need to protect the public, a longer sentence of **15 years** was appropriate. Held. The long sentences he had served had done nothing to deter him. Even without resorting to s 2(2)(b) of the 1991 Act (longer than commensurate sentences now governed by the Powers of Criminal Courts (Sentencing) Act 2000, s 80(2)(b)), **10 years** was justified for this armed robbery. The judge was right that the s 2(2)(b) power should be exercised. It is clear from his record the letter to the jeweller, he is likely to commit further offences of this very serious kind. The sub-section requires that the court 'shall' pass such sentence 'as is in the opinion of the court necessary to protect the public from serious harm from the offender'. Since a previous 15 year sentence did not deter him from re-offending, it is difficult to see how the necessary period of protection required should be any shorter. The sentence was an entirely proper one.

R v Adams and Harding [2000] 2 Cr App Rep (S) 274. See also ***Armed with firearm – Security guards carrying money***

Armed with firearm – Post Offices

146.14   *R v Woodruff and Hickson* [1998] 1 Cr App Rep (S) 424. The defendants W and H were convicted of conspiracy to rob, robbery, having a firearm with intent and having an imitation firearm with intent. The conspiracy to rob was based on 4 months of observations when the two were seen visiting Post Offices and watching deliveries of cash take place. Vans carrying money were also followed. For the robbery W and H posed as customers in a Post Office. They were armed with a loaded handgun, an imitation handgun and a bottle of ammonia. They waited till the security guard had finished delivering the cash and then entered the secure area. An assistant tried to intervene and W produced a loaded gun and H banged his head against the window. £33,500 was taken. Their defence was it was a theft not a robbery. The judge said they were professionals who carried out the robbery meticulously. W was 61 and H was 54. In 1969 W had received 14 years for armed robbery. In 1979 he received 15 and 18 years for armed robberies. In 1976 H had received 12 years for robbery. In 1985 he had received 6 years for handling. W was mentally ill. Held. No distinction should be drawn between a robbery that takes place in a bank, a security van, a Post Office van or a sub-Post Office. Post Offices are soft targets staffed by defenceless men and women. It is a reasonable inference that they would have used the gun if need arose. As the conspiracy was not carried out it should be treated as one robbery. **15 years** not 17.

For sentencing principles about Post Offices, see *Post Offices*

Armed with firearm – Security guards carrying money

146.15   *R v Devlin and Cotter* [1997] 1 Cr App Rep (S) 68. The defendants D and C pleaded guilty to robbery. Both wearing crash helmets and brandishing guns, attacked a security guard when he was collecting money from a store. They ordered the guard to lie on the floor, which he refused to do. He was struck on the arm with a gun. Two bags each containing £20,000 were taken. The two then drove off chased by the guard in his van. The guard managed to ram their vehicle but the two escaped and were caught later by police. D had driven recklessly. Both guns were found to be loaded. The defendants admitted the offence in interview. D was 20 and had become a successful licensee until he bought new premises, which led to serious debt. C was 48 and had health problems. Both were of good character and expressed remorse. Held. They had no option but to plead guilty. This is not in the same category as cases where sawn-off shotguns and ammonia are carried, and firearms discharged. The starting point was not more than 12 years. A 2 year discount was given for the plea. The sentence of **10 years** was at the top of the bracket but was not manifestly excessive.

R v Adams and Harding [2000] 2 Cr App Rep (S) 274. The defendant H was convicted of two counts of robbery, GBH with intent, attempted robbery and making use of a firearm to avoid arrest. On the three robbery matters he was also convicted of possessing a firearm with intent to commit robbery. On the last robbery there were two counts of firearms with intent. The defendant A was convicted of the last robbery and with the two firearm counts. The first robbery was on a Securicor guard who was delivering money to a Building Society. The guard was shot in the lower leg and foot and £20,000 was stolen. The second was an attempted robbery of another Securicor guard who was delivering money to the Midland Bank. A handgun was used and the guard was forced to hand over an empty cash box. In the third robbery another Securicor guard was delivering £25,000 cash to Lloyds Bank. A Webley revolver which was adapted to fire shotgun cartridges was produced by H and the cash box taken. Police officers intervened and H pointed a revolver at an officer. A was standing nearby with a stun gun in his pocket. A and H were arrested. They both had been involved in an earlier armed robbery. H received 12 years and A 8 years. As a result both received automatic life. Held. If it hadn't been life **25 years** could not be considered manifestly excessive for H. Because of the previous for armed robbery **16 years** notional determinate sentence was not wrong for A.

A-G's Reference (No 84 of 2001) [2002] 2 Cr App Rep (S) 226. The defendant pleaded guilty at the first opportunity to attempted robbery and having a firearm with intent to resist arrest. In the evening, Securicor guards were supplying cash machines in Regent Street in London. The defendant approached and was disguised with a cap with ear flaps and a scarf. He held out a firearm in front of him at arms length from a guard. It was a few inches from the guard's chest and he said, 'Give me the money.' The guard was scared and dropped the cartridge with £22,000 in it and then tried to apprehend the defendant in a headlock. The gun was pressed to his chest and a violent struggle ensued. With the help of his colleague they wrestled the defendant to the ground and with the help of some American students and other helpers the gun and money were put out of reach. The police arrived and the defendant continued to struggle. The defendant tried to bite a hand of a student. The firearm was a double action revolver with four bullets in the chamber. The ejector rod was bent and the cylinder axis pin missing so it could not be operated in the normal way. However, it could be fired by holding the cylinder manually. He said another had supplied him with the firearm and the man drove him to the cash dispenser. The prosecution agreed there must have been a second man. He was now 23 with no convictions and favourable references. A psychologist said he was clinically anxious and depressed and was assessed as someone who was very compliant. A prison report said he was, 'very timid, nervy and very vulnerable.' Held. Personal factors in relation to offences of this gravity can have only a very small effect in determining what the appropriate sentence is. We would have expected a sentence for these two offences of **at least 8 years**. Because it was a reference, the progress he is making in prison **5 years** for the attempt and 1 consecutive for the firearm making **6 years** not 2 and 1 consecutive.

Armed with firearm – Series of robberies

146.16 *R v Turner* [1975] 61 Cr App Rep 67. The court is alive to the problems arising when men are kept in prison for very long periods of time. On the other hand it is only just that those who are making a career out of crime should receive more serious punishment than those who have committed only one grave crime. Something must be added to the sentence for those who have committed more than one robbery but the maximum total sentence should not be more than **18 years**. The maximum refers to crimes that are not 'wholly abnormal.'

R v Adams and Harding [2000] 2 Cr App Rep (S) 274. See **Armed with firearm – Security guards carrying money**

Armed with firearm – Shops, public houses etc

146.17 *A-G's Reference (No 56 of 1999)* [2000] 1 Cr App Rep (S) 401. The defendant pleaded guilty to robbery, having a firearm with intent, burglary and making off without payment. He stayed at a guesthouse and left without paying. The owners discovered a wallet containing £50 had been stolen from the private quarters. A week later he went to a public house, drank 2 pints and left. A few minutes later he returned and ordered a drink. He approached the barmaid from behind and said, 'Open the fucking till.' He took money and told the barmaid to go upstairs. Once upstairs he bound her hands and ankles with tape and flex. Referring to the gun he said, 'You don't think this is fucking real?' and fired it against the wall. He taped her mouth and threatened to come back with friends if she gave the police his description or said anything about him. When arrested he threatened to kill the officers but later admitted the offences. The defendant was 39. In 1984 he was made the subject of a hospital order with a restriction order for robbery, aggravated burglary, burglary and ABH. He had tied up a man, inflicted multiple cuts and poured hot water into the wounds. The robbery was with a large spanner when the victim was threatened, bound and gagged. The medical report said there was no formal medical illness but he had an obsessional aspect to his personality with compulsive thoughts. He ruminated about revenge and had considerable difficulty in controlling anger. The writer thought, 'the threats to the officers were important. The offences were a mixture of a desire for money and a need to assert himself aggressively. He had longstanding personality difficulties. He was a very inadequate man who finds it impossible to live a settled life and was untreatable. He is a significant and ongoing risk to the public. The risk is unpredictable and ever present.' The report was based on a great deal of material about him. Held. An appropriate determinate sentence was **9 years**. He presents a serious danger to the public for an indeterminate time. A **life sentence with 4½ years specified** substituted for 6 years.

See also *R v Banks* [2001] 1 Cr App Rep (S) 39. Notional determinate sentence assessed at 12 years.

Armed with firearm – Victim injured

146.18 *R v Adams and Harding* [2000] 2 Cr App Rep (S) 274. See *Armed with firearm – Security guards carrying money*

Attempted robbery – Automatic life

146.19 *R v Buckland* [2000] 2 Cr App Rep (S) 217 – LCJ. Attempted robbery is not a 'serious offence' for the purposes of Crime (Sentences) Act 1997, s 2 (automatic life).

Automatic life, is it?

146.20 Powers of Criminal Courts (Sentencing) Act 2000, s 109(2) and (5) The court shall impose a life sentence (for his second) serious offence.

Robbery where, at some time during the commission of the offence, the offender had in his possession a firearm or imitation firearm is a serious offence within the meaning of that Act.

A-G's Reference (No 71 of 1999) [1999] 2 Cr App Rep (S) 369. Section 109(5)(h) includes joint enterprise. Whether the offence falls within para (h) depends on the basis of the offender's participation. If he was party to a robbery which to his knowledge involved the possession of a firearm it qualifies. If a firearm was produced or used contrary to his own understanding and belief about the robbery we doubt it would qualify. Here he didn't carry the firearm but he knew of it so he qualified.

Banks, security guards etc (no firearms)

146.21 *R v Exley and Day* [2000] 2 Cr App Rep (S) 189. The defendant D pleaded guilty to robbery on re-arraignment. Police kept a cash delivery under observation where a guard and a police officer disguised as a guard pretended to deliver cash to a bank. Two men ran up and the officer was sprayed with corrosive liquid from a bottle. Both men ran to a waiting car which was driven off by D. A police car blocked the exit and the three men ran off. D had convictions. Held. The getaway driver is an important feature in the offence of robbery. His role was pivotal to the success of it. **7 years** consecutive to 1 year for an unrelated wounding count was not excessive.

A-G's Reference (No 20 of 2000) [2001] 1 Cr App Rep (S) 178. The defendant pleaded guilty to robbery at a late stage, and to being carried in a taken conveyance, going equipped, TDA, theft, driving whilst disqualified and other lesser charges. A witness outside a store saw four men in a car pulling scarves over their faces while a guard was delivering cash to the store. As the guard removed the cash bags from the van the rear door of the van was pushed against his back trapping his legs. He pushed the door open and saw three men including the defendant. They had hold of his trolley. He grabbed one of the bags and was hit on the hand by what he thought was a screwdriver. The men carried another screwdriver. The three went to the front of the van and one called out, 'Go and get some more.' The guard managed to lock the door and the men escaped in the car. The guard's finger and back were sore. £2,250 in coins was stolen. Only the defendant was arrested. The car was taken the night before. A nearby house had been used as a safe house. The defendant was 23 and most if not all the offences were committed whilst he was on bail. He had convictions but they were not for serious offences. For some of the other offences he received in total 12 months consecutive to the robbery sentence. Held. Men collecting or delivering cash are particularly vulnerable. Offences committed against them are prevalent. Courts should impose substantial custodial sentences. Bearing in mind it was a reference and the principles of totality **4½ years** not 3 for the robbery consecutive to the 12 months.

Commercial/industrial premises

146.22   *R v Ginley* [2002] EWCA Crim 209, [2002] 2 Cr App Rep (S) 277 The defendant was convicted of manslaughter and attempted robbery. The 57-year-old victim and his disabled wife were helping out at their frozen food warehouse. Because of ill health they were semi retired and their sons had taken the business over. In 1987 the victim had had a triple bypass and his wife was paralysed down one side and in a wheelchair. In the late morning the defendant and another entered the warehouse. One pulled a balaclava down over his face and demanded to know where the safe was. He put a knife with a 10" blade to the victim's throat and put him in a headlock. There was a scuffle in which the victim was prodded in the ribs a number of times with the knife. The wife pointed to the safe in the office and picked up a walking stick to go to her husband's aid. The second man who was masked grabbed her stick and pushed her in her wheelchair to the other side of the office away from the panic button. The victim shouted the police were on their way and the robbers left believing the panic button had been pressed. The victim then pressed the panic button and the police attended quickly. The victim gave the number of the car to an officer, collapsed and died of a heart attack. The pathologist said, 'death could have occurred at any time but trauma and excitement could precipitate a heart attack. More likely than not the victim would have been alive had it not been for the struggle.' The defendant was 21 when sentenced and had convictions but none for violence. Held. The judge quite rightly took the view that this was a robbery of an extreme kind. It was a prepared robbery. There was nothing wrong with **9 years** for the robbery without considering the death. The 3 years extra for the death was wholly appropriate. **12 years** upheld.

Death is caused

See MANSLAUGHTER – *Burglars/Robbers/Thieves, by*

Defendant aged 10–13 – Domestic robberies

146.23 *R v Lindsay* [1998] 2 Cr App Rep (S) 230. The defendant pleaded guilty to robbery and two counts of burglary. He was 13 when the offences were committed and when he was sentenced. The offences took place within 5 weeks. The burglaries were daytime domestic burglaries. The occupiers returned home to find drawers etc had been rifled. In the first burglary a video and cash were stolen. In the second jewellery and cash worth about £2,000 was taken. He was arrested and released. A week later he and another robbed a 14-year-old schoolboy on his paper round. The boy was pushed and one of the robbers produced a knife and demanded his Walkman. The earphones were pulled from his neck. The defendant had been cautioned for robbery and ABH. He had had a disruptive home life and had been permanently excluded from school. The judge sentenced him on the basis the other had the knife. The report from where he was detained was in part positive but also said he was abusive and aggressive. Considering *R v Fairhurst* (1986) 8 Cr App Rep (S) 346 and *R v Wainfur* [1997] 1 Cr App Rep (S) 43, **2 years** detention in all not 3.

Defendant aged 10–13 – Street robbery

146.24 *R v McKay* [2000] 1 Cr App Rep (S) 17. The defendants M, A, and T pleaded guilty to robbery and ABH as an alternative to s 18 GBH. L was convicted of false imprisonment and ABH. A 15-year-old boy was approached on a railway station platform by two girls and a boy, M, A and T aged then 13, 14 and 13 respectively. They demanded money and cigarettes and threatened to beat him up. The boy handed over 42p and two cigarettes. T said, 'Let's punch and kick him.' M and T kicked him about the face. A joined in and scratched him. L then 16 got off a train and asked what was going on and the four then attacked him. The victim was hit with a padlock and chain. M got a piece of wood and hit him on the legs with it. The boy ran away and they caught him and carried on beating him. As trains came in they crowded round him and pretended he was drunk. L took the padlock and chain off the others and also stopped one of then using a broken bottle on the boy. A lighter was put to the boy's hair and it was singed. A bicycle was thrown at him. His coat was taken from him. The whole incident lasted 35–40 minutes and the four left. The victim was in hospital for 5 days. He was unable to leave his home for a month. He had extensive bruising to the face, eyes, nose, mouth, back, shoulder and hands. One eye was swollen shut. The pictures were alarming and it was possible to see chain marks and probable footprints. M and L had no findings of guilt. A and T had cautions. When sentenced they were 14, 14, 16, and 17. The defence suggested that the serious feature was the assault and not the robbery. No custodial sentence were available for the assault for those who were 14. Held. It was a merciless attack on a defenceless harmless youth. It was one single incident. The removal of the coat underlines that. It was appropriate to rely on Children and Young Persons Act 1933, s 53(3), (now Powers of the Criminal Courts (Sentencing) Act 2000, s 91). The sentences of **2 years** detention (one being a YOI order) for M, T, and A were within the appropriate range. As L made serious efforts to prevent the attack becoming absolutely disastrous his sentence was reduced from 21 months to **15 months**.

R v T and F [2001] 1 Cr App Rep (S) 294. The defendant F pleaded guilty to robbery. The defendant T pleaded guilty to handling. The victim was walking home when F grabbed her from behind and pressed a closed penknife into her neck. F demanded her handbag and dragged and pushed her over a small fence. The victim fell and F grabbed her bag off her shoulder and ran off. The defendants both then 13 were arrested and T pointed out a bin where the bag was found. £15 and cash was missing. T admitted being given £5. A month later the victim still had a fear of being out alone. F's mother died in childbirth. Her father's whereabouts was unknown. F came to the UK to live with her step-grandmother and grandfather several years before. Because of her behaviour they were unable to look after her. She had placements with foster parents and in local authority residential units. She was difficult, absconded and took part in petty offending and anti-social behaviour. While on remand in a secure unit she made good progress. A psychologist said she was in dire need of therapeutic help. Her social worker said that a detention and training order would mean she would leave the secure unit where she was doing well. Held. Taking into account her age and the mitigation **18 months** not 2½ years' detention.

Defendant aged 14–15 – Armed with firearm – Shops, public houses, petrol stations etc

146.25   See *R v W* [2002] 2 Cr App Rep (S) 528.

Defendant aged 14–15 – Armed with firearm – Imitation – Shops, public houses, petrol stations etc

146.26   *R v Brown and Roberts* [2001] EWCA Crim 1455, [2002] 1 Cr App Rep (S) 274. The defendants B and R were convicted of robbery, possession of an offensive weapon and common assault. R demanded a cigarette from a man who was walking across a supermarket car park. The man refused their request and shouted abuse. R produced a knife and lunged at him. The man seized his wrist and twice got the better of him while R was swinging a knife and the incident ended. Within minutes they entered the supermarket's petrol station having changed into dark clothes and put on balaclava helmets. R was holding a knife at least 9' long and B had an imitation gun which was quite realistic. They shouted, 'Give us your fucking money.' Some £10 notes were handed over to R while B banged his gun on the till. When interviewed they denied involvement. They were now 17 but then they were 15. At trial they relied on alibis. B had a long record starting when he was 10. Regularly he had committed a large number of offences including burglary, handling, ABH, threatening words, common assault, criminal damage, theft and vehicle interference etc. While on bail for the robbery he was convicted with R of ABH in which he struck the victim with a leather belt and both received 10 months detention and training order. R's record started at 11 and paralleled Bs. Both abused alcohol and drugs. B's offending was said to be impulsive with no thought of the consequences to him or others. His risk assessment was high with a real possibility of harm to others being caused. B and R had family difficulties and B was living with R's family. Held. The court must carefully consider the principles in *R v Storey* (1984) 6 Cr App Rep (S) 104 but will apply them in light of the sentencing practice developed since then. The court has to be prepared in appropriate cases to make examples of juveniles who commit these types of offences. **6 years** detention was severe but fully merited.

Defendant aged 14–15 – Domestic

146.27   *R v Pinkney* [1998] 1 Cr App Rep (S) 57. The defendant pleaded guilty at the first opportunity to attempted robbery. The defendant then 15 and two others went to the home of an elderly lady who lived in a flat in an old peoples' complex intending to commit burglary. He carried a knife which he held close to her face when she answered the door. She called for help and the three ran away. She was greatly upset and was taken to hospital for a check up. Four months later he voluntary attended the police station and eventually admitted his role and took police to where the knife was recovered. He showed genuine remorse and increasing signs of maturity. Held. It is inappropriate to impose detention under s 53(2) (now the Powers of the Criminal Courts (Sentencing) Act 2000, s 91) on a person of this age unless no other course is suitable. So 30 months under s 53(2) reduced to **2 years** YOI.

Defendant aged 14–15 – Series of robberies

146.28 *R v Barker* [2001] 2 Cr App Rep (S) 75. The defendant pleaded guilty to three sets of offences. The first in time was robbery and theft. The second was robbery and the third was robbery, false imprisonment and threatening to damage property. The first started when a taxi with a passenger slowed down to make a turn. four youths started to kick the taxi and the driver stopped. The defendant then 14 attempted to drag the passenger from the cab while another attacked him. The defendant took his luggage and ran off with it. His watch was taken and the driver who was trying to help the passenger lost a bag with £45 in it. The luggage was recovered. Ten days later a taxi called at a pub to pick up a fare called Barker. Three got in and when the taxi reached the destination the defendant walked round to the driver's side and leant though the window. He refused to pay the fare and was brandishing a knife. The driver was searched and between £70 to £80 was taken. Three days later the defendant was arrested and he denied the offence. He was bailed. Thirteen days later he rushed into a discount store where a 21 year old was working on her own. A 12 year old was in the store. He ran straight to the assistant carrying a knife and demanded money. She refused to give him any money and he became angry. She moved to the back of the shop and he threatened to slash her. He lashed out at her demanding the till be opened. The panic alarm was pressed and the police arrived quickly. He jumped over the counter and threw milk bottles at the front door. The young girl ran out and the assistant was prevented from leaving. Police used CS gas but were prevented from entering because the defendant threatened to slash the assistant. She was forced to write a note saying please leave and a threat to burn the shop down. He sprayed lighter fuel at the victim. He lit the can turning it into a small blowtorch. He closed the front door, locked the shutters and a siege began. He blamed the assistant for him being locked up for 3 months. He took £65 in cash and started a number of fires. He pointed two small imitation handguns which were owned by the victim's father at the police. Two hours 10 minutes after he arrived he surrendered. The 12 year old was very distressed. The father of the assistant suffered emotionally, and the victim suffered from shock, bruising and swellings. The defendant had four convictions for assaulting a police officer, three for threatening behaviour, and one of affray, ABH, common assault, attempted robbery, assault with intent to rob, damaging property being reckless whether life was endangered and having an offensive weapon. When 13 he threw a concrete slab at a bus injuring a passenger. Also when 13 he threatened a man with a knife. The attempted robbery was on someone sitting in a motor vehicle when he wore a stocking mask and brandished a knife. His past offences were frequently violent and involved weapons. He was in breach of a supervision order and he was excluded from school. He was almost illiterate and innumerate, but since his sentence he had made huge efforts to catch up. Held. The discount for the store offences has to be limited. Because of his age and the authorities **6 years** detention not 10.

Defendant aged 14–15 – Street robbery

146.29 *R v Fenemore* [1998] 1 Cr App Rep (S) 167. The defendant pleaded guilty to robbery. In the afternoon, a 61-year-old lady was walking along a road. The defendant then aged 14 attempted to grab her bag and pushed her forward. She fell and hit her head. He took her handbag and her shopping bag. She had a bruised and swollen eye and a cut to the head. The bag was recovered but the purse with £10 in it was missing. The defendant was arrested and admitted the offence. He said he didn't intend to hurt her. He was of good character but during the considerable delay before the sentence he had committed criminal damage and common assault. He was placed on supervision. He came from a caring family but had become involved with drugs. His YOI report said he had been fighting only a few days after his sentence and had absconded. Held.

Even considering his youth, for this cowardly act by a young thug against a 61-year-old lady **18 months** YOI was not a day too long.

R v Deegan [1998] 1 Cr App Rep (S) 291. The defendant pleaded guilty to attempted robbery. At 4.30pm the 65-year-old victim entered a subway holding her handbag. The defendant when 14, and another boy followed her. As she left the subway the defendant pulled the straps of her bag. She pulled against them so forcibly she fell over and felt pain to her leg and shoulder. She was dragged along the ground for a foot or so but did not release the bag. The boys laughed and ran off. The victim was taken to hospital and found to have a dislocated shoulder and fracture of her femur. She was in hospital for over a month and was unlikely to make a full recovery. He had a disturbed domestic background and had no convictions. He wrote a letter to the victim apologising for the offence. Held. **2 years** detention was severe but warranted.

R v Manghan and Manghan [2000] 1 Cr App Rep (S) 6. The defendants P and B who were brothers pleaded guilty to robbery and five counts of theft. They targeted old ladies, jostled them and stole their purses or handbags. The first offence was on a 77-year-old woman on a bus and she lost her purse. The next day they distracted the bus driver and pushed the victim up the front of the bus. Her purse was stolen. On the same day they operated in precisely the same was on a woman aged 70. The next day two other women were attacked. One was 69 and the other 77. They both lost their purse and one was very upset. On the same day they jostled an elderly lady and stole her purse. This was the robbery. P was interviewed and said, 'Fuck the old ladies. I don't give a fuck about them.' He was 16 and had four findings of guilt and a conviction mostly for dishonesty. He had received 15 months for burglary. B was then 14 had two findings of guilt and two convictions of a relatively minor nature. The defendants said they needed the money for drugs. Held. Even with young defendants it was proper to include a deterrent element. Because of their age and the plea **4 years** detention for P and **3½ years** for B not 5 for both.

R v McKay [2000] 1 Cr App Rep (S) 17. The ages of the defendants were 13–15. For a summary see *Defendant 10–13 – Street robbery*

R v S J-R and G [2001] 1 Cr App Rep (S) 377. The defendant J-R pleaded guilty to robbery and G was convicted of robbery. They were both 14. The victim aged 14 was walking home and saw J-R, G and another youth S. He increased his speed. S shouted out for him to stop and G grabbed him by the collar and punched him in the face. The victim was led into an alleyway. He was surrounded and they demanded money. G produced a knife and held it to the victim's throat. The contents of his bag were tipped onto the ground. A pen, pencil and pencil sharpener were taken. The three walked off. The victim suffered from nightmares, became withdrawn and was frightened to go out alone. His school results suffered. Previously he had been happy go lucky and successful. J-R was of excellent character. He bitterly regretted his actions. His risk of re-offending was low. G was the ringleader. In recent years he had aggressive and problematic behaviour. He did not attend school. Held. The judge was right to bear in mind the increase in street robbery. The effects on the victims can be disastrous as in this case. J-R's sentence was reduced from 20 months to **15 months** detention. G's sentence was reduced from 3 years to **30 months**.

R v Joseph [2001] EWCA Crim 304, [2001] 2 Cr App Rep (S) 398. The defendant was convicted of attempted robbery. At 11.40pm the victim was walking home carrying his lap top computer. The defendant then 14 and two others approached him. He was asked for 10p and one of them flicked off his glasses. One of the three jumped on them and they broke. The defendant asked him if he wanted a fight and punched him in the face and headbutted him six or seven times. He told the others to take the victim's wallet and computer. He also produced a knife and the victim ran off. The victim was chased, tackled and fell to the ground. He held onto his computer as the group tried to take it off him. Eventually the victim managed to run away. The incident had lasted between 5 and 10 minutes. The victim had swelling to his jaw, bruising to his eye and scratches to his face. He needed 5 stitches for a cut above his eye. A tooth was chipped and his ribs were sore. The laptop was damaged and he had to replace his glasses. The defendant had no convictions and was a hard working student. The probation officer said the offence was out of character. The judge said he was a big lad and bigger than the victim. Held. A balance is required between the youth of the defendant and deterrence and the effect of a long sentence upon the perception of the defendant. The sentence of **3 years** detention was not manifestly excessive.

See also *R v Sahadeo* [2002] EWCA Crim 784, [2002] 2 Cr App Rep (S) 563.

Defendant aged 14–15 – Taxi drivers etc

146.30 *R v Hilden* [1999] 1 Cr App Rep (S) 386. The defendant pleaded guilty to robbery, three burglaries, a theft and making off without payment. He asked for three matters including a burglary to be taken into consideration. When he was 15 he directed a taxi to a quiet place and demanded money from the driver. He held a razor at the driver's neck. The driver said he hadn't any until he saw he had been cut and handed over £35. The defendant ran off. The driver was bleeding heavily and was taken to hospital. He had a 1" cut to his hand and a 5" cut on his cheel and a 4 ½" cut to his neck. When arrested the defendant made a full admission. He said he had not meant to cut the driver. His offending began when he was 12. The offences included burglary, intimidating witnesses and offences involving motor vehicles. He had eight appearances at the Youth Court usually for a plurality of offences sometimes as many as 10 or 12. He had a depressing family history. His father was in prison for his second rape offence. His mother and stepfather were alcoholics. There was a history of abuse. Held. The injuries were dreadful. Because of his age **4 years** not 5

Defendant aged 16–17 – Armed with firearm – Imitation – Banks

146.31 *R v Jephson* [2001] 1 Cr App Rep (S) 18. The defendant pleaded guilty to attempted robbery. A hoax call was made to the police to set the robbery up. [The content and purpose is not revealed.] The defendant then 17 with two others entered a bank. She did not attempt to conceal her face. Her co-defendant pointed an imitation gun, which fired small pellets at the bank clerk. Money was demanded and she held out a bag. No money was handed over and the three left. One of the victims had received counselling. She became depressed and was on medication. She was unable to return to work. Another victim suffered from anxiety. The defendant had no convictions and lived in a stable home. The risk of re-offending was described as low. She expressed her remorse and wrote to the victim saying she appreciated the misery she had caused. The co-defendants who were older received 5 years' detention and imprisonment. Held. 5 years for the co-defendants could not be criticised. As she stood further away from the planning and to some extent had been caught up rather than joined up in their enterprise **4 years** detention not 5.

Defendant aged 16–17 – Armed with firearm – Imitation – Post Offices etc

146.32 *A-G's Reference (Nos 52 to 55 of 1999)* [2000] 1 Cr App Rep (S) 450. The defendants T, L, B and J pleaded guilty to robbery. L also pleaded to attempted robbery. After 1½ hours reconnaissance and careful planning the four defendants entered a sub-Post Office and newagency. They were dressed in camouflage clothing and wore masks. T had a hammer, which he used to smash the security video. Two imitation firearms were carried. There were four customers and four members of staff. They shouted, 'Get to the floor.' A firearm was waved and those inside were terrified. Two of the staff were working in the Post Office part and they were told to 'Open the fucking door.' The guns were pointed at them and they opened the door. It was opened and the staff left leaving the keys inside. The door closed and they demanded the door to be opened again. The staff tried to explain that couldn't be done as the keys were inside. The guns were discharged and one of the staff thought her colleague had been shot. The demands and the explanations continued till they left. One had demanded the till be opened and £200 was taken. They ran to a hostel because there was no getaway transport. The defendants were arrested and the guns recovered. They were both blank firing pistols and one had a live round in it. They were granted bail. Eight months later L confronted a boy who went to the same school as him. L and his friends bullied him. L asked to use his mobile phone and tried to grab it. He tried to run from L but was followed. L produced a Stanley knife and held it to his stomach. The boy thinking he was to be stabbed broke free and escaped. T and B were 17, J 16 and L 15 years old. T had no previous convictions, B had been cautioned, J had a conviction and a caution. L had been dealt with for violence. L received an indication that on a plea to the attempted robbery he would receive a concurrent sentence. Held. Had they been adults the sentences would be in the region of **10 years**. Bearing in mind their youth and the mitigation **7 years** would be appropriate. Because it was a reference **5 years** detention not 2.

For sentencing principles about Post Offices, see *Post Offices*

Defendant aged 16–17 – Armed with firearm – Imitation – Street etc robbery

146.33   Old case. *A-G's Reference (No 47 of 1996)* [1997] 2 Cr App Rep (S) 194.

Defendant aged 16–17 – Armed with firearm – Imitation – Trains

146.34   *A-G's Reference (Nos 7–10 of 2000)* [2001] 1 Cr App Rep (S) 166. The defendants K and W pleaded guilty to two robberies and were convicted of an attempted robbery. The defendant W also pleaded guilty to possessing an imitation firearm with intent. The defendants S and P were convicted of attempted robbery and two robberies. The boys then all aged 16 travelled on the Amersham part of the London Underground. K threw a bottle at the victim N aged 17. W had a gun which was waved in the N's face. N pushed it away and moved to the next carriage. He told two other boys C aged 18 and S aged 16 who had seen what had happened who also became victims that it was an imitation gun. The defendants moved as well and swore and abused the victims. N was asked if he had any money. N showed them his wallet was empty. C's rucksack was searched and W asked him to produce his wallet. £8 was taken from it. W searched S's rucksack and £35 was taken from his wallet. The victims were told they would be shot if they reported what had happened. W told them that he knew they attended Amersham College which he had discovered from their belongings. K had convictions and was in breach of a supervision order. He had been given 2 months' custody for an offence committed after the robbery. S was of good character. P at the time of the robbery had a conviction for which he was conditionally discharged and since then he had been convicted of theft. W had convictions and was in breach of a supervision order. He had been cautioned for ABH and the possession of an air weapon. K received 4 months' detention. S and P were given 80 and 90 hours' CSO. W was given a combination order with 100 hours' CSO. S had failed to comply with his CSO. Breach proceedings were instituted and he was given another 20 hours. No hours had been completed. P performed no hours of his CSO and breach proceedings were instituted against him. W had completed his CSO. Held. *A-G's Reference (No 6 of 1994)* [1995] 16 Cr App Rep (S) 343 applies to offences committed on trains and other forms of public transport. Save in wholly exceptional circumstances robberies committed against young people on public transport must be met by custodial sentences. **18 months** for W and **12 months** for the rest would have been appropriate. Taking into account it was a reference, the mitigation and that W had completed his CSO **12 months** in a YOI for W and K and **6 months** detention for S and P.

Defendant aged 16–17 – Domestic

146.35   *A-G's Reference (No 30 of 1997)* [1998] 1 Cr App Rep (S) 349. The defendant pleaded guilty to robbery having previously denied it. He had earlier pleaded guilty to aggravated vehicle-taking. When 16 with two others he took a car and was a passenger when it was driven at speed on minor roads. The police chased it and it crashed. When on bail for that offence he and another at night entered the ground floor flat of an 85-year-old lady suffering from diabetes and high blood pressure. She was in bed and got up because she heard noises. She tried to use the telephone but the intruders had disconnected it. One entered her room wearing a mask and demanded her keys. She said she didn't have any but the demand was repeated and he threatened to kill her. She hit him with her stick and he became angry and frantic. He pushed her backwards and downwards across the bed and onto the floor. He put his foot on her chest and she told him where the keys were. The robbers stole a TV and some keys. A taxi driver saw them and was suspicious and called the police. He and one of his passengers asked them what they were doing. One of the robbers said he had a gun and told them to get on the fucking floor. He tried to kick out the taxi's lights. The robber was overpowered. The defendant said he had been drinking. The old lady suffered pains to her chest and some bruising but no lasting injury. The basis of plea was he hadn't struck the lady. The prosecution said they couldn't prove which intruder did. He had convictions for robbery and assault and was the subject of a supervision order. He had not served a custodial sentence. Held. Had the defendant contested the case **5 years** would have been appropriate. As he pleaded **4 years** would have been appropriate. Because it was a reference **3 years** detention substituted for 8 months. The 4 months consecutive sentence for the vehicle offence was quashed.

R v Roberts [1999] 2 Cr App Rep (S) 194. The defendant pleaded guilty to robbery. When 17 he and another knocked on the door of a 52-year-old man who was disabled with arthritis of the spine and neck. The victim was pushed the length of the hallway and pinned against the wall. The victim protested and was punched. He was dragged into the living room by his wrist causing bruising to wrist and his forearm. The other youth began to dismantle electrical equipment and the victim protested. He was pushed violently against the wall. His head was banged and his face pushed backwards. Because of his arthritis he was in considerable pain. He was told that if he did anything he would be slashed to pieces and would be killed. They claimed he owed someone some money. He was also slapped and told if he informed the police he'd be cut up and killed. They demanded money. £60 was handed over. They stole property worth about £1,500 and left. The victim had trouble sleeping and felt unable to return to his flat. The defendant had previous convictions for theft but none for violence. There was a Newton hearing and in all material respects he was disbelieved. Held. Because of his age and the discount for the plea, albeit reduced, **4 years** not 6.

Defendant aged 16–17 – Post Offices

146.36   *A-G's Reference (No 79 of 2001)* [2001] EWCA Crim 1925, [2002] 1 Cr App Rep (S) 460. The defendant pleaded guilty to robbery. He and his co-defendant were under police observations. The co-defendant, W entered a Post Office and grocer's shop pretending to make an enquiry about a savings account. The shop was staffed by a 62, 67 and 79 year old. He re-entered wearing a mask with the defendant who had zipped up his jacket up to conceal the lower part of his face and wore a baseball cap.

They rushed in and W seized the manageress of the grocer's department's coat and put a knife with an 8" blade to her back. She was pushed towards the sub-Post Office and her face was pushed against the wall. He said, 'Give me the money or I'll stab her'. She was petrified, screaming, crying and shouting. The defendant took the money that was passed through the security hatch while the woman was held with the knife now at her throat. Police officers entered the shop and the defendant tried to escape by running into the street. They were arrested. £1,000 was found in their possession. The manageress had to give up her job. The defendant had previous convictions for dishonesty and possession of drugs. He was on bail for a comparatively minor robbery, offences of burglary and possession of heroin. After receiving 12 months YOI, a Youth Court sentenced him to 4 months consecutive for those offences. Since his sentence he had taken a grip on his life and cleared himself of his drug problem. He was due to be released in the not too distance future. Held. Despite the mitigating features we would have expected **3 to 3½ years** detention. Taking into account it was a reference and the sentence imposed by the magistrates **2½ years** substituted.

For sentencing principles about Post Offices, see *Post Offices*

Defendant aged 16–17 – Shops

146.37   *R v B* [2001] 1 Cr App Rep (S) 303. The defendant pleaded guilty to robbery. He, when 16 went into the shop part of a service station in the evening with a mask on. The cashier saw him holding a bag which was later discovered to contain a plastic imitation gun. He asked for cash and she told him not to be stupid. She thought it was a joke and went though the door behind the counter. When she came back he had gone. He had no convictions and was depressed with suicidal thoughts. Reports indicated the offence was a cry for help. Held. It was a serious offence but **12 months** detention and training not 18 would be sufficient.

Defendant aged 16–17 – Street etc robberies

146.38   *R v Mills Re King* (1998) 2 Cr App Rep (S) 128 at 136 – LCJ. The defendant pleaded guilty to robbery and was committed for sentence for three counts of theft. He when 17 watched the victim aged 18 withdraw money from a cash point. He then ran up with another and held a serrated knife to his stomach and demanded money. The youth refused and he was thrown to the ground and the defendant and the other went though his rucksack and stole a computer and a packet of cigarettes. The thefts were car stereos with nine TICs relating to thefts from cars. The judge passed 3 years and 6 months detention for the thefts which was wrong because committals cannot be dealt with by what was then s 53 orders [now the Powers of Criminal Courts (Sentencing) Act 2000, s 91]. The defendant had two appearances for shoplifting on his record. Held. 3 years detention was entirely right. The consecutive detention sentences were quashed and replaced with consecutive sentences in a YOI of 6 months (making 3 ½ in all).

R v Mills Re Maloney [1998] 2 Cr App Rep (S) 128 at 138 – LCJ. The defendant pleaded guilty to two robberies and was committed for sentence for five shopliftings. He robbed a Swiss tourist guide of her shoulder bag by pushing her in the back which caused her to fall to the ground. The bag contained £120 and 330 Swiss francs. He was arrested when he tried to exchange the francs. He denied the offence and was bailed. Next he and three other youths picked on two 15-year-old schoolboys who were on holiday in an arcade. Money was demanded and one of the youths (not the defendant) pushed a sharp object into the ribs of one of the boys saying it was a gun. It was probably his finger. A boy handed over £10 but the robbery was caught on video. Two of the other youths received supervision orders. The third youth received 12 months at a YOI. Held. There was nothing wrong with **18 months** detention for the first robbery.

However there was insufficient material to say he was the ringleader so **12 months** detention not 18 months consecutive so **30 months** in all.

R v Mills Re Howe [1998] 2 Cr App Rep (S) 128 at 142 – LCJ. The defendant pleaded to robbery and threatening behaviour. The threatening behaviour was with others in a pub when and they were challenged about their ages. There was an unpleasant scene and someone not the defendant produced what appeared to be a gun. An air pistol was later found. He was arrested and released on bail. About 7 weeks later he and another robbed a 74-year-old lady in a tunnel under a railway. He drove passed her on his bicycle and brushed passed her. His accomplice tried to take her bag and she spun round. She hit her head on the wall and fell to the floor. She crawled out of the tunnel on her hands and knees and was taken to hospital. She had a fractured femur and a cut on the forehead requiring stitches. She also sustained psychological injuries and was frightened to leave her home. He had a conviction for robbery, aggravated vehicle-taking, attempted burglary and various convictions for dishonesty. His risk of re-offending was assessed as high, although the report said he showed remorse and suggested probation. **2½ years** detention was lenient.

R v Manghan and Manghan [2000] 1 Cr App Rep (S) 6. The defendants P and B who were brothers pleaded guilty to robbery and 5 counts of theft. They targeted old ladies, jostled them and stole their purses or handbags. The first was on a 77-year-old woman on a bus and she lost her purse. The next day they distracted the bus driver and pushed the victim up the front of the bus. Her purse was stolen. On the same day they operated in precisely the same was on a woman aged 70. The next day two other women were attacked. One was 69 and the other 77. They both lost their purse and one was very upset. On the same day they jostled an elderly lady and stole her purse. This was the robbery. P was interviewed and said, 'Fuck the old ladies. I don't give a fuck about them.' He was 16 and had four findings of guilt and a conviction mostly for dishonesty. He had received 15 months for burglary. B was then 14 had two findings of guilt and two convictions of a relatively minor nature. They said they needed the money for drugs. Held. Even with young defendants it was proper to include a deterrent element. Because of their age and the plea **4 years** detention for P and **3½ years** detention for B not 5 for both.

A-G's Reference (No 21 of 1999) [2000] 1 Cr App Rep (S) 197. The defendant pleaded guilty at the first opportunity to attempted robbery. The victim aged 69 was walking along the pavement when the defendant then 17 ran up behind him and pushed him to the ground. The defendant stood over him and demanded his wallet. The victim shouted for help and the defendant placed his hand over the victim's mouth. He continued to demand the wallet. Two members of the public in a car stopped and shouted out and the defendant ran off. In a long chase he was caught. The victim had an orbital fracture to his eye socket, a cut above the eye requiring three stitches, swelling and bruising. There was some permanent disfigurement. He felt unable to use public transport and felt uncomfortable in the presence of strangers. He lost confidence and had difficulty in sleeping. The defendant was of good character with references. He had spent 4 months in custody before sentence. Held. The appropriate sentence for an adult of good character would be **3 years**. Taking into account his age and that it was a reference **18 months** YOI not probation.

A-G's Reference (Nos 57 and 58 of 1999) [2000] 1 Cr App Rep (S) 502 – LCJ. The defendant L was convicted at the Youth Court of robbery, burglary (both offences involving the defendant G) and shoplifting. She pleaded guilty to attempted robbery. G was convicted of another robbery on the same victim, possession of cannabis and theft. They were committed for sentence. L when 16 and G when 15 followed the victim aged 12 and demanded her jacket. They grabbed her arm and L pulled the jacket off.

There had been long term intimidation of her by the two defendants. Three months later they went to the victim's home and demanded money. They entered uninvited and stole shopping vouchers worth £30 and left. Two days later G confronted the victim in a park, searched her and removed £30. Police arrested the two and cannabis was found on G. L's shoplifting was of goods worth £95 and G's theft was bedding from her children's home. The attempted robbery was on a 43-year-old woman who was walking home. Someone grabbed her handbag and tried to snatch it. A struggle ensued and the victim was dragged to the ground. At that point L joined in and both tried to wrench the handbag from her grasp. The victim was kicked. A motorist disturbed them and the two made off. L had been convicted of damage to property, common assault, disorderly behaviour and a drugs offence. She was conditionally discharged. She had had limited contact with her family. She had been on remand for 6 weeks The probation officer said she had made positive steps to make a fresh start and a custodial sentence might have a serious and detrimental effect on her ability to protect herself from more sophisticated offenders. She said she was a damaged individual who had attempted suicide. She had been effected by media interest because the victim had committed suicide although the prosecution did not suggest the two defendants were responsible for it. G had convictions for affray, two shopliftings, disorderly behaviour, two ABHs and other assaults. Her upbringing was turbulent and her response to supervision was poor. She was pregnant. However there were signs of improvement. Since sentence she had demonstrated a high level of commitment and was showing signs of responsibility. Held. We don't view these offences just through the eyes of the defendants. Supervision orders were unduly lenient. Parents are incensed when their children are victimised by others. Custody of some months was required. Taking into account the time passed, their co-operation with the authorities and the pregnancy it would be destructive and cruel to impose custody now.

A-G's Reference (Nos 11 and 12 of 2000) [2001] 1 Cr App Rep (S) 30. The defendants F and T pleaded guilty at the first opportunity to five counts of robbery. They when 16 with three others of similar ages robbed five 15-year-old schoolboys who were sitting by a river. They went up to them and asked the boys about three other boys and left. Five minutes later they approached the victims from behind and F who was the largest held a kitchen knife with an 8" blade to a boy's throat. The knife poked into the boy's Adam's apple. He told the others not to move or, 'He's going to get it.' The others joined in the attack. T took £10 from one boy. T wore no disguise unlike the others. F demanded a boy's wallet and took £16 and his watch worth £25. His hands and neck were checked for jewellery. The second victim was struck in the stomach and his mobile and wallet were taken. His shirt was pulled to check for jewellery. He was straddled and punched five or six times to the head causing bruising. The third victim had his wallet snatched which contained £20 and a door key. He was punched near his eyebrow and his wrists, socks and neck were checked. He was threatened again. The fourth victim was forced to hand over his watch. The fifth was robbed at knifepoint. A different knife with a 3" blade was poked into his neck and he thought he was going to be stabbed. £9 was taken and he was told to jump in the river. The robberies were interrupted by the stolen mobile phone being called and the attackers ran away. The second and the third victims received bruises. T was not personally involved with the violence. T had no convictions and made full admissions to the police. His risk assessment for re-offending was described as very low. F was treated as of good character. Both showed remorse and had references etc. T was due to be released in 9 days time and had employment to go to. Held. Attacks of this kind are very frightening indeed. The offence is rife. The effect on them of being sentenced twice is likely to be very much greater than in the case of older and more experienced offenders. The sentences substituted were very substantially reduced. The effective sentences substituted were F **18 months** YOI not 8 and T **12 months** YOI not 6. Because of the change in the sentences for young offenders, lesser sentences starting for the Court of Appeal ruling were imposed.

R v Lang [2001] 2 Cr App Rep (S) 175. The defendant pleaded guilty to two robberies, handling and theft. He then 17 approached an 18-year-old boy and asked to see his ring and bracelet. A man with the defendant started to shout and swear at the victim threatening to cut off his finger if he didn't remove the ring. The bracelet was taken and the victim was forced to remove his ring. The other man said, 'If you tell anyone I'm going to put a gun to your head and blow your head off.' This was the handling count. Six days later the defendant and another ran up to two 14-year-old boys and the defendant demanded one of the boy's rings. When the boy refused he threatened to stab him. The victim pretended he couldn't remove it and the defendant pulled it off. He also took a bracelet. Next he pulled down his collar and saw a gold chain which he also took. The victim said it was a Christmas present and the defendant said, 'I don't care. It's my Christmas present now.' The total value of the items was £300. This was one of the robbery counts. The other attacker pointed a screwdriver at the other boy and asked him for jewellery. He threatened to stab that boy and searched him. A £325 bracelet was taken. This was the theft count. The next day the defendant and two others followed two brothers aged 13 and 15 and another. They asked for money and jewellery and the boys said they didn't have any. One of the attackers put a screwdriver into a boy's cuff and threatened to stab him if he was lying. After pushing and shoving a hat was taken. The older brother feared he would be stabbed and was very frightened. When arrested he made limited admissions. He had 22 previous convictions predominately for dishonesty. There was one robbery and one common assault. He had received comparatively short custodial sentences. He abused ecstasy and alcohol. Held. The number and nature of the offences called for a strong deterrent sentence. The appeal over the **3½ years** detention sentence had no merit.

A-G's Reference (Nos 19, 20 and 21 of 2001) [2002] 1 Cr App Rep (S) 136. There was an attempted robbery and a robbery. A 16 year old was not involved in the death of one of the victims. Following a plea the equivalent of 4 years was not unduly lenient. See MANSLAUGHTER – *Burglars/Robbers/Thieves, by*

Defendant aged 16–17 – Street etc robberies – Mobile phones

146.39   *A-G's Reference (Nos 4 and 7 of 2002)* [2002] EWCA Crim 127, [2002] 2 Cr App Rep (S) 345 and *R v Q* – LCJ. A reference and an application for leave to appeal were listed together. The defendant Q was convicted of robbery. The victim aged 14 was on his paper round. The defendant aged 17 approached him wearing surgical gloves and holding a claw hammer above his head. He said, 'Give me your fucking 'phone now.' The victim handed it over and it was worth about £80. He was a persistent offender, (no details given) and was on bail. The judge said the message needs to go out that to those that do this that they will serve a custodial sentence of a substantial length. A deterrent sentence is demanded. Held. The judge was absolutely right. Punishment will be severe. Custodial sentences will be the only option unless there are exceptional circumstances irrespective of age and lack of previous convictions. **3 years** detention substituted for 4 years. That would not have happened if there had been violence used, or there was more than 1 offence or if the defendant had been older.

Defendant aged 16–17 – Taxi drivers

146.40   *A-G's Reference (Nos 35 and 37 of 1997)* [1998] 1 Cr App Rep (S) 344. The defendants T and A were convicted of attempted robbery. The two then aged 16 and 18 and another travelled in a minicab at night and when they reached their destination they held, punched and kicked the driver. One pulled out the radio supply point. The driver managed to drive off causing the two defendants to fall from the car. No money was taken. The driver had a sore neck for a couple of days and was bruised. T had been placed on probation 3 months before and was responding well to the order. T was sentenced to 240 hours' community service and A to 4 months' detention. T had only completed 6¾ hours of his order in 2½ months. It was A's first custodial sentence and he was the sole carer of his mother who had a brain tumour. Held. Personal mitigation can only be of very limited relevance when a taxi driver is attacked in the middle of the night, save in the really exceptional case. It was of little relevance that no money was taken and it was an attempt. Bearing in mind particularly the age of the defendants, that there is a 2 year maximum for YOI detention for someone now 17, that it was a reference and that A was due to be released at the end of next week, **18 months** for T and **2 years** for A

A-G's Reference (Nos 7–10 of 2000) [2001] 1 Cr App Rep (S) 166. The defendants K and W pleaded guilty to two robberies and were convicted of an attempted robbery. The defendant W also pleaded guilty to possessing an imitation firearm with intent. The defendants S and P were convicted of attempted robbery and two robberies. The boys then all aged 16 travelled on the Amersham part of the London Underground. K threw a bottle at the victim N aged 17 and W waved a gun in the N's face. N pushed it away and moved to the next carriage. He told two other boys – C aged 18 and S aged 16 – who had seen what had happened and became victims, that it was an imitation gun. The defendants moved as well and swore and abused the victims. N was asked if he had any money. N showed them his wallet was empty. C's rucksack was searched and W asked him to produce his wallet. £8 was taken from it. W searched S's rucksack and £35 was taken from his wallet. The victims were told they would be shot if they reported what had happened. W told them that he knew they attended Amersham College which he had discovered from their belongings. K had convictions and was in breach of a supervision order. He had been given 2 months' custody for an offence committed after the robbery. S was of good character. P at the time of the robbery had a conviction for which he was conditionally discharged and since then he had been convicted of theft. W had convictions and was in breach of a supervision order. He had been cautioned for ABH and the possession of an air weapon.

K received 4 months' detention. S and P were given 80 and 90 hours' CSO. W was given a combination order with 100 hours' CSO. S had failed to comply with his CSO. Breach proceedings were instituted and he was given another 20 hours. No hours had been completed. P performed no hours of his CSO and breach proceedings were instituted against him. W had completed his CSO. Held. *A-G's Reference (No 6 of 1994)* (1994) 16 Cr App Rep (S) 343 applies to offences committed on trains and other forms of public transport. Save in wholly exceptional circumstances robberies committed against young people on public transport must be met by custodial sentences. **18 months** for W and **12 months** for the rest would have been appropriate. Taking into account it was a reference, the mitigation and that W had completed his CSO **12 months** in a YOI for W and K and **6 months** detention for S and P.

Defendant aged 18–20

146.41   Where age is not treated as significant eg where the defendant has convictions the cases for defendants who are 18–20 are listed in the general categories.

A-G's Reference (Nos 35 and 37 of 1997) [1998] 1 Cr App Rep (S) 344. The defendants T and A were convicted of attempted robbery. The two then aged 16 and 18 and another travelled in a minicab at night and when they reached their destination they held, punched and kicked the driver. One pulled out the radio supply point. The driver managed to drive off causing the two defendants to fall from the car. No money was taken. The driver had a sore neck for a couple of days and was bruised. T had been placed on probation 3 months before and was responding well to the order. T was sentenced to 240 hours' community service and A to 4 months detention. T had only completed 6¾ hours of his order in 2½ months. It was A's first custodial sentence and he was the sole carer of his mother who had a brain tumour. **Held.** Personal mitigation can only be of very limited relevance when a taxi driver is attacked in the middle of the night, save in the really exceptional case. It was of little relevance that no money was taken and it was an attempt. Bearing in mind particularly the age of the defendants, that there is a 2 year maximum for YOI detention for someone now 17, that it was a reference and that A was due to be released at the end of next week, **18 months** for T and **2 years** for A.

Defendant aged 18–20 – Armed robbery

146.42 *R v Brownbill and Dorian* [1999] 2 Cr App Rep 331. The defendants B and D both then 18 pleaded guilty to robbery and possession of a firearm on arrest. D had also pleaded guilty at the Magistrates' Court to aggravated vehicle taking. In the incident he was a passenger. At about 21.45, the defendants burst in to a convenience store wearing balaclava helmets. D pointed a gun at the owner and demanded the till be open and B was armed with a knife. D seized £220 cash from the till and some cigarettes. B seized some bottles of spirits. The total value of goods stolen was £500. An off duty police officer pursued them and they were caught. The property was recovered and the gun found. It was unloaded damaged air pistol. They both admitted the offence. B had convictions including non-domestic burglary and wounding with intent for which he received 18 months detention. He was in breach of his licence. D had convictions for burglary and motor vehicle offences but had not had a custodial sentence. B's risk assessment was high. The judge sentenced B to automatic life with 4½ years specified based on ⅔ of 7 years. D was sentenced to 7 years' detention. **Held.** It was a very serious robbery. If they had been adults 7 years would have been fully justified. Because of their age the sentence for D was reduced to **6 years** detention. B's specified period was reduced to 3 years (being half 6 years).

Defendant aged 18–20 – Street etc robberies – Mobile phones

146.43 *A-G's Reference (Nos 4 and 7 of 2002)* [2002] EWCA Crim 127, [2002] 2 Cr App Rep (S) 345 and *R v Q* – LCJ. The defendant was convicted of robbery and assault with intent to commit robbery. The defendant then aged 18 with two others confronted two 16-year-old victims as they were walking in a town centre. The defendant grabbed one and demanded his mobile. He threatened to stab him and produced a knife which he pointed at his chest. His mobile and bus pass was stolen. The second victim was asked for jewellery and his mobile. A threat to stab him was made and his hand was jabbed causing a small cut. The defendant and another each headbutted him. A member of the public intervened and the robbery was abandoned. The defendant was the ringleader and was of good character. **Held.** The appropriate detention was **4 years** not 6 months. Because it was a reference **3½ years** substituted.

Domestic premises

146.44 *R v Gabbidon and Bramble* [1997] 2 Cr App Rep (S) 19. The defendant G pleaded guilty to robbery. He was convicted of wounding with intent to resist apprehension. B was convicted of three robberies and assault with intent to resist apprehension. B was comfortably over 6' tall. He was 37 and a professional burglar. He had 12 burglary convictions and two aggravated burglary conviction since he was 14. For the last three offences he had received 6 years. On his release from a period in custody when he was acquitted he was the subject of surveillance. The defendant entered the home of a mother who was at home with her two young children and a woman friend. He had a mask on and carried a crowbar. He demanded jewellery and the adults handed over their rings. They were pulled upstairs. Following the robbery both women had slept badly and had been very scared in the home.

Three nights later, B entered another home where another mother lived with her husband, her children aged 2 years and 7 months and their nanny. He demanded property. The nanny managed to lock herself into the library and call the police. This did not seem to effect the defendant. The defendant threatened to hurt the baby. He pushed the husband who was holding the baby but the husband saved the baby from injury. The defendant left 20 seconds before the police arrived with cash, credit cards and a handbag. All three adults suffered from trauma.

Five days later B and G entered the home of a couple aged 66 and 69 who were entertaining an 82 year old. B had a handkerchief across his face and carried a crowbar. The husband tried to hit B but was pushed to the floor where B held a screwdriver to his eye. B attacked the 82 year old and held him down. B threatened to shoot them and G demanded the safe be opened. The wife opened the safe because she was so frightened about the older man. Her ring and watch were taken as well as the jewellery in the safe. The couple's main worry was that the older man would be killed. The husband had bruises and was in a great deal of pain. G was chased by police who caught him when he leapt onto a fence. They seized his legs and he kicked out. He raised a metal jemmy and brought it down on the head of a policeman with some force. There was a lot of blood and the officer required three stitches.

All three incidents terrified the occupants and had the potential for long term trauma. G was 32 and had 16 burglar convictions. The judge said B gloried in the effect he could produce terror. G received 16 years for the robbery and 1 year consecutive for the wounding. B received 21, 22, and 27 years concurrent for the robberies with 6 months concurrent for the assault. B's sentences was made longer than commensurate under the then Criminal Justice Act 1991, s 2(2)(b). The judge had considered 18 years suitable for the B's overall figure and added 50% under the then s 2(2)(b). G's sentence was not made longer than commensurate. Held. We have conducted a full review of the authorities. The case falls to the top of the range although not the very worst of their kind. The very worst are those involving firearms and where gratuitous violence to the extent of torture is used. Top of the range sentences must correlate sensibly and fairly with the indeterminate sentences of life for comparable murders, ie in 'robberies that went wrong.' Here the burglars wished the houses to be occupied to increase their haul by causing fear to open safes etc. The trauma of the victims can cause lasting psychological damage. The judge was under a duty to extend B's sentences. There was a clear need to protect the public. The 18 years and 9 years consecutive sentence for B was out of scale. Without extending the sentence **15 years** would have been appropriate. To reflect the need to protect the public, 5 additional years was right making 20 years in all. The correct sentence for G would have been **12 years** with **9 years** on a plea and 12 months consecutive for the GBH. Therefore G's sentence was reduced from 17 to **10 years**.

Domestic premises – Victim over 65 – Guideline remarks

146.45   *R v O'Driscoll* (1986) 8 Cr App Rep (S) 121 – LCJ. There is a tendency for burglars to select as victims elderly or old people living on their own. It is plain why. First of all they are not likely to offer much resistance, and the chances are they have got not inconsiderable sums of money concealed about the house. Where thugs, because that is what they are, select as their victims old folk and attack them in their own homes and then torture them – that is what happened here – in order to try to make them hand over their valuables in this most savage fashion, then this sort of sentence (15 years) will be the sort of sentence they can expect. One hopes this court may have some effect in protecting these old folk from this sort of savage, sadistic, cruel and greedy attack.

A-G's Reference (Nos 32 and 33 of 1995) [1996] 1 Cr App Rep (S) 346 – LCJ. Both defendants pleaded to aggravated burglary. One also pleaded guilty to attempted robbery. The general effect of the cases is that where an elderly victim, living alone, is attacked by intruders and is injured the likely sentence will be in **double figures**. We wish to stress that attacks on elderly people in their homes are particularly despicable and will be regarded by the court as deserving severe punishment. Elderly victims living alone are vulnerable, not only because of their lack of assistance but also because of their own weakness and isolation. Any attack on such a person is cowardly and can only be expected attract a very severe punishment indeed.

R v Dunn [2001] EWCA Crim 1146, [2002] 1 Cr App Rep (S) 95. We bear in mind the principles in *R v O'Driscoll* (1986) 8 Cr App Rep (S) 121.

Domestic premises – Victim over 65

146.46 *R v Hearne* [1999] 1 Cr App Rep (S) 333. The defendant pleaded guilty to robbery. The defendant got to know a 90-year-old lady when cleaning her windows. He offered to help her when she moved home. It was agreed he would get £10 and any furniture she didn't want. After some discussions about tea-chests he inexplicably pushed her on her bed. He told her to be quiet and pulled one of her jumpers over her face and knotted it. He said, 'Keep quiet I want your money.' He took £30 and ran off. She went after him. Eight hours later he went to the police station and confessed to the crime and said he spent the money on crack. He had character witnesses. Held. Generally 5 years is not a day too long. However, here **3 years** instead.

R v Collins [2001] EWCA Crim 586, [2001] 2 Cr App Rep (S) 433. The defendant was convicted of robbery. The defendant called at the victim's flat pretending to be from the Water Board. He was let in and 4–5 minutes later the defendant's brother who was also pretending to be a workman was let in. The victim, aged 86 became suspicious and they asked for £25 for work done. The victim went upstairs to get money from his safe. The brother went to the safe and the defendant pushed the victim onto the bed and tried to put a gag into his mouth. That failed but he was held down for about 5 minutes while the brother rifled the safe. They took five watches, a ring, some commemorative coins and £60. The defendant was 29 with convictions for 13 burglaries and attempted burglaries, three for robbery and had received four custodial sentences one of which was 6 years. Held. **12 years** was at the top end but not manifestly excessive. There was a significant element of deterrent.

A-G's Reference (No 113 of 2001) [2002] EWCA Crim 143, [2002] 2 Cr App Rep (S) 269. The defendant pleaded guilty to five counts of robbery on the date his case was listed for trial. The victims were all elderly and attacked in their own homes after dark. He had been released from prison for 5 months. He was masked and they were terrified. He demanded money and he put his hand over two of their mouths. He brushed passed one and caused her to fall. Another victim was tied up. Money and small items were taken. The offences were on two separate nights just 2 weeks apart. The defendant had 17 court appearances for 35 offences. They included robbery, rape, burglary, assault, theft, possession of offensive weapons, motor vehicle offences and unlawful sexual intercourse. In 1988 he gained entry to an 85-year-old lady's house by pretending to be a police officer. He bound gagged and raped her. In 1989 he broke into an 81-year-old lady's flat at 1am. He tied her up, gagged her and searched for money. She was raped at gunpoint. In 1989 he received 18 years for offences of robbery and rape. He was 47 with a long history of drink and drug abuse. The risk of re-offending was assessed as exceptionally high. He believed he had caused his victims little harm and refused to take part in programmes for offence focused work. The judge was not satisfied the offences were violent and sentenced him in total to 9½ years. Held. Bearing in mind the ages of the victims and what was done to each of them, the real possibility of fractures, asphyxia and cardiac arrest each was a violent offence. **Life** substituted.

Domestic premises – Victim over 65 – Victim injured or attacked

146.47   *R v Owen* [1998] 1 Cr App Rep (S) 52. The defendant pleaded guilty to robbery. He rang the doorbell of an 88 year old widow and she made it clear she did not want him to come in. Yet he made his way in and demanded money. He opened her handbag and rifled her chest of drawers. She tried to telephone for help and he threw the telephone into the hallway. He gripped her forearm tightly and ordered her upstairs. She refused to go and he left. She was bruised and had a swollen arm. She was also shaken and very frightened. Her gold watch was stolen. He visited friends who on hearing what he had done called the police. The police found him drunk and recovered the watch. He was 32 and had convictions for criminal damage, making hoax calls to the fire and police services, burglary involving a 70-year-old blind man and a robbery involving a 90 and 87 year old when they were threatened with a knife or screwdriver. He had been released from prison for 8 months and was liable to be recalled for 11 months. Doctors said he suffered from chromosome abnormality and targeted the elderly. He was considered extremely dangerous. Held. A **life** sentence was inevitable to protect the public. If a determinate sentence had been passed it would have been **9 years**.

A-G's Reference (No 1 of 1999) [1999] 2 Cr App Rep (S) 398. The defendant pleaded guilty to five robberies. In all of them the defendant had forced his way into the homes of elderly people. The first robbery was on a 71 year old who was pushed to the floor when he opened his door. He was then pushed into his sitting room where the defendant demanded money. The defendant shouted and said he was on drugs. He obtained £230 and pulled out the telephone wires. Eight months later he returned and pushed the same victim to the floor. He took cash from his pockets and £130 in all. The victim was threatened with a radio. The telephone wires were cut and the victim was very distressed. The second robbery was on an 88-year-old man. The defendant was wearing a balaclava and pushed the victim over. The victim had £215 taken from his pockets and his wrist was hurt. 3½ weeks later he returned and climbed through a window and seized the same victim's arms and stole £110. The other robbery was on an 84-year-old woman who suffered from a heart condition. She lived with her lodger aged 79. He entered their home wearing a balaclava and demanded money. The lodger tried to push him out and a struggle ensued. The lodger fell to the floor and the woman was pushed in the chest and stumbled. He took £40 from her purse and she suffered an anginal attack. She said she was in total fear.

The defendant was arrested and said the money was for drugs. He expressed remorse. Held. He had targeted the homes of the elderly. Attacks on the elderly in their homes were despicable and deserved severe punishment. They are vulnerable not only because they lack assistance and support but because of their weakness and feeling of isolation. Fear and anxiety are ever present and that blights the future. The first visit to the victims was worth **6 years** and the second visit **8 years**. The total should have been 8. Because it was a reference **6 years** not 4. [His age and character is not revealed.].

A-G's Reference (No 89 of 1999) [2000] 2 Cr App Rep (S) 382. The defendant was convicted of robbery. The victim, D lived alone and was 69 years old and frail. The defendant had robbed him previously. The defendant knocked on his door and forced his way in. He demanded money and produced a knife. The victim was pushed to the floor and sat upon. The defendant pushed his Adam's apple with a lot of pressure. The telephone cable was ripped from the wall and wrapped around his neck. The victim was in pain and passed out. The incident had lasted about 15 minutes. When he came to he found £120 and a £20 souvenir coin was stolen. The victim was taken to hospital and found to have redness to the front of his neck. The defendant was 32 and had 29 convictions. In 1979 there were two burglaries and other offences for which he received 9 months youth custody. In 1987 there were three robberies, a residential burglary, three thefts and a blackmail for which he received 5 years. Except for the burglary the victim was D. In 1991 the defendant received 3 years for robbery and a non-residential burglary. In 1993 he received 7 years for a robbery and two burglaries. The 1993 convictions all involved the same 64-year-old victim and each involved a knife. He was on licence. **Held.** The sentence should have been in **double figures** even though the injuries were not the gravest. Applying *A-G's Reference (No 1 of 1999)* [1999] 2 Cr App Rep (S) 398 the starting point was 10 years. Because it was a reference **8 years** not 6. The powers should have been exercised about the breach of the licence. 443 days were ordered to run consecutive.

A-G's Reference (No 48 of 2000) [2001] 1 Cr App Rep (S) 423. The defendant pleaded guilty to robbery. Police watched the defendant paying attention to elderly pedestrians near sheltered accommodation. He was seen trying to open a door and a window. He approached the victim aged 79 in the street and was told he couldn't come into the block because of incidents in the past. The defendant pushed past the victim and went in. He was seen by a witness inside to be agitated and he claimed to be delivering pizzas. He went to the victim's flat and when the door was opened he forced his way in. The victim was pushed and fell on the floor face down. The defendant went through his pockets and took £24. The victim was then punched on the mouth and nose. The sideboard was searched and the defendant left. The victim suffered from pains in his ribs and tenderness. The defendant was 36 and had been convicted of 49 offences. They started when he was 13 and were mostly for burglary or theft. In 1993 he had received 5 years for robbery, residential burglary, burglary and theft. In 1996 he received 3 extra years for three robberies committed about the time of the 1993 offences. They were on elderly victims who had been assaulted in their own homes. Thirteen months after the defendant had been released from that sentence he committed this offence. **Held.** The sentences for a single offence when a defendant had pleaded guilty range between **4 and 7 years**. **4 years** was lenient but not unduly lenient. It fell at the bottom of the range which are permissible. One factor in the decision is as it was 4 years he would have to serve a greater proportion of the sentence and be subject to more stringent conditions on his release.

R v Dunn [2001] EWCA Crim 1146, [2002] 1 Cr App Rep (S) 95. The defendant pleaded guilty to robbery, an attempted robbery and two counts of theft. The robbery was on a husband aged 86 and wife aged 78. The husband suffered from cancer and had heart problems. They lived in housing for the elderly. At about 10.30pm while the wife went to check the front door the defendant entered the living room where the husband was. The defendant started to open drawers and cupboards. When the wife returned she told him to leave and he said, 'I want some money or I'll kill you.' He continued searching. She told him to leave her husband alone and he repeated his threats and demand. She told him to kill her and he grabbed her by the throat, squeezed and dug his fingers into her neck causing marks to her neck. She had breathing difficulties and eventually he let go and left. Both the victims found the incident frightening and she felt unable to leave the house at all for 2 weeks. About 2½ hours later he entered the bedroom of his next victims by climbing in through a window. One of them, the wife, jumped out of bed and as she screamed for her husband tried unsuccessfully to push the defendant out. He knocked her to the floor, raised his fist and said, 'Where's the money? I want money.' The husband got out of bed and seized a walking stick. He repeatedly struck the defendant who kicked out at him. The defendant tried to leave by the front door but it was locked The husband continued to hit him and the defendant jumped out of the window. The wife suffered scratches and her hand was sore. She feared the defendant would return. Nothing was taken but some ornaments of great sentimental value were damaged. The thefts were from supermarkets. The defendant had a substantial record but no convictions for violence. Held. The **10 year** sentence was severe but in all the circumstances justifiably so.

Old cases. *R v Lee* (1994) 16 Cr App Rep (S) 60.

Drug abstinence order

146.48   Powers of Criminal Courts (Sentencing) Act 2000, s 58A(1). Where a person is 18 or over the court may make an order requiring the offender to abstain from misusing specified Class A drugs and provide, when instructed to do so a sample to ascertain whether he has any specified Class A drugs in his body. (3) The court must be of the opinion the offender is dependant or has a propensity to misuse specified Class A drugs and the offence is a trigger offence or the misuse of any specified Class A drug caused or contributed to the offence in question. (7) An order shall be for not less than 6 months and not more than 3 years. (9) No order shall be made unless the court has been notified that arrangements for implementing the order are available. [Criminal Justice and Court Services Act 2000, Sch 6 specifies robbery as a trigger offence.]

Life sentence – General principles

146.49   *R v Baker* [2001] 1 Cr App Rep (S) 191. Held. *R v Chapman* [2000] 1 Cr App Rep (S) 377 held that a discretionary life sentence imposed for the purposes of public protection and not for the purposes of pure retribution or deterrence had to be passed under the longer than commensurate sentence provisions for violent or sexual offences.

See also ***Automatic life, is it?*** and ***Attempted robbery – Automatic life***

Life sentence was appropriate, a

146.50   *A-G's Reference (No 56 of 1999)* [2000] 1 Cr App Rep (S) 401. The defendant pleaded guilty to robbery, having a firearm with intent, burglary and making off without payment. He stayed at a guesthouse and left without paying. The owners discovered a wallet containing £50 had been stolen from the private quarters. A week later he went to a public house drank 2 pints and left. A few minutes later he returned and ordered a drink. He approached the barmaid from behind and said, 'Open the fucking till.' He took the money and told the barmaid to go upstairs. Once upstairs he bound her hands and ankles with tape and flex. Referring to the gun he said, 'You don't think this is fucking real?' and fired it against the wall. He taped her mouth and threatened to come back with friends if she gave the police his description or anything about him. When arrested he threatened to kill the officers and later admitted the offences. The defendant was 39. In 1984 he was made the subject of a hospital order with a restriction order for robbery, aggravated burglary, burglary and ABH. He had tied up a man, inflicted multiple cuts and poured hot water into the wounds. The robbery was with a large spanner when the victim was threatened, bound and gagged. The medical report said there was no formal medical illness but he had an obsessional aspect to his personality with compulsive thoughts. He ruminated about revenge and had considerable difficulty in controlling anger. The writer thought the threats to the officers were important. The offences were a mixture of a desire for money and a need to assert himself aggressively. He had longstanding personality difficulties. He is a very inadequate man who finds it impossible to live a settled life and is untreatable. He is a significant and ongoing risk to the public. The risk is unpredictable and ever present. The report was based on a great deal of material about him. Held. An appropriate determinate sentence was **9 years**. He presents a serious danger to the public for an indeterminate time. A **life sentence** with 4½ years specified substituted for 6 years.

A-*G's Reference (No 113 of 2001)* [2002] EWCA Crim 143, [2002] 2 Cr App Rep (S) 269. See *Domestic premises – Victim over 65*

Longer than commensurate sentences (frequently wrongly called extended sentences) – Is it a violent offence?

146.51   Powers of Criminal Courts (Sentencing) Act 2000, s 80(2)(b) . . .the custodial sentence shall be. . .where the offence is a violent or sexual offence, for such longer term (not exceeding the maximum) as in the opinion of the court is necessary to protect the public from serious harm from the offender. [Previously the Criminal Justice Act 1991, s 2(2)(b).]

Powers of Criminal Courts (Sentencing) Act 2000, s 161(3). . . .a violent offence is an 'offence which leads, or is intended or likely to lead, to a person's death or physical injury to a person. '

R v Cochrane (1994) 15 Cr App Rep (S) 708. The defendant pleaded guilty to robbery. Held. The definition of a violent offence does not require that the physical injury be serious. It does not include psychological harm. Here no injury was actually done. Sometimes shock may amount to ABH. This was not that case. The defendant denied he intended to cause physical injury. The judge accepted that. It was not necessary to show that injury was a necessary or probable consequence. The only issue was whether the acts were likely to lead to physical injury. Here it could have done if the shopkeeper had resisted or the defendant had lost control. 6 years was arguably too high if the sentence was commensurate with the facts of the offence. However, it was a perfectly proper sentence for a man foreseeably likely to cause serious harm to the public.

R v Palin (1995) 16 Cr App Rep (S) 888 – LCJ. A robbery was committed with an imitation weapon. Held. Considering *R v Cochrane* (1994) 15 Cr App Rep (S) 708 and the statutory definition of 'violent offence' the Act did not apply.

R v Johnson [1998] 1 Cr App Rep (S) 126. The defendant pleaded guilty to three robberies and a s 20 wounding which were concerning four separate attacks on minicab drivers. He had three previous convictions for robbery. The defence contended that in the three robberies there was no evidence that he intended injury to the victims. The judge passed a longer than commensurate sentence. Held. Applying *R v Cochrane* (1994) 15 Cr App Rep (S) 708 the judge was entitled to come to that view. In little more than a week four drivers were subjected to attacks with a knife. In three of the attacks the defendant produced a knife to reinforce demands for money and/or jewellery. In one case a driver was stabbed in the chest. One driver was told he would be killed.

R v Blades [2000] 1 Cr App Rep (S) 463. The defendant pushed a 74-year-old woman in the middle of the back causing her to fall to the ground. She sustained cuts and bleeding to her knees. The judge was mindful of the psychological harm caused to old victims by attacks of this kind. Held. Injuries of this kind should be regarded as serious. The section did apply.

R v Grady [2000] 2 Cr App Rep (S) 468. The defendant entered an off-licence and threatened an assistant with two knives. She was uninjured but was in a considerable state of shock. The judge said the offence was worth **7 years** but made it 11 years as a longer than commensurate sentence. Held. It was entirely a question of fact for the judge to decide whether the offence was a 'violent offence.' To establish that physical injury was intended where none ensued will be difficult in most cases, but to find it was likely is a very different matter. Applying *R v Cochrane* (1994) 15 Cr App Rep (S) 708 the judge was entirely justified in saying it was a violent offence. **11 years** was not too high. For further details see *Shops off-licences, estate agencies etc*

R v Baker [2001] 2 Cr App Rep (S) 191. Held. *R v Palin* (1995) 16 Cr App Rep (S) 888 held that robbery carried out by a man with an imitation firearm was not a 'violent offence.' That decision is binding. The life sentence must be quashed.

A-G's Reference (No 113 of 2001) [2002] EWCA Crim 143, [2002] 2 Cr App Rep (S) 269. The defendant pleaded guilty to five counts of robbery. The victims were all elderly and attacked in their own homes after dark. He was masked and they were terrified. He demanded money and he put his hand over two of their mouths. He brushed passed one and caused her to fall. Another victim was tied up. The judge was not satisfied the offences were violent. Held. Bearing in mind the ages of the victims and what was done to each of them, the real possibility of fractures, asphyxia and cardiac arrest each was a violent offence. The defendant was lucky not to have caused physical injury and this demonstrates its likelihood.

R v Bowmer (11 December 2001, unreported). [It was not a violent offence here.]

Longer than commensurate sentences, how much extra?

146.52 *R v Avis Re Goldsmith* [1998] 2 Cr App Rep (S) 178 at 192 – LCJ. The defendant pleaded guilty to attempted robbery and having a firearm with intent to commit an indictable offence. In June 1997, he entered a jeweller's shop and asked to see a ring. He left returning an hour later and again asked to see the ring. He produced a starting pistol threatening to shoot the jeweller if he did not open the till. The jeweller tried to 'bluff him'. The gun was fired into the ceiling and Goldsmith left the shop. He was arrested nearby. The gun was a .22 pistol capable of firing .22 pellets. The jeweller and his wife were terrified. The defendant later wrote to the jeweller expressed the hope that he had not been too upset. He suggested that if the jeweller had been on his own he might have shot him but that he wouldn't do that in front of a lady. He advised that the next time someone came to rob him with a gun, he should let them take what was there. The defendant was 49 and was a persistent armed robber. In 1968 he had two convictions for assault with intent to rob involving arms. In 1971, he was sentenced to 2 years for offences that included using a firearm with intent to resist arrest. In 1979, he went to prison for 6 years for offences that included possession of a firearm and ammunition. In 1985 he was sentenced to 15 years for six armed robberies or attempted robberies and in 1994 he was sentenced to 8 years concurrent for armed robbery. He was released in August 1996. The judge said that viewed in isolation 10 years' imprisonment was the correct sentence but when he considered the need to protect the public, a longer sentence of 15 years was appropriate. Held. The long sentences he had served had done nothing to deter him. Even without resorting to s 2(2)(b) of the 1991 Act (extending sentences), 10 years was justified for this armed robbery. The judge was right that the s 2(2)(b) power should be exercised. It is clear from his record and the letter to the jeweller, he is likely to commit further offences of this very serious kind. The sub-section requires that the Court 'shall' pass such sentence 'as is in the opinion of the court necessary to protect the public from serious harm from the offender'. Since a previous 15 year sentence did not deter him from re-offending, it is difficult to see how the necessary period of protection required should be any shorter. The sentence was an entirely proper one.

R v Winfield [1999] 2 Cr App Rep (S) 116. The defendant was convicted of robbery. He and two others were in a public house. One followed the victim, who had drunk about 5 pints, into the lavatory. The victim's gold chain was seized and there was a struggle. The victim received a bite on the finger. The defendant and the other man joined them and all three kicked and punched the victim. The door was closed to stop those who had heard the commotion from entering. The victim became unconscious and lost his gold chain, his bracelet, a gold watch, a ring and £30. Police found him covered in blood with a boot mark on his forehead. At hospital he was found to have a 2" cut to his head and bruising to his temple, nose, cheek and near his eye. He stayed there for a few days. The defendant had a bad record (details not given). The judge found the defendant was not the instigator but the No 2. He was given an extended sentence of 8 years. Held. There is substance in the criticism that he was no more involved than the third man and should have been sentenced on that basis. Ordinarily the offence would warrant 5 years. The court had to balance the need to protect the public and ensure the sentence is not out of all proportion to the nature of the offending. It must also ensure there is no double counting. Double counting is when a sentence has a deterrent factor built in and is extended without taking into account that existing deterrent factor. That deterrent factor caters for the necessity to protect the public. **6 years** not 8.

R v Blades [2000] 1 Cr App Rep (S) 463. The defendant made a late guilty plea to robbery. An elderly victim was pushed over in the street and her handbag was stolen. He had very many previous convictions and was on licence for similar offences. Held. The offence was worth 4–5 years. A 2 year extension was appropriate so **7 years** plus 1 year consecutive for the breach of licence. For more details see *Street etc robbery – Victim over 65*

See also LONGER THAN COMMENSURATE SENTENCES

Mobile phones

See *Street robbery – Mobile phones*

Persistent offenders

146.53 *R v Taylor* [2001] EWCA Crim 2188, [2002] 1 Cr App Rep (S) 490. The defendant pleaded guilty to robbery. Three months after his release from custody he and another entered a small village Post Office and general store. They had stocking masks and were carrying knives and a hammer. They pushed the terrified victim to the back and held the knives to his throat. One was a large thick knife for cutting meat. They threatened to chop off the defendant's head and asked for the safe keys. They were given the keys to the front door to delay them. When they realised they demanded the correct keys and threatened him again. He said there was a time lock on the safe and handed them £10 from his pocket. They asked if he had any jewellery or watches and armed police entered the shop. There was £18,000 in the safe and the victim was terrified. The defendant said he had a serious crack and heroin habit. He had an appalling record with 25 offences for theft and kindred matters. In 1991 he had two convictions for robbing a taxi driver. He received 2½ years. In 1996 he robbed a post office with an imitation firearm. The firearm was a toy gun in a bag and his accomplice had a cucumber in a bag to look like a firearm. He received 7 years. The co-defendant had 39 offences of theft and kindred matters but no convictions for robbery. He received 6 years and the judge said he hadn't drawn any real distinction between the culpability of the two defendants. There were 684 days unexpired on his licence. The judge said severe deterrent sentences were necessary. Held. We agree with the judge about deterrent sentences. He was entirely correct to treat this offence as an extremely serious offence. Courts will protect these vulnerable premises. The offence was aggravated by the very substantial knife. The disparity between his sentence, (twice as much) and the co-defendant was a little too great so **10 years** substituted. The 684 days were not reduced and were to remain consecutive.

Post Offices

146.54 *A-G's Reference (No 9 of 1989)* [1990] 12 Cr App Rep (S) 7 – LCJ. Businesses such as small Post Offices coupled with sweet-shops are particularly susceptible to attack. They are easy targets. The courts must provide such protection as they can for those who carry out the public service of operating those Post Offices and sweet-shops, which fulfil a very important public function. The only way in which the court can do that is to make it clear that if people do commit this sort of offence, then, inevitably a severe sentence containing a deterrent element will be imposed to persuade others it is not worth a candle.

A-G's Reference (No 7 of 1992) (1993) 14 Cr App Rep (S) 122 – LCJ. It has to be realised that corner shops, sub-Post Offices etc are very often staffed by only one person, who may be unable to defend himself or herself. It is unlikely there will be any sophisticated security there, and it is a prime target for someone who wants to enrich himself quickly and successfully. It is therefore very important that the courts should indicate by the sentences passed that that type of offence will be punished severely.

R v Woodruff and Hickson [1998] 1 Cr App Rep (S) 424. No distinction should be drawn between a robbery that takes place in a bank, a security van a post office van, or a sub Post Office. Post Offices are soft targets staffed by defenceless men and women.

R v Taylor [2001] EWCA Crim 2188, [2002] 1 Cr App Rep (S) 490. See **Persistent offenders**

Public servants (Doctors etc)

146.55 *A-G's Reference (No 45 of 2000)* [2001] 1 Cr App Rep (S) 413. The defendant pleaded guilty to false imprisonment and robbery. A doctor visited a female patient who was a heroin addict and the also defendant's girlfriend. He explained to the defendant and the patient that he was not going to prescribe any medication. They explained their displeasure and then the doctor tried to leave. The defendant's activity caused the doctor to ask, 'Are you barring my exit.' The defendant replied, 'I've done 7 years and I'll do it again.' The defendant then armed himself with a large knife and held the knife at the doctor's chest. He demanded the doctor's bag. The doctor who was frightened gave the defendant two tablets. The defendant demanded a sleeping pill, which he was given. The doctor was allowed to leave but was in a highly distressed condition. Fortunately the doctor had a driver who became suspicious and called the police who arrived. The defendant appeared to be under the influence of drink or drugs or both and the police found him incoherent. The defendant had an appalling record including offences of violence and dishonesty. He was on licence at the time. Held. A sentence of **4 or 5 years** would be appropriate. However, as it was a reference the **30 month** sentence was not altered.

Security vehicles etc

146.55 *A-G's Reference Nos 65–6 of 2001* (26 October 2001, unreported). The defendant S was convicted of robbery. Before trial the defendant H changed his plea to guilty. Four men were involved in the robbery of a security van. The guard was attacked by two of them who were not S or H. The two were wearing balaclava helmets and were armed with an axe and a machete. The guard was struck on the head with the axe. Fortunately, because of his protective headgear, he suffered no injury. He was also hit on the arm causing no more than a graze. A security box with £3,268 in cash was stolen. S then 20 was the getaway driver and H then 19, sat beside him wearing a balaclava helmet throughout the robbery. H's basis of plea was that when the two assailants got out of the car he was unaware that weapons were to be used. When he saw the weapons he decided not to go with the other two and he remained in the car. H had convictions for criminal damage, having an air rifle, theft of a bicycle and three offences of possession of cannabis with intent to supply and a similar offence involving amphetamine. He had served 6 months' detention for breach of probation. S had convictions, mainly for burglary and theft but included interfering with a motor vehicle and going equipped for theft, affray and ABH. He had served three custodial sentences. The longest one was 2 years 3 months. Held. It has to be recognised that since *A-G's Reference (Nos 72 and 73 of 1995)* [1996] 2 Cr App Rep (S) 438 sentences have increased for these sort of serious offences where weapons are used. Where young men choose to arm themselves with weapons capable of causing really serious injury they must expect very long sentences. The more so if they make use of them. The proper sentence for S who received 6 years was **8 years** detention. Because it was a reference 7 years instead. The basis of plea for H was supported by the fact he just remained in the car. Courts ought to encourage people who at the last minute decide not to go through with a criminal enterprise and who withdraw their own involvement even if they remain a party to what is going on. Having regard to that factor, his plea and his bad criminal record, his sentence of **4 years** cannot be unduly lenient.

Series of robberies

146.57   *R v Brown* [1998] 2 Cr App Rep (S) 257. The defendant pleaded guilty to unlawful wounding and robbery; two counts of offering to supply drugs; six counts of robbery; and an attempted robbery. The defendant approached a man in the street and took £10. He used a knife and caused a wound to the man's cheek. He was arrested and bailed. He offered two plain clothes officers ecstasy and cannabis. He was arrested and found to have neither. He was released on bail. The other robberies were on minicab drivers who were threatened with a knife and had money and other items taken. The last was where after he had threatened a driver with a knife a struggle took place and the defendant fled empty handed. He was picked out at ID parades. He had only recently been released from prison. For all but two of the robberies he was on bail twice. In 1982 he received 3 years for robbery, in 1993 he received 2 years for robbery, in 1993 he was convicted of 13 offences of which 4 were robbery and received 2 years and also in 1993 he was convicted of 6 offences 4 of which were robbery and received 4 years. Those robberies were very similar to the latest offences. He received 4 years for the street robbery, 6 years for the robberies and 3 years for the attempt consecutive making 13 years in all. The judge made it an extended sentence. The defence did not suggest the making of the extended sentences was wrong. Held. Without considering the powers to extend the worrying features of this case meant a sentence of between 6 or 7 years would be justified even after a guilty plea. None of the sentences could be faulted but the total should be **10 years** not 13.

R v Ebanks [1998] 2 Cr App Rep (S) 339. The defendant pleaded guilty to five robberies and asked for 15 robberies and three attempted robberies to be taken into consideration. The robberies followed a similar pattern and were committed between January and April 1997. He entered small shops and demanded money. There was no actual violence but he was extremely aggressive. He always threatened the staff with a knife and told them they would be cut. One example was on Tie Rack. It was not an impulsive robbery. He waited till there was one assistant. He entered the shop and moved about aggressively causing a display cabinet to fall to the ground. He passed the assistant a note saying, 'Put the money in the bag or I will cut you.' He was holding a Stanley knife. The assistant was very frightened and he made sure he got all the money there was. He was caught red handed in another shop and identified on ID parades. He co-operated with the police. In all about £6,000 was taken. He was 33 and had dishonesty and drug convictions going back to 1981. In 1994 he received 6 years for two robberies and possession of an imitation firearm with intent with seven robbery TICs. There was 13 months left on his licence to run. Held. The number of offences was a very relevant factor. **15 years** was severe but not manifestly excessive.

Series of robberies – Returning to rob the same person again

146.58   *A-G's Reference (No 1 of 1999)* [1999] 2 Cr App Rep (S) 398. The defendant pleaded guilty to 5 robberies. In all of them the defendant had forced his way into the homes of elderly people. The first robbery was on a 71–year-old man who was pushed to the floor when he opened his door. He was then pushed into his sitting room where the defendant demanded money. The defendant shouted and said he was on drugs. He obtained £230 and pulled out the telephone wires. Eight months later he returned and pushed the same victim to the floor. He took cash from his pockets and £130 in all. The victim was threatened with a radio. The telephone wires were cut and the victim was very distressed. The second robbery was on an 88 year old. The defendant was wearing a balaclava and pushed the victim over. The victim had £215 taken from his pockets and his wrist was hurt. 3½ weeks later he returned and climbed through a window and seized the same victim's arms and stole £110. The other robbery was on an 84-year-old woman who suffered from a heart condition. She lived with her lodger aged 79. He entered their home wearing a balaclava and demanded money. The lodger tried to push him out and a struggle ensued. The lodger fell to the floor and the woman was pushed in the chest and stumbled. He took £40 from her purse and she suffered an anginal attack. She said she was in total fear. The defendant was arrested and said the money was for drugs. He expressed remorse. Held. He had targeted the homes of the elderly. Attacks on the elderly in their homes were despicable and deserved severe punishment. They are vulnerable not only because they lack assistance and support but because of their weakness and feeling of isolation. Fear and anxiety are ever present and that blights the future. The first visit to the victims was worth **6 years** and the second visit **8 years**. The total should have been 8. Because it was a reference **6 years** not 4.

Shops, off-licences, take away restaurants, estate agencies etc – Guideline remarks

146.59   *A-G's Reference (No 7 of 1992)* [1993] 14 Cr App Rep (S) 122 – LCJ. It has to be realised that corner shops, sub-post offices etc are very often staffed by only one person, who may be unable to defend him or herself. It is unlikely there will be any sophisticated security there, and it is a prime target for someone who wants to enrich himself quickly and successfully. It is therefore very important that the courts should indicate by the sentences passed that that type of offence will be punished severely.

Shops, off-licences, take away restaurants, estate agencies etc – Cases

146.60   *A-G's Reference (No 18 of 1997)* [1998] 1 Cr App Rep (S) 151 – LCJ. The defendant pleaded guilty to robbery and common assault. When aged 25 the defendant entered a video shop with his face covered. He knocked a 15-year-old friend of the assistant to the floor and went to the back of the shop and threatened the assistant aged 19. He took money from the till and demanded that the safe be opened. He was told there was no safe but the demand was repeated. As the assistant opened the safe he was told to do it faster and was grabbed by the back of the neck. The assistant's forehead was banged into a shelf. Money was passed over and the defendant left. He punched a man who was on the way to the shop. The two victims inside the shop were shaken and frightened. He was arrested and admitted the offence in interview. He claimed he was drunk. He had no convictions. The pre-sentence report said he presented a high risk of harm to the public and a corresponding risk of re-offending. He was sentenced to a combination order of 90 hours' community service and attendance at a Violent Offender Programme for up to 60 days. Since the order the defendant attended the community service activities and the course. The probation officer expressed concern that custody might reverse the progress that had been made. Held. We respect the considerations, which led the judge to make the order he did, but the sentence was unduly lenient. Staff who work in these premises must be entitled to rely on the protection of the courts. There is a need to deter and these offences call for serious punishment. Making every allowance for the mitigation if there had been a trial less than **3 years** would not be proper. As he pleaded guilty the minimum sentence is **2 years**. Taking into account that it was a reference and the developments since then **1 year** substituted.

R v Ebanks [1998] 2 Cr App Rep (S) 339. The defendant pleaded guilty to five robberies and asked for 15 robberies and three attempted robberies to be taken into consideration. The robberies followed a similar pattern and were committed between January and April 1997. He entered small shops and demanded money. There was no actual violence but he was extremely aggressive. He always threatened the staff with a knife and told them they would be cut. One example was on Tie Rack. It was not an impulsive robbery. He waited till there was one assistant. He entered the shop and moved about aggressively causing a display cabinet to fall to the ground. He passed the assistant a note saying, 'Put the money in the bag or I will cut you.' He was holding a Stanley knife. The assistant was very frightened and he made sure he got all the money there was. He was caught red handed in another shop and identified on ID parades. He co-operated with the police. In all about £6,000 was taken. He was 33 and had dishonesty and drug convictions going back to 1981. In 1994 he received 6 years for two robberies and possession of an imitation firearm with intent with seven robbery TICs. There was 13 months left on his licence to run. Held. The number of offences was a very relevant factor. **15 years** was severe but not manifestly excessive.

A-G's Reference (No 67 of 1998) [1999] 2 Cr App Rep (S) 152. The defendant pleaded guilty to robbery. He entered a Co-Op without any disguise. He went to the till and said, 'Give me the notes.' The assistant thought he was joking and he showed her a note, which said, 'Give me the notes because I have a gun pointing right at you.' His hand was in his pocket and seemed to be pointing something. She was very frightened and handed over £250. He was arrested and found with £130. He was of good character and had financial and marital problems. He had always been in work until a few years before when he lost his job. A business he set up failed. He was depressed and had turned to alcohol. He received 6 months and was due to be released in about 2 weeks. Held. The bracket is **4 to 5 years**. Taking into account it was a reference and his anticipated release **3½ years** instead.

R v Bishop [2000] 1 Cr App Rep (S) 89. The defendant pleaded guilty to two counts of attempted robbery. He changed his plea a month before the trial. He entered an estate agent, which acted as a building society wearing a false beard and hat, which covered most of his face. He went to the cashier and said, 'CS gas, give me all your money.' He was pointing a small aerosol at her. The cashier said she didn't have any money. He repeated the demand and she repeated the reply. He then left. 1¼ hours later he entered a village general store wearing the same disguise. He tried the same ploy with the can again. When the proprietor went for the panic button he fled. He was driven away by the co-defendant. He had no convictions. He was under severe personal stress. The driver of the getaway car received 2 years. The defence said there was disparity and the sentence was excessive. Held. We need to protect the staff in small premises, who tend to be vulnerable women. He was carrying a purported weapon. It appears wholly out of character. There is some force in the disparity point but not much. **3 years** not 5. (The case is listed under **Shops** because the amount of money on the premises makes it more similar to a shop than a building society.)

A-G's Reference (No 68 of 1999) [2000] 2 Cr App Rep (S) 50. The defendant was convicted of attempted robbery. He was unexpectedly made redundant and he spent the day drinking. He set off to walk home and was shouting loudly in the street. He entered an estate agency smelling strongly of drink and asked to shelter from the rain. He was told he could. A couple of minutes later he suddenly approached an assistant and said, 'You've been fucking stupid.' His hand was in his pocket and the victims thought it was a gun. He told her and her colleague to get in the back and demanded cash. He swore and seized the woman assistant round the neck and again pushed his fingers in his pocket so it appeared to be a weapon. He pointed it to the side of her head. They thought he was deranged and he said, 'Get the cash or she's dead.' She was told to get on the floor. The male assistant found the petty cash tin but there was no key so the defendant threw it to the ground. That assistant was also ordered to get on the floor. He tried to find a cupboard to put the female assistant in but there wasn't one. She was pushed into a hallway and she managed to escape. The defendant then fled leaving his rucksack. The defendant said he had no recollection of the incident and said he was sorry. No injury was caused. He was 33 with no violent convictions and no convictions in the 1990s. A report said at the time he was severely depressed and his mother extremely ill. At the trial only the male assistant was required to give evidence and his account was not challenged. He was sentenced to 6 months and there was a hearing to consider whether the sentence should be increased. He had been released on a tag which was removed about a month ago. Held. The normal sentence would have been **3 years**. Taking into account the 'triple jeopardy' **2 years** substituted.

R v Grady [2000] 2 Cr App Rep (S) 468. The defendant was convicted of robbery. He entered an off licence and pulled a balaclava or mask over his face. He went to the counter and said, 'Open the door I've got a knife.' The assistant saw a small knife in his hand and opened the counter door. She was forced to open a wall safe and a bag was taken which did not contain much. The defendant demanded that the main safe be opened. The assistant deliberately took the wrong key and she was unable to open the safe. He continued to demand the safe be opened and said, 'I'll give you 5.' She also saw a larger knife with a 14" blade. He was handed two cash bags from the till float. The defendant lost the knifes and said, 'Where's my fucking knives you bitch.' The defendant then left and £559 was found to have been taken. The victim was left in a considerable state of shock. He had an appalling record including offences of robbery with knives and one on the same premises. He had received 12 years for robberies and 5 years shortly after his release. The judge said the offence was worth **7 years** but made it 11 years as an extended sentence. Held. It was entirely a question of fact for the judge to decide whether the offence was a 'violent offence. Applying *R v Cochrane* (1994) 15 Cr App Rep (S) 708 the judge was entirely justified in saying it was a violent offence. **11 years** was not too high.

A-G's Reference (No 16 of 2000) [2001] 1 Cr App Rep (S) 144. The defendant pleaded guilty to robbery and possession of 2½ ecstasy tablets. He went to a cashier in a video hire shop wearing a balaclava and gloves and carrying an 8" knife and a bag. He demanded money and banged on the counter. The knife was pointed at the victim in a threatening way. She had difficulty in opening the till and the defendant became impatient and shouted for her to hurry. Eventually the till was opened and over £300 was taken. He left the shop and caused the glass panel in the door to shatter cutting the finger of woman from another shop who was trying to lock the door. After the robbery he was in a stressed state. He expressed remorse. He was in breach of a combination order for two ABHs and two common assaults. That was a fight in a pub.

He had been released from prison and was now said to be free of drink and drugs. Held. We would have expected the sentence to be **5 or 6 years**. Taking into account it was a reference and that he had been released **4 years** not 9 months consecutive to the 1 month for the breach.

A-G's Reference (No 78 of 2001) (25 July 2001, unreported). [We'd expect 4 years for this robbery by two people with a knife.]

Shops, off-licences, take away restaurants, estate agencies etc – Injuries caused

146.61   *A-G's Reference (No 58 of 1996)* [1997] 2 Cr App Rep (S) 233. The defendant pleaded guilty to attempted robbery after the count had been amended. He also pleaded guilty to four shoplifting counts and possession of cannabis. The defendant entered an off licence with another. Both were worse for drink. He had earlier been banned from the shop. He asked for money and when the request was refused he jumped onto the counter. He was pushed off. Then he climbed over the counter and his leg was grabbed. He punched the owner twice and he was punched back. He produced a brick and he was disarmed. The co-defendant tried unsuccessfully to steal from the till. They both fled. He was arrested nearby. The owner and his wife had scratches, bruises etc but no serious injuries. The defendant had many previous convictions including two for assaulting police officers, affray and criminal damage. He had been released from prison 3 days before. He was starting to address his alcohol problem. Held. The normal bracket for these offences is **3 to 7 years**. Taking into account that it was a reference and that he was due to be released in 2 weeks time **3½ years** not 18 months with 3 months consecutive for the other offences unaltered.

A-G's Reference (No 17 of 2000) [2001] 1 Cr App Rep (S) 96. The defendant pleaded guilty to ABH. He was convicted of two assaults with intent to rob. He and another entered a take away restaurant and enquired about the menu. Suddenly the defendant sprayed ammonia from a plastic bottle into the owner's face. She screamed in shock, suffered pains in the eye and had difficulty in breathing. Both men went to the staff side of the counter and looked for cash. The co-owner arrived and was also sprayed with ammonia. He partly protected his face with his arm. It caused him considerable pain to one eye. The men ran off with nothing. The victims went to hospital for treatment. The bottle was left behind and contained ammonia with strength at the top range for household solutions. His defence was he complained about food, which had been eaten by his brother and had been threatened and chased by the owners. He had been sentenced on 14 occasions before for theft, burglary, robbery, handling and possession of a firearm. He had received 30 months' youth custody and 8 years' imprisonment. At the time of his arrest he had failed to attend for a handling matter. Held. There was no mitigation. Taking into account his record we would have expected a sentence in the order of **6 years**. As it was a reference **4½ years** substituted for 30 months.

A-G's Reference (No 22 of 2001) [2001] EWCA Crim 1174, [2002] 1 Cr App Rep (S) 46. The defendant pleaded guilty to robbery and going equipped for theft. At 11am he went into a newsagent and waited for the customers to leave. Then he went behind the counter where the assistant was and held a knife to her throat. Her blouse was pulled up and she was pushed to the floor. He twisted her wrist and put his foot on her elbow. He took a money bag and left. Outside the shop people detained him. £205 was found in the money bag. The victim said she had injuries but there was no evidence as to their nature. The knife had been bought for the robbery the day before. He was now 20 with no convictions. Two weeks before he had left home after an argument with his parents. He had no where to stay and no money. Remorse and shame was expressed. He was sentenced to a combination order and had done what was required by the order. 22 hours' CSO had been performed. Employment had been obtained. Held. Allowing for his age, no record, remorse and there were no serious injuries caused the proper sentence was **3 years**. Because it was a reference and the efforts he had made during his combination order **18 months** YOI instead.

Street etc robbery (including premises open to the public) – Guideline remarks

146.62   *A-G's Reference (No 6 of 1994)* (1994) 16 Cr App Rep (S) 343 at 345 – LCJ. Street robberies make the public afraid to walk out alone. The public require protection. There must be an element of deterrence to protect the public. Even a first offender must expect a period of custody.

R v Edward and Larter (1987) Times, 3 February – LCJ. The defendants were convicted of robbery and received 5 years. Held. Judges should impose long sentences on muggers who attack others particularly women at night in urban areas. The amount of money was beside the point. [This case has been recently relied on by the Court of Appeal.]

A-G's Reference (Nos 19, 20 and 21 of 2001) [2001] EWCA Crim 1432, [2002] 1 Cr App Rep (S) 136. There can be little doubt that the two forms of criminal conduct which causes the public most concern are domestic burglary and street robberies. The effect of such offences goes way beyond the dreadful trauma suffered by the immediate victim and causes large sections of the public to alter their lifestyle to seek to avoid the danger. People are afraid to go out of their homes.

Street etc robbery (including premises open to the public) – Cases

146.63   *R v Luck and Woollard* [1999] 1 Cr App Rep (S) 248. The defendant L pleaded guilty to four robberies and an attempted robbery and W pleaded guilty to five robberies and an attempted robbery. W was then 17 years old and L 16. In the first incident L pleaded to one robbery and W to two robberies. A 14-year-old schoolboy was intimidated by three youths with what looked like a knuckle-duster. Threats were made by one of them that another boy had ripped someone's tongue out and stabbed someone. The victim handed over £10 and the group left. The returned and extracted another £10. The victim's friend was threatened that he would be pushed through the wall. He handed over £1 and was told if he didn't hand over more the shit would be kicked out of him. Nothing was handed over and he was not attacked.

A week later W and six other youths surrounded a 17-year-old boy near the scene of the earlier robbery. They took his packet of cigarettes and searched him taking £13. They tried to rob his younger brother of his jacket but he resisted and they gave up. W pleaded guilty to robbery of them both. The same day seven youths surrounded a 16 year old and others. The boy's wallet was taken. He didn't resist as he had an injured hand. Another boy was told that if he didn't hand over money he would be knifed. No knife was produced and nothing taken. L pleaded guilty to the attempt and W to the robbery. They were arraigned and W pleaded guilty to all his matters and L only one but changed the pleas later. They were bailed. Five months later L and W attacked C a 16 year old and a 14 year old in a shopping centre. C's neck was seized and he was told they had a knife. The boys handed over their bags. L had convictions for two offences of criminal damage, assault, three burglaries, theft, handling and vehicle taking. Several were committed when he was on bail and he was subject to a supervision order. W had convictions for shoplifting, vehicle taking, theft and threatening words. Held. They had been given every opportunity. Their **3½ years** detention (under different provisions) was not manifestly excessive.

A-G's Reference (No 34 of 1999) [2000] 1 Cr App Rep (S) 322 – LCJ. The defendant pleaded guilty to robbery 4 months after the PDH hearing. The defendant who had partly covered his face with a shirt came up to the victim in a park and grabbed him by his jacket. He also grabbed hold of a valuable gold chain, which was round his neck. The defendant produced a hypodermic syringe, which appeared to contain a brown liquid and accused the boy of selling drugs to his brother. He held the syringe about a foot away from his neck and threatened to give him AIDS if he didn't get the chain off. The boy was terrified and the syringe was moved close to the boy's legs in a stabbing motion. Eventually the chain was undone. The defendant ran off with it. The next day he went to the shop where the boy worked and asked if he was accusing him of being the robber. He warned the boy not to make trouble for himself. He was arrested and gave an alibi. He was 25 and had convictions for burglary, common assault, drink/drive and failing to provide a specimen. They were all drug related. He didn't co-operate with a probation order and was given CSO for the breach, which he breached again and he then served a short period of custody. There were reports from drug rehabilitation units, which said 'He was committed to overcoming his addiction and was doing his utmost to sort out his life. He arranged his own interviews and all tests were negative. To interfere with the programme would jeopardise the recovery. He was now in a residential unit. The progress was very good. The stay would be for up to 9 months funded by the council.' The risk to the public was now described as being very low. He was given **18 months' suspended** and a suspended sentence supervision order. Held. What distinguishes this from the normal case of a defendant saying they will cure themselves is that here he has taken vigorous, persistent, constructive and determined action. That made it exceptional so the sentence could be suspended. The sentence did not fall outside the options open to the judge.

A-G's Reference (No 30 of 2001) [2001] EWCA Crim 1319, [2002] 1 Cr App Rep (S) 164. The defendant pleaded guilty to two counts of robbery on the day his trial was listed. At about 2.10am he when 25 and another spoke to the victim. They then lurked in an alleyway and tripped him up. He was pushed into the alleyway and pinned down. The other man held a knife to his neck. They demanded his wallet and he was rolled over so his pockets could be searched. They found nothing and took his watch. He was made to stand so they could check for his wallet and then they walked off laughing. The victim was very shaken and had a small nick in his neck from the knife. About 10 minutes later the next victim was dragged into an alleyway by the same two. The other man raised a knife to the victim's face and demanded his wallet. They searched his pockets and took his mobile and his wallet containing £5–10 and some bank cards. The other man asked for his PIN number and moved the knife closer to his throat. The number was given and they ran off. The attack had lasted about 30 seconds. Shortly after £110 was drawn from the victim's bank account. The defendant then surrendered himself to the police and identified his accomplice. When interviewed he said he was no more than a look out, although he did search the men's pockets. He said the money was for drugs but he didn't receive any. The defendant was said to be in fear of the other man. He was injured and said that they were caused by the other man and that was why he gave himself up. He had convictions for minor offences of dishonesty, four common assaults and driving offences. The risk of re-offending was described as significant. Held. 12 months was unduly lenient. A proper sentence could not be less than **3 years**. As it was a reference **2½ years** substituted.

See also *R v Ezair* (14 November 2001, unreported). 3 years and 1 year consecutive upheld for defendant who robbed students in a city were there were over 700 robberies of students in that area.

Street etc robbery (including premises open to the public) – Injuries caused

146.64 *A-G's Reference (No 44 of 1997)* [1998] 2 Cr App Rep (S) 105. The defendants H and B pleaded guilty to robbery. B approached a 44-year-old alcoholic in a telephone box. He had been drinking and ignored him. When the victim left the box he was invited to a park for a drink. As he passed the entrance to the park H seized him round the neck and pulled him to the ground. He was kicked about the head and body by B and his wallet was taken. It contained £20, credit cards a driving licence and a rail ticket. Beer was poured over him to make it look as if he had had too much to drink. The victim was concussed with a bruised, cut and swollen face. B was the instigator and ringleader. H was then 17. B was now 21. B had convictions for criminal damage and common assault. H received a combination order with 100 hours' community service and B was ordered to perform 240 hours' community service, £500 compensation and £350 costs. H had completed 82 hours of the community service, had demonstrated a commitment to CSO and had obtained work. He also had references. B had completed 25 hours of his CSO. Held. For an adult even on a plea of guilty **3 years** would generally be appropriate. Because of H's age and his steps to rehabilitate himself the sentence which was unduly lenient would not be altered. Taking into account it was a reference **2 years** substituted for B.

R v Winfield [1999] 2 Cr App Rep (S) 116. The defendant was convicted of robbery. He and two others were in a public house. One followed the victim who had drunk about 5 pints into the lavatory. The victim's gold chain was seized and there was a struggle. The victim received a bite on the finger. The defendant and the other man joined them and all three kicked and punched the victim. The door was closed to stop those who had heard the commotion from entering. The victim became unconscious and lost his gold chain, his bracelet, a gold watch, a ring and £30. Police found him covered in blood with a boot mark on his forehead. At hospital he was found to have a 2″ cut to his head and bruising to his temple, nose, cheek and near his eye. He stayed there for a few days. The defendant had a bad record (details not given). The judge found the defendant was not the instigator but the No 2. He was given an longer than commensurate sentence of 8 years. Held. There is substance in the criticism that he was not more involved than the third man. Ordinarily the offence would warrant **5 years**. We must ensure the sentence is not out of all proportion to the nature of the offending and there is no double counting. Double counting is when a sentence has a deterrent factor built in and is extended without taking into account that existing deterrent factor. That deterrent factor caters for the necessity to protect the public. **6 years** not 8.

A-G's Reference (Nos 24 and 25 of 2000) [2001] 1 Cr App Rep (S) 237. The defendants E and M were convicted of robbery. They stopped an 18 year old who was running for a bus. They pretended to be police officers and dragged him to a dark alley. One held him while the other punched him. He was forced to the ground. They took £14 cash from his wallet. Police on the roof of a nearby building saw it and arrested the defendants. The victim suffered bruising and his spectacles were bent. The lenses were scratched. At the trial they claimed the victim made a racist remark and he was chased and had fallen over. E was now 30 and had nine court appearances for offences including ABH and robbery. M was now 31 and had 9 court appearances when he was aged 10 to 20. They were all for minor dishonesty. He was brought up in care. Both were sentenced to 6 months and had been released. Held. The differences between the defendants did not require different sentences. We would have expected **4 years** imprisonment. Because it was a reference and they had been released **3 years** substituted.

A-G's Reference (Nos 19, 20 and 21 of 2001) [2001] EWCA Crim 1432, [2002] 1 Cr App Rep (S) 136. There was an attempted robbery and a robbery. For those adults not involved in the death of one of the victims the appropriate sentence was **6 years**. See MANSLAUGHTER – *Burglars/Robbers/Thieves, by*

Street etc robbery – Mobile phones – Guideline remarks

146.65 *A-G's Reference (Nos 4 and 7 of 2002)* [2002] EWCA Crim 127, [2002] 2 Cr App Rep (S) 345 and R v Q – LCJ. A Home Office Study shows a marked increase in mobile thefts and robberies. In 2000 there were 470,000 thefts and robberies including attempts from those 16 or over. There were 15,000 from those aged 11–15. The risk of theft for those aged between 11 to 16 is five times higher. Offences have at least doubled in 2 years. We have to adopt a robust sentencing policy. Punishment will be severe. Custodial sentences will be the only option unless there are exceptional circumstances irrespective of age and lack of previous convictions. The authorities indicate the sentencing bracket is **18 months to 5 years**. Without a weapon the upper limit is **3 years**. If there the defendant has a number of convictions or there is a substantial violence the upper limit may be **more than the 3 and 5 years**.

Street etc robbery – Mobile phones

146.66   *A-G's Reference (Nos 4 and 7 of 2002)* [2002] EWCA Crim 27, [2002] 2 Cr App Rep (S) 345 – LCJ. The defendant S pleaded guilty to three robberies and two thefts. The defendant who was on bail, approached a 14-year-old boy who was with five friends and grabbed him by the collar. The victim was dragged to the nearby shopping centre, pushed against a wall and searched. The defendant threatened to beat him up if he did not hand over his mobile phone. The victim was then pushed to the floor. The robbery ended. About a month later he stole a mobile phone and jewellery. About another month later the defendant was with another who approached the victim. He asked to borrow his mobile phone because 'he had been mugged.' The victim said he didn't have one. The defendant pulled up his top to cover his nose and mouth and joined them. He told the victim not to be stupid and not to look at them. They took his phone and unclipped his watch. The other youth took his gold chain. The items were worth £175. The victim was frightened. The next day he blocked the path of an 18 year old in the street. The defendant accused him of stealing his mobile and was asked to prove his was a different type and then when it was shown the defendant tried to seize it. The defendant's accomplice ran off with it. The defendant then threatened to beat the victim up if he did not give him some money. He was given some money and then ran off. He was 19 and had three convictions including stealing a bicycle when he scuffled with the owner. He spent 93 days in custody and the judge gave him a community rehabilitation order with 60 hours of community punishment. Held. **4 years' detention** was the starting point. The plea reduced it to 3 years and because it was a reference **2½ years** substituted.

stead.

The sentences have gone up. Ignore all cases before the *A-G's Reference (Nos 4 and 7 of 2002)*.

Street etc robbery – Vehicles, attacking people in their

146.67   *A-G's Reference (Nos 53–57 of 2001)* (31 July 2001, unreported). [The appropriate sentences would have been at 6 at the very least, 4½ years, 3 and 3 years.]

Street etc robbery – Victim over 65

146.68   *A-G's Reference (No 48 of 1998)* [1999] 2 Cr App Rep (S) 48. The defendant pleaded guilty at the first opportunity to attempted robbery and handling. The victims of the attempted robbery were a married couple aged 82 and 78. They walked to their car after collecting their pensions. As they reached the car the defendant who was then 19 demanded the wife's purse. He was armed with two walking sticks. She got in the car and locked it. He then demanded money from the husband. The defendant raised his hand and the husband saw a black metal barrel. The husband said he was sure it was a gun from his years in the RAF. He told the defendant not to waste his time and the defendant ran away. The couple said they were shaken by the incident. The defendant was arrested and the officer found a weight bar. He also had a number of cigarette lighters, which had been stolen, in a burglary. In interview he admitted the attempted robbery and having the weight bar at the time. He also said he had been drinking and taking pills and was absolutely desperate for money. He was released on bail and committed further offences, which were dealt with in the Magistrates' Court. He had convictions for theft and a non-domestic burglary. He was sentenced to a combination order with a 100 hours' CSO. He attended twice and then for 3½ months failed to attend. Held. A sentence in the region of **3 years** was appropriate. Because of his age and that it was a reference **2 years** detention substituted.

R v Buck [2000] 1 Cr App Rep (S) 42. The defendant pleaded guilty to two robberies after the judge had ruled the ID evidence admissible. Both victims had to attend the court expecting to give evidence. The defendant watched the first victim aged 77, collect her pension and he followed her. He grabbed her round the neck from behind and threw her to the ground. He dragged her down a path to some bushes. She banged her head and became dazed. He took the pension book with the money still in it. She had a cut to her elbow and a bruise to her leg and forehead. An hour and a half later the next victim aged 79 collected her pension. As she was walking along the street the defendant grabbed her handbag and the strap broke. He ran off with it. The defendant was 29 with 52 offences of burglary, theft, handling and six drug-related offences. He had served 5 custodial sentences. The judge gave him 6 years on each concurrent. Held. The appropriate individual sentences are **5 years and 4**. The individual sentences would be **3 years each but consecutive**.

R v Blades [2000] 1 Cr App Rep (S) 463. The defendant made a late guilty plea to robbery. The defendant pushed a 74-year-old woman in the middle of the back causing her to fall to the ground. She sustained cuts and bleeding to her knees. He grabbed her handbag which contained £11. The defendant was arrested and the bag returned. In 1991 he brandished a gun in a burger restaurant and demanded the takings. He received 5 years. In 1994 he snatched cash and banking documents from a victim in a wheelchair (9 months). One year after his release and within 33 days, he committed two street robberies and two street thefts and another street offence. The victims were a care worker, a mother with a 2-month-old baby, a disabled woman and a 82 and 72-year-old woman respectively He received 4 years and was on licence for it at the time of the new offence. There was 1 year to run. He was 33. The pre-sentence report said he was addicted to crack and the offence was committed when his drug use was out of control. The judge was mindful of the psychological harm caused to old victims by attacks of this kind. He was sentenced to a longer than commensurate sentence of 10 years but there was no order about the breach of licence. Held. The offence was worth **5 years**. A 2 year extension was appropriate so 7 years plus 1 year consecutive for the breach of licence making **8 years**.

R v Howe and Graham [2001] EWCA Crim 768, [2001] 2 Cr App Rep (S) 479 – LCJ. The defendants H and G pleaded guilty to robbery. Their cases were unrelated but heard together because they were similar. H and another approached the victim aged 73 as she was walking. She was pushed which caused her to stagger back. She didn't fall but her handbag with personal items and £14 was taken. The two ran off. Two passers-by followed them and asked them for the bag. H used insulting words and one of them was hit on her face. The 73 year old was very shocked and upset. H was 24 with 107 convictions and 28 TICs since he was 14. They included 26 burglaries, 15 thefts and a robbery. He had eight custodial sentences one of which was for 5 years. He was in breach of probation and a conditional discharge. The judge sentenced him to 5 years on the basis he struck the passer-by. This was denied and there was no Newton hearing. G approached his victim aged 76 as she was walking alone from behind. He pushed her and she turned and screamed. She tried to hang onto her bag but

G eventually got it off her and ran away. It contained cash and personal items. He was 26 and had eight previous court appearances. His convictions included two for robbery which was one incident. The defence said he was in dire financial straits and had not eaten for several days. He received 4 years. Held. In each case the handbag was snatched with no more force than necessary. No threats or weapons were used. The striking of the passerby should have been ignored. Both sentences should be **4 years**.

R v Simpson [2002] EWCA Crim 25, [2002] 2 Cr App Rep (S) 234 – LCJ. The defendant made an early guilty plea to manslaughter and two robberies. The first victim, an 89-year-old lady was returning to her flat after picking up her pension and doing some shopping. As she was walking up the stairs to the flat the defendant pulled her shopping bag firmly backwards. It contained her purse with £6 in it. She tried to resist and he gave it a heavier pull. She fell backwards and slid down the concrete stairs. He ran off with the bag. She was found to have a fracture to her neck and femur. A plate and screws were inserted. The operation appeared straight forward but she suffered two consequential chest infections and died about a month after the robbery. Almost immediately after the first robbery, the defendant 'thumped' a 76-year-old lady in the back and then pulled at her bag. It contained her pension book, documents and purse. The victim had just returned from collecting her pension. He pulled at it until she let go and drove away. The defendant was now 40 with convictions going back to the early 70s. Over the years he had been in and out of prison for dishonesty and driving offences. In 1995 he received 4 years for two robberies and one of the victims was an 83 year old lady who was followed from picking up her pension and knocked to the ground. The second robbery was similar. After the manslaughter offence he was sentenced to 3 years for burglary and serious driving offences. He needed £200 a day for heroin. Held. These offences are mean beyond words, easy to commit, highly prevalent and dangerous both to life and limb of the elderly victims. When they are committed by dangerous acts and death occurs severe sentences are called for. There can be no fault with the sentence of **7 years** for the robberies because of his record and the circumstances. The 10 years for the manslaughter as an overall sentence could not be faulted. The sentences remained consecutive to the sentence he was serving.

A-G's Reference (No 108 of 2001) [2002] EWCA Crim 193, [2002] 2 Cr App Rep (S) 294. See *Victim seriously injured*

Street etc robbery – Victim taken to a cash machine

146.69   *R v Targett and Watkins* [1999] 2 Cr App Rep (S) 282. The defendants T and W pleaded guilty to robbery and false imprisonment. They followed a man into a public lavatory. The man went into a cubicle, which had no lock. They pushed the door open despite effort by the victim to stop them and T threatened him with a Swiss Army knife. The victim was sitting on the lavatory with his trousers down. T demanded his wallet saying he was a crack head and he'd use the knife. The wallet was examined and the man was allowed to dress. They took £5. They saw his credit cards and asked him how much he could obtain from a cash machine. He said £30. They told him he was to be taken to a cash machine and T said he had a gun and he wasn't afraid to use it. W told the victim to remove his jewellery and two rings and a watch worth about £40. They were stolen. The victim was taken to a cash machine and told again that T was not afraid to use the gun. He was unable to obtain any money either inside or outside the bank. On his way to another machine the victim was able to escape into a shop. The incident had lasted about 20 minutes. They were arrested soon afterwards. T was 33 and W 41 with records (details not given). They were both addicted to various substances. The judge said that without a guilty plea 9 years would have been appropriate. Held. The judge was right to consider the offence was more serious than a straightforward street robbery. **6 years** was at the top of the bracket but was not manifestly excessive.

R v Gordon and Foster [2001] 1 Cr App Rep (S) 200. The defendants G and F pleaded guilty at the first opportunity to robbery and ABH. A 17-year-old student in the street at night asked the defendants what the time was. G grabbed him by the throat and pinned him against the wall. He was asked if he had anything on him. The victim said, 'Nothing,' and he was told that wasn't good enough and was made to empty his pockets. G punched him and repeated the demand. F stood close by as if to hide what was going on. The victim handed over some keys and loose change. His wallet was taken and F looked through it. The victim was so frightened he handed over his bank card. F grabbed his arm and together they took him to the nearest cash point. On the way he was further threatened. They discovered he only had £1.70 in the account. He was taken round the side of the bank and was punched and headbutted. The victim managed to escape. He had a swollen and cut lip and swelling to his head. He also suffered from dizzy spells. G was 26 with 6 convictions including ABH. F was 28 and had been sentenced 13 times largely for dishonesty. The offences included ABH and possession of a bladed article. Held. **5 years** was not manifestly excessive.

Taxi drivers etc – Guideline remarks

146.70 *A-G's Reference (No 38 of 1995)* [1996] 2 Cr App Rep (S) 103 – LCJ. Taxi drivers are particularly vulnerable; they operate alone and they are at the whim of the passenger to be taken where the passenger asks. It is this court's job to see they are properly protected and anyone who is minded to attack a taxi driver must receive a substantial sentence of imprisonment.

Taxi drivers etc – Cases

146.71 *R v Johnson* [1998] 1 Cr App Rep (S) 126. The defendant pleaded guilty to three robberies, a s 20 wounding and two TDA counts. The first minicab driver drove the defendant and felt something sharp near his ribs. It was a knife. The defendant demanded money and took over £50 in notes and £15 in loose change. He also demanded his gold chains and took them as well. He ran off taking the car keys. Six days later the defendant produced a knife on the second minicab driver. He stabbed him in the chest and ran off. He was in hospital for 5 days. The same evening he grabbed another minicab driver by the hand and produced a knife. He pushed it into his stomach and demanded money and jewellery. He took £86. The driver kicked him to stop him driving off and the defendant lunged at him with a knife. The defendant drove off in the car. The next evening the defendant and another were in another minicab and the driver was directed to a dead-end street. The defendant grabbed the driver from behind and forced his neck against the headrest. The other man produced a knife, which was held against his chest. They demanded money and said if he resisted he would be killed. His wallet containing about £50 and has mobile was taken. He was forced out of the car and they drove off in it. The defendant was 29 with three previous convictions for robbery. One was in 1993 and the other two were in 1994. He received 5 years concurrent on each and was released 3 months before the fist minicab robbery. The judge sentenced him to 10 years. Held. He had deliberately targeted minicab drivers because they were vulnerable. He either used a knife or was a party to the use of a knife. He was prepared to use violence on the one who was wounded. 7 years for the robberies cannot be faulted. The sentence as an overall sentence cannot be faulted.

R v Okee and West [1998] 2 Cr App Rep (S) 199. The defendants O and W pleaded guilty at the last minute to robbery. W used a minicab a number of times to move his belongings from his hostel to his new address. O helped him. At the end of the last journey W seized the ignition key and the driver struggled and seized it back. The driver got out and the two manhandled him and tried to hit him. The victim dodged the blows. Then O hit him causing injury to the driver's forehead and kept hold of him while W went to the car and stole money from the ashtray. In interviewed they concocted contradictory lies. O was 20 and had two convictions for robbery. For the last one he received 3 years. W was 21 and had an attempted robbery conviction for which he received 3 years. The judge passed a 4½ year sentence saying with no plea it would have been 5 years. The defence said there was insufficient credit given. Held. Those who run their not guilty pleas to the wire should know that the discount will be substantially and visibly reduced. The 10% discount here was ample. However, the starting point is too high. **3 years 9 months** detention and imprisonment substituted.

R v Brown [1998] 2 Cr App Rep (S) 257. The defendant pleaded guilty to unlawful wounding and robbery; two counts of offering to supply drugs; six counts of robbery; and an attempted robbery. The defendant approached a man in the street and took £10. He used a knife and caused a wound to the man's cheek. He was arrested and bailed. He offered two plain clothes officers ecstasy and cannabis. He was arrested and found to have neither. He was released on bail. The other robberies were on minicab drivers who were threatened with a knife and had money and other items taken. The last was where after he had threatened a driver with a knife, a struggle took place and the defendant fled empty handed. He was picked out at ID parades. He had only recently been released from prison. For all but 2 of the robberies he was on bail twice. In 1982 he received 3 years for robbery, in 1993 he received 2 years for robbery, in 1993 he was convicted of 13 offences of which 4 were robbery and received 2 years and also in 1993 he was convicted of six offences four of which were robbery and received 4 years. Those robberies were very similar to the latest offences. He received 4 years for the street robbery, 6 years for the robberies and 3 years for the attempt consecutive making 13 years in all. The judge passed a longer than commensurate sentence. The defence did not suggest the making of the longer than commensurate sentences was wrong. Held. Without considering the powers to extend the worrying features of this case mean a sentence of between 6 or 7 years would be justified even after a guilty plea. None of the sentences could be faulted but the total should be **10 years** not 13.

See also *Armed with firearm – Imitation – Taxi drivers etc*

Trains, buses etc

146.72 *A-G's Reference (Nos 35 and 36 of 2000)* [2001] 1 Cr App Rep (S) 327 – LCJ. The defendant H aged 27 pleaded guilty to two robberies. The defendant D was convicted of robbery. The defendants approached the victims G aged 15 and F aged 16 and another at a railway station. They called out to them in a hostile manner. H got G in a loose headlock and asked him if he had a mobile. G said 'No.' H took £2 in change which had been proffered. A train arrived and the defendants and the victims entered different carriages. After the train left the station the defendants moved to the victims' carriage. There was another intimidating verbal exchange and D tried to persuade H to leave them alone. One boy got away but the defendants blocked the other two from leaving. The victims ran to the other end of the carriage and were chased. H pushed G into a seat and demanded his fucking money. G handed over his wallet containing £20. H searched F and took his mobile phone and camera. These were returned. The train arrived at a station and defendants told the victims they would have to travel back to London with them but F was able to tell staff at the a station what had happened. D gave a false name, failed to attend an ID parade and failed to answer to his bail. H expressed remorse. H had convictions mainly for dishonesty and was on probation. He had drug and alcohol problems. D's record was similar and he was on probation for assaulting a police officer. Held. Applying *A-G's Reference (Nos 7-10 of*

2000) [2001] 1 Cr App Rep (S) 166 the starting point for H is **3 years** and for D is **30 months**. Taking into account it was a plea and a reference **2 years** not 4 months for H. Taking into account D was involved in one offence 2 years for him.

R v Dikko [2002] EWCA Crim 292, [2002] 2 Cr App Rep (S) 380. The defendant pleaded guilty to robbery. The victim was near the terminus of a London Underground journey and was alone in a carriage when the defendant came through the connecting door. The defendant sat next to her and said in an authoritative manner that she was going to give him everything she had. Frightened she took out her purse and he took her keys, bankcards and cash and demanded to know her PIN number which she gave him. He said he would not hurt her. She asked for her keys and he gave them back. He demanded details of her car and she was very frightened because he showed her what appeared to be a handle of a knife in his waist band. The train arrived at its destination and he left and withdrew £400 from her account. He was arrested and denied the offence in interview. He was 19 with 5 non-relevant convictions, (details not given). Held. The public is entitled to travel unaccompanied in safety. The victim was in terror. **3 years** YOI was unimpeachable.

Victims, elderly

See **Domestic premises – Victim over 65** and **Street robbery – Victim over 65**

Victim seriously injured

146.73   *R v Evans* [2000] 1 Cr App Rep (S) 454. The defendant pleaded guilty to robbery. He entered an antiques shop and took out a bottle or gas container which he used as a cosh. He struck the 59-year-old lady that ran the shop with it on the side of her face. She was propelled back against a wall and fell unconscious. He then stole jewellery from the cabinets worth about £1,200 and left her bleeding and unconscious on the floor. The incident was recorded on CCTV. She was found by another shopkeeper. She was taken to hospital and found to have blood over the surface of the brain. There was bruising to the brain. Her scalp was injured. She was in hospital for 11 days. She had loss of hearing, problems with her balance and she would never be able to return to work. Her hearing in her right ear and her sense of taste and smell would never recover. She had difficulty with strangers and her quality of life had been very seriously and permanently impaired. He was 30 with convictions in South Africa but was treated as of good character. He had no mental illness. His behaviour had changed after a motor accident. Held. The injuries were horrific, but **8 years** not 10.

R v Hooley [2001] 2 Cr App Rep (S) 105. The defendants H, R and F pleaded guilty to robbery. The R and F had changed their pleas. The defendants had all used the village store which the victim aged 62 managed. Shortly after 10pm F entered the store with some tape and a balaclava. The victim took the cash drawers to the back of the shop where F was waiting wearing a mask and hat and holding an iron bar in a threatening way. He had picked up the bar in the shop. He asked for money and the victim turned to go to the office. F struck him with the bar on the shoulder and the victim fell to his knees. He was made to open the safe and hand over the money. The next thing he remembered after being unconscious for ½ hour was crawling to a take away. The defendants had done nothing to assist him. He was in intensive care for 3 weeks. He had broken ribs on both sides of his chest. His lung was punctured. He had bruising on his shoulder and arms. His jaw and cheekbones were fractured and plates had to be inserted. There was a cut to his eye and his eye socket had been knocked slightly backwards. He required a tracheotomy. An expert said, 'He had been subjected to kicking and/or stamping with substantial force. He had been punched and hit with a weapon like an iron bar.' H said F was in the shop for about ½ hour and then H and R stole £1,600 in cash, a large quantity of cigarettes and the CCTV. Previously he had lied about his involvement. The property was divided and items were burnt. H was sentenced on the basis that he did not believe any violence was to be used and his role was that of a lookout. H was 21 with ten convictions including offences of violence and dishonesty. R was 29 with three convictions including affray and ABH. F was 30 with eight convictions including four for violence. He had not served a prison sentence. The judge said it was well planned and ruthlessly executed. Held. **10 years** not 13 for H and **8 years** not 11 for H and R.

A-G's Reference (No 108 of 2001) [2002] EWCA Crim 193, [2002] 2 Cr App Rep (S) 294. The defendant made an early guilty plea to robbery. When 19 she approached an 88-year-old lady from behind and pulled her shopping bag. The victim held on and there was a struggle in which the victim swung round and fell to the ground. The defendant seized the bag and ran off but was detained by the public. While they waited for police to arrive she made two attempts to run off. The purse contained £17. The victim had a wound to her head and her shoulder was broken in four places. She needed a major operation, which effectively provided a new shoulder. There was also a hairline fracture to the pelvis. She was eventually released from hospital but would have to live in a home rather than independently. The defendant was interviewed and said it was easy money and she was desperate for drugs. There were no relevant convictions and she was 6 months pregnant. She showed remorse. Held. We would have expected **3½ years** YOI taking into account the injuries, the victim was targeted and the defendant's pregnancy. As it was a reference **2½ years** YOI not 18 months.

See also **OFFENCES AGAINST THE PERSON ACT 1861, S 18** – *Robbery, and*

Withdrawing from robbery plan

146.74   *A-G's Reference (Nos 65–6 of 2001)* (26 October 2001, unreported). H pleaded guilty to robbery of a guard of a security van. H then 19 sat beside the getaway driver wearing a balaclava helmet throughout the robbery. H's basis of plea was that when the two assailants who attacked the guard got out of the car he was unaware that weapons were to be used. When he saw the weapons he decided not to go with the other two and he remained in the car. Held. The basis of plea for H was supported by the fact he just remained in the car. Courts ought to encourage people who at the last minute decide not to go through with a criminal enterprise and who withdraw their own involvement even if they remain a party to what is going on.

See also **BURGLARY – AGGRAVATED**

147   SCHOOL, FAILURE TO SECURE REGULAR ATTENDANCE

147.1   Parent with child who fails to attend regularly.

Education Act 1996, s 444(1)
Summary only. Maximum Level 3 £1,000.

Parent who knows child is failing to attend regularly, and fails to cause him to attend.

Education Act 1996, s 444 (1A)[1]
Summary only. Maximum 3 months and/or Level 4 £2,500.

For both offences there is power to make a parenting order under the Crime and Disorder Act 1998, s 8.

Sentencing trends. In 2002 parents have been sent to prison under the new aggravated offence (section 1A). This had been received with judicial, journalist and government approval. Prison sentences are likely to continue to be passed but only where there has been repeated failure to respond to non-custodial alternatives.

1   In force 1 March 2001. Criminal Justice and Courts Services Act 2000, s 72.

Magistrates' Court Sentencing Guidelines September 2000 – Section 444(1)

147.2   Entry point. Is a discharge or a fine appropriate? Examples of aggravating factors for the offence are harmful effect on other children in the family, lack of parental effort to ensure attendance and parental collusion. Examples of mitigating factors for the offence are parent has complained of bullying, drugs etc, parental unawareness and physical or mental health of child. Examples of mitigation are age, health (physical or mental), subsequent co-operation with the Education Authority and genuine remorse. Consider a parenting order where appropriate. **Starting point fine B**. (£100 when defendant has £100 net weekly income. See page 334 for table showing fines for different incomes.)

For details about the guidelines see MAGISTRATES' COURT SENTENCING GUIDELINES at page 331.

148   SENTENCES SERVED FOR WHICH THE CONVICTION WAS LATER QUASHED

148.1   *R v Exley and Day* [2000] 2 Cr App Rep (S) 189. The defendant is not entitled to any discount when sentenced for another offence.

149   SEX OFFENDER ORDER, BREACH OF

149.1   Crime and Disorder Act 1998, s 2(8)

Triable either way. On indictment maximum 5 years. Summary maximum 6 months and/or £5,000.

Guideline remarks

149.2   *R v Brown* [2002] EWCA Crim 724, [2002] 1 Cr App Rep (S) 1. The police obtained a Sex Offender Order for the defendant. Held. It would be wholly illogical if, against that background (an order for the protection of children) a judge did not have the protection of children foremost in his mind. The remarks in *B v Chief Constable of Avon and Somerset Constabulary* [2001] 1 All ER 562 were obiter. The actual quality of the acts which considered the breach are by no means the only consideration in determining its seriousness.

Children, order made to protect

149.3   *R v Brown* [2002] EWCA Crim 724, [2002] 1 Cr App Rep (S) 1. The defendant was convicted of three breaches of a Sex Offender Order. Shortly before his release the police obtained a Sex Offender Order for him which prohibited him from contact, communication, association or befriending children under 16. On the evening of his release he spoke to a 14 year old and was with him for over an hour. He occasionally put his arm around the boy's shoulder. Next morning he waved a £5 note towards a 13 year old and later approached and made a sexual remark to a 14-year-old boy. He was 35 with some 'run of the mill' and six sex convictions. They were two indecent assaults on a female under 16, gross indecency with a child and outraging public decency for which he received 18 months. He had apparently an irresistible attraction to children. The judge said he posed a very serious risk to children. Held. The breaches were serious because of the speed they took place and the number. **3 years** was not manifestly excessive.

Police officers, conduct directed towards

149.4 *R v Beech* [2002] EWCA Crim 951, [2002] 1 Cr App Rep (S) 7 – LCJ. The defendant made a late guilty plea to breaching his Sex Offender Order. The order prohibited him from being drunk in any other place than a dwelling and using threatening, abusive or insulting words etc towards any female. The day after it was made he was released. He stayed at police accommodation as he was prepared to co-operate with them and because of the local media publishing inaccurate details about him. He and police officers visited a number of pubs and had a considerable amount to drink. His behaviour deteriorated and he was taken into custody. While there he was abusive and threatening in particular to a woman police sergeant. It was a torrent of abuse and threats including, 'Bitch, I'm going to shag you and bury you, you whore.' She found it frightening and unnerving. He apologised. He was 37 and had one court appearance for sex offences namely rape and indecent assault for which he received 9 years. There were also 13 appearances for drugs, assault, affray, harassment and threatening behaviour etc. A dyssocial personality disorder which was exacerbated by alcohol and illicit substances was diagnosed. His risk of re-offending was assessed as extremely high and he presented a serious risk of harm to the public particularly women. The judge identified a history of failing to comply with court orders. He was due to be released in a few days. Held. There is no doubt the defendant finds it very difficult to behave in a manner which is other than extremely antisocial. It was precisely this sort of behaviour the order was designed to avoid. In normal circumstances even for someone with the defendant's background 12 months would not be proportionate for these remarks, however distressing they were to the sergeant. However, we can take into account the risk he poses himself and the public. It is important the arrangements for his release are in place so **12 months** is not manifestly excessive. The public are entitled to be protected.

See also SEX OFFENDERS' REGISTER

150 SEX OFFENDERS' REGISTER

150.1 Sex Offenders Act 1997, ss 1–6

The requirements are not listed as they concern the operation of a sentencing provision which for reasons of space are not included in the book. The only matter that is listed is whether the registration can impact on the length of the sentence.

Can the need to register contribute to a reduction in sentence

150.2 *A-G's Reference (No 50 of 1997)* [1998] 2 Cr App Rep (S) 155. The sentencing judge thought 9 months was appropriate for two counts of indecent assault. He said, 'That would require registration for 10 years which would be an absurd additional burden. I have no discretion.' He passed a 6 month sentence which required 7 years of notification. Held. The judge was wrong to reduce the sentence. It is the duty of judges to implement the sentencing powers that have been given to them by Parliament.

See also SEX OFFENDER ORDER, BREACH OF

SEXUAL INTERCOURSE

For sexual intercourse with a girl under 13, see **SEXUAL OFFENCES ACT 1956, S 5**

For permitting premises to be used by a girl under 13 or under 16 for sexual intercourse see **SEXUAL OFFENCES ACT 1956, SS 25 AND 26**

151   SEXUAL INTERCOURSE – BREACH OF TRUST

151.1   Sexual Offences (Amendment) Act 2000, s 1

Triable either way. On indictment maximum 5 years. Summary maximum 6 months and/or £5,000.

The defendant must notify the police within 14 days (or 14 days from his release from imprisonment) his name and home address etc, any change and addresses where he resides for 14 days or more in any 12 month period[1]. See **SEX OFFENDERS' REGISTER**

1   Sex Offenders Act 1997, ss 1 and 2.

Teachers

151.2   *R v Hubbard* [2002] EWCA Crim 494, [2002] 2 Cr App Rep (S) 473. The defendant pleaded guilty to three counts of abuse of trust on a 15-year-old pupil of his. He was head of department at a secondary school. She was vulnerable but sexually experienced and found him easy to talk to about her personal problems. Consensual sexual intercourse took place on three occasions. It was revealed because she told her friends. The defendant was 43 and was full of remorse. His marriage ended in divorce. Held. This Act is to protect girls like this. **2 years** was not manifestly excessive. The judge was entitled to extend his licence by 2 years.

152   SEXUAL OFFENCES ACT 1956, S 5

152.1   Having unlawful sexual intercourse with a girl under 13.

Indictable only. Maximum sentence for full offence 10 years, and for an attempt 7 years.

It is a specified offence for automatic life.

The defendant must notify the police within 14 days (or 14 days from his release from imprisonment) his name and home address etc, any change and addresses where he resides for 14 days or more in any 12 month period[1]. See **SEX OFFENDERS' REGISTER**

1   Sex Offenders Act 1997, ss 1 and 2.

Crown Court statistics England and Wales – Crown Court – Males 21+ – Unlawful Sexual intercourse with a girl under 13

152.2

Year	Plea	Total Numbers sentenced	Type of sentence%						Average length of custody[1] (months)
			Discharge	Fine	Community sentence	Suspended sentence	Custody	
2000	Guilty	20	0%	0%	10%	0%	90%	36.2
	Not guilty	6	0%	0%	0%	0%	100%	49

1   Excluding life sentences. Source: Crime and Criminal Justice Unit, Home Office Ref: IOS416-02.

Guideline remarks

152.3 *R v Watkins* [1998] 1 Cr App Rep (S) 410. The significance of an 11-year-old girl consenting is limited.

Victim aged 10–12

152.4 *R v Murray* [1998] 1 Cr App Rep (S) 395. The defendant pleaded guilty to unlawful sexual intercourse with a girl under the age of 13. He met the victim, who was 12, near his home as she took a short cut. She approached the defendant and asked him for a cigarette. A conversation took place between the two and the victim consented to have sexual intercourse with the defendant. The girl had had sex before. The defendant was 40 and had a conviction for indecent assault on a woman in 1996. In 1985 he was convicted of indecent assault on his 9-year-old stepdaughter. The sentencing judge noted that the defendant was unable to contain his sexual appetite and took advantage of a solitary girl. Held. She was vulnerable and the age difference is appalling. **4 years** was a reasonable sentence.

Victim aged 10–12 – Breach of trust

152.5 *R v Watkins* [1998] 1 Cr App Rep (S) 410. The defendant pleaded guilty to three counts of unlawful sexual intercourse with a girl under the age of 13 and one count of incitement to unlawful sexual intercourse with a girl under 13. The defendant was friendly with the 11-year-old daughter of his neighbour. He asked her whether she would like to label some items for a car boot sale. He bought her cigarettes, cake and chips. Later she went with a youth, Hill, to the defendant's home. The defendant showed the victim a pornographic video and then told the victim to remove her trousers. The defendant had sexual intercourse with the girl and next actively encouraged Hill to also engage in sexual intercourse with her. He then told her if she told anyone he would get his brother to kill her. He had sex with the girl on two other occasions. The defendant was 55 and had convictions, but none of a sexual nature. He was of limited intelligence. The sentencing judge noted that an offence of this type was the most serious type of unlawful sexual intercourse. Held. Unlawful sexual intercourse with a girl under 13 carries a maximum sentence of life, as would rape on a girl under 13. The sentence must reflect that the significance of an 11-year-old girl consenting is limited. This was not the very worse case of its kind and there was no extreme degradation, therefore 7 years not 10 years was appropriate. Had it been a fight 10 years would have been appropriate. **6 years** concurrent for the incitement count remained.

R v Ssejjuko [1998] 2 Cr App Rep (S) 262. The defendant pleaded guilty to sexual intercourse and indecent assault on a girl aged 11. He was acquitted of rape on the same girl. In late 1996 he touched her breasts over her clothing. He said that was with her consent and she was flirtatious with him. In January 1997, he went in the early hours to the mother's house when the mother was out and insisted he be let in. He woke the victim up. Sexual intercourse took place. He said she was flirtatious, encouraging and consenting. He was 26 and of good character and expressed remorse. The judge said he knew she was a virgin and it must have been painful for her as he caused her internal injuries. He also said there was a degree of breach of trust because the mother had on numerous occasions let him and his girlfriend look after her children. Held. The judge was right in his observations but his view about the defendant's perception of her age was wrong. Considering the authorities **2 years and 3 months concurrent** not 3 years and 3 months consecutive.

R v JCM [2001] EWCA Crim 2971, [2002] 2 Cr App Rep (S) 99. The defendant was convicted of sexual intercourse of a girl aged 12 and was found not guilty of rape. The parents of three children went out for the evening leaving them with victim who was

12 years 8 months, the defendant's 19-year-old brother and another. During the evening the defendant and a friend arrived and beer and cider were drunk. The defendant took the victim upstairs put his hand inside her trousers, touched her vagina and had intercourse with her which lasted 2 minutes. The victim told the parents. When interviewed the defendant denied the offence. He was sentenced on the basis he knew she was 12, he knew she had a very great deal to drink and was greatly affected by it, that he was sexually experienced and persuaded her to agree, she was a virgin and he was in breach of trust. The defendant was 20 and immature. The risk of re-offending was assessed as high with a high risk of harm to young females. Since sentence he was considered a suicide risk. The defence said there was no breach of trust. Held. In the broad view there was a breach of trust to enter their home and interfere with the victim. **3½ years** detention was not manifestly excessive.

R v Fidler [2001] 1 Cr App Rep (S) 349. The defendant was convicted of unlawful sexual intercourse with an 11-year-old girl. He was acquitted of rape. He was the boyfriend of the victim's mother and stayed intermittently at the home. He was a father figure to the girl. The defendant had intercourse with the girl in December 1998 and made her pregnant. The girl's child was born only 10 days after her mother had given birth to the defendant's child also. The child's birth was very traumatic, as she was not expecting it till it happened. When interviewed he said he was aware she had started having periods. The defendant, who was 24 and had IQ of only 66 which is in the bottom 1%. He had three previous convictions for theft from graves and had served a prison sentence. The sentencing judge said that this was a grave offence and was not substantially less serious than rape. Held. The defendant knew that the girl had started her periods and was therefore at risk of becoming pregnant. He had a duty to treat the girl with paternal care rather than to seduce her. It was a grave case and he was in a position of trust. However, taking into account his IQ **3½ years** not 7 years.

Old cases. *R v Polley* [1997] 1 Cr App Rep (S) 144.

153   SEXUAL OFFENCES ACT 1956, S 6

153.1   Triable either way. On indictment maximum 2 years. Summary maximum 6 months and/or £5,000.

The defendant must notify the police within 14 days (or 14 days from his release from imprisonment) his name and home address etc, any change and addresses where he resides for 14 days or more in any 12 month period[1]. See **SEX OFFENDERS' REGISTER**

1   Sex Offenders Act 1997, ss 1 and 2.

Crown Court statistics England and Wales[1] *– Crown Court – Males 21+ – Unlawful Sexual intercourse with a girl under 16*

153.2

Year	Plea	Total Numbers sentenced	Type of sentence%					Average length of custody (months)
			Discharge	Fine	Community sentence	Suspended sentence	Custody	
2000	Guilty	79	8%	3%	24%	5%	61%	10.7
	Not guilty	11	0%	0%	0%	0%	100%	14.4

1   Excluding committals for sentence. Source: Crime and Criminal Justice Unit, Home Office Ref: IOS416-02.

Guideline case

153.3   *R v Bayliss* [2000] 1 Cr App Rep (S) 412. The attitude of society to teenage prostitution and the taking of sexually suggestive and explicit photographs of under-age girls has changed since the *R v Taylor* (1977) 64 Cr App Rep 182 became the guideline case for unlawful sexual intercourse.

Old case. *R v Taylor* (1977) 64 Cr App Rep 182. [Best ignored as so much has changed since then.]

General

153.4   *R v Offord* [1999] 1 Cr App Rep (S) 327. The defendant pleaded guilty to two counts of unlawful sexual intercourse with a 15-year-old girl. Over 3 months there was consensual sex eight times. They were discovered when the girl's mother found a love letter he had written to her. He was 36, married with three children and four stepchildren. The judge said he took the initiative and in a sense had corrupted her. He was treated as of good character. A psychiatrist said he was an inadequate, vulnerable man with a very disadvantaged childhood. Held. This was a serious offence by a man of mature years. **15 months** was not manifestly excessive.

R v Hancocks [2000] 1 Cr App Rep (S) 82. The defendant pleaded guilty to unlawful sexual intercourse with a 13-year-old girl, indecent assault and indecency with a child. The victim, who was almost 14, met the defendant as she was going to meet a friend. The victim did not have any money for the bus so asked the defendant for 37 pence. He asked the victim how old she was and was told 13. He offered her money if she would return to his flat with him. The defendant ordered a taxi and they went to a supermarket where he bought the victim some lager and cigarettes. After the two went back to the defendant's flat he began to undress her and performed oral sex on her. The victim then engaged in sexual intercourse with the defendant. He then performed oral sex on her again and she masturbated him. He tried to make her stay by holding her arm saying he wanted to have sex again. She managed to get free and run out. The defendant, who was 52 years of age, had previous convictions, though none for sexual offences. He expressed remorse but his risk of re-offending was assessed as high. Held. The maximum is 2 years. Taking account of the defendant's guilty plea and that he was not in a position of trust **9 months** not 18 months was appropriate.

Breach of trust

153.5   *R v Lane* [1999] 1 Cr App Rep (S) 415. The defendant pleaded guilty at the Magistrates' Court to unlawful sexual intercourse with a girl who was aged 15 and two counts of indecent assault. He was doing building work for the mother of friend of the victim. He met the friend, the victim and another girl and showed them his penis. The victim telephoned the defendant and initiated a sexually explicit conversation. He met her and one of her friends and took them to a secluded lane where they consented to masturbate him. On a separate occasion the defendant took the two girls to his house and the victim consented to sexual intercourse with him on two occasions during the same day. Later in the month he drove the two other girls aged 14 and 15 to a canal where they masturbated him of their own volition. He touched one girl's breasts and kissed the other girl's breasts over her clothing. These were the indecent assault matters. The defendant was 31 and had two previous convictions though neither were of a sexual nature. Held. Important consideration should have been given to the extent to which the victim agreed to and encouraged the behaviour of the defendant. It may be said he was in a position of trust but that did not seriously aggravate the offence here. The indecent assaults were at the bottom of the scale. **9 months** not 15 months was appropriate.

R v Goy [2001] 1 Cr App Rep (S) 43. The defendant pleaded guilty to unlawful sexual intercourse with a 15 year old. She was a baby-sitter for the defendant's daughter and stepdaughter. After she had put the children to bed he knelt between her legs and they kissed. Intercourse lasted about 3–4 minutes and he withdrew without ejaculating. It did not appear that she resisted him. The defendant, who was 24, had one previous conviction for burglary of a non-dwelling. Held. The aim of the legislation is to ensure that girls are protected. The victim was 15½ so there was not a vast discrepancy in age between them so **3 months** not 9 months.

A-G's Reference No 80 of 2000 [2001] 2 Cr App Rep (S) 72. The defendant pleaded guilty to indecent assault and four counts of unlawful sexual intercourse with a 13-year-old girl. She was a virgin and met the defendant, as he was the stepbrother of a friend of her sister. She suggested sex and he was initially reluctant, as he didn't want to hurt her. The two began a sexual relationship. There was pressure on the girl not to see him but they ran away using a milk delivery van he used for work. Within hours police discovered them. The defendant, who was more than twice the victim's age, contacted the victim after he had been charged, which was a breach of his bail conditions. As a consequence the defendant served 22 days' imprisonment. He was sentenced to 100 hours' CSO which he had almost completed. Held. A custodial sentence should have been made at the first instance, however the defendant had served a period of imprisonment, and as it was a reference the **community service order** was undisturbed.

R v Reeves [2001] EWCA Crim 1053, [2002] 1 Cr App Rep (S) 52. The defendant pleaded guilty to attempted unlawful sexual intercourse with a 15-year-old girl. There were two short attempts. He was 30 and of good character. **18 months** was not manifestly excessive.

R v Garrity [2001] EWCA Crim 953, [2002] 1 Cr App Rep (S) 38. **12 months** not 18 for a 30-year-old man who pleaded guilty to unlawful sexual intercourse with a 13-year-old girl. He was 60 and of good character. The girl was vulnerable and damaged and had a mental age of 7–8. Had there been a trial and no remorse 2 years would not have been inappropriate.

Victim becomes pregnant

153.6   *R v Clement* [2000] 2 Cr App Rep (S) 153. The defendant pleaded guilty to three counts of unlawful sexual intercourse with girls under the age of 16. The defendant, who was 26 years of age, had sexual intercourse with a 14-year-old girl at her home during her parents' absence. A few days later he had sex with her in his van. The victim told him her true age and he said it did not matter. The girl became pregnant. He took two other girls out in his van and had sexual intercourse with one of them off the road in an overgrown area. She was 13 years old and said it was painful. It lasted a few minutes and she said she wasn't ready for it. He stopped and went back to the van and told the other girl who was also 13 that he wanted to talk to her. The same thing happened to that girl. During the sex she twice asked him to leave her alone. He continued and then took the girls back and told them not to tell anyone. He had a borderline personality disorder. The judge gave him 1½, 1½ and 1 year consecutive. He gave him maximum credit for his early plea. Held. This was a campaign of sexual intercourse against underage girls, one of whom became pregnant. Nevertheless **3 years** not 4.

154   SEXUAL OFFENCES ACT 1956, SS 25 AND 26

154.1   Section 25: Permitting a girl under 13 to use premises for sexual intercourse Indictable only. Maximum sentence life.

Section 26: Permitting a girl under 16 to use premises for sexual intercourse

Triable either way. On indictment maximum 2 years. Summary maximum 6 months and/or £5,000.

Girl aged 13–15

154.2 *R v Sisson* [2001] EWCA Crim 1706, [2002] 1 Cr App Rep (S) 353. The defendant pleaded guilty to permitting premises to be used by a girl under 16 for sexual intercourse. The defendant who lived in Newcastle upon Tyne was a female friend of the mother of a girl T. T then aged 15 was a regular and welcome visitor to the defendant's home. The defendant accessed Internet chat rooms and a met a man from Hastings. She introduced T to the chat room and T met a man, M. T gave her age on the Internet as 17. The defendant told M that T was only 15. The man from Hastings travelled to Newcastle to meet T and M decided to join him. The defendant took them to her home where T was babysitting. M had sex with T. The next day T and the two men spent the afternoon together and then went to the defendant's home. T telephoned her parents to say she had been asked to baby-sit and she would be staying overnight. M again had sex with T. The girl had been given a quarter bottle of schnapps and some vodka and was encouraged to have sexual discussions with M. After a Newton hearing in which T gave evidence the judge found that T had been put under pressure to go into the bedroom. The defendant was 32 and had a child aged 11 who was severely disabled with autism and two younger children who were being looked after her husband while the defendant was in prison. The judge found the defendant obtained a degree of pleasure of a perverted nature from what had occurred and it was a very gross breach of trust. Also she had set it up and put her under pressure to take part. Held. It was obvious why the men were travelling to Newcastle. **14 months** was a severe sentence but it was justified.

SLAUGHTERHOUSES

See ENVIRONMENTAL OFFENCES – *Slaughterhouses and animal incinerators*

155 SOCIAL SECURITY FRAUD/HOUSING BENEFIT FRAUD ETC

155.1 Social Security Administration Act 1992, s 112

Summary only. Maximum sentence 3 months and/or Level 5 fine (£5,000).

Many offences can also be charged under the Theft Act 1968, false instruments, forgery etc. See also THEFT ETC

Guideline case

155.2 *R v Stewart* (1987) 85 Cr App Rep 66 – LCJ. Welfare benefit offences are easy to commit and difficult and expensive to track down. However, it must be remembered that they are non-violent, non-sexual and non-frightening crimes. In some cases immediate unsuspended imprisonment (or youth custody) is unavoidable. The sentence will depend on an almost infinite variety of factors, only some of which it is possible to forecast. The factors are (i) a guilty plea; (ii) the amount involved and the length of time over which the defalcations were persisted in (bearing in mind that a large total may in fact represent a very small amount weekly); (iii) the circumstances in which the offence began (eg there is a plain difference between a legitimate claim which becomes false owing to a change of situation and on the other hand a claim which is false from the very beginning); (iv) the use to which the money is put (the provision of household necessities is more venial than spending the money on unnecessary luxury); (v) previous character; (vi) matters special to the offender, such as illness, disability, family difficulties, etc; (vii) any voluntary repayment of the amounts overpaid. Before sentencing the offender the court should consider (i) whether a custodial sentence is really necessary? The fraud cases dealt with in the Crown Court are likely to be relatively serious and a non-custodial sentence may often be inappropriate; (ii) if a custodial sentence is necessary, can the court make a community service order as an equivalent to imprisonment, or can it suspend the whole sentence? (The law for suspending sentences has changed since these guidelines were issued.) It seems to us that a suspended sentence or (especially) a community service order may be an ideal form of punishment in many of these cases; (iii) if not, what is the shortest sentence the court can properly impose? We do not think that the element of deterrence should play a large part in the sentencing of this sort of case in the Crown Court.

Magistrates' Court Sentencing Guidelines September 2000

155.3   Entry point. Is it serious enough for a community penalty? Consider the impact on the victim. Examples of aggravating factors for the offence are fraudulent claims over a long period, large amount, organised group offence and planned deceptions. Examples of mitigating factors for the offence misunderstanding the regulations, pressured by others and small amount. Examples of mitigation are age, health (physical or mental), co-operation with the police, voluntary compensation and genuine remorse. Give reasons if not awarding compensation.

For details about the guidelines see **MAGISTRATES' COURT SENTENCING GUIDELINES** at page 331.

Top of the range offences – Guideline case

155.4   *R v Stewart* [1987] 85 Cr App Rep 66 –LCJ. At the top of the range, requiring substantial sentences, perhaps of **2½ years and upwards**, are the carefully organised frauds on a large scale in which considerable sums of money are obtained, often by means of frequent changes of name or address or of forged or stolen documents. These offenders are in effect professional fraudsmen, as is often apparent from their previous records. They have selected the welfare departments as an easy target for their depredations and have made a profitable business out of defrauding the public in this way. The length of the custodial sentence will depend in the first instance on the scope of the fraud. Of course, as in all fraud cases, there may be a variety of mitigating circumstances and in particular a proper discount for a plea of guilty should always be given.

Compensation – Guideline remarks

155.5   *R v Stewart* (1987) 85 Cr App Rep 66 – LCJ. So far as compensation is concerned, where no immediate custodial sentence is imposed, and the amount of overpayment is below, say, £1,000 or thereabouts, a compensation order is often of value. This will usually only be the case when the defendant is in work. Counsel for the Crown must be equipped with the relevant information to enable the court to come to a proper conclusion on this matter. [Since 1987 the value of money has fallen considerably.]

Compensation – Will the department attempt to recover the sum? Duty to ascertain

155.6   *R v Stewart* (1987) 85 Cr App Rep 66 – LCJ. It may well be advisable as a first precaution for the court to inquire what steps the department proposes to take to recover their loss from the offender. Counsel for the Crown should be equipped to assist the court on this aspect of the matter.

Over £1,000 under £20,000 – Guideline Case

155.7   *R v Stewart* (1987) 85 Cr App Rep 66 – LCJ. A short term of up to about **9 or 12 months** will usually be sufficient in a contested case where the overpayment is less than, say, £10,000. (Since 1987 the value of money has fallen considerably.)

R v Smethurst (23 November 1998, unreported). In *Clark* [1998] 2 Cr App Rep (S) 95 which was a breach of trust case using *R v Barrick* (1985) 7 Cr App Rep (S) 142 this Court accepted that the figure in *Barrick* of £10,000 was now out of date, taking into account the change in the value of money. A figure of £17,500 was accepted as a realistic modern equivalent. We can see no logical reason not to apply a similar updating to the figure in *Stewart*. [The value of money has fallen again since then.]

Over £1,000 under £10,000 –Cases

155.8   *R v Rosenburg* [1999] 1 Cr App Rep (S) 365. The defendant was convicted of 9 counts of obtaining property by a deception. The defendant claimed income support on the basis of an alleged degenerate arthritic condition and that he wasn't working or receiving income. In fact he was running an agency for dancers. The paperwork for the business was found at his house and £22,000 was paid into a bank account and £21,000 into her wife's bank account during the period. He received rent from two properties let to tenants and during the period sold a Porsche car and a villa in Spain. The loss in the counts was £2,500, which were treated by the judge as specimens for a total loss of about £30,000 over a 2½ year period. Held. *R v Clark* [1996] 2 Cr App Rep (S) 351 meant he had to sentenced for the £2,500 loss only. **2 years** not 2½ years.

R v Evans [2000] 1 Cr App Rep (S) 144. The defendant was convicted of 20 counts of furnishing false information and procuring the execution of securities by deception. She had earlier pleaded guilty to four further similar counts. Over 4½ years she was involved in a housing benefit fraud involving 11 different claims, which were repeated over and over again. The prosecution said they were sample counts for a £25,000 fraud. The total loss in the 24 counts was £2,807. She gave a slightly wrong National Insurance number, an address that did not exist, false details of employers, a variety of false names and submitted false tenancy agreements. She was 32 and had two dishonesty convictions. The judge described it as a highly sophisticated, professional fraud and that she was the major player. Held. Because of earlier authorities the court was not able to sentence on the basis of sample counts. Therefore **2 years** not 3.

£10,000 and up to £20,000

155.9   *R v Ellison* [1998] 2 Cr App Rep (S) 382. The defendant pleaded guilty to five counts of obtaining money by a deception. He asked for 88 matters to be taken into consideration. From 1992 to 1996 the defendant claimed income support for himself and his family. He claimed his wife was not working but she was working although not earning very much. The over payment was £10,948. He was of good character and made early admissions to the offences. He made some efforts to repay the money. There was no luxurious living. **10 months** in total not 15.

R v Smethurst (23 November 1998, unreported). The defendant pleaded guilty to three offences of obtaining property by deception and two offences of false accounting. He asked for 84 similar offences to be taken into consideration. Between 1991 and 1996 the defendant defrauded the DSS of £12,258.60. He had started legitimately to claim benefit for himself and his partner in February 1990, but when his partner started to work in April 1991 he failed to disclose that. She continued in work until October

1996. He was interviewed on three occasions. He admitted that his wife had been working, but initially claimed that he did not think that she was earning sufficient to affect their entitlement to benefit. Later he admitted that he knew he should have reported that she was working and that he realised that, if he had done so, it would have reduced the benefits they were receiving. He was 44 and had a number of minor convictions for dishonesty as a young man, but he fell to be treated as if he was of good character. There were two character references. **9 months** not 21.

R v Bendris [2000] 2 Cr App Rep (S) 183. The defendant pleaded guilty to conspiracy to obtain property by a deception. Over 4½ years he claimed Income Support for a fictitious male using a document that the person had entered the UK in 1994 and a false passport with the defendant's photograph on it. After just over 3 years his brother continued the scheme with the defendant signing a new claim form to give substance to the conspiracy. The amount claimed was in excess of £10,000. He was 35 and had one conviction in 1998 for obtaining by a deception for which he received a non-custodial sentence. Held. Applying *R v Ellison* [1998] 2 Cr App Rep (S) 382 **10 months** not 15.

See also TAX FRAUD

SOLDIERS

See ARMED FORCES, MEMBERS OF

156   SOLICITORS

156.1   There is no tariff for defendants who are solicitors. The fact a defendant is a solicitor may or may not be relevant to the sentence. Where the offence is committed as part of the defendant's work as a solicitor it is likely to be a factor. In a case of careless driving it is likely to be irrelevant. Frequently the case of a solicitor defendant will involve a breach of trust and a loss of reputation and employment. The court should approach those factors in the same way as non-solicitor defendants. An example of the way a court deals with solicitor defendants is *R v Neary* [1999] 1 Cr App Rep (S) 431.

See also MONEY LAUNDERING – *Solicitors*

SPECIMEN

See FAILING TO PROVIDE A SPECIMEN

157   SPEEDING

157.1   Road Traffic Act 1988, s 89(1)

Summary only. Maximum Level 3 fine, £1,000. Level 4 (£2,500) if on motorway. Discretionary disqualification. Obligatory endorsement. 3–6 points.

Magistrates' Court Sentencing Guidelines September 2000

157.2   Entry point. Is a discharge or a fine appropriate? Examples of aggravating factors for the offence are LGV, HGV, PCV, PSV, or minicabs, location/time of day/visibility, serious risk and towing caravan or trailer. Examples of mitigation for the offence are emergency established and limit changed (eg from 40 to 30 mph). Examples of mitigation are co-operation with police and fixed penalty not taken up for valid reason. Consider disqualification until test is passed where appropriate. New drivers 6 points. **Starting point fine A or B depending on speed**. (A = £50 fine when defendant has £100 net weekly income. B = £100 fine. See page 334 for table showing fines for different incomes.)

Legal speed limit	Excessive speed mph	Fine	Guideline penalty points
20–30 mph 40–50 mph 60–70 mph	Up to 10 mph Up to 15 mph Up to 20 mph	A	3
20–30 mph 40–50 mph 60–70 mph	From 11–20 mph From 16–25 mph From 21–30 mph	A	4 or 5 or Disqualify for up to 42 days
20–30 mph 40–50 mph 60–70 mph	From 21– 30mph From 26–35 mph From 31–40 mph	B	6 or Disqualify for up to 56 days

For details about the guidelines see MAGISTRATES' COURT SENTENCING GUIDELINES at page 331.

158   STALKING

158.1   Offences Against the Person Act 1861, ss 18, 20 and 47

For penalties see ABH and OFFENCES AGAINST THE PERSON ACT 1861, SS 18, 20

ABH

158.2   *R v Smith* [1998] 1 Cr App Rep (S) 138. The defendant was convicted of ABH. The defendant developed an obsession with a woman with whom he had had a relationship. She made it clear the relationship was completely over. Over 4 years he telephoned her, sent her offensive letters, watched her, loitered outside her place of work, followed her, confronted her even after she told him how distressed she was. He was warned by her employers, the police and was bound over by the Magistrates' Court on several occasions. He brought County Court proceedings against her, which were dismissed and the judge warned him. The psychiatrist said the victim suffered clinical depression, which would require a year's treatment. He also said she would remain mentally scarred for life. The defendant was not mentally ill but had suffered depression at one stage. The judge, unlike the reports, was satisfied he still presented a risk to the victim. Held. Here the judge was entitled to disagree with the writers of the reports. The defendant had no previous convictions. **21 months** substituted for 2½ years.

R v Haywood [1998] 1 Cr App Rep. (S) 358. The defendant pleaded guilty to two counts of ABH and then later pleaded to another ABH. The defendant developed an obsession with a nurse with whom he had had a relationship. After their relationship broke down he shouted at her, he telephoned her, appeared outside her house, hammered on the door, sent a frightening note to her, wrote to her employers saying she was stealing drugs from the hospital and threw a rock through her window. She obtained an injunction and he put her obituary in the local paper. Notices were put up at her place of work, windows broken, her windscreen shattered, and many taxis ordered for her. She became mentally and physically ill. He was arrested and pleaded guilty. It had been over a 2 month period. When in custody he ordered another taxi and arranged for a firm of undertakers to send her a letter treating her as a client. He was convicted of two counts (one before and one after his arrest) of ABH and sentenced to **3 years and 1 year consecutive.** On the day he was sentenced the victim received another letter containing a picture of a gravestone with her details on it saying she died in pain. She continued to receive threatening and frightening letters. He instructed solicitors to falsely claim property from her and telephone messages were left at her place of work. She believed she was going to be killed. He had no other convictions. For these later matters he was sentenced to 3 years consecutive. The first 3 year sentence was reduced to 2 so making the sentence **6 years** not 7 years.

R v Notice [2000] 1 Cr App Rep (S) 75. The defendant was convicted of ABH. The victim aged 48 worked as a manager at a building society. He looked into her office most weekdays, mouthed obscenities at her, watched her leave work and left a note under her windscreen. The company then installed cameras and a security guard. She started to keep a log. The defendant continued to stare and make lewd remarks. He banged on her car roof in stationary traffic and approached her in the street saying he loved her. She was moved to another branch. The defendant was arrested but 7 months later he spoke to her in a street in an aggressive tone. She was counselled for distress and a psychiatrist said she suffered from a generalised anxiety state. The defendant claimed she was harassing him. He had convictions for minor matters including three cases of indecent exposure. He was not mentally ill. There was 19 months between the first and last incident with 16 specified incidents. **15 months** not 2 years.

Wounding (Offences Against the Person Act 1861, s 20)

158.3   Old case. *R v Burstow* [1997] 1 Cr App Rep 144.

STATEMENTS, GIVING FALSE

For the making of false witness statements see **PERVERTING THE COURSE OF JUSTICE/CONTEMPT OF COURT ETC** – *Statement, making a false witness*

STOP

See **FAILING TO STOP/FAILING TO REPORT**

159   SUPPLY OF DRUGS (CLASS A, B AND C)

159.1   Misuse of Drugs Act 1971, s 4(3)(a)–(c) and 5(3)

Triable either way unless the defendant could be sentenced to a 7 year minimum sentence under the Powers of Criminal Courts (Sentencing) Act 2000, s 110(2) when the offence is triable only on indictment. On indictment maximum Life for Class A drugs, 14 years for Class B drugs and 5 years for Class C drugs. Summary maximum 6 months and/or £5,000 for Class A and B drugs and 3 months and/or £2,500 for Class C drugs.

Specified offence for minimum 7 years for third Class A drug trafficking offence.

The categories listed are not the determining factor. What matters is the scale of the dealing, which is not solely determined by the amount of drugs found[1]. As the Court of Appeal has determined that courts are not to distinguish between drugs in the same class[2] all the cases about drugs in the same class can be used to estimate the likely sentence. So if the drug you are considering is heroin, cases for cocaine and ecstasy will provide assistance.

This chapter is divided up into **General, Amphetamine, Cannabis, Cocaine, Ecstasy, Heroin, LSD, Opium, Steroids** and **Permitting premises to be used for the supply of drugs**.

1   *R v Singh* (1988) 10 Cr App Rep (S) 402 at 406.
2   *R v Thompson* [1997] 2 Cr App Rep (S) 223.

Crown Court statistics England and Wales[1] – Crown Court – Males 21+ – Production, supply and possession with intent to supply a controlled drug
159.2

Year	Plea	Total Numbers sentenced	Type of sentence%					Average length of custody[2] (months)
			Discharge	Fine	Community sentence	Suspended sentence	Custody	
Class A								
2000	Guilty	2,092	0%	0%	10%	2%	87%	39
	Not guilty	438	0%	0%	2%	0%	95%	59.1
Class B								
2000	Guilty	1,377	2%	3%	30%	5%	60%	17.1
	Not guilty	270	0%	1%	14%	3%	81%	24
Class C								
2000	Guilty	18	11%	6%	22%	6%	56%	19.1
	Not guilty	3	0%	0%	33%	0%	67%	33

1   Excluding committals for sentence. Source: Crime and Criminal Justice Unit, Home Office Ref: IOS416-02.
2   Excluding life sentences.

Class A – Guideline cases

159.3   *R v Aramah* (1982) 76 Cr App Rep 190 – LCJ. The sentence will largely depend on the degree of involvement, the amount of trafficking and the value of the drugs being handled. It is seldom that a sentence of less than 3 years [now increased, see *R v Singh* (1998) below]will be justified and the nearer the source of supply the defendant is shown to be, the heavier will be the sentence. There may well be cases where sentences similar to those appropriate to large scale importers may be necessary. It is unhappily all too seldom that those big fish amongst the suppliers get caught.

R v Singh (1988) 10 Cr App Rep (S) 402 at 406 – LCJ. The starting point for possession with intent to supply Class A drugs 'is in general **5 years at least**.' following a conviction. It should be noted . . . that the assistance which can be derived from the amount of the drug actually found in the possession of the defendant is limited. It is the scale and nature of the dealing which are the material factors.

Class B – Guideline case

159.4   *R v Aramah* (1982) 76 Cr App Rep 190 – LCJ. Class B particularly cannabis. The supply of massive quantities will justify sentences in the region of **10 years** for those playing anything more than a subordinate role. Otherwise the bracket should be between **1 to 4 years** imprisonment, depending on the scale of the operation. Supplying a number of smaller sellers – wholesale if you like – comes at the top of the bracket. At the lower end will be the retailer of a small amount to a customer. Where there is no commercial motive (for example, where cannabis is supplied at a party), the offence may well be serious enough to justify a custodial sentence.

Magistrates' Court Sentencing Guidelines September 2000 – Class A and B

159.5   Entry point. Are Magistrates' sentencing powers appropriate? Consider the impact on the victim. Example of aggravating factors for the offence are commercial production, large amount, deliberate adulteration, venue, eg prison or educational establishment, sophisticated operation and supply to children. An example of a mitigating factor for the offence is small amount. Examples of mitigation are age, health (physical or mental), co-operation with the police, and genuine remorse. Consider forfeiture and destruction.

For details about the guidelines see MAGISTRATES' COURT SENTENCING GUIDELINES at page 331.

General

Assisting the authorities

159.6   *R v Aramah* (1982) 76 Cr App Rep 190 at 192. It is particularly important that offenders should be encouraged to give information to the police, and a confession of guilt coupled with considerable assistance to the police can properly be marked by a substantial reduction.

Believing the drugs to be of a different class

159.7   *R v Young* [2000] 2 Cr App Rep (S) 248. The defendant pleaded guilty to possession with intent to supply heroin and cannabis. She went to visit her boyfriend who was a prisoner serving life. She was told she was to be searched and she produced two balloons from her underwear containing the drugs. The heroin was 10.7 grams of unknown purity (worth at street value £900 and £1,000) and the cannabis was 25.9 grams. She was told it was a one off and she would be paid £75. She was shocked to learn one contained heroin. She was 45 with no convictions. She had a number of problems. Two sons lived with her and one of them had considerable difficulties. An older son suffered from muscular dystrophy and she had four other sons. She was described as vulnerable, lonely and suffered from low esteem. She was not in good health. She was sentenced on the basis she may not have known it was heroin and she thought it was cannabis. Held. Smuggling drugs into prison is an offence of extreme gravity. It is becoming more prevalent. Had she known it was heroin she could have expected a sentence of 5 years. **2½ years** was entirely correct.

R v Ngiam [2002] 1 Cr App Rep (S) 150. The defendant pleaded guilty to possessing 50 kgs of heroin (at 47%) with intent to supply. She was sentenced on the basis she thought it was cannabis and she was a courier. Held. The fact she believed it was cannabis was a mitigating factor but it did not mean the judge was obliged to sentence her as if it was cannabis.

Class A – Large scale conspiracy

159.8   *A-G's Reference (Nos 90 and 91 of 1998)* [2000] 1 Cr App Rep (S) 32. The defendants S and F pleaded guilty to a conspiracy to supply Class A and Class B drugs. The prosecution case was that the conspiracy from February to September 1997 was to supply large quantities of drugs to wholesalers. They were organisers and brokers. Police put a bug in F's car and police heard reference to amphetamine, ecstasy and cocaine. There was also reference to 50,000 pills, 100 kg, a ton of cannabis, 200 kgs of cannabis and sums of money up to £250,000. There was evidence of F taking large quantities of money to Ireland and Holland. There as mass of observation material and links with those connected with drugs. The defendant S after an extended period of legal argument pleaded on a limited basis, which was not accepted by the prosecution. There was a Newton hearing and the defence accepted the prosecution evidence. F had pleaded earlier. S was 42 and of good character. F was 54 and had a conviction for importing 600 kgs of cannabis for which he received 10 years. Held. Had the offence been contested **14 years** would have been appropriate. With an early plea **12 years** would have been appropriate. Because it was a reference **10 years** each not 6 for S and 5 for F.

Death is caused

159.9   *R v Lucas* [1999] 1 Cr App Rep (S) 78. The defendant pleaded guilty to supplying heroin. He bought three £10 bags of heroin and then joined his girlfriend at home. They drank and he injected himself with heroin. He passed the syringe to his girlfriend. He then went to the local shop to buy beer and left her apparently asleep. On his return he couldn't rouse her and called an ambulance. The paramedics arrived and she was already dead. She was found to have 3½ times the legal limit of alcohol for drivers and a high level of unmetabolised heroin which suggested she died shortly after injecting herself. Death was thought to have been caused by a combination of drugs and alcohol. The defendant was interviewed and made a frank confession. He said she had only used heroin twice before. There was genuine remorse. Following the death he made a number of suicide attempts. He was now drug free. He was 36 with no relevant convictions. He had abused drugs and alcohol for many years. He had been treated from time to time for depression and had not always been very well. **3 years** not 5.

R v Ashford [2000] 1 Cr App Rep (S) 389. The defendant pleaded guilty to supplying heroin at the Magistrates' Court. The defendant was living at a bail hostel and another resident who was very drunk asked for some heroin. The defendant said no, but later after being pestered gave him some. The other resident took it and died during the night. He was sentenced on the basis heroin was not the cause of death. Death was caused by asphyxia after vomit had been swallowed. The defendant had served five custodial sentences for dishonesty. He expressed remorse. The prison report said he was traumatised by the death and he was displaying a very high motivation to address his drug problem. **2 years** not 3.

R v Bull [2000] 2 Cr App Rep (S) 195. The defendant pleaded guilty at the first opportunity to supplying ecstasy. He gave two ecstasy tablets to his sister's boyfriend without charge. The boyfriend and the sister went to a nightclub where they stayed several hours. He drank a number of double whiskeys as well as a lot of water. He was seen to be sweating a lot. The two came home at 2.30pm. He was found dead the next morning. He died of heart failure. It was discovered he had an abnormality of the heart and ecstasy contributed to the heart failure. If he hadn't taken the ecstasy it is unlikely he would have died. When questioned by the police the defendant admitted he had given him the tablets. The defendant was 21 and lived with his parents. He was in regular employment and working hard. He had no convictions and had a deep sense of remorse, which led to a depressive illness and a suicide attempt. Held. He must not receive a disproportionate sentence because of the tragic and appalling consequences of the supply. **9 months** not 18.

R v Dorosz [2001] EWCA Crim 769, [2001] 2 Cr App Rep (S) 476. The defendant pleaded guilty at the first opportunity to two counts of supplying heroin and administering heroin so as to endanger life (Offences Against the Person Act 1861, s 23). The victim visited his flat. At the request of the victim he injected her with heroin. Later she injected herself. One evening she brought heroin and cocaine to his flat. They both injected themselves with heroin and cocaine probably four or five times. He probably gave her two of them and she gave herself the rest. He asked her several times whether she was alright and she always said she was. She seemed to be enjoying it. Apart from one occasion he always put the heroin in the syringe to ensure she was taking less than he was. He left her to sleep on the sofa. In the morning he rang his workplace to say he was unwell and went back to bed. He woke again at 1pm and could not wake her. He called for an ambulance and she could not be resuscitated. Police arrived and he gave them above account although in less detail. An expert said she possibly died from heroin and cocaine. He also said she had taken heroin up her nose, which the defendant said he had not seen. He was 28 and of good character. He gave a full account to the coroner although he was not obliged to. He was arrested 2 months later. He was a computer programmer, which rewarded well. He had developed a fascination with altered states of the mind and had abused drugs including heroin from time to time. He had impressive character witnesses. He was genuinely remorseful and the pre-sentence report said that the event had been devastating for him. Held. There were many factors in his favour. **2½ years** on each count concurrent not 3½.

R v Anderson [2001] EWCA Crim 2613, [2001] All ER (D) 147 (Nov). On a guilty plea the range is 2½ to 3½ years.

See also **MANSLAUGHTER** – *Drug abuse*

Defendant under 18 – Class A

159.10 *R v JM* [2001] 1 Cr App Rep (S) 101. The defendant pleaded guilty to two counts of possession of heroin with intent to supply. The defendant then aged 16 was stopped on his bicycle. He was searched and police found two bags containing 55 grams of heroin at 28–9% purity in his pocket. He was heard to shout out to some youths to contact his mother about a leak which was interpreted as a coded message indicating there were drugs at his home. Police found 13 grams of heroin of 30% purity there. The total was the equivalent of 19 grams at 100% purity. They also seized £9,170 in cash. He had no convictions. The pre-sentence report indicated that he was naïve and had fallen in with bad company. He was keen to demonstrate that he had changed his attitude and keen to pursue his education. On remand he was described as a model resident. Held. This was a serious offence. It was trafficking for a substantial profit. Even taking into account the substantial mitigation **3 years** detention was not manifestly excessive.

R v Hussain [2001] EWCA Crim 246, [2001] 2 Cr App Rep (S) 273. The defendant pleaded guilty to possession of heroin with intent to supply and supplying heroin. An undercover police officer contacted the defendant then aged 15 on his mobile phone and arranged to meet him so he could be supplied with three wraps. The defendant went to the meet on his bicycle and was arrested when he arrived. Six wraps of heroin containing 1.04 grams were found on him. Their value was £100. £57.96 was found at his home. When interviewed he said he had sold 8–10 wraps for £10 before. He said he had found the drugs. He agreed the money at his home was drug profits. He was treated as being of good character. He came from a good home. Held. The judge was right to include an element of deterrent in the sentence. **2 years' detention and training** not 3 years detention.

R v Coudjoe [2001] EWCA Crim 3015, [2002] 2 Cr App Rep (S) 205. The defendant pleaded guilty on the day of his intended trial to possession of heroin and cocaine with intent to supply. Then 15, the defendant was seen by police acting suspiciously and he was searched. In his second and under pair of tracksuit bottoms police found nine wraps of heroin containing 913 mgs at 44% purity and seven wraps of crack cocaine at 56% purity. In his coat pocket was 118 mgs of heroin at 46% purity. He was on bail at the time. The pre-sentence report indicated he did not take hard drugs and had a blasé attitude to the dangers of supplying them. His risk of re-offending was assessed as significant. He had two non-drug relatively minor convictions. His account was rejected in a Newton trial. He was sentenced on the basis that he was going to supply friends. He was not sentenced on the basis he was going to trade on the street. Held. A severe sentence was called for but because of his youth **18 months** detention not 30.

Determining the scale of the supply

159.11   *R v Singh* (1988) 10 Cr App Rep (S) 402 at 406 – LCJ. It should be noted . . . that the assistance which can be derived from the amount of the drug actually found in the possession of the defendant is limited. It is the scale and nature of the dealing which are the material factors.

R v Djahit [1999] 2 Cr App Rep (S) 142. The defendant pleaded guilty to possession of heroin with intent to supply and possession of cannabis. The police arrived to execute a search warrant at his shop and adjoining flat. Two bags of heroin were found in a door panel near his kitchen. Two further bags were found in a kitchen cupboard. A small amount of heroin was found in one of his socks. The total weight was 21.5 grams with a street value of £2,150. The purity was not ascertained. £6,005, a list of names and addresses, a set of scales and bags were found. The defendant accepted the paraphernalia belonged to him and the list did not. Held. One count of possession with intent to supply does not prevent the judge from taking into account the admitted level of dealing as reflected by the sums of money and drugs paraphernalia found. If, however, there is a dispute about the level of dealing and no conviction on a count which reflects dealing over a period of time, then the sentencing judge must exercise care, see for example *R v Canavan* [1998] 1 Cr App Rep (S) 243; *R v Thompson and Smith* [1997] 1 Cr App Rep (S) 289 and *R v Johnson* (1984) 6 Cr App Rep (S) 227.

R v Brown [2000] 1 Cr App Rep (S) 300. The defendant was convicted of being concerned in the supply of controlled drugs and possession with intent to supply. The counts were based on one occasion. The defendant's car was stopped and he was searched. Police found five small bags of cannabis and nearly £700. At his home in his sister's room there were scales, 100 self sealing bags, £7,520 in cash and two Building Society account books in her name. £43,000 was in the accounts. There was no scientific link between any of the money and the defendant. The judge sentenced him on the basis of 'the wider picture.' He was sentenced on the basis of a period of 33 months with profits of £33,000. Held. The judge was bound to sentence for the single offence. The prosecution could have avoided the difficulties if they had drafted six substantive counts against him which the sister faced (assisting another to retain the proceeds of drug trafficking). The sentence was reduced from 3½ years to 9 months consecutive on each making **18 months**.

R v Morris [2001] 2 Cr App Rep (S) 297 at para 18. The amount of Class A or B drug with which a defendant is involved is a very important but not solely the determinative factor in sentencing. Evidence as to the scale of dealing can come from many sources other than the amount with which a defendant is directly connected.

Distinction, don't draw a distinction between drugs in the same class

159.12   *R v Thompson* [1997] 2 Cr App Rep (S) 223. The defendant pleaded guilty to two counts of supplying ecstasy. The judge sentenced him on the basis that ecstasy was more serious than other Class A drugs so passed a higher sentence than the guidelines. Held. The court has said on a number of occasions that there should be no distinction between the various drugs in a class. The sentence was reduced.

Drug abstinence order

159.13 Powers of Criminal Courts (Sentencing) Act 2000, s 58A(1). Where a person is 18 or over the court may make an order requiring the offender to abstain from misusing specified Class A drugs and provide, when instructed to do so a sample to ascertain whether he has any specified Class A drugs in his body. (3) The court must be of the opinion the offender is dependant or has a propensity to misuse specified Class A drugs and the offence is a trigger offence or the misuse of any specified Class A drug caused or contributed to the offence in question. (7) An order shall be for not less than 6 months and not more than 3 years. (9) No order shall be made unless the court has been notified that arrangements for implementing the order are available. [Criminal Justice and Court Services Act 2000, Sch 6 specifies supplying Class A drugs and possession of Class A drugs with intent to supply as trigger offences.]

Drug gang using violence

159.14 *R v Brocklesby* [1999] 1 Cr App Rep (S) 80. The defendants D and P were brothers and were convicted of conspiracy to supply heroin and crack cocaine, wounding Andrew Mournian (s 18), falsely imprisoning Andrew Mournian, ABH on Philip Parker, falsely imprisoning Philip Parker, kidnap and falsely imprisoning Natham Burton and kidnapping and falsely imprisoning Anthony Newton. D was also convicted of wounding Philip Parker (s 18) and having a sawn-off shotgun with intent to cause fear to Philip Parker. The two defendants were the organisers and principles of a highly successful and lucrative heroin and crack cocaine business. They only supplied individual users but engaged others to do the selling. [The judgment may be missing a 'not' before 'only in the preceding sentence.] They had hundreds of customers and made an estimated minimum of £8,000 a week. The blatant drug dealing was only possible because of the fear they and their henchmen generated. The fear was generated by extreme violence, nothing short of a reign of terror involving guns and knives in order to protect the empire and discourage or punish those perceived to be informers. P was more prominent. Andrew Mournian was thought possibly to have been an informer. He was held prisoner and D slashed his arm with a knife and threatened to stab him in the eye. P tried to break his leg with the back of an axe. He was punched and kicked with D saying, 'Let's fucking kill him.' D sewed up each arm with ordinary thread because of the loss of blood. This caused great pain and distress. D also bit his nose making threats.

Later D and another attacked Philip Parker a drug addict by throwing knives at and into his leg. The blade came out the other side. The knife was held to his eye and threats to kill him were made. A knife was thrown which fractured his ankle. A sawn-off shotgun was held at his head moved a few inches and discharged. After returning from hospital he was accused of stealing money. He was punched and kicked. His face was burnt with a soldering iron. His tooth was damaged with a knife. He smashed a glass window trying to escape and cut himself badly. Natham Burton aged 17, was a customer and owed them money. He was kidnapped off the street and taken to a house. He was threatened with knives and knives were thrown at his feet. The defendants set others on to him to punch and kick him. He managed to escape through a window. Anthony Newton was taken by force to a house. He was punched and told he was a police informer. He was hit with knives and head butted. He fell backwards into a bath, which contained water. P told D to electrocute him. A radio with mains leads was held over the bath. Newton managed to run to a nearby house but was caught and attacked again. He was imprisoned overnight. A police officer found him next day.

The defendants were arrested. D was 31 with an extensive criminal past. He had convictions for robbery, violence, firearms and drugs. P had a similar record and some of the offences had been committed jointly. Their longest sentences were 5 and 4½ for robbery respectively. D received 7 years for the drug conspiracy and 7 years for one of the kidnapping offences and 7 years for the firearm offence all consecutive making 21 years in all. P was sentenced to 9 years for the drug conspiracy and 6, 3 and 4 years consecutive for the other incidents making 22 years in all. Held. The only question was whether the totals were manifestly excessive for this campaign of terror, designed to protect the lucrative drug operation. These were two gangsters who cared nothing for those they hurt. They used fear, violence and brutality to a quite dreadful extent. They showed no mercy. We are quite satisfied the sentences were not excessive.

R v Smith Re S [2001] EWCA Crim 1812, [2002] 1 Cr App Rep (S) 386 at 394. The defendants C and S pleaded guilty to kidnapping. A drugs deal went wrong and one of those involved, J and his family fled fearing J would take the blame for the money and drugs which disappeared. J was arrested and bailed. S, C and another kidnapped J and drove him along a motorway demanding the return of the drugs and the money. They 'thumped' him and threatened to kill him and throw him out of the moving car. C made a number of calls on his mobile suggesting someone who might enjoy torturing J for fun. J was handcuffed and taken to a building where he was assaulted. After the three left he remained a prisoner for 24 hours until a ransom was paid. J made a statement to the police, which contained false details about the culprits and said he didn't want any action taken. Later he gave a full and true statement. There was considerable delay before sentence. **3 years** not 4.

R v Bediako and Martin [2001] EWCA Crim 1967, [2001] All ER (D) 109 (Aug). Manslaughter, two counts of kidnapping and two counts of false imprisonment. Held. 7 years reduced from 14.

Entrapment (and similar situations)

159.15   *R v Springer* [1999] 1 Cr App Rep (S) 217. The defendant pleaded guilty at the Magistrates' Court to three charges of supplying heroin and was committed to the Crown Court. The defendant was a suspected drug dealer. The police tested their suspicions by making three telephone calls. He was asked, 'Have you got anything.' He replied, 'Yeah,' and arrangements were made to meet him. In response to each call a meeting was arranged and about 1.5 grams of heroin was supplied. The calls were recorded and the meetings were videoed. The defence argued that he was entitled to a discount because of entrapment. Held. There was a need for the police to adopt this method of detection. There was need for there to be more than one supply to provide evidence he was a dealer. This was not a case of entrapping a suspect into supplying drugs who would otherwise never have engaged in that activity. *R v Underhill* [1979] 1 Cr App Rep (S) 270 at 272 applied. Here there was legitimate police activity and not activity that could provide mitigation or a reduction at all. (For further details see later in this section *Heroin – Class A – Street dealer*)

R v Tonnessen [1998] 2 Cr App Rep (S) 328. The defendant pleaded guilty to supplying heroin. The defendant was approached by a man who claimed to know her. He was accompanied by two others who turned out to be from the *News of the World*. They said they worked for a Sheikh and they were instructed to buy drugs. She was a heroin addict and a cannabis user and said they were widely available. They said they wanted to buy heroin and asked her whether she was prepared to get it for them. They gave her £50 and she bought four wraps of heroin. She and a friend spent the rest of the evening with them. Immediately after her name and photograph appeared in the paper. The police felt obliged to arrest her and she admitted the offence. After the publicity she was assaulted and received a threat to her life. She was 31 and had already served a prison sentence for an unrelated offence. She had no supply convictions. She suffered from a serious pre-cancerous condition. The judge did not refer to the involvement of agents provocateurs and appeared not to have taken it into account. The defence said there could be considerable mitigation where it can be shown that the offence would not otherwise have been committed. It is legitimate for policemen to entrap criminals. When the entrapment is by journalist even more consideration and more weight should be given. Held. We consider there is substance in those submissions. However it merited immediate custody. We cannot ignore she was set up. If these men had been police officers that would provide mitigation. Different considerations must apply to investigatory journalists. Their purpose was perfectly honourable. But we feel the public would be left with a sense of unease by the identification in the paper. The consequences were most unfortunate. It is appropriate to reflect the entrapment in the sentence. It should have been expressly mentioned in the remarks. In the exceptional circumstances we reduce the sentence from **12 months** to 6.

R v Mayeri [1999] 1 Cr App Rep (S) 304. The defendant pleaded guilty at the earliest opportunity to four counts of supplying ecstasy. One tablet was involved in each case. Four undercover police officers approached him in a nightclub and he agreed to sell them a tablet for £10. He claimed there was an element of entrapment. The defendant relied on *R v Tonnessen* [1998] 2 Cr App Rep (S) 328. Held. The entrapment argument is not a good one. Where undercover officers discover a man is prepared to sell drugs by approaching him it is not a matter the courts need normally take into account as amounting to entrapment. It might be said 'Seller beware.' These premises are frequently used to sell drugs.

Indictment/Charge, must restrict yourself to what is alleged in

159.16 *R v Twisse* [2001] 2 Cr App Rep (S) 37. We recognise the importance of only sentencing for the criminality proved or admitted. This established principle of law is now reinforced by the European Convention of Human Rights, art 6. If the prosecution can prove the defendant has been acting as a supplier over a substantial time it can put the court in a position to sentence properly by one of three ways. (1) charging a number of offences of supply or possession supply at different dates; (2) charging a conspiracy over a prescribed period; (3) charging him with being concerned in the supply over a specified period contrary to the Misuse of Drugs Act 1971, s 4(3)(b). If the indictment is not drawn as we have suggested and the defendant does not ask for offences to be taken into consideration judges should refrain from drawing inferences to the extent of the defendant's criminal activities, even if those inferences are inescapable having regard to admissions made or equipment found. In other words a defendant charged with one offence of supply cannot receive a more substantial sentence because it is clear he has been dealing for 9 months: but the court is not required to blind itself to the obvious. If he claims that the occasion in question was an isolated transaction, that submission can be rejected. He can be given the appropriate sentence for that one offence without the credit he would receive if he really were an isolated offender.

Informing on the defendant, family

159.17 *R v Catterall* (1993) 14 Cr App Rep (S) 724. The defendant's father called the police because he and his wife were concerned the defendant was under the influence of drink or drugs. They did it entirely in the interests of their son. Held. His father and mother care so much about his future they were prepared to disclose the offences to the police. They are likely to support his efforts to give up his habit. The court should take those facts into account and give him a further discount. The sentence will be reduced from 4 years to **2 years**, a reduction entirely due to his father's action.

R v Ferrett [1998] 2 Cr App Rep (S) 384. The defendant pleaded guilty to four counts of supplying ecstasy, a count of supplying amphetamine and two counts of supplying cannabis. A teenage girl died after taking ecstasy and amphetamine. The defendant's mother and others told the police he might have been the supplier of the drugs. The defendant was interviewed and denied supplying the deceased but admitted supplying another. He was 18 when sentenced and of good character. Held. A total of **5 years** would have been appropriate. However applying *R v Catterall* [1993] 14 Cr App Rep (S) 724 he is entitled to a further discount because of the credit due to his family for taking the course they did. So **4½ years** YOI not 7. (For further details see **Ecstasy – Class A – *Retail supply***)

Innocuous substances, material turns out to be

159.18 *R v Porter* [1999] 2 Cr App Rep (S) 205. The defendant pleaded guilty to attempting to possess amphetamine with intent to supply at the Magistrates' Court. Police watched someone walk from a car to the defendant at a railway station. They shook hands and walked to the car. The defendant got in and left shortly after carrying a plastic bag. The police stopped him and he struggled. In the bag were 4,063 tablets and he said they were speed (ie amphetamines). In fact the tablets were not a controlled drug. If they had been amphetamine they would have been worth between £8,000 and £12,000. When interviewed he said his job was to travel from Wales and collect the drugs. He was 27. **12 months** not 30.

Persistent Class A supplier etc – Minimum 7 years

159.19 Powers of Criminal Courts (Sentencing) Act 2000, s 110. Where a person is convicted of a class A drug trafficking offence committed after 30 November 1999 and was 18 or over and he has been convicted of two other class A drug trafficking offences one of which was committed after he had been convicted of the other the court shall impose a sentence of imprisonment of at least 7 years except where the court is of the opinion that there are particular circumstances which relate to any of the offences or to the offender which would make it unjust. [This section is summarised and is slightly amended by Criminal Justice and Court Services Act 2000.]

Persistent Class A supplier etc – Minimum 7 years – Plea of guilty

159.20 Powers of the Criminal Courts (Sentencing) Act 2000, s 152(3). Where a sentence is to be imposed under the Powers of the Criminal Courts (Sentencing) Act 2000, s 110 after a plea of guilty nothing in that section shall prevent the court from imposing a sentence of 80% or more of the minimum period. [Section summarised. The section means if s/he pleads guilty the court can impose a sentence, which is 80% or more of the minimum term.]

R v Brown [2000] 2 Cr App Rep (S) 435. The defendant pleaded guilty at the first opportunity to supplying crack cocaine, supplying heroin and possession of cocaine. Police were conducting a drugs operation in the Kings Cross area of London and the defendant gave an officer a piece of paper with a telephone number on it and told them to call it if they wanted drugs. An officer rang the number and the defendant told them where they should meet. Two officers went to flat as directed and one purchased 164 mgs of crack for £20 and another officer asked for heroin and crack but was told there was no crack left and was given 105 mgs of heroin for £20. When the defendant was arrested nearly 3 months later he had 1.6 mgs of crack on him. He was 45 and had three convictions for supplying drugs, two of which were for Class A drugs. He also had two convictions for possession of an offensive weapon and one for possession of a bladed article. He was sentenced to 6½ years for the supply counts with 6 months consecutive for a breach of a CSO. There was a concurrent sentence for the possession offence. The defence said either the Judge started too high or failed to give the full 20% discount for the guilty plea. Held. We agree and as he didn't indicate which we adjust the supply sentence to **5 years 8 months** and because of totality the 6 months should run concurrently.

Persistent Class A supplier etc – Minimum 7 years – Unjust, meaning

159.21   *R v Hickson* [2001] EWCA Crim 1595, [2002] 1 Cr App Rep (S) 298. One is not looking for exceptional circumstances; one is looking at the particular circumstances of the offence and the offender.

Persistent Class A supplier etc – Minimum 7 years – Cases

159.22   *R v Harvey* [2000] 1 Cr App Rep (S) 368. The defendant was convicted of supplying two small wraps of heroin. Each was worth £20. He had been arrested in a police drugs operation in the Kings Cross area of London. He was on bail for drug offences at the time. He was 57 with convictions going back to 1962. The first 16 appearances were for dishonesty. From March 1997 they included drug offences. Those included possessing cannabis with intent to supply, conspiracy to supply drugs, a possession of heroin with to supply (for which he received 6 years) and supplying heroin (for which he received 4 years). The judge imposed the 7 year minimum sentence saying that would not be unjust. Held. Applying *R v Munson* (23 November 1998, unreported) (where a defendant in very similar circumstances save that that defendant made a late guilty plea had his 7 year sentence described as a 'tough sentence, but. . .a deliberately tough sentence.' and one that was not manifestly excessive.) The sentence is not manifestly excessive. Parliament has chosen 7 years as the standard penalty on a third conviction, which meets the conditions in the section. The object is plainly to require courts to impose a sentence of at least 7 years where but for the section they would not or might not do so. The judge was entitled to pass the **7 years** minimum sentence.

[Since this case was decided the rules about the imposition of mandatory sentences have been considered under the Human Rights legislation by *R v Offen (No 2)* [2001] 1 Cr App Rep 372. Those changes are not dealt with here.]

R v Stenhouse [2000] 2 Cr App Rep (S) 386. The defendant pleaded guilty to supplying heroin on four separate occasions. A police officer called a number and was told to ring back in 15 minutes. He did so and spoke to the defendant. They agreed to meet. The defendant was given £10 and the undercover officer was given a wrap, which contained 52 mgs of heroin. The other offences were similar. He had convictions for possession of drugs and 2 for supplying Class A drugs. The last conviction was in 1997 for supplying one methadone tablet for which he was given probation at the Magistrates' Court. He had been in custody from December 1998 to July 1999 when he was released because of the Custody Time Limit provisions. He was sentence in December 1999 to the 7 year minimum term. Since his arrest he had made valiant attempts to conquer his drug addiction. Held. His efforts to break his drug habit were rare and he should be encouraged to continue with his efforts. The sentence because of the combination of circumstances was unjust so **3 years** substituted.

Pretending innocuous material was a prohibited drug

159.23   *R v Chambers and Barnett* [1999] 1 Cr App Rep (S) 262. The defendants C and B pleaded guilty to offering to supply ecstasy and going equipped to cheat. The defendants went to a rave with some innocuous tablets. They tried to sell them as ecstasy. B tried to sell one to an undercover police officer. C was 26 with no convictions. B was 19 with a conviction for deception. It was contended it was a deception case not tainted by any stain of the Drug Trafficking Act offences. Held. We don't entirely agree with that submission as it still contributed to the raves plus drug scene which the police and courts are trying to stamp out. However, no damage and possibly some good would have been done to the purchases. **12 months** imprisonment and YOI not 18 months.

R v Cargill [1999] 2 Cr App Rep (S) 421. The defendant pleaded guilty to offering to supply cocaine. Police mounted a surveillance operation in Moss Side. There were 13 days of video evidence and he appeared in only one of them. Because there was no link with others being sentenced the Court of Appeal decided to look at the facts of his case in isolation. An undercover officer approached someone and asked for 'a stone.' He said he had none and the defendant approached and sold her a wrap for £20. It was 208 grams of paracetamol. The defendant later accepted a stone meant crack cocaine. He was 38 and had been addicted to drugs particularly cocaine for some time. He had a long list of convictions mainly for dishonesty to finance his addiction. He was in breach of his licence following his release from a 2½ year sentence for robbery. There were 224 days left to serve. He had no drug convictions. Held. It was an important the sentence reflected that what was sold was not a controlled drug. 18 months was too long. **12 months** substituted.

R v Tugwell [2001] EWCA Crim 719, [2001] 2 Cr App Rep (S) 501. The defendant pleaded guilty to possession of cannabis and ecstasy and two counts of offering to supply fake ecstasy. Held. Supplying fake drugs is not simply a case of obtaining money by fraud but it involves a lesser degree of criminality than supplying real drugs.

R v McNab [2001] EWCA Crim 1605, [2002] 1 Cr App Rep (S) 304. The defendants Mc, L, B and M were convicted of conspiracy to offer to supply ecstasy. The conspiracy was to offer people in nightclubs large amounts of fake ecstasy, which in fact contained various mixtures of ketamine, ephedrine and caffeine. They were non-controlled and but did have dangerous side effects. Tablet presses were imported from Thailand and the pills were given dove and other motifs to make them look like ecstasy. M was the main player. L operated the laboratory company and was the financial backer and controller of the conspiracy. There were four tablet factories. B played a main part liasing between L's company and the various makers of the tablets. He also organised deliveries and the provision of minders. Mc was involved in the Scottish end and played a slightly smaller part. The judge said the lowest figure for the value of the tablets ran into six figures and the potential into seven figures. It was a fraud on a massive scale. Held. The judge was right to start by looking at the sentences for drug trafficking rather than fraud. It is not just a fraud. These drugs were not harmless. There is a danger that people who buy fake pills may not find the effect they want and then when they buy the real thing they take increased quantities and put themselves in serious danger even death. To suggest the purchasers are not innocent victims because they were buying illegal drugs is misguided. They are the real victims of the drugs trade even if they are not innocent. The 2 year maximum for ketamine is not a material factor. It couldn't relate to a conspiracy of this size. There can be no criticism of M's **11 years** and L and B's **9 years**. (Mc received 3 years and 11 months and only appealed his conviction.)

See also **Cocaine – Class A** – *Offering to supply/Deceiving the buyer* and **Ecstasy – Class A** – *Offering to supply/Deceiving the buyer*

Prisoners, supply to – Class A – Cocaine or heroin – Guideline remarks

159.24   *R v Bower* [2001] EWCA Crim 2040, [2002] 1 Cr App Rep (S) 483. The message has to go out to those who succumb to threat or persuasion to take drugs into prison that if they do so they will lose their liberty for a very long time indeed. Good character and absence of previous convictions notwithstanding.

Prisoners, supply to – Class A – Cocaine or heroin – Cases

159.25   *R v Prince* [1996] 1 Cr App Rep (S) 335. The defendant pleaded guilty to possessing heroin and methadone with intent to supply. The heroin count was a specimen count. The defendant's son was a heroin addict and in prison. He supplied the son twice with heroin. His flat was searched and police found ten wraps of heroin (27% purity) weighing 0.49 grams in total. He admitted he was going to supply his son with the wraps. They also found some methadone, which he said he was going to supply his son's girlfriend. He was 59 with effectively no convictions. He was not in good health. Held. The supply of Class A or indeed any drugs to a prisoner is a most serious offence. A lengthy custodial sentence was required. **5 years** was right. [Although this an old case it is regularly used by the Court of Appeal when appeals are heard.]

R v Slater [1998] 2 Cr App Rep (S) 415. The defendant pleaded guilty to possessing heroin and dihydrocodeine (Class B) with intent to supply. He went to visit his brother in prison and officers found 198 mg of heroin and ten dihydrocodeine tablets on him. He said they were for his brother. He was 20 and had convictions and had had a custodial sentence (9 months). There were no drug convictions (not drug-related and not stated). He was on probation. The pre-sentence report said he was maturing and had huge family problems. His mother was ill and he had to do many of her duties. He was very much influenced by his elder brothers and had been able to stop taking drugs. Held. It is a most serious offence particularly for Class A. Taking into account all the mitigation **3 years** detention was not manifestly excessive.

R v Batt [1999] 2 Cr App Rep (S) 223. The defendant was convicted of possessing heroin with intent to supply. She went to prison to smuggle 4.9 grams of heroin to her son. She was 60. She fought her case on the basis she had been threatened. She was suffering from depression and was at serious risk of having a nervous breakdown and possible suicide attempts. She had an unfortunate background. She has been traumatised by a series of events, which have occurred in her family. Two of her sons were imprisoned for robbery. Another son had a serious accident in Germany such that they considered turning off his life support machine. He has severe brain damage and will require 24 hour nursing for the rest of his life. She is playing a major part in that. That has left her in a vulnerable and exhausted state. Another son suffered a brain haemorrhage and died leaving a wife and two children. She was unable to come to terms with that. Her daughter suffers from epilepsy. Her brother aged 69 who lives next door to her is disabled. She had served the equivalent of a year in prison. The defence did not contend the 3 year sentence was wrong but asked for the sentence to be suspended as an act of mercy. Held. The rejection of the defence of duress does not mean there was no element of pressure. We have well in mind the case of *R v Prince* [1996] 1 Cr App Rep (S) 335. This is an exceptional case. We do not want to undermine the seriousness of the offence as set out in *R v Prince* [1996], but the factors here enable us to take an exceptional course. We don't criticise the judge but she has now served a significant period in custody. 3 years was in no way inappropriate. However, **2 years suspended** substituted.

R v Ellingham [1999] 2 Cr App Rep (S) 243. The defendant pleaded guilty to possessing heroin with intent to supply at the Magistrates' Court. She went to visit her boyfriend in prison. When she was searched the drugs were found in her mouth. It was 0.1 grams with a street value of £10. She admitted it in interview. She said her boyfriend had said he would kill himself in a call 2 days earlier. She was 20 and of good character. Held. Her good character was of comparatively little mitigating significance. The sentence of **3 years** YOI was not excessive applying *R v Prince* [1996] 1 Cr App Rep (S) 335.

R v Appleton [1999] 2 Cr App Rep (S) 289. The defendant pleaded guilty to possessing heroin with intent to supply and three counts of possessing Class B drugs. He was a serving prisoner who had his cell searched. Officers found two plastic wraps, each containing ten foil wraps of heroin (total of 0.74 grams at 32%), two foil wraps of heroin (0.15 grams at 31%) and a cling film wrap of 0.56 grams of amphetamine sulphate. He was arrested and admitted the offences. He was sentenced on the basis that he was looking after the drugs for someone else. He was 29 and was nearing the end of a 7 year sentence for robbery, ABH, using a firearm to resist arrest and possessing a firearm. He had four court appearances before that mainly for dishonesty. There were no convictions for drugs. Held. The court supports a policy of giving long additional sentences to those involved with drugs in prison. They will be dealt with severely as shown in *R v Prince* [1996] 1 Cr App Rep (S) 335. The fact he was minding them rather than dealing does not necessarily mean a shorter sentence. Those who mind the drugs prevent the real dealers being caught. Those that do the minding and them protect the dealer cannot receive any mercy. It would be different if the person was prepared to name the dealer and assist the police. Otherwise we see little reason to reduce the sentence. The **5 years** sentence was entirely appropriate and we do not wish to alter the message we wish to send out by saying the total sentence of 12 years is too long.

R v Hamilton [2000] 1 Cr App Rep (S) 91. The defendant pleaded guilty to possession with intent to supply 6.02 grams of heroin. On Christmas Eve she visited an associate of her husband in prison. The associate was serving 6 years for drugs' offences. A sniffer dog gave a positive indication and later she handed over a knotted condom with the heroin from her mouth. She was arrested and admitted the offence in interview. She was 32 and of good character. She was the sole carer of her three children aged 15, 10 and 9. The youngest had both physical and learning difficulties, which had led to behavioural problems. Her husband had indicated that if she help him with the associate he would spend Christmas with her. That time was a particularly difficult time of year as it was the anniversary of the death of her 2-year-old son who died in a cot death tragedy. She was on anti-depressant medication and receiving bereavement counselling. Held. Mitigation features happen in almost every case. It is often the wife, the ex-wife or the mother of children who is selected. Applying *R v Prince* [1996] 1 Cr App Rep (S) 335 there were not here exceptional circumstances for the sentence to be suspended. **2 years** upheld.

R v Cowap [2000] 1 Cr App Rep (S) 284. The defendant pleaded guilty to possession with intent to supply ½ gram of cocaine. Previously she had pleaded not guilty and the case had been listed for trial. She went to visit her ex-boyfriend in prison. An officer noticed something in her mouth. She struggled but the drugs were retrieved. The cocaine was 96% pure and worth between £40 and £50. She was 31 and unemployed. She had quite an appalling record for unrelated offences mainly for dishonesty and prostitution. She was addicted to heroin and/or cocaine. The judge said considering her background she was well aware of the risks she was taking. Held. Even taking into account her late plea and the pressure from her former boyfriend **4 years** could not be criticised.

R v Young [2000] 2 Cr App Rep (S) 248. The defendant pleaded guilty to possession with intent to supply heroin and cannabis. She went to visit her boyfriend who was a prisoner serving life. She was told she was to be searched and she produced two balloons from her underwear containing the drugs. The heroin was 10.7 grams of unknown purity (worth at street value £900 and £1,000) and the cannabis was 25.9 grams. She was told it was a one off and she would be paid £75. She was shocked to learn one contained heroin. She was 45 with no convictions. She had a number of problems. Two sons lived with her and one of them had considerable difficulties. An older son suffered from muscular dystrophy and she had four other sons. She was described as vulnerable, lonely and suffered from low esteem. She was not in good health. She was sentenced on the basis she may not have known it was heroin and she thought it was cannabis. Held. Smuggling drugs into prison is an offence of extreme gravity. It is becoming more prevalent. Had she known it was heroin she could have expected a sentence of 5 years. **2½ years** was entirely correct.

R v Bower [2001] EWCA Crim 2040, [2002] 1 Cr App Rep (S) 483. The defendant pleaded guilty to supplying 340 mgs of heroin to her boyfriend in prison. She was observed passing it to him on CCTV. Its street value was £28. In interview she said her boyfriend had threatened her with violence. She was 18 and of good character. The pre-sentence report and the psychiatrist's report said she was quiet, shy and vulnerable and that the boyfriend was older and of a violent disposition. In prison she was doing extremely well, obtaining qualifications and rebuilding her relationship with her mother. Held. **2 years** YOI was severe but not manifestly excessive.

Prisoners, supply to – Class A – Prison officers

159.26 *R v Whenman* [2001] EWCA Crim 328, [2001] 2 Cr App Rep (S) 395. The defendant pleaded guilty to three counts of supplying heroin and possession with intent to supply heroin. They were specimen counts representing 15–20 transactions. They all related to the same prisoner. The defendant was arrested and said the prisoner had some information on him and he was pressurised first to supply cannabis and then heroin. He said threats were made which included violence to younger members of his family. A package was sent to an address and the defendant was called and told where to go. He collected it and took it to the prison kitchen and passed the package over in the whites room. He received no payment. Police found one of the packages and it contained 4 grams of heroin. The defendant was 45 and of good character. The risk of re-offending was assessed as significant. He had three character witnesses and a certificate for nomination for a prison award. Held. The supply of Class A drugs to a serving prisoner is a most serious offence, *R v Prince* [1996] 1 Cr App Rep (S) 335. We have considered the mitigating and aggravating features and **7 years** was not excessive.

Prisoners, supply to – Cannabis

159.27 *R v Freeman* [1997] 2 Cr App Rep (S) 224 – The defendant pleaded guilty to possessing cannabis resin with intent to supply. He went to a prison to visit an inmate. He was found to have a packet with two balloons filled with in all 11 grams. of cannabis resin worth £15. He was 33 with many previous for dishonesty and had been sentenced to custody twice; one of which was for attempted burglary for which he got 6 months. He had no drug convictions. In 1993 he suffered severe injuries to his leg caused by a car accident. The condition was permanent and he was badly disabled. Held. Taking drugs into prison is serious and deterrent sentences are required. Considering *R v Aramah* (1982) 4 Cr App Rep (S) 407, which said the bracket for small scale dealing in cannabis resin was 1–4 years, **15 months** not 21.

R v Doyle [1998] 1 Cr App Rep (S) 79. The defendant pleaded guilty to possessing cannabis resin with intent to supply. She went to visit her boyfriend in prison and she was strip searched after a sniffer dog made a detection. 8.7 and 10.4 grams of cannabis resin was found in her underclothes. It was worth about £70. She was under a fair amount of emotional pressure because she had found him very depressed and possibly suicidal when she had visited him before. She was 28 and had lost both her jobs, which had caused her and her elderly parents difficulty and distress. She is now unable to pay the mortgage on the parents' house and the parents were in poor health. She had no convictions. Held. The need to deter is of very great importance. Taking into account the extenuating circumstances **12 months** not 18.

R v Farooqi [1999] 1 Cr App Rep (S) 379. The defendant pleaded guilty to possessing cannabis with intent to supply at the Magistrates' Court. He went to visit a friend in prison. A sniffer dog alerted the staff and a £15 wrap of cannabis was found. It contained 1.91 grams. He admitted the offence. He said the previous night he had been given the package by three men who threatened to harm his family if he didn't carry out their instructions. He was 22 and single. He lived with his parents and was unemployed. As a juvenile he had a conviction for robbery for which he was fined. In 1996 he was convicted of possessing cannabis and obstructing the police. In 1997 he was convicted of blackmail and he was given a combination order. He had been the victim of a violent assault and suffered from depression and headaches. The risk of re-offending was described as minimal. Held. Even where the quantity is small the offence should be treated seriously. A sentence of **12 months** is likely to be passed even on a plea. 6 months is not the tariff in these cases. The appeal must be dismissed.

Purity – What is required?

159.28   *R v Morris* [2001] 2 Cr App Rep (S) 297. We have considered a large number of authorities. The relevant principles are the amount of Class A or B drug with which a defendant is involved is a very important but not solely the determinative factor in sentencing. Evidence as to the scale of dealing can come from many sources other than the amount with which a defendant is directly connected. Amounts should generally be based on the weight of drug involved at 100% purity, not its street value: see *R v Aramah* (1982) 4 Cr App Rep (S) 407 at 409 and *R v Ronchetti* [1998] 2 Cr App Rep (S) 100 at 104 as to cannabis*; R v Aranguren* (1994) 99 Cr App Rep 347 at 351 as to cocaine; *R v Warren and Beeley* [1996] 1 Cr App Rep 120 at 123A as to ecstasy and *R v Wijs* [1999] 1 Cr App Rep (S) 181 at 183 as to amphetamine. But, in some circumstances, reference to the street value of the same weight of different drugs may be pertinent, simply by way of cross check. Eg 1 kg of LSD is worth very much more than 1 kg of heroin, and 1 kg of amphetamine is worth very much more than 1 kg of cannabis. Weight depends on purity. The purity of drugs such as cocaine and heroin, and amphetamine powder, can be appropriately determined only by analysis. The weight of drugs such as ecstasy, in tablet, or LSD, in dosage, form, can generally be assessed by reference to the number of tablets or doses and, currently, an assumed average purity of 100 mgs of ecstasy (*R v Warren and Beeley* [1996] 1 Cr App Rep (S) 233 at 236) and 50 micrograms of LSD (*R v Hurley* [1998] 1 Cr App Rep (S) 299 at 304) unless prosecution or defence, by expert evidence, show the contrary (*R v Warren and Beeley* [1996] 1 Cr App Rep (S) 233 at 236, and *R v McPhail* [1997] 1 Cr App Rep (S) 321 at 322) Purity analysis is essential for sentencing purposes for cases of importation, or in other circumstances, where 500 grams or more of cocaine, heroin or amphetamine are seized. It may be desirable in cases where quantities less than 500 grams of those substances are seized. But, bearing in mind the cost of purity analysis and that analysis may cause delay, purity analysis will not generally be required where a defendant is in possession of only a small consistent with either personal use or only limited supply to others. In such a case the court can be expected to sentence only on the basis of a low level of retail dealing, but taking into account all the other circumstances of the particular case. But, as purity can indicate proximity to the primary source of supply, if there is reason for the prosecution to believe that a defendant in possession of a small quantity of drugs is close to the source of supply and is wholesaling rather than retailing, it will be necessary for purity analysis to be undertaken before a court can be invited to sentence on this more serious basis. In the absence of purity analysis or expert evidence, it is not open to a court to find or assume levels of purity, except in the case of ecstasy and LSD in the circumstances to which we have referred.

Retailing, low level – Class A

159.29   *R v Djahit* [1999] 2 Cr App Rep (S) 142. The appropriate sentence following a trial for low level retailing of a Class A drug, with no relevant previous convictions, ie selling to other addicts in order to be able to buy drugs for his own consumption and to earn enough to live very modestly is about 6 years. A plea at the earliest opportunity will reduce the sentence by about ¼ to ⅓. Personal circumstances may reduce it further. If the defendant is able to show that he is no longer addicted to Class A drugs then a reduction may also be appropriate.

R v Twisse [2001] 2 Cr App Rep (S) 37. It has been said that the *R v Djahit* [1999] (see above) decision does not lie entirely comfortably alongside what has been said in a number of other cases which suggest a longer sentence. We have looked at a wide range of reported cases, which suggest a longer sentence. All indicate a sentence of between **5 and 7 years**: in other words the offender may expect about 6 years which can be increased or mitigated. We are persuaded it is not necessary to review the existing tariff. As has been pointed out in *R v Djahit* the present level of sentencing does seem to bear a sensible relationship with those importing quantities of drugs.

Retailing to the vulnerable or young

159.30   *R v Djahit* [1999] 2 Cr App Rep (S) 142. Selling to the vulnerable or the young will increase the sentence, see *R v Barnsby* [1998] 2 Cr App Rep (S) 222 and *R v Doyle* (1988) 10 Cr App Rep (S) 5. Introducing people to heroin will also increase the sentence, see *R v Singh* (1988) 10 Cr App Rep (S) 402.

R v Kitching [2000] 2 Cr App Rep (S) 194. The defendant was convicted of five charges of supplying cannabis resin and herbal cannabis. He was a cleaner at Ampleforth School. Pupils approached him for cannabis and he supplied a 17 year old with £10's worth and £45's worth for which he charged £5 delivery. He supplied a 15 year old with £18.50's worth. Another 17 year old was sold £20's worth on two occasions. A 16 and 17 year old were each supplied with £20's worth. One of the pupils informed the school and the defendant was arrested. He was 28 and of good character. Held. The judge was in error to describe the offences as committed in breach of trust. The offences were very serious which merited immediate custody. This was less serious than *R v Nolan* (1992) 13 Cr App Rep (S) 144 so **18 months** on each concurrent not 2 years.

Warehouseman – Class A

159.31   *R v Harvey* [1997] 2 Cr App Rep (S) 306. The defendant pleaded guilty to possessing ecstasy with intent to supply. He and his co-defendant were working in a café and police searched the premises and found 900 ecstasy tablets. The defendant had started work there the night beforehand was so short of cash he was living in his car. He was told the drugs belonged to a drug baron and understood he would be in danger if he didn't comply with the request to assist. Following a Newton hearing the judge indicated that the basis for sentence was that the café was a wholesale distribution point where the 900 tablets were split for onward dispatch. The defendant was neither an organiser nor a chief. He was a warehouseman with a duty to repackage the goods for later collection. There was nothing to suggest this wasn't his first occasion he was involved, but there was clearly substantial trust placed in him. He did it for an undisclosed benefit, which might have been to keep his job. He was desperately short of money. The judge found he had made no benefit. The previous convictions were disregarded. He had spent his youth in children's homes. Held.

Because of the plea, his personal circumstances and the sentence on the co-defendant **3½ years** not 5.

For basic principles about the different drugs see CANNABIS, ECSTASY, HEROIN, LSD and OPIUM

Amphetamine – Class B

159.32 *R v Wijs Re Rae* [1999] 1 Cr App Rep (S) 181 at 185. The defendant pleaded guilty to two counts of possessing cannabis and a count of possessing temazepan. He was convicted of possessing amphetamine with intent to supply. Police officers stopped a vehicle in which he was a passenger. He gave false answers. Inside a carrier bag under the seat in front of him was found a large block of amphetamine. It had a dry weight of 606 grams (95% pure), the equivalent at 100% purity of 575 grams and a street value of £75,600. He was 32 and had a long criminal record stretching back to 1979, which included drug convictions in 1980 and 1984. In 1989 he was sentenced to 7 years for robbery. The judge said he was a medium wholesaler, right at the start of the chain. Held. We are in full agreement with the observations of the judge but **3 years** not 5.

R v Horrigan [2001] EWCA Crim 1957, [2001] All ER (D) 17 (Sep). The defendant D pleaded guilty to two counts of being concerned in the supply of cannabis and a similar count for supplying amphetamine P pleaded guilty to five counts of supplying amphetamine. The pleas were entered at the first opportunity. They and other co-defendants were members of a family, which sold drugs. The police decided to make test purchases. D was at his father's home. The house had a padlocked gate through which cannabis was passed. Police made two £10 test purchases on different days. P sold the drug from his home. Those who wanted heroin were directed to two other family members. P sold them £10 deals of amphetamine on 4 different days. He appeared to get it from a box with 3–4 oz of it in it. Police found scales and small bags at P's house. D was 22 and P 41. D was said to be assisting in his father's 'shop.' P accepted dealing for 3 weeks. D had many convictions before 1997 for petty offences but only two for driving whilst disqualified since. P had a long list of convictions, which had always been dealt with at the Magistrates' Court. Neither had any drug convictions. Held. D's sentence reduced from 15 to 9 months on each concurrent and P's from 4 to **3 years** on each concurrent.

See also AMPHETAMINE

Cannabis – Class B

Cannabis – Class B – Large scale dealing – Couriers

159.33 *R v Netts* [1997] 2 Cr App Rep (S) 117. The defendant was convicted of possessing 94 kgs of cannabis resin with intent to supply. Police stopped his car and in the boot were two large laundry bags and a cardboard box, which together contained 94 kgs of cannabis resin with a street value of just over £250,000. He was arrested. He was 36, married with two children and of good character. He was sentenced on the basis he was a courier and not an organiser. **5 years** not 7.

R v Fairburn and McCarthy [1998] 2 Cr App Rep (S) 4. The defendants F and M pleaded guilty to possession of cannabis with intent to supply. The defendants put some boxes from F's garage to M's car. The police pounced and found five boxes, which contained 93 kgs of herbal cannabis worth, wholesale over £200,000 and retail £320,000. F told police he had agreed to look after the cannabis and expected to receive £14,000. He had picked them up and driven them to his garage. He had received a telephone call and as a result went to a public house where he met M. One of the boxes was to be his payment. M said he was to be paid £300. F was 43 and M

25. F had two unrelated convictions. In 1992 M had been convicted of possession with intent to supply and was given a community service order. F had some real problems in recent years including being seriously injured in a road accident and depression. M had weaned himself off drugs and had started to attend college with hopes of obtaining a degree. The case was delayed because of M making two serious attempts at suicide. F was ordered to pay £67,300 under the DTA provisions. It was accepted M had no assets. The judge said they were trusted and valued members of a distribution chain and he said that he was not giving a lot of credit for the plea because it was entered late and the case was overwhelming. Held. We agree with his approach over the discount for the plea. F's involvement was at a relatively high level. M should be sentenced on the basis his job was to drive them for A to B. In light of *R v Netts* [1997] 2 Cr App Rep (S) 117 and the other circumstances **5 years** not 6 for F and **3½ years** not 5 for M.

R v Freeder [2000] 1 Cr App Rep (S) 25. The defendant was convicted of possessing cannabis resin with intent to supply. Police saw the defendant speeding and followed him. He was stopped and they noticed he was nervous. He could not supply an address so he was arrested. At the police station officers became suspicious of the back seat and when it was removed they found 48 kgs of cannabis resin. It was discovered the car had arrived from Spain 7 days earlier with another driver. At Portsmouth a detector drug had not indicated a presence of drugs. The defendant had arrived at Gatwick 8 days before his arrest. He denied all knowledge of the drugs. In 1988 he received 15 months for possession with intent to supply cannabis. In 1996 in Morocco he received 2 years for possession of cannabis with intent to export it. His arrest was shortly after his release from that offence. The judge said he was passing a draconian sentence because of the size of the operation. **5 years** not 7.

R v Odey [2001] EWCA Crim 465, [2001] 2 Cr App Rep (S) 388. The defendant pleaded guilty to possession of cannabis with intent to supply and dangerous driving. Police tried to stop the defendant in a van because a door was not secure and he was not wearing a seat belt. He accelerated away and drove at speed and dangerously until he lost control of the van and skidded into a lamppost. He then ran off and fell. He said it was because the van was stolen but in fact there were 143 kgs of cannabis worth about £400,000 in the back. Police found £2,000 in cash at his home. He was interviewed and refused to comment. He had received no benefit. The basis of plea was that he was a courier on a single occasion. He was 35 and had no drug convictions. He had not served a custodial sentence. Held. We anticipate he was expecting some significant financial benefit. 5 years would have been appropriate if he had contested the case, but because of the plea **3 years 9 months** substituted for 5.

Cannabis – Class B – Large scale dealing – Organisers and others

159.34   *A-G's Reference Nos 19 to 22 of 1997* [1998] 1 Cr App Rep (S) 164. The defendants J, T, M and R pleaded to a conspiracy to supply cannabis. J was the most involved and was responsible for securing a safe and secure store for the cannabis and providing couriers and assistance for its onward transmission. M was his right hand man and was closely involved with the movement and storage of the cannabis. T was recruited as a courier and for the acquisition of motor vehicles and insurance. R was a courier and a supplier. J rented a barn saying he wanted to store electrical equipment. He, M and R made it secure so the owner did not have a key. Drugs were then stored there. The police found 17 kgs of cannabis in the barn and 195 kgs of cannabis and some scales in a van outside. £29,505 was found at J's home with smaller sums on the others. T had acquired from drug money a Vauxhall Lotus Carlton for M and a Land Rover Discovery for his brother J. A notebook at J's home revealed very large drug dealing. M provided a vehicle for T and R to deliver drugs. The cannabis in the barn and van was worth £334,000 to a retailer and £1.6m to a retailer. Held. J was the leader of the South Nottinghamshire cannabis supply corporation. On a plea of not guilty the correct sentence would have been **at least 10 years** and on a plea **8 or 9 years**. Because it was a reference **7 years** not 4. M should have been given on a contested case **at least 8 years probably more**. On a plea the least sentence was **7½ years**. As it was a reference **6 years** substituted. T and R should have got at least 4 years on a trial and 3 years on a plea. R had been released from prison and was working well in his job. Taking into account it was a reference **2½ years** would have been appropriate. Although 2 years was unduly lenient for T and R it too close to 2½ to alter the sentence.

R v Cunnington [1999] 2 Cr App Rep (S) 261. The defendant pleaded to possessing cannabis with intent to supply. The police watched him drop off what they believed were drugs at his parents' address. Two days later they arrested him as he was driving to that address. Two holdalls were found in his vehicle, which together contained fifteen 1 kg blocks of cannabis. Five further blocks were found at his parents' address, which were identical to the others. The street value was over £100,000. £900 was found in the defendant's home. The defendant was 45 and traded in oriental crafts and wood carvings. He had convictions dating from 1973 to 1984. His last four convictions were drug related and included supplying Class A drugs for which he received 6 months suspended. He had never been to prison before. He was not the ringleader. **4 years** not 5.

R v Chisholm [1999] 2 Cr App Rep (S) 443. The defendants C, F, Wa, K, Wr and T pleaded guilty to conspiracy to supply cannabis and to a lesser extent amphetamine. The Crown dropped a count referring to supplying Class A drugs after difficulties including witness problems became apparent. Pleas were entered after a 5–6 week pre-trial hearing. C ran a major supply organisation for Class B drugs in the North-East under the cover of his business in sale and repair of vehicles. His right-hand man and chief of staff was K, Wa and Wr were helpers and took part in the day to day running of the yard. They cut the amphetamine, couriered the drugs and money and looked after them. T supplied the drugs to Teeside and F purchased the drugs from C and sold them to South Tyneside. F was described as a sort of area manager. The offence lasted for 15 months. Police mounted a surveillance operation. with observation posts and covert listening devices. Police picked up conversations referring to 60 kgs in Spain, £250,000 in the boot of a car and 45 drums, 50, 100, 300, 200 kgs of either cannabis or amphetamine. The sentencing judge referred to the conspiracy as being on a massive scale and one never seen before in that part of the world. C was 39 and had a bad record with 14 appearances in court. He had received 5 years in 1989 but had no drug related convictions. F was 42 with a dismal record including two crimes of violence. He had no drug convictions. Wa was 35 with a number of previous convictions including one for drugs. K was 41 with 40 previous convictions, but none for drugs. Wr was 36 with a better record than the first four. T was 49 with virtually no convictions. C relied on the limited confiscation order of £40,000, indicating limited assets, the judge's remark that the defendant's were entitled to explore the legality of the covert operation, the fact that the Crown would not have accepted a plea to Class B until then and 11 years on a plea did not leave enough room for more serious cases. Held. 11 years gave a discount of less than 25% from the maximum. The judge must have pitched it too high. C's sentence was reduced to **10 years**. That wasn't regarded as tinkering. Because F's involvement was over only 2½ months and the reduction made for C his sentence was reduced from 7 to **5½ years**. Wa's sentence was reduced from 7 to **6 years**. Because of the reduction for C. K's sentence was reduced from 8 to **7 years** and Wr's and T's sentence was reduced from 7 to **6 years**.

Cannabis – Class B – Small retail dealer

159.35   *R v Fantom* [1999] 2 Cr App Rep (S) 275. The defendant pleaded guilty to possessing cannabis with intent to supply, supplying cannabis resin and possession of cannabis and amphetamines. For 3 months the defendant had supplied a boy aged 17 with cannabis. The police searched his flat and found £1,000 in cash and three pieces of cannabis, a smoking pipe, a set of scales, some glucose powder, a roll of cling film and some amphetamine. They searched him and found two pieces of cannabis. £145 in cash was found in a wallet. He was interviewed and said he used cannabis everyday and admitted selling it to whoever came to the flat. The cannabis weighed 137.6 grams. He was 29 with 17 unrelated previous convictions. Held. The *R v Aramah* (1982) 76 Cr App Rep 190 guidelines suggest 1 to 4 years. Here **2 years** not 3.

R v Kitching [2000] 2 Cr App Rep (S) 194. The defendant was convicted of five charges of supplying cannabis resin and herbal cannabis. He was a cleaner at Ampleforth School. Pupils approached him for cannabis and he supplied a 17 year old with £10's worth and £45's worth for which he charged £5 delivery. He supplied a 15 year old with £18.50's worth. Another 17 year old was sold £20's worth on two occasions. A 16 and 17 year old were each supplied with £20's worth. One of the pupils informed the school and the defendant was arrested. He was 28 and of good character. Held. The judge was in error to describe the offences as committed in breach of trust. The offences were very serious which merited immediate custody. This was less serious than *R v Nolan* (1992) 13 Cr App Rep (S) 144 so **18 months** on each concurrent not 2 years.

R v Horrigan [2001] EWCA Crim 1957, [2001] All ER (D) 17 (Sep). The defendant D pleaded guilty to two counts of being concerned in the supply of cannabis and a similar count for supplying amphetamine P pleaded guilty to five counts of supplying amphetamine. The pleas were entered at the first opportunity. They and other co-defendants were members of a family, which sold drugs. The police decided to make test purchases. D was at his father's home. The house had a padlocked gate through which cannabis was passed. Police made two £10 test purchases on different days. P sold the drug from his home. Those who wanted heroin were directed to two other family members. P sold them £10 deals of amphetamine on 4 different days. He appeared to get it from a box with 3–4 oz of it in it. Police found scales and small bags at P's house. D was 22 and P 41. D was said to be assisting in his father's 'shop.' P accepted dealing for 3 weeks. D had many convictions before 1997 for petty offences but only two driving whilst disqualified since. P had a long list of convictions, which had always been dealt with at the Magistrates' Court. Neither had any drug convictions. Held. D's sentence reduced from 15 to **9 months** on each concurrent and P's from 4 to **3 years** on each concurrent.

R v Barber [2001] EWCA Crim 2267, [2002] 1 Cr App Rep (S) 548. The defendant pleaded guilty before venue to possessing cannabis with intent to supply, possession of cannabis and possession of cannabis with intent to supply. Police officers executed a search warrant at a Golf Club intending to search the defendant's locker. The defendant arrived and his car was searched and police found twelve 9 oz bars of cannabis resin. He had £167 on him and he said it was 3 kgs worth and it was fractionally under 3 kgs. At the police station he said there was a lump of cannabis at his home and police found 37.4 grams of cannabis resin there. At his mothers house they found 144 grams and £26,000 in a holdall. In the kitchen they found 46.5 grams and a set of scales. When interviewed he said he had bought the cannabis resin in the car that morning for £3,650. He admitted dealing and to making £550 profit per kg. In 1998 he had two convictions for possessing cannabis and in 1999 a conviction for possessing cocaine. He received fines. The pre-sentence report said he was displaying a high level of motivation in favour of not offending again. Held. He deserved more than a ⅓ discount because his plea was before venue. **2½ years** not 3½.

Cannabis – Class B – Social supply

159.36   *R v Roberts* [1998] 1 Cr App Rep (S) 155. The defendant pleaded guilty to possessing cannabis with intent to supply, producing cannabis and possession of cannabis. On 26 September 1996 the defendant was stopped by police and found to have a tin containing about 3 grams of cannabis bush. In his accommodation was found a set of scales, three packets of hemp seeds, £245 in cash, four cannabis plants, a sachet containing 1 gram of cannabis bush and two dolls containing four wraps with 10.74 grams of cannabis in them. He said he had been selling to mainly friends making £20 per oz so he did not have to pay for his cannabis. He had sold about 1 to 1½ oz a week that summer. He was sentenced on the basis he sold only to friends. He was 20 and was a student at Leeds University with no convictions. The sentencing judge granted him a certificate to appeal and he obtained bail. Held. The case passed the custody threshold. It was commercial supply albeit at the bottom end. It is important for people to know that if they are University students or others if they dabble even in small scale supply they are likely to lose their liberty. For deterrent reasons it was necessary to impose a custodial sentence. Applying *R v Black* (1992) 13 Cr App Rep (S) 262, **2 months** YOI on each concurrent not 6 months.

R v Luke [1999] 1 Cr App Rep (S) 389. The defendant pleaded guilty to supplying 6.8 grams of cannabis and possessing with intent to supply 84 grams. The defendant was a university student and was of good character. He had references. There was a written basis of plea, which said the first matter, was to a friend who had asked for it and he had initially refused to supply it. This was the first time he had sold it. The second amount was to be used by his flat mates. They had put the money together and some money was outstanding. He was holding the drugs till he was paid for. It was purchased in that amount as it was cheaper and it would mean others could concentrate on their revising. He was visiting a drug project to cure himself of his drug habit. **4 months** not 9 months.

See also **CANNABIS**

Cocaine – Class A

Cocaine – Class A – Flat, dealing from (including telephone sales from flat)

159.37   *R v Day* [2000] 2 Cr App Rep (S) 312. The defendant pleaded guilty to two counts of supplying cocaine and possessing cannabis resin. He was convicted of possessing ecstasy. There was a police operation and undercover officers telephoned the defendant and arranged meetings. On two separate occasions £50's worth of cocaine was sold. A search was made of the defendant's flat and 37.7 grams of cannabis and eight ecstasy tablets were found. Held. There was no material difference between this case and *R v Howard* [1996] 2 Cr App Rep (S) 273 where the sentence was reduced to 4 years. **4 years** for the supply counts not 5½. [The other sentences remained shorter and concurrent.]

Cocaine – Class A – Offering to supply/Deceiving the buyer

159.38   *R v Cargill* [1999] 2 Cr App Rep (S) 421. The defendant pleaded guilty to offering to supply cocaine. Police mounted a surveillance operation in Moss Side. There were 13 days of video evidence and he appeared in only one of them. Because there was no link with others being sentenced the Court of Appeal decided to look at the facts of his case in isolation. An undercover officer approached someone and asked for 'a stone.' He said he had none and the defendant approached her and sold her a wrap for £20. It was 208 grams of paracetamol. The defendant later accepted a stone meant crack cocaine. He was 38 and had been addicted to drugs particularly cocaine for some time. He had a long list of convictions mainly for dishonesty to finance his addiction. He was in breach of his licence following his release from a 2½ year sentence for robbery. There were 224 days left to serve. He had no drug convictions. Held. It was an important the sentence reflected that what was sold was not a controlled drug. 18 months was too long. **12 months** substituted. Although the judge when he activated the 224 days left to serve didn't say whether they were consecutive or concurrent they should be served consecutively. The amount should be 6 months consecutive not 224 days.

See also *Pretending innocuous material was a prohibited drug*

Cocaine – Class A – Street dealing etc

159.39 *R v Cargill* [1999] 2 Cr App Rep (S) 72. The defendant pleaded guilty to four counts of supplying crack cocaine, possessing crack cocaine with intent to supply and simple possession at the Magistrates' Court. A police operation was mounted to combat drugs. An undercover officer sought to purchase drugs and called the defendant's mobile number. A meeting was arranged and 1.4 grams of crack cocaine was bought for £100. This occurred three further times. The defendant struggled violently on arrest and said, 'I'm only trying to make a living.' Eleven rocks of crack cocaine were found in his car. He was of good character. The sentencing judge referred to the defendant's activities being sufficient to trigger the police operation. Held. We do not think that is a permissible inference, as it is far more likely that his name cropped up when they were looking into far more serious dealers. That fact and *R v Howard* [1996] 2 Cr App Rep (S) 273 persuades us to reduce the sentence from 6 to **5 years**.

R v Walker [1998] 2 Cr App Rep (S) 245. The defendant pleaded guilty at his first appearance to three counts of supplying crack cocaine. In August 1994 he was sentenced to 3 years for supplying crack cocaine. Two months after his release he was seen by an officer in Brixton conducting an undercover drugs operation. The officer asked if he had any crack. The officer was asked to follow him and he did. A short distance away the defendant broke off a piece of crack from a large piece and sold it to the officer for £50. It weighed 321 mgs. A few days later there was another meeting and two wraps were sold for £40 each. Their total weight was 253 mgs. The next day he sold 197 mgs of crack for £20 to another undercover officer. That wrap was spat from his mouth. He was arrested 3 months later and lied in his interview. The risk of re-offending was described as considerable, although there were some indications that he was trying to lead a more settled life. The judge sentenced him to 3 years 11 months consecutive to 16 months for being in breach of his licence for the previous supply offence. The sentenced had been varied because the judge had misstated his parole position. Held. The **3 years 11 months** sentence was entirely proper. He could not have complained if it had been longer. These offences were committed in flagrant breach of his licence. Some judges might have given a reduction for the 3 months after the offences when he was not offending but the judge could not be criticised for not doing so. The total was not excessive.

R v Iqbal [2000] 2 Cr App Rep (S) 119. The defendant pleaded guilty at the earliest opportunity to possessing crack cocaine, possessing crack cocaine with intent to supply and a bail offence. Police were in plain clothes trying to reduce drug supply. The defendant asked an officer, 'What do you want?' The officer replied, 'Rocks.' The defendant spat out two rocks of crack cocaine into his hand and was arrested. The cocaine was 0.694 grams at 80% purity. He produced 15 clingfilm wrapped packages of crack cocaine from his sock. Their weight was 2.9 grams at 83% purity. He was of good character. Held. The cases indicate that notwithstanding the mitigation in this case the level of sentencing for first offenders for this offence is of the order of **4½ years** which is what he received albeit at the upper end of the tariff. It was not manifestly excessive.

A-G's Reference (No 84 of 2000) [2001] EWCA Crim 166, [2001] 2 Cr App Rep (S) 336. The defendant pleaded guilty to two charges of supplying crack cocaine at the Magistrates' Court. A police operation was set up to combat drugs in Peckham. Audio and video tape was used The defendant asked an undercover officer if he wanted 'weed.' The officer said he wanted a rock. He gave the defendant £20. The defendant then disappeared and returned with 247 mgs of crack at 60% purity. Two weeks later he sold another rock which was again 247 mgs and 58% purity. He was arrested and declined to answer questions. He had arrived in this country 2 weeks before the first sale. He had quickly become addicted to cocaine. He was 29 with no convictions. Held. For those of good character who plead guilty to supplying more than once to an undercover officer the sentencing bracket is **4–5 years**. Personal qualities play a comparatively small part in determining the appropriate sentence. Taking into account that it was a reference and he had already been released **3 years** not 9 months.

R v Beevor [2001] EWCA Crim 620, [2001] 2 Cr App Rep (S) 362. The defendant pleaded guilty to two counts of possession of cocaine, two counts of possession of heroin, supplying heroin, supplying cocaine, possessing heroin with intent to supply and possessing cocaine with intent to supply. Police stopped his car and 68 mgs of crack cocaine was found in his pocket. He had £279 in cash and a mobile telephone. He admitted he had been out that night selling heroin and cocaine. His home was searched and 81 wraps were found containing a total of 7.67 grams of heroin and 25 grams, which contained 3.48 grams of cocaine. The purity was 27%. There was also ½ gram of heroin and 185 mgs of cocaine. He said he was a runner. He said he used the mobile for dealing and had been dealing for about 2 weeks because he couldn't pay his mortgage. For the last 2 years he had had a drug habit. He was spending £40 a day. He was 32 with no convictions. His family had paid £2,500 for a clinic for him. He was remorseful and the risk of him re-offending was described as low. The judge said he had been totally honest with the police. Held. The level of sentence for supplying and possession with intent to supply is in general on a conviction 5 years at least, *R v Singh* (1988) 10 Cr App Rep (S) 402 at 406. The sentence largely depended on the degree of involvement, the amount of trafficking and the value of the drugs. The purity of the drugs needed consideration. Personal mitigation however strong does not necessarily reduce the sentence below a certain level. **4 years** not 5.

Ecstasy – Class A

Ecstasy – Class A – Minder etc of the drugs

159.40   *R v Harris* [1998] 1 Cr App Rep (S) 38. The defendant pleaded guilty to possessing ecstasy with intent to supply. Police searched his home address and found seven plastic bags containing 705 ecstasy tablets with a street value of between £5,600 and £10,500. He said he had minded the drugs for 10 days and thought he would be paid £50. He would not identify the person who asked him to mind them. The sentencing judge said that a minder performs an essential service to the dealer and is often close to the dealer. Held. The position of a minder will depend upon the amount of drugs involved and what inferences can be drawn from the surrounding circumstances. There may well be circumstances when the minder is more seriously involved than the courier. Bearing in mind the authorities **4 years** not 5.

Old case. *R v Spalding* [1995] 16 Cr App Rep (S) 803.

Ecstasy – Class A – Offering to supply/Deceiving the buyer

159.41   *R v Chambers and Barnett* [1999] 1 Cr App Rep (S) 262. The defendants C and B pleaded guilty to offering to supply ecstasy and going equipped to cheat. The defendants went to a rave with some innocuous tablets. They tried to sell them as ecstasy. B tried to sell one to an undercover police officer. C was 26 with no convictions. B was 19 with a conviction for deception. It was contended it was a deception case not tainted by any stain of the Drug Trafficking Act offences. Held. We don't entirely agree with that submission as it still contributed to the raves plus drug scene which the police and courts are trying to stamp out. However, no damage and possibly some good would have been done to the purchases. **12 months** imprisonment and detention not 18 months.

R v Tugwell [2001] EWCA Crim 719, [2001] 2 Cr App Rep (S) 501. The defendant pleaded guilty to possession of cannabis and ecstasy and two counts of offering to supply ecstasy. At the Glastonbury pop festival two undercover officers wanting to buy ecstasy approached him. He sold four tablets to one officer at £30 and eight to another for £40. They were innocuous zinc tablets. He told the police this in interview. The other drugs were found on him. He was 35 with 12 court appearances. The convictions were for dishonesty including robbery and burglary. Held. He was not duped. Supplying fake drugs is not simply a case of obtaining money by fraud but it involves a lesser degree of criminality than supplying real drugs. This distinction was not reflected in the sentence. **15 months** not 2 years for the supply counts.

R v McNab [2001] EWCA Crim 1605, [2002] 1 Cr App Rep (S) 304. [The defendants were convicted of offering to supply large quantities of ecstasy. 9 years and 3 years 11 months upheld.]

See also ***Pretending innocuous material was a prohibited drug***

Ecstasy – Class A – Retail supply

159.42   *R v Wright* [1998] 2 Cr App Rep (S) 333. The defendant pleaded guilty to possession with intent to supply ecstasy and supplying ecstasy. Police searched the co-defendant's premises and found him, the defendant and another. Police found in the defendant's jean's pocket 53 ecstasy tablets. A piece of paper with names and amounts in the defendant's writing was also found. He was arrested and claimed the tablets were for personal use. There was a Newton hearing and the judge determined it was commercial supply – retailing on a moderate scale not wholesaling. He was 24 with one possession of amphetamine caution in 1994 and in 1995 possession of amphetamine and two offences of possession of cannabis. **4 years** was not manifestly excessive.

R v Ferrett [1998] 2 Cr App Rep (S) 384. The defendant pleaded guilty to four counts of supplying ecstasy, a count of supplying amphetamine and two counts of supplying cannabis. A teenage girl died after taking ecstasy and amphetamine. The defendant's mother and others told the police he might have been the supplier of the drugs. The defendant was interviewed and denied supplying the deceased but admitted supplying another. The police interviewed several of his friends and they admitted receiving drugs from the defendant. Some of the drugs were supplied near a school to pupils aged 15. The defendant denied it but admitted to the probation officer that he had supplied drugs for about a year and made about £80 a week. The judge did not attribute the girl's death to him. He was 18 when sentenced and of good character. There were eight character references. Following his detention his risk of re-offending was assessed as very low. Held. A total of 5 years would have been appropriate. However, he is entitled to a further discount because of the credit due to his family for taking the course they did. So **4 ½ years** YOI not 7.

Ecstasy – Class A – Retail supply – Sales in nightclubs

159.43   *R v Skidmore* [1997] 1 Cr App Rep (S) 15. The defendant pleaded guilty to offering to supply ecstasy. She and her co-defendant went to a nightclub. When she arrived at the club she learnt that her co-defendant had 50 pills and she agreed to help sell them. She thought they were ecstasy. She collected £50 from a customer and asked two others if they wanted to buy any. A security officer called the police who found her co-defendant had 43 tablets and almost £200 on her. The tablets were found to contain no prohibited drug. She showed remorse. She was 22 and had no convictions. She was a swimmer of Olympic standard who hoped to join the army. **2 years** was well within the tariff for this offence.

R v Thompson [1997] 2 Cr App Rep (S) 223. The defendant pleaded guilty to two counts of supplying ecstasy. The defendant was watched in a nightclub by plain-clothes police officers, who saw him being approached by a number of people and something being exchanged. The defendant approached one of them and asked, 'Are you sorted?' The officer relied, 'No, what have you got?' He said, 'E's,' and told her they were £10 each. She paid for two. Two other plain-clothes police officers were approached and asked if they needed to be sorted out. They asked for two ecstasy tablets and were directed to the defendant. They were able to buy two further tablets. The defendant was arrested and was found to have £495 and a small piece of cannabis resin on him. He also had £150 in his bedroom at his parents' address. He was 20 and in employment. He had a conviction for possession of cannabis and ecstasy. He expressed remorse and appeared to have changed his lifestyle since his arrest. The judge sentenced him on the basis that ecstasy was more serious than other Class A drugs. Held. There should be no distinction between the various drugs in a class. Because he did so **4 years** not 5 detention.

R v Patel [1998] 1 Cr App Rep (S) 170. The defendant pleaded guilty to being concerned in the supply of ecstasy. It was based on one act only. Police officers attended a nightclub, which the defendant was involved with her brother in promoting. She was also responsible for running the disco that night. The police were able to buy ecstasy at £20 a time from the defendant's boyfriend. Later they approached her about buying pills and she said no problem and took them over to her boyfriend where they were able to obtain some. She was arrested and said she did not know her part was against the law. The judge said the aggravating features were that she was part of the management and she was living with her boyfriend and had full knowledge of what was going on. The boyfriend pleaded and received 3 years. She was 26 and of good character. Held The sentence of **12 months** was wholly appropriate. She was permitting and encouraging her boyfriend to sell drugs. Sentences will be severe and have a considerable element of deterrent.

R v Mayeri [1999] 1 Cr App Rep (S) 304. The defendant pleaded guilty at the earliest opportunity to four counts of supplying ecstasy. One tablet was involved in each case. Four undercover police officers approached him in a nightclub and he agreed to sell them a tablet for £10. He named his supplier. He was 22 and of good character. There was a 9 month wait before he was sentenced. He claimed there was an element of entrapment. The defendant relied on *R v Tonnessen* [1998] 2 Cr App Rep (S) 328. Held. The entrapment argument is not a good one. Where undercover officers discover a man is prepared to sell drugs by approaching him it is not a matter the courts need normally take into account as amounting to entrapment. It might be said 'Seller beware.' These premises are frequently used to sell drugs. There has to be a considerable element of deterrence. **2 years** was entirely justified.

R v Robotham [2001] EWCA Crim 580, [2001] 2 Cr App Rep (S) 323. The defendant pleaded guilty to two counts of supplying ecstasy and possession of amphetamine. He was seen acting suspiciously by staff in a nightclub. He was taken to be searched and he produced 0.45 grams of amphetamine. He was told police would be called and he said he had 40–50 ecstasy tablets on him. When the police came he tried to run. A bag with 56 ecstasy tablets and fragments of about five more was found on the floor. He had £285 cash on him. His home was searched and 32 more tablets, glucose and plastic bags similar to the one found in club were found. He was 32 with many previous including ones for possession of drugs. Held. **4½ years** was entirely correct.

R v Kesler [2001] EWCA Crim 825, [2001] 2 Cr App Rep (S) 542. The defendant pleaded guilty to supplying ecstasy and possessing ecstasy with intent to supply at the Magistrates' Court. Police officers kept observation on the defendant outside a public house where members of the public approached him. Over an hour he was watched having short conversations with people and then he would put his hands in his pocket. He gave one female something which she put in her mouth. This was the first charge. Shortly after he was searched and police found 40 ecstasy tablets. He admitted he supplied the female with ecstasy. He was 22 and had no drug supply convictions. His convictions included robbery, dishonesty and possession of cannabis. He said he was under pressure because of debts. The judge gave a modest discount for the plea because he was caught red-handed. Held. **4 years** was not manifestly excessive.

R v Hendry [2001] EWCA Crim 2231, [2002] 1 Cr App Rep (S) 534. The defendant pleaded guilty to three counts of supplying ecstasy, possessing ecstasy with intent to supply and possession of an offensive weapon. The defendant worked unpaid as a doorman at a pub. Three police officers asked for ecstasy and he supplied them with three pills for £10. Six days later he supplied them another three more and 2 weeks later he supplied them with another two. His car was searched and police found 63 pills and a rubber handled extendable baton. The basis of plea was he had bought tablets for a friend who declined to accept them. He said he was selling them off cheaply to get rid of them. He was then 24 with convictions but none for drugs. Reports spoke well of him. Held. These were persistent supplies with a drug store available but **4 years** not 5.

Ecstasy – Class A – Sales to friends

159.44   *R v Kramer* [1997] 2 Cr App Rep (S) 81. The defendant pleaded guilty to offering to supply ecstasy and possession of ecstasy and cannabis resin. The doorman of a nightclub noticed the defendant appeared to be dealing in drugs. He had a bag with 34 tablets in it and £80, which he had hid behind a fire extinguisher. Three white tablets and 3.43 grams of cannabis resin were found at his flat. All the tablets except one found at the flat contained a stimulant but were not ecstasy. The one was ecstasy. He was 20 and a student at Leeds University and he said he bought 40 ecstasy tablets for £8 each. His friends had put him in funds and it was the lottery of the lecture timetable, which determined which student bought the drugs. He was sentenced on the basis sales were to be at cost price. He was of exemplary character. It was unlikely that he would be able to resume his course. Held. 12 months was below the norm for this offence. The fact he had been granted bail cannot force the court's hand. Our duty is to uphold deterrent sentences. The appeal fails.

R v Pettet [1998] 1 Cr App Rep (S) 399. The defendant aged then 19 pleaded guilty to possessing 20 tablets of ecstasy with intent to supply. He asked for one matter to be taken into consideration. Police officers searched the car the defendant and others were in. They found a bag of white powder, a bag of cannabis, finger scales and £160 in cash. Under a seat was a bag of tablets. He and the others were arrested and the defendant said he and his friends pooled their money to purchase ecstasy and he and his co-accused had made frequent purchases every few weeks for several months. He had spent the evening collecting the money for some ecstasy, which he had ordered earlier in the week. He had one caution for possession of drugs but no convictions. He was working as a trainee electrician and was held in high regard by those who knew him. He was sentenced on the basis he had made no profit. The sentence would mean he would just miss the opportunity to attend an electrical course for his training Held. On the face of it 12 months detention was lenient. Taking into account the mitigation and that it was not an isolated offence the sentence was entirely appropriate. [Unfortunately the report does not give details about the tablets found in the car.]

R v Wakeman [1999] 1 Cr App Rep (S) 222. The defendant pleaded guilty to offering to supply ecstasy, possession of ecstasy, two counts of possession of cocaine and two counts of possession of cannabis. Police kept watch outside a nightclub. They approached the defendant and he took something from his pocket and put it in his mouth. He began to walk away and the police held him. He was chewing something and was told to spit it out. Eventually he spat out what turned out to be six tablets of ecstasy. He was arrested and was found to have ½ gram. of cocaine and nearly 2 grams of cannabis resin. At his house there was found a list, which he said were lists of pills which he was to get for friends. There were 14 names on it. In another list there were 18 names and 19 amounts in figures. He said it was money he owed friends so they might buy pills from him. The prosecution accepted that there had been no supply of drugs against the list and the money he had lent was to supply drugs in the future. Also the customers were friends who were existing users of ecstasy. The defendant was then just 21. Held. The basis of plea was wholly artificial. There was evidence that he was a drug dealer. All too often pleas are tendered on an artificial basis. It puts the judge in difficulty. We have to accept that basis now. Where there is supplying to friends and here where there is just an offer to supply the sentence will be less than usual sentence for commercial supply. **18 months** not 2 years.

R v Busby [2000] 1 Cr App Rep (S) 279. The defendant pleaded guilty to possession of ecstasy and amphetamines with intent to supply. He entered a nightclub and was found to have 14 ecstasy tablets and four amphetamine tablets. He said he and his two friends had bought the drugs between them. He was going to give them their share. They were expecting to be in clubs for the best part of 24 hours. The defendant was then 27and a self employed electrician. He had two Public Order Act convictions. The court considered *R v Denslow* [1998] Crim LR 566 where two heroin users bought together £300 worth of heroin. The dealer gave it to the defendant who gave half to his friend. He had been absolutely discharged for the supply count. The Court of Appeal said a count of supply would hardly ever be justified. Held. We don't doubt that observation. Possession of Class A drugs carries a maximum sentence of 7 years. This was not a trivial or technical offence. Possession on behalf of others to enable them to commit offences is more serious than possession simply for oneself. Trying to take the drugs into a nightclub through the security check is more serious. Custody was appropriate. 9 months was too long for someone who pleaded guilty at the first opportunity and had a lot to lose by way of home, standing and employment. The fact of imprisonment was a very large part of the punishment. Taking into account *R v Ollerenshaw* [1999] 1 Cr App Rep (S) 65, **6 months** substituted.

R v Robertson [2000] 1 Cr App Rep (S) 514. The defendant pleaded guilty at the earliest opportunity to possession of ecstasy with intent to supply and possession of a cannabis. The defendant was driving his car when police stopped him. Drugs were found in the car. The police searched his home and found 28 ecstasy tablets. Some were divided into wraps of six, five and three tablets. Quantities and names were found on notepaper. 14.33 grams of cannabis and drug paraphernalia were found. The basis of plea was that he was going to supply 20 of the tablets to the five persons on the list on a non profit making basis. He was of good character and was in extremely good and profitable employment which was now lost. He had purchased property on a mortgage. Held. Because of *R v Byrne* [1996] 2 Cr App Rep (S) 34 and *R v Wakeman* [1999] 1 Cr App Rep (S) 222, **12 months** instead of 18.

R v Bull [2000] 2 Cr App Rep (S) 195. The defendant pleaded guilty at the first opportunity to supplying ecstasy. He gave two ecstasy tablets to his sister's boyfriend without charge. The boyfriend and the sister went to a nightclub where they stayed several hours. He drank a number of double whiskeys as well as a lot of water. He was seen to be sweating a lot. The two came home at 2.30pm. He was found dead the next morning. He died of heart failure. It was discovered he had an abnormality of the heart and ecstasy contributed to the heart failure. If he hadn't taken the ecstasy it is unlikely he would have died. When questioned by the police the defendant admitted he had given him the tablets. The defendant was 21 and lived with his parents. He was in regular employment and working hard. He had no convictions and had a deep sense of remorse, which led to a depressive illness and a suicide attempt. Held. He must not receive a disproportionate sentence because of the tragic and appalling consequences of the supply. **9 months** not 18.

R v Bennett [2001] All ER (D) 11 (Aug). **1 year** not 3 on a plea for 21 pills.

R v Edwards [2001] EWCA Crim 2185, [2001] All ER (D) 271 (Oct). Social supply. The defendant was convicted of possession 29½ pills and he pleaded to supplying cocaine. **2 years** not 3.

See also ECSTASY

Heroin – Class A

Heroin – Class A – 1 to 10 kgs (at 100%)

159.45 *A-G's Reference Nos 64 and 65 of 1997* [1999] 1 Cr App Rep (S) 237. The defendants O and H pleaded guilty at the earliest opportunity to a conspiracy to supply heroin. Police officers saw the two walking along the street. O was carrying a large green holdall. It was searched and was found to contain large amount of drugs. H had £310 cash at his home and a relatively small amount of drugs. O had £520 in cash and packaging bags used to distribute heroin at his home. The total drugs seized from the bag and his home was over 3½ kgs of heroin. At 100% it was 1½ kgs of heroin. H said he didn't know what was in the bag and had been asked to look after it by another for about a week or two. He knew it was drugs. O said he knew it was heroin and that he was going to dump it. They were said to be high up the ladder of distribution. The prosecution accepted they were couriers. O was 28 and H was 40. O was of good character and H had no drug's convictions. Both had references. H had had some depressive illnesses in prison. Held. People who deal in Class A drugs must be dealt with severely to punish and deter. Taking into account the mitigation and that it was a reference **6 years** not 30 months.

Heroin – Class A – 10 to 50 kgs (at 100%)

159.46 *R v Sehitoglu and Ozakan* [1998] 1 Cr App Rep (S) 89. The defendants S and O made early pleas to conspiracy to supply heroin. The defendants were subject to a surveillance operation. S and O were seen carrying holdalls After arrests police found in a flat 44 kgs of heroin (24 kgs at 100% purity), three semi-automatic pistols, two silencers which fitted two of the guns and some live ammunition. The drugs were worth £7–8m. At another flat police found hydraulic presses and moulds for the compression of heroin into blocks. They were arrested and S had about £1,100 on him. £28,290, £3,500 and £1,680 in cash were found elsewhere. A card was found which was consistent with large scale drug dealing. Neither had convictions. S was 27 and O was 28. S gave information and evidence in a linked murder case, which his part had been crucial. He had also given information and assistance in a significant drugs conspiracy. He was due to give evidence in that case and he was described as the lynch pin in both cases. He and his family were very seriously at risk. The police were satisfied his account was true and accurate. The judge started at 25 for S and reduced it to 15 because of the assistance he had given. Held. The case falls into the highest category of drug trafficking. O was not right at the top of the conspiracy. On a trial the sentence for O and S would be in the region of **24 years**. Because of his plea **18 years** for O not 25 years. The information, assistance, evidence, given and the risks to S and his family mark this as a case where the maximum possible reduction should be made. Applying *R v King* (1985) 7 Cr App Rep (S) 227 the reduction for S should be ⅔ off the starting figure before one considers the plea. The sentence should then be reduced to **8 years**.

R v Altun [1998] 2 Cr App Rep (S) 171. The defendant was convicted of possessing 12.3 kgs of heroin with intent to supply. It was 5.8 kgs at 100%. Its wholesale value was £300,000. Police discovered the heroin in a clothing factory in London. As the police arrived the defendant made off. He was arrested in a hotel and found to have £2,000 cash on him. His fingerprints were found on some of the packages of heroin. The lease of the factory was in his name but he sublet it to another. He was 36 with no convictions and came to this country in 1988. The judge said he didn't know the part the defendant played and there was no evidence to show his role was other than a custodian. However, the value of the drugs showed he must have been a trusted member of the organisation having sophisticated involvement indicated by the cash found and that he registered at the hotel in a false name. The defence said he should be sentenced as a custodian. Held. The defendant was closer to the source of the supply than a mere minder of the drugs. However, **14 years** not 16.

R v Ngiam [2001] EWCA Crim 1332, [2002] 1 Cr App Rep (S) 150. The defendant pleaded guilty to possessing 50 kgs of heroin (at 47%) with intent to supply. Police stopped the car she was driving and found a large suitcase in the boot. It was padlocked and she said it wasn't hers. She was sentenced on the basis she thought it was cannabis and she was a courier. She had a conviction for importing 24 ecstasy tablets and some cannabis cigarettes. For that she received probation. Held. The fact she believed it was cannabis was a mitigating factor but it did not mean the judge was obliged to sentence her as if it was cannabis. If she thought it was heroin the appropriate sentence would be in the region of **15–20 years**. **6 years** was not manifestly excessive.

Heroin – Class A – Couriers

159.47 *A-G's Reference Nos 64 and 65 of 1997* [1999] 1 Cr App Rep (S) 237. The defendants O and H pleaded at the earliest opportunity to a conspiracy to supply heroin. Police officers saw the two walking along the street. O was carrying a large green holdall. It was searched and was found to contain large amount of drugs. H had £310 cash at his home and a relatively small amount of drugs. O had £520 in cash and packaging bags used to distribute heroin at his home. The total drugs seized from the bag and his home was over 3½ kgs of heroin. At 100% it was 1½ kgs of heroin. H said he didn't know what was in the bag and had been asked to look after it by another for about a week or two. He knew it was drugs. O said he knew it was heroin and that he was going to dump it. They were said to be high up the ladder of distribution. The prosecution accepted they were couriers. O was 28 and H was 40. O was of good character and H had no drug's convictions. Both had references. H had had some depressive illnesses in prison. Held. People who deal in Class A drugs must be dealt with severely to punish and deter. Taking into account the mitigation and that it was a reference **6 years** not 30 months.

Heroin – Class A – Flat or shop, dealing from

159.48   *R v Weeks* [1999] 2 Cr App Rep (S) 16. The defendant pleaded guilty to nine counts of supplying heroin. Police kept his flat under observation for 9 days. They saw between 20 and 25 callers a day. He was arrested and the police found £245 and a wrap of heroin. Items consistent with handling drugs were found. He immediately admitted his involvement and said he had a drug habit, which cost him £100 a day. He said he was selling for someone else and was paid in drugs. He kept three bags for every ten he sold. He said he had been dealing for between 2 and 2½ months and selling to up to 30 callers a day. He was 24 and had convictions for burglary and aggravated vehicle taking. He had no convictions for drugs. In light of the authorities and the mitigation **5 years** not 7.

R v Djahit [1999] 2 Cr App Rep (S) 142. The defendant pleaded guilty to possession of heroin with intent to supply and possession of cannabis. He had indicated his plea shortly after his PDH when he had pleaded not guilty. The police arrived to execute a search warrant at his shop and adjoining flat. The defendant was arrested. Two bags of heroin were found in a door panel near his kitchen. Two further bags were found in a kitchen cupboard. A small amount of heroin was found in one of his socks. The total weight was 21.5 grams with a street value of £2,150. The purity was not ascertained. £6,005, a list of names and addresses, a set of scales and bags were found. The defendant accepted the paraphernalia belonged to him but the list did not. Cannabis was found at his home address. The defendant had no convictions. The pre-sentence report indicated that he had been to a Dependency Unit and had become 'clean.' Held. He should have been given a full discount for his plea of guilty. The correct sentence for low level retailing is about 6 years. He appears to have solved his problems with heroin. The proper sentence was **4 years** not 6.

R v Williams [2000] 2 Cr App Rep (S) 308. The defendant D pleaded guilty to a conspiracy to supply cocaine and another conspiracy to supply heroin. The defendant W and J pleaded not guilty to the same counts. Three months later they changed their pleas to guilty. Police targeted W and his and B's address in Oxford. They saw a large number of visitors to W's address who stayed for a very short period of time. Some times they would not enter the premises. On a few occasions small packages were seen to be exchanged for money. An undercover officer made a number of test purchases and was supplied with cocaine and heroin from the three defendants. W's address was searched. W was in the attic throwing drug deals out of the window. Heroin worth £6,000 with a purity between 32 and 57% was found. A set of electric scales was found at J's address. W was the principle figure. Each defendant had a bad record. W's assessment of re-offending was described as high. W's basis for plea was that he started to sell drugs to pay off a debt. He had let a supplier use his address till about 4 weeks before he was arrested when he supplied the drugs. He had six regular customers who were friends. J's basis was that he had not made any money out of the dealing. J's role was described as not marginal. D's risk assessment for re-offending was described as high until she overcame her drug dependency. The judge said he wanted to send a clear message to dealers who were agents of death and destruction. He expressed the gravest concerns about Class A drugs in Oxford. He said it was a medium sized operation. He rejected W's assertion there were only six regular customers. Held. Because the judge decided not to hear evidence about the factual disputes between the Crown and the defence he was bound to sentence on the basis of plea submitted by the defendants. Applying *R v Djahit* [1999] 2 Cr App Rep (S) 142 the sentences were too long. The judge was in the best situation to judge the relative culpability of the defendants. W's sentence reduced from 8 to **6½ years**. J's reduced from 6 to 5 years and D's from 5 to **3½ years**.

R v Twisse [2001] 2 Cr App Rep (S) 37. The defendant pleaded guilty at the first opportunity to three counts of supplying heroin and offering to supply cocaine. Undercover officers rang the defendant's telephone number and as a result another man supplied the officer with a wrap of heroin. This was not in any count in the indictment. The next day another call was made and the officers were asked to come to an address and were supplied by the defendant with 0.342 grams of heroin at 36% purity. It cost £30 and the officers paid £15 and a video in part exchange. The next day there was another telephone call and visit and they were supplied again by the defendant with 0.273 grams of heroin at 35% purity. The value was £25 and they paid £15 and gave him two T-shirts. The next day they rang again and asked for heroin and cocaine. They were invited to the house and the defendant offered to sell them cocaine. The officer asked for heroin and was supplied with two wraps at £20 each. They contained 0.204 and 0.207 grams of heroin at 23% and 28 % purity. A search warrant was executed and the defendant and his associate were arrested. He was frank in interview and said he had been dealing for 9 months. He said he bought drugs and used some himself and sold the rest. He had three previous convictions. They were a supply conviction and two possession convictions including one a month before the first sale. On that occasion the defendant had been conditionally discharged for possessing heroin. He said he was now drug free. The defence said it was on a small scale, he made no real profit and following *R v Djahit* [1999] 2 Cr App Rep (S) 142 the starting point was 6 years. Held. You have to bear in mind the horrific picture of what it is like to live near someone trafficking in drugs. Supply is likely to cause offence and very often a good deal of fear. It did seem he made little profit. This was a team effort. **5 years** not 6.

R v Morris [2001] 2 Cr App Rep (S) 297. The defendant was convicted of possessing heroin with intent to supply and possessing cocaine with intent to supply. He had pleaded guilty to simple possession of ecstasy and the drugs he was convicted of. Police officers stopped the defendant, as he was about to get into a car. They searched him, and his flat. They found 23 ecstasy tablets, 23.37 grams of cocaine, the street value was up to £2,200, 42.5 grams of heroin the street value was up to £3,400. The appellant was arrested and interviewed and claimed the drugs were for his own use. He was 35 years of age and had nine previous court appearances mostly for robbery, sometimes including firearms. In 1993, he was sentenced to 11 years for attempted robbery and carrying a firearm with intent to commit an indictable offence. He was released on licence in 1998. He was ordered to serve the whole 1,670 days of the unexpired term of the 11 year sentence. (That was illegal, as the maximum is the time from the breach to the end of the sentence.[1]) The defence said the total was too long and the sentence was too high for one without a purity analysis. Held. Had the purity been known the defendant could not have been treated more favourably than he was and a sentence of less than 5 years would not have been appropriate. We agree with the observations in *R v Djahit* [1999] 2 Cr App Rep (S) 142, and **5 years** for possession of two different Class A drugs, with intent to supply, cannot be excessive following a trial. The judge when considering the unexpired term of the licence did not pay sufficient regard either to the defendant's history following his release or to the principle of totality. 2½ years consecutive substituted for an order to serve the whole term.

1   Criminal Justice Act 1991, s 40A(4)(b) and (5).

Heroin – Class A – Friends etc

159.49   *R v Lucas* [1999] 1 Cr App Rep (S) 78. The defendant pleaded guilty to supplying heroin. He bought three £10 bags of heroin and then joined his girlfriend at home. They drank and he injected himself with heroin. He passed the syringe to his girlfriend. He then went to the local shop to buy beer and left her apparently asleep. On his return he couldn't rouse her and called an ambulance. The paramedics arrived and she was already dead. She was found to have 3½ times the legal limit of alcohol for drivers and a high level of unmetabolised heroin which suggested she died shortly after injecting herself. Death was thought to have been caused by a combination of drugs and alcohol. The defendant was interviewed and made a frank confession. He said she had only used heroin twice before. There was genuine remorse. Following the death he made a number of suicide attempts. He was now drug free. He was 36 with no relevant convictions. He had abused drugs and alcohol for many years. He had been treated from time to time for depression and had not always been very well. **3 years** not 5.

R v Giunta [2000] 1 Cr App Rep (S) 365. The defendant pleaded guilty to possession of heroin with intent to supply, various possession of drug counts and production of cannabis. Police searched his home and found 120.9 grams of heroin of various purity worth £4,300 and small amounts of cannabis, methadone, 50 temazepan tablets and an ecstasy tablet. There was also a cannabis plant, £765 in cash, some scales and a card with figures on it. He was interviewed and said all the drugs were his for his personal use but he had supplied and would supply fellow drug addicts. He had a long standing habit, which he had to finance. He had just a drink drive conviction. He was assessed as being of high risk for re-offending. He had a good reference from his employer and from the prison. He received 5 years for the supply count and short concurrent sentences for the other counts. **5 years** was not manifestly excessive.

R v Ashford [2000] 1 Cr App Rep (S) 389. The defendant pleaded guilty to supplying heroin at the Magistrates' Court. The defendant was living at a bail hostel and another resident who was very drunk asked for some heroin. The defendant said no, but later after being pestered gave him some. The other resident took it and died during the night. He was sentenced on the basis heroin was not the cause of death. Death was caused by asphyxia after vomit had been swallowed. The defendant had served five custodial sentences for dishonesty. He expressed remorse. The prison report said he was traumatised by the death and he was displaying a very high motivation to address his drug problem. **2 years** not 3.

R v Smythe [2000] 1 Cr App Rep (S) 547. The defendant pleaded guilty to possession of heroin with intent to supply. Police officers saw the defendant approach a woman on a bicycle. They spoke and there was an exchange of articles. The police approached and the defendant cycled off. He then discarded the bicycle and ran off. He threw away a wrap which was found to contain 1.82 grams of heroin of unknown purity worth £182. 0.21 grams of heroin was found at his house with £700, a pager and a mobile. He was 22 with 12 court appearances mainly for dishonesty. There were two drug possession appearances and three custodial sentences. The basis of plea was that he and two friends had clubbed together to buy the heroin and he was the one to approach the dealer. Held. It was regrettable that there was no written basis of plea. Also that matters like the money and the mobile etc. were opened which run contrary to the basis of plea. 4½ years was a tariff sentence for a relatively low level dealer with a similar record to the defendant and allowing credit for the plea. This was a case when a purchase was not made in the presence of the others. **2 years** substituted.

R v Underdown [2001] EWCA Crim 1088, [2002] 1 Cr App Rep (S) 50. The defendant pleaded guilty to four counts of supplying heroin and possession of heroin with intent to supply on the first day of his trial. They were specimen counts covering 2 months activity. The purchasers were heroin users and lived in Aberaman in South Wales. They asked for heroin and after initially refusing to help them he regularly sold them heroin bought in Bristol. He then moved in with them. When the premises were searched heroin worth between £400 and £560 was found. He had no relevant convictions and had character witnesses. He had not had a custodial sentence before. **5 years** not 6.

Heroin – Class A – Intermediary etc

159.50   *R v Tonnessen* [1998] 2 Cr App Rep (S) 328. The defendant pleaded guilty to supplying heroin. The defendant was approached by a man who claimed to know her He was accompanied by two others who turned out to be from the *News of the World*. They said they worked for a Sheikh and they were instructed to buy drugs. She was a heroin addict and a cannabis user and said they were widely available. They said they wanted to buy heroin and asked her whether she was prepared to get it for them. They gave her £50 and she bought four wraps of heroin. She and a friend spent the rest of the evening with them. Immediately after her name and photograph appeared in the paper. The police felt obliged to arrest her and she admitted the offence. After the publicity she was assaulted and received a threat to her life. She was 31 and had already served a prison sentence for an unrelated offence. She had no supply convictions. She suffered from a serious pre-cancerous condition. The judge did not refer to the involvement of agents provocateurs and appeared not to have taken it into account. The defence said there could be considerable mitigation where it can be shown that the offence would not otherwise have been committed. It is legitimate for policemen to entrap criminals. When the entrapment is by journalist even more consideration and more weight should be given. Held. We consider there is substance in those submissions. However, it merited immediate custody. We cannot ignore she was set up. If these men had been police officers that would provide mitigation. Different considerations must apply to investigatory journalists. Their purpose was perfectly honourable. But we feel the public would be left with a sense of unease by the identification in the paper. The consequences were most unfortunate. It is appropriate to reflect the entrapment in the sentence. It should have been expressly mentioned in the remarks. In the exceptional circumstances we reduce the sentence from **12 months** to 6.

Heroin – Class A – Minder etc of the drugs

159.51   *R v Appleton* [1999] 2 Cr App Rep (S) 289. The defendant pleaded guilty to possessing heroin with intent to supply and three counts of possessing Class B drugs. He was a serving prisoner who had his cell searched. Officers found two plastic wraps, each containing ten foil wraps of heroin (total of 0.74 grams at 32%), two foil wraps of heroin (0.15 grams at 31 %) and a cling film wrap of 0.56 grams of amphetamine sulphate. He was arrested and admitted the offences. He was sentenced on the basis that he was looking after the drugs for someone else. Held. The fact he was minding them rather than dealing does not necessarily mean a shorter sentence. Those who mind the drugs prevent the real dealers being caught. Those that do the minding and them protect the dealer cannot receive any mercy. It would be different if the person was prepared to name the dealer and assist the police. [For further details see *Prisoners, supply to*.]

Old cases. *R v Arif* (1994) 15 Cr App Rep (S) 895.

Heroin – Class A – Street dealer

159.52   *R v Springer* [1999] 1 Cr App Rep (S) 217.   The defendant pleaded guilty at the Magistrates' Court to three charges of supplying heroin and was committed to the Crown Court. The defendant was a suspected drug dealer. The police tested their suspicions by making three telephone calls. He was asked, 'Have you got anything.' He replied, 'Yeah,' and arrangements were made to meet him. In response to each call a meeting was arranged and about 1.5 grams of heroin was supplied. The calls were recorded and the meetings were videoed. The defendant was 30. He had suffered the death of his father and his marriage had broken down. His new partner became terminally ill. He was at a low ebb and he began to take heroin and cocaine. He had previous for simple possession of drugs. He began to supply to finance his addiction. He suffered from sickle cell anaemia. The defence argued that he was entitled to a discount because of entrapment. Held. There was a need for the police to adopt this method of detection. There was need for there to be more than one supply to provide evidence he was a dealer. This was not a case of entrapping a suspect into supplying drugs who would otherwise never have engaged in that activity. *R v Underhill* [1979] 1 Cr App Rep (S) 270 at 272 applied. Here there was legitimate police activity and not activity that could provide mitigation or a reduction at all. As the evidence was overwhelming it was legitimate for the judge not to give the full credit for the plea. The disease was no basis to sentence him more favourably than other defendants. The sentence of **4 years** was not manifestly excessive.

R v Barnsby [1998] 2 Cr App Rep (S) 222. The defendant pleaded guilty to four counts of supplying heroin. Outside a Drug Rehabilitation Centre, officers conducting an undercover drugs operation approached the defendant. He supplied two wraps of heroin to one officer and two further wraps to another officer. The next day he offered to supply an officer with a wrap and he fetched it from inside the centre. Later the same officer was supplied with another wrap. All the wraps had cost £10. The total weight was 484 mgs at about 50% purity and 238 mgs at 100% purity. He was arrested and after being shown the video he accepted his guilt. He was 36 and had been a heroin addict for the last 10 years. He had several previous convictions including possession of amphetamine in 1987 and possession of methadone in 1997. He was placed on probation each time. The judge said that the need to deter other drug dealer for the protection of all those vulnerable people using the centre took priority over the defendant's personal circumstances Held. The judge was right. There was nothing wrong with **5½ years**.

R v Stenhouse [2000] 2 Cr App Rep (S) 386. The defendant pleaded guilty to supplying heroin on four separate occasions. A police officer called a number and was told to ring back in 15 minutes. He did so and spoke to the defendant. They agreed to meet. The defendant was given £10 and the undercover officer was given a wrap, which contained 52 mgs of heroin. The other offences were similar. He had convictions for possession of drugs and two for supplying Class A drugs. The last conviction was in 1997 for supplying one methadone tablet for which he was given probation at the Magistrates' Court. He had been in custody from December 1998 to July [1999] when he was released because of the Custody Time Limit provisions. He was sentence in December [1999] to the 7 year minimum term. Since his arrest he had made valiant attempts to conquer his drug addiction. Held. His efforts to break his drug habit were rare and he should be encouraged to continue with his efforts. The sentence because of the combination of circumstances was unjust so **3 years** substituted.

A-G's Reference Nos 58-9 of 2001 [2001] All ER (D) 402 (Jul). We would have expected 6 years if it had been fought.

LSD

Guidelines

159.53   *R v Hurley* [1998] 1 Cr App Rep (S) 299 – LCJ. It is wrong to consider some Class A drugs merit lesser sentences than others. Assuming the unit (the square containing the drug) is approximately 50 micrograms of pure LSD, the sentence for 25,000 units should in the ordinary case be **10 years** plus. For 250,000 or more units the sentence should ordinarily be **14 years plus**. Adjustment may be needed where it is shown the amount in the square varies significantly from the 50 micrograms figure. Where the seizure is of tablets or crystal in a form which permits a precise amount to be ascertained easily, then work out the number of 50 micrograms units which could be produced from that quantity and then implement the guidelines.

Cases

159.54   *R v Hurley* [1998] 1 Cr App Rep (S) 299 – LCJ. The defendant pleaded guilty to possessing LSD with intent to supply. He travelled from America and arranged for sheets of paper to be sent from California to a house, which he had access to. He received them and collected materials so he could impregnate the paper in a flat, which he had rented. The materials were trays, a perforating board, and measuring jugs, He successfully impregnated at least 319 sheets with each sheet having about 900 such impregnated squares which would give a total of 287,000 units of LSD. He was arrested. His home address in California was also searched and items were found which indicated he had a comparable operation in that country. His passport showed seven short trips to the United Kingdom and Peru in the last few years. A Newton hearing was held about the number units he intended to produce and the retail value of the units. The judge concluded that the 319 sheets were to be divided into 287,000 units, but rounded it down to 280,000 units. He decided the retail price was £3.75 per square and thus estimated the projected sale receipts to be over £1m. He described this operation as 'a very highly organised and professional enterprise' and as a 'massive drugs operation'. He said the credit for his plea must take into account that the evidence was overwhelming. The defendant had a number of 'very impressive written references.' and had various medical afflictions Held. The defendant was very heavily involved. The average LSD content of the squares was 31 micrograms, which fell substantially below the 50 micrograms average content, which we have treated as the standard unit. The number of squares should be notionally reduced to reflect that. The judge perhaps gave inadequate credit for the plea. Had this case been contested the appropriate sentence would have been **12 or 13 years**. With the plea of guilty the appropriate sentence was **10 years**.

See also **LSD**

Opium – Class A

Opium – Class A – Guidelines

159.55   *R v Mashaollahi* [2001] 1 Cr App Rep (S) 330. The current classification of opium as a Class A drug is on the premise that it was to be regarded as being every bit as harmful as other Class A drugs. Weight for weight, where street value is concerned, heroin is considered to be approximately eight times more valuable than opium. On this basis, a consignment of 40 kgs of opium at 100% purity would be equivalent in value to five kgs of heroin at 100% purity, importation of which, under the current sentencing guidelines, attracts a sentence of 14 years and upwards on a contested case. There is at least the remote possibility that opium might be imported to convert it into morphine or heroin. In those cases base the sentence on the amount of heroin or morphine that could be produced from the opium seized. We understand that the ratio to apply in these circumstances would be 10:1 ie ten kgs of opium would be needed to produce one kg of morphine or heroin assuming average levels of purity. The guideline for the possession of opium with intent to supply should be based on weight, cross-checked with street value to ensure that at least an approximate equivalence with heroin and cocaine is maintained. Because opium is the natural extract from the poppy and not a drug adulterated with other material the court should assume that it is unadulterated and of 100% purity. Should the defence wish, by way of mitigation, to persuade a judge that the active ingredient was of a lesser percentage it is open to them to call the appropriate evidence. If the judge is presented with evidence which persuades him that a calculation based on the equivalent street value of heroin or cocaine would produce an unacceptably high sentence for opium offences, he would be entitled to disregard any cross-check based on the street value of heroin or cocaine. For importing 40 kgs or more of opium the sentence should be 14 years and upwards, and for 4 kgs or more the sentence should be ten years and upwards. There is one exception and that is where the importation of opium was carried out for the purpose of conversion into morphine or heroin the appropriate sentence should be based on the equivalent value of those drugs. [As this was a supply case it is a pity the court did not give guidelines about supply other than figures for importation from which a discount could be made.]

Opium – Class A – Cases

159.56   *R v Mashaollahi* [2001] 1 Cr App Rep (S) 330. The defendant pleaded guilty to possessing opium with intent to supply. The opium was 28 kgs of raw opium and 2 kgs in sticks, probably representing some degree of adulteration. The street value of the consignment lay somewhere between £295,000 and £342,000. He was of good character. Held. Applying our guidelines it will be seen that the total importation fell into the ten years and upwards bracket. Having regard to the plea, the good character, and of somewhat less impact, the fact that he was acting as a warehouseman, we reduce the sentence from 14 years to **9 years**. [These are the only facts about the individual case recorded in the judgment.]

See also OPIUM

Steroids

Class C

159.57   For an old case before steroids were made a Class C drug see *R v Wilson* [1998] 1 Cr App Rep (S) 364 (best ignored)

Permitting premises to be used for the supply etc of drugs

159.58   Misuse of Drugs Act 1971, s 8(b)

Class A drugs – Supply

159.59   Triable either way unless the offence could qualify for a minimum 7 year sentence when the offence is triable only on indictment.

On indictment maximum sentence 14 years for Class A and B drugs and 5 years for Class C drugs. Summary maximum 6 months or £5,000 for Class A and B drugs and 3 months and £2,500 for Class C drugs.

The offence will qualify for a minimum sentence of 7 years for the third Class A drug trafficking offence[1].

1   Applying Drug Trafficking Act 1994, s 1(1)(a) which defines a drug trafficking offence as doing or being concerned in. . . supplying a controlled drug where the. . . supply contravenes section 4(1) of the Misuse of Drugs 1971. (Section 4(1) does not create an offence.)

Addicts permitting dealing

159.60   *R v Kilby* [2001] EWCA Crim 2468, [2002] 2 Cr App Rep (S) 20. The defendant pleaded guilty to permitting premises to be used for the supply of heroin and attempted possession of heroin. Over 4 days he allowed his home to be used for the supply of heroin to gour heroin addicts. There was no corruption or profit. He was frank with the police. He was 30 and for 11 years had been a heroin addict with convictions for supply and possession with intent to supply cannabis. There were a large number of other offences including theft. A drug treatment and testing order failed. **2 years** not 3.

R v Sykes [2001] EWCA Crim 2781, [2002] 2 Cr App Rep (S) 83. The defendant pleaded guilty to permitting premises to be used for the supply of heroin, possession of heroin and obstructing a constable. The prosecution dropped a supply count. Police went to his room at a hostel for the homeless to search it. He blocked the door and became quite aggressive. There was a struggle which no doubt gave the five other people in the room time to discard drugs they had onto the floor. They were small amounts consistent with personal use. The defendant had a single wrap of heroin on him. It was conceded the people all used heroin and were used to supplying each other by way of exchange or gift. He was 39 and a long-standing heroin addict and had a number of convictions mostly for dishonesty but including possession with intent to supply a kg of cannabis. In 1998 he received 6 years for various burglaries including one where an 80-year-old lady was struck a number of times with a metal bar. He was in breach of his licence for that and 12 months consecutive for it was imposed. Held. The offence was to facilitate the use and exchange of heroin and was not to be equated with supply. Different considerations would apply if it was effectively a retail outlet. Taking into account his obstruction it was still too much so **3 years** not 4.

Failing to take steps to stop dealing

159.61   *R v Coulson* [2001] 1 Cr App Rep (S) 418. The defendant pleaded guilty to permitting premises to be used for the supply of heroin. A drug dealer and his accomplice dealt with drugs at the defendant's flat with his full knowledge. Police raided the flat and found a large amount of cash, drug paraphernalia and 16.7 grams of heroin at 30% purity. The defendant was arrested and said he knew what was going on and was scared. He had a long list of convictions. 33 were for dishonesty. He had served five custodial sentences. Held. *R v Bradley* [1997] 1 Cr App Rep (S) 59 was substantially different. In that case the supply was very limited and this defendant's record is much worse. It is no precedent for reducing the **30 months** sentence. Without people like the defendant it would be difficult for people like this dealer to carry on their business. The appeal was dismissed.

R v Brock and Wyner [2001] 2 Cr App Rep (S) 249. The defendants B and W were convicted of permitting premises to be used for supplying Class A drugs. W was the director and B the project manager of a charity drop-in centre for the homeless. It provided shelter, food, clothing, washing, advice and medical care. Police recorded videos of obvious dealing on and off the premises. The prosecution was that anyone working there would have seen the activity and they were unwilling to take steps to stop it. W said she did have policies to stop it and she was there only there 30% of the time. There was a policy of no non-prescribed drugs being allowed on the premises. A document said that it was not an offence to fail to pass on information to the police except for terrorism etc. The police were members of an Advisory Group at the centre and they complained about the problem. A policy of bans for those involving drugs was formulated. A centre logbook showed the presence of people on the banned list. Police said the centre was unhelpful with information after someone died of drugs there. Also they said there was a lack of supervision. Three dealers gave evidence. One said it was a 'smack dealers paradise.' They had a system of signals to warn each other about the staff. Another said staff saw it going on. When the police were called the staff told them in advance. The third said he had never been warned off and there were 10 other dealers at one time. It wasn't necessary to be worried about the staff and deals were done openly. When he arrived 40–50 people rushed up to him. After the defendant's arrest fundamental changes were made. They were both 49 and with impeccable characters. They had character evidence in the highest terms. There was a 2½ year wait for trial and they had been in custody after sentence for 7 months before being granted bail. Held. This was serious because the drugs were Class A, there were several suppliers and the dealing may make their funding difficult when these refuges are vital for the homeless. They were also aware of the police concerns. However, there was no commercial gain and there was no evil motive. They were caring. The appropriate sentence would have been **18 months** not 4 and 5 years. In future longer may be appropriate. As they had served the equivalent of **14 months** it was not necessary to return them to custody for the 2 months.

R v Setchall [2001] EWCA Crim 1758, [2002] 1 Cr App Rep (S) 320. The defendant pleaded to permitting premises to be used for supplying heroin at the earliest opportunity. She was a single mother with three children aged 11, 4 and 1 years old. Police executed a search warrant at her home and found small quantities of heroin and cannabis. When interviewed she admitted that a long-standing friend of hers had become a heroin addict. She unsuccessfully tried to stop him and found that he was supplying heroin from her house to feed his and his girlfriend's addiction. She did not take steps to prevent it and it lasted 3 months. She co-operated with the police. In December 1998 she was given 12 months probation for permitting premises to be used for smoking cannabis and possession of a prohibited weapon. The judge said the offence was misguided loyalty and he appreciated it would have been difficult to stop it. He started at 18 to 24 months and reduced it to 12 months. Held. There was no evidence of profit. She was vulnerable and was used by those she tried to help. 18 months before she committed a similar offence and it should have served as a warning. There was no option but to send her to prison. There were no exceptional circumstances to suspend the sentence. The judge started too high. Because of her personal mitigation, early plea and frankness **4 months** substituted.

R v Williams [2001] EWCA Crim 2362, [2002] 1 Cr App Rep (S) 532. The defendant pleaded guilty to permitting premises to be used for supplying cocaine and possession of cocaine with intent to supply. She shared her house with her partner who was a Class A drug supplier. Police exercised a search warrant and she was searched. Police found a small amount of crack on her. She said she was carrying it for her partner because she was less likely to be searched than he was. It was said it was very difficult for her to do anything to arrest his activity. She was a mother of two young children. Held. She had little opportunity to exercise any will in the matter. The more serious offence was the possession with intent. **8 months** on each concurrent not 18 months and 3 months concurrent.

Premises used specifically for dealing

159.62   *R v Fitzpatrick* [2001] 1 Cr App Rep (S) 15. The defendant pleaded guilty to permitting premises to be used for supplying heroin. Undercover officers were escorted by guides to the defendant's flat to buy heroin on four occasions. On most of the occasions the purchase money was given to a guide. The money would be pushed through the letter box and a hand would then pass the drugs back through a letter box. There were a number of people in the flat besides the defendant. Officers entered the flat and found the defendant there and he was arrested. The defendant was the tenant of the flat and a heroin user. He was a diabetic and suffered from epilepsy. Held. Where a person is a regular dealer or provides facilities for others to carry on an established course of dealing over a substantial period sentences ought to reflect that. There was a significant difference between this case and *R v Bradley* [1997] 1 Cr App Rep (S) 59 as in that case the supply might be called social. This was a retail outlet for all and sundry. It was used for an established business of supplying heroin. It is important that he was not himself actively involved in the supply of heroin. He took a passive role. He did not make a profit. Taking these matters into account and that his co-accused received 2 years, **3 years** substituted for 4½.

Prostitution, and

159.63 *R v Bradley* [1997] 1 Cr App Rep (S) 59. The defendant pleaded guilty to permitting premises to be used for supplying cocaine, possessing cocaine and permitting premises to be used for habitual prostitution. The defendant was a tenant of a flat in the 'red light' district of Walsall. Over 6 or 7 years he had allowed his premises to be used as a brothel. As a by-product the premises had been used for smoking crack cocaine for 'a number of years.' Drug dealers had come to use the premises for the supply of drugs. The case against him was based on admissions he made. No drugs were found on the premises when the police raided them. In 1988 he had a conviction for supplying drugs for which he received 3 months at the Magistrates' Court. There were no previous convictions after that. The defence contended that the supply of drugs was very limited and *R v Gregory* (1992) 14 Cr App Rep (S) 403 meant 4 years was too long. Held. We should interfere on the basis of the submission. **2 years** substituted. [The other sentences remained lesser and concurrent.]

See also **DRUG USERS**

160 TACHOGRAPH AND OTHER DRIVERS' HOURS OFFENCES

160.1 Transport Act 1968, ss 96(11), 97(1), 97A, 97AA, 98 and 99(5)

Contravening permitted driving time; using vehicle without proper recording equipment; driver failing to return proper recording sheet; forging etc the seals on recording equipment, contravening records regulations and making etc false record etc.

Sections 97AA and 99(5) are triable either way. On indictment maximum 2 years. Summary maximum £5,000.

Sections 96(11), 97(1), 97A and 98 are summary only. The maximum fines are Level 4 (£2,500), Level 5 (£5,000), Level 4 and Level 4 respectively.

Magistrates' Court Sentencing Guidelines September 2000
160.2

Tachograph	Penalty points	Maximum penalty	Owner/operator	Driver or owner/driver
Not properly used	–	Level 5	C	B
Falsification or fraudulent use	–	Level 5	C	B
For an owner/driver, take net turnover into account as appropriate.				

Starting point fine B is £100 and starting point fine C is £150 when defendant has £100 net weekly income. See page 334 for table showing fines for different incomes.

For details about the guidelines see **MAGISTRATES' COURT SENTENCING GUIDELINES** at page 331.

Guideline remarks

160.3 *R v McCabe* (1989) 11 Cr App Rep (S) 154. These offences were serious and caused danger to the public. The very fact that employees or drivers may regard them as bureaucratic interference with their livelihood was a reason for imposing a significant sentence.

Falsifying or failing to keep proper records

160.4 *R v Saunders* [2001] EWCA Crim 93, [2001] 2 Cr App Rep (S) 301. The defendants S, H and W pleaded guilty at the Magistrates' Court to eleven, ten and six charges of making a false entries respectively. They were over 5, 5 and 6 months respectively. They were all drivers from the same company. Following a fatal accident which had nothing to do with the defendants police made enquires at their haulage company which revealed the offences. On two occasions H drove 380km on top of the mileage he had recorded. When interviewed the defendants made no comment. They were 39, 38 and 45 respectively. S and H were of good character and W had convictions but during the 1990s there was an improvement. He had no convictions of this kind. Each had family responsibilities. Six other drivers who faced fewer charges were prosecuted for the same offence and were given financial penalties. Held. Each had a financial motive for the offences, the extra wages. Members of the public were put in danger. The sentences need to be significant. **8 months** on each was not manifestly excessive.

Interfering with equipment to stop true recordings

160.5 *R v Potter* [1999] 2 Cr App Rep (S) 448. The defendant pleaded guilty to five offences of making a false record [Transport Act 1968, s 99(5)], two offences of failing to use recording equipment [Transport Act 1968, s 97(1)(a)(iii)] and two offences of failing to have a daily rest period [Transport Act 1968, s 96(11)(a)] at the Magistrates' Court. He had an accident for which he wasn't to blame and his lorry was examined. The policeman was suspicious about the tachograph and arranged for it to be examined by an expert who discovered that a switch had been fitted which enabled the clock to run while there was no recording of speed and distance travelled. Earlier tachographs were found at his home address and in interview he admitted he had switched off the device. He said the device was installed 4 years previously and he had used it sparingly. The tachograph records were compared with his driver's journal. He was a 51-year-old owner-driver of good character with a substantial record of charitable works. Held. His positive good character militates very much in his favour. **3 months** not 9.

Persons in authority – Guideline remarks

160.6 *R v Raven* [1988] 10 Cr App Rep (S) 354. The defendant was concerned in the management of a haulage company. He pleaded guilty to six charges of making false entries on a driver's sheet. The judge said, 'The deliberate alteration of tachographs with a view to profit is a shocking state of affairs. One only needs to have regard to the news on an almost daily basis to realise how important it is that safety regulations with regard to the use of heavy vehicles on the road are complied with and it must be obvious that those who come before the courts charged with effectively fraud but which give rise to matters of public danger, as these offences have done, must understand there will be serious consequences when and if they come to light. Where it is done for profit it dangerous and unfair competition for other traders.' Held. We agree with those comments.

R v McCabe (1989) 11 Cr App Rep (S) 154. Where someone in authority was corrupting employees the offence was more serious than when committed by the employees and demanded a severe sentence to discourage others.

R v Saunders [2001] EWCA Crim 93, [2001] 2 Cr App Rep (S) 301. We agree with the comments in *R v Raven* [1988] 10 Cr App Rep (S) 354.

See also **ROAD TRAFFIC**

161 TAKING MOTOR VEHICLES

161.1 Theft Act 1968, s 12

Summary only. Triable on indictment as an alternative to theft. Maximum sentence 6 months and/or Level 5 (£5,000). There is power to commit for sentence with an either way offence[1].

The offence carries discretionary disqualification. No mandatory points.

1 Criminal Justice Act 1988, s 41.

Crown Court statistics England and Wales[1] – Crown Court – Males 21+ – Theft or unauthorised taking of motor vehicles

161.2

Year	Plea	Total Numbers sentenced	Type of sentence%					Average length of custody (months)
			Discharge	Fine	Community sentence	Suspended sentence	Custody	
2000	Guilty	79	4%	3%	33%	5%	56%	14.9
	Not guilty	24	0%	4%	25%	0%	71%	16.9

1 Excluding committals for sentence. Source: Crime and Criminal Justice Unit, Home Office Ref: IOS416-02.

Drug abstinence order

161.3 Powers of Criminal Courts (Sentencing) Act 2000, s 58A(1): Where a person is 18 or over the court may make an order requiring the offender to abstain from misusing specified Class A drugs and provide, when instructed to do so a sample to ascertain whether he has any specified Class A drugs in his body. (3) The court must be of the opinion the offender is dependant or has a propensity to misuse specified Class A drugs and the offence is a trigger offence or the misuse of any specified Class A drug caused or contributed to the offence in question. (7) An order shall be for not less than 6 months and not more than 3 years. (9) No order shall be made unless the court has been notified that arrangements for implementing the order are available. [Criminal Justice and Court Services Act 2000, Sch 6 specifies the Theft Act 1968, s 12 as a trigger offence.]

Magistrates' Court Sentencing Guidelines September 2000

161.4 Entry point. Is it serious enough for a community penalty? Consider the impact on the victim. Examples of aggravating factors for the offence are group action, pre-meditated, related damage, professional hallmarks and vulnerable victim. Examples of mitigating factors for the offence are misunderstanding with the owner, soon returned and vehicle belonged to family or friend. Examples of mitigation are health (physical or mental), co-operation with police, voluntary compensation and genuine remorse. Give reasons for not awarding compensation.

For details about the guidelines see MAGISTRATES' COURT SENTENCING GUIDELINES at page 331.

See also AGGRAVATED VEHICLE-TAKING

TAKING THE LAW INTO YOUR OWN HANDS

See also FALSE IMPRISONMENT – *Taking the law into your own hands* and BURGLARY – AGGRAVATED – *Revenge attack on a burglar*

162   TARIFF, CHANGE IN TARIFF YEARS LATER

Can you appeal?

162.1   *R v Graham* [1999] 2 Cr App Rep (S) 312. The defendant was convicted of importing 665 kgs of cannabis in 1994. He received 12 years. In 1996 his appeal against conviction and sentence was dismissed. The Court of Appeal issued new guidelines for sentencing in cannabis cases in *R v Ronchetti* [1998] 2 Cr App Rep (S) 100. The defendant's case was referred to the Court of Appeal by the Criminal Cases Review Commission and it was argued that the sentence should be 10 years. Held. The Commission was set up to refer possible miscarriages of justice to the Court of Appeal. It has an unfettered power to refer sentencing cases to the Court of Appeal. A defendant sentenced on the prevailing tariff cannot be described as a victim of a miscarriage of justice. An alteration in the statutory maxima or minima penalty cannot give rise to a legitimate grievance. Changes do not have retrospective effect.

163   TAX FRAUD

This section is in two parts, **Tax Fraud** and **Duty Evasion**.

Tax Fraud

163.1   Many different offences and penalties but in particular:

Cheating the Public Revenue

Contrary to common law so penalty at large (maximum life) and triable only on indictment.

Value Added Tax Act 1994, s 72

Knowingly concerned in or taking steps with a view to the fraudulent evasion of VAT.

Triable either way. On indictment maximum 7 years. Summary maximum 6 months and/or £5,000 or three times the VAT whichever is greater.

Crown Court statistics England and Wales[1] – Crown Court – Males 21+ – Revenue law offences

163.2

Year	Plea	Total Numbers sentenced	Type of sentence%					Average length of custody (months)
			Discharge	Fine	Community sentence	Suspended sentence	Custody	
2000	Guilty	34	0%	3%	6%	26%	65%	17.8
	Not guilty	9	0%	11%	0%	0%	89%	18.8

1   Excluding committals for sentence. Source: Crime and Criminal Justice Unit, Home Office Ref: IOS416-02.

Guideline remarks

163.3   *R v Thornhill* (1980) 2 Cr App Rep (S) 320 – LCJ The defendant pleaded guilty to failing to deduct tax from employees' wages. The loss was £3,278. Held. Defrauding the Inland Revenue is a serious offence because it means defrauding the vast body of honest taxpayers. Those that plead guilty may well receive immediate imprisonment. **3 months** not 6 partly because his business might fail.

A-G's Reference (Nos 86 and 87 of 1999) [2001] 1 Cr App Rep (S) 505. The length of sentence will depend on a number of factors, the amount of tax evaded, the period of time the evasion took place, the efforts made to conceal the fraud, whether others were drawn in and corrupted, the character of the defendant, his personal gain, his plea and the amount recovered.

Value £1,000–£100,000

163.4   *R v Wells* [1999] 1 Cr App Rep (S) 371. The defendant pleaded guilty to being knowingly concerned in the fraudulent evasion of VAT at the Magistrates' Court. His demolition company, which was registered for VAT, failed and he was left substantially in debt. Soon afterwards he borrowed £12,000 and opened a wine bar. Shortly after that his wife who looked after the administration and the accounts left him. Those duties fell to him and his experience of that was limited. He worked hard and the bar prospered although he was being pressed for payment of the debts. He was made bankrupt but because of the success of the wine bar the Receiver allowed the business to continue and it prospered. He was told by his accountant to register the company for VAT and sent him the forms. He didn't register although he was obliged to. Over 17 months the tax evaded was £28,000. Until he lost the tenancy the Customs didn't charge him. Then seeing no opportunity to recover the money they did charge him. He was 36 and of good character. Held. Sentences of 12 months or more are appropriate for this kind of fraud even on a plea. **8 months** fully took into account the delay.

R v Rogers [2001] EWCA Crim 1680, [2002] 1 Cr App Rep (S) 337. The defendant was convicted of two offences of cheating the Inland Revenue. He was an unqualified accountant and provided accounting services for contractors and sub-contractors in the building trade. Sub-contractors holding 715 vouchers were able to receive their money gross. Contractors under the SC60 scheme deducted tax at source and remunerated the sub-contractor net. The defendant on behalf of his clients submitted false SC60 forms indicating tax had been paid which had not been and then applied for the tax allowances. The profits were split equally between the contractor, the sub-contractor and the defendant. The extent of the fraud was in the region of £1m. The judge said, 'the fraud was your idea, you masterminded it and led it throughout. You recruited vulnerable people and there was the possibility of corrupting young people. You were motivated by greed and had shown no remorse. In the witness box you were scheming, manipulative and dishonest. The only mitigation was you would be left with nothing and have to start again.' The defendant was 41 with no relevant convictions. Held. This was not mere evasion but positive cheating on a grand scale and over several years, all masterminded by the defendant. There was no benefit from a guilty plea and there were several aggravating features. The sentence of **7 years** was severe but not manifestly excessive. [The judgment does not accurately record the defence submissions.]

Old cases. *R v Rogers* (1994) 16 Cr App Rep (S) 720; *R v Aziz* [1996] 1 Cr App Rep (S) 265.

Value over £1m

163.5   A-*G's Reference (Nos 86 and 87 of 1999)* [2001] 1 Cr App Rep (S) 505 [for facts see Unreported case Re conviction judgment 23 October]. The defendants W and S were convicted of two offences of cheating the Inland Revenue, conspiracy to cheat and two offences of false accounting. The offences were over a 3 year period. W was convicted of another false accounting count. The defendants were involved in the sale of a distance learning course. They claimed copyright so it would be tax free. Payments were sent to an off shore company which they had set up after receiving legitimate tax advice. Some payments were diverted to another company. Documents were concealed during audits. The investigators raided their premises in 1996 and during the investigation W and another agreed to repay £200,000. The prosecution claimed it was window dressing and the defendants' knew it couldn't be treated as copyright payments. The total loss with interest was £1,979,808. W received not less than £500,000 and S not less than £200,000. The money was spent on property including a house for W bought for £423,428 and for S a flat costing £120,000 and another for S costing £49,000, cars including a Bentley for W costing £77,000 and credit card purchases for W of £17,872 and for S of £26,074. W was 53 and had earlier problems with the Inland Revenue [not it appears convictions]. S was 46 and of good character. She also had health problems. The trial lasted 4 months in which the judge said he would not be imposing imprisonment. He fined W £694,000 [following the quashing of one conviction £534,00] and S £106,000 [now £86,000]. There was a £16m compensation order. The financial penalties had been paid. Held. W's sentence should have been in the region of 4½ years. As S was less involved and not involved in one of the counts which was a separate venture, the appropriate sentence was 18 months to 2 years. Taking into account the delay, that it was a reference and all the factors **18 months** for W and **6 months** for S.

Old case. *R v Alibhai* [1992] 13 Cr App Rep (S) 682.

Confiscation orders

163.6   Criminal Justice Act 1988, s 72(5). The court shall leave the (confiscation) order out of account in determining the appropriate sentence.

R v Andrews [1997] 1 Cr App Rep (S) 279. The defendant who was sentenced for a £300,000 tax fraud was ordered to pay a £¼m confiscation order. The Court of Appeal reduced the sentence because of the large order.

R v Rogers [2001] EWCA Crim 1680, [2002] 1 Cr App Rep (S) 337. *R v Andrews* [1997] 1 Cr App Rep (S) 279 was decided without reference to s 72(5) and the court cannot reduce a sentence because of the confiscation order.

See also SOCIAL SECURITY FRAUD/HOUSING BENEFIT FRAUD ETC

Duty Evasion

163.7   Customs and Excise Management Act 1979, s 170(2)

Triable either way. On indictment maximum sentence 7 years. Summary maximum 6 months and/or £5,000 or three times the value of the goods which ever is greater.

There are powers to forfeit the goods and cars, ships etc used in duty evasion.

Guideline case

163.8   *R v Dosanjh* [1999] 1 Cr App Rep (S) 107. Cross-channel liquor and tobacco smuggling is a source of major loss to the Inland Revenue. Minor offenders may merely have their goods seized and forfeited. Sometimes a civil penalty, akin to a parking ticket and contestable before the VAT and Duties Tribunal, may be imposed under s 170A of the Act. Sometimes an offence may be compounded by payment instead of prosecution under s 152(a). The illicit import of alcohol and tobacco is often associated with other criminal activities involving gangs. There has, in recent times, been an increase in violence towards and intimidation of Customs officers and ferry staff. Illicit alcohol and tobacco can pass more readily to underaged consumers and such goods are often transported in overloaded vehicles, to the hazard of other road users. Legitimate traders are unfairly deprived of business. The courts need to distinguish between three broad categories of offenders: those who import comparatively small quantities on a few occasions; those who, acting on their own, or possibly with one other, persistently import greater quantities, and those in organised gangs, involved in importation on a large commercial scale. There is a need for a deterrent element in sentencing, particularly when significant amounts of duty are evaded by repeated organised expeditions, which lead to distribution on a commercial scale. In those cases, good character and personal circumstances will be of comparatively little mitigating significance. In an appropriate case the court should also consider a deprivation order under s 43 of the Powers of Criminal Courts Act 1973 [now the Powers of the Criminal Courts (Sentencing) Act 2000, s 143]. Consideration should also be given to disqualifying drivers under s 44 of the same 1973 Act [disqualification when vehicle used for the purposes of crime now governed by the Powers of Criminal Courts (Sentencing) Act 2000, s 147]. Justices also have a power in relation to the revocation of licences, where licensees are involved.

R v Flaherty and McManus [2000] 1 Cr App Rep (S) 250. *R v Dosanjh* [1999] 1 Cr App Rep (S) 107 does not intend that the starting point should be fixed solely by the duty involved. Nor does it lay down a hard and fast rule that where more than £1m is involved the top sentence will be **7 years**. Consider the level of involvement and the aggravating and mitigating factors.

Guideline remarks

163.9   *R v Ollerenshaw* [1999] 1 Cr App Rep (S) 65. The maximum is **7 years** and sentenced close to that have been imposed. Those who evade significant amounts should expect to go to prison. Aggravating features are playing an organisational role, making repeated importations, continuing when warned and importing more than one dutiable item eg alcohol *and* tobacco.

R v Latif [1999] 1 Cr App Rep (S) 191. The principle factor in any case will be the duty lost.

Old cases. Ignore all cases before *R v Ollerenshaw* [1999] 1 Cr App Rep (S) 65.

Magistrates' Court Sentencing Guidelines September 2000

163.10   Entry point. Are Magistrates' sentencing powers appropriate? Examples of aggravating factors for the offence are organiser, more than one journey, commercial operation, sophisticated operation and importing 2+ dutiable goods. Examples of mitigating factors for the offence are supply to restricted group and small quantity of goods. Examples of mitigation are age, health (physical or mental), co-operation with the police, voluntary payment of duty and genuine remorse. [Note. It should perhaps read co-operation with customs and not police.]

For details about the guidelines see **Magistrates' Court Sentencing Guidelines** at page 331.

Deprivation orders

163.11   *R v Dosanjh* [1999] 1 Cr App Rep (S) 107. In an appropriate case the court should also consider a deprivation order under s 43 of the Powers of Criminal Courts Act 1973 [now the Powers of the Criminal Courts (Sentencing) Act 2000, s 143].

Disqualification from driving

163.12   *R v Dosanjh* [1999] 1 Cr App Rep (S) 107. Consideration should also be given to disqualifying drivers under s 44 of the Powers of Criminal Courts Act 1973 [disqualification when vehicle used for the purposes of crime now governed by the Powers of Criminal Courts (Sentencing) Act 2000, s 147].

Value less than £10,000

163.13   *R v Dosanjh* [1999] 1 Cr App Rep (S) 107. Cases involving less than £10,000 will frequently be dealt with by magistrates. When the amount evaded is in thousands of pounds, custody will generally be called for, and, on a plea of guilty, sentences up to **6 months** will be appropriate;

R v Latif [1999] 1 Cr App Rep (S) 191. The two defendants, M and N were brothers and they made an early guilty plea to evading duty on 154 cartons of cigarettes. They were committed for sentence. The defendants flew to Stockholm and back to London. Each journey was via Prague. They obtained green-edged EC baggage tags in Stockholm and 154 cartons of cigarettes in Prague. At Heathrow their luggage was searched and the cigarettes found. In interview they admitted the offence and told the probation officer that the bulk would be sold on. Both were of good character. M was 40 with a wife and three children. N was 32 and had a wife and two children. They had been in regular work and expressed remorse. They were considered unlikely to re-offend and were suitable for community service. Held. The principle factor in any case will be the duty lost. Custody was right to deter others. Applying *R v Dosanjh* [1999] 1 Cr App Rep (S) 107, **6 months** not 9. [Unfortunately the report does not refer to the value of the duty lost.]

Value £10,000–£100,000

163.14   *R v Ollerenshaw* [1999] 1 Cr App Rep (S) 65. The defendant pleaded guilty to three counts of evasion of excise duty. Police officers stopped a van because they thought it was overweight and found it was laden with cigarettes and alcohol. There were 500 cigars, almost 20,000 cigarettes, 10 kgs of rolling tobacco, 49 litres of spirits, 165 litres of beer and 1.5 litres of wine. He said he had bought it duty free across the Channel and intended selling them to his family and friends. He said he had made about ten trips between Dover and Calais in all and five trips from Sheffield to Dover. He said on two of the trips he had been warned by Customs. He also said the profit was about £1,000. The evaded duty amounted to some £10,000. He was 46, unemployed and effectively of good character. Held. When a court is considering imposing a comparatively short period of custody that is 12 months or less it should ask itself particularly when the defendant has not previously served a sentence of custody whether a shorter period might be equally effective. Applying that **9 months** not 12.

R v Dosanjh [1999] 1 Cr App Rep (S) 107. For amounts between £10,000 and £100,000, sentences **between 6 months and 2 years** will generally be appropriate on a guilty plea.

Value £100,000–£500,000

163.15   *R v Mann* [1998] 2 Cr App Rep (S) 275. The defendant pleaded guilty to conspiracy over 7 months to evade duty on beer. The loss to the revenue was between £374,000 and £385,000 and when it was sold the VAT loss would bring the total loss figure to about £½m. Beer was bought in cash in France and driven back to the UK. It was taken to a public house, which had once been owned and operated by the defendant till he had been made bankrupt. The pub was owned by others but managed by the defendant. The beer was stored in a large shipping container. The defendant took the most active part in the affair, playing the 'office manager' and organiser. He was not the head of the conspiracy although he had recruited others. He received the beer, helped to package it and saw to its onward dispatch. He also travelled to France in the vans. At his home was £11,500. He was 53 and of good character. He was of high standing in the Sikh community. He had once owned three pubs. The judge accepted that his bankruptcy had made him extremely vulnerable to suggestions from others. Held. It was a well organised and lucrative conspiracy. **3 years** was not manifestly excessive.

R v Dosanjh [1999] 1 Cr App Rep (S) 107. The defendant pleaded guilty to evasion of duty. Police stopped a van because it seemed to be overweight. The defendant was a passenger. A large number of cans of beer were found. His home was searched and a total of about 86 litres of spirits, 68 litres of wine, 4,500 cigarettes and 8 litres of beer were found. The defendant said they were from duty free shops. At his house were names and telephone numbers of off-licences. There were also receipts of goods for off-licences. Inquiries revealed that the defendant had made a total of 82 trips across the channel between November 1995 and September 1996 in a variety of vans or mini buses that had been hired in his name. On two occasions, customs officials in Dover had stopped the defendant, and alcohol and cigarettes had been confiscated. The total duty evaded was £164,000. The defendant was now 26 years of age with a conviction for driving while disqualified and a forgery offence but no convictions for an offence of this kind. **Held.** For amounts between £100,000 and £500,000, **2 to 3 years** on a guilty plea, and **up to 4 years**, following a trial, will generally be appropriate. It was repeated wholesale importation in a van hired in his name, despite two previous warnings. **3 years** was at the top of the bracket which we have indicated, following a guilty plea. It was not so manifestly excessive that this court should interfere.

Value £500,000–£1m

163.16   *R v Dosanjh* [1999] 1 Cr App Rep (S) 107. For amounts in excess of £500,000, sentences in the region of **4 years, increasing to the maximum of 7 years**, when a million pounds or more in duty is evaded, will be appropriate, following a trial, with a suitable discount for a plea of guilty.

R v Lee [2001] EWCA Crim 2652, [2002] 2 Cr App Rep (S) 41. The defendant changed his plea to guilty for seven counts of duty evasion which were specimen counts. The EU had introduced an anti dumping duty to protect the EU market from cheap imports from countries with state subsidies or cheap labour. Between August 1994 and September 1997 a company of which the defendant was the beneficial owner arranged with a Hong Kong supplier to purchase Chinese silicon which was subject to the duty. The defendant's company was registered in Liberia and administered in Jersey. The silicon was sold to a company who had contracted to buy silicon of either Western or Australian origin. The defendant stipulated that the silicon should be packaged in plain bags and that Hong Kong should appear as the port of loading. He forged certificates showing the silicon was Australian. 1,960 metric tonnes of silicon was imported in at least 33 importations. The defendant was not responsible for the payment of the duty but the duty evaded was £600,000. He was sentenced on the basis that at the beginning but for a very short time he thought he was buying Australian silicon. His profit was $200,000. He was 51 and of good character. The case meant he could no longer trade in metal and he had lost his livelihood. **Held.** The appropriate starting point was **4 years**. **30 months** was not manifestly excessive.

Value £1m–£5m

163.17   *R v Dosanjh* [1999] 1 Cr App Rep (S) 107. For amounts in excess of £500,000, sentences in the region of **4 years, increasing to the maximum of 7 years**, when a million pounds or more in duty is evaded, will be appropriate, following a trial, with a suitable discount for a plea of guilty. In exceptional cases, where very many millions of pounds in duty are evaded, consecutive sentences may be appropriate; alternatively, it may be appropriate to charge conspiracy to cheat, which is capable of attracting higher sentences than those already indicated.

R v Flaherty and McManus [2000] 1 Cr App Rep (S) 250. The defendants F and M pleaded guilty to evasion of duty. From November 1996 to February 1997 F was involved in removing spirits intended for exports from bonded warehouses. M was involved from the very end of November to February. Fraudulent paper was used and the goods were sold at less than half price. F organised the storage space and some of the documentation. M organised the distribution, signed dockets, hired vehicles etc. The Customs mounted a surveillance operation and the duty evaded was estimated to be £1.2m. F was 41, of good character and a model prisoner. M was 45 with convictions including 1 for deception for which he received 18 months. He also was a model prisoner. The defence contended that there were others more involved and the Judge had been wrong to start at 7 years. Held. The judge started at 7 years and then reduced it because of their relatively subordinate roles. There was no fault in **4 years** for F and **5 years** for M.

Value over £5m

163.18   *R v Dosanjh* [1999] 1 Cr App Rep (S) 107. For amounts in excess of £500,000, sentences in the region of **4 years, increasing to the maximum of 7 years**, when £1m pounds or more in duty is evaded, will be appropriate, following a trial, with a suitable discount for a plea of guilty. In exceptional cases, where very many millions of pounds in duty are evaded, consecutive sentences may be appropriate; alternatively, it may be appropriate to charge conspiracy to cheat, which is capable of attracting higher sentences than those already indicated.

R v Towers [1999] 2 Cr App Rep (S) 110. The defendant pleaded guilty to six counts of being concerned in dealing with goods for which duty had not been paid. He asked for 59 (or 62) similar offences to be taken into account. Over a year he diverted high value goods such as alcohol from bonded warehouses to the black market. He used forged documents, aliases and set up 13 companies to facilitate the fraud. The loss was over £6m. He wasn't the only principle and was involved in the paperwork. He was 53 and had a number of convictions including nine for deception in 1986 for which he received 5 years. Held. This crime is prevalent. The judge could not be faulted for the course he took in imposing 5 years on one count and 2 years consecutive for the other counts making 7 years which was the maximum sentence. However, it could be reduced to **6 years** because of matters raised when we cleared the court.

A-G's Reference (No 90 of 1999) [2001] EWCA Crim 424, [2001] 2 Cr App Rep (S) 349. The defendant pleaded guilty at an early stage to conspiracy to cheat the Inland Revenue and assisting another to obtain the benefit of criminal conduct by money laundering. There was a massive conspiracy to cheat the Inland Revenue of £18m of alcohol and tobacco duty over 3 years. 800 containers of dutiable goods were bought, transported, stored and sold. The second conspiracy was the laundering of the proceeds. He was a director of two French companies and deceived the French tax authorities. He also produced false accounts to support the fraud. The organising brains of the conspiracy pleaded guilty and was sentenced to 9 years. Afterwards the defendant continued the conspiracies and set up other companies to assist. He visited the organiser in prison. He was also involved in printing the false documents. To launder the proceeds he invested in French properties through off shore companies. His payment was £1,700 a month. At the start he was 23 or 24 years old and was of good character with excellent references. He had a degree in accountancy and was married and his wife suffered from ill health. His benefit was assessed at £100,000 and a confiscation order of just over £1,000 was made. Others received 5, 4 and 3 years for conspiracy to cheat. Four years had elapsed since his arrest. Held. 2 years suspended for 2 years was unduly lenient. We would have expected **3½ to 4 years**. Because of the delay, that it was a reference and he had received a non-custodial sentence **18 months** instead.

TDA

See **TAKING MOTOR VEHICLES**

164 TELEPHONE OFFENCES

164.1 Various offences including dishonesty offences and the Telecommunications Act 1984, ss 42 and 42A

Fraudulent use of a telecommunications system and possession or supply of anything for fraudulent purposes in connection with a telecommunication system.

Triable either way. On indictment maximum 5 years. Summary maximum 6 months and/or £5,000.

Harassment

See HARASSMENT, S 4 (OR PUBLIC NUISANCE) – *Telephone calls*

Landline phones, obtaining cheaper or free calls from

164.2   Old case. *R v Aslam* [1996] 2 Cr App Rep (S) 377.

Mobile phones, chipping

164.3   *R v Stephens* [2002] EWCA Crim 136, [2002] 2 Cr App Rep (S) 291. The defendant pleaded guilty at the Magistrates' Court to having items in his custody and control (s 42A). A search warrant was executed at his address and in his workshop were found 75 mobiles which could be encoded and chips some of which could be used for encoding and computer equipment. These chips could modify mobiles to obtain free calls. He was frank and co-operative from his arrest and he said he had copied a system from the Internet. He sold the chips for about £10 and had made about £500. He was in employment earning a reasonable sum but had debts. There were two spent dishonesty convictions. It was very difficult to arrive at a figure for the loss but £11,000 was suggested. The potential was enormous. There was a delay of about a year. Held. Taking into account *R v Barber* [2002] 1 Cr App Rep (S) 548 (about more than a 1/3 off for a plea before venue) **12 months** not 18.

For offences connected with mobiles see DANGEROUS DRIVING – *Magistrates' Court Sentencing Guidelines September 2000*; DEATH BY DANGEROUS DRIVING, CAUSING – *Mobile phone, defendant using;* ROBBERY – *Street robbery – Mobile phones*

TENANTS

See HARASSMENT AND UNLAWFUL EVICTION OF TENANTS

165 TERRORISM

165.1   Defendants are frequently indicted under the Explosive Substances Act 1883, ss 2 and 3.

Indictable only. Maximum life.

Guideline case

165.2   *R v Martin* [1999] 1 Cr App Rep (S) 477 – LCJ. The defendants were convicted of conspiracy to cause explosions likely to endanger life or cause serious injury to property. They planned to attack electricity sub-stations with 37 bombs. Held. This crime was clearly abnormal within Lawton LJ's description in *R v Turner* (1975) 61 Cr App Rep 67 at 90. We fully agree with the extract from *R v Byrne* (1975) 62 Cr App Rep 159 at 163. The reported cases show that the most severe sentences have been passed in cases involving a deliberate threat to human life. For example: *R v Hindawi* (1988) 10 Cr App Rep (S) 104: **45 years**; *R v Basra* (1989) 11 Cr App Rep (S) 527: **35 years**; *R v Kinsella* (1995) 16 Cr App Rep (S) 1035: **35, 25, 16 years**; *R v Al-Banna* (1984) 6 Cr App Rep (S) 426: **30, 35 years**; *R v Mullen* (1991) 12 Cr App Rep (S) 754: **30 years**; *R v Taylor and Hayes* (1995) 16 Cr App Rep (S) 873: **30 years**; *R v McGonagle and Heffernan* [1996] 1 Cr App Rep (S) 90: **25, 23 years**; and *R v Al-Mograbi and Cull* (1980) 70 Cr App Rep (S) 24: **12 years** (but the defendant pleaded guilty, was aged 19 and 'had she been of full adult age, the sentence might well have been 20 years or more.' The current level of sentencing in cases concerning terrorist explosions appeared to be in the range of 20 to 35 years. But there are some cases, which fall outside the bracket, either above or below. The appropriate sentence will plainly depend on a large number of factors, including the likely result of any explosion, the target, the role, the nature, size and likely effect of any explosive device, the motivation and, where death, injury, or damage has been caused, the nature and extent of the death, injury and damage. When imposing sentences for conspiracies of this sort, the courts should remind themselves of the term actually served for murder, particularly murder in its more aggravated forms. But there can be no precise equivalence and conduct threatening the democratic government and the security of the state, and the daily life and livelihood of millions of people, has a seriousness all of its own. For conspiracies directed purely to the destruction of property the starting point should be somewhat wider than 'below 20 years'. In some cases below 15 will be appropriate. In a case such as this it would be unrealistic to ignore the threat to life and limb, since had the conspirators' plan been implemented it seems probable that some injury and loss of life would have resulted, whether intended or not. It is not appropriate to recast English sentencing practice to bring it into line with that in Northern Ireland, even assuming the level of sentences there are lower.

Guideline remarks

165.3 *R v Byrne* (1975) 62 Cr App Rep 159 at 163. The defendants appealed their sentences under s 3 of the Explosives Act 1923. Held. Clearly conduct which is likely to endanger life is more grave than conduct which is likely to cause serious injury to property. In a particular case it may well be that the conduct is likely to do both; in other cases, conduct, although it is likely to do both, is more likely to endanger life than cause serious injury to property or vice versa. The maximum sentence should be reserved for the case with the type of explosive device which has, as its primary purpose (and I stress primary) to endanger life. It is unnecessary for us to specify what kind of explosive device we have in mind. Explosive devices differ considerably. A device which is primarily designed to endanger life may well attract the maximum sentence (then 20 years). On the other hand, if the primary purpose of the device is not to endanger life but to cause serious injury to property then a sentence less than the maximum may be appropriate. The deterrent aspect of sentences for using or conspiring to use explosive devices designed primarily to endanger life should be made clear.

Arson

165.4 *R v Cruickshank and O'Donnell* (1994) 16 Cr App Rep (S) 728 – LCJ. The two defendants pleaded guilty to conspiracy to commit arson with intent to cause, or being reckless as to, damage. They planted and set off a series of incendiary devices in shops in Leeds in order to advance the interests of Irish republicanism. They did not aim to inflict physical injury but to damage property to a very considerable extent. Held. If all the devices in the five shops had ignited, the damage would have been enormous and the City would have looked like a City in the blitz. The emergency services would have been stretched to, and possibly beyond, their limits. £45,000 worth of damage was caused in one store. There would have been a high risk of injury to watchmen, firemen, bomb-disposal men, shop staff and the public generally. The gravamen of what was done was not an attack on an individual, but on the community as a whole. It had a political motivation. It must be clearly understood by activists for whatever cause, that to seek to de-stabilise the community or exert pressure must be met with severe deterrent sentences. Applying *R v Byrne* (1975) 62 Cr App Rep 159, **11 years** not 15 and **16 years** not 20.

Bombs – Lives at risk

165.5 *R v McCardle* [1999] 1 Cr App Rep (S) note at 482 – High Court Judge at Crown Court. The defendant was convicted of conspiracy to cause an explosion. He was a member of PIRA and the explosion was at Canary Wharf. Held. You did not intend to kill anyone, or cause really serious injury to anyone, nor did you personally appreciate the risks of those consequences. However, objectively there was a substantial risk of both death and injury and this conspiracy did, in fact, result in two deaths and many injuries, some of such a severity that the victims' lives will be permanently marred if not ruined. In addition, the conspiracy resulted in damage in excess of £150m and engendered terror and misery for many people. I accept that others did the planning and I make some allowance for that. The fact that there were deaths and serious injuries, whether or not you intended them, whether or not you appreciated the risk, is a serious aggravating feature of this offence. The law does and always should recognise, as one factor in sentencing, the consequences for others and I reject the submission that the deaths should be disregarded in determining the sentence for this offence. **25 years**.

R v Martin [1999] 1 Cr App Rep (S) 477 – LCJ. The defendants were convicted of conspiracy to cause explosions likely to endanger life or cause serious injury to property. They planned to attack electricity sub-stations with 37 bombs. The court reviewed past cases at the Court of Appeal and the Crown Court. Held. The judge was fully entitled to take the view that it called for a sentence of the utmost severity. The political, economic and social threat presented by this conspiracy was, perhaps, as great as in any of the cases we have considered. However, some weight must be given to the fact that death and injury, although likely, was not its primary object. Some reduction should be made in the sentence of 35 years. That sentence means, in real years, a minimum of 17½ years and a maximum of 23 years and 4 months: that is the sort of term served by the perpetrator of a murder with severely aggravating features. **28 years** substituted.

R v Abedin (2002) Times, 28 February – High Court Judge at Crown Court. The defendant was convicted of conspiracy to cause an explosion. As a result of a long surveillance operation, MI5 nipped in the bud a plot that would have caused immense risk to life. The defendant who had extreme Islamic views had used a house and an industrial unit to stockpile bomb-making material. The defendant was born in Bangladesh and was 27. **20 years**. [Treat news reports with care.]

166 THEFT ETC

166.1 Theft Act 1968, s 1

Triable either way. On indictment maximum sentence 7 years. On summary maximum 6 months and/or £5,000. There is power to make a restitution order under the Powers of Criminal Courts (Sentencing) Act 2000, s 148. If the offence is theft or attempted theft of a motor vehicle the offence carries discretionary disqualification.

The cases listed include cases of obtaining money etc by deception, forgery, false accounting, making or using a false instrument and public nuisance where the essence of those offences is theft.

Crown Court statistics England and Wales[1] – Crown Court – Males 21+ – Theft

166.2

Year	Plea	Total Numbers sentenced	Type of sentence%					Average length of custody (months)
			Discharge	Fine	Community sentence	Suspended sentence	Custody	
From the person								
2000	Guilty	786	6%	4%	30%	3%	57%	11.7
	Not guilty	139	3%	6%	25%	0%	65%	18.1
In a dwelling not automatic machine or meter								
2000	Guilty	54	7%	0%	26%	4%	63%	11.3
	Not guilty	7	0%	0%	57%	0%	43%	34
Theft by employee								
2000	Guilty	157	6%	3%	32%	7%	52%	11.1
	Not guilty	41	2%	5%	22%	5%	66%	14.4
Theft or unauthorised taking from Mail								
2000	Guilty	6	17%	17%	17%	0%	33%	16.5
	Not guilty	4	0%	0%	25%	0%	75%	10.7
Abstracting electricity								
2000	Guilty	3	0%	0%	100%	0%	0%	0
	Not guilty	5	0%	0%	60%	0%	40%	4.6
Theft from vehicle								
2000	Guilty	29	3%	0%	24%	3%	69%	10.6
	Not guilty	9	0%	0%	0%	0%	100%	22.3
Theft from shops								
2000	Guilty	465	10%	7%	30%	1%	51%	8.9
	Not guilty	111	16%	16%	27%	0%	40%	8.1
Theft of pedal cycle								
2000	Guilty	5	20%	0%	0%	0%	60%	6
Theft from automatic machine or meter								
2000	Guilty	9	22%	0%	67%	0%	11%	6
	Not guilty	4	50%	0%	0%	0%	50%	6.5
Forgery of drug prescriptions								
2000	Guilty	12	8%	0%	25%	8%	58%	21.9
	Not guilty	2	0%	0%	100%	0%	0%	0
Other forgery								
2000	Guilty	174	6%	4%	27%	7%	54%	15
	Not guilty	40	3%	5%	33%	5%	55%	27.1

Crown Court statistics England and Wales[1] *– Crown Court – Males 21+ – Fraud by a company director*

Year	Plea	Total Numbers sentenced	Type of sentence%					Average length of custody (months)
			Discharge	Fine	Community sentence	Suspended sentence	Custody	
2000	Guilty	29	0%	7%	24%	10%	59%	24.2
	Not guilty	12	0%	0%	8%	17%	75%	30.4

1 Excluding committals for sentence. Source: Crime and Criminal Justice Unit, Home Office Ref: IOS416-02.

Magistrates'CourtSentencingGuidelinesSeptember2000

166.3 Entry point. Is it serious enough for a community penalty? Consider the impact on the victim. Examples of aggravating factors for the offence are high value, planned, sophisticated, adults involving children, organised team, related damage and vulnerable victim. Examples of mitigating factors for the offence are impulsive action and low value. Examples of mitigation are age, health (physical or mental), co-operation with police, voluntary compensation and genuine remorse. Give reasons for not awarding compensation.

For details about the guidelines see MAGISTRATES' COURT SENTENCING GUIDELINES at page 331.

Advance fee fraud

166.4 *R v Boothe* [1999] 1 Cr App Rep (S) 98. See *Value £100,001–£1m*

R v Iwuji [2001] 1 Cr App Rep (S) 456. The defendant pleaded guilty to conspiracy to defraud. The victim who was employed in Saudi Arabia received a fax regarding blocked funds in Nigeria. He contacted the sender of the fax who claimed to be a highly placed official in the Nigerian National Petrol Corporation. The sender said there was $30.5m from an over invoiced contract which was available to be transferred to an account abroad. The victim received false documents purportedly from the Petrol Corporation, the Ministry of Finance at the Funds Disbursement Unit in Lagos and the Central Bank of Nigeria. There were a number of telephone calls and faxes. The victim was asked to pay an administration fee of £5,500, and asked to travel to London. He did so and was met by a chauffeur and was driven to the defendant who was posing as Dr Moore. Eventually he paid the fee and was told the cheque had been stopped because of the lack of a VAT receipt. He was shown a number of forged documents including a cheque for $30.5m. He was told to pay $305,000 and he contacted the police who conducted an undercover operation and the defendant was arrested. The defendant was involved in planning the fraud by using false cheques, false documents and creating a false organisation in London. Accommodation and cars were hired. He was 28. In 1996 he received 30 months for possessing false instruments with intent to use. It involved cloned credit cards. Held. He is a determined fraudster who failed to heed the warning of his last sentence. Because of that and that he was attempting to obtain a larger figure than *R v Boothe* [1999] 1 Cr App Rep (S) 98 there can be no criticism of **3½ years**.

Airport baggage handlers

166.5 *R v Dhunay* (1986) 8 Cr App Rep (S) 107. For persistent pilfering from luggage at airports the starting point is **3 years**.

Alternatives to custody

166.6   *R v Kefford* [2002] EWCA Crim 519, [2002] 2 Cr App Rep (S) 495 – LCJ. In the case of economic crimes, eg obtaining undue credit by fraud, prison is not necessarily the only appropriate form of punishment. Particularly in the case of those who have no record of previous offending, the very fact of having to appear before a court can be a significant punishment. Certainly, having to perform a type of community punishment can be a very salutary way of making it clear that crime does not pay, particularly if a community punishment order is combined with a curfew order.

Betting, connected with/Sporting

166.7   *R v Chee Kew Ong* [2001] 1 Cr App Rep (S) 404. The defendant pleaded on the first day of his trial to conspiracy to cause a public nuisance. The plan was to interfere with the lighting in a Premier Division football match so those placing bets in the Far East could make large sums of money. If the lights go out the match is abandoned and the bookmakers pay out on the then score. The defendant and another were prime movers in this country. They recruited a security guard at the ground who for £20,000 gave the defendant who was an electrical engineer access to the control room. Before the match started the defendants were arrested. The defendants were expected to gain substantial money. The Club would have incurred substantial financial loss estimated to be a six figure sum. He was of good character. Held. The practice of interfering with an important sporting fixture should be discouraged by severe sentences. **4 years** was not manifestly excessive.

Car ringing

See *Vehicles – Car ringing*

Charging for work that is not necessary or not done

166.8   *R v Hafeez and Gibbs* [1998] 1 Cr App Rep (S) 276. The defendant G changed his plea to guilty to conspiracy to obtain property by deception. G expressed a willingness to give evidence for the prosecution against H and another and the other two then changed their pleas to guilty. Over 7 months H, G and others agreed to defraud customers about work done and goods supplied in the garage trade. There were 10 loser witnesses who lost about £10,000. The prosecution case was that there were very substantially more vehicles involved than those belonging to the 10. Vehicles were deliberately damaged eg a car was put in fourth or fifth gear to burn out the clutch. This was called 'hitting.' All members of staff were instructed in 'hitting' cars. Bills were inflated. H was the prime mover who had invented the scheme and he owed and operated a number of businesses in the garage trade. G was an account clerk who had been involved for a comparatively short period of time. However he was a manager who did instruct employees to defraud customers. H was of good character and a family man. He had borrowed money so a compensation order of £10,000 could be paid. G was also of good character and had a supportive letter from the Council about his valuable work as a foster parent. Held. It was complex and audacious. It was more serious than the framework in *R v Barrick* (1985) 7 Cr App Rep (S) 142. H involved a large number of other people and conducted a substantial business on a deeply dishonest basis. **3 years** was not excessive. The offer to give evidence weighs heavily in G's favour. His sentence reduced from 18 to **12 months**.

Charging for work that is not necessary or not done or overcharging – House repairs

166.9   *R v Stewart* [1997] 1 Cr App Rep (S) 71. The defendant pleaded guilty to conspiracy to steal and doing an act tending to pervert the course of justice. Over

6 days he and three or four others stole £13,900 from a 66-year-old lady who lived alone. She was told the house was in danger of falling down. She agreed to repairs and the thieves took her to banks and building societies to withdraw the cash. They took all her savings. Very little work was done to the house apart from rough painting over some cracks. That work was valued at £100. The defendant came in at a late stage. During the court proceedings he claimed the identity of his brother for nearly 7 months. He also produced false alibi evidence. The defendant was 47 and had an appalling record. He had a number of convictions for dishonesty and three for attempting to pervert the course of justice. **4 years** and 3 months consecutive was not manifestly excessive.

R v Flynn [1998] 2 Cr App Rep (S) 413. The defendant pleaded guilty to four counts of obtaining property by deception and two counts of procuring the execution of a valuable security by a deception. He obtained £6,200 from three elderly people by overcharging them for building works. The first victim was charged £3,360 for re-pointing, re-plastering and damp proofing etc. His work was only worth £500 and it was below standard. The second victim paid £1,740 for work on her roof tiles. He accompanied her to the bank and that amount was all the money she had. The work was only worth £190. The third victim was partly blind and she gave him £1,100 for work which was worth about £250–£350. He was 32 with a long record. In 1990 he received 2 years for similar offences with a burglary. The risk of re-offending was described as clear. The judge said the offences were carefully planned and he deliberately chose vulnerable old victims. Held. These were mean and unpleasant deceptions. His previous offending made it more serious. **4 years** not 6.

R v Ball and Ball [2001] 1 Cr App Rep (S) 171. The defendants A and N were father and son and jointly indicted. N pleaded guilty to two counts of obtaining money transfers by deception, one count of obtaining property by deception and one attempt. A was convicted of the three counts and the attempt count was left on the file. They told an 80-year-old widow that they had done work for her before and urgent work was needed on her roof. They said the side of the roof needed stripping out and the tiles needed mastic coating etc. The cost was £4,095. She paid £3,000 in cash and £1,095 in a cheque after they drove her to her bank. She was next told two beams in the roof needed replacing and that would cost £800. To pay for it she had to obtain a bank loan. Next they said the chimney stacks needed lowering because they were dangerous. The cost would be £1,200. Her stepson was present and informed the police. A was 42 and had spent convictions. N was 23 with convictions for dishonesty but it wasn't a bad record. Held. The victim was elderly, vulnerable and targeted. The offences were cowardly and courts will take a very serious view of them and impose substantial sentences. **4 years** for A and **3 years** for N were severe but not excessive.

See also *R v Seymour* [2002] EWCA Crim 444, [2002] 2 Cr App Rep (S) 442.

Charity offences

166.10   *R v Pippard and Harris* [2001] EWCA Crim 2925, [2002] 2 Cr App Rep (S) 166. The defendants were convicted of conspiracy to obtain money by deception. They set up a bogus charity, Helping Kids and kept the money collected. A genuine charity's name was usurped and one of the signatures of a local secretary was transferred to give the charity authenticity. That charity's number was misused on literature and put on the badges of those who collected the money. The defendants recruited collectors who were often the wives of serving officers to collect from pubs, ensuring the collectors made the contact and not the defendants. Small amounts were obtained and it was impossible to say how much. Both defendants had clean records and had good army service. Imprisonment would have serious consequences for their families. The judge said it was vital that public confidence in charities should be maintained so people continue to give to charities and that deterrent sentences were necessary. Held. It was a thoroughly dishonest scheme exploiting the public's goodwill. We agree with the judge's comments. **2 years** was consistent with the court's duty to stamp out dishonesty of this kind.

See also **FRAUD** – *Charity fraud*

Cheques

166.11   *R v Osinowo* (23 October 2001, unreported). The defendant pleaded guilty on re-arraignment to handling. He also pleaded guilty to a bail offence for which he was fined. He allowed another, Q to use his bank account to pay in cheques. The victim discovered her chequebook had been taken and a cheque for £4,700 was paid into his bank account. He was charged and a verdict of not guilty was entered for that. Police searched his home and discovered a blank cheque. He said Q gave it to him. No attempt had been made to use the cheque. The defendant was a 23-year-old student of good character when the offence was committed. Since then he had been given a community service order and had not performed any work. His pre-sentence report said that that another order would not be appropriate. Held. The offence of handling is always serious and that certainly applies to cheques. A short custodial sentence was right and the judge was justified in suspending it. However, **4 months suspended** not 12.

Credit card offences – Guideline remarks

166.12   *R v Aroride* [1999] 2 Cr App Rep (S) 406. Fraudulent use of credit cards or information about credit cards is a serious offence, since it undermines and exploits the modern system of telephone transactions using credit cards. Immediate and substantial terms of imprisonment will generally be called for. [This remark appears to relate to telephone ordering.]

Credit card offences

166.13   *R v Aroride* [1999] 2 Cr App Rep (S) 406. The defendant pleaded guilty to attempting to obtain property by a deception at the Magistrates' Court. He acquired a copy of someone else's credit card statement. He then ordered some Porsche wheels and tyres worth £3,000 on the telephone and to pay for them gave the other person's name and card number. It was arranged the wheels should be delivered to the other person's house. The seller was suspicious and the wheels were in fact delivered by two plain clothes policemen who met the defendant outside the property. The defendant said he was the other person and signed a receipt. He denied he had made the telephone call. After pleading guilty he failed to attend the next hearing. The defendant was about 23 and a student who was short of money. Held. There was nothing wrong with an 8 month sentence. However, as the judge had not mentioned the credit for the plea the sentence was reduced to **7 months** consecutive to the bail sentence.

Credit facilities, obtaining

166.14   *R v Mills* (2002) Times, 30 January – LCJ. The defendant pleaded guilty to two offences of obtaining services by deception. She completed an application for credit at a store and claimed that the Merseyside Fire Service had employed her for 3 years. This was untrue. Credit facilities were granted. For 12 months she had made the minimum payments. She made no more payments. With interest and charges, the account was £5,682.66 in debt. She also purchased goods to the value of £714 from another store. A 10% deposit was paid. She applied for credit to finance the balance. In her application she claimed to have been employed by Allwood Joinery for 6 years.

This was quite untrue. Some months after a finance company issued a credit card to the appellant, which she then used. She said she had not knowingly applied for, or expected to receive, the card. By the time that account was closed, it was approximately £5,438 in debit, and only £43.76 had been paid. She was arrested and when interviewed she admitted that she had made the false representations on each application. She had borrowed £4,000 from her mother to pay off part of the debt. She was 33 years of age and the sole carer of two children aged 11 and 4. She had no previous convictions or cautions and had references. They said that she did voluntary work at a local charity shop and gave her time to a voluntary agency assisting parents with young children. A pre-sentence report recommended a community sentence. The judge said, 'Those who commit offences of this kind, knowing perfectly well that there is really no chance of them ever being able to pay for the goods concerned, go to prison.' Held. The appellant was deeply sorry for the way she had behaved and the offences had been committed to provide for her children. The first factor that has to be take into account is that apart from 'the clang of the prison door' type of sentence, which gives a prisoner the opportunity of knowing what is involved in imprisonment, the ability of the prison service to achieve anything positive in a short prison sentence is very limited. Secondly, with a mother who is the sole supporter of two young children, you must consider them if the sole carer is sent to prison. Finally, take into account the current situation with the female prison population. Since 1993 there has been a remarkable increase. Short prison sentences are always difficult for the prison service to accommodate. The ability to imprison mothers close to their homes in the community is difficult. The difficulties in the prison population to which we have referred does not mean that if an offence is such that it is necessary to send an offender to prison, they should not be sent to prison. But in a borderline case, where the offence does not in particular involve violence but is one with financial consequences to a commercial concern, it is very important to take into account the facts to which we have referred. The courts should strive to avoid sending people like her to prison and instead use punishments in the community. It is true that obtaining credit is easy. Commercial concerns are entitled to the protection of the courts. It was wrong in principle to send her to prison. The minimum period should be passed for this category of offending. If it was necessary to send her to prison, all that would be required was the clang of the prison door. One month not 8 months should have been imposed. It would have been right to impose a **community punishment** order in this case then but now we will make a community rehabilitation order for 6 months.

Company frauds

See COMPANY FRAUDS AND FINANCIAL SERVICES OFFENCES

Confidence tricks

166.15 *R v Salathiel* [1998] 1 Cr App Rep (S) 338. The defendant Sa was convicted of six offences of obtaining by deception. The defendant Sm pleaded guilty to six theft and deception counts and the third defendant M pleaded guilty to three. Over nearly 3 years, the main victim who was in his 50s and lived with his parents was systematically swindled by the three defendants using false names. Sa befriended him and told him she needed a kidney operation and that gypsies were not covered by the Health Service. He gave her £1,000 and said he would repay him from a legacy, which was expected shortly. This was followed by another request and payment of £1,000. £850 was then given for a poll tax bill. £4,000 was obtained to make up the £10,000 needed for the operation. The victim then became fond of Sa and believed she would marry him. Sa introduced Sm to the victim and Sm said she needed money for a divorce. The victim obtained a bank loan for £2,000 and paid the money over. Sa said she needed a further operation and the victim sold £1,300 of shares to pay the £1,700 requested. The victim borrowed £6,910 from his aunt to pay the various sums. Sa said the money would be paid back. The victim then discussed marrying M and he obtained a legacy of £28,000 and paid the aunt back. The money was paid to her estate as she had died. £26,500 was handed over for a caravan and site for them to live together. Sm also obtained £2,000 so she could buy a caravan to live near them. Finally Sm and M visited him. M had a black eye and they claimed all their inheritance had been taken in a mugging. They asked to take some ornaments, which he agreed to. While he cuddled with M, S took ornaments, which he hadn't agreed to give them. He called the police who discovered Sm and M had obtained £1,500 from a woman on the promise of an inheritance. The judge described Sa as scheming, greedy and heartless and the instigator. The judge said the case ranks among the gravest because of the number of people involved, the length of time it operated and the amount of money obtained from very vulnerable people. The judge sentenced Sa to **5 years**, M to **4 years** and Sm to **3 years**. Held. We endorse his tariff.

Drug abstinence order

166.16 Powers of Criminal Courts (Sentencing) Act 2000, s 58A(1). Where a person is 18 or over the court may make an order requiring the offender to abstain from misusing specified Class A drugs and provide, when instructed to do so a sample to ascertain whether he has any specified Class A drugs in his body. (3) The court must be of the opinion the offender is dependant or has a propensity to misuse specified Class A drugs and the offence is a trigger offence or the misuse of any specified Class A drug caused or contributed to the offence in question. (7) An order shall be for not less than 6 months and not more than 3 years. (9) No order shall be made unless the court has been notified that arrangements for implementing the order are available. [Criminal Justice and Court Services Act 2000, Sch 6 specifies theft, obtaining property by a deception and going equipped to steal as trigger offences.]

Electricity or gas (including abstracting electricity)

166.17 *R v Hughes* [2000] 2 Cr App Rep (S) 399. The defendant pleaded guilty to criminal damage, and two counts of theft of gas. A gas engineer went to the defendant's home and found that the gas meter had been removed so the gas supply by-passed the meter. The engineer capped the internal supply. About five months later another engineer found the cap had been removed and a home-made connection had been fitted. Gas was leaking from that connection. The defendant admitted that he had by-passed the system and said that he intended to pay for the gas when he could. He also claimed there was also a problem with his benefits, which had been suspended. The defendant was 36. He had been in the army and had been a lorry driver. Currently he was unable to work due to clinical depression. The previous year he had been sentenced to 2 months imprisonment for three fraudulent benefit offences. He was on probation for possession of a Class B drug. The pre-sentence report referred to the break up of his marriage and recommended probation. A custodial sentence was inevitable. However, the theft sentences were reduced from 6 months each to 3 months each. The 2 months criminal damage sentence was unchallenged and the all the sentences remained concurrent.

Endorsement

166.18 Road Traffic Act 1991, s 26 and Sch 2, para 32. The relevant entries were removed from the Road Traffic Offenders Act 1988 so endorsement was no longer applicable for stealing a motor vehicle.

Financial services

See COMPANY FRAUDS AND FINANCIAL SERVICES OFFENCES

Handbag thefts

See *Pickpocket/Theft from persons in public places*

Making off without payment

See MAKING OFF WITHOUT PAYMENT

Persistent offenders

166.19   *R v Mullins* [2000] 2 Cr App Rep (S) 372. The defendant pleaded guilty to theft and was committed for sentence. An undercover police officer posed as a customer in a shoe shop. Another officer kept watch. The defendant seized the bag and gave it to an accomplice. The defendant was arrested. He was 34 and had 36 appearances (the report says convictions) for 44 offences. Most of them were for dishonesty and mostly related to the defendant's drug addiction. He had been to prison three times in the last year for theft. He suffered from epilepsy and hepatitis C. **3 years** was severe but it was not excessive.

R v Richardson [2000] 2 Cr App Rep (S) 373. The defendant pleaded guilty to theft and false imprisonment. The defendant at night visited the victim, a lady of 89 whom he knew. He asked to use the lavatory. She followed him. She said he should leave. He refused and appeared to be on drugs. He was aggressive and threatened to hurt her. He pushed her into her sitting room and forced her into an armchair. He tied a jumper over her face. He asked for £20. On a number of occasions she attempted to get out of the chair but he pushed her back. She was repeatedly threatened that she would be hurt if she told anyone about him. She allowed him to make a call for a taxi. When the taxi arrived he snatched her bag and stole £20. He tore the telephone wire from the wall. Because the telephone did not work and she could not manage the steps in the dark she had to stay in all night unable to contact anyone. Before the police started to look for him he went to a police station and confessed to a robbery. His account was very similar to the victim, although he claimed to have told her he wasn't going to hurt her. The defendant was very anxious she should not have to go to court and therefore did not contest her account. He had a bad record with 12 appearances in the last 10 years seven of which were for robbery. He had three convictions for burglary, three convictions for theft in a dwelling house and three convictions for theft from a person. He expressed remorse. The reason for his offending was crack cocaine. It was so serious a DTT order was inappropriate. In light of the mitigation **4 years** not 5 years substituted.

R v Dolphy [1999] 1 Cr App Rep (S) 73. The defendant was convicted of stealing £287. An elderly lady picked up her pension at the Post Office. He distracted her attention and stole £287. The defendant had convictions for dishonesty over 25 years. He had shortly been released from a three year sentence for three counts of theft totalling £1,500. They were all thefts from persons. **4 years** was severe but not excessive.

Pickpocket/Theft from persons in public places – Guideline remarks

166.20   *R v Gwillim-Jones* [2001] EWCA Crim 904, [2002] 1 Cr App Rep (S) 19. A handbag may contain within it credit cards, diaries, telephone numbers, and personal items. The theft of a handbag may cause both inconvenience and distress to the victim, quite out of proportion to the intrinsic value of the handbag itself or any cash within it.

Pickpocket/Theft from persons in public places – Persistent offenders – Guideline remarks

166.21 *R v Spencer and Carby* (1994) 16 Cr App Rep (S) 482. Where the offender has a long history of pickpocketing and can properly be considered a professional pickpocket, the sentences may well be in terms of years. Professional pickpocketing must be deterred. Both of these men fall into that category. They have not been deterred by short sentences. These offences can properly be viewed as more serious by reason of the appallingly long records of each for pickpocketing.

Pickpocket/Theft from persons in public places – Persistent offenders – Cases

166.22 *R v Mullins* [2000] 2 Cr App Rep (S) 372. The defendant pleaded guilty to theft and was committed for sentence. An undercover police officer posed as a customer in a shoe shop. Another officer kept watch. The defendant seized the bag and gave it to an accomplice. The defendant was arrested. He was 34 and had 36 appearances (the report says convictions) for 44 offences. Most of them were for dishonesty and mostly related to the defendant's drug addiction. He had been to prison three times in the last year for theft. He suffered from epilepsy and hepatitis C. **3 years** was severe but it was not excessive.

R v Dolphy [1999] 1 Cr App Rep (S) 73. The defendant was convicted of stealing £287. An elderly lady picked up her pension at the Post Office. He distracted her attention and stole £287. The defendant had convictions for dishonesty over 25 years. He had shortly been released from a three year sentence for three counts of theft totalling £1,500. They were all thefts from persons. **4 years** was severe but not excessive.

R v Bolt [1999] 2 Cr App Rep (S) 202. The defendant pleaded guilty to theft. His accomplice stole a handbag from the floor of a pub near a customer and the two drove off together. The police caught them. He was 28 and had an appalling record. There were 30 convictions since he was 11. He had been sentenced to 3 and 5 years. This offence was committed 3 months after his release from the 5 years. The judge ignored the defence version that it was an impulse theft. Held. The judge should have indicated his view to counsel. An impulse theft is worth **12 months** not 2 years. There was no reason he should not serve the remainder of the earlier sentence.

R v Jarrett [2000] 2 Cr App Rep (S) 166. The defendant changed his plea to guilty of theft. He and another took a hotel guest's purse from her bag while she was waiting at reception. They were so close she felt uncomfortable. Security staff saw them and they were arrested The purse was recovered. The defendant was 37 with numerous convictions including burglary, theft and attempted theft. He had nine convictions for stealing handbags or their contents and had been out of trouble for 2 years. Held. These offences are prevalent. People need to be protected especially from people like the defendant who can be described as a professional pickpocket. **18 months** was well within the appropriate range.

R v Gwillim-Jones [2001] EWCA Crim 904, [2002] 1 Cr App Rep (S) 19. The defendant was convicted of attempted theft. The defendant sat on a barstool and dragged a woman's handbag towards him using his foot. Another customer who saw it grabbed him. The police arrested him. Seven weeks before he was placed on probation for two thefts of handbags or purses from women in pubs. He was placed on probation. He had 100 convictions for theft and seemed to target ladies handbags in pubs and shopping areas. Every type of penalty had been tried. None seemed to have any effect. He was 47 Held. He was plainly a professional. It is necessary for professional handbag thieves to know if they are caught they will receive severe sentences. **3 years** was appropriate.

Police officers as defendants

166.23   *R v Roberts* [1999] 1 Cr App Rep (S) 381. The defendant was convicted of stealing a watch. He was a police constable with 19 years' service attached to CID with the temporary rank of detective constable. After a search, property including two watches was taken to a police station. It was lodged in a property store. Sometime later another officer noticed the defendant wearing one of the watches. He found the watch was missing from the store and reported it. When questioned the defendant said he was going to replace it and had mislaid his watch. No owner could be traced as all those questioned denied any knowledge of the watch. The watch was worth about £90. He was sentenced on the basis it was a moment of madness. He was 41 with a family and had lost his job. Held. There can be no compromise on the standard of integrity the public requires of serving policemen in relationship to the performance of their duties. Applying *R v Ollerenshaw* [1999] 1 Cr App Rep (S) 65 **2 months** not 4.

See also **POLICE OFFICERS**

Shoplifting

166.24   *R v Howells Re Glowacki* [1999] 1 Cr App Rep (S) 335 at 340 – LCJ. The defendant pleaded guilty to theft. The defendant and two women entered a store and were seen to be acting suspiciously. They were watching the staff and the defendant was continually covering the movements of the two women. The police were informed and the three were stopped as they left. They were arrested and the women were found to have two pairs of jeans and a number of bottles of perfume and after-shave concealed in apron-type bags under their skirts. The value was £449. He denied the offence when interviewed. He was 22 and was a polish citizen who had applied for political asylum. He was not permitted to work. He had failed to co-operate with the probation service and had failed to answer to his bail. The women absconded. Held. This was an organised and deliberate shoplifting expedition. However it did not justify a custodial sentence. Community service would have been appropriate with a clear explanation of the consequences for non-compliance. Taking into account the time served (34 days) **conditional discharge** not 6 months.

Telephone boxes (including going equipped to steal)

166.25   *R v Ferry and Wynn* [1997] 2 Cr App Rep (S) 42. Both defendants pleaded guilty to going equipped to steal from telephone boxes in a rural area. The plea was entered just before a trial was to take place. The two were seen in a telephone box. A passer-by told the police who later stopped their car. Inside the car were tools including a screwdriver, a cordless drill, a ratchet and surgical gloves. A BT investigator said that some of them had been specially modified for telephone box fraud. Also found was a map with nine red dots, which corresponded to telephone box locations. Several of those boxes had signs of attempted theft. Wynn also pleaded guilty to attempted theft of another telephone box when he was on bail for the Ferry offence. He was also in breach of a conditional discharge for attempted theft of another telephone box. He had a handling conviction. Held. As Wynn was the prime mover 12 months for the going equipped and 6 months consecutive for the attempted theft with 12 months concurrent for the conditional discharge matter was not wrong (18 months in all). Ferry, who was 28, had a long record of dishonesty offences including up to 20 for thefts. He had a heroin problem. **6 months** not 12 imprisonment.

Old cases. *R v Arslan* (1993) 15 Cr App Rep (S) 90; *R v Costello* (1993) 15 Cr App Rep (S) 240.

Vehicles, entering into them

166.26   *A-G's Reference (No 48 of 1999)* [2000] 1 Cr App Rep (S) 472 – LCJ. The defendant pleaded guilty to conspiracy to steal. During a 9 month period he stole tools from vans during the night. Each loss was between £100 to £3,000 and he was arrested and bailed twice. He co-operated with the police and admitted involvement in 25 thefts. In all, the property stolen was worth £25,000. He was 28 and had a long list of convictions including burglary and some which were similar to this offence. He looked after his disabled father who was 'highly dependant' on him. The defendant had been addicted to amphetamines but had voluntarily sought help at a clinic. The judge recognised he had made a determined effort to conquer his drug problem and the public interest was best served by a course of treatment. He was placed on **probation** for 2 years with a condition of attendance at a centre for 30 days. Although there had been one lapse back into drug taking the latest reports were positive. One said he had attended regularly at the centre and the writer considered a custodial sentence would be counterproductive. Held. If he had been convicted the ordinary sentence would have been 18 months to 2 years. With a guilty plea and his mitigation a sentence in the order of 12 months would have been in no way excessive. Sentencing courts must retain an element of discretion. The sentence was merciful and one open for the judge to pass so not unduly lenient.

R v Burns (26 September 2002, unreported). The defendant pleaded guilty to theft. He was seen sitting in a minibus owned by a charity and the police were called. He told them he was looking for somewhere to sleep. He was searched and they found a carton of fruit juice, keys to the minibus and a fuel card. The basis of plea was he found the bus unlocked and entered it to sleep. He took the juice and intended to drive the bus. He had no intention of using the fuel card. His pre-sentence report offered no community penalty as the hostel he was satying at was no longer willing to house him because of his behaviour. He had failed to respond to a previous community penalty. Held. The offence had not crossed the custody threshold. The difficulty is finding a non-custodial sentence which can realistically be imposed on the defendant. **Conditional discharge for 12 months** not 3 months.

Vehicles, car ringing cases (including handling)

166.27   *R v Evans* [1996] 1 Cr App Rep (S) 105. The judge said, 'Car crime is rampant and police resources are so limited they can only deal with a small proportion of the car crimes reported. The public are sick to death of having to subsidise the activities of people like you by ever increasing insurance premiums and having to suffer the heartache of the loss of an expensive piece of property and large sums of money which they hardly ever get back.' Held. We agree. For a ringleader on a fight **4–5 years** would not be excessive even when the defendant is of good character. For a lieutenant on a fight **3 years** notwithstanding good character.

R v Dennard and Draper [2000] 1 Cr App Rep (S) 232. The first defendant WD was convicted of conspiracy to steal. The second defendant JD pleaded guilty to six counts of handling and one count of obtaining property by a deception. It was a car ringing case. 33 vehicles were involved of which 23 were stolen. Vans were obtained so their identities could be used and vans were stolen. 15 transactions were referred to. WD was 50. JD was 30 and treated as a secondary actor in the conspiracy. WD was JD's father-in-law. They were both treated as of good character. The judge considered WD the mastermind who kept his distance from the actual dirty work. Held. Because WD was given the maximum sentence his 7 years was reduced to **5 years**. JD sentence was reduced from 4 years to **3 years**.

See also *A-G's Reference (Nos 110–1 of 2001)* [2002] EWCA Crim 586, [2002] 2 Cr App Rep (S) 546.

Value hard to quantify

166.28   *A-G's Reference (No 48 and 49 of 1997)* [1998] 2 Cr App Rep (S) 392. The two defendants pleaded guilty to conspiracy to steal and one of them pleaded guilty to an earlier residential burglary. They had originally been charged with conspiracy to rob. Police surveillance revealed that the two had among other matters followed a Royal Mail van, driven slowly passed a security van, and were seen outside two Post Offices. They were also seen driving two stolen cars and two balaclavas were found hidden in a car. The prosecution said it was a protracted conspiracy to steal from compounds, factories, security vans and Post Offices. The basis of plea was that they had targeted premises but there was to be no force or threats. One defendant was 35, with a number of previous convictions including burglary and robbery. The other was 28 with previous convictions including s 20 GBH, attempted burglary, going equipped for burglary and burglary. Held. Because of the basis of plea the chance of serious theft taking place was very small. **2 years** would have been appropriate. However, it was not appropriate to alter sentences of **14 and 15 months**.

Value less than £1,000

166.29   *R v Burns* (26 September 2002, unreported). The defendant pleaded guilty to theft. He was seen sitting in a minibus owned by a charity and the police were called. He told them he was looking for somewhere to sleep. He was searched and they found a carton of fruit juice, keys to the minibus and a fuel card. The basis of plea was he found the bus unlocked and entered it to sleep. He took the juice and intended to drive the bus. He had no intention of using the fuel card. His pre-sentence report offered no community penalty as the hostel he was satying at was no longer willing to house him because of his behaviour. He had failed to respond to a previous community penalty. Held. The offence had not crossed the custody threshold. The difficulty is finding a non-custodial sentence which can realistically be imposed on the defendant. **Conditional discharge for 12 months** not 3 months.

Value £1,000–£100,000

See also *R v Vanderwell* [1998] 1 Cr App Rep (S) 439.

Value £100,001–£1m

166.30   *R v Boothe* [1999] 1 Cr App Rep (S) 98. The defendant pleaded guilty to attempting to obtain property by deception and having a false instrument. The victim a US businessman received an unsolicited letter purporting to be from the Government of Nigeria inviting his company to receive $17.5m in excess fees in return for which he would receive 30% commission. He received faxes apparently from the Nigerian Government and the Central Bank of Nigeria. As a result he paid £17,000 legal fees, cable charges of $14,000, $26,150 for an Insurance Release Bond, $25,000 signing fees, $25,500 handling charges, a further sum for VAT, $3,124 for postage $28,000 insurance fees, a $13,500 security charge and stamp duty fees as well as two fountain pens and two fax machines. He contacted the US Secret Service and they asked him to continue to go along with the arrangements. He did so and was told by the fraudsters to go to London and pay $200,000 VAT to Gary Boothe. As arranged he met the defendant who produced further documents from the Central Bank of Nigeria. It was arranged the money would be exchanged the following day. They met again the next day and $200,000 was exchanged for some documents and a forged cheque for $17.5m. Police then arrested him and he had an ID card for the Central Bank of Nigeria on him. In interview he said he was a lawyer for the Bank and he believed the cheque was genuine. He was 31. Held. This advance fee fraud was at that time prevalent. This was not a breach of trust case but guidance can be obtained from those cases. The victim was a greedy and willing participant in this scam, but that does not destroy the defendant's criminality. The defendant came late into the scheme. **2½ years** in all not 3½.

Breach of trust

Breach of trust – Guideline case

166.31   *R v Barrick* [1985] 7 Cr App Rep (S) 142 – LCJ. Where a person in a position of trust, for example, an accountant, solicitor, bank employee or postman, has used that privileged and trusted position to defraud his partners or clients or employers or the general public of sizeable sums of money. He will usually, as in this case, be a person of hitherto impeccable character. It is practically certain, again as in this case, that he will never offend again and, in the nature of things, he will never again in his life be able to secure similar employment with all that that means in the shape of disgrace for himself and hardship for himself and also his family. It was not long ago that this type of offender might expect to receive a term of imprisonment of 3–4 years, and indeed a great deal more if the sums involved were substantial. More recently, however, the sentencing climate in this area has changed, and certainly so far as solicitors are concerned, has changed radically. Professional men should expect to be punished as severely as the others; in some cases more severely. We make the following suggestions. In general a term of immediate imprisonment is inevitable, save in very exceptional circumstances or where the amount of money obtained is small. Despite the great punishment that offenders of this sort bring upon themselves, the court should nevertheless pass a sufficiently substantial term of imprisonment to mark publicly the gravity of the offence. The sum involved is obviously not the only factor to be considered, but it may in many cases provide a useful guide. Where the amounts involved cannot be described as small but are less than £17,500, terms of imprisonment ranging from the very short up to about **21 months** are appropriate. Cases involving sums of between about £ 17,500 and £100,000 will merit a term of about **2–3 years**. Cases involving between £100,000 and £250,00 will merit **3–4 years**. Cases involving £250,00 and £1m will merit **5–9 years** and cases over £1m will merit **10 years or more**. The terms suggested are appropriate where the case is contested. In any case where a plea of guilty is entered, however, the court should give the appropriate discount. Where sums are exceptionally large, and not stolen on a single occasion, or the dishonesty is directed at more than one victim or groups of victims, consecutive sentences may be called for. As already indicated, the circumstances of cases will vary almost infinitely. The court will no doubt wish pay regard to: (i) the quality and degree of trust reposed in the offender including his rank; (ii) the period over which the fraud or the thefts have been perpetrated; (iii) the use to which the money or property dishonestly taken was put; (iv) the effect upon the victim; (v) the impact of the offences on the public and public confidence; (vi) the effect on fellow-employees or partners; (vii) the effect on the offender himself; (viii) his own history; (ix) those matters of mitigation special to himself such as illness; being placed under great strain by excessive responsibility or the like; where, as sometimes happens, there has been a long delay, say over two years, between his being confronted with his dishonesty by his professional body or the police and the start of his trial; finally, any help given by him to the police. [As adapted by *R v Clark* [1998] 2 Cr App Rep (S) 95 (judgment 27 November 1997) which is itself now over 5 years old.]

R v Roach [2001] EWCA Crim 992, [2002] 1 Cr App Rep (S) 43. The defendant stole money from a housebound 80 year old who she was employed to look after. Held. The guidelines in *Clark* and *Barrick* involved theft in breach of trust from employees, charitable bodies or other organisations of that kind. They are not directly in point at all in this case.

R v Hale [2001] EWCA Crim 1329, [2002] 1 Cr App Rep (S) 205. Because of a number of aggravating factors the judge passed a longer sentence (2 years instead of 21 months) than in *R v Clark* [1998] 2 Cr App Rep 137. Held. The judge was entirely justified in what he did. Sentencing is not a matter of mathematical calculation and guideline cases are intended simply as guidelines.

Breach of trust – Magistrates' Court Sentencing Guidelines September 2000

166.32   Entry point. Are magistrates' sentencing powers appropriate? Consider the impact on the victim. Examples of aggravating factors for the offence are casting suspicion on others, committed over a period, high value, organised team, planned, senior employee, sophisticated and vulnerable victim. Examples of mitigating factors for the offence are impulsive action low value, previous inconsistent attitude by employer, single item and unsupported junior. Examples of mitigation are age, health (physical or mental), co-operation with police, voluntary compensation and genuine remorse. Give reasons for not awarding compensation.

For details about the guidelines see **MAGISTRATES' COURT SENTENCING GUIDELINES** at page 331.

Breach of trust – Value £100–£1,000

166.33   *R v Randhana* [1999] 2 Cr App Rep (S) 209 – LCJ. The defendant pleaded guilty to four counts of theft and one attempt (two at the Magistrates' Court and three at the Crown Court). The defendant then 18 was a checkout girl at Tesco and conducted a £50 cash back transaction without a customer being there. There was a random till check and she admitted a colleague had shown her how to obtain cash by retaining a receipt and typing the customer's details into the till and signing the freshly created receipt for cash back. She admitted doing that for a £50.70 transaction. A check was made and two similar transactions came to light. The four transactions were for about £50 and the total was some £200. There was one unsuccessful attempt. All the transactions were within a month. She was of good character and was soon to take her first year exams of a business degree course at Luton University. Held. Immediate custody was necessary but **2 months** YOI not 6. .

Breach of trust – Value £1,001–£5,000

166.34   *R v Mangham* [1998] 2 Cr App Rep (S) 344. The defendant pleaded guilty to using a false instrument with intent and obtaining a money transfer by deception. The defendant was employed by an agency and one of her charges was a 95-year-old lady. She obtained the lady's National Savings passbook and forged her signature on a form enabling a cheque for £2,500 to be obtained. Four months later she did the same again obtaining another £2,500. She admitted it and pleaded at the first opportunity. She said the money went on domestic bills and presents for her family. She had two children aged 13 and 15. She had a previous conviction for theft, again as an employee and again in breach of trust. It was a cruel deception requiring a substantial sentence. Because of the plea **18 months** not 2 years.

R v Whitehouse and Morrison [1999] 2 Cr App Rep (S) 259. The defendants W and M pleaded guilty to theft at the Magistrates' Court. W was employed by a haulage company and two lorries were left overnight at the locked depot full of clothing. The two defendants and two others entered the compound and took 35 boxes of clothing worth £17,700 and loaded them into a van they had hired earlier. The property was rapidly distributed. Police found some of the clothing hidden under a rug on the back seat of the car. As a result of what was said by one of the occupants of the car, police went to W's home and recovered 13 of the stolen boxes. W said he had sold some of the clothing for £700 in order to pay off debts. He also indicated that part of the motive was revenge against his employers who were not continuing his employment after a trial period. M was arrested and said he had loaded the van with 25 boxes and he had not had his cut from the proceeds. W was sentenced as the prime mover who had used his knowledge of the security procedures to effect the offence. He had recruited the others and used a stolen key. M was sentenced on the basis he had played a major part. W was 24 with three previous spent convictions for theft. M was also 24 and had a variety of dishonest convictions in the early 1990s. Held. The element of revenge was an aggravating factor which took W outside the guidelines in *Barrick* and *Clark*. **2 years** for W and **18 months** for M were severe but not manifestly excessive.

Breach of trust – Value £5,001–£10,000

166.35   *R v Barrick* (1985) 7 Cr App Rep (S) 142 – LCJ. Where the amounts involved cannot be described as small but are less than £17,500, terms of imprisonment ranging from the very short up to about **21 months** are appropriate when the case is contested. [As adapted by *R v Clark* [1998] 2 Cr App Rep (S) 95.]

R v Ross-Goulding [1997] 2 Cr App Rep (S) 348. The defendant pleaded guilty to theft and forgery. A care assistant was employed to look after a patient suffering from multiple sclerosis. She opened the patient's mail and read it to her because the patient found it difficult to read. £8,000 was taken from her building society account. She admitted the offence saying she had financial difficulties including a £9,000 car loan. She had forged her signature. The defendant was 33, with three children and living on benefits. The children's father did not provide any financial help. There were no previous convictions. She had married before the court hearing. This was not a straightforward *Barrick* case. She was preying on someone who could not look after themselves. **15 months** was not excessive.

R v Feakes [1998] 2 Cr App Rep (S) 295. The defendant pleaded guilty to five counts of theft. The defendant was treasurer of the church restoration fund. Over a 3½ year period he stole £9,594 from the fund. He drew the cheques and forged the other signature on the cheque. He had become besotted with a woman who produced four children but no financial support. He was terrified she would leave him, which she frequently threatened to do unless he provided for them adequately. He had no previous convictions and had given maximum co-operation from the outset. About £3,000 had been repaid. Applying *R v Clark*, **9 months** not 15.

R v Griffiths [2000] 1 Cr App Rep (S) 240. The defendant pleaded guilty to theft, false accounting, making a false instrument and using a false instrument at the Magistrates' Court. The defendant was treasurer of a football club. He provided falsified accounts, (the false accounting count). He forged an insurance certificate so he could pretend the premises were insured, (the using a false instrument count). To satisfy members he produced a bank statement indicating there was a balance in the club account of over £9,000. It was faxed to the bank and the bank reply said no such account existed, (the making a false instrument count). When bills weren't paid the police were called. When interviewed about the matter he agreed that between £7,300 and £7,500 had been stolen, (the theft count). It was over an 8 year period. He was 44 and a man with a good character with various references. It was said he tried to live up to the lifestyle of some of his friends. He owed £40,000 in loans and on credit card bills. He was humiliated in the community and was likely to lose his job and be divorced. He was depressed but had an exemplary prison report. The amount of money is only the starting point. It is not the sole consideration. It was over a long period and he had fobbed off the committee with a series of lies reinforced by the falsification of the accounts and other documents. Applying *R v Clark* it would be difficult to justify more than 18 months for the theft after a trial. The total sentence should have been 12 not 21 months. So **12 months** for the theft and 9 months concurrent for the other counts.

R v James [2000] 1 Cr App Rep (S) 285. The defendant pleaded guilty to two counts of theft. She was a Post Office counter clerk. She stole twice. The total appears to be £7,318, (although the judgment is contradictory). She hid the theft by inflating the computerised records. She was a single parent with daughters aged 15 and 7. She was in debt. She denied it till the day of her trial. She had one spent dishonesty conviction. Applying *R v Clark* [1998] 2 Cr App Rep (S) 95, **9 months** substituted for 14 months.

R v Donaldson [2002] EWCA Crim 2854, [2002] 2 Cr App Rep (S) 140. The defendant pleaded guilty to theft, attempting to obtain property by deception and two counts of obtaining property by a deception. She asked for six offences to be taken into consideration. She was employed by a carer to a 90 year old who was at home after being released from hospital. The old lady needed 24-hour care. The defendant stole £3,300 in cash from a drawer and blank cheques. She forged the lady's signature on the cheques and tried to pay them into her bank account. She left her employment without notice. The banks were suspicious and the deception failed. She next started work caring for an 88-year-old lady who was immobile. Her employer allowed her to withdraw £250 in cash for her wages and housekeeping expenses. However, on six occasions she exceeded the limit and withdrew between £400 and £600 totalling £3,300. She then left that employment without notice the next day. She was questioned by the police and denied the offences and then failed to return to the police station when on bail. When she was next arrested she admitted the offences. She was 36 of good character with an unsettled background. In 1996 she suffered from postnatal depression. Her son went into care and her mother died. Held. These offences are serious and despicable but **18 months** not 2½ years.

Breach of trust – Value £10,001–£100,000

166.36   *R v Barrick* (1985) 7 Cr App Rep (S) 142 – LCJ. Where the amounts involved cannot be described as small but are less than £17,500, terms of imprisonment ranging from the very short up to about **21 months** are appropriate. Cases involving sums of between about £ 17,500 and £100,000 will merit a term of about **2–3 years**, when the case is contested. [As adapted by *R v Clark* [1998] 2 Cr App Rep (S) 95.]

R v Husbands [1998] 2 Cr App Rep (S) 428. The defendant pleaded guilty to theft and two offences of obtaining property by deception. Just before she left her employment with the National Westminster Bank she sent a letter to the bank which purported to be signed by a customer of the bank asking for a service card. She then made an unauthorised transfer of £10,000 that customers account. Over the following year she obtained £22,603 from cash machines and through the Switch system using the service card. She had paid off loans, debts, gone to America and had had six months in Barbados. She expressed remorse and had no previous convictions. Applying *R v Clark* and giving credit for the guilty plea **18 months** not 2 years' imprisonment. A £500 compensation order and £200 prosecution costs not challenged.

R v Kerr [1998] 2 Cr App Rep (S) 316. The defendant was convicted of procuring the execution of a valuable security by deception. The defendant lived in a bungalow owned by a lady now 86 with a memory that had deteriorated. His wife asked to buy the property and an offer of £70,000 was made. The lady was agreeable to sell but her daughter who was due to inherit the property valued it and was given a higher value. The daughter tried to obtain a power of attorney but it was unsuccessful and the owner decided not to sell. The defendant managed to obtain the title deeds of the property from the owner and a transfer form from the Land Registry. He drafted a deed of gift and filled in the transfer form and forged the signature of the owner. The witness to the signature said there was no signature when she signed. The documents were sent to the Land Registry. The Land Registry wrote to the owner asking her to confirm the transfer. She never replied and the police were informed. The defendant was arrested and maintained the owner wanted the transfer without solicitors and the documents were genuine. He was 33 with an outstanding work record and no convictions. The owner gave evidence at the committal and the trial. The house was valued between £70,000 and £110,000. Held. The deception was practised on the Land Registry, which makes the case equivalent to a breach of trust case. **3 years** was not manifestly excessive.

R v Kefford [2002] EWCA Crim 519, [2002] 2 Cr App (S) 495 – LCJ. The defendant pleaded guilty to 12 thefts and asked for nine offences of false accounting to be taken into consideration. When 23 he made withdrawals from customer's accounts at the Building Society he worked at. He took windfall payments and signed a slip in their name. £11,120 was obtained. After he stopped it there were 5 months before he was detected. When interviewed he made an immediate confession. He had no convictions. He sold his home and paid the money back. He was under financial strain because of buying the house. He stopped when his finances improved. Held. **12 months** not 18 would have been the appropriate starting point. Because of the mitigation **4 months** not 12.

Breach of trust – Value £100,000–£1m

166.37   *R v Barrick* [1985] 7 Cr App Rep (S) 142 – LCJ. Cases involving between £100,000 and £250,00 will merit **3 to 4 years** would be justified. Cases involving £250,00 and £1m will merit **5–9 years**, when the case is contested. (As adapted by *R v Clark* [1998] 2 Cr App Rep (S) 95.)

R v Clark [1998] 2 Cr App Rep (S) 95. The defendant pleaded guilty to two counts of theft. The defendant was the bursar of the Royal Academy in London and treasure of his local church. He stole £400,000 from the Royal Academy and £29,000 from the church over a four year period. He spent the money on house improvements, horses, school fees and an extravagant life. He made immediate admissions and co-operated fully with the police. He did not contest the civil proceedings and was made bankrupt. He repaid about £120,000 by selling his house. He had no previous convictions. The offences were aggravated by the degree of trust placed in him, the four year period of the thefts, and the use he had made of the money. **3 years** and 1 year consecutive not 5 on each concurrent.

R v Neary [1999] 1 Cr App Rep (S) 431. The defendant pleaded guilty at the first opportunity to 12 counts of theft. Since 1971 he had been a solicitor who became a senior partner in a distinguished firm. In the early 1990s his property interests, business and consultancy work gave him a 'very great income'. However, he was badly affected by the property crash. He managed a family trust fund, which had property which was let to Glasgow District Council. The defendant kept the rents and failed to pay the lessor and the lease was forfeited. The fund lost between £800,000 and £1.1m. He spent the money on a business venture, repaying a bank loan, reducing his overdraft etc. The amount stolen was £135,230. In a property company he was entrusted to manage he stole £153,500 using 2/3 of the money to pay off a loan. The total loss was £288,730, which was stolen between November 1991 and November 1992. When interviewed he denied the offences and about 9 months later in 1994, he left the country. In 1997 he returned voluntarily and the proceedings against him started. From then he co-operated with the authorities. He was of previous unblemished character with an impressive array of testimonials including references to his charity work. In 1995 he was made bankrupt. The defendant had been an international rugby player. He had played for England 43 times and had been captain for 2 years. Held. *R v Clark* [1998] 2 Cr App Rep (S) 95 only provides guidelines. Each case has its own special features. It was a very serious continuing breach of trust by a man in a very senior position. **5 years** was not manifestly excessive.

Breach of trust – Value more than £1m

166.38   *R v Barrick* [1985] 7 Cr App Rep (S) 142 – LCJ. Cases over £1m will merit **10 years or more**, when the case is contested. [As adapted by *R v Clark* [1998] 2 Cr App Rep (S) 95.]

Victim believes plan is dishonest but is tricked as to who the victim is

See *Advance fee frauds*

Victim over 70

166.39   *R v Mangham* [1998] 2 Cr App Rep (S) 344. The defendant pleaded guilty to using a false instrument with intent and obtaining a money transfer by deception. The defendant was employed by an agency and one of her charges was a 95-year-old lady. She obtained the lady's passbook to her National Savings and forged her signature on a form enabling a cheque for £2,500 to be obtained. Four months later she did the same again obtaining another £2,500. She admitted it and pleaded guilty at the first opportunity. She said the money went on domestic bills and presents for her family. She had two children aged 13 and 15. She had a previous conviction for theft again as an employee and again in breach of trust. It was a cruel deception requiring a substantial sentence. Because of the plea **18 months** not 2 years.

R v Richardson [2000] 2 Cr App Rep (S) 373. The defendant pleaded guilty to theft and false imprisonment. The defendant at night visited the victim, a lady of 89 who he knew. He asked to use the lavatory. She followed him. She said he should leave. He refused and appeared to be on drugs. He was aggressive and threatened to hurt her. He pushed her into her sitting room and forced her into an armchair. He tied a jumper over her face. He asked for £20. On a number of occasions she attempted to get out of the chair but he pushed her back. She was repeatedly threatened that she would be hurt if she told anyone about him. She allowed him to make a call for a taxi. When the taxi arrived he snatched her bag and stole £20. He tore the telephone wire from the wall. Because the telephone did not work and she could not manage the steps in the dark she had to stay in all night unable to contact anyone. Before the police started to look for him he went to a police station and confessed to a robbery. His account was very similar to the victim, although he claimed to have told her he wasn't going to hurt her. The defendant was very anxious she should not have to go to court and therefore did not contest his account. He had a bad record with 12 appearances in the last 10 years seven of which were for robbery. He had three convictions for burglary, three convictions for theft in a dwelling house and three convictions for theft from a person. He expressed remorse. The reason for his offending was crack cocaine. Held. It was so serious a DTT order was inappropriate. In light of the mitigation **4 years** not 5 years substituted.

R v Hale [2002] 1 Cr App Rep (S) 205. The defendant pleaded guilty to 11 counts of obtaining by a deception, one theft and asked for 68 offences to be taken into consideration. He took over a care home and was unable to buy it outright so paid £12,500 a month rent. In June 1999 the arrears stood at £40,000 and he was given notice to quit. The home was effectively closed down and 30 or so residents were relocated. A number of residents had entrusted him with their pension books and between 2 September and 8 October 1999 he continued to cash their pensions. He was arrested with about £1,400 and the pension books. In all he had taken about £13,000. In interview he claimed to have no memory of it and that he was suffering from depression. The money was used to fund his cocaine habit. It was his third home he had bought or leased. As a result of an Inland Revenue investigation he lost everything including his home. The Benefits Agency refunded the pensioners except for those that had died. He had convictions for theft and forgery. Because of a number of aggravating factors the judge passed a longer sentence (2 years instead of 21 months) than in *R v Clark* [1998] 2 Cr App Rep (S) 137. Held. The judge was entirely justified in what he did. Sentencing is not a matter of mathematical calculation and guideline cases are intended simply as guidelines. **2 years** was not excessive.

R v Roach [2002] 1 Cr App Rep (S) 44. The defendant pleaded guilty to three specimen counts of obtaining a money transfer by deception. She was employed as a carer for an 80-year-old lady who was housebound. The defendant collected her pension, paid her bills and did her shopping. She asked the victim to sign blank cheques and the victim expected her bills to be paid. Over 15 months she wrote 26 cheques to herself and stole £2,875. The amounts varied between £40 and £250. The money was used to repay a loan to enable her father who lived in Jamaica and was dying of cancer to visit England. Because other members of her family were not working much of the burden of supporting the family fell on her. She lost her job but obtained work with another carer shortly after. She was 27 and during the period of the obtaining she was convicted of social security fraud. She was ordered to perform 100 hours' community service for that. Held. The distinctive feature is the exploitation of particularly vulnerable people. The contemporaneous sentence for the social security offending was an aggravating feature. The *Clark* guidelines are not directly on point at all. **18 months** was entirely appropriate.

THREATENING BEHAVIOUR

See PUBLIC ORDER ACT OFFENCES, S 4 ETC

167   THREATS TO KILL

167.1   Offences Against the Person Act 1861, s 16

Triable either way. On indictment maximum 10 years. Summary maximum 6 months and/or £5,000.

It can be a violent offence for the purposes of passing a longer than commensurate sentence [Powers of Criminal Courts (Sentencing) Act 2000, s 80(2)] and an extended sentence (extending the licence) [Powers of Criminal Courts (Sentencing) Act 2000, s 85(2)(b)]

Guideline remarks

167.2   *A-G's Reference (No 84 of 1999)* [2000] 1 Cr App Rep (S) 213 – LCJ. It is relevant to regard the vulnerability of the party threatened and most important the reality of the threat – the likelihood, in the view of the party threatened, that the threat will be carried out and the extent the party is put in genuine fear. It is very relevant to consider whether the party making the threat is known to be violent, and whether the party making the threat is known to have some grudge or animus or grievance which may cause him to act.

R v Tucknott [2001] 1 Cr App Rep (S) 318. Although at first instance sentences of in excess of 5 years have been passed, this court has not approved a sentence of more than 5 years on a plea of guilty. It may be that a higher sentence could be justified in a special case but the reason for this general position is plain: concern lest at higher figures the offence of threats is placed too high in the scale of violent crime. Judges have to consider the safety of the public.

Domestic/ex partners etc

167.3 *R v Healy* [1998] 1 Cr App Rep (S) 107. The defendant pleaded guilty to threatening to kill. The defendant's relationship of 10 years broke up and he was asked to leave because of his drinking. Two months later he left and the two remained on good terms. Well over a year later she received telephone calls from him during the night and he visited her house shouting abuse and damaging her property. Her car tyres were slashed and an egg was thrown over her car. About 6 months later there was an attempted arson on her house. Two months later in the early evening her electricity went off and she reset it. Twenty minutes later he entered her sitting room carrying a Swiss Army-type knife, which he pointed at her. He told her not to activate her panic alarm and showed her a plastic tie wrap. He said, 'This is for me and I've got something else for you. Today is the day I'm going to kill myself and kill you. I just want to talk to you.' He threw the knife into her lap and said, 'Take that.' She was able to leave and activate the alarm. The police came and discovered the outside light and the telephone wires had both been severed. Police found him sitting in the living room drinking beer. He said, 'Don't worry it is just domestic.' He was arrested and said, 'We've just been having a chat for God's sake.' In interview he said he had lain under the bed for a while and he had not meant to harm her. He wanted to surprise her and talk to her. He did want to kill them both but could not do it. The victim was extremely fearful and her GP said she was suffering from depression and serious anxiety because of his behaviour. He was 53 with one assault conviction in 1983 for which he was conditionally discharged. He was not mentally ill but was dependent on alcohol. Held. The fact it arises out of a so called domestic incident affords no mitigation. Because of the plea **3 years** not 5.

R v Wilson [1998] 1 Cr App Rep (S) 341. The defendant pleaded guilty to four counts of making threats to kill. The defendant had persistently said it was necessary to kill his wife if she was seen partly undressed even by a doctor. He said he kept knives hidden in the house so he could kill her and mutilate her so her sexual parts would be unrecognised to police or pathologists. In May 1996, he visited his psychiatrist and told him that he thought his wife had gone to see a doctor and he would have to go home and kill her. The doctor said it would be better if he was admitted to hospital but if he was not willing to be admitted he would have to tell the police. The doctor believed the threats were serious and his wife and the police were informed. The defendant was admitted as an inpatient and also in May, he told his son that he was going to kill his wife and then himself. At first the son didn't treat the threat seriously but later he treated it very seriously. In August 1996, the defendant discussed separation from his wife with a key worker at the hospital and told him he would not accept that and would have to break into her house and kill her. On another occasions he said he intended to kill his wife. In September 1996 when still an inpatient he was taken by a friend to a pub where the he told the friend that he was going to do her and himself in. The defendant was concerned that his wife would not speak to him on the 'phone. The friend told him not to be stupid and he said, 'I can cut her up, I've done butchery and nobody would recognise her. In November he was arrested and told police he was thinking of killing his wife and himself. His wife found two knives in the house, which the defendant said a butcher had given him and that they were for cutting up meat. He was 58 and had trained as a butcher. A psychiatrist said he had no mental condition, which would permit a mental health disposal, but he had an abnormal personality. The original psychiatrist said the threats were serious and posed a real and dangerous threat to the wife. A mental nurse had no doubt that given the opportunity to carry out the threats he would. The wife was petrified. He was given a longer than commensurate 4 year sentence. Held. The threats did fall within the *R v Richart* (1995) 16 Cr App Rep (S) 977 definition so it was a violent offence enabling that sentence to be passed. The judge correctly made it longer than commensurate. It was necessary to protect the public and in particular the wife. **4 years** was appropriate.

R v Mill [1999] 2 Cr App Rep (S) 28. The defendant pleaded guilty to threats to kill and common assault. The defendant had a relationship with someone he met at a drug rehabilitation clinic. The next year it was over and she formed a new relationship. Over 3½ years later he barged his way into her flat. He was very angry and she tried to calm him down. He rushed past her into the kitchen, grabbed hold of a bread knife, and returned to the living room where over an hour he made various threats to her, backed up with the knife. He said things like, 'Don't do anything stupid, I'll kill you, I don't care what happens to me.' He pulled the telephone from its socket. He drank from a bottle of wine he had brought with him. He then reconnected the phone and allowed Miss Graham to ring a friend who came to the flat who realised something was wrong, and left very shortly after. Eventually she persuaded the defendant that they should go to the local off-licence to get some more drink. He put the knife up his sleeve and they went off to the off-licence where they bought some more drink and returned to the flat. He continued to threaten her, who felt she could not make good her escape, being afraid of him with the knife up his sleeve. Later she suggested they should go to a pub and he again put the knife up his sleeve. At the pub she managed to run out shout for help in another pub. She rushed behind the bar but he caught up with her, assaulted her and then ran off. He had a very large number of convictions going back to 1976. Except for the first offence they were not for violence. Most of them were for theft, mainly shoplifting. Since being remanded in custody he has withdrawn from drugs, and has approached a residential drug rehabilitation project about receiving treatment when he is at liberty. **3 years** not 4.

R v Hasgular [2001] 1 Cr App Rep (S) 122. The defendant pleaded guilty to making a threat to kill and ABH. He separated from his wife and she stayed in the matrimonial home with their three children. Six months later she started a relationship with someone else and he moved in. 11 months later at 3am she woke up to find the defendant in her bedroom carrying a knife. The defendant walked round the bed and put the knife to the throat of the new man. The point went in and he started to bleed. He punched him, forced him out of bed and walked him to the door. The defendant put his arms round his neck and the knife to his throat and threatened to kill him. One of the children was at the door crying as the defendant took the man downstairs. The wife told the child to 'phone the police. The defendant told the man he intended to rape him and said he had bought all the furniture. He swung the knife at him and slightly cut his face. The wife came downstairs and told him to put the knife away which he did. She went to make some coffee and gave him a cigarette. The police arrived and the defendant seized his son. Eventually he was persuaded to drop the knife and he was arrested. The new man had an 8″ superficial scratch across the cheek and a superficial wound on his neck. The defendant was 30 and of good character. He spoke Turkish and had difficulty in speaking English. He also had some medical problems. Held. Although he desisted the threats were very real. It could be said **3 years** was stern but it was not manifestly excessive. The other sentence remained 1 year concurrent.

R v Tucknott [2001] 1 Cr App Rep (S) 318. The defendant pleaded guilty to four counts of making threats to kill. There was one count for his latest girlfriend and three against her and her new partner. At all time he was a serving prisoner. In April 1998 he met and moved in with the victim. The relationship was turbulent. He was possessive, drunken and violent. After they parted in February 1999 he started harassing her. Later he broke into her home, slashed her clothes and put a brick through the window. He was arrested and sentenced to 21 months for harassment, burglary, theft and criminal damage. He was sent to a prison near her and she visited him notwithstanding he had written to the Governor of the prison saying she wished nothing more to do with him. He said she was playing mind games with him. The first threat was that the victim was worth less than the one he had killed and she was messing him about and he would kill her. He was moved and the authorities tried to stop him ringing her on the telephone. He got round this by asking others to ring her and then pass the phone over to him. In a call he discovered about the new boyfriend and slashed his wrists with a razor blade. The other threats were made to prison officers when they escorted him to hospital for the wounds. He threatened to kill them both on his release by giving them an overdose or shooting them. It was his third serious relationship to end in violence. The first was in 1983 when he was convicted of ABH and put on probation. The second was the killing of his partner with a knife after a 4 year drunken and turbulent relationship. He was convicted of manslaughter on the basis of diminished responsibility and was sentenced to 7 years. He served 5 and was released in 1996. In 1997 he was the subject of three probation orders. One was for threatening behaviour and two were for drink/drive. He was 40. Doctors said he was suffering from a personality disorder but thought he probably wasn't treatable and the probation board thought he should be detained in a secure unit for the protection of the public. His risk of re-offending was assessed as high. Held. Judges have to consider the safety of the public. There is a difficulty here. The court could not make a hospital order or pass a longer than normal sentence. **5 years** not 8.

R v Burke (26 July 2001, unreported). The defendant pleaded gulity to breach of a restraining order and criminal damage and later he made a belated plea to threats to kill. He had a 6 year stormy relationship with the one of the victims. He harassed her and in 1994 stabbed her. For that he was convicted of wounding with intent and received 4 years. On his release he resumed the relationship and it remained extremely stormy. Many incidents were reported to the police and she feared for her life. In May 2000 the relationship ended and in August 2000 he was sentenced to 3 months for harassment and a restraining order was made. Because of time served on remand he was released immediately. The victim was so scared she stayed overnight with friends and visited her disabled elderly mother during the day. Five days after the order was made he entered the mother's flat from the garden. He pushed the arthritic lady to the ground, used foul and abusive language and threatened to shoot both victims. The flat was ransacked and he damaged a window, a table, china ornaments, a clock, a gas fire, a kettle and electrical equipment. The mother went outside to get help and he told her he was going to shoot her daughter and her current boyfriend. He also said, 'I've got a gun. Do you want to see it.' He then sat on a wall until the police arrived. When he was charged he threatened to repeat his behaviour. He was 37 with 23 convictions and had had ten periods of custody. As well as the offences already mentioned he had convictions for GBH with intent, assault on police, two affrays and two threatening words or behaviours. Held. The offences were in breach of the court order. It was permissible to make the 2 years for the breach of the order consecutive to the threats to kill, because the threats to kill were outside the flat after the breach offence was committed. The total of **5 years** was appropriate but the criminal damage sentence should be made concurrent not consecutive.

Longer than commensurate sentences (frequently wrongly called extended sentence)

167.4   Powers of Criminal Courts (Sentencing) Act 2000, s 80(2)(b). . . . the custodial sentence shall be. . .where the offence is a violent or sexual offence, for such longer term (not exceeding the maximum) as in the opinion of the court is necessary to protect the public from serious harm from the offender. [Previously the Criminal Justice Act 1991, s 2(2)(b).]

Powers of Criminal Courts (Sentencing) Act 2000, s161(3) . . . a violent offence is an 'offence which leads, or is intended or likely to lead, to a person's death or physical injury to a person.'

R v Richart (1995) 16 Cr App Rep (S) 977. Threats to kill could in some circumstances be a 'violent offence.' Here where the threats were made in the post or over the telephone and the threats did not lead to injury there was no evidence that they were intended or likely to lead to physical injury. It therefore did not apply.

R v Wilson [1998] 1 Cr App Rep (S) 341. The defendant pleaded guilty to four counts of making threats to kill. The defendant had persistently said it was necessary to kill his wife if she was seen partly undressed even by a doctor. A psychiatrist said he had no mental condition, which would permit a mental health disposal, but he had an abnormal personality. A mental nurse had no doubt that given the opportunity to carry out the threats he would. The wife was petrified. Held. Whether a particular offence amounted to a violent offence depended on the circumstances. The threats did fall within the *R v Richart* (1995) 16 Cr App Rep (S) 977 definition. The definition comprises two ingredients, there has to be an intention and a likelihood of a person's death, the intention of the defendant at the time, and whether what he intended was likely to lead to a person's death or physical injury to the person. (For more details see *Domestic*.)

R v Tucknott [2001] 1 Cr App Rep (S) 318. The defendant pleaded guilty to four counts of making threats to kill to his ex-partner and her new boyfriend. At all time he was a serving prisoner. It was his third serious relationship to end in violence. The second was the killing of his partner with a knife after a 4 year drunken and turbulent relationship. He was convicted of manslaughter on the basis of diminished responsibility and was sentenced to **7 years**. Doctors said he was suffering from a personality disorder but thought he probably wasn't treatable and the probation thought he should be detained in a secure unit for the protection of the public. His risk of re-offending was assessed as high. Held. Judges have to consider the safety of the public. There is a difficulty here. The court could not make a hospital order or pass a longer than normal sentence. We urge this offence to be made a 'violent offence.'

R v Birch (23 October 2001, unreported). The defendant made threats to a prison officer but no violence was used. It did not apply.

See also LONGER THAN COMMENSURATE SENTENCES

Obsessional behaviour to the opposite sex

167.5 *R v Jones* [2001] EWCA Crim 2235, [2002] 1 Cr App Rep (S) 536. The defendant pleaded guilty to putting another in fear contrary to s 4, threats to kill and making a threat to kill. The defendant met the victim whilst she was modelling. She refused his offer to take her out. She received a call and letters every few weeks from him. They were not threatening but she became worried. At Christmas she received a diamond necklace which she returned saying it was too expensive. A week later he turned up on her doorstep with flowers. She shut the door on him and felt sick. She then received long rambling letters and she contacted the police. They didn't caution the defendant but the letters ceased for about a year. After that he sent very abusive, vile and sick letters. The letters referred to injecting the victim's sister with AIDS and said for example 'We're going to rape your mum' and 'we will destroy your family and burn them alive.' They threatened to kill her and her mother received two letters threatening to burn her house down, cutting her brake cables and putting acid on her door handle etc. Except for work the victim didn't leave the house and she couldn't sleep properly. She refused to be on her own in the flat and had now no social life. She gave up modelling. The sister and her husband were deeply disturbed.

The defendant went out once with victim in the last count. She found him creepy and said she to him she didn't want to see him again. She stated receiving text messages in which the defendant pretended he was dying of cancer. They continued at all hours every other day for 3 weeks or more and then stopped and started again. She then received a quite vile letter referring to cutting brake lines, raping her mother, putting superglue in her eyes and petrol in her letter box etc. She told the police and the defendant was arrested. He was 28 with one conviction that could be ignored. He showed some remorse but blamed the victims. The pre-sentence report considered he was likely to re-offend and cause pain. The psychiatric report said he was obsessive but not mentally ill and he thought the events were likely to be repeated. Held. There were aggravating features: the genuine fear that the threats would be carried out and the repetition. Taking into account the plea, there was no actual violence and there was no breach of a court order 4 years on the first two matters cannot be described as excessive. However, the **1 year** on the third matter will be made concurrent not consecutive.

Persistent offender

167.6   *R v Shepherd* [1998] 1 Cr App Rep (S) 397. The defendant pleaded guilty to making a threat to kill. He dialled 999 and police sent a unit to him. He was found to be agitated and said he intended to kill Paul Carlton his former landlord. He also said he had access to firearms and that the victim owed him £700. He was arrested and admitted the offence. He said he called the police to be arrested before he could carry out his threat. He was now 44 with a bad record for dishonesty and a 'staggering' record for threatening to kill. In 1987 he received 4 years and in 1990 5 years for it. He was then sentenced for attempted robbery and other offences. In 1996 he received 2 years for threatening to kill Paul Carlton, the same victim. The offence was committed 2 days after his release from that sentence. He suffered from a severe personality disorder and an explosive temper and was regarded as a potential threat to the public. He had no family and no skills. Held. This was not a gesture to secure a return to prison but a real threat. The judge was entitled to find he posed a real danger to the public. **5 years** consecutive to 12 months for the unserved part of his earlier sentence was not excessive.

Police officers etc, to

167.7   *R v Penny* [1998] 1 Cr App Rep (S) 389. The defendant pleaded guilty at the Magistrates' Court to four counts of threats to kill and three counts of using a telephone system to send obscene messages. He was also committed for sentence for petty theft, deception involving £5, two counts of damaging police property and threatening to kill. The defendant made repeated telephone calls to a police station over 6 months. He phoned a particular woman and they went from aggressive to obscene. He threatened to tear out her throat. From an outgoing person she became changed and frightened to answer the phone. There were direct threats to kill, to come after her and to inject her daughters with HIV infected blood. Police were very concerned that he would carry out the threats. He was interviewed and admitted the threats. He was 25 with convictions for violence and misusing the telephone system. He was subject to two probation orders. A psychiatrist said he suffered from a delusional disorder that he was being persecuted by the police. After sentence a report said that he was now stable and no longer required treatment in the hospital wing of the prison. Held. He had been given repeated non-custodial sentences because of his mental fragility. Those chances were thrown away. **4 years** was at the severe end of the available bracket but not manifestly excessive.

R v Orwin [1999] 1 Cr App Rep (S) 103. The defendant pleaded guilty to threats to kill and possession of ammunition. Police were called at about 1am to a domestic dispute of his and went to the next door house and found his partner and a small baby. She told them about it and the police tried to enter his house by knocking on the locked front door and shouting through the letterbox. They spoke with the partner who gave them permission to enter by force. There were further unsuccessful attempts to enter until an officer broke a pane of glass in the kitchen and gained entry. That officer shouted, 'It's the police, come downstairs.' There was no reply and the officer again asked the defendant to come down. The defendant said, 'Who is it? Burglars?' and the officer said, 'No, police officers, we need to speak to you.' The defendant said, 'Fuck off burglars, I've got a gun.' After being told it was the police and to calm down the defendant said, 'If you come in here I will blow your fucking heads off, I have a 12 bore shotgun.' He was again told they were police and the defendant said, 'I've got a shotgun and I will shoot you.' The officers withdrew and at 10.30am they went to his house and he opened the door and was arrested. They searched the house and ammunition was found. In interview he denied the dispute and threatening the officers. He was 25. Held. He did not have a gun. **18 months** not 4 years.

R v Gidney [1999] 1 Cr App Rep (S) 138. The defendant pleaded guilty to seven counts of threats to kill. She asked for two other offences to be taken into consideration. In 1996 she received psychiatric treatment and came into contact with a male nurse. In January 1997 she was arrested by two police officers for threatening to stab them. In May 1997 she was convicted of affray and was sentenced to 18 months. In July 1997 the two officers received threatening and abusive letters from her saying that on her release she was going to wait outside the police station with a knife and kill them. In August 1997 the nurse received two threatening and abusive letters from her saying that she would put a 9' blade in his and his wife's back and she'd be 'back inside for two murders'. In September 1997 she wrote a similar letter to the nurse again. She was arrested and said she meant what she had written. A week later, she sent similar letters to the two officers. She also made threats against prison officers which she had not carried out. She was 23 with convictions for violence and threatening behaviour since 1992. A report said the letters were attention seeking and she was unlikely to be organised enough to carry out the threats when she was released. Another said she was extremely dangerous with an extremely high risk of re-offending. A third report said she was suffering from an 'organic personality disorder' and hospital treatment was not appropriate. **3½ years** not 5.

Prison officers, to

167.8 *R v Birch* [2001] EWCA Crim 2400, [2002] 1 Cr App Rep (S) 544. The defendant was convicted of two counts of threats to kill. He was serving a sentence of 18 months for threatening to kill, of using violence to cause entry to premises and common assault. 5½ months later he threw a cup of very hot coffee over the probation officer when the officer was explaining his release conditions. He said: 'I'll kill anyone that gets in my way. IRA, no surrender.' He was placed on report by Prison Officer Rowland and lost 28 days and had 14 days in cellular confinement. During the hearing it was claimed he made a number of threats to Rowland. He was acquitted of that allegation. Nine days after the coffee incident Rowland was checking the defendant's cell in the segregation unit. He said to her, 'Officer Rowland you're fucking dead you are.' He was again made the subject of report and sent to Dartmoor. In the course of that procedure he was seen by two prison officers to form his hand into a pistol shape, point it at his temple and make a silent explosive sound by puckering his lips. As he did it, he stared intently at Rowland and the officers thought it was plainly directed at her, although she did not actually see it herself. Rowland took the threats seriously. The defendant was 29 and had a bad record. He had seven convictions for ABH, one for common assault, one for battery, one for assaulting a police officer and the convictions for which he was serving. He admitted to multi-drug abuse. He had an untreatable personality disorder. Held. The judge was faced with a very difficult sentencing problem and we sympathise with his desire to protect the public. He was unable to impose an extended sentence. He was compelled to pass a longer than commensurate sentence, which was commensurate with the gravity of the offences. He contested the case so the sentencing judge could make an assessment of him. He was able to take into account the element of risk. **2½ years** not 4.

Racist defendants

167.9   *R v Mati* [1999] 2 Cr App Rep (S) 238. The defendant pleaded guilty on re-arraignment to two counts of threats to kill. The victim lived at No 8 and the defendant No 10 in a block of flats. The victim woke up and smelt burning and found a lighted cigarette burning outside her flat which caused no damage. However, painted on her door was, 'fucking black bastard pakki coon we are goin to come'n'kill u both, fucking pakkis u are going to fucking die.' She informed the police. Five days later a brick was thrown at the victim's window with a note attached with threats to petrol bomb the flat unless she moved and threats to kill. More racist threats had been painted on her door. The victim was very frightened and went to stay with friends. She suffered a good deal from being homeless and had sleepless nights. Police arrested the defendant and found paint and racist material. He denied the offences. He was 24 and had no relevant convictions. He was black and came from Fiji and had psychological problems which were treatable. The psychiatrist referred to lack of social skills and very low self esteem. The defendant saw himself as ugly, unintelligent with nothing to offer people. Held. This could not be said to be a campaign against those from ethnic minorities. It was a very serious case but unusual. **4 years** not 5.

Victims of the defendant's earlier crimes and their relatives, to

167.10   *A-G's Reference (No 84 of 1999)* [2000] 1 Cr App Rep (S) 213 – LCJ. The defendant was convicted of two counts of threatening to kill. Between 1975 and 1990 the defendant lived with a woman and used violence against her. When the relationship ended he continued to molest her, displaying 'obsessive possessiveness.' In 1992 he killed her in a frenzied knife attack and tried to burn her body while she was alive but unconscious. He pleaded guilty to manslaughter on the basis of diminished responsibility. He received 2 years on account of cancer and because he acted out of almost insane jealousy. On his release for no rational reason he began to blame the deceased's brother and sister, Pamela for her death. He made threats towards the family and every Christmas left flowers on her grave, which contained threats against the brother and sister. In 1998 he made an unprovoked attack on the brother in a town centre. Ten months later the defendant who was with his son approached the brother in a supermarket and said, 'I mean what I say you will die.' He raised his voice and said, 'I have killed your sister and I'm going to kill you, that's a promise. And that fucking cow Pamela's going too. I'll kill you both.' The brother was terrified and took the threats seriously. The sister was similarly terrified and confined herself to her home because of fear. When arrested he told police, 'Don't get me wrong. I'd love to kill the pair of them.' and '. . .when I do get out today. I'll kill him.' He denied making the threats in the supermarket. There was no remorse or undertaking to desist. He was 56 and was cured of his cancer. His convictions went back to 1954 but there was more dishonesty than violence. He had served his sentence of 15 months on remand and had been released with no repetition for 3 months. Held. It is relevant to regard the vulnerability of the party threatened and most important the reality of the threat – the likelihood, in the view of the party threatened, that the threat will be carried out and the extent the party is put in genuine fear. It is very relevant to consider whether the party making the threat is known to be violent, and whether the party making the threat is known to have some grudge or animus or grievance which may cause him to act. Here there was a record of the most proven violence. There was an obsessive grudge against the brother and sister and a prolonged obsession-enough to inspire fear in anyone. The protection of the victims must be of paramount concern. Following a trial the appropriate sentence was 3½–4 years. Taking into account it was a reference and that he had been released **3 years** substituted.

For index of racist crimes see **RACIST OFFENCES**

168 TOTALITY OF THE CUSTODIAL SENTENCE

Basic rule

168.1 *R v Stevens* [1997] 2 Cr App Rep (S) 180. Although it may be proper to make a sentence consecutive to one passed on an earlier occasion, particularly where the second offence was committed on bail for the first offence, the court must nevertheless have regard to the total sentence to be served.

R v Watts [2000] 1 Cr App Rep (S) 460. Rule restated. The sentence was adjusted accordingly.

TOWN AND COUNTRY PLANNING

See **PLANNING OFFENCES**

TRADE DESCRIPTIONS OFFENCES/TRADE MARK OFFENCES

See **COPYRIGHT/TRADE MARK OFFENCES/TRADE DESCRIPTIONS OFFENCES**

TRUANTS

See **SCHOOL, FAILURE TO SECURE REGULAR ATTENDANCE**

169 TV LICENCE EVASION

169.1 Wireless Telegraphy Act 1949, s 1
Summary only. Maximum fine Level 3 (£1,000).

Magistrates' Court Sentencing Guidelines September 2000

169.2 Entry point. Is a discharge or a fine appropriate? An examples of an aggravating factor for the offence is failure to respond to payment opportunities. Examples of mitigation for the offence are accidental oversight, confusion of responsibility, licence immediately obtained and very short unlicensed use. Examples of mitigation are age, health (physical or mental). **Starting point fine A.** (£50 when defendant has £100 net weekly income. See page 334 for table showing fines for different incomes.)

For details about the guidelines see MAGISTRATES' COURT SENTENCING GUIDELINES at page 331.

VALUE ADDED TAX

See TAX FRAUD

170 VEHICLE INTERFERENCE

170.1   Criminal Attempts Act 1981, s 9

Summary only. Maximum sentence 3 months and/or Level 4 fine (£2,500).

Magistrates' Court Sentencing Guidelines September 2000

170.2   Entry point. Is it serious enough for a community penalty? Consider the impact on the victim. Examples of aggravating factors for the offence are disabled passenger vehicle, emergency service vehicle, group action, planned and related damage. An example of a mitigating factor for the offence is impulsive action. Examples of mitigation are age, health (physical or mental), co-operation with the police, voluntary compensation and genuine remorse. Give reasons if not awarding compensation.

For details about the guidelines see MAGISTRATES' COURT SENTENCING GUIDELINES at page 331.

171 VICTIMS

Victim fears she will contact AIDS from sex attack

171.1   *R v Malcolm* (1987) 9 Cr App Rep. (S) 487. The victim was raped and feared she might contract AIDS. There was no evidence she had. The judge added 2 years to the sentence because of the fear. Held. That was not justified.

R v Twigg (1988) Times, 8 June. The defendant was convicted of inciting a boy to commit an act of gross indecency with a woman. There was no evidence the woman had AIDS. Held. The risk the woman had AIDS was so slight it should be ignored. Because of the judge's remarks about it the sentence was reduced.

Victim impact statements etc

171.2   *R v Perks* [2000] Crim LR 606 judgment 19 April 2002. The defendant pleaded guilty to robbery. The judge's papers included a document from the CPS, which said; 'The actions of this greedy, self-indulgent irresponsible mindless and spoilt thug has FOREVER ruined the carefree life of a caring woman. What about the victim of this crime, she is totally and utterly innocent, yet she is going to pay for someone else's crime, for the rest of her life. WHY? JAIL HIM! AND MAKE AN EXAMPLE OF HIM TO OTHERS WHO THINK THAT DRUGS ARE SOCIALLY ACCEPTABLE - THEY ARE NOT!!' It was from the victim's husband and was not disclosed to the defence. Held. The court shares the concern of defence counsel about the document. A number of propositions can be derived from the authorities: (1) a sentencer must not make assumptions, unsupported by evidence, about the effects of an offence on the victim; (2) if an offence has had a particularly damaging or distressing effect upon a victim, this should be known to and taken into account by the court when passing sentence; (3) evidence of the effects of an offence on the victim must be in proper form, a s 9 witness statement, an expert's report or otherwise, duly served upon the defendant or his representatives prior to sentence; (4) evidence of the victim alone should be approached with care, the more so if it relates to matters which the Defence cannot realistically be expected to investigate. It is to be hoped that in future 'victim impact statements' will be in proper form as envisaged by this court in *R v Hobstaff* (1993) 14 Cr App Rep (S) 605.

Practice Direction (Victim Personal Statements) [2002] 1 Cr App Rep (S) 482. Police officers will tell the victim about their chance to make a Victim Personal Statement. It shall be served on the defence, considered by the court and taken into account. The sentencer must not make assumptions unsupported by evidence about the effects of an offence on the victim. The court must pass the appropriate sentence taking into account so far as the court considers appropriate the consequences to the victim.

See the articles: Reparation: sentencing and the victim [1999] Crim LR 470; Victim Impact statements [1999] Crim LR 545 and Victims and the Criminal Justice System [2000] Crim LR 5.

Victims, the views of

171.3   *R v Hayes* (1999) Times, 5 April judgment 22 February 1999. (Notwithstanding the case name this was an A-G's Reference.) The defendant pleaded guilty to robbing his great-grandmother aged 95. The 2 had an affectionate relationship and he went to her house wearing a mask, pushed her in the chest and caused her to stumble back and slide to the floor. He put her hand in her bag and stole her purse. She suffered some bruising. When re-interviewed he admitted the offence and said he had been ripped off in a drugs transaction. He was then 17 and lived with his grandmother. He showed profound remorse and was having difficulty in coping with custody. He had served 3 months. His great grandmother had forgiven him and they had resumed their normal relationship. His grandmother was finding it difficult to cope without him. He was normally kind and considerate. The two ladies did not feel anger towards him but were concerned for his welfare. He was given probation. Held. The sentence cannot depend on the wishes of those most affected by the crime. Crimes perpetrated against vengeful victims would be sentenced differently and much more severely than identical crimes committed against merciful victims. What is more, there are many crimes with more than one victim, and different victims of the same crime might, and sometimes do, take very different views. Many victims simply do not want to have the responsibility or be subject to the inevitable pressures that would be created on them if their views were reflected in the sentencing process. That, many of them feel, is a matter for the court, and they are right. The responsibility rests with the sentencing judge. He has an overall view of current sentencing considerations. None of that means or implies that the victim is to be ignored. An essential consideration is to assess the impact of the particular crime on the individual victim or victims. Rarely, the court is required to consider a refinement of this principle which arises when the imposition of a custodial sentence will add to the distress and concern suffered by the victim. That is a factor to which the court must also pay attention. The weight to be attached to it in a particular case and its practical impact on the sentencing decision depends of course on the crime itself and all the very many differing facets of the case which the judge has to balance. Here the judge balanced the relevant considerations and was merciful. We should be profoundly troubled if it were thought that a judge who tempered justice with mercy was not acting appropriately, or that even serious crimes never admitted in exceptional circumstances exceptional sentences. The sentence was courageous and justified but not unduly lenient.

R v Perks [2000] Crim LR 606 judgment 19 April 2002. The opinions of the victim and the victim's close relatives on the appropriate level of sentence should not be taken into account. The court must pass what it judges to be the appropriate sentence having regard to the circumstances of the offence and of the offender subject to two exceptions: (i) where the sentence passed on the offender is aggravating the victim's distress, the sentence may be moderated to some degree; (ii) where the victim's forgiveness or unwillingness to press charges provide evidence that his or her psychological or mental suffering must be very much less than would normally be the case.

See the article: The Place of Victims' preferences in the Sentencing of 'their' offenders. [2002] Crim LR 689.

For statements of principle about the relatives of those who die (who are both positive and negative to the defendant) see **Death by Dangerous Driving, Causing –** *Victims* and *Victims, the views of the relatives of the* and **Rape –** *Victim says she does not want the defendant sent to prison/has forgiven him*

Victim of sex assault will lose contact with father, stepfather etc

171.4   *A-G's Reference (No 2 of 2001)* [2001] EWCA Crim 1015 [2001] 2 Cr App Rep (S) 524. The defendant pleaded guilty to seven counts of indecent assault against his stepdaughter when she was between the ages of 8 and 15. Held. The loss through imprisonment of her stepfather will bear hardly upon her and that can be taken into account.

Violent and Sexual Offenders

See also **Extended Sentences** and **Longer Than Commensurate Sentences**

172   Violent Disorder

172.1   Public Order Act 1986, s 2

Triable either way. On indictment maximum 5 years. Summary maximum 6 months and/or £5,000.

Crown Court statistics England and Wales[1] – Crown Court – Males 21+ – Violent Disorder

172.2

Year	Plea	Total Numbers sentenced	Type of sentence%					Average length of custody (months)
			Discharge	Fine	Community sentence	Suspended sentence	Custody	
2000	Guilty	233	2%	6%	27%	4%	61%	15.5
	Not guilty	66	0%	6%	21%	0%	67%	19.7

1   Excluding committals for sentence. Source: Crime and Criminal Justice Unit, Home Office Ref: IOS416-02.

Magistrates' Court Sentencing Guidelines September 2000

172.3 Entry point Are magistrates' sentencing powers appropriate? Consider the impact on the victim. Examples of aggravating factors for the offence are busy public place, fighting between rival groups, large group, people put in fear, planned vulnerable victims. Examples of mitigating factors for the offence are impulsive, nobody actually afraid and provocation. Examples of mitigation are age, health (physical or mental), co-operation with the police, voluntary compensation and genuine remorse. Consider committal. Give reasons if not awarding compensation.

For details about the guidelines see MAGISTRATES' COURT SENTENCING GUIDELINES at page 331.

Guideline remarks

172.4 *R v Hebron and Spencer* (1989) 11 Cr App Rep (S) 226. The two defendants were sentenced for violent disorder. They were involved in a serious New Year's Eve disturbance. Held. In cases of violent crowd disorder, it is not only the precise individual acts that matter. It is the fact that the defendant is taking part in violent disorder, threatening violence against other people, and is part and parcel of the whole threatening and alarming activity.

R v Tyler (1993) 96 Cr App Rep 332. Two defendants were convicted of riot and two of violent disorder. After a poll tax demonstration buildings were damaged and police attacked. Held. It is not the individual act that is the essence of the offence here. It is the using of violence in circumstances where so many people are present as to cause or inspire fear in the general public. One must look at the individual act in the context of that fear. When it occurs in a busy street the dangers are obvious.

Late night violence

172.5 *R v Howells Re Shanoor* [1999] 1 Cr App Rep (S) 335 at 346 – LCJ. The defendant pleaded guilty to violent disorder. In the early hours there was violence outside a nightclub not instigated by the defendant. However, he was in the middle of it and the CCTV showed him punch one man who had his back to him and who was behaving violently to others. There was then a brief struggle between them and the defendant walked away while others continued fighting. When interviewed he admitted that he punched the man with no lawful excuse. He had no convictions but did have a Public Order Act 1986, s 4 caution in 1996. He was employed as a head chef and had testimonials and was described as remorseful and ashamed. The risk of him re-offending was described as low. Held. This was not so serious as to call for a custodial sentence. It could have been punished by community service. Because of time served **conditional discharge** not 6 months.

WASTE

See ENVIRONMENTAL OFFENCES – *Waste, unauthorised keeping, treating or depositing*

173 WATER

173.1 Various penalties and statutes and regulations.

Water Industry Act 1991, s 70(1)

Supplying water unfit for human consumption.

Triable either way. On indictment maximum unlimited fine. Summary maximum a fine of £5,000.

R v Yorkshire Water Services Ltd [2001] EWCA Crim 2635 [2002] 2 Cr App Rep (S) 37. The company pleaded guilty to 17 counts of supplying water unfit for human consumption. There were four incidents between May and November 1998 when work was being carried out which resulted in water to households became so discoloured or smelly that the water was unfit for human use, but with no bacteriological risk to health. The first incident was when the Water Company was installing metres to correct leakage. A main valve had been closed for some months and when it was reopened heavily contaminated water flowed affecting 165 properties over 4 days. The second incident was when during a pressure test air was drawn into the system causing the water to be filthy. 930 properties were affected for up to 2 days. There was a lack of proper procedures. The third incident was caused by a failure to warn customers that water would be unfit when an old disused reservoir was put back into use. There was extreme discoloration affecting 2,204 properties over 2 days. There was bad planning. The last incident was caused by pump tests on two boreholes, which caused sediment, that the treatment process could not cope with. The faults were worst here because there was a failure of the automatic control system, an operator error, a communications failure and a similar incident the year before. 6,500 properties were potentially affected over 2 days. The errors for the four incidents had been corrected at considerable cost and in certain cases compensation was paid. Held. We adopt the considerations in *R v F Howe & Son (Engineers) Ltd* [1999] 2 Cr App Rep 37. When sentencing the court had to have in mind; (1) the degree of culpability; (2) the damage caused together with the ill effects both physical and economical; (3) the defendant's record including any failure to heed warnings and recommendations; (4) the balance that might have to be struck between fitting censure and the counter-productive effect, where a water authority was endeavouring to carry out work in connection with the water supply of imposing too great a financial penalty; (5) the attitude and performance of the water authority after the events in question; and (6) the need to determine the penalty for each incident and divide it up rather than tot up the amounts from the counts in the indictment. The number of complaints should not be used as a multiplier when deciding the penalty. Bearing in mind the level of costs and the penalties awarded in other Crown Court cases the fines for the four incidents would be £18,000, £18,000, £14,000 and £30,000 making **£80,000** not £119,000 with £125,598 costs undisturbed indictment.

See also Environmental Offences

174   Withdrawing From Plan

It should be encouraged

174.1   *A-G's Reference (Nos 65 and 66 of 2001)* (26 October 2001, unreported). H. pleaded guilty to robbery of a guard of a security van. H then 19 sat beside the getaway driver wearing a balaclava helmet throughout the robbery. H's basis of plea was that when the two assailants who attacked the guard got out of the car he was unaware that weapons were to be used. When he saw the weapons he decided not to go with the other two and he remained in the car. Held. The basis of the plea for H was supported by the fact he just remained in the car. Courts ought to encourage people who at the last minute decide not to go through with a criminal enterprise and who withdraw their own involvement even if they remain a party to what is going on.

WITNESSES

For interfering with witnesses see **PERVERTING THE COURSE OF JUSTICE/CONTEMPT OF COURT ETC** *– Witness interference – Guideline remarks*

WOUNDING

See **OFFENCES AGAINST THE PERSON ACT 1861, S 18** and **OFFENCES AGAINST THE PERSON ACT 1861, S 20**

175   YOUNG OFFENDERS

Defendant under 18

The clash between marking the seriousness of the offence and the welfare of the child

175.1   *R v W* [1999] 1 Cr App Rep (S) 488. The defendant was convicted of indecent assault on a 12-year-old girl. He was acquitted of attempted rape. The victim was walking home in the early evening when the defendant caught up with her and started to kiss her. The defendant, who was aged 13, then put his hand down the victim's clothes and touched her vaginal area. The victim pulled his hand away and attempted to escape whereupon the defendant tripped her over, pulled her jogging bottoms down and simulated sexual intercourse on her. The defendant had no previous convictions. Held. These cases are extremely difficult to deal with. It is extremely important that if any woman, whatever age, and in particularly if a child, is sexually assaulted then that is an extremely serious matter and must be dealt with by appropriate punishment. On the other hand when the attacker is no more than a child, the overriding consideration is to do the best to see what can be done to assist him, but at the same time to mark the seriousness of the offence. Here the two principles clash. It was a gratuitous assault but a supervision order rather than **8 months** was appropriate.

INDEX